Lars Powers
Mike Snell

# Microsoft® Visual Studio 2008

# UNLEASHED

**SAMS** | 800 East 96th Street, Indianapolis, Indiana 46240 USA

# Microsoft® Visual Studio 2008 Unleashed

Copyright © 2008 by Pearson Education, Inc.

ISBN-13: 978-0-672-32972-2
ISBN-10: 0-672-32972-7

*Library of Congress Cataloging-in-Publication Data*

Powers, Lars.
   Microsoft Visual Studio 2008 unleashed / Lars Powers and Mike Snell.
      p. cm.
   ISBN 978-0-672-32972-2 (pbk.)
   1. Microsoft Visual studio. 2. Microsoft .NET Framework. 3. Application software—Development. I. Snell, Mike. II. Title.
   TK5105.8885.M57P692 2008
   006.7'882—dc22
                                   2008017300

Printed in the United States of America
First Printing June 2008

## Trademarks

All terms mentioned in this book that are known to be trademarks or service marks have been appropriately capitalized. Sams Publishing cannot attest to the accuracy of this information. Use of a term in this book should not be regarded as affecting the validity of any trademark or service mark.

## Warning and Disclaimer

Every effort has been made to make this book as complete and as accurate as possible, but no warranty or fitness is implied. The information provided is on an "as is" basis. The authors and the publisher shall have neither liability nor responsibility to any person or entity with respect to any loss or damages arising from the information contained in this book.

## Bulk Sales

Sams Publishing offers excellent discounts on this book when ordered in quantity for bulk purchases or special sales. For more information, please contact

**U.S. Corporate and Government Sales**

**1-800-382-3419**

**corpsales@pearsontechgroup.com**

For sales outside of the U.S., please contact

**International Sales**

**international@pearson.com**

**Editor-in-Chief**
Karen Gettman

**Executive Editor**
Neil Rowe

**Acquisitions Editor**
Brook Farling

**Development Editor**
Mark Renfrow

**Managing Editor**
Kristy Hart

**Project Editors**
Kristy Hart
Anne Goebel

**Copy Editor**
Cheri Clark

**Senior Indexer**
Cheryl Lenser

**Proofreader**
Water Crest
Publishing

**Technical Editor**
Todd Meister

**Publishing Coordinator**
Cindy Teeters

**Cover Designer**
Gary Adair

**Composition**
Jake McFarland

The Safari® Enabled icon on the cover of your favorite technology book means the book is available through Safari Bookshelf. When you buy this book, you get free access to the online edition for 45 days. Safari Bookshelf is an electronic reference library that lets you easily search thousands of technical books, find code samples, download chapters, and access technical information whenever and wherever you need it.

To gain 45-day Safari Enabled access to this book:

▶ Go to http://www.samspublishing.com/safarienabled
▶ Complete the brief registration form
▶ Enter the coupon code F6LR-PGTM-NL83-DMMI-TLYE

If you have difficulty registering on Safari Bookshelf or accessing the online edition, please e-mail customer-service@safaribooksonline.com.

# Contents at a Glance

# Table of Contents

# About the Authors

**Lars Powers** is an ISV Technical Advisor on the Microsoft Developer and Platform Evangelism team. He works with Microsoft's largest global ISV partners to help them craft solutions on top of Microsoft's next-generation technologies. Prior to joining Microsoft, Lars was an independent consultant providing training and mentoring on the .NET platform.

**Mike Snell** runs the Solutions division at CEI (www.ceiamerica.com). Mike and his team deliver architecture, consulting, and mentoring to clients looking to build great enterprise and commercial software. Mike is also a Microsoft Regional Director (www.theregion.com).

# Dedication

*To Cheryl, Kelsey, and Carson: a simple "thank you" for being there when I needed you.*

*—Lars Powers*

*To Carrie, Allie, and Ben. Thanks for your understanding for the many long weekends spent in my office and for having to split up the rock band to get this book done. We can fire up the Xbox again.*

*—Mike Snell*

# Acknowledgments

We would like to thank the great team at Sams Publishing for their many valuable contributions and helping us get this book completed. This includes our copy editor, Cheri Clark; our technical editor, Todd Meister; our development editor, Mark Renfrow; our two project editors, Kristy Hart and Anne Goebel; and, finally, our two acquisitions editors, Brook Farling and Neil Rowe.

Mike Snell: I would also like to thank the architects on my team for their insight and for hearing me out on a number of topics that are included in this book. In addition, I would like to thank my good friend and co-author, Lars Powers. This was yet another great experience working together.

Lars Powers: I would like to thank the various members of the Microsoft Developer and Platform Evangelism team worldwide. I can honestly say that this is the smartest, most motivated group of folks that I have ever worked with, and it is my pleasure to call this team my professional home. I'd also like to thank my co-author, Mike, for first convincing me to embark on this project and then for being a solid peer and partner during the writing and editing process. Lastly, and with apologies to Jason Olsen: For the Developers!

And finally, we would like to thank the various teams at Microsoft responsible for bringing Visual Studio and the Visual Studio Team System concepts to life.

# We Want to Hear from You!

As the reader of this book, *you* are our most important critic and commentator. We value your opinion and want to know what we're doing right, what we could do better, what areas you'd like to see us publish in, and any other words of wisdom you're willing to pass our way.

You can email or write me directly to let me know what you did or didn't like about this book—as well as what we can do to make our books stronger.

*Please note that I cannot help you with technical problems related to the topic of this book, and that due to the high volume of mail I receive, I might not be able to reply to every message.*

When you write, please be sure to include this book's title and author, as well as your name and phone or email address. I will carefully review your comments and share them with the author and editors who worked on the book.

**E-mail**:     feedback@samspublishing.com

**Mail**:       Neil Rowe
           Executive Editor
           Sams Publishing
           800 East 96th Street
           Indianapolis, IN 46240 USA

# Reader Services

Visit our website and register this book at www.informit.com/title/9780672329722 for convenient access to any updates, downloads, or errata that might be available for this book.

# Introduction

The release of Visual Studio 2005 and Visual Studio Team Systems marked a major revision to the .NET development experience. It brought us code snippets, custom project templates, refactoring, data binding wizards, smart tags, modeling tools, automated testing tools, and project and task management—to name just a few features.

Visual Studio 2008 builds on these tools and provides additional core changes and additions to the Visual Studio integrated development environment (IDE). The languages have many new improvements, the Framework has a number of additions, and the tools have been significantly enhanced. For instance, Visual Studio 2008 includes such things as Windows Presentation Foundation (WPF) for building richer client solutions, Windows Communication Foundation (WCF) to help build more dynamic service-oriented solutions, and Windows Workflow Foundation (WF) to enable structured programming around business processes. In addition, there are language enhancements such as the Language Integrated Query (LINQ) and team systems enhancements such as code metrics, performance profiling, and a revised team build system. All of these tools are meant to increase your productivity and success rate. This book is meant to help you unlock the many tools built into Visual Studio so that you can realize these gains.

## Who Should Read This Book?

Developers who rely on Visual Studio to get work done will want to read this book. It provides great detail on the many features inside the latest version of the IDE. The book covers all the following key topics:

- ▶ Understanding the basics of solutions, projects, editors, and designers
- ▶ Writing macros, add-ins, and wizards
- ▶ Debugging with the IDE
- ▶ Refactoring code
- ▶ Sharing code with team members and the larger community
- ▶ Writing ASP.NET applications
- ▶ Writing and consuming web services and using the Windows Communication Foundation (WCF)
- ▶ Coding with Windows forms and with Windows Presentation Foundation (WPF)
- ▶ Working with data and databases
- ▶ Creating and hosting workflow-based applications using Windows Workflow Foundation (WF)

- ▶ Using team collaboration and the Visual Studio Team System products

- ▶ Modeling applications

- ▶ Testing applications at both the system and unit test level

- ▶ Managing source code changes and builds

This book is not a language book; it is a tools book. If you are trying to understand Visual Basic or C#, you will want a companion book that focuses on those subjects. If you can write C# or Visual Basic code, this book will radically help you to optimize your productivity with Visual Studio. Again, this book is not a primer on the .NET languages. However, we do cover the new language features (such as LINQ) in both C# and Visual Basic. We also try to provide simple examples that can be read by developers of both languages. By and large, however, this book has one primary focus: detailing and explaining the intricacies of the Visual Studio 2008 IDE to enable developers to be more productive.

# How Is This Book Organized?

You can read this book cover to cover, or you can pick the chapters that apply most to your current need. We sometimes reference content across chapters, but for the most part, each chapter can stand by itself. This organization allows you to jump around and read as time (and interest) permits. There are four parts to the book; each part is described next.

## Part I: An Introduction to Visual Studio 2008

The chapters in this part provide an overview of what to expect from Visual Studio 2008. Readers who are familiar only with prior versions of Visual Studio will want to review these chapters. In addition, we cover the new language enhancement for the 2008 versions of VB and C#.

## Part II: An In-Depth Look at the IDE

This part covers the core development experience relative to Visual Studio. It provides developers with a base understanding of the rich features of their primary tool. The chapters walk through the many menus and windows that define each tool. We cover the base concepts of projects and solutions, and we explore in detail the explorers, editors, and designers.

## Part III: Writing and Working with Code

Part III builds on the topics discussed in Part II by digging into the powerful productivity features of Visual Studio 2008. These chapters investigate the developer productivity aids that are present in the IDE, and discuss how to best use Visual Studio for refactoring and debugging your code.

## Part IV: Extending Visual Studio

For those developers interested in customizing, automating, or extending the Visual Studio IDE, these chapters are for you. We explain the automation model and then document how to use that API to automate the IDE through macros. We also cover how you can extend the IDE's capabilities by writing your own add-ins.

## Part V: Creating Enterprise Applications

Part V focuses on how to work with the IDE tools to write your applications. Each chapter provides an in-depth overview of how to use Visual Studio to help you design and develop an application. We cover writing applications using ASP.NET, web services and WCF, Windows forms, WPF, WF, and working with data and databases.

## Part VI: Visual Studio Team System

Finally, Part VI discusses the special set of Visual Studio versions collectively referred to as Visual Studio Team System (VSTS). We devote an entire chapter to each individual VSTS edition: Development Edition, Architecture Edition, Test Edition, and Database Edition. We also explore, in-depth, the key concepts of team collaboration, work item tracking, and version control using the VSTS client editions in conjunction with the Team Foundation Server product. And lastly, we discuss the concept of automated builds within the context of Visual Studio Team System.

# Conventions Used in This Book

The following typographic conventions are used in this book:

Code lines, commands, statements, variables, and text you see onscreen appears in a monospace typeface.

Placeholders in syntax descriptions appear in an *italic monospace* typeface. You replace the placeholder with the actual filename, parameter, or whatever element it represents.

*Italics* highlight technical terms when they're being defined.

A code-continuation icon is used before a line of code that is really a continuation of the preceding line. Sometimes a line of code is too long to fit as a single line on the page. If you see ➡ before a line of code, remember that it's part of the line immediately above it.

The book also contains Notes, Tips, and Cautions to help you spot important or useful information more quickly.

# PART I

# An Introduction to Visual Studio 2008

## IN THIS PART

# A Quick Tour of Visual Studio 2008

Windows Vista marked the release of the .NET Framework 3.0. This release included many great new features for the Windows developer. Among them was the initial release of Windows Presentation Foundation (WPF), Windows Communication Foundation (WCF), and Windows Workflow Foundation (WWF). However, Visual Studio remained unchanged. You could use these new features but they were not "built in" to the IDE. Instead, you had to use extensions to build applications on these .NET Framework elements and Visual Studio 2005.

Visual Studio 2008 represents a re-synch of the development tools and the .NET Framework. The .NET Framework evolves from 3.0 (released with Vista) to 3.5, an incremental release that ships with Visual Studio 2008. The IDE now natively supports WPF, WCF, and WWF out of the box. In addition, there are many other new bells and whistles including direct Office application support, CardSpace, LINQ, a large revision to ASP.NET, the CLR add-in framework, and more. In addition to Visual Studio, SQL Server will get an update in 2008.

> **NOTE**
>
> Although Visual Studio 2008 represents a major, milestone release, it is by no means the end for Visual Studio. On the heels of 2008 will be a large revision to Microsoft's developer collaboration tool, Visual Studio Team Systems and Team Foundation Server.

If you've been doing this very long, you've come to expect a new release like Visual Studio 2008 to come with new programming models, unfamiliar terms, fresh dialog boxes, and new ways to view code; it can be hard to find your footing on what seems to be unfamiliar ground. This chapter represents what to expect as a first encounter with Visual Studio 2008. We will first do a run-through of the tool to help you get your bearing. We'll then help you sort through the Visual Studio product line. Let this chapter serve as your map of what's great in 2008; it will get you moving in the right direction.

> **NOTE**
>
> Part I, "An Introduction to Visual Studio 2008," is broken into three chapters. This chapter covers what's new inside the tools and documents the product line. Chapter 2, "A Quick Tour of the IDE," is an introduction to getting the tool installed, running it, and creating that first project. It also serves to familiarize you with the basics of the IDE. In Chapter 3, ".NET Framework and Language Enhancements in 2008," we will cover the language and .NET Framework enhancements that are part of the 2008 release.

# Some Welcome Enhancements to the IDE

Visual Studio 2008 and the .NET Framework 3.5 introduce hundreds of new features to an already full-featured toolset. This latest version is about increasing developer productivity when writing applications targeted at the new version of the .NET Framework. This includes expanded project types, a reduction in mundane tasks, and ever-evolving aspects of team-oriented software engineering. This section and those that follow highlight these enhancements that promise to make your work life easier. Of course, we will go over each of these items in greater detail throughout the book; think of the content in this chapter as your "executive overview" for the hurried developer.

## Use a Single Tool for Many Jobs

Many of us work in environments that include applications built on various versions of the .NET Framework. This becomes even more prevalent as more versions are released. For example, you may have an existing application in production built on .NET 2.0. You may be writing a new application on .NET 3.5. However, if your production application requires occasional maintenance, you do not want to have to keep two versions of Visual Studio on your machine.

Visual Studio 2008 supports the ability to target a specific version of the .NET Framework for an application. This means you can use a single tool to develop against many applications built on various .NET Framework flavors. Setting the .NET Framework version of an application will appropriately set the toolbox, project types, available references, and even IntelliSense inside the IDE to be in synch with the chosen .NET Framework version. Figure 1.1 shows creating a new application with Visual Studio 2008 and selecting the .NET Framework version (upper-right corner).

Notice the Add Reference dialog in Figure 1.2. It shows adding a reference to a Windows application that targets .NET Framework 2.0. In this instance, any component that is part of the 3.0 or 3.5 version of the .NET Framework is disabled (grayed out).

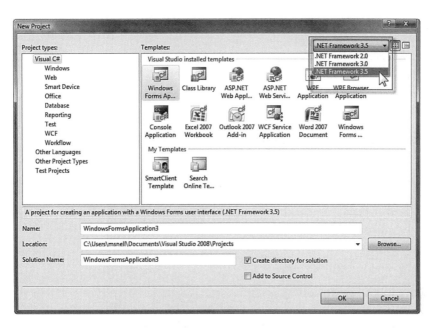

FIGURE 1.1    Creating an application that targets a specific version of the .NET Framework.

FIGURE 1.2    Adding a reference to .NET Framework 2.0 application.

You can also decide to move your application to a different (hopefully newer) version of the .NET Framework. You can do so inside the project properties dialog (right-click your project file and select Properties). Figure 1.3 shows an example. Notice the Target Framework drop-down. You can change this and the IDE will then reset IntelliSense, reference, your toolbox, and more to the newly selected target framework.

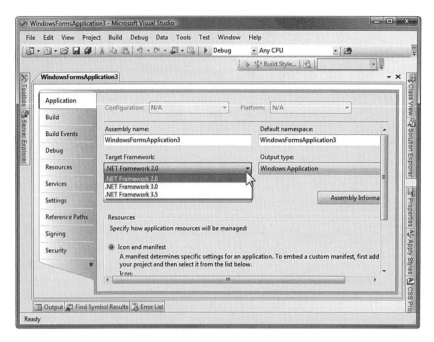

FIGURE 1.3    Resetting the target framework of a Windows application.

Of course, you can use Visual Studio 2008 to open an existing application built on a prior version of the .NET Framework. When doing so, you have the option of upgrading or keeping it tied to the existing .NET Framework version. These features serve to help you upgrade to the advantages of 2008 and continue to work with applications built on an older version of the .NET Framework.

**NOTE**

The Framework setting is per project. Therefore, you can create a single solution that contains multiple projects and each can target a different version of the .NET Framework.

## Cleaner Windows

There have been a number of improvements to the overall management and access of the many Windows inside the IDE. Many user interface elements have a new look and new features.

### The IDE Navigator

Developers can now navigate open windows in the IDE without touching a mouse. This keeps your fingers on the keyboard and can lead to greater productivity. Visual Studio 2008 provides a couple of options here. The first is a simple Window switching hotkey.

Suppose you have a number of code windows open in the IDE. To navigate forward (left to right) through them, you can use the key combination Ctrl+- (minus sign). This is for the standard development settings in the IDE; your settings may differ. To go backward (right to left), you use Ctrl+Shift+- (minus sign). This provides faster Window switching without your having to scroll with the mouse or search through your solution.

You can get similar results using a new visual aid called the IDE Navigator. This tool is similar to the Alt+Tab feature of Windows that allows for fast application switching. To access it, you use Ctrl+Tab (and Ctrl+Shift+Tab). You use this key combination to open the dialog and navigate open code Windows and active tool Windows. Figure 1.4 shows the result. Notice that active files are cycled through on the right.

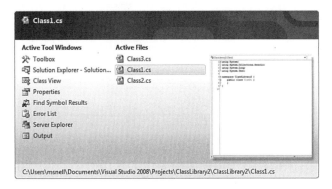

FIGURE 1.4     The IDE Navigator in action.

**TIP**

To change the keyboard combinations assigned to the IDE navigator, select the menu option Tools, Options. Under the Environment node, select Keyboard. Here you can set keyboard shortcut keys. You will want to change the settings assigned to `Window.NextDocumentWindowNav` and `Window.PreviousDocumentWindowNav`.

Alternatively, you can access the IDE Navigator directly using Alt+F7. This brings up the tool with the active tool windows list selected. You can jump between the lists using the right- and left-arrow keys.

### Improved Docking

In prior versions, it was often difficult to get your code or tool window to dock correctly in the IDE. In 2008, docking windows is much improved. There are new icons and visualizations that make this process very simple. Figure 1.5 shows an example of docking the

Server Explorer window on top of the Toolbox pane. You can see that there are options to move this window to the left of the toolbox, below it, and so on. Selecting each option shows a visual representation of the results before you release your mouse button.

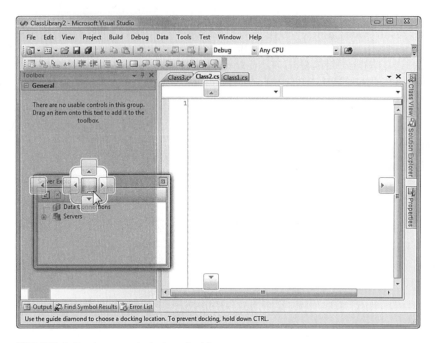

FIGURE 1.5     Improved window docking.

### Standard Dialogs

Another welcome change to the IDE is the use of Windows standard dialog boxes for doing such tasks as opening a file, saving something, or printing code. In prior version of Visual Studio, the IDE had its own versions of these common tasks. However, this only made things confusing because most Windows users are accustomed to working using specific tools.

As an example, consider Figures 1.6 and 1.7. Figure 1.6 is the Open File dialog in Visual Studio 2005. This dialog was specific to Visual Studio. Figure 1.7 shows the same dialog in Visual Studio 2008. Notice that the dialog is the same dialog you would get in any other Windows-based application.

### Choose Your Font

There is a new setting called Environment Font inside the Options dialog (Tools menu) under the Environment node, Fonts and Colors. This option allows you to set the font for the entire IDE to the selection of your choice. Figure 1.8 shows selecting this option from the list.

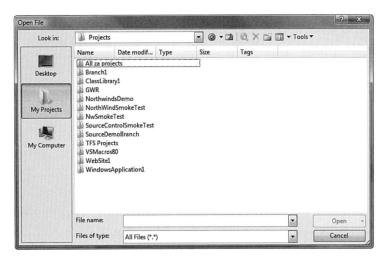

FIGURE 1.6    The Open File dialog in Visual Studio 2005.

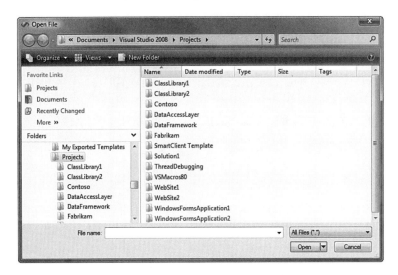

FIGURE 1.7    The Open File dialog in Visual Studio 2008.

Changing this font changes your IDE. For example, suppose you set the Environment Font to Courier New, 8pt. This changes dialogs, menus, and more. Figure 1.9 shows the results of such a change.

## Keep Your Settings

Many of you have customized your IDE to fit your exact needs. These settings can be painful to have to re-create. Thankfully, Visual Studio 2008 supports settings migration. If, for example, you already have Visual Studio 2005 installed, Visual Studio 2008 will allow you to migrate these settings on startup.

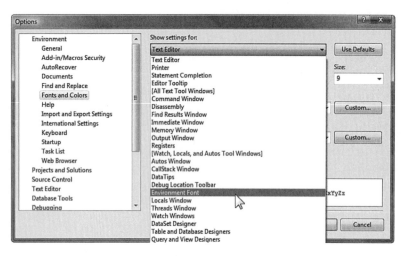

FIGURE 1.8    Setting the Environment Font.

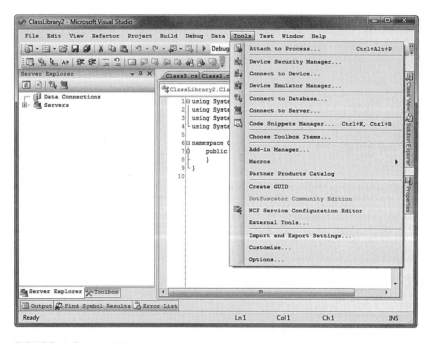

FIGURE 1.9    The IDE with a new font setting.

Alternatively, if you are upgrading to a new computer or want to share your Visual Studio 2008 settings, you can do so using the Import and Export Settings tool. This option is available from the Tools menu in both Visual Studio 2005 and 2008. It is a wizard that allows you to import settings, export them to a file, or reset your settings to one of the IDE defaults. Figure 1.10 shows an example of exporting settings.

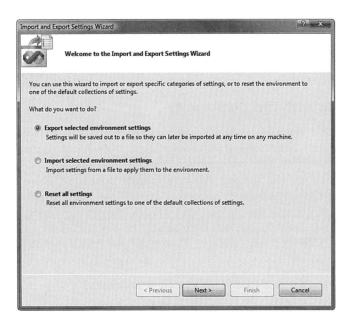

FIGURE 1.10   Exporting your settings.

When you export or import settings, you can select those you want to apply. Figure 1.11 shows the second step in the export process. Notice you can pick and choose those items you want to export.

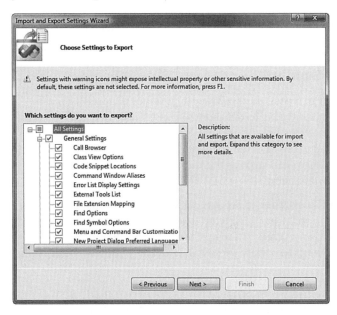

FIGURE 1.11   Selecting the settings you want to export.

The final step when exporting is to save the file as a .vssettings file. This file can then be shared among users. It can also be used to migrate settings from one PC and one IDE version to another. With it, you can rerun the Import and Export Settings Wizard, choosing to import settings from a file.

## Share (and Consume) Code with the Community

Writing code is often a community thing. The developer community is broad and, for the most part, supportive of one another. Chances are, if you are having a problem, someone else has had the same issue. You can often reach out across the Internet and find solutions, components, sample code, articles, and the like that help to solve your issue. There is some kinship among developers that attracts them to posting sample code, newsgroup answers, and tips. Perhaps it is as simple as knowing that they may be the next in line to need an answer to a critical question, or maybe it's just the need to show off to one another. Either way, Visual Studio 2008 continues the community support that was built into 2005.

You can still author components targeted at the development community. In 2008, however, you can now indicate whether your components are targeted at both 2005 and 2008 or simply one or the other.

Another change to the community features is the simplification of the community menu items into a couple of menu items under the Help menu. The first menu item links directly to MSDN Forums and replaces Ask a Question and Check Question Status. This allows you to link to the forums and work directly with the features there. The second item is Report a Bug. This menu option replaces Send Feedback.

For more information on the community features of Visual Studio 2008 (and MSDN Forums), see Chapter 7, "The .NET Community: Consuming and Creating Shared Code."

## Expanded Class Designer Support

The Class Designer was introduced in Visual Studio 2005. It provides a graphical means for writing and modifying classes. You can use it to define new classes and their relationships, add properties and methods to those classes, and modify elements within a property or method; it even allows for the refactoring of code. A change to a given method name within the Class Designer, for instance, will change the method's name as well as update all the method's callers to use the new name.

Visual Studio 2008 now provides Class Designer support for C++ applications. You can use it to visualize classes and their relationships. This includes seeing native C++ inheritance structures, enums, template classes, and more. There are, however, some limitations. If you are a C++ developer, you will want to review these inside of the production documentation.

The Class Designer is an integral part of Visual Studio Professional Edition and above. However, we cover it in detail inside the Visual Studio Team System part of the book, Chapter 26, "Development Edition."

# Develop User Applications

.NET has quickly become pervasive throughout the entire Windows product world. It took only a few short years, but it is now fair to say that .NET is everywhere; Windows programming and .NET programming are now synonymous. Many of the user applications we interact with have some if not all of their base in .NET. This includes web applications, rich clients built on Windows, mobile applications, Office solutions, smart clients that work across the Web, and more. The good news is that the .NET developer is in high demand, and you can leverage your skills to target a wide audience.

Figure 1.12 shows the New Project dialog in Visual Studio 2008; it serves as an example of the myriad of user solutions that are possible with .NET.

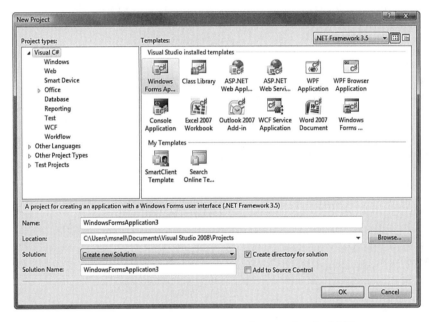

FIGURE 1.12   The many application faces of Visual Studio 2008.

Although Figure 1.12 shows many project templates, it does not represent a road map with respect to user applications. The .NET developer has many choices for creating the user experience using both Visual Studio and the new Expressions Studio (discussed later in the chapter). The following list is meant to provide an overview of the presentation technologies available to the .NET developer:

- ▶ **ASP.NET**—This allows you to build web-based (and browser-based) solutions using HTML, AJAX, and server-side processing.

- ▶ **NetCF**—The .NET Compact Framework 3.5 runs on small devices and allows you to build applications that target these mobile devices.

▶ **Sliverlight**—This is Microsoft's new solution for developing highly interactive solutions experiences that combine video and animation, delivered across the Web for both Windows and Mac.

▶ **VSTO**—Visual Studio Tools for Office allows you to build solutions based on the Office productivity tools (including Outlook and SharePoint).

▶ **WinForms**—These are Windows forms used to deliver business applications and tools built on the windows platform. WinForms applications can be stand-alone or data-driven. In addition, WinForm applications may connect to web services, leverage resources on the client, and more.

▶ **WPF**—Windows Presentation Foundation combines WinForms, XAML, Smart Clients, 3D graphics, and more to allow you to create the richest, most fully featured client solutions that run on Windows. WPF applications can be delivered similar to a WinForms application. In addition, they can exist as a browser-hosted solution that runs in a security sandbox.

▶ **XNA**—This technology allows you to build Xbox games using Visual Studio (a topic for another book).

Each of these technologies is supported by Visual Studio 2008. With them, you have many options for creating user applications. This section highlights a number of development improvements in Visual Studio 2008 with respect to developing the user experience.

> **NOTE**
>
> There are many new client options in Visual Studio 2008. We highlight them all here. However, these and more are covered in greater detail throughout the rest of the book. Chapter 14, "Creating ASP.NET Applications," covers ASP.NET; Chapter 15, "Building Windows Forms Applications," is about standard Windows forms; Chapter 16, "Creating Richer, Smarter User Interfaces," focuses squarely on WPF; Chapter 17, "Creating Rich Browser Applications," discusses AJAX and XBAP applications; and Chapter 21, "Developing Office Business Applications," covers creating solutions based on Microsoft Office.

## Enhance the Web Developer's Productivity

The vast majority of applications built these days involve some semblance of a web component—be it a full-blown browser-based, web application; a smart client that works across the Web; a web service; or otherwise. In fact, the line between a traditional rich client and a web application is blurring. Technologies such as AJAX (Asynchronous JavaScript and XML), Web Services, Smart Clients, and XAML (Extensible Application Markup Language) have ensured this. You can now build rich user experiences as your needs dictate. Of course, Microsoft has remained suitably focused on expanding Visual Studio's capabilities with respect to web development.

Web developers want tools that help them through the common functions of building their application. Let's face it, the HTML, CSS, and XML standards can sometimes be a pain to follow by memory and by hand. Instead, we want tools that guide us. And of course, as soon as we want to work with code, we want to be able to access the entire related source and massage it as necessary. Visual Studio 2008 builds on recent (2005) enhancement. It's a step forward in adding productivity to the web development day. We highlight many of these advancements in the following sections.

> **NOTE**
>
> We will cover many of the items that follow (and more) in greater detail in Chapter 14.

### Create a Richer Web Interface

AJAX represents the capability to leverage the ubiquitous support for JavaScript in web browsers to create a more interactive user experience. Client applications built to leverage AJAX still have a client-server paradigm. However, with AJAX the client can update portions of a given page without appearing to have posted back to the server (of course, it typically does). In addition, most AJAX-enabled applications put more processing on the client for things like toggling sections of a page, working with tabs, auto-completing data entry, popping up dialogs, and more. The result is a step forward in interactivity for a user.

AJAX is not a Microsoft-specific technology. It represents more of a programming model. However, Microsoft released the AJAX Extensions for Visual Studio targeting both the 2003 and 2005 versions. These controls allowed developers to more easily create AJAX experiences. These controls have been enhanced and are now incorporated into Visual Studio 2008 and the .NET Framework 3.5. Figure 1.13 shows the controls inside the Visual Studio Toolbox.

FIGURE 1.13   The AJAX Extensions in Visual Studio 2008.

These controls allow you to create a page that can receive partial, asynchronous updates (using `UpdatePanel`) and show update progress (using `UpdateProgress`). They also allow you to create your own controls and features that implement AJAX without having to write the client-side JavaScript.

In addition to these controls, Visual Studio 2008 supports IntelliSense, code comment documentation, and client-side debugging for JavaScript. It also contains the Microsoft AJAX Library, which is a JavaScript common library that supports object-oriented development for JavaScript. For a detailed overview of these items, AJAX, and more, see Chapter 17.

---

**Microsoft Silverlight**

Microsoft's Silverlight is another exciting client technology for the Web. Silverlight allows for an even greater user experience delivered through the browser. You use it to create media-rich, highly interactive experiences. Silverlight requires a browser add-on (or plug-in). It works with Windows, Mac, and Linux in a wide variety of browsers. Silverlight does not ship with Visual Studio 2008; however, the Silverlight extensions for Visual Studio are available as a plug-in to the tool.

---

### Work with an Expanded Toolbox

Visual Studio 2008 provides a rich set of tools and controls for the web developer. It still supports the standard controls for ASP.NET and HTML. This includes labels, text boxes, buttons, and the like. In addition, the validation, data, WebParts, and login controls are all still present. There are, of course, enhancements to many of these controls. However, here we focus on introducing the new controls for the ASP.NET developer.

There are three ASP.NET user interface controls that should be highlighted to the web developer: ListView, DataPager, and LinqDataSource. The first of these, ListView, is a control that simplifies the display of repeating data. The ListView control is driven based on user templates. In this way, you can easily configure how you want your UI to behave during operations such as view, edit, add, and delete. In addition, the ListView supports sorting, paging, and, of course, data binding. Figure 1.14 shows the Configure ListView screen. Here you can choose a default Runtime View layout, visual styles, and more.

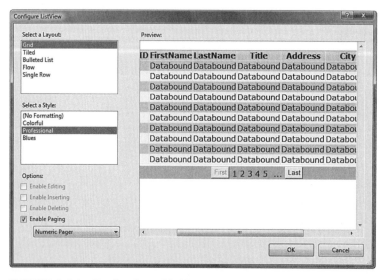

FIGURE 1.14   Configuring a ListView control.

The ListView control is template driven. You, of course, have complete access to the layout and control of these templates. In addition, the control can assist in setting up the appropriate template. Figure 1.15 shows the ListView Tasks. Notice that you can change the Current View shown in the WebForm designer to another template view.

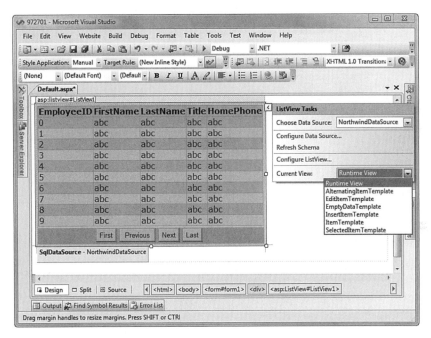

FIGURE 1.15    The ListView Tasks.

Figure 1.16 shows the template view for the EditItemTemplate. Again, the template layout source is available for you to customize. In fact, in this example, we put the form labels and controls into a table for a cleaner look. Notice too that the record navigation is available from within these templates. This allows your users to cycle through sections of their data and make appropriate updates.

Another new control in 2008 that we'd like to highlight is the DataPager control. This control allows you to manage the paging of data and the UI associated with that paging. You can use this control by itself or embed it as part of another control you create. In fact, the ListView control mentioned previously already uses the DataPager control. You can associate other, data-bound controls to a DataPager by using the DataPager's PagedControlID property (the given control must implement the IPageableItemContainer interface).

You have full control over the customization, layout, and behavior of the DataPager. Figure 1.17 shows the DataPager Fields editor (accessed from the control's Tasks window). Notice that you can set appearance and behavior for all items associated with a given DataPager layout.

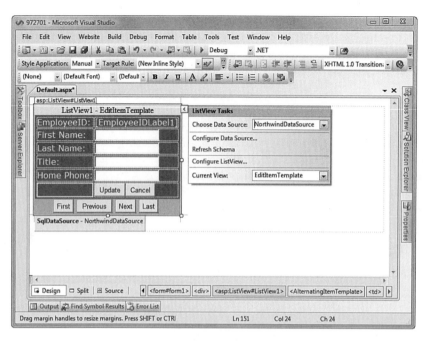

FIGURE 1.16    The EditItemTemplate form designer layout.

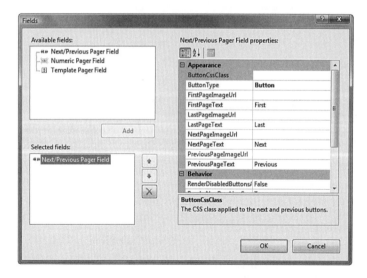

FIGURE 1.17    The DataPager Fields editor.

The final new ASP.NET control we will highlight here is the LinqDataSourceControl. LINQ (Language Integrated Query) is a new programming model introduced in Visual Studio 2008. It combines database query and .NET language. In this way, you can write strongly typed code (and not just simple strings) to query your data. This includes writing queries with full IntelliSense support that is based on your data. In addition, LINQ can work with data from various data sources including SQL Server, XML, and many more. For a richer overview of this new technology, check out Chapter 18, "Working with Databases."

The LinqDataSourceControl gives you the ability to bind controls using the LINQ technology in a familiar construct as other ASP.NET data sources. You can use the LinqDataSourceControl to gain access to database data, in-memory collections of data, data-source classes, and more. When you connect with these data sources, the LinqDataSourceControl allows you to write your data interaction using the power of LINQ. Your database query code for selecting, grouping, ordering, filtering, updating, inserting, and deleting will all be strongly typed and based on LINQ. In fact, the LinqDataSourceControl writes this code for you. Figure 1.18 shows an example of configuring a LinqDataSourceControl to connect and work with a LINQ data class.

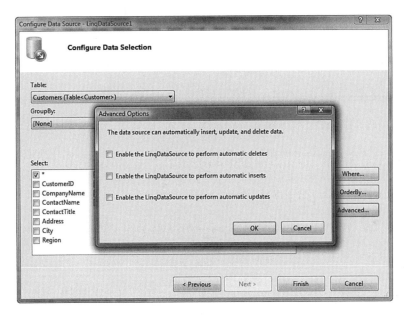

FIGURE 1.18    The LinqDataSource Configure Data Source Wizard.

### Develop and Design at the Same Time

Most web form developers switch between the Source and Design view of a web form many times during its development. The Source view allows you full access to editing the XHTML of the page. Design view lets you see the page develop and gives access to the many shortcuts attached to controls in the designer. Visual Studio 2008 makes this switching much easier. It provides a Split view. With it, you can see both the XHTML and the Designer. Figure 1.19 shows an example.

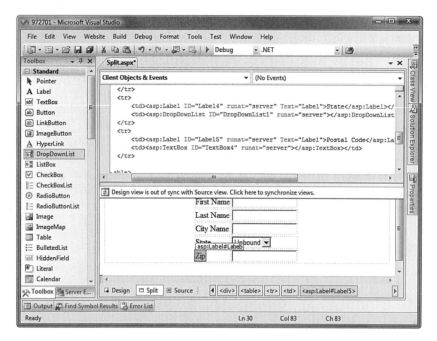

FIGURE 1.19   The Web Form Designer Split view.

Split view tries to keep both the source and the design in synch. This works when you drag items from the toolbox to either the Source or the Design view panes. However, the Design view can get out of synch when you are doing a lot of edits to your source. In these cases, the Design view indicates that it is out of synch (see the middle of Figure 1.19). A click on the Designer and everything is back in synch. This new view can make developing your web forms more intuitive and more productive.

### Create and Manage Your Look

Styles and style sheets have been part of the web development world for years now. They help ensure a consistent look and feel that can be managed centrally. The CSS (cascading style sheet) specification also continues to evolve; it allow you to do more and more with the visual display of our applications. Of course, this introduces additional elements, attributes, and complexity. Thankfully, Visual Studio 2008 introduces better tools for creating and managing both inline styles (styles defined directly in your XHTML source) and style sheets (.css files).

One such tool is the Manage Styles pane available to the web form developer. Figure 1.20 shows the pane in action. From here you can attach a style sheet to a web form, create a new style, preview styles, and more. Notice the Options button and related menu. These options help you control which styles you want to see and how you want to see them.

Also revised for 2008 is the New Style/Modify Style dialog. Here you can create or modify a style based on the appropriate CSS spec (through 2.1). This dialog has been revamped to give you access to new features and make things a bit more intuitive. You can access this

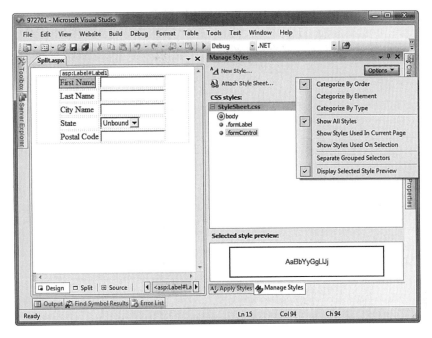

FIGURE 1.20   Managing styles in your application.

dialog from the Build Style button on the Style Sheet toolbar, from within a style sheet, or from within the Manage Styles pane using the New Style option. Figure 1.21 shows an example of the New Style dialog as accessed from the Manage Styles pane.

You can quickly apply styles to the elements on your page using the Apply Styles pane. Here you can see all the styles define on your form or the attached style sheet. Each style is shown with a visual representation for quick access. To apply the style, you simply select the form element and click the style. Figure 1.22 shows an example of this feature. Notice too that the ToolTip text for a style shows its CSS definition.

The final, new style management item we will cover here is the CSS Properties pane. Here you can quickly see the properties of a given style and manage them as you would the properties of a control. Figure 1.23 shows the use of this pane. Notice that you can work with styles defined within your web form. Each style is also grouped or available alphabetically. This can make things a bit easier for those who do not like to hunt through IntelliSense when defining styles.

### Centrally Manage Navigation and Design

Visual Studio 2005 introduced the capability to create master pages. These pages centralized the management of a site's design and navigation elements. In addition, master pages are supported by the designer, which allows for a richer design experience (and replaced the need for include files that were only seen in a browser). A developer is able to see the page in the context of the site's central design while in design mode.

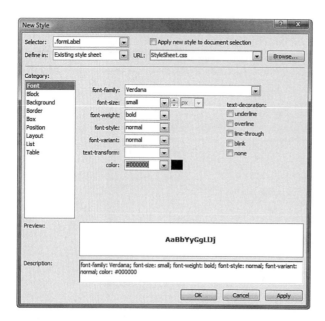

FIGURE 1.21    Creating or modifying a style.

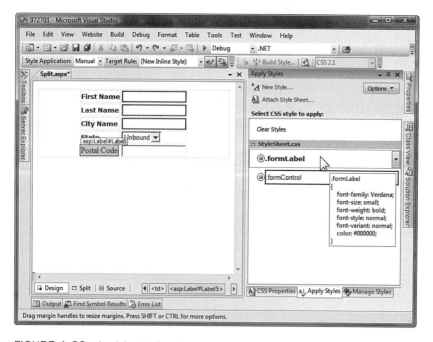

FIGURE 1.22    Applying styles to your source.

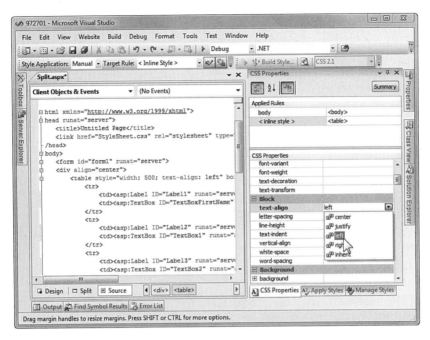

FIGURE 1.23   Editing the properties of a given style.

One drawback, however, was that you could have only one level of master page. You could not nest master pages inside of each other and view the results in the designer. For example, a common scenario is to define a main master page to contain your site's frame, navigation, footer information, and the like. You might then create separate, sub–master pages for various content types. These sub–master pages would have their own, central design elements in addition to those defined by the main master page. Again, this scenario is not supported in 2005.

Thankfully, Visual Studio 2008 does support this scenario. With it, you can select an existing master page when creating a new master page. Figure 1.24 shows doing just that. Previously, during creation of a master page, this option was disabled.

With the new, nested master page, you can define master content inside the content placeholder defined by the main master page. You then add a new content placeholder inside your nested page. Pages based on this nested master page will put their content inside this area. Of course, you can go multiple levels deep with nested master pages. The designer will then show your various master pages during design. Figure 1.25 shows a simple example of an .aspx page created from a nested master page.

## Smarter Clients

Rich clients are having a bit of a renaissance in 2008. The line between a web-based and Windows-like user experience continues to blur thanks to many UI advancements in terms of technology and tools. We have already discussed AJAX. Here we look at how

2008 allows you to create richer, smarter clients with Microsoft's new Windows Presentation Foundation (WPF).

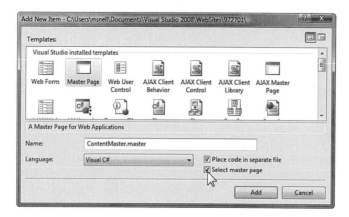

FIGURE 1.24    Selecting the master page for a new, sub–master page.

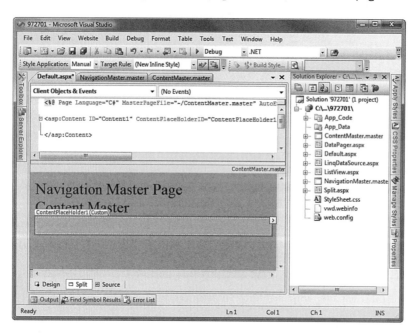

FIGURE 1.25    A page created from a nested master page.

WPF is both an addition to the .NET Framework and a set of tools with which developers can create richer solutions for the Web. The presentation code itself is based on XAML (Extensible Application Markup Language). The UI XAML is created using the Visual Studio WPF designer (or a similar tool called Expression Blend). The XAML is then run by the .NET CLR. Because it is processed on the client and not bound by HTML, it runs as a vector-based, hardware-accelerated user experience. The result is an extremely rich and interactive experience that supports both 2D and 3D graphics.

Visual Studio provides a familiar experience for creating WPF solutions. You first define a WPF project and add WPF forms to the project. When creating your solution, you select a project type based on whether the application will run as a browser add-in or as an installed desktop client. Figure 1.26 shows the WPF project templates. Selecting WPF Application will create a basic WPF application that is pushed to or installed on a client. It may have access to local resources on the client.

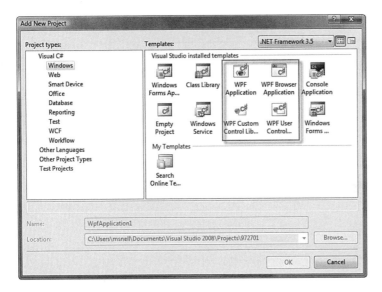

FIGURE 1.26   Creating a new WPF project with Visual Studio 2008.

The WPF Browser Application, on the other hand, is meant to be deployed through a URL and run as a browser extension. The application, called an XBAP (XAML browser application), runs inside a sandbox. It does not have rights to the client machine and is cleaned up as part of the browser's cache. It does not require a download provided that the user has the .NET Framework 3.5 on their machine. It can work with the browser's cookies and is supported by both IE and Firefox.

Making the wrong choice here is not too problematic. You can move the WPF forms between application types. Note that the other two application types highlighted in Figure 1.26 are WPF User Controls and WPF Custom Control Library. Both are for creating reusable controls for WPF applications.

The next step in building your WPF form is to simply open it and drag and drop UI controls onto a design surface. One big difference for Windows developers, however, is that you now have control over the form layout code (or XAML). This is more akin to designing a web form with Visual Studio. Figure 1.27 shows the XAML designer in action.

Notice that the XAML controls are listed in the toolbox on the left. While they are similar to Windows and web controls, they are a new set of controls just for WPF. Also, notice how the designer has a split view between the design surface and the XAML. These stay in synch as you develop your code. Finally, the properties window shown on the left provides a similar experience when you're editing the many properties of a XAML control.

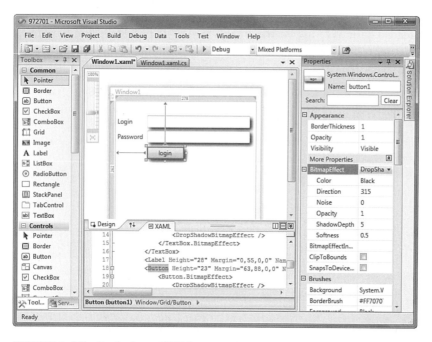

FIGURE 1.27    Designing a WPF form.

We cover the designer in greater detail in Chapter 16. Here we focus on the forms engine, the controls, event programming, debugging support, deployment, IntelliSense, configuration, and more inside of WPF.

### Designers and Developers

When discussing WPF, it's important to note the work that went into the technology and tools to support a strong designer-developer workflow. It's understood that traditionally developers have been left to try to "design" the UI. It goes without saying that developers have not exactly shined as UI designers.

However, even in scenarios where designers were employed on projects, the design would often fall short or the implementation would be an arduous process. Designers had their own tools that did not talk with those of the developers. A design was often provided to the development team as a picture or some basic HTML. Developers were often left to try to realize the intricacies of the design while having to concern themselves with coding the solution. In the end, nobody was happy. The design was never exactly what was envisioned and developers would spend too much time trying to get the look right.

WPF tries to right this wrong. It keeps the UI markup (XAML) as totally separate from the implementation code (C# or VB). In addition, Microsoft has provided design tools that let designers create real user interfaces that can be leveraged by the development team. There are no more "lost in translation" issues. Instead, a designer can create or open a WPF UI element, edit it using the power of Expression Blend (they do not have to learn Visual Studio), and save it back to the solution or send it to a developer. The developer can then open the same item inside of Visual Studio and begin responding to key UI events with their code. This back-and-forth can continue as the UI builds up over time. Nobody's code gets stepped on; everyone focuses on their strength.

Figure 1.28 shows a sample of the Expression Blend tool. Notice that the same .xaml file (WFP form) is open here. Designers can use a tool with which they are more familiar to lay out the UI and apply visual techniques such as 3D and animation. Also notice that the C# project file is being used to maintain continuity between the solutions. After the designers are finished, their save goes right back to the development team. They can even test their UI in the context of the application by building and running the project.

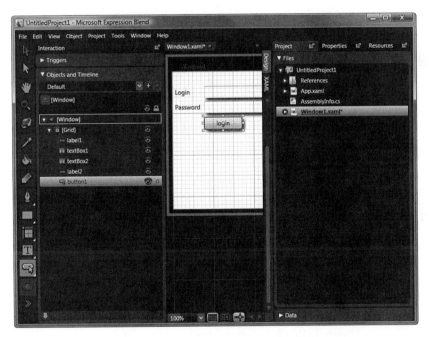

FIGURE 1.28   Designing a WPF form inside of Expression Blend.

**Expression Blend**

Microsoft's Expression Blend is a sister tool to Visual Studio 2008. It gives designers the ability to create rich WPF (XAML) forms, animations, and more—all without code. You can also use it to build Silverlight applications.

Expression Blend is entirely built on WPF. It provides a great example of exactly what is possible with this technology.

Although the Expression suite of products is outside the scope of this book, you should be aware of these tools. We will provide an overview of them in the later section "The Visual Studio Product Line."

### Making a Choice

The many options for developing rich user experiences on Windows invariably leads to the question: "What is the right UI technology for my next Windows application?" Of course, the answer depends on your specific scenario. When making your decision, you should keep the intent of each technology in mind.

WPF is a Windows technology that requires the .NET Framework on the client. It can run in a browser sandbox or as a fully featured Windows application. You should leverage WPF when you need to create a rich user experience with high design aesthetics, want a low cost of installation and update, and require distributed connectivity.

Sliverlight, on the other hand, requires only a browser plug-in. The browser plug-in runs a mini version of the CLR on the client. In this way, you still can write your code in C# or VB and have access to bits of the .NET Framework. Silverlight is a very lightweight, cross-platform version of WPF. Its core strength is video, animation, and sound (multimedia). Think of Silverlight as an alternative to Adobe's Flash product.

Lastly, Windows forms still has a place in creating installed, business applications that connect with the operating system, leverage resources on the client, connect to databases, and more. They offer standard, workman-like user experiences for data entry, file manipulation, configuration, and related task-oriented solutions. They are easy to develop and do not typically involve much work from a design perspective.

## Office-Based Solutions

Developers have been able to customize Office for a long time now; some of us still remember writing Excel macros on Windows 3.1 or automating Word with Word Basic. Visual Studio 2008 is another step forward for Office development. The tools are now are built into the IDE. With them, you can create Office-based projects and solutions that leverage Word, Excel, Project, Visio, PowerPoint, Outlook, SharePoint, and InfoPath.

There are project templates for all the Office products. In fact, you can create solutions for both Office 2003 and 2007. Figure 1.29 shows the New Project dialog for Office solutions. These are Visual Basic templates but the same exist for C#.

> **NOTE**
>
> Visual Studio Tools for Office (VSTO) is not part of Visual Studio Professional Edition. It is no longer a separate product. Visual Studio 2008 ships with the new VSTO 3.0. This should increase the awareness of these tools and their usage.

There are a few scenarios that would lead you to create an application based on Office. The most common is when you need to extend a line-of-business (LOB) application to provide functionality inside the common, information-worker productivity tools of Office. A LOB typically has a lot of rich data and some workflow.

For example, you may work with a financial, manufacturing, or payroll application. Each of these fills a specific need. However, users may need to work with the data that is housed inside the application and make key decisions that feed back into these systems. This work is often done through cut-and-paste and is often not captured by the systems. Users lose productivity switching back and forth between the Office tools and the LOB. This is where you should consider creating an Office Business Application (OBA) to help bridge this gap.

### Develop Documents, Templates, and Add-Ins

Notice the many templates in Figure 1.29. There are three separate templates for Excel 2007, for example. Each of these templates provides a specific purpose. Office application templates allow you to create solutions built on a single document, a document template, or as an add-in to the given Office application. The following list provides a brief overview of these three project subtypes:

▶ **Document**—Document projects allow you to build a solution based on a specific document. There are typically not multiple instances of the document. As an example, suppose you have an Excel document that needs to read and write project resource billing information from and to an ERP system. This document might be updated weekly as part of a resource meeting. The data should be up-to-date and changes should feed the billing system. In this instance, you would create a solution based on this single document.

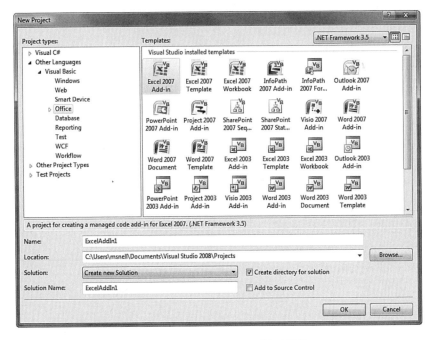

FIGURE 1.29   The many project templates inside VSTO.

▶ **Template**—An Office Template project is one that is based on an Office template file (an Excel `.xltx`, for example). Creating a solution based on an Office template file gives you the flexibility to provide users with assistance when creating a new instance of a given template. You might push common document templates out to your users. When a user creates a new instance, the template may reach into data housed in other systems to help the user fill out the details of the document. You might then, in turn, capture the results in a database after routing the template through a basic SharePoint workflow.

▶ **Add-in**—An Add-in project allow you to extend the features and functionality of a given Office application. You create Add-ins to offer additional productivity and solutions inside a given application. You might, for example, write an Outlook Add-in that allows users to more easily file and categorize their email.

Whichever template you choose, Visual Studio 2008 provides a rich, design-time experience for building your Office solution. As an example, Figure 1.30 shows the Visual Studio 2008 design experience building a solution for a Word 2007 Template. In this example, a user is creating a quote for training. The fields in the document pull from a LOB database that includes customer information, resource data, and common pricing.

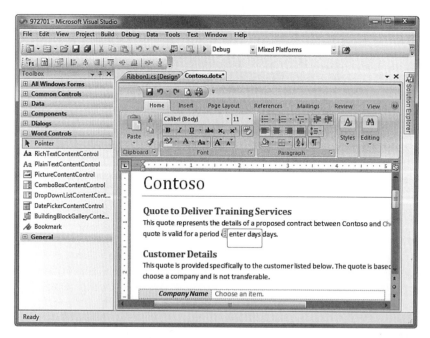

FIGURE 1.30    Designing a Word 2007 Template project in Visual Studio 2008.

VSTO 3.0 also provides design support for working with the Office 2007 Ribbon. In this way, your application can behave like the rest of Office. You can embed productivity features and aids on your own tab of the Office Ribbon. Figure 1.31 shows a simple example. The features here apply to the document template discussed previously. In this example, a developer provides specific features based on the document template and accessed by the user directly from Word's Ribbon.

FIGURE 1.31   Customizing the Microsoft Office Ribbon.

### Create SharePoint Solutions

SharePoint has become nearly as ubiquitous as Office. Companies are leveraging it for knowledge management, collaboration, and business process automation. Of course, this inevitably means customization and extension by developers. If you customized SharePoint using the existing tools for Visual Studio prior to 2008, you know that this presented a big challenge. The design-time support was not there, configuration was difficult, and debugging was very challenging.

Visual Studio 2008 presents a much richer toolset for SharePoint developers. With it, you can create SharePoint workflows (see the project templates back in Figure 1.29) and build WebParts based on ASP.NET. In addition, the debug experience has been reduced from approximately 15 to 5 steps in the IDE. SharePoint development is now a first-class consideration inside the IDE. This should streamline the process for extending SharePoint and help meet the business demand this collaboration product has generated.

This section highlighted many of the new features in VSTO 3.0 for Visual Studio 2008. There are many more advancements, however. These include access to open XML formats, the capability to add features to existing Outlook forms, custom task panes in Word and Excel, data binding, and improved deployment and security. We cover all of these and more in Chapter 21.

## Target Mobile Devices

Visual Studio 2008 continues to extend the power to write applications that target mobile devices. This latest version allows you to build applications on a wide variety of technologies and devices. You can build solutions based on Windows Mobile 2003, Windows CE 5.0 and 6.0, and Windows Mobile 5.0 and 6.0 for both Smartphone and Pocket PC. In addition, you can target many devices and device types that leverage these operating systems and related versions of the .NET Compact Framework.

The IDE provides the forms designers, code editors, and debugging support for building mobile applications. You start with a Smart Device project. You can then select your Target Platform, the target version of the .NET Compact Framework (NetCF), and the project template type (forms application, class library, control, and so on). Figure 1.32 shows an example. Here the application is targeting Windows Mobile 5.0 and the latest version of NetCF.

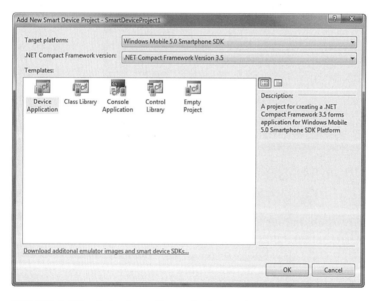

FIGURE 1.32    Selecting a Smart Device project template.

Designing Windows Mobile forms is a familiar process. There is a set of device controls in the toolbox. You select a control and drop it on a Mobile form. The form looks and acts like the device you are targeting. Figure 1.33 is an example of the design experience. This example is a simple customer search form. Notice the menus at the bottom of the screen. You use these menus to allow the user to work with the form from the major keys on the phone (of course, a Smartphone has no stylus or mouse).

As you develop your application, you can deploy and test it against device emulators. This allows you to debug your application and see how it behaves on a simulated device. Visual Studio 2008 ships with the basic emulators for Smartphones and Pocket PC. However, there are more than 20 device emulators available for download. Figure 1.34 shows the application deployed and running on the basic Smartphone emulator. From here, you can interact with the application and debug your code.

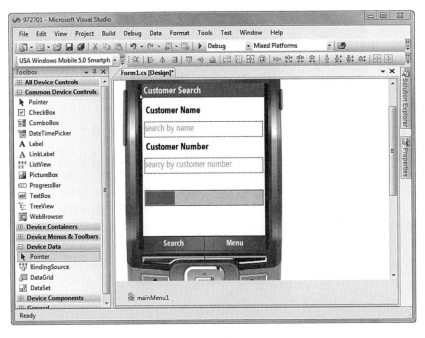

FIGURE 1.33   Designing a Smartphone form.

FIGURE 1.34   Running a mobile application in a device emulator.

A big addition for 2008 is the capability to write unit tests for mobile device applications. You can now create these tests using the standard unit test framework built into Visual Studio as of 2005. These unit tests behave the same way. In addition, they can integrate with Team System products (like Team Test) and publish test data to Team Foundation Server.

The Compact Framework 3.5 provides some welcome enhancements. These include support for LINQ data binding, Windows Communication Foundation, better compression, advancements in sound, better security management, and more.

# Write Connected, Service-Oriented Solutions

Many business applications involve specific processes, or workflows, around documents, records, and related data. These business processes typically involve staged review and approval by business personnel; they might also require communication between various systems. A business process is also typically long-running—meaning the process is not a simple, single execution but rather a multistep process that has to "wait" before moving to the next step.

Building these processes into business application was typically a lot of custom development work with little guidance, or it meant tying your application to third-party tools. Web services helped but developers lacked an easy way to build them with support for multiple protocols, different transports, strong security, and transactional support.

Visual Studio 2008 now provides in-the-box (and in the .NET Framework) support for building business processes as workflows and reliably integrating them with other applications, systems, and partners. This section takes a look at Windows Workflow (WF) for defining reusable business process and Windows Communication Foundation (WCF) for unlocking that business process across system boundaries.

> **NOTE**
>
> We will highlight .NET Framework and language enhancements (as opposed to IDE enhancements) to support communication and workflow in Chapter 3.

## Develop an Application/Business Process

A workflow represents a set of actions (called activities) that are taken based on one another, business rules and conditions, and user actions. Workflows typically model business processes and often involve user interaction. Windows Workflow provides a framework, tools, and an engine for enabling workflows in your application. With it, you can create a workflow and know that it will run wherever the .NET Framework is installed.

You interact with workflows from within your application. This could be any type of application (Windows, ASP.NET, console, service, and so on). You typically submit data to the workflow and you might get a response, or you might use the workflow to kick off certain tasks or activities in your business process. The workflow can also persist itself during long-running transactions and then rehydrate on demand.

Two principal workflow types are built into Visual Studio 2008: sequential workflows and state-machine workflows. A sequential workflow follows a series of steps from top to bottom (as you design). Each step is gated based on the prior step and perhaps a set of conditions. A state-machine workflow, on the other hand, responds to different states (think status) being passed into the workflow. The states provide the gates between other states and may also trigger certain events.

You choose your workflow type at design type. There are both sequential and state-machine templates. Figure 1.35 shows an example of the workflow templates built into Visual Studio 2008. Notice also the SharePoint workflow templates. These provide the same workflows with extra hooks for SharePoint developers.

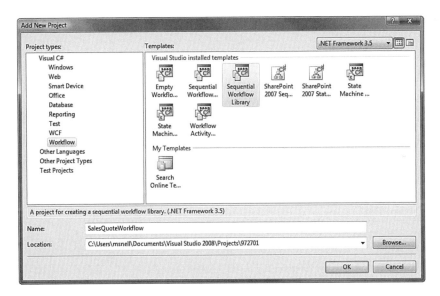

FIGURE 1.35   Creating a sequential workflow application.

Building a workflow is a very visual process. The thought behind this is that workflows themselves are traditionally illustrated as a set of steps (boxes) and connections (arrows). You still have access to code, but the designer provides a strong visual tool for building both sequential and state-machine workflows. With it, you can indicate a start and end point, add activities to the diagram, and configure each activity in terms of its task.

Figure 1.36 shows a sequential workflow inside Visual Studio. On the left are the workflow activity shapes. You use these to visually represent your workflow. Each shape has a set of properties that require developer configuration. This simple workflow example allows for the approval of a sales quote. There is an if/then condition set to determine whether the sales quote requires approval. If so, the quote waits (or listens) for approval. The quote is then either approved or rejected by a user. If the user does not respond in a timely manner, a timeout message is sent. You can follow this workflow through the visual representation in the diagram.

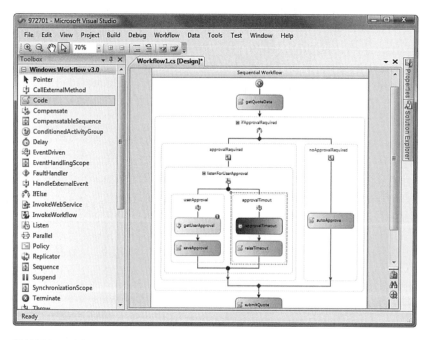

FIGURE 1.36    Designing a sequential workflow.

The workflow toolset also includes a basic rules and conditions editor. This editor allows you to set and manage workflow rules. These rules are then output as XML to be configured at runtime should the need arise. Figure 1.37 shows an example of the rules editor. In this dialog, the sales quote value condition from the previous example is being set. This condition is then attached to the if/then activity in the diagram.

**NOTE**

See Chapter 20, "Embedding Workflow in Your Applications," for a more detailed discussion of the Windows Workflow tools.

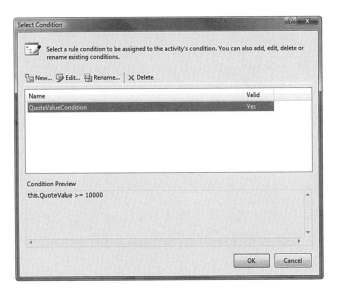

FIGURE 1.37   Defining workflow rules and conditions.

## Create and Consume Services

Most organizations have multiple systems, each designed for a specific purpose. They may have a financial system, HR, order management, inventory, customer service, and more. These applications each house specific business processes. However, most organizations need to unlock these business processes from their application and reuse them as part of an integrated solution. This is where service-oriented solutions have helped. By exposing an application's business process as a service, multiple clients can take advantage of that process.

The promise of code reuse has been with us a long time. However, service-oriented code reuse became very popular with the advent of web services. The ubiquitous nature of HTTP and port 80 coupled with XML-based interfaces allowed for a new level of communication between application boundaries. Developers began wrapping key business functions as services and calling them from multiple clients.

Visual Studio 2008 and the .NET Framework 3.5 represent another step forward in this service-oriented paradigm. With these tools, you can create services based on Microsoft's Windows Communication Foundation. WCF is a framework which recognizes that developers need multiple layers of communication (not just the SOAP protocol carried over an HTTP transport), require strong security, often need to support transactions, and do not want to write all the plumbing code to do so.

You create WCF services as a code library, as a workflow, or as a web service application. Figure 1.38 shows the new project templates listed under the WCF project types. From here you can indicate that your web service contains a workflow (think business process) or simply create a service library that will call custom code you write.

FIGURE 1.38    Selecting a WCF project type.

You can also still create .asmx web services through the web project templates. This same template area also provides access to the new, WCF Service Application template. With it, you can create a WCF service that is configured similarly to a web service.

WCF is all about configuration. It frees you from having to write all the service plumbing code. Instead, you can focus on the functionality of your service. For example, you can add service endpoints to your service depending on which communication stack you intend to support (HTTP, TCP/IP, MSMQ, Named Pipes, and so on). Figure 1.39 shows the WCF configuration editor. Notice how the binding support for an endpoint is a configuration (and not coding) task.

---

**NOTE**

See Chapter 19, "Service-Oriented Applications," for a more detailed discussion of the tools for Windows Communication Foundation and web services.

---

# Work with Data

Data is the domain of the business developer. It makes sense then that the number one tool and framework for business development continues to provide new and better ways of accessing and exposing that data. Data access is everywhere inside Visual Studio and the .NET Framework. Here we highlight some of the new things you will encounter in the 2008 version.

---

**NOTE**

Data access is covered in more detail in Chapter 18.

---

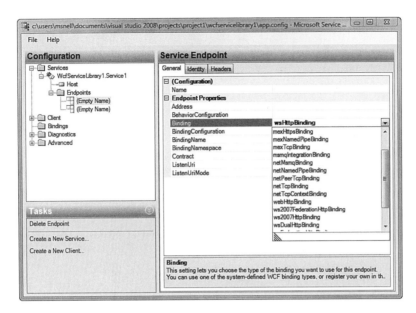

FIGURE 1.39    Configuration of a WCF service.

## Design Your Data

A typed dataset allows you to create a .NET class that is based on your database table semantics but works as a dataset behind the scenes. Typed datasets have been part of Visual Studio for a while now. You can auto-generate them based on table schemas and edit the code used to query, update, insert, and delete data.

Visual Studio 2008 provides additional design-time support for typed datasets. You can create a typed dataset file (.xsd) and use the Toolbox and Server Explorer to build the dataset. Figure 1.40 shows an example of this. Tables from the Server Explorer were added to the design surface to build the dataset.

In addition, the typed dataset in 2008 now supports hierarchical updates. This feature allows you to save data in multiple, related tables through the typed dataset. In Figure 1.40, this would mean you could edit both the employee details and the related territories and update as a single process.

## Map Objects to Relational Data

Most business applications rely on data that is stored in relational databases. Databases have a well-known structure of tables, columns, and relationships. This structure makes for a nice storage and reporting mechanism. However, there is often a mismatch between the needs of an object-oriented, .NET developer and the database technology. The object developer thinks in terms of objects, properties, methods, relationships, encapsulation, and the like. A lot of time is spent converting data from a database into an object-oriented structure and back again. In addition, developers are asked to write code in Structured Query Language (SQL) and .NET.

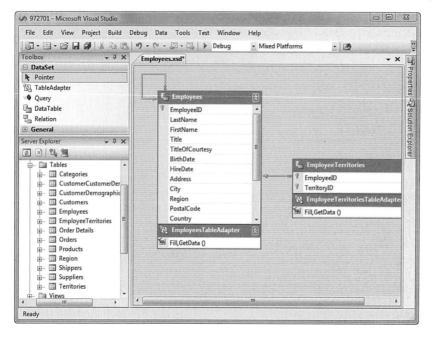

FIGURE 1.40    Building a typed dataset with the dataset designer.

LINQ, which we introduce in Chapter 3, is a technology that helps bridge this gap. It provides a means to work with database records as objects. It also allows you to write your queries using .NET (C# and VB). On top of LINQ is an object relational (O/R) designer for SQL Server called LINQ to SQL. With it, you can design and build .NET classes based on database schemas. In this way, you can quickly take database concepts and convert them to object-oriented ones.

You use a Visual Studio template to create a LINQ to SQL class. You can add such a class to any project type (web, Windows, class library, and so on). Figure 1.41 shows the Add New Item dialog with the LINQ to SQL Classes template selected.

You can then use the O/R Designer to build your LINQ class. You first use Server Explorer to open a connection to the database with which you are working. You can then drag and drop tables from the database onto the design surface. The designer understands (and enforces) the table relationships. It maps tables to classes and columns to properties.

Figure 1.42 shows an example of the designer. Here there is a customer class with an association link to the customer's orders. Notice also the methods listed on the right side of the diagram. These were created by dragging stored procedures from Server Explorer to the designer. A developer may now work with these classes and methods in a similar manner as they would with other .NET objects.

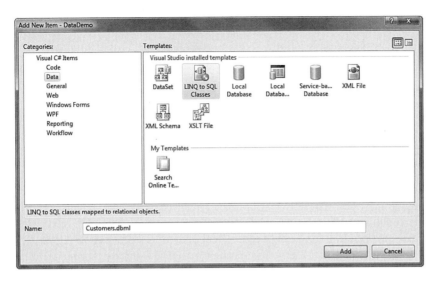

FIGURE 1.41   Creating a new LINQ to SQL class.

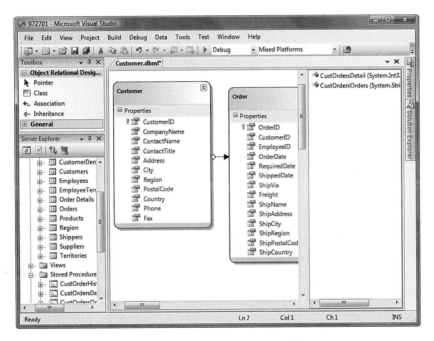

FIGURE 1.42   Mapping database relationships to objects.

## Build Occasionally Connected Applications

Many applications written these days require access to data both on- and offline. For example, you might need report data or customer service records when traveling or at a customer site. You cannot always rely on being connected. Developers have been dealing with this issue in various ways. The latest version of Visual Studio provides data synchronization services to provide a common, easy solution to this difficult problem.

Data synchronization allows you to synch and cache data between a central database and a user's client system. The cache is a version of SQL Server Compact Edition (CE). Microsoft is already taking advantage of these services in Vista, Office, and even their Zune software. You too can take advantage of these services in your applications.

Looking back at Figure 1.41, you will notice a template called Local Databa.... This template is actually called Local Database Cache. With it, you create a .sync file to configure how synchronization should happen between a local data store and a server. Opening the local database cache file in Visual Studio opens the Configure Data Synchronization dialog. Here you can set up tables that should be cached on a client, set up the server database, and configure the client database information. Figure 1.43 shows an example of this dialog.

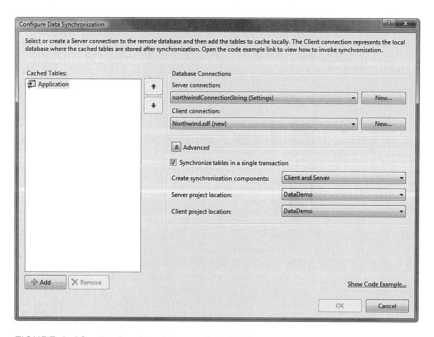

FIGURE 1.43    Configuring data synchronization.

The Cached Tables area of the Configure Data Synchronization dialog allows you to define which tables will be synchronized. Figure 1.44 shows an example of adding tables to this list. Here you configure how synchronization happens for each table. Synchronization services are discussed further in Chapter 18.

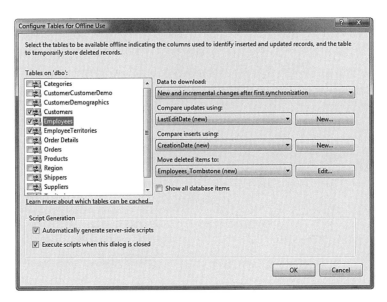

FIGURE 1.44    Adding and configuring table synchronization.

# The Visual Studio Product Line

Like the 2005 version, Visual Studio 2008 comes in many flavors; each is baked for a different appetite. There is a recipe targeted at the hobbyist to the enterprise architect, the beta tester to the operations guy—and, oh yeah, there are morsels for the developer too! Sorting through all the Visual Studio products and editions can be confusing. We hope the following aids you in your Visual Studio flavor selection.

## Express Editions

Microsoft offers the Visual Studio Express Editions on a per-language basis (VB, C#, C++, Web, SQL). These editions are free, downloadable, low-barrier to entry versions targeted directly at the novice, hobbyist, student, or anyone else looking to write some code without breaking the bank. There is even an edition targeted at video game developers. Along with the editions are tutorials, videos, sites, fun projects, and more.

The Express Edition can be seen as Microsoft's answer to all the "freeware" tools available to today's developers. After all, if you are a college student looking to put up a buddy's website, you are more likely to look for the low-cost solution. Of course, five years down the road when you're making decisions for your company, Microsoft wants to be sure you've had a chance to work with its products. The Expression Edition fits this niche nicely.

These editions purposely do not have all the power of their professional patriarch (a Class Designer, unit testing, enterprise templates, XSLT support, source code control, 64-bit support, and so on). However, they do have full language support (like LINQ) and access to the .NET Framework items like WPF.

The Express Editions also have a more streamlined user experience that does not expose the full complexity (or power) of the professional editions. However, developers will be able to create client/server form-based applications, websites, and even web services using these tools.

---

**NOTE**

For more information regarding the Visual Studio Express Editions or to download one of these editions, you can visit Microsoft's site at the following URL: http://www.microsoft.com/express/default.aspx.

---

## Standard Edition

The Standard version of Visual Studio is the base-level entry point for professional developers. This edition is similar in nature to the Express Editions. However, it contains all the .NET languages in a single package. In addition, it gives developers an expanded feature set over the Express versions. These additional capabilities include the following:

- Multiproject solution support

- Multitargeting support for working with .NET 2.0, 3.0, and 3.5

- Design support for creating Web, Windows, WPF, and Ajax User Experiences

- Database design tools for working with databases beyond SQL Express Edition

- Windows Communication Foundation (WCF) and Windows Workflow (WF) support

- Visual modeling via the visual Class Designer

- Support for XML editing including XSLT

- Click-once deployment tool

- Capability to write, record, and run macros

- Support for creating and using Visual Studio add-ins

- Conversion Wizard for converting legacy projects to 2008

- SQL Server 2005 Express included

- Compatibility with Visual Source Safe (VSS)

## Professional Edition

Most corporate developers and consultants will find a home within one of the professional editions of Visual Studio. In fact, you may already have a version of Visual Studio depending on what license you bought and when. Visual Studio Professional gives you all the language support (including VB, C#, C++), everything in the Standard Edition, and, of course, the whole host of new enhancements we've discussed in this chapter.

The primary differences between standard and professional (besides the MSDN packaging) is a set of features that you do not get in the standard edition. The following features ship only with the professional version (and above):

- ▶ Visual Studio Tools for Office (VSTO)

- ▶ SQL Server 2005 Developer Edition

- ▶ Capability to build software for mobile devices

- ▶ Class Designer and Object Test Bench

- ▶ Crystal Reports

- ▶ Unit Testing (no longer just a Team Edition feature)

- ▶ Server Explorer

Outside of these additional features, the Professional Edition is packaged as part of an MSDN subscription. Visual Studio Professional is packaged with various MSDN flavors. This change started with the 2005 version. You can now buy Visual Studio Professional as follows (listed from the fewest features/applications to the most):

- ▶ **Visual Studio Professional only (without MSDN)**—Includes just Visual Studio Professional as discussed.

- ▶ **Visual Studio Professional with MSDN Professional**—Includes Visual Studio as discussed. In addition, you get access to older versions of Visual Studio. You also get Visual Source Safe. The MSDN subscription provides developer licenses for Windows and Window Server, Virtual PC, SDKs, driver development kits, and more. You also get two technical support incidents and access to managed newsgroups.

- ▶ **Visual Studio Professional with MSDN Premium**—Includes all the preceding with the following extras: includes Expression Web and Blend; adds developer licenses for SQL Server and other application platforms (BizTalk, Commerce Server, and many more); provides licenses for working with Microsoft Dynamics (GP, CRM, POS, and so on); includes licenses for Microsoft Office Systems 2007 (including Visio, Groove, Word, Excel, and many more).

**NOTE**

For more information regarding the professional editions of Visual Studio, you can visit Microsoft's site at the following URL: http://msdn2.microsoft.com/en-us/subscriptions/ aa718657.aspx.

## Team Systems

Team Systems is a set of integrated, software development life-cycle tools. Microsoft released the first versions of its Team Systems products in 2005. These included versions of Visual Studio targeted at various members of the software development life cycle. In the middle is a centralized management and reporting server called Team Foundation Server. By all accounts, these tools were a great success. Microsoft has built on this success with the release of Visual Studio Team Systems 2008.

### The Client Tools

The Visual Studio Team System editions are targeted to roles within the software development life cycle. These roles include developer, architect, tester, and database developer. In addition, there are client access licenses available for project managers and other interested parties. However, the aforementioned roles each represent versions of Team Systems that can be purchased.

It's important to note that each role-based version of Team Systems comes with Visual Studio 2008 Professional. It also comes with MSDN Premium (as defined previously). The Team System client tools also give you access to the central Team Foundation Server (purchased separately). What makes each of these products unique and significant, however, is what additional goodies they do and do not contain. The intent is a targeted set of tools to different roles on the project. The following list outlines the features that drive these products to their target users:

- **Visual Studio Team System Development Edition**—Targeted at most developers, this version includes static code analysis, code profiling, dynamic code analysis, code metrics, code analysis check-in policies, unit testing, and code coverage analysis. These tools help developers with verifying, testing, and checking their code against common issues.

- **Visual Studio Team System Database Edition**—Targeted at developers who need to work closely with and manage database development, this edition enables you to create database projects, generate sample data, compare schemas, compare data, do database-level unit testing, and more.

- **Visual Studio Team System Architect Edition**—Designed for the software architect, this product improves design and design validation of distributed systems. Features include the System Designer, Application Designer, Logical Datacenter Designer, Deployment Designer, and a Settings and Constraints Editor.

- **Visual Studio Team System Test Edition**—Targeted at the software tester, this edition includes the capability to create unit tests and see code coverage analysis. Its real strength for testers, however, is its capability to manage and create web, load, manual, generic, and ordered tests. In addition, there is the Team System 2008 Test Load Agent. This is a separate product that works with Team Test to generate massive load for various load-testing scenarios.

- **Visual Studio Team Suite**—For those who must have it all (and have unlimited budgets), this product is the everything-but-the-kitchen-sink option. It includes all the features of Team Architect, Developer, Database Developer, and Test in a single package. Microsoft also understands that there are those among our ranks who can't stand to not have it all. For them, Microsoft has created Team Suite—the full IDE experience that transcends all team roles.

> **NOTE**
>
> We cover Team Systems features in great depth in Part VI of this book, "Visual Studio Team System."

### The Server

Team Foundation Server (TFS) is at the center of Team Systems. While the client tools enable great functionality, the server allows you to assign work, report statistics, and track the overall health of your project. Project information is synchronized among architects, developers, testers, project managers, and operations.

The functionality behind Team Foundation Server revolves around project management and source control. Project management and tracking are accomplished through work items. A *work item* can be a task on the project, an issue or bug, a software requirement, a feature, or a test scenario. In general, a work item represents a generic unit of work on the project. Of course, work items are customizable and can have states, new fields, and business rules associated with them. Work items can also be driven by a methodology. Finally, work items play a central part in ensuring project team communication and reporting.

The source control features in Team Foundation Server include enterprise-class features such as change sets, shelving, automatic build rules, the capability to associate work items to changed source, parallel development, a source control policy engine, branching, checkpoints, and more.

Surrounding these project management and source control features are a build management engine, a reporting infrastructure, and a project portal. The build tools allow for both automatic, scheduled builds and on-demand builds. Builds are reported against, documented, automatically tested, and analyzed for code coverage and churn (as an example). The reporting engine and project portal combine to further enhance the view into the project by team members. Built on Windows SharePoint Services (WSS), it delivers the latest test and build reports, documentation, announcements, and quality analysis.

> **NOTE**
>
> You purchase TFS as you would any other Microsoft Server product (such as Microsoft SQL Server or Microsoft BizTalk Server). For more information on licensing TFS, see http://msdn2.microsoft.com/en-us/vsts2008/products/bb933758.aspx.

## The Expression Tools

A sister product line to Visual Studio is the new Microsoft Expression tools. These will, undoubtedly, get a lot of attention in upcoming releases. The tools are targeted at designers' build applications on the Microsoft platform. They offer rich design experiences for building Web, Windows, and Silverlight applications. The tools are also built to enable workflow between designers and developers.

It is important that you are aware of these tools so that you know where you might use them and because they work with Visual Studio projects and project files and offer some similar capabilities (but in different ways). A high-level overview of these tools is listed here:

▶ **Expression Blend**—Used to create WPF interfaces based on XAML. You can also use it to create Silverlight applications.

▶ **Expression Design**—Allows a designer to create vector-based illustrations that include drawing, text, and more.

▶ **Expression Web**—A design tool for creating ASP.NET Web Forms and websites.

▶ **Expression Encoder**—A tool for encoding video and audio and publishing the same to Silverlight applications.

▶ **Expression Media**—A tool for organizing and managing design assets (files) into visual catalogs.

▶ **Expression Studio**—Includes the full set of Expression tools. For those designers who need it all.

**NOTE**

For more information on the Expression products (not covered further in this book), see http://www.microsoft.com/expression/default.aspx.

# Summary

A new release of Visual Studio means a lot to all the various development camps out there. Visual Studio touches developers who write code in C++, C#, Visual Basic, and many other languages. Literally millions of developers boot up and launch their favorite tool every day. They spend the vast majority of their working hours, days, weeks, and months architecting and building solutions with the tool. This chapter oriented you to some of the many new possibilities available with this latest version.

CHAPTER 2

# A Quick Tour of the IDE

When you're traveling on unfamiliar ground, it's often wise to consult a tour guide. At a minimum, a quick check of the map is in order before you set out for new adventures. The same holds true for approaching a new development tool the size and breadth of Visual Studio 2008. It is wise to familiarize yourself a bit with the tool before starting that first project off on the wrong foot.

This chapter is meant to be your quick, to-the-point guide. It serves to orient you before you set out. We'll cover the basics of installation; booting up the IDE; and getting to know the layout of the tool in terms of projects, editors, and designers. Let's get started.

## Installing Visual Studio

The installation of Visual Studio 2008 remains similar to that of previous versions. The application plays host to many tools. Depending on your purchase, a subset of these items will be available for your selection during install (see Chapter 1, "A Quick Tour of Visual Studio 2008"). If you are fortunate enough to own the Team Suite Edition, you'll be presented with the full set of options. Figure 2.1 shows the setup options selection dialog box for Visual Studio Professional.

### Choosing a Language

Setting up your development machine should be relatively straightforward. We suggest that the ordinary developer keep language installs to a primary language and perhaps one backup. You might use a secondary language for viewing sample code from MSDN or similar sites. Typically, this means if your primary language is Visual Basic, you install C# as a secondary language (and vice versa). This solves the problem of finding a great bit of code you want to embed in your project only to discover it's not available in your chosen language. Additionally, Visual Studio 2008 lets you configure your primary language (see the next section). Choosing to install many languages, most of which you do not intend to use, not only takes up hard drive space, but also can clutter your environment with too many choices. We do, however, recommend installing the full MSDN help system. There is always a possibility of finding a solution to a problem you are having inside an item targeted at a different language.

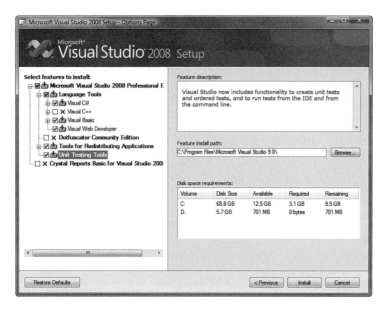

FIGURE 2.1    Visual Studio 2008 Setup Options page.

## Configuring Your Development Environment

Booting the new IDE for the first time will result in a dialog box asking you to choose your environment settings. As Visual Studio becomes the central tool for so many developers, testers, architects, and even project managers, it's harder and harder to satisfy them all with a single tool. To aid in this dilemma, Microsoft has created an entire set of environment settings that are configured for the usual developer type. For instance, if you set your environment to C#, the New Project dialog box will automatically highlight C# projects above other languages. Figure 2.2 shows the available options.

Only your first use of Visual Studio will launch the default settings dialog box. On subsequent visits, you'll go straight to the tool. However, you might consider switching your environment settings if you do a lot of switching from one language to another or if you switch roles. For example, C# developers might use the C# development settings most of the time. They might then toggle to the Tester or Project Management Settings if they intend to do a lot of testing for the project.

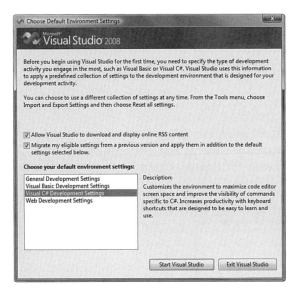

FIGURE 2.2    The Environment Settings options dialog box.

You manage your environment settings from the Tools menu's Import and Export Settings option. Figure 2.3 shows the first screen in this wizard. This screen allows you to choose to execute either a settings export or an import.

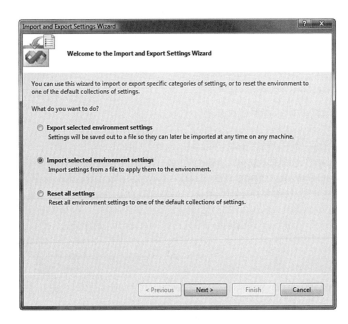

FIGURE 2.3    The Import and Export Settings Wizard.

**TIP**

If you are like most developers, you are probably particular about your environment setup. There is nothing worse than having to work on a machine that has a different IDE configuration. You can be thankful that you can use the Import and Export Settings Wizard to take your IDE settings with you.

You can choose from several setting collections when importing. There are a few default collections, including those based on language and role (such as web developer and tester). In addition, you can browse to a custom settings file. Figure 2.4 shows the import settings collection options.

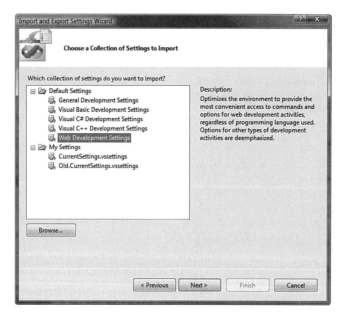

FIGURE 2.4    Choosing a collection of settings for import.

Another key screen to the Import and Export Settings Wizard is the settings selection screen. On this screen, you decide which options are important for import. This allows you to pick and choose settings you plan to import. For example, you may love the way a friend has configured her code editor in terms of font and contrasting colors, but you do not want all her other settings, such as her keyboard configurations. Figure 2.5 provides a glimpse at the granular level to which you can manage your environment settings.

**TIP**

A great feature of the import and export settings tool is the capability to move help favorites. These favorites are abstracted from your default web browser favorites. In addition, they can travel with you from machine to machine, so you do not have to spend valuable development time digging through the help file for a particularly important topic.

FIGURE 2.5   Choosing settings to import.

# The Start Page

When you first get into the Visual Studio 2008 IDE, you are presented with the Start Page for the tool. This feature looked promising in previous versions but now seems to be actually useful in Visual Studio 2008. Figure 2.6 shows an example of the new Start Page.

The Start Page contains a number of web parts. Starting from the upper left, there is the Recent Projects area. From here, you can launch a project you were recently working on or create a new one. Moving down, you see the Getting Started area. This web part is useful if you are looking for learning opportunities with the tool. This can be a great place to set out exploring with a starter kit, what's new, or the "How do I...?" question-and-answer section. Below this is the headlines area for Visual Studio. Here, you are notified of recent releases or can provide feedback to Microsoft yourself. Finally, in the middle of the page are the headlines and offers from MSDN. This area can be useful to peruse at project startup—especially if you find yourself spending too much time on the project and feel yourself losing touch with the goings-on in the development world.

## Startup Options

If you just don't like the Start Page or prefer to launch directly into the project you'll be spending the next few months of your life working on, you can customize what happens when the IDE boots. From the Options dialog box (Tools, Options), choose the Environment node and then the Startup leaf. Figure 2.7 shows some of the options available at startup.

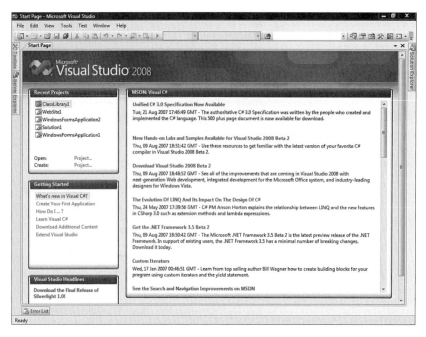

FIGURE 2.6    The Visual Studio 2008 Start Page.

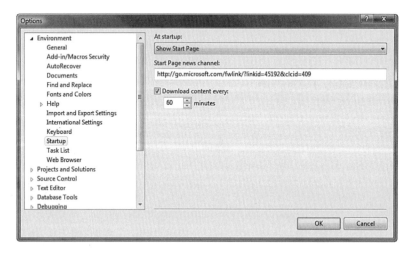

FIGURE 2.7    Startup options.

From here, you can configure where to get your start page news items. You can also tell the environment to load the last solution, show the new or open project dialog boxes, open your browser's home page, or do nothing (show an empty environment). You can also configure how often your content is automatically refreshed from the server.

# Your First Project

The next, natural step is to create your first project. Doing so will quickly expose you to some of the basic project and file management features within the IDE. From the File menu, you're given the option to create a new project or website. Projects are simply templates that group files for Windows, Office, mobile, and similar executable applications (see Chapter 4, "Solutions and Projects"). You can also create web projects that you mix with other compiled projects. A website creates a set of web files that get promoted and managed as files (and not complied code).

Figure 2.8 shows a sample website inside the IDE. We chose C# as the target language of this website. Notice that the IDE layout is relatively generic. You should expect a similar experience for your first few applications (until you've customized things). In the following sections, we will break down the many items on this screen; it might be useful to refer to this graphic to provide overall context as we discuss a given item.

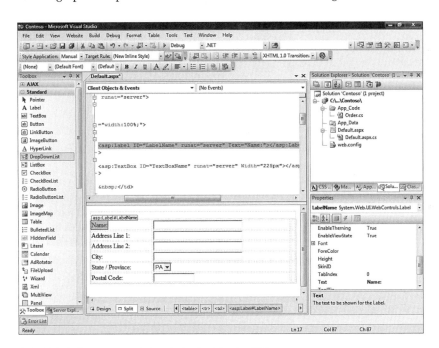

FIGURE 2.8    A basic C# website inside the IDE.

# The Menu Bar

If you've been working with previous versions, you should find the Visual Studio 2008 menu bar to be standard fare. It is very intuitive; options are where you'd expect them; and new menus appear depending on your place within the IDE, the tools you've chosen to install, and your default language. For example, a Refactor menu appears when you are in the C# code editor; the Project menu shows up when you have a project open; and the

File menu configures itself differently depending on Visual Basic or C#. Table 2.1 lists (from left to right across the IDE) some of the more common menus, along with a description of each.

---

**NOTE**

Note that each menu screenshot in Table 2.1 was taken using the C# menu default settings. In each case, Visual Basic has an equivalent, albeit slightly different, menu. In addition, the keyboard shortcut callouts in the menu items are also those of C#. Visual Basic developers will recognize a lot of them as the same. All of them can be customized to an individual developer's preference.

---

TABLE 2.1    Visual Studio 2008 Menus

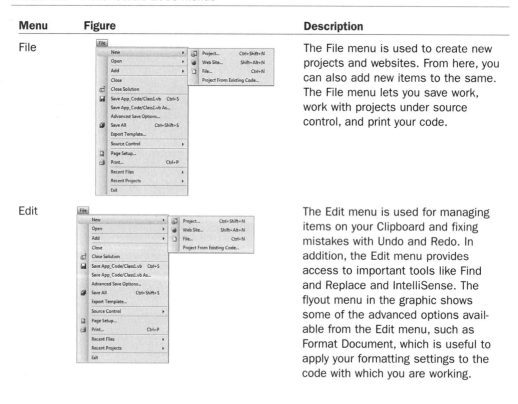

| Menu | Figure | Description |
|------|--------|-------------|
| File | | The File menu is used to create new projects and websites. From here, you can also add new items to the same. The File menu lets you save work, work with projects under source control, and print your code. |
| Edit | | The Edit menu is used for managing items on your Clipboard and fixing mistakes with Undo and Redo. In addition, the Edit menu provides access to important tools like Find and Replace and IntelliSense. The flyout menu in the graphic shows some of the advanced options available from the Edit menu, such as Format Document, which is useful to apply your formatting settings to the code with which you are working. |

TABLE 2.1   Continued

| Menu | Figure | Description |
|------|--------|-------------|
| View | | The View menu provides access to the multitude of windows available in Visual Studio. If you lose your way (or window) in the tool, the View menu is the best place to look to find your bearings. From here, you can access the Server Explorer, Solution Explorer, Task List, and other key windows of the IDE. The flyout menu shows the Other Windows option—the many, many windows of Visual Studio 2008. |
| Refactor | | The Refactor menu (C# only) provides access to options such as renaming code elements, extracting code from a method to a new method, and promoting local variables to parameters. See Chapter 9, "Refactoring Code," for more information on refactoring. |
| Website | | The Website menu is available only when you're working with web applications. It provides access to add new items, add references to your web application, copy your website to a deployment location, and work with project dependencies. You can also set the start page for the application and access ASP.NET configuration options for the given website. |
| Project | | The Project menu is similar to the Website menu but is available to non–web-based projects. From here, you can add new items and references to your projects, set the startup project, and change the build order for projects in your solution. In addition, you can access the Properties for a given project. This will allow you to set things such as the version of the .NET Framework you are targeting, the default namespace, and many more items. |

TABLE 2.1   Continued

| Menu | Figure | Description |
|------|--------|-------------|
| Build | 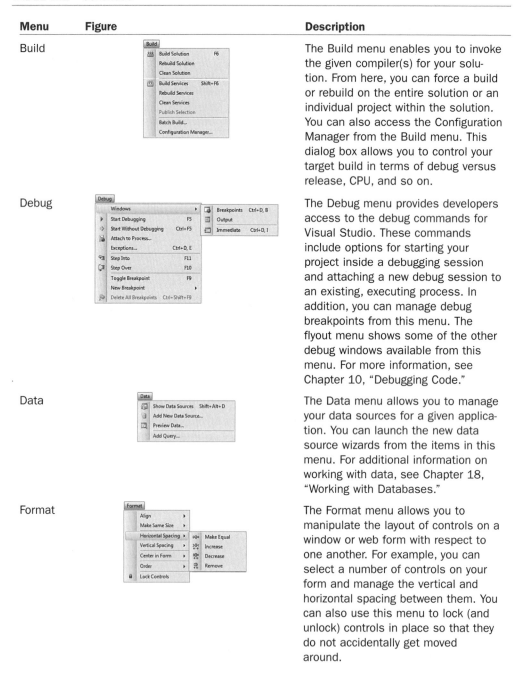 | The Build menu enables you to invoke the given compiler(s) for your solution. From here, you can force a build or rebuild on the entire solution or an individual project within the solution. You can also access the Configuration Manager from the Build menu. This dialog box allows you to control your target build in terms of debug versus release, CPU, and so on. |
| Debug | | The Debug menu provides developers access to the debug commands for Visual Studio. These commands include options for starting your project inside a debugging session and attaching a new debug session to an existing, executing process. In addition, you can manage debug breakpoints from this menu. The flyout menu shows some of the other debug windows available from this menu. For more information, see Chapter 10, "Debugging Code." |
| Data | | The Data menu allows you to manage your data sources for a given application. You can launch the new data source wizards from the items in this menu. For additional information on working with data, see Chapter 18, "Working with Databases." |
| Format | | The Format menu allows you to manipulate the layout of controls on a window or web form with respect to one another. For example, you can select a number of controls on your form and manage the vertical and horizontal spacing between them. You can also use this menu to lock (and unlock) controls in place so that they do not accidentally get moved around. |

TABLE 2.1    Continued

| Menu | Figure | Description |
|------|--------|-------------|
| Tools | | The Tools menu provides access to many of the tools that ship with Visual Studio. This includes managing Visual Studio Add-Ins and Macros that extend your environment (see flyout menu). You can also access tools for performance, connecting to other servers and applications, and managing your IDE settings. The items in this tool menu are covered in depth throughout the book. |
| Table | | The Table menu (available when in design view for a web form) is used exclusively for adding and manipulating tables on a web form. From here, you can create a new table, insert rows into an existing table, and resize table items. |
| Test | | The Test menu enables you to manage tests in Visual Studio. For example, you can use options on this menu to create a new test, manage existing tests, and measure test effectiveness. You can also launch test runs from here. See Chapter 28, "Test Edition," for more information on testing with Visual Studio. |
| Window | | The Window menu allows you to manage the open windows in the IDE. You can hide windows, close all open windows, and turn an existing window such as the Solution Explorer from a docked window into a tabbed document. |

TABLE 2.1    Continued

| Menu | Figure | Description |
|------|--------|-------------|
| Help | | The Help menu provides direct access to all the help options available from Visual Studio. For example, you can turn on dynamic help from the Help menu; doing so will have the IDE tracking your context and providing help as you need it. The Help menu also takes you to the MSDN forums, and lets you report a bug, review samples, and more. Finally, you can check for updates from here and, of course, access the help library. |

The Figure column for Help shows a menu with the following items:

Help
- How Do I            Ctrl+F1, H
- Search              Ctrl+F1, S
- Contents            Ctrl+F1, C
- Index               Ctrl+F1, I
- Help Favorites      Ctrl+F1, F
- Dynamic Help        Ctrl+F1, D
- Index Results       Ctrl+F1, T
- MSDN Forums
- Report a Bug
- Samples
- Customer Feedback Options...
- Register Product
- Check for Updates
- Technical Support
- About Microsoft Visual Studio

# The Many Toolbars

Visual Studio 2008 includes more than 30 toolbars. If you use a set of commands often, there is a good chance that there is a matching toolbar to group those commands. As a result, a large percentage of the toolbars are highly specialized. For example, if you are working with the Class Designer, you would, of course, use the Class Designer toolbar to manage class groups or change screen magnification. Or if you are building a SQL Query, you would use the Query Designer toolbar. We will not cover each of these toolbars here because they are highly specialized. Instead, we will stick to a quick tour and cover the common ground here and save the sidetracks for the upcoming chapters.

## The Standard Toolbar

The Standard toolbar is present at all times during your IDE sessions (unless, of course, you customize things or turn it off). It provides quick access to all the commands you'll use over and over. The standard commands are on the top left: Create New Project, Add New Item, Open, and Save. These are followed by Cut, Copy, Paste, and Undo. Figure 2.9 shows the Standard toolbar undocked from the IDE.

**TIP**

We suggest you learn the keyboard equivalents for such standard commands as Cut, Copy, Past, Undo, and the like. You can then remove these toolbar icons from the toolbar to save precious screen real estate for commands that have you reaching for the mouse anyway (and have harder-to-remember shortcut keys).

FIGURE 2.9    The Standard toolbar in Visual Studio 2008.

Additional items worth mentioning include the two navigation commands on the toolbar. These are the icons that look like a document (or code file) with a blue arrow on them. One icon's arrow points left and the other's points right. These navigation buttons allow you to move backward and forward through your code and your solution. They keep track of special lines in your code or windows you have visited and provide one-click access up and down this line.

The button to the right of the navigation commands (the one that is a green arrow) is often called the Run or Play button. This will initiate a build of your project and launch you into debug mode. Moving to the right (downward in the graphic), you see options for initiating a search within your code. This capability can be handy for quickly finding the place where you left off or the place you are looking for. To the right of this are icons for quick access to displaying one of the many windows of Visual Studio. Just as with the View menu, these icons give you quick access to the Solution Explorer, Properties window, Object Browser, Toolbox, and so on. You even have an icon for Other Windows, which gives access to even more windows.

## Customizing Toolbars

In the event that the standard toolbars that ship with Visual Studio don't meet your needs, you can create custom ones that do. To do so, you select the Tool menu's Customize item or right-click a toolbar in the IDE and select Customize. This launches the Customize dialog as shown in Figure 2.10. From here, you select which toolbars to show, indicate icon size for toolbar items, turn on and off tips and shortcut keys, and more.

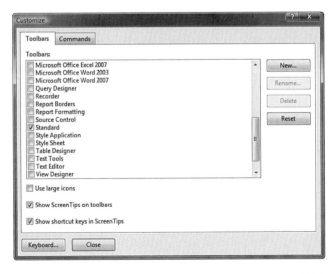

FIGURE 2.10   The Customize dialog in Visual Studio 2008.

To customize a toolbar, first make sure the Customize dialog is open. Then simply grab toolbar items (icons) and move them around and delete them as necessary. You can also use the Commands tab (see Figure 2.11) to add specific commands to a given toolbar. If things get messed up, you can use the Reset button from the Toolbars tab to revert to the default state.

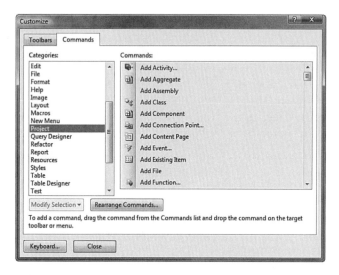

FIGURE 2.11   The Customize dialog's Commands tab.

The New button enables you to create new toolbars to group existing commands. This gives you a great deal of customization options. Once it's clicked, you name your new toolbar and use the Commands tab to add items. You can also drag commands off other toolbars and place them on your new one.

You can also configure your keyboard shortcut combinations from the Customize dialog. Use the Keyboard button to bring up the Options dialog to the environment's keyboard options screen. Figure 2.12 shows an example. First, you find a command in the list; next, you press a shortcut key to map (or remap) a combination. Notice that if the option is already assigned a shortcut key, Visual Studio warns you before you make the reassignment.

We recommend that you do some of your own exploration into the many toolbars (and toolbar customization options) within Visual Studio. Often their usefulness presents itself only at the right moment. For instance, if you are editing a Windows form, having the Layout toolbar available to tweak the position of controls relative to one another can be a very valuable timesaver. Knowing that these toolbars are available will increase the likelihood that you'll benefit from their value.

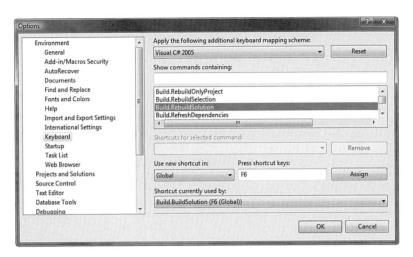

FIGURE 2.12   Options dialog keyboard assignments.

# The Toolbox

The Visual Studio 2008 Toolbox provides access to the many controls when you're building both Web and Windows forms. It also provides access to nearly anything that can be
dragged onto one of the many designers used for creating forms, XML schemas, classes,
and more. As an example, if you are building a web form, the Toolbox provides the many
controls, grouped for easier access, which can be added to the form. New for 2008 are the
AJAX controls. These are used for creating rich, browser-based applications (covered in
Chapter 17, "Creating Rich Browser Applications"). Furthermore, if you are working with a
text editor, the Toolbox allows you to save clips of text for quick access.

Figure 2.13 shows the Toolbox in a standard configuration (undocked from the IDE) for
building a web form. Note that the "Standard" group of controls is closed up to highlight
some additional control groups. Note that these controls are covered throughout the
book. They are first covered in Chapter 6, "Introducing the Editors and Designers."
However, the bulk are covered in Chapter 14, "Creating ASP.NET Applications," and
Chapter 15, "Building Windows Forms Applications."

## TIP

You can customize the Toolbox to your liking. For example, you can add your own
groups (called *tabs*). You can also configure the Toolbox to show more icons on the
screen at a time. As you familiarize yourself with the various standard controls, you can
turn off their text descriptions and simply show them as icons. To do so, right-click the
control group (tab) and uncheck List View. Figure 2.14 illustrates the additional screen
real estate you will gain in doing so.

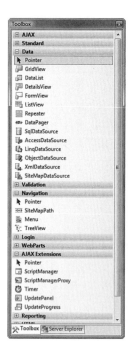

FIGURE 2.13    The Visual Studio Toolbox configured for a web form.

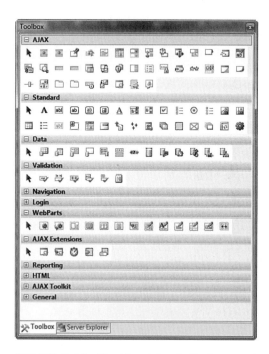

FIGURE 2.14    The Visual Studio Toolbox configured for more screen real estate.

# The Visual Designers

Visual Designers are the canvases that you work on using the mouse to create items such as forms via drag, drop, move, resize, and the like. Visual Studio 2008 ships with many such Visual Designers. Together, they allow you to build the items that make up your application (and understanding of it). Items include Windows forms, web forms, class diagrams, XML schemas, and more.

The Visual Designers all work mostly the same way. First, they take center stage within the IDE as tabbed windows surrounded by various menus, toolbars, and panes. Second, you use the Toolbox as your palette to place items on the designer. You then configure each item's many properties using the Properties window.

Figure 2.15 shows the Windows Forms Designer in action (the middle, highlighted tab). Note that the Toolbox is on the left and the Properties window is on the bottom right. Additionally, many of the designers have their own toolbars. Note that this graphic that the Layout toolbar is shown when you're working with forms. This allows you to easily position controls relative to one another. We will cover the majority of the visual designers in depth in the coming chapters. You can also get a better overview from Chapter 6, "Introducing the Editors and Designers."

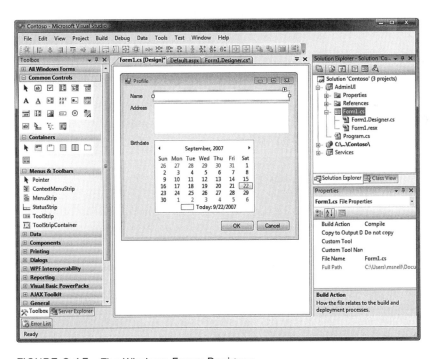

FIGURE 2.15    The Windows Forms Designer.

# The Text Editors

Visual Studio 2008 has several text editors or word (code) processors. Each text editor is based on a common core that provides the basic set of functionality for each editor such as the selection margin, the capability to collapse nested items, and colorization. Each editor derives from this core and is customized to give you the editors for code (C#, VB, and so on), the XML editor, the HTML (or aspx) editor, and the style sheet editor.

## The Code Editors

The code editor, for our money, is where the magic happens. It is here that you get down to business leveraging your favorite language to define objects and their functionality. Of course, you can write code outside the Visual Studio editor, but why would you? You can also write a novel using Notepad or do your taxes by hand. A good code editor means higher productivity, plain and simple. And Visual Studio has some of the best code editors around.

The code editor is front and center when you're working on code. It handles indentation and whitespace to make your code clean and readable. It provides IntelliSense and statement completion to free you from having to look up (or memorize) every object library and keyword. It groups code into blocks; it provides color codes for keywords and comments; it highlights errors; it shows new code relative to previously compiled code. All in all, the Visual Studio code editor does quite a bit to keep you productive.

### The C# Code Editor

Figure 2.16 shows the C# code editor. Some items to note include the following:

▶ The code is grouped into logical sections along the left side. You can use the minus signs to close up a whole class, method, property, or similar group. This capability allows you to hide code you are not working on at the moment. You can also create your own custom, named regions to do the same thing.

▶ New code is signaled inside the section groups with a colored line. Yellow is used for new code that has yet to be saved. The highlighted line turns green after a save and disappears after you close and reopen the file. This feature allows you (and the editor) to track where you have made changes to code during your current session.

▶ The name of the open code file is listed as the code window's tab across the top. The asterisk indicates that the code has changed since the last time it was saved.

▶ IntelliSense is invoked as you type. You can use the arrow keys to quickly find the item in the list. Hovering over the item shows details for the given item (tip text to the right). You can press the Tab key to complete the item from IntelliSense.

▶ The code is highlighted in various colors. By default, keywords are blue, comments are green, text is black, types you create are light blue, string values are red, and so on.

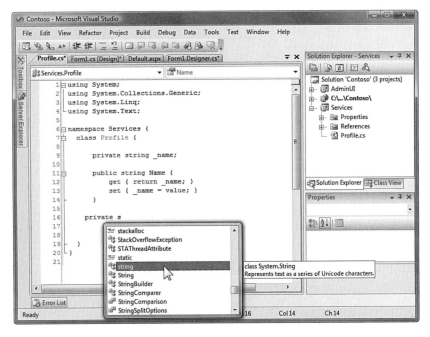

**FIGURE 2.16**   The C# code editor.

▶ The two drop-downs at the top of the code editor allow you to navigate between the classes in the file (left-side drop-down) and methods, fields, and properties within a given class (right-side drop-down).

### The Visual Basic Code Editor

The Visual Basic code editor works much the same way as the C# editor. Figure 2.17 shows the same code as in Figure 2.16 written inside the Visual Basic code editor. Some of the differences between the editors are as listed here:

▶ Horizontal lines are used to separate methods and properties within the editor.

▶ The IntelliSense drop-down list is filtered into a common subset and all the possible values.

▶ The code navigation drop-downs at the top of the code editor allow you to navigate the entire, active object hierarchy (including events). The left-side drop-down shows namespaces, objects, and events. The right-side drop-down shows all methods for the given type, including those you have not yet overridden. The items you have implemented are highlighted as bold within the list.

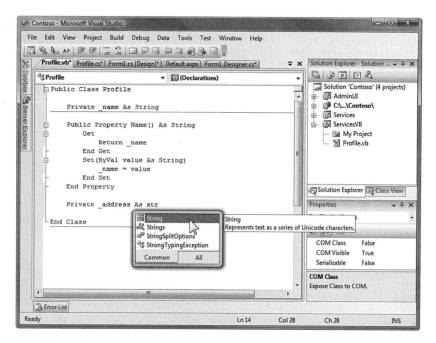

FIGURE 2.17    The Visual Basic code editor.

## Editor Customizations

Nearly every aspect of the text and code editors can be customized to your every whim. From our experience, it seems no two developers see their code the same way. You can use the Options dialog (Tools, Options) to change the editor's background color or the color and font of various text within the editor. You can also turn on line numbering, and manage indenting (tabs) and whitespace. The full list of customizations for the text editor is large. You can set language and editor-specific options.

Figure 2.18 shows the Options dialog box set for Fonts and Colors. From here, you can tweak the many display items in the editor in terms of their color, font, and font size.

If you dig a little deeper in the Options dialog box, you will come across the Text Editor node in the option tree. From here, you can manipulate even more settings for the text editor. For example, you can remove the horizontal procedure separators in the Visual Basic editor or turn off the automatic reformatting of code by the editor.

Even better, you can control how the editor automatically formats your code inside the C# editor. If you like to see all your curly braces on separate lines or prefer them to start on the line that starts the block, you can do so from here. Figure 2.19 shows some of the options available for formatting C# inside the editor.

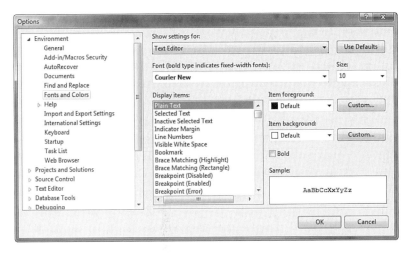

FIGURE 2.18    The Options dialog box set to Fonts and Colors.

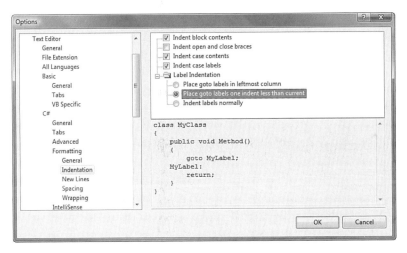

FIGURE 2.19    Controlling code formatting from the Options dialog box.

# The Solution Explorer

The Solution Explorer allows you to group and manage the many files that make up your application. A solution simply contains multiple projects (applications). A project groups files related to its type. For instance, you can create a website, Windows Form application, class library, console application, and more. The files inside the project containers represent your code in terms of forms, class files, XML, and other related items.

The Solution Explorer is the place where you typically start when adding a new item (class, image, form) to your application. It is also used to access these items. Double-clicking an item in the Solution Explorer opens the given designer or editor associated with the type of file you request. For example, opening a file with the extension .cs opens the C# code editor. Finally, you also use the Solution Explorer during source control scenarios to check items in and out of the source database.

Figure 2.20 shows the Solution Explorer undocked from the IDE. Note that a single solution is open (that is the limit), and the solution contains a few applications (called *projects*). One is a Windows form application (AdminUI); another is a website (Contoso); the project at the bottom is a class library (Services). The Solution Explorer is covered in depth in Chapter 4, "Solutions and Projects."

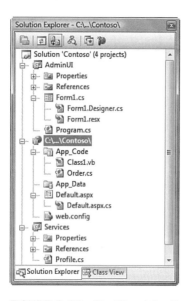

FIGURE 2.20   The Visual Studio 2008 Solution Explorer.

# The Properties Window

It seems that with every new release and every new tool, programming becomes less and less about writing code and more and more about dragging, dropping, and configuring. The many tools, controls, and rich designers that free us from the repetitive code also now require our attention in the form of maintenance. This work is typically done through the manipulation of the literally hundreds of properties that work in concert to define our application. This is where the Properties window comes into play. It allows us to control the size, appearance, and behavior of our controls. Furthermore, the Properties window groups common properties into sets for easier access. Finally, the Properties window also gives us access to connecting the events for a given control to the code inside our application.

Figure 2.21 shows the Properties window (undocked from the IDE) for a button control. Note that, by default, the window groups similar properties into sections via banded categories, such as Appearance. You can turn off this capability and list properties in alphabetic order by clicking the AZ icon on the property toolbar. Another item worth noting is the lightning bolt icon also on the toolbar. This gives you access to the events for the given control.

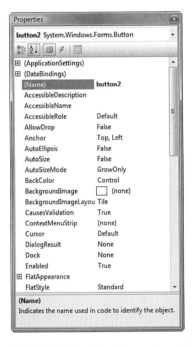

FIGURE 2.21   The Properties window in Visual Studio 2008.

# Managing the Many Windows of the IDE

To round out our whirlwind tour, we thought it important to provide you guidance on customizing and managing the plethora of windows available within the IDE (lest they leave you with a postage-stamp-size window in which to write your code). To manage these windows, you really need to know only two skills: pinning and docking.

## Pinning

*Pinning* refers to the process of making a window stick in the open position. It is called pinning in reference to the visual cue you use to perform the act: a pushpin (refer to the Toolbox title bar in Figure 2.22). Pinning is imperative because you sometimes want full-screen real estate for writing code or designing a form. In this case, you should unpin (hide) the various extraneous windows in your IDE. Note that when a window is unpinned, a vertical tab represents the window (see the Solution Explorer tab in

Figure 2.22). Moving the mouse near this tab will result in the window unfolding for your use. After you use it, however, it will go back to its hiding spot.

Alternatively, you might be working to drop controls on that form. In doing so, you might want to pin (stick open) the Toolbox window (see Figure 2.22). This keeps open just the window you are working with and closes everything else.

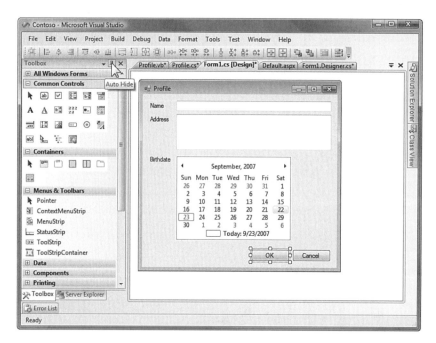

FIGURE 2.22    Pinned and unpinned windows in the IDE.

## Docking

*Docking* is the process of connecting windows to various sticky spots within the IDE. Typically, this means docking to the left, top, right, or bottom of the IDE. For example, the Toolbox is, by default, docked to the left side of the IDE. You may prefer to put it at the bottom of the screen, docked below the active designer (see Figure 2.23).

You can also dock windows to one another. For example, you may want to dock the Properties window below the Solution Explorer. Or you may want the Properties window to be a tab within the same window to which the Solution Explorer is docked (see Figure 2.23).

To help with docking, Visual Studio 2008 has revamped the visual cues and helpers that first appeared in 2005. First, you start with a pinned window (you cannot dock unpinned windows). You click and hold the title bar with the mouse. You then drag the window to where you want to dock it. Visual Studio will display some docking icons.

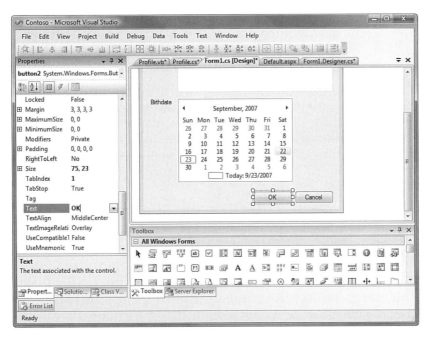

FIGURE 2.23   Some docking options in the IDE.

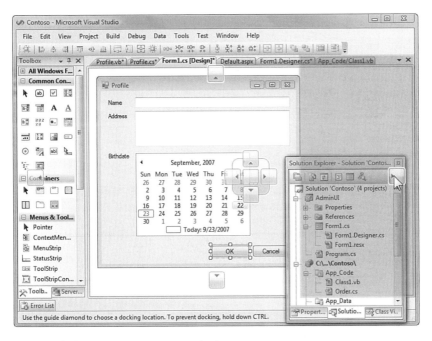

FIGURE 2.24   A window being docked.

Four icons are at the edge of the IDE, one each at the left, top, right, and bottom. These icons are used for docking the window at the given edge of the IDE. Using these icons will result in the window being docked across the full length (or width) of the IDE. Figure 2.24 shows the window housing the Solution Explorer and related tabs being docked to the full right side of the IDE.

There is also an icon in the middle of the IDE. This icon is used for docking the selected window relative to the other windows in the IDE. For example, you might want to dock the Solution Explorer to the right side of the IDE but above the Toolbox. You would do so with the rightmost icon inside this center group. Finally, the centermost icon in the center group is used for docking a window to another window as a tabbed item (as in the Class View pane at the bottom of Figure 2.20).

Of course, you can also undock items. This is simply the process of floating windows off by themselves (outside, or on top of, the IDE). To do so, you simply grab (click with the mouse) a pinned window by the title bar and move it off to the side of the IDE or just don't choose a docking icon.

Finally, when working with a floating window, you can right-click the title bar and tell Visual Studio how the window should behave. Figure 2.25 shows the available options. A docked window provides a down-arrow menu for access to the same features. The Floating option indicates that the window will float wherever you put it, on top of the IDE. This can be useful if you find yourself moving windows about but do not want to constantly trigger the docking options. You turn off this option by choosing Dockable (default state). You can also add a window to the center of your IDE to behave just like a designer or code editor. This is the Tabbed Document option.

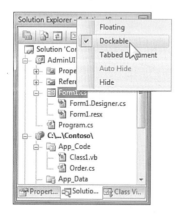

FIGURE 2.25    The IDE window options.

## Summary

The whirlwind tour is over. We've covered the basics of installation, your first project, and the standard items you'll encounter when journeying out on your own. We hope you've found your bearings and can begin pushing onward.

# CHAPTER 3

# .NET Framework and Language Enhancements in 2008

Most of this book focuses on unlocking the productivity promises of the Visual Studio IDE. However, it's important that we also cover some of the recent advances in the .NET languages and the Framework. These items (the IDE, the languages, and the Framework) typically ship from Microsoft in concert. That is, when a new version of the IDE is released such as Visual Studio 2008, you can expect changes to the primary .NET languages and a new version of the .NET Framework. Therefore, any discussion of a new version of the IDE would be incomplete without at least some coverage of the elements that have been bundled with it.

> **NOTE**
>
> Microsoft recently extended the .NET Framework without releasing a new version of the IDE. This new version (3.0) was released with Windows Vista. Developers wanting to target this version of the .NET Framework could do so by using various developer extension packs for Visual Studio 2005. The 2008 version of the IDE, however, allows developers to select a version of the .NET Framework for their given application. This feature is called multi-targeting and may lead to more independent releases of the .NET Framework and the IDE.

This chapter covers the enhancements relative to both Visual Basic .NET and C#. In addition, it highlights some of the key advances made in the latest version of the .NET Framework.

Our assumption is that most readers have some base-level understanding of either VB or a C-based language prior to the 2008 version. In addition, you should have an overall grasp of the .NET Framework. This chapter therefore assumes that you have some working knowledge of the 2003/2005 versions of the languages and .NET Framework. In this way, we can focus this chapter on the advances for 2008 (VB 9, C# 3, and the .NET Framework 3.5). This approach should give you insight into the enhancements that you should focus on in the 2008 version.

# An Overview of the Visual Studio 2008 IDE Enhancements by .NET Language

Most current .NET developers know that programming includes much more than just language. As a result, when a new edition is released, it is understood that it will include language enhancements, framework additions, and changes to the way you write code. Visual Studio 2008 is no different. It releases in step with the .NET Framework 3.5, VB 9, and C# 3.0. The sections that follow cover many of the VB and C# language additions for 2008. This section, however, highlights some of the key IDE enhancements specific to your .NET language of choice.

## VB IDE Enhancements

As in past versions of Visual Basic, the language is only a part of the story. Visual Basic is about both language and productivity tools. It's worth noting some of the nonlanguage, but VB-specific, productivity enhancements that ship with the 2008 version. These are highlighted as listed here:

▶ **Improved IntelliSense**—The latest version of VB has IntelliSense built-in every-where, every time you type. Simply type a letter in the code window and the tool guesses (almost always right) at what you are trying to accomplish. The performance is also much improved over prior editions. In addition, VB has much stronger ToolTips to help you code.

▶ **VB Power Pack Controls**—The VB team is working to add the RAD back into the language and reduce the shock of moving from VB 5/6 to the .NET version. Therefore, they have created off-cycle releases (between 2005 and 2008) of controls that provide additional productivity such as printing, line and shape, and a DataRepeater. In addition, they are committed to continuing to release power pack controls. For more info, search MSDN for "Visual Basic Power Packs."

▶ **Refactor!**—As a rule, we do not cover third-party tools for Visual Studio in this book. However, this one is worth mentioning because Microsoft has made it a key part of VB by striking a deal to offer the Refactor! product from DevExpress free to all licensed VB .NET developers. Visual Studio refactoring is covered in Chapter 9, "Refactoring Code." However, we cover only the refactoring built into IDE. That refactoring, of course, is primarily for the C# developers out there. With this deal, VB developers get a lot of existing and many new (2008 only) refactoring tools.

▶ **Interop Forms Toolkit**—Microsoft continues to provide help to the developers out there still working with VB 6 code. The Interop Forms Toolkit is a new set of tools that allow you to keep your existing code in VB 6 and write new code for the same application using .NET. The toolkit provides interop support between the two environments so that you can begin using .NET without having to rewrite your entire application.

**3**

## C# IDE Enhancements

The C# language takes another step forward in the 2008 release; we'll discuss this shortly. However, the code writing and editing process is also improved with this recent release. Like VB, C# has some language-specific IDE features that aid in writing and editing code. These new features include the following:

▶ **Improved IntelliSense**—The latest version of C# has an improved IntelliSense engine. This new version puts IntelliSense nearly everywhere you type. It includes statement completion, more helpful Quick Info ToolTips, and faster performance. In addition, the IntelliSense works with all the great new language features in C# that we'll discuss shortly. These include implicitly typed variables, extension methods, query expressions, lambda expressions, partial methods, and more.

▶ **Refactoring**—Visual Studio 2005 introduced refactoring to the toolset of the C# developer. In 2008, the refactoring tools are extended to support the many new features of the language, including query expressions, extension methods, and lambda expressions. Renaming, extracting methods, and other refactoring tools work as well with these new features as they did with the previous C# language syntax. In addition, the refactoring tools now provide additional options and warnings to make sure you don't end up with some unintended consequences when making changes to working code. See Chapter 9 for more on refactoring.

▶ **Code Formatting**—The C# code editor continues to improve the formatting of your code and the control over how that formatting gets applied. For example, the formatting engine understands things like query expressions. When you write one, it will automatically line up keywords such as From and Where under one another to improve the readability of your code.

▶ **Organize Your Using Declarations**—As your code ages, you might notice that the using declarations sometimes become a little unwieldy. The C# editor has a new feature to help you manage these declarations. There is now an Organize Usings menu option available from both the Edit menu and the context menu when you right-click on a using declaration. You can use the options on this menu to sort your using declarations by namespace and to clean your code of any unused usings declarations. Figure 3.1 shows the options available from this menu.

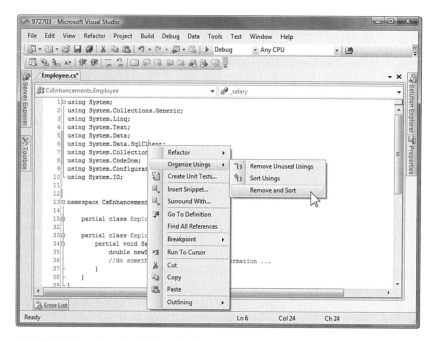

FIGURE 3.1    Organize Usings declarations.

# .NET Language Additions in 2008

The .NET languages pick up a number of enhancements as a result of updates made to the Common Language Runtime (CLR). Although there are a few specific enhancements to Visual Basic and to C#, the big (and majority of) advancements made in 2008 apply to both languages. Therefore, we cover language enhancements as a group and provide examples in both languages. If a given addition is language specific, it will be indicated as such. The .NET language additions covered here include the following:

▶ Local Type Inference (also called Implicit Typing)

▶ Object Initializers

▶ Extension Methods

▶ Anonymous Types

▶ Lambda Expressions

▶ Partial Methods

▶ Language Integrated Query (LINQ)

▶ Friend Assemblies

- ▶ XML Language Support (VB only)

- ▶ Unused Event Arguments (VB only)

- ▶ Automatically Implemented Properties (C# only)

Many of these new language features serve to support an important new feature, Language Integrated Query (LINQ), which we also cover here (and elsewhere in the book). However, each language feature is useful on its own and should be understood clearly. Therefore, each is covered in detail in the coming sections. Examples are provided in both C# and VB (when applicable).

## Infer a Variable's Data Type Based on Assignment

In the latest versions of Visual Basic and C#, you can define variables without explicitly setting their data type. And, when doing so, you can still get the benefits of strongly typed variables (compiler checking, memory allocation, and more). The compilers have been improved to actually infer the data type you intend to use based on your code. This process is called *local type inference*, or *implicit typing*.

As an example, consider the following lines of code. Here you create a variable of type String and assign a value.

**C#**

```
string companyName = "Contoso";
```

**VB**

```
Dim companyName As String = "Contoso"
```

Now, let's look at the same line of code using type inference. You can see that you do not need the string portion of the declaration. Instead, the compiler is able to determine that you want a string and strongly type the variable for you. In C#, this is triggered by the new keyword, var. This should not be confused with the var statement in languages such as JavaScript. Variables defined as var will be strongly typed. In VB, you still simply use the Dim statement but omit the data type.

**C#**

```
var companyName = "Contoso";
```

**VB**

```
Dim companyName = "Contoso"
```

These two lines of code are equivalent in all ways. Although in the second example no data type was declared, one is being declared by the compiler. This is not a return to a generalized data type such as Variant or Object. Nor does this represent late-binding of the variable. Rather, it is simply a smarter compiler that strongly types the variable by choosing a data type based on the code. You get all the benefits of early-bound variables while saving some keystrokes.

For example, take a look at Figure 3.2. This is the VB compiler in action (the C# compiler does the same thing). You can see that even at development time, the compiler has determined that this variable is of type System.String.

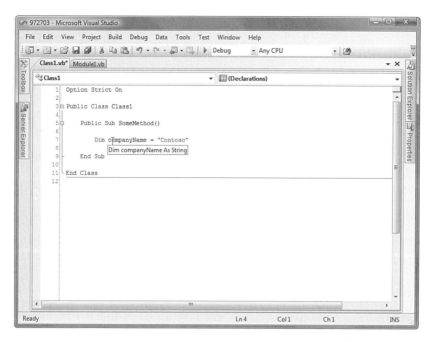

FIGURE 3.2    Type inference in action.

There are a few things for you to be aware of when using type inference. The first is that it requires your local variable to be assigned a value in order to do the compiler typing. This should not be a big deal because if your variable is not assigned it is not used.

The second item you should consider is that type inference works only with local types. It does not work with class-level variables (also called fields) or static variables. In these cases, using local type inference will result in an error being thrown by the compiler in C#. In VB, you would get the same error provided that Option Strict is set to On. If you are not using Option Strict in your VB code, the variable will not be strongly typed. Instead, the variable will be assigned the generic, Object data type.

Local type inference can be useful in other declaration scenarios as well. This includes defining arrays, creating variables during looping, defining a variable inside a Using statement, and defining a variable that contains the result of a function call. In each of these cases, the compiler can infer your data type based on the context of the code. As another example, the following code creates a Using statement and infers the type of the variable cnn.

C#

```
using (var cnn = new System.Data.SqlClient.SqlConnection()) {
  //code to work with the connection
}
```

VB

```
Using cnn = New System.Data.SqlClient.SqlConnection
  'code to work with the connection
End Using
```

In Visual Basic, you can turn local type inference off and on for a given file. By default, a new VB code file is set to allow type inference. However, if you want to turn it off at the file level, you can do so by setting Option Infer Off at the top of the code file.

## Create an Object and Set Its Properties with a Single Line of Code

There is now a shortcut for both declaring an instance of a class and setting the initial value of all or some of its members. With a single line of code, you can instantiate an object and set a number of properties on that object. During runtime, the object will first be created and then the properties will be set in the order in which they appear in the initialization list. This new feature is called *object initializers*.

Let's look at an example. Suppose you have a class called Employee that has a number of properties like FirstName, LastName, FullName, Title, and the like. Using object initialization, you can both create an instance of this class and set the initial values of some (or all) of the Employee instance's properties. To do so, you first construct the object. In Visual Basic, you follow this construction with the With keyword (C# does not require an equivalent indicator). You then place each property initialization inside a set of curly braces. Examples are as shown here:

C#

```
Employee emp = new Employee { FirstName = "Joe",
  LastName = "Smith", Title = "Sr. Developer" };
```

VB

```
Dim emp As New Employee With {.FirstName = "Joe", _
  .LastName = "Smith", .Title = "Sr. Developer"}
```

This single line of code is the equivalent of first creating an Employee class and then writing a line of code for each of the listed properties. Notice that in VB, you need to proceed the initialization using the With keyword; you also access each property using a dot. In C#, you do not need the dot or a keyword indicator.

Of course, you can also use object initialization with parameterized constructors. You simply pass the parameters into the constructor as you normally would. You then follow the constructor with the initialization. For example, suppose that the Employee class had a constructor that took the first and last name respectively. You could then create the object with the parameters and use object initialization for the Title as shown here:

**C#**

```
Employee emp = new Employee("Joe", "Smith")
  { Title = "Sr. Developer" };
```

**VB**

```
Dim emp As New Employee("Joe", "Smith") With _
  {.Title = "Sr. Developer"}
```

Object initialization also allows you to write some code in the initialization. In addition, with VB you can use properties of the object you are initializing to help initialize other properties. This is not valid in C#. The C# compiler does not allow you to access the variable until the assignment is complete. To see an example of this, the following code initializes an Employee object and sets the Employee.FullName property by concatenating the first and last names. Notice that the VB code uses the object itself.

**C#**

```
Employee emp = new Employee { FirstName = "Joe",
  LastName = "Smith", FullName = "Joe" + " Smith"};
```

**VB**

```
Dim emp As New Employee() With {.FirstName = "Joe", _
  .LastName = "Smith", _
  .FullName = .FirstName & " " & .LastName}
```

You can also nest object initialization. That is, if a given property represents another object, you can create the other object as part of the initialization. You can also nest an initialization of the other object within the initialization of the first object. A simple example makes this clear. Suppose that the Employee class has a property called Location. The Location property may point to a Location object that includes the properties for City and State. You could then create the Employee object (along with the nested Location object) as shown here:

**C#**

```
Employee emp = new Employee { FirstName = "Joe",
  LastName = "Smith", Location = new Location
  { City = "Redmond", State = "WA" } };
```

**VB**

```
Dim emp As New Employee() With {.FirstName = "Joe", _
  .LastName = "Smith", _
  .Location = New Location With _
  {.City = "Redmond", .State = "Washington"}}
```

## Add Methods to Existing Classes

You can now add custom features to an existing type as if the type always had the custom features. In this way, you do not have to recompile a given object, nor do you have to create a second, derived object to add these features. Rather, you can add a method to an existing object by using a new compiler feature called *extension methods*.

Doing so is a bit different between VB and C#. In VB, you first import the System.Runtime.CompilerServices namespace into your code file. Next, you mark a given Sub or Function with the <Extension()> directive. Lastly, you write a new Sub or Function with the first parameter of the new method being the type you want to extend. The following shows an example. In this example, we extend the Integer type with a new method called DoubleInSize:

**VB**

```
Imports System.Runtime.CompilerServices


Public Module IntegerExtensions
    <Extension()> _
    Public Function DoubleInSize(ByVal i As Integer) As Integer
        Return i + i
    End Function
End Module
```

The C# compiler does not require the same import or method attribute. Instead, you first create a static class. Next, you create a static method that you intend to use as your extension. The first parameter of your extension method should be the type you want to extend. Additionally, you apply the this modifier to the type. Notice the following example. In it, we extend the int data type with a new method called DoubleInSize.

**C#**

```
namespace IntegerExtensions {
    public static class IntegerExtensions{
        public static int DoubleInSize(this int i) {
            return i+i;
        }
    }
}
```

To use an extension method, you must first import (using in C#) the new extension methods into a project. You can then call any new method as if it had always existed on the type. The following is an example in both VB and C#. In this case, a function called DoubleInSize that was added in the preceding example is being called from the Integer (int) class.

**VB**

```
Imports IntegerExtensions


Module Module1
    Sub Main()
        Dim i As Integer = 10
        Console.WriteLine(i.DoubleInSize.ToString())
    End Sub
End Module
```

**C#**

```
using IntegerExtensions;


namespace CsEnhancements {
    class Program {
        static void Main(string[] args) {
            int i = 10;
            Console.WriteLine(i.DoubleInSize().ToString());
        }
    }
}
```

## Create an Instance of a Nonexistent Class

You can now create an object that does not have a class representation at design time. Instead, an unnamed (anonymous) class is created for you by the compiler. This feature is called *anonymous types*. Anonymous types provide crucial support for LINQ queries. With them, columns of data returned from a query can be represented as objects (more on this later). Anonymous types get compiled into class objects with read-only properties.

Let's look at an example of how you would create an anonymous type. Suppose you want to create an object that had both a Name and a PhoneNumber property. However, you do not have such a class definition in your code. You could create an anonymous type declaration to do so as shown here:

**VB**

```
Dim emp = New With {.Name = "Joe Smith", _
   .PhoneNumber = "123-123-1234"}
```

**C#**

```
var emp = new { Name = "Joe Smith",
   PhoneNumber = "123=123=1234" };
```

Notice that the anonymous type declaration uses object initializers (see the previous discussion) to define the object. The big difference is that there is no strong typing after the variable declaration or after the New keyword. Instead, the compiler will create an anonymous type for you with the properties Name and PhoneNumber.

There is also the Key keyword in Visual Basic. It is used to signal that a given property of an anonymous type should be used by the compiler to further define how the object is treated. Properties defined as Key are used to determine whether two instances of an anonymous type are equal to one another. C# does not have this concept. Instead, in C# all properties are treated like a VB Key property. In VB, you indicate a Key property in this way:

```
Dim emp = New With {Key .Name = "Joe Smith", _
   .PhoneNumber = "123-123-1234"}
```

You can also create anonymous types using variables (instead of the property name equals syntax). In these cases, the compiler uses the name of the variable as the property name and its value as the value for the anonymous type's property. For example, in the following code, the Name variable is used as a property for the anonymous type:

**VB**

```
Dim name As String = "Joe Smith"
Dim emp = New With {name, .PhoneNumber = "123-123-1234"}
```

**C#**

```
string name = "Joe Smith";
var emp = new {name, PhoneNumber = "123=123=1234" };
```

## Write Simple, Unnamed Functions Within Your Code

In the latest version of the .NET languages, you can write simple functions that may or may not be named, execute in-line, and return a single value. These functions exist *inside* your methods and not as separate, stand-alone functions. These functions are called *lambda expressions*. It's useful to understand lambda expressions because they are used behind the scenes in LINQ queries. However, they are also valid outside of LINQ.

Let's take a look at an example. Suppose you want to create a simple function that converts a temperature from Fahrenheit to Celsius. You could do so within your Visual

Basic code by first using the keyword Function. Next, you can indicate parameters to that function (in this case, the Fahrenheit value). Lastly, you write an expression that evaluates to a value that can be returned from the lambda expression. The syntax is as follows:

**VB**

```
Dim fahToCel = Function(fahValue As Integer) ((fahValue - 32) / 1.8)
```

The C# syntax is a bit different. In C#, you must explicitly declare a delegate for use by the compiler when converting your lambda expression. Of course, you declare the delegate at the class-level scope. After you have the delegate, you can write the expression inside your code. To do so, you use the => operator. This operator is read as "goes to." To the left side of the operator, you indicate the delegate type, a name for the expression, and then an = sign followed by any parameters the expression might take. To the right of the => operator, you put the actual expression. The following shows an example of both the delegate and the expression:

**C#**

```
//class-level delegate declaration
delegate float del(float f);

//lambda expression inside a method body
del fahToCel = (float fahValue) => (float)((fahValue - 32) / 1.8);
```

Notice that in both examples, we assigned the expression to a variable, fahToCel. By doing so, we have created a delegate (explicitly converting to one in C#). We can then call the variable as a delegate and get the results as shown here:

**VB**

```
Dim celcius As Single = fahToCel(70)
```

**C#**

```
float celcius = fahToCel(-10);
```

Alternatively, in Visual Basic, we could have written the function in-line (without assigning it to a variable). As an example, we could have written this:

**VB**

```
Console.WriteLine((Function(fahValue As Integer) ((fahValue - 32) / 1.8))(70))
```

Notice in this last example that the function is declared and then immediately called by passing in the value of 70 at the end of the function.

The C# language has its own quirk too. Here you can write multiple statements inside your lambda expression. You do so by putting them inside curly braces and setting off each statement with a semicolon. The following example has two statements inside the lambda expression. The first creates the new value; the second writes it to a console window. Notice too that the delegate must be of type void in this instance and that you still must call the lambda expression for it to execute.

C#

```
//class level delegate declaration
delegate void del(float f);

del fahToCel = (float fahValue) => { float f =
  (float)((fahValue - 32) / 1.8); Console.WriteLine(f.ToString()); };
fahToCel(70);
```

Lambda expressions are used in LINQ queries for things such as the Where, Select, and Order by clauses. For example, using LINQ, you can write the following statement:

VB

```
Dim emps = From emp In db.employees
  Where(emp.Location = "Redmond")
  Select emp
```

C#

```
var emps = from emp in db.employees
  where emp.Location == "Redmond"
  select emp;
```

This LINQ code gets converted to lambda expressions similar to this:

VB

```
Dim emps = From emp In db.employees
  .Where(Function(emp) emp.Location = "Redmond")
  .Select(Function(emp) emp)
```

C#

```
var emps = from emp in db.employees
  where (emp => emp.Location == "Redmond"
  select (emp => emp);
```

## Add Business Logic to Generated Code

A partial method (like a partial class) represents code you write to be added as a specific method to a given class upon compilation. This allows the author of a partial class to define a method stub and then call that method from other places within the class. If you provide implementation code for the partial method stub, your code gets called when the stub would be called (actually the compiler merges your code with the partial class into a single class). If you do not provide a partial method definition, the compiler goes a step further and removes the method from the class along with all calls to it.

The partial method (and partial class) was created to aid in code generation and should generally be avoided unless you are writing code generators or working with them because they can cause confusion in your code.

Of course, Visual Studio has more and more code generation built in. Therefore, it is likely you will run into partial methods sooner or later. In most cases, a code generator or designer (such as LINQ to SQL) generates a partial class and perhaps one or more partial methods. The Partial keyword modifier defines both partial classes and partial methods. If you are working with generated code, you are often given a partial class that allows you to create your own portion of the class (to be merged with the code-generated version at compile time). In this way, you can add your own custom business logic to any partial method defined and called by generated code.

Let's look at an example. The following represents an instance of a partial class, Employee. Here there is a single property called Salary. In addition, there is a method marked Partial called SalaryChanged. This method is called when the value of the Salary property is modified.

**VB**

```
Partial Class Employee

    Private _salary As Double

    Property Salary() As Double
        Get
            Return _salary
        End Get
        Set(ByVal value As Double)
            _salary = value
            SalaryChanged()
        End Set
    End Property

    Partial Private Sub SalaryChanged()
    End Sub

End Class
```

C#

```
partial class Employee {

    double _salary;

    public double Salary {
        get {
            return _salary;
        }
        set {
            _salary = value;
            SalaryChanged();
        }
    }

    partial void SalaryChanged();

}
```

The former code might represent code that was created by a code generator. The next task in implementing a partial method then is to create another partial Employee class and provide behavior for the SalaryChanged method. The following code does just that:

VB

```
Partial Class Employee
    Private Sub SalaryChanged()
        Dim newSalary As Double = Me.Salary
        'do something with the salary information ...
    End Sub
End Class
```

C#

```
partial class Employee {
    partial void SalaryChanged() {
        double newSalary = this.Salary;
        //do something with the salary information ...
    }
}
```

When the compiler executes, it replaces the SalaryChanged method with the new partial method. In this way, the initial partial class (potentially code-generated) made plans for a method that might be written without knowing anything about that method. If you decide to write it, then it gets called at the appropriate time. However, it is optional. If you do not provide an implementation of the partial method SalaryChanged, the compiler strips out the method and the calls to the method—as if had never existed.

## Access and Query Data Using the .NET Languages

A lot of what is special about Visual Studio 2008 from a language perspective has to do with a new feature set called LINQ (for Language-Integrated Query). LINQ is a new programming model that takes advantage of many of the features just discussed. It provides language extensions that are meant to change the way you access and work with data. With it, you can work with your data using object syntax and query collections of objects using VB and C#.

You can use LINQ to map between data table and objects (see Chapter 18, "Working with Databases"). In this way, you get an easier, more productive way to work with your data. This includes full IntelliSense support based on table and column names. It also includes support for managing inserts, updates, deletes, and reads.

The last of these, reading data, is a big part of LINQ in that it has built-in support for easily querying collections of data. Using LINQ features, you can query not only your data but any collection in .NET. There are, of course, new keywords and syntax for doing so. Query operators that ship with Visual Basic, for example, include Select, From, Where, Join, Order By, Group By, Skip, Take, Aggregate, Let, and Distinct. The C# language has a similar set of keywords. And, if these are not enough, you can extend the built-in query operators, replace them, or write your own.

You use these query operators to query against any .NET data that implements the IEnumerable or IQueryable interface. This may include a DataTable, mapped SQL Server objects, .NET collections including Generics, DataSets, and XML data.

Let's look at an example. Suppose you had a collection of employee objects called employees and you wanted to access all the employees at a specific location. To do so, you might write the following function:

C#

```csharp
public static List<Employee> FilterEmployeesByLocation(
  List<Employee> employees, string location) {

  //LINQ query to return collection of employees filtered by location
  var emps = from Employee in employees
             where Employee.Location.City == location
             select Employee;

  return emps.ToList();
}
```

VB

```vb
Public Function FilterEmployeesByLocation( _
  ByVal employees As List(Of Employee), _
  ByVal location As String) As List(Of Employee)
```

```
'LINQ query to return collection of employees filtered by location
Dim emps = From Employee In employees _
          Where Employee.Location.City = location

Return emps.ToList()
End Function
```

Take a look at what is going on in the previous listing. The function takes a list of employee objects, filters it by a region passed to it, and then returns the resulting list. Notice that to filter the list, we create a LINQ, in-memory query called emps. This query can be read like this: Looking at all the employee objects inside the employees collection, find those whose city matches the city passed into the function. Finally, the emps.ToList() method call in the return statement converts the in-memory query results into a new collection.

This is just a brief overview of LINQ. There are many things going on here, such as compile-time checking and schema validation—not to mention the new LINQ language syntax. You will undoubtedly want to spend more time with LINQ in the months to come.

## Split an Assembly Across Multiple Files

The 2005 version of C# introduced the concept of Friend assemblies. This feature allows you to combine assemblies in terms of what constitutes internal access. That is, you can define internal members but have them be accessible by external assemblies. This capability is useful if you intend to split an assembly across physical files but still want those assemblies to be accessible to one another as if they were internal. Visual Basic developers now have this same feature as of the 2008 version.

> **NOTE**
>
> Friend assembles *do not* allow for access to private members.

You use the attribute class InternalsVisibleToAttribute to mark an assembly as exposing its internal members as friends to another assembly. This attribute is applied at the assembly level. You pass the name and the public key token of the external assembly to the attribute. The compiler will then link these two assemblies as friends. The assembly containing InternalsVisibleToAttribute will expose its internals to the other assembly (and not vice versa). You can also accomplish the same thing by using the command-line compiler switches.

Friend assemblies, like most things, come at a cost. If you define an assembly as a friend of another assembly, the two assemblies become coupled and need to coexist to be useful. That is, they are no longer a single unit of functionality. This can cause confusion and increase management of your assemblies. It is often easier to stay away from this feature unless you have a very specific need.

## Work with XML Directly Within Your Code

You can now embed XML directly within your Visual Basic code. This can make creating XML messages and executing queries against XML a simple task in VB. To support this feature, VB allows you to write straight XML when using the data types called `System.Xml.Linq.XElement` and `System.Xml.Linq.XDocument`. The former allows you to create a variable and assign it an XML element. The latter, `XDocument`, is used to assign a variable to a full XML document.

> **NOTE**
>
> What we cover here is how VB allows you to write XML code. The two objects (`XElement` and `XDocument`) are still important additions to C# developers. However, C# developers will work with the properties and methods of these objects directly and not write and parse XML directly within a code editor.

Writing XML within your code is a structured process and not just simple strings assigned to a parsing engine. In fact, the compiler uses LINQ to XML behind the scenes to make all of this work. Let's look at a simple example. The following code creates a variable, emp, of type `XElement`. It then assigns the XML fragment to this variable.

```
Dim emp As XElement = <employee>
                        <firstName>Joe Smith</firstName>
                        <title>Sr. Developer</title>
                        <company>Contoso</company>
                        <location state="WA">Redmond</location>
                      </employee>
```

You can create a similar fragment as an `XDocument`. You simply add the XML document definition (`<?xml version="1.0"?>`) to the header of the XML. In either scenario, you end up with XML that can be manipulated, passed as a message, queried, and more.

In most scenarios, however, you would not want to hard-code your XML messages in your code. You might define the XML structure there, but the data will come from other sources (variables, databases, and so on). Thankfully, Visual Basic also supports building the XML using expressions. To do so, you use an ASP-style syntax, as in `<%= expression %>`. In this case, you indicate to the compiler that you want to evaluate an expression and assign it to the XML. For XML messages with repeating data, you can even define a loop in your expressions. As an example, let's look at building the previous XML using this syntax. Suppose you have an object e that represents an employee. In this case, you might write your `XElement` assignment as shown here:

```
Dim e As Employee = New Employee()
Dim emp As XElement = <employee>
                        <firstName><%= e.FirstName %></firstName>
                        <lastName><%= e.LastName %></lastName>
```

```
<title><%= e.Title %></title>
<company><%= e.Company %></company>
<location state=<%= e.Location.State %>>
    <%= e.Location.City %>
</location>
</employee>
```

## Remove Unused Arguments from Event Handlers (VB Only)

Visual Basic now allows you to omit unused and unwanted arguments from your event handlers. The thought is that this will make for cleaner reading code. In addition, it allows you to assign methods directly to event handlers without trying to determine the proper event signature.

As an example, suppose you had the following code to respond to a button click event:

```
Private Sub Button1_Click(ByVal sender As System.Object, _
                          ByVal e As System.EventArgs) Handles Button1.Click
    'your code here
End Sub
```

You could remove the event handlers from this code (or never put them in). Your new code would function the same and look as follows:

```
Private Sub Button1_Click() Handles Button1.Click
    'your code here
End Sub
```

## Create an Automatically Implemented Property (C# Only)

The latest version of C# allows for a simplified property declaration called *auto-implemented properties*. With this feature, you can simply declare a property without having to declare a local, private field to back the property. Instead, the compiler will do this for you. This can be useful when you do not need logic inside the property's accessors.

As an example, suppose you want a property on the Employee class called Name. You can declare this property without setting a private field variable as shown here:

```
public string Name { get; set; }
```

Notice that there is no logic in the get or set statements. Instead, the compiler will create an anonymous field to back the property for you. In addition, the IntelliSense built into the C# code editor makes this property declaration even faster. Simply type prop to stub out a code snippet based on the automatically implemented property syntax.

# .NET Framework 3.5 Enhancements

Many new classes and features are provided by the .NET Framework 3.5. This latest version layers on top of the prior version. The .NET Framework 2.0 (and SP1) added many new base classes, interfaces, generics, and more. The interim release (.NET Framework 3.0) that shipped with Windows Vista layered in support for Windows Presentation Foundation (WPF), Windows Communication Foundation (WCF), and Windows Workflow Foundation (WF). This latest version continues to build on that release. The 3.5 version the .NET Framework includes LINQ, a revision to ASP.NET, the Add-In Framework, SQL Synch Services, and more.

Of course, we cannot begin to cover all of these features in depth in this limited space. Therefore, we will simply highlight some of the key additions and enhancements that fuel this version of the .NET Framework. Many of these items are covered in more depth throughout the book.

> **NOTE**
>
> If you've installed 2.0, SP 1 for 2.0, 3.0, or SP 1 for 3.0, the good news is that 3.5 will install side by side with prior versions of the framework.

▸ **ASP.NET**—The .NET Framework 3.5 includes many new enhancements for the ASP.NET web developers. The `System.Web` namespace that backs ASP.NET includes many new classes and controls. For example, the framework now directly supports AJAX programming with the ScriptManager and UpdatePanel controls. There is also a new control for displaying data called ListView, a data-source object called `LinqDataSource` for working with LINQ data, and a `DataPager` object for controlling how records are paged in your application. For more on the ASP.NET framework enhancements, see Chapter 1, "A Quick Tour of Visual Studio 2008," and Chapter 14, "Creating ASP.NET Applications."

▸ **LINQ**—We've mentioned LINQ a few times already; it's worth noting, however, that LINQ is built into the .NET Framework. This includes the `System.Linq` namespace that defines standard LINQ query operators and types. The `System.Data.Linq` namespace holds the connection between databases and the LINQ subsystem. There are more LINQ-related namespaces too. These include `System.Data.Linq.Mapping` for handling the O/R mapping between SQL and LINQ (see Chapter 18) and `System.Xml.Linq` for working between XML and the LINQ subsystem. Of course, many of the controls in the framework have also been updated to work with LINQ.

▸ **Add-In Framework**—The `System.AddIn` namespace is new to the .NET Framework 3.5. It provides classes and methods for developers looking to build applications that can be extended based on a common add-in framework. For example, the `AddInStore` class allows for the discovery and management of add-ins. The framework also provides versioning, isolation, activation, and sandboxing. If you are building a new application and hope to allow for add-ins, you want to dig in deeper on this namespace.

▶ **ClickOnce Improvements**—ClickOnce application deployment continues to improve in this latest version of .NET. This includes the capability to deploy an application from multiple locations and third-party branding on your ClickOnce deployment dialogs.

▶ **Windows Communication Foundation (WCF)**—The new `System.ServiceModel` encapsulates what is known as WCF. With it you can easily create service-based applications that work across multiple protocols, transports, and message types. WCF is a major component of .NET 3.5 and is covered more in Chapter 20, "Embedding Workflow in Your Applications." However, some highlights included in WCF are the following: expose and consume RSS and ATOM feeds with the `System.ServiceModel.Syndication` namespace; communicate with AJAX operations using the JavaScript Object Notation (JSON) data format built into WCF's `System.Runtime.Serialization.Json` namespace; and use the WCF web programming model to create REST (representational state transfer) services to communicate directly across HTTP (without SOAP). In addition, WCF contains the new identity management system called CardSpace.

▶ **Windows Presentation Foundation (WPF)**—WPF provides a new presentation technology for Windows applications. This technology is spread throughout the `System.Windows` namespace and includes support for creating Windows applications based on XAML, XBAP, vector graphics, and both 2D and 3D scenarios. For more information, see Chapter 16, "Creating Richer, Smarter User Interfaces," and Chapter 17, "Creating Rich Browser Applications."

▶ **Windows Workflow Foundation (WF)**—The `System.Workflow` namespace first introduced in .NET 3.0 has been extended (and integrated into Visual Studio) in the 3.5 release. WF allows you to create both sequential and state-driven workflows for your applications, host them, persist them, and more. WF is also now integrated with WCF. Therefore, you can easily expose and call a workflow as a WCF service. For more on WF, see Chapter 20.

▶ **Tracing and Diagnostics**—The `System.Diagnostics` namespace contains the new `EventSchemaTraceListener` class to allow for cross-domain, cross-thread, cross-computer, end-to-end, lock-free logging and tracing.

▶ **Pipe Streams**—The new `System.IO.Pipes` namespace provides support for both named and anonymous pipe communication. With it, you can write code that communicates at the pipe level across processes and across computers. For example, the `NamedPipeServerStream` class can be used to allow read and write communication across a named pipe. The `NamedPipeClientStream` provides client support for communicating with pipe servers.

▶ **Threading Improvements**—There is a new class called `ReaderWriterLockSlim` in the `System.Threading` namespace that provides better performance and reduced deadlock scenarios.

▶ **Time Zone Additions**—There are two new types that help you work with applications that need to understand multiple time zones. These classes are `System.DateTimeOffset` and `TimeZoneInfo`. The `DateTimeOffset` structure represents an exact point in time. The offset indicates how the time differs from UTC (Universal Coordinated Time). You use this new class when you need precision and date/time arithmetic.

The `TimeZoneInfo` class is a welcome enhancement that represents a date and time in a given time zone. You can use this class to reliably represent the same date and time in any other time zone. In addition, you can use the class to create custom time zones if needed.

▶ **Peer-to-Peer Networking Support**—The .NET Framework finally has its own peer-to-peer networking support. This can be found in the `System.Net.PeerToPeer` namespace. With it, you can create an application that works without a server and instead communicates from one client (peer) to another (similar to Microsoft's Groove application). Application scenarios supported by this new namespace include tracking where peers are (online or offline), what they might be doing, interacting (messaging) with peers, managing peer contacts, discovering new peers, and more.

▶ **Sync Services for ADO.NET**—Shipping with Visual Studio 2008 is Microsoft's Sync Services. With it you can build an application that works both online and offline. These types of applications are referred to as *occasionally connected applications* (OCA). You use Sync Services (and its related tools) to indicate which data should be available when a user is offline. When connected, the Sync Services works to synchronize user changes with database changes.

The Sync Services for ADO.NET is part of the `Microsoft.Synchronization.Data` namespace. Notice that this is not part of `System` and therefore not a principal part of the .NET Framework but an add-on library from Microsoft. The ADO.NET services are actually a part of what is called the Microsoft Sync Framework. This framework provides synchronization services for data (ADO.NET), file and folders (the File System), and RSS/ATOM feeds (FeedSync).

▶ **Windows Vista Support**—The Windows Forms engine has been updated to give your applications Vista support. This means that upgrading your applications will give them that Vista appearance. In addition, you now have access to the common dialogs (`System.Windows.Forms.FileDialog`) in Vista. For example, the `OpenFileDialog` and `SaveFileDialog` support the same interface you see in Windows Vista for opening and saving files.

▶ **.NET Compact Framework**—A new version of the .NET Compact Framework also ships with 3.5. This framework is used on distributed, mobile devices such as SmartPhones and Windows Mobile/CE devices. This faster version of the framework provides support for WCF, LINQ, and improved debugging and diagnostics.

# Summary

This chapter presented the core enhancements to the .NET languages that ship with Visual Studio 2008. These additions should help you write more and better code during your development day. We covered compiler inference of your data type, object initialization upon construction, adding method implementation code to a code-generated partial method, and many more topics. These advancements made to both C# and VB work to further evolve the .NET toolset and help increase your productivity and abilities.

Finally, this chapter briefly covered some of the new items inside the .NET Framework 3.5. Clearly, there is a lot that is new. The Framework is becoming so large that developers (and books) are often forced to specialize in a particular area. We suggest that you look at our list of enhancements and then jump off to your own specialty area for further exploration.

3

# PART II

# An In-Depth Look at the IDE

## IN THIS PART

# Solutions and Projects

$S$*olutions* and *projects* are the containers Visual Studio uses to house and organize the code you write within the IDE. Solutions are virtual containers; they group and apply properties across one or more projects. Projects are both virtual and physical in purpose. Besides functioning as organizational units for your code, they also map one to one with compiler targets. Put another way, Visual Studio turns projects into compiled code. Each project will result in the creation of a .NET component (such as a DLL or an EXE file).

In this chapter, we will cover the roles of solutions and projects in the development process. We'll see how to create solutions and projects, examine their physical attributes, and discuss ways to best leverage their features.

## Understanding Solutions

From a programming perspective, everything that you do within Visual Studio will take place within the context of a solution. As we mentioned in this chapter's introduction, solutions in and of themselves don't do anything other than serve as higher-level containers for other items. Projects are the most obvious items that can be placed inside solutions, but solutions can also contain miscellaneous files that may be germane to the solution itself, such as "read me" documents and design diagrams. Really, any file type can be added to a solution. Solutions can't, however, contain other solutions. In addition, Visual Studio will load only one solution at a time. If you need to work on more than one solution concurrently, you need to launch another instance of Visual Studio.

So what do solutions contribute to the development experience? Solutions are useful because they allow you to treat various different projects as one cohesive unit of work. By grouping multiple projects under a solution, you can work against those projects from within one instance of Visual Studio. In addition, a solution simplifies certain configuration tasks by allowing you to apply settings across all the solution's child projects.

You can also "build" a solution. As mentioned previously, solutions themselves aren't compiled, per se, but their constituent projects can be built using a single build command issued against the solution. And solutions are also a vehicle for physical file management: Because many items that show up in a solution are physical files located on disk, Visual Studio can manage those files in various ways (delete them, rename them, move them). So it turns out that solutions are very useful constructs within Visual Studio.

The easiest way to explore solution capabilities and attributes is to create a solution in the IDE.

## Creating a Solution

To create a solution, you first create a project. Because projects can't be loaded independent of a solution within Visual Studio, creating a project will cause a solution to be created at the same time.

> **NOTE**
>
> There actually is a way to create a blank, or empty, solution without also creating a project. If you expand the Other Project Types node that appears in the Project Types list, you will see an option for Visual Studio Solutions. This contains a Blank Solution template. Blank solutions are useful when you are creating a new solution to house a series of already-existing projects; the blank solution obviates the need to worry about extra, unneeded projects being created on disk.

Launch the New Project dialog box by using the File menu and selecting the New, Project option (shown in Figure 4.1) or by using the Ctrl+Shift+N keyboard shortcut.

The New Project dialog box is displayed with defaults for the project name, location, and solution name (see Figure 4.2). We'll take a detailed look at the various project types offered there when we discuss projects later in this chapter. Notice that at the bottom of the dialog box, a Solution Name field is displayed. This field allows you to customize the name of your solution before creating the solution. Just clicking OK at this point does two things: A project of the indicated type and name is created on disk (at the location specified), and a solution, with links to the project, also is created on disk using the provided name.

Assuming that you have selected something other than the Blank Solution project type, Visual Studio now displays the newly created solution and project in the Solution Explorer window (we cover the Solution Explorer in depth in Chapter 5, "Browsers and Explorers"). In effect, Visual Studio has created the solution hierarchy shown in Figure 4.3.

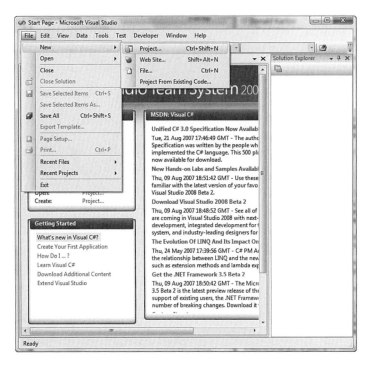

FIGURE 4.1   The File, New, Project menu.

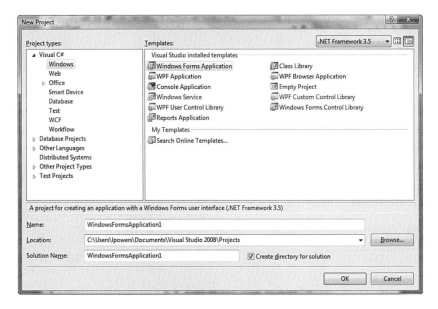

FIGURE 4.2   The New Project dialog box.

FIGURE 4.3     A simple solution hierarchy.

Assuming that you have accepted the default locations and left the Create Directory for Solution box checked, the physical directory/file structure is created as shown in Figure 4.4.

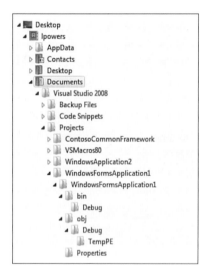

FIGURE 4.4     The solution file hierarchy.

In this example, the first `WindowsFormsApplication1` folder holds the solution file and has a subfolder for each project. The second `WindowsFormsApplication1` folder contains the new Windows forms project. The source files are placed in the root of this folder, and any compiled output files sit underneath the `bin` directory and then under the specific build configuration (for example, `Debug` or `Release`).

---
**CAUTION**

By default, the solution is named after the project. There is potential for confusion here because you now have two folders/entities named `WindowsFormsApplication1`. One refers to the solution; the other, the project. This is not an ideal way to physically organize your code on disk. It is recommended that you give the solution itself a unique name during the project creation process by simply overriding the default name given in the Solution Name field (see Figure 4.2).

---

**The Solution Definition File**

Visual Studio stores solution information inside two separate files: a solution definition file and a solution user options file. For the preceding example, Visual Studio created the solution definition file `WindowsFormsApplication1.sln` and the solution user options file `WindowsFormsApplication1.suo` in the indicated folder.

The solution definition file is responsible for actually describing any project relationships in the solution and for storing the various solution-level attributes that can be set. The solution user options file persists any customizations or changes that you, as a Visual Studio user, might have made to the way the solution is displayed within the IDE (such as whether the solution is expanded or which documents from the solution are open in the IDE). In addition, certain source control settings and other IDE configuration data are stored here.

The solution user options file is, by default, marked as a hidden file, and its content is actually binary. Because its internal structure is not publicly documented, we won't attempt to dissect it here. The solution definition file, however, is simply a text file. Listing 4.1 shows the file content for a fairly complex sample solution.

LISTING 4.1   Sample Solution File

```
Microsoft Visual Studio Solution File, Format Version 10.00
# Visual Studio 2008
Project("{FAE04EC0-301F-11D3-BF4B-00C04F79EFBC}") = "Contoso.Fx.Integration",
➥"ClassLibrary1\Contoso.Fx.Integration.csproj", "{DA0BA585-76C1-4F5E-B7EF-
57254E185BE4}"
EndProject
Project("{FAE04EC0-301F-11D3-BF4B-00C04F79EFBC}") = "Contoso.Fx.Common", "Contoso.
➥Fx.Common\Contoso.Fx.Common.csproj", "{A706BCAC-8FD7-4D8A-AC81-249ED61FDE72}"
EndProject
Project("{FAE04EC0-301F-11D3-BF4B-00C04F79EFBC}") = "Contoso.Fx.Analysis",
➥"Contoso.Fx.Analysis\Contoso.Fx.Analysis.csproj", "{EB7D75D7-76FC-4EC0-A11E-
➥2B54849CF6EB}"
EndProject
Project("{FAE04EC0-301F-11D3-BF4B-00C04F79EFBC}") = "Contoso.Fx.UI",
➥"Contoso.Fx.UI\Contoso.Fx.UI.csproj", "{98317C19-F6E7-42AE-AC07-72425E851185}"
EndProject
Project("{2150E333-8FDC-42A3-9474-1A3956D46DE8}") = "Architecture Models",
➥"Architecture Models", "{60777432-3B66-4E03-A337-0366F7E0C864}"
    ProjectSection(SolutionItems) = postProject
        ContosoSystemDiagram.sd = ContosoSystemDiagram.sd
    EndProjectSection
EndProject
Project("{FAE04EC0-301F-11D3-BF4B-00C04F79EFBC}") = "Contoso.UI.WindowsForms.
➥OrderEntry", "Contoso.UI.WindowsForms.OrderEntry\Contoso.UI.WindowsForms.
➥OrderEntry.csproj", "{49C79375-6238-40F1-94C8-4183B466FD79}"
```

LISTING 4.1    Continued

```
EndProject
Project("{2150E333-8FDC-42A3-9474-1A3956D46DE8}") = "Class Libraries", "Class
➥Libraries", "{E547969C-1B23-42DE-B2BB-A13B7E844A2B}"
EndProject
Project("{2150E333-8FDC-42A3-9474-1A3956D46DE8}") = "Controls", "Controls",
➥"{ED2D843C-A708-41BE-BB52-35BFE4493035}"
EndProject
Global
    GlobalSection(SolutionConfigurationPlatforms) = preSolution
        Debug|Any CPU = Debug|Any CPU
        Release|Any CPU = Release|Any CPU
    EndGlobalSection
    GlobalSection(ProjectConfigurationPlatforms) = postSolution
        {DA0BA585-76C1-4F5E-B7EF-57254E185BE4}.Debug|Any CPU.ActiveCfg = Debug| Any
➥CPU
        {DA0BA585-76C1-4F5E-B7EF-57254E185BE4}.Debug|Any CPU.Build.0 = Debug| Any CPU
        {DA0BA585-76C1-4F5E-B7EF-57254E185BE4}.Release|Any CPU.ActiveCfg = Release
➥|Any CPU
        {DA0BA585-76C1-4F5E-B7EF-57254E185BE4}.Release|Any CPU.Build.0 = Release|
➥Any CPU
        {A706BCAC-8FD7-4D8A-AC81-249ED61FDE72}.Debug|Any CPU.ActiveCfg = Debug| Any
➥CPU
        {A706BCAC-8FD7-4D8A-AC81-249ED61FDE72}.Debug|Any CPU.Build.0 = Debug| Any CPU
        {A706BCAC-8FD7-4D8A-AC81-249ED61FDE72}.Release|Any CPU.ActiveCfg = Release
➥|Any CPU
        {A706BCAC-8FD7-4D8A-AC81-249ED61FDE72}.Release|Any CPU.Build.0 = Release
➥|Any CPU
        {EB7D75D7-76FC-4EC0-A11E-2B54849CF6EB}.Debug|Any CPU.ActiveCfg = Debug| Any
➥CPU
        {EB7D75D7-76FC-4EC0-A11E-2B54849CF6EB}.Debug|Any CPU.Build.0 = Debug| Any CPU
        {EB7D75D7-76FC-4EC0-A11E-2B54849CF6EB}.Release|Any CPU.ActiveCfg = Release
➥|Any CPU
        {EB7D75D7-76FC-4EC0-A11E-2B54849CF6EB}.Release|Any CPU.Build.0 = Release
➥|Any CPU
        {98317C19-F6E7-42AE-AC07-72425E851185}.Debug|Any CPU.ActiveCfg = Debug| Any
➥CPU
        {98317C19-F6E7-42AE-AC07-72425E851185}.Debug|Any CPU.Build.0 = Debug| Any CPU
        {98317C19-F6E7-42AE-AC07-72425E851185}.Release|Any CPU.ActiveCfg = Release
➥|Any CPU
        {98317C19-F6E7-42AE-AC07-72425E851185}.Release|Any CPU.Build.0 = Release
➥|Any CPU
        {49C79375-6238-40F1-94C8-4183B466FD79}.Debug|Any CPU.ActiveCfg = Debug| Any
➥CPU
        {49C79375-6238-40F1-94C8-4183B466FD79}.Debug|Any CPU.Build.0 = Debug| Any CPU
```

```
        {49C79375-6238-40F1-94C8-4183B466FD79}.Release¦Any CPU.ActiveCfg = Release
➥¦Any CPU
        {49C79375-6238-40F1-94C8-4183B466FD79}.Release¦Any CPU.Build.0 = Release
➥¦Any CPU
    EndGlobalSection
    GlobalSection(SolutionProperties) = preSolution
        HideSolutionNode = FALSE
    EndGlobalSection
    GlobalSection(NestedProjects) = preSolution
        {ED2D843C-A708-41BE-BB52-35BFE4493035} = {E547969C-1B23-42DE-B2BB-
➥A13B7E844A2B}
        {EB7D75D7-76FC-4EC0-A11E-2B54849CF6EB} = {E547969C-1B23-42DE-B2BB-
➥A13B7E844A2B}
        {A706BCAC-8FD7-4D8A-AC81-249ED61FDE72} = {E547969C-1B23-42DE-B2BB-
➥A13B7E844A2B}
        {DA0BA585-76C1-4F5E-B7EF-57254E185BE4} = {E547969C-1B23-42DE-B2BB-
➥A13B7E844A2B}
        {98317C19-F6E7-42AE-AC07-72425E851185} = {ED2D843C-A708-41BE-BB52-
➥35BFE4493035}
    EndGlobalSection
EndGlobal
```

At the beginning of the file are references to the projects that belong to the solution. The references contain the project's name, its GUID, and a relative path to the project file itself (more on project files in a bit).

You can also see some of the various configuration attributes applied to the solution: The Debug and Release settings, for instance, show up here. Note that this project contains several solution folders: Architecture Models, Class Libraries, and Controls. They are represented in the solution file in much the same way as projects. In fact, the only difference is that they do not have a relative file path associated with them.

## Working with Solutions

After you have created a solution, the primary vehicle is in place for interacting with your code base. In essence, this boils down to controlling the way its constituent projects and files are built and deployed. Solutions also provide functionality outside the scope of projects. The primary tool for manipulating solutions and projects is the Solution Explorer. This tool is discussed in depth in Chapter 5. Here, we will look at the general procedures used to manage solutions by using the menu system in Visual Studio; keep in mind that most of the commands and actions discussed here can be initiated from the Solution Explorer.

**Solution Items**

In practice, the content you will add most often to a solution is project related. But items can be added directly to a solution as well. Collectively, the term *solution items* refers to any nonproject file that is attached to a solution. Because we know that solutions can't be compiled, it stands to reason that files added at the solution level serve no practical purpose from a compilation perspective. There are various reasons, however, that you may want to add solution items to your solution. For instance, this is a convenient way to store documentation that applies to the solution as a whole. Because you can add any type of file to a solution, this could take the form of documents, notes to other developers, design specifications, or even source code files from other solutions that may have some impact or bearing on the work at hand.

By default, Visual Studio supports a few types of solution items that can be created directly from within the IDE. They are grouped within four categories. Within each category are various file types that can be generated by Visual Studio. Table 4.1 shows the supported types.

TABLE 4.1    File Types Supported Within a Solution by Add New Item

| Category | Item Type | File Extension |
|---|---|---|
| General | Text file | `.txt` |
| | Style sheet | `.css` |
| | XML schema | `.xsd` |
| | Bitmap file | `.bmp` |
| | Cursor file | `.cur` |
| | Visual C# class | `.cs` |
| | Visual Basic class | `.vb` |
| | HTML page | `.html` |
| | XML file | `.xml` |
| | XSLT file | `.xsl` |
| | Icon file | `.ico` |
| | Native resource template | `.rct` |
| Test Run Configuration | Test run configuration | `.testrunconfig` |

**NOTE**

Keep in mind that you are in no way limited as to the type of file you can add to a solution. Even though Visual Studio supports only a limited number of file types that can be created within the IDE, you always have the option of creating a file *outside* the IDE and then adding it to a solution by using the Add Existing Item command.

Figure 4.5 shows the Add New Item – Solution Items dialog box that appears when you try to add a new item to a solution.

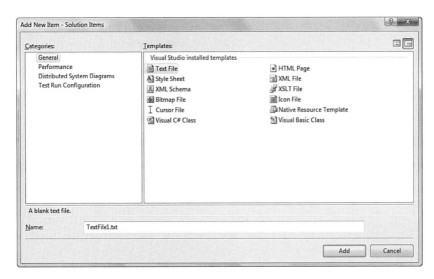

FIGURE 4.5    Adding a new solution item.

**Solution Folders**

To assist in organizing the various files in your solution, you can use *solution folders*. Solution folders are virtual folders implemented entirely within Visual Studio. Creating a solution folder does not cause a physical file folder to be created on disk; these folders exist solely to provide another grouping level within the solution. Solution folders can be nested and are especially useful in large solutions that contain many different projects and miscellaneous files. For example, you may want to group all of your web service projects under a single solution folder called Services while grouping the Windows forms elements of your solution under a UI folder. On disk, files added to a virtual folder are physically stored within the root of the solution directory structure.

Beyond providing a way to visually group items, solution folders also allow you to apply certain commands against all the projects contained within an individual folder. For example, you can "unload" all the projects within a virtual folder by issuing the unload command against the virtual folder (this will make the projects temporarily unavailable within the solution, and can be useful when trying to isolate build problems or solution problems). After unloading the projects in a folder, another right-click on the solution folder will allow you to reload the projects.

### Solution Properties

Several solution-level properties can be set from within the IDE. The Solution Property Pages dialog box gives you direct access to these properties and allows you to do the following:

▶ Set the startup project of the solution (this project will run when you start the debugger)

▶ Manage interproject dependencies

▶ Specify the location of source files to use when debugging

▶ Modify the solution build configurations

You launch this dialog box from the View, Property Pages menu or with the keyboard shortcut Shift+F4. On this dialog, the property page categories are represented in a tree view to the left; expanding a tree node reveals the individual property pages available.

**Specifying the Startup Project**   Figure 4.6 shows the Startup Project property page. The Startup Project property page indicates whether the startup project should be the currently selected project, a single project, or multiple projects.

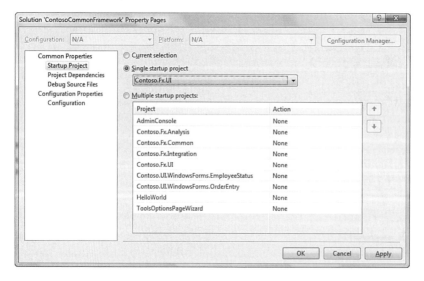

FIGURE 4.6   The Startup Project property page.

The default, and most typically used option, is to specify a single startup project. The project to run is specified in the drop-down box. If Current Selection is selected, the project that currently has focus in the Solution Explorer will be considered the startup project.

You can also launch multiple projects when the debugger is started. Each project currently loaded in the solution will appear in the list box with a default action of None. Projects set to None will not be executed by the debugger. You can also choose from the actions Start and Start Without Debugging. As their names suggest, the Start action will cause the indicated project to run within the debugger; Start Without Debugging will cause the project to run, but it will not be debugged.

**Setting Project Dependencies**   If a solution has projects that depend on one another—that is, one project relies on and uses the types exposed by another project—Visual Studio will need to have a build order of precedence established among the projects. As an example, consider a Windows application project that consumes types that are exposed by a class library project. The build process will fail if the class library is not built first within the build sequence.

Most of the time, Visual Studio is able to determine the correct sequence. Sometimes, you may need to manually indicate that a project is dependent on other, specific projects. To supply this information, you use the Project Dependencies property page (see Figure 4.7). By selecting a project in the drop-down, you can indicate which other solutions it depends on by placing a check mark on any of the projects shown in the Depends On list.

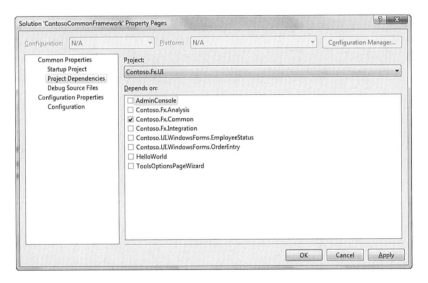

FIGURE 4.7   Project dependencies.

**Source File Location for Debugging**   In certain situations, you may need to explicitly point the Visual Studio debugger at source files to use when the debugger executes. One such scenario occurs when you are trying to debug a solution that references an object on a remote machine. If the source is not available locally for that remote object, you can explicitly point Visual Studio at the source files.

The Debug Source Files property page (see Figure 4.8) has two different list boxes. The top box contains a list of folders that hold source code specific to your debugging scenario. The bottom list box allows you to indicate specific files that the debugger should ignore (that is, should not load) when debugging.

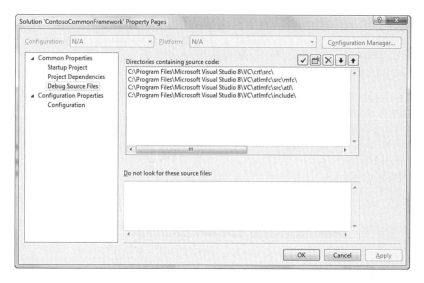

FIGURE 4.8    Source file locations.

To add an entry to either box, first place your cursor within the box and then click on the New Line button (upper right of the dialog box). This will allow you to enter a fully quali-fied path to the desired folder. You remove an entry by selecting the item and then click-ing on the Cut Line button. The Check Entries button allows you to double-check that all entries point to valid, reachable folder paths.

If the loaded solution has any Visual C++ projects, you will probably see several items already added into the Directories Containing Source Code list box.

**Build Configuration Properties**    Build configurations are covered in depth in Chapter 10, "Debugging Code." On the Build Configuration property page (see Figure 4.9), you indi-cate how Visual Studio will build the projects contained within the solution. For each project, you can set a configuration and platform value. In addition, a check box allows you to indicate whether to build a particular project.

See Chapter 10 for information on how to effectively use build configurations in your development.

Now that we have covered the concept of a solution in depth, let's examine the role of projects within Visual Studio.

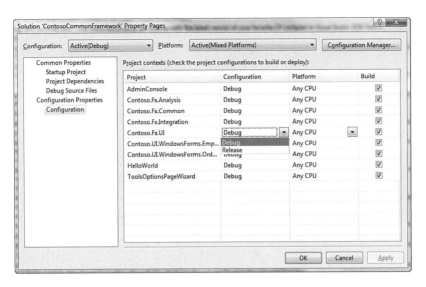

FIGURE 4.9 Build configuration properties.

# Getting Comfortable with Projects

Projects are where all the real work is performed in Visual Studio. A project maps directly to a compiled component. Visual Studio supports various project types. Let's reexamine the project creation process.

## Creating a Project

As we saw earlier when discussing solution creation, you create projects by selecting the New, Project option from the File menu. This launches the New Project dialog box (see Figure 4.10).

Table 4.2 shows some of the various project types supported in Visual Studio out of the box.

TABLE 4.2   Supported Project Types

| Type | Language | Template |
|------|----------|----------|
| Database | Visual Basic, Visual C# | SQL Server Project |
| Office | Visual Basic, Visual C# | Excel Workbook |
| | | Excel Template |
| | | Word Document |
| | | Word Template |
| Smart Device | Visual Basic, Visual C# | Pocket PC – Device Application |
| | | Pocket PC – Control Library |

TABLE 4.2   Continued

| Type | Language | Template |
|------|----------|----------|
| | | Pocket PC – Empty Project |
| | | Pocket PC – Class Library |
| | | Pocket PC – Console Application |
| | | Smartphone 2003 – Device Application |
| | | Smartphone 2003 – Console Application |
| | | Smartphone 2003 – Class Library |
| | | Smartphone 2003 – Empty Project |
| | | Windows CE 5.0 – Device Application |
| | | Windows CE 5.0 – Control Project |
| | | Windows CE 5.0 – Empty Project |
| | | Windows CE 5.0 – Class Library |
| | | Windows CE 5.0 – Console Application |
| | Visual C++ | ATL Smart Device Project |
| | | MFC Smart Device Project |
| | | Win32 Smart Device Project |
| | | MFC Smart Device ActiveX Control |
| | | MFC Smart Device DLL |
| Test | Visual Basic, Visual C# | Test Project |
| Web | Visual Basic, Visual C# | ASP.NET Web Application |
| | | ASP.NET AJAX Server Control |
| | | ASP.NET Server Control |
| | | ASP.NET Web Service Application |
| | | ASP.NET AJAX Server Control Extender |
| | | WCF Service Application |
| Windows | Visual Basic, Visual C# | Windows Application |
| | | Windows Control Library |
| | | Console Application |
| | | Empty Project |
| | | Class Library |
| | | Web Control Library |
| | | Windows Service |

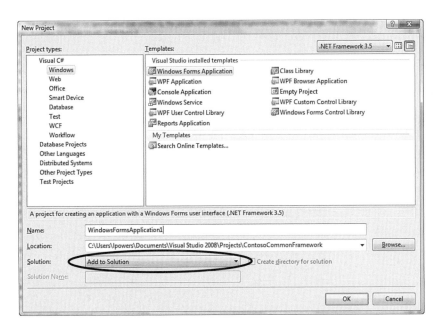

FIGURE 4.10    Adding a project to the current solution.

**NOTE**

Visual Studio supports the capability to create new project types and templates. Because Visual Studio is extensible in this fashion, the list of project types that you see in your particular copy of Visual Studio can vary greatly depending on the Visual Studio SKU you have installed, and any add-ins, extensions, or "Starter Kits" you may have installed on your PC.

As outlined previously, creating a new project will also create a new containing solution. However, if you are creating a project and you already have a solution loaded in the IDE, the New Project dialog box will offer you the opportunity to add the new project to the existing solution. Compare Figure 4.10 with Figure 4.2; notice that there is a new option in the form of a drop-down box that allows you to indicate whether Visual Studio should create a new solution or add the project to the current solution.

### Website Projects

Developers have two different ways to create web projects within Visual Studio 2008: web application projects are created using the New Project dialog that we just discussed. Website projects are created in a slightly different fashion. Instead of selecting File, New, Project, you select File, New, Web Site. This launches the New Web Site dialog box (see Figure 4.11).

As with other project types, you initiate website projects by selecting one of the predefined templates. In addition to the template, you also select a target source language and

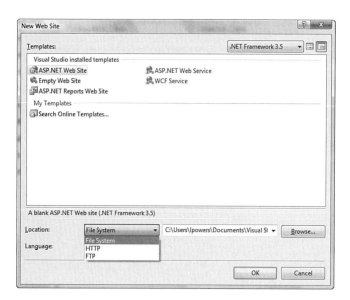

FIGURE 4.11    Creating a new website project.

the location for the website. The location can be the file system, an HTTP site, or an FTP site. Unlike other project types, websites are not typically created within the physical folder tree that houses your solution. Even selecting the file system object will, by default, place the resulting source files in a Web Sites folder under the Visual Studio 2008 projects folder.

---

**NOTE**

The *target source language* for a website project simply represents the default language used for any code files. It does not constrain the languages you can use within the project. For instance, a website project created with C# as the target language can still contain Visual Basic code files.

---

After you have created the website, you manage and maintain it just like the other project types within the IDE.

You may be wondering about the difference between a web application project and a website project. One key difference is the way that these two different project types are built. Web application projects use the same build model as the other .NET project types; that is, all the code in the project is compiled into a single assembly. Website projects, on the other hand, support a dynamic build model in which the code for a particular page is generated at runtime the first time a user hits the page. In this model, each page has its own assembly. There are many other differences between the two project types that we will discuss in depth in Chapter 14, "Creating ASP.NET Applications."

## Working with Project Definition Files

As with solutions, projects also maintain their structure information inside a file. These files have different extensions depending on their underlying language. Table 4.3 shows the various extensions that Visual Studio uses to identify project files.

TABLE 4.3    Project File Extensions

| Project File Extension | Language |
| --- | --- |
| .vbproj | Visual Basic |
| .csproj | Visual C# |
| .vcproj | Visual C++ |

Each project definition file contains all the information necessary to describe the source files and the various project properties and options. This includes the following:

► Build configurations

► Project references and dependencies

► Source code file locations/types

Visual Basic and Visual C# project definition files are based on the same schema. Listing 4.2 contains a snippet from a Visual C# project definition file.

LISTING 4.2    Contents of a Visual C# Project Definition File

```
<Project DefaultTargets="Build" xmlns="http://schemas.microsoft.com/
➥developer/msbuild/2003">
  <PropertyGroup>
    <Configuration Condition=" '$(Configuration)' == '' ">Debug</Configuration>
    <Platform Condition=" '$(Platform)' == '' ">AnyCPU</Platform>
    <ProductVersion>8.0.50215</ProductVersion>
    <SchemaVersion>2.0</SchemaVersion>
    <ProjectGuid>{E22301F1-5AD6-4514-A05D-266158AB1CAB}</ProjectGuid>
    <OutputType>WinExe</OutputType>
    <AppDesignerFolder>Properties</AppDesignerFolder>
    <RootNamespace>WindowsApplication2</RootNamespace>
    <AssemblyName>WindowsApplication2</AssemblyName>
  </PropertyGroup>
  <PropertyGroup Condition=" '$(Configuration)|$(Platform)' == 'Debug|AnyCPU' ">
    <DebugSymbols>true</DebugSymbols>
    <DebugType>full</DebugType>
    <Optimize>false</Optimize>
    <OutputPath>bin\Debug\</OutputPath>
    <DefineConstants>DEBUG;TRACE</DefineConstants>
    <ErrorReport>prompt</ErrorReport>
```

LISTING 4.2    Continued

```
    <WarningLevel>4</WarningLevel>
  </PropertyGroup>
  <PropertyGroup Condition=" '$(Configuration)|$(Platform)' == 'Release|AnyCPU' ">
    <DebugType>pdbonly</DebugType>
    <Optimize>true</Optimize>
    <OutputPath>bin\Release\</OutputPath>
    <DefineConstants>TRACE</DefineConstants>
    <ErrorReport>prompt</ErrorReport>
    <WarningLevel>4</WarningLevel>
  </PropertyGroup>
  <ItemGroup>
    <Reference Include="System" />
    <Reference Include="System.Data" />
    <Reference Include="System.Deployment" />
    <Reference Include="System.Drawing" />
    <Reference Include="System.Windows.Forms" />
    <Reference Include="System.Xml" />
  </ItemGroup>
  <ItemGroup>
    <Compile Include="Form1.cs">
      <SubType>Form</SubType>
    </Compile>
    <Compile Include="Form1.Designer.cs">
      <DependentUpon>Form1.cs</DependentUpon>
    </Compile>
    <Compile Include="Program.cs" />
    <Compile Include="Properties\AssemblyInfo.cs" />
    <EmbeddedResource Include="Properties\Resources.resx">
      <Generator>ResXFileCodeGenerator</Generator>
      <LastGenOutput>Resources.Designer.cs</LastGenOutput>
      <SubType>Designer</SubType>
    </EmbeddedResource>
    <Compile Include="Properties\Resources.Designer.cs">
      <AutoGen>True</AutoGen>
      <DependentUpon>Resources.resx</DependentUpon>
    </Compile>
    <None Include="Properties\Settings.settings">
      <Generator>SettingsSingleFileGenerator</Generator>
      <LastGenOutput>Settings.Designer.cs</LastGenOutput>
    </None>
    <Compile Include="Properties\Settings.Designer.cs">
      <AutoGen>True</AutoGen>
      <DependentUpon>Settings.settings</DependentUpon>
      <DesignTimeSharedInput>True</DesignTimeSharedInput>
```

```
    </Compile>
  </ItemGroup>
  <Import Project="$(MSBuildBinPath)\Microsoft.CSharp.targets" />
</Project>
```

This project definition file would look relatively the same as a Visual Basic or Visual J#
project. Visual C++ project files, however, use an entirely different schema. For complete-
ness, and to contrast with the Visual Basic/Visual C# content, Listing 4.3 shows a sample
Visual C++ project definition file in its entirety.

LISTING 4.3   Visual C++ Project Definition File

```
<?xml version="1.0" encoding="Windows-1252"?>
<VisualStudioProject
    ProjectType="Visual C++"
    Version="8.00"
    Name="Contoso.Fx.UI.BrowserShim"
    ProjectGUID="{BE574BF5-7FDA-46F2-A42E-4A35E5E338A0}"
    RootNamespace="ContosoFxUIBrowserShim"
    Keyword="MFCActiveXProj"
    SignManifests="true">
    <Platforms>
        <Platform Name="Win32" />
    </Platforms>
    <ToolFiles>
    </ToolFiles>
    <Configurations>
        <Configuration Name="Debug¦Win32" OutputDirectory="Debug"
            IntermediateDirectory="Debug" ConfigurationType="2"
            UseOfMFC="2" CharacterSet="1">
            <Tool Name="VCPreBuildEventTool" />
            <Tool Name="VCCustomBuildTool" />
            <Tool Name="VCXMLDataGeneratorTool" />
            <Tool Name="VCWebServiceProxyGeneratorTool" />
            <Tool
                Name="VCMIDLTool"
                PreprocessorDefinitions="_DEBUG"
                MkTypLibCompatible="false"
                TypeLibraryName="$(IntDir)/$(ProjectName).tlb"
                HeaderFileName="$(ProjectName)idl.h"
                ValidateParameters="false"
            />
            <Tool
                Name="VCCLCompilerTool"
                Optimization="0"
```

LISTING 4.3    Continued

```
                PreprocessorDefinitions="WIN32;_WINDOWS;_DEBUG;_USRDLL"
                MinimalRebuild="true"
                BasicRuntimeChecks="3"
                RuntimeLibrary="3"
                TreatWChar_tAsBuiltInType="true"
                UsePrecompiledHeader="2"
                WarningLevel="3"
                Detect64BitPortabilityProblems="true"
                DebugInformationFormat="4"
            />
            <Tool Name="VCManagedResourceCompilerTool" />
            <Tool
                Name="VCResourceCompilerTool"
                PreprocessorDefinitions="_DEBUG"
                Culture="1033"
                AdditionalIncludeDirectories="$(IntDir)"
            />
            <Tool Name="VCPreLinkEventTool" />
            <Tool
                Name="VCLinkerTool"
                RegisterOutput="true"
                OutputFile="$(OutDir)\$(ProjectName).ocx"
                LinkIncremental="2"
                ModuleDefinitionFile=".\Contoso.Fx.UI.BrowserShim.def"
                GenerateDebugInformation="true"
                SubSystem="2"
                TargetMachine="1"
            />
            <Tool Name="VCALinkTool" />
            <Tool Name="VCManifestTool" />
            <Tool Name="VCXDCMakeTool" />
            <Tool Name="VCBscMakeTool" />
            <Tool Name="VCFxCopTool" />
            <Tool Name="VCAppVerifierTool" />
            <Tool Name="VCWebDeploymentTool" />
            <Tool Name="VCPostBuildEventTool" />
        </Configuration>
        <Configuration
            Name="Release|Win32"
            OutputDirectory="Release"
            IntermediateDirectory="Release"
            ConfigurationType="2"
            UseOfMFC="2"
            CharacterSet="1"
            >
```

```
<Tool Name="VCPreBuildEventTool" />
<Tool Name="VCCustomBuildTool" />
<Tool Name="VCXMLDataGeneratorTool" />
<Tool Name="VCWebServiceProxyGeneratorTool" />
<Tool
    Name="VCMIDLTool"
    PreprocessorDefinitions="NDEBUG"
    MkTypLibCompatible="false"
    TypeLibraryName="$(IntDir)/$(ProjectName).tlb"
    HeaderFileName="$(ProjectName)idl.h"
    ValidateParameters="false"
/>
<Tool
    Name="VCCLCompilerTool"
    Optimization="2"
    PreprocessorDefinitions="WIN32;_WINDOWS;NDEBUG;_USRDLL"
    MinimalRebuild="false"
    RuntimeLibrary="2"
    TreatWChar_tAsBuiltInType="true"
    UsePrecompiledHeader="2"
    WarningLevel="3"
    Detect64BitPortabilityProblems="true"
    DebugInformationFormat="3"
/>
<Tool Name="VCManagedResourceCompilerTool" />
<Tool
    Name="VCResourceCompilerTool"
    PreprocessorDefinitions="NDEBUG"
    Culture="1033"
    AdditionalIncludeDirectories="$(IntDir)"
/>
<Tool Name="VCPreLinkEventTool" />
<Tool
    Name="VCLinkerTool"
    RegisterOutput="true"
    OutputFile="$(OutDir)\$(ProjectName).ocx"
    LinkIncremental="1"
    ModuleDefinitionFile=".\Contoso.Fx.UI.BrowserShim.def"
    GenerateDebugInformation="true"
    SubSystem="2"
    OptimizeReferences="2"
    EnableCOMDATFolding="2"
    TargetMachine="1"
/>
<Tool Name="VCALinkTool" />
<Tool Name="VCManifestTool" />
```

LISTING 4.3    Continued

```xml
                <Tool Name="VCXDCMakeTool" />
                <Tool Name="VCBscMakeTool" />
                <Tool Name="VCFxCopTool" />
                <Tool Name="VCAppVerifierTool" />
                <Tool Name="VCWebDeploymentTool" />
                <Tool Name="VCPostBuildEventTool" />
            </Configuration>
        </Configurations>
        <References></References>
        <Files>
            <Filter Name="Source Files"
                Filter="cpp;c;cc;cxx;def;odl;idl;hpj;bat;asm;asmx"
                UniqueIdentifier="{4FC737F1-C7A5-4376-A066-2A32D752A2FF}">
                <File RelativePath=".\Contoso.Fx.UI.BrowserShim.cpp"></File>
                <File RelativePath=".\Contoso.Fx.UI.BrowserShim.def"></File>
                <File RelativePath=".\Contoso.Fx.UI.BrowserShim.idl"></File>
                <File RelativePath=".\Contoso.Fx.UI.BrowserShimCtrl.cpp">
                </File>
                <File RelativePath=".\Contoso.Fx.UI.BrowserShimPropPage.cpp">
                </File>
                <File RelativePath=".\stdafx.cpp">
                    <FileConfiguration Name="Debug|Win32"    >
                        <Tool Name="VCCLCompilerTool"
                            UsePrecompiledHeader="1" />
                    </FileConfiguration>
                    <FileConfiguration Name="Release|Win32">
                        <Tool Name="VCCLCompilerTool"
                            UsePrecompiledHeader="1" />
                    </FileConfiguration>
                </File>
            </Filter>
            <Filter
                Name="Header Files"
                Filter="h;hpp;hxx;hm;inl;inc;xsd"
                UniqueIdentifier="{93995380-89BD-4b04-88EB-625FBE52EBFB}">
                <File RelativePath=".\Contoso.Fx.UI.BrowserShim.h"></File>
                <File RelativePath=".\Contoso.Fx.UI.BrowserShimCtrl.h"></File>
                <File RelativePath=".\Contoso.Fx.UI.BrowserShimPropPage.h">
                </File>
                <File RelativePath=".\Resource.h"></File>
                <File RelativePath=".\stdafx.h"></File>
            </Filter>
            <Filter Name="Resource Files"
```

```
    Filter="rc;ico;cur;bmp;dlg;rc2;rct;bin;rgs;gif;jpg;jpeg;jpe;resx;tiff;tif;
➡png;wav"
            UniqueIdentifier="{67DA6AB6-F800-4c08-8B7A-83BB121AAD01}">
            <File RelativePath=".\Contoso.Fx.UI.BrowserShim.ico"></File>
            <File RelativePath=".\Contoso.Fx.UI.BrowserShim.rc"></File>
            <File RelativePath=".\Contoso.Fx.UI.BrowserShimCtrl.bmp"></File>
        </Filter>
        <File RelativePath=".\ReadMe.txt"></File>
    </Files>
    <Globals></Globals>
</VisualStudioProject>
```

## Working with Projects

As source code containers, projects principally act as a settings applicator. They are used to control and organize your source code files and the various properties associated with the whole build and compile process (we cover the build process in depth in Chapter 10). As with solutions, projects can contain various different items that are germane to their development. Projects are language specific. You cannot mix different languages within a specific project. There is no similar limitation with solutions: A solution can contain many projects, each one in a different language.

### Project Items

After a project is created, it will, by default, already contain one or more project items. These default items will vary depending on the project template you selected and on the language of the project. For instance, creating a project using the C# Windows application template would result in the formation of a Form1.cs file, a Form1.Designer.cs file, and a Program.cs file. Projects are also preconfigured with references and properties that make sense for the given project type: The Windows application template contains a reference to the System.Windows.Forms assembly, whereas the class library template does not.

Projects, like solutions, can also have subfolders within them that you can employ to better manage and group project items. Unlike solutions, the folders you create within a project are physical; they are created on disk within your project directory structure. These are examples of physical project items. Source code files are also physical in nature.

Projects can also contain virtual items—items that are merely pointers or links to items that don't actually manifest themselves physically within your project structure. They are, for example, references to other assemblies, database connections, and virtual folders (virtual folders are described in Chapter 5). Figure 4.12 illustrates a fully described solution and project.

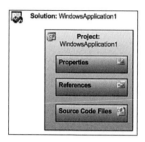

FIGURE 4.12    Project structure.

## Project Properties

Like solution properties, project properties are viewed and set using a series of property pages accessed through the Project, Properties menu. These property pages are hosted within a dialog box referred to as the *Project Designer*. Figure 4.13 shows the Project Designer that is displayed for a sample Visual Basic class library project. Different languages and different project types will actually surface different property pages within the Project Designer. For instance, the Application property page for a Visual Basic project looks different and contains slightly different information than an identical Visual C# project (although the basic intent of the page remains unchanged).

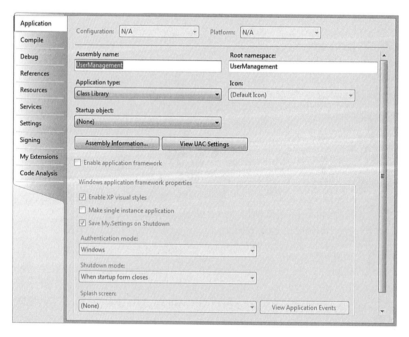

FIGURE 4.13    Setting properties using the Project Designer.

In general, you use project properties to control the following:

▶ General project attributes such as the assembly name and project type

▶ The way that the project will be built/compiled

▶ Debugger configuration for the project

▶ Resources used by the project

▶ Signing and security settings

Let's examine some of the more common project property pages and discuss briefly the options that can be set on each.

**Application**   The Application property page allows you to set the assembly name, root/default namespace, application/output type, and startup object. For Windows forms applications, authentication modes and visual styles are also controlled via this property page. Note that the options available in this dialog will depend on the project type and the chosen language.

▶ **Assembly Name**—This is the filename of the assembly that the project is compiled into. Typically, it defaults to the project name. The extension used is determined by the output type of the project.

▶ **Root/Default Namespace**—This specifies a namespace to be used by any types declared within the project. This can also be declared manually in code.

▶ **Output Type**—Displayed as Application Type for Visual Basic projects, this value determines the fundamental project type (for example, class library, Windows application, console application).

▶ **Startup Object**—This object is used to set the entry point for the project. For Windows applications, this will be the default form (or in the case of C#, the program entry point for the form) that should be launched when the application is executed. For console applications, this will be the main subroutine procedure that implements the console. Class library projects do not have an entry point and will be set to (Not set).

▶ **Icon**—This is the icon to associate with the assembly. It is not pertinent to class library or web projects.

▶ **Resource File**—This text box can be used to specify a path and filename for a resource file. Resource files contain nonexecutable content, such as strings, images, or even persisted objects, that need to be deployed along with an application.

▶ **Visual Styles**—The Enable XP Visual Styles check box allows you to indicate whether the application will support XP themes when the user interface is rendered. This option is not applicable for non-Windows application projects.

▶ **Windows Application Properties**—Visual Basic provides a series of properties that apply specifically to Windows application projects. These properties allow you to set the splash screen associated with the project, the authentication mode supported by the project (Windows or application-defined), and the shutdown mode of the project. The shutdown mode specifies whether the application should shut down when the initial form is closed or when the last loaded form in the application is closed.

**Build**  The Build property page is used with Visual C# projects to tweak settings associated with build configurations. Using this dialog box, you can select whether the DEBUG and TRACE constants are turned on, and you can specify conditional compilation symbols. Settings that affect the warning and error levels and the build output are also housed here. For more exploration of the options available here, see Chapter 10.

**Build Events**  Visual Studio will trigger a pre- and post-build event for each project. On the Build Events page, you can specify commands that should be run during either of these events. This page also allows you to indicate when the post-build event runs: always, after a successful build, or when the build updates the project output. Build events are particularly useful for launching system tests and unit tests against a project that has just been recompiled. If you launch a suite of, say, unit tests from within the post-build event, the test cycle can be embedded within the build cycle.

---

**NOTE**

If you specify commands in the pre- or post-build events, Visual Studio will create a batch file for each event and place it into the bin/debug directory. These files, titled PreBuildEvent.bat and PostBuildEvent.bat, will house the commands you enter on the Build Events property page. In the event of an error running the build event commands, you can manually inspect and run these files to try to chase down the bug.

---

**Compile (VB Only)**  The Compile property page is used by Visual Basic projects to control which optimizations will be performed during compile and also to control general compilation options for the output path and warnings versus errors raised during the compilation process.

▶ **Compile Options**—You use the Option Strict, Option Explicit, and Option Infer drop-downs to turn on or off these settings. You can also control whether the project will perform binary or text compares with the Option Compare drop-down.

▶ **Compiler Conditions**—Visual Basic allows you to customize the level of notification provided upon detecting any of a handful of conditions during the compilation process. For instance, one condition defined is Unused Local Variable. If this condition is detected in the source code during the compile, you can elect to have it treated as a warning or an error, or to have it ignored altogether.

▶ **Build Events**—Visual Basic allows you to access the Build Events property page (see the preceding section for an explanation) via a Build Events button located on this screen.

▶ **Misc Compile Options**—You can choose to disable all compiler warnings, treat all warnings as errors, and generate an XML documentation file during the compile process. This will result in an XML file with the same name as the project; it will contain all the code comments parsed out of your source code in a predefined format.

**Debug**    The Debug property page allows you to affect the behavior of the Visual Studio debugger.

▶ **Start Action**—You use this option to specify whether a custom program, a URL, or the current project itself should be started when the debugger is launched.

▶ **Start Options**—You use this option to specify command-line arguments to pass to the running project, set the working directory for the project, and debug a process on a remote machine.

▶ **Enable Debuggers**—You use the check boxes in this section to enable or disable such things as support for debugging unmanaged code, support for SQL stored procedure debugging, and use of Visual Studio as a host for the debugger process.

**Publish**    The Publish property page enables you to configure many ClickOnce-specific properties. You can specify the publish location for the application, the install location (if different from the publish location), and the various installation settings, including prerequisites and update options. You can also control the versioning scheme for the published assemblies.

**References (Visual Basic)**    The References property page is used within Visual Basic projects to select the assemblies referenced by the project and to import namespaces into the project. This screen also allows you to query the project in an attempt to determine whether some existing references are unused. You do this by using the Unused References button.

**Reference Paths (Visual C#)**    The Reference Paths property page allows you to provide path information meant to help Visual Studio find assemblies referenced by the project. Visual Studio will first attempt to resolve assembly references by looking in the current project directory. If the assembly is not found there, the paths provided on this property page will be used to search for the assemblies. Visual Studio will also probe the project's obj directory, but only after attempting to resolve first using the reference paths you have specified on this screen.

**Resources**    *Resources* are items such as strings, images, icons, audio, and files that are embedded in a project and used during design and runtime. The Resources property page allows you to add, edit, and delete resources associated with the project.

**Security**    For ClickOnce applications, the Security property page allows you to enforce code access security permissions for running the ClickOnce application. Various full-trust and partial-trust scenarios are supported.

**Settings**    *Application settings* are dynamically specified name/value pairs that can be used to store information specific to your project/application. The Settings property page allows you to add, edit, and delete these name/value pairs.

4

Each setting can be automatically scoped to the application or to the user, and can have a default value specified. Applications can then consume these settings at runtime.

**Signing**    The Signing property page allows you to have Visual Studio code sign the project assembly—and its ClickOnce manifests—by specifying a key file. You can also enable Delay signing from this screen.

# Summary

Solutions and projects are the primary vehicles within Visual Studio for organizing and managing your code. They allow you to divide and conquer large solutions, and they provide a single point of access for various settings (at both the solution and project levels). Solutions are the top-level container, and the first work item that Visual Studio creates when creating a new code project.

To summarize what we have learned about solutions:

- ▶ Solutions can be built (triggering a build of each of its projects) but cannot be compiled.

- ▶ Visual Studio can load only one solution at a time; to work on multiple solutions concurrently, you must have multiple copies of Visual Studio running.

- ▶ You can create folders within a solution to help group its content; these folders are virtual and do not represent physical file folders.

- ▶ Solutions are primarily used to group one or more projects together. Projects within a solution can be a mix of the various supported languages and project types.

- ▶ Solutions cannot contain other solutions.

- ▶ Besides projects, solutions can also contain miscellaneous files (called solution items) that typically represent information pertinent to the solution (readme files, system diagrams, and the like).

Although solutions are an important and necessary implement, it is the Visual Studio project that actually results in a compiled .NET component. Projects are created and based on templates available within the IDE that cover the various development scenarios, ranging from web application development to Windows application development to smart device development.

To summarize what we have learned about projects:

- ▶ Projects exist to compile code into assemblies.

- ▶ Projects are based on a project template; project templates define the various artifacts, references, and so on that make sense for the project's context.

▶ Like solutions, projects also support subfolders to help you better organize your code. These folders are actual, physical folders that are created on disk.

▶ Projects contain project items. They can be source code files, references, and other items such as virtual folders and database connections.

We have seen how solutions and projects are physically manifested; in the next chapter, we will cover the primary Visual Studio tools used to interact with solutions and projects.

4

# Browsers and Explorers

Visual Studio provides a cohesive and all-encompassing view of your solutions, projects, and types within your projects by exposing them to you via *browsers* and *explorers*. These windows (which are confusingly also referred to as *view windows*) attempt to provide a visually structured representation of a large variety of elements—some code-based, others not.

In general, you access and display these windows through the View menu. Some of these windows, such as the Solution Explorer and Class View, are staples of a developer's daily routine. Others touch on elements that are used during specific points within the development cycle or by more advanced Visual Studio IDE users.

In this chapter, we will examine each of the basic browser/explorer windows in detail.

> **NOTE**
>
> As with many Visual Studio features, the actual browser and explorer tools available to you vary according to the Visual Studio version; we will cover the ones specific to Visual Studio Team System in their respective chapters in the last part of this book.

## Solution Explorer

The Solution Explorer is the primary tool for viewing and manipulating solutions and projects. It provides a simple but powerful hierarchical view of all solution and project items, and it allows you to interact with each item directly via context menus and its toolbar.

Using Solution Explorer, you can launch an editor for any given file, add new items to a project or solution, and reorganize the structure of a project or solution. In addition, the Solution Explorer provides instant, at-a-glance information as to the currently selected project; the startup project for the solution; and the physical hierarchy of the solution, its projects, and their child items.

The Solution Explorer is simply another window hosted by Visual Studio. It can be docked, pinned, and placed anywhere within the Visual Studio environment. It is composed of a title bar, a toolbar, and a scrollable tree-view region (see Figure 5.1).

FIGURE 5.1    The Solution Explorer.

The tree view provides a graphics- and text-organizational view of the currently loaded solution. Figure 5.1 shows all the various items and projects represented for a thirteen-project solution loaded in the IDE.

## Visual Cues and Icons

Each item in the Solution Explorer is represented by a name and by an icon. Table 5.1 summarizes which icon is used to represent the supported item types.

TABLE 5.1    Solution Explorer Item Types and Icons

| Icon | Item | Notes |
|---|---|---|
| | About Box | Visual Basic only. |
| | Application Diagram | |
| | ASP.NET Web Site | This represents the root node for an ASP.NET website project. |
| | Bitmap File | |
| | Class Diagram | |
| | Component Class | |
| | Custom Control | |
| | DataSet | |
| | Dialog | Visual Basic only. |
| | Folder | Solution folders or project folders. |
| | Global Application Class | |
| | HTML Page | |
| | Icon File | |
| | Interface (Visual Basic) | |
| | Interface (Visual C#) | |
| | Logical Datacenter Diagram | |
| | Master Page | Web projects only. |
| | Module | Visual Basic only. |
| | My Project File | Visual Basic equivalent to the C# Properties folder. |
| | Partial Class | |
| | Project Reference | Visual C# only. |
| | Properties Folder | Visual C# equivalent to the Visual Basic My Project File folder. |
| | References Folder | Visual C# only. |
| | Resources Folder | |
| | Settings Folder | |
| | Site Map | Web projects only. |
| | Skin File | Web projects only. |
| | Solution | This is the topmost, root node visible within Solution Explorer. |

TABLE 5.1    Continued

| Icon | Item | Notes |
|------|------|-------|
| | Style Sheet | |
| | System Diagram | |
| | Text File | |
| | User Control | Any class that inherits directly from the `UserControl` class. |
| | User Control (Web) | Class that inherits from TODO. |
| | VBScript/JScript File | |
| | Visual Basic Class File | |
| | Visual Basic Project | This is the root node for a Visual Basic project. |
| | Visual C# Project | This is the root node for a Visual C# project. |
| | Visual C# Class File | |
| | Web Configuration File | |
| | Web Form (.aspx) | |
| | Web Service | |
| | Windows Form | Refers to a file containing a class that implements the Form class. |
| | Windows Form (Inherited) | |
| | Windows Form (MDI Parent) | Visual Basic only. |
| | Web Project | |
| | XML File | |
| | XML Schema File | |
| | XSLT File | |

**NOTE**

The icons shown in Table 5.1 are a representative list of icons that correspond to specific project and solution items within the IDE. Other files added to a project or solution will be represented by the icon associated with their file type. For example, a Word document will be represented by the standard Word document icon in the Solution Explorer.

## Icon Overlays

To provide a visual cue about the status of a particular item, the Solution Explorer will overlay an additional graphical element over the item icon. These overlays are called *signal icons*. For example, when source code control is enabled, the Solution Explorer visually indicates whether an item is checked out via a graphical overlay. Table 5.2 describes the version control signal icons used by the Solution Explorer to indicate the current version control status of the item. Note that the version control state of an item is dependent on the actual version control system you are using (for instance, Visual Source Safe or Team Foundation Source Control).

TABLE 5.2    Version Control Signal Icons

| Icon | Description |
| --- | --- |
| 🄾 | Item not found. The item was specified as part of the solution/project, but can't be located. |
| 🔒 | Checked in. The item is under source code control and is currently checked in. |
| ✔ | Checked out (exclusive). The item is under source code control and is currently checked out exclusively. |
| ✔ | Checked out (shared). The item is under source code control and is currently checked out in a shared mode. |
| ⊘ | Disabled. The item is located within a project that is under source control, but this item could not be added to source control. |
| ✎ | Editable. The item is available for editing. |
| ⊖ | Excluded. The item has been specifically excluded from version control. |
| ↰ | Orphaned. The item has been orphaned within the version control system because one or more dependency links have been broken. |
| ✚ | Pending Add. The item is scheduled to be added to the source control system during the next check-in. |
| 🔒 | Read Only. The item is not available for editing (this is the opposite of Editable). |

The Solution Explorer supports different management actions depending on whether you are currently interacting with a solution or a project. In fact, supported commands may vary by project type as well. As an example, the Copy Web Project command button is available for web projects but not class library projects, whereas the Properties command button is available for all item types.

Table 5.3 shows the various toolbar command buttons supported by the Solution Explorer, along with their specific context.

TABLE 5.3 Solution Explorer Toolbar Buttons

| Icon | Context | Description |
|---|---|---|
|  | All | Properties button. Launches the solution properties dialog. |
|  | Solution, solution item, solution folder | Add New Solution Folder button. Creates a new solution folder in the currently loaded solution. |
|  | Project, project item | Refresh. Refreshes the solution explorer's tree view of the project. |
|  | Web project, web project item | Nest Related Files. Visual Studio has the capability to group certain project item constructs together. This is most commonly done with items such as code behind files. This is a toggle button: Clicking it "on" causes related files to be nested underneath the "parent" file. Clicking it "off" causes all files to show up at the same level under the project. |
|  | Project, project item | View Class Diagram. Creates a class diagram project item and launches the viewer for that item. All the types contained within the project will be automatically added to the diagram. |
|  | Web project, web project item | Copy Web Site. Copies the website to a specified location (available only for web projects). |
|  | Web project, web project item | ASP.NET Configuration. Launches a browser to the ASP.NET Web Site Administration tool. This is useful for setting up global security parameters and application-specific options. |
|  | Solution, solution item, project, project item (only if items in the solution are currently hidden) | Unhide All. Unhides any hidden items in the solution. |
|  | Project code files | View Code. Opens the current item in the code editor. |
|  | Project code files with a UI (Windows Form or Web Form) | View Designer. Opens the designer for the currently selected item. |

## Managing Solutions

Clicking on the solution in Solution Explorer will immediately expose all the valid management commands for that solution. You access these commands through either the Solution Explorer toolbar or the context menu for the solution (which you access by right-clicking on the solution). Through the toolbar and the solution's context menu, the Solution Explorer allows you to do the following:

- ▶ View and set the properties for a solution

- ▶ Build/rebuild a solution

- ▶ Directly launch the configuration manager for a solution

- ▶ Set project dependencies and build order

- ▶ Add any of the various Visual Studio–supported solution and project items

- ▶ Add the solution to the source control

You can initiate some of these actions by using the Solution Explorer toolbar; you can access the balance in the context menu for a solution, as shown in Figure 5.2.

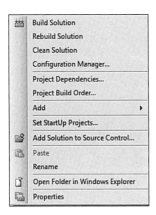

FIGURE 5.2   The solution context menu.

## Managing Projects

Just as with solutions, Solution Explorer provides various ways to manage projects within a solution. They include these:

- ▶ Opening a project item

- ▶ Building or rebuilding a project

- ▶ Adding items to a project

▶ Adding a reference to a project

▶ Cutting, pasting, renaming, or deleting a project within the solution tree

▶ Unloading a project

> **NOTE**
>
> The current startup project for a solution is indicated with a bold font (as is the OrderEntry project in Figure 5.1). If multiple projects are selected as startup projects, the solution name is instead bolded.

The default action when you double-click an item is to open it within its default editor or designer. Multiple select and drag-and-drop operations are also supported. For instance, multiselecting several code files allows you to open them simultaneously in their editor windows.

You can move and copy items within a solution, within a project, or between projects through the standard drag and drop using the left mouse button. You can also drag certain items from within a project and drop them onto a suitable designer surface. This is an easy way, for instance, to add classes to a class diagram: Simply highlight the code files that contain the types you want to add and drag them onto the class diagram designer window.

# Class View

The Class View window is similar in design and function to the Solution Explorer window. It, too, provides a hierarchical view of project elements. However, the view here is not based on the physical files that constitute a solution or project; rather, this window provides a view of the various namespaces, types, interfaces, and enums within a project.

The Class View window is composed of four major visual components: a toolbar, a search bar, a tree view of types (called the *objects pane*), and a members pane, as shown in Figure 5.3.

## Toolbar

The Class View window's toolbar provides easy access to command buttons for adding virtual folders, moving forward and back through the objects pane items, and controlling which objects are displayed.

Table 5.4 describes the various Class View toolbar buttons.

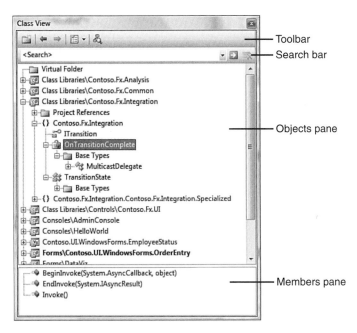

FIGURE 5.3   The Class View window.

TABLE 5.4   Class View Toolbar Buttons

| Icon | Description |
| --- | --- |
| | Class View New Folder. Creates a virtual folder used to organize objects within the objects pane. |
| | Back. Causes the previously selected item to become the currently selected item. |
| | Forward. Causes the most recently selected item to become the currently selected item. This button is available only after you've used the Back button. |
| | Class View Settings. Displays a drop-down that allows selection of object types to display within the objects pane and the members pane. The available options include these:<br>Show Base Types<br>Show Derived Types<br>Show Project References<br>Show Hidden Types and References<br>Show Public Members<br>Show Protected Members<br>Show Private Members<br>Show Other Members<br>Show Inherited Members |
| | View Class Diagram. Creates a class diagram project item and launches the viewer for that item. All the types contained within the project are automatically added to the diagram. |

## Search Bar

The search bar is a drop-down text box that provides a quick and easy way to filter the objects shown in the objects pane. When a search term (such as type name or namespace name) is entered, the Class View window will clear the objects pane and then repopulate it with only those objects that match the search term. Figure 5.4 shows the results of a search for ITransition.

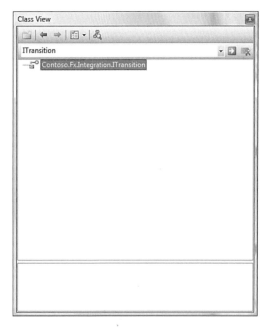

FIGURE 5.4    Filtering the objects pane.

To restore the objects pane and remove the filter, click on the Clear Search button to the right of the Search button.

Recent search terms are saved for reuse in the drop-down list.

## Objects Pane

The objects pane encloses a tree of objects grouped, at the highest level, by project. Each object is identified by an icon and by its name. Expanding a project node within the tree will reveal the various types contained within that project. Further parent-child relationships are also visible, such as the namespace-to-class relationship and the type-to-parent-type relationship.

Table 5.5 shows the icons used in the objects pane.

TABLE 5.5   Objects Pane Icons

| Icon | Description |
|------|-------------|
|  | Class/Struct |
|  | Delegate |
|  | Enum |
|  | Namespace |
|  | Module |
|  | Interface |

Certain signal images are also overlaid on top of these icons to visually represent scope and access information for each object. These access type signal icons are shown in Table 5.6.

TABLE 5.6   Scope/Access Signal Icons

| Icon | Description |
|------|-------------|
|  | Private |
|  | Internal/Friend |
| (n/a) | Public |
|  | Protected |

The depth of the various levels shown for each object will be dictated by the view settings in place at the time. For instance, turning on the Show Base Types option will append an additional base type level to the tree for each type. The objects pane's principal duty is to allow quick and easy navigation back and forth through the object tree for each project. It exposes, in other words, an object-oriented view of each project.

Right-clicking within the objects pane will display the shortcut menu. The menu is essentially identical to the shortcut menu exposed by the Solution Explorer, with the exception of various Sort and Group By selections. These are the Sort options available here:

▶ **Sort Alphabetically**—The projects, namespaces, and types in the objects pane will be sorted in ascending, alphabetic order.

▶ **Sort by Object Type**—The types in the objects pane will be alphabetically sorted by their general classification (for example, in the following order: classes, enums, interfaces, structs).

▶ **Sort by Object Access**—The types will be sorted by their access modifier (public, private, protected, and so on).

▶ **Group by Object Type**—Another folder level will be added to the tree for each distinct object type present. For example, if a project contains both class and interface types, a class folder and an interface folder will be displayed in the objects pane tree, with their correlated types contained within.

## Members Pane

The members pane reacts to the selection(s) made in the objects pane by displaying all the members—properties, events, constants, variables, enums—defined on the selected type. Each member has a distinctive icon to immediately convey information such as scope and type; even member signatures show up here (note that the same signal icons used by the objects pane, and documented in Table 5.7, are used here as well).

The members pane is ideal for quickly visualizing type behavior and attributes: Just select the class/type in the objects pane and browse its members in the members pane.

TABLE 5.7    Members Pane Icons

| Icon | Description |
| --- | --- |
| 🔳 | Constant |
| 🔷 | Method/Function |
| 🔲 | Property |
| 🔵 | Field |

**NOTE**

Many developers will find that the bulk of their development tasks are more easily envisioned and acted on here within the Class View window rather than in the Solution Explorer window. The available actions among the two are virtually identical, and the Class View window provides a much more code-focused perspective of your projects. Developers can spelunk through inheritance trees and see, at a glance, the various members implemented on each defined type within their project. The con to using the Class View is that source code control information is not visually surfaced here.

The members pane also exposes a context menu that has invaluable tools for browsing and editing code. For one, you can directly apply the Rename refactoring to a selected member. Other capabilities exposed here include the capability to immediately view the definition code for a member, to find every code location where the selected member is referenced, and to launch the Object Browser with the primary node for the member already selected for you.

The capability to alter the filter and display settings is also presented here. Figure 5.5 illustrates all the available commands on this menu.

FIGURE 5.5    The members pane context menu.

# Server Explorer

The Server Explorer window serves two purposes: It exposes various system services and resources that reside on your local machine and on remote machines, and it provides access to data connection objects. As with the other Visual Studio explorer windows, the systems, services, resources, and data connections are viewed in a graphical tree format. Systems appear under a top-level Servers node (your local machine will show up by default), and data connections appear under a top-level Data Connections node.

> **NOTE**
>
> The Server Explorer window content and configuration are not specific to a solution or project. Server Explorer settings are preserved as part of the IDE environment settings and are thus not subject to change on a per-solution (or project) basis.

A toolbar appears at the top of the Server Explorer window, providing one-click access to the Add Data Connection and Add Server functions (see Figure 5.6). You can also force a refresh of the window contents (a button is also provided to cancel the refresh because querying remote machines may be a lengthy process).

> **NOTE**
>
> The Express and Standard editions of Visual Studio do not have support for servers within the Server Explorer window; they are limited to data connections only. In fact, these versions of Visual Studio actually refer to this window as the Data Explorer window.

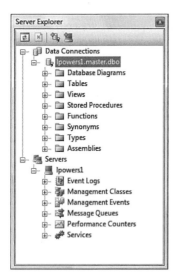

FIGURE 5.6    The Server Explorer window.

## Data Connections

Data Connections represent a physical connection to a local or remote database. Through an established connection, you can gain access to and manipulate the various objects within a database. Each category of object will show up as a folder node under the Data Connections node. The tree items under each node allow you to directly interact with their physical database counterparts through a suite of designers and editors collectively referred to as *Visual Database Tools*. These tools are covered in depth in Chapter 18, "Working with Databases."

The following objects are exposed in the Server Explorer:

▶ Tables

▶ Views

▶ Stored procedures

▶ Functions

▶ Synonyms

▶ Types

▶ Assemblies

In general, you can create new database objects, edit or delete existing ones, and, where appropriate, query data from a database object (such as a table or view).

---

**NOTE**

The level of functionality and the number of object types you can access through the Server Explorer depend on both the version of Visual Studio you are using and the version of the database you are connecting to. In other words, not all functions are supported across all databases. The Visual Database Tools interact most effectively with Microsoft SQL Server, although most basic functions are supported against a variety of other relational databases.

---

## Server Components

The Servers node in Server Explorer exposes various remote or local services and resources for direct management or use within a Visual Studio project. In essence, it is a management console for server-based components. By default, your local machine will be visible here as a server; to add other servers, right-click on the Servers node and select Add Server or simply click on the Connect to Server button in the Server Explorer toolbar. A dialog box will prompt you for a computer name or IP address for the server; this dialog box also supports the capability to connect via a different set of credentials.

Under the Servers node, the following component categories will appear as child nodes:

- ▶ Event Logs
- ▶ Management Classes
- ▶ Management Events
- ▶ Message Queues
- ▶ Performance Counters
- ▶ Services

Other component categories may also choose to register for display under the Servers node; the preceding list, however, represents the default, out-of-the-box functionality provided by Visual Studio 2008.

### Event Logs

Under the Event Logs node, you can administer the separate application, security, and system event logs for the connected server. This includes clearing event log entries or drilling into and inspecting individual event log entries. Highlighting an event log or event log entry causes its properties to display in the Visual Studio property window, enabling you to view and edit their values. If you drag and drop one of the event logs into a project, a `System.Diagnostics.EventLog` or `System.Diagnostic.EventLogEntry` component instance will automatically be created.

**Management Classes**

The items under the Management Classes node represent various Windows Management Instrumentation (WMI) classes. Each of these classes maps to a logical or physical entity associated with a server. The available classes here are shown in Table 5.8.

TABLE 5.8    WMI Management Class Nodes

| Title | WMI Class |
| --- | --- |
| Desktop Settings | Win32_Desktop |
| Disk Volumes | Win32_LogicalDisk |
| My Computer | Win32_ComputerSystem |
| Network Adapters | Win32_NetworkAdapter |
| Network Connections | Win32_NetworkConnection |
| NT Event Log Files | Win32_NTEventLogFile |
| Operating Systems | Win32_OperatingSystem |
| Printers | Win32_Printer |
| Processes | Win32_Process |
| Processors | Win32_Processor |
| Services | Win32_Service |
| Shares | Win32_Share |
| Software Products | Win32_Product |
| System Accounts | Win32_SystemAccount |
| Threads | Win32_Thread |

A thorough discussion of WMI is beyond the scope of this chapter and this book; in summary, however, each of these nodes exposes various WMI class property groups (such as precedents, antecedents, settings, dependents), and, in turn, each of these property groups will expose a span of commands, enabling you to directly affect a resource on the server. One simple example of how you might use this capability is to set access information for a share exposed on a remote server. When you expand nodes in the Server Explorer down to the share (via the Disk Volumes node), access to the share information is gained via the shortcut menu on the share. In this example, you would select the SetShareInfo action, which initiates a WMI dialog box allowing you to change various share attributes such as the description and maximum allowed users.

**Management Events**

The Management Events node contains a list of event queries; essentially, these are "listeners" that you establish to periodically poll the WMI eventing system on the server. These event queries are established through a dialog box (see Figure 5.7; you launch the dialog box by selecting Add Event Query on the shortcut menu). When an event is created, a child node to the Management Events node is created, and under this node, actual event instances will appear.

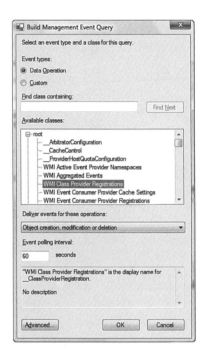

FIGURE 5.7    Creating a Management Event query.

### Message Queues

If message queuing is installed on the target server, the Message Queues node displays all the available message queues, along with any messages currently residing in each queue.

### Performance Counters

Every performance counter installed on the target computer can be viewed in the Performance Counters node. Each performance counter is displayed within its category. Performance counter instances, if available, are also displayed.

### Services

Each installed service is enumerated under the Services node.

### Programming with Server Explorer

Beyond allowing you to examine and manipulate data connections and server resources, the Server Explorer serves another task: By dragging and dropping items from the Server Explorer onto a Visual Studio design surface, you can quickly create components in code that directly reference the item in question. As an example, dragging the Application Log node (from Servers, Event Logs) onto an existing Windows form will create a

`System.Diagnostics.EventLog` component instance that is preconfigured to point to the application log. You can then immediately write code to interact with the event log component. You could use the same process to quickly embed message queue access into your application or read from/write to a performance counter. Table 5.9 lists the various possible drag-and-drop operations, along with their results.

TABLE 5.9    Server Explorer Drag and Drop

| Under This Node... | Dragging This... | Does This |
| --- | --- | --- |
| Event Logs | Event Log Category (e.g., Application or System) | Creates a `System.Diagnostics.EventLog` component instance, configured for the appropriate event log |
| Management Classes | Management Class instance | Creates the appropriate WMI/CIMv2 component instance |
| Management Events | Management Event Query | Creates a `System.Management.ManagementEventWatcher` component instance |
| Message Queues | Message Queue instance | Creates a `System.Messaging.MessageQueue` component instance for the selected queue |
| Performance Counters | Performance Counter or counter instance | Creates a `System.Diagnostics.PerformanceCounter` component instance, configured for the appropriate counter |
| Services | Service | Creates a `System.ServiceProcess.ServiceController`, provisioned for the indicated service |

**NOTE**

Data connection items in the Server Explorer cannot be dragged onto a design surface. For more information regarding drag-and-drop development of database solutions, see Chapter 18.

# Object Browser

The Object Browser is similar in functionality and look and feel to the Class View window. It provides a hierarchical view of projects, assemblies, namespaces, types, enums, and interfaces. Unlike the Class View window, however, the Object Browser is capable of a much wider scope of objects. In addition to the currently loaded projects, the Object Browser is capable of displaying items from the entire .NET Framework, up to and including COM components and externally accessible objects. This is a great tool for finding and inspecting types, regardless of where they are physically located.

## Changing the Scope

You can use the toolbar's Browse drop-down to filter or change the scope of the objects displayed within the Object Browser. The scoping options offered are shown in Table 5.10.

TABLE 5.10   Object Browser Scoping Options

| Scope | Effect |
| --- | --- |
| All Components | This is a superset of the other scopes offered. Selecting this will show all types and members within the .NET Framework, the current solution, any libraries referenced by the current solution, and any individually selected components. |
| .NET Framework | Shows all objects within a specific version of the .NET Framework (e.g., .NET Framework 2.0, .NET Framework 3.0). |
| My Solution | Shows all objects with the currently loaded solution, including any referenced components. |
| Custom Component Set | Shows any objects specifically added to the custom component set. |

### Editing the Custom Component Set

A *custom component set* is a list of components that you manually specify. Using a custom list might be useful in situations in which you want to browse a list of components from a variety of different "buckets." Instead of wading through each of the other scopes, you could include only those types that you care about in the component list.

You add to the custom component list by selecting the Edit Custom Component Set option in the Browse drop-down or by clicking on the ellipses to the right of the drop-down. This will launch an editor dialog box in which you can add or remove entries in this list (see Figure 5.8).

Adding a component to the set is as easy as selecting from one of the prepopulated object lists (available via the .NET, COM, or Projects tabs) or by browsing directly to the container assembly via the Browse tab. You can select an object or objects and then click the Add button. The current set members show up at the bottom of the dialog box. You can also select a current member and remove it from the list by clicking the Remove button.

## Browsing Objects

The Object Browser consists of a toolbar and three different panes: an objects pane, a members pane, and a description pane. Again, the similarity here to the Class View window is obvious. The toolbar, objects pane, and members pane function identically to the Class View objects pane and members pane. You click down through the tree view to view each individual object's members; the toolbar aids in navigating deep trees by providing a Forward and Back button. Figure 5.9 shows the Object Browser in action.

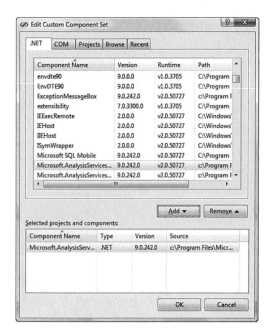

FIGURE 5.8 Editing the custom component set.

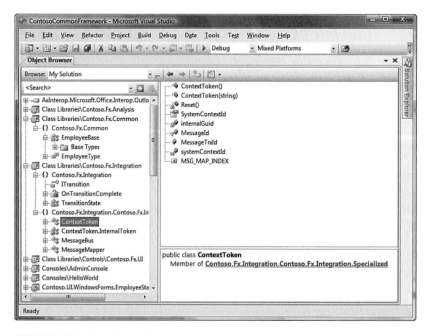

FIGURE 5.9 The Object Browser.

The hierarchical relationships, icons, and actions possible within the panes are the same (and therefore we won't rehash them here). The description pane, however, is a new concept.

### Description Pane

When an item is selected in either the Object Browser's objects pane or members pane, the description pane will provide detailed information about the selected item. The data provided is quite extensive, and includes the following:

▶ The name of the selected object

▶ The name of the parent of the selected object

▶ Code comments and in-line help associated with the selected object

Where possible, the description pane will embed hyperlinks within the data that it displays to allow you to easily navigate to related items. As an example, a declared property of type `string` might show the following description:

```
public string SystemContextId { set; get; }
    Member of Contoso.Fx.Integration.ContextToken
```

Note the use of hyperlinking: Clicking on the string identifier navigates to the `string` data type within the Object Browser window. Similarly, clicking on the Contoso.Fx.Integration.ContextToken hyperlink navigates the browser to the class definition for the `ContextToken` class.

> **TIP**
>
> You can click on an assembly in the objects pane and quickly add it as a reference to the current project by clicking on the Add to References button, located on the Object Browser's toolbar.

# Document Outline

The Document Outline window (opened from the View, Other Windows menu) exposes a hierarchical view of elements residing on a Windows form or web form. This window is a fantastic tool for "re-parenting" form items or changing the z-order of a control within its parent. In addition, it assists with understanding the exact logical structure of a form that may have a lot happening on it from a visual perspective.

Figures 5.10 and 5.11 show the Document Outline windows for a simple web form and a slightly more complicated Windows form.

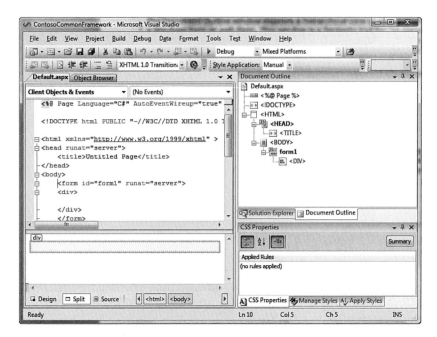

FIGURE 5.10   A web form.

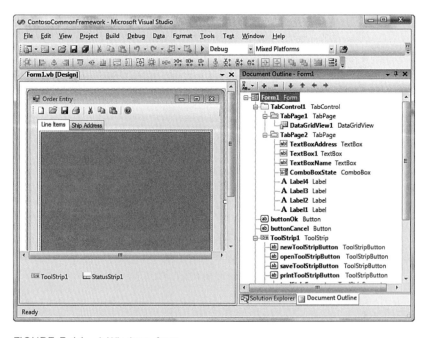

FIGURE 5.11   A Windows form.

The Document Outline toolbar allows you to control the display of the types within the tree view and also facilitates reordering and repositioning elements within the outline. Table 5.11 shows the toolbar commands available in the Document Outline window.

TABLE 5.11    Document Outline Toolbar Commands

| Icon | Description |
|------|-------------|
| | Type Name Display Style. This drop-down button allows you to control how type names are displayed in the tree view: <br> None—No type names are displayed. <br> Short—The local, unqualified type name is displayed. <br> Long—The fully qualified type name is displayed. |
| | Expand All. Causes all the parent nodes to expand. |
| | Collapse All. Causes all the parent nodes to collapse. |
| | Move Down in Container. Moves the currently selected item down one place within its order in the current container. |
| | Move Up in Container. Moves the currently selected item up one place within its order in the current container. |
| | Move Out of Current Container. Moves the currently selected item out of its current container and places it in the next, higher container (or within the root level if no container exists). |
| | Move into Next Container. Moves the currently selected item out of its current container (or root level) and into the next container. |

### Editing Elements

The Document Outline makes it easy to instantly jump from the hierarchical element view directly to the underlying code for an item. If an item is currently being edited in the designer/code window, it will be highlighted within the outline tree. Conversely, selecting an item within the outline view will cause the item to be selected/highlighted within the designer/code window.

Besides using the toolbar commands in Table 5.11, you can use drag-and-drop actions within the tree view to move elements around in the outline.

## Summary

In this chapter, we have seen that browsers and explorers are Visual Studio windows that typically provide a hierarchical view of their content. They tend to share common interface elements (tree views, toolbars, and elements), and they are, in effect, the primary means to visualize and interact with project elements within the IDE.

Browsers and explorers provide simple point-and-click interfaces for

- ▶ Visualizing and organizing your solutions and projects on a file-by-file basis.
- ▶ Visualizing and organizing your projects on a type-by-type, class-by-class basis.
- ▶ Querying and interacting with server resources such as databases, performance counters, and message queues.
- ▶ Browsing through type libraries.

Although certain browsers/explorers touch underlying concepts that are fairly deep and complicated (WMI, for instance), they are all geared toward a common goal: extending the reach of the IDE as a rapid application development tool for tasks beyond simple code file editing.

# CHAPTER 6

# Introducing the Editors and Designers

Although Visual Studio provides an impressive array of functionality for nearly all areas of the development process, its editors and designers are the real heart of the IDE. They are the bread-and-butter tools of the programmer: They enable you to write code, edit resources, design forms, and construct schemas. And, of course, each of these tools has key features designed to boost your productivity and the quality of your output.

This chapter is squarely focused on using these editors and designers to create solutions within the IDE.

## The Basics

Broadly speaking, a Visual Studio editor is a text editor (think word processor) that enables you to write specific output efficiently (Visual Basic code, HTML, XAML, and so on). A designer, on the other hand, is a *visual* editor, enabling you to work with visual concepts directly instead of text. Many document types are supported by both designers and editors: You can build a form, for instance, by using the drag-and-drop convenience of the Windows Forms designer or by handcrafting the code within a text editor; or you can build an XML file using the same mechanisms.

The Visual Studio text editor provides the core text-editing functionality for all the editors. This functionality is then inherited and added upon to create editors specific for a given document type. Thus, you have a code editor for source code files, an XML editor for markup, a CSS editor for style sheets, and so on.

Likewise, designers manifest themselves in ways specific to their role. The HTML designer is part text editor and part graphical tool, and the Windows and web forms designers are superb WYSIWYG form builders.

## The Text Editor

There are a few text-editing features that we all take for granted: selecting parts of an existing body of text, inserting text into a document, copying and pasting text, and so on. As you would expect, the text editor window supports all of these features in a way that will be familiar to anyone who has used a Windows-based word processor.

You select text, for instance, by using the following familiar actions:

1.  Place the cursor at the start of the text you want to select.
2.  While holding down the left mouse button, sweep the mouse to the end of the text you want selected.
3.  Release the left mouse button.

In addition to this "standard" selection method, the Visual Studio text editor supports "column mode" selection. In column mode, instead of selecting text in a linear fashion from left to right, line-by-line, you drag a selection rectangle across a text field. Any text character caught within the selection rectangle is part of the selected text. This is called *column mode* because it allows you to create a selection area that captures columns of text characters instead of just lines. The procedure is largely the same:

1.  Place the cursor at the start of the text you want to select.
2.  While holding down the Alt key *and* the left mouse button, expand the bounds of the selection rectangle until it includes the desired text.
3.  Release the left mouse button and the Alt key.

After you've selected text, you can copy, cut, or drag it to a new location within the text editor. As with text selection, the commands for cutting, copying, and pasting text remain unchanged from their basic, standard implementation in other Windows applications: You first select text and then cut or copy it using the Edit menu, the toolbar, or the text editor's shortcut menu.

By dragging a text selection, you can reposition it within the current text editor; place it in another, previously opened text editor window; or even drag the selection into the command or watch windows.

### Line Wrapping and Virtual Space

The default behavior of the text editor is not to automatically wrap any text for you. In other words, as you type, your text or code will simply keep trailing on to the right of the editor. If you exceed the bounds of the currently viewable area, the editor window will simply scroll to the right to allow you to continue typing. However, the text editor window can behave more like a word processor, in which the document content is typically constrained horizontally to its virtual sheet of paper.

**TIP**

With word wrapping turned on, Visual Studio will automatically wrap your text onto the next line. You can also have the IDE place a visual glyph which indicates that a wrap has taken place. Both of these options are controlled on the Options dialog box, under the Text Editor, All Languages, General page (shown in Figure 6.1).

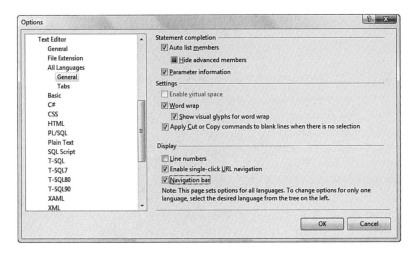

FIGURE 6.1   Editor Options dialog box.

If you override the default behavior, turn wrapping on, and then type a line of code that exceeds the editor's width, you can see that the editor window (see Figure 6.2) automatically wraps the source to fit within the boundaries of the window and provides an icon to the far right of the editor to indicate that a wrap has taken place. Word wrapping is useful for keeping all of your code in plain sight (without the need for scrolling horizontally).

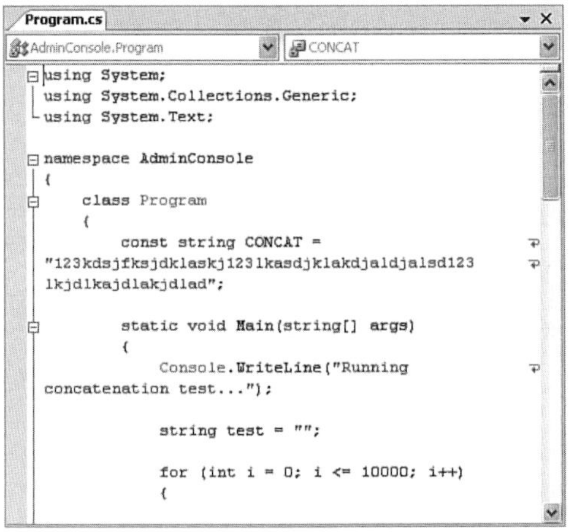

FIGURE 6.2   Word wrapping in the editor.

The other option on the Text Editor Options dialog box, Enable Virtual Space, is a mutually exclusive feature to word wrapping. That is, you can enable virtual space *or* word wrapping, but not both. Virtual Space refers to the capability to type text anywhere within the editor window without entering a bunch of spaces or tabs in the text area. This feature is useful in situations in which you want to place, for example, a code comment to the right of a few lines of code. Instead of tabbing each code comment over (or padding spaces before them) to get them to indent and line up nicely, you can simply place the cursor at the exact column within the text editor where you want your comments to appear. See Figure 6.3 for an example; the code comments in the screenshot were not preceded by any spaces or tabs. They were simply typed directly into their current positions.

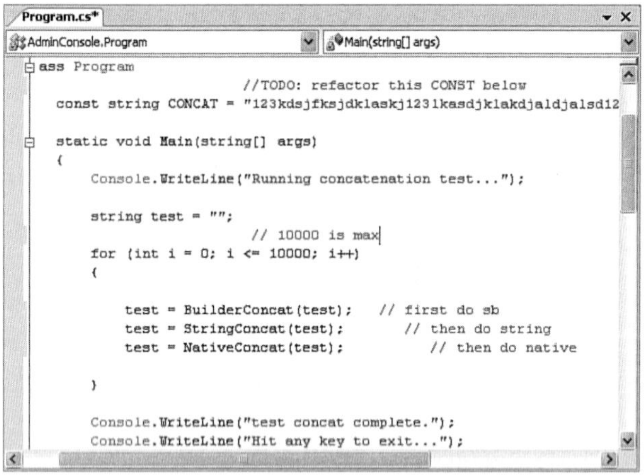

FIGURE 6.3    Virtual spacing in the editor window.

## Visual Studio Designers

Designers are much more visual in nature than the text editors within Visual Studio; they provide a graphical perspective of a particular solution artifact. Thus, a form will appear within a designer just as it would to the end user: as visual constructs made up of buttons, borders, menus, and frames. The code to implement the items shown in a designer is actually written by Visual Studio itself.

Like the various editors, the designers are all similar in form and function. They occupy space within the tabbed documents area of the IDE (just as the editors do). They may take on different behaviors depending on their target use. The Windows Forms designer and the component designer both appear nearly the same, but there are subtle differences in their usage.

# Coding with the Code Editor

Writing code and creating other syntax-based files are really all about typing text. The text editor window is the Visual Studio tool directly mapped to the task of creating source code text files. It is the keystone of development inside the IDE. It supports text entry and basic text operations such as selecting text regions, dragging and dropping text fragments, and setting tab stops. With basic text features alone, the editor would be sufficient to code with. However, the features layered on top for debugging, code formatting, code guidance, and customization really make this tool shine.

As we mentioned previously, the text editor actually has a few different personalities within the IDE. The code editor is designed to support creating and editing of source code files, the XML editor is targeted at XML files, and the CSS editor is targeted at CSS files. Although there may be subtle differences in the way that code or markup is displayed in these windows, they all share the user interface and the same set of editing functionality.

> **TIP**
>
> Each editor type is fully customizable. Just fire up the Options dialog box (by choosing Tools, Options) and locate the Text Editor node. Under this node are separate pages that allow customization of each editor type.

## Opening an Editor

There are two ways to launch a text editor (or any other editor in the IDE, for that matter). The first way involves using the Solution Explorer: Select an existing code file, text file, or other type file and double-click on the file. If it is a code file, you can also right-click on it and select View Code. The file content is loaded into a new editor window.

The second way to launch an editor window is to choose File, New, File. This launches the New File dialog box. Selecting a code template from this dialog box launches a code editor prefilled with the initial code stubs relevant to the template selected.

> **TIP**
>
> The text editor windows live as tabbed windows front-and-center within the IDE. If multiple code editors are open, they will each be accessible by their tab. If a lot of editors are open at one time, finding the window you are looking for by cycling through the tabs may be cumbersome. There are four ways to quickly locate and select a code editor window. First, you can use Solution Explorer. Double-clicking on the code file again within the Solution Explorer will select and display the associated code editor window. Second, you can use the Window menu. Each open code editor window is shown by name in the windows list under the Window menu. Third, to the far right of the editor tabs, right next to the Close icon, is a small drop-down button in the image of an arrow. Clicking on the arrow drops down a list of all open editor windows, allowing you to select one at will. And finally, Visual Studio has its own version of the Windows switcher: Hold down the Ctrl key and tap the Tab key to cycle through a list of all windows open in IDE.

## Writing Code in the Code Editor

Because the code editor's primary purpose is "word processing" for source code, let's first look at writing the simplest of routines—a "Hello, World" function—from the ground up using the code editor.

Figure 6.4 shows a code editor with an initial stubbed-out console file. This was produced by creating a new Visual C# Console project using the Solution Explorer. Double-clicking on the Program.cs file within that new project displays the source code for this console application.

FIGURE 6.4    The initial template console code.

As you can see, Visual Studio, as a result of the template used for creating the project, has already filled in some code:

```
using System;
using System.Collections.Generic;
using System.Linq;
using System.Text;

namespace HelloWorld
{
    class Program
    {
        static void Main(string[] args)
        {
        }
    }
}
```

To demonstrate the code editor in action, you will create a console application that outputs the "Hello, World!" string to the console window.

Within the Main routine, add the following:

```
Console.WriteLine("Hello, World!");
```

To begin writing the code, you simply place your cursor in the window by clicking within the Main routine's braces, press Enter to get some space for the new line of code, and type the Console.WriteLine syntax.

These and other productivity enhancers are discussed at great length in the next chapter. Here, we will focus on the basics of editing and writing code in the editor window.

Now that you have seen the code editor in action (albeit for a very simple example), you're ready to dig more into the constituent components of the editor window.

## Anatomy of the Code Editor Window

Editor windows, as you have seen, show up as tabbed windows within the IDE and are typically front-and-center visually in terms of windows layout. As you can see with the code editor window in Figure 6.5, each text editor window consists of three primary regions: a code pane, a selection margin, and an indicator margin. There are also both horizontal and vertical scrollbars for navigating around the displayed file.

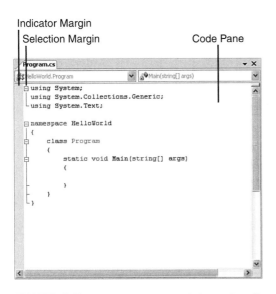

FIGURE 6.5   The components of the code editor window.

These regions, and their functionality, remain the same for all editor types within the IDE.

The code editor adds an additional set of UI elements that are not present with the other editors: Two drop-down boxes at the top of the code editor window enable you to quickly navigate through source code by selecting a type in the left drop-down and then selecting a specific type member (property, field, function, and so on) in the right drop-down (these drop-downs are called *class* and *method name*, respectively, in Visual Basic). This will jog the current cursor location directly to the indicated type.

> **NOTE**
>
> The type drop-down displays only those types that are declared in the file currently displayed in the editor; it won't display a list that is global to the entire solution, project, or even namespace. Likewise, the type member drop-down displays only members for the selected type.

### The Code Pane

The code pane is the place where the document (source code, XML, and so on) is displayed and edited. This region provides basic text-editing functionality, in addition to the more advanced productivity features of the editor, such as IntelliSense.

Right-clicking within the code pane provides a shortcut menu (see Figure 6.6) that includes standard cut, copy, and paste verbs, along with an assortment of other handy editing actions.

FIGURE 6.6   Code editor shortcut menu for a WinForms file.

### The Indicator Margin

The indicator margin is the slim, gray-colored margin to the far left of the editor. This margin area is used to mark a line of code that contains a breakpoint or bookmark. Figure 6.7 shows the "Hello, World" example with a bookmark placed on the Main routine and a breakpoint placed on the Console.WriteLine command.

Clicking within the indicator margin will toggle a breakpoint on or off for the line of code you have selected (we cover more on the topic of breakpoints later in this chapter and in Chapter 10, "Debugging Code").

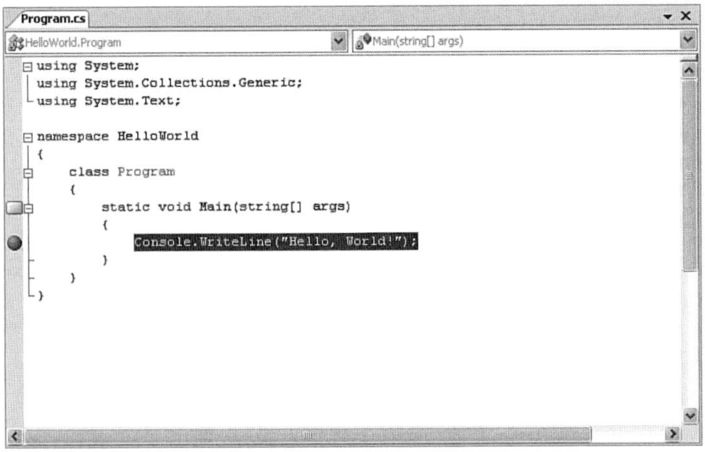

FIGURE 6.7   A bookmark and a breakpoint.

## The Selection Margin

The selection margin is a narrow region between the indicator margin and the editing area of the code pane. It provides the following:

▶ The capability to select an entire line of text by clicking within the selection margin.

▶ A visual indication—via colored indicator bars—of those lines of code that have changed during the current editing session.

▶ Line numbers if this option has been turned on. See the following section, where we discuss customizing the text editor's behavior.

You can clearly see the "changed text" indicator and line numbers in action in Figure 6.8.

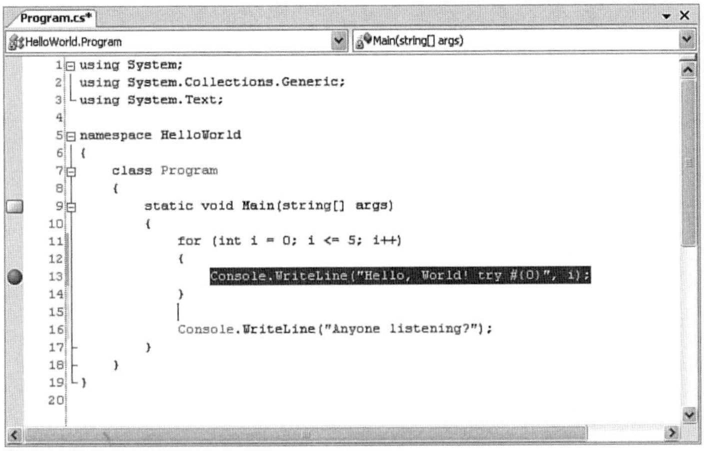

FIGURE 6.8   Changed text indicators.

---

**TIP**

Visual Studio provides a dedicated toolbar for the text editor. You can view this toolbar by selecting View, Toolbars, Text Editor. It exposes buttons for the Member List, Quick Info, Parameter List, and Word Completion IntelliSense features, in addition to indenting, commenting, and bookmark navigation buttons. The navigation buttons are arguably the most useful here because they provide easily accessible forward and back navigation through your code.

---

## Code Navigation Tools

As the lines of code in any given project increase, effectively navigating through the code base—that is, quickly and easily finding lines of interest among the potentially thousands or even millions of lines of code—becomes an issue.

The text editor comes equipped with several tools to help you mark lines of code, search and replace text across source files, and, in general, maintain your situational awareness from within a long code listing.

### Line Numbering

As we mentioned in the discussion of the text editor's selection margin, line numbering can be enabled for any given document loaded into an editor. This option is controlled in the Options dialog box within the Text Editor, All Languages, General page, or selectively under the individual languages and their General page.

By themselves, line numbers would be fairly useless. The capability to immediately jump to a line of code completes the equation and provides some real benefit from a navigation perspective. While within a text editor, press the Ctrl+G key combination to jump to a line of code. This triggers the Go To Line dialog box (see Figure 6.9), which provides a text box for specifying the line number to jump to and even indicates the valid "scope" for the jump by providing a line number range for the current document. Entering a valid line number here will move the current cursor position to the start of that line.

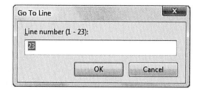

FIGURE 6.9    Jumping to a line.

### Bookmarks

Bookmarks tackle the problem of navigating through large code files. By placing a bookmark on a line of code, you can instantly navigate back to that line of code at any time. When dealing with a series of bookmarks, you can jump back and forth through the bookmarked lines of code. This turns out to be a surprisingly useful feature. If you are a developer who is dealing with a large base of source code, there will inevitably be points of interest within the source code that you want to view in the editor. Recall that the text editor window does provide a means of navigating via type and member drop-downs; these are not, however, the best tools for the job when your "line of interest" may be an arbitrary statement buried deep within a million lines of code.

Bookmarks are visually rendered in the indicator margin of the text editor (refer to Figure 6.8; a bookmark appears on line 9).

To add a bookmark or navigate through your bookmarks, you use either the text editor toolbar or the Bookmarks window.

You can view the Bookmarks window, shown in Figure 6.10, by choosing View, Other Windows, Bookmark Window. You will notice that this window provides a toolbar for bookmark actions and provides a list of all available bookmarks, along with their actual physical location (filename and line number within that file).

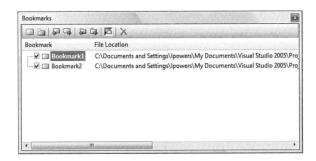

FIGURE 6.10    The Bookmarks window.

To toggle a bookmark for a given line of code, you first place your cursor on the desired line within the text editor and then click on the Toggle Bookmark button. The same process is used to toggle the bookmark off. Using the Forward and Back buttons within the bookmarks window will jump the text editor's cursor location back and forth through all available bookmarks.

**TIP**

Use the Bookmarks window to navigate through code across projects. You are not limited to bookmarks placed within a single code file; they can, in fact, be in *any* loaded code file. The list of bookmarks in this window is also a useful mechanism for quickly toggling a bookmark on or off (via the check box next to the bookmark) and for assigning a meaningful name to a bookmark. Right-clicking on a bookmark allows you to rename it something more meaningful than "Bookmark7."

**Bookmark Folders**    One interesting feature with the Bookmarks window is the capability to create a bookmark folder. This is an organizational bucket for related bookmarks. For instance, you may want to place bookmarks for a specific math algorithm under a folder called MathFuncs. To do this, you would first create a folder by using the New Folder button on the toolbar. You can rename the folder to whatever makes sense for your particular scenario. Then you can create a bookmark and drag and drop it into the folder.

See Figure 6.11 for a look at a populated Bookmarks window. Note that two folders are in use, in addition to bookmarks being shown for various source code files.

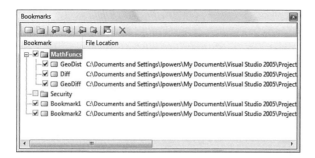

FIGURE 6.11    The Bookmarks window with folders.

## Searching Documents

The text editor window provides an extensive search-and-replace capability. Three primary methods of searching are supported: Quick Find (ideal for finding text fragments within the current document or set of open documents), Search In Files (ideal for finding text in a file residing anywhere with a folder structure), and Find Symbol (ideal for searching on objects or members by name). All of these search mechanisms are triggered through the Find and Replace window; a drop-down button on the Find and Replace window will control the mode of the window, which directly maps to the three search methods just itemized.

This same window is used to perform text substitution. This Replace functionality has two different modes that equate to the first two search modes. Thus, you have Quick Replace, which functions in a similar fashion to Quick Find, and Replace In Files, which functions in a similar fashion to Search In Files.

That makes a total of five different function modes for the Find and Replace tool:

- ▶ Quick Find
- ▶ Find In Files
- ▶ Find Symbol
- ▶ Quick Replace
- ▶ Replace In Files

Let's take a closer look at each of these search-and-replace modes individually.

### Quick Find/Quick Replace

Figure 6.12 illustrates the Find and Replace window in Quick Find mode. You have three pieces of information to fill in here: what you are searching for, what you want to search in, and the options to use to fine-tune your search parameters.

FIGURE 6.12    Quick Find mode.

The Find What drop-down, obviously, specifies the string to search for. This drop-down will hold the last 20 strings used in a Find operation, making it easy to reuse a previous search: Just select it from the list.

The Look In drop-down sets the scope of the search. For Quick Find searches, you have a few options to choose from:

- ▶ **Current Document**—This option indicates the currently active document within the text editor.

- ▶ **Selection**—If a portion of a document is selected within a text editor, this option will limit the search to only the selected text.

- ▶ **All Open Documents**—With this option, the search will be performed across any open documents.

- ▶ **Entire Solution**—This option expands the search to include all files within the solution.

- ▶ **Current Type**—If the cursor is currently positioned within an object or namespace code block, the "current type" option will allow you to search within that code block. Note that this option will use the name of the code block itself and won't display as "current type." Consider this example: A code editor window is open, and the cursor is placed within the definition for a class called `MessageBus`, within the `Contoso.Fx.Integration` namespace. The Look In drop-down will display an option called `Contoso.Fx.Integration.MessageBus` to limit the scope of the search to just this class. If the cursor is not positioned within a code block, this option will simply not display.

**Fine-Tuning Your Search**    Below the Look In control is a series of check boxes for fine-tuning the search. The effects these options have on your search are self-explanatory:

▶ Match Case causes the search to be executed against the exact case you used in the Find What drop-down.

▶ Match Whole Word forces the search to match only on the entire string as entered in the Find What drop-down.

▶ Search Up causes the search to move from bottom to top in a document (as opposed to the default top-to-bottom search).

▶ Search Hidden Text (selected by default) searches code regions that are currently not visible (in other words, collapsed code regions, a hidden outline region, design time metadata, and so on).

▶ Use Wildcards/Use Regular Expressions changes how the search engine performs matching on the Find What string. A standard search does a character match for the target string. You can also, however, use wildcard conventions (such as `Message*` to find any string starting with the text `Message`) or a full-blown regular expression to perform even more intricate searches. You would enter a regular expression as the Find What string.

---

**TIP**

If you elect to use wildcards or regular expressions for your search, there is a tool that can help you to write the correct syntax for the search phrase. If the Use check box is selected, a small button located directly to the right of the Find What drop-down will become enabled. This button will display the expression builder: a fly-out menu of expression syntax choices along with their descriptions. The context of this menu will change depending on whether you have indicated Wildcard or Regular Expressions.

---

**Finding Search Results**    After you have specified all the criteria for your search, the Find Next button at the bottom of the search window launches the search. Any matches within the scope specified are highlighted for you within the document. Clicking on the Find Next button moves to the next match until no more matches are found.

You also have the option of placing a bookmark against any matches. Just click the Bookmark All button.

**Replacing Text**    You set the Quick Replace mode (see Figure 6.13) by clicking on the right-most of the two mode buttons (in the same fashion that you set Quick Find mode). The Quick Replace process is virtually identical to Quick Find; a single additional field, used to specify the replacement text, is added to the dialog box. The Find What, Look In, and Find Options fields all remain the same in form and function.

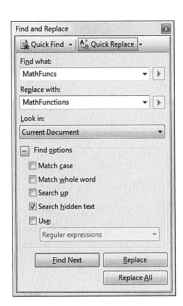

FIGURE 6.13   Quick Replace mode.

Two buttons are added to the dialog box to initiate the string replacement: Replace, which replaces the first instance found with the Replace With text, and Replace All, which replaces all instances found with the Replace With text. Note that any replacements made can always be undone via the Undo command under the Edit menu. These two buttons take the place of the Bookmark All button, which is not available in this mode.

**NOTE**

Although a complete discussion of regular expressions is outside the scope of this book, you should note that the Replace With box is capable of supporting tagged expressions. For more information on how you might use this to your advantage during replace operations, consult a regular expression reference manual and look at the MSDN Regular Expressions help topic for Visual Studio.

### Find In Files/Replace In Files

Figure 6.14 depicts the Find and Replace dialog box in Find In Files mode. The operation of this mode is similar to Quick Find, with a few minor differences. You still have to specify the "what" and the "where" components of the search. And you still can fine-tune your search, although you lose the Search Up and Search Hidden options because they don't make sense for a file-based search. The major differences with this mode are (1) the available search scopes you can specify in the Look In drop-down and (2) the way search results are displayed. Let's look at these two differences in turn.

FIGURE 6.14    Find In Files mode.

The search scope is notable in that it allows you to select the entire solution as your search target (in addition to the scopes supported for Quick Find). In addition, notice that you now have a Choose Search Folders button located just to the right of the Look In drop-down.

**Building Search Folder Sets**    Clicking the Choose Search Folders button launches a dialog box; this dialog box allows you to build up a set of directories as the scope of the search. You can name this folder set and even set the search order for the directories. Figure 6.15 captures this dialog box as a search set called ClassLibCode is built. You can see that three directories have been added to the set and that you can add more by simply browsing to the folder with the Available Folders control and adding them to the Selected Folders list.

**The Find Results Window**    With Quick Find, the search results are simply highlighted (or bookmarked) right within the text editor window. The Find In Files mode displays its search results in a separate, dedicated Find Results window (see Figure 6.16). You can redirect the output to one of two results windows by selecting either the Find Results 1 Window or Find Results 2 Window option at the bottom of the Find and Replace dialog box. These windows are identical; two options provided here allow you to keep different search results separate and avoid the confusion that the commingling of matches would cause if you were constrained to just one output window.

In Figure 6.16, you see the results of a simple search conducted across all the files in a solution. The interior of the Find Results window provides the following information:

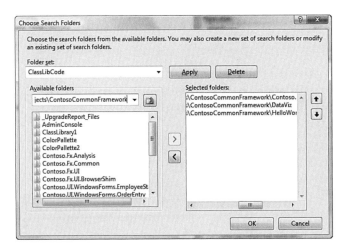

FIGURE 6.15    Building a Search Folder set.

FIGURE 6.16    The Find Results window.

▶ A description of the search performed (for example, `Find all "MessageBus"`, `Subfolders, Find Results 1, "Entire Solution"`).

▶ The matches returned from the search. Match information includes the file path and name, the line number within the file, and a verbatim repeat of the line of code containing the match.

▶ A summary of the find results, including the number of matching lines of code, the number of files containing matches, and the total number of files searched.

Double-clicking on one of the results lines in the window will jog the cursor location directly to the matching line within the editor. Note that this window has a toolbar. From left to right, the buttons on this toolbar allow you to do the following:

▶ Jump to the matched line of code within the text editor. (First place your cursor on the match inside the Find Results window, and then click on the Go to the Location of the Current Line button.)

▶ Move back and forth through the list of matches. Each matched item is highlighted in the Find Results window and in the Text Editor window.

▶ Clear the Find Results window.

▶ Cancel any ongoing searches.

**Replacing In Files**   The Replace In Files mode builds from the Find In Files mode by providing all the same functionality and adding back the ability to cycle through matching results in the Text Editor window. Replace, Replace All, and Skip File buttons also make an appearance in this mode (see Figure 6.17).

FIGURE 6.17    Replace In Files mode.

We've already covered the Replace and Replace All functions. Each file that matches the search phrase will be opened in a separate text editor window, and the replacements will be made directly in that window. If you're performing a Replace All, the replacements will be made and then saved directly into the containing file. You also have the option, via the Keep Modified Files Open After Replace All check box, to have Visual Studio keep any files touched open inside their respective text editors. This allows you to selectively save or discard the replacements as you see fit.

You can elect to skip files during the search-and-replace process by using the Skip File button. This button is available only if more than one file has been selected as part of the search scope. Clicking this button tells the search engine to skip the current file being processed and continue with the next in-scope file.

**Find Symbol**
The last search mode supported by the Find and Replace dialog box is called Find Symbol. It is used to search out lines of code in which a symbol is defined, referenced, or used.

This tighter search scope makes this the preferred mechanism for, say, finding all places where a class called `CustomAnalyzer` is referenced. You could use the other Find modes to locate this text, but the Find Symbol algorithm's tighter scope is much more relevant to this kind of search because it will not rove over any nonsymbol text in the document. In addition, the Find Symbol function uses reflection and the compiler to find symbol references; this is not a simple text search with a different scope.

The Find Symbol search also has two other distinguishing characteristics over the normal Find/Replace. It is able to search external components even in the absence of source code. As an example, you can opt to select .NET Framework in the Look In drop-down. Figure 6.18 shows the results of searching for the String symbol in the framework itself.

FIGURE 6.18   The Find Symbol Results window.

The second difference with Find Symbol is the capability to immediately jump to a referenced object's definition or browse its definition using the object browser. You can access both of these functions, Go To Definition and Browse Definition, by right-clicking on any of the matches displayed in the results window.

> **NOTE**
>
> If you are searching for a symbol within a library where you do not have access to the source code, the option to view the symbol's definition in source (for example, Go To Definition) will obviously not be available. However, you can still leverage the Browse Definition function to instantly pull the definition open in the object browser. It turns out that this is a great way to understand and explore libraries not of your own creation.

**Incremental Search**

Incremental Search functions without the aid of a dialog box. With a text editor open, select Edit, Advanced, Incremental Search (or press Ctrl+I). While Incremental Search is active, you will see a visual pointer cue composed of binoculars and a down arrow. If you start typing a search string, character-by-character, the first match found will be highlighted within the text editor window itself. With each successive character, the search string is altered and the search itself is reexecuted. The current search string is displayed on the Visual Studio status bar. Figure 6.19 illustrates an Incremental Search in progress; the characters *MESSA* have been entered, and you can see the first match flagged within the text editor.

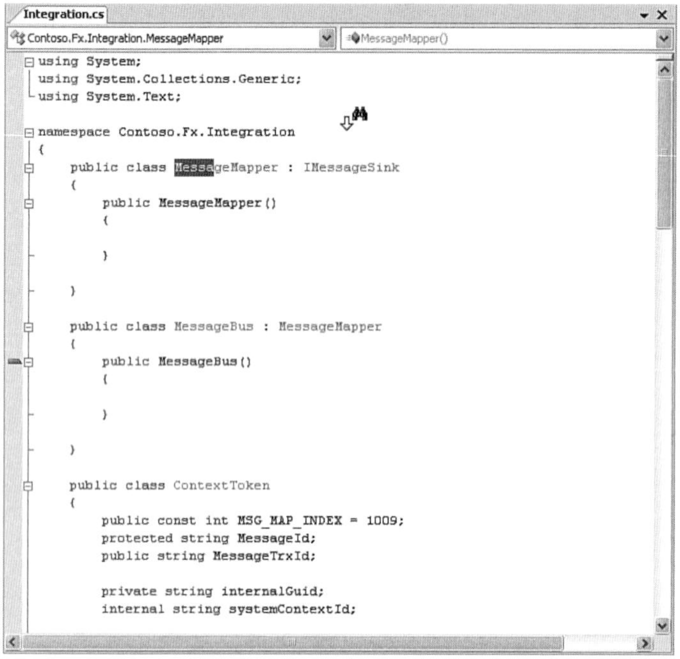

```csharp
using System;
using System.Collections.Generic;
using System.Text;

namespace Contoso.Fx.Integration
{
    public class MessageMapper : IMessageSink
    {
        public MessageMapper()
        {

        }
    }

    public class MessageBus : MessageMapper
    {
        public MessageBus()
        {

        }
    }

    public class ContextToken
    {
        public const int MSG_MAP_INDEX = 1009;
        protected string MessageId;
        public string MessageTrxId;

        private string internalGuid;
        internal string systemContextId;
```

FIGURE 6.19    Incremental Search.

By default, the search function works from the top of the document to the bottom, and from left to right. You can reverse the direction of the search by using the Ctrl+Shift+I key combination.

To jump to the next match within the document, use the Ctrl+I key combination.

Clicking anywhere within the document or pressing the Esc key cancels the Incremental Search.

---

**NOTE**

Incremental Searches are always performed in a manner that is not case-sensitive and will always match on substrings.

---

## Debugging in the Text Editor

The text editor—more specifically, the code editor—has several interactive features that facilitate the code debugging process. Debugging activities within the text editor primarily center on breakpoints and runtime code control. We will cover general Visual Studio debugging in greater detail in Chapter 10.

A breakpoint is simply a location (for example, a line of code) that is flagged for the debugger; when the debugger encounters a breakpoint, the currently executing program is paused immediately before executing that line of code. While the program is in this paused state, you can inspect the state of variables or even affect variable state by assigning new values. You can also interactively control the code flow at this point by skipping over the next line of code or directly to another line of code and continuing from there— all of this without actually leaving the IDE.

### Setting a Breakpoint

To set a breakpoint using the code editor, first locate the line of code you want to pause on and then click on that line of code within the indicator margin. This will set the breakpoint, which can now be visually identified by a red ball in the indicator margin. Hovering over the breakpoint indicator margin will show a ToolTip indicating some basic information about that breakpoint: the code filename, the line number within that code file, the type you are in (if any), and the line number within that type.

In Figure 6.20, a breakpoint has been set within a class called MessageMapper. The ToolTip information shows that you are on line 3 in the MessageMapper type, but within the overall code file (Integration.cs), you are on line number 9.

FIGURE 6.20   Setting a breakpoint.

Clicking on the breakpoint again will remove it.

The breakpoint we have set is a simple one in that it will suspend the program on that line of code without regard for any other variable or factor. Simple breakpoints are, however, only the tip of the iceberg. Breakpoints support an extensive set of conditions used to fine-tune and control what will actually trigger the breakpoints. For instance, you can set a breakpoint to activate the state of a variable or the number of times program execution will "hit" the breakpoint. You also can configure conditional breakpoints by simply pointing and clicking within the code editor window.

### Configuring a Breakpoint

Right-clicking on the breakpoint indicator will reveal the context menu (see Figure 6.21) for configuring the breakpoint.

FIGURE 6.21   Configuring a breakpoint.

It is from here that you can indicate special conditions for triggering the breakpoint and even disable or enable the breakpoint. Disabling the breakpoint, rather than deleting it, keeps its location intact if you ever need to reenable it.

---

**TIP**

Visual Basic actually provides a command word that allows you to programmatically trigger a breakpoint within your code. The Stop statement, like a breakpoint, will suspend execution of the executing code. This capability is useful when you're running the application outside the IDE. Any time a Stop statement is encountered during runtime, the Visual Studio debugger will launch and attach to the program.

Although C# doesn't have an equivalent statement to Visual Basic's Stop command, you can use the Debugger class to achieve the same thing: simply call Debugger.Break to force a breakpoint programmatically. The Debugger class lives in the System.Diagnostic namespace.

---

### Controlling the Flow of Running Code

When a program is run within the IDE, it will continue along its path of execution through the code base until it hits a breakpoint or Stop statement, is paused manually, or terminates either by reaching the end of its code path or by a manual stop.

---

**TIP**

The VCR-like controls and their shortcut keys (available under the Debug menu or on the Debug toolbar) are, by far, the easiest way to start, pause, or stop code within the IDE.

---

When a breakpoint is hit, the code editor will visually indicate the line of code where execution has paused. Figure 6.22 shows a slightly modified version of the "Hello, World" program, suspended at a breakpoint. A yellow arrow in the indicator margin flags the next statement that will execute when you resume running the program. In this case, because the breakpoint is also here, the next statement indicator appears in the margin embedded within the breakpoint glyph.

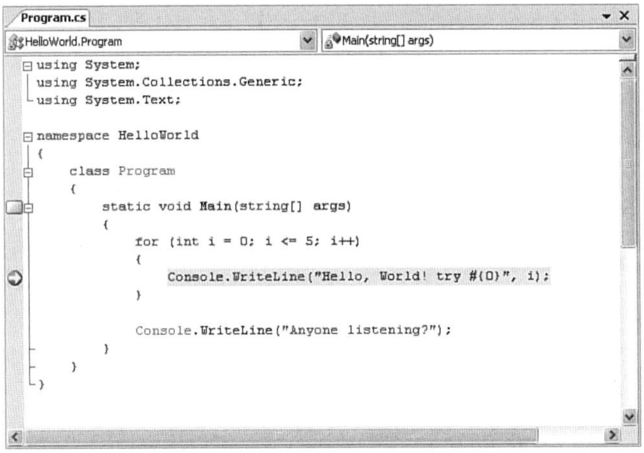

```csharp
using System;
using System.Collections.Generic;
using System.Text;

namespace HelloWorld
{
    class Program
    {
        static void Main(string[] args)
        {
            for (int i = 0; i <= 5; i++)
            {
                Console.WriteLine("Hello, World! try #{0}", i);
            }

            Console.WriteLine("Anyone listening?");
        }
    }
}
```

FIGURE 6.22    Stopping at a breakpoint.

When execution is paused, you can change the next line of code to be executed. By default, of course, this will be the line of code where operations were paused (recall that execution stops just before running the line of code matched with the breakpoint). But you can manually specify the next line of code to run by right-clicking on the target line and then selecting Set Next Statement.

In Figure 6.23, this feature has been used to jump out of the WriteLine loop. Normal flow through the code has been circumvented, and instead of continuing to spin through the for loop, the program will immediately execute the line of code just after the loop. You can see the arrow and highlighting which show that the next line of code and the breakpoint are no longer at the same location within the code file.

You can also create a sort of virtual breakpoint by selecting Run To Cursor from the editor's context menu. This will cause the program to run until it hits the line of code that you have selected, at which point it will pause much as if you had set a breakpoint there.

## Printing Code

To print the current text editor's contents, select Print from the File menu. The Print dialog box is fairly standard, allowing you to select your printer and set basic print properties. Two Visual Studio–specific options bear mentioning here. The Print What section in this dialog box controls whether line numbers will be produced in the printout and whether collapsed regions will be included in the printed content.

### Colors and Fonts

By default, the font colors and markup that you see in the text editor window will be sent to the printer as is (assuming that you are printing to a color printer). If you so desire, you can tweak all these settings from the Fonts and Colors page in the Options dialog box (see Figure 6.24).

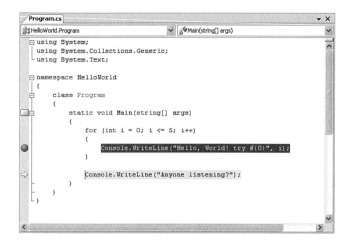

FIGURE 6.23    Setting the next run statement.

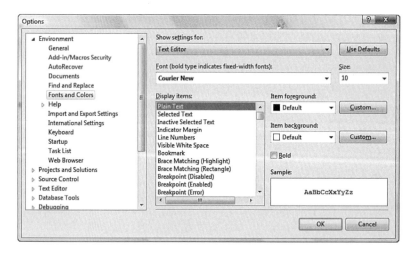

FIGURE 6.24    The Fonts and Colors Options dialog box.

This is the same dialog box used to control font and color settings for many of the IDE's constituent parts. You access the printer settings by selecting Printer in the Show Settings For drop-down at the top of the dialog box.

Figure 6.25 provides a snapshot of output produced by printing a code file.

```
C:\Documents and Settings\lpowers\My ...\HelloWorld\Program.cs                          1

1  using System;
2  using System.Collections.Generic;
3  using System.Text;
4
5  namespace HelloWorld
6  {
7      class Program
8      {
9          static void Main(string[] args)
10         {
11             for (int i = 0; i <= 5; i++)
12             {
13                 Console.WriteLine("Hello, World! try {0}", i);
14             }
15             Console.WriteLine("Anyone listening?");
16         }
17     }
18 }
19
```

FIGURE 6.25    Code printout.

## Using the Code Definition Window

The code definition window is a "helper" window that works in close conjunction with the code editor window by displaying definitions for symbols selected within the code editor. It is actually a near clone of the code editor window, with one big exception: It is read-only and does not permit edits to its content.

The code definition window content is refreshed anytime the cursor position is moved within the code editor window. If the cursor or caret is placed in a symbol/type, the code definition window shows you how that symbol is defined.

Figure 6.26 shows an open code editor and a code definition window; the cursor in the editor is positioned on an internal field, _state, defined within the class InternalToken.

The code definition window has reacted to the cursor position by showing the source code that actually defines the type of the _state field. You can see from the figure that the code definition window is a fairly featured adaptation of a text editor window: It supports bookmarks, breakpoints, and various navigation aids. Although you cannot edit code using this window, you are not prevented from copying code out of the window.

You can open a code definition window by using the View menu.

# Creating and Editing XML Documents and Schema

The text editor is equally adept, and just as productive, at editing documents with XML content—including XML schemas. The XML editor is launched whenever you open a file with the .xml extension inside of Visual Studio. It is also launched for .xsl files and .config files, and is always available when you use the Open With command in the Solution Explorer against any item in a project.

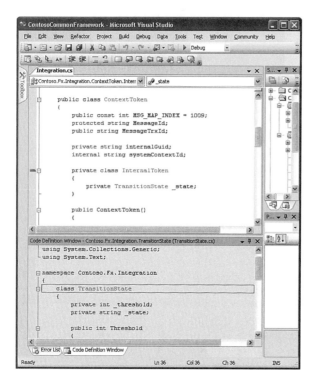

FIGURE 6.26    The code definition window.

Because XML documents contain structured content involving the concepts of nodes and tags, attributes, and node containership, the XML editor supports document outlining in a similar fashion to the code editor: You can expand or collapse nodes within the editor to expose or hide a node's content (see Figure 6.27). And just as with the code editor, syntax checking and IntelliSense are fully supported by the XML editor. The XML editor is aware of the syntactical requirements for the current document and provides appropriate IntelliSense and formatting help where possible.

Using the XML Editor, you can also carry out these actions:

▶ Edit XSD schema documents

▶ Generate a schema document from an XML document

▶ Edit XSLT style sheets

▶ Edit Document Type Definition (DTD) documents and XML-Data Reduced (XDR) documents

▶ Insert XML snippets

For a proper treatment of the various editing, validation, and productivity aids available in this editor, see Chapter 8, "Working with Visual Studio's Productivity Aids." Here, let's explore two of the core XML functions: schema generation and XSLT style sheet editing.

FIGURE 6.27    Editing an XML schema document.

## Inferring Schema

The XML Editor can automatically generate an XML schema document (XSD) based on a valid XML document. While the XML document is open, select Create Schema from the XML main menu. This creates an XSD document and opens it in the XML editor (as a separate document). From there, you can make any needed changes to the XSD document and save it to disk. You can also include it in your project at this point.

> **NOTE**
>
> If you run the Create Schema command against an XML document that already contains a DTD or XDR schema, the XML inference algorithm will use these schemas as the basis for the conversion as opposed to the actual data within the XML document.

## Editing XSLT Style Sheets

XSLT files are XML files, so the process of editing an XSLT style sheet is the same as that described for editing an XML document. There are, however, a few additional features specific to XSLT documents. For one, keywords are recognized and shaded appropriately in the editor just as with a code document. Second, the XML editor will automatically process the current state of the document against the standard schema for XSLT style sheets and will show any validation errors to you directly. And finally, Visual Studio is fully aware of any script embedded in an XSLT document. You can set breakpoints within a script block, and there is full debug support for script enabling you to step through code, see the current state of variables, and so forth. Figure 6.28 shows an XSLT style sheet with a breakpoint set within a section of embedded script.

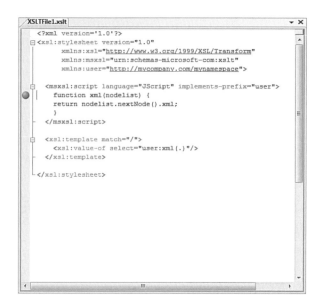

FIGURE 6.28   Debugging script embedded into an XSLT document.

### Running XSLT Against XML

After a style sheet has been created and attached to an XML document, you can execute that XSLT style sheet and view the output within a new editor window. To attach the XSLT sheet to the XML document, use the Properties window for the XML document and set the Stylesheet property. Entering the full path and filename of the XSLT in this property will attach the style sheet. Alternatively, you can manually code the style sheet into the XML document's prolog section by typing an xml-stylesheet Processing Instruction prolog into the document, like this:

```
<?xml-stylesheet type='text/xsl' href='myxsl.xsl'?>
```

When a style sheet is associated, selecting the Show XSLT Output option from the XML menu will run the transforms against the XML document and show you the results in a separate editor window.

# Working with Cascading Style Sheets

The CSS Editor allows you to build and edit cascading style sheet documents. Because CSS documents are, at their core, text documents, the editor doesn't need to provide much more than standard text-editing features to be effective. There are, however, a few built-in tools available from the editor that allow you to add style rules and build styles using dialog boxes as opposed to free-form text entry.

## Adding Style Rules

Right-click within the CSS editor to access the shortcut menu. From there, select the Add Style Rule option. The Add Style Rule dialog box allows you to input an element, class-name, or class ID and even define a hierarchy between the rules. Committing the change from this dialog box will inject the necessary content into the CSS editor to create the rule.

## Defining Style Sheet Attributes

After you've added a style to the CSS document by either writing the style syntax manually or using the aforementioned Add Style Rule dialog box, you can edit the attributes of that style using the Style Builder dialog box. You launch this dialog box by right-clicking anywhere within the previously entered style section and then selecting the Build Style option. When you use this dialog box, it is possible to fully describe the style across several different categories from font to layout to list formatting.

# Developing Windows Client Applications

There are two principal .NET technologies used to develop Windows client application: Windows Forms (WinForms) and Windows Presentation Foundation (WPF). Both of these technologies are essentially a set of classes and user interface controls exposed by the .NET Framework that enable developers to quickly build out applications that are installed, and run, under the Microsoft Windows operating system.

The WinForms classes and components are a mature technology, and they represent the current mainstream of client application development under .NET. WPF, on the other hand, is a brand-new technology that looks to provide a huge leap forward in crafting applications that must blend multimedia, document, and high-impact user interface elements together.

WPF uses a markup language called XAML (Extensible Application Markup Language) to describe application objects, property values, and behavior. In this respect, it is very similar to a web application that uses HTML to describe the various elements of a web page. WPF as a technology heavily leverages vector graphics and graphics hardware acceleration to display an application's user interface.

Visual Studio has supported WinForms for years now. Visual Studio 2008, on the other hand, is the first version of Visual Studio that provides designers and editors for constructing WPF applications.

Regardless of the type of client application you need to build, the process is much the same: Both the WinForms designer and the WPF designer enable drag-and-drop development, and both have project templates available in Visual Studio.

## Creating a Windows Forms Project

The process of building a Windows Forms application starts the same as all other project types within Visual Studio: You select the Windows Application project template from the New Project dialog box and set up the location for the applications source. From there, Visual Studio will stub out an initial project, and the Windows Forms designer will load, as shown in Figure 6.29.

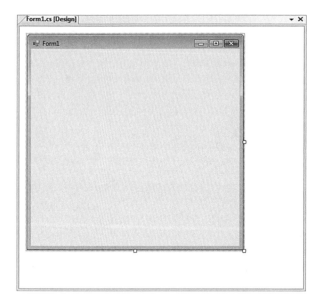

FIGURE 6.29    Initial form in the Windows Forms designer.

As you can see from the figure, a design-time "mock-up" of the actual form is visible within the designer. This is the canvas for your user interface. Using this canvas, you can add controls and visual elements to the form, tweak the look and feel of the form itself, and launch directly to the code that is wired to the form. To investigate how the designer works, start with a simple design premise: Say you want to take the blank form that Visual Studio generated for you and create a login dialog box that allows users to input a name and password and confirm their entries by clicking an OK button. A Cancel button should also be available to allow users to dismiss the form.

**NOTE**

Don't get confused about the various representations that a form can have, such as message box or dialog box. From a development perspective, they are all windows and are therefore all forms.

The designer in this exercise allows you, the developer, to craft the form and its actions while writing as little code as possible. Using drag-and-drop operations and Property dialog boxes, you should be able to customize the look and feel of the application without ever dealing with the code editor.

### Customizing the Form's Appearance

There are a few obvious visual elements in the designer. For one, the form itself is shown complete with its borders, title bar, client area, and Min/Max/Close buttons. In addition, you can see grab handles at the bottom, right, and bottom-right corner of the form. The grab handles are used to resize the form. To change other attributes of the form, you use the property grid for the form. The property grid enables you to set the background color, border appearance and behavior, title text, and so on.

In Figure 6.30, the title of the form has been changed to Login, and the border behavior has been changed to match a dialog box as opposed to a normal, resizable window.

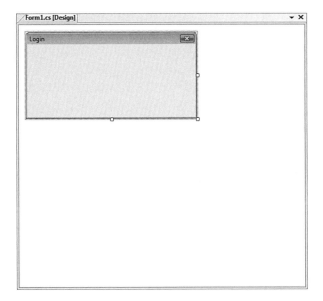

FIGURE 6.30   Editing the form's size and title.

### Adding Controls to a Form

Controls are adornments to a form that have their own user interface. (There is such a thing as UI-less controls; we'll cover such controls in this chapter in the section "Authoring Components and Controls.") They provide the principal interaction mechanism method with a form. Put another way, a form is really just a container for the various controls that will implement the desired functionality for the form.

You can add controls to a form quite easily by dragging and dropping them from the toolbox. Continuing the metaphor of the designer as a canvas, the toolbox is the palette.

**The Toolbox**   The toolbox is a dockable window within the IDE; it is viewable only when you are editing a project element that supports toolbox functionality. To make sure that the toolbox is visible, select it from the View menu (or use the Ctrl+W, X shortcut).

The toolbox groups the controls in a tabbed tree. Simply expand the tab grouping (such as Common Controls or Menus & Toolbars), and you will see a list of the available controls. In this case, you want two text box controls to hold the login ID and password text, a few label controls to describe the text box controls, and the OK and Cancel buttons to commit or cancel the entries. All of these controls can be located under the Common Controls tab (see Figure 6.31).

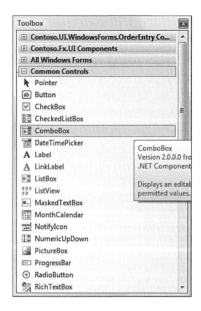

FIGURE 6.31   The toolbox.

To place a control on the form, drag its representation from the toolbox onto the form. Some controls, referred to as *components*, don't actually have a visual user interface. The timer is one example of a component. When you drag a component to a form, it is placed in a separate area of the designer called the *component tray*. The component tray allows you to select one of the added components and access its properties via the Properties window.

**TIP**

The toolbox is customizable in terms of its content and arrangement. You can add or remove tabs from the toolbox, move controls from one tab to another through simple drag and drop, and even rename individual items within the toolbox. To perform many of these actions, bring up the toolbox context menu by right-clicking on a tab or an item.

**Arranging Controls**   When you are designing a form, control layout becomes an important issue. You are typically concerned about ensuring that controls are aligned either horizontally or vertically, that controls and control groups are positioned with equal and common margins between their edges, that margins are enforced along the form borders, and so on.

The designer provides three distinct sets of tools and aids that assist with form layout. First, you have the options available to you under the Format menu. With a form loaded in the designer, you can select different groups of controls and use the commands under the Format menu to align these controls vertically or horizontally with one another, standardize and increase or decrease the spacing between controls, center the controls within the form, and even alter the controls' appearance attributes so that they are of equal size in either dimension.

The other layout tools within the designer are interactive in nature and are surfaced through two different modes: snap line and grid positioning. You can toggle between these two modes via the Windows Forms Designer Options dialog box (choose Tool, Options and then the Windows Forms Designer tab). The property called LayoutMode can be set to either SnapToGrid or SnapLines.

*Using the Layout Grid*   The layout grid is, as its name implies, a grid that is laid on top of the form. The grid itself is visually represented within the designer by dots representing the intersection of the grid squares. As you drag and move controls over the surface of the grid, the designer will automatically snap the control's leading edges to one of the grid's square edges.

**TIP**

Even with the grid layout turned on, you can circumvent the snapping behavior by selecting a control, holding down the Ctrl key, and using the arrow keys to move the control up, down, right, or left one pixel at a time.

The size of the grid squares (and thus the spacing of these guide dots) is controlled by the GridSize property (also located in the Options dialog box). A smaller grid size equates to a tighter spacing of guide dots, which in turns equates to more finely grained control over control placement.

Figure 6.32 shows the login form with the layout grid in evidence. Note that the grid was used to make sure that

▶ The text boxes are aligned with one another (and are the same length).

▶ The labels are aligned vertically with the text boxes and horizontally with each other.

▶ The buttons are aligned vertically and have an appropriate buffer area between their control edges and the form's border.

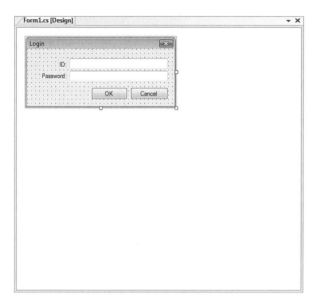

FIGURE 6.32 The layout grid.

*Using Snap Lines* Snap lines are a slightly more intelligent mechanism for positioning controls. With snap lines, there is no grid visible on the form's surface. Instead, the designer draws visual hints while a control is in motion on the form.

Figure 6.33 illustrates snap lines in action; this figure shows the process of positioning the OK button.

Note that the control—in this case, an OK button—has "snapped" into a position that is located a set distance away from the form border (indicated by the thin blue line extending down from the button to the form edge). The button snap position also sufficiently spaces the control from its neighboring Cancel button, as indicated by the thin blue line extending from the right edge of the button to the left edge of the Cancel button. The snap line algorithm has also determined that you are trying to create a row of buttons and thus need to vertically align the current control to its neighbor. This is actually done using the interior text of the buttons; the thin pink line running under the text of both buttons clearly shows that they are perfectly aligned.

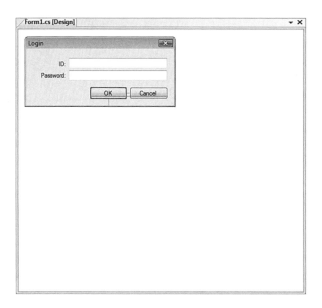

FIGURE 6.33  Using snap lines.

The snap line algorithms automatically take into account the recommended margins and spacing distances as discussed in the Windows User Interface Guidelines written and adopted by Microsoft. This feature takes the guesswork out of many layout decisions and helps to ensure some commonality and standards adherence within the Windows Forms applications.

**NOTE**

Changes made to the layout modes of the designer typically do not take effect immediately. You may need to close the designer and reopen it after making a change (such as switching between SnapLine mode and SnapToGrid mode).

**Resizing Controls and Editing Attributes**   When a control is in place on its parent form, you can interact with the control in various ways. You can set control properties using the Properties window. You also can alter the sizing and shape of the control by dragging the grab handles on the sides of the control.

### Writing Code

Although the designer excels at enabling developers to visually construct a user interface, its capability to actually implement behavior is limited. You can use the designer to place a button, but responding to a click on the button and reacting in some way are still the domain of code.

At the code level, a form is simply a class that encapsulates all the form's behavior. For simplicity and ease of development, Visual Studio pushes all the code that it writes via the designer into clearly marked regions and, in the case of Windows forms, a separate code file. The file is named after the primary form code file like this: *FormName.Designer.language extension*. As an example, the login form is accompanied by a Login.Designer.cs file that implements the designer-written code.

Listing 6.1 shows what Visual Studio has generated in the way of code to implement the changes made through the designer.

LISTING 6.1   Windows Forms Designer–Generated Code

```
namespace Contoso.UI.WindowsForms.OrderEntry
{
    partial class Login
    {
        /// <summary>
        /// Required designer variable.
        /// </summary>
        private System.ComponentModel.IContainer components = null;

        /// <summary>
        /// Clean up any resources being used.
        /// </summary>
        /// <param name="disposing">true if managed resources should be disposed;
        /// otherwise, false.</param>
        protected override void Dispose(bool disposing)
        {
            if (disposing && (components != null))
            {
                components.Dispose();
            }
            base.Dispose(disposing);
        }

        #region Windows Form Designer generated code

        /// <summary>
        /// Required method for Designer support - do not modify
        /// the contents of this method with the code editor.
        /// </summary>
        private void InitializeComponent()
        {
            this.label1 = new System.Windows.Forms.Label();
            this.label2 = new System.Windows.Forms.Label();
            this.textBoxID = new System.Windows.Forms.TextBox();
            this.textBoxPassword = new System.Windows.Forms.TextBox();
```

```
this.buttonCancel = new System.Windows.Forms.Button();
this.buttonOk = new System.Windows.Forms.Button();
this.SuspendLayout();
//
// label1
//
this.label1.AutoSize = true;
this.label1.Location = new System.Drawing.Point(61, 23);
this.label1.Name = "label1";
this.label1.Size = new System.Drawing.Size(17, 13);
this.label1.TabIndex = 0;
this.label1.Text = "ID:";
//
// label2
//
this.label2.AutoSize = true;
this.label2.Location = new System.Drawing.Point(26, 46);
this.label2.Name = "label2";
this.label2.Size = new System.Drawing.Size(52, 13);
this.label2.TabIndex = 1;
this.label2.Text = "Password:";
//
// textBoxID
//
this.textBoxID.Location = new System.Drawing.Point(85, 20);
this.textBoxID.Name = "textBoxID";
this.textBoxID.Size = new System.Drawing.Size(195, 20);
this.textBoxID.TabIndex = 2;
//
// textBoxPassword
//
this.textBoxPassword.Location = new System.Drawing.Point(85, 46);
this.textBoxPassword.Name = "textBoxPassword";
this.textBoxPassword.Size = new System.Drawing.Size(195, 20);
this.textBoxPassword.TabIndex = 3;
//
// buttonCancel
//
this.buttonCancel.DialogResult =
   System.Windows.Forms.DialogResult.Cancel;
this.buttonCancel.Location = new System.Drawing.Point(205, 72);
this.buttonCancel.Name = "buttonCancel";
this.buttonCancel.Size = new System.Drawing.Size(75, 23);
this.buttonCancel.TabIndex = 4;
this.buttonCancel.Text = "Cancel";
```

LISTING 6.1    Continued

```
        //
        // buttonOk
        //
        this.buttonOk.Location = new System.Drawing.Point(124, 72);
        this.buttonOk.Name = "buttonOk";
        this.buttonOk.Size = new System.Drawing.Size(75, 23);
        this.buttonOk.TabIndex = 5;
        this.buttonOk.Text = "OK";
        //
        // Login
        //
        this.AcceptButton = this.buttonOk;
        this.AutoScaleDimensions = new System.Drawing.SizeF(6F, 13F);
        this.AutoScaleMode = System.Windows.Forms.AutoScaleMode.Font;
        this.CancelButton = this.buttonCancel;
        this.ClientSize = new System.Drawing.Size(292, 109);
        this.Controls.Add(this.buttonOk);
        this.Controls.Add(this.buttonCancel);
        this.Controls.Add(this.textBoxPassword);
        this.Controls.Add(this.textBoxID);
        this.Controls.Add(this.label2);
        this.Controls.Add(this.label1);
        this.FormBorderStyle =
            System.Windows.Forms.FormBorderStyle.FixedDialog;
        this.MaximizeBox = false;
        this.MinimizeBox = false;
        this.Name = "Login";
        this.ShowInTaskbar = false;
        this.SizeGripStyle = System.Windows.Forms.SizeGripStyle.Hide;
        this.Text = "Login";
        this.ResumeLayout(false);
        this.PerformLayout();

    }

    #endregion

    private System.Windows.Forms.Label label1;
    private System.Windows.Forms.Label label2;
    private System.Windows.Forms.TextBox textBoxID;
    private System.Windows.Forms.TextBox textBoxPassword;
    private System.Windows.Forms.Button buttonCancel;
    private System.Windows.Forms.Button buttonOk;
  }
}
```

## Creating a Windows Presentation Foundation Project

Windows Presentation Foundation projects behave much like WinForms projects do. In fact, one of the design goals for the WPF designer and editor was to act in ways that would be familiar to developers who are used to Windows Forms development. Just as we previously did with our WinForms project, we start the development and design process by selecting a template—WPF Application—from the File, New Project dialog.

Two XAML files are automatically created within the project: `Window1.xaml`, which represents the main window for the app, and `App.xaml`, which represents the application itself. These are analogous to the `Form1.cs`/`Form1.vb` and `Program.cs`/`Module1.vb` files created in a new Windows Forms project.

The first difference you will notice with WPF projects is that, by default, you are presented with two different panes: In one pane, you see the design surface for the window, and in another you see an editor that contains the XAML declarations for the form. This design view is actually the same that is used for web applications (which we will investigate as part of the next topic). See Figure 6.34 for a look at the `Window1` file loaded in the IDE.

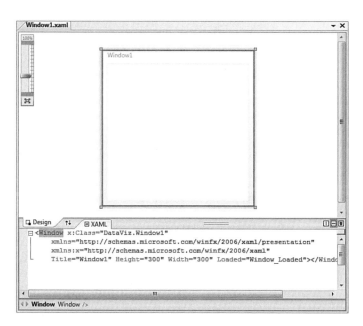

FIGURE 6.34   The initial window in the WPF designer.

Each of these panes is simply a different view of the same window: a visual view and a text/XML view. I can add a button to the window, for example, by dragging it from the toolbox onto the design surface, or by typing the XAML declaration directly into the XAML pane like this:

```
<Button Height="23.07" Name="button1" Width="75.362">Button</Button>
```

Both the design and the XAML view are kept in sync with one another automatically.

Because WPF is based on vector graphics, you can zoom in and out in the designer using the slider control in the upper left of the designer. Figure 6.35 shows the Window1 form, with a button, zoomed in at 10x.

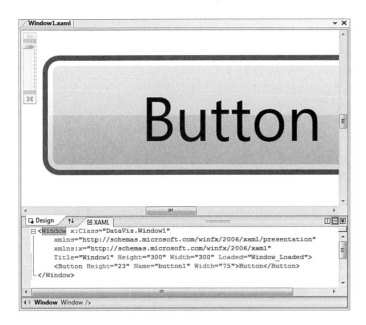

FIGURE 6.35    Zooming in on a WPF element.

### Using the Split Panes

You have control over how the design and XAML panes are displayed and positioned within the IDE. There is a small button flagged with two-way arrows that, when pressed, swaps the position of the two panes. You can also change the panes from a horizontal to a vertical orientation (or vice versa) by clicking on the Horizontal Split or Vertical Split button. And, finally, you can collapse either pane by clicking on the Collapse/Expand Pane button.

There is one other feature of interest that is unique to the WPF designer: You can navigate back and forward through objects that you have selected by using the forward and back selectors shown in the bottom area of the designer. The controls for pane management, object navigation, and view zoom are highlighted for you in Figure 6.36.

### Adding Controls

WPF windows are populated with controls by using the same drag-and-drop action from the toolbox. Control positioning and sizing is aided through snap lines and sizing boxes that look a bit different than their WinForms counterparts but perform the same tasks (see Figure 6.37).

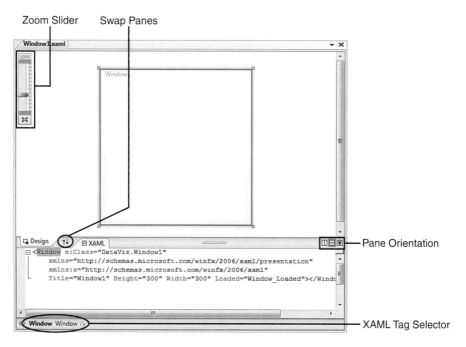

FIGURE 6.36    WPF editor controls.

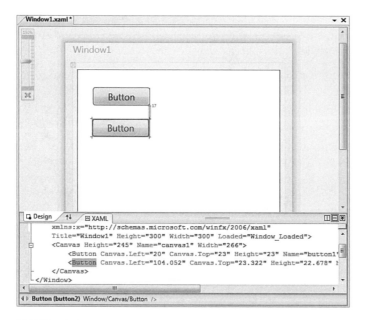

FIGURE 6.37    Control positioning guidelines.

We cover WPF development in more depth in Chapter 16, "Creating Richer, Smarter User Interfaces."

# Developing Web Forms

Web forms represent the user interface element to a web application. Traditionally with .NET, the term *web form* is used to refer specifically to pages processed dynamically on the server (using ASP.NET). We use a broader definition here and use the term to refer to any web page, static or dynamic, that can be developed and designed within the Visual Studio IDE.

The HTML designer (also referred to as the Web designer) is the sister application to the Windows Forms and WPF designers; it allows you to visually design and edit the markup for a web page. As with the two client application designers, it works in conjunction with the HTML designer and source view to cover all the bases needed for web page design. We will cover the entire web application development process in depth in Chapter 14, "Creating ASP.NET Applications"; in the following sections, we will simply cover the basics of the web designers and editors.

## Designing a Web Form Application

Web page design starts first with a web project. As previously discussed, there are two different ways for you to construct a web page or website with Visual Studio. Both of these approaches are represented by their own unique project templates. Specifically, we are talking about "web application" versus "website" projects. In Chapter 4, we broached some of the core differences between these two project types; even more detail is waiting for you in Chapter 14. However, because the actual construction of a web page with the Web designer remains exactly the same between the two project types, we will concentrate here on illustrating our points by walking through a "website" project.

Select File, New Web Site, and from the dialog box, select the ASP.NET Web Site option. After you set the source code directory and source language, click OK to have Visual Studio create the project and its initial web page.

The Web designer looks similar to the WPF designer; it has a design surface that acts as a canvas, allowing objects from the toolbox to be placed and positioned on its surface. Although they look slightly different from the pane controls we saw in the WPF designer, they have the same basic functions. You can work in a "split" mode in which the designer and markup editor are visible in separate panes, or you can elect to work strictly with either the designer or the editor open.

Now examine what happens when you try to mimic the login form that was previously built using Windows forms. (There is actually a prebuilt login form component that you could use here; for the sake of demonstrating the development process, however, we will go ahead and cobble together our own simplistic one for comparison's sake.)

### Adding and Arranging Controls

The process of adding and arranging controls doesn't change from the Windows Forms designer process. Simply drag the controls from the toolbox onto the designer's surface. In this case, you want two labels, two text boxes, and an OK button (because this isn't a dialog box, you can dispense with the Cancel button). Changing control properties is also handled the same way via the Properties window. You can select the labels and command buttons and set their text this way.

---

**NOTE**

As you add controls to a web page, you should note that the default layout mode is relative. That is, controls are not placed at absolute coordinates on the screen but instead are placed relative to one another. Absolute positioning is accommodated via style sheets. For instance, you can select a label control, edit its style properties, and select Absolutely Position as the position mode. This will now allow you to range freely over the form with the control.

---

A formatting toolbar is provided by default; it supplies buttons for common text formatting actions such as changing font styles, colors, paragraph indenting, and bulleting.

To line up control edges the way you want, you can press Shift+Enter to insert spacing between the controls as necessary (this will generate a break tag, <br>, in the HTML). In this case, a break was added between the first text box and the second label, and between the second text box and the first button. Figure 6.38 shows the design in progress. The text boxes don't line up and you will probably want to apply a style for the label fonts and buttons; but the general layout and intent are evident. Note that the designer provides a box above the currently selected control that indicates both the control's type and the instance name of the control on the page.

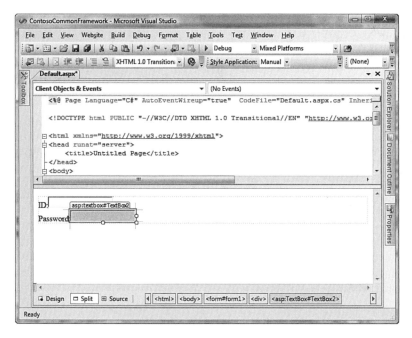

FIGURE 6.38   Creating a web form.

**TIP**

As a further aid for control alignment, be sure to turn on either the ruler, the positioning grid, or both; they are accessed from the View menu, under Ruler and Grid.

### Editing Markup

As controls and other elements are added and manipulated on the designer's surface, HTML is created to implement the design and layout. As a designer or developer, you are free to work at either the visual level with the designer or the text/source level with the HTML Source Editor. Like the other editors within Visual Studio 2008, the HTML Source Editor supports IntelliSense and other interactive features for navigating and validating markup.

Looking back at Figure 6.38, you can see the markup generated by the designer when the controls were added to the login page.

As with the other designer/editor pairs, you can write your own HTML and see it implemented immediately in the design view. The HTML editor has a toolbar as well: The HTML source editing toolbar provides quick access to code "forward and back" navigation, commenting, and schema validation options (we'll discuss this specific part in the section "Browser Output and Validation").

One key feature realized with the HTML editor is source format preservation: The HTML source editor works very hard to respect the way that you, the developer, want your markup formatted. This includes the placement of carriage returns and whitespace, the use of indentation, and even how you want to handle word and line wrapping. In short, Visual Studio will never reformat HTML code that you have written!

**Working with Tables**    HTML tables provide a quick and easy way to align controls on a web page. With Visual Studio 2008, there is a dedicated Insert Table dialog box that provides extensive control over table layout and appearance. To place a table onto the design surface, select Insert Table from the Layout menu. The Insert Table dialog box supports custom table layouts in which you specify the row and column attributes and the general style attributes such as borders and padding. Through this dialog box, you can also select from a list of preformatted table templates.

After you've added a table to the designer, it is fully interactive for drag-and-drop resizing of its columns and rows.

**Formatting Options**    In addition to preserving the format of HTML that you write, Visual Studio 2008 provides fine-grained control over how the designer generates and formats the HTML that it produces. You use the HTML page and its subpages in the Options dialog box (Tools, Options, Text Editor, HTML) to configure indentation style, quotation use, word wrapping, and tag casing (see Figure 6.39).

Settings can be applied globally for all markup, or you can set options on a per-tag basis by clicking the Tag Specific Options button (Text Editor, HTML, Format). As an example, this level of control is useful if your particular coding style uses line breaks within your

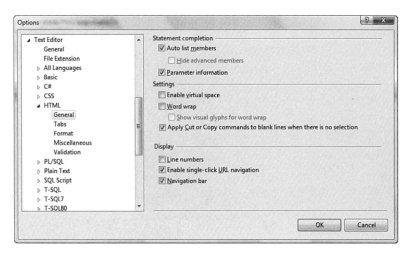

FIGURE 6.39   HTML formatting options.

table column tabs (<td>), but not with your table row tags (<tr>). In Figure 6.40, the tr tag is being set to support line breaks before and after the tag, but not within the tag.

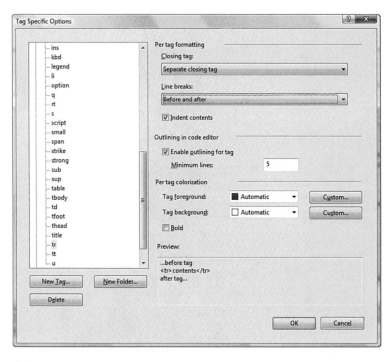

FIGURE 6.40   Setting HTML formatting at the tag level.

**Managing Styles and Style Sheets**

Visual Studio 2008 introduces a brand-new set of tools for managing styles and cascading style sheets. The Manage Styles and Apply Styles windows are both used to perform common style editing tasks, including applying a style to the current HTML document, or attaching/detaching a cascading style sheet file to/from the current HTML document. The third tool, the CSS Properties window, enumerates all the CSS properties for the currently selected page element, allowing for quick changes for any of the property values.

A typical workflow for editing styles might look like this:

> open a web page
>
> define a new style
>
> apply the style
>
> tweak the style

Figure 6.41 shows the Manage Styles window, and its capability to itemize and preview any of the formatting elements within a style sheet. The Options button at the upper right of the window is used to control the way that the list of elements within a style sheet is shown (by order, by type, and so on), or to filter the elements that are shown (all, only those used in the current page, and so on).

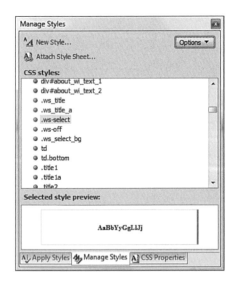

FIGURE 6.41    The Manage Styles window.

Both the Manage Styles window and the Apply Styles window show up by default whenever you are editing a web page, and can be reopened via the Format, CSS Styles menu. The CSS properties window is available off of the View menu.

**Browser Output and Validation**

The result of all the design effort put into an HTML document is its final rendering within a browser. With various flavors of browsers in use supporting various levels of HTML specifications (including XHTML), it is difficult to ensure that the page's design intent actually matches reality. Visual Studio's browser target settings help with this problem by enabling you to easily target a specific HTML standard or *browser*. As you type HTML into the source editor, Visual Studio will validate the syntax on the fly against your selected browser target. If a piece of markup violates the rules of your particular validation target, it will be flagged by the familiar red squiggly line (complete with a ToolTip explaining the exact violation), and the error will be listed within the Task List window.

The target can be selected on the HTML designer or source editor toolbar: Just pick the target from the drop-down.

> **NOTE**
>
> The validation rules for a given browser or standard can actually be customized to support targets that may not ship out of the box with Visual Studio.

**Standards Compliance**    The HTML code generated by the HTML designer is, by default, XHTML compliant; tags, for instance, are well formed with regard to XHTML requirements. Using the various XHTML validation targets will help you to ensure that the code you write is compliant as well.

Visual Studio also focuses on providing compliance with accessibility standards—those standards that govern the display of web pages for persons with disabilities. You launch the Accessibility Checker by using the Check Page for Accessibility button on the HTML Source Editing or Formatting toolbars.

Figure 6.42 shows the Accessibility Validation dialog box. You can select the specific standards you want to have your HTML validated against. You can also select the level of feedback that you receive (errors, warnings, or a text checklist). Each item flagged by the checker will appear in the Task List window for resolution. For more details on the two standards supported here (WCAG and Access Board Section 508), see their respective websites: http://www.w3.org/TR/WCAG10/ and http://www.access-board.gov/508.htm.

FIGURE 6.42    Setting accessibility validation options.

# Authoring Components and Controls

Referring to our earlier discussion of Windows forms, components are nonvisual controls or classes. This is a good generic definition, but a more specific one is this: A component is any class that inherits from `System.ComponentModel.IComponent`. This particular interface provides support for designability and resource handling. If you need a designable control that does not have a user interface of its own, you will work with a component. And in Visual Studio, the component designer is the tool used to develop components.

Controls are similar in function but not form: A control is a reusable chunk of code that *does* have a visual element to it.

## Creating a New Component or Control

You kick off the process of authoring a component by using the Add New Item dialog box (from the Project menu). Selecting Component Class in this dialog box will add the stub code file to your current project and will launch the component designer. To start control development, you use the Add New User Control dialog box.

> **NOTE**
>
> Essentially two different "types" of controls can be authored within Visual Studio: custom controls and user controls. Custom controls inherit directly from the `System.Windows.Forms.Control` class; they are typically code intensive because you, the developer, are responsible for writing all the code necessary to render the control's visual portion. User controls (sometimes called *composite controls*) inherit from the `System.Windows.forms.UserControl` class. User controls are advantageous because you can build them quickly by compositing other controls together that are already available in the toolbox. These controls already have their user interface portion coded for you.

Both the control and the component designers work on the same principles as the Windows Forms designer: The designers allow you to drag an object from the toolbox onto the design surface.

Assume that you need a component that will send a signal across a serial port every *x* minutes. Because Visual Studio already provides a timer and a serial port component, which are accessible from the toolbox, you can use the component designer to add these objects to your own custom component and then leverage and access their intrinsic properties and methods (essentially, using them as building blocks to get your desired functionality).

Figure 6.43 shows the component designer for this fictional custom component. Two objects have been added: a timer and a process component.

A similar scenario can be envisioned with a user control. You can take the example of a login "form," consisting of two text boxes, two labels, and two buttons, and actually make

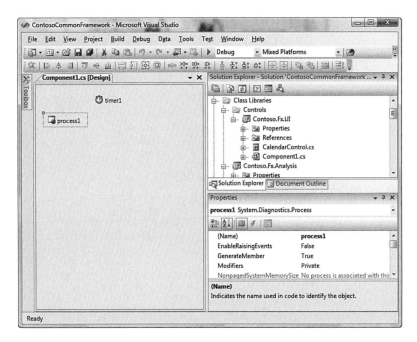

FIGURE 6.43   The component designer.

that a control—one that can be easily included in the toolbox and dropped onto a Windows form or web form.

## Further Notes on Writing Component Code

Because the component has no visual aspect to it, you don't have the layout and formatting features that you see with the Windows Forms designer. However, the concept of drag-and-drop programming is alive and well. Visual Studio, behind the scenes, injects the code to programmatically add the given class to the component's container. From there, you can edit the various objects' properties, double-click an object to get to its code, and so on.

When you simply drag the timer and process objects over from the toolbox, Visual Studio aggregates these objects into the component by automatically writing the code shown in Listing 6.2.

LISTING 6.2   Component Designer–Generated Code

```
namespace Contoso.UI.WindowsForms.OrderEntry
{
    partial class Component1
    {
        /// <summary>
        /// Required designer variable.
        /// </summary>
```

LISTING 6.2    Continued

```
        private System.ComponentModel.IContainer components = null;


        /// <summary>
        /// Clean up any resources being used.
        /// </summary>
        /// <param name="disposing">true if managed resources should be
        /// disposed; otherwise, false.</param>
        protected override void Dispose(bool disposing)
        {
            if (disposing && (components != null))
            {
                components.Dispose();
            }
            base.Dispose(disposing);
        }


        #region Component Designer generated code

        /// <summary>
        /// Required method for Designer support - do not modify
        /// the contents of this method with the code editor.
        /// </summary>
        private void InitializeComponent()
        {
            this.components = new System.ComponentModel.Container();
            this.timer1 = new System.Windows.Forms.Timer(this.components);
            this.serialPort1 = new System.IO.Ports.SerialPort(this.components);

        }

        #endregion

        private System.Windows.Forms.Timer timer1;
        private System.IO.Ports.SerialPort serialPort1;



    }
}
```

Writing code "behind" one of the objects placed on the component designer canvas is easy: Double-click the object's icon, and the code editor is launched. For instance, double-clicking on the timer icon on the designer surface causes the timer1_Tick routine to be created and then launched in the code editor.

# Summary

Visual Studio provides a full array of editors and designers. They cover the gamut of solution development activities from WYSIWYG positioning of graphical controls to finely tuned text editing for a certain language, syntax, or markup.

This chapter described how to leverage the basics within these editors and designers. It also described how the editor and designer relationship provides two complementary views of the same solution artifact, in effect working together to provide you, the developer, with the right tool for the right task at hand.

In subsequent chapters, we'll look at the more advanced options and productivity features available within these tools and even look at end-to-end development efforts involved in building a web application or Windows forms application.

# CHAPTER 7

# The .NET Community: Consuming and Creating Shared Code

The .NET community is a large and diverse group. Take a quick look across the Internet and you will find countless bits of content and help for building applications. Microsoft added several new community features to the prior version, Visual Studio 2005. These features help you quickly gain access to information, sample code, and productivity aids provided by other developers and communities out there. Visual Studio helps to package this content, manage it, and streamline access to it.

This chapter covers how developers can take advantage of the community capabilities of Visual Studio 2008. You will learn how to customize your community content to provide the right mix, how to get community support, and how to find and consume code from the developer community. Finally, you will also learn how you can bundle your own code samples and productivity aids for sharing with the community.

## The Community Features of Visual Studio

Software development has become a more connected experience. Web services, RSS feeds, websites, and the like now provide access to rich content well beyond what was once stored on a local hard drive or network. This content is no longer simply supplied by and managed by Microsoft. Microsoft provides a huge amount of developer help, samples, and information, but they also recognize the contributions of the greater .NET community. Visual Studio 2008 provides a link to this content. Its goal is to provide developers with important (and targeted) product, development, and learning information where they will find it: in the IDE. The intent is to increase productivity and best practices by connecting developers with information.

The Visual Studio team built these connections and features into the IDE so as to be intuitive and unobtrusive yet readily available. You do not have to go searching to find and connect to your community. Rather, these communities are delivered to you through your development tool. If you are looking to find specific information, explore what is available, or publish your own community content, you can do so directly from within Visual Studio 2008. The following sections illustrate what is available from the IDE in terms of the Visual Studio Start Page and the Help menu.

> **NOTE**
>
> Visual Studio 2005 provided the Community menu. The features exposed by this menu have been rolled into the Help menu. This cleans up the toolbar and provides a single source for finding development aid and information.

## The Visual Studio Start Page

Developers new to Visual Studio 2008 will first encounter the IDE through the Start Page. The Start Page acts as a simple portal to your development experience and includes links to your favorite community. The four principal parts to the Start Page are Recent Projects, Getting Started, Visual Studio Headlines, and the MSDN news channel. Figure 7.1 shows a sample of the Start Page in the IDE.

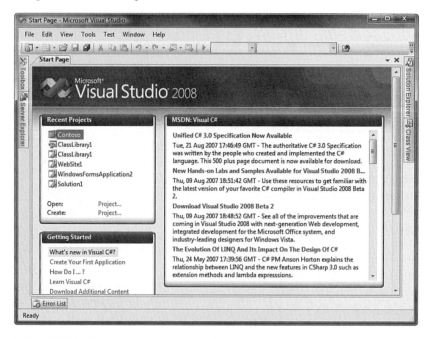

FIGURE 7.1   The Visual Studio Start Page.

Notice that the sample Start Page (or portal) shown in Figure 7.1 is for a developer who has set default settings in the IDE to Visual C# Development Settings. The Start Page (and other items in the IDE such as toolbars and layout) will change to reflect the setup of your default profile in the IDE. For example, if you select Web Development Settings, your MSDN news channel will be set to the ASP.NET news, and the Getting Started information will be targeted to an ASP.NET developer. Now let's look at each section on the home page.

### Recent Projects

The Recent Projects section of the Start Page provides a list of projects you have been working on. This allows you to easily access one or more projects in which you are currently engaged. Of course, clicking on a project in this list opens that project for editing. Figure 7.2 shows an example of a Recent Projects list.

FIGURE 7.2    The Recent Projects list from the Start Page.

Note that the Recent Projects list also contains links to open and create other projects not in the list. Using these links, you can quickly start a new project, create a new website, or browse to another project not listed here. Having quick access to these features makes the Start Page more useful as a launch point for your daily development work.

### Getting Started

The Getting Started section of the Start Page provides developers who are new to Visual Studio 2008 (or those looking to learn something new) a common place to start. The links in this list typically revolve around creating a new project, using a template or starter kit, answering a question, or learning something new. This feature can be a great launch point for doing your own exploration. Figure 7.3 shows an example of the Getting Started section from the C# Start Page. Of course, this section changes based on your developer profile (VB, C#, C++, Web, and so on).

FIGURE 7.3   The Getting Started list from the Start Page.

From Figure 7.3, you can see that the Getting Started block provides links directly to MSDN in terms of what's new and similar learning opportunities. You can also connect directly to community-related websites or download add-ins and starter kits.

### Visual Studio Headlines

The Visual Studio Headlines section of the Start Page shows announcements and headlines relative to Visual Studio. Figure 7.4 shows an example. You can see here that the feature contains headlines and links to MSDN content. These headlines are important bits of information for the developer regarding product updates, changes, and the like.

FIGURE 7.4   Visual Studio Headlines from the Start Page.

### Start Page News Channel

The news channel information is located inside the main section on the Start Page. In Figure 7.1, this section was titled MSDN: Visual C#. Figure 7.5 provides a closer look at some of the content that is included in this news channel. The news channel shown in this graphic is specific to Visual Studio. This information includes announcements on new books, new betas, new tools, webcasts, and more. It helps keep you informed even if you do not have time for browsing MSDN.

Content for the news channel is targeted to the concerns of a particular Visual Studio developer. You can choose from various news channels. The default news channel gets set through your developer profile (VB, C#, C++, Web, and so on).

**Customizing the News Channel**   The news channel information comes to the IDE via RSS feeds. If you are unfamiliar with RSS, you should be aware that RSS stands for Rich Site Summary, or Really Simple Syndication, or RDF Site Summary, depending on which definition you use. The gist is that RSS is meant to provide an XML-structured list that contains summaries and links to key information found within a particular site. With this technology, Visual Studio users can get the published summary of key news items for a particular development center on MSDN.

To customize the Start Page news channel, you use the Options dialog box (which you access by choosing Tools, Options). You select the Environment item from the tree view on the left side of the dialog box. Under Environment, you select the Startup leaf. This will present you with a couple of options, as shown in Figure 7.6.

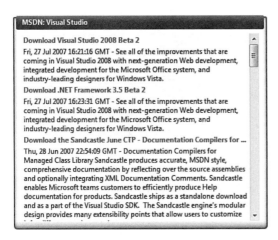

FIGURE 7.5   The Start Page news channel.

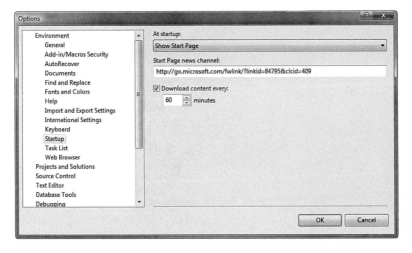

FIGURE 7.6   Customizing the Start Page news channel.

The dialog box's first option allows you to choose what happens when Visual Studio starts. Of course, we suggest you continue showing the Start Page by default. However, you can also open the last project on which you were working or show one of the open project dialog boxes.

> **TIP**
>
> If you choose not to see the Start Page when your IDE starts, you can still navigate there. You do so by either using the Start Page toolbar icon, shown in Figure 7.7, or choosing View, Other Windows, Start Page from the menus.

FIGURE 7.7    Accessing the Start Page using the toolbar icon.

The second option, Start Page News Channel, is the focus of our attention. Here, you can set a URL to an RSS feed. This allows for easy customization and connection to any RSS channel. Changing this setting will change the data that is displayed in the news channel section of the Start Page.

Some common news channels and their URLs are listed in Table 7.1. They correspond to the MSDN developer centers Microsoft has created. There are many more developer centers (and RSS feeds) than those listed in the table. For more, look at http://msdn2. microsoft.com/developercenters.

TABLE 7.1    Common RSS Feeds for the VS Start Page

| Description | URL |
| --- | --- |
| *Development with MS Products & Platforms* | |
| *Architecture and the .NET Framework* | |
| .NET Framework | http://msdn.microsoft.com/netframework/rss.xml |
| Architecture | http://msdn.microsoft.com/architecture/rss.xml |
| Patterns & Practices | http://msdn.microsoft.com/practices/rss.xml |
| Mobile | http://msdn.microsoft.com/windowsmobile/rss.xml |
| Security | http://msdn.microsoft.com/security/rss.xml |
| *Web Development* | |
| ASP.NET | http://msdn.microsoft.com/asp.net/rss.xml |
| Silverlight | http://msdn.microsoft.com/silverlight/rss.xml |
| Web Services | http://msdn.microsoft.com/webservices/rss.xml |
| *Visual Studio and Languages* | |
| Visual Studio | http://msdn.microsoft.com/vstudio/rss.xml |
| Team System | http://msdn.microsoft.com/vstudio/teamsystem/rss.xml |
| C# News | http://msdn.microsoft.com/vcsharp/rss.xml |
| VB News | http://msdn.microsoft.com/vbasic/rss.xml |

| Description | URL |
|---|---|
| *Development with MS Products & Platforms* | |
| C++ News | http://msdn.microsoft.com/visualc/rss.xml |
| Microsoft Office | http://msdn.microsoft.com/office/rss.xml |
| SQL Server | http://msdn.microsoft.com/sql/rss.xml |
| BizTalk | http://msdn.microsoft.com/biztalk/rss.xml |
| Windows Vista | http://msdn.microsoft.com/windowsvista/rss.xml |

**TIP**

Each URL listed in Table 7.1 not only points to an RSS feed that can be put into Visual Studio, but also provides a link to the related developer center on Microsoft's website. Simply remove the `rss.xml` from the link and you have the URL to the related developer center.

## The Help Menu

Visual Studio 2008 has combined the features found in the Community menu in 2005 with the Help menu. The Help menu provides access to help. It also provides quick access to things like the MSDN forums, online content, samples, and more. You can quickly search for an answer to a question, report a bug with Visual Studio or the framework, and access code samples. Figure 7.8 shows the Help menu. We will cover the relevant items in this menu in the following sections.

FIGURE 7.8   The Visual Studio 2008 Help menu.

### MSDN Forums

The MSDN Forums button on the Help menu allows you to search the community forums for answers to questions you might have about Visual Studio or the .NET Framework and related languages. When you click this button, Visual Studio launches the Microsoft Document Explorer for MSDN and navigates to a general search page for the MSDN Community Forums. Figure 7.9 shows an example of this search page.

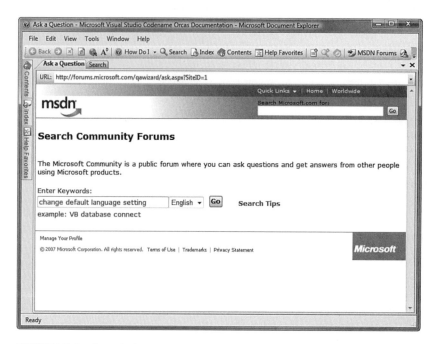

FIGURE 7.9    Search for an answer to your question.

The MSDN Community Forums allow developers to find information relevant to a common problem or post specific issues and receive feedback from the community. The intent of these moderated forums is to provide a community of developers to aid other developers.

When you reach out to the MSDN forums, you start the process of getting an answer to your question by first searching to find out whether your question was already asked (and possibly already answered). As an example, Figure 7.9 shows a question pertaining to changing the default language for Visual Studio. When you click the Go button, MSDN searches the community forum for relevant matches. Figure 7.10 shows the matches returned by the sample question.

In this example, the results show that someone has already asked a similar question. The green icon with a check mark next to the post indicates that this item was an answer to a question. When you ask a question and receive a reply that answers your question, you are able to mark that reply as an "Answer." This makes it much easier to find real answers to your questions and not have to filter through a large number of replies that did not really answer the question. Of course, if you do want to see the complete thread (and all related replies), you can do so by selecting the item in the list. Figure 7.11 shows an example of the thread. Notice how the answer is clearly highlighted. You can also use the Alert Me button to receive alerts when a new post is added to the discussion thread (more on this a bit later).

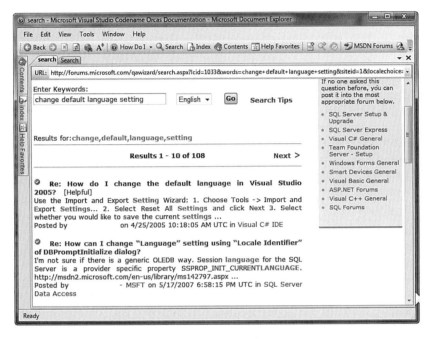

FIGURE 7.10    Community Forum search results.

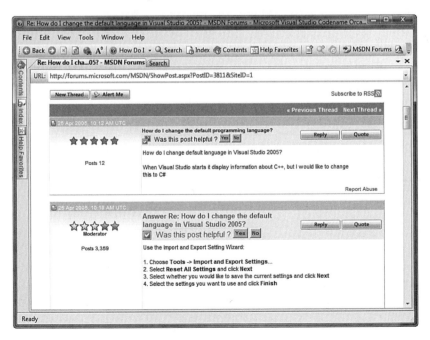

FIGURE 7.11    Community Forum answers.

**Starting a New Thread**  Sometimes when you ask a question, you cannot find an answer. In these cases, you can post the question to the appropriate community forum. If, for example, you cannot find your answer in the search results, you can use the links on the right side of the page (see Figure 7.10) to navigate to the appropriate forum.

You would navigate to the Visual Studio General Forum if you were unable to find the answer to the question on changing the default language in the IDE. Clicking this link will take you to the main page for this forum. From here, you can click the New Thread button (in the left corner of Figure 7.11) to post the question to the community. You must have a Windows Live account. Your new question/thread will be added to the appropriate forum and marked unanswered. Typically, each forum has a group of people who peruse these unanswered questions and try to provide assistance.

**Navigating Forums and Topics**  The MSDN Community Forums are organized into a wide variety of high-level forum categories. These categories include web development, .NET, XML, Smart Devices, and, of course, Visual Studio. Figure 7.12 shows the Community Forums home page.

Each forum category is further refined by the actual forums in the given category. You click on a forum category to navigate to the forums list for the given category. You can find forums that may be of particular interest to you in the Visual Studio category. Figure 7.13 shows the main page for the Visual Studio forums. From here, you can find forums on setup and installation, MSBuild, the debugger, the Class Designer, and many other IDE topics.

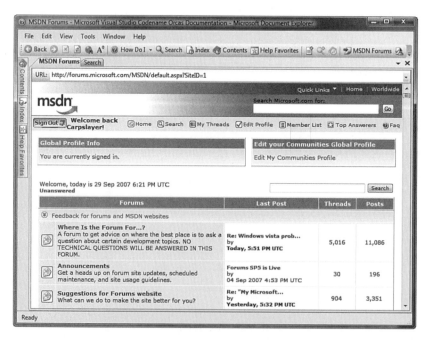

FIGURE 7.12  The Community Forums home page.

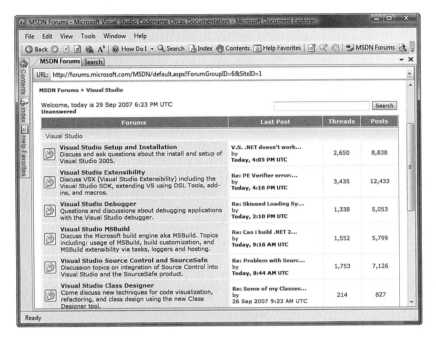

FIGURE 7.13   The Visual Studio Forums home page.

Selecting a given forum will take you to the main page for that forum. From here, you can find information such as announcements, FAQs, the five most-viewed answers, and, of course, actual topics that have been posted to the forum. As an example, Figure 7.14 shows some of the topics found on the Visual Studio Source Control and SourceSafe Forum.

You may have noticed the many icons next to each topic in Figure 7.14. These icons help you to navigate through topics. When doing so, you quickly learn that not all topics are questions and not all questions are answered.

The icons next to each topic help guide you to the content held within a given topic. For instance, a check mark over a document icon indicates that the topic is an answer to a question. Popular items also have a sun attached to their icon. There are many icons with which you will want to become familiar. Figure 7.15 shows the icons and what they mean next to a given topic.

**Managing Your Thread/Topic Alerts**   Typically, when you start a new thread or post a new question, you will ask to receive alerts when someone replies to your post or answers your question. In addition, if you find a topic that is of particular interest, you can request to be alerted when new posts are made to the thread. The MSDN Community Forums enable you to receive these alerts via email, instant messenger, or a mobile device. This capability allows the community to stay in touch with its participating members without forcing them to constantly log in and check for activity.

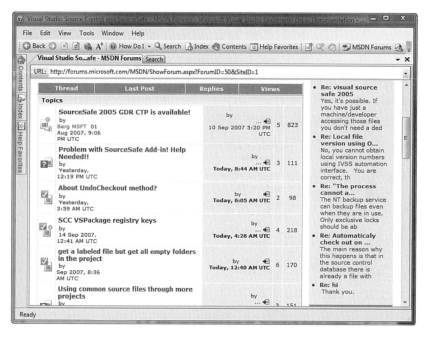

FIGURE 7.14    Forum topics.

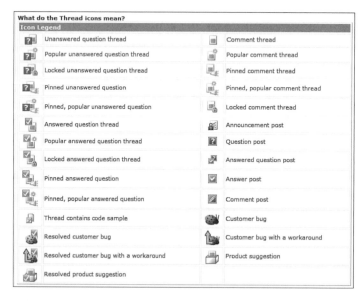

FIGURE 7.15    Topic icon legend.

Figure 7.16 shows some of the options you have for managing forum alerts. You can get to these options by clicking My Threads in the topmost toolbar, then selecting My Subscriptions. There is a button at the bottom of this screen to change your Alert settings. Notice that there are basic options and custom delivery options. The latter (shown) allows for alerts to be sent based on your MSN Messenger status. If you are logged in, you can get an IM; if not, the alert can be forwarded to your email or phone.

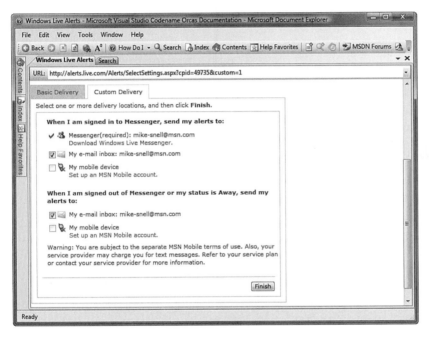

FIGURE 7.16   Microsoft Forum alert settings.

### Customer Feedback Options

Most developers we've met love to work with cool software and are always looking for ways it might be improved. This holds especially true for their tools, the biggest of which is Visual Studio. Selecting the Customer Feedback Options menu item from the Help menu will give you the option to allow Microsoft to collect data and identify usage trends with Visual Studio. Figure 7.17 shows this dialog. You can see that this is an anonymous collection of data.

**Report a Bug or Make a Suggestion**   Often you'll think of something that would make for a great addition or perhaps you'll find a flaw (or bug) in the software. Using the Report a Bug item on the Help menu, you can post your suggestions and log any bugs you find.

The process for reporting bugs and making suggestions is similar to that of starting a new thread in the MSDN forums. That is, the process starts by first searching for a similar suggestion or bug. This helps to reduce the creation of duplicate submissions.

FIGURE 7.17    The Customer Experience Improvement Program.

If you do find an item similar to the one you had planned to post, you can rate the item, validate it, or post a comment/workaround. Rating allows Microsoft to prioritize an item in terms of its importance. Both the number of people rating the item and the rating itself help to influence how the item is prioritized. You can also add comments to a suggestion or bug. Adding your comments to an item allows you to provide similar evidence or clarification to a reported bug or suggestion.

Microsoft actively monitors these lists. In fact, most items are marked with Microsoft comments and closed or resolved in new builds and service packs. In addition, if you find a bug for which you know a workaround, you can attach your workaround to the item. This is another way the .NET community can help itself.

Finally, you can help the Visual Studio team by trying to validate a specific item. Typically, this involves following the "steps to reproduce" as posted by the person who logged the issue. You mark an item as either Can or Can't Validate. This allows the Visual Studio team to know that more than one person is experiencing the issue. Figure 7.18 shows the Feedback summary information across the top of the page. This table contains links to the features we've discussed in this section.

### Search

The Search menu option on the Help menu links you to the search feature inside the MSDN help system. Of course, this search tool covers your local help files. However, it also reaches out to MSDN Online and the Codezone Community sites (see the section "Codezone Community") to give you a wider coverage for your search results.

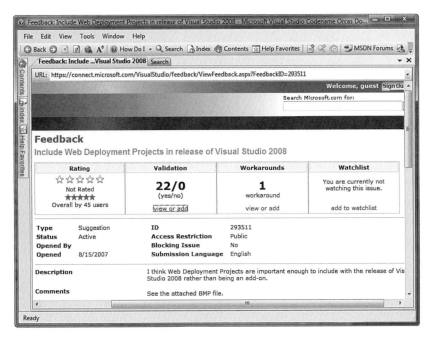

FIGURE 7.18   The Feedback table.

Selecting Search from the Help menu opens the MSDN Search screen. Figure 7.19 shows an example. A number of parameters control your search. Content type is a big one. It allows you to narrow your search to just controls, templates, samples, and more. You can also set the development language you are referring to in your search and the technology. Development language indicates that you are looking for community content that is targeted at a particular language (C#, VB, HTML, C++, and so on). Of course, as with all the options, you can select more than one. The technology parameter allows you to narrow your search to a particular set of technologies, such as ASP.NET, SQL Server, and Windows Forms. There are a large number of technologies on which you can search.

When you execute a search, the results are grouped by where they came from. This includes your local help, MSDN online, the Codezone community, and the forums (questions). Figure 7.20 shows the results for a particular search. We will look at using these community results in the coming sections.

**Managing Search Options**   You have some degree of control over Search through the Options dialog box. From inside the MSDN documentation, you can access these settings by choosing Tools, Options. You then select the Online item under the Help node. Figure 7.21 provides an example. You can navigate to this same set of options from within Visual Studio (choose Tools, Options and then select the Help node under Environment).

These help options allow you to set your order of preference in terms of local versus online help. In addition, you can choose the help provider(s) you want to search. This includes turning on and off individual Codezone communities.

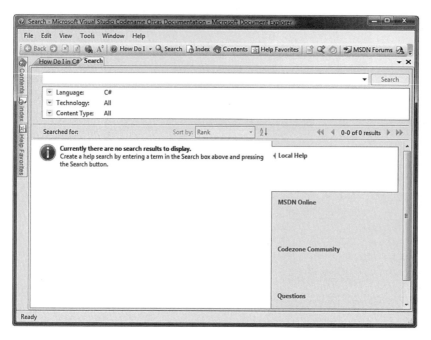

FIGURE 7.19    The MSDN Search screen.

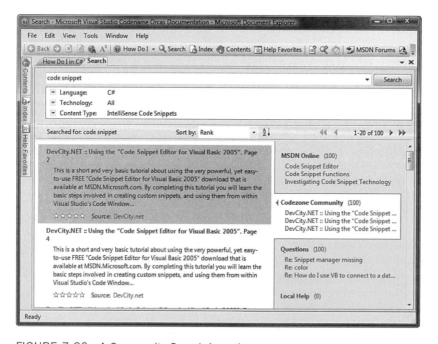

FIGURE 7.20    A Community Search in action.

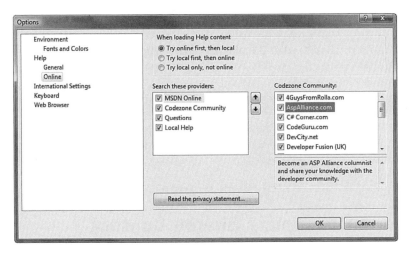

FIGURE 7.21    The Search Options dialog.

If you use a proxy server on your network, you may have problems with the search function. Authentication to the proxy may not be getting passed from the help system. Fortunately, a quick search of the community forums provided an answer to this issue.

A potential solution is to change the help system's application configuration file located at `Program Files\Common Files\Microsoft Shared\Help 8\dexplore.exe.config`. You can modify this file in one of two ways. If your computer is a stationary desktop, you add the following element to the `<system.net>` node:

```
<defaultProxy enabled="true" useDefaultCredentials="true">
  <proxy bypassonlocal="True" proxyaddress="http://yourproxy"/>
</defaultProxy>
```

If you use a laptop and have a proxy script that controls when and when not to use the proxy, you add the following element:

```
<defaultProxy enabled="true" useDefaultCredentials="true">
  <proxy autoDetect="true" usesystemdefault="true" scriptLocation=
➥"file://c:/yourfile"/>
</defaultProxy>
```

**Codezone Community**    The Codezone community is a link to Microsoft's list of independent .NET resources. These resources include sites dedicated to the .NET community, individual experts, user groups, and the like. Having these sites helps to broaden access to communities outside just the Microsoft resources. These communities typically publish articles, blogs, code snippets, independent forums, and so on.

Codezone (http://www.codezone.com) membership is granted by the Visual Studio and .NET teams. This membership policy helps to ensure the quality of the sites. Codezone community members' content is indexed and made searchable through the Search feature as discussed previously.

---

**NOTE**

For a link to many of the Visual Studio community sites, visit the MSDN Community Center (http://msdn2.microsoft.com/en-us/community/). Here, in addition to Codezone and Codezone sites, you can access other blogs, Channel 9, newsgroups, webcasts, and the like.

---

# Discovering and Consuming Shared Content

We have all been given programming tasks in which we *just know* someone must have already tackled the problem, and we've all faced tight deadlines. In these cases, it is often wise to hit the Internet to find out whether there is community content you can use to your advantage. At a minimum, you may find a partial solution that can speed your development effort and increase your understanding of how you might solve your particular problem.

Visual Studio provides a formal mechanism for publishing, finding, and consuming shared content. In the following sections, we will look at discovering and leveraging this content. We will then demonstrate how you can be an active participant in this community.

## Examining Shared Content Types

Visual Studio provides a number of code-sharing opportunities. For example, you might download a project template that defines an observer or singleton pattern, perhaps you'll find a code snippet that inserts a common method for accessing a database, or maybe you'll write a timesaving add-in or macro to share with the community. Visual Studio allows developers to write these types of extensions and more. Table 7.2 describes the many content types that provide opportunities for community sharing and consumption in Visual Studio 2008.

TABLE 7.2    Shared Content Types

| Content | Description |
| --- | --- |
| Project Template | Project templates are the sets of files that define a new project. When you create a new project using Visual Studio, you are asked to select a project template. Visual Studio allows for the creation of your own project templates and the consumption of the same. |
| Starter Kit | Starter kits are just like project templates but typically include additional documentation and step-by-step instructions. |

| Content | Description |
|---|---|
| Item Template | Item templates are files that you want to be able to reuse across projects. When you use Visual Studio to add a new item to your project, you are selecting and adding an item template. Item templates define the contents and structure of new items when added to a project. Visual Studio allows you to create and consume custom item templates. |
| Code Snippet | Code snippets are bits of code that you can add to the Visual Studio IntelliSense feature. You can create your own code snippets and share them with your community. A number of useful snippets are also available for download. We cover creating a custom code snippet in Chapter 8, "Working with Visual Studio's Productivity Aids." |
| Sample | A number of MSDN sample applications are available for download and installation. These files are typically .zip files and come in multiple languages (C# and VB being the most common). In addition, a number of samples are available when installing Visual Studio. |
| Control | Controls can be both user and custom controls written for .NET. They may be free to the community and include source code, or they may be made for commercial purposes. You can write and share your own controls using Visual Studio. |
| Add-Ins & Macros | Add-ins and macros are typically extensions and enhancements to the development environment. Visual Studio supports the creation and sharing of these items. We cover macros in great depth inside Chapter 12, "Writing Macros"; add-ins are covered in Chapter 13, "Writing Add-Ins and Wizards." |

## Finding the Right Content

The first trick to leveraging the knowledge that exists out there is finding it. You have already seen the search feature that is built into the Visual Studio help system. However, it is worth noting that one of the search options is Content Type. This allows you to filter your search based on what you are looking for. For example, if you are looking only for a control or a code snippet, you can limit the search to content that has been tagged as such. Figure 7.22 shows the Content Type drop-down options.

## Installing and Storing Shared Content

Visual Studio 2008 provides a tool called the Visual Studio Content Installer. Its role is to both allow content consumers to easily install content and help content creators package their content (more on this later). The Content Installer is invoked when you run a .vsi (Visual Studio Installer) file. The Content Installer is a wizard that walks you through installing shared content. The dialog boxes in the wizard are slightly different depending on what type of content you are installing. For example, Figure 7.23 shows the tool installing a code snippet. Visual Studio 2008 uses the content type to determine where to store your content (macro, add-in, snippet, and so on).

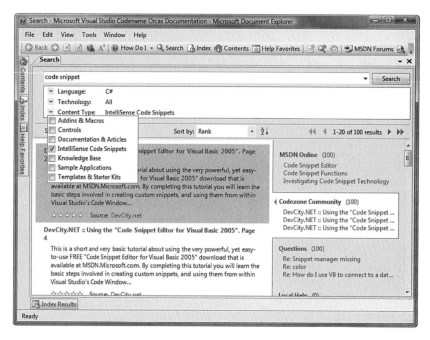

FIGURE 7.22    A Content Type search.

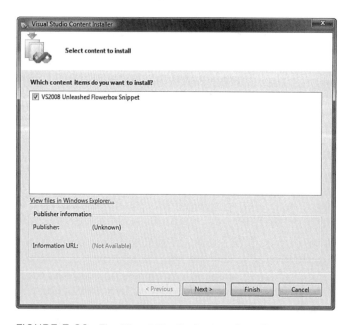

FIGURE 7.23    The Visual Studio Content Installer.

Content that is not a macro, an add-in, or a snippet gets installed in one of the appropriate Visual Studio locations. There are paths for projects, project templates, and item templates. Figure 7.24 shows the Options dialog box that can be used to manage these paths. Note that if you have a lot of varied project and item templates, you may choose to set these paths to a network share.

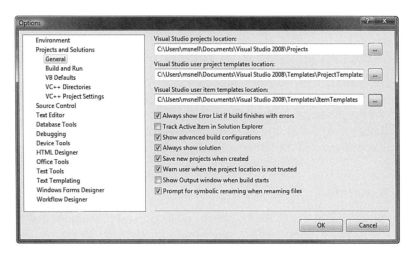

FIGURE 7.24    Setting project and item template storage locations.

We will examine this tool more closely in the upcoming section, where we discuss how you can create and package your own content.

> **TIP**
>
> Microsoft has created a new community site for open-source projects. This site is called CodePlex (www.codeplex.com). It replaces the now-deprecated gotdotnet.com. You can find a number of projects and samples here. You can also start a new open-source project or participate in an existing one. One such project worth checking out is the Power Toys for Visual Studio Packet Installer project. It offers an easy installation and management tool for the many open-source enhancements available for Visual Studio.

## Participating in the Community

No matter how good Visual Studio gets, most developers often think of great additions or extensions to the existing functionality. These extensions may simply be project specific, or they may apply to all Visual Studio users. Of course, developers also like to write code. Therefore, it is not surprising that some go so far as to write their own custom extensions (add-ins, snippets, macros, and the like). This feat is often successful for single, personal use. The trouble comes when you want to share your timesaving creation with the rest of the team. Often, you end up writing a page of installation instructions and doing one-on-one troubleshooting with each developer as he or she installs your "timesaver."

Visual Studio 2008 offers a solution in the form of a packaging mechanism that allows developers to publish, exchange, and install Visual Studio content. Previously, we looked at consuming community content. Now we will demonstrate how you can package your own creations and exchange them with team members, with friends, or through community websites.

## Creating Shared Items (Project and Item Templates)

In other chapters, we demonstrate how to create snippets, macros, and add-ins (see Table 7.2 for chapter references). What we have not covered is creating project and item templates. These items are very useful for large teams that want to disseminate standards and provide guidance. Rather than dedicating an entire chapter to these two items, we will cover them here as creating shared content.

## Creating Project Templates

Project templates are what appear in Visual Studio's New Project dialog box. Projects are grouped by project type (C#, VB, Windows, Office, and so on). In addition, the templates themselves are split between Visual Studio installed templates and My Templates. The latter refers to the custom templates you install. Figure 7.25 shows the New Project dialog box in action. You choose a project type or group and then the actual templates themselves.

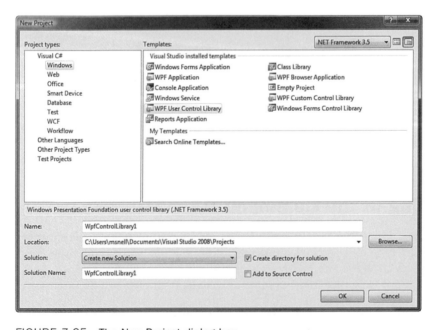

FIGURE 7.25    The New Project dialog box.

You can create a project template manually or use the Visual Studio Export Template Wizard. It simply makes the task of putting together the right XML files and zipping your project slightly easier. To create a project template, you follow these basic steps:

1. Create a project in Visual Studio (or start with an existing project).
2. Determine where (if any) parameters should exist in your template.
3. Choose the Export Template option from the File menu.
4. (Optional) Edit the .vstemplate XML.

Next, let's look at each of these steps.

### Step 1: Create Your Project
Most templates you create will start with an existing Visual Studio template (or an empty project). Typically, developers look to templates to enforce standards and practices and provide guidance to teams. Therefore, the hardest part of creating a project template is defining the template itself in terms of what content should go into it. As an example, perhaps your team uses a common set of libraries, resources, or controls. You can define a project template that has these items either built in or referenced.

### Step 2: Determine Project Parameters
Project parameters define the items that are set by default when Visual Studio sets up a new project based on the given template. For example, when you create a new project, the namespace of the code files is set to the namespace of the project. This is a project parameter. Visual Studio uses a number of *reserved template parameters* for this purpose. Table 7.3 provides an overview of these parameters.

TABLE 7.3  Reserved Template Parameters

| Content | Description |
| --- | --- |
| clrversion | The version of the Common Language Runtime (CLR). |
| GUID[1-10] | A unique project ID. You can set up to 10 project IDs using GUID1, GUID2, and so on. |
| itemname | The name of the given item that the user types into the Add New Item dialog box—for example, MyNewClass.cs. |
| machinename | The user's computer name. |
| projectname | The name of the given project that the user types into the Add New Project dialog box—for example, MySmartClient. |
| registeredorganization | The Registry key value for the organization set during Windows installation. |
| rootnamespace | The namespace that will be set as the root for the current project. |
| safeitemname | Similar to the itemname but with all unsafe characters and spaces removed. |
| safeprojectname | Similar to the projectname but with all unsafe characters and spaces removed. |

TABLE 7.3   Continued

| Content | Description |
| --- | --- |
| time | The current time on the user's computer. |
| userdomain | The domain the user has logged in to. |
| username | The name of the active user. |
| year | The current year as represented by the user's computer. |

The Export Template Wizard helps you with these parameters. After you define them manually in your code, the Export Template Wizard will pick up the settings.

As an example, suppose you have a project template titled SmartClient. When a user chooses to create a project based on this template, you want the template to behave as another template in the dialog box. For instance, you want the project's namespace to be defined as the project name the user has chosen.

To implement parameters in the template, you define the parameter's position within the code. In the namespace example, you must use the reserved template parameter safeprojectname in place of the actual namespace defined throughout the code files in the project. This indicates to Visual Studio that when a new project is created, the namespace should be set to the safe project name as defined by the user. The following code example shows how to define the code:

```
namespace $safeprojectname$ {
    class Framework {
```

> **NOTE**
>
> Your code will not build with these parameters in place. Therefore, it is best to debug your code before setting up parameters.

Now that you've defined your parameters, the Export Template Wizard will pick them up and place them in the .vstemplate XML file. We will look at this in step 3.

**Defining Custom Parameters**   In addition to the aforementioned Visual Studio parameters, you can define your own custom parameters to be passed to your templates. The process is similar to using the reserved template parameters. You first define the parameters using the $parameter$ syntax in your code as shown here:

```
string myCustomValue = "$CustomParameter1$";
```

You then edit the .vstemplate XML to include a <CustomParameters> node in which you define your replacements. We will look at this XML in more detail in the next major section; however, the following defines a custom parameter in the .vstemplate file:

```
<TemplateContent>
```

```
    ...
    <CustomParameters>
        <CustomParameter Name="$CustomParameter1$" Value="Some Custom Value"/>
    </CustomParameters>
</TemplateContent>
```

Visual Studio will replace the content of the custom parameter when a user creates a new instance of the project template. In the preceding example, the value of the variable myCustomValue will be set to Some Custom Value.

> **NOTE**
>
> The Export Template Wizard does not recognize custom parameters. You will have to edit the .vstemplate XML manually to include the CustomParameters node.

### Step 3: Export Your Template

Now that you have defined your template and decided on template parameters, the next step is to run the Export Template Wizard. This wizard is used for both project and item templates. You access it from the File menu.

Figure 7.26 shows the first step in the wizard. Here, you are asked to choose the template type (project or item). You then must select a project from within the current, open Visual Studio solution. This project will serve as the basis for your template.

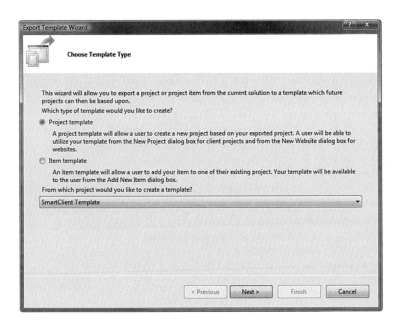

FIGURE 7.26 The Export Template Wizard.

The next step in the Export Template Wizard allows you to define a few additional parameters for your template. You can set an icon for the template, indicate a name and description that show up in the New Project dialog box, and also choose the location where your template will be placed. Figure 7.27 shows an example of this dialog box.

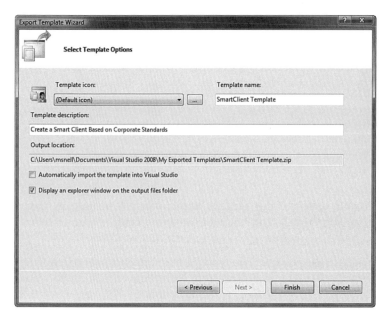

FIGURE 7.27    Export Template options.

Notice that in the dialog box shown in Figure 7.27 the option Automatically Import the Template into Visual Studio is not checked. This is for two reasons. First, you want to edit the .vstemplate file the wizard generates, and second, you want to package the template for installation (we will look at this topic in the next major section). By default, the template is created in the directory ...\Documents\Visual Studio 2008\My Exported Templates\. The file is created as a .zip file (as are all Visual Studio templates).

### Step 4 (Optional): Edit the .vstemplate XML
A fourth, optional step in the process is to edit the .vstemplate XML. The Export Template Wizard generates a default .vstemplate for you. You can open the .zip file, edit the XML, rezip (compress) the file, and place it directly into the template folder or package for installation. Listing 7.1 shows a sample .vstemplate file.

LISTING 7.1    A Sample .vstemplate File

```
<VSTemplate Version="2.0.0"
  xmlns="http://schemas.microsoft.com/developer/vstemplate/2005" Type="Project">
  <TemplateData>
    <Name>Smart Client</Name>
```

```
    <Description>Corporate standard smart client template</Description>
    <ProjectType>CSharp</ProjectType>
    <ProjectSubType>
    </ProjectSubType>
    <SortOrder>1000</SortOrder>
    <CreateNewFolder>true</CreateNewFolder>
    <DefaultName>Smart Client</DefaultName>
    <ProvideDefaultName>true</ProvideDefaultName>
    <LocationField>Enabled</LocationField>
    <EnableLocationBrowseButton>true</EnableLocationBrowseButton>
    <Icon>__TemplateIcon.ico</Icon>
  </TemplateData>
  <TemplateContent>
    <Project TargetFileName="Smart Client.csproj" File="Smart Client.csproj"
      ReplaceParameters="true">
      <ProjectItem ReplaceParameters="true"
        TargetFileName="Framework.cs">Framework.cs</ProjectItem>
    </Project>
  </TemplateContent>
</VSTemplate>
```

Notice that the wizard added the `ReplaceParameters` attribute to the `ProjectItem` node and set its value to `true`. This setting indicates to Visual Studio that it should swap any parameters in the target file during project creation. In the example, `Framework.cs` is the target file containing the parameters ($safeprojectname$).

---

**TIP**

You can actually create templates that contain multiple projects. To do so, you still create a `.vstemplate` file for each project in the solution. You then create a `.vstemplate` root file that describes the multiproject template. The data inside this XML is used by the New Project dialog box. The file also contains pointers to each individual project's `.vstemplate` file.

---

### Installing the Template

Finally, all that is left to do is to package the template into a `.vsi` file (see the next section) for sharing. You can then install it. Figure 7.28 shows an example of a newly installed template under the My Templates subsection. Also, notice that the item should be installed for C#, Windows applications. This is done through the `.vsi` file. Again, we will cover this topic in the following section.

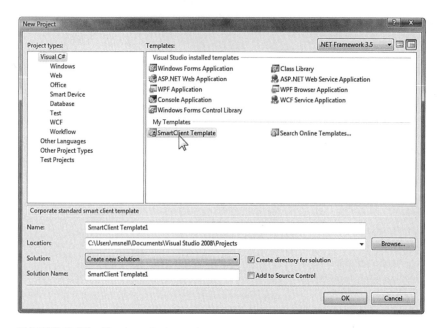

FIGURE 7.28    The installed template in the New Project dialog box.

Finally, when the project is generated, Visual Studio inserts the safe filename for the project namespace. Recall that this was the reserved parameter you had set. The following code is inserted into Framework.cs:

```
namespace My_New_Smart_Client_App {
    class Framework {
```

## Creating Item Templates

Item templates represent the various items or files you can add to Visual Studio projects. Selecting Add New Item opens a dialog box that allows you to select from the various Visual Studio items (class files, for example). You can also create your own, custom items. Custom items could be timesaving devices that stub out the shell of a class or a fully implemented, specific type of class, for instance. Figure 7.29 shows the Add New Item dialog box with the custom item, DataFramework, in the My Templates section.

The good news is that you create item templates the same way you create project templates. You start with an existing item, edit it, and then use the Export Template Wizard to create an item template from the item. In step 1 of the wizard, you choose item template (see Figure 7.26). You then select the files in your project you want to use to generate item templates. Note that you can also define the same set of parameters for item templates that you can for project templates.

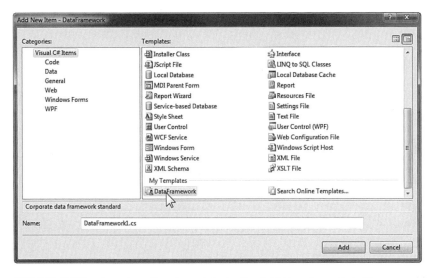

FIGURE 7.29    A custom item template in the Add New Item dialog box.

## Packaging Your Creation

As mentioned previously, Visual Studio 2008 provides a tool called the Visual Studio Content Installer. The role of this tool is to help developers install content that is targeted at the Visual Studio IDE. This content takes the form of Visual Studio content files (with the .vsi extension). After you've bundled your creation inside one of these files, the tool can easily install the content into the IDE. The good news is that creating these files is a relatively straightforward process.

Of course, the first step is to define and debug your creation (see Chapter 11, "Introducing the Automation Object Model," Chapter 12, "Writing Macros," and Chapter 13, "Writing Add-ins and Wizards," for more information on extending Visual Studio). Creations such as project and item templates, add-ins, macros, and code snippets can all be bundled as .vsi files. When you are ready to share your creation, you need to follow these steps (we will elaborate on them later):

1. Create a .VSContent file that contains XML describing your content.

2. Gather the file or files that define your creation.

3. Compress your files into a .zip file.

4. Rename the .zip file using the .vsi extension.

5. Optional: Sign your .vsi file.

This process is the same no matter the content type. You follow the same steps for macros, add-ins, and snippets. The install tool gets its information regarding your contents through the settings of your .VSContent XML file. Now let's explore this file in detail.

### The Elements of a VSContent File

The VSContent file is an XML structure that contains elements for all pertinent items needed by the Visual Studio Content Installer. Your content is defined by a Content node (or element). This element is meant to define a single item of content you want to share (such as a macro file or control defined in a .dll file). Listing 7.2 presents the high-level structure of the VSContent file. This is neither a real example nor the official XSD. Rather, it serves to present the elements and their relations to one another.

LISTING 7.2    The Structure of a .VSContent File

```
<VSContent xmlns="http://schemas.microsoft.com/developer/vscontent/2008">
  <Content>
    <FileName></FileName>
    <DisplayName></DisplayName>
    <Description></Description>
    <FileContentType></FileContentType>
    <ContentVersion></ContentVersion>
    <Attributes>
      <Attribute name="" value=""/>
    </Attributes>
  </Content>
</VSContent>
```

> **TIP**
>
> The actual XSD that defines the structure of a VSContent file is a bit lengthy to reprint here. However, if you would like to examine the XSD file that defines the structure for valid VSContent XML, you can do so. The file is stored at C:\Program Files\ Microsoft Visual Studio 8\Xml\Schemas\1033\ and is named vscontent.xsd.

You can point to multiple content types and their associated files using a single .vsi file. You do so by creating multiple instances of the Content element, one for each item you want to share. For example, a single .vsi file could contain a Content node that installs a code snippet and another Content node that points to a .vsmacro file containing macros.

Each element inside Listing 7.2 is covered in depth in Table 7.4. We will walk through an actual example of creating and using a VSContent file in the following section.

TABLE 7.4   Elements of a VSContent File

| Element | Description |
|---------|-------------|
| FileName | This element represents the name of the file that contains the item to be installed as the content. |
|  | A single `Content` element can contain multiple `FileName` elements, depending on the situation. For example, you may define a VSContent file to install an add-in. The add-in might contain both an `.Addin` file and a `.dll` file. |
| DisplayName | This is the name of your content. The Visual Studio Content Installer displays this name when users install your creation. |
| Description | This element is used as the ToolTip text for your content inside the Visual Studio Content Installer. |
| FileContentType | This represents the type of content defined by the given `Content` node. This value is enumerated and therefore must be one of the following settings: `Addin, Macro Project, Code Snippet, VSTemplate, Toolbox Control`. |
| ContentVersion | This element represents a version number for your content. The only valid setting at this time is `1.0`. All other settings will result in an error. |
| Attributes | This element is used to group `Attribute` elements. |
| Attribute | You can use attributes to further define code snippet and VSTemplate content. These settings are discussed further in the next section. |

**Using Attributes to Define VSTemplates and Code Snippets**   The `Attribute` element inside the VSContent file provides the Visual Studio Content Installer additional information for content types that include project templates, item templates, and code snippets. The `Attributes` node is not used for the content types `Addin, Macro Project`, and `Toolbox Control`.

The `Attribute` element consists of a name/value pair. You set the name and value of the element using XML attributes in the following format:

```
<Attribute name="" value=""/>
```

Both the `name` and the `value` attributes are defined with enumerated values. These enumerated values define the possible setting combinations you can define for code snippets and templates.

For code snippets, only the value `lang` is applicable for the `name` attribute. Setting the `lang` attribute on code snippets allows you to indicate the development language to which the snippet applies. Possible entries for the `value` attribute when defined with `lang` include `csharp, jsharp, vb`, and `xml`. For example, if your code snippet is meant to work with Visual Basic, you would define your attribute as shown here:

```
<Attribute name="lang" value="vb"/>
```

When defining content of type VSTemplate, you can use the following enumerated items for the name attribute:

- ▶ **TemplateType**—Defines the type of template your content represents. Values are either Project for project templates or Item for item templates.

- ▶ **ProjectType**—Defines the type of project contained in your template. Possible enumerated items for the value attribute are Visual Basic, Visual C#, Visual J#, and Visual Web Developer.

- ▶ **ProjectSubType**—Defines the subcategory in which your template is placed in the New Project dialog box. Possible entries include Windows, Office, Smart Device, Database, Starter Kits, and Test.

Recall the Smart Client project template you created earlier. Listing 7.3 represents the VSContent file used to define the installation for the Smart Client. Notice the three attribute definitions. This combination allows for the configuration shown in Figure 7.28 (the New Project dialog box).

LISTING 7.3    The VSContent File for the Smart Client Example

```
<VSContent xmlns="http://schemas.microsoft.com/developer/vscontent/2008">
  <Content>
    <FileName>Smart Client.zip</FileName>
    <DisplayName>Smart Client</DisplayName>
    <Description>Install a smart client project template</Description>
    <FileContentType>VSTemplate</FileContentType>
    <ContentVersion>1.0</ContentVersion>
    <Attributes>
      <Attribute name="TemplateType" value="Project"/>
      <Attribute name="ProjectType" value="Visual C#"/>
      <Attribute name="ProjectSubType" value="Windows"/>
    </Attributes>
  </Content>
</VSContent>
```

### An Example: Packaging a Macro

As with most things, the best way to understand the Visual Studio content packaging process is to work through a real example. In this case, we will take a few of the macros defined in Chapter 12 and bundle them for sharing with the community.

**Step 1: Create the VSContent File**    After you've debugged and tested your creation, the first step in packaging it is to define the VSContent file. For this example, we've created a macro file that contains a few macros from previous chapters, including the InsertTemplateFlowerbox macro that places common comment structure above the Visual Basic Subs and Functions, the ResizeIDE macro, and others. The name of the macro file is VS2008_Unleashed.vsmacros.

An easy way to define the VSContent file is to open the Visual Studio IDE, select the File menu, New option, and then select the File option. In the resulting dialog box, select XML File. Remember, the VSContent file is nothing more than an XML file with a special extension in the filename (VSContent). In this way, you can create and edit your VSContent file directly in Visual Studio. You will have to edit the filename from .xml to VSContent. However, using Visual Studio allows you to take advantage of the built-in XML editor that includes IntelliSense.

The first step in defining the content of this file is to set the XML namespace (xmlns) to the proper schema. You do this by adding the following root node to the file:

```
<VSContent xmlns="http://schemas.microsoft.com/developer/vscontent/2005">
```

After you've done this, Visual Studio will recognize the intended structure for the XML and guide you through defining additional elements. Figure 7.30 shows an example of creating the VSContent file inside the IDE. Note that for the example, you define the FileName element to point to the macro file. You also must set the FileContentType to the enumerated value Macro Project. This ensures that the example is installed in the proper location for macros.

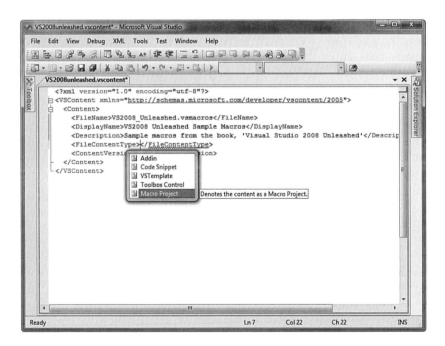

FIGURE 7.30    Defining the VSContent file inside the IDE.

**Step 2: Gather Files That Define Your Creation**    The next step is to place all your files into a single directory where they can easily find each other. You need to include in your bundle any files that are called out in the VSContent file (.vsmacros, .dll, .addin) and the VSContent file itself. For some files and projects, you may have to dig a little. For this macro project, the .vsmacros file created as a new macro project is stored in the VSMacros80 folder. This folder exists inside the path ...\Documents\Visual Studio 2008\Projects\.

In this example, you create a folder named VS2008 Unleashed Macros. In it, you place the macro file named VS2008_Unleashed.vsmacros and the VSContent file named VS2008_Unleashed.vscontent.

---

**TIP**

If you are creating a macro project and want to include it in a .vsi file, you will first need to find it! By default, Visual Studio stores custom macro projects in the folder ...\Documents\Visual Studio 2008\Projects\VSMacros80\.

---

**Step 3: Compress (Zip) Files**    The process of compressing the files should be familiar to all developers. You can use Window's built-in capability to compress files, or you can use a compression tool. In this example, use the Windows compression tool. You select the .vsmacros and VSContent files, right-click, and then choose Send To, Compressed (Zipped) Folder.

**Step 4: Rename the .zip File to .vsi**    The result of step 3 was the creation of a file named VS2008unleashed.zip. Now you're ready for the easiest step. Right-click the .zip file and choose Rename from the context menu. Remove the .zip extension and replace it with .vsi. That's it. If you are on a machine with Visual Studio installed, the new file will take on the .vsi icon (used for both .vsi and VSContent files). Figure 7.31 shows an example of these files and their icons.

**Installing the Sample Content**    All that remains is to distribute the .vsi file to the intended audience. Of course, it would be prudent to do a couple of test installations first. Let's look at the Visual Studio Content Installer tool in action.

First, in Figure 7.31, notice that both the .vsi and the VSContent files are Visual Studio Content Installer (VSContentInstaller.exe) files. They have the same icon. The reason is that both can be used to install the content.

There are some differences between the two, however. The .vsi file is fully self-contained. It does not require additional files for installation, whereas the VSContent file must exist in a directory that also contains the related content files. In addition, when you run the VSContent file, you are not warned about the lack of a signature (if one is lacking). Therefore, you might think that there is a bug or that these files are more appropriate for internal installations. The .vsi file, on the other hand, prompts you with a security warning dialog box if the content is not signed by a publisher. This, along with the single file and compression factor, seems to make the .vsi file ideal in larger, distributed scenarios.

Let's examine the installation process for the .vsi file. First, you double-click the file to invoke the Visual Studio Content Installer. Figure 7.32 shows the example loaded in the tool.

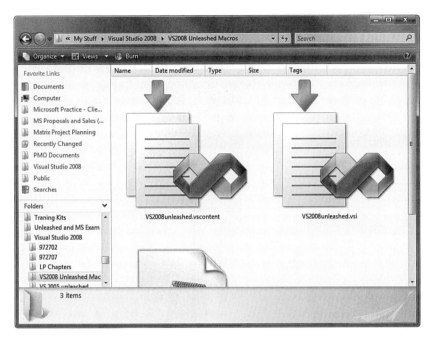

FIGURE 7.31   The packaged files.

FIGURE 7.32   The Visual Studio Content Installer.

From this screen, you can select View Files in Windows Explorer to examine the files that will be installed by the .vsi. Also, notice that the Publisher Information section is blank. The reason is that the bundle is not signed. When you click the Next button, the tool prompts you with a warning regarding the lack of signature. Figure 7.33 shows this warning. Again, this warning is not shown if you are installing from the VSContent file directly. For now, click Yes and move on. In the sidebar, we will discuss signing your work.

FIGURE 7.33     The No Signature Found warning.

## Signing Your Work

To sign your .vsi files with Authenticode, you must get a valid software publisher certificate (.spc) from a certificate authority (CA). Of course, this requires that you have a company set up and that you fill out an application as such. Visual Studio does have a few test tools to help developers understand the process before working with a CA. These tools include the following:

▶ Zip to Exe Conversion Tool (MakeZipExe.exe)
▶ Certificate Creation Tool (MakeCert.exe)
▶ Software Publisher Certificate Test Tool (Cert2spc.exe)
▶ Sign Tool (SignTool.exe)

The vision for these tools is as follows: You use the MakeZipExe.exe tool to convert your .zip file to an .exe file (because code signing requires an .exe or a .dll). You then use the SignTool.exe to sign the resulting .exe. You then convert this file into a .vsi file for publication.

If you do not have a valid certificate from a CA, you can create a test certificate (not to be used for publishing) with the `MakeCert.exe` tool. You then must convert this certificate into a software publisher certificate (`.spc`) using the `Cert2spc.exe`.

Next, the installer prepares you to finish the installation. Figure 7.34 shows an example. When you click the Finish button, the installer writes the files to the appropriate folders based on content type. If the given file already exists, the installer prompts you to find out whether you want it left as is or overwritten.

FIGURE 7.34    Finishing the installation.

When you click Finish, the installer finishes its job and reports back. Figure 7.35 shows a successful installation.

## Publishing Your Creation

You can publish your `.vsi` files to your coworkers, friends, team, or other developers. You also can post them on a network share, email them, or drop them on a content-sharing website such as CodePlex (www.codeplex.com) or similar community sites.

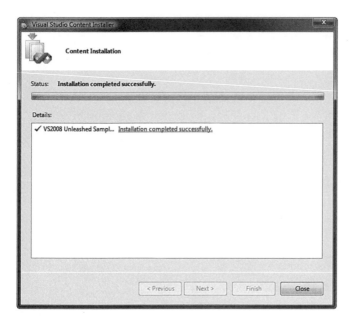

FIGURE 7.35    A successful installation.

## Summary

This chapter presented the many community options inside Visual Studio 2008. Developers can expect to feel part of a larger community that surrounds .NET. Microsoft has tried to build in a community to .NET. You see it with the Start Page inside Visual Studio, in the options on the Help menu, and within the capability to search the community from the MSDN help system.

Don't forget that being part of the developer community means giving back to it once in a while. Visual Studio provides the tools to make that happen. You can create and share project and item templates, code snippets, macros, add-ins, and controls. After you've created these items, Visual Studio provides the Visual Studio Content Installer framework in which to package your shared content for distribution. Now, the next time you write a great timesaving macro or snippet, you will have the know-how to package it up and share it with others.

# PART III

# Writing and Working with Code

## IN THIS PART

# CHAPTER 8

# Working with Visual Studio's Productivity Aids

In Chapter 6, "Introducing the Editors and Designers," we discussed the basic capabilities of the designers and editors in Visual Studio 2008. In this chapter, we will travel a bit deeper into their capabilities and those of other Visual Studio tools by examining the many productivity aids provided by the IDE. Many of these productivity enhancers are embedded within the text editors. Others are more generic in nature. But they all have one common goal: helping you, the developer, write code quickly and correctly.

If you recall from Chapter 6, in our coverage of the editors we used a very basic code scenario: a console application that printed "Hello, World!" to the console. In Figure 8.1, you see what the final code looks like in the code editor window.

If you have followed along by re-creating this project and typing the "Hello, World!" code in Visual Studio, you will notice that the productivity features of the code editor have already kicked into gear. For one, as you start to type code into the template file, the code editor has tabbed the cursor in for you, placing it at a new location for writing nicely indented code.

Second, as you type your first line of code, Visual Studio reacts to your every keystroke by interpreting what you are trying to write and extending help in various forms (see Figure 8.2). You are given hints in terms of completing your in-progress source, provided information on the members you are in the process of selecting, and given information on the parameters required to complete a particular method. These features are collectively referred to as *IntelliSense,* and we will explore its forms and functions in depth in this chapter.

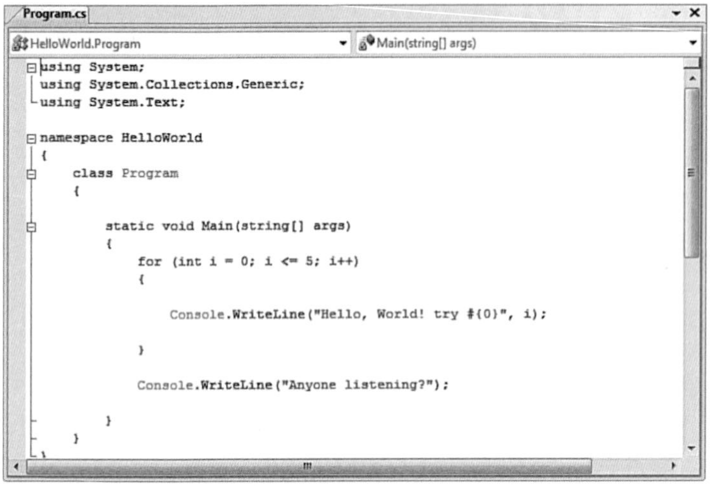

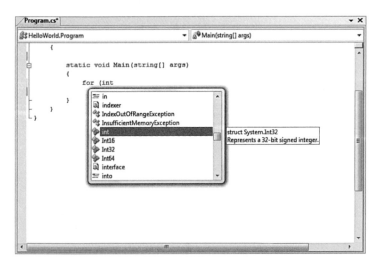

FIGURE 8.1    "Hello, World" in the code editor.

FIGURE 8.2    IntelliSense in action.

As you type, the IDE is also constantly checking what you have written with the compiler. If compile errors exist, they are dynamically displayed for you in the output window.

So, for this one simple line of code, Visual Studio has been hard at work improving your coding productivity by doing the following:

- ▶ Intelligently indenting the code

- ▶ Suggesting code syntax

- ▶ Displaying member descriptions to help you select the correct code syntax

- ▶ Visually matching up delimiting parentheses

- ▶ Flagging code errors by constantly background-compiling the current version of the source code

These features subtly help and coach you through the code-writing process by accelerating the act of coding itself.

# Basic Aids in the Text Editor

The text editor user interface has several visual constructs that help you with common problem areas encountered during the code-writing process. These basic aids provide support for determining what has changed within a code document and what compile problems exist in a document. Additionally, the discrete syntax elements for each individual language are visually delineated for you using colored text.

## Change Tracking

When you are in the midst of editing a source code file, it is tremendously useful to understand which lines of code have been committed (that is, saved to disk) and which have not. Change tracking provides this functionality: A yellow vertical bar in the text editor's selection margin will span any lines in the editor that have been changed but not saved. If content has been changed and subsequently saved, it will be marked with a green vertical bar in the selection margin.

By looking at the yellow and green tracking bars, you can quickly differentiate between:

- ▶ Code that hasn't been touched since the file was loaded (no bar)

- ▶ Code that has been touched and saved since the file was loaded (green bar)

- ▶ Code that has been touched but not saved since the file was loaded (yellow bar)

Change tracking is valid only for as long as the editor window is open. In other words, change tracking is significant only for the current document "session"; if you close and reopen the window, the track bars will be gone because you have established a new working session with that specific document.

Figure 8.3 shows a section of a code file displaying the change tracking bars.

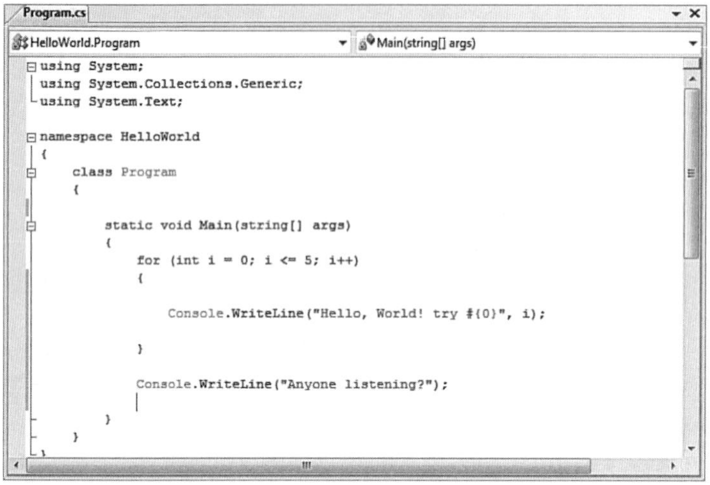

FIGURE 8.3    Change tracking.

## Coding Problem Indicators

The Visual Studio compiler works in conjunction with the code editor window to flag any problems found within a source code document. The compiler can even work in the background, enabling the editor window to flag problems as you type (as opposed to waiting for the project to be compiled).

Coding problems are flagged using "squiggles": wavy, color-coded lines placed under the offending piece of code. These squiggles are the same mechanism Microsoft Word uses to flag spelling and grammar problems. The squiggle colors indicate a specific class of problem. Table 8.1 shows how these colors map to an underlying problem.

TABLE 8.1    Coding Problem Indicator Colors

| Color | Problem |
| --- | --- |
| Red | Syntax error; the code will not compile because of the syntax requirements and rules of the language. |
| Blue | Semantic error; this is the result of the compiler not being able to resolve the type or code construct within the current context. For instance, a type name that doesn't exist within the compiled context of the current project is flagged with a blue squiggle. Typically, these are good indicators for typos (for example, misspelling a class name). |
| Purple | Warning; the purple squiggle denotes code that has triggered a compiler warning. |

Hovering the mouse pointer over the problem indicator will reveal the actual compiler error or warning message, as demonstrated in Figure 8.4.

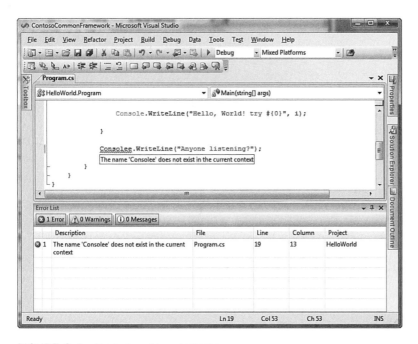

FIGURE 8.4   Coding problem indicators.

## Active Hyperlinking

Text editors support clickable hyperlinks within documents; clicking on a link launches a browser redirected at the URL. One great use of this feature is to embed URLs for supporting documentation or other helpful reference information within code comments.

## Syntax Coloring

The text editor can parse and distinctly color different code constructs to make them that much easier to identify on sight. As an example, the code editor window, by default, colors any code comments green. Code identifiers are black, keywords are blue, strings are colored red, and so on.

In fact, the number of unique elements that the text editor is capable of parsing and coloring is immense: The text editor window recognizes more than 100 different elements. And you can customize and color each one of them to your heart's content through the Fonts and Colors section, under the Environments node in the Options dialog box. Do you like working with larger fonts? Would a higher contrast benefit your programming activities? How about squeezing more code into your viewable screen real estate? These are just a few reasons you might stray from the defaults with this dialog box.

8

Figure 8.5 shows the fonts and colors page in the Options dialog box that allows you to specify foreground and background colors for code, HTML, CSS, or other elements. Select the element in the Display Items list and change its syntax coloring via the Item Foreground and Item Background drop-downs.

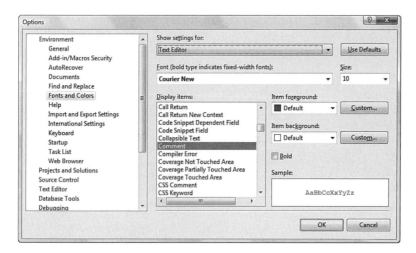

FIGURE 8.5    Setting font and color options.

---

**NOTE**

The dialog box shown in Figure 8.5 actually enables you to control much more than the syntax coloring for the text editor; you can change the coloring schemes used in all the different windows within Visual Studio. The item you select in the Show Settings For drop-down will determine the portion of the IDE you are customizing and will alter the list of items in the Display Items list.

You can always use the Use Defaults button at the upper right of the dialog box to restore the default coloring schemes.

---

## Outlining and Navigation

Certain documents, such as source code files and markup files, have a natural parent-child aspect to their organization and syntax. XML nodes, for instance, can contain other nodes. Likewise, functions and other programming language constructs such as loops and try/catch blocks act as a container for other lines of code. Outlining is the concept of visually representing this parent-child relationship.

# Code Outlining

Code outlining is used within the code editor; it allows you to collapse or expand regions of code along these container boundaries. A series of grouping lines and expand/collapse boxes are drawn in the selection margin. These expand/collapse boxes are clickable, enabling you to hide or display lines of code based on the logical groupings.

---

**TIP**

Both Visual Basic and C# provide a way to manually create named regions of code via a special region keyword. Use `#region`/`#endregion` (`#Region` and `#End Region` for Visual Basic) to create your own artificial code container that will be appropriately parsed by the code outliner. Because each region is named, this is a handy approach for organizing and segregating the logical sections of your code. In fact, to use one example, the code generated for you by the Windows Forms Designer is automatically tucked within a "Windows Forms Designer generated code" region.

One quick way to implement a region is with Surround With: In the editor, highlight the code that you want to sit in a new region, right-click on the highlighted text, select Surround With from the context menu, and then select #region (or #Region for VB).

---

Code outlining is best understood using a simple example. First, refer to Figure 8.1. This is the initial console application code. It contains a routine called Main, a class declaration, a namespace declaration, and several using statements. The code outline groupings that you see in the selection margin visually indicate code regions that can be collapsed or hidden from view.

Because the class declaration is a logical container, the selection margin for that line of code contains a collapse box (a box with a minus sign). A line is drawn from the collapse box to the end of the container (in this case, because you are dealing with C#, the class declaration is delimited by a curly brace). If you click on the collapse box for the class declaration, Visual Studio will hide all the code contained within that declaration.

Figure 8.6 shows how the editor window looks with this code hidden from view. Note that the collapse box has changed to a plus sign, indicating that you can click on the box to reshow the now-hidden code, and that the first line of code for the class declaration has been altered to include a trailing box with ellipses.

The HTML Editor also supports outlining in this fashion. HTML elements can be expanded or collapsed to show or hide their containing elements.

### Using the Outlining Menu

Several code outlining commands are available under the Edit, Outlining menu (see Figure 8.7).

- ▶ **Toggle Outlining Expansion**—Based on the current cursor position in the editor window, hides or unhides the outline region.

- ▶ **Toggle All Outlining**—Hides or unhides all outline regions in the editor.

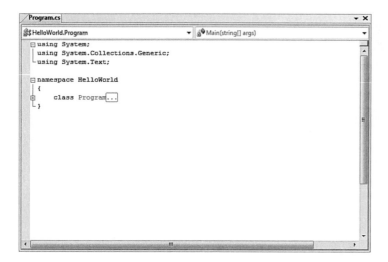

FIGURE 8.6    A collapsed outline region.

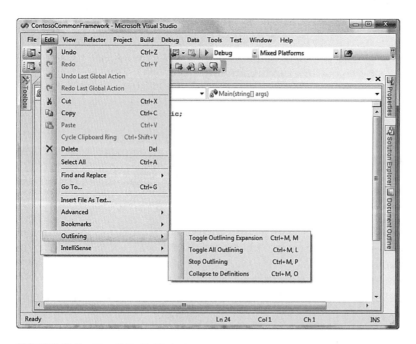

FIGURE 8.7    The Edit, Outlining menu.

▶ **Stop Outlining**—Turns off automatic code outlining (any hidden regions will be expanded). This command is available only if automatic outlining is turned on.

▶ **Stop Hiding Current**—Removes the outline for the currently selected region. This command is available only if automatic outlining has been turned off.

▶ **Collapse to Definitions**—Hides all procedure regions. This command is useful for distilling a type down to single lines of code for all of its members.

▶ **Start Automatic Outlining**—Enables the code outlining feature. This command is available only if outlining is currently turned off.

Code outlining is a convenience mechanism: By hiding currently irrelevant sections of code, you decrease the visible surface of the code file and increase code readability. You can pick and choose the specific regions to view based on the task at hand.

> **TIP**
>
> If you place the mouse pointer over the ellipses box of a hidden code region, the contents of that hidden region will be displayed to you in a ToolTip-style box; this is done without your having to actually expand/reshow the code region.

## HTML Navigation

One problem with large or complex web pages is that navigation through the HTML can be problematic with multiple levels and layers of tag nesting. Envision a page containing a table within a table within a table. When you are editing the HTML (through either the designer or the editor), how can you tell exactly where you are? Put another way, how can you tell where the current focus is within the markup hierarchy?

### Using the Tag Navigator

The tag navigator is Visual Studio's answer to this question. The navigator appears as a series of buttons at the bottom of the web page editor, just to the right of the designer/editor tabs. A bread-crumb trail of tags is shown (as buttons) that leads from the tag which currently has focus all the way to the outermost tag. If this path is too long to actually display within the confines of the editor window, it is truncated at the parent tag side; a button enables you to display more tags toward the parent.

Figure 8.8 picks up a scenario we dealt with in Chapter 6: an HTML login page. While you're editing the OK button in the sample login page, the tag navigator shows the path all the way back to the parent enclosing <html> tag.

Each tag button displayed by the navigator can be used to directly select the inclusive or exclusive contents of that tag. A drop-down triggered by the tag button will contain options for selecting the tag or selecting the tag content. The former will cause the tag itself, in addition to all of its enclosed content, to be selected. The latter will exclude the tag begin and end, but will still select all of its enclosed content.

The navigator is a great mechanism for quickly moving up and down within a large HTML documents tag tree.

### Using the Document Outline Window

The Document Outline window displays a tree-view representation of the HTML elements on a page. This hierarchical display is also a great navigation tool because it allows you to

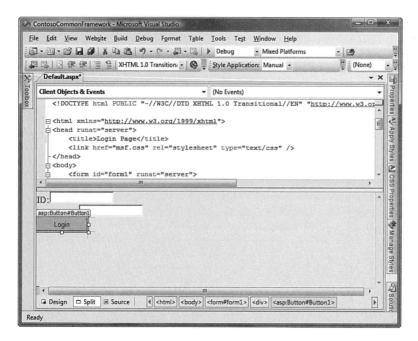

FIGURE 8.8    The tag navigator.

take in the entire structure of your web page in one glance and immediately jump to any of the elements within the page.

To use the Document Outline window, choose Document Outline from the View, Other Windows menu. Figure 8.9 shows a sample outline window. Elements within the head, page, and body elements are displayed, in addition to script and code elements.

Clicking on an element will navigate to that element (and select it) within the designer window, and, of course, you can expand or collapse the tree nodes as needed.

# Smart Tags and Smart Tasks

*Smart tags* and *smart tasks* (the terms can essentially be used interchangeably) are menu- or IntelliSense-driven features for automating common control configuration and coding tasks within the IDE. Designers and editors both implement smart tags in various scenarios. In the following sections, we will examine a few of the ways that smart tags make your life easier, starting first with the HTML designer.

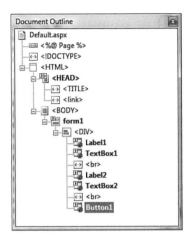

FIGURE 8.9   The Document Outline window.

## HTML Designer

As controls are placed onto the HTML designer, a pop-up list of common tasks appears. These tasks, collectively referred to as *smart tasks*, allow you to "set the dials" for a given control to quickly configure it for the task at hand.

You use the common tasks list to quickly configure a control's properties, as well as walk through common operations you might perform with it. For example, when you add a GridView control to a web page, a common task list appears that allows you to quickly enable sorting, paging, or editing for the GridView. When you add a TextBox control to a web page, a common task list appears that enables you to quickly associate a validation control with the control.

The Windows Forms designer also plays host to smart tags.

## Windows Forms Designer

With the Windows Forms designer, the functionality of smart tags remains consistent; they do, however, take a slightly different form. A form control that supports this functionality shows a smart tag glyph somewhere within its bounds (typically to the top right of the control). This glyph, when clicked, opens a small drop-down of tasks. Figure 8.10 contains a snapshot of the smart tag in action for a tab control.

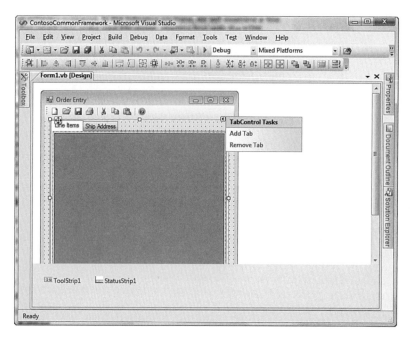

FIGURE 8.10    A TabControl smart tag.

## Code Editor

Smart tags can also appear within code. One example can be found on interfaces. Normally, implementing an interface is a fairly code-intensive task. You have to individually create a member to map to each member defined on the interface. The smart tag in this case allows you to automatically create those members using two different naming modes:

- ▶ **Explicit naming**—Members have the name of the derived interface.

- ▶ **Implicit naming**—Member names do not reference the name of the derived interface.

See Figure 8.11 to view this smart tag in action.

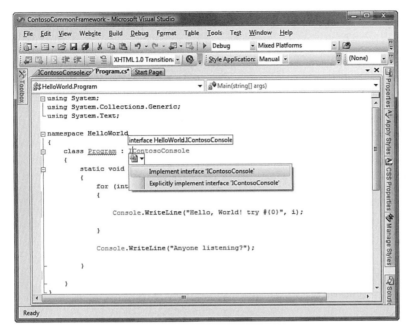

FIGURE 8.11   An implement interface smart tag.

# IntelliSense

IntelliSense is the name applied to a collection of different coding aids surfaced within the text editor window. Its sole purpose is to help you, the developer, write a syntactically correct line of code *quickly*. In addition, it tries to provide enough guidance to help you write lines of code that are correct *in context*—that is, code that makes sense given the surrounding lines of code.

As you type within the text editor, IntelliSense is the behind-the-scenes agent responsible for providing a list of code fragments that match the characters you have already entered, highlighting/preselecting the one that makes the most sense given the surrounding context, and, if so commanded, automatically inserting that code fragment in-line. This saves you the time of looking up types and members in the reference documentation and saves time again by inserting code without your having to actually type the characters for that code.

We'll spend a lot of time in this section discussing IntelliSense in the context of editing code, but you should know that IntelliSense also works with other document types such as XML documents, HTML documents, and XSLT files.

**TIP**

Attaching a schema to an XML document is beneficial from an IntelliSense perspective. The schema is used to further enhance the capabilities of the List Members function (see the "List Members" section later in this chapter).

There are many discrete pieces to IntelliSense that seamlessly work in conjunction with one another *as you are writing code.* You can also trigger all of these IntelliSense features directly from the Edit, IntelliSense menu, or by pressing Ctrl+space. And many of them can be found as well on the text editor's context menu, or by right-clicking anywhere in the editor window. Let's look at them one by one.

## Complete Word

Complete Word is the basic timesaving kernel of IntelliSense. After you have typed enough characters for IntelliSense to recognize what you are trying to write, a guess is made as to the complete word you are in the process of typing. This guess is then presented to you within a list of possible alternatives (referred to as the *completion list*) and can be inserted into the code editor with one keystroke. This is in contrast to your completing the word manually by typing all of its characters.

Figure 8.12 illustrates the process: Based on the context of the code and based on the characters typed into the editor, a list of possible words is displayed. One of these words is selected as the most viable candidate; you may select any entry in the list (via the arrow keys or the mouse). Pressing the Tab key automatically injects the word into the editor for you.

**NOTE**

Complete Word takes the actual code context into account for various situations. For instance, if you are in the midst of keying in the exception type in a `try`/`catch` block, IntelliSense displays only exception types in the completion list. Likewise, typing an attribute triggers a completion list filtered only for attributes; when you're implementing an interface, only interface types are displayed; and so on. This IntelliSense feature is enabled for all sorts of content: Beyond C# and Visual Basic code, IntelliSense completion works for other files as well, such as HTML tags, CSS style attributes, `.config` files, and HTML script blocks, just to name a few. Visual Basic offers functionality with Complete Word that C# does not: It provides a tabbed completion list, in which one tab contains the most commonly used syntax snippets, and the other contains *all* the possible words.

You can manually invoke Complete Word at any time by using the Ctrl+space or Alt+right-arrow key combinations.

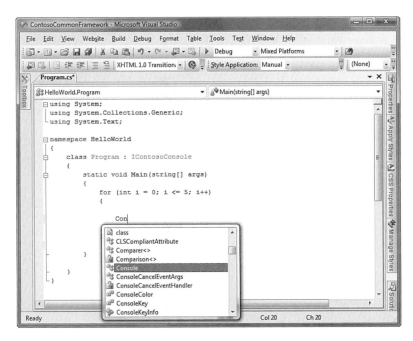

FIGURE 8.12    IntelliSense: Complete Word.

---

**TIP**

Holding down the Ctrl key while the completion list is displayed makes the list partially transparent. This is useful if, during the process of selecting an item from the list, you need to see any of the lines of code that may be hidden behind the list.

---

## Quick Info

Quick Info displays the complete code declaration and help information for any code construct. You invoke it by hovering the mouse pointer over an identifier; a pop-up box displays the information available for that identifier.

Figure 8.13 shows Quick Info being displayed for the Console.ReadLine function. You are provided with the declaration syntax for the member, a brief description of the member, and a list of its exception classes. The description that shows up in the Quick Info balloon also works for code that you write: If you have a code comment associated with a member, IntelliSense parses the comment and uses it to display the description information.

## List Members

The List Members feature functions in an identical fashion to Complete Word; for any given type or namespace, it displays a scrollable list of all valid member variables and functions specific to that type. To see the List Members function in action, perform the following steps in an open code editor window:

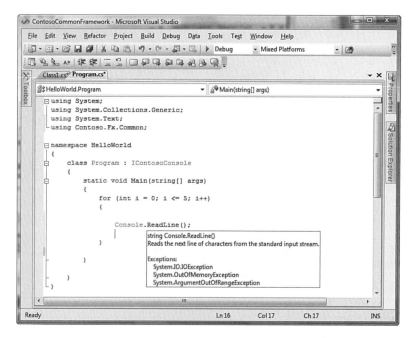

FIGURE 8.13    IntelliSense: Quick Info.

1. Type the name of a class (Ctrl+spacebar will give you the IntelliSense window with possible class names).

2. Type a period; this indicates to IntelliSense that you have finished with the type name and are now "scoped in" to that type's members.

3. The list of valid members is now displayed. You can manually scroll through the list and select the desired member at this point, or, if you are well aware of the member you are trying to code, you can simply continue typing until IntelliSense has captured enough characters to select the member you are looking for.

4. Leverage Complete Word by pressing the Tab key to automatically insert the member into your line of code (thus saving you the typing effort).

This feature also operates in conjunction with Quick Info: As you select different members in the members list, a Quick Info pop-up is displayed for that member.

---

**NOTE**

IntelliSense maintains a record of the most frequently used/selected members from the List Members and Complete Word functions. This record is used to help avoid displaying or selecting members that you have rarely, if ever, used for a given type.

---

## Parameter Info

Parameter Info, as its name implies, is designed to provide interactive guidance for the parameters needed for any given function call. This feature is especially useful for making function calls that have a long list of parameters and/or a long overload list.

Parameter Info is initiated whenever you type an opening parenthesis after a function name. To see how this works, perform these steps:

1. Type the name of a function.

2. Type an open parenthesis.

3. A pop-up box shows the function signature. If there are multiple valid signatures (for example, multiple overloaded versions of this function), you can scroll through the different signatures by using the small up- and down-arrow cues. Select the desired signature.

4. Start typing the actual parameters you want to pass in to the function.

   As you type, the parameter info pop-up continues coaching you through the parameter list by bolding the current parameter you are working on. As each successive parameter is highlighted, the definition for that parameter appears.

In Figure 8.14, the second parameter for the `Console` object's `SetWindowPosition` function is currently being entered.

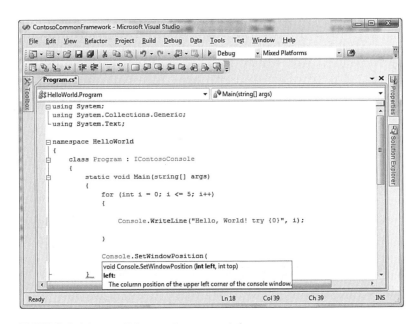

FIGURE 8.14    IntelliSense: Parameter Info.

## Organize Usings

Organize Usings is a C#-only IntelliSense item. It encapsulates two separate functions: Remove Unused Usings and Sort Usings. It also provides a third command, Remove and Sort, that combines the two actions into one. All three commands live under the Organize Usings menu item on the editor shortcut menu, or under the main Edit, IntelliSense menu.

The Remove Unused Usings function is a great aid for uncluttering your code. It parses through the current body of code and determines which Using statements are necessary for the code to compile; it then removes all other Using statements. The Sort command is straightforward as well: It simply rearranges all of your Using statements so that they appear in A–Z alphabetical order by namespace.

## Code Snippets and Template Code

Code snippets are prestocked lines of code available for selection and insertion into the text editor. Each code snippet is referenced by a name referred to as its *alias*. Code snippets are used to automate what would normally be non–value-added, repetitive typing. You can create your own code snippets or use the default library of common code elements provided by Visual Studio.

### Using the Code Snippet Inserter

You insert snippets by right-clicking at the intended insertion point within an open text editor window and then selecting Insert Snippet from the shortcut menu. This launches the Code Snippet Inserter, which is a drop-down (or series of drop-downs) that works much like the IntelliSense Complete Word feature. Each item in the inserter represents a snippet, represented by its alias. Selecting an alias expands the snippet into the active document.

Each snippet is categorized to make it easier to find the specific piece of code you are looking for. As an example, to insert a constructor snippet into a C# class, we would right-click within the class definition, select Visual C# from the list of snippet categories, and then select ctor. Figure 8.15 shows this workflow in process; note that as you select a snippet category, a placeholder is displayed in the text editor window to help establish a "bread-crumb" trail.

After the constructor snippet is expanded into the text editor, you will still, of course, have to write meaningful code inside of the constructor; but, in general, snippets eliminate the process of tedious coding that really doesn't require much intellectual horsepower to generate.

Figure 8.16 shows the same process being followed for a Visual Basic code window. The process is identical with the exception that Visual Basic makes more extensive use of categories.

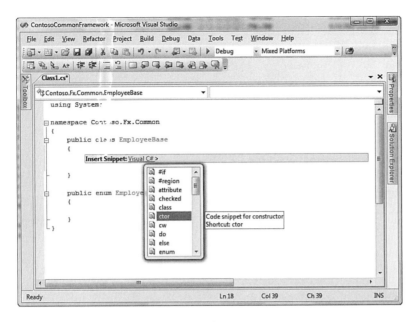

FIGURE 8.15    The C# `ctor` code snippet.

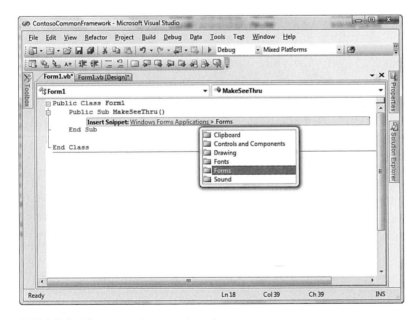

FIGURE 8.16    Visual Basic code snippets.

**TIP**

A quick, alternative way to display the Code Snippet Inserter is to type a question mark and then press the Tab key. This works only with Visual Basic code documents.

Visual Basic also exhibits slightly different behavior than C# after a snippet has been expanded into the code window. Figure 8.17 shows the results of drilling down through multiple categories and, in this example, selecting the Create Transparent Windows Form snippet. Notice that the inserter has injected the template code into the Visual Basic code for you, but the inserter (at least in this case) wasn't intelligent enough to know the name of the form you are trying to make transparent.

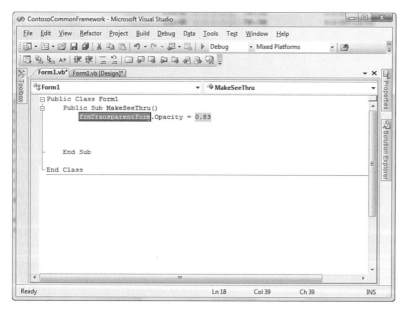

FIGURE 8.17   A form transparency snippet.

The snippet code has the form name filled in with a default, dummy name that is already highlighted. You merely start typing the form name you need, and it replaces the dummy name. The opacity value is also a dummy value that you can quickly correct at this time.

**TIP**

Snippets may have one or more placeholder values: fragments of code that you will want and probably need to change. You can cycle through each of the placeholder values by pressing the Tab key. When a placeholder is highlighted (in blue), you can start typing to replace the syntax with something that makes sense for your specific code context.

### Surrounding Code with Snippets

C# and XML documents have one additional style of code snippets that bears mentioning: Surround With snippets. Surround With snippets are still snippets at their core (again, these are simply prestocked lines of code), but they differ in how they are able to insert themselves into your code.

Using a Surround With snippet, you can stack enclosing text around a selection with the text editor. As an example, perhaps you have a few different class declarations that you would like to nest within a namespace. When you use the Surround With snippet, this is a simple two-step process: Highlight the class definitions and fire up the Code Snippet Inserter. This time, instead of selecting Insert Snippet from the shortcut menu, you select Surround With. The insert works the same way, but this time has applied the snippet (in this case, a namespace snippet) in a different fashion. Compare the before and after text shown in Figures 8.18 and 8.19. We have encapsulated the class definitions within a new namespace that sits within yet another namespace—all with just a few mouse clicks.

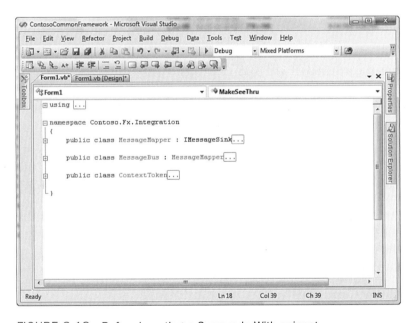

FIGURE 8.18    Before inserting a Surrounds With snippet.

### Creating Your Own Code Snippets

Because code snippets are stored in XML files, you can create your own snippets quite easily. The key is to understand the XML schema that defines a snippet, and the best way to do that is to look at the XML source data for some of the snippets included with the IDE.

Snippets are stored on a per-language basis under the install directory for Visual Studio. For example, the Visual Basic snippets can be found, by default, in the folders under the

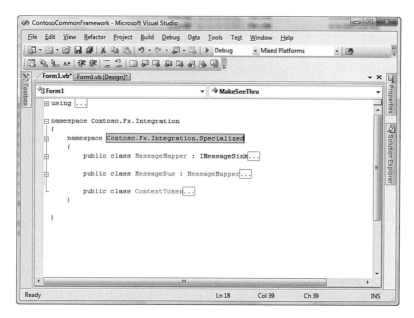

FIGURE 8.19    After inserting a Surrounds With snippet.

C:\Program Files\Microsoft Visual Studio 9.0\Vb\Snippets directory. Although snippet files are XML, they carry a .Snippet extension.

**The XML Snippet Format**    Listing 8.1 provides the XML for the C# constructor snippet.

LISTING 8.1    C# Constructor Snippet

```xml
<?xml version="1.0" encoding="utf-8" ?>
<CodeSnippets  xmlns="http://schemas.microsoft.com/VisualStudio/2005/CodeSnippet">
    <CodeSnippet Format="1.0.0">
        <Header>
            <Title>ctor</Title>
            <Shortcut>ctor</Shortcut>
            <Description>Code snippet for constructor</Description>
            <Author>Microsoft Corporation</Author>
            <SnippetTypes>
                <SnippetType>Expansion</SnippetType>
            </SnippetTypes>
        </Header>
        <Snippet>
            <Declarations>
                <Literal Editable="false">
                    <ID>classname</ID>
                    <ToolTip>Class name</ToolTip>
                    <Function>ClassName()</Function>
```

```
            <Default>ClassNamePlaceholder</Default>
        </Literal>
    </Declarations>
    <Code Language="csharp"><![CDATA[public $classname$ ()
{
    $end$
}]]>
        </Code>
    </Snippet>
  </CodeSnippet>
</CodeSnippets>
```

The basic structure of this particular snippet declaration is described in Table 8.2. A more complete schema reference is available as a part of the Visual Studio MSDN help collection; it is located under Integrated Development Environment for Visual Studio, Reference, XML Schema References, Code Snippets Schema Reference.

TABLE 8.2   XML Snippet File Node Descriptions

| XML Node | Description |
|---|---|
| <CodeSnippets> | The parent element for all code snippet information. It references the specific XML namespace used to define snippets within Visual Studio 2008. |
| <CodeSnippet> | The root element for a single code snippet. This tag sets the format version information for the snippet (for the initial release of VS 2008, this should be set to 1.0.0). Although multiple CodeSnippet elements are possible within the parent <CodeSnippets> element, the convention is to place one snippet per file. |
| <Header> | A metadata container element for data that describes the snippet. |
| <Title> | The title of the code snippet. |
| <Shortcut> | Typically, the same as the title, this is the text that will appear in the code snippet insertion drop-downs. |
| <Description> | A description of the snippet. |
| <Author> | The author of the snippet. |
| <SnippetTypes> | The parent element for holding elements describing the snippet's type. |
| <SnippetType> | The type of the snippet: Expansion, Refactoring, or Surrounds With. You cannot create custom refactoring snippets. This property is really used to tell Visual Studio where the snippet can be inserted within the editor window: Expansion snippets insert at the current cursor position, whereas Surrounds With snippets get inserted before and after the code body identified by the current cursor position or selection. |
| <Snippet> | The root element for the snippet code. |
| <Declarations> | The root element for the literals and objects used by the snippet. |

8

TABLE 8.2    Continued

| XML Node | Description |
| --- | --- |
| `<Literal>` | A string whose value can be interactively set as part of the snippet expansion process. The `Editable` attribute on this tag indicates whether the literal is static or editable. The `ctor` snippet is an example of one without an editable literal; contrast this with the form transparency snippet that you saw—an example of a snippet with an editable literal that allows you to set the form name as part of the snippet insertion. |
| `<ID>` | A unique ID for the literal. |
| `<ToolTip>` | A ToolTip to display when the cursor is placed over the literal. |
| `<Function>` | The name of a function (see Table 8.3) to call when the literal receives focus. Functions are available only in C# snippets. |
| `<Default>` | The default string literal to insert into the editor. |
| `<Code>` | An element that contains the actual code to insert. |

The trick to writing a snippet is to understand how literals and variable replacement work. Say that you wanted to create a C# snippet that writes out a simple code comment indicating that a class has been reviewed and approved as part of a code review process. In other words, you want something like this:

```
// Code review of ContextToken.
//    Reviewer: Lars Powers
//    Date: 1/1/2006
//    Approval: Approved
```

In this snippet, you need to treat four literals as variable; they can change each time the snippet is used: the class name, the reviewer's name, the date, and the approval. You can set them up within the declarations section like this:

```
<Declarations>
    <Literal Editable="False">
        <ID>classname</ID>
        <ToolTip>Class name/type being reviewed</ToolTip>
        <Function>ClassName()</Function>
        <Default>ClassNameGoesHere</Default>
    </Literal>
    <Literal Editable="True">
        <ID>reviewer</ID>
        <ToolTip>Replace with the reviewer's name</ToolTip>
        <Default>ReviewerName</Default>
    </Literal>
    <Literal Editable="True">
        <ID>currdate</ID>
        <ToolTip>Replace with the review date</ToolTip>
```

```
        <Default>ReviewDate</Default>
    </Literal>
    <Literal Editable="True">
        <ID>approval</ID>
        <ToolTip>Replace with Approved or Rejected</ToolTip>
        <Default>Approved</Default>
    </Literal>
</Declarations>
```

Notice that you are actually calling a function to prepopulate the class name within the snippet. Functions are available only with C# (with a subset also available in J#); they are documented in Table 8.3. The rest of the literals rely on the developer to type over the placeholder value with the correct value.

TABLE 8.3  Code Snippet Functions

| Function | Description |
|---|---|
| GenerateSwitchCases (*enumliteral*) | Creates the syntax for a switch statement that includes a case statement for each value defined by the enumeration represented by *enumliteral* (C#/J#). |
| ClassName() | Inserts the name of the class containing the code snippet (C#/J#). |
| SimpleTypeName (*typename*) | Takes the type name referenced by *typename* and returns the shortest name possible given the using statements in effect for the current code block. |
| | Example: SimpleTypeName(System.Exception) would return Exception if a using System statement is present (C#). |
| CallBase (*parameter*) | Is useful when stubbing out members that implement or return the base type: When you specify get, set, or method as the parameter, a call will be created against the base class for that specific property accessor or method (C#). |

You should also provide some basic header information for the snippet:

```
<Header>
    <Title>review</Title>
    <Shortcut>review</Shortcut>
    <Description>Code review comment</Description>
    <Author>L. Powers</Author>
    <SnippetTypes>
        <SnippetType>Expansion</SnippetType>
    </SnippetTypes>
</Header>
<Snippet>
```

At this point, the snippet is syntactically complete. Although this snippet is writing comments into the editor, the same exact process and structure would apply for emitting code into the editor. If you wanted to write a Surrounds With snippet, you would change the <SnippetType> to Surrounds With.

Now, you need to make Visual Studio aware of the snippet.

**Adding a Snippet to Visual Studio**    You can use Visual Studio's own XML editor to create the XML document and save it to a directory (a big bonus for doing so is that you can leverage IntelliSense triggered by the XML snippet schema to help you with your element names and relationships). The Visual Studio installer creates a default directory to place your custom snippets located in your Documents folder: *user*\Documents\Visual Studio 2008\Code Snippets\Visual C#\My Code Snippets. If you place your XML template here, Visual Studio will automatically include your snippet for use.

The Code Snippets Manager, which is launched from the Tools menu, is the central control dialog box for browsing the available snippets, adding new ones, or removing a snippet (see Figure 8.20). As you can see, the review snippet shows up under the My Code Snippets folder.

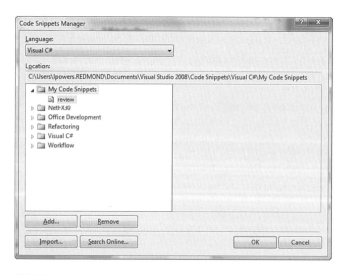

FIGURE 8.20   The Code Snippets Manager.

You can also opt to include other folders besides the standard ones. To do so, click on the Add button to enter additional folders for Visual Studio to use when displaying the list of snippets.

Figure 8.21 shows the results of the custom snippet.

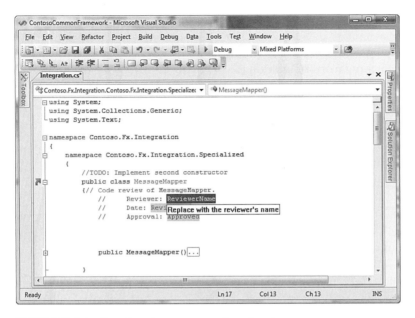

FIGURE 8.21   Results of a custom code snippet.

### Snippets in the Toolbox

Although this capability is technically not part of the official code snippet technology within Visual Studio, you can also store snippets of code in the toolbox. First, select the text in the editor and then drag and drop it onto the toolbox. You can then reuse this snippet at any time by dragging it back from the toolbox into an open editor window.

## Brace Matching

Programming languages make use of parentheses, braces, brackets, and other delimiters to delimit function arguments, mathematical functions/order of operation, and bodies of code. It can be difficult to visually determine whether you have missed a matching delimiter—that is, if you have more opening delimiters than you have closing delimiters—especially with highly nested lines of code.

*Brace matching* refers to visual cues that the code editor uses to make you aware of your matching delimiters. As you type code into the editor, any time you enter a closing delimiter, the matching opening delimiter and the closing delimiter will briefly be highlighted. In Figure 8.22, brace matching helps to indicate the matching delimiters for the interior `for` loop.

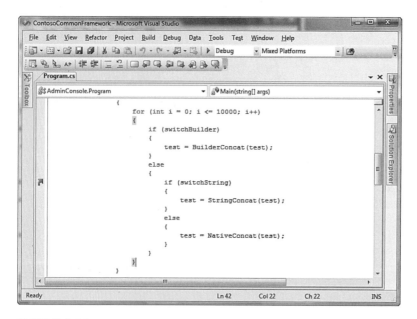

FIGURE 8.22   Brace matching.

---

**TIP**

You also can trigger brace matching simply by placing the cursor directly to the left of an opening delimiter or the right of a closing delimiter. If you are browsing through a routine congested with parentheses and braces, you can quickly sort out the matching pairs by moving your cursor around to the various delimiters.

---

Although this feature is referred to as brace matching, it actually functions with the following delimiters:

▶ Parentheses: ( )

▶ Brackets: [ ], <>

▶ Quotation marks: " "

▶ Braces: {}

In the case of C#, brace matching also works with the following keyword pairs (which essentially function as delimiters using keywords):

▶ # region, #endregion

▶ #if, #else, #endif

▶ case, break

▶ default, break

▶ for, break, continue

▶ if, else

▶ while, break, continue

## Customizing IntelliSense

Certain IntelliSense features can be customized, on a per-language basis, within the Visual Studio Options dialog box. If you launch the Options dialog box (located under the Tools menu) and then navigate to the Text Editor node, you will find IntelliSense options confusingly scattered under both the General and IntelliSense pages.

Figure 8.23 shows the IntelliSense editor Options dialog box for Visual C#.

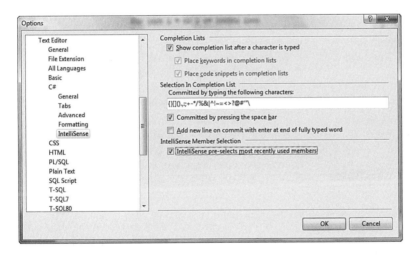

FIGURE 8.23    IntelliSense options.

Completion Lists in this dialog box refer to any of the IntelliSense features that facilitate autocompletion of code, such as List Members and Complete Word. Table 8.4 itemizes the options available in this dialog box.

TABLE 8.4    IntelliSense Options

| Option | Effect |
| --- | --- |
| Show Completion List After a Character Is Typed | This causes the Complete Word feature to automatically run after a single character is typed in the editor window. |
| Place Keywords in Completion Lists | If this box is checked, language keywords will be displayed within the completion list. As an example, for C#, this would cause keywords such as `class` or `string` to be included in the completion list. |
| Place Code Snippets in Completion Lists | Checking this box will place code-snippet alias names into any displayed completion lists. |
| Committed by Typing the Following Characters | This check box contains any of the characters that will cause IntelliSense to execute a completion action. In other words, typing any of the characters in this text box while a completion list is displayed will cause IntelliSense to insert the current selection into the editor window. |
| Committed by Pressing the Space Bar | Checking this adds the space character to the list of characters that will fire a completion commit. |
| Add New Line on Commit with Enter at End of Fully Typed Word | Checking this box will cause the cursor to advance down an entire line if you fully type a word in the IntelliSense list box. This is useful for those scenarios in which fully typed keywords are unlikely to be followed on the same line with other code. |
| IntelliSense Pre-selects Most Recently Used Members | If this box is checked, IntelliSense will maintain and use a historical list of the most frequently used members for a given type. This "MFU" list is then used to preselect members in a completion list. |

# The Task List

The Task List is essentially an integrated to-do list; it captures all the items that, for one reason or another, need attention and tracking. The Task List window then surfaces this list and allows you to interact with it. To show the window, select the View menu and choose the Task List entry. Figure 8.24 illustrates the Task List window displaying a series of user tasks. Tasks belong to one of three categories—comment tasks, shortcut tasks, and user tasks—and only one category can be displayed at a time.

The drop-down at the top of the Task List window enables you to select the current category. Each category will have slightly different columns that it shows for each task category type, but they will all have a Priority column and a Description column. For instance, user tasks and shortcut tasks provide a check box that is used to track task completion; shortcut and comment tasks display a filename and line number; and so on.

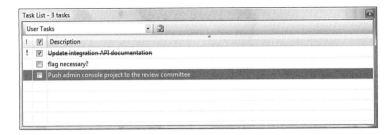

FIGURE 8.24    The Task List window.

You can sort the tasks by any of the columns shown in the list. Right-clicking on the column headers provides a shortcut menu that allows you to control the sort behavior, as well as which columns (from a list of all supported columns) should be displayed.

## Comment Tasks

Comment tasks are created within your code. Placing a code comment with a special string literal/token will cause Visual Studio to add that comment to the comment task list. Three of these tokens are defined by Visual Studio: HACK, TODO, and UNDONE. To see these tasks in your task window, ensure that you have selected "Comments" from the drop-down at the top of the task list.

As an example, the following C# code would result in four different comment tasks in the task list:

```
namespace Contoso.Fx.Integration.Specialized
{
    //TODO: Implement second constructor
    public class MessageMapper : IMessageSink
    {
        public MessageMapper()
        {
        }
    }

    //TODO: Check on IMap interface implementation
    public class MessageBus : MessageMapper
    {
        public MessageBus()
        {
            //UNDONE: MessageBus ctor
        }
    }
```

```
//HACK: re-write of TokenStruct
public class ContextToken
{
    public ContextToken()
    {
    }
    public ContextToken(string guid)
    {
    }
}
}
```

Double-clicking on the comment task will take you directly to the referenced comment line within the editor window.

### Custom Comment Tokens

If needed, you can add your own set of tokens that will be recognized as comment tasks. From the Tools, Options dialog box, select the Task List page under the Environment section; this dialog box provides options for adding, editing, or deleting the list of comment tokens recognized by the task list.

In Figure 8.25, a REVIEW token has been added to the standard list. Note that you can also set a priority against each of the tokens and fine-tune some of the display behavior by using the Task List Options check boxes, which control whether task deletions are confirmed, and by setting whether filenames or complete file paths are displayed within the task list.

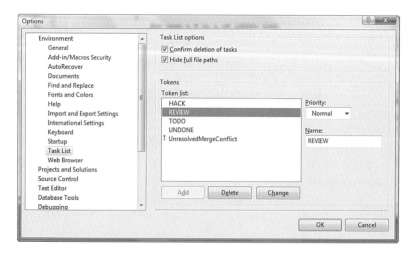

FIGURE 8.25    Adding a custom comment task token.

## Shortcut Tasks

Shortcut tasks are actually links to a line of code. You add them using the Bookmarks menu by placing the cursor on a line within the editor and then selecting Edit, Bookmarks, Add Task List Shortcut. The actual content of that line of code shows up as the task description.

Double-clicking on the task takes you directly to the bookmarked line within the editor window.

## User Tasks

User tasks are entered directly into the task window. A Create User Task button appears next to the category drop-down on the Task List window (refer to Figure 8.24); this button adds a new entry within the list. You can type directly into the description column to add the task's title.

Unlike shortcut and comment tasks, user tasks aren't linked to a specific line of code.

> **NOTE**
>
> Visual Studio's automation model provides complete control over task lists. Using the exposed automation objects such as `TaskList` and `TaskListEvents`, you can, for example, programmatically add or remove tasks from the list; respond to a task being added, edited, or even selected; and control the linking between a task and an editor.

# Summary

Visual Studio 2008 carries a staggering number of features designed to boost your productivity. This chapter described the many facets of the IntelliSense technology, ranging from statement completion to the new code snippet technology, and you learned how to work with the various IntelliSense features to both write code faster and improve the quality of your code.

We covered how to navigate and browse through sometimes complicated and congested code files.

We also introduced code snippets and discussed the different types of code snippets and their usefulness.

Last, we covered how to use the Task List window to its fullest potential, to help organize and track the various to-do items inherent with any programming project.

From a productivity standpoint, Visual Studio 2008 truly is more than the sum of its parts: In synergy with one another, each of these features knocks down substantial hurdles and pain points for developers, regardless of their background, skill level, or language preference.

# CHAPTER 9

# Refactoring Code

Whether or not you realize it, if you are like most developers, you are always refactoring code. Every time you change your code to reduce duplication or rename items for the sake of clarity, you are refactoring. Refactoring is simply putting a name to a common development task. The strict definition of the term is "a change made to the internal structure of software to make it easier to understand and cheaper to modify without changing its observable behavior." That is, refactoring does not add features to the application. Instead, it improves the general maintenance of the code base.

The term *refactoring* has received a large amount of attention. A number of good books have been written touting the many benefits of refactoring code as you are building your application. This is when you are closest to the code and thus able to quickly make these maintenance-type changes. Many of these books are on the subject of extreme programming. Refactoring has become one of the key tenets of the extreme programmer. In extreme programming, your code base builds feature by feature to satisfy a series of tests. This can result in code that works wonderfully but does not look as though it was designed as a cohesive unit. To combat this problem, you would be wise to go over the code base at frequent intervals and thus improve the general quality of the code (remove duplication, create common interfaces, rename items, put things into logical groups, and so on).

A new set of features has arisen inside code editors to aid with refactoring. These features have their basis in a real need. No developer wants to introduce errors into a relatively stable code base simply for the sake of improving maintenance—especially when running a tight schedule. Imagine explaining to your manager or client that the large spike in bugs is a result of sweeping changes you made to the code to improve future maintenance and readability. We can be thankful that the C# editor inside Visual Studio 2008 provides a reliable set of refactoring tools. These tools let you make changes to the code base without the concern of creating more problems than you are solving.

### Refactoring for the VB Developer

We are focusing this chapter on the refactoring tools built into Visual Studio 2008. These tools (with the exception of Rename) are strictly for the C# code editor. Fortunately, Visual Basic developers do have an option for refactoring. A third-party development house, DevExpress (http://www.devexpress.com), struck a deal with Microsoft to include a version of its product for all Visual Studio 2008 VB .NET developers. We do not cover this tool in this book, but users should find many similarities between the two products.

### Refactoring for the Database Developer

There are a couple of features built into Visual Studio for refactoring database elements. We cover these in Part 6, "Visual Studio Team System," in Chapter 29, "Database Edition."

## Visual Studio Refactoring Basics

The Visual Studio refactoring tools work to ensure that you see the promises of refactoring: increased reuse of your code, fewer rewrites, reduced duplication, and better readability. These tools work to instill confidence in the edits they make to your code. They do so by using a common refactoring engine based on the C# compiler rather than string matching and search-and-replace. The engine and compiler work together to cover the entire code base (and its references) to find all possible changes that need to be made as part of a given refactor operation. The engine even searches out code comments and tries to update them to reflect new type names. In addition, you can preview changes to your code before they happen. This adds further to your comfort level with the modifications these tools are making to your code.

Table 9.1 presents a high-level overview of the many refactoring operations that are possible with the C# editor. We will cover each of them in detail in the coming sections. First, however, we will cover some of the common elements of the refactoring process. These elements include both invoking a refactoring tool inside Visual Studio and previewing the refactoring changes as they happen.

TABLE 9.1   Refactoring Tools Inside the Visual Studio 2008 C# Editor

| Tool | Description |
| --- | --- |
| Rename | Renames fields, properties, namespaces, methods, types, and local variables. |
| Extract Method | Creates a new method using existing code within an existing method. |
| Promote Local to Parameter | Moves an internal, local member (variable) of a method to a parameter of the method. |
| Reorder Parameters | Changes the order of parameters for a given method and updates all callers. |
| Remove Parameters | Removes a parameter from a method and updates callers. |
| Encapsulate Field | Quickly creates a property from an existing field. |
| Extract Interface | Creates an interface from an existing class or structure. |

## Invoking the Refactoring Tools

The refactoring tools are available from wherever you work on your C# code inside Visual Studio. You can invoke them in several ways. For example, if you are working inside the code editor, you can invoke the Rename tool using a smart tag. You can also select and right-click code to reveal the refactoring options; these same options are available on the menu bar through the Refactor menu. Finally, you can refactor directly from the Class Designer as you edit and change various items within a given class.

### Using the Refactor Menu (and Right-Click)

The most common place to invoke the refactoring commands is from the actual refactoring menu. This menu item is added to the IDE when you have a C# code window open and active. Figure 9.1 shows the menu being invoked. Note that the portion of code you are trying to refactor is highlighted in the IDE. In this case, we want to rename the class Product because we have determined that all our products are books. Therefore, we will rename the class Product to Book.

This same menu is available via a right-click within the editor. Again, you highlight a word or section of code (or simply position the cursor accordingly) and then right-click. The top item in this menu is Refactor. This menu folds out to reveal the full Refactor menu (as shown in Figure 9.2).

### Refactoring in the Code Window via Smart Tags

The smart tag was originally introduced in Microsoft Office. As discussed in Chapter 8, "Working with Visual Studio's Productivity Aids," the goal of the smart tag is simple: Try to understand what the user is typing and offer additional, "smart" functionality. For example, as you type in the Word editor, it tries to understand what you've typed. The editor then provides you with additional functionality and the ability to control formatting options based on that information.

FIGURE 9.1    The Refactor menu in action.

FIGURE 9.2    The Refactor menu invoked via a right-click with the mouse.

The C# code editor provides a similar smart tag feature. The editor detects your typing and understands when you have made a change to your code that is the equivalent of a refactor. In these cases, the editor creates a smart tag that can be used to invoke the refactoring tool. This allows you to stay in the code editor but still take advantage of the increased productivity and reduced error rate that the refactoring tool can provide.

As an example, suppose you have a property named Id. You want to rename this item to Identifier. You open the class file and position your cursor near the property name. You then type the new property name. The C# code editor detects your change and underlines the final character of the changed name. Figure 9.3 shows an example of this. Notice the small rectangle beneath the *r* in *identifier*.

```
public int Identifier {
```

FIGURE 9.3    Renaming a property invokes a smart tag for refactoring.

This small rectangle hovering under the change is your visual cue that the C# code editor thinks it can help you. You can position your mouse cursor next to the rectangle to reveal an in-line menu that indicates how the editor might help. Figure 9.4 shows the smart tag as it is invoked relative to the previous example.

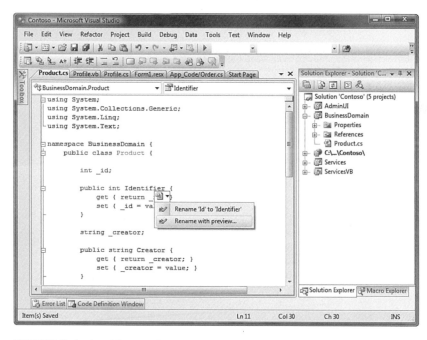

FIGURE 9.4    Invoking a refactor via a smart tag.

**TIP**

You can also invoke smart tags without grabbing for the mouse. To do so, press the key combination Shift+Alt+F10.

### Using the Class Designer to Refactor

Visual Studio 2008 provides a Visual Designer for working with classes. This Class Designer allows you to view the contents of your classes and their relationships. It can also be used as a productivity tool: You can create new classes and modify existing classes directly within the designer.

### Class Designer Coverage

Note that the class designer is included in the professional version of Visual Studio. However, we cover it in Chapter 27, "Architecture Edition." This allows us to cover the Visual Studio modeling tools in a single chapter.

The Visual Studio Class Designer exposes the refactoring tool when you're working with C# classes. This ensures that code modifications made using this Visual Designer take full advantage of refactoring. For instance, suppose you want to rename a property from within the Class Designer but also want to make sure that the references to that property are automatically updated. You can do so by right-clicking the property within the Class Designer and choosing the Refactor menu's Rename option. Figure 9.5 shows refactoring from directly within the Class Designer.

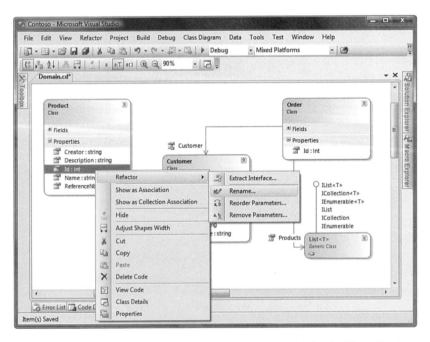

FIGURE 9.5    Invoking refactoring from within the Visual Studio Class Designer.

## Previewing Changes

As you become comfortable with the refactoring tools, you may decide to simply let them do their thing without much oversight on your part. However, if you are like most developers, no one (or no tool) touches your code without your consent. Fortunately for us, the refactoring tools provide a preview option. This option lets you follow the tool through its changes and, in turn, accept or reject a given change.

The Preview Changes dialog box is invoked as an option (check box) on a given refactoring operation (or, in the case of a smart tag, from a second menu item on the smart tag menu). Figure 9.6 provides an example of selecting the Preview Reference Changes option from the Rename refactor operation.

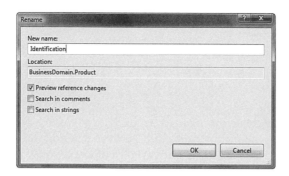

FIGURE 9.6   Invoking a refactor operation with Preview Reference Changes.

After the refactoring operation is invoked with Preview Changes, Visual Studio presents you with the Preview Changes dialog box. The top portion of this dialog box lists all the changes the given refactor operation intends to make. This list is presented as a tree, with the outer branch representing where you intend to originate the change. The leaves under this branch are all files where changes will happen. Nested beneath the filenames are the actual places within the code where a change will be made. You use this list to select each item you would like to preview. Figure 9.7 shows an example of the changes required in our simple example of changing the Id property of the Product object.

As each item in the Preview Changes tree is clicked, the corresponding code is displayed below the tree in the Preview Code Changes section of the dialog box. This allows developers to quickly review where changes will be made. To prevent a given change, you can simply uncheck the item in the tree view. Of course, you can prevent entire file changes by unchecking farther up in the hierarchy at the file level. When you are finished with your preview and satisfied with the proposed changes, you simply click the Apply button to commit the changes to your code.

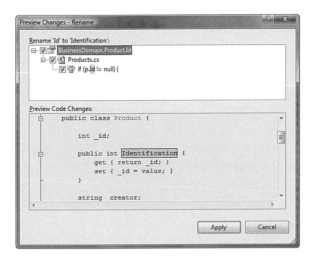

FIGURE 9.7    Previewing changes of a Rename operation.

# Rename

Renaming code elements is the most common refactoring operation. In fact, while Rename is part of the C# editor, a similar rename feature exists in both the VB editor and the Team Systems Database Developer tool. Here we stick to our coverage of the C# refactoring tools. However, both the VB and database rename operations work in a similar fashion.

In a typical refactoring session, renaming often makes up the bulk of the work. However, most renaming happens outside the normal refactoring window. Developers do not typically wait until the code base is operational and say to themselves, "Okay, now I will go back and rename these 10 items for clarity." Although this does happen, the more likely scenario is that as you build your application, you consistently rename items to correct mistakes or make things clearer and more readable. Of course, as the code base builds, renaming classes, methods, fields, and the like becomes more and more difficult without introducing new bugs into your code.

Therefore, the capability to rename items with the confidence that you will not introduce bugs into your code is paramount. With the C# editor, you can rename all relevant code items including namespaces, classes, fields, properties, methods, and variables. The compiler helps make sure that your code does not get broken and that all source code references are found. In fact, the Rename operation can even search through your code comments and update them accordingly.

## Accessing the Rename Operation

You can rename from many places within the IDE. In the previous "Invoking the Refactoring Tools" section, we looked at accessing Rename from the Refactor menu, a right-click, a smart tag, and the Class Designer. You can also access Rename from the Object Browser, Solution Explorer, and Class View. In addition, if you use the Properties dialog box to change the name of a control you've placed on a form, the Rename operation is invoked behind the scenes and the control gets renamed appropriately.

From the Object Browser, you can access the Rename operation only from the Refactor menu. Of course, you need to be browsing your own types in your solution. You simply select the item you want to rename and then click the Refactor menu. Figure 9.8 shows an example of the Object Browser and Rename operation (top of screen shot) working together.

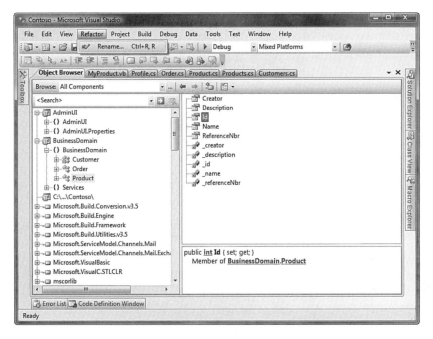

FIGURE 9.8    Accessing the Rename operation from the Object Browser.

You can rename within the Solution Explorer for filenames that equate to class names. For instance, if you select a file named Customer, right-click, and choose Rename, Visual Studio will rename the file. In addition, it will search the code within the file for any class that has the same name as the file. So if you have a Customer class and a Customer.cs file, a Rename operation will rename the file as well as the class (and all references to the class). Note that although an undo on the Rename operation will roll back a change, in the case of a filename change, Undo reverts the code but does not change the filename back to its original name.

Finally, you can rename from within Class View. This can be helpful if you look at your code from a namespace and object perspective (rather than simply files). To do so, you right-click the item you want to rename and select the Rename option. Figure 9.9 shows an example of renaming the Id property of the Product object from within Class View. Note that renaming a class from within Class View has no effect on the filename for the file that contains the class. This is consistent with other renaming options (the exception being the Solution Explorer Rename).

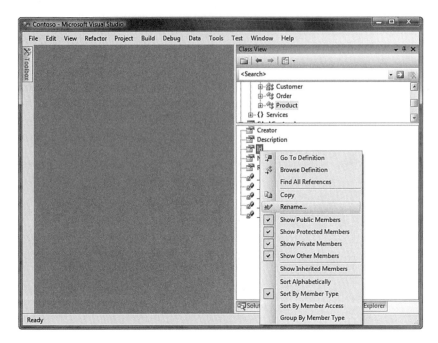

FIGURE 9.9    Accessing Rename from the Class View.

---

**TIP**

You can access the Rename operation from a set of command keys. Past versions of Visual Studio introduced the concept of *chords.* They are like traditional keyboard commands, but you press (or *play*) them in sequence. For instance, to invoke the Rename operation without touching your mouse, position your cursor over what you want to rename. Then press the sequence Ctrl+R, Ctrl+R. Pressing this combination in sequence will bring up the Refactoring, Rename dialog box relative to the code element behind your cursor.

---

## Working with the Rename Dialog Box

The Rename dialog box allows you to specify a few options when invoking a given Rename refactor operation. Refer to Figure 9.6 for an example of the dialog box. The two text boxes on the form allow you to define the rename itself. In the New Name section, you indicate the new name of the element to be renamed. The Location text box indicates the namespace of the element to be renamed. Of course, all referenced locations will also be searched.

The Rename dialog box also presents developers with a few options when doing a rename. The three check boxes below the Location text box allow you to set the options as described in Table 9.2.

TABLE 9.2    The Rename Dialog Box Options

| Option | Description |
|---|---|
| Preview Reference Changes | This option allows you to indicate whether you want to preview the changes before they are applied to your code. This capability can be especially useful if you are renaming for the first time or you intend to rename items inside strings or comments. |
| | Renaming strings and comments does not use the compiler. Instead it uses string matching (see Figure 9.10 for an example). In this case, previewing a change before applying it can be especially helpful. For example, you may want to rename a type, but not similar text in a label. |
| Search in Comments | This option allows you to indicate whether the Rename operation should search your comments for possible textual references that should be renamed. Comments often refer to types and hence need to be synced with changes. |
| | Figure 9.10 shows the Preview Changes – Rename dialog box with both a `Strings` folder and a `Comments` folder expanded in the tree. Note that the string matching is case-sensitive. Therefore, you may want to be vigilant when writing comments that refer to types. |
| Search in Strings | This preference allows you to indicate whether the Rename operation should search inside your literal strings for references to a given item name. String literals include constants, control names, form names, and so on. This capability is most useful if there is a tight coupling between your code and the elements within your user interface. Again, this too is case-sensitive. |

# Extract Method

When developers go back and take a look at their code, perhaps during a periodic code review or after a particularly long session of heads-down development, they often find methods that are too long or coarse-grained, contain duplicate code, or are just poorly organized. A common thing to do is pass over the code and create fine-grained, discrete methods to reduce these issues and make for a more readable, reusable, and maintainable code base.

The problem, of course, is that doing this is time-consuming and often introduces bugs into the code. The C# code editor in Visual Studio 2008 provides an Extract Method refactoring tool to ensure a quick, bug-free experience when you're working to better organize your code. With this tool, you can create a new method using existing code.

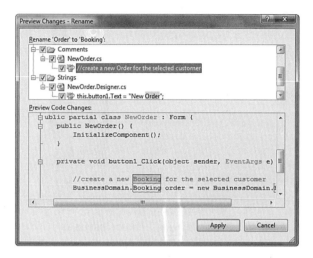

FIGURE 9.10    The Preview Changes – Rename dialog box.

## Accessing the Extract Method Refactor

To access the Extract Method refactor operation, you first must select a portion of code to refactor. You then can use the Refactor menu and select the Extract Method menu item. You can also invoke the Extract Method from the context menu via a right-click.

### TIP

To invoke the Extract Method operation from the keyboard, first select the section of code you want to extract. Next, play the chord Ctrl+R, Ctrl+M.

## Extracting Methods

With the Extract Method operation, you can create (or extract) a new method from multiple lines of code, a single line, or an expression within a given line of code. In each case, the method is created immediately following the method from which the code was extracted. The extracted code is replaced by a call to the new method.

Listing 9.1 provides an example of a typical, overlong method. We've added line numbers for reference purposes. When you're reviewing code, methods such as these are common and exactly what you should be looking for. The method is designed as a static call that returns a given customer's Order object based on the customer's ID number and the order ID number. However, the order, the order line items, and the customer details are all retrieved from discreet database calls and stored in domain-specific objects. These objects are then stored on the order as properties.

LISTING 9.1    A Long Static Method

```
01  public static Order GetCustomerOrder(int customerId, int orderId) {
02
03    DataAccess.DAL dal = new DataAccess.DAL();
04    Order order = new Order();
05
06    //get order details
07    System.Data.DataTable dtOrder = dal.GetData("customerOrder", orderId);
08
09    //validate order against customer
10    if (customerId != (int)dtOrder.Rows[0]["customer_id"]) {
11      throw new ApplicationException("Invalid order for the given customer.");
12    }
13    order.Id = (string)dtOrder.Rows[0]["id"];
14
15    //get order items
16    List<OrderItem> items = new List<OrderItem>();
17    System.Data.DataTable dtItems = dal.GetData("orderItems", orderId);
18    foreach (System.Data.DataRow r in dtItems.Rows) {
19      OrderItem item = new OrderItem((int)r["product_id"], orderId);
20      item.Name = (string)r["name"];
21      item.Description = (string)r["description"];
22      item.Quantity = (int)r["quantity"];
23      item.UnitPrice = (double)r["unit_price"];
24      items.Add(item);
25    }
26    order.Items = items;
27
28    //get customer details
29    System.Data.DataTable dtCustomer = dal.GetData("customer", customerId);
30    Customer cust = new Customer(customerId);
31    cust.Name = (string)dtCustomer.Rows[0]["name"];
32    order.Customer = cust;
33
34    return order;
35  }
```

Opportunities for method extraction inside this one method are numerous. You might consider extracting the call to initialize the Order object, the call to get order items, and the call to get customer details. Doing so will result in better organized code (thus, more readable), more opportunities for reuse, and an easier-to-maintain code base. Let's look at doing these extractions.

First, you'll extract the call that sets up the order. Knowing what to select for extraction requires a bit of experience with the tool. In this case, extract lines 3–13. This takes the code from the DataAccess setup through the order initialization. However, doing so confuses the Extract Method operation somewhat because you are setting up both a DataAccess object and an Order object in the first two operations. The Extract Method understands you need these two objects later in your method. Therefore, it will create both objects as *out* parameters of the method. What you want is the method to return an instance of the Order object and set up its own DataAccess object. You can accomplish this with the following steps:

1. Select lines 4–13 (order creation through initialization).
2. Select the Extract Method refactor operation (menu, right-click, or keyboard chord).
3. Visual Studio presents the Extract Method dialog box, as shown in Figure 9.11. This dialog box presents the new method name (NewMethod by default) and the method signature. If the method signature does not look right, you can cancel the operation and refine your code selection. In this case, the method is static; returns an Order object; and takes customerId, orderId, and DataAccess objects. We do not want the latter in our function signature but will deal with this momentarily.

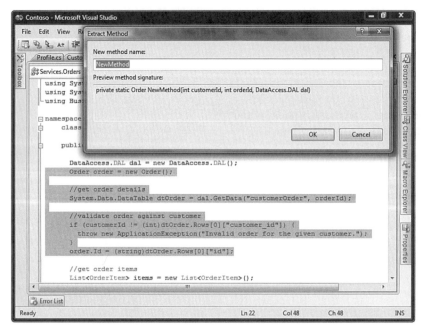

FIGURE 9.11   Extracting code from an existing method to a new method.

4. Rename the method to something meaningful. In this case, rename it to InitCustomerOrder.
5. Click the OK button to allow the method to be extracted.
6. The new method is created, and the old method is replaced by the following call:

```
Order order = InitCustomerOrder(customerId, orderId, dal);
```

---

**NOTE**

Extracted methods are created as private by default.

---

You still have one issue with the extracted method: It takes an instance of `DataAccess` when you would prefer that it created its own instance. Fortunately, you can use another refactoring operation to deal with this issue. In this case, use the Remove Parameters refactor. This refactoring operation is covered later in this chapter. It is important to point out that removing the parameter results in removing it from both the method signature and the call to the method. It does not, however, put the call to create that `DataAccess` object inside the new method (nor does it remove it from the old method). You must take these steps manually.

Next, let's extract the call to get order items. Begin by selecting lines 16–25 (see Listing 9.1). Note that we do not want to select the call to set the order's property (line 26); we simply want to return an object that represents all line items for a given order. Figure 9.12 shows the selection and method extraction. In this case, name the new method `GetOrderItems`. After the method is extracted, it is replaced by the following call to the new method:

```
List<OrderItem> items = GetOrderItems(orderId, dal);
```

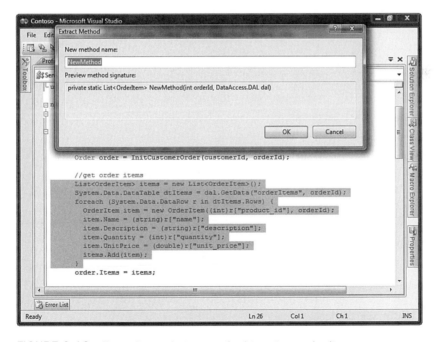

FIGURE 9.12  Extracting code to a method to return order items.

Again you have the issue with the `DataAccess` object being passed into the new method. You solve this issue in the same manner as you did previously.

Finally, let's look at extracting the portion of the method that gets the customer details. By now, this procedure should be reasonably straightforward. You select the code (lines 29–31) and choose the Extract Method operation. You name the new method `GetCustomer` and deal with the extracted `DataAccess` parameter.

The newly organized (and much shorter) method looks like Listing 9.2. In addition, you now have three new tight, discreet methods that you may be able to reuse in the future (and perhaps make public). These new methods can be found in Listing 9.3.

LISTING 9.2   The Static Method After the Extractions

```
public static Order GetCustomerOrder(int customerId, int orderId) {

  Order order = InitCustomerOrder(customerId, orderId);

  //get order items
  List<OrderItem> items = GetOrderItems(orderId);
  order.Items = items;

  //get customer details
  Customer cust = GetCustomer(customerId);
  order.Customer = cust;

  return order;
}
```

LISTING 9.3   The Extractions

```
private static Customer NewMethod(int customerId) {
  DataAccess.DAL dal = new DataAccess.DAL();
  System.Data.DataTable dtCustomer = dal.GetData("customer", customerId);
  Customer cust = new Customer(customerId);
  cust.Name = (string)dtCustomer.Rows[0]["name"];
  return cust;
}

private static List<OrderItem> GetOrderItems(int orderId) {
  List<OrderItem> items = new List<OrderItem>();
  DataAccess.DAL dal = new DataAccess.DAL();
  System.Data.DataTable dtItems = dal.GetData("orderItems", orderId);
  foreach (System.Data.DataRow r in dtItems.Rows) {
    OrderItem item = new OrderItem((int)r["product_id"], orderId);
```

```
    item.Name = (string)r["name"];
    item.Description = (string)r["description"];
    item.Quantity = (int)r["quantity"];
    item.UnitPrice = (double)r["unit_price"];
    items.Add(item);
  }
  return items;
}

private static Order InitCustomerOrder(int customerId, int orderId) {

  Order order = new Order();

  //get order details
  DataAccess.DAL dal = new DataAccess.DAL();
  System.Data.DataTable dtOrder = dal.GetData("customerOrder", orderId);

  //validate order against customer
  if (customerId != (int)dtOrder.Rows[0]["customer_id"]) {
    throw new ApplicationException("Invalid order for the given customer.");
  }
  order.Id = (string)dtOrder.Rows[0]["id"];
  return order;
}
```

---

**NOTE**

Extract Method does not allow you to choose where to put the extracted method. Many times you might find a bit of code that really needs to be extracted into a method of another, different class. For this, you have to extract the method and then move things around manually.

---

**Extracting a Single Line of Code**

Sometimes, you might want to extract a single line of code or a portion of a line of code as its own method. For example, you may have a calculation that is done as part of a line of code but is common enough to warrant its own method. Alternatively, you might need to extract an object assignment to add additional logic to it. In either case, the C# code editor supports this type of extraction.

Let's look at an example. Suppose you have the following line of code that calculates an order's total inside a loop through the order items list:

```
total = total + item.Quantity * item.UnitPrice;
```

You may want to extract the portion of the assignment that calculates a line item's total (quantity * unit price). To do so, you simply select the portion of code and invoke the Extract Method refactor. Figure 9.13 shows this operation in action.

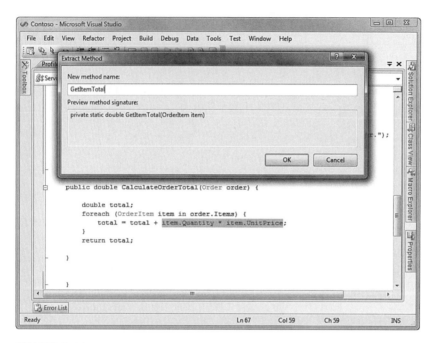

FIGURE 9.13    Extracting a portion of a line of code.

Notice that, by default, the new method would like an instance of OrderItem. You may prefer to pass both quantity and unit price instead. You would have to make this change manually. You could do so by creating the variables in the new method and doing a Promote Local to Parameter refactor (covered later in this chapter). Alternatively, if quantity and unit price were assigned to variables before the extraction was done, you would get a new method that accepted these parameters (instead of an OrderItem instance). Figure 9.14 demonstrates this fact.

The resulting refactor replaces a portion of the line of code with the following:

```
total = total + GetItemTotal(qty, unitPrice);
```

It also adds the new method as follows:

```
private static double GetItemTotal(int qty, double unitPrice) {
  return qty * unitPrice;
}
```

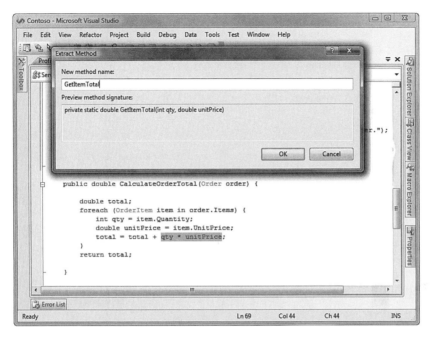

FIGURE 9.14   An alternative extraction of a portion of a line of code.

## Generate Method Stub

You can get Visual Studio to automatically generate a method stub for you. This is not strictly a refactoring operation but can provide some similar increases in productivity. The scenario where this is applicable is as follows. Suppose you are writing code that calls a method off one of your objects. However, that method does not exist. You can still write code to make the call to the nonexistent method. Visual Studio will then recognize that this method does not exist and provide you with a smart tag (see Figure 9.15) to create the method.

Clicking on the smart tag will result in Visual Studio extracting the method call to a newly generated method in the target assembly and class. Figure 9.16 shows the new method. Note that Visual Studio even provided a readable name for the method's parameter. This name was based on the variable inside the calling method.

# Extract Interface

When classes contain the same subset of members, it can be useful to define a common contract that each class shares. This, of course, is done via an interface. Some basic advantages to defining interfaces are that your code becomes more readable, is easier to maintain, and operates the same for like members. However, developers often don't realize the

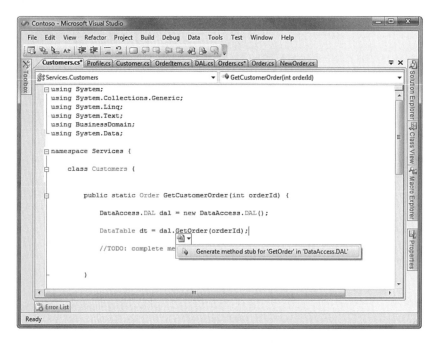

FIGURE 9.15    Generate a method stub for a nonexistent method.

FIGURE 9.16    The generated method stub.

commonality between their classes until after those classes are coded. This makes creating interfaces sometimes a painful operation.

The C# editor in Visual Studio 2008 provides the Extract Interface refactoring operation to make this process easier. It allows you to take an existing class or struct and automatically generate a matching interface that the existing class will then implement.

## Accessing the Extract Interface Refactor

To access the Extract Interface refactor operation, you first must position your cursor in a class, a struct, or another interface that contains the members you want to extract. You then can use the Refactor menu and select the Extract Interface menu item. You can also invoke Extract Interface from the context menu via a right-click and from the Class Designer.

## Extracting Interfaces

To better understand the Extract Interface operation, let's look at an example. Suppose you review your code and notice that a number of your domain objects share similar properties and methods. Let's say the objects Customer, Vendor, Manufacturer, SalesAgent, and Product all contain properties for Id, Name, and Description and methods for Load, Save, and Delete. In this case, you should consider extracting this commonality into a standard interface that each of your domain objects would implement. Let's look at how the Extract Interface refactoring operation aids in this regard.

First, you position your cursor on the target class whose members you want to extract. In the example, choose the Customer class. Invoking the Extract Interface operation presents a dialog box named the same. Figure 9.17 shows this dialog box relative to the example.

FIGURE 9.17   Extracting an interface.

Notice that you first define a name for the interface. By default, the tool names the interface with the name of the class preceded by the letter *I* for interface—in this case,

`ICustomer`. Of course, we are going to use our interface across our domain, so we will change this to `IDomainObject`.

The Extract Interface dialog box also shows the generated name and the new filename for the interface. The generated name is simply the fully qualified name of the interface. This will be used by the class for implementation of the interface. The New File Name text box shows the C# filename for the interface. All extracted interfaces result in the creation of a new file. The tool tries to keep the filename in sync with the interface name.

The last thing to do is select which members of the object you want to publish as an interface. Of course, only public members are displayed in this list. For this example, select the following public members: `Id`, `Name`, `Description`, `Load`, `Save`, and `Delete`.

Clicking the OK button generates the interface. The only change that is made to the `Customer` class is that it now implements the new interface, as in the following line of code:

```
public class Customer : BusinessDomain.IDomainObject
```

The interface is then extracted to a new file. Listing 9.4 shows the newly extracted interface.

LISTING 9.4   The Extracted Interface

```
using System;
namespace BusinessDomain {
    interface IDomainObject {
        void Delete();
        string Description { get; set; }
        int Id { get; set; }
        void Load(int id);
        string Name { get; set; }
        void Save();
    }
}
```

The next step in the example is to go out to each additional domain object and implement the new interface. This has to be done without the benefit of refactoring. However, Visual Studio does provide a smart tag for implementing an interface. Figure 9.18 shows the smart tag that results from typing **: IDomainObject** after the `Vendor` class declaration.

In this case, you have two options: implement the interface or explicitly implement the interface. The former checks the current class to see whether there are implementations that apply. The latter generates code that explicitly calls the interface items. It puts all this code inside a region for the given interface. This capability can be very useful if you're stubbing out a new class based on the interface. The following lines of code provide an example of an explicit interface member declaration:

```
void IDomainObject.Load(int id) {
  throw new NotImplementedException();
}
```

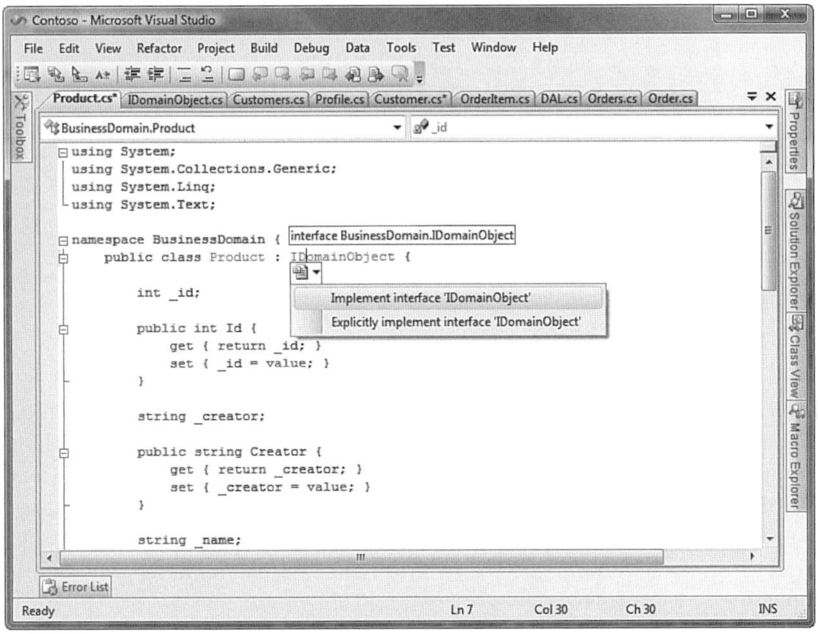

FIGURE 9.18   Implementing an interface.

# Refactor Parameters

You sometimes need to change your method signatures by removing an item, by adding a local variable as a parameter, or by reordering the existing parameters. These changes require that all calls to the method also be changed. Doing this manually can introduce new bugs into the code. For example, suppose you want to swap the order of two parameters with the same type (int, for example). If you forget to change a call to the method, it may still work; it just won't work right. These bugs can be challenging to find. Therefore, Visual Studio provides refactoring operations for removing, promoting, and reordering parameters.

## Remove Parameters

The Remove Parameters refactor operation allows you to select one or more parameters from a given method, constructor, or delegate and have it removed from the method. It also works to update any callers to the method and remove the value passed to the parameter.

You invoke the Remove Parameters operation by positioning your cursor inside the method signature and then selecting the Remove Parameters menu item from the Refactor menu. You can also get to this operation through the context menu (right-click). In addition, this operation is available from the Class Designer from inside both the class designer and the Class Details window.

---

**TIP**

To invoke the Remove Parameters operation from the keyboard, first position your cursor in the method that contains the parameters you want to remove. Next, play the keyboard chord Ctrl+R, Ctrl+V.

---

Let's look at an example. Suppose you have a method with the following signature:

```
public static Order GetCustomerOrder(int customerId, int orderId)
```

This method returns an Order object based on both a customer and an order identification number. Suppose you determine that the order ID is sufficient for returning an order. In this case, you invoke the Remove Parameters refactor and are then presented with the Remove Parameters dialog box (see Figure 9.19). Method parameters are listed at the top. To remove one, you select it and click the Remove button. The item to be removed is then updated with a strikethrough. If you change your mind, you can use the Restore button to cancel individual parameter removals.

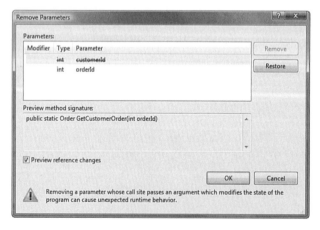

FIGURE 9.19    The Remove Parameters dialog box.

When you are ready to make the removal, you can choose to preview the changes or simply apply them all at once. The preview option works the same as other previews. It simply shows you each change in a tree view and allows you to see the details behind the change. You can, of course, also uncheck specific changes. When finished, you apply the final set of removals to your code.

> **CAUTION**
>
> It is common to declare a local variable inside a method and pass that local variable as a call to another method. If you use the refactoring operation to remove the parameter on the method you are calling, the local variable still exists in your calling method. Be careful to make sure that this is what you intended; if not, you will have to remove the local variable manually.

## Promote Local to Parameter

One common developer activity is to take a variable from within a method and make it a parameter of the method. As an example, you might look up a value inside a method and assign that value to a local variable. Instead of doing the lookup inside the method, you might want to have the value passed to the method (perhaps you would use the Extract Method refactor to push the value assignment to a new method).

This change of taking a local variable and creating a parameter can be done automatically via the Promote Local Variable to Parameter refactoring operation. It allows you to select a local member of a given method and promote it to a parameter of the method. The tool also works to update any callers of the method.

You invoke the Promote Local Variable to Parameter operation by positioning your cursor on a line of code that declares a variable. You then select the Promote Local Variable to Parameter menu item from the Refactor menu. You can also get to this operation through the context menu (right-click).

> **TIP**
>
> To invoke the Promote Local Variable to Parameter operation from the keyboard, first position your cursor on the line of code that contains the variable declaration. Next, play the keyboard chord Ctrl+R, Ctrl+P.

> **NOTE**
>
> You can promote locals only where they have been initialized. Otherwise, the operation gives an error because it does not know how to update callers to the method. In fact, if the declaration and initialization are on separate lines of code, you cannot use the refactor operation. This refactoring method works best when both declaration and initialization (assignment) are done on the same line.

Let's walk through an example. Suppose you have a method that takes an order ID and returns an Order object, as in the following method signature:

```
public static Order GetCustomerOrder(int orderId)
```

When looking through this method, you notice that there is a variable assignment that retrieves a customer ID as follows:

```
int customerId = GetCustomerId(orderId);
```

Suppose you determine that looking up a customer ID from an order ID is very inefficient for a couple of reasons. First, you already should know the customer ID before calling the method. Second, you plan to look up the order inside this method. By looking up the customer ID from the order, you look up the order twice. Therefore, you identify this variable assignment as a good candidate for promoting to the method signature. To do so, you first must right-click the line of code that does the assignment and then choose Promote Local Variable to Parameter from the Refactor context menu.

In this case, there is no preview of the change. Instead, Visual Studio does the refactor. The assignment is removed from the method. The method signature is changed to read as follows:

```
public static Order GetCustomerOrder(int orderId, int customerId)
```

In addition, clients who called into this method also get updated. In this case, a call to `GetCustomerOrder` would now include the code that previously did the variable assignment, `GetCustomerId(orderId)`. The following is an example:

```
Order newOrder = Customer.GetCustomerOrder(odrId, GetCustomerId(orderId));
```

One negative here is the code contained in this example defined the Order ID variable with the name `odrId` (see the preceding code line). Refactoring used the variable assignment code, which defined order ID as `orderId`. This will result in a compile error that you will have to fix manually because you now have a variable called `orderId` that you did not declare. Of course, this would not be the case with constants or in situations in which you use consistent variable names within methods to mean the same thing.

### Some Promoting Tips

Constants work as the best type of local variable for promoting to parameters. The reason is that there is no issue with updating calling clients. If you have a local variable with a constant value assigned, you can update callers with that set value.

When you promote a variable that includes an object call in the assignment, however, you will get the warning dialog box shown in Figure 9.20. Promoting a variable whose assignment is the result of a call to another method requires that callers which require an update as a result of the promotion should also be able to call the object that does the assignment.

As an example, suppose you have the variable declaration and assignment as follows:

```
int CustomerId = GetCustomerFromOrder(orderId);
```

If you promote `CustomerId` to a parameter, callers to the method will have to have a reference to the object that contains `GetCustomerFromOrder`. If they do not, you will end up

FIGURE 9.20   A promoting warning.

with a compiler error (and hence the warning). Whether this is an issue depends on how you've organized your code and reference.

When you promote a local variable as a parameter, the parameter is attached to the end of the function signature. This may be your intention. However, you might want to order things differently for better code readability and maintenance. To do so, you would then combine the Reorder Parameters refactor with the promotion. We will look at this operation next.

## Reorder Parameters

You move parameters around in a method typically just for readability and maintenance. You might want the more important parameters to appear first on the method signature, or you might try to keep the order similar across like methods or overloads. The Reorder Parameters refactor operation allows you to change the order in which parameters exist on a given method, constructor, or delegate. It also works to update any callers to the method and rearrange the parameters passed on the call.

You invoke the Reorder Parameters operation by positioning your cursor inside the method signature that contains the parameters you want to reorder and then selecting the Reorder Parameters menu item from the Refactor menu. You can also get to this operation through the context menu (right-click). In addition, this operation is available from the Class Designer.

| TIP |
| --- |
| To invoke the Reorder Parameters operation from the keyboard, first position your cursor in the method that contains the parameters you want to rearrange. Next, play the keyboard chord Ctrl+R, Ctrl+O. |

Let's look at an example. Suppose you just ran the Promote Local Variable example that promoted a customer ID local to a parameter of the method. The following is the method signature for reference:

```
private static Order InitCustomerOrder(int orderId, int customerId)
```

This method is called `InitCustomerOrder`. Suppose that because the `customer` parameter comes first in the method name, you want to make that the first parameter of the method. To do so, you position the cursor on the method and invoke the Reorder Parameters refactor. This presents the Reorder Parameters dialog box.

This dialog box allows you to modify the order of the parameters on the given method. At the top, it lists all the parameters of the method. To the right of this list, there are two buttons. The up-arrow button moves the selected parameter in the list up. The down arrow does the opposite. You use these buttons to get the order of the parameters the way you want them. Figure 9.21 shows this example loaded into the Reorder Parameters dialog box.

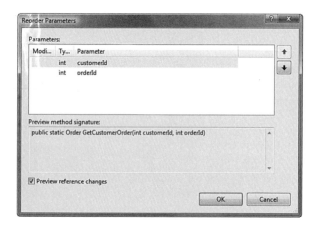

FIGURE 9.21    The Reorder Parameters dialog box.

Notice that as you change parameter order, the resulting method signature is displayed below the parameter list. You also have the option to preview any changes that will be made to callers of the method. Clicking the OK button applies the changes to both the method and its callers.

# Encapsulate Field

It's common to have a private field in your object from which you need to create a property. These fields might have been built as private because they were used only internally to the object. Alternatively, a developer may have simply defined a public field instead of encapsulating it as a property. In either case, if you need to make an actual property out of a field, you can do so with the Encapsulate Field refactor operation.

## Accessing Encapsulate Field

The Encapsulate Field operation allows you to quickly generate properties from a given field. Properties, of course, allow you to protect the field from direct access and to know when the given field is being modified or accessed. To encapsulate a field, you simply position your cursor over the field and select the Encapsulate Field option from the Refactor menu. You can also do so from the context menu (right-click) or the Class Designer.

**TIP**

To invoke the Encapsulate Field operation from the keyboard, first position your cursor on the field that you want to encapsulate. Next, play the keyboard chord Ctrl+R, Ctrl+F.

## The Encapsulate Field Dialog Box

The Encapsulate Field dialog box, shown in Figure 9.22, allows you to set a few options for this refactor. First, it presents the field you are refactoring in a read-only text box. Next, it allows you to define a name for the new property. The good news is that the tool will try to name your property correctly. For example, if you have a private field named _rating, the tool will choose Rating for the property name by default.

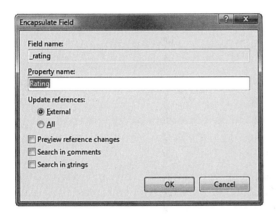

FIGURE 9.22    The Encapsulate Field dialog box.

An additional option on this dialog box is the choice of which references you would like to have updated. This refers to existing references to the field. Suppose you have a public field. This field may be called both from within the object that defines the field and by other, external objects. You may want to force external callers to use the new property. For this, you would use the External setting. In this case, the object that contains the field would still reference the local, private field (and not the property). Setting the Update Reference option to All results in both the external and internal callers using the property.

When you apply the encapsulation, the tool changes your internal field to private (if it was not already private) and then generates a property. The property includes both get and set accessors for the field. If the field was declared as read-only, the encapsulation generates only a get accessor.

Let's look at the code. Suppose you have the following field declaration:

```
private int _rating;
```

You want to encapsulate this private into a public property. Figure 9.22 shows the selected options for the encapsulation. The code that is generated is as follows:

```
private int _rating;
public int Rating {
    get { return _rating; }
    set { _rating = value; }
}
```

In addition, should you choose the All value for the update references option in the Encapsulate Field dialog, your internal callers to the field (the field was private) would be updated to use the property internally.

## Summary

This chapter showed how the refactoring tools built into the C# editor for Visual Studio 2008 can greatly increase productivity and decrease unwanted side effects (bugs) when you're making sweeping changes to your code to improve maintenance, reuse, and readability. The refactoring tools use the compiler and not text searching. This improves confidence in and reliability of the tools.

These tools can be accessed using the keyboard, the Refactor menu, a context menu, the Class Designer, and elsewhere. Actual refactoring operation access, of course, depends on code selection context.

The refactoring tools allow you to change your code in many ways. You can easily rename items in your code. You can take existing lines of code and extract them to new methods. Your objects can be used as the basis to define new interfaces. Method signatures can be modified using the Remove, Promote Local Variable, and Reorder refactoring operations. Finally, you can take existing fields and quickly encapsulate them into properties.

# Debugging Code

Today's developers may spend as much time debugging their code as they do writing it. This is due in some part to the nature of today's highly dependent and distributed applications. These applications are built to leverage existing functionality, frameworks, building blocks, libraries, and so on. In addition, they often communicate with other applications, services, components, databases, and even data exchanges. Developers also demand more assistance from their debugger to help increase their productivity. The Visual Studio 2008 debugger addresses these needs by offering some great debugging scenarios. Some highlights include the following:

▶ Breakpoint and tracepoint management

▶ Visualizers and debugger DataTips

▶ Edit and Continue for both VB and C# developers

▶ Just-my-code debugging

▶ The Exception Assistant

▶ Debugging support at design time

▶ Client-side script debugging

▶ Support for debugging WCF applications

▶ Debugging support for LINQ

▶ Remote debugging

We will cover all of these features and more in this chapter. Of course, if you are just getting started with .NET, more than just this list is new to you. The Visual Studio debugger has been evolving since the first release of .NET, which provided a unified debugger with the capability to debug across languages. In this chapter, we will start by covering the basics of debugging an application. We will then discuss the Visual Studio 2008 debugger in depth.

# Debugging Basics

A typical scenario for a developer is to start building a screen or form and build up the code that surrounds it. In addition, the developer may rely on a framework or a few building blocks that provide added functionality. The application may also communicate with a services layer and most often a database. Even the most typical applications have a lot of moving parts. These moving parts make the task of finding and eliminating errors in the code all the more complex. The tools that help you track down and purge errors from your code not only have to keep up with this complexity, but also must ease the effort involved with the debugging process. In the following sections, we will cover how a developer would use the tools built into Visual Studio 2008 to debug a typical development scenario.

## The Scenario

We want to define an application scenario that we can use both to introduce the basics of debugging and to function as a base for us to build on throughout the chapter when demonstrating the many features of the debugging tools. In this scenario, imagine you are writing a web page that allows customers to view and edit their profiles. This page will offer new functionality to a larger, existing application. The following are some of the conditions that surround this application scenario:

▶ The customers' profiles are stored in a SQL 2005 database.

▶ A data access library abstracts all access to the database.

▶ A web service exists to provide the customers' profile information.

Your task is to write a page using the web service to return profile information for customers. The page should display customer profile information and allow a user to edit this data. You will also need to write changes to a customer profile back to the database using the data access library. The application you will be debugging in this scenario is written in C#. However, the debugging tools in Visual Studio are equally applicable to both C# and Visual Basic. That is, everything we discuss here applies to both languages unless specified otherwise.

## The Many Phases of Debugging

Nearly every time developers open the IDE, they are in some way debugging their code. The line between debugging and writing code, in fact, is becoming more and more blurred. For example, the code editor helps eliminate errors in your code as you write it.

It highlights items where errors are present and allows you to fix them. You are then both writing and debugging simultaneously.

In addition, the compiler acts as another debugging tool. The first time you click the Run button, the compiler checks your code and reports a list of errors for you to fix before continuing. This is debugging. The steps or phases of the debugging process include the following:

▶ **Coding**—The editor helps you by pointing out issues and possible resolutions.

▶ **Compiling**—The compiler checks your code and reports errors before continuing.

▶ **Self-checking**—You run the application in debug mode and step through screens and code to verify functionality.

▶ **Unit testing**—You write and run unit tests to check your application.

▶ **Code analysis**—You run the Static Code Analyzer to verify that your application meets project standards.

▶ **Code review**—Your code is reviewed by a peer or an architect and issues are logged accordingly.

▶ **Responding to bug**—When a bug has been logged against the code, you must re-create and debug a specific scenario.

In this chapter, we will concentrate on two of these phases: self-checking and responding to bugs. These are the two phases in which developers will get the most use of the debugging tools built into Visual Studio. We will therefore assume that the code is written and compiles. Let's start by looking at how to self-check the code.

> **NOTE**
>
> Code reviews are another important tool for debugging your application. They help ensure that you are meeting standards and refactoring out things like duplicate code. The Visual Studio Static Code Analyzer can help. This tool is covered in Chapter 26, "Development Edition."

## Debugging the Application (Self-Checking)

In this scenario, you have just started writing a web page to edit a customer's profile. Assume that you've laid out the page, connected to the profile web service, and written the code to save a user's profile to the database. You now need to start self-checking your work to make sure that everything operates as you expect.

The first step is to start your application in debug mode. This will allow you to break into your code if an error occurs. In development, this is typically your default setting. You first invoke debug mode by clicking the Run button (the green arrow on either the Standard or the Debug toolbar). Figure 10.1 shows the sample application about to be run in debug mode for the first time. Notice the cursor hovering over the Run button.

FIGURE 10.1    Starting the debugger.

### Enabling Debugging on a Website

This example is a web application. As such, it requires you to set up debugging on server-side code whose errors and information are output to a remote client. Of course, in the vast majority of cases, developers code and debug on a single development machine. However, sometimes you may have to debug a process on a test server.

In either case, you have to enable debugging through a setting in the configuration file (web.config) for your application. Visual Studio will prompt you to enable debugging when you first press the Run button. Figure 10.2 shows this prompt. Clicking the OK button adds the configuration file to the application and starts the debugging session.

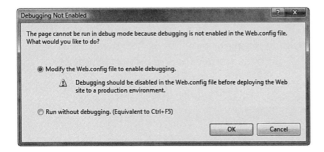

FIGURE 10.2    Allowing Visual Studio to enable debugging.

**NOTE**

It is important that you turn off debugging in your config file before deploying your web application to production. Having debugging enabled in a production environment is a security risk. With debugging enabled, ASP.NET writes the details of your errors to a web page. These details provide valuable clues to would-be hackers about how your application is put together. In some instances, the error could include user credentials that are being used to access secured resources.

To turn off debug mode, you must edit the web configuration file. Specifically, you edit the `Compilation` element under the `system.web` node. You set `debug` equal to `false` (as in off). The following is an example of the XML with debug mode turned on:

```
<system.web>
  <compilation debug="true"/>
    ...
</system.web>
```

### Starting in Debug Mode

The most typical scenario for starting a debug session is just clicking the Run button on the toolbar. This works with all application types including Windows and ASP.NET. This action instructs Visual Studio to compile the application and bring up the initial form or page.

Applications can also be started without debugging; this includes both Windows and ASP.NET applications. This capability is useful if you intend to attach to a running process or simply want to walk through an application as a user might see it (without breaking into the IDE). You use the Debug menu, Start Without Debugging option to start your application without attaching it to the Visual Studio Debugger. Figure 10.3 shows an example of invoking this action.

You can also start by stepping into code, line by line. This approach is useful if you want to see all of your code as it executes (rather than just errors). You might desire this if you are getting some unexpected behavior. Stepping line by line gives you an exact understanding of what is going on with your code (rather than just your assumed understanding).

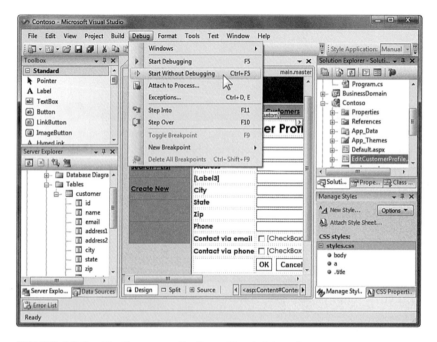

FIGURE 10.3    Starting an application without debugging.

Stepping into code on a web form is typically done by first opening the main source. You then right-click and select the Run to Cursor option from the shortcut menu. Figure 10.4 shows an example. This command tells Visual Studio to run the application until it gets to this point. At that time, the IDE will open into debug mode, where you can step through each line of code (or continue, and so on).

**Breaking on an Error**

Not everything you find in debug mode is an error that results in a break in the code. Often, issues arise just because you're looking at the behavior of the application. For example, a control could be out of place, the tab order could be wrong, and so on. For these items, you still have to rely on your eyes. The debugging tools in Visual Studio help you respond to hard errors in your code.

By default, when unhandled exceptions occur in your code, the debugger will break execution and bring up the IDE with the offending code highlighted. The key in that sentence is "unhandled exceptions." They represent places in your code where you do not have try-catch blocks to manage an exception. This is typically a good default setting. However, you often need to see handled exceptions as well.

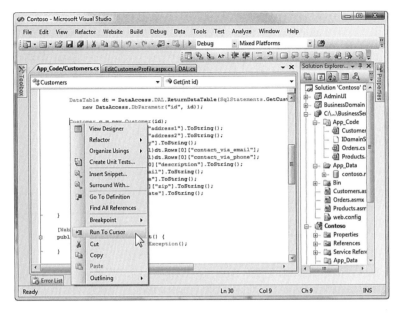

FIGURE 10.4    After selecting Run to Cursor, you can start debugging.

Fortunately, the errors that result in a break in the IDE are a configurable set. For example, you may handle a specific exception in your code and not want to be dumped to the IDE every time it occurs. Rather, you want to be notified only of those especially exceptional conditions. The Exceptions dialog box allows you to manage the set of exceptions you're concerned with. You access this dialog box by choosing Debug, Exceptions (or pressing Ctrl+D, E in C# or Ctrl+Alt+E in VB). Figure 10.5 shows the dialog box.

In the Exceptions dialog box, the various exceptions are categorized by namespace for easy access (there is also a Find feature). The two columns of check boxes are of primary interest: one for Thrown and one for User-unhandled. Notice that, by default, the setting for all exceptions in the .NET Framework is User-unhandled. This indicates that the debugger should break execution only when a given exception is thrown and it is not handled by your code.

Adding Thrown to the mix will tell the debugger to break execution even if you have code to handle a given exception. The debugger will react by breaking on the line of the exception, before your handler is called. If you intend to use this option, you should consider simply setting it at the category level. For example, you might toggle Thrown for the entire category Common Language Runtime Exceptions. Setting up more granularity is certainly possible. However, doing so often results in more confusion as the debugger breaks in different places depending on the given exception thrown.

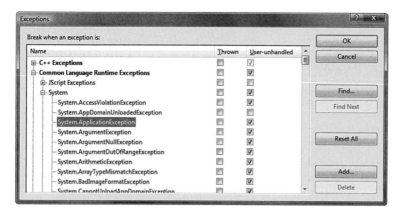

FIGURE 10.5    Determining where Visual Studio breaks.

### Debugging an Error

The first step in debugging your application is to click the Run button. Your application is then running in debug mode. As it happens, the sample application we discussed in our scenario throws an exception upon its initial startup. The debugger responds by breaking into the code and showing the offending line. Figure 10.6 shows a typical view of the editor when it breaks on an error.

There are a few items to point out about the standard debug session shown in Figure 10.6. First, Visual Studio has highlighted the line on which the error was thrown. You can see this clearly by the arrow and the highlighted text.

Next, notice the window in the upper right of the image. This is the Exception Assistant. It provides details on the exception and offers tips for troubleshooting and fixing the given issue. From this window, you can access a few actions, including searching online help for more information on the exception.

At the bottom of the screen are a few additional helpful windows. The Locals window on the left automatically shows the value assigned to all local variables in the code where the exception was thrown. This gives you easy access to key information that might be contributing to the issue. Notice that to the right of this window is an inactive tab called Watch 1 (bottom of screen). This is a watch window; it keeps track of any custom watch scenarios you set up (more on this later).

The window on the bottom right of the screen is the Call Stack. It shows the order in which various components of an application were called. You can look at the Call Stack to find out how you got to where you are. You can also use it to navigate to any code referenced in the stack. Finally, the inactive tab next to this gives you access to the Immediate Window. The Immediate Window allows you to type in code commands and get the results in the editor (more on this to come).

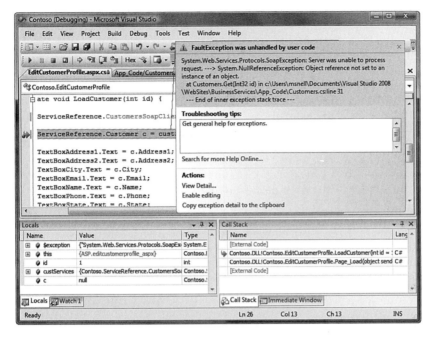

FIGURE 10.6    The debugger breaking on execution.

**Debugging Different Processes**    After you examine your error, you can see that it is being thrown inside the web service process. The code called by the web service is being run in a separate process from that of the startup application (the web user interface). When you debug an application, you debug (or shadow) a running process such as an executable (.exe). Visual Studio, by default, considers the startup application's process as the primary process being debugged.

To debug code that is running in a different process (such as the web service process), you must both have the source code and be attached to the executing process (running a debug build). If all the code for a given application is in a single solution, Visual Studio will automatically attach to each process. In our example, this includes both the web user interface process and the web service process. Therefore, in this case, you do not need to manually attach to another process. This is new to Visual Studio 2008.

The debugger will not, however, automatically break into the IDE on errors raised outside of the startup process. Instead, it will respect breakpoints you set inside code executing in other processes. If an error is thrown in a separate process (and no related breakpoints exist in that process), the debugger will break into the IDE inside the process that called into the process that threw the error. Therefore, in our example from Figure 10.6, you see that the error is in code contained in a library that is called by the web service. The web service is contained in a separate web server process from that of the executing startup application (web user interface). To debug this error, then, you need to set a breakpoint in the web service or near the referenced code.

**NOTE**

Recall that you need to enable debugging for web applications using the configuration file (web.config). This holds true for web service applications as well. Refer to Figure 10.2 for details.

Sometimes you will need to manually attach to an already running process. You might want to attach the IDE to a running web server, or you may have a service application to which you want to bind debugging. Whatever the scenario, Visual Studio allows you to attach to the process and begin a debug session. To attach to a running process, like a web server, you choose the Attach to Process option from the Debug menu. This brings up the dialog box shown in Figure 10.7.

In Figure 10.7, notice that any currently attached processes are grayed out. This is a visual indicator that you are already attached to a given process. To connect the Visual Studio debugger to this process, you simply highlight it and click the Attach button. You are now debugging both processes and can therefore set a breakpoint in the related code where an error might be occurring.

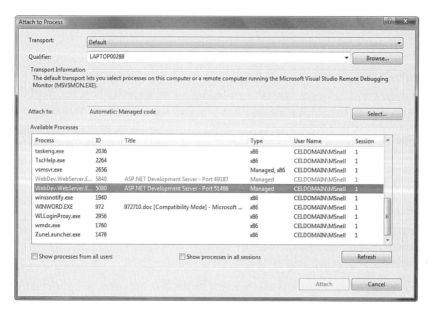

FIGURE 10.7    Attaching debugging to a running process.

**Setting a Breakpoint**    To get the debugger to break into your code when it reaches a specific line, you set a breakpoint on that line. You do so by clicking on the indicator bar for the given line. Alternatively, you can right-click on the line and choose Insert Breakpoint from the Breakpoint context menu. In the example, the error may be coming from the code that gets the customer data from the database. Therefore, you need to navigate to the DataAccess project, open the DAL.cs file, and set a breakpoint, as shown in Figure 10.8.

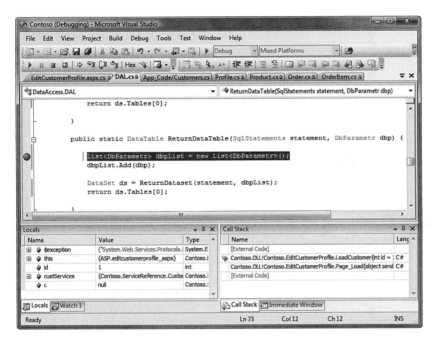

FIGURE 10.8  Setting a breakpoint.

**Continuing the Debugging**    After you've navigated off the executing code during a debug session, it can often be hard to find your way back. The line that was executing could be buried in any one of the open code windows. Thankfully, you can use the Show Next Statement button (yellow arrow icon) on the Debug toolbar to take you back. This will return you to the line that was executing when the debugger broke.

In the example, rerun the call to the web service so that you can now hit your breakpoint and step through the code. To do so, you must move the current execution point in the code. You can accomplish this by right-clicking the line where you want execution to start (or rerun) and selecting Set Next Statement from the context menu. Figure 10.9 shows this menu option.

Now that you have backed up the execution point, you are ready to continue the debugging. You can do this by clicking the Run button again. This is essentially indicating that you are done with the break and want to continue execution.

**Stepping to Find the Error**    In the example, the debugger will break execution as soon as it hits the breakpoint in the web service process. This will allow you to step through the code. To step line by line through the code, you can click the Step Into button on the Debug toolbar (or press the F11 function key). This will execute the code one line at a time, allowing you to view both execution flow and the state of the application as code executes. Doing so with the example allows you to see the error. It seems that an instance of the `DataSet` object was not set prior to trying to fill it with data.

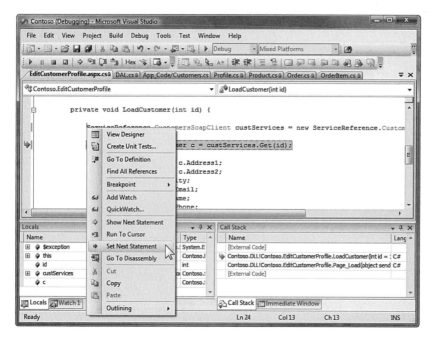

FIGURE 10.9    The Set Next Statement option.

In most scenarios, you can make this fix during the debug session and continue stepping through or running the code. Unfortunately, in this example you cannot make the change while debugging. You cannot invoke Edit and Continue when the debugger is attached to another process (whether attachment was automatic or manual). Figure 10.10 shows the message you get when you try.

FIGURE 10.10    An Edit and Continue error with an attached process.

So instead of using Edit and Continue, you can bookmark the line where you want to make the change using the Text Editor toolbar. You then click the Stop button on the Debug toolbar to stop the debug session. The code change can now be made.

To continue through self-checking, you would next restart the debugging process. However, before this, you may want to clear the breakpoint you set. To do so, select the Breakpoints toolbar item from the Debug toolbar. This brings up the Breakpoints window, as shown in Figure 10.11. From this window, you can view all breakpoints in the application. Here, you select and clear the breakpoint by clicking the Delete button from the toolbar on the Breakpoints pane. Finally, you click the Run button to continue the debug, self-check session.

FIGURE 10.11   The Breakpoints window.

## Debugging Basics Summary

This scenario walked through the many phases of debugging a simple error. This example was meant to introduce the basics of doing debugging in Visual Studio 2008. If you are familiar with prior IDE versions, you probably noticed a lot of similarities. Walking through the scenario demonstrated the many tools inside the debugging environment, including the Debug toolbar and menu, the Breakpoints window, the watch window, and so on. Now that you have a grasp of the basics, in the next section we intend to explore these debug elements in greater detail.

# The Visual Studio Debugger

The debugger built into Visual Studio 2008 is one of the largest and most complex tools in the IDE. With such a large feature-set area, we cannot cover every scenario you will encounter. However, we hope to expose the most commonly applicable features in this section. We will continue to work with the customer profile scenario for our previous example.

## The Debug Menu and Toolbar

The Debug menu and its related toolbar provide your first-level access to starting debug sessions, stepping into code, managing breakpoints, and accessing the many features of debugging with Visual Studio. There are two states to the debug menu: at rest (or inactive) and in debug mode. Figure 10.12 shows the menu in the at-rest state.

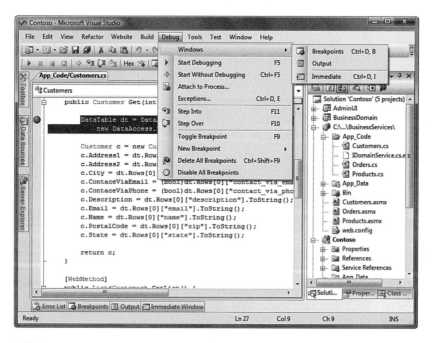

FIGURE 10.12    The Debug menu at rest.

In the at-rest state, the Debug menu provides features to start a debug session, attach code to a running process, or access some of the many debug windows. Table 10.1 lists all the features available from the Debug menu at rest.

TABLE 10.1    Debug Menu Items at Rest

| Menu Item | Description |
|---|---|
| Windows, Breakpoints | Opens the Breakpoints window in the IDE. This window provides access to all the breakpoints in the option solution. |
| Windows, Output | Shows the Output window in the IDE. The Output window is a running log of the many messages that are emitted by the IDE, the compiler, and the debugger. Therefore, the information transcends just debug sessions. |
| Windows, Immediate | Opens the Immediate window in the IDE. This window allows you to execute commands. For example, during application design, you can call your methods directly from the Immediate window. This will start the application and enter directly into a debug session. |
| Start Debugging | Starts your application in debug mode. |
| Start Without Debugging | Starts your application without connecting the debugger to the executing process. In this mode, the developer sees what users would see (instead of breaking into the IDE for errors and breakpoints). |
| Attach to Process | Allows you to attach the debugger (and your code) to a running process (executable). If, for example, you started the application without debugging, you could then attach to that running process and begin debugging. |
| Exceptions | Opens the Exceptions option dialog box. This dialog box allows you to choose how the debugger breaks on any given exception. |
| Step Into | Starts the application in debug mode. For most projects, clicking the Step Into command invokes the debugger on the first executing line of the application. In this way, you can step into the application from the first line. |
| Step Over | When not in a debug session, the Step Over command simply starts the application the same way clicking the Run button would. |
| Toggle Breakpoint | Toggles the breakpoint on or off for the current, active line of code in a text editor. The option is inactive if you do not have a code window active in the IDE. |
| New Breakpoint, Break at Function | Brings up the New Breakpoint dialog box. This dialog box allows you to indicate a function name to define for which to create a breakpoint. This can be useful if you know a function's name but do not want to search your code files for it. |
| New Breakpoint, New Data Breakpoint | This option is available only for native, C++ applications. It allows you to define a breakpoint that breaks into the IDE when a value in a specific memory location changes. |
| Delete All Breakpoints | Removes all breakpoints from your solution. |
| Disable All Breakpoints | Disables (without removing) all the breakpoints in your solution. |

When the debugger is engaged and you are working through a debug session, the state of the Debug menu changes. It now provides several additional options over those provided by the at-rest state. These options include those designed to move through the code, restart the session, and access even more debug-related windows. Figure 10.13 shows the Debug menu during a debug session.

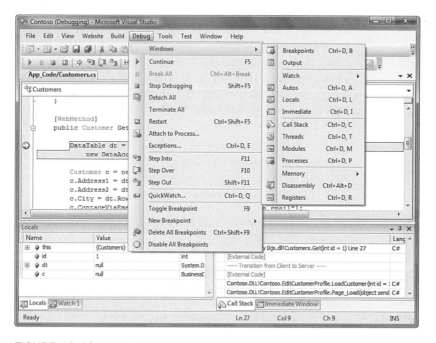

FIGURE 10.13    The Debug menu during a debug session.

Let's look at the many options provided by the Debug menu during a debug session. Table 10.2 presents the many items available from the debug menu in this state. When reading through the table, refer to the preceding figures to get context on any given item.

### The Debug Toolbar

The Debug toolbar provides quick access to some of the key items available on the Debug menu. From here, you can manage your debug session. For example, you can start or continue a debug session, stop an executing session, step through lines of code, and so on.

Figure 10.14 presents the Debug toolbar during an active debug session. In design mode, the Continue button would read Start Debugging, and a number of these items would be disabled. We have added callouts for each item on the toolbar. You can cross-reference these callouts back to Table 10.2 for further information.

TABLE 10.2   Debug Menu Items for an Active Debug Session

| Menu Item | Description |
|-----------|-------------|
| Windows, Breakpoints | Allows you to open the Breakpoints window during a debug session. |
| Windows, Output | Opens the Output window during an active debug session in order to read output messages emitted by the compiler and debugger. |
| Windows, Watch | Opens one of many possible watch windows in the IDE. Watch windows represent items and expressions you are keeping a close eye on through a debug session. |
| Windows, Autos | Opens the Autos window. This window shows variables (and their value) in the current line of code and the preceding line of code. |
| Windows, Locals | Opens the Locals window in the IDE. This window shows variables in the local scope (function). |
| Windows, Immediate | Opens the Immediate window where you can execute a command. |
| Windows, Call Stack | Shows the list of functions that are on the stack. Also indicates the current stack frame (function). This selected item is what defines the content from the Locals, watch, and Autos windows. |
| Windows, Threads | Shows the Threads window in the IDE. From here, you can view and control the threads in the application you are debugging. |
| Windows, Modules | Shows the Modules window in the IDE. This window lists the DLLs and EXEs used by your application. |
| Windows, Processes | Shows the Processes window in the IDE. This window lists the processes to which the debug session is attached. |
| Windows, Memory | Opens the Memory window for a view at the memory used by your application. This is valid only when address-level debugging is enabled from the Options dialog box. |
| Windows, Disassembly | Opens the Disassembly window. This window shows the assembly code corresponding to the compiler instructions. This is valid only when address-level debugging is enabled from the Options dialog box. |
| Windows, Registers | Opens the Registers window so that you can see register values change as you step through code. This is valid only when address-level debugging is enabled from the Options dialog box. |
| Continue | Continues executing the application once broken into the IDE. The application continues running on the active line of code (the breakpoint, a line that threw an error, or a line set using Set Next Statement). |

10

TABLE 10.2    Continued

| Menu Item | Description |
| --- | --- |
| Break All | Allows you to break the application into the debugger manually (without having to hit a breakpoint) during a debug session. The application will break on the next line that executes. This capability is useful to gain access to the debug information such as watch windows. It can also be used to gain access to the debug session when your application appears to have hung. |
| Stop Debugging | Terminates the debugging session. It also terminates the process you are debugging, provided that the process was started by Visual Studio. |
| Detach All | Detaches the debugger from the executing process. This allows your application to continue running after the debugger is through with it. |
| Terminate All | Stops debugging and terminates all processes to which you are attached. |
| Restart | Stops the debugging session and restarts it. Similar to clicking both Stop Debugging and Start Debugging in sequence. |
| Attach to Process | Allows you to attach the active debug session to one or more additional processes such as an executing web server or a Windows service. |
| Exceptions | Brings up the Exceptions dialog, which allows you to manage how the IDE breaks on specific exception types in the .NET Framework and other libraries. |
| Step Into | Step Into advances the debugger a line. If you choose to "step into" a function, the debugger will do so line by line. |
| Step Over | Functions the same as Step Into with one major difference: If you choose to "step over" a function, the line calling the function will be executed (along with the function), and the debugger will set the next line after the function call as the next line to be debugged. |
| Step Out | Tells the debugger to execute the current function and then break back into debugging after the function has finished. This capability is useful if you step into a function but then want to have that function just execute and yet return you to debug mode when it is complete. |
| QuickWatch | Brings up the QuickWatch window when the debugger is in break mode. The QuickWatch window shows one variable or expression you are watching and its value. |
| Toggle Breakpoint | Turns an active breakpoint on or off. |
| New Breakpoint | Brings up the New Breakpoint dialog box (see Table 10.1 for more information). |
| Delete All Breakpoints | Deletes all breakpoints in your solution. |

TABLE 10.2    Continued

| Menu Item | Description |
|-----------|-------------|
| Disable All Breakpoints | Disables breakpoints in the solution without deleting them. You can also disable individual breakpoints. This capability is very useful if you want to keep the breakpoints around for later but simply don't want to hit that one at the moment. |
| Enable All Breakpoints | Enables all breakpoints that have been disabled due to a call to Disable All Breakpoints. |

**NOTE**

In Figure 10.14, the Breakpoints window icon on the right of the figure with the callout "Debug Windows" actually is a drop-down menu. This menu provides access to the many debug windows that are available to developers. See Figure 10.13 for a sample of the menus you can access from this toolbar item.

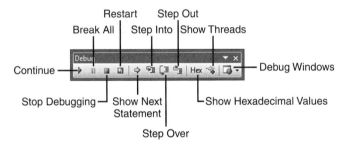

FIGURE 10.14    The Debug toolbar during break mode.

## Debug Options

You can control the many debugging options in Visual Studio through the Options dialog box. The Debugging node on the options tree provides access to these debugging switches. Figure 10.15 shows the general debugging settings in the Options dialog (Tools, Options).

The general settings list provides access to turn on and off many debugging options. These options include all the following:

▶ Turn on and off breakpoint filters

▶ Enable or disable the warning dialog box associated with clearing all breakpoints

▶ Turn on or off the Exception Assistant

▶ Enable or disable just-my-code debugging

▶ Require source code to exactly match that being debugged (or not)

▶ And many more

We will cover the features behind these options throughout the chapter.

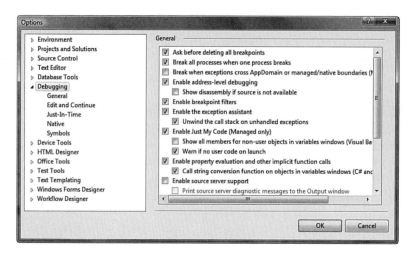

FIGURE 10.15    The Debug Options dialog box.

The options dialog provides access to even more debug-related settings. For instance, you can control how Edit and Continue works (you can also turn off this feature). There are settings for which type of code (Managed, Native, Script) is enabled for just-in-time debugging. You also have the option for using additional debug symbol files (.pdb and .dbg). These files can be helpful if you do not have the source code associated with a particular library you need to debug, such as Windows source or a third-party component.

These many options help you customize your debug experience. However, as we debug code in this chapter, we are assuming the default options for the debugger.

## Stepping In, Out, and Over Code

Probably the most common debug operation for developers is stepping through their code line by line and examining the data emitted by the application and the debugger. Code stepping is just that, examining a line, executing the line, and examining the results (and then repeating the process over and over). Because this is such a dominant activity, becoming efficient with the step operations in Visual Studio is important for maximizing the use of your time during a debug session. Here, we will cover each of the stepping options and provide examples accordingly.

### Beginning a Debug Session (Stepping into Code)

The Step Into command is available from the Debug menu and toolbar (you can also press F11 as a shortcut). There are two behaviors commonly associated with this one command.

The first is related to when you invoke the command for an application that is not currently running in debug mode. In this case, the application will be compiled and started, and the first line will be presented to you in the debug window for stepping purposes. This is, in essence, stepping into your application. Figure 10.16 shows a Windows form application in debug mode as the result of a call to Step Into.

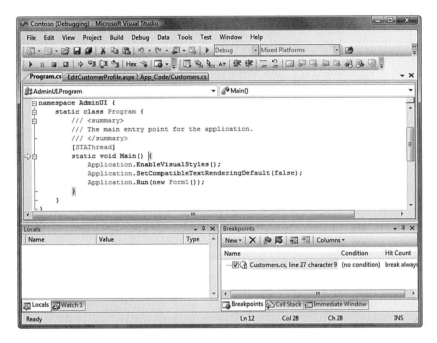

FIGURE 10.16    Using Step Into to start an application.

**NOTE**

For web applications, using Step Into or Step Over does not work the same. Instead, your application simply runs in debug mode in the case of websites. The debugger does not break on the first line of your application. To do this, you must set a breakpoint or choose the Run to Cursor option (see the following section).

A call to the Step Over command (Debug menu, toolbar, or F10) while your application is at rest will result in the same behavior as Step Into. That is, your application (provided it is not a website) will be compiled and started in a debug session on the first line of code.

**Run to Cursor**    One of the more handy (and overlooked) features of the debug toolset is Run to Cursor. This feature works the way it sounds. You set your cursor position on some code and invoke the command. The application is compiled and run until it hits the line of code where your cursor is placed. At this point, the debugger breaks the application and presents the line of code for you to step through. This capability is especially handy because this is how many developers work. They are looking at a specific line (or lines) of code and want to debug this line. They do not need to start from the first line and often do not want to be bothered with breakpoints. The Run to Cursor feature is therefore an efficient means to get the debugger on the same page as you. Figure 10.17 shows this feature being invoked from the context menu.

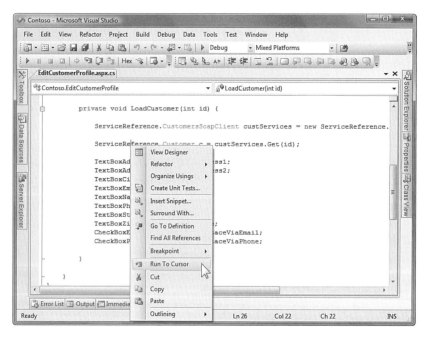

FIGURE 10.17    Invoking the Run to Cursor command.

Run to Cursor works even if the user is required to activate some portion of the code prior to the code's reaching the cursor position. In this way, it really is an invisible, temporary breakpoint. For instance, consider an example in which users are presented with a default web page. From here, they can select to edit their profile as an option. If you set the Run to Cursor command on a line inside the edit profile screen, the debugger will still execute the application and wait until the user (tester or developer) invokes the given line of code.

**Start Debugging**    You can also start your debug session by selecting the Start Debugging option (green "play" arrow) from the Debug menu or toolbar (or F5). This starts a debug session but does not break into code unless an exception occurs or a breakpoint is encountered. This is a common operation for developers testing their code without wanting to walk through it or those who use a lot of breakpoints.

**Break All**   If your application is running and you want to enter break mode, you can do so at any time by invoking the Break All command from the Debug menu or toolbar (or Ctrl+Alt+Break). The Break All feature is represented by the pause icon on the toolbar. Clicking this button stops your application on the next executing line and allows you to interrogate the debugger for information. The Break All command is especially useful if you need to break into a long-running process or a loop that seems to have stalled your application.

### Walking Through Your Code

During a debug session, you have basically three options for moving through your code. You can step into a line or function, step over a given function, or step out of a function. Let's look at each option.

**Step Into**   The Step Into command (F11 for C# and F8 for VB) allows you to progress through your code one line at a time. Invoking this command will execute the current line of code and position your cursor on the next line to be executed. The important distinction between stepping into and other similar commands is how Step Into handles lines of code that contain method calls. If you are positioned on a line of code that calls into another method in your solution, calling Step Into will take you to the first line inside that method (provided you have the appropriate debug symbols loaded).

As an example, look at Figure 10.18. It shows an example of a web service making a call to a data access library's method named `ReturnDataTable`. In this case, both projects are loaded in the solution; thus, you have access to their debug symbols. Therefore, a call to Step Into will result in your stepping into the first line of `ReturnDataTable`.

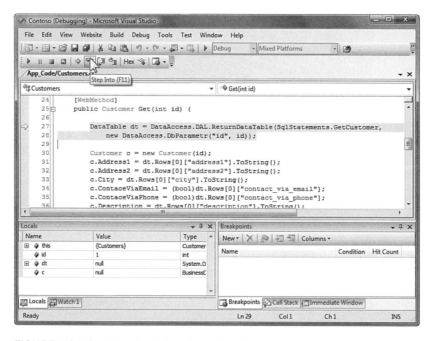

FIGURE 10.18   Stepping into a line of code.

Figure 10.19 shows stepping into this method. Notice that you are now positioned to step line by line through the method. Of course, when you reach the end of this method, the debugger will return you to the next line in the calling function (line 30 in the web service depicted in Figure 10.18).

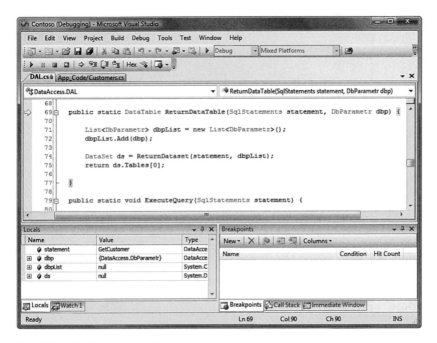

FIGURE 10.19   The results of stepping into a function.

**Step Over**   The Step Over command (F10 for C# and Shift+F8 for VB) allows you to maintain focus on the current procedure without stepping into any methods called by it. That is, calling Step Over will execute line by line but will not take you into any function calls, constructors, or property calls.

As an example, consider Figure 10.18. Here, the debugger is positioned on the call to ReturnDataTable. If you called the Step Over command, the ReturnDataTable function would execute without your stepping through it. Instead, the next line to execute in step mode would be the line following the call to ReturnDataTable (line 30). Of course, any exception thrown by the function you step over will result in the debugger breaking into your code (and the function) as normal.

**Step Out**   The Step Out command (Shift+F11 and Ctrl+Shift+F8 for VB) is another useful tool. It allows you to tell the debugger to finish executing the current method you are debugging but return to break mode as soon as it is finished. This is a great tool when you get stuck in a long method you wished you had stepped over. In addition, you may step into a given function only to debug a portion of it and then want to step out.

As an example, refer again to Figure 10.19. Recall that you stepped into this method from the code in Figure 10.18. Suppose that you start stepping through a couple of lines of code. After you take a look and verify that a connection is made to the database, you simply want to have the function complete and return to debugging back in the calling function (line 30 of Figure 10.18). To do so, you simply invoke Step Out.

**Continuing Execution**

When you are in a debug session, the Start Debugging (or Run) command changes to Continue. The Continue command is available when you are paused on a given line of code in the debugger. It enables you to let the application continue to run on its own without stepping through each line. For example, suppose you walked through the lines of code you wanted to see, and now you want to continue checking your application from a user's perspective. Using Continue, you tell the application and debugger to keep running until either an exception occurs or a breakpoint is hit.

**Ending a Debug Session**

You can end your debug session in few ways. One common method is to kill the currently executing application. This might be done by closing the browser window for a web application or clicking the Close (or ×) button of a Windows application. Calls in your code that terminate your application will also end a debug session.

There are also a couple of options available to you from the Debug window. The Terminate All command kills all processes that the debugger is attached to and ends the debug session. There is also the Detach All option. Figure 10.20 shows both options in the toolbar. Detach All simply detaches the debugger from all running processes without terminating them. This capability can be useful if you've temporarily attached to a running process, debugged it, and want to leave it running.

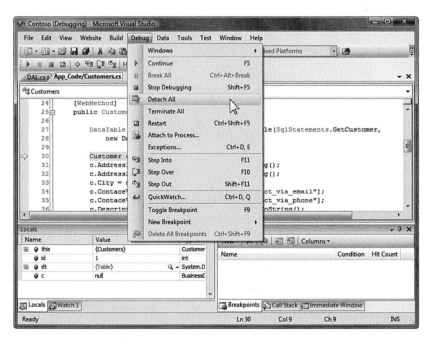

FIGURE 10.20   Detaching from a process.

## Indicating When to Break into Code

You control the debugger through breakpoints and tracepoints. With these, you can tell the debugger when you are interested in breaking into code or receiving information about your application. Breakpoints allow you to indicate when the debugger should stop on a specific line in your code. Tracepoints were first introduced in Visual Studio 2005. They are a type of breakpoint that allows you to perform an action when a given line of your code is reached. This typically involves emitting data about your application to the output window. Mastering the use of breakpoints will reduce the time it takes to zero in on and fix issues with your code.

### Setting a Breakpoint

The most common method of setting a breakpoint is to first find the line of code on which you want the debugger to stop. You then click in the code editor's indicator margin for the given line of code. Doing so will place a red circle in the indicator margin and highlight the line of code as red. Of course, these are the default colors; you can change the look of breakpoints in the Tools, Options dialog box under the Environment node, Fonts and Colors.

There are a few additional ways to set breakpoints. For instance, you can right-click a given line of code and choose Insert Breakpoint from the Breakpoint context menu. You can also choose New Breakpoint from the Debug menu (or press Ctrl+D, N in C# or Ctrl+B in VB). This option brings up the New Breakpoint dialog box in which you can set a function breakpoint.

**Setting a Function Breakpoint**   A function breakpoint is just a breakpoint that is set through the New Breakpoint dialog box. It is called a *function breakpoint* because it is typically set at the beginning of the function (but does not need to be). From the New Breakpoint dialog box, you can manually set the function on which you want to break, the line of code in the function, and even the character on the line.

If your cursor is on a function or on a call to a function when you invoke this dialog box, the name of the function will automatically be placed in the dialog box. You can also type a function name in the dialog box. Figure 10.21 shows the New Breakpoint dialog box in action. Notice that you can manually set the line and even the character on the line where the breakpoint should be placed.

---

**NOTE**

If you specify an overloaded function in the New Breakpoint dialog box, you must specify the actual function on which you want to break. You do so by indicating the correct parameter types for the given overload. For example, the current LoadCustomer takes a customer ID as an int. If you had an overload that also looked up a customer by name (as a string), you would indicate this overload in the Function field as LoadCustomer(string).

---

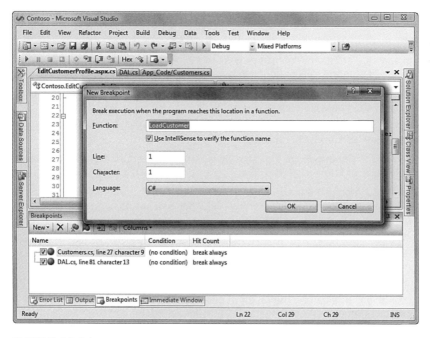

FIGURE 10.21    The New Breakpoint dialog box.

### Recognizing the Many Breakpoints of Visual Studio

Visual Studio 2008 has a number of breakpoint icons. These icons allow you to easily recognize the type of breakpoint associated with a given line of code. For instance, a round, filled circle is a common breakpoint, whereas a round, hollow circle represents a common breakpoint that has been disabled. We've provided Table 10.3 for reference purposes. It shows some of the more common icons associated with breakpoints and presents a description of each.

### Working with the Breakpoints Window

The Breakpoints window in Visual Studio provides a convenient way to organize and manage the many conditions on which you intend to break into the debugger. You access this window from the Debug menu or toolbar (or by pressing Ctrl+D, B in C# or Ctrl+Alt+B in VB). Figure 10.22 shows the Breakpoints window inside Visual Studio.

**The Breakpoints Window Toolbar**    The Breakpoints window has its own toolbar that allows you to manage the breakpoints in the window. The commands available from the toolbar are described in detail in Table 10.4.

**Managing Each Individual Breakpoint**    The Breakpoints window also gives you access to each individual breakpoint. It serves as a launching point for setting the many options associated with a breakpoint. For example, you can disable a single breakpoint by toggling the check box associated with the breakpoint in the list. In addition, you can set the many properties and conditions associated with a breakpoint. Figure 10.23 shows both a disabled tracepoint and the context menu associated with an individual breakpoint.

TABLE 10.3   The Breakpoint Icons

| Icon | Description |
|---|---|
|  | This icon indicates a standard, enabled breakpoint. When the debugger encounters this line of code, it will stop the application and break into debug mode. |
|  | This icon indicates a standard tracepoint. When the debugger hits this line of code, it will perform the action associated with the tracepoint. |
|  | The plus icon inside the breakpoint indicates an advanced breakpoint that contains a condition, hit count, or filter. |
|  | The plus icon inside the tracepoint indicates an advanced tracepoint that contains a condition, hit count, or filter. |
|  | An empty or hollow breakpoint indicates a disabled breakpoint. The breakpoint is still associated with the line of code. However, the debugger will not recognize the disabled breakpoint until it has been reenabled.<br><br>Hollow icons are associated with types of breakpoint icons such as tracepoints, advanced items, and even breakpoint errors and warnings. In all conditions, the hollow icon indicates that the item is disabled. |
|  | Represents a breakpoint warning indicating that a breakpoint cannot be set due to a temporary condition. This can be the result of debugging not being enabled for a website or debug symbols not being loaded. These icons are set by Visual Studio. |
|  | Represents a tracepoint warning (see preceding description). |

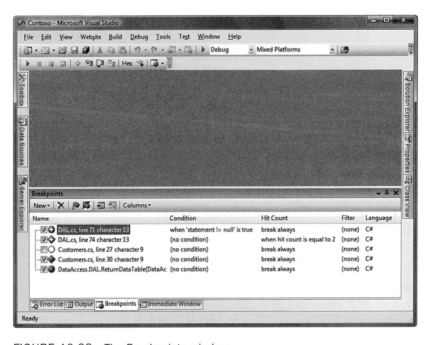

FIGURE 10.22   The Breakpoints window.

TABLE 10.4   The Breakpoints Window Toolbar

| Item | Description |
|------|-------------|
| ![New▾ / Break at Function... Ctrl+D, N / New Data Breakpoint...] | Brings up the new Breakpoints window, allowing you to set a breakpoint at a function. |
| ![X] | Allows you to delete the selected breakpoint in the list. |
| ![delete all icon] | Deletes all breakpoints in the window. |
| ![toggle icon] | Toggles all breakpoints as either on or off. If even one breakpoint in the list is enabled, clicking this icon the first time will disable it (and all others that are enabled). Clicking it a second time (or when all breakpoints are disabled) will enable all breakpoints. |
| ![source icon] | Allows you to go to the source code associated with the selected breakpoint. |
| ![disassembly icon] | Allows you to go to the disassembly information associated with the selected breakpoint. |
| ![Columns menu] | Allows you to choose which columns you want to view in the Breakpoints window. Each column provides information about a given breakpoint. For example, you can see information on the condition associated with each breakpoint, the filename, the function, the filter, the process, and so on. |

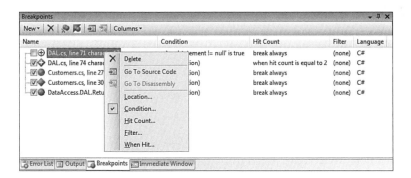

FIGURE 10.23   Managing an individual breakpoint.

Notice that from this context menu, you can delete the breakpoint and navigate to its related source code. More important, however, is the access to setting the conditions and filters associated with the breakpoint. We will cover using each of these options next.

### Breaking Based on Conditions

Often, setting a simple breakpoint is not sufficient (or efficient). For instance, if you are looking for a particular condition to be true in your code—a condition that seems to be causing an exception—then you would prefer to break based on that condition. This saves the time of constantly breaking into a function only to examine a few data points and determine that you have not hit your condition.

There are five types of conditions you can add to a breakpoint: Location, Condition, Hit Count, Filter, and When Hit. You add a condition to a breakpoint from within the Breakpoints window. Select a given breakpoint and then right-click. This brings up the context menu for the given breakpoint. Figure 10.24 shows an example. You can see that each condition is listed for the breakpoint. The following sections highlight the conditional options available for breakpoints.

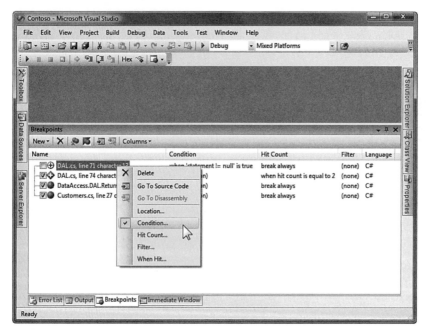

FIGURE 10.24    Accessing breakpoint conditional features.

**Setting a Breakpoint Condition**    A breakpoint condition allows you to break into the debugger or perform an action (tracepoint) when a specific condition is either evaluated as true or has changed. Often, you know that the bug you are working on occurs only based on a very specific condition. Breakpoint conditions are the perfect answer for troubleshooting an intermittent bug.

To set a condition, you select the breakpoint on which you want to apply a condition. You then choose the Condition option from the context (right-click) menu. This will bring up the Breakpoint Condition dialog box, as shown in Figure 10.25. Notice that when setting the condition, you have access to IntelliSense (you can invoke IntelliSense by either clicking a dot or pressing Ctrl+spacebar).

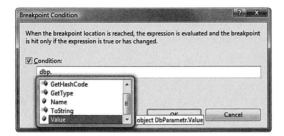

FIGURE 10.25   Setting a breakpoint condition.

When you set a condition, you have two options: Is True and Has Changed. The Is True option allows you to set a Boolean condition that, when evaluated to true, results in the debugger's breaking into the given line of code.

For an example, refer to the sample application. Suppose that you are notified of an error that happens only for a specific customer. You might go to the Customer service class and set a breakpoint inside the Get function. You might then add the Is True condition, id=1234, to the breakpoint (where id is the parameter to the method). This will tell the debugger not to stop on this line of code unless this condition is met. Figure 10.26 shows this condition in the dialog box. It also presents the two options available for conditions.

FIGURE 10.26   The Breakpoint Condition dialog box.

The Has Changed option tells the debugger to break when the value of an expression changes. The first pass through your code sets the value for the first evaluation. If the value changes after that, the debugger will break on a given line. This capability can be useful when you have fields or properties with initial values and you want to track when those values are being changed. In addition, Has Changed can be useful in looping and if...then scenarios in which you are interested in only whether the results of your code changed a particular value.

> **TIP**
>
> Your breakpoint information is persisted between debug sessions. That is, when you close Visual Studio for the day, your breakpoints are still there when you return. This validates the time you might spend setting some sophisticated debugging options. They can remain in your application and be turned on and off as required.

**Breaking on Location**    You can edit a breakpoint to break based on a specific location in a file. Most breakpoints already work this way. That is, they automatically know the file, line number, and character on which to break. However, there are times when you might want to edit this information. For example, suppose your code is slightly out of synch with the running build. You may need to edit your breakpoints to break on a different line of code.

Figure 10.27 shows an example of the File Breakpoint window as accessed from the Location option on the breakpoint context menu. You might also use this feature to quickly set a breakpoint on a specific line without searching your source code.

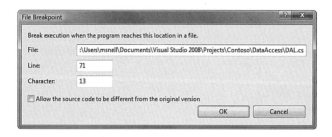

FIGURE 10.27    The File Breakpoint location dialog.

**Setting a Breakpoint Filter**    Breakpoint filters allow you to specify a specific machine, process, or thread on which you want to break. For instance, if your error condition seems to happen only on a certain machine or within a certain process, you can debug this condition specifically with a filter. Filters are most useful in complex debugging scenarios in which your application is highly distributed.

To use this feature, you can specify the machine by name, the process by name or ID, or the thread by name or ID. You can also specify combinations with & (and), ¦¦ (or), and ! (not). This allows you to get to a specific thread on a specific process on a certain machine. Figure 10.28 shows the dialog box in which you set breakpoint filters. In this figure, the breakpoint is being configured to stop provided that the running process is the development web server (WebDev.WebServer.EXE).

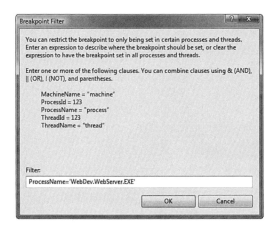

FIGURE 10.28   The Breakpoint Filter dialog box.

**Using a Hit Count with a Breakpoint**   Using the Hit Count command, you can tell the debugger that you want to break when a given line of code is reached a number of times. Typically, you can find a better condition than breaking based on Hit Count. However, This feature is useful in those cases in which you can't determine the actual condition but know that when you pass through a function a certain number of times, something bad happens. In addition, the Hit Count option might be more useful in tracepoint scenarios in which you are emitting data about what is happening in your code. You might want to write that data only periodically.

Figure 10.29 shows the Breakpoint Hit Count dialog box. Notice that this screenshot was taken during an active debug session. You can add any of these conditions to breakpoints during an active debug session. In addition, notice that the current hit count is set to one (1). You have the option to click the Reset button and turn the hit count back to zero and continue debugging from that point.

This dialog box also provides a few options for setting the actual hit count. In the drop-down list under When the Breakpoint Is Hit, the following options are available:

- Break Always (the default and does not invoke the hit count option)
- Break When the Hit Count Is Equal To
- Break When the Hit Count Is a Multiple Of
- Break When the Hit Count Is Greater Than or Equal To

**TIP**

You can combine all the breakpoint conditions we've discussed on a single breakpoint. For example, you may add a condition and a filter to a given breakpoint. Doing so allows you to create even more specific scenarios for debugging your application using breakpoints.

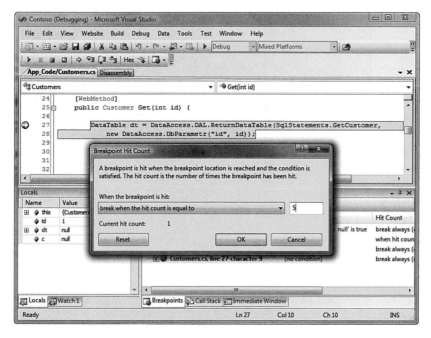

FIGURE 10.29    Setting a breakpoint hit count.

## Working with Tracepoints (When Hit Option)

Tracepoints allow you to emit data to the Output window or run a Visual Studio macro when a specific breakpoint is hit. You then have the option to break into the debugger (like a regular breakpoint), process another condition, or just continue executing the application. This capability can be very useful if you want to keep a running log of what is happening as your application runs in debug mode. You can then review this log to get valuable information about specific conditions and order of execution when an exception is thrown.

You can set tracepoints explicitly by right-clicking a line of code and choosing Insert Tracepoint from the Breakpoint menu. In addition, selecting the When Hit command from the context menu (see Figure 10.24) for a breakpoint in the Breakpoints window will bring up a tracepoint dialog box, which is titled When Breakpoint Is Hit, as shown in Figure 10.30.

The options available for the When Breakpoint Is Hit dialog box include printing a message to the output window, running a macro, and continuing execution. You can choose any combination of these options. The first, printing a message, allows you to output data about your function. There are a number of keywords you can use to output data, such as $FUNCTION for the function name and $CALLER for the name of the calling function. A list of keywords is shown in the instructional text within the dialog box in Figure 10.28. You can also output your specific variable values. You do so by enclosing the variable names in curly braces.

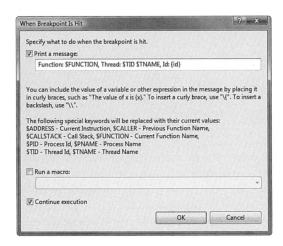

FIGURE 10.30   Setting a tracepoint.

The Continue execution option allows you to indicate whether this is a true tracepoint or a breakpoint that contains a tracing action. If you choose to continue, you get only the trace action (message and/or macro). If you indicate not to continue, you get the trace action, plus the debugger stops on this line of code, just as with a regular breakpoint. This is essentially applying a When Hit action to a standard breakpoint.

Finally, when you select the Run a Macro option, the dialog box gives you a list of all the macros loaded in your environment for selection.

You can also combine tracepoint actions with conditions. When you do so, the action fires only when the breakpoint condition is met.

As an example, we have set a tracepoint inside the web service `Customers.Get()` (see Figure 10.30). This tracepoint prints a message to the output window when the line of code is hit and simply continues executing the application. The message we intend to print is as follows:

```
Function: $FUNCTION, Thread: $TID $TNAME, Id: {id}
```

This message will print the function name, the thread ID and name (if any), and the value of the variable, `id`. Figure 10.31 shows two passes through the tracepoint output in the Output window.

FIGURE 10.31    The results of a tracepoint.

## Viewing Data in the Debugger

After the debugger has thrown you into break mode, the next challenge is to filter all the data your application is emitting. Getting to the right data will help you find problems faster and fix them faster. Visual Studio tries to make the data available where you want it. For example, DataTips show you variable values right in the code editor. There are many similar examples in the way Visual Studio shows debugging data when and where you need it. We will cover these and more throughout the following sections.

### Watching Variables

A common activity in a debug session is to view the values associated with the many types in your application. There are various windows available to help you here. The two most obvious are the Locals and Autos windows.

**Locals Window**    The Locals window shows all the variables and their values for the current debug scope. This gives you a view of everything available in the current, executing method. The variables in this window are set automatically by the debugger. They are organized alphabetically in a list by name. In addition, hierarchy is also shown. For example, if a given variable relates to object type, that object's members are listed inside the variable (as a tree-based structure).

Figure 10.32 shows an example of the Locals window. In it, you can see the sample application paused inside the `Customer.Get` service method. Notice that the customer variable (c) is expanded to show the various properties and fields associated with this object. As values are set, the results are shown in the Value column.

---

**TIP**

You can edit a value in the Locals or Autos window. To do so, right-click the variable and choose Edit Value from the context menu. You can then change the value of the variable directly from within the window (similar to changing variable values using the Immediate window).

---

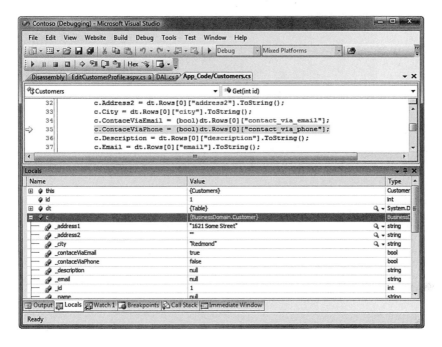

FIGURE 10.32   The Locals window.

**The Autos Window**   Often, viewing all the locals provides too many options to sort through. This can be true when there is just too much in scope in the given process or function. To home in on the values associated with the line of code you are looking at, you can use the Autos window. This window shows the value of all variables and expressions that are in the current executing line of code or in the preceding line of code. This allows you to really focus on just the values you are currently debugging.

Figure 10.33 shows the Autos window for the same line of code as was shown in Figure 10.32. Notice the difference in what is shown. Also, notice that Visual Studio has even added specific expressions that differ from the code to the watch list. For example, the call to dt.Rows[0]["contact_via_email"] is shown as an item in the Autos window.

**The Watch Windows**   The Visual Studio Watch windows allow you to set a custom list of variables and expressions that you want to keep an eye on. In this way, you decide the items in which you are interested. The Watch windows look and behave just like the Locals and Autos windows. In addition, the items you place in Watch windows persist from one debug session to another.

You access each Watch window from the Debug menu or toolbar. The four Watch windows are named Watch 1, Watch 2, Watch 3, and Watch 4. Having four Watch windows allows you to set up four custom lists of items you want to monitor. This capability can be especially helpful if each custom list applies to a separate scope in your application.

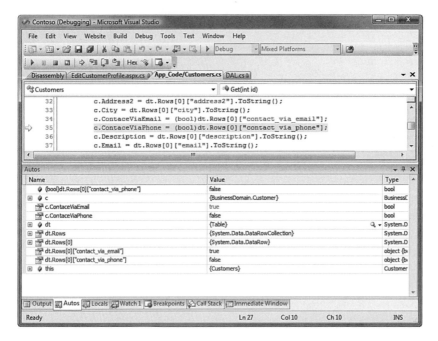

FIGURE 10.33   The Autos window.

You add a variable or an expression to the Watch window from either the code editor or the QuickWatch window. If you are in the code editor, you select a variable or highlight an expression, right-click, and choose the Add Watch menu item. This will take the highlighted variable or expression and place it in the Watch window. You can also drag and drop the highlighted item into a Watch window.

**QuickWatch**   The QuickWatch window is very similar to the other Watch windows. However, it allows you to focus on a single variable or expression. The QuickWatch window has been used less often since DataTips were introduced in 2005. From the QuickWatch window, you can write expressions and add them to the Watch window. When writing your expression, you have access to IntelliSense. Figure 10.34 shows the QuickWatch window.

The item you add to QuickWatch will be evaluated when you click the Reevaluate button. Clicking the Add Watch button will send the variable to the Watch 1 window.

### DataTips

DataTips allow you to highlight a variable or an expression in your code editor and get watch information right there in the editor. This feature is more in tune with how developers work. For example, if you are looking at a line of code, you might highlight something in that line to evaluate it. You could do this by creating a QuickWatch. However, you can also simply hover over the item and its data will simply unfold in a DataTip.

FIGURE 10.34   The QuickWatch window.

Figure 10.35 provides an example. Here, the cursor is positioned over the variable that is of type Customer. Clicking on the plus sign to expand this variable unfolds the many members of the object. You can scroll through this list using the arrow at the bottom of the window. You can also right-click any member in the list and edit its value, copy it, or add it to the watch window. The magnifying glass icon next to the items in the list allows you to select a specific visualizer for a given item (more on visualizers shortly).

You can also select an expression and have it evaluated as a DataTip. For example, if you select the portion of line 34 in Figure 10.35 that reads (bool)dt.Rows[0]["contact_via_email"], a DataTip will show this variable and its value of true.

---

**TIP**

The DataTips window can often get in the way of viewing code. Sometimes, you need to see the DataTips and the code underneath. In this case, holding the Control (Ctrl) key will make the DataTips window transparent for as long as you press it.

---

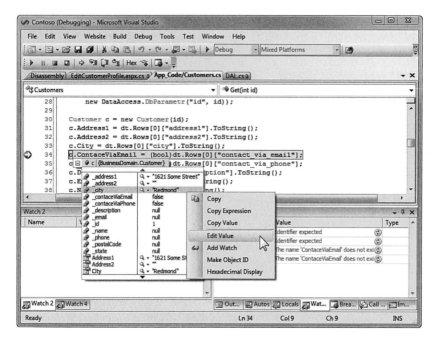

FIGURE 10.35   The DataTips window.

## Visualizing Data

When you are looking at variable values, what you really want to get to is the data behind the object. Sometimes this data is obscured by the object model itself. For example, suppose you are looking for the data that is contained in a DataSet object. To find it, you have to dig many layers deep in a watch window or a DataTip. You have to traverse the inner workings of the object model just to get at something as basic as the data contained by the object. If you've spent much time doing this, you know how frustrating it can be.

Visual Studio offers a quick, easy way to access the data contained in an object. It does so through a tool called a *visualizer*. Visualizers are meant to present the object's data in a meaningful way.

A few visualizers ship with Visual Studio by default, including these:

▶ **HTML**—Shows a browser-like dialog box with the HTML interpreted as a user might see it.

▶ **XML**—Shows the XML in a structured format.

▶ **Text**—Shows a string value in an easy-to-read format.

▶ **DataSet**—Shows the contents of the DataSet, DataView, and DataTable objects.

There is also a framework for writing and installing visualizers in Visual Studio. You can write your own and plug them into the debugger. You can also download additional visualizers and install them. The possibilities of visualizers are many—as many ways as there are to structure and view data. A few ideas might be a tree-view visualizer that displays hierarchical data or an image visualizer that shows image data structures.

You invoke a visualizer from one of the many places you view data values. This includes watch windows and DataTips. Visualizers are represented by a magnifying glass icon. Refer back to Figure 10.35 to see an example of launching a visualizer using this icon. Rather than digging through the object hierarchy to get at the data, you can invoke the DataSet visualizer right from a DataTip. Figure 10.36 shows the visualizer in action for the customer DataSet object in the sample application.

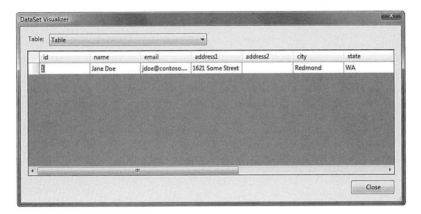

FIGURE 10.36    The DataSet Visualizer.

## Using the Edit and Continue Feature

Edit and Continue allows you to change code as you debug without killing your debug session. You can make a modification to a line of code or even fix a bug and keep working in break mode. Visual Basic developers who worked in versions prior to .NET should recall this powerful tool. Its absence in .NET made it one of the most requested features. The good news is that Edit and Continue was added in 2005 to both Visual Basic and C#. In 2008, this feature was also added to Visual C++.

There is no trick to invoking Edit and Continue. You simply make your code change during a debug session and then keep running through your code with a Step command or Continue.

The feature is turned on by default. If it is turned off, you can reenable it using the Options dialog box available from the Tools menu.

Not all code changes you make are eligible for Edit and Continue. In fact, it should be used only in minor fixes. Any major additions to your code should not be done in debug mode just as a best practice. If your change is within the body of a method, it has a higher likelihood of passing the Edit and Continue test. Most code changes outside the method body require the debugger to restart. Some common changes that are not eligible for Edit and Continue include these:

▶ Changing code on the current, active statement

▶ Changing code on any calls on the stack that lead to the current, active statement

▶ Adding new types, methods, fields, events, or properties

▶ Changing a method signature

For a more exhaustive list, search MSDN for "Edit and Continue." From there, you can link to the Edit and Continue documentation for your chosen language. You can then select the link, titled "Supported Code Changes." Here you can review the full list of supported and unsupported changes for your chosen language.

# Advanced Debugging Scenarios

Debugging can sometimes be a complex process. We've looked at many of the straightforward scenarios presented by Windows and Web applications. However, debugging remote processes and multithreaded applications, for example, present their own needs in terms of configuration and tools. This section presents a few of the more common, advanced debugging scenarios you will encounter.

## Remote Debugging

Remote debugging allows you to connect to a running application on another machine or domain and debug that application in its environment. This is often the only way to experience errors that are occurring on specific hardware. We've all heard the developer's cry, "Works on my machine." Remote debugging helps those developers figure out why their application doesn't work in other environments.

In various scenarios, remote debugging makes a lot of sense. They include debugging SQL server–stored procedures, web services, web applications, remote services or processes, and so on.

The hardest part about doing remote debugging is getting it set up properly. The actual debugging is no different from the debugging we've discussed thus far. However, the setup requires you to jump through a lot of hoops in terms of installation and security. These hoops are necessary because you do not, by default, want developers to easily connect debug sessions to applications on your servers.

There is some good news. Visual Studio tries to minimize and simplify the setup and configuration of remote debugging. Microsoft has written the Remote Debugging Monitor (`msvsmon.exe`) for this purpose. However, developers will still find the setup tasks somewhat arduous (but rewarding when finished). We will not cover the setup in great detail here because it is often environment-specific. We suggest querying MSDN for "Remote Debugging" to get the full walk-through and troubleshooting advice for your specific situation.

We do offer the following, however, as a set of high-level tasks that you will need to complete to get remote debugging working:

1. Install the remote debugging monitor (`msvsmon.exe`) on the remote machine being debugged. You install it using the setup application, `rdbsetup.exe`. You can also run it from a file share.

2. Configure remote debugging permissions. Typically, this means one of two things. You can set up identical accounts (username and password) on both machines (debugging and server). The debugging account may be local or a domain account. However, the server account should be a local account. Alternatively, you can give your user account administrative access to the machine being debugged. This is often a security risk that should not be taken lightly.

3. Run the remote debugging monitor on the remote machine. This is a Windows application (with a GUI). You can also set the monitor to run as a Windows service. This capability can be useful for specific server scenarios and ASP.NET remote debugging.

4. If your debug machine is running XP with SP2, you will have to configure your security policy and firewall for remote debugging (see the MSDN documentation "How to: Set Up Remote Debugging"). If you are running Windows Vista, you may have to elevate privileges when running Visual Studio (run as Administrator).

5. Run Visual Studio on your debug machine as you would to debug any process. Open the project that contains the source for the process you want to debug.

6. Attach to the running process on the remote machine using Attach to Process. You will have to browse to the machine you want to debug and find the process running on that machine.

As you can see, getting remote debugging set up can be a challenge. However, if you have a test environment that you typically debug, the setup should be a one-time operation. From there, you should be able to debug in a more realistic environment as well as walk through SQL stored procedures.

## Debugging WCF Services

For the most part, you debug a web service (or Windows Communication Foundation service) using the same tools and techniques we've discussed to this point. The key to debugging services is properly attaching to them. There are basically two options for this. The first option is to step into a service directly from within code you are debugging (a client calling a service). The second option is to attach to a service that has already been called by a client. Let's look at these options.

### Stepping Into a WCF Service

You can step directly into a WCF service provided that your calling code (or client) has a two-way contract with the service. This is called a Duplex Contract. Such a contract allows the client and the service to communicate with one another. Each can initiate calls. This is useful when your server needs to call back to the client or raise events on the client. You use the `ServiceContractAttribute` to set this up (see Chapter 19, "Service-Oriented Applications," for more information).

Your client must also be synchronous for this to work. That is, the client cannot make a call to the WCF service asynchronously and then begin doing something else. Instead, it must call and wait.

### Attaching to a WCF Service

You can use the Attach to Process option (covered earlier) to debug both WCF and Web Services (.asmx). In these cases, the service is already running typically in a process outside of your current debug environment. To attach and debug to this process, you must make sure you have the code for the service loaded inside of Visual Studio. Next, the service process must be hosted by IIS or the ASP.NET Development Server. Finally, the service must have been invoked by a WCF-based client to gain access to its execution.

## Debugging Multithreaded Applications

A multithreaded application is one in which more than a single thread is running in a given process. By default, each process that runs your application has at least one thread of execution. You might create multiple threads to do parallel processing. This can significantly improve performance, especially when run on today's multicore processors and hyperthreading technology. However, multithreading comes at a cost. The code can be more complex to write and more difficult to debug. If you've ever written a multithreaded application, you already know this.

Fortunately, Visual Studio provides a few tools that make the job a bit easier. We will not cover coding a multithreaded application here; rather, we will cover the debug options available to you for debugging one. The following lists these tools and features:

- Ability to view threads in your source during a debug session
- The Debug Location toolbar used to view processes, threads, and flagged threads
- The Thread window used to work with a list of threads in your application
- Breakpoint filters that allow you to set a breakpoint for an individual thread

Let's look at each of these features in more detail.

### Discovering and Flagging Threads

Visual Studio allows you to visualize the threads in your application in debug mode. When you are stopped on a breakpoint, your application is paused and you are debugging the active thread. At this time, the other threads in your application are still there. However, they may not be visible. To see them in the debug menu, you can use the Show Threads in Source option from the Debug menu, as shown in Figure 10.37.

FIGURE 10.37   Show/hide threads in source option.

Selecting this option will highlight other threads that exist in your code. These lines of code are highlighted for you in the indicator margin (or gutter) of the code window during a debug session. The icon used to highlight these items looks like two wavy lines (or cloth threads). Figure 10.38 shows an example.

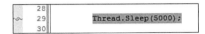

FIGURE 10.38   A thread highlighted in the indicator margin.

Notice the graphic on the left of line 29. This indicates that a thread exists at this location in your source code. Hovering over this indicator shows the thread (or threads) that are referenced by the indicator. Each thread is shown by its ID number (in brackets) and name (if any). Figure 10.39 shows an example.

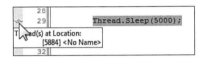

FIGURE 10.39   Hovering over a thread indicator.

**TIP**

Naming threads can help you better identify them when debugging. To name a thread, you use the Threading namespace. Specifically, call the Name property of the Thread class.

Now that you've found a thread, you might want to flag it for further monitoring. This simply helps group it with the threads you want to monitor versus those you do not care about. You can flag a thread right from the indicator margin. To do so, right-click the indicator and choose the Flag option on the context menu. Figure 10.40 shows an example.

FIGURE 10.40   Flagging a thread.

You can unflag threads the same way. You can also flag threads directly in the Thread window. Flagged threads provide special grouping in both the Thread window and the Debug Location toolbar. We will cover these features next.

## Managing Debug Processes and Threads

You can switch between the processes you are debugging and the threads within those processes by using the Debug Location toolbar. This toolbar is shown in Figure 10.41. On the left is the Process list. Here you can select a process to view details about that process, including executing threads. Many multithreaded applications are run within a single process, however.

FIGURE 10.41   The Debug Location toolbar.

The Thread list on the toolbar shows a list of threads for the selected process. This list is highlighted in Figure 10.41. Notice that threads are shown with their ID, name, and flag indicator. You can select a thread in this list to jump to source code associated with the thread. If no source code is associated with a selected thread, the thread name will be shown as red when selected. You can filter this list to show only flagged threads by toggling the second button to the right of the Thread list (shown with two flags). The first button to the right simply flags (or unflags) the current, active thread. Finally, the list on the right shows the call stack. The active stack frame in the call stack is what gets shown in the debug windows (watch, local, autos, and so on).

You can also manage threads from within the Threads window (Debug menu, Windows, Threads). Here you will see all threads listed for a given process. Figure 10.42 shows an example. Notice that the left of the list shows flagged threads. Here we have flagged the two threads in a sample application. Notice also that these threads are named. This allows for easy recognition in the Name column.

| | ID | Category | Name | Location | Priority | Suspend |
|---|---|---|---|---|---|---|
| | 6064 | Worker Thread | <No Name> | | Highest | 0 |
| | 5704 | Worker Thread | Instance caller | ServerClass.InstanceMethod | Normal | 0 |
| | 4480 | Worker Thread | Static caller | ServerClass.StaticMethod | Normal | 0 |
| | 4156 | | ame> | | Normal | 0 |
| | 2984 | | ame> | | | 0 |
| | 2696 | | ame> | | Normal | 0 |
| | 532 | | ystemEvents | | Normal | 0 |

Copy
Select All
Hexadecimal Display
Hide Threads in Source
Switch To Thread
Rename
Freeze
Unflag
Unflag All Threads

FIGURE 10.42   The Threads window.

There are several options available from the Threads window. They are shown in the context menu in Figure 10.42. Notice the option Switch to Thread. This allows you to switch the active thread being debugged. The active thread is shown with a yellow arrow in the thread list (to the right of the flag). Switching active threads will change the debug context and content in the debug windows. You can also Freeze (or pause) threads using this context menu. This is equivalent to suspending a thread.

### Breaking Based on a Specific Thread

You can also decide to break on a line of code based on the calling thread. To do so, set a breakpoint and choose a breakpoint filter (covered earlier). Figure 10.43 shows an example. You can choose to break based on the thread ID or its name. In this case, the breakpoint will be hit based on the latter option. Of course, this requires that you give the thread a name within your code.

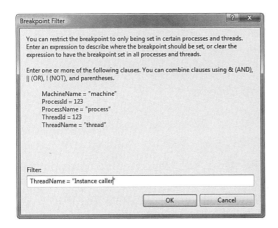

FIGURE 10.43    Setting a breakpoint filter based on a thread.

## Debugging a Client-Side Script

Visual Studio lets you debug your client-side VBScript and JScript. To do so, you must enable script debugging in the browser. This can be done using the menu, via Tools, Internet Options, inside Internet Explorer. From the Internet Options dialog, select the Advanced tab and then navigate to the Browsing category. Figure 10.44 shows an example. Here you will want to uncheck the box Disable Script Debugging (checked by default).

Next, set breakpoints inside your `.aspx` or `.html` files within your `<script>` blocks. You can then stop on these lines and debug them with Visual Studio. There are some limitations, however. If you are having trouble, review "Limitations on Script Debugging" in the MSDN documentation.

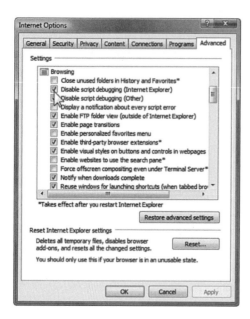

FIGURE 10.44    Enable script debugging in Internet Explorer.

# Summary

This chapter presented the Visual Studio 2008 debugger. We covered setting breakpoints in code as well as setting conditions for when those breakpoints are hit. We discussed stepping through code after hitting that breakpoint. In addition, we presented tracepoints, which perform an action (such as printing a message to the output window) when a line of code is hit in the debugger. The chapter also examined the many ways you can see the data presented by the debugger, including the watch windows, visualizers, and DataTips. Finally, we covered advanced debugging scenarios presented by remote processes, web services, multithreaded applications, and client-side script.

The Visual Studio 2008 debugger is sure to speed your overall development effort. This is a key skill to have. Honing your skills with the debugging tools is yet another way to unlock additional productivity.

# PART IV

# Extending Visual Studio

## IN THIS PART

# Introducing the Automation Object Model

Visual Studio is built to be "extensible." It ships with its own API to enable you, the developer, to control many of the pieces of the IDE.

The API is called the *Visual Studio automation object model*, and understanding its capabilities is the key to unlocking your ability to program and control the IDE itself by writing code in the form of macros and add-ins (discussed in Chapter 12, "Writing Macros," and Chapter 13, "Writing Add-ins and Wizards").

In this chapter, we discuss the layout and structure of the automation object model. We map the various objects in the object model to their IDE counterparts, delve into the various ways to interact with these objects through managed code, and, we hope, start to see a glimpse of the possibilities in terms of Visual Studio customization.

To drive home the object model concepts and place them in context, we have provided various code snippets and listings, nearly 100% of which are written in Visual Basic. The reason is that Visual Basic is the language of macros (other languages are not supported), and macros are by far the easiest and quickest way to reach out and touch elements of the IDE. As such, macros are a perfect vehicle for exploring and understanding the object model. In Chapters 12 and 13, we'll move beyond the object model and work to understand how to use, write, and run macros and add-ins (add-ins don't suffer from the Visual Basic limitation, so we'll switch gears and provide most of our add-in code using C#).

Don't worry too much about the mechanics of writing an add-in or macro at this point; concentrate instead on understanding the automation objects and how they are referenced and used. For the ambitious, know that the code listings here can be pasted directly into the Macros IDE Editor and run as is.

# An Overview of the Automation Object Model

The automation object model is a structured class library with a top-level root object called DTE (or DTE2; more on this in a bit), which stands for Development Tools Environment. By referencing the assembly that implements the DTE/DTE2 object, you can instance this root object and use its members and child classes to access the IDE components.

## Object Model Versions

The automation object model is actually implemented across three different, complementary primary interoperable assemblies: EnvDTE, EnvDTE80, and EnvDTE90. EnvDTE is the original automation assembly distributed with Visual Studio .NET 2003. EnvDTE80 was the library distributed with Visual Studio 2005, and EnvDTE90 is distributed with Visual Studio 2008. The reason for multiple assemblies is simple: They help balance the need for new features against the need to preserve backward compatibility. For instance, with Visual Studio 2008, Microsoft was faced with a common design decision: replace or upgrade the previous assembly shipped with Visual Studio 2005 (EnvDTE80) and risk introducing incompatibilities with current macros and add-ins, or ship a new assembly that could be leveraged in cases in which the new functionality was desired (existing code would still target the previous, unchanged library).

The latter path was chosen, and thus EnvDTE90 (90 represents version 9.0) contains automation types and members that are new to Visual Studio 2008, while EnvDTE80 (for Visual Studio 2005) and EnvDTE (for older versions of Visual Studio) provide the base level of functionality and backward compatibility.

Within the EnvDTE90 assembly, you will find types that supersede their predecessors from the EnvDTE80 assembly, and the same is true for types within EnvDTE80 that supersede types implemented in EnvDTE. In these cases, the type name has been appended with a number to indicate the revised version. Thus, we have DTE and DTE2; Solution, Solution2, and Solution3; and so on.

Table 11.1 provides a side-by-side listing of some of the most important types implemented in the EnvDTE libraries. This type list is incomplete; it should be considered for reference only. This table is useful, however, for identifying some of the newly minted types in the new automation assembly; in the next section, we'll see how these types can be organized into broad Visual Studio automation categories and how they map onto physical IDE constructs.

TABLE 11.1   Partial List of Automation Types

| Type | Description |
|---|---|
| AddIn | Represents a VS add-in. |
| Breakpoint, Breakpoint2 | Represents a debugger breakpoint. |
| BuildDependencies | For the selected project, represents a collection of BuildDependency objects. |
| BuildDependency | For the selected project, the projects that it depends on for a successful build. |
| BuildEvents | Exposes a list of events relevant to a solution build. |
| Command | Represents a command action in the IDE. |
| Commands, Commands2 | A collection of all commands supported in the IDE. |
| CommandWindow | Represents the command window. |
| Configuration | Represents a project's configuration properties. |
| Debugger, Debugger2, Debugger3 | Represents the Visual Studio debugger. |
| DebuggerEvents | Exposes events from the debugger. |
| Document | Represents an open document in the IDE. |
| Documents | A collection of all open documents in the IDE. |
| DTE | Represents the IDE; this is the top-level, root object for the automation object model. |
| EditPoint | Represents a text operation point within a document. |
| Events | Exposes all automation events. |
| ExceptionGroups | Represents the exception grouping categories supported by Visual Studio (new to Visual Studio 2008). |
| Find | Represents the Find capability for text searches in the IDE. |
| HTMLWindow, HTMLWindow3 | Represents an HTML document window. |
| OutputWindow | Represents the Output window. |
| Program, (Process2) | Represents a program running within the IDE; useful for examining process and threads within the program. EnvDTE80 functionality is provided by the Process2 object. |
| Project | Represents a project loaded in the IDE. |
| ProjectItem | Represents an item contained within a given project. |
| ProjectItems | A collection of all items contained within a project. |
| Property | Represents a generic property for an object (this can be used across various objects in the automation library). |
| SelectedItem | Represents projects or project items that are currently selected in the IDE. |
| Solution, Solution2, Solution3 | Represents the solution currently loaded in Visual Studio. |

## 11

TABLE 11.1    Continued

| Type | Description |
|------|-------------|
| `SourceControl,` `SourceControl2` | Represents the source control system of record within Visual Studio. |
| `TaskItem` | Represents an item in the Task List window. |
| `TaskItems, TaskItems2` | A collection of all items in the Task List window. |
| `TaskList` | Represents the Task List window. |
| `Template` | Represents a Visual Studio template (new to Visual Studio 2008). |
| `TextDocument` | Represents a text file open in the IDE. |
| `TextPane, TextPane2` | Represents a pane within an open text editor window. |
| `TextWindow` | Represents a text window. |
| `ToolBox` | Represents the Toolbox window. |
| `ToolBoxItem,` `ToolBoxItem2` | Represents an item within the Toolbox window. |
| `ToolBoxTab,` `ToolboxTab2,` `ToolboxTab3` | Represents a tab of items on the Toolbox window. |
| `Window, Window2` | Represents, generically, any window within the IDE. |
| `Windows, Windows2` | A collection of all windows within the IDE. |

## Automation Categories

Because any automation effort with Visual Studio starts with the object model, you should first understand how it maps onto the IDE constructs and determine the exact capabilities it exposes.

In general, you can think of the object model classes as being organized into categories that directly speak to these IDE concepts:

- ▶ Solutions and projects
- ▶ Windows and command bars (toolbars and menu bars)
- ▶ Documents
- ▶ Commands
- ▶ Debugger
- ▶ Events

Each of the objects in these categories touches a different piece of the IDE, and access to each object is typically through the root-level DTE2 object.

# The DTE/DTE2 Root Object

The DTE/DTE2 object represents the tip of the API tree. You can think of it as representing Visual Studio itself, with the objects under it mapping to the various constituent parts of the IDE.

As mentioned previously, DTE2 is the most current version of this, with DTE providing compatibility with previous versions. In this chapter, unless we specifically need to differentiate between their capabilities, we will generically refer to the DTE and DTE2 objects as simply DTE.

The DTE properties are used to gain a reference to a specific IDE object (or collection of objects). Methods on the object are used to execute commands in the IDE, launch wizards, or close the IDE.

Table 11.2 shows the major properties and methods defined on the DTE2 object; they have been organized within the six object categories itemized in the preceding section.

TABLE 11.2   DTE2 Properties and Methods for IDE Access

| Category | Property | Description |
|---|---|---|
| Commands | Commands | Returns a collection of Command objects; in general, a command is an action that can be carried out within the IDE such as opening or saving a file. |
| Debugger | Debugger | Returns the debugger object. |
| Documents | ActiveDocument | Returns a Document object representing the currently active document. |
| Documents | Documents | Returns a collection of Document objects representing all open documents. |
| Event Notification | Events | Returns the Events object for handling event notifications. |
| Solutions and Projects | ActiveSolutionProjects | Returns a collection of the Project objects representing the projects that are currently selected within the Solution Explorer. |
| Solutions and Projects | Solution | Returns the Solution object for the currently loaded solution. |
| Windows and Command Bars | ActiveWindow | Returns a Window object representing the window within the IDE that currently has focus. |
| Windows and Command Bars | CommandBars | Returns a collection of CommandBar objects representing all the toolbars and menu bars. |
| Windows and Command Bars | MainWindow | Returns a Window object representing the IDE window itself. |

TABLE 11.2    Continued

| Category | Property | Description |
|---|---|---|
| Windows and Command Bars | StatusBar | Returns a `StatusBar` object representing Visual Studio's status bar. |
| Windows and Command Bars | ToolWindows | Returns a `ToolWindows` instance, which in turns provides access to a few of the most prominent tool windows: the command window, error list, output window, Solution Explorer, task list, and toolbox. |
| Windows and Command Bars | WindowConfigurations | Returns a collection of `WindowConfiguration` objects; these objects represent the various window layouts in use by Visual Studio. |

| Category | Method | Description |
|---|---|---|
| Commands | ExecuteCommand | Executes an environment command. |
| — | LaunchWizard | Starts the identified wizard with the given parameters. |
| — | Quit | Closes Visual Studio. |

**NOTE**

The mechanics of referencing and instancing a DTE object change slightly depending on whether you are writing an add-in or a macro, so we'll cover the specifics in the macro and add-in sections in Chapters 12 and 13.

In summary, the DTE object is a tool for directly interacting with certain IDE components and providing access to the deeper layers of the API with its property collections. If you move one level down in the API, you find the major objects that form the keystone for automation.

# Solution and Project Objects

The Solution object represents the currently loaded solution. The individual projects within the solution are available via Project objects returned within the Solution.Projects collection. Items within a project are accessed in a similar fashion through the Project.ProjectItems collection.

As you can see from Figure 11.1, this hierarchy exactly mirrors the solution/project hierarchy that we first discussed in Chapter 4, "Solutions and Projects."

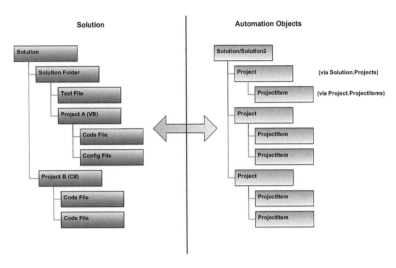

FIGURE 11.1   Mapping the solution/project hierarchy.

There are some mismatches here—solution folders, for instance, are treated as projects—but for the most part, the object model tree closely resembles the solution project tree that you are used to.

The Solution object and Solution2 object members allow you to interact with the current solution to perform common tasks such as these:

▶ Determining the number of projects in the solution (Count property)

▶ Adding a project to the solution based on a project file (AddFromFile method)

▶ Creating a new solution or closing the current one (Create and Close methods)

▶ Saving the solution (SaveAs method)

▶ Removing a project from the solution (Remove method)

You can also directly retrieve a reference to any of the projects within the currently loaded solution by iterating over the Solution.Projects collection. As an example of interacting with the Solution and Project objects, this Visual Basic code snippet removes the first project from the current solution:

```
Dim sol As Solution = DTE.Solution
Dim proj As Project = sol.Projects.Item(1)

If proj.Saved Then
            sol.Remove(proj)
Else
    ...
End If
```

Table 11.3 provides the combined list of the most commonly used properties and methods implemented by Solution3.

TABLE 11.3    Primary Solution/Solution2/Solution3 Type Members

| Property | Description |
| --- | --- |
| AddIns | Returns a collection of AddIn objects associated with the current solution. |
| Count | A count of the project within the solution. |
| DTE | A reference back to the parent DTE object. |
| FullName | The full path and name of the solution file. |
| Globals | Returns the Globals object, a cache of variables used across the solution. |
| IsOpen | Indicates whether a solution is open. |
| Projects | Returns a collection of Project objects representing all the projects within the solution. |
| Properties | Returns a collection of Property objects that expose all the solution's properties. |
| Saved | Indicates whether the solution has been saved since the last modification. |
| SolutionBuild | Returns a reference to a SolutionBuild object; this is the entry point to the build automation objects applicable for the current solution. |
| **Method** | **Description** |
| AddFromFile | Adds a project to the solution using an existing project file. |
| AddFromTemplate | Takes an existing project, clones it, and adds it to the solution. |
| AddSolutionFolder | Creates a new solution folder in the solution. |
| Close | Closes the solution. |
| Create | Creates an empty solution. |
| FindProjectItem | Initiates a search for a given item in one of the solution's projects. |
| GetProjectItem-Template | Returns the path to the template used for the referenced project item. |
| GetProjectTemplate | Returns the path to the template used for the referenced project. |
| Item | Returns a Project instance. |
| Open | Opens a solution (using a specific view). |
| Remove | Removes a project from the solution. |
| SaveAs | Saves the solution. |

## Controlling Projects in a Solution

One of the things that the `Solution` object is good for is retrieving references to the various projects that belong to the solution. Each `Project` object has its own set of useful members for interacting with the projects and their items. By using these members, you can interact with the projects in various, expected ways, such as renaming a project, deleting a project, and saving a project.

See Table 11.4 for a summary of the most common `Project` members.

TABLE 11.4   Primary `Project` Object Members

| Property | Description |
| --- | --- |
| AddIns | Returns a collection of `AddIn` objects associated with the current solution. |
| Count | Returns a count of the project within the solution. |
| DTE | Provides a reference back to the parent `DTE` object. |
| FullName | Provides the full path and name of the solution file. |
| IsOpen | Indicates whether a solution is open. |
| Projects | Returns a collection of `Project` objects representing all the projects within the solution. |
| Properties | Returns a collection of `Property` objects that expose all the solution's properties. |
| Saved | Indicates whether the solution has been saved since the last modification. |
| SolutionBuild | Returns a reference to a `SolutionBuild` object. This is the entry point to the build automation objects applicable for the current solution. |
| **Method** | **Description** |
| AddFromFile | Adds a project to the solution using an existing project file. |
| AddFromTemplate | Takes an existing project, clones it, and adds it to the solution. |
| AddSolutionFolder | Creates a new solution folder in the solution. |
| Close | Closes the solution. |
| Create | Creates an empty solution. |
| FindProjectItem | Initiates a search for a given item in one of the solution's projects. |
| Item | Returns a `Project` instance. |
| Open | Opens a solution (using a specific view). |
| Remove | Removes a project from the solution. |
| SaveAs | Saves the solution. |

## Accessing Code Within a Project

Beyond the basic project attributes and items, one of the cooler things that can be accessed via a `Project` instance is the actual code within the project's source files. Through the `CodeModel` property, you can access an entire line of proxy objects representing the code constructs within a project. For instance, the `CodeClass` interface allows you to examine *and edit* the code for a given class in a given project.

> **NOTE**
>
> Support for the different `CodeModel` entities varies from language to language. The MSDN documentation for each `CodeModel` type clearly indicates the source language support for that element.

After grabbing a `CodeModel` reference from a `Project` instance, you can access its `CodeElements` collection (which is, not surprisingly, a collection of `CodeElement` objects). A `CodeElement` is nothing more than a generic representation of a certain code structure within a project. The `CodeElement` object is generic, but it provides a property, `Kind`. This property is used to determine the exact native type of the code object contained within the `CodeElement`.

The `CodeElement.Kind` property is an enumeration (of type `vsCMElement`) that identifies the specific type of code construct lurking within the `CodeElement` object. Using the `Kind` property, you can first determine the true nature of the code element and then cast the `CodeElement` object to its strong type. Here is a snippet of C# code that does just that:

```
if (element.Kind == vsCMElement.vsCMElementClass)
 {
         CodeClass myClass = (CodeClass)element;
 }
```

For a better grasp of the code model hierarchy, consider the C# code presented in Listing 11.1; this is a "shell" solution that merely implements a namespace, a class within that namespace, and a function within the class.

LISTING 11.1   A Simple Namespace and Class Implementation

```
using System;
using System.Collections.Generic;
using System.Text;

namespace MyNamespace
{
    class MyClass
    {
        public string SumInt(int x, int y)
        {
```

```
            return (x + y).ToString();
        }
    }
}
```

If you map the code in Listing 11.1 to the code object model, you would end up with the structure shown in Figure 11.2.

To get an idea of the complete depth of the code model tree that can be accessed through the `CodeElements` collection, consult Table 11.5; this table shows all the possible `vsCMElement` values, the type they are used to represent, and a brief description of the type.

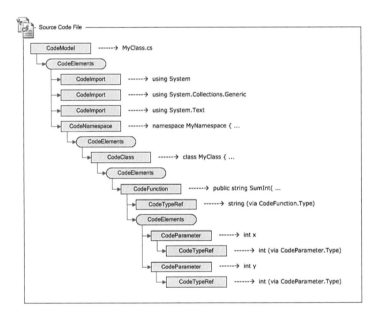

FIGURE 11.2   A simple code model object hierarchy.

TABLE 11.5   Mapping the `vsCMElement` Enumeration Values

| Enumeration Value | Type | Description |
| --- | --- | --- |
| vsCMElementAssignmentStmt | | An assignment statement |
| vsCMElementAttribute | | An attribute |
| vsCMElementClass | CodeClass | A class |
| vsCMElementDeclareDecl | | A declaration |
| vsCMElementDefineStmt | | A define statement |
| vsCMElementDelegate | CodeDelegate | A delegate |
| vsCMElementEnum | CodeEnum | An enumeration |

TABLE 11.5    Continued

| Enumeration Value | Type | Description |
| --- | --- | --- |
| vsCMElementEvent | CodeEvent | An event |
| vsCMElementEventsDeclaration | | An event declaration |
| vsCMElementFunction | CodeFunction | A function |
| vsCMElementFunctionInvokeStmt | | A statement invoking a function |
| vsCMElementIDLCoClass | | An IDL co-class |
| vsCMElementIDLImport | | An IDL import statement |
| vsCMElementIDLImportLib | | An IDL import library |
| vsCMElementIDLLibrary | | An IDL library |
| vsCMElementImplementsStmt | | An implements statement |
| vsCMElementImportStmt | CodeImport | An import statement |
| vsCMElementIncludeStmt | | An include statement |
| vsCMElementInheritsStmt | | An inherits statement |
| vsCMElementInterface | CodeInterface | An interface |
| vsCMElementLocalDeclStmt | | A local declaration statement |
| vsCMElementMacro | | A macro |
| vsCMElementMap | | A map |
| vsCMElementMapEntry | | A map entry |
| vsCMElementModule | | A module |
| vsCMElementNamespace | CodeNamespace | A namespace |
| vsCMElementOptionStmt | | An option statement |
| vsCMElementOther | CodeElement | A code element not otherwise identified in this enum |
| vsCMElementParameter | CodeParameter | A parameter |
| vsCMElementProperty | CodeProperty | A property |
| vsCMElementPropertySetStmt | | A property set statement |
| vsCMElementStruct | CodeStruct | A structure |
| vsCMElementTypeDef | | A type definition |
| vsCMElementUDTDecl | | A user-defined type |
| vsCMElementUnion | | A union |
| vsCMElementUsingStmt | CodeImport | A using statement |
| vsCMElementVariable | | A variable |
| vsCMElementVBAttributeGroup | | A Visual Basic attribute group |
| vsCMElementVBAttributeStmt | | A Visual Basic attribute statement |
| vsCMElementVCBase | | A Visual C++ base |

# Windows

The visible, content portion of Visual Studio is represented by `Window` objects. `Window` objects are instances of open windows within the IDE such as the Solution Explorer, the Task List window, an open code editor window, and so on. Even the IDE itself is represented by a `Window` object.

Any given window is either a document window or a tool window. Document windows host documents that are editable by the Text Editor. Tool windows contain controls that display information relevant to the current context of the IDE; the Solution Explorer and Task List windows are examples of tool windows, and a VB source code file open in an editor is an example of a document window.

## Referencing Windows

If you need to retrieve an instance of a specific window, you have a few different options, each optimal for a given situation. For starters, the main IDE window is always available directly from the `DTE` object:

```
Dim IDE As Window
IDE = DTE.MainWindow
```

Obviously, if you need to perform a specific action against the IDE window, this is your quickest route.

The `DTE.ActiveWindow` property also provides direct and quick access to a `Window` object, in this case the currently active window:

```
Dim CurrentWindow As Window
CurrentWindow = DTE.ActiveWindow
```

The tool windows within the IDE—that is, the command window, the error list window, the output window, the Solution Explorer, the Task List window, and the toolbox—also have a direct way to retrieve their object model instances: You use the `DTE.ToolWindows` property. This property returns a `ToolWindows` object that exposes a separate property for each of the tool windows.

This Visual Basic code grabs a reference to the Task List window and closes it:

```
Dim taskwin As Window


taskwin = DTE.ToolWindows.TaskList
taskwin.Close()
```

And finally, the fourth way to access an IDE window is through the `DTE.Windows` collection; this collection holds an entry for each IDE window. You can access a window from the collection either by using an integer representing the window's position within the collection, or by providing an object or a string that represents the window you are trying to retrieve.

The following code grabs a handle to the Solution Explorer window:

```
Dim windows As Windows2 = DTE.Windows
Dim window As Window = windows.Item(Constants.vsWindowKindSolutionExplorer)
```

## Interacting with Windows

Table 11.6 itemizes the properties and methods available on each `Window` object.

TABLE 11.6   Window Object Members

| Property | Description |
| --- | --- |
| AutoHides | A Boolean flag indicating whether the window can be hidden (applies only to tool windows). |
| Caption | The title/caption of the window. |
| Collection | The Windows collection that the current Window object belongs to. |
| CommandBars | A CommandBars collection of the command bars implemented by the window. |
| ContextAttributes | A collection of ContextAttribute objects; they are used to associate the current context of the window with the Dynamic Help window. |
| Document | If the Window object is hosting a document, this returns a reference to the document. |
| DTE | A reference to the root DTE object. |
| Height | The height of the window in pixels. |
| IsFloating | A Boolean flag indicating whether the window is floating or docked. |
| Left | The distance, in pixels, between the window's left edge and its container's left edge. |
| Linkable | A Boolean flag indicating whether the window can be docked with other windows. |
| LinkedWindowFrame | Returns a reference to the Window object that is acting as the frame for a docked window. |
| LinkedWindows | A collection of Window objects representing the windows that are linked together within the same frame. |
| Object | Returns an object proxy that represents the window and can be referenced by name. |
| ObjectKind | A GUID indicating the type of the object returned from Window.Object. |
| Project | A Project instance representing the project containing the Window object. |

| Property | Description |
|---|---|
| ProjectItem | A `ProjectItem` instance representing the project item containing the `Window` object. |
| Selection | Returns an object representing the currently selected item in the window (for document windows, this might be text; for tool windows, this might be an item in a list; and so on). |
| Top | The distance, in pixels, between the window's top edge and its parent's top edge. |
| Visible | A Boolean flag indicating whether the window is visible or hidden. |
| Width | The width of the window in pixels. |
| WindowState | Gets or sets the current state of the window (via a `vsWindowState` enum value: `vsWindowStateMaximize`, `vsWindowStateMinimize`, `vsWindowStateNormal`). |
| **Method** | **Description** |
| Activate | Gives the window focus. |
| Close | Closes the window; you can indicate, with a `vsSaveChanges` enum value, whether the window's hosted document should be saved or not saved, or whether the IDE should prompt the user to make that decision. |
| SetSelectionContainer | Passes an array of objects to the Properties window when the `Window` object has focus. This property is mainly used for custom tool windows where you need to control what is displayed in the Properties window. |
| SetTabPicture | Specifies an object to use as a tab image; this image is displayed whenever the window is part of a tab group within the IDE. |

Beyond the basics (such as using the `Height` and `Width` properties to query or affect a window's dimensions, or setting focus to the window with the `SetFocus` method), a few properties deserve special mention:

▶ The `Document` property gives you a way to programmatically interact with the document that the window is hosting (if any).

▶ The `Project` and `ProjectItem` properties serve to bridge the `Window` portion of the API with the `Project`/`Solution` portion; in a similar vein as the `Document` property, you can use these properties to interact with the project that is related to the window, or the project item (such as the VB code file, text file, or resource file).

▶ If you are dealing with a tool window, the `SetTabPicture` method provides a way to set the tab icon that is displayed when the tool window is part of a group of tabbed windows (for instance, the Toolbox window displays a wrench and hammer picture on its tab when part of a tabbed group).

▶ Again, specifically for tool windows only, the SetSelectionContainer can be used to supply one or more objects for display within the Properties window. This capability is useful if you have a custom window where you need to control what is displayed in the Properties window when the window has focus (all the standard VS windows already do this for you).

Listing 11.2 contains a simple macro illustrating the use of the Window object; in this example, each window is queried to determine its type, and then a summary of each window is output in a simple message box.

LISTING 11.2    VB Macro for Querying the Windows Collection

```
Imports EnvDTE
Imports EnvDTE80
Imports System.Diagnostics
Imports System.Windows.Forms


Public Module MacroExamples

    Public Sub InventoryWindows()
        ' Get collection of all open windows
        Dim windows As Windows2 = DTE.Windows

        ' Count the nbr of open windows
        Dim windowCount As Integer = windows.Count

        ' Local vars for looping and holding window and string
        ' results
        Dim idx As Integer
        Dim results As String
        Dim window As Window2

        results = windowCount.ToString + " windows open..." + vbCrLf

        ' Iterate the collection of windows
        For idx = 1 To windowCount

            window = windows.Item(idx)
            Dim title As String = window.Caption

            ' If the window is hosting a document, a valid Document
            ' object will be returned through Window.Document
            If Not (window.Document Is Nothing) Then
```

```
            ' Write this out as a document window
            Dim docName As String = window.Document.Name
            results = results + "Window '" + title + "' is a document window"
                + vbCrLf
        Else
            ' If no document was present, this is a tool window
            ' (tool windows don't host documents)
            results = results + "Window '" + title + "' is a tool window"
                + vbCrLf
        End If

    Next

    ' Show the results
    MessageBox.Show(results, "Window Documents", MessageBoxButtons.OK, _
        MessageBoxIcon.Information)

    End Sub

End Module
```

---

**NOTE**

If you want to embed your own custom control inside a tool window, you have to write an add-in and use the `Windows.CreateToolWindow` method. We cover this scenario in Chapter 13.

---

## Text Windows and Window Panes

Text windows have their own specific object abstraction in addition to the generic `Window` object: The `TextWindow` object is used to represent text editor windows. To obtain a reference to a window's `TextWindow` object, you retrieve the `Window` object's value and assign it into a `TextWindow` type:

```
Dim textWindow As TextWindow
textWindow = DTE.ActiveWindow.Object
```

The `TextWindow` object doesn't provide much functionality over and above the functionality found in the `Window` type; its real value is the access it provides to window panes.

Text editor windows in Visual Studio can be split into two panes; with a text editor open, simply select Split from the Window menu to create a new pane within the window. The `TextWindow.ActivePane` property returns a `TextPane` object representing the currently active pane in the window, and the `TextWindow.Panes` property provides access to all the panes within a text window:

```
' Get pane instance from collection
Dim newPane As TextPane2
newPane = textWindow.Panes.Item(1)

' Get currently active pane
Dim currPane As TextPane2
currPane = textWindow.ActivePane
```

One of the more useful things you can do with the `TextPane` object is to scroll the client area of the pane (for example, the visible portion of the document within the pane) so that a specific range of text is visible. This is done via the `TextPane.TryToShow` method.

Here is the definition for the method:

```
Function TryToShow( Point As TextPoint, Optional How As vsPaneShowHow, _
    PointOrCount As Object)
```

The `TextPoint` parameter represents the specific location within the text document that you want visible in the text pane (we discuss `TextPoint` objects in depth later in this chapter, in the section "Editing Text Documents"). The `vsPaneShowHow` value specifies how the pane should behave when scrolling to the indicated location:

- ▶ `vsPaneShowHow.vsPaneShowCentered` causes the pane to center the text/text selection in the middle of the pane (horizontally and vertically).

- ▶ `vsPaneShowHow.vsPaneShowTop` places the text point at the top of the viewable region in the pane.

- ▶ `vsPaneShowHow.vsPaneShowAsIs` shows the text point as is with no changes in horizontal or vertical orientation within the viewable region in the pane.

The last parameter, the `PointOrCount` object, is used to specify the end of the text area that you want displayed. If you provide an integer here, this represents a count of characters past the original text point; if you provide another text point, the selection is considered to be that text that resides between the two text points.

The `TextPane` object is also used to access the Incremental Search feature for a specific window pane. Listing 11.3 shows an example of this feature in action.

LISTING 11.3    Controlling Incremental Search

```
Imports EnvDTE
Imports EnvDTE80
Imports Microsoft.VisualStudio.CommandBars
Imports System.Diagnostics
Imports System.Windows.Forms
```

```
Public Module MacroExamples

    Public Sub IncrementalSearch()
        ' Grab references to the active window;
        ' we assume, for this example, that the window
        ' is a text window.
        Dim window As Window2 = DTE.ActiveWindow

        ' Grab a TextWindow instance that maps to our
        ' active window
        Dim txtWindow As TextWindow = window.Object

        ' Get the active pane from the text window
        Dim pane As TextPane2 = txtWindow.ActivePane

        ' Using the active pane, get an IncrementalSearch object
        ' for the pane
        Dim search As IncrementalSearch = pane.IncrementalSearch

        ' Try to find our IMessageMapper interface by looking
        ' for the string "IM"
        ' Configure the search:
        '    search forward in the document
        '    append the chars that we are searching for
        '    quit the search
        search.StartForward()
        search.AppendCharAndSearch(AscW("I"))
        search.AppendCharAndSearch(AscW("M"))

        ' To remove us from incremental search mode,
        ' we can call IncrementalSearch.Exit()...
        'search.Exit()

    End Sub
End Module
```

## The Tool Window Types

In addition to having a `Window` object abstraction, each default tool window in the IDE—the command window, output window, Toolbox window, and Task List window—is also represented by a discrete type that exposes methods and properties unique to that tool window. Table 11.7 lists the default tool windows and their underlying type in the automation object model.

TABLE 11.7    Tool Windows and Their Types

| Tool Window | Type |
| --- | --- |
| Command window | CommandWindow |
| Output window | OutputWindow |
| Task List window | TaskList |
| Toolbox window | ToolBox |

To reference one of these objects, you first start with its Window representation and then cast its Window.Object value to the matching type. For instance, this VB snippet starts with a Window reference to the Task List window and then uses that Window object to obtain a reference to the TaskList object:

```
Dim windows As Windows = DTE.Windows
Dim twindow As Window = _
    DTE.Windows.Item(EnvDTE.Constants.vsWindowKindTaskList)
```

### Tasks and the Task List Window

The TaskList object enables you to access the items currently displayed in the Task List window; each item in the window is represented by its own TaskItem object. The TaskItem object exposes methods and properties that allow you to manipulate the task items. For instance, you can mark an item as complete, get or set the line number associated with the task, and change the priority of the task.

You remove tasks from the list by using the TaskItem.Delete method and add them by using the TaskItems.Add method. The Add method allows you to specify the task category, subcategory, description, priority, icon, and so on:

```
Dim tlist As TaskList = CType(twindow.Object, TaskList)


tlist.TaskItems.Add("Best Practices", "Coding Style", _
    "Use of brace indenting is inconsistent", _
    vsTaskPriority.vsTaskPriorityMedium, _
    vsTaskIcon.vsTaskIconUser, True, _
    "S:\ContosoCommonFramework\Contoso.Fx.Common\Class1.cs", _
    7, True, True)
```

Table 11.8 provides an inventory of the TaskItem members.

Listing 11.4 contains a short VB macro demonstrating the use of the TaskList, TaskItems, and TaskItem objects to iterate the tasks and toggle their completed status.

TABLE 11.8  `TaskItem` Members

| Property | Description |
|---|---|
| Category | The category of the task. |
| Checked | A Boolean flag indicating whether the task is marked as completed (a check mark appears in the check box next to the task). |
| Collection | The `TaskList` collection that the current `TaskItem` object belongs to. |
| Description | The description of the task. |
| Displayed | A Boolean flag indicating whether the task is currently visible in the Task List window. |
| DTE | A reference to the root `DTE` object. |
| FileName | The name of the file associated with the task (if any). |
| IsSettable | By passing in a `vsTaskListColumn` enum value to this property, you can determine whether that column is editable. |
| Line | The line number associated with the task. |
| Priority | A `vsTaskPriority` value indicating the task's priority level. Possible values include `vsTaskPriorityHigh`, `vsTaskPriorityMedium`, and `vsTaskPriorityLow`. |
| SubCategory | The subcategory of the task. |
| **Method** | **Description** |
| Delete | Removes the task from the Task List window. |
| Navigate | Causes the IDE to navigate to the location (for example, file and line) associated with the task. |
| Select | Selects or moves the focus to the task within the Task List window. |

LISTING 11.4  Toggling Task Item Completion

```
Imports EnvDTE
Imports EnvDTE80
Imports Microsoft.VisualStudio.CommandBars
Imports System.Diagnostics
Imports System.Windows.Forms


Public Module MacroExamples

    Public Sub ToggleAllTasks()

        ' Reference the windows collection
        Dim windows As Windows = DTE.Windows
```

LISTING 11.4    Continued

```
        ' Pluck the task list window from the collection
        Dim twindow As Window = _
            DTE.Windows.Item(EnvDTE.Constants.vsWindowKindTaskList)

        ' Convert the window object to a TaskList instance by
        ' casting its Object property
        Dim tlist As TaskList = CType(twindow.Object, TaskList)

        ' Iterate all of the task items in the task list
        For Each task As TaskItem In tlist.TaskItems
            ' Toggle the "completed" check mark on each item
            task.Checked = Not task.Checked
        Next


    End Sub
End Module
```

**The Toolbox**

Four objects are used to programmatically interface with the toolbox:

- ▶ **ToolBox**—An object representing the toolbox itself.

- ▶ **ToolBoxTabs**—A collection representing the tab panes on the toolbox.

- ▶ **ToolBoxItems**—A collection representing the items within a tab on the toolbox.

- ▶ **ToolBoxItem**—A discrete item displayed within a toolbox tab.

Figure 11.3 illustrates the Toolbox object hierarchy.

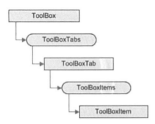

FIGURE 11.3    Toolbox object hierarchy.

These objects are used primarily to add, remove, or alter the items hosted by the toolbox. For instance, you can easily add a custom tab to the toolbox by using the ToolBoxTabs collection:

```
Dim tBox As ToolBox
Dim myTab As ToolBoxTab
tBox = DTE.Windows.Item(Constants.vsWindowKindToolbox).Object
myTab = tBox.ToolBoxTabs.Add("My TBox Tab")
```

You can also add items to any tab with the ToolBoxItems.Add method, which accepts a name for the item to add, a "data" object representing the item, and a vsToolBoxItemFormat enum, which specifies the format of the item. The Add method uses the vsToolBoxItemFormat to determine how to interpret the "data" object value. For instance, if you wanted to add a .NET control to the tab created in the preceding code snippet, you could accomplish that with just one line of code:

```
myTab.ToolBoxItems.Add("ContosoControl", _
        "C:\Contoso\Controls\CalendarControl.dll", _
        vsToolBoxItemFormat.vsToolBoxItemFormatDotNETComponent)
```

Notice that the item, in this case, is represented by a path to the assembly that implements the control and that it has an item format of vsToolBoxItemFormatDotNET-Component.

Listing 11.5 contains a VB function that adds a tab to the toolbox, adds a control and a text fragment to the tab, and then removes the tab.

LISTING 11.5   Adding and Removing Items in the Toolbox Window

```
Imports EnvDTE
Imports EnvDTE80
Imports Microsoft.VisualStudio.CommandBars
Imports System.Diagnostics
Imports System.Windows.Forms


    Public Sub AddAToolBoxTab()
        Dim toolBox As ToolBox
        Dim tabs As ToolBoxTabs
        Dim tab As ToolBoxTab
        Dim tabItems As ToolBoxItems
        Dim win As Window

        Try
            ' Get a reference to the toolbox
            win = DTE.Windows.Item(Constants.vsWindowKindToolbox)
            toolBox = win.Object

            ' Get a reference to the toolbox tabs collection
            tabs = toolBox.ToolBoxTabs
```

LISTING 11.5   Continued

```
            ' Add a new tab to the ToolBox
            tab = tabs.Add("New ToolBox Tab")

            ' Make the added tab the active tab
            tab.Activate()

            tabItems = tab.ToolBoxItems

        With tabItems
            ' Add a piece of text to the toolbox.
            ' Clicking on the text will add it to
            ' the active document...
            .Add("Code Comment", _
                "This is some text to add to the toolbox", _
                vsToolBoxItemFormat.vsToolBoxItemFormatText)

            'Now add a control to the toolbox.
            'When adding a control, you need to specify
            'the path to the assembly; you can add all
            'classes from the assembly (shown below)
            'or just one of the classes (see MSDN
            'docs for that syntax)
            .Add("My Login Control", _
                "C:\MyComponents\Contoso\LoginControl.dll", _
                vsToolBoxItemFormat.vsToolBoxItemFormatDotNETComponent)

            'For demonstration purposes, let's remove
            'the items that we had just added, and then
            'remove the newly created tab...

            'Put up a messagebox to confirm the deletes
            MessageBox.Show("Click OK to delete the tab and added items.", _
                "Delete Toolbox Tab Items", MessageBoxButtons.OK, _
                MessageBoxIcon.Information)

            'Delete the tab
            tab.Delete()

        End With

    Catch ex As Exception
        MsgBox("Error: " & ex.ToString())
    End Try

End Sub
```

**Executing Commands in the Command Window**

The command window is a tool window used to execute IDE commands or aliases. IDE commands are essentially ways to tell the IDE to perform some action. Some commands map directly to menu items (such as File Open), whereas others don't have menu equivalents.

The `CommandWindow` object permits you to programmatically pipe commands into the command window and execute them. You can also output a text string (for informational purposes) to the window and clear its current content:

```
' Get a reference to the command window
Dim cmdWindow As CommandWindow = _
   DTE.Windows.Item(Constants.vsWindowKindCommandWindow).Object


' Display some text in the command window
cmdWindow.OutputString("Hello, World!")


' Clear the command window
cmdWindow.Clear()
```

Listing 11.6 shows how to programmatically execute commands in the `CommandWindow` object.

LISTING 11.6    Executing Commands in the Command Window

```
Imports EnvDTE
Imports EnvDTE80
Imports Microsoft.VisualStudio.CommandBars
Imports System.Diagnostics
Imports System.Windows.Forms


Public Module MacroExamples

    Public Sub ExecCommandWindow()
        Dim cmdWindow As CommandWindow = _
            DTE.Windows.Item(Constants.vsWindowKindCommandWindow).Object

        ' Display some text in the command window
        cmdWindow.OutputString("Executing command from the automation OM...")

        ' Send some command strings to the command window and execute
        ' them...

        ' This command will start logging all input/output in the
        ' command window to the specified file
        cmdWindow.SendInput("Tools.LogCommandWindowOutput cmdwindow.log", True)
```

LISTING 11.6   Continued

```
      ' Open a file in a code editor:
      '    1. We use an alias, 'of', for the File.OpenFile command
      '    2. This command takes quote-delimited parameters (in this case,
      '       the name of the editor to load the file in)
      Dim cmd As String = "of "
      cmd = cmd &
"""C:\Contoso\ContosoCommonFramework\Integration\Integration.cs"""
      cmd = cmd & "/e:""CSharp Editor"""

      cmdWindow.SendInput(cmd, True)

      cmdWindow.SendInput("Edit.Find MessageTrxId", True)

      ' Turn off logging
      cmdWindow.SendInput("Tools.LogCommandWindowOutput /off", True)


    End Sub
End Module
```

**Output Window**

The output window displays messages generated from various sources in the IDE. A prime example is the messages generated by the compiler when a project is being built. For a deeper look at the functionality provided by the output window, see Chapter 10, "Debugging Code."

The output window is controlled through three objects:

▶ OutputWindow is the root object representing the output window.

▶ OutputWindowPanes is a collection of OutputWindowPane objects.

▶ OutputWindowPane represents one of the current panes within the output window.

Using these objects, you can add or remove panes from the output window, output text to any one of the panes, and respond to events transpiring in the window.

The following VB code fragment retrieves a reference to the output window and writes a test string in the Build pane:

```
Dim outWindow As OutputWindow = _
DTE.Windows.Item(Constants.vsWindowKindOutput).Object

Dim pane As OutputWindowPane = _
    outWindow.OutputWindowPanes.Item("Build")

pane.OutputString("test")
```

Using the OutputWindowPane object, you can also add items simultaneously to a specific output pane and the Task List window. The OutputWindowPane.OutputTaskItemString method writes text into the output window and simultaneously adds that text as a task to the Task List window:

```
Dim output As String = "Exception handler not found"
Dim task As String = "Add exception handler"
pane.OutputTaskItemString(output, _
    vsTaskPriority.vsTaskPriorityMedium,  "", vsTaskIcon.vsTaskIconNone, _
    "", 0, task, True)
```

Because most of the output window actions are conducted against a specific pane, most of the useful methods are concentrated in the OutputWindowPane object. For your reference, the OutputWindowPane members are itemized in Table 11.9.

TABLE 11.9   OutputWindowPane Members

| Property | Description |
|---|---|
| Collection | The OutputWindowPanes collection that the current OutputWindowPane object belongs to. |
| DTE | A reference to the root DTE object. |
| Guid | The GUID for the output window pane. |
| Name | The name of the output window pane. |
| TextDocument | A TextDocument object representing the window pane's content. |
| **Method** | **Description** |
| Activate | Moves the focus to the output window. |
| Clear | Clears the contents of the window pane. |
| ForceItemsToTaskList | Writes all task items not yet written to the Task List window. |
| OutputString | Writes a string to the output window pane. |
| OutputTaskItemString | Writes a string to the output window pane and simultaneously adds a task to the Task List window. |

Listing 11.7 demonstrates controlling the output window by adding a new pane to the window, writing text into that pane, and then clearing its content.

LISTING 11.7   Writing to the Output Window

```
Imports EnvDTE
Imports EnvDTE80
Imports Microsoft.VisualStudio.CommandBars
Imports System.Diagnostics
Imports System.Windows.Forms
```

LISTING 11.7    Continued

```
Public Module MacroExamples

    Public Sub WriteToOutputWindow()

        ' Grab a reference to the output window
        Dim outWindow As OutputWindow = _
            DTE.Windows.Item(Constants.vsWindowKindOutput).Object

        ' Create a new pane in the output window
        Dim pane As OutputWindowPane = _
            outWindow.OutputWindowPanes.Add("New Pane")

        pane.OutputString("Text in the 'New Pane'")

        pane.Clear()

    End Sub
End Module
```

## Linked Windows

Tool windows can be positioned in various ways within the IDE: You can float tool windows around within the overall IDE container; you can dock a tool window to one of the sides of the IDE; you can join windows together and pin and unpin them; and so on (see the section "Managing the Many Windows of the IDE" in Chapter 2, "A Quick Tour of the IDE," for an introduction to window layout).

A *linked window* refers to two or more tool windows that have been aggregated together. Figure 11.4 shows one common example of this: The toolbox and Solution Explorer window have all been joined together in a common frame. Each window that is part of the frame can be viewed by clicking on its tab.

By joining together two or more tool windows, you actually create an additional window object—called a *linked window* or *window frame*—that functions as the container for its hosted tool windows and is available as a part of the DTE.Windows collection.

By using the Window.LinkedWindows and Window.WindowFrame properties and the Windows2.CreateLinkedWindowFrame method, you can programmatically link and unlink any available tool windows. The Visual Basic code in Listing 11.8 demonstrates this process by doing the following:

1. You grab the window objects for the Toolbox window and the Solution Explorer window.

2. You programmatically join these two windows together, effectively creating the linked window shown in Figure 11.4.

**3.** After joining the windows together, you get a reference to the newly created linked window and use its `LinkedWindows` property to unlink the windows that were previously just linked together.

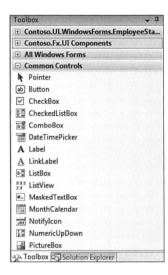

FIGURE 11.4   Linked windows.

LISTING 11.8   Linking and Unlinking Tool Windows

```vb
Imports EnvDTE
Imports EnvDTE80
Imports System.Diagnostics
Imports System.Windows.Forms


Public Module MacroExamples

    Public Sub LinkUnLink()
        Dim windows As Windows2 = DTE.Windows

        ' Grab references to the solution explorer and the toolbox
        Dim solExplorer As Window2 = _
            windows.Item(Constants.vsWindowKindSolutionExplorer)
        Dim toolbox As Window2 = windows.Item(Constants.vsWindowKindToolbox)

        ' Use the Windows2 collection to create a linked window/window
        ' frame to hold the toolbox and solution explorer windows
        Dim windowFrame As Window2
        windowFrame = windows.CreateLinkedWindowFrame(solExplorer, _
            toolbox, vsLinkedWindowType.vsLinkedWindowTypeTabbed)
```

LISTING 11.8    Continued

```vb
    ' At this point, we have created a linked window with two tabbed
    ' "interior" windows: the solution explorer, and the toolbox...

    MessageBox.Show("Press OK to Unlink the windows", "LinkUnLink", _
        MessageBoxButtons.OK, MessageBoxIcon.None)

    ' To unlink the windows:
    '    — Use the window frame's LinkedWindows collection
    '    — Remove the window objects from this collection

    windowFrame.LinkedWindows.Remove(toolbox)
    windowFrame.LinkedWindows.Remove(solExplorer)


  End Sub
End Module
```

# Command Bars

A command bar is a menu bar or toolbar; from an object model perspective, these are represented by `CommandBar` objects. Because menu bars and toolbars are hosted within a window, you reference specific `CommandBar` objects via the `Window` object, through the `Window.CommandBars` property. In turn, every `CommandBar` plays host to controls such as buttons and drop-downs. Figure 11.5 shows the Solution Explorer tool window with its command bar highlighted.

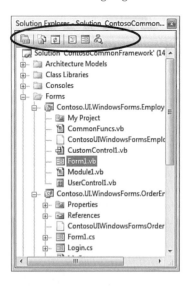

FIGURE 11.5    The Solution Explorer tool window and its command bar.

Note that there are six buttons hosted on the command bar.

> **NOTE**
>
> Unlike the `Windows` collection, which holds only an instance of each open window, the `CommandBars` collection holds instances for every single registered command bar, regardless of whether the command bar is currently being shown in the window.

The VB code in Listing 11.9 queries the `CommandBar` object for the Solution Explorer window and prints out the `CommandBar` objects that it finds.

LISTING 11.9   Querying the `CommandBar` Object

```vb
Imports EnvDTE
Imports EnvDTE80
Imports Microsoft.VisualStudio.CommandBars
Imports System.Diagnostics
Imports System.Windows.Forms


Public Module MacroExamples

    Public Sub QueryCommandBar()
        Dim windows As Windows2 = DTE.Windows

        ' Grab reference to the solution explorer
        Dim solExplorer As Window2 = _
            windows.Item(Constants.vsWindowKindSolutionExplorer)

        ' Retrieve the solution explorer's command bar object
        Dim cmdBar As CommandBar = CType(solExplorer.CommandBars(1), CommandBar)

        ' Start building our output string
        Dim output As String = "Command bar contains: " + vbCrLf

        ' Get a reference to the controls hosted in the
        ' command bar
        Dim controls As CommandBarControls = cmdBar.Controls

        ' Count integer
        Dim i As Integer = 1

        ' Iterate the controls in the command bar
        For Each control As CommandBarControl In controls
```

LISTING 11.9 Continued

```
        If control.Enabled Then

            output = output + i.ToString() + " " + _
                control.Type.ToString() + _
                ": " + control.Caption + vbCrLf

            i = i + 1

        End If

    Next

    MessageBox.Show(output, "Solution Explorer Command Bar", _
        MessageBoxButtons.OK)

    End Sub
End Module
```

Correlate the results in Figure 11.6 with Figure 11.4: Four buttons are visible on the tool window, and the code has found six items in the CommandBarControls collection (which is returned through the CommandBar.Controls property). Removing the following check against the Enabled property would result in many more controls produced in the message box:

```
If control.Enabled Then
```

Notice in Listing 11.9 that you have to explicitly cast the object returned from the Window.CommandBars property. This is, interestingly, not a strongly typed property, and it returns an Object instead of an actual CommandBars instance.

FIGURE 11.6 Controls found in the command bar.

11

**TIP**

Use the CommandBar.Type property to determine whether a command bar is a toolbar or a menu bar. A value of MsoBarType.msoBarTypeNormal indicates that the command bar is a toolbar, whereas a value of MsoBarType.msoBarTypeMenuBar indicates that the command bar is a menu bar.

The CommandBar object properties and methods are documented in Table 11.10.

**NOTE**

Previous versions of Visual Studio actually relied on a Microsoft Office assembly for the CommandBar object definition (Microsoft.Office.Core). Visual Studio 2005 and later versions provide their own implementation of the CommandBar object that is defined in the Microsoft.VisualStudio.CommandBars namespace, although you will find some types that carry their nomenclature over from the MS Office assembly, such as the various MsoXXX enums.

TABLE 11.10   CommandBar Members

| Property | Description |
| --- | --- |
| AdaptiveMenu | For menu bars, this Boolean flag indicates whether the command bar has *adaptive menus* enabled. (Adaptive menus, sometimes referred to as *personalized menus*, are menus that alter their drop-down content based on projected or actual usage by the user; the intent is to display only those commands that are useful on the menu and hide the other nonessential commands.) |
| Application | An object representing the parent application to the command bar. |
| BuiltIn | A Boolean flag used to distinguish between built-in and custom command bars. |
| Context | A string indicating where the CommandBar is saved (the format and expected content of this string are dictated by the hosting application). |
| Controls | A CommandBarControls collection containing CommandBarControl objects; each of these objects represents a control displayed by the command bar. |
| Creator | An integer value that identifies the application hosting the CommandBar. |
| Enabled | A Boolean flag indicating whether the command bar is enabled. |
| Height | The height of the command bar in pixels. |
| Index | The index of the command bar in the command bar collection. |
| Left | The distance, in pixels, between the left side of the command bar and the left edge of its parent container. |
| Name | The name of the command bar. |
| NameLocal | The localized name of the command bar. |

TABLE 11.10    Continued

| Property | Description |
|----------|-------------|
| Parent | An object that is the parent of the command bar. |
| Position | An `MsoBarPosition` enum value used to get or set the position of the command bar (for example, `MsoBarPosition.msoBarTop`). |
| Protection | An `MsoBarProtection` enum value that identifies the protection employed against used modification (for example, `MsoBarProtection.msoBarNoMove`). |
| RowIndex | An integer representing the docking row of the command bar. |
| Top | The distance, in pixels, between the top of the command bar and the top edge of its parent container. |
| Type | The type of the command bar (as an `MsobarType` enum value; for example, `MsoBarType.msoBarTypeNormal`). |
| Visible | A Boolean flag indicating whether the command bar is currently visible. |
| Width | The width of the command bar in pixels. |
| **Method** | **Description** |
| Delete | Removes the command bar from its parent collection. |
| FindControl | Enables you to retrieve a reference to a control hosted by the command bar that fits various parameters such as its type, ID, tag, and visibility. |
| Reset | Resets one of the built-in command bars to its default configuration. |
| ShowPopup | Displays a pop-up representing a command bar. |

# Documents

`Document` objects are used to represent an open document in the IDE. To contrast this abstraction with that provided by the `Window` object: A `Window` object is used to represent the physical UI aspects of a document window, whereas a `Document` object is used to represent the physical document that is being displayed within that document window.

A document could be a designer, such as the Windows Forms designer, or it could be a text-based document such as a readme file or a C# code file open in an editor.

Just as you get a list of all open windows using the `DTE.Windows` collection, you can use the `DTE.Documents` collection to retrieve a list of all open documents:

```
Dim documents As Documents = DTE.Documents
```

The `Documents` collection is indexed by the document's `Name` property, which is, in effect, the document's filename without the path information. This makes it easy to quickly retrieve a `Document` instance:

```
Dim documents As Documents = DTE.Documents
Dim readme As Document = documents.Item("ReadMe.txt")
```

Using the Document object, you can do the following:

- ▶ Close the document (and optionally save changes)
- ▶ Retrieve the filename and path of the document
- ▶ Determine whether the document has been modified since the last time it was saved
- ▶ Determine what, if anything, is currently selected within the document
- ▶ Obtain a ProjectItem instance representing the project item that is associated with the document
- ▶ Read and edit the contents of text documents

Table 11.11 contains the member descriptions for the Document object.

TABLE 11.11   Document Members

| Property | Description |
| --- | --- |
| ActiveWindow | The currently active window associated with the document (null or Nothing value indicates that there is no active window). |
| Collection | The collection of Document objects to which this instance belongs. |
| DTE | The root-level DTE object. |
| Extender | Returns a Document extender object. |
| ExtenderCATID | The extender category ID for the object. |
| ExtenderNames | A list of extenders available for the current Document object. |
| FullName | The full path and filename of the document. |
| Kind | A GUID representing the kind of document. |
| Name | The name (essentially, the filename without path information) for the document. |
| Path | The path of the document's file excluding the filename. |
| ProjectItem | The ProjectItem instance associated with the document. |
| Saved | Indicates whether the solution has been saved since the last modification. |
| Selection | An object representing the current selection in the document (if any). |
| Windows | The Windows collection containing the window displaying the document. |
| **Method** | **Description** |
| Activate | Moves the focus to the document. |
| Close | Closes the document. You can indicate, with a vsSaveChanges enum value, whether the window's hosted document should be saved or not saved, or whether the IDE should prompt the user to make that decision. |
| NewWindow | Opens the document in a new window and returns the new window's Window object. |

TABLE 11.11   Continued

| Property | Description |
| --- | --- |
| Object | Returns an object proxy that represents the window and can be referenced by name. |
| Redo | Reexecutes the last user action in the document. |
| Save | Saves the document. |
| Undo | Reverses the last used action in the document. |

## Text Documents

As we mentioned, documents can have textual or nontextual content. For those documents with textual content, a separate object—TextDocument—exists. The TextDocument object provides access to control functions specifically related to text content.

If you have a valid Document object to start with, and if that Document object refers to a text document, then a TextDocument instance can be referenced from the Document.Object property like this:

```
Dim doc As TextDocument
doc = myDocument.Object
```

Table 11.12 contains the TextDocument members.

TABLE 11.12   TextDocument Members

| Property | Description |
| --- | --- |
| DTE | The root-level DTE object. |
| EndPoint | A TextPoint object positioned at the end of the document. |
| Parent | Gets the parent object of the text document. |
| Selection | Returns a TextSelection object representing the currently selected text in the document. |
| StartPoint | A TextPoint object positioned at the start of the document. |
| **Method** | **Description** |
| ClearBookmarks | Removes any unnamed bookmarks present in the document. |
| CreateEditPoint | Returns an edit point at the specific location (if no location is specified, the beginning of the document is assumed). |
| MarkText | Bookmarks lines in the document that match the specified string pattern. |
| ReplacePattern | Replaces any text in the document that matches the pattern. |

---

**TIP**

A text document is represented by both a `Document` instance and a `TextDocument` instance. Nontext documents, such as a Windows form open in a Windows Forms designer window, have a `Document` representation but no corresponding `TextDocument` representation. Unfortunately, there isn't a great way to distinguish whether a document is text-based during runtime. One approach is to attempt a cast or assignment to a `TextDocument` object and catch any exceptions that might occur during the assignment.

---

Two `TextDocument` methods are useful for manipulating bookmarks within the document: `ClearBookmarks` removes any unnamed bookmarks from the document, and `MarkText` performs a string pattern search and places bookmarks against the resulting document lines. A simple macro to bookmark `For` loops in a VB document is presented in Listing 11.10.

LISTING 11.10    Bookmarking For Loops in a VB Document

```
Imports EnvDTE
Imports EnvDTE80
Imports Microsoft.VisualStudio.CommandBars
Imports System.Diagnostics
Imports System.Windows.Forms


Public Module MacroExamples

    ' Bookmark all 'For' tokens in the current
    ' document
    Public Sub BookmarkFor()
        Dim doc As Document
        Dim txtDoc As TextDocument

        ' Reference the current document
        doc = DTE.ActiveDocument

        ' Retrieve a TextDocument instance from
        ' the document
        txtDoc = doc.Object

        ' Call the MarkText method with the 'For' string
        Dim found As Boolean = _
            txtDoc.MarkText("For", vsFindOptions.vsFindOptionsFromStart)
```

LISTING 11.10    Continued

```
        ' MarkText returns a boolean flag indicating whether or not
        ' the search pattern was found in the textdocument
        If found Then
            MessageBox.Show("All instances of 'For' have been bookmarked.")
        Else
            MessageBox.Show("No instances of 'For' were found.")
        End If
    End Sub
End Module
```

The other key functionality exposed by the `TextDocument` object is the capability to read and edit the text within the document.

### Editing Text Documents

From a Visual Studio perspective, text in a text document actually has two distinct "representations": a virtual one and a physical one. The physical representation is the straight, unadulterated code file that sits on disk. The virtual representation is what Visual Studio presents on the screen: It is an *interpreted* view of the text in the code file that takes into account various editor document features such as code outlining/regions, virtual spacing, and word wrapping.

Figure 11.7 shows this relationship. When displaying a text document, Visual Studio reads the source file into a text buffer, and then the text editor presents one view of that text file to you (based on options you have configured for the editor).

Text in a document is manipulated or read either on the buffered text or on the "view" text that you see in the editor. There are four different automation objects that enable you to affect text; two work on the text buffer and two work on the editor view.

For the text buffer:

▶ `TextPoint` objects are used to locate specific points within a text document. By querying the `TextPoint` properties, you can determine the line number of the text point, the number of characters it is offset from the start of a line, the number of characters it is offset from the start of the document, and its display column within the text editor window. You can also retrieve a reference to a `CodeModel` object representing the code at the text point's current location.

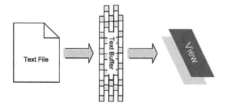

FIGURE 11.7    Presentation of text documents within the IDE.

▶ The EditPoint object inherits from the TextPoint object; this is the primary object used for manipulating text in the text buffer. You can add, delete, or move text using edit points, and they can be moved around within the text buffer.

And, for the editor view:

▶ The VirtualPoint object is equivalent to the TextPoint object except that it can be used to query text locations that reside in the "virtual" space of the text view (virtual space is the whitespace that exists after the last character in a document line). VirtualPoint instances are returned through the TextSelection object.

▶ The TextSelection object operates on text within the text editor view as opposed to the text buffer and is equivalent to the EditPoint interface. When you use the TextSelection object, you are actively affecting the text that is being displayed within the text editor. The methods and properties of this object, therefore, end up being programmatic approximations of the various ways that you would manually affect text: You can page up or page down within the view; cut, copy, and paste text; select a range of text; or even outline and expand or collapse regions of text.

Because the VirtualPoint object is nearly identical to the TextPoint object, and the TextSelection object is nearly identical to the EditPoint object, we won't bother to cover each of these four objects in detail. Instead, we will focus on text buffer operations using EditPoint and TextPoint. You should be able to easily apply the concepts here to the text view.

Because EditPoint objects expose the most functionality and play the central role with text editing, we have provided a list of their type members in Table 11.13.

Now let's look at various text manipulation scenarios.

TABLE 11.13    EditPoint2 Members

| Property | Description |
| --- | --- |
| AbsoluteCharOffset | The number of characters from the start of the document to the current location of the edit point. |
| AtEndOfDocument | Boolean flag indicating whether the point is at the end of the document. |
| AtEndOfLine | Boolean flag indicating whether the point is at the end of a line in the document. |
| AtStartOfDocument | Boolean flag indicating whether the point is at the beginning of the document. |
| AtStartOfLine | Boolean flag indicating whether the point is at the start of a line in the document. |
| CodeElement | Returns the code element that maps to the edit point's current location. |
| DisplayColumn | The column number of the edit point. |
| DTE | Returns the root automation DTE object. |

TABLE 11.13    Continued

| Property | Description |
|----------|-------------|
| Line | The line number where the point is positioned. |
| LineCharOffset | The character offset, within a line, of the edit point. |
| LineLength | The length of the line where the edit point is positioned. |
| Parent | Returns the parent object of the EditPoint2 object. |
| **Method** | **Description** |
| ChangeCase | Changes the case of a range of text. |
| CharLeft | Moves the edit point to the left the specified number of characters. |
| CharRight | Moves the edit point to the right the specified number of characters. |
| ClearBookmark | Clears any unnamed bookmarks that exist on the point's current line location. |
| Copy | Copies a range of text to the Clipboard. |
| CreateEditPoint | Creates a new EditPoint object at the same location as the current EditPoint object. |
| Cut | Cuts a range of text and places it on the Clipboard. |
| Delete | Deletes a range of text from the document. |
| DeleteWhitespace | Deletes any whitespace found around the edit point. |
| EndOfDocument | Moves the edit point to the end of the document. |
| EndOfLine | Moves the edit point to the end of the current line. |
| EqualTo | A Boolean value indicating whether the edit point's AbsoluteCharOffset value is equal to another edit point's offset. |
| FindPattern | Finds any matching string patterns in the document. |
| GetLines | A string representing the text between two lines in the document. |
| GetText | A string representing the text between the edit point and another location in the document. |
| GreaterThan | A Boolean value indicating whether the edit point's AbsoluteCharOffset value is greater than another edit point's offset. |
| Indent | Indents the selected lines by the given number of levels. |
| Insert | Inserts a string into the document, starting at the edit point's current location. |
| InsertFromFile | Inserts the entire contents of a text file into the document starting at the edit point's current location. |
| LessThan | Returns a Boolean value indicating whether the edit point's AbsoluteCharOffset value is less than another edit point's offset. |

TABLE 11.13    Continued

| Property | Description |
|---|---|
| LineDown | Moves the point down one or more lines. |
| LineUp | Moves the point up one or more lines. |
| MoveToAbsoluteOffset | Moves the edit point to the given character offset. |
| MoveToLineAndOffset | Moves the edit point to the given line and to the character offset within that line. |
| MoveToPoint | Moves the edit point to the location of another EditPoint or TextPoint object. |
| NextBookmark | Moves the edit point to the next available bookmark in the document. |
| OutlineSection | Creates an outline section between the point's current location and another location in the document. |
| PadToColumn | Pads spaces in the current line up to the indicated column number. |
| Paste | Pastes the contents of the Clipboard to the edit point's current location. |
| PreviousBookmark | Moves the edit point to the previous bookmark. |
| ReadOnly | Returns a Boolean flag indicating whether a text range in the document is read-only. |
| ReplacePattern | Replaces any text that matches the provided pattern. |
| ReplaceText | Replaces a range of text with the provided string. |
| SetBookmark | Creates an unnamed bookmark on the edit point's current line in the document. |
| StartOfDocument | Moves the edit point to the start of the document. |
| StartOfLine | Moves the edit point to the beginning of the line where it is positioned. |
| TryToShow | Attempts to display the point's current location within the text editor window. |
| Unindent | Removes the given number of indentation levels from a range of lines in the document. |
| WordLeft | Moves the edit point to the left the given number of words. |
| WordRight | Moves the edit point to the right the given number of words. |

**Adding Text**    EditPoint objects are the key to adding text, and you create them either by using a TextDocument object or by using a TextPoint object.

A TextPoint instance can create an EditPoint instance in its same exact location by calling TextPoint.CreateInstance. With the TextDocument type, you can call the CreateEditPoint method and pass in a valid TextPoint.

Because TextPoint objects are used to locate specific points in a document, a TextPoint object is leveraged as an input parameter to CreateEditPoint. In essence, the TextPoint object tells the method where to create the edit point. If you don't provide a TextPoint object, the edit point will be created at the start of the document.

This code snippet shows an edit point being created at the end of a document:

```
Dim doc As Document = DTE.ActiveDocument
Dim txtDoc As TextDocument = doc.Object

Dim tp As TextPoint = txtDoc.EndPoint
Dim ep As EditPoint2 = txtDoc.CreateEditPoint(tp)
' This line of code would have the same effect
ep = tp.CreateEditPoint
```

After creating an edit point, you can use it to add text into the document (remember, you are editing the buffered text whenever you use an EditPoint object). To inject a string into the document, you use the Insert method:

```
' Insert a C# comment line
ep.Insert("// some comment")
```

You can even grab the contents of a file and throw that into the document with the EditPoint.InsertFromFile method:

```
' Insert comments from a comments file
ep.InsertFromFile("C:\Contoso\std comments.txt")
```

**Editing Text**    The EditPoint object supports deleting, replacing, cutting, copying, and pasting text in a document.

Some of these operations require more than a single point to operate. For instance, if you wanted to cut a word or an entire line of code from a document, you would need to specify a start point and end point that define that range of text (see Figure 11.8).

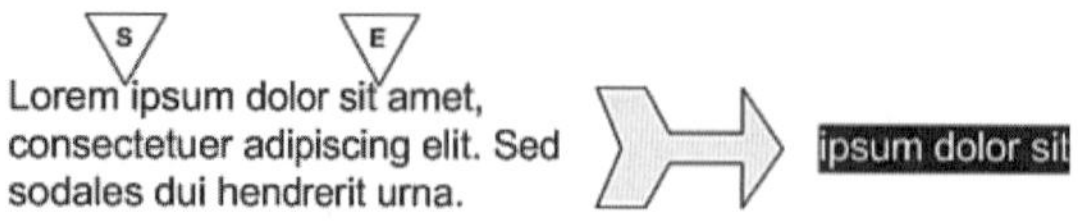

FIGURE 11.8    Using points within a document to select text.

This snippet uses two end points, one at the start of a document and one at the end, to delete the entire contents of the document:

```
Dim doc As Document = DTE.ActiveDocument
Dim txtDoc As TextDocument = doc.Object

Dim tpStart As TextPoint = txtDoc.StartPoint
Dim tpEnd As TextPoint = txtDoc.EndPoint

Dim epStart As EditPoint2 = txtDoc.CreateEditPoint(tpStart)
Dim epEnd As EditPoint2 = txtDoc.CreateEditPoint(tpEnd)
epStart.Delete(epEnd)
```

Besides accepting a second `EditPoint`, the methods that operate on a range of text will also accept an integer identifying a count of characters. This also has the effect of defining a select. For example, this snippet cuts the first 10 characters from a document:

```
epStart.Cut(10)
```

**Repositioning an `EditPoint`**      After establishing an `EditPoint`, you can move it to any given location in the document by using various methods. The `CharLeft` and `CharRight` methods move the point any number of characters to the left or right, whereas the `WordLeft` and `WordRight` methods perform the same operation with words:

```
' Move the edit point 4 words to the right
epStart.WordRight(4)
```

The `LineUp` and `LineDown` methods jog the point up or down the specified number of lines. You can also move `EditPoints` to any given line within a document by using `MoveToLineAndOffset`. This method also positions the point any number of characters into the line:

```
' Move the edit point to line 100, and then
' in 5 characters to the right
epStart.MoveToLineAndOffset(100, 5)
```

The macro code in Listing 11.11 pulls together some of the areas that we have covered with editing text documents. This macro and its supporting functions illustrate the use of `EditPoints` to write text into a document. In this case, the macro automatically inserts a comment "flowerbox" immediately preceding a routine. To accomplish this, the macro goes through the following process:

1. A reference is obtained for the current document in the IDE.
2. The active cursor location in that document is obtained via the `TextDocument.Selection.ActivePoint` property.

3. An `EditPoint` is created using the `VirtualPoint` returned from the `ActivePoint`.

4. A second `EditPoint` is then created; these two points are used to obtain the entire content of the routine definition line.

5. The routine definition is then parsed to try to ferret out items such as its name, return value, and parameter list.

6. A string is built using the routine information and is inserted into the text document using an `EditPoint`.

LISTING 11.11   Inserting Comments into a Text Window

```
Imports EnvDTE
Imports EnvDTE80
Imports Microsoft.VisualStudio.CommandBars
Imports System
Imports System.Collections
Imports System.Diagnostics
Imports System.Text
Imports System.Windows.Forms


Public Module MacroExamples

    ' This routine demonstrates various text editing scenarios
    ' using the EditPoint and TextPoint types. If you place your
    ' cursor on a subroutine or function, it will build a default
    ' "flower box" comment area, insert it immediately above the
    ' sub/function, and outline it.
    '
    ' To use:
    '    1) put cursor anywhere on the Sub/Function line
    '    2) run macro
    '    The macro will fail silently (e.g., will not insert any
    '    comments) if it is unable to determine the start
    '    of the Sub/Function
    '
    Public Sub InsertTemplateFlowerbox()

        ' Get reference to the active document
        Dim doc As Document = DTE.ActiveDocument
        Dim txtDoc As TextDocument = doc.Object
        Dim isFunc As Boolean

        Try
            Dim ep As EditPoint2 = txtDoc.Selection.ActivePoint.CreateEditPoint()
```

```
        ep.StartOfLine()
        Dim ep2 As EditPoint2 = ep.CreateEditPoint()
        ep2.EndOfLine()

        Dim lineText As String = ep.GetText(ep2).Trim()

        If InStr(lineText, " Function ") > 0 Then
            isFunc = True
        ElseIf InStr(lineText, " Sub ") > 0 Then
            isFunc = False
        Else
            Exit Sub
        End If

        ' Parse out info that we can derive from the routine
        ' definition: the return value type (if this is a function),
        ' the names of the parameters, and the name of the routine.
        Dim returnType As String = ""
        If isFunc Then
            returnType = ParseRetValueType(lineText)
        End If

        Dim parameters As String() = ParseParameters(lineText)
        Dim name As String = ParseRoutineName(lineText)
        Dim commentBlock As String = BuildCommentBlock(isFunc, name, _
➥_returnType, parameters)

        ' Move the edit point up one line (to position
        ' immediately preceding the routine)
        ep.LineUp(1)

        ' Give us some room by inserting a new blank line
        ep.InsertNewLine()

        ' Insert our comment block
        ep.Insert(commentBlock.ToString())

    Catch ex As Exception

    End Try

End Sub
Private Function BuildCommentBlock(ByVal isFunc As Boolean, _
    ByVal name As String, _
    ByVal returnType As String, ByVal parameters As String())
```

LISTING 11.11    Continued

```vb
        Try
            Dim comment As StringBuilder = New StringBuilder()

            ' Build up a sample comment block using the passed in info
            comment.Append("'''''''''''''''''''''''''''''''''''''''''''''''''''''''")
            comment.Append(vbCrLf)
            comment.Append("' Routine: " + name)
            comment.Append(vbCrLf)
            comment.Append("' Description: [insert routine desc here]")
            comment.Append(vbCrLf)
            comment.Append("'")
            comment.Append(vbCrLf)
            If isFunc Then
                comment.Append("' Returns: A " & returnType & _" [insert return
➥value description here]")
            End If
            comment.Append(vbCrLf)
            comment.Append("'")
            comment.Append(vbCrLf)
            comment.Append("' Parameters:")
            comment.Append(vbCrLf)
            For i As Integer = 0 To parameters.GetUpperBound(0)
                comment.Append("'        ")
                comment.Append(parameters(i))
                comment.Append(": [insert parameter description here]")
                comment.Append(vbCrLf)
            Next
            comment.Append("'''''''''''''''''''''''''''''''''''''''''''''''''''''''")

            Return comment.ToString()

        Catch ex As Exception
            Return ""
        End Try

    End Function
    Private Function ParseRetValueType(ByVal code As String) As String
        Try
            ' Parse out the return value of a function (VB)
            ' Search for 'As', starting from the end of the string
            Dim length As Integer = code.Length
            Dim index As Integer = code.LastIndexOf(" As ")

            Dim retVal As String = code.Substring(index + 3, length - (index + 3))
```

```vbnet
            Return retVal.Trim()

    Catch ex As Exception

            Return ""
        End Try
    End Function
    Private Function ParseParameters(ByVal code As String) As String()
        Try
            ' Parse out the parameters specified (if any) for
            ' a VB sub/func definition
            Dim length As Integer = code.Length
            Dim indexStart As Integer = code.IndexOf("(")
            Dim indexEnd As Integer = code.LastIndexOf(")")

            Dim params As String = code.Substring(indexStart + 1, _indexEnd
➥ (indexStart + 1))

            Return params.Split(",")

    Catch ex As Exception
            Return Nothing
        End Try
    End Function
    Private Function ParseRoutineName(ByVal code As String) As String
        Try
            Dim name As String
            Dim length As Integer = code.Length
            Dim indexStart As Integer = code.IndexOf(" Sub ")
            Dim indexEnd As Integer = code.IndexOf("(")

            If indexStart = -1 Then
                indexStart = code.IndexOf(" Function ")
                If indexStart <> -1 Then
                    indexStart = indexStart + 9
                End If
            Else
                indexStart = indexStart + 5
            End If

            name = code.Substring(indexStart, indexEnd - indexStart)

            Return name.Trim()

    Catch ex As Exception
            Return ""
```

LISTING 11.11   Continued

```
        End Try
    End Function
End Module
```

# Command Objects

Every action that is possible to execute through the menus and toolbars in Visual Studio is generically referred to as a *command*. For example, pasting text into a window is a command, as are building a project, toggling a breakpoint, and closing a window.

For each command supported in the IDE, there is a corresponding Command object; the DTE.Commands collection holds all the valid Command object instances. Each command is keyed by a name that categorizes, describes, and uniquely identifies the command. The "paste" command, for instance, is available via the string key "Edit.Paste". If you wanted to retrieve the Command object mapping to the paste command, you would pull from the Commands collection using that string key:

```
Dim commands As Commands2 = DTE.Commands
Dim cmd As Command = commands.Item("Edit.Paste")
```

You can query a command's name via its Name property:

```
' name would = "Edit.Paste"
Dim name As String = cmd.Name
```

Table 11.14 contains the members declared on the Command interface.

TABLE 11.14   Command Members

| Property | Description |
| --- | --- |
| Bindings | The keystrokes that can be used to invoke the command. |
| Collection | The Commands collection that the Command object belongs to. |
| DTE | A reference to the root-level DTE object. |
| Guid | A GUID that identifies the command's group. |
| ID | An integer that identifies the command within its group. |
| IsAvailable | A Boolean flag that indicates whether the command is currently available. |
| LocalizedName | The localized name of the command. |
| Name | The name of the command. |
| **Method** | **Description** |
| AddControl | Creates a control for the command that can be hosted in a command bar. |
| Delete | Removes a named command that was previously added with the Commands.AddNamedCommand method. |

The list of all available commands is extremely long (nearly 3,000 total), and it is therefore impossible to cover every one of them here, or even a large portion of them. To get an idea, however, of the specific commands available, you can visit the dialog box used to customize the Visual Studio toolbars. If you select the Customize option from the View, Toolbars menu, and then click on the Commands tab, you can investigate all the various commands by category (see Figure 11.9). Another alternative would be to programmatically iterate the DTE.Commands collection and view them that way. In fact, in Chapter 13, we use this as one scenario for showcasing add-in development.

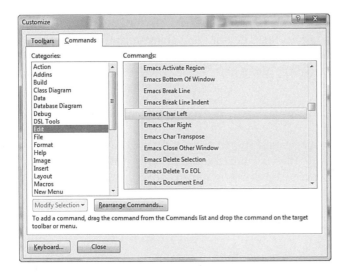

FIGURE 11.9   Using the Customize dialog box to view commands.

So, although we can't cover all the commands, you can learn how to perform common tasks with the Command objects such as executing a command, checking on a command's current status, and even adding your own commands to the command library.

## Executing a Command

Commands can be executed in two ways. The DTE object has an ExecuteCommand method you can use to trigger a command based on its name:

```
DTE.ExecuteCommand("Window.CloseDocumentWindow")
```

The Commands collection is also a vehicle for launching commands through its Raise method. Instead of using the command's name, the Raise method uses its GUID and ID to identify the command:

```
Dim commands As Commands2 = DTE.Commands
Dim cmd As Command = commands.Item("Window.CloseDocumentWindow")
Dim customIn, customOut As Object

commands.Raise(cmd.Guid, cmd.ID, customin, customout)
```

Some commands accept arguments. The Shell command is one example. It is used to launch an external application into the shell environment and thus takes the application filename as one of its parameters. You can launch this command by using the ExecuteCommand method like this:

```
Dim commands As Commands2 = DTE.Commands
Dim cmd As Command = commands.Item("Tools.Shell")
Dim arg1 = "MyApp.exe"

DTE.ExecuteCommand(cmd.Name, arg1)
```

The Raise method also works with arguments: The last two parameters provided to the Raise method are used to specify an array of arguments to be used by the command and an array of output values returned from the command.

## Mapping Key Bindings

Most commands can be invoked by a keyboard shortcut in addition to a menu entry or button on a command bar. You can set these keyboard shortcuts on a per-command basis by using the Command.Bindings property. This property returns or accepts a SafeArray (essentially an array of objects) that contains each shortcut as an element of the array.

Key bindings are represented as strings with the following format:
"[scopename]::[modifier+][key]".

Scopename is used to refer to the scope where the shortcut is valid, such as Text Editor or Global. The modifier token is used to specify the key modifier such as "Ctrl+", "Alt+", or "Shift+" (modifiers are not required). And the key is the keyboard key that will be pressed (in conjunction with the modifier if present) to invoke the command.

To add a binding to an existing command, you first need to retrieve the current array of binding values, add your binding string to the array, and then assign the whole array back into the Bindings property like this:

```
Dim commands As Commands2 = DTE.Commands
Dim cmd As Command = _
    commands.Item("File.SaveSelectedItems")

Dim bindings() As Object

bindings = cmd.Bindings

' Increase the array size by 1 to hold the new binding
ReDim Preserve bindings(bindings.GetUpperBound(0) + 1)
```

```
' Assign the new binding into the array
bindings(bindings.GetUpperBound(0)) = "Global::Shift+F2"

' Assign the array back to the command object
cmd.Bindings = bindings
```

> **NOTE**
>
> You can create your own named commands that can be launched from a command bar in the IDE (or from the command window for that matter). The Command object itself is added to the Commands collection by calling Commands.AddNamedCommand. The code that will run when the command is executed will have to be implemented by an add-in. We'll cover this scenario in Chapter 13.

# Debugger Objects

The automation object model provides a Debugger object that allows you to control the Visual Studio debugger. A Debugger instance can be obtained through the DTE.Debugger property:

```
Dim debugger As EnvDTE.Debugger
debugger = DTE.Debugger
```

With a valid Debugger object, you can do the following:

▶ Set breakpoints

▶ Start and stop the debugger for a given process

▶ Control the various execution stepping actions supported by the debugger such as Step Into, Step Over, and Step Out

▶ Issue the Run to Cursor command to the debugger

▶ Query the debugger for its current mode (for example, break mode, design mode, or run mode)

The following code starts the debugger if it isn't already started:

```
Dim debugger As Debugger2
debugger = DTE.Debugger

If debugger.CurrentMode <> dbgDebugMode.dbgRunMode Then
    debugger.Go()
End If
```

# Automation Events

If your macro or add-in needs to be notified when a certain event occurs, various event objects are supported in all the automation object categories previously discussed. There are events for windows, events for editors, events for projects, and so on. For every event supported by the IDE, a corresponding class in the automation model allows you to hook the event and take action if the event is raised. The event objects tree is rooted in the DTE.Events property, as depicted in Figure 11.10.

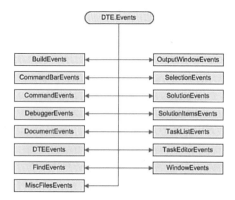

FIGURE 11.10    Event types.

Because events are handled differently depending on whether you are working with code in an add-in or code in a macro, we will wait until the next chapter to cover the details of handling events. The basic premise, however, is fairly simple: You obtain a reference to the event object that you are interested in and then write an event handler that responds to one of that object's published events.

This code, for instance, is how you might handle the "build complete" event from inside a Visual Basic add-in:

```
Dim WithEvents bldevents As BuildEvents
bldevents = DTE.Events.BuildEvents
```

After instantiating a BuildEvents object, you now have to write the actual event handler:

```
Private Sub bldevents_OnBuildDone(ByVal Scope As EnvDTE.vsBuildScope, _
    ByVal Action As EnvDTE.vsBuildAction) Handles bldevents.OnBuildDone
        " Code to handle the event goes here
    End Sub
```

# Summary

The Visual Studio automation object model is a deep and wide API that exposes many of the IDE components to managed code running as a macro or an add-in. In this chapter, we documented how this API is organized and described its capabilities in terms of controlling the Visual Studio debugger, editors, windows, tool windows, solutions, and projects.

We also discussed the eventing model exposed by the API and looked at the API's capabilities with regard to accessing the underlying code structure for a project, issuing commands inside the IDE, and editing text documents programmatically.

Using the methods and properties expressed on the automation objects, you can automate common tasks in the IDE and extend Visual Studio in ways that address your specific development tool needs.

In the next chapter, we will directly build on the concepts discussed here and specifically walk you through the process of writing macros that talk to the automation objects.

# CHAPTER 12

# Writing Macros

In the preceding chapter, we examined the API available for developers to customize, tweak, and control various portions of the Visual Studio IDE. This chapter takes that knowledge and shows you how to write macros that leverage the automation object model.

A macro's purpose is to provide you with an approach for writing your own task automation applets. In previous chapters, you saw many IDE features that automate repetitive tasks. The built-in refactoring support, IntelliSense word completion, code snippets, and others certainly fall into that category. And as you develop solutions with Visual Studio, you will find yourself performing additional repetitive tasks that beg for a solution. Macros are the means to that end: They are Visual Basic routines that interact with the automation object model to control various aspects of the IDE. Although macros can certainly be complex pieces of logic, their real value lies in the fact that it is relatively simple to write short, quick routines that take some of the manual pain away from the development process. Macros aren't used so much to add new functionality to the IDE as to batch together actions in the IDE and enable a single invocation point for those actions.

If you think about the common tasks that you perform while developing a Visual Studio solution, the macro's value lies in its capability to help you automate those tasks where it makes sense. Chapter 11, "Introducing the Automation Object Model," included a macro sample that inserts a comment "flowerbox" at the start of a function or subroutine. The goal with that macro was to reduce the time required to fully comment routines. That particular macro wasn't complicated, nor did it solve a particularly egregious software engineering problem. Its intent, rather, was to take a small edge off a very manual component to the code-writing process: commenting your code. So the macro development process really starts with first identifying an opportunity for automation. The next step is to understand the IDE objects you will have to touch to effect a solution. The final step is tying those objects together with Visual Basic code in the form of a macro.

We have already covered two of the three pieces of knowledge that enable you to become proficient with macros: We discussed the automation object model in-depth in the preceding chapter, and we summarized the scenarios in which macros shine. The third and final piece is understanding the mechanics of writing a macro from start to finish and then executing the macro in the IDE.

Macros can be handcrafted or generated for you by recording certain actions within the IDE. In fact, Visual Studio even has a separate macro development environment—the Macros IDE—designed to help you quickly develop macro solutions.

## Recording a Macro

The simplest way to create a macro is to record one: Just turn on Visual Studio's macro recorder and perform a series of actions in the IDE. The macro recorder will turn your IDE interactions into macro code.

To start recording a macro, select Tools, Macros, Record TemporaryMacro (or press Shift+Ctrl+R). This immediately starts the recorder; a small toolbar, as shown in Figure 12.1, appears at this point to enable you to control the recording.

FIGURE 12.1   The Macro Recorder toolbar.

The three buttons on the toolbar enable you to pause and resume the recording, stop the recording, or cancel the recording. Pausing the recording does just that: The recorder stops recording your actions in the IDE, although it still remains active. Clicking the button a second time resumes recording. If you stop the recording, this causes the macro code to be generated and saved for later execution. Canceling the recording stops the recorder but does not save the macro.

With the recorder running, perform a series of actions in the IDE. Suppose that you want to have an easy way to expand all the project nodes (and their subnodes) in the Solution Explorer window. To record this action, you simply start the recorder, and then click on each of the project items in the Solution Explorer to expand them in their tree view. When you are finished going through every project and project item, click on the Stop Recording button. The macro is stored at this point as a "temporary" macro. It is not saved to disk at this stage, but you can immediately run it by selecting Run Temporary Macro from the Tools, Macros menu.

> **NOTE**
>
> Only one temporary macro is stored at a time in Visual Studio. This means that if you record another temporary macro, it simply replaces the current temporary macro. If you want to have the macro around for a while, you can store it on disk by selecting Tools, Macros, Save TemporaryMacro. If the Macro Explorer is not already displayed, this selection will show it.

## Using the Macro Explorer

The Macro Explorer is the central tool within the IDE for managing macros. Macros are organized in projects and modules. For instance, the temporary macro that you just created shows up under the MyMacros project, under a module called RecordingModule, and it is called TemporaryMacro.

If you have selected to save the temporary macro, Visual Studio will automatically place that TemporaryMacro node in edit mode with the name highlighted. This is your cue to type in a name for the macro. Pressing Enter will commit the name change and cause the macro to be saved to disk. If you don't change the name, it will not be saved.

Using the Macro Explorer, you can rename or delete macros and run macros.

To execute a macro, just double-click on its node in the Macro Explorer. This immediately runs the macro's code. While a macro is running, you see an animated icon and a status message on Visual Studio's status bar (see Figure 12.2).

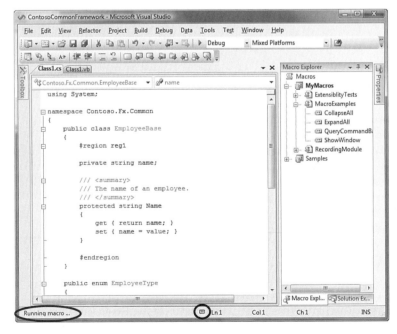

FIGURE 12.2   A running macro.

---

**TIP**

Macros don't have any default or prebuilt notification mechanism that tells you when the macro has completed or if the macro has encountered an error. If you want to track a macro's progress, you need to edit the macro accordingly so that it outputs messages to the output window, through message boxes or other means.

---

To see the Visual Basic code responsible for implementing the macro, you right-click on the macro in the Macro Explorer and select Edit. This launches the Macro IDE. You can also launch the IDE by selecting Tools, Macros, Macros IDE (or pressing Ctrl+F11). The code generated by our prior recording attempt is shown in Listing 12.1. The commands for deleting or renaming a macro, macro module, or macro project are also located on the right-click menu in the Macro Explorer.

LISTING 12.1    Recorder-Generated Macro Code

```
Option Strict Off
Option Explicit Off
Imports System
Imports EnvDTE
Imports EnvDTE80
Imports EnvDTE90
Imports System.Diagnostics


Public Module RecordingModule

    Sub TemporaryMacro()
DTE.ActiveWindow.Object.GetItem("ContosoCommonFramework\Architecture
➥Models").UIHierarchyItems.Expanded = True
DTE.ActiveWindow.Object.GetItem("ContosoCommonFramework\Class Libraries").
➥UIHierarchyItems.Expanded = True
DTE.ActiveWindow.Object.GetItem("ContosoCommonFramework\Class
➥Libraries\Contoso.Fx.Analysis\Properties").UIHierarchyItems.Expanded = True
DTE.ActiveWindow.Object.GetItem("ContosoCommonFramework\Class
➥Libraries\Contoso.Fx.Analysis\References").UIHierarchyItems.Expanded = True
DTE.ActiveWindow.Object.GetItem("ContosoCommonFramework\Class
➥Libraries\Contoso.Fx.Common\Properties").UIHierarchyItems.Expanded = True
DTE.ActiveWindow.Object.GetItem("ContosoCommonFramework\Class
➥Libraries\Contoso.Fx.Common\References").UIHierarchyItems.Expanded = True
DTE.ActiveWindow.Object.GetItem("ContosoCommonFramework\Class
➥Libraries\Contoso.Fx.Integration\Properties").UIHierarchyItems.Expanded = True
DTE.ActiveWindow.Object.GetItem("ContosoCommonFramework\Class
➥Libraries\Contoso.Fx.Integration\References").UIHierarchyItems.Expanded = True
DTE.ActiveWindow.Object.GetItem("ContosoCommonFramework\Consoles\AdminConsole").
➥UIHierarchyItems.Expanded = True
```

```
DTE.ActiveWindow.Object.GetItem("ContosoCommonFramework\Consoles\HelloWorld").
➥UIHierarchyItems.Expanded = True
DTE.ActiveWindow.Object.GetItem("ContosoCommonFramework\Consoles").
➥UIHierarchyItems.Expanded = True
DTE.ActiveWindow.Object.GetItem("ContosoCommonFramework\Consoles\AdminConsole\
➥Properties").UIHierarchyItems.Expanded = True
DTE.ActiveWindow.Object.GetItem("ContosoCommonFramework\Consoles\AdminConsole\
➥References").UIHierarchyItems.Expanded = True
DTE.ActiveWindow.Object.GetItem("ContosoCommonFramework\Consoles\HelloWorld\
➥Properties").UIHierarchyItems.Expanded = True
DTE.ActiveWindow.Object.GetItem("ContosoCommonFramework\Consoles\HelloWorld\
➥References").UIHierarchyItems.Expanded = True
DTE.ActiveWindow.Object.GetItem("ContosoCommonFramework\Consoles\HelloWorld\
➥XMLSchema1.xsd").UIHierarchyItems.Expanded = True
DTE.ActiveWindow.Object.GetItem("ContosoCommonFramework\Forms").UIHierarchyItems.
➥Expanded = True
DTE.ActiveWindow.Object.GetItem("ContosoCommonFramework\Forms\Contoso.UI.
➥WindowsForms.TestHost\Properties").UIHierarchyItems.Expanded = True
DTE.ActiveWindow.Object.GetItem("ContosoCommonFramework\Forms\Contoso.UI.
➥WindowsForms.TestHost\References").UIHierarchyItems.Expanded = True
DTE.ActiveWindow.Object.GetItem("ContosoCommonFramework\Forms\Contoso.UI.
➥WindowsForms.TestHost\Form1.jsl").UIHierarchyItems.Expanded = True
DTE.ActiveWindow.Object.GetItem("ContosoCommonFramework\C:\...\PortalSite\").
➥UIHierarchyItems.Expanded = True
    End Sub
End Module
```

**12**

# Writing Macros with the Macro IDE

The Macros IDE, shown in Figure 12.3, is essentially a specialized version of Visual Studio, trimmed down and streamlined to support the macro development process.

Immediately, you can see that this is, in fact, the Visual Studio user interface that you are by now used to working with. Everything behaves the same: Tool windows can be docked, can float, can be pinned, and so on. The code editor window that you use to edit your macro code works the same with IntelliSense, outlining, and all the other productivity aids you have come to expect. Although the Macros IDE behaves identically to the full-blown Visual Studio IDE, there are some differences. For instance, it has only a subset of the tool windows and document windows supported in the full IDE. Language support in the code editor is limited strictly to Visual Basic (because that is the only macro language supported), and you can't design forms or any similar artifact here.

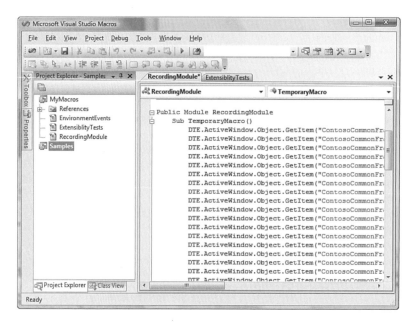

FIGURE 12.3    The Macros IDE.

## Working with Macro Projects

The Project Explorer tool window works on the same principles as the Solution Explorer; it presents a tree view of your work items. In the case of macros, the tree nodes are organized like this: project -> module. Individual macros are displayed in the code editor window (note that this is essentially the same as the Macro Explorer view, with the exception that the Macro Explorer's tree shows each individual macro by name).

In our case, we recorded a temporary macro, and it shows up under the MyMacros project, in the module named RecordingModule. If you look back at Figure 12.3, you will see a portion of the code that was created when the macro was recorded; it is all contained in a Visual Basic sub called TemporaryMacro().

---

**TIP**

When you use the macro recorder, the code that it emits is automatically stored in the MyMacros project. To change this, just right-click any other macro project in the Macro Explorer and select Set as Recording Project.

---

Macro projects map one-to-one with a folder on disk; they are not the same as Visual Studio projects. By default, you have a MyMacros project (which maps to the folder MyMacros under Documents\Visual Studio 2008\Projects\VSMacros80) and a Samples project (which maps to a Samples folder under the same directory tree). Within each macro project directory, there will be a .vsmacros file whose name is the same as the project directory's name. Thus, there is a `Samples.vsmacros` file in the `Samples` folder, and a `MyMacros.vsmacros` file in the `MyMacros` folder.

The `.vsmacro` file contains all the code for the individual macros (and modules) within the project that it maps to. This is a huge difference from the way that Visual Studio works with project files: A macro does not map to its own file like a project item does in, say, a Visual Basic class library project.

### Sharing Macros

You might be surprised to learn that the default, native storage format for macros is binary. Technically, the `.vsmacros` file is a COM-structured storage file; within this file resides all the source code for every macro in the project. To share a specific macro module with others, you can export the module to a Visual Basic (`.vb`) file. To do so, perform the following steps:

1. Right-click the macro module in the Macros IDE Project Explorer.

2. Select Export *ModuleName*. The Export File dialog box launches (see Figure 12.4).

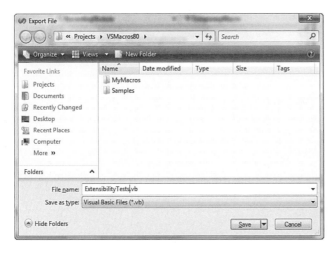

FIGURE 12.4     Exporting a macro module.

3. Select a location and filename, and the macro code will be written into the file in plain text.

After a macro module has been exported, you can physically share it with other developers by simply passing the file around. Importing a previously exported macro file is easy: From the Macros IDE, you select Project, Add Existing Item and select the macro `.vb` file to import; this places it into the macro project currently selected in the Project Explorer.

By sharing the entire `.vsmacros` file, you can also share entire macro projects at a time. It is often helpful in this scenario to change the default storage format from binary to text. You accomplish this from the primary Visual Studio IDE by first selecting a macro project in the Macro Explorer and then, in the property window, changing the Storage Format property from Binary to Text (see Figure 12.5).

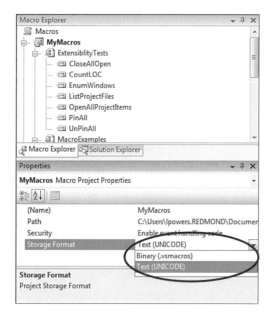

FIGURE 12.5    Changing the storage format for a macro project.

Immediately after changing this property value, Visual Studio converts the single binary macro project file to a series of plain-text files. Each module is represented by its own .vb file at this stage. See Figure 12.6 for a look at the files in the MyMacros folder, after the MyMacros project has been converted to text.

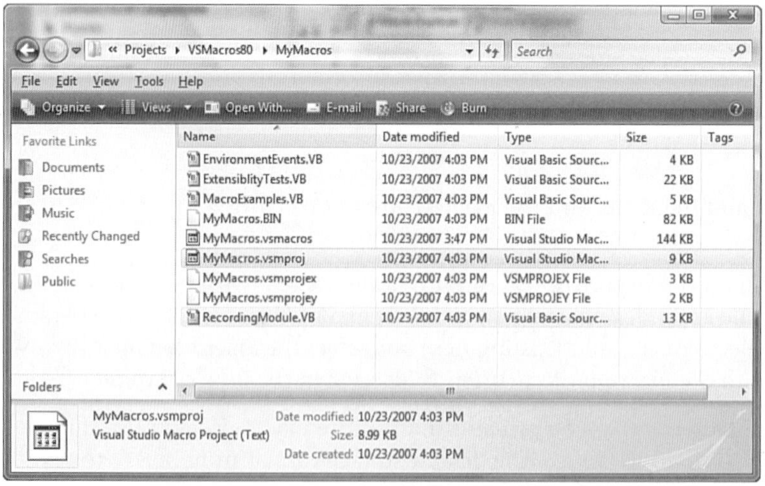

FIGURE 12.6    A macro project stored as text.

### Adding a Project

Confusingly, the capability to add a macro project is not present in the Macros IDE. In other words, there is no File, Open command for opening a .vsmacro file. There is, however, a way to do this in the Visual Studio IDE: Select Tools, Macros, Load Macro Project. From there, you simply browse for the .vsmacros file that contains the project you want to load. If you want to create a new, empty macro project, select Tools, Macros, New Macro Project.

After a macro project has been added, it is immediately accessible in the Macros IDE.

## Writing a Macro

If you revisit the code in Listing 12.1 that was generated for you when you recorded your Solution Explorer node expansions, you can see that it is straightforward, and represents a verbatim replay of what you manually accomplished in the Solution Explorer window. The macro references each individual item in the Explorer window by using the `ActiveWindow.Object.GetItem` method, passing in the object's name to get a `UIHierarchyItem` reference. From there, it is a simple property set to expand all the items below (by setting `UIHierarchyItems.Expand = True`).

The code is complete and works, but it's probably not exactly what you were looking for. For instance, it references the projects and project items that you expanded by their path and name. This means that the macro is certainly not generic (it would work only with this specific Contoso sample solution), and even then the code is fairly brittle: If you add or remove a project or project item, the macro won't know and will still try to set the prior item's `Expanded` property. To really make the macro useful, you want to rework the code here. The advantage of using the recorder is that it produces, if nothing else, a valid starting point for macro development. In fact, it has highlighted the use of an object, `UIHierarchyItem`, which we did not discuss in the preceding chapter. An eye for general program structure would tell you that there should be a way to refactor these lines of code into a loop, recursively expanding nodes out in the tree until all have been expanded. Perhaps instead of just expanding or collapsing nodes, you could also try toggling the `Expanded` property on this object.

You edit macro code using the code editor just as you would edit any other document with Visual Studio. To rework this macro, you can start by establishing a *recursive* helper routine that takes in a `UIHierarchyItem` object, toggles its `Expanded` property to `True`, and calls itself for each sub item found in the `UIHierarchyItems` collection:

```
For Each subNode As UIHierarchyItem In node.UIHierarchyItems
    ExpandNodes(subNode)
Next
node.UIHierarchyItems.Expanded = True
```

> **NOTE**
>
> Unlike the editors in the main Visual Studio IDE, the text editor in the Macros IDE auto-
> matically saves the file you are editing when you close it. This is done without any
> prompting whatsoever. Unless you undo changes you have made while editing, they are
> committed after you close the editor, regardless of whether you have explicitly saved
> them.

Then, to kick things off, you need a parent, controlling routine that instantiates a window object (representing the Solution Explorer) and grabs the root-level UIHierarchy object from the window. From there, you loop the first level of nodes in the tree and call down into the recursive routine:

```
Dim tree As UIHierarchy
Dim explorer As Window2

explorer = DTE.Windows.Item(Constants.vsWindowKindSolutionExplorer)

tree = explorer.Object

For Each node As UIHierarchyItem In tree.UIHierarchyItems
    ExpandNodes(node)
Next
```

To go one step further, if you modify the recursive routine to take in a Boolean value, you now have a general-purpose routine that can either expand or collapse a series of nodes. Putting it all together, you end up with two macros: One expands all nodes in the Solution Explorer tree, and one collapses all nodes in the Solution Explorer tree. In Listing 12.2, you see these two macros as public subroutines called ExpandAll and CollapseAll. The private routine ExpandCollapseNodes is called by both of the macros.

LISTING 12.2    Macro: Expand/Collapse All Solution Explorer Nodes

```
Imports EnvDTE
Imports EnvDTE80
Imports Microsoft.VisualStudio.CommandBars
Imports System
Imports System.Collections
Imports System.Diagnostics
Imports System.Text
Imports System.Windows.Forms


Public Module MacroExamples

    ' Expands all nodes in the Solution Explorer
```

```
Public Sub ExpandAll()
    Dim tree As UIHierarchy
    Dim explorer As Window2

    ' Reference to the solution explorer window
    explorer = DTE.Windows.Item(Constants.vsWindowKindSolutionExplorer)

    ' Reference to the UIHierarchy object obtained from the
    ' solution explorer window
    tree = explorer.Object

    ' Iterate the top level nodes, call recursive routine to
    ' expand each node
    For Each node As UIHierarchyItem In tree.UIHierarchyItems
        ExpandCollapseNodes(node, True)
    Next

End Sub

' Collapses all nodes in the Solution Explorer
Public Sub CollapseAll()
    Dim tree As UIHierarchy
    Dim explorer As Window2

    ' Reference to the solution explorer window
    explorer = DTE.Windows.Item(Constants.vsWindowKindSolutionExplorer)

    ' Reference to the UIHierarchy object obtained from the
    ' solution explorer window
    tree = explorer.Object

    ' Iterate the top level nodes, call recursive routine to
    ' expand each node
    For Each node As UIHierarchyItem In tree.UIHierarchyItems
        ExpandCollapseNodes(node, True)
    Next

End Sub

' Recursive routine for expanding or collapsing all of the sub nodes
' of a given UIHierarchyItem
Private Sub ExpandCollapseNodes(ByRef node As UIHierarchyItem, _
    ByVal expanded As Boolean)
  For Each subNode As UIHierarchyItem In node.UIHierarchyItems
        ' Re-call this routine with the new subnode as the parent node
        ExpandCollapseNodes(subNode, expanded)
```

12

LISTING 12.12    Continued

```
        Next

        ' Perform the collapse/expansion
        node.UIHierarchyItems.Expanded = True

    End Sub
End Module
```

Compared with the code that the macro recorder emitted for you, there isn't a whole lot of similarity; but again, the recorded code *was* useful from an education perspective, alerting you to the approach and concept of using the UIHierarchy/UIHierarchyItem/ UIHierarchyItems objects to handle the node expansion.

## Debugging

The debug experience with macros is similar to that of debugging other Visual Studio projects (which we covered in-depth in Chapter 10, "Debugging Code"). The runtime debugger in the Macros IDE supports all the familiar concepts of breakpoints and the Step Into and Step Over commands.

If you were unsure of your recursive code, you might choose to place a breakpoint in the recursive routine and monitor the progress of the macro. The Macros IDE also supports the Error List window, which flags any syntax errors for you. See Figure 12.7 for a glimpse of a breakpoint and the Error List window in the Macros IDE.

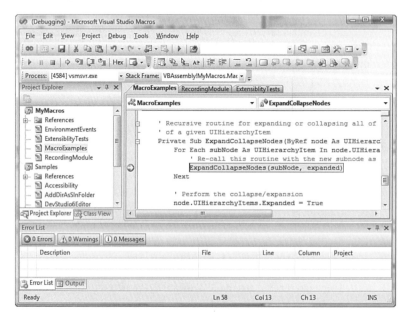

FIGURE 12.7    Debugging a macro.

**NOTE**

If debugging is taking place in the Macros IDE, the main IDE will be inaccessible. You won't be able to perform tasks in the main IDE.

## Handling Events

We covered the individual event classes in Chapter 11; every event exposed in the IDE is available via these automation classes. To handle an event in a macro, you need to have two things: an event definition and an event handler.

Every macro project has, by default, an `EnvironmentEvents` module. This module is automatically created for you every time you create a new macro project, and it implements event definitions for many of the automation events. If you need to handle any of the following event categories, the event definition is already taken care of for you:

▸ Core DTE events

▸ Document events

▸ Window events

▸ Task List events

▸ Search events

▸ Output window events

▸ Selection events

▸ Build events

▸ Solution events

▸ Solution item events

▸ File events

▸ Debugger events

▸ Project events

▸ Keypress events

▸ Code model events

Listing 12.3 shows the `EnvironmentEvents` source code (generated by Visual Studio) that is responsible for implementing these event definitions.

LISTING 12.3   EnvironmentEvents Module

```
Option Strict Off
Option Explicit Off
Imports EnvDTE
Imports EnvDTE80
```

LISTING 12.3    Continued

```vb
Imports System.Diagnostics

Public Module EnvironmentEvents

#Region "Automatically generated code, do not modify"
'Automatically generated code, do not modify
'Event Sources Begin
    <System.ContextStaticAttribute()> _
    Public WithEvents DTEEvents As EnvDTE.DTEEvents

    <System.ContextStaticAttribute()> _
    Public WithEvents DocumentEvents As EnvDTE.DocumentEvents

    <System.ContextStaticAttribute()> _
    Public WithEvents WindowEvents As EnvDTE.WindowEvents

    <System.ContextStaticAttribute()> _
    Public WithEvents TaskListEvents As EnvDTE.TaskListEvents

    <System.ContextStaticAttribute()> _
    Public WithEvents FindEvents As EnvDTE.FindEvents

    <System.ContextStaticAttribute()> _
    Public WithEvents OutputWindowEvents As EnvDTE.OutputWindowEvents

    <System.ContextStaticAttribute()> _
    Public WithEvents SelectionEvents As EnvDTE.SelectionEvents

    <System.ContextStaticAttribute()> _
    Public WithEvents BuildEvents As EnvDTE.BuildEvents

    <System.ContextStaticAttribute()> _
    Public WithEvents SolutionEvents As EnvDTE.SolutionEvents

    <System.ContextStaticAttribute()> _
    Public WithEvents SolutionItemsEvents As EnvDTE.ProjectItemsEvents

    <System.ContextStaticAttribute()> _
    Public WithEvents MiscFilesEvents As EnvDTE.ProjectItemsEvents

    <System.ContextStaticAttribute()> _
    Public WithEvents DebuggerEvents As EnvDTE.DebuggerEvents

    <System.ContextStaticAttribute()> _
    Public WithEvents ProjectsEvents As EnvDTE.ProjectsEvents
```

```
    <System.ContextStaticAttribute()> _
    Public WithEvents TextDocumentKeyPressEvents As
        EnvDTE80.TextDocumentKeyPressEvents

    <System.ContextStaticAttribute()> _
    Public WithEvents CodeModelEvents As EnvDTE80.CodeModelEvents

    <System.ContextStaticAttribute()> _
    Public WithEvents DebuggerProcessEvents As EnvDTE80.DebuggerProcessEvents

    <System.ContextStaticAttribute()> _
    Public WithEvents DebuggerExpressionEvaluationEvents As
        EnvDTE80.DebuggerExpressionEvaluationEvents
'Event Sources End
'End of automatically generated code
#End Region

End Module
```

### Writing the Event Handler

In addition to defining the various event objects for you, the IDE can also be leveraged to insert the actual event handler skeleton code for you. First, open the `EnvironmentEvents` module in the code editor. Then use the type drop-down (the leftmost drop-down at the top of the code editor) to select the event class you want. Figure 12.8 shows the process of selecting the `SolutionEvents` type.

When you have the type selected, the declarations drop-down (the drop-down at the upper right of the code editor) holds a list of the events defined for that event object. If you were interested in receiving notification, for example, every time a solution was opened, you would select the `Opened` event. Immediately after you select this event, the event handler code is injected into the code editor. In this case, the following code results from the selection:

```
Private Sub SolutionEvents_Opened() Handles SolutionEvents.Opened


End Sub
```

You can leave this code as is in the `EnvironmentEvents` module (a reasonable practice), or you can cut and paste it into any other module in the project. With the event handler in place, you just need to worry about writing the code that deals with the event.

Every time a macro project that contains event handlers is loaded in Visual Studio, a security dialog box is displayed (shown in Figure 12.9).

This dialog box merely alerts you to the fact that the macro contains event interception code and enables you to disable the event objects in the macro; the latter is probably a

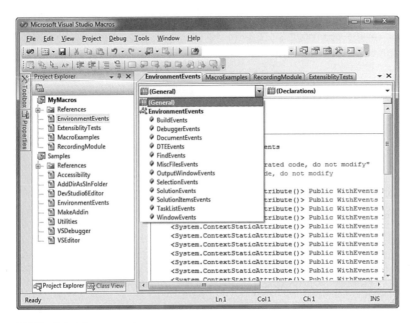

FIGURE 12.8    Selecting a macro event type.

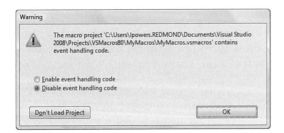

FIGURE 12.9    Loading a macro project with events.

good idea when you're opening a macro from an untrusted source. You also have the option to simply abort the project load process by clicking on the Don't Load Project button at the lower left in the security dialog box.

### Adding a New Event Declaration

If you need access to an event that isn't predeclared for you in the EnvironmentEvents module, it is possible to add the event declaration manually. As a demonstration, let's add a new event handler for the WindowHiding event exposed by the WindowVisibilityEvents class. This event, which is not included by default, tells you whenever a tool window in the IDE is hidden.

First, you need to add the event declaration somewhere within the macro project. The obvious location would be the EnvironmentEvents module; this keeps all the event code in one spot. Just remember to place any manual event declarations outside the region marked as "Automatically generated code, do not modify". Here is the event declaration for the WindowVisibilityEvents class:

```
<System.ContextStaticAttribute()> _
Public WithEvents WindowVisibilityEvents As EnvDTE80.WindowVisibilityEvents
```

Now for the event handler: Just as you did in the previous example, select the type WindowVisibilityEvents in the type drop-down and the event WindowHiding in the members drop-down. This will create a skeleton event handler routine (to which you have the display of a message box):

```
Private Sub WindowVisibilityEvents_WindowHiding(ByVal Window As _
        EnvDTE.Window) Handles WindowVisibilityEvents.WindowHiding

        MessageBox.Show("WindowHiding fired for " & Window.Caption)

End Sub
```

### Initializing the Event Object

Although you have declared the event object and have written the event handler, you still aren't finished: You also need to initialize the event object. The macro runtime itself has two events you need to hook to ensure that the event object is initialized correctly every time the macro runtime starts or resets itself. Without this step, the event object is syntactically complete but won't receive any events from the main IDE.

There are two events you need to concern yourself with, both exposed by the DTEEvents class. The first is DTEEvents.OnMacrosRuntimeReset; this event is fired whenever the runtime is reset for any reason. Because a runtime reset causes all global state to be cleared, including event connections, this would essentially prevent any event interception from happening if you didn't initialize the event object as a step in the reset process.

Handling this event is the same as handling any other: You use the type and member drop-downs to generate the skeleton code for you, and then you insert the code that you need to initialize the event object:

```
Private Sub DTEEvents_OnMacrosRuntimeReset() Handles _
    DTEEvents.OnMacrosRuntimeReset
     WindowVisibilityEvents = CType(DTE.Events, Events2).WindowVisibilityEvents
End Sub
```

The second event you need to hook is the DTEEvents.OnStartupComplete event. This event is fired when the runtime and macro environment has completed its startup process:

```
Private Sub DTEEvents_OnStartupComplete() Handles DTEEvents.OnStartupComplete
    WindowVisibilityEvents = CType(DTE.Events, Events2).WindowVisibilityEvents
End Sub
```

By initializing the event object every time the runtime starts or resets itself, you ensure that you maintain a viable, active link to the eventing engine in the IDE.

To test the event handler, you simply switch to the main IDE and close or hide any of the tool windows by clicking on their Close button. If you have done everything correctly, you will see the message box shown in Figure 12.10.

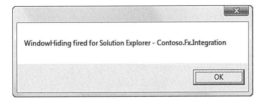

FIGURE 12.10   Catching the `WindowHiding` event.

---

**TIP**

If you have added a new event declaration to your macro project and are unable to get its event handler to fire, a few things may have gone wrong. First, make sure that you have correctly added the event class initialization code to both the `OnStartup-Complete` and `OnMacrosRuntimeReset` events. Second, you may need to unload and reload your macro project to establish the "wiring" for your event. To unload the macro project, shut down the Macros IDE (if it is open), and from the Main IDE's Macro Explorer window, right-click on the macro project that you have added the event(s) to and select Unload Macro Project. Then add the macro project back in by right-clicking the root Macros node in the Macro Explorer and selecting Load Macro Project. Make sure you select Enable Event Handling Code in the security dialog box that triggers when you try to load the project.

---

## Invoking Macros

From the discussion of the Macro Explorer, you know that one way to run a macro is to simply double-click on the specific macro in the Explorer window. And we have also covered macro invocation based on an event within the IDE. Another common scenario you will want to support with certain macros is a way to trigger a macro from the main IDE through toolbar buttons, menu items, and keyboard shortcuts.

### Triggering Macros from Toolbars and Menus

If you wanted to provide quick access to the node expansion and node collapse macros, you could assign them as toolbar buttons or menu items in the main IDE. You do this through the Customize dialog box as shown here:

1. Display the dialog box by selecting Tools, Customize.
2. Select the Commands tab.

3. Select the Macros category in the categories list. Each individual macro in all the currently loaded macro projects will be displayed in the commands list box (following the format [*Macro Project Name*].[*Macro Module Name*].[*Macro Subroutine Name*]).

4. With the macro selected, drag it onto any of the visible toolbars or menus (see Figure 12.11).

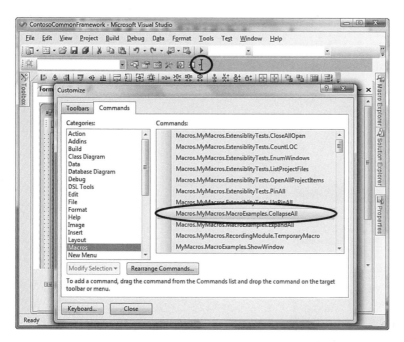

FIGURE 12.11    Drag the macro from the list to the toolbar or menu.

After you add the button or menu item, the item will remain highlighted/selected; if you now click on the Modify Selection button in the Customize dialog box, a drop-down menu (displayed in Figure 12.12) appears that enables you to change the appearance of the button or menu item.

Using this interactive drop-down, you can change the text that appears for the item, assign a picture to the item, or even "paint" your own picture using the Button Editor (see Figure 12.13). You launch the Button Editor dialog box by selecting the Edit Button Image option from this drop-down.

### Assigning Keyboard Shortcuts to Macros

To launch a macro via a keyboard shortcut, you need to assign the key sequence to the macro using the Options dialog box as described here:

1. Open the Options dialog box by selecting Tools, Options.

2. Under the Environment node, select the Keyboard page.

3. In the Keyboard settings page, select the macro in the list of commands (you can filter this list by typing the name of the macro or by just typing **macros** in the text

box labeled Show Commands Containing). Each macro is listed by its macro project, module name, and then macro name.

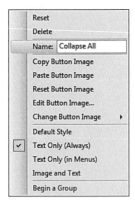

FIGURE 12.12　The Modify Selection drop-down.

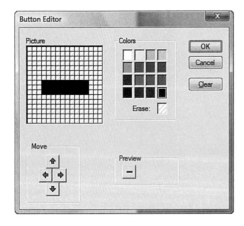

FIGURE 12.13　Assigning a button image.

4. Put the cursor in the Press Shortcut Keys text box and then press the key or keys you want to use to trigger the macro (see Figure 12.14).

5. Click on the Assign button; your macro can now be launched through the key combination that you entered.

**NOTE**

Visual Studio already has many different key combinations assigned to its various actions and commands. If you happen to press a key combination that is already in use, the command that currently uses that key combination is displayed in the drop-down at the bottom of the Options dialog box (see Figure 12.14). At this point, you can either choose a different set of keys to use, or you can overwrite the key assignments. Overwriting is probably not a good idea if you are replacing one of the more common commands: cut, open file, and so on.

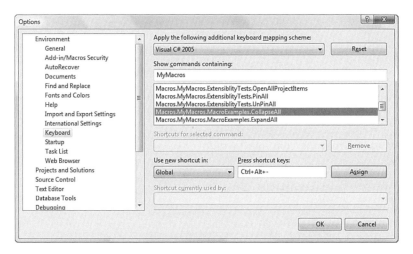

FIGURE 12.14    Assigning a keyboard shortcut to a macro.

### Running Macros from the Command Window

As you have seen from the steps to trigger a macro via toolbar/menu and keyboard short-cut, each macro is exposed in the IDE via a command (see the section "Command Objects" in Chapter 11). The command window is purpose-built to execute commands, so macros can be run from the command window prompt as well.

With your cursor at the prompt in the command window, just type the letter m to trigger the window's IntelliSense and thus display a list of all macros. Scroll down and select the macro you want to run; then press Enter. The macro will execute.

**Macros with Parameters**    Although, in general, it makes sense for macros to execute without any required user interaction, it may sometimes be beneficial to write macros that accept parameters as part of their function/sub definition.

Consider the ResizeIDE macro in Listing 12.4. It takes in width and height values as parameters and then resizes the main IDE window according to those values.

LISTING 12.4    Resizing the IDE

```
Option Strict Off
Option Explicit Off
Imports EnvDTE
Imports EnvDTE80


Public Module MacroExamples

    Public Sub ResizeIDE(Optional ByVal width As Integer = 800, _
        Optional ByVal height As Integer = 600)
        Dim ide As Window2 = DTE.MainWindow
```

LISTING 12.4    Continued

```
        ide.Width = width
        ide.Height = height


    End Sub
End Module
```

If you were to call this macro from the command window, you would have to pass these parameters in like this:

```
Macros.MyMacros.MacroExamples.ResizeIDE(800, 600)
```

> **NOTE**
>
> If you write a macro that accepts parameters, those parameters must be declared as optional, and you must provide default values for the parameters. Although you won't receive any errors, if you write a macro with nonoptional parameters, the macro won't be registered. You won't see it in the Macro Explorer, and you won't be able to run the macro.

# Summary

In this chapter, we described how to leverage the power of Visual Studio's automation APIs to create macros, add-ins, and wizards.

You saw that the macro recorder gives you a quick entry point into driving various components of the IDE, that the Macro Explorer provides a central place to manage your macro collections, and that Visual Studio provides a fully featured integrated development environment built specifically for macro development. Using these tools, you can record basic macros and use them as a starting point for more complicated macros, or you can craft macros from scratch using the Visual Basic programming language.

# CHAPTER 13

# Writing Add-ins and Wizards

If macros represent the quick and easy approach to automation, then add-ins are their more complex, and more powerful, counterparts. Add-ins are compiled projects written in Visual Basic, Visual C#, even Visual C++. Add-ins are useful for covering more advanced extensibility scenarios up to and including surfacing your own custom forms, tool windows, and designers in the IDE.

Another related topic we will tackle in this chapter is that of creating and customizing Visual Studio wizards. Wizards are launched anytime you create a new project or add an item to a project. These wizards typically present one or more dialog boxes to capture preferences from the user and then use those preferences to create a project structure, generate default code, or perform even more complicated tasks. Wizards work in conjunction with template files to drive the initial structure for a code file or an entire project. The entire framework for wizards and templates is available to customize to fit your particular needs.

In the two preceding chapters, you have seen how the Visual Studio automation API is organized, and how you can write macros that interact with that API. Macros are an ideal way to control various items in the IDE. Within a macro, you have access to the entire automation object model, macros are easy to write, and they come complete with their own development environment. Even with all of these positives, however, there are limitations as to what a macro can do:

▶ A macro can't be used to create and display custom tool windows.

▶ A macro is incapable of exposing any sort of user interface beyond simple dialog boxes and message boxes.

▶ A macro can't implement a property page hosted in the Options dialog box.

▶ A macro can't dynamically enable or disable menu and toolbar items in the IDE.

▶ A macro can't be compiled and distributed as an executable binary.

Visual Studio add-ins can do all this and more. Put simply, add-ins present deeper IDE integration options to developers. So, what exactly is an add-in? An add-in is a compiled DLL containing a COM object that implements a specific interface, `IDTExtensibility2`, which provides the add-in with a direct connection to the IDE. As we have mentioned previously, you can write add-ins in your managed language of choice. Because we have spent so much time working with Visual Basic syntax in the macro world, in this chapter all the add-in examples are done in C#.

# Creating Your First Add-in Project

The simplest way to get started with add-ins is to jump right in by running the Add-in Wizard. As with the macro recorder, the wizard will give you a starting point for implementing your own add-ins, and by examining the code that the Add-in Wizard creates, you can learn a great deal about the makeup of an add-in.

The Add-in Wizard is launched whenever you try to create a new project of the type Visual Studio Add-in. From the File, New Project dialog box, select the Extensibility node in the project types tree (in Other Project Types, Extensibility). From here, you can see two project templates: Visual Studio Add-in and Shared Add-in (see Figure 13.1).

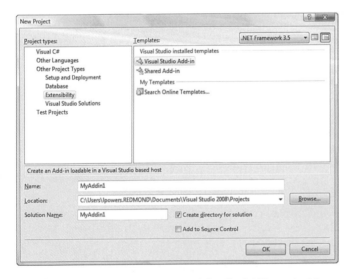

FIGURE 13.1    Selecting the Visual Studio Add-in project type.

We'll touch on the differences between these two project types in a bit; for now, we are interested in the Visual Studio Add-in template.

Clicking OK will start the Add-in Wizard.

## Setting Add-in Parameters

The Add-in Wizard will collect all the information needed to define the core parameters for the add-in project: the language you want to develop in, the application host, and runtime information about the add-in such as a description, and information for the About box. Let's briefly examine each of the wizard pages.

### Selecting a Language

After an initial welcome page, the first piece of information you need to provide is the language you want to use for developing the add-in (see Figure 13.2).

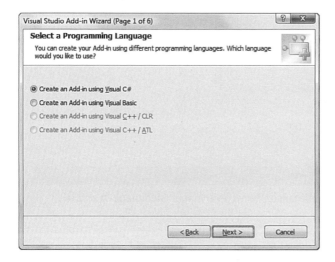

FIGURE 13.2   Picking your add-in language.

The list of languages available will depend on two things:

▶ The languages installed as part of your Visual Studio package

▶ The type of add-in (shared or Visual Studio)

Visual Studio add-ins support Visual C#, Visual Basic, and both managed and unmanaged Visual C++.

### Picking an Application Host

After selecting a language, you are presented with a question about "application hosts." This screen is really just asking where you want the add-in to run.

Because you have indicated that this is a Visual Studio Add-in and not a shared add-in, your host options essentially are the Visual Studio IDE or the Macros IDE. Visual Studio

2008 has the capability to target multiple versions of the IDE. For instance, if you have Visual Studio 2005 installed side by side with Visual Studio 2008, you will have the option to host your add-in in both IDEs. See Figure 13.3, noting that options are displayed for both versions of Visual Studio.

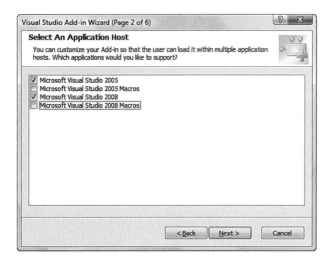

FIGURE 13.3    Selecting the application host.

---

**NOTE**

This is a good time to discuss the differences between a Visual Studio add-in and a shared add-in. A *shared add-in* is the moniker given for add-ins hosted inside a Microsoft Office application, such as Microsoft Word or Microsoft Excel. A *Visual Studio add-in* can be hosted only within the Visual Studio or Macros IDE. If you run through the Add-in Wizard for a shared add-in, you will find that the page which asks you to select an application host (or hosts) will be populated with a list of the installed Microsoft Office applications; you won't be able to select Visual Studio as an application host for a shared add-in.

---

### Describing the Add-in

The name and description you enter on page 3 of the wizard (see Figure 13.4) are visible in the Add-in Manager when the add-in is selected. This information is intended to give users an idea as to the add-in's functionality and purpose.

### Setting Add-in Options

The next wizard page, shown in Figure 13.5, allows you to specify various add-in options. You can indicate whether you want the add-in to appear in the Tools menu, when you want the add-in to load, and whether the add-in could potentially display a modal dialog box during its operation.

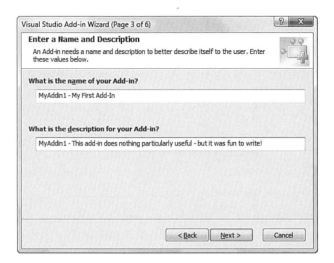

FIGURE 13.4     Giving the add-in a name and description.

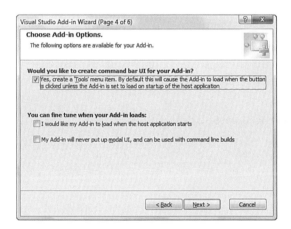

FIGURE 13.5     Setting add-in options.

### Setting About Box Information

The second-to-last wizard page captures the text that Visual Studio will display in its About box (see Figure 13.6).

This is the place to include such details as where users can contact the author of the add-in, support and licensing information, copyright and version information, and so on.

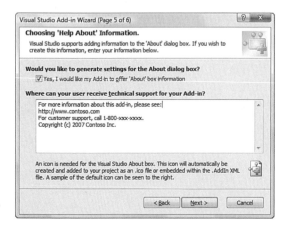

FIGURE 13.6    Entering text for the Visual Studio About box.

**Finishing the Wizard**

The last page of the wizard contains a summary of the options that you have selected. After you click the Finish button, the wizard will start creating the code for your add-in based on all the selections you have made in the wizard.

Because add-ins are DLLs, the Add-in Wizard will create the add-in source as part of a class library project in the IDE. The primary code file that is created implements a class called Connect. This class inherits from all the necessary COM interfaces to make the add-in work in the context of the IDE.

Listing 13.1 shows the Connect class as it was generated by the Add-in Wizard.

LISTING 13.1    Code Generated by the Add-in Wizard

```
using System;
using Extensibility;
using EnvDTE;
using EnvDTE80;
using Microsoft.VisualStudio.CommandBars;
using System.Resources;
using System.Reflection;
using System.Globalization;

namespace MyAddin1
{
    /// <summary>The object for implementing an Add-in.</summary>
    /// <seealso class='IDTExtensibility2' />
    public class Connect : IDTExtensibility2, IDTCommandTarget
    {
        /// <summary>Implements the constructor for the Add-in object.
        /// Place your initialization code within this method.</summary>
```

```
public Connect()
{

}

/// <summary>Implements the OnConnection method of the
/// IDTExtensibility2 interface. Receives notification that
/// the Add-in is being loaded.</summary>
/// <param term='application'>Root object of the host
/// application.</param>
/// <param term='connectMode'>Describes how the Add-in
/// is being loaded.</param>
/// <param term='addInInst'>Object representing this
/// Add-in.</param>
/// <seealso class='IDTExtensibility2' />
public void OnConnection(object application,
  ext_ConnectMode connectMode,
  object addInInst, ref Array custom)
{
  _applicationObject = (DTE2)application;
  _addInInstance = (AddIn)addInInst;
  if(connectMode == ext_ConnectMode.ext_cm_UISetup)
  {
    object []contextGUIDS = new object[] { };
    Commands2 commands =
      (Commands2)_applicationObject.Commands;

    string toolsMenuName;

    try
    {
      //If you would like to move the command to a different
      // menu, change the word "Tools" to the English version
      // of the menu. This code will take the culture, append
      // on the name of the menu, then add the command to
      // that menu. You can find a list of all the top-level
      // menus in the file CommandBar.resx.
      string resourceName;
      ResourceManager resourceManager =
        new ResourceManager("MyAddin1.CommandBar",
        Assembly.GetExecutingAssembly());

      CultureInfo cultureInfo =
        new CultureInfo(_applicationObject.LocaleID);

      if(cultureInfo.TwoLetterISOLanguageName == "zh")
```

LISTING 13.1    Continued

```
          {
            System.Globalization.CultureInfo
              parentCultureInfo = cultureInfo.Parent;
            resourceName =
              String.Concat(parentCultureInfo.Name, "Tools");
          }
          else
          {
            resourceName =
              String.Concat(cultureInfo.TwoLetterISOLanguageName,
                "Tools");
          }
          toolsMenuName = resourceManager.GetString(resourceName);
      }
      catch
      {
          //We tried to find a localized version of the word
          // Tools, but one was not found. Default to the en-US
          // word, which may work for the current culture.
          toolsMenuName = "Tools";
      }

      //Place the command on the Tools menu.
      //Find the MenuBar command bar, which is the top-level
      // command bar holding all the main menu items:
      Microsoft.VisualStudio.CommandBars.CommandBar
        menuBarCommandBar =
        ((Microsoft.VisualStudio.CommandBars.CommandBars)
        _applicationObject.CommandBars)["MenuBar"];

      //Find the Tools command bar on the MenuBar command bar:
      CommandBarControl toolsControl =
        menuBarCommandBar.Controls[toolsMenuName];

      CommandBarPopup toolsPopup =
          (CommandBarPopup)toolsControl;

      //This try/catch block can be duplicated if you wish to
      // add multiple commands to be handled by your Add-in,
      // just make sure you also update the QueryStatus/Exec
      // method to include the new command names.
      try
      {
          //Add a command to the Commands collection:
          Command command =
```

```csharp
        commands.AddNamedCommand2(_addInInstance,
        "MyAddin1", "MyAddin1",
        "Executes the command for MyAddin1", true, 59,
        ref contextGUIDS,
        (int)vsCommandStatus.vsCommandStatusSupported+
        (int)vsCommandStatus.vsCommandStatusEnabled,
        (int)vsCommandStyle.vsCommandStylePictAndText,
        vsCommandControlType.vsCommandControlTypeButton);

    //Add a control for the command to the Tools menu:
    if((command != null) && (toolsPopup != null))
    {
        command.AddControl(toolsPopup.CommandBar, 1);
    }
}
catch(System.ArgumentException)
{
    //If we are here, then the exception is probably because
    //a command with that name already exists. If so there
    //is no need to recreate the command and we can safely
    //ignore the exception.
    }
}
}

/// <summary>Implements the OnDisconnection method of the
/// IDTExtensibility2 interface. Receives notification that the
/// Add-in is being unloaded.</summary>
/// <param term='disconnectMode'>Describes how the Add-in is being
/// unloaded.</param>
/// <param term='custom'>Array of parameters that are host application
/// specific.</param>
/// <seealso class='IDTExtensibility2' />
public void OnDisconnection(ext_DisconnectMode disconnectMode,
  ref Array custom)
{
}

/// <summary>Implements the OnAddInsUpdate method of the
/// IDTExtensibility2 interface. Receives notification when the
/// collection of Add-ins has changed.</summary>
/// <param term='custom'>Array of parameters that are host application
/// specific.</param>
/// <seealso class='IDTExtensibility2' />
public void OnAddInsUpdate(ref Array custom)
{
}
```

LISTING 13.1    Continued

```csharp
/// <summary>Implements the OnStartupComplete method of the
/// IDTExtensibility2 interface. Receives notification that the host
/// application has completed loading.</summary>
/// <param term='custom'>Array of parameters that are host application
/// specific.</param>
/// <seealso class='IDTExtensibility2' />
public void OnStartupComplete(ref Array custom)
{
}


/// <summary>Implements the OnBeginShutdown method of the
/// IDTExtensibility2 interface. Receives notification that the host
/// application is being unloaded.</summary>
/// <param term='custom'>Array of parameters that are host application
/// specific.</param>
/// <seealso class='IDTExtensibility2' />
public void OnBeginShutdown(ref Array custom)
{
}


/// <summary>Implements the QueryStatus method of the IDTCommandTarget
/// interface. This is called when the command's availability is
/// updated</summary>
/// <param term='commandName'>The name of the command to determine
/// state for.</param>
/// <param term='neededText'>Text that is needed for the
/// command.</param>
/// <param term='status'>The state of the command in the user
/// interface.</param>
/// <param term='commandText'>Text requested by the neededText
/// parameter.</param>
/// <seealso class='Exec' />
public void QueryStatus(string commandName,
  vsCommandStatusTextWanted neededText,
  ref vsCommandStatus status,
  ref object commandText)
  {
    if(neededText ==
      vsCommandStatusTextWanted.vsCommandStatusTextWantedNone)
    {
      if(commandName == "MyAddin1.Connect.MyAddin1")
      {
        status =
          (vsCommandStatus)vsCommandStatus.vsCommandStatusSupported
          |vsCommandStatus.vsCommandStatusEnabled;
```

```
                return;
            }
        }
    }

    /// <summary>Implements the Exec method of the IDTCommandTarget
    /// interface. This is called when the command is invoked.</summary>
    /// <param term='commandName'>The name of the command to
    /// execute.</param>
    /// <param term='executeOption'>Describes how the command should
    /// be run.</param>
    /// <param term='varIn'>Parameters passed from the caller to the
    /// command handler.</param>
    /// <param term='varOut'>Parameters passed from the command handler
    /// to the caller.</param>
    /// <param term='handled'>Informs the caller if the command was
    /// handled or not.</param>
    /// <seealso class='Exec' />
    public void Exec(string commandName,
      vsCommandExecOption executeOption,
      ref object varIn, ref object varOut,
      ref bool handled)
    {
        handled = false;
        if(executeOption ==
           vsCommandExecOption.vsCommandExecOptionDoDefault)
        {
            if(commandName == "MyAddin1.Connect.MyAddin1")
            {
                handled = true;
                return;
            }
        }
    }
    private DTE2 _applicationObject;
    private AddIn _addInInstance;
  }
}
```

At this stage, the add-in doesn't actually *do* anything. You still have to implement the custom logic for the add-in. What the wizard has done, however, is implement much (if not all) of the tedious plumbing required to do the following:

▶ Wire the add-in into the IDE.

▶ Expose it on the Tools menu.

▶ Intercept the appropriate extensibility events to make the add-in work.

Now that you have a baseline of code to work with, you're ready to examine the source to understand the overall structure and layout of an add-in.

# The Structure of an Add-in

The first thing to notice is that the Connect class inherits from two different interfaces: IDTCommandTarget and IDTExtensibility2.

```
public class Connect : IDTExtensibility2, IDTCommandTarget
```

The IDTCommandTarget interface provides the functionality necessary to expose the add-in via a command bar. The code to inherit from this interface was added by the wizard because the Yes, Create a Tools Menu Item box was checked on page 4 of the add-in wizard.

The IDTExtensibility2 interface provides the eventing glue for add-ins. It is responsible for all the events that constitute the life span of an add-in.

## The Life Cycle of an Add-in

Add-ins progress through a sequence of events every time they are loaded or unloaded in their application host. Each of these events is represented by a method defined on the IDTExtensibility2 interface. These methods are documented in Table 13.1.

TABLE 13.1 **IDTExtensibility2** Methods

| Method | Description |
| --- | --- |
| OnAddInsUpdate | Called whenever an add-in is either loaded or unloaded |
| OnBeginShutdown | Called if Visual Studio is shut down while an add-in is loaded |
| OnConnection | Called when an add-in is loaded |
| OnDisconnection | Called when an add-in is unloaded |
| OnStartupComplete | Called when the add-in loads if this add-in is set to load when Visual Studio starts |

The diagrams in Figure 13.7 and Figure 13.8 show how these methods (which really represent events) fall onto the normal load and unload path for an add-in.

If you look back at the template code for the add-in, you can see that each one of these IDTExtensibility2 methods has been implemented. The OnDisconnection, OnAddInsUpdate, OnStartupComplete, and OnBeginShutdown methods are empty; the wizard has merely implemented the method signature. The OnConnection method, however, already has a fair bit of code to it before you even lift a hand to modify or add to the wizard-generated code.

Now you're ready to investigate what happens in each of the IDTExtensibility2 methods.

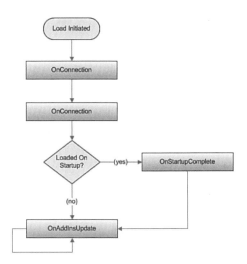

FIGURE 13.7    Load sequence of events.

FIGURE 13.8    Unload sequence of events.

### OnAddInsUpdate

The OnAddInsUpdate method is called when any add-in is loaded or unloaded from Visual Studio; because of this, the OnAddInsUpdate method is primarily useful for enforcing or dealing with dependencies between add-ins. If your add-in depends on or otherwise uses the functionality contained in another add-in, this is the ideal injection point for containing the logic that deals with that relationship.

Here is the OnAddInsUpdate method as implemented by the Add-in Wizard:

```
/// <summary>Implements the OnAddInsUpdate method of the IDTExtensibility2
/// interface. Receives notification when the collection of Add-ins has
/// changed.</summary>
/// <param term='custom'>Array of parameters that are host application
/// specific.</param>
/// <seealso class='IDTExtensibility2' />
public void OnAddInsUpdate(ref Array custom)
{
}
```

> **TIP**
>
> Because you don't know which add-in has triggered the `OnAddInsUpdate` method, you would need to iterate through the `DTE.AddIns` collection and query each add-in's `Connected` property to determine its current state.

### OnBeginShutdown

OnBeginShutdown is called for every running add-in when Visual Studio begins its shutdown sequence. If an IDE requires any cleanup code (including perhaps resetting IDE settings that have been changed during the add-in's life), you would place that code within this method.

A user may elect to cancel Visual Studio's shutdown process. OnBeginShutdown will fire regardless of whether the Visual Studio shutdown process was successful. This forces you, as an add-in author, to always assume that Visual Studio has, in fact, terminated and therefore act accordingly in your code.

Here is the OnBeginShutdown method:

```
/// <summary>Implements the OnBeginShutdown method of the
///IDTExtensibility2 interface. Receives notification that the host
///application is being unloaded.</summary>
/// <param term='custom'>Array of parameters that are host
application specific.</param>
/// <seealso class='IDTExtensibility2' />
public void OnBeginShutdown(ref Array custom)
{
}
```

### OnConnection

OnConnection indicates that an add-in has been loaded:

```
public void OnConnection(object application, ext_ConnectMode connectMode,
    object addInInst, ref Array custom)
```

It accepts four parameters. The first parameter, `application`, is the most important; it provides a reference to the DTE object representing the IDE. You know from Chapter 11, "Introducing the Automation Object Model," that the DTE object is the key to accessing the entire automation object model. With macros, the DTE object is held as a global variable. For add-ins, the OnConnection method is the sole provider of this object, thus providing the crucial link between the add-in and its host IDE.

The second parameter, `connectMode`, is an ext_ConnectMode enumeration. It indicates exactly how the add-in was loaded (see Table 13.2 for a list of the possible ext_ConnectMode values).

TABLE 13.2  **ext_ConnectMode** Members

| Member | Description |
| --- | --- |
| ext_cm_AfterStartup | The add-in was loaded after Visual Studio was started. |
| ext_cm_CommandLine | The add-in was loaded from the command line. |
| ext_cm_External | n/a (Visual Studio 2008 does not use this value.) |
| ext_cm_Solution | The add-in was loaded with a Visual Studio solution. |
| ext_cm_Startup | The add-in was loaded when Visual Studio started. |
| ext_cm_UISetup | The add-in was loaded for UI setup (this represents the initial load of an add-in). |

The addInInst parameter is actually a reference to the add-in itself. And last, the custom parameter is an empty Array object. This array is passed by reference and can be used to pass parameters into and out of the add-in.

The Add-in Wizard has taken the first two parameters, explicitly cast them to their underlying types, and assigned them into two class fields for later reference:

```
_applicationObject = (DTE2)application;
_addInInstance = (AddIn)addInInst;
```

The next block of code examines the ext_ConnectMode value. If this is the first time the add-in was loaded (for example, ext_ConnectMode is equal to ext_cm_UISetup), then the code does two things: It creates a Tools menu entry for the add-in, and it creates a custom, named command to launch the add-in (this named command is called when you select the add-in from the Tools menu).

```
if(connectMode == ext_ConnectMode.ext_cm_UISetup)
{
        object []contextGUIDS = new object[] { };
        Commands2 commands = (Commands2)_applicationObject.Commands;
    string toolsMenuName;

    try
    {
        //If you would like to move the command to a different menu, change the
        // word "Tools" to the English version of the menu.
        //  This code will take the culture, append on the name of the menu,
        //   then add the command to that menu. You can find a list of all
        // the top-level menus in the file
        //  CommandBar.resx.
        ResourceManager resourceManager = new _
                ResourceManager("MyFirstAddin.CommandBar", _
                Assembly.GetExecutingAssembly());
        CultureInfo cultureInfo = new _
                System.Globalization.CultureInfo(_applicationObject.LocaleID);
```

13

```
        string resourceName = String.Concat(cultureInfo.TwoLetterISOLanguageName,
                            "Tools");
        toolsMenuName = resourceManager.GetString(resourceName);
    }
    catch
    {
        //We tried to find a localized version of the word Tools, but one
        //was not found.
        //   Default to the en-US word, which may work for the current culture.
        toolsMenuName = "Tools";
    }
    //Place the command on the Tools menu.
    //Find the MenuBar command bar, which is the top-level command bar holding
    //all the main menu items:
    Microsoft.VisualStudio.CommandBars.CommandBar menuBarCommandBar = _
        ((Microsoft.VisualStudio.CommandBars.CommandBars)__
        applicationObject.CommandBars)["MenuBar"];

    //Find the Tools command bar on the MenuBar command bar:
    CommandBarControl toolsControl = menuBarCommandBar.Controls[toolsMenuName];
    CommandBarPopup toolsPopup = (CommandBarPopup)toolsControl;

    //This try/catch block can be duplicated if you wish to add multiple commands
    //to be handled by your Add-in,
    // just make sure you also update the QueryStatus/Exec method to include
    // the new command names.
    try
    {
        //Add a command to the Commands collection:
        Command command = commands.AddNamedCommand2(_addInInstance, _
                    "MyFirstAddin", "MyFirstAddin", _
                    "Executes the command for MyFirstAddin", true, 59, _
                    ref contextGUIDS,
                    (int)vsCommandStatus.vsCommandStatusSupported
                     +(int)vsCommandStatus.vsCommandStatusEnabled,
                     (int)vsCommandStyle.vsCommandStylePictAndText,
                      vsCommandControlType.vsCommandControlTypeButton);

        //Add a control for the command to the Tools menu:
        if((command != null) && (toolsPopup != null))
        {
            command.AddControl(toolsPopup.CommandBar, 1);
        }
    }
    catch(System.ArgumentException)
    {
```

```
    //If we are here, then the exception is probably because a command with
    //that name already exists. If so there is no need to recreate the
    //command and we can
    //  safely ignore the exception.
}
```

**TIP**

You can see that the Add-in Wizard is quite liberal with its code comments; when you set out to write your own add-in, it is often useful to read the auto-generated comments and simply copy/paste relevant code snippets to duplicate functionality that the wizard has generated for you.

### OnDisconnection

OnDisconnection fires when the add-in is unloaded from Visual Studio. This is the opposite action from that signaled by the OnConnection method. As with OnConnection, an enumeration—ext_DisconnectMode—is provided to this method that indicates how the unload action was initiated. For a list of the possible ext_DisconnectMode values, see Table 13.3.

TABLE 13.3  **ext_DisconnectMode** Members

| Member | Description |
|---|---|
| ext_dm_HostShutdown | The add-in was unloaded because Visual Studio was shut down. |
| ext_dm_SolutionClosed | The add-in was unloaded because the solution was closed. |
| ext_dm_UISetupComplete | The add-in was unloaded after UI setup was complete. |
| ext_dm_UserClosed | The add-in was manually or programmatically unloaded. (This is used only if Visual Studio is still running; otherwise, ext_dm_HostShutdown will be used.) |

Here is the OnDisconnection method:

```
/// <summary>Implements the OnDisconnection method of the IDTExtensibility2
///interface. Receives notification that the Add-in is being
///unloaded.</summary>
/// <param term='disconnectMode'>Describes how the Add-in is being
/// unloaded.</param>
/// <param term='custom'>Array of parameters that are host application
/// specific.</param>
/// <seealso class='IDTExtensibility2' />
public void OnDisconnection(ext_DisconnectMode disconnectMode, ref Array custom)
{
}
```

**OnStartupComplete**

If an add-in is set to load automatically during Visual Studio startup, the OnStartupComplete method will fire after that add-in has been loaded.

Here is the OnStartupComplete method:

```
/// <summary>Implements the OnStartupComplete method of the IDTExtensibility2
/// interface. Receives notification that the host application has completed
/// loading.</summary>
/// <param term='custom'>Array of parameters that are host application
/// specific.</param>
/// <seealso class='IDTExtensibility2' />
public void OnStartupComplete(ref Array custom)
{
}
```

## Reacting to Commands

Add-ins can react to commands issued within the IDE. If you recall from the discussion on commands in Chapter 11, and in Chapter 12, "Writing Macros," this is done through the concept of "named commands." A named command is really nothing more than an action that has a name attached to it. You already know that Visual Studio comes with its own extensive set of commands that cover a wide variety of actions in the IDE. Using the Commands/Commands2 collection, you can create your own named commands by using the AddNamedCommand2 method.

To repeat the dissection of the OnConnection method, the wizard has created a body of code responsible for creating a new named command, adding it to the Tools menu, and then reacting to the command. The IDTCommandTarget.Exec method is the hook used to react to an issued command. Here is its prototype:

```
void Exec (
    [InAttribute] string CmdName,
    [InAttribute] vsCommandExecOption ExecuteOption,
    [InAttribute] ref Object VariantIn,
    [InAttribute] out Object VariantOut,
    [InAttribute] out bool Handled
)
```

To handle a command issued to an add-in, you write code in the Exec method that reacts to the passed-in command.

CmdName is a string containing the name of the command; this is the token used to uniquely identify a command, and thus is the parameter you will examine in the body of the Exec method to determine whether and how you will react to the command.

ExecuteOption is a vsCommandExecOption enumeration that provides information about the options associated with the command (see Table 13.4).

TABLE 13.4  **vsCommandExecOption** Members

| Member | Description |
|---|---|
| vsCommandExecOptionDoDefault | Performs the default behavior |
| vsCommandExecOptionDoPromptUser | Obtains user input and then executes the command |
| vsCommandExecOptionPromptUser | Executes the command without user input |
| vsCommandExecOptionShowHelp | Shows help for the command (does not execute it) |

The VariantIn parameter is used to pass any arguments needed for the incoming command, and VariantOut is used as a way to pass information back out of the add-in to the caller.

Lastly, Handled is a Boolean that indicates to the host application whether the add-in handled the command. As a general rule, if your add-in processed the command, it will set this to true. Otherwise, it will set it to false, which is a signal to Visual Studio that it needs to continue to look for a command invocation target that *will* handle the command.

The code to handle the Tool menu command looks like this:

```
/// <summary>Implements the Exec method of the IDTCommandTarget
///interface. This is called when the command is invoked.</summary>
/// <param term='commandName'>The name of the command to execute.</param>
/// <param term='executeOption'>Describes how the command should
///be run.</param>
/// <param term='varIn'>Parameters passed from the caller to the command
/// handler.</param>
/// <param term='varOut'>Parameters passed from the command handler to
/// the caller.</param>
/// <param term='handled'>Informs the caller if the command was handled
/// or not.</param>
/// <seealso class='Exec' />
public void Exec(string commandName, vsCommandExecOption executeOption,
    ref object varIn, ref object varOut, ref bool handled)
{
    handled = false;
    if(executeOption == vsCommandExecOption.vsCommandExecOptionDoDefault)
    {
        if(commandName == "MyFirstAddin.Connect.MyFirstAddin")
        {
            handled = true;
            return;
        }
    }
}
```

## Managing Add-ins

Visual Studio add-ins are controlled with the Visual Studio Add-in Manager. It allows you to do two things: load and unload any registered add-in and specify how an add-in can be loaded. To access the Add-in Manager (see Figure 13.9), select Tools, Add-in Manager.

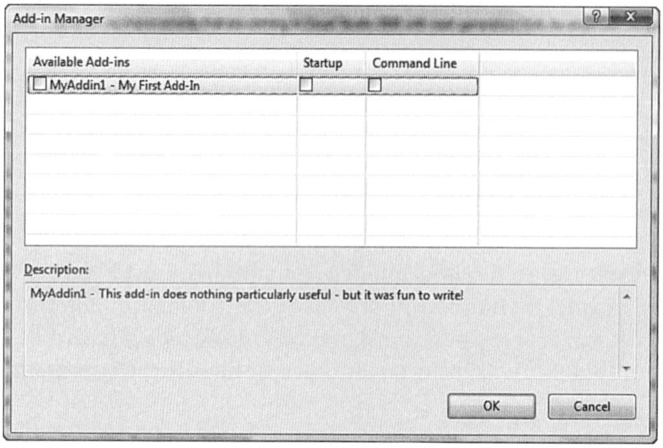

FIGURE 13.9    Managing add-ins.

This dialog box will always display a list of any available add-ins on the local machine. Checking or unchecking the box next to an add-in's name will cause the add-in to immediately load or unload. The Startup check box determines whether the add-in will load automatically when Visual Studio is started. The Command Line check box performs the same action if Visual Studio is started via the command line (such as when you are launching Visual Studio as part of an automated build scenario).

### Add-in Automation Objects

To programmatically manage add-ins, you use the DTE.AddIns collection, which contains an AddIn instance for every currently registered add-in (whether or not it is loaded).

You can directly reference add-ins from the DTE.AddIns collection by using their name like this:

```
AddIn addIn = this.DTE.AddIns.Item("MyFirstAddIn");
```

With a valid add-in object, you can use its properties to determine whether it is loaded, query its name, or retrieve the add-in's ProgID:

```
bool isLoaded = addIn.Connected;
string name = addIn.Name;
string id = addIn.ProgID;
```

---

**NOTE**

We use the term *registered* to denote an add-in that has been installed on the local machine and registered with Visual Studio. In versions before Visual Studio 2005, this meant that a Registry entry was created for the add-in. This concept was replaced in 2005 with XML files: Visual Studio looks for XML files with an `.addin` extension to determine the list of add-ins available to be loaded (an add-in is "loaded" when it has been connected to, and loaded within, an application's host process). These `.addin` files are created for you automatically by the Add-in Wizard, but they can be easily created or edited by hand as well. To get a feeling for the information and structure of these files, look in the `Visual Studio 2008\Addins` folder under your local `Documents` directory. Each registered add-in will appear here; you can explore an add-in file by loading it into Visual Studio, Notepad, or any other text editor.

---

# A Sample Add-in: Color Palette

To cap this discussion of add-ins, let's look at the process of developing a functioning add-in from start to finish. The add-in will be a color picker. It will allow users to click on an area of a color palette, and the add-in will then emit code to create an instance of a color structure that matches the selected color from the palette. Here is a summary list of requirements for the add-in:

▶ In a tool window, it will display a visual color palette representing all the possible colors.

▶ As the mouse pointer is moved over the palette, the control will display the Red, Green, and Blue values for the point directly under the mouse pointer.

▶ If a user clicks on the palette, it will take the current RGB values and emit C# or VB code into the currently active document window to create a new color structure that encapsulates the given color.

▶ The selection of language (for example, C# or VB) will be a configurable property of the control.

## Getting Started

To start the development process, you will create a new solution and a Visual Studio Add-in Project called `ColorSelectorAddIn`. The Add-in Wizard will create a code base for you inside a `Connect` class just as you saw earlier in this chapter. The `Connect` class is the place where all the IDE and automation object model–specific code will go.

In addition to the core add-in plumbing, you will also need to create a `User Control` class that encapsulates the user interface and the processing logic for the add-in.

## Creating the User Control

First, you can work on getting a user control in place that has the functionality you are looking for. After you have a workable control, you can worry about wiring that control into Visual Studio using the Connect class created by the Add-in Wizard.

Add a user control (called PaletteControl) to the add-in project by selecting Project, Add User Control. After the control is added, you'll place nine controls on the user control design surface. First, add a picture box; this will be used to display the palette of colors, stored as a simple bitmap in a resource file (in this case, we're using a color palette from a popular paint program as our source for the bitmap). With the palette in place, you now need six label controls to display RGB values (and label them as such) per the requirements. And finally, in the finest tradition of gold-plating, you'll also add a picture box that repeats the current color selection and a label that shows the code you would generate to implement that color in a color structure.

Figure 13.10 provides a glimpse of the user control after these controls have been situated on the designer.

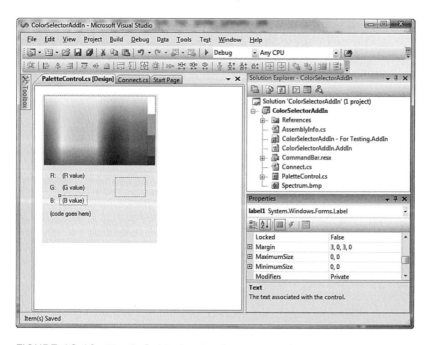

FIGURE 13.10   The **PaletteControl** user control.

### Handling Movement over the Palette

With the UI in place, you can now concentrate on the code. First, you can add an event handler to deal with mouse movements over the top of the palette picture box. With the

MouseMove event handler, you can update your label controls and the secondary picture box instantly as the pointer roves over the palette bitmap:

```
public PaletteControl()
{
    InitializeComponent();
    this.pictureBoxPalette.MouseMove +=
        new MouseEventHandler(pictureBoxPalette_MouseMove);
    this.pictureBoxPalette.Cursor = System.Windows.Forms.Cursors.Cross;
}

void pictureBoxPalette_MouseMove(object sender, MouseEventArgs e)
{
    // Get the color under the current pointer position
    Color color = GetPointColor(e.X, e.Y);

    // Update the RGB labels and the 2nd pic box
    // using the retrieved color
    DisplayColor(color);

    // Generate our VB or C# code for the Color
    // structure
    SetCode(color, _generateVB);
}
```

### Looking at the Code Generation Properties

The PaletteControl class will expose two properties: Code is a string property that holds the color structure code generated when the palette is clicked on, and GenerateVB is a Boolean that specifies whether the control should generate Visual Basic code (GenerateVB = true) or C# code (GenerateVB = false). Here are the field and property declarations for these two properties:

```
string _code = "";
public string Code
{
    get { return _code; }
}

bool _generateVB = false;
public bool GenerateVB
{
    get { return _generateVB; }
}
```

**Implementing the Helper Routines**

Whenever the mouse pointer moves over the picture box region, you need to capture the color components of the point directly below the cursor (GetPointColor), update the label controls and the secondary picture box control to reflect that color (DisplayColor), and then generate the code to implement a matching color structure (SetCode). Here are the implementations of these routines:

```csharp
/// <summary>
/// Returns a Color structure representing the color of
/// the pixel at the indicated x and y coordinates.
/// </summary>
/// <param name="x"></param>
/// <param name="y"></param>
/// <returns>A Color structure</returns>
private Color GetPointColor(int x, int y)
{
    // Get the bitmap from the palette picture box
    Bitmap bmp = (Bitmap)pictureBoxPalette.Image;
    // Use GetPixel to retrieve a color
    // structure for the current pointer position
    Color color = bmp.GetPixel(x, y);

    // Return the color structure
    return color;
}

/// <summary>
/// Displays the RGB values for the given color. Also sets
/// the background color of the secondary picture box.
/// </summary>
/// <param name="color">The Color to display</param>
private void DisplayColor(Color color)
{
    // pull out the RGB values from the
    // color structure
    string R = color.R.ToString();
    string G = color.G.ToString();
    string B = color.B.ToString();
    // set our secondary picture box
    // to display the current color
    this.pictureBoxColor.BackColor = color;
    // display RGB values in the label
    // controls
    this.labelRValue.Text = R;
    this.labelGValue.Text = G;
    this.labelBValue.Text = B;
```

```
}

/// <summary>
/// Generates a string representing the C# or VB code necessary to
/// create a Color structure instance that matches the passed in
/// Color structure. This string is then assigned to this
/// user control's _code field.
/// </summary>
/// <param name="color">The color to represent in code.</param>
/// <param name="isVB">Boolean flag indicating the language
/// to use: false indicates C#, true indicates VB</param>
private void SetCode(Color color, bool isVB)
{
    // Read in add-in settings from registry
    SetPropFromReg();

    string code = "";

    if (isVB)
    {
        code = "Dim color As Color = ";
    }
    else
    {
        code = "Color color = ";
    }

    code = code + "Color.FromArgb(" + color.R.ToString() + ", " +
        color.G.ToString() + ", " +
        color.B.ToString() + ");";

    _code = code;
    this.labelCode.Text = _code;

}
/// <summary>
/// Reads a registry entry and sets the language output fields
/// appropriately.
/// </summary>
private void SetPropFromReg()
{
    RegistryKey regKey =
        Registry.CurrentUser.OpenSubKey(@"Software\Contoso\Addins\ColorPalette");
    string codeVal = (string)regKey.GetValue("Language", "CSharp");

    if (codeVal == "CSharp")
```

```
    {
        _generateVB = false;
    }
    else
    {
        _generateVB = true;
    }
}
```

### Signaling a Color Selection

Because you will need some way for the control to indicate that a user has selected a color (for example, has clicked on the palette), you will also define an event on the user control class that will be raised whenever a click is registered in the palette picture box:

```
public event EventHandler ColorSelected;

protected virtual void OnColorSelected(EventArgs e)
{
    if (ColorSelected != null)
        ColorSelected(this, e);
}

private void pictureBoxPalette_Click(object sender, EventArgs e)
{
    OnColorSelected(new EventArgs());
}
```

> **TIP**
>
> To isolate and test the user control, you may want to add a Windows forms project to the solution and host the control on a Windows form for testing. Just drop the control onto the form and run the forms project.

With the user control in place, you are ready to proceed to the second stage of the add-in's development: wiring the user control into the IDE.

## Finishing the Connect Class

The Connect class already has the basic add-in code; now it's time to revisit that code and add the custom code to drive the user control. You'll want the add-in to integrate seamlessly into the development environment, so you can use a tool window to display the user control that you previously created.

Harking back to the discussions of the automation object model, you know that the Windows2 collection has a CreateToolWindow2 method, which allows you to create your own custom tool windows.

> **NOTE**
>
> Prior versions of Visual Studio required you to create a shim control (using C++) that would host a control for display in a tool window. The tool window, in turn, would then host the shim. With Visual Studio 2005 and beyond (and the improved Windows2.CreateToolWindow2 method), this is no longer necessary. Now you can directly host a managed user control in a tool window.

Here is the method prototype:

```
Window CreateToolWindow2 (
    AddIn Addin,
    string Assembly,
    string Class,
    string Caption,
    string GuidPosition,
    [InAttribute] out Object ControlObject
)
```

### Displaying the Tool Window and User Control

Because you want the tool window to be created and displayed after the add-in has loaded, this `CreateToolWindow2` method call will be placed in the `Connect.OnConnection` method. First, you set up a local object to point to the `DTE.ToolWindows` collection:

```
// The DTE.ToolWindows collection
Windows2 toolWindows= (Windows2)_applicationObject.Windows;
```

Then you need an object to hold the reference to the tool window that you will create:

```
// Object to refer to the newly created tool window
Window2 toolWindow;
```

And finally, you need to create the parameters to feed to the `CreateToolWindow2` method:

```
// Placeholder object; will eventually refer to the user control
// hosted by the user control
object paletteObject = null;

// This section specifies the path and class name for the palette
// control to be hosted in the new tool window; we also need to
// specify its caption and a unique GUID.
Assembly asm = System.Reflection.Assembly.GetExecutingAssembly();
string assemblyPath = asm.Location;
string className = "ColorSelectorAddIn.PaletteControl";
string guid = "{62175059-FD7E-407a-9EF3-5D07F2B704E8}";string caption = "Palette
Color Picker";
```

13

Note that we have hard-coded a GUID to pass in to the `CreateToolWindow2` method. Because our user control is a managed code control, and it will be hosted in a native COM component (all tool windows in Visual Studio are COM-based), the add-in infrastructure needs some way to establish a viable calling interface for the control. This is done through the use of the GUID parameter. We will also need to "label" the user control with the GUID by placing a `Guid` attribute just before our PaletteControl class declaration like this:

```
namespace ColorSelectorAddIn
{
    [Guid("62175059-FD7E-407a-9EF3-5D07F2B704E8")]
    public partial class PaletteControl : UserControl
    { ... }
}
```

You can use Visual Studio to generate your GUID by selecting Tools, Create GUID, and then selecting Registry Format. You can then directly copy and paste this into your code window.

With that in place, you are only a few lines of code away from creating and displaying the tool window:

```
// Create the new tool window with the hosted user control
toolWindow = (Window2)toolWindows.CreateToolWindow2(_addInInstance, assemblyPath,
    className, caption, guid, ref paletteObject);

// If tool window was created successfully, make it visible
if (toolWindow != null)
{
    toolWindow.Visible = true;
}
```

### Capturing User Control Events

The add-in is missing one last piece: You need to react whenever the user clicks on the palette by grabbing the generated code (available from the `PaletteControl.Code` property) and inserting it into the currently active document. There are two tasks at hand. First, you need to write an event handler to deal with the click event raised by the `PaletteControl` object. But to do that, you need a reference to the user control. This is the purpose of the `paletteObject` object that you pass in as the last parameter to the `CreateToolWindow2` method. Because this is passed in by reference, it will hold a valid instance of the `PaletteControl` after the method call completes and returns. You can then cast this object to the specific `PaletteControl` type, assign it to a field within the `Connect` class, and attach an event handler to the `PaletteControl.ColorSelected` event:

```
// retrieve a reference back to our user control object
_paletteControl = (PaletteControl)paletteObject;

// wire up event handler for the PaletteControl.ColorSelected event
```

```
_paletteControl.ColorSelected +=
    new System.EventHandler(paletteControl1_ColorSelected);
```

> **TIP**
>
> Getting a reference to the user control can be a bit tricky. If the user control is not a part of the same project as your add-in class, `CreateToolWindow2` will return only a null value instead of a valid reference to the user control. If you want to develop your user control outside the add-in project, you have to make sure that the user control is fully attributed to be visible to calling COM components. See the topic "Exposing .NET Framework Components to COM" in MSDN for details on how this task is accomplished.

### Inserting the Generated Code

You react to the `ColorSelected` event by grabbing the content of the `PaletteControl.Code` property and writing it into the currently active document. Again, you will use your automation object model knowledge gained from the preceding chapter to make this happen. The `DTE.ActiveDocument` class will hold a reference to the currently active document. By using an edit point, you can easily write text directly into the text document:

```
TextDocument currDoc = (TextDocument)_applicationObject.ActiveDocument.Object("");
EditPoint2 ep = (EditPoint2) currDoc.Selection.ActivePoint.CreateEditPoint();
ep.Insert(_paletteControl.Code);
ep.InsertNewLine(1);
```

## Exposing Add-in Settings

The final step is to make the add-in's language choice a configurable option. Users should be able to indicate whether they want the add-in to emit C# or Visual Basic code. To do this, you need to have a user interface in the form of an Options page (that will display in the Options dialog box), and you need a place to persist the option selections.

### Creating the Option Page UI

Add-ins can reference an Options page that will appear in the Tools Options dialog box. Again, as you did with the custom tool window, you will build a user control to implement the logic and the user interface for the Options page.

You start by adding a new user control to the existing add-in project. For this example, call this class `PaletteControlOptionPage`. Adding a label control and two radio button controls will enable you to indicate the language preference for the palette add-in. Figure 13.11 shows the design surface of the Options page.

The user control for the Options page needs to inherit from `IDTToolsOptionsPage`:

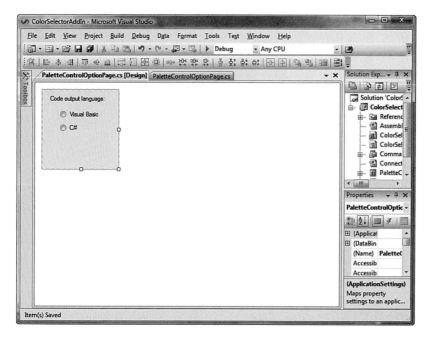

FIGURE 13.11    The Options page user control.

```csharp
public partial class PaletteControlOptionPage : UserControl, IDTToolsOptionsPage
{
    public PaletteControlOptionPage()
    {
        InitializeComponent();
    }
}
```

The IDTToolsOptionsPage interface defines five methods, outlined in Table 13.5.

TABLE 13.5    **IDTToolsOptionsPage** Members

| Member | Description |
| --- | --- |
| GetProperties | Returns a properties object in response to calling DTE.Properties for this specific Options page |
| OnAfterCreated | Fires after the Tools Options page is created for the first time |
| OnCancel | Fires if the user clicks on the Cancel button on the Tools Options dialog box |
| OnHelp | Fires if the user clicks on the Help button on the Tools Options dialog box |
| OnOK | Fires if the user clicks on the OK button on the Tools Options dialog box |

These methods are called as the Options page progresses through its normal sequence of states, as you can see in Figure 13.12.

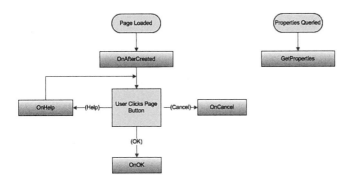

FIGURE 13.12   The Tools Options page action sequence.

By placing code within these methods, you can read in and store any configuration changes that a user makes through the Options page. In this case, you can keep things simple: Read in a value from a Registry entry as part of the OnAfterCreated method and update that same entry as part of the OnOK method:

```
public void OnAfterCreated(DTE DTEObject)
{
    // read our current value from registry
    // TODO: we should really include contingency code here for creating
    // the key if it doesn't already exist, dealing with unexpected values,
    // exceptions, etc.
    RegistryKey regKey =
        Registry.CurrentUser.OpenSubKey(@"Software\Contoso\Addins\ColorPalette");
    string codeVal = (string)regKey.GetValue("Language", "CSharp");

    if (codeVal == "CSharp")
    {
        this.radioButtonCSharp.Checked = true;
        this.radioButtonVB.Checked = false;
    }
    else
    {
        this.radioButtonCSharp.Checked = true;
        this.radioButtonVB.Checked = false;
    }
```

```
}
public void OnOK()
{
    string codeValue = "CSharp";    // our default value

    if (this.radioButtonVB.Checked)
    {
        codeValue = "VB";
    }

    // update the registry with the new setting
    RegistryKey regKey =
       Registry.CurrentUser.OpenSubKey(@"Software\Contoso\Addins\ColorPalette");
    regKey.SetValue("Language", codeVal);
}
```

> **NOTE**
>
> It is up to you to decide where and how you persist your add-in's settings. The Registry is one logical place; you could also elect to store your settings in an XML file that is deployed along with your binaries.

### Registering the Options Page

The registration mechanism for an Options page is the same as that for an add-in: The .addin file is used. By adding a few lines of XML, you can indicate to Visual Studio that an Options page exists with the custom add-in. You can do this easily by editing the .addin file right in Visual Studio (because it is automatically created as part of the project).

To include the necessary XML registration information, edit the .addin file and place the following XML before the closing </extensibility> tag:

```
<ToolsOptionsPage>
  <Category Name="Color Palette">
    <SubCategory Name="Code Generation">
      <Assembly>C:\Users\lpowers\My Documents\Visual Studio 2008\Projects\
      PaletteControlAddIn\PaletteControlAddIn\bin\PaletteControlAddIn.dll</Assembly>
      <FullClassName>PaletteControlAddIn.PaletteControlOptionPage </FullClassName>
    </SubCategory>
  </Category>
</ToolsOptionsPage>
```

You use the Category tag to specify the name of the option category displayed in the Tools Options dialog box. The SubCategory tag specifies the subnode under that category. The Assembly tag provides a path to the add-in's DLL file, and the FullClassName tag contains the full name for the add-in class.

With this final step complete, the add-in is fully functional. You can compile the project and then immediately load the add-in using the Add-in Manager. Figure 13.13 shows the add-in in action, and a complete code listing for the `Connect`, `PaletteControl`, and `PaletteControlOptionPage` classes (in that order) is provided in Listings 13.2, 13.3, and 13.4. The complete source code for this add-in can be downloaded at the SAMS site.

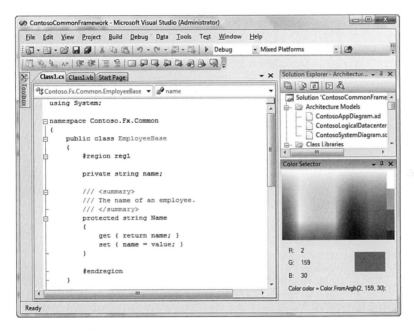

FIGURE 13.13    The Color Selector add-in.


LISTING 13.2    The **Connect** Class

```
using System;
using Extensibility;
using EnvDTE;
using EnvDTE80;
using Microsoft.VisualStudio.CommandBars;
using System.Resources;
using System.Reflection;
using System.Globalization;
using System.Windows.Forms;

namespace ColorSelectorAddIn
{
```

LISTING 13.2    Continued

```
/// <summary>The object for implementing an Add-in.</summary>
/// <seealso class='IDTExtensibility2' />
public class Connect : IDTExtensibility2, IDTCommandTarget
{
    #region Fields

    private DTE2 _applicationObject;
    private AddIn _addInInstance;
    private PaletteControl _paletteControl;

    #endregion

    /// <summary>Implements the constructor for the Add-in object.
    /// Place your initialization code within this method.</summary>
    public Connect()
    {
    }

    #region Events and Event Handlers

    private void paletteControl1_ColorSelected(object sender, EventArgs e)
    {
        try
        {
            TextDocument currDoc =
              (TextDocument)_applicationObject.ActiveDocument.Object("");
            EditPoint2 ep = (EditPoint2)
              currDoc.Selection.ActivePoint.CreateEditPoint();
            ep.Insert(_paletteControl.Code);
            ep.InsertNewLine(1);
        }

        catch (Exception ex)
        {
            MessageBox.Show("Exception caught: " + ex.ToString());
        }

    }

    #endregion

    /// <summary>Implements the OnConnection method of the
    /// IDTExtensibility2 interface. Receives notification that the Add-in
    /// is being loaded.</summary>
    /// <param term='application'>Root object of the host application.
```

```
///</param>
/// <param term='connectMode'>Describes how the Add-in is being
/// loaded.</param>
/// <param term='addInInst'>Object representing this Add-in.</param>
/// <seealso class='IDTExtensibility2' />
public void OnConnection(object application,
    ext_ConnectMode connectMode,
    object addInInst, ref Array custom)
{
    _applicationObject = (DTE2)application;
    _addInInstance = (AddIn)addInInst;

    if(connectMode == ext_ConnectMode.ext_cm_UISetup)
    {
        object []contextGUIDS = new object[] { };
        Commands2 commands = (Commands2)_applicationObject.Commands;
        string toolsMenuName;

        try
        {
            string resourceName;
            ResourceManager resourceManager =
              new ResourceManager("ColorSelectorAddIn.CommandBar",
                Assembly.GetExecutingAssembly());

            CultureInfo cultureInfo =
                new CultureInfo(_applicationObject.LocaleID);

            if(cultureInfo.TwoLetterISOLanguageName == "zh")
            {
                System.Globalization.CultureInfo parentCultureInfo =
                    cultureInfo.Parent;
                resourceName = String.Concat(parentCultureInfo.Name,
                                            "Tools");
            }
            else
            {
                resourceName =
                    String.Concat(cultureInfo.TwoLetterISOLanguageName,
                      "Tools");
            }
            toolsMenuName = resourceManager.GetString(resourceName);
        }
        catch
        {
            //We tried to find a localized version of the word Tools,
            //but one was not found.
```

13

LISTING 13.2    Continued

```
            //  Default to the en-US word, which may work for the
            //  current culture.
            toolsMenuName = "Tools";
        }


        //Place the command on the Tools menu.
        //Find the MenuBar command bar, which is the top-level command
        // bar holding all the main menu items:
        Microsoft.VisualStudio.CommandBars.CommandBar
          menuBarCommandBar =
              ((Microsoft.VisualStudio.CommandBars.CommandBars)
    _          applicationObject.CommandBars)["MenuBar"];


        //Find the Tools command bar on the MenuBar command bar:
        CommandBarControl toolsControl =
          menuBarCommandBar.Controls[toolsMenuName];
        CommandBarPopup toolsPopup = (CommandBarPopup)toolsControl;


        //This try/catch block can be duplicated if you wish to add
        // multiple commands to be handled by your Add-in, just make
        // sure you also update the QueryStatus/Exec method to include
        // the new command names.
        try
        {
            //Add a command to the Commands collection:
            Command command = commands.AddNamedCommand2(_addInInstance,
              "ColorSelectorAddIn", "ColorSelectorAddIn",
              "Executes the command for ColorSelectorAddIn", true, 59,
              ref contextGUIDS,
              (int)vsCommandStatus.vsCommandStatusSupported+
                (int)vsCommandStatus.vsCommandStatusEnabled,
              (int)vsCommandStyle.vsCommandStylePictAndText,
              vsCommandControlType.vsCommandControlTypeButton);


            //Add a control for the command to the Tools menu:
            if((command != null) && (toolsPopup != null))
            {
                command.AddControl(toolsPopup.CommandBar, 1);
            }
        }
        catch(System.ArgumentException)
        {
            //If we are here, then the exception is probably because a
            //command with that name already exists. If so there is no
            //need to recreate the command and we can safely ignore the
```

```
            //exception.
       }
}

#region Create Tool Window

// The DTE.ToolWindows collection
Windows2 windows = (Windows2)_applicationObject.Windows;

// Placeholder object; will eventually refer to the user control
// hosted by the user control
object paletteObject = null;

// This section specifies the path and class name for the palette
// control to be hosted in the new tool window; we also need to
// specify its caption and a unique GUID.
Window toolWindow;
Assembly asm = System.Reflection.Assembly.GetExecutingAssembly();
string assemblyPath = asm.Location;
string className = "ColorSelectorAddIn.PaletteControl";
string guid = "{62175059-FD7E-407a-9EF3-5D07F2B704E8}";
string caption = "Color Selector";

try
{

  // Create the new tool window and insert the user control in
  // it.
    toolWindow = windows.CreateToolWindow2(_addInInstance,
        assemblyPath, className, caption, guid,
        ref paletteObject);

    // If tool window was created successfully, make it visible
    if (_toolWindow != null)
    {
        _toolWindow.Visible = true;
    }

    // retrieve a reference back to our user control object
    _paletteControl = (PaletteControl)paletteObject;

    // wire up event handler for the PaletteControl.ColorSelected
    //event
    _paletteControl.ColorSelected +=
        new System.EventHandler(paletteControl1_ColorSelected);

}
```

13

LISTING 13.2　Continued

```
        catch (Exception ex)
        {
            MessageBox.Show("Exception caught: " + ex.ToString());
        }

        #endregion

    }

    /// <summary>Implements the OnDisconnection method of the
    /// IDTExtensibility2 interface. Receives notification that
    /// the Add-in is being unloaded.</summary>
    /// <param term='disconnectMode'>Describes how the Add-in
    /// is being unloaded.</param>
    /// <param term='custom'>Array of parameters that are host
    /// application specific.</param>
    /// <seealso class='IDTExtensibility2' />
    public void OnDisconnection(ext_DisconnectMode disconnectMode,
        ref Array custom)
    {
    }

    /// <summary>Implements the OnAddInsUpdate method of the
    /// IDTExtensibility2 interface. Receives notification when
    /// the collection of Add-ins has changed.</summary>
    /// <param term='custom'>Array of parameters that are host
    /// application specific.</param>
    /// <seealso class='IDTExtensibility2' />
    public void OnAddInsUpdate(ref Array custom)
    {
    }

    /// <summary>Implements the OnStartupComplete method of the
    /// IDTExtensibility2 interface. Receives notification that
    /// the host application has completed loading.</summary>
    /// <param term='custom'>Array of parameters that are host
    /// application specific.</param>
    /// <seealso class='IDTExtensibility2' />
    public void OnStartupComplete(ref Array custom)
    {
    }

    /// <summary>Implements the OnBeginShutdown method of the
    /// IDTExtensibility2 interface. Receives notification that
    /// the host application is being unloaded.</summary>
```

```
/// <param term='custom'>Array of parameters that are host
/// application specific.</param>
/// <seealso class='IDTExtensibility2' />
public void OnBeginShutdown(ref Array custom)
{
}


/// <summary>Implements the QueryStatus method of the
/// IDTCommandTarget interface. This is called when the
/// command's availability is updated</summary>
/// <param term='commandName'>The name of the command to
/// determine state for.</param>
/// <param term='neededText'>Text that is needed for the
/// command.</param>
/// <param term='status'>The state of the command in the
/// user interface.</param>
/// <param term='commandText'>Text requested by the neededText
/// parameter.</param>
/// <seealso class='Exec' />
public void QueryStatus(string commandName,
    vsCommandStatusTextWanted neededText, ref vsCommandStatus status,
    ref object commandText)
{
    if(neededText ==
        vsCommandStatusTextWanted.vsCommandStatusTextWantedNone)
    {
        if(commandName ==
            "ColorSelectorAddIn.Connect.ColorSelectorAddIn")
        {
            status = (vsCommandStatus)
                    vsCommandStatus.vsCommandStatusSupported
                  ¦vsCommandStatus.vsCommandStatusEnabled;
            return;
        }
    }
}

/// <summary>Implements the Exec method of the IDTCommandTarget
/// interface. This is called when the command is invoked.</summary>
/// <param term='commandName'>The name of the command to
/// execute.</param>
/// <param term='executeOption'>Describes how the command should
/// be run.</param>
/// <param term='varIn'>Parameters passed from the caller to the
/// command handler.</param>
/// <param term='varOut'>Parameters passed from the command handler
```

LISTING 13.2   Continued

```
        /// to the caller.</param>
        /// <param term='handled'>Informs the caller if the command was
        /// handled or not.</param>
        /// <seealso class='Exec' />
        public void Exec(string commandName, vsCommandExecOption executeOption,
            ref object varIn, ref object varOut, ref bool handled)
        {
            handled = false;
            if(executeOption ==
                vsCommandExecOption.vsCommandExecOptionDoDefault)
            {
                if(commandName ==
                    "ColorSelectorAddIn.Connect.ColorSelectorAddIn")
                {
                    handled = true;
                    return;
                }
            }
        }

    }
}
```

LISTING 13.3   The **PaletteControl** Class

```
using System;
using System.Collections.Generic;
using System.ComponentModel;
using System.Drawing;
using System.Data;
using System.Runtime.InteropServices;
using System.Text;
using System.Windows.Forms;
using Microsoft.Win32;

namespace ColorSelectorAddIn
{
    [Guid("62175059-FD7E-407a-9EF3-5D07F2B704E8")]
    public partial class PaletteControl : UserControl
    {
        #region Fields

        string _code = "";
        bool _generateVB = false;
```

```
#endregion

#region Properties

public string Code
{
    get { return _code; }
}

public bool GenerateVB
{
    get { return _generateVB; }
}

#endregion

#region Ctor(s)

public PaletteControl()
{
    InitializeComponent();
    this.pictureBoxPalette.MouseMove += new
      MouseEventHandler(pictureBoxPalette_MouseMove);
    this.pictureBoxPalette.Cursor = System.Windows.Forms.Cursors.Cross;
}

#endregion

#region Event Handlers and Delegates

void pictureBoxPalette_MouseMove(object sender, MouseEventArgs e)
{
    // Get the color under the current pointer position
    Color color = GetPointColor(e.X, e.Y);

    // Update the RGB labels and the 2nd pic box
    // using the retrieved color
    DisplayColor(color);

    // Generate our VB or C# code for the Color
    // structure
    SetCode(color, _generateVB);
}
```

LISTING 13.3    Continued

```csharp
    public event EventHandler ColorSelected;

    protected virtual void OnColorSelected(EventArgs e)
    {
        if (ColorSelected != null)
            ColorSelected(this, e);
    }

    private void pictureBoxPalette_Click(object sender, EventArgs e)
    {
        OnColorSelected(new EventArgs());
    }

    #endregion

    #region Private Routines

    /// <summary>
    /// Returns a Color structure representing the color of
    /// the pixel at the indicated x and y coordinates.
    /// </summary>
    /// <param name="x"></param>
    /// <param name="y"></param>
    /// <returns>A Color structure</returns>
    private Color GetPointColor(int x, int y)
    {
        // Get the bitmap from the palette picture box
        Bitmap bmp = (Bitmap)pictureBoxPalette.Image;
        // Use GetPixel to retrieve a color
        // structure for the current pointer position
        Color color = bmp.GetPixel(x, y);

        // Return the color structure
        return color;
    }

    /// <summary>
    /// Displays the RGB values for the given color. Also sets
    /// the background color of the secondary picture box.
    /// </summary>
    /// <param name="color">The Color to display</param>
    private void DisplayColor(Color color)
    {
        // pull out the RGB values from the
        // color structure
```

```csharp
        string R = color.R.ToString();
        string G = color.G.ToString();
        string B = color.B.ToString();

        // set our secondary picture box
        // to display the current color
        this.pictureBoxColor.BackColor = color;

        // display RGB values in the label
        // controls
        this.labelRValue.Text = R;
        this.labelGValue.Text = G;
        this.labelBValue.Text = B;
    }

    /// <summary>
    /// Generates a string representing the C# or VB code necessary to
    /// create a Color structure instance that matches the passed in
    /// Color structure. This string is then assigned to this
    /// user control's _code field.
    /// </summary>
    /// <param name="color">The color to represent in code.</param>
    /// <param name="isVB">Boolean flag indicating the language
    /// to use: false indicates C#, true indicates VB</param>
    private void SetCode(Color color, bool isVB)
    {
        // Read in add-in settings from registry
        SetPropFromReg();

        string code = "";

        if (isVB)
        {
            code = "Dim color As Color = ";
        }
        else
        {
            code = "Color color = ";
        }

        code = code + "Color.FromArgb(" + color.R.ToString() + ", " +
            color.G.ToString() + ", " +
            color.B.ToString() + ");";

        _code = code;
        this.labelCode.Text = _code;
    }
```

LISTING 13.3    Continued

```csharp
        /// <summary>
        /// Reads a registry entry and sets the language output fields
        /// appropriately.
        /// </summary>
        private void SetPropFromReg()
        {
            try
            {
                RegistryKey regKey =
                  Registry.CurrentUser.OpenSubKey(@"Software\Contoso\Addins\
➡ ColorPalette");
                string codeVal = (string)regKey.GetValue("Language", "CSharp");

                if (codeVal == "CSharp")
                {
                    _generateVB = false;
                }
                else
                {
                    _generateVB = true;
                }
            }
            catch (Exception ex)
            {
                // error reading the registry; default to C#
                _generateVB = false;
            }
        }
        #endregion
    }
}
```

LISTING 13.4    The **PaletteControlOptionPage** Class

```csharp
using System;
using System.Collections.Generic;
using System.ComponentModel;
using System.Drawing;
using System.Data;
using System.Text;
using System.Windows.Forms;
using EnvDTE;
using Microsoft.Win32;
```

```
namespace ColorSelectorAddIn
{
    public partial class PaletteControlOptionPage : UserControl,
      IDTToolsOptionsPage
    {
        public PaletteControlOptionPage()
        {
            InitializeComponent();
        }

        #region IDTToolsOptionsPage Members

        public void GetProperties(ref object PropertiesObject)
        {
            throw new NotImplementedException();
        }

        public void OnAfterCreated(DTE DTEObject)
        {
            // read our current value from registry
            // TODO: we should really include contingency code here for
            // creating the key if it doesn't already exist, dealing with
            // unexpected values, exceptions, etc.
            RegistryKey regKey =
              Registry.CurrentUser.OpenSubKey(@"Software\Contoso\Addins\
➥ ColorPalette");
            string codeVal = (string)regKey.GetValue("Language", "CSharp");

            if (codeVal == "CSharp")
            {
                this.radioButtonCSharp.Checked = true;
                this.radioButtonVB.Checked = false;
            }
            else
            {
                this.radioButtonCSharp.Checked = true;
                this.radioButtonVB.Checked = false;
            }
        }


        public void OnCancel()
        {
            throw new NotImplementedException();
        }
```

LISTING 13.4    Continued

```
    public void OnHelp()
    {
        throw new NotImplementedException();
    }

    public void OnOK()
    {
        string codeValue = "CSharp";      // our default value

        if (this.radioButtonVB.Checked)
        {
            codeValue = "VB";
        }

        // update the registry with the new setting
        RegistryKey regKey =
            Registry.CurrentUser.OpenSubKey(@"Software\Contoso\Addins\
➡ ColorPalette");

        regKey.SetValue("Language", codeValue);

    }

    #endregion
    }
}
```

**NOTE**

If you have add-ins that were written for a previous version of Visual Studio, you will need to make some minor updates to the source code to fully migrate features over to Visual Studio 2008. Detailed migration steps are provided in the Visual Studio MSDN documentation. Search for the article "How to: Update Visual Studio 2005 Add-ins to Visual Studio 2008."

# Creating a Visual Studio Wizard

Visual Studio makes heavy use of wizards to help guide developers through various tasks. The Add-in Wizard that we discussed in the previous sections is one such example of a New Project Wizard (it is launched when you try to create a new add-in project). There are also wizards for adding new items to projects. You can modify the existing Project/Add New Item wizards or create your own wizard complete with its own user interface.

In the following sections, we will focus on understanding the wizard landscape and creating a custom Add New Item Wizard.

## Examining the Wizard Structure

Each wizard consists of two major components: a class that contains the code (and user interface) for the wizard and a .vsz file that provides information about the wizard to Visual Studio.

### The IDTWizard Interface

To hook into Visual Studio's wizard engine, your Wizard class must implement the EnvDTE.IDTWizard interface. The IDTWizard defines a single method, Execute, that is called by Visual Studio whenever the wizard is launched. Here is the prototype for the IDTWizard.Execute method (in C#):

```
void Execute (
    Object Application,
    int hwndOwner,
    ref Object[] ContextParams,
    ref Object[] CustomParams,
    out wizardResult retval
)
```

The arguments passed to the Execute method are used to link the wizard to the Visual Studio environment and to pass relevant data to the wizard:

- ▶ **Application**—A DTE instance for the Visual Studio IDE.

- ▶ **hwndOwner**—A handle to the parent window; this window will "parent" any user interface elements created by the wizard.

- ▶ **ContextParams**—For New Project/Add New Item wizards, an array of objects used to pass information about the type of wizard that was launched and various data necessary for the wizard to function, such as project name and install directory.

- ▶ **CustomParams**—An array of objects used to carry any custom parameters you define for your wizard.

- ▶ **wizardResult**—A wizardResult enumeration value that indicates the results of the wizard.

The ContextParams parameter's content will vary depending on the type of wizard. For instance, for a New Project Wizard, the third value in the ContextParams array represents the location where the project file is stored (called the LocalDirectory). But for an Add Item Wizard, the third value in the array is a pointer to a ProjectItems collection. Table 13.6 maps the various array elements to the three different wizard types.

TABLE 13.6 **ContextParams** Values

| Index | NewProject Wizard | AddSubProject Wizard | AddItem Wizard |
|---|---|---|---|
| 0 | WizardType enum | WizardType enum | WizardType enum |
| 1 | Project name | Project name | Project name |
| 2 | Local directory | ProjectItems object | ProjectItems object |
| 3 | VS install directory | Local directory | Local directory |
| 4 | FExclusive flag (create new solution or use current) | Name of added item | Name of added item |
| 5 | Solution name | VS install directory | VS install directory |
| 6 | Silent flag (run with or without UI) | Silent flag | Silent flag |

To determine the results of the wizard, you look at the value placed in the wizardResult parameter. Table 13.7 lists the wizardResult enum values.

TABLE 13.7 **wizardResult** Enumeration Values

| Member | Description |
|---|---|
| wizardResultBackOut | The user exited the wizard by clicking on the Back button. |
| wizardResultCancel | The wizard was canceled. |
| wizardResultFailure | The wizard startup failed. |
| wizardResultSuccess | The wizard startup succeeded. |

The core content of the Execute method is entirely up to you. Within the body of the Execute method, you will need to implement all the code necessary to do the work of the wizard and display its UI to the user.

---

**NOTE**

Although you probably think of wizards as a series of pages accessed by Next and Back navigation buttons, a wizard in Visual Studio's terms is nothing more than a COM object that implements IDTWizard. In fact, a wizard doesn't need to display a user interface at all. It could, for instance, merely use the parameters passed to it to do some work and then quit.

---

### The .vsz and .vsdir Files

If you recall from our discussion of add-ins, every add-in uses an .addin file to register the add-in with Visual Studio. The .vsz files are the equivalent for wizards; they make Visual Studio aware of the wizard and its implementing class.

Here is a complete, sample .vsz file:

```
VSWizard 8.0
Wizard=ContosoWizard.AddNewClassWizard
Param=
```

The VSWizard line in this file identifies the version information for the wizard. The number 9.0 equates to Visual Studio 2008, and prior version numbers map to prior Visual Studio releases.

> **NOTE**
>
> The .vsz file format has not changed at all since Visual Studio 2003, so the version number is largely irrelevant; many of the wizards included with Visual Studio 2008 are labeled as version 6 files!

After the version number, a class ID is provided for the wizard. And finally, there are one or more (optional) Param lines. These lines define any custom parameters that you want sent to the wizard. Any parameters defined here will come across in the CustomParams parameter in the Execute method.

Visual Studio has a specific folder hierarchy that it uses for storing wizard .vsz files; the folder where you place the .vsz file will dictate exactly where the option to launch the wizard will appear. As an example, if you wanted to create an Add Item Wizard for both Visual Basic and Visual C#, you would need to place a copy of the .vsz file into both the Visual Basic and the C# folders. If Visual Studio 2008 was installed in its default location, that would mean placing the wizard files here:

```
C:\Program Files\Microsoft Visual Studio 9.0\VC#\CSharpProjectItems
C:\Program Files\Microsoft Visual Studio 9.0\VB\VBProjectItems
```

If you were creating a New Project Wizard, the files would be placed in the VC#\CSharpProjects and the VB\VBProjects folders.

Wizard folders may also contain a .vsdir file. This file is used to provide Visual Studio with icon and other resource information about a particular wizard. The .vsdir file is also a plain-text file. Each line in the file represents a specific .vsz file/wizard and provides multiple fields (separated by the pipe character, |) with optional information about the wizard. Table 13.8 documents the valid fields for each .vsdir line, in order of their appearance. The optional fields are noted.

## 13

TABLE 13.8   **.vsdir** Record Fields

| Field | Description |
|---|---|
| Relative Path | The relative path to the wizard's .vsz file. |
| Class ID | The Class ID of the wizard component in GUID format. Optional. |
| Localized Name | The localized name of the wizard that will appear in the Add Item dialog box. Optional. |
| Sort Priority | A number used to provide a relative grouping number for the wizard in the display dialog boxes. A wizard with a value of 1 will be displayed next to other 1 wizards, and so on. |
| Description | The description of the wizard. This will appear whenever the wizard is selected in the Add Item dialog box. |
| DLL Path | A full path to the assembly containing the wizard's icon. |
| Icon Resource id | A resource identifier that points within the DLL to the icon to be displayed. |
| Flags | One or more bitwise values used to control certain wizard behaviors. See the MSDN documentation for a complete list. Optional. |
| Name | The name of the wizard to be displayed in the Name field of the dialog box (unlike the Localized Name, this field is required). |

Here is a simple .vsdir file example with one wizard record:

```
CSharpContosoDataClass.vsz ¦ ¦ ¦1¦Create a new Contoso storage class¦c:\Con-
tosoFramework\Wizards\DataClassWizard.dll¦ ¦ ¦Contoso Data Class
```

**TIP**

The .vsdir record provides a way to associate an icon resource to the wizard by allowing you to specify a DLL path and an icon resource ID. There is also a simpler way to accomplish this: Just create an .ico file, give it the same name as the wizard's .vsz file, and place it in the same directory.

## Creating an Add New Item Wizard

Here are the basic steps for creating a wizard:

1. Create a new class library project; in this project, create a new class that implements the IDTWizard interface.

2. In the wizard class, write the code in the Execute method to perform the wizard's tasks and display its UI.

3. Create a .vsz file for the wizard.

4. Create or edit a .vsdir file to reference the new wizard and the .vsz file.

To solidify these concepts, let's look at them in action. We'll follow the development of a wizard from start to finish. In this case, the wizard will be a C# Add Item Wizard. Its purpose will be to collect some basic data from the user and then create a Tools Options page class (much like you manually did earlier in the chapter) that has been customized in accordance with the user's input into the wizard dialog box.

### Implementing the `Execute` Method

The `Execute` method needs to do two things: display a Windows Forms dialog box to capture preferences such as class name; and process those preferences, generate a class that implements a Tools Options page, and add that class to the current project.

**Creating the Dialog Box**    First, the dialog box: It should look roughly like the dialog box in Figure 13.14 (there is nothing special about the implementation of this form, so we won't bother to detail all of its code here).

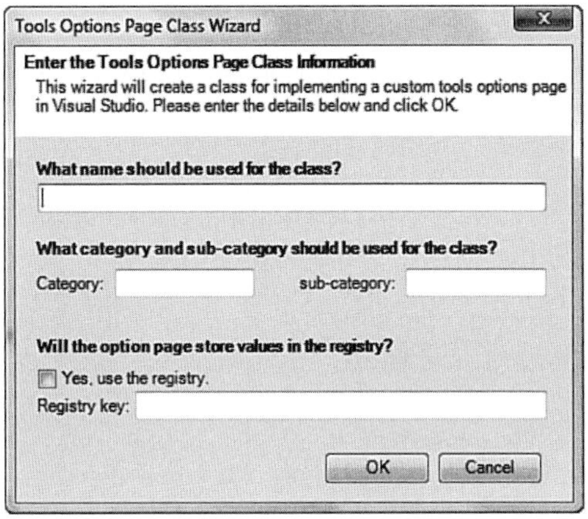

FIGURE 13.14    The wizard form.

When the user clicks on the OK button, you should set several properties on the form that mirror the selections made on the dialog box. For instance, if you implement this form as a class called `WizardDialog`, you will want a `WizardDialog.ClassName` property, a `WizardDialog.Category` property, and so on. The last thing to do when the OK button is clicked is to set the form's `DialogResult` property. The `Execute` method on the wizard (which we will examine in a moment) will query the `DialogResult` property to determine whether the user has committed the wizard or canceled it. Here is a look at the OK and Cancel button click event handlers:

```
private void buttonOK_Click(object sender, EventArgs e)
{
    // assign screen control values to our public
```

```
    // fields
    this.ClassName = this.textBoxClassName.Text;
    this.Category = this.textBoxCategory.Text;
    this.SubCategory = this.textBoxSubCategory.Text;
    this.UseRegistry = this.checkBoxUseRegistry.Checked;
    this.RegKey = this.textBoxRegKey.Text;

    // indicate dialog was accepted
    this.DialogResult = DialogResult.OK;
}

private void buttonCancel_Click(object sender, EventArgs e)
{
    // indicate dialog was cancelled
    this.DialogResult = DialogResult.Cancel;
}
```

**Using a Template File**    There are two approaches here to creating the Tools Options page class: You could generate every line of code using either the Code DOM API or brute-force string creation/concatenation, or you could use a template file. The template file approach is a bit simpler and probably more efficient as well, so that is the approach we describe here (and the topic of templates in Visual Studio is explored in-depth in the next chapter).

The class template is a file that looks just like any other user control. Using the standard code created for a user control class, you substitute key areas with string placeholders. For instance, the class name is specified within the wizard, and thus something you will want to replace in the template class:

```
public class %TemplateClassName% : UserControl, IDTToolsOptionsPage
{
    ...
}
```

You will also want the IDTToolsOptionsPage members—such as OnAfterCreated, OnOK, and so on—represented in the class. For most of these methods, you will leave a simple System.NotImplementedException call to remind the user to fill in code as necessary. For OnAfterCreated and OnOK, however, you want the option of including a line of code to open the indicated Registry key:

```
public void OnAfterCreated(DTE DTEObject)
{
    // read our current value from registry
    // TODO: Include code to read from registry here
    %StartRegistryCode%
```

```
    RegistryKey regKey = Registry.CurrentUser.OpenSubKey(@"%TemplateRegKey%");
    %EndRegistryCode%
}
public void OnOK()
{
    //TODO: include code to save options
    // update the registry with the new setting
    %StartRegistryCode%
    RegistryKey regKey = Registry.CurrentUser.OpenSubKey(@"%TemplateRegKey%");
    %EndRegistryCode%
}
```

Again, you use placeholders here: The %StartRegistryCode% and %EndRegistryCode% delimits the OpenSubKey line of code. If the user unchecks the User Registry check box in the wizard, you will eliminate everything between these two placeholders (including the placeholders themselves). The %TemplateRegKey% is used as a token for the Registry key value; this is something else that you collect from the user in the wizard's dialog box.

**Executing the Wizard**   The Execute method will open the wizard form and, if the user has not canceled the dialog box, will use the form's properties to call into a few internal routines responsible for generating the output class:

```
public void Execute(object Application, int hwndOwner, ref object[] ContextParams,
    ref object[] CustomParams, ref wizardResult retval)
{
    // instance the dialog for the wizard
    WizardDialog dlg = new WizardDialog();

    // show the dialog
    dlg.Show();

    // process the wizard results
    if (dlg.DialogResult == DialogResult.OK)
    {
        // Load template file, replace tokens, return content
        // as string
        string classContent = ReplaceTokens(dlg.ClassName, dlg.Category,
            dlg.SubCategory, dlg.UseRegistry, dlg.RegKey);

        // Put the returned string content into a file and
        // add the file to the current project
        // (3rd element of ContextParams is the current project's
```

```
            // items collection)
            ProjectItems projItems = (ProjectItems)ContextParams[2];
            AddFile(classContent, projItems);

            retval = wizardResult.wizardResultSuccess;

        }
        // wizard was canceled; no action required
        else
        {
            retval = wizardResult.wizardResultCancel;
        }
    }
```

To react to the user clicking OK, you call three separate internal routines. The first, ReplaceTokens, opens the template class file and replaces the tokens (because this is a simple string substitution process, we won't reproduce the code here).

The second routine, AddFile, writes the new class content into a new file and adds it to the current project. Because this code may not be entirely obvious, here is one approach:

```
private void AddFile(string className, string classContent,
    ProjectItems projItems)
{
    // determine path to project files
    string fileName =
        Path.GetDirectoryName(projItems.ContainingProject.FileName);

    // use path and class name to build file name for class
    fileName = fileName + className + ".cs";

    // save class file into project folder
    using (TextWriter writer = new StreamWriter(fileName, false))
    {
        writer.Write(classContent);
        writer.Close();
    }

    // add the newly created file to the current project
    projItems.AddFromFile(fileName);

}
```

Last, you call UpdateXML; this routine opens the .addin file and adds the appropriate <ToolsOptionsPage> node to the XML content:

```csharp
private void UpdateXml(ProjectItems projItems, string category,
    string subCategory)
{
    // create string XML snippet
    string xml = "";
    xml += "<ToolsOptionsPage>\r\n";
    xml += "    <Category Name=\"" + category + "\">\r\n";
    xml += "        <SubCategory Name=\"" + subCategory + "\">\r\n";
    xml += "            <Assembly></Assembly>\r\n";
    xml += "            <FullClassName></FullClassName>\r\n";
    xml += "        </SubCategory>\r\n";
    xml += "    </Category>\r\n";
    xml += "</ToolsOptionsPage>\r\n";
    xml += "</Extensibility>";

    // iterate items in the project, looking for the
    // .addin file
    string projName = projItems.ContainingProject.FullName;
    foreach (ProjectItem itm in projItems)
    {
        if (itm.Name == projName + ".addin")
        {
            // open the .addin file's document object
            itm.Document.Activate();
            TextDocument txtDoc = (TextDocument)itm.Document.Object("");
            TextRanges nullObj = null;
            // add in the cat/sub-cat XML snippet
            txtDoc.ReplacePattern("</Extensibility>", xml,
                (int)vsFindOptions.vsFindOptionsFromStart,
                ref nullObj);

        }
    }
}
```

At this point, the wizard code is complete.

### Creating the `.vsz` and `.vsdir` Files

All that is left is to create the `.vsz` file and add an entry to the `.vsdir` file. The `.vsz` file is straightforward:

```
VSWizard 8.0
Wizard=ContosoWizards.ToolsOptionsPageWizard
Param=
```

The record you add to the .vsdir file looks like this:

```
ToolsOptionsPageWizard.vsz ¦ ¦ ¦1¦Create a new Tools Options Page class¦c:\Con-
tosoFramework\Wizards\ToolsOptionsPageWizard.dll¦ ¦ ¦Contoso Options Page Class
```

With that, the wizard is fully functional and can be selected from the Add Item dialog box.

## Summary

In this chapter, we described how to leverage the power of Visual Studio's automation APIs to create add-ins and wizards.

You investigated the nearly unlimited potential for extending Visual Studio by using add-ins that call into the automation API and expose their interfaces in a variety of ways, including custom tool windows and dialog boxes.

And you also saw how to once again leverage the ubiquitous automation object model and the built-in wizard engine to create your own custom wizards for adding new projects, adding new project items, or executing nearly any other type of step-by-step process within Visual Studio.

# PART V

# Creating Enterprise Applications

## IN THIS PART

W eb development continues to be a major focus in the latest release of Visual Studio. As with its predecessors, the 2008 release continues to evolve the .NET web development experience. The new tool is packed with additional design productivity enhancements, and there are new and improved controls, better IntelliSense, and support for LINQ—just to name a few features. These additions and improvements are meant to provide web developers more confidence and control when building their next web application with .NET.

This chapter is focused on helping web developers leverage ASP.NET to create browser-based applications whose code runs on a server. These types of applications offer the broadest possible reach for web developers by targeting applications to work cross-browser and cross-platform with HTML-based compatibility. Of course, web development continues to evolve beyond the browser. For more information on such things as XBAP, AJAX, and Silverlight, see Chapter 17, "Creating Rich Browser Applications." If you are looking to develop XAML-based applications using Microsoft's WPF, see Chapter 16, "Creating Richer, Smarter User Interfaces."

We'll start by covering the basics of defining Visual Studio web projects and creating simple web forms. From there we'll move on to more advanced topics and demonstrate how you might build a cohesive user interface for your ASP.NET application that includes master pages, themes, Web Parts, and data binding. Lastly, we'll spend some time covering the major set of controls built into ASP.NET.

---

**NOTE**

ASP.NET is a huge topic. We are not able to dig in on its every aspect. Instead, we concentrate on areas where you can leverage Visual Studio to increase your productivity in building web-based user interfaces. This is a key topic for all web developers.

We expect that as you build your ASP.NET interface, you will discover places that require further exploration. To that end, we will try to point out some of them as we move through the chapter. Some examples include membership, user profiles, caching, website administration, and cross-page posting.

---

# The Basics of an ASP.NET Website

Websites in Visual Studio start with a website project. The website project represents a connection between Visual Studio, the development version of your website (see Chapter 4, "Solutions and Projects," for more information), and a web server, be it local or otherwise. What is meant by *website*, however, continues to evolve and expand.

Simple HTML sites with just text, hyperlinks, and a few images are rarely created anymore or even discussed seriously as websites. Instead, .NET has pushed the definition of website well beyond the original ASP model that combined HTML with some server-side script. Nowadays, a website means user-interactive web forms; compiled code that links those web forms to a middle tier; master pages, styles, and themes that control the look of a site; configuration for such things as security, membership, and caching; database connectivity and data binding; and so on. The Visual Studio 2008 tools bring these concepts together to allow you to create rich, modern websites that offer an ever-higher degree of user interaction. In the following sections, we examine the makeup of the modern website and discuss how you create and configure them.

## Creating a New Web Application Project

A web application project represents a template for a new site. This template helps define default directories, configuration, web forms, and other related files and settings. Visual Studio ships with a number of website templates. These templates allow you to define a few different versions of a website. You can also use these templates as a basis to define your own custom templates (see Chapter 7, "The .NET Community: Consuming and Creating Shared Code," for more information on creating custom templates).

Beginning with Visual Studio 2005, websites are no longer considered just another Visual Studio project (like a Windows forms or a class library application). Instead, websites have been elevated and given their own status inside Visual Studio. To create one, you choose the New Web Site option from the File menu. This launches the New Web Site dialog box, which is different from your standard new project dialog box. Figure 14.1 shows an example of this dialog. We'll look at the many items that make defining a website a unique process.

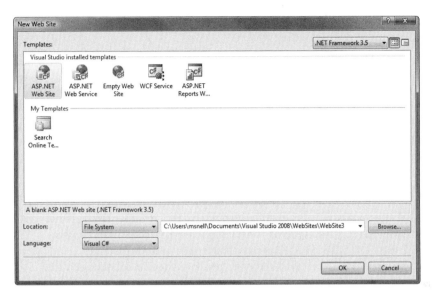

FIGURE 14.1   Creating a new website.


### Selecting a Visual Studio Website Template

Visual Studio installs five ASP.NET templates by default. You pick a template based on your needs. However, the majority of sites will be built with the standard template, ASP.NET Web Site. These are the five default ASP.NET templates:

- ▶ **ASP.NET Web Site**—Represents the standard ASP.NET website and starts with an App_Data directory, a `Default.aspx` web form, and a `web.config` file. Of course, additional folders and files can be added as you build out your site. This is the template most commonly used to start a new website from scratch.

- ▶ **ASP.NET Web Service**—Represents a site focused on creating an XML-based web service (see Chapter 19, "Service-Oriented Applications," for more details). The template includes a service called `Service.asmx` that includes code for a basic web service, an App_Code directory to house the service's class files, an App_Data folder for housing data to which ASP.NET has access, and a `web.config` file for managing site configuration.

- ▶ **Empty Web Site**—Represents a website project devoid of all folders and files. You use this project container as a starting point. It does not presume folders and files. Instead, you explicitly add these items yourself as required.

- ▶ **WCF Service**—Used to create a website that contains WCF services (see Chapter 19 for more details). Like the Web Service project template, the WCF Service contains the standard App_Code, App_Data, and Web.config files. However, the service file is a

`Service.svc` file. This service stubs out a class that implements a configurable, WCF-based (and not simply XML-based) service.

▶ **ASP.NET Reports Web Site**—Creates a site for building web-based reports using the Microsoft Report Viewer tools. Creating this site will not only create an initial report in your project and set appropriate references to Microsoft's report libraries, but also launch a wizard to walk you through configuring the first report. This includes connecting to the data source, selecting data, and setting display options. You can then run reports in a web browser. The report viewer includes options for exporting reports as Excel and PDF.

---

**TIP**

Visual Studio 2005 developers will note that the Personal Web Starter Kit template no longer ships with Visual Studio 2008 Professional. This template allowed you to create a fully functional site in just a few clicks. However, starter kits have evolved and expanded. There are now many more available and, therefore, they do not ship with the tool. Developers using Visual Web Developers Express Edition and Visual Studio 2008 Professional can take advantage of these starter kits. They include kits for blogs, portals, e-commerce, small business, clubs, wikis, and many more. You can find out about these sites at http://www.asp.net/community/projects.

---

### Choosing a Website Location

In older versions of Visual Studio (before 2005), you were essentially stuck (or boxed in) when creating a location for your development website. You had to be running Internet Information Services (IIS) locally, and you had to store your web application inside the wwwroot folder structure. This model caused a number of problems. The first was that typically your application was spread all over your machine. You would have your solution file and `.dll` projects inside one directory and your web application buried on your C: drive in a special directory. The second was that this model forced development managers to allow IIS servers on every developer desktop (or not get work done). This typically broke standard policy. There were many more issues too around IIS versioning, deployment, and more.

Visual Studio 2005 solved these issues. Options for connecting to the development version of an application were vastly expanded. You can now work with your application using a local IIS server (or not). You might instead want to work against the file system and use a local development web server (instead of a local instance of IIS). Or you may need to work against a remote server and connect to it via FTP or HTTP. Let's look at configuring these many website location options using Visual Studio 2008.

You define the location for your website (and consequently how you want to access it) when you first create it or connect to it. Recall that in Figure 14.1, there is a drop-down list next to the Location option (bottom left). This list contains the values File System, HTTP, and FTP. Each of these locations requires you to enter the appropriate location of your website and provide the appropriate credentials in order to create (or open) your site.

Clicking the Browse button lets you navigate to the site's intended location. This button launches the Choose Location window. In the following sections, we'll look at the many options of this dialog box.

**File System**    The first option you have at the top of the Choose Location window is File System. This allows you to choose any directory on your machine in which to store the contents of your website. You can use this dialog box to navigate the file system and select or create a new folder to contain your site. Figure 14.2 shows this dialog box for selecting a folder. The Create New Folder button is in the upper-right corner (along with the Delete button).

If you choose File System for your local website development, you do not need to have IIS on your machine. Instead, Visual Studio recognizes the content in the file system directory as a website and runs a local instance of ASP.NET Development Server. This server mimics IIS and can be run and killed on an as-needed basis. You end up with an instance for each website you are currently running, debugging, or even building with Visual Studio.

Each development server instance is listed in your system tray. You can right-click an instance of the development server and navigate to the site it serves via a web browser, stop the server, or view its details. An example of the development server details window is shown in Figure 14.3. Here you can see the virtual and physical paths of the server, the port number, and the root URL. You also have the option to stop the running server using the Stop button.

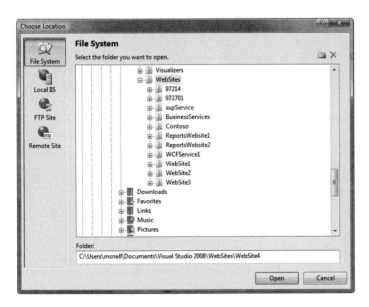

FIGURE 14.2    Creating a website stored on the file system.

FIGURE 14.3    The ASP.NET Development Server details window.

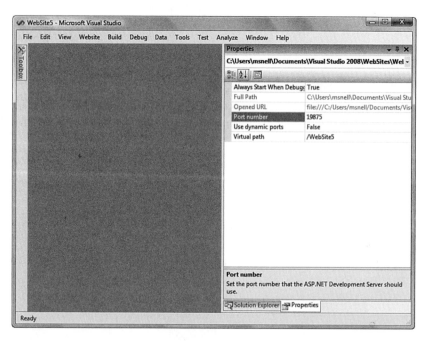

FIGURE 14.4    Forcing a port number for the development server.

**Local IIS**    Visual Studio 2008 still allows you to configure a web application to use a local
instance of IIS. This capability gives you the benefit of being able to run the server even
when you're not developing. It also lets you have more control over the configuration of

your site using the IIS administration tool. However, in most scenarios, running a local version of IIS on a developer's machine is less than desirable. It takes up valuable system resources and often violates internal policies by exposing an extra server to the network.

To configure a local version of IIS, select the Local IIS option. Figure 14.5 shows the dialog box with this option selected. Note that here IIS is not installed locally on the machine. You can see that if you are running Visual Studio on Windows Vista, you have some work to do. You must get all the IIS components installed. Then, you must configure Visual Studio to run with the elevated privileges of Administrator. Again, this typically is not a good idea.

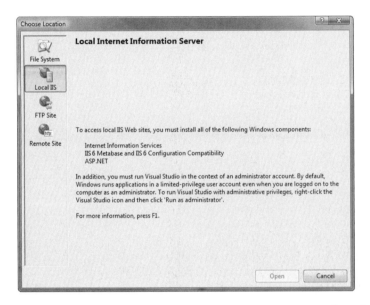

FIGURE 14.5    Creating a site to run on an uninstalled, local version of IIS.

To install these options locally on Windows Vista, you will want to open the Control Panel. From here you can select Uninstall Program. You are then given the option to add or remove Windows components. Select this option and you will be presented with the Windows Features dialog shown in Figure 14.6. Find Internet Information Services and make sure you have it installed along with ASP.NET.

You should now see more options in your new website dialog for the Local IIS selection (see Figure 14.7). First, you can see three buttons in the upper-right corner of the dialog box. In order, these buttons allow you to create a new web application, create a new virtual directory, and delete a selected item. If you choose to create a new virtual directory, you are asked to define a directory name and a folder location where you want to store the site. You are not bound to wwwroot. Instead, you can create your site using any folder. You can also choose to connect to this site via Secure Sockets Layer (SSL). This capability is useful if you need to encrypt sensitive information between the development machine and the server.

FIGURE 14.6    Installing IIS and ASP.NET on Windows Vista.

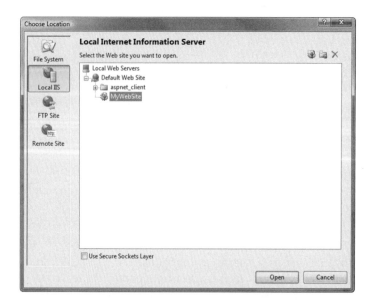

FIGURE 14.7    Creating a website on a local version of IIS.

**TIP**

If running Windows Vista, you need to run Visual Studio with Administrator privileges in order to connect to IIS. To do so, right-click the shortcut to Visual Studio and choose Run as administrator.

**FTP Site**    Another option is to work with your site across FTP (File Transfer Protocol). The New Website dialog allows you to indicate where on a given FTP server your site should (or does) exist. To do so, you must enter the address of the server and the port and provide appropriate credentials. All FTP constraints apply to FTP sites; this means, for example, that passwords are not secure. Figure 14.8 shows the FTP website settings. Note that sites created using FTP are run in debug mode using the local ASP.NET Development Server. FTP is simply used to retrieve and store the files. Of course, you might have a web server that serves up the files from the FTP server. This server is independent and is not seen by Visual Studio.

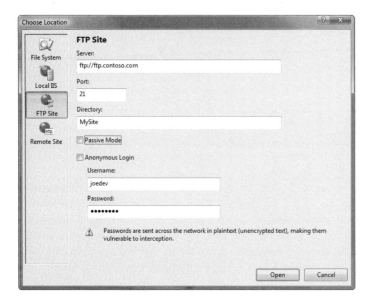

FIGURE 14.8    Defining a website with FTP.

**Remote HTTP Site**    Finally, you can choose to communicate with a web server across HTTP for defining your website. This is typically a remote web server where you are doing shared development. The development server must have FrontPage Server Extensions applied to allow this type of connectivity from Visual Studio. Figure 14.9 shows an example of configuring a site's location to be a remote IIS server.

### Choosing a Default Programming Language

Visual Studio 2008 allows you to mix the languages you use to develop the items in your site. When you create a web form or a class file, you determine the language in which each individual item is written. However, when you create a new site, you set a default language for the site. This default language is set in the New Web Site dialog box (recall Figure 14.1, bottom left). Setting this value tells Visual Studio how to generate your template. In addition, it sets the initial value for the setting that controls the default language of any new items being added to your site.

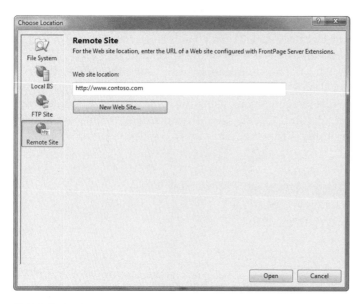

FIGURE 14.9    Creating a website on a remote server.

Figure 14.10 shows a website with mixed code. There are two web files: one with a code-behind written in VB and one with a C# code-behind. Also, notice that the App_Code directory contains a C# class file. If you need to mix VB class files, you might consider putting them in another class library. However, you can do so in the same website: You simply need to put the code into another folder as shown by the More Code folder in Figure 14.10. The compiler groups code by folder; therefore, all code in a given folder must be of the same type.

### Understanding the File Makeup of Your Website

A number of files go into the definition of an ASP.NET website. In addition, Visual Studio 2008 adds various "special" directories. The following sections provide a reference for the many directories and files that define a .NET website.

**Directories**    ASP.NET defines a number of folders that it uses to organize and recognize various files that make up your application. These folders have reserved names that mean something special to ASP.NET; therefore, you should use them appropriately.

You add an ASP.NET directory to your application via the context menu (right-click) for the site. Choose Add ASP.NET Folder from this menu. Figure 14.11 shows a web application with each of these special folders defined. Each of these directories is listed in Table 14.1, along with a basic explanation of their usage.

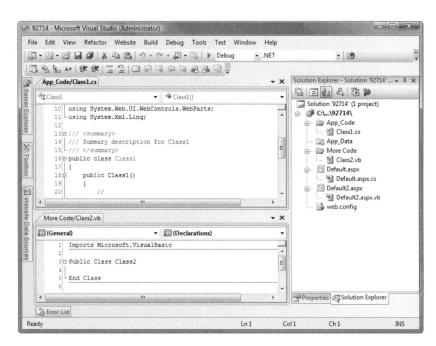

FIGURE 14.10    A website with mixed VB and C# files.

FIGURE 14.11    The ASP.NET special directories.

TABLE 14.1    ASP.NET Directories

| Directory | Description |
| --- | --- |
| Bin | This folder contains the compiled code (.dll files) that your application references. This might include external class libraries or controls you want to embed into your application (without embedding the source). |
| App_Code | This folder houses the class files that help define your application. For example, you could choose to put your business object or data access classes in this directory. All code in this directory is compiled into a single library. This includes code in any subdirectories. Therefore, all code in the directory must be of the same language. |
| App_Data | This directory contains data files used by your applications. This can be SQL Express files (.mdf), XML data, Excel files, and so on. |
| App_GlobalResources | This folder contains the resource files (.resx and .resources) that make up your application. You use resource files to abstract such things as string-based text and images from your actual application. In this way, your application reads from a resource file instead of being hard-coded with these values. This helps you support multiple language user interfaces, design-time changes, and related issues. |
| App_LocalResources | This folder also contains resource files. However, these files are specific to a page or control. They are not global to the entire application scope. |
| App_WebReferences | This folder is used to house and maintain references to web services. The files inside the folder include web service contracts (.wsdl) and schemas (.xsd) and other related items. |
| App_Browsers | This folder contains browser definition files (.browser). These files are typically used for mobile application support. Each .browser file defines the various capabilities for a given browser. This helps your user interface render appropriately for a specific device. |
| App_Themes | This folder contains subfolders that each define a specific theme (look and feel) for your application. Each theme folder contains one or more skin (.skin) files, a style (.css) sheet, and any theme-based images. See "Creating a Common Look and Feel," later in this chapter, for more on themes. |

**Files**    Numerous files and file types define a typical ASP.NET website. Of course, there are files that you use often, such as web forms, user controls, classes, and configuration files; and then there are those that are rarer, such as skins, master pages, resources, and site maps. Table 14.2 lists some of the more common files that might exist in any given ASP.NET web application.

TABLE 14.2    ASP.NET Files

| File Extension | Description |
| --- | --- |
| .aspx | Defines an ASP.NET web form. This is the most common ASP.NET file. See "Creating Web Pages," later in this chapter. |
| .asmx | Defines an ASP.NET XML-based web service. See Chapter 19. |
| .ascx | Represents an ASP.NET user control. User controls allow you to define your own version or combination of controls and reuse them throughout your site. |
| .asax | Creates a global application class. This allows you to define code inside events that fire when IIS starts or stops an application, an error occurs, or a user initiates or terminates a session. |
| .cs/.vb | Defines a class file. The extension .cs is a C# class file. The .vb extension is a class written in Visual Basic. |
| .master | Represents a master page. A master page is used to define common elements that might appear on multiple pages within a website. These might include menu items, navigation, headers, footers, and other related items. See "Master Pages," later in this chapter. |
| .config | Represents a configuration file for your web application. You use the configuration file to manage settings such as debugging and to store application-specific data (such as an encrypted connection string to a database). |
| .css | Represents a cascading style sheet. It stores the styles of your application or theme. See "Style Sheets," later in this chapter. |
| .dbml | Is a LINQ to SQL class file. You create such a file to provide a class file that exposes LINQ queries against a given SQL database. |
| .rdlc | Allows you to create a web-based report that leverages the Microsoft reporting technology. |
| .sitemap | Allows you to create a file that defines a map of your website. Sitemaps are used for various navigation controls within ASP.NET. |
| .svc | Represents a WCF service. See Chapter 19 for more information. |
| .skin | Represents a skin for one or more controls in your application. A skin is defined for an application theme. See "Themes and Skins," later in this chapter. |

14

You add a new ASP.NET file to your application by right-clicking your site and selecting Add New Item. Figure 14.12 shows the Add New Item dialog box. The many files that are available to your site are also listed as item templates. Visual Studio will take care to place each file in a special directory if applicable.

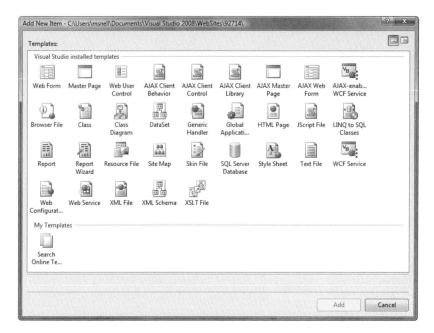

FIGURE 14.12    Adding an ASP.NET file to your website.

## Controlling Project Properties and Options

ASP.NET applications have their own set of properties and configuration options. These properties control how an application works, gets built, works with the debugger, and so on. You access the properties for your website through the Property Pages dialog box. You can open this dialog by right-clicking your website and selecting the Property Pages option. The following sections cover the many options of this dialog box.

### References

The references in your application define the code that your application uses by reference. You add references to other projects in your solution, other .NET namespaces in the .NET Framework, third-party controls, and other .NET libraries. The code you reference is compiled into a .dll file and exists on its own. It may or may not be installed in the Global Assembly Cache (GAC). Figure 14.13 shows the References portion of the Property Pages dialog box.

Each current reference for the website is listed along with its associated reference type. The figure shows the standard references for a new website in ASP.NET. You will notice that System.Core is referenced along with System.Xml.Linq, System.Web.Extensions, and System.Data.DataExtensions. All of these items are stored in the GAC as indicated by the Type column. You can also see the version being referenced (in this case, 3.5). From this dialog box, you can also add a new reference, remove an existing reference, or refresh (update) the reference.

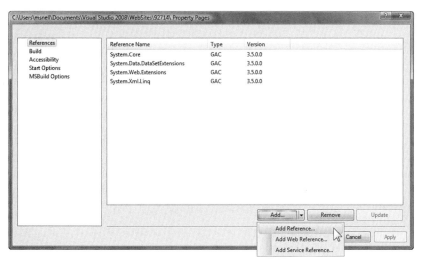

FIGURE 14.13   Managing web application references.

**Adding a New Reference**   You can add three types of references to your ASP.NET applications (as shown in Figure 14.13): a standard reference to a .NET class library (Add Reference), a reference to an XML web service (Add Web Reference), or a reference to a WCF service (Add Service Reference). We cover the two service-type references in Chapter 19. When you add a standard reference, you are making a connection to a .dll file that exists as part of another application or another project. Establishing this reference places a copy of the compiled .dll file into your website's bin directory. The namespaces, classes, and methods inside this .dll file will then be available for you to code against. The compiler will also check your application against any referenced .dlls to ensure that you are not breaking type constraints, method signatures, and the like.

Figure 14.14 shows the Add Reference dialog box. You can use the tabs across the top of the dialog box to find the specific item you want to reference. If, for example, you are looking to reference a namespace from the .NET Framework, you would select the .NET tab. This tab will locate items installed in your GAC such as those in the System or Microsoft namespace. You can also set references to COM components, browse for .dll files, set references to other projects, and view recent references.

Note that the items under the Projects tab represent those that exist in the current solution. These references work like any other with one exception. For your convenience, items marked as a project reference are automatically refreshed when those projects are recompiled.

**Build**

The Build page of the Property Pages dialog box allows you to control how your application is built using Visual Studio 2008. Figure 14.15 shows the options that are available.

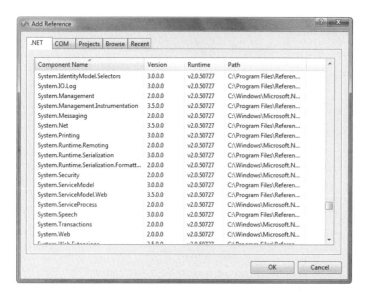

FIGURE 14.14    Adding a new reference to your web application.

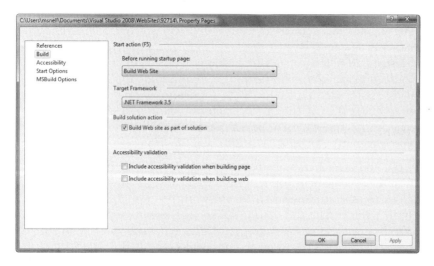

FIGURE 14.15    Controlling the build options for your site.

**Start Action**    The Start Action section of the Build page allows you to define how your application is compiled when you run it from the IDE. There are three options in this drop-down: No Build, Build Page, and Build Web Site (the default). Let's look at each of these options.

The No Build option tells the IDE to just launch the site in a browser without doing any compilation. In this instance, as pages and items are accessed, they are built. Instead of the errors showing in the IDE before you run the application, the errors are displayed in the browser as you find them.

---

**TIP**

The No Build capability can be great when you have a large application that contains pages that you are not working on or that have errors (and you intend to avoid). It also speeds the startup time because no pages are precompiled.

---

The Build Page option tells the IDE to compile only the current startup page or the page you're working on. This capability is very useful if you work on only one page at a time. If the IDE finds errors, they are shown in the IDE before the page launches.

Last, the Build Web Site option, the default setting, tells the IDE to build the entire website and all dependent projects before launching into the browser. This capability can be helpful if you are working on a small site by yourself. However, it can also cause longer build times on larger projects.

**Target Framework**    New to 2008 is the Target Framework option. This feature allows you to indicate (and change) the version of the .NET Framework your application targets. This means you can write ASP.NET applications using Visual Studio 2008 that target .NET 2.0, 3.0, or 3.5. Flipping this option will compile and check your application against the target version of the .NET framework. When your application runs, it will call code in the given target framework.

**Build Solution Action**    There is a single option under Build Solution Action in the Build page for the professional edition of Visual Studio. Build Web Site as Part of Solution indicates whether Visual Studio should include the website as part of the solution's build. The default for this setting is true (or checked). In this case, when you choose Build Solution from the Build menu, the website will also be built.

There is another option (not shown) for developers running Visual Studio Team System Development Edition. This option, Enable Code Analysis, indicates whether you want to have the website analyzed by Visual Studio for performance, unused variables, naming standards, and so on. This can be a great tool for ensuring that developers are adhering to common .NET coding standards.

**Accessibility Validation**    The Accessibility Validation options in the Build page allow you to have Visual Studio check your web application for conformance with accessibility standards. These standards ensure that your application will work for people with disabilities. The actual standards are covered in the next section. Here, you have two options for enabling validation: for the entire site or for just the current startup page. If these options are enabled, Visual Studio displays accessibility issues in the IDE when you run the application.

**Accessibility**

The Accessibility page of the Property Pages dialog box allows you to define what checks should be done relative to your site's conformance. Figure 14.16 shows the options for configuring the checks. There are three levels of checks based on two standards: the W3C's Web Content Accessibility Guidelines (WCAG) 1 and 2, and the U.S. government's standards for accessibility (Access board section 508).

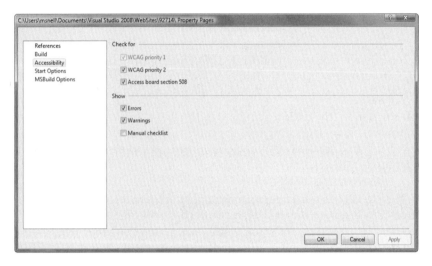

FIGURE 14.16    Managing accessibility options.

---

**TIP**

Visual Studio checks only your HTML pages for accessibility standards compliance upon build. It does not check ASP.NET controls because those controls emit their own HTML. However, most, but not all, of this HTML is standards-compliant. If you need to verify that the final HTML output is 100% standards-compliant for accessibility, you need to know a few things. First, many of the ASP.NET controls should be safe and of no concern. There is, however, a list of controls that need to be configured properly for accessibility. These can be found in MSDN by searching for ASP.NET Controls and Accessibility. This also indicates those controls to stay away from.

A quick way to verify an entire ASP.NET as accessible-compliant is to run the page in a web browser, view the HTML source, copy the HTML from the page, and embed it as a separate HTML file in your solution. Visual Studio will then check to ensure that this new page is compliant on build.

For more information on building accessible applications, see "Walkthrough: Creating an Accessible Web Application" on MSDN.

---

### Start Options

The Start Options page in the Property Pages dialog box allows you to define what happens when you start (or run) your application. Figure 14.17 shows the many options available. We'll look at each in the following sections.

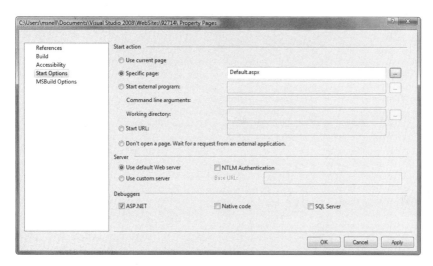

**FIGURE 14.17**   Configuring the startup options for your application.

**Start Action**   The Start Action section of the Start Options page is useful for defining what happens when a page is loaded when you start your application through the IDE. The first option, Use Current Page, tells the IDE to start the application using the current, active page in the IDE. This capability can be great for developers who work on one standalone page at a time. The next option, Specific Page, allows you to set a startup page. This is akin to right-clicking a page and choosing Set as Start Page. The third option, Start External Program, allows you to specify an .exe file to run (instead of the browser) when you start the application. The Start URL option allows you to send the browser to a different URL when running your application. This capability can be useful when debugging a web service. You might launch a client that uses your web service, for example. Finally, you can use the last option to tell Visual Studio to wait for a request (don't start anything). This, too, can be useful for a web service scenario.

**Server**   The Server section of the Start Options page allows you to specify a server to be launched for your application. Most applications will leave this set to Use Default Web Server. This represents the file system websites. For scenarios that use IIS or FTP, you will specify a URL to the actual server.

**Debuggers**   The Debuggers group of options on the Start Options page allows you to set the enabled debuggers used when running your application. By default, only ASP.NET is enabled. You can choose to turn off this setting. You can also add both Native code and SQL Server debuggers to the mix.

**MSBuild Options**

The final page in the Property Pages dialog box, MsBuild Options, allows you to control precompiling of your application. These options are specific to using the MSBuild compilation tool from the command line. Figure 14.18 shows an example. From here, you can set your precompilation output folder and manage related settings.

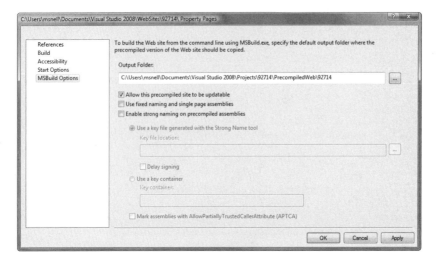

FIGURE 14.18    Managing the options related to MSBuild and ASP.NET.

**NOTE**

You can get the same results from the Publish Web Site option in the IDE as you would with the MSBuild command-line application.

## Creating Web Pages

ASP.NET web pages (also called web forms) make up the bulk of any given website. You create web pages to define your user interface. Web pages in ASP.NET have both a designer component and an event model. The designer allows you to define the controls and look of a given web page. The event model is used on the server to respond to user interaction (or events posted back to the server over HTTP). This section looks at the basics of both the web page's designer and its event model.

### Adding a Web Page to Your Website

The first step to working with web pages is adding one or more to your website. To do so, you use the Add New Item dialog box and select Web Form from the item templates. Figure 14.19 shows an example of adding a CustomerEdit.aspx page to a website.

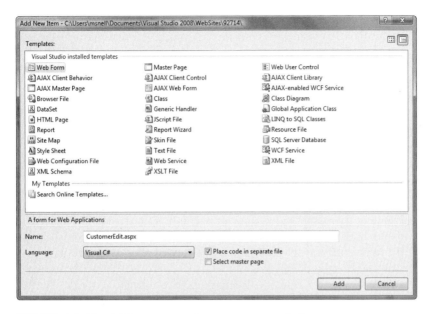

FIGURE 14.19    Adding a new web page to your website.

You have a few options when adding a new web page to your site. First, you can set the page's name. It is best to use a standard naming scheme and to make sure that the name also references the page's primary function. Web page names must be unique in a given directory. A good standard might be to indicate the data with which the page works followed by a user action for the page. In our example, this is `CustomerEdit.aspx`. The second option is the language on which the web form is based. Your website is typically either all C# or VB. However, it can be made up of a mixture of both languages. When you create a new page, the default language is chosen based on the default language for your website. However, you can use the drop-down at the bottom of the Add New Item dialog to choose a different language for the page.

Next, you can indicate whether you want the code for the web page to be in a separate file. ASP.NET allows you to create a web form as a single file. This form will include both ASP markup and server-side code. In fact, you also get VB or C# IntelliSense inside the markup editor for these types of forms.

The dominant setting (and default) for most professional developers is code-behind (Place Code in Separate File). Putting code in a new file allows you to manage that code independently of the UI markup. This can be a much cleaner development experience. In addition, ASP.NET puts your code into what is called a *partial class*. This partial class contains only the code that you write. Code that is emitted by the tool or framework is not part of this file. Your code and the tool-emitted code are combined together during compilation. In this way, you are not burdened by code that is really not yours.

The final option on the Add New Item dialog when adding a Web Form is Select Master Page. This setting tells the IDE that you want your new web form to use a master page for its default content and layout. We will look at master pages later in this chapter.

### Adding Controls to Your Web Page

You add controls to a web page by dragging them from the Visual Studio Toolbox to the web page. In the page designer, there are multiple views of your form: design, source, and split view. The design view allows you to build your form using drag-and-drop with a visual editor (or designer). This is similar to building a Windows form. As you drag items onto the page, you see a visual representation of what they will look like at runtime. This includes their layout with respect to one another. You can select an item on a page and use the property editor to change the look and behavior of the element.

Figure 14.20 shows a page in the design view. Notice the Toolbox on the left. This is the source of controls you can add to your page. In the center of the figure is the actual design surface. Notice that the Save button is selected. The properties for the Save button are shown on the right. You can use the property editor to make changes to how the control looks and acts. These changes are stored inside the markup for the page.

FIGURE 14.20   Adding a control to the design view of an ASP.NET page.

The source view allows you to see (and edit) the markup related to a web page. Here you can still drag controls from the Toolbox onto the editor, but instead of a visual representation, you get the markup code that represents the given item. You can then use the markup editor to change the values inside the markup. This includes setting property values and changing layout information. Of course, Visual Studio provides IntelliSense for doing so. Figure 14.21 shows the same page in source view as we looked at previously. Notice that the button's properties are available for edit from IntelliSense. This may be a more familiar experience for coders.

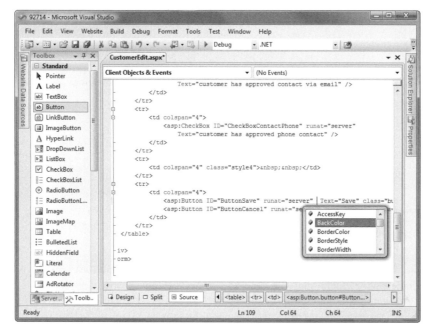

FIGURE 14.21    Editing a control in the source view of an ASP.NET page.

The third view is new for Visual Studio 2008, split view. This gives you both markup and the visual design surface. The two try to stay in synch with one another. If you make a change in the source view, for example, the design view will try to update itself or wait for you to click on it and then update. This can be very useful if you do things both visually and through code (and have a big monitor). You end up doing a lot less switching back and forth between views. Figure 14.22 shows an example of the same page we've been looking at, now in split view. Notice how in both views it knows that the Save button is selected.

Note that you can shift among these three views using the options at the bottom of the form design window. Here you see buttons for design, split, and source views.

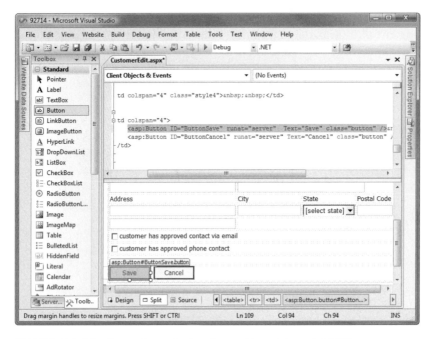

FIGURE 14.22    Using the split view for working with an ASP.NET page.

---

**TIP**

You can change how Visual Studio brings up your web forms. You can choose between viewing in source view and viewing in design view by default. To do so, choose Options from the Tools menu. You then select the HTML Designer node from the tree. Figure 14.23 shows an example of this window. The Start Pages In group box allows you to modify this setting.

---

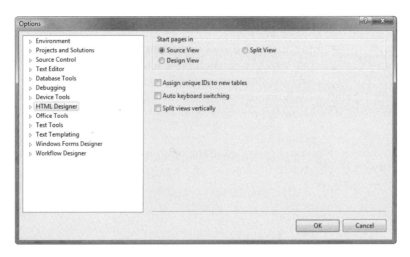

FIGURE 14.23    Choosing a default view for web pages.

### Responding to Events

When you write ASP.NET web pages, it is important to understand how the event model works. The event model represents how events are fired on the server when users make requests (or trigger actions). The ASP.NET event model is different from the standard Windows form event model because it combines events that process on a server with the nature of a web application delivered inside a web browser.

An ASP.NET page has less of an event model and more of a life cycle. The life cycle has a series of stages through which a page goes. In each stage, there is typically one or more events that gets fired. The life cycle stages of an ASP.NET page are shown in Figure 14.24.

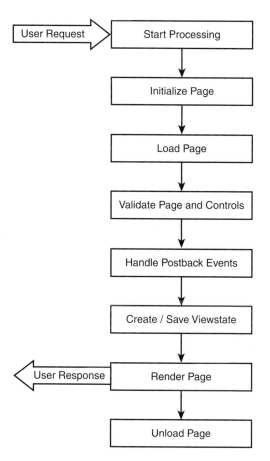

FIGURE 14.24   The life cycle of an ASP.NET page.

Each stage in Figure 14.24 is described here:

1. **User Request**—A user makes a request for a given page.

2. **Start Processing**—ASP.NET determines whether the page life cycle needs to be executed or a version of the page can be returned from cache.

3. **Initialize Page**—ASP.NET initializes the page and makes each control on the page available from a code perspective. However, the controls at this point are not matched to any viewstate and no postback data has been loaded.

4. **Load Page**—ASP.NET loads the page, connects controls to their viewstate information, and connects data from the postback to each control.

5. **Validate Page and Controls**—After the page has been loaded, it gets validated. This means calling out to each control and ensuring that the `Validation` method is fired. Finally, the Page's `IsValid` property gets set at this stage based on the results.

6. **Handle Postback Events**—If the user's request is posting back data to the page (instead of a simple request), then at this point any postback-related events are called, such as a button's click event.

7. **Create/Save Viewstate**—ASP.NET begins the process of sending the response back to the user. The first thing is to create the ViewState data and embed it inside the response.

8. **Render Page**—At this stage, ASP.NET generates all the HTML for the page and writes it to an output stream.

9. **User Response**—A response is sent back to the user that made the request.

10. **Unload Page**—ASP.NET unloads the page and discards it from memory.

As a page moves through this life cycle, a series of events are triggered. These events are where you place your code. It is important to understand this life cycle to help you understand the events, when they are fired, and what is available to you inside these events. You want to be sure to get the right code in the right event for the right job. Let's take a look at the basics of the web page event model. The following lists the key events in the page life cycle in the order in which they are fired:

1. **Page PreInit**—This is the first event for which you might write code. The `PreInit` event is useful if you are creating controls dynamically, setting a master page dynamically, or setting a page's theme dynamically.

2. **Page Init**—This event is called to create the controls used by the web page. It also initializes the properties of these controls. This event is typically created automatically by the IDE to set properties of controls on a given page.

3. **Page Load**—This event is called when the page is loaded and after the controls are initialized. This is a common event for web developers to use. You can use this event to determine whether a user is requesting a page or executing a postback (submitting data). You then call the appropriate code based on this information.

4. **Control Specific Event(s)**—Next, the page framework executes the event or events that are associated with the control the user used to submit the form (if any).

For example, if a user clicked a button on your form, the button's click event is called (after page load).

5. **Page Pre Render**—This event is called just before the final rendering of the page is sent back to the browser. You can use this event to make changes to the page after all events are called.

6. **Page Unload**—This is the last event that is called for the page (after the page is rendered). You use this event to do cleanup. For example, you might close page-level connections or do some form of logging. You cannot, however, make any changes that will affect the response to the user. That was completed in the rendering stage (see Figure 14.24).

These steps represent the basic event model for a page. However, there are additional events for the page. In addition, user controls have their own events that are called during the control-specific event stage. Master pages can also add default processing for all pages. Understanding the events in any given page will always help when you're debugging or trying to achieve a specific result.

> **NOTE**
>
> For more information on what happens inside the ASP processing framework, see "ASP.NET Application Life Cycle Overview" on the MSDN website. This article provides a detailed view of how ASP.NET works with user requests and renders a page. It also covers application- and session-specific events (inside `global.asax`).

**Adding Page Event Handlers**     There are a couple of ways to ensure that your event handlers are called by ASP.NET when a page executes. First, you can call them automatically. If you set the `AutoEventWireup` page-level attribute to `True`, then ASP.NET will find events that follow the `Page_Event` naming convention and automatically call them at their appropriate time. This approach can be convenient but requires you to recall each event's name so that you can define it appropriately.

You can also explicitly bind page events to methods in your code. In this way, you can use your own event names. You can also let Visual Studio generate the event names. You can add events to a page from the designer in a similar way you would bind events to controls: from the Properties window. However, to access a page's events, you must be in the Component Designer for the page. The Component Designer is another design view for a page. It is used to add components to the page such as event logging. You get to the component designer by right-clicking a page and choosing View Component Designer. After you have it open, you then open that page's Properties window. From there, you can select the lightning bolt icon to show all events for the page. Figure 14.25 shows an example.

The right side of the figure shows the properties for the `CustomerEdit.aspx` page. Notice that the lightning bolt icon is selected from the Properties toolbar. This shows the events (and not the properties). You can double-click an event in this list to generate a method stub for the given event. You can also choose a method from your code and explicitly bind that to an event.

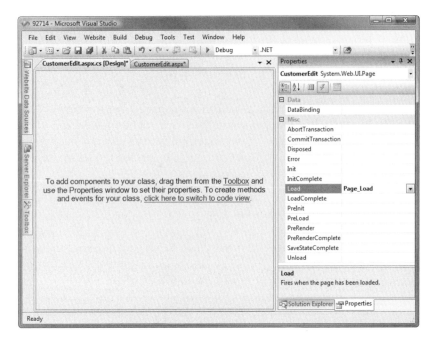

FIGURE 14.25    Using the Component Designer to add events to a page.

**Adding Control Event Handlers**    You add events to controls in a similar manner. There is no component designer (thankfully) for a control. You simply select the control on a given page and view its properties in the Properties window. From the Properties window, you can select the lightning bolt icon to show all the events for the given control. You then double-click an event to add it to your code-behind.

Most events you add to a control will be Action events. These are events that are based on user actions (such as button click). There are, however, other events. These events are typically used for special purposes and control developers only. Figure 14.26 shows adding an event to the Click action of the Save button.

# Designing Your User Interface

There is a lot that goes into building a good web user interface. So much so that some solid planning is typically in order before you start dragging controls onto forms. Your first step should be to consider your options, the needs of the users, and your maintenance requirements. You then put this information into some sort of design plan. Your design plan should include the following:

▶ Determine the type of information and user activity your site needs to support. You might make a list of the screen types in your system. For example, you might have pages that display report data, others that allow users to do data entry, still others that do searches, and so on. This will help you when deciding on the style elements required of your site.

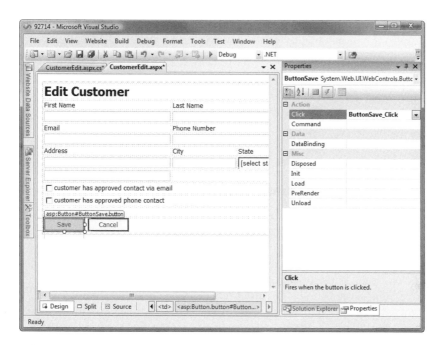

FIGURE 14.26   Adding an event to a control.

▶ Decide whether you need to plan for multiple-language and culture information. This can have a big impact on how you build out the content items (such as labels, menu text, and the like) of your pages.

▶ Define the key areas of your site and how users will navigate among them. This is often referred to as your site's taxonomy or sitemap.

▶ Determine what items will go on all pages. This might include navigation, logos, design elements, footer information, and more. For example, you might make the key areas of your site into top-level menu items that go on all pages.

▶ Determine the style elements for your site. Or at least define the items that need to be stylized. As an example, you may determine that you need a consistent way to show page titles, navigation items, buttons, column headers, table data, and so on. Getting these items documented allows you to plan for these upfront. You may also pass the list on to a designer and have the designer build out the styles for the application.

▶ Decide whether you will support multiple themes or user-configurable options. You might, for example, need to rebrand your site depending on the user accessing it. In this case, you need to think about themes. You might also need to allow user customization of layout and content. In this case, you should consider using some of the portal controls.

These and many more decisions go into the planning of a good, web-based UI. Thinking through the items upfront will pay big dividends down the road by saving you a lot of frustrating rework.

When you have your plan, Visual Studio 2008 is there to help. It allows you to create master pages for determining a common look and feel. There are controls for managing links and menus. You can support themes through skin files and style sheets. You can even allow users to participate in the customization of their layout using Web Parts. The following sections demonstrate the many features of ASP.NET that go into creating web UIs.

## Determining Page Layout and Control Positioning

An important consideration when building your web pages is deciding how controls are placed on a page. This is a big topic that continues to evolve. Many websites rely on tables of information for their layout. Each item on the page is in a table of columns and rows. Other sites place items on a page such that they do not move. If items overlap (such as when font sizes are increased), they show as overlap. There are others that build a page with no real layout at all at design time. They then rely on style sheets to apply a layout of the controls at runtime. And, of course, there are pages and sites that mix these options depending on the situation. The following list is meant to describe your options in more detail:

▶ **Flow Layout**—If you are comfortable with the dynamic nature of a web page in a browser, you may prefer to control your positioning through flow layout. This refers to your controls moving with the flow of the page. This capability is great if you intend to lay out your page with tables and place your controls within table cells. Things are lined up with respect to how their neighbors are lined up. If an item moves down, for example, anything below that item also moves down in a relative fashion. This is the default setting in Visual Studio 2008.

▶ **Absolute Positioning**—If you are used to building Windows forms, you may be more comfortable controlling the positioning of each individual item. In this case, you drag an item onto the form and move it around relative to other items. Where you drop it is where it gets positioned (and where it stays). In addition, with absolute positioning, items get positioned based on their parent container. For example, if you put a button inside a div tag and set the position of the button to 5 pixels from the top and 5 pixels from the left, the 5 pixels in each case are counted from the bounds of the div tag (and not the page).

▶ **Relative Positioning**—This combines a flow layout with absolute positioning. With relative positioning, items are placed within the flow of a page. However, if you set an item's top and left properties, the distance defined by these properties gets calculated based on the item's relative position on the page.

▶ **CSS Positioning**—This is a more advanced positioning option. Items are typically laid out on a page using flow layout. However, each item has a specific style defined either on the page or in a style sheet (preferred). The style has positioning information defined, including margins, heights, widths, and the like. This can be more complicated to set up. However, you then can easily change the layout of a page by changing the style sheet (and not the page itself).

You may have situations in which you need to mix both flow and absolute layouts in a single page. For example, you could define a page that flows based on tables. Inside a given cell, you might set a panel control. This panel control might be set to allow only absolute positioning for items within the panel. Alternatively, you might add an image to a page that uses flow layout or CSS positioning. You might indicate that the image should be positioned as absolute or relative similar to how you would embed an image in a Word document.

Whichever path you choose, you will want to be consistent. You should define your layout strategy as part of your design plan. All the pages in the site should behave in a similar manner to make your maintenance easier. In addition, most pages are dependent on other pagelike items (such as master pages and user controls). For this reason, you might want all of these items to be laid out on a page in the same way.

**Setting How Controls Are Positioned**

By default, Visual Studio is set to lay out items on your page using flow layout. That is, as you drag items from the Toolbox to the designer, the items will be placed relative to one another. If you are using tables to lay out your page or CSS positioning, this should be fine for your needs. Figure 14.26, presented earlier, shows a page in flow layout using a table.

You may run into a situation in which you need to absolute-position an item on a page that uses flow layout. For example, suppose in Figure 14.26 that we wanted to embed our company logo on the right side of the page. We could try to fit it in the table but would most likely be frustrated doing so because things can get out of line quickly. Instead, we can select the image and from the Format menu choose the Position option. This brings up the Position dialog, shown in Figure 14.27.

The Position dialog allows you to indicate how a given, selected item should be positioned on the page. You can see that this is similar to positioning a graphic in a Word document. You choose the wrapping style and the positioning style—in our case, Absolute positioning. Do not worry too much about the location information. You can change this just by dragging the item around.

Figure 14.28 shows the same image being dragged around the page. Notice that the IDE shows you the vertical and horizontal centers as lines up and down the designer. This helps you line up an item. If we were lining up a button or text box, the IDE would also show margin and space indicators to assist you.

If you intend to use absolute positioning for your entire page, you do not want to have to manually select each item and choose Position from the Format menu. This would be tedious indeed. Instead, you can set an option that tells Visual Studio how to add controls to a page by default. You set this choice within the Options dialog box (Tools, Options). Here you navigate to the HTML Designer/CSS Styling node. Figure 14.29 shows an example. There is a check box highlighted. Selecting this check box indicates that from this point forward all controls should be added to a page using absolute positioning.

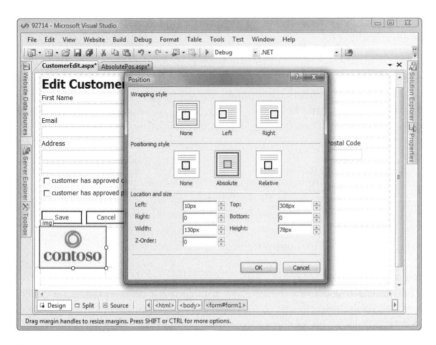

FIGURE 14.27   Setting a single element to absolute positioning on a page that uses flow layout.

FIGURE 14.28   Positioning an item absolutely.

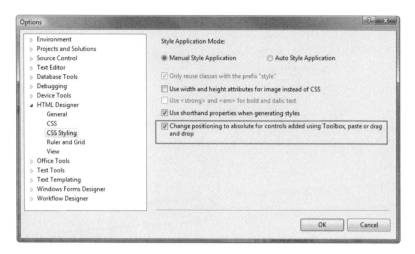

FIGURE 14.29    Selecting absolute positioning for all controls added to a site.

When you lay out a page using absolute positioning, all items must be put in their exact spot. For this reason, you must worry about margins and spacing issues. For example, Figure 14.30 shows the start of a page being built with absolute positioning. Here the Cancel button is being positioned to the right of Save and under the First Name TextBox. You can see the margin indicators. However, if additional items need to be added between the TextBox and the buttons, each button will have to be moved and repositioned. With flow layout, the items would just move or you would insert a row in the table.

When an item is absolute-positioned on a page, the designer is simply changing the item's style behind the scenes. That is, it is setting the positioning details for each item using the style tag. For example, the following code shows the markup for one of the TextBox items in Figure 14.30:

```
<asp:TextBox ID="TextBox1" runat="server" CssClass="inputBox"
  style="z-index: 1; left: 275px; top: 91px; position: absolute">
</asp:TextBox>
```

You can see here that all that is happening is that the position attribute is set to absolute and the left and top positions are set. For this reason, items in the markup for absolute positioned pages do not typically follow in the order in which they exist on the screen. Rather, they are put into the markup in the order in which they are added to the page.

Also, notice that the code indicated something called z-index. This allows you to do layering in your output. Each item is on a layer (in this case, layer 1). Layers may overlap one another.

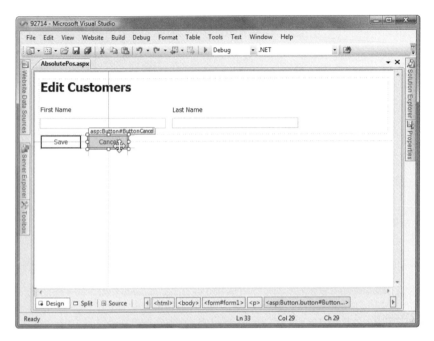

FIGURE 14.30    Building an entire page using absolute positioning.

---

**NOTE**

Visual Studio 2008 does not provide the same feature set for absolute positioning as was found in 2005. Specifically, in 2008 you can no longer select multiple items on the web form designer and work with them as a group. In addition, gone are the options on the Format menu for making two or more items the same size or aligning them to one another. In addition, not all items when dragged from the Toolbox automatically implement absolute positioning. Whereas such things as TextBox and Button do, Label and CheckBox do not. Instead, for these items you must manually set the absolute positioning style and then you can work with them in the designer.

We suspect that this reduced support for absolute positioning may be for a couple of reasons. The first reason is that Microsoft rewrote a lot of the layout engine to be more compliant with CSS. The second is that absolute positioning has fallen somewhat out of favor. Most new sites are being built using flow layout (with tables) or with CSS positioning.

---

## Creating a Common Look and Feel

When you create a website, you want the pages to look as if they all belong to one application. The navigation should be standard, the colors and fonts should match for like items, and sizing should be consistent. Users should not feel as though they are jumping sites simply by navigating from one page to the next. In addition, you don't want to have to manage this consistency across every single page in the site. This would be extremely tedious when you need to make a change to, for example, how all buttons in your site look.

Thankfully, you have the tools to support a consistent look across pages and make the management of it all much easier. Visual Studio 2008 provides increased support for building styles, managing them, and applying them to your pages. In addition, you can leverage style sheets at the site level, master pages, and themes. Let's take a look at all of these.

### Styles and Style Sheets Basics

Styles and style sheets allow you to define a common look and behavior. You can then apply that common look to multiple items within your page and application. In this way, if you decide to change something, you can change it in one place and all the places that use the style will be updated.

**Inline Styles**    A style simply defines the look of a given item. You can create inline styles that use the style attribute on a given form element to indicate how that element looks. In the following code, there is an inline style that sets the font, font size, and color for a label control:

```
<asp:Label ID="Label1" runat="server" Text="Edit Customer"
  style="font-family: Arial; font-size: large; color: Blue">
</asp:Label>
```

Inline styles do not offer much in the way of reuse. Instead, you have to define the style for every item on every page. This is okay for the occasional, unique circumstance. However, it quickly becomes unmanageable if you are trying to keep like items on like pages looking alike. In these cases, it's best to abstract the style definition from the item. You can do so by putting the style definition in a style class.

**Page-Level Styles**    A style class can be defined in one of two places: in the page itself or in a style sheet linked to the page. If you define a style class in the page itself, it is applicable to only that page (and not the rest of the pages in the site). Styles defined at the page level are embedded in the <head> section of the XHTML. For example, the following markup abstracts the same style discussed previously into a page-level style:

```
<head runat="server">
    <title>Edit Customer</title>
    <style type="text/css">
        .titleText
        {
            font-family: Arial;
            font-size: large;
            color: Blue;
        }
    </style>
</head>
```

14

To apply this style to the form element, you set its `Class` (for HTML controls) or `CssClass` (for ASP.NET controls) property as shown here:

```
<asp:Label ID="Label1" runat="server" Text="Edit Customer"
  CssClass="titleText"></asp:Label>
```

**Element Styles (Style Rules)**   You can create a style rule for an HTML element. This style rule will then apply for all HTML elements (and their related ASP.NET counterpart) of the given type automatically. That is, you do not have to assign the style to the element; it will simply pick up the style.

As an example, suppose you want to manage how hyperlinks on your site look when a user hovers the mouse pointer over them. To do so, you can define a style inside a style sheet for the anchor tag's hover (`A:hover`) behavior. Inside the style, you might set the color, name, and size of the font. You might also turn off underlining when a user hovers over the link. After you've defined this style, you apply it to the page. All anchor tags on the page will then use the given style definition. The following code shows an example:

```
a:hover
{
    font-family: Tahoma;
    font-size: 10pt;
    color: #0099FF;
    text-decoration: none;
}
```

**Style Sheets**   A style sheet represents a file that houses a set of styles to be applied to a page. In this way, you can abstract all your styles away from a page, centralize them, and manage them as a group. A style sheet file has the `.css` extension. Inside the file you can add element styles and your own style classes. The code for these styles looks just like the code we've shown thus far.

Once the style sheet is defined, you link a page to a style sheet. You can do so by dragging the style sheet to the form designer or by adding the following code to the <head> section of the page:

```
<head runat="server">
  <link href="StyleSheetMaster.css" rel="stylesheet" type="text/css" />
  <title>Edit Customer</title>
</head>
```

The Visual Studio designer will show applicable styles during design. This way, you can see how your application will look as you build it.

## The Style Toolset

Thus far, we've looked at the basics of styles and style sheets. Of course, there is a lot more to creating styles, managing them, and applying them to your site. Thankfully, Visual Studio has a number of tools built-in to help us work with styles. Let's examine these tools.

**Creating a Style Sheet**   You can add one or more style sheets to an application through the Add New Item dialog box (refer to Figure 14.19). You can open a style sheet in the Visual Studio code editor. When you do, Visual Studio presents a Style Sheet toolbar, the Styles menu, and the actual contents of the style sheet. Figure 14.31 shows these items.

The middle pane of Figure 14.31 shows the contents of the style sheet. You can manually edit the style sheet from here. Of course, being able to edit it requires you to have a decent working understanding of CSS. Of course, there is also IntelliSense to help guide you. As with anything, the more you work with it, the more familiar you will become. You can also right-click inside a style here to gain access to building the style using the Modify Style dialog (more on this topic in a moment).

The Style Sheet toolbar has just a few options. The first one on the left launches the Add Style Rule dialog box. The second option opens the Modify Style dialog. The next button allows you to view the results in a browser window. Finally, the drop-down allows you to set a CSS standard that you want to target.

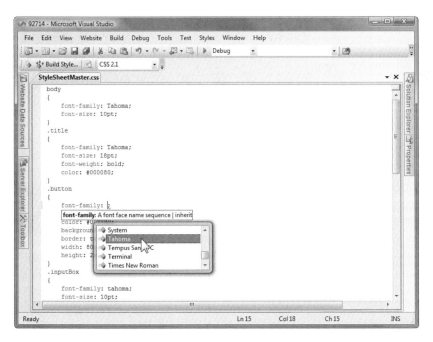

FIGURE 14.31   Working with a style sheet in the IDE.

**Building a Style**   You can code a style directly using the editor or you can use the Modify Style dialog to do so. Visual Studio 2008 has enhanced the Modify Style dialog to provide better access to key style attributes. This tool generates the correct markup for your style.

You can access the Modify Style dialog box by right-clicking inside an existing style, by selecting the Build Style option from the Style menu, or by clicking on the Build Style option on the Style toolbar. Figure 14.32 shows an example. This figure represents the many options for controlling the font on a style. The Modify Style dialog box has many more options, such as backgrounds, tables, and borders. In addition, the Layout and Position items allow you to control how CSS positioning works.

Clicking the OK button on the Modify Style dialog saves your changes back to the style sheet. Changes are saved as they appear at the bottom of the dialog in the Description box.

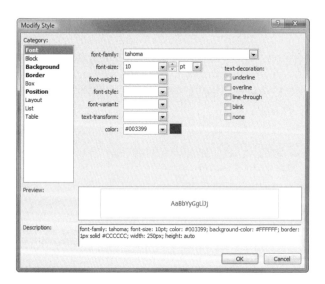

FIGURE 14.32   Building your style markup.

**Creating a Style Rule**   A style rule defines a style for an element or a class. You can create a new style rule by typing it directly into the editor (using the correct syntax, of course). You can also define a style rule by using the Add Style Rule dialog box. You access this dialog box by right-clicking in the style sheet editor pane, by clicking the leftmost button on the Style Sheet toolbar, or by selecting the Add Style Rule option on the Style menu. This dialog box is useful in that it lists the many HTML elements for which you can define styles. It also allows you to define a style hierarchy. Figure 14.33 shows an example.

After you click OK, the style is saved back to the style sheet. You can then edit the style's contents as you would build any other style (see the previous section, "Building a Style").

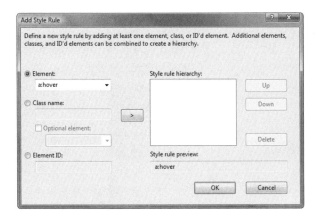

FIGURE 14.33    Adding a style rule.

**Managing Styles**    Visual Studio 2008 has a new Manage Styles pane. This pane allows you to see the styles for a given page, create a new style, attach a new style sheet, apply a style, and more. This makes applying styles to your page a fluid and fast process.

You can access the Manage Styles pane from the View menu (View, Manage Styles). By default, the pane loads to the right side of the IDE. Figure 14.34 shows the Manage Styles pane loaded for the `EditCustomer.aspx` page.

There are a number of items to note here. The first is that the pane shows all styles for the page. This includes those defined on the page and those linked to the page through a style sheet. In fact, you can drag items that are defined on the current page into the style sheet (and vice versa). Visual Studio will move the code for you. Notice too that you can see a preview for the style selected. You also get the style's definition by hovering over it.

The Attach Style Sheet button lets you select an existing style sheet and attach (link) it to the page. Clicking the New Style button launches the New Style dialog. This is a version of the Modify Style dialog discussed previously. Notice that the top of the dialog is different. Here you can indicate the location of where you intend to define your new style (Current Page, New Style Sheet, or Existing Style Sheet). Figure 14.35 shows an example.

The Options button (top-right corner of the Manage Styles pane) allows you to filter how the styles are shown in the list. Options include categorize styles by element, type, or order. You can also indicate that you want to see all styles, only those used on the current page, or only those used inside the items currently selected on the page.

Finally, you can right-click a style in the menu and execute one of many options. These include applying the style to the selected item in the designer and navigating to the code behind the style. You can also modify the style, delete it, or make a new style by copying the selected style. Figure 14.36 shows the right-click menu options for a given style.

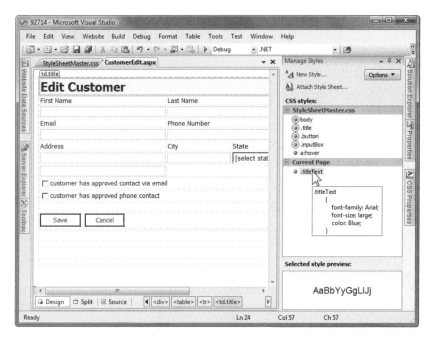

FIGURE 14.34    Managing styles in your site.

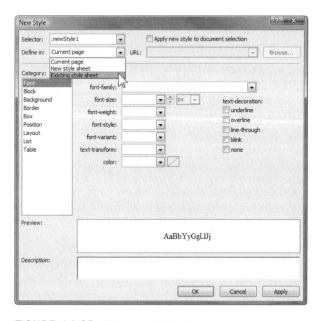

FIGURE 14.35    The New Style dialog.

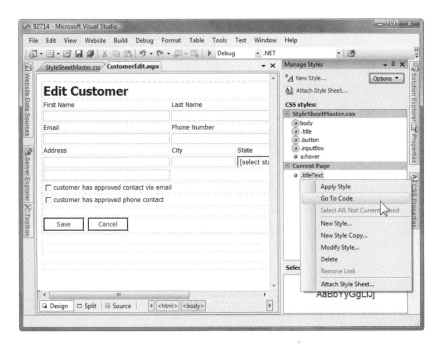

FIGURE 14.36   The right-click menu for a style.

**Applying a Style**   There are many ways in which you can apply a style to a given element on a page. We've seen a couple already. In the previous section, you saw that you could select a style in the Style Manager pane and choose the Apply Style option from the context menu (refer to Figure 14.36). There is also a pane similar to Style Manager called Apply Styles (View, Apply Styles).

The Apply Styles pane behaves similarly to the Style Manager. One difference is that you can see a visual representation of the style on the style name. Figure 14.37 demonstrates this. You simply click on the style name to apply it to your selection.

Another way to apply styles to your elements is in the markup itself. The good news is that both styles defined on the page and those linked as a style sheet are available inside IntelliSense. Figure 14.38 shows this.

Lastly, you can also set an item's style inside the Property window. Simply select an item and view its properties. The property CssClass will provide you a drop-down of all styles available for the given element.

**Editing Styles**   There are various ways in which you can edit styles. You can simply right-click the code and choose Build Style to open the Modify Style dialog. In addition, Visual Studio 2008 has the new CSS Properties pane (View, CSS Properties) for editing styles.

The CSS Properties pane allows you to see all the properties of a given style in a property editor form. Figure 14.39 illustrates this.

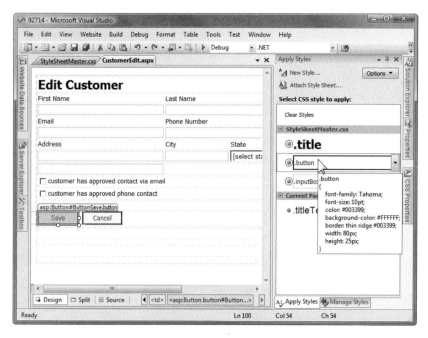

FIGURE 14.37    Applying styles using the Apply Styles pane.

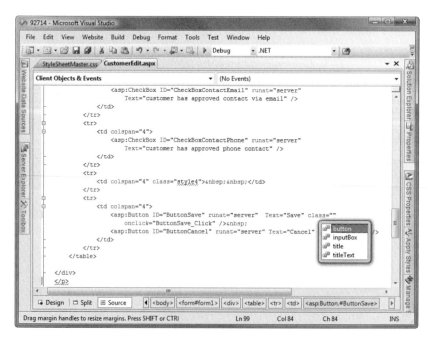

FIGURE 14.38    Using IntelliSense to select your style.

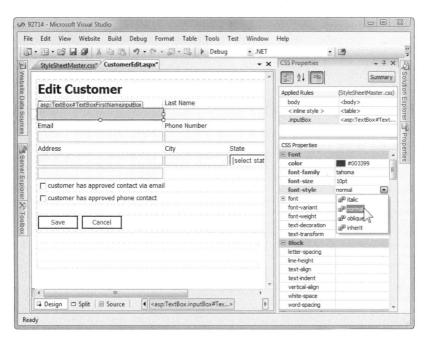

FIGURE 14.39   Editing a style using the CSS Properties pane.

Notice that a TextBox is selected. The CSS Properties pane then shows the rules and their style information for the selected item. You can then edit the properties of the given style from this pane. An edit to a style here applies to wherever the style is defined. In this example, the edit is to the .inputBox style defined on the StyleSheetMaster.css file. The edit will show up immediately in the design window. It will also be stored back in the .css file.

### Master Pages

Master pages were first introduced in Visual Studio 2005. They allow you to visually design a common look for your application in one file and then use that look across other files. This way you can centralize such things as navigation, headers, and footers. In addition, when you derive a page from a master file, Visual Studio displays the contents of both pages at once inside the designer. This helps developers see how their page looks in the context of the overall site as they build it.

**Creating a Master Page**   You add a master page to your project through the Add New Item dialog box. You can have multiple master pages in your application. This capability can be especially useful if your application has more than one default layout (or look) for certain areas of the site. It is most common to have a master page that includes common navigation, common graphics, and a common footer. You can also nest master pages within one another (more on this to follow).

A master page defines the main HTML for the page. This includes the opening and closing HTML tags, head, body, and form. Inside the master page are one or more `ContentPlaceHolder` controls. These controls indicate areas on the page where content pages (pages that derive from the master) may place their content.

Master pages also have their own code-behind file. This file should contain all code that relates to the workings of the master page itself. If there are working controls on the page, a menu for example, their code would go inside this code-behind file. In addition, the master page has its own set of page events (just like a standard `.aspx` page).

Figure 14.40 shows an example of a master page. Notice that this master page is laid out as a table using flow layout. The cell in the center row contains a `ContentPlaceHolder` control. This is the only place where content pages that use the master page can add their content.

**Creating a Content Page**   Users do not access master pages directly. Instead, they call the content pages that derive from the master. When they do, .NET combines the contents of both pages and returns a single response as if there were only one page.

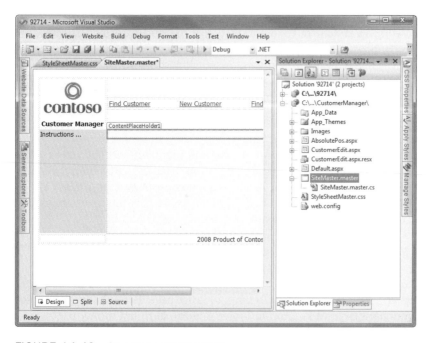

FIGURE 14.40   Creating a master page.

You create a content page by selecting a master when adding a web page to your site. When you do, there is an option titled Select Master Page at the bottom of the dialog box (recall Figure 14.19). Selecting this option will present you with available master pages in your application.

When your content page opens, you will see the content of the master page in the background. In the foreground will be the `ContentPlaceHolder` controls. This is where you will add controls specific to your page. This provides a separation of functionality between what belongs to your page and what belongs to the master. You work with the page as you would any other ASP.NET web page. You add controls to the form and write event code in the code-behind file.

> **NOTE**
>
> Control layout and positioning can be important when you work with content areas. If, for example, you have turned on absolute positioning, the content placeholder acts more as a guide. Due to the nature of this layout option, the content placeholder cannot restrict you from placing your controls anywhere on the page. The flow layout option, however, has the opposite effect. Controls will be allowed only inside the content areas unless otherwise marked as absolute positioned.

Figure 14.41 shows an example. This web page was created to edit a customer's profile; it is based on the application's master page. Notice that the content page has the same extension as any web form (`.aspx`).

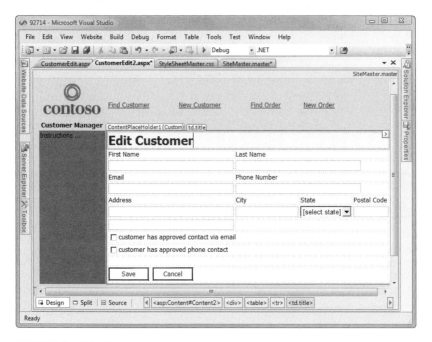

FIGURE 14.41   Creating a content page.

**TIP**

You can use the `Master` object to reference the master page from the code within your content page's code-behind file. For example, suppose you want to set the instruction text on the master page from within each content page. You would need to find the control used by the master page for the instruction text. You could then set the appropriate property on this control. The code to find the control on a master page would look like the following:

```
Label lb = (Label)this.Master.FindControl("LabelInstructions");
```

**Nesting Master Pages**   Prior to 2008, you could have only one level of master page. You could not nest one inside the other and view the results in the designer. Visual Studio 2008 supports this scenario. With it, you can create a master page. You can then create another master page and select a master page from which it derives. In this way, you build up a master page hierarchy. See Chapter 1, "A Quick Tour of Visual Studio 2008," for a basic example of a nested master page.

### Themes and Skins

Visual Studio 2005 introduced the concept of themes for web pages and an entire website. This feature allows you to define one or more specific looks for the controls that make up your application. After you do, you can then switch between them based on user preference, company affiliation, or similar factors.

At first glance, it seems that themes provide nearly the same experience as style sheets. However, themes go a few steps further. First, they leverage style sheets. Each theme can have an associated style sheet. Themes can also be applied in such a way as to work with an existing style sheet or to override it (see "Applying a Theme to a Site or Page," later in this chapter). The next difference is that themes allow you to embed graphic files as part of the themes. In this way, you can switch from one set of graphics to another based on a theme's name. Style sheets cannot do this. Themes also allow you to define skin files for your ASP.NET controls. These skin files enable you to set property values of a control that fall outside mere styles (these property values must be nonbehavioral, however). Lastly, a theme for a page can be set (and changed) at runtime. You can modify a property of the `Page` object to do so. This allows for fast switching of your site's look.

**NOTE**

Only one theme can apply to a site at any given time (unlike style sheets).

**Creating a Theme**   Themes are created inside the `App_Themes` folder. Each theme gets its own theme folder. The name of the theme is the name of the folder (which must be unique). This ensures that there is no confusion when applying a theme. You apply it based on the folder's name.

As an example, suppose you are building an application to manage customer details and orders. Assume that this application is accessed from multiple company sites. Therefore, company A would manage its customers, and company B would manage its customers. In this scenario, the site owner might define a different theme for each company. Perhaps the theme is based on each company's colors, fonts, and graphics.

To create a theme, you typically follow a standard set of steps:

1. You must first create the App_Theme directory. You can do so through the context menu. You choose Add ASP.NET Folder and then Theme. Alternatively, you might add a skin file to your application through the Add New Item dialog and then Visual Studio will create the App_Theme directory automatically for you to house the .skin file.

2. When you have the App_Theme directory, you can right-click on it to add a new theme folder. This can again be found under the Add ASP.NET Folder menu. You will want to name this folder with the name of your theme.

3. Next, you add the files that make up your theme. These files typically include a style sheet, any images or resources, and a skin file.

Figure 14.42 shows the folder and file structure based on the example we discussed here. There are three themes: one for company A, one for company B, and a noncompany theme (ThemeMain).

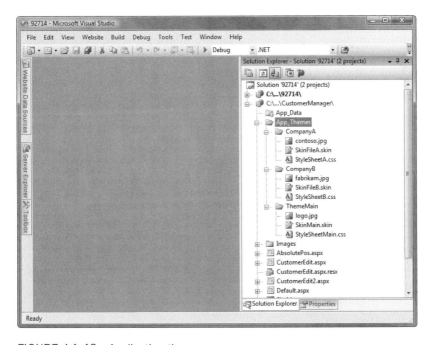

FIGURE 14.42   Application themes.

**Creating a Skin File**    We have already discussed style sheets. What we need to look at now is defining a skin file. You can have one or more skin files in your theme. You might want to create a new skin file for each control you intend to skin. Alternatively, you may want to define a single skin file for your entire theme. The choice is yours.

Inside the skin file are control skin definitions called *skins*. You declare each skin just as you would write the markup for a given control on a web page. The syntax is similar. However, you omit the property assignments for the control that do not pertain to the skin.

There are two types of skin definitions: named skins and unnamed skins. A named skin is created by using the attribute SkinId. This allows you to define a unique name for the skin declaration. In this case, only controls in your site with this same SkinId will be affected by the skin declaration. On the other hand, unnamed skins apply to all controls of a similar type. For example, if you want all your button controls to look a similar way, you create an unnamed skin for the button control. When you apply the skin to a page, all buttons will pick up this look. Let's look at an example.

For this example, say you want to define a few skins to define your theme. You will define named skins for the customer logo on the master page and the title labels on each screen. You will then create unnamed skins for label, text box, button, and grid view controls.

Listing 14.1 shows the sample skin file. At the top are the named skins. Notice the use of the SkinId attribute. Again, this attribute will be used when this skin is applied to specific instances of these types of controls (image and label in this case). Below this are the skins that apply to standard controls. There is one for all buttons, labels, text boxes, and grid views. Notice that the GridView definition includes definitions for the many parts of the control. You nest these definitions within the GridView definition as you would on any ASP.NET page.

You also need a similar file for company B. To create it, you copy and paste this file to that company's directory. You then make minor edits to the image skin and the fonts and colors of the other skin definitions. We will next look at applying these skins to the pages in the site.

LISTING 14.1    The Company A Skin File

```
<%— named skins —%>
<asp:Image runat="server" SkinID="CustomerLogo"
 ImageUrl="~/App_Themes/CompanyA/contoso.jpg"/>

<asp:Label runat="server" SkinID="TitleLabel"
 Font-Names="Arial Black"
 Font-Size="X-Large" />

<%— default, control skins —%>
<asp:Button runat="server" Width="80px" Height="24px"
 BackColor="#FFFFFF" ForeColor="MidnightBlue"
```

```
 Font-Name="Tahoma" Font-Size="10pt"
 BorderColor="#003399" BorderStyle="Solid" />

<asp:Label runat="server" ForeColor="MidnightBlue"
 Font-Names="Arial" Font-Size="Small" />

<asp:TextBox runat="server" Width="265px" BackColor="White"
 BorderColor="MidnightBlue" BorderStyle="Solid" BorderWidth="1px"
 Font-Names="Arial" Font-Size="Small" />

<asp:GridView runat="server" CellPadding="4" ForeColor="#333333" GridLines="None">
 <FooterStyle BackColor="#5D7B9D" Font-Bold="True" ForeColor="White" />
 <RowStyle BackColor="#F7F6F3" ForeColor="#333333" />
 <EditRowStyle BackColor="#999999" />
 <SelectedRowStyle BackColor="#E2DED6" Font-Bold="True" ForeColor="#333333" />
 <PagerStyle BackColor="#284775" ForeColor="White" HorizontalAlign="Center" />
 <HeaderStyle BackColor="#5D7B9D" Font-Bold="True" ForeColor="White" />
 <AlternatingRowStyle BackColor="White" ForeColor="#284775" />
</asp:GridView>
```

**TIP**

There is not much tool support for defining skin declarations. You are forced to manually enter this markup. However, a common shortcut can be to create a page that includes each control in the theme. You then use the designer to edit the controls on the page. Finally, you copy this markup from the page to the skin declaration and then delete any unwanted declaration code (including the ID tag).

**Applying a Theme to a Site or Page**  There are a few ways in which you can apply a theme. Each is meant to provide a different level of control. For example, you can set a global theme for an entire server. You can configure a theme for just one website. You can also choose to configure a theme at the individual page level. Finally, you can apply a single skin to a single control. You can see that these levels go from the very macro (server) to the granular (control). Most websites will fall somewhere in the middle, like applying a theme at the page or site level.

You apply a theme at the page level by using the @ Page directive inside the page's markup. You have a couple of options here. You can decide that your theme should always trump all control settings. That is, if a developer explicitly sets a control value and that value is overridden by the theme, then the theme takes precedence. This type of declaration would look like the following:

```
<%@ Page Theme="MyPageTheme" %>
```

Alternatively, you can set what is called a `StyleSheetTheme` at the page level. This indicates that the theme applies only where controls do not have explicit overriding values. In the previous declaration, the theme would override local control settings. Using the `StyleSheetTheme`, you can set the theme to apply only to control settings that are not explicitly set. That is, if the control has a value for a given attribute, that value is used. If it does not, the theme's value is used. You set this type of theme for the page as shown here:

```
<%@ Page StylesheetTheme="MyPageTheme" %>
```

You can define the theme for an entire website through the configuration file. This allows you to set a theme and then change it without recompiling your code. To do so, you add the `Theme` or `StylesheetTheme` (see the preceding example) attributes to the `pages` element inside the `system.web` node. The following is an example:

```
<system.web>
  <pages theme="MySiteTheme" />
</system.web>
```

To define just the style sheet theme, you would use the following:

```
<system.web>
  <pages stylesheetTheme=" MySiteTheme" />
</system.web>
```

You can also set a theme inside your code. This capability can be useful if you are allowing users to choose their theme or you are dynamically setting a theme based on some user information. Recall the example with two companies: company A and company B. Remember, a theme file was defined for each. If you determine within your code that a member of company A, for example, has logged in, then you would set the theme this way:

```
Page.Theme = "CompanyA"
```

Figure 14.43 shows an example of the theme defined in Listing 14.1.

Figure 14.44 shows the theme switched to that of company B.

---

**TIP**

You can make changes to a theme file or skin without recompiling your site. These changes will simply be applied on the next browser refresh.

---

To set a theme for a single control, you use the `SkinID` attribute of the control. This ID can be set to reference a particular skin inside a skin file. The skin definition would have the same skin ID as the one used inside the markup. The markup for this looks like this:

```
<asp:SomeControl runat="server" ID="ControlID" SkinID="MySkinId" />
```

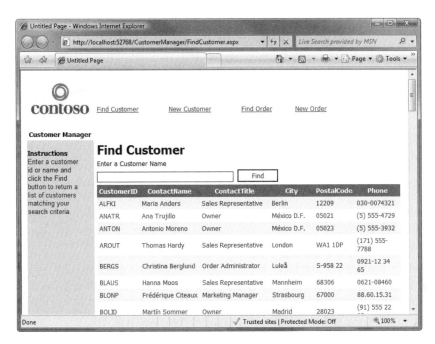

FIGURE 14.43    Company A's theme applied.

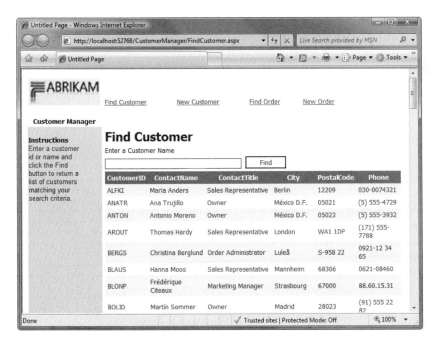

FIGURE 14.44    Company B's theme applied.

## 14

You can set the skin ID from the markup or by using the Properties window for a given control open in the designer. This window will provide a drop-down list of skins that are available for the given control type. You can also set the skin ID programmatically. The following is an example:

```
SomeControl.SkinId = "MySkinId"
```

## Creating a User-Configurable UI

ASP.NET provides support for creating a user interface that can be configured and personalized by each individual user of a site. As an example, if you have ever worked with Microsoft Office SharePoint Server (MOSS) or visited MSN.com, you will notice that blocks of functionality define a given page. These blocks can be removed, added, moved around, and configured by users. To enable this functionality, the blocks all must work together as part of a portal framework. .NET has just such a framework built into the product.

The following sections provide an overview of creating a configurable user interface using the Web Part controls. We will walk through the basics of building a Web Part page that allows users to monitor customers in a customer management application. In doing so, we will cover the many basics of Web Parts. We will not, however, be able to cover everything. Web Parts is a big topic. This section should get you started in the right direction.

> **NOTE**
>
> The Web Part controls built into Visual Studio also rely on the personalization features of ASP.NET. For this reason, they require you to run a version of the ASPNETDB database. This will be installed for you when you run your first Web Part page. The database, by default, is a SQL Express database and requires SQL Express on your machine.

### Working with the Web Part Controls

ASP.NET includes many Web Part controls and classes; the Visual Studio Toolbox alone defines 14 Web Part controls (see Figure 14.45). In addition, the `System.Web.UI.WebControls.WebParts` namespace contains nearly 100 classes. These controls and classes work together to manage the structure of a Web Part page, its personalization and configuration, and the presentation itself.

When you create a basic Web Part page, you typically work with three types of controls: the `WebPartManager`, `WebPartZone`, and presentation controls themselves. The first control, `WebPartManager`, is actually required of all Web Part pages. It is the control responsible for managing the Web Parts on the page. You must define this control on each Web Part page and can define only one per page. The `WebPartManager` is responsible for tracking the controls and their zones throughout the page. It also manages the state that a page might be in, such as view or edit mode.

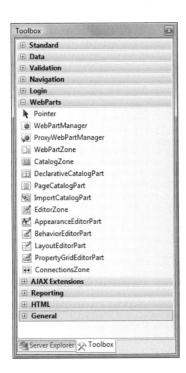

FIGURE 14.45    The Web Part controls.

The second control, WebPartZone, enables you to manage the layout or "zones" of your page. A zone represents an area of the page where controls or features can be placed. To understand zones, you can think of your page in terms of horizontal and vertical content zones. For example, you may have a zone at the top of your page that presents the header for the application. Beneath this, you may have two vertical zones. The leftmost zone may be used for links and navigational controls. The middle zone may contain content Web Parts. Finally, you may have another zone at the bottom of the page to manage footer-type content.

Figure 14.46 shows an example of a Web Part page broken into zones. Of course, you can define any number of zones and lay them out as you like. This is simply one example.

> **NOTE**
>
> Zones also have associated styles. Each zone provides a common UI for controls within the zone. That is, they define a header, title, border, button style, and so on. This is known as the "chrome" for the controls in a given zone.

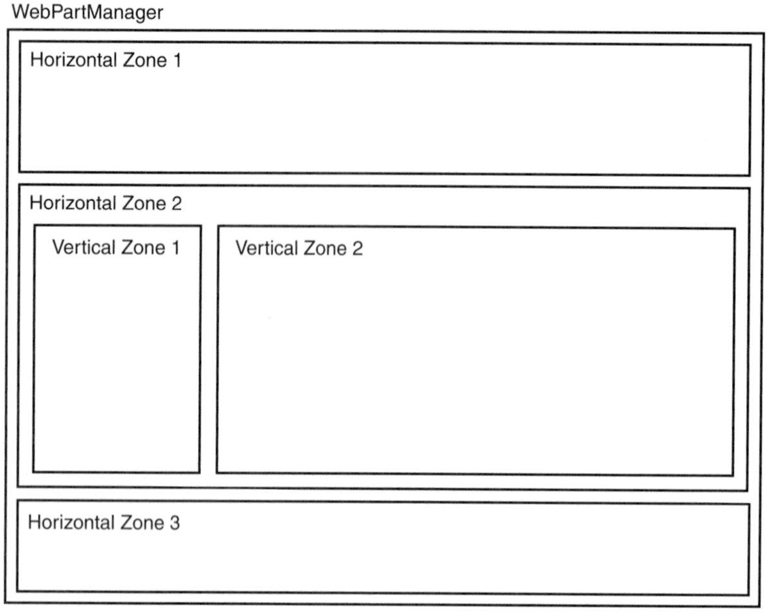

WebPartManager

FIGURE 14.46   An example of Web Part zones for a page.

Last, you put controls into each zone of the Web Part page. These controls can be any .NET control that you want to be managed by the zone. You can also create your own user controls and Web Parts that can be placed in these zones. The advantage of the latter is that you can provide configuration capabilities for Web Parts. This allows users to edit a given Web Part's properties from within the web browser (similar to how Microsoft's SharePoint product works).

Table 14.3 provides a brief reference to the primary controls that are used to manage a Web Part page. Each of these controls can be found on the Visual Studio Toolbox (see Figure 14.45). These controls are all zone controls (except the manager control). As such, they constrain what type of control should be added to the given zone.

### Creating a Web Part Page

You create a Web Part page using any standard web form (.aspx). For the following example, create a form titled MonitorCustomer.aspx. The next step is to drag a WebPartManager control onto this form. This control has no visual appearance on the form. Instead, it is simply necessary to create a Web Part page.

**TIP**

Inside the form designer, you can decide to show or hide controls that have no visual appearance. To do so, you use the View menu, Visual Aids submenu and check or uncheck the option ASP.NET Non-Visual Controls. Nonvisual controls show up as gray boxes inside the designer. The box typically contains a control's name and ID.

TABLE 14.3    The Web Part Zone Controls

| Control | Description |
| --- | --- |
| WebPartManager | This control tracks the zones on the page and the Web Part controls that are in those zones. Each Web Part page requires one (and only one) instance of this control. |
| CatalogZone | This control defines a zone that contains one or more CatalogPart controls. The CatalogPart control provides a list of Web Parts that are available for the page. When a user is editing the page, this zone is enabled. Users then use the CatalogPart control to select one or more Web Part objects and drag them into WebPartZones. |
| WebPartZone | You use this control for defining the primary zones of your user interface. You can add ASP.NET controls and Web Part controls into these zones. Most Web Part pages define two or more WebPartZones. |
| EditorZone | You use this zone for providing an area for users to edit and configure a given Web Part. The editor for a Web Part is defined as an EditorPart control. This zone contains these types of controls. |

**Defining Zones**    Next, you add the zones to the page. Recall that the zones define where your Web Parts can exist and how they look and are sized. You can lay out your zones inside a table, use absolute positioning to place zones in specific areas, or use relative positioning. If you allow users to hide or close the controls in a zone, you might consider a table or relative positioning. If, on the other hand, your zones are static, you would use absolute positioning.

Before adding the Web Parts, you will want to add an HTML table to the page and create three rows: the top for the page title, the middle to house your Web Parts, and the bottom for a footer. Inside the middle row, define a new HTML table with three columns. Each column will contain a zone for the page. The left zone will contain Web Parts related to customers, the middle zone will contain information related to orders and statistics, and the rightmost zone will allow users to modify the Web Parts displayed on the page. At this point, your form should look something like the one defined in Figure 14.47.

Next you must lay out the zones inside the center row's HTML table. You can follow these steps to do so:

1. Place a WebPartZone control inside the first column of the table.

2. Set the HeaderText property of the first control to Customer Links. This allows people editing the page to see a zone name (and, you hope, your intentions for the zone).

3. Set the first control's ID property to WebPartZoneCustomerLinks.

4. Repeat steps 1 to 3 for the middle column in the row. This time, call the Web Part zone Customer Statistics. This will take up the most screen area and allows users of this screen to find orders and view stats.

5. Add a `CatalogZone` control to the rightmost column of the middle row. This Web Part will allow users to customize what they see on the screen.

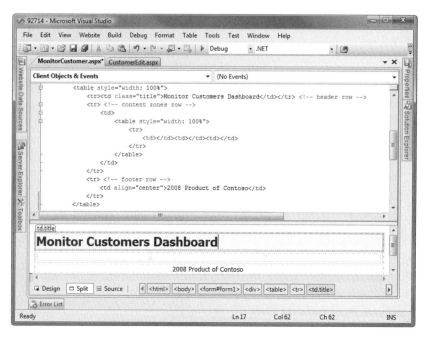

FIGURE 14.47    The initial layout of your Web Part page.

At this point, your Web Part page should look something like what's shown in Figure 14.48.

The next step is to define the chrome for the Web Parts that are placed in the zones. Chrome refers to the styles such as header, links, and buttons. There are a lot of styles you can set for a given zone and its Web Parts. These include styles for when there is an error, styles for when things are inactive, and many more. These styles can configure this through numerous properties of the zone. You can also use the smart tag associated with the control to autoformat the zone. Figure 14.49 shows an example of the AutoFormat dialog box. On the left are possible formats. On the right is a preview showing how the Web Parts in the zone will look. This preview is based on actual content for the zone.

Use the AutoFormat option to set the chrome for each zone control. Set the customer links and customer statistics zones to Professional. Set the page Catalog Zone to Colorful.

**Adding Web Parts to Zones**    Now you're ready to add Web Parts to the zones you have defined. There are few ways to go about this. You can create actual controls that implement the `WebPart` class. This allows the most flexibility for creating Web Parts. It also allows you to create user configuration for your Web Parts. This configuration is shown when a user edits a given Web Part. This also happens to be the most involved method. Of course, it is recommended for portal developers. Alternatively, a quick way to create

Web Parts is through the use of user controls or regular ASP.NET controls. For instance, when you drag a control like a `Label` onto the form, ASP.NET will define a Web Part around the given control. This makes for an easy way to create Web Parts.

FIGURE 14.48 The Web Part zones added to the page.

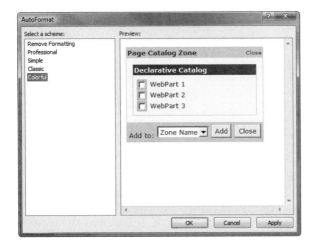

FIGURE 14.49 Setting the chrome for a zone.

For the example, you will implement the latter method. You will first create a Customer Links Web Part. This Web Part will provide a series of links used to manage a customer. The following outlines the process for creating this Web Part:

1. Drag an ASP Label control inside the WebPartZone control for customer links.

2. This label will be automatically turned into a WebPart control. You can see this in the markup. The <ZoneTemplate> element is added inside the <asp:WebPartZone> node. Inside this goes the Label control you added to the form.

3. Set a title for the Web Part. To do so, add the title attribute to the Label control. This attribute is picked up by ASP and applied to the Web Part.

4. Add a few links within the confines of the <asp:Label> declaration. The final markup looks something like Listing 14.2. Here we omitted the style information that would normally go inside the Web Part zone; this omission is for the sake of clarity.

LISTING 14.2    The Customer Links Web Part

```
<asp:WebPartZone ID="WebPartZoneCustomerLinks" runat="server">
  <ZoneTemplate>
    <asp:Label title="Customer Links" ID="Label1" runat="server" Text="Label">
      <a href="FindCustomer.aspx">Find Customer</a><br />
      <a href="FindOrder.aspx">Find Order</a><br />
      <a href="CustomerDiscounts.aspx">Customer Discounts</a><br />
    </asp:Label>
  </ZoneTemplate>
</asp:WebPartZone>
```

Repeat this method for a few more Web Parts. For our example, create Active Shoppers, Help, Edit Mode indicator, Find Customer Orders, and Top Products Web Parts to round out the dashboard. You can try creating a couple of these as user controls (for more information on user controls, skip ahead to the "Working with the ASP.NET Controls" section later in this chapter). Also, try building out one or two of these Web Parts as tables nested inside a Label control. Figure 14.50 shows what your page should now look like inside the designer.

**Enabling Users to Configure the Page**    There are many options available for allowing users to customize the look and behavior of Web Parts. You can create editors for your controls that allow for full configuration on a per-control basis. You might have Web Parts that can connect (or talk to) other Web Parts. They typically require some sort of configuration. You might allow users to pick from a catalog of controls in order to determine which controls they would like to see on the page. It is also common to allow users to minimize, close, and move your controls from zone to zone. Here we look at a couple of these options.

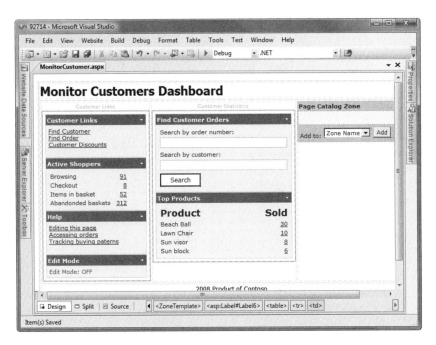

FIGURE 14.50   The Web Parts inside the designer.

First, let's configure our Web Part page to allow users to add Web Parts to the page as they see fit. This way users can determine which Web Parts they want to see on the page and where they want to see them. The following list defines the steps required to modify our Web Part page to allow for this level of user customization:

1. We start with a Web Part page that includes two label-based Web Parts: Active Shoppers and Find Customer Orders. The page also contains three user control Web Parts: Help, Customer Links, and Top Products. It is these last three that we are going to make user optional. A user will be able to add and remove these items from the page. Your first step is to remove them from the page. We will add them back in a moment.

2. You use the `CatalogZone` Web Part to enable the management of a group (or catalog) of Web Parts. When the page was first laid out, we added this Web Part to the right-most zone. If you do not have it, add it.

3. Next, inside the `CatalogZone` Web Part add a `DeclarativeCatalogPart`. The control indicates that you will declare all Web Parts that are managed in the zone. There are similar Web Parts like `PageCatalogPart`, which manages all Web Parts on the page.

4. The next step is to declare the Web Parts that will be managed inside the catalog. You do so by putting each user control's (or Web Part's) definition inside the `DeclarativeCatalogPart` section. Your markup should look like the following:

```
<asp:CatalogZone ID="CatalogZone1" runat="server"
  HeaderText="Manage Web Parts">
```

```
<ZoneTemplate>
  <asp:DeclarativeCatalogPart Title="Select a Web Part"
    ID="DeclarativeCatalogPart1" runat="server">
    <WebPartsTemplate>
      <uc1:TopProducts title="Top Products" ID="TopProducts1"
        runat="server" />
      <uc2:HelpControl title="Help" ID="HelpControl1" runat="server" />
      <uc3:CustomerLinks title="Customer Links" ID="CustomerLinks1"
        runat="server" />
    </WebPartsTemplate>
  </asp:DeclarativeCatalogPart>
</ZoneTemplate>

</asp:CatalogZone>
```

5. The final step is to allow the user to enable editing to turn this catalog on. We will use a LinkButton control to do so. Add a LinkButton control to the bottom right of the page. Create an event handler for the LinkButton control's click event. Inside this event handler, you need to toggle the display state of the page between Browse (normal view) and Catalog (user Web Part selection view). The following code does just that:

```
protected void LinkButtonChangeContent_Click(object sender, EventArgs e) {
  if (LinkButtonChangeContent.Text == "Change Content") {
    //EditorZoneMain.
    WebPartManagerMain.DisplayMode =
      WebPartManagerMain.SupportedDisplayModes["Catalog"];
  } else {
    WebPartManagerMain.DisplayMode =
      WebPartManagerMain.SupportedDisplayModes["Browse"];
  }
}
```

That is it. You should now be able to run the page and allow user selection for these three Web Parts. Figure 14.51 shows the page running in the browser. The user has clicked the Change Content LinkButton in the bottom right to bring up this Web Part manager. The user can select a Web Part and indicate to which zone on the page it should be added. Notice too that the Top Products Web Part has already been added to the page by the user. Finally, the user can choose to add multiple versions of the same Web Part to the page if they like.

Another common user customization is to allow for the moving of Web Parts between the zones and above and below one another. When the user is in the catalog mode, as in the prior example, this feature is enabled. However, there are times when you will add this feature for users but require another level of trust to add and remove Web Parts from the page.

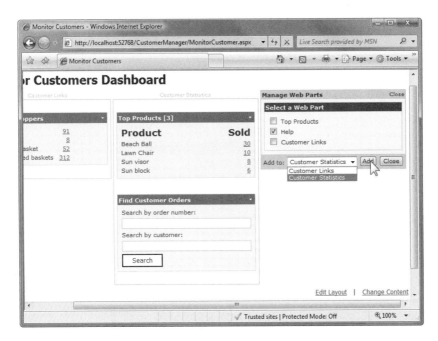

FIGURE 14.51   Using the Web Part catalog at runtime.

You need to take a few steps to enable users to change only the layout of a Web Part page:

1. Add an `EditorZone` control to the page. Adding this control creates a zone where you can put `EditorParts`. It is typical for you to show this zone when your page is in edit mode. In the example, assume that you are using the zone but do not intend to display it to users.

2. Add the `LayoutEditorPart` control to the `EditorZone` you just created. This Web Part allows for the page's layout to be edit-enabled.

3. Create a `LinkButton` control for allowing a user to turn on edit mode for the page. The design of your form should look something like that shown in Figure 14.52.

4. Next you need to write some code for the `LinkButton`'s click event. This code is similar to our prior example. The following is an example:

```
protected void LinkButtonEditPage_Click(object sender, EventArgs e) {
  if (LinkButtonEditPage.Text == "Edit Layout") {
    //EditorZoneMain.
    WebPartManagerMain.DisplayMode =
      WebPartManagerMain.SupportedDisplayModes["Edit"];
    LinkButtonEditPage.Text = "Finish Edit";
  } else {
    WebPartManagerMain.DisplayMode =
      WebPartManagerMain.SupportedDisplayModes["Browse"];
```

```
        LinkButtonEditPage.Text = "Edit Layout";
    }
}
```

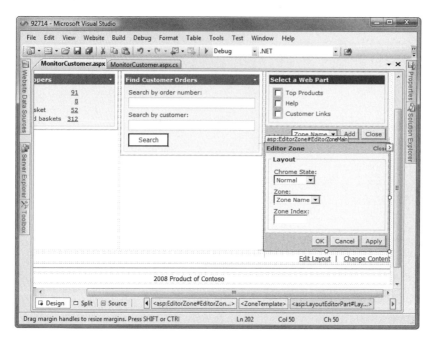

FIGURE 14.52   Designing the layout options for a user.

You can now run the page and view the results. When you click the Edit Layout LinkButton, the page will go into Edit mode. Here a user can move controls between zones, rearrange them, and toggle their close versus open state. Figure 14.53 shows this in action.

**TIP**

Web part personalization is persisted from session to session. If users (or developers) close controls, you need to give them a way to get them back. You can write some code to reset personalization for a page. You might give the user a reset link, for example. Inside the event for this link, you would add code that resembles the following line:

```
WebPartManagerMain.Personalization.ResetPersonalizationState()
```

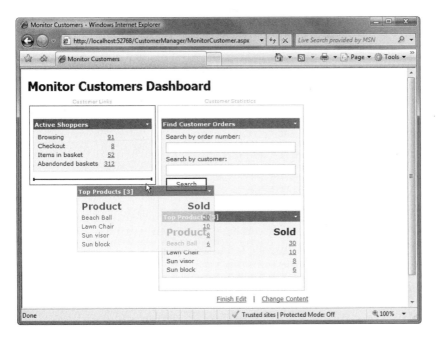

FIGURE 14.53   The page edit mode at runtime.

# Working with the ASP.NET Controls

Visual Studio 2008 and the new version of ASP.NET introduce a few new controls and a number of control enhancements. We have already covered a few of the ASP.NET controls in this chapter, such as Web Parts, labels, and buttons. Our intent for the following sections is to provide broad coverage of the many other controls in ASP.NET. This includes the standard controls as well as controls for validation, login, navigation, and data. We also spend some time discussing user-defined controls.

> **NOTE**
>
> See Chapter 17 for coverage of the AJAX controls.

## An Overview of the ASP.NET Controls

Controls render your user interface to the user's browser. ASP.NET controls are considered *server controls*. Server controls have a few basic tenants. They exist at design time (on the Toolbox) and allow you to manipulate their layout and properties. They also have associated classes in the .NET Framework. The code in your site creates instances of these classes for manipulating a given control. In addition, all server control processing happens on the web server. That is, the code of the control executes (along with your code) and emits its HTML to be sent to the user's browser. When the user posts the page back to the server,

ASP.NET rebuilds the controls and then reprocesses them to build a response back to the user.

---

**NOTE**

ASP.NET also supports the standard HTML controls. By default, these items are not available on the server. However, you can mark any of them as `runat="server"` to be able to work with them in your code-behind class. In general, if you do not think you will ever need access to a control on the server, it's wise to simply use the HTML controls.

---

### The ASP.NET Control Features

The ASP.NET server controls are a set of abstract controls that render their UI in many different forms back to a user's browser. They can emit HTML and JavaScript. They store state between requests and some work with databases. The following list outlines some of the key features found inside the ASP.NET control model:

▶ **XHTML Compliance**—The ASP.NET controls are sent back to the user's browser as standard HTML. All controls generate XHTML 1.1–compliant markup. This ensures that there are fewer surprises when your pages are being viewed in a web browser.

▶ **Browser Detection and Adaptive Rendering**—The ASP.NET controls can also adapt their markup output based on the requesting browser. Therefore, they can be both XHTML-compliant and browser-specific. This feature works by default for ASP.NET controls. This can save a lot of time because you don't have to try to code around the various browser types.

▶ **Event Model**—All the ASP.NET controls have the same server-side event model. You can write code to be called when a user triggers an event on the page such as pulling down a drop-down or clicking a button.

▶ **Client Event Model**—The set of ASP.NET controls can participate in client-side events. That is, you can work to emit JavaScript as part of the control's rendering and call that JavaScript as part of the client's (browser's) event model.

▶ **State Maintenance**—ASP.NET controls (including the HTML controls) automatically maintain state between round trips to the server. For example, suppose that a user enters a value into a TextBox and posts the page to the server. If you send the response back to the user, the user's entry is still maintained inside the control. This saves you from having to code this feature into your pages when doing operations such as validation processing on the server.

▶ **Data Binding**—Many of the ASP.NET controls can be bound to data in your application. The data-binding model allows you to bind to many data sources such as a database, a business object, XML, and so on. In most scenarios, the binding requires little coding on your part.

▶ **Template-Based Layout**—Some of the ASP.NET controls provide templates to allow developers to define their layout. For example, you can use the `ListView` control to create a template that defines how the control renders when a user is editing data versus displaying it.

▶ **Skins and Style Support**—We have already described how themes and style sheets can be used to change the look of a site. Each ASP.NET control has support for both skins and CSS styles.

▶ **Data Entry**—ASP.NET controls support layout that makes data entry easier. You can, for example, define a tab order for the controls on a page; you can set the focus to a given control; you can even assign a hotkey (or access key) to a given control. All of this is done through properties on the control. The controls themselves generate JavaScript on the client to enable these features.

▶ **Validation**—There are validation controls built into ASP.NET. The server controls work with these validation controls and ASP.NET to provide a cohesive validation model for your pages. For example, you can group a set of validation controls and manage validation at the group level (think sections of your page).

This list represents some of the basic features of the ASP.NET control set. In addition, each control has its own set of features. You will want to experiment with each control to determine what works best for your situation. In the following sections, we will discuss many of these controls.

## The ASP.NET Standard Controls

There is a large set of what are called Standard controls in ASP.NET. These appear on the Toolbox in the Standard group. Most pages you build will draw heavily from this list. It includes label, text box, button, check box, radio button, calendar, and many more controls.

At design time, you drag one of these controls from the Toolbox onto the designer. You can then work with the control using the Properties dialog. Each control has a host of properties for controlling appearance, behavior, accessibility, and more.

Figure 14.54 shows the Standard control list on the left. In the center, you can see controls for labels, text box, button, and check box. Notice that a text box has been selected. On the right is the property window for this text box. To access the events for a given control, you click the lightning-bolt icon on this property window.

There are many standard controls. Table 14.4 provides a list of a number of these, along with a brief description of its use.

FIGURE 14.54    The ASP.NET standard controls.

TABLE 14.4    The Standard Controls

| Control | Description |
| --- | --- |
| Label | Use this control to provide text-based information to a user. You need a Label control only if you intend the text to be dynamic (set at runtime). If you have static text, you can typically just type it into the page using standard HTML formatting. |
| TextBox | Use this control to allow a user to enter text-based data on your page. The TextBox control has the property TextMode. Use this property to indicate that the user's entry is a single line (default), multiple lines, or a password. |
| Button | Use the Button control when you expect a user to trigger an action on the page such as save, reset, or cancel. There are also the LinkButton and ImageButton controls. LinkButton behaves like a button but looks like a hyperlink. ImageButton is similar: It behaves like a button but you set an image to define its look. |
| HyperLink | Use this control when you need to work with a hyperlink at runtime. You might, for example, set the NavigateUrl property dynamically based on data in the system. If you simply need a static link on the page, you can use the anchor tag (<a />) in HTML. |

| Control | Description |
|---|---|
| DropDownList | Use this control to provide a list of options from which a user can select. You can bind the list to data. You can also respond to a user selecting an item from the list. If you have a lot of options from which a user might need to choose, consider the ListBox control. There is also the CheckBoxList control for a list of multi-select items and the RadioButtonList for a list of mutually exclusive items. |
| CheckBox | Use this control when you want to allow a user to set a setting (yes or no, on or off). Again, there is an HTML equivalent if you do not need server-side processing. |
| RadioButton | Use this control to provide a user with a group of items from which they may select only one. Use the GroupName property to group a set of radio buttons that need to work together. |
| Image | Use this control when you need to populate an image on your page dynamically (using the ImageUrl property). Static images can use the HTML <img /> tag. There is also an ImageMap control that allows you to define sections of an image from which you can respond differently to user interaction. |
| Table | Use the Table control to build out tables dynamically in your code. If your tables are static, consider the HTML table control. |
| Calendar | Use this control when you need to allow a user to see a set of dates and select one. Use the SelectionMode property to allow a user to select a day, a week, or a month. |
| MultiView | Use this control when you want to provide multiple views to a user based on the user's selection or the state of the system. For example, you might implement a read-only view and an edit view of the same data. Each view requires that you drag a View control onto the multiview. You then add the controls you want to display for the given view to this View control. You can get similar results with multiple Panel controls. However, the MultiView control provides additional management features for you. |
| Wizard | The Wizard control is similar to MultiView. However, it provides the additional capabilities needed for a wizard moving from step to step (or view to view) and back again. |

## Validation Controls

A set of validation controls is provided with ASP.NET. These controls allow you to indicate how user input should be validated for a page before the page is processed. In this way, you can ensure that a user has entered data in all the required fields and validate that this data meets your application's constraints.

Controls are always validated on the server and will prevent an ASP.Page from processing if validation fails (see the page life cycle discussed previously). The controls can emit JavaScript to be run on the client too (the EnableClientScript property is set to True by default). In this way, a user is notified of any page-level validation errors before having to submit the page to the server.

To use the validation controls, you drag them onto your form like any other control. You want to place them near the control they validate because they provide textual clues to the user as to what is wrong with the page. A standard process is to put the validation control to the right of the control it validates. You then set the ControlToValidate property of the validation control to another control on your form (the one you want to validate).

You then typically set the Text and ErrorMessage properties of the validation control. The Text property indicates the text that should be displayed by the validation control if the validation fails. The ErrorMessage property indicates the error message that should be displayed to the user inside a ValidationSummary control for the page. The ValidationSummary groups all error messages for a user in a single area.

As an example, take a look at Figure 14.55. Here you can see the validation control group in the Toolbox to the left. The page has a ValidationSummary control at the top (under Edit Customer). You can also see that both the first name and the email text boxes have an associated validation control. The validation control for the email text box is selected. This is a RegularExpressionValidator control. With it you can use pattern matching to validate whether the user has entered a compliant email address. To the right, you can see this control's properties.

FIGURE 14.55   Using the ASP.NET validation controls.

Table 14.5 lists the validation controls provided in ASP.NET, along with brief descriptions of each.

TABLE 14.5   The Standard Controls

| Control | Description |
| --- | --- |
| RequiredFieldValidator | Use this control for required fields on your page. You might combine a required field validation control with another control listed here. |
| RangeValidator | Use this control to validate whether a user's input is between a specified range. Use the Type property to indicate what type of range to validate, such as string, integer, double, date, or currency. |
| RegularExpressionValidator | Use this control to validate the pattern of the user's entry. You set the ValidationExpression property to a valid regular expression to do so. In addition, there are built-in regular expressions in Visual Studio. Clicking the ellipsis button in this property will allow you to set standard regular expressions for such things as postal codes, email addresses, and phone numbers. |
| CompareValidator | Use this control to compare the user's input and validate based on this comparison. You can compare the input of the control being validated to a static value, another control, or a data type. Comparing to a data type allows you to ensure that the user has entered a valid value that can be converted to a given data type. Use the Type property to set this comparison. |
| CustomValidator | Use this control to write your own custom validation controls. You can write server-side validation and emit JavaScript to validate on the client. |
| ValidationSummary | Use this control to provide a summary of any validation errors raised by the page. The validation control's ErrorMessage property value will end up in the summary for each validation control that fails on the page. |

## The Login Controls

ASP.NET has a built-in set of login controls. These controls are meant to provide a complete low-code (sometimes no-code) solution for managing and authenticating users inside web applications.

By default, the login controls use what is called *ASP.NET Membership*. This feature allows these controls to work with an authentication database and related features without your writing code. Membership allows for the creation of users and groups and the management of user data (including passwords). The membership services inside ASP.NET can work with a SQL Express database or Active Directory. You can also write your own custom provider that can be plugged into the model.

We will look at configuring membership in a moment. First, let's examine the many login controls. Figure 14.56 shows a list of all these controls in the Toolbox. Each control has a purpose and is aptly named.

FIGURE 14.56    The login controls for ASP.NET.

Table 14.6 provides a brief overview of these many controls.

### Configuring User Authentication

You can create a login page (or control) by dropping the login control directly on a form. After you place it, you can begin to set the properties that define your application's security. Figure 14.57 shows an example. Notice that the login control provides access to the Administer Website link. This link takes you to the Web Site Administration Tool (WSAT) for your site, where you can begin to define your authentication.

> **NOTE**
>
> By default, user data is sent to the server from the client as plain text. Therefore, you should enable SSL and HTTPS for securing your site.

The WSAT is a web-based tool that allows you to configure your site, including security. Figure 14.58 shows the home page of the tool. From here, you can access the Security tab, define application configuration (turn on tracing, for example), and select an administration provider. The default administration provider is configured for SQL Express. This is the place where the configuration data (such as users) for your site is stored.

TABLE 14.6    The Login Controls

| Control | Description |
|---------|-------------|
| Login | This control provides the primary interface for challenging users for their credentials (usernames and passwords). You can format the look of the control as well as display other links and messages such as authentication errors. |
| | The control is set up to work with ASP.NET Membership by default. If you configure it, you do not need to write code. However, if you want to write your own code, you can use the `Authenticate` event to write your custom scheme. |
| LoginView | This control allows you to define two views of information: a view for users who are logged in to your application and a view for anonymous users. You add controls to each view to define what users see based on their current status. |
| PasswordRecovery | This control is used for users to recover their passwords. Typically, you configure this control to email users their passwords. However, there are additional options as well. |
| LoginStatus | This control shows the authentication status of the current user. Users are either logged in or not. If they are, the control enables them to log out. If they are not logged in, the control gives them the opportunity to do so. |
| LoginName | This control displays the username of the currently logged-in user. |
| CreateUserWizard | This control allows users to create their own accounts or helps in password recovery. Users can request an account (and fill in their details) with this control. |
| ChangePassword | This control allows users to enter their current passwords and new passwords. The control can then validate the passwords and make the change if successful. |

You can use the WSAT to change from Windows security to Internet security. The former is best when working on a LAN environment. The latter is required for most public-facing, secure sites. After you configure your security model to that of Internet, ASP.NET switches you over to using the membership database for user storage.

You can use the Security tab, shown in Figure 14.59, inside WSAT to configure the users, roles, and access for this database. Notice the three groups at the bottom of the screen: Users, Roles, and Access Rules. These groups provide links for managing the accounts in your system. Your login control will automatically respect the information configured here.

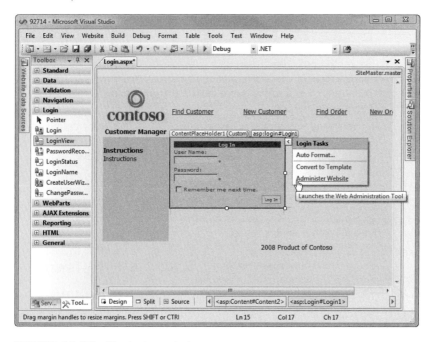

FIGURE 14.57    The login control.

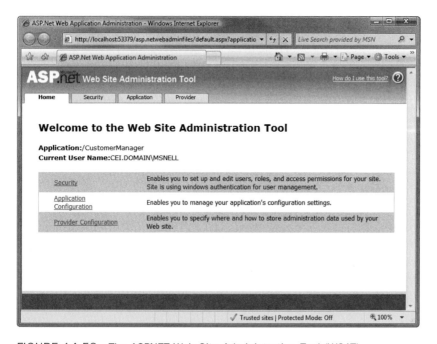

FIGURE 14.58    The ASP.NET Web Site Administration Tool (WSAT).

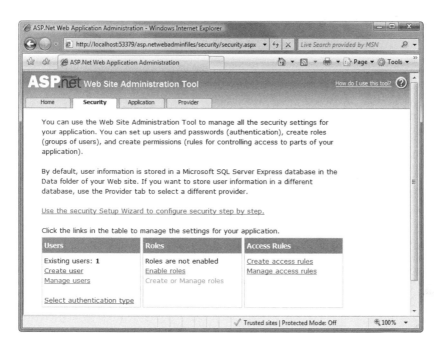

FIGURE 14.59    Managing users and roles for your site.

## Site Navigation Controls

It can be easy to become lost on a lot of websites out there. If you don't provide good user navigation, chances are that users will complain (or stop visiting). ASP.NET provides a few controls to help deal with defining and controlling navigation. The controls include the following:

▶ **Menu**—You can use this control to create menus for your web page with Visual Studio. The menus support submenus and fly-out menus. You can even bind your menus to an XML data source.

▶ **SiteMapPath**—This control allows you to leave *cookie crumbs* as users navigate your site. That is, you can tell them where they came from and where they are. When you do so, users can use this list to jump backward to a place they just were.

▶ **TreeView**—This control could always show hierarchical data. However, it can also be bound to an XML representation of your site called a *site map*. In this way, you can quickly define a navigation structure for your site that is updated in a single place.

### Using the SiteMapPath Control

Recall that the SiteMapPath control is used to orient users in your site. You control this orientation definition through the use of a .sitemap file. You add this file to your site through the Add New Item dialog box. Inside it, you define the logical hierarchy of your site by nesting pages inside `siteMapNode` elements.

For example, if users start at a home page, this would be your outermost node. As they navigate into your site, you create nested nodes. Listing 14.3 shows a simple example that includes a three-tier definition: Home, Find Customer, Edit Customer. This makes a logical progression through the sample site.

LISTING 14.3   A **.sitemap** File

```
<siteMap xmlns="http://schemas.microsoft.com/AspNet/SiteMap-File-1.0" >
  <siteMapNode url="Default.aspx" title="Home"  description="">
    <siteMapNode url="FindCustomer.aspx" title="Find Customer"
      description="">
      <siteMapNode url="EditCustomer.aspx" title="Edit Customer"
        description="" />
    </siteMapNode>
  </siteMapNode>
</siteMap>
```

Figure 14.60 shows the results users see in their browser. In this case, the `SiteMapPath` control was added to the master page so that it appears throughout the site. The control automatically picks up the content of the `Web.sitemap` file.

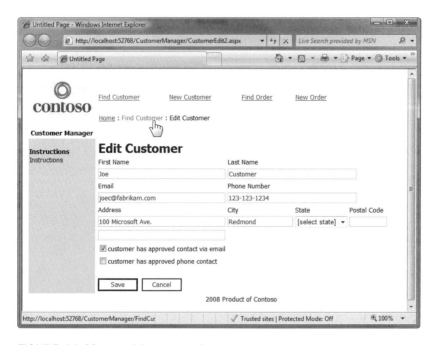

FIGURE 14.60   The **SiteMapPath** control in action.

## Data Controls

ASP.NET has a full set of controls that you can use for working with, displaying, and binding to data. These controls are meant to work with little to no additional code. Instead of writing code, you should be able to configure the controls to behave as you want. Figure 14.61 shows a list of all the data controls in the Toolbox.

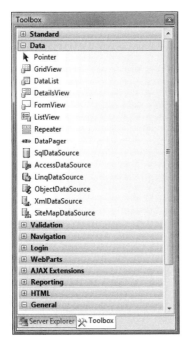

FIGURE 14.61    The data controls in ASP.NET.

Table 14.7 provides a brief overview of each of these controls.

> **NOTE**
>
> We cover ways to work with data and databases in Chapter 18, "Working with Databases." See "Data Binding with Web Controls" in this chapter.

## User Controls

If you still can't find the perfect control, Visual Studio provides you with the framework to create your own controls. You can take the simple approach and define a *user control*. This is a file that you can design like a page and then use across other pages.

TABLE 14.7    The Data Controls

| Control | Description |
| --- | --- |
| GridView | This control is for binding to and working with tabular data. The control works with multiple data sources. It also allows sorting, paging, edit, add, and delete features. |
| DataList | You use this control when you want to control how your data is displayed and formatted. You can use this control with templates to gain control over when and how your data is displayed. |
| DetailsView | This control lets you display a single row of data (or row detail). You can display this row as an editable set of fields inside a table. The DetailsView control can be used in conjunction with the GridView control to obtain a master-detail editing structure. |
| FormView | This control offers the same features as the DetailsView control with the added benefit of being able to define the templates that make up the display of a given row. |
| ListView | This control is new in 2008. It simplifies the display of repeating data. The ListView control is driven based on user templates. In this way, you can configure how you want your UI to behave during operations such as view, edit, add, and delete. In addition, the ListView supports sorting, paging, and, of course, data binding. Refer to Chapter 1 (Figures 1.14 through 1.16), for more on the ListView control. |
| Repeater | This control is a container for repeating data. You use the Repeater control with a template to indicate how the contents of the repeated data should be displayed. This ListView control can be a better alternative to Repeater. |
| DataPager | This control is new to 2008. This control allows you to manage the paging of data and the UI associated with that paging. You can use this control by itself or embed it as part of another control. This control was also discussed in Chapter 1. |
| Data Source Controls | Several data source controls are available in ASP.NET. These sources can be configured to work with the source data and execute select, update, new, and delete methods. You use a data source control to bind to other controls (such as a GridView). The ASP.NET data source controls allow access to SQL Server data, Microsoft Access data, data contained in objects, XML data, data defined as a .sitemap file, and LINQ data. |

You add a user control to your project from the Add New Items dialog. User controls have the extension .asx. You define a user control by dragging other form elements to the page. In this way, user controls are composed of one or more existing ASP.NET controls. For example, you might create a simple user control to provide a list of common links. The benefit is reuse. You can now use this user control across multiple pages in the site but manage it centrally.

In addition, user controls are shown inside the designer. So when you drag a user control from the solution explorer to a page, you see its representation in design view. However, when a user control exists on a page, you work with it as a single control. It too can expose properties like other controls. However, if you need to work with the inner workings of the user control, you have to open it in the designer.

User controls also have their own code-behind file for processing their own events. In this way you can also abstract and centralize the code for user controls from the rest of your page.

> **NOTE**
>
> If a user control is still not right and you want to provide design-time support for the Toolbox, configuration, and the Properties window, then you can create a *custom control*. Custom controls follow the same framework as the existing ASP.NET controls. You can even subclass and extend an existing control and turn it into your own custom version.

## Summary

In this chapter, we described how to create a web application and build web forms. In addition, we looked at how to leverage the new features of ASP.NET to create a consistent (sometimes configurable) user interface. We also looked at the many controls in ASP.NET. Some key points in this chapter include the following:

▶ You can create a website using a local built-in server. You can also create your site on a remote server using HTTP (and IIS) or FTP.

▶ The website project property pages allow you to set what happens when you start your application from Visual Studio (among other things).

▶ You can create themes to switch the look and feel of your site without writing code or recompiling. The themes contain style sheets, images, and skin files.

▶ Web parts allow you to define a user-configurable user interface. You lay out this interface with zones and place Web Parts inside these zones.

▶ ASP.NET ships with login controls, Membership provider, and WSAT to help you manage the authentication of users on your site.

▶ Data controls inside ASP.NET make data binding, editing, and updating easier (often requiring no code).

# CHAPTER 15

# Building Windows Forms Applications

One of the core goals for Visual Studio is enabling rapid Windows Forms construction. Using the Windows Forms Designer, the Controls Toolbox, and the various common controls provided by the .NET Framework, this chapter will serve as your guide to the drag-and-drop creation of rich form-based applications. Specifically, we'll look at how best to leverage the built-in capabilities of the Forms Designer and the Visual Studio project system to quickly build a baseline form from scratch.

We won't worry about the code behind the form at this point; instead, the focus will be on the user interface and Visual Studio's inherent Rapid Application Development (or RAD) capabilities with the Windows Forms Designer. In other words, we will focus on the design-time capabilities of the IDE as opposed to the runtime capabilities of the form and control classes.

## The Basics of Form Design

Designing the appropriate user interface for a Windows application is still part art and part science. In the Windows Forms world, a user interface is a collection of images, controls, and window elements that all work in synergy. Users absorb information through the UI and also use it as the primary vehicle for interacting with the application.

The task in front of any developer when creating a user interface is primarily one of balance: balancing simplicity of design with the features that the application is required to implement. Also thrown in the mix is the concept of standards, both formal and experiential.

> **NOTE**
>
> Although we use the term *developer* in this chapter, much of the UI design and layout process is actually squarely in the camp of the *designer*. Although many development teams don't have the luxury of employing a full-time UI designer (developers handle this area on many teams), this is rapidly becoming a key competitive differentiator as software development firms look to distinguish their applications and rise above their competitors at the "look and feel" level.

## Considering the End User

You simply can't start the design process unless you understand how the application will be used and who its intended audience is. Even applications that surface similar feature sets might need to provide significantly different user experiences. An application designed to store medical information might have the same data points and functions but would likely have a different persona if it was designed for the ordinary consumer as opposed to a physician or registered nurse.

Use cases and actual usability labs are both great tools for understanding user expectations, and they provide great data points for preserving that function versus simplicity of design balance.

### Location and Culture

Location and culture figure into the equation as well. The typical form application used in the United States would cater to this culture's expectations by anticipating left-to-right, top-to-bottom reading habits. In this environment, the most important elements of the UI are typically placed in the most prominent position: top and left in the form. Other cultures would require this strategy to change based on right-to-left and even bottom-to-top reading traits.

Most controls in Visual Studio 2008 directly support right-to-left languages through a `RightToLeft` property. By setting this property to an appropriate `RightToLeft` enum value, you can indicate whether the control's text should appear left to right or right to left, or should be based on the setting carried on the parent control. Even the `Form` class supports this property.

Beyond the `RightToLeft` property, certain controls also expose a `RightToLeftLayout` property. Setting this Boolean property will actually affect the overall layout within the control. As an example, setting `RightToLeftLayout` to `True` for a `Form` instance will cause the form to mirror its content.

> **TIP**
>
> Search for "Best Practices for Developing World-Ready Applications" in MSDN for more detailed information on how to design an application for an international audience.

In addition, simple things such as the space allocated for a given control are impacted by language targets. A string presented in U.S. English might require drastically more space when translated into Farsi. Again, many controls support properties designed to overcome this design issue; setting the AutoSize property on a control to True will automatically extend the client area of the control based on its contained text.

## Understanding the Role of UI Standards

Applications must also strive to adhere to any relevant standards associated with their look and feel. Some standards are documented for you by the platform "owner." Microsoft, for example, has a set of UI design guidelines documented within MSDN. The book *Microsoft Windows User Experience,* published by Microsoft Press, is included in its entirety within MSDN. By tackling topics such as "Data-Centered Design," "Input Basics," and "Design of Graphic Images," this book provides a structured baseline of UI design collateral for Windows application developers.

Design guidelines and UI standards are often specific to a given platform. The current look and feel expected from a Windows application trace primarily back to the "new" design that debuted with Windows 95. Windows XP further refined those expectations. Now, Windows Vista—the next-generation operating system from Microsoft—features an entirely new set of user experience guidelines.

Visual Studio 2008 surfaces some of these design guidelines and standards to make it easy to develop conforming interfaces. For instance, default button heights match the recommended standard, and Visual Studio assists developers with standard control positioning relative to neighboring controls by displaying snaplines as you move controls on the form surface. We cover this topic more fully later in this chapter.

### De Facto Standards

Sometimes the influence of a particular application or suite of applications is felt heavily in the UI design realm. One example here is Microsoft Outlook. There are various applications now in the wild that mimic, for instance, the structure and layout of Microsoft Outlook even though they are not, per se, email applications. The Microsoft Outlook designers struck a vein of usability when they designed its primary form, and now other companies and developers have leveraged those themes in their own applications. A similar comment can be made about the visual appearance of the "Ribbon" toolbar made popular with Microsoft Office 2007.

Although there are limits, Visual Studio enables developers to achieve the same high-fidelity UIs used in Microsoft Office and other popular applications. In fact, if you look at the official Windows Forms website, you'll see demo applications written with Visual Studio, showcasing how you can develop replicas of the Microsoft Outlook, Quicken, or even Microsoft Money facades (visit the "Downloads" page at http://www.windowsclient.net).

## Planning the User Interface

Before you embark on the design process in Visual Studio, it is probably a decent idea to first draft a mock-up of the form's general landscape. This can be a simple pen and paper sketch; what we are looking for is a simple, rough blueprint for the application.

As a sample scenario, consider a Windows Forms application written for Contoso customer service representatives. The application needs to expose a hierarchical list of orders placed with Contoso, and it should allow the reps to search on orders and edit data.

### Preliminary Design

A few basic components have been established as de facto standards for a Windows form: Menus, toolbars, and status bars are all standard fare and can certainly be leveraged within this fictional order application.

Beyond those staples, you know that you need to list orders on the screen and also provide for a region that will show order details. By borrowing liberally from an existing layout theme a la Microsoft Outlook, you might arrive at a tentative form layout plan like the one shown in Figure 15.1.

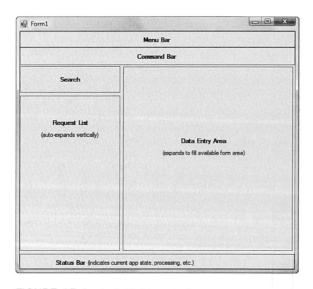

FIGURE 15.1    An initial layout plan.

It is important to pay some attention to the concept of resizing: How will the form's constituent controls respond relative to one another when a user resizes the form? What if a control element is resized because of a language change or a change in the underlying data? By fleshing out some of the resizing design intent now, you can save a mountain of work later. The prototype sketch in Figure 15.1 includes some simple text to remind you how to accommodate the different form regions during resizing.

# Creating a Form

Although there are many different ways of approaching form design, the starting point for all of them within Visual Studio is the Windows Application project template. From the New Project dialog box, select this template, give the project an appropriate name, and click OK (see Figure 15.2).

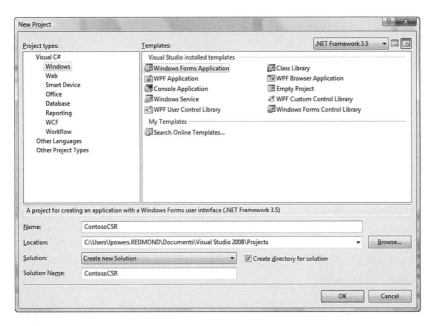

FIGURE 15.2    Creating a new Windows Forms project.

## The Windows Forms Application Project Type

Windows Forms Application projects consist of a default form class and, in the case of C#, a default static Program class. After creating the project, you are immediately presented with a blank, default form opened in the Windows Forms Designer. For a refresher on the basic capabilities and components of the Windows Forms Designer, reference Chapter 6, "Introducing the Editors and Designers."

### Setting the Startup Form

Although the default project creates only a single form, you can, of course, add multiple forms at any time. This then raises the question of how to indicate at design time which form you initially want displayed at runtime (if any). There are two methods:

> ▶ For Visual Basic projects, the startup form is set using the Project Properties dialog box. The Startup Object drop-down in this dialog box contains a list of all valid form objects. You simply select the form you want launched on startup, and you're all set.

▶ For Visual C# projects, a slightly more complex approach is needed. The notion of a C# startup object is simply any class that implements a `Main()` method. Within the body of the `Main` method, you need to place a line of code that passes in a form instance to the `Application.Run` method, like this: `Application.Run(new OrderForm())`. Assuming that you have a class that implements `Main` and code that calls `Application.Run` in that `Main` method, you can then select the specific startup object via the Project Properties dialog box. The `Program` class, which is created for you during the project creation process, already implements the `Main` method, and will by default run the default form (`Form1`) on startup.

### Inheriting Another Form's Appearance

If your form will look similar to another form that you have already developed, you have the option of visually inheriting that other form's appearance. Visual Studio provides an Inherited Form project item template to help you along this path.

To create a form that visually inherits another, select Project, Add New Item. In the Add New Item dialog box, select the Inherited Form item type. The Inheritance Picker dialog box then lists the available forms within the current project that you can inherit from. Note that you also have the option of manually browsing to an existing assembly if you want to inherit from a form that doesn't appear in the list. After you select the base form, Visual Studio will create the new form class; its code will already reflect the base class derivation.

## Form Properties and Events

A form is like any other control: You can use the Properties window in the IDE to control its various properties. Although we won't touch on all of them here, you will want to consider a few key properties as you begin your form design process.

### Startup Location

You use the form's `StartPosition` property to place the form's window on the screen when it is first displayed. This property accepts a `FormStartPosition` enumeration value; the possible settings are documented in Table 15.1.

TABLE 15.1  **FormStartPosition** Enumeration Values

| Value | Description |
|---|---|
| CenterParent | Centers the form within its parent form. |
| CenterScreen | Centers the form within the current display screen. |
| Manual | The form will position itself according to the Form.Location property value. |
| WindowsDefaultBounds | Positions the form at the Windows default location; the forms bounds are determined by the Windows default as well. |
| WindowsDefaultLocation | Positions the form at the Windows default location; the form's size is determined by the Form.Size property (this is the default setting). |

## Appearance

Given our discussion on the priority of UI design, it should come as no surprise that the appearance of the form is an important part of the overall application's user experience. For the most part, the default appearance property values are sufficient for the typical application. You should set the ForeColor and BackColor properties according to the color scheme identified for your application. Note that when you add controls to the form, most of them have their own individual ForeColor values set to mimic that of the form.

Some properties allow you to implement a more extravagant user interface. The Opacity property allows you to implement transparent or semitransparent forms. This capability might be useful for situations in which users want to see a portion of the screen that actually sits behind the form's window. In addition to the Opacity property, you use the Form.BackgroundImage property to set an image as the form's background. This property is best used to display subtle color gradients or graphics not possible with just the BackColor property.

Keeping in mind our goal of rapidly crafting the form, most of the activities within the designer described in this chapter consist of tweaking the form's properties and adding controls from the Toolbox to the form.

## Form Events

Forms inherit the same event-driven architecture as other controls do. Certain public events defined on the Form class are useful as injection points across the continuum of a form's life.

Figure 15.3 shows the various stages (and corresponding events) from form inception to close. To react to a form event, you first need to create an event handler.

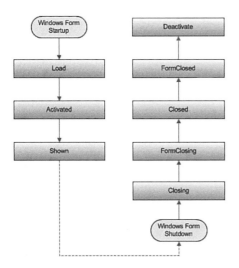

FIGURE 15.3    The events in the life of a Windows form.

**Creating an Event Handler**    Visual Studio's Properties window provides a speedy mechanism for defining an event handler. First, select the form of interest. Then click on the Events button in the Properties window's toolbar. The window will now show a list of every event defined on the form. Double-clicking on the event will create a blank event handler routine and open it in the code editor for you. The event handler will have the correct arguments list and will follow established standards for event handler naming (typically, `object_eventname`).

Figure 15.4 depicts the form events within the Properties window.

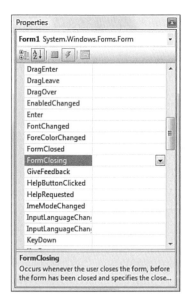

FIGURE 15.4    Form events in the Properties window.

With the form in place, you can start placing controls onto its surface.

# Adding Controls and Components

When you are building a form-based application, the user interface design really involves three separate tools within Visual Studio: the Forms Designer tool, which provides the canvas for the form; the Toolbox, which contains the controls to be placed onto the canvas; and the property browser, which is used to affect the form and its child controls, appearance, and behavior. This triad of IDE tools provides the key to rapid form construction with Visual Studio, especially as it relates to building a form's content.

The term *control* technically refers to any .NET object that implements the `Control` class. In practice, we use the term to refer to the visual controls hosted by a form. This is in contrast to a *component,* which has many of the same characteristics of a control but doesn't expose a visual interface. A button is an example of a control; a timer is an example of a component.

Controls and components alike live in the Toolbox window (see additional coverage of the Toolbox in Chapter 6). Adding either a control or a component to a form is as easy as dragging its likeness from the Toolbox and dropping it onto the form's surface.

After you place a control on a form, the Windows Forms Designer will paint the control onto the form to give you a WYSIWYG view of how the form will look at runtime. As we noted in Chapter 6, components are handled in a slightly different fashion. The Forms Designer has a special region called the *component tray*; any components placed onto the form are represented here. This allows you to interact in a point-and-click fashion with the component as you would with a control but doesn't place a representation onto the form itself because a component has no visual aspect to it.

Figure 15.5 highlights the component tray area of the Windows Forms Designer.

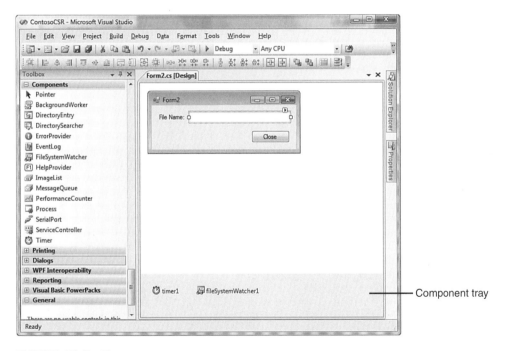

FIGURE 15.5   The component tray.

15

---

**TIP**

The Toolbox is customizable: You can add or remove controls from the Toolbox within any of the Toolbox tabs. Right-click anywhere in the interior of the Toolbox window and select Choose Items. This launches the Choose Toolbox Items dialog box; from here, you can select or deselect the Toolbox control population. If a control doesn't show up in the .NET Framework Components tab or the COM Components tab of the dialog box, you can browse to the control's assembly and add it directly.

---

## Control Layout and Positioning

When a few controls are on a form, the Windows Forms Designer is able to help automate some of the more common layout tasks, such as aligning a group of controls vertically to one another. We again refer you to Chapter 6 to see how you can leverage these productivity tools. But these layout functions, although nice from a design perspective, do nothing for you at runtime.

As previously noted, a control's runtime behavior within its parent form is an important area that needs attention if you are to implement your form according to your design intent. That is, you not only want controls to look a certain way, but also want them to act a certain way when the form is resized.

The simplest way to underscore the issue presented during a form resize is to look at a few figures. Figure 15.6 shows the simplest of forms: a label, a text box, and OK and Cancel buttons. The controls on the form have been carefully placed to maintain equal spacing, the controls are nicely aligned in the vertical and horizontal planes, and, in short, this form looks just like the developer intended it to look.

FIGURE 15.6    Controls aligned on a form.

But then a user becomes involved. Figure 15.7 shows the results of resizing the form horizontally and vertically.

FIGURE 15.7    Form resize effects on design.

This appearance is clearly not what was intended; the nice clean design of the form has failed to keep up with the form's size. Perhaps the user resized the form in an attempt to get more room to type in the text box. Or perhaps the user tiled this application's window with other applications, causing its size to change. Whatever the reason, it is clear that further intervention by the developer is needed to keep the design "valid," regardless of the size of the form.

Just by viewing the before and after figures, you can decide on a strategy and answer the question "What should happen when a user resizes the form?" Figure 15.8 is a snapshot of the ideal; the text box has "kept pace" with the resize by horizontally extending or shrinking its width. The command buttons have kept their alignment with one another and with the text box, but they have not altered their overall dimensions. Plus, the label has stayed in its original location.

FIGURE 15.8    Reacting to a form resize.

Every form object has a resize event that fires whenever the form boundary size changes (most commonly as the result of a user dragging the form's border to increase or decrease the size of the form). Because every control has positioning properties such as `Top`, `Left`, `Height`, and `Width`, you could implement a brute-force approach to achieving the form shown in Figure 15.8. By writing several lines of code for each control, you can manually move or redimension the controls in response to the form size and the position of the other controls. But this approach is tedious at best and results in brittle code that has to be touched every time the layout and placement of controls are tweaked.

Thankfully, the Visual Studio Windows Forms Designer, in conjunction with some standard control properties, allows you to take all the common resize optimizations into account during the layout of the form. By *anchoring* and *docking* your controls, you can dictate their position relative to one another and to their position within the borders of the form.

### Anchoring

*Anchoring*, as its name implies, is the concept of forcing a control's left, top, right, or bottom border to maintain a static, anchored position within the borders of the form. For instance, anchoring a label control to the top and left of a form (this is the default) will cause the label to maintain its exact position regardless of how the form is resized. Each control's `Anchor` property can be set to any combination of `Top`, `Left`, `Bottom`, and `Right`. The control's property browser provides a convenient property editor widget, shown in Figure 15.9, which graphically indicates the sides of the control that are anchored.

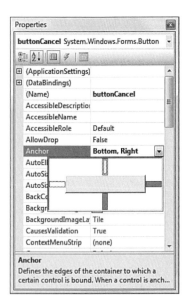

FIGURE 15.9    Setting the **Anchor** property.

Anchoring opposite sides of a control has an interesting effect. Because each side must maintain its position relative to the sides of the form, the control itself will stretch either vertically or horizontally depending on whether the Top and Bottom or Right and Left anchors have been set. In fact, this is the exact behavior you want with the text box: You want its width and height to adjust whenever the form is resized. By anchoring all sides of the control, you get the behavior shown in Figure 15.8; the control has automatically adjusted its dimensions with no code required from the developer.

> **NOTE**
>
> By default, controls are typically anchored on their top and left sides. You may be wondering what happens if no anchors are specified at all. In that case, the control will maintain its exact position regardless of form resize actions. This is, in effect, the same behavior as top and left anchors would have because forms have their top leftmost points as their "origin."

Anchoring also solves the positioning problem with the command buttons. If you change their Anchor property to Bottom, Right, they will anchor themselves to the bottom right of the form, which is consistent with their recommended placement on a form. Because you aren't anchoring opposing sides of the control, you aren't forcing the buttons to resize; they are merely repositioned to keep station with the right and bottom edge of the form. Contrast this with the anchoring performed for the text box: Because you anchored all sides, you are not only keeping a uniform border between the edge of the text box and the form, but also causing the text box to stretch itself in both dimensions.

## Docking

For the simple form in Figure 15.8, you can implement most of your layout logic using the Anchor property. But if you refer to the overall plan for the CSR screen (see Figure 15.1), you can see that you have some positioning needs that would be cumbersome to solve using anchors. For instance, the data entry region of the form should automatically expand vertically and horizontally to fill any space left between the list of requests, the status bar, and the command bar. This is where the concept of *docking* comes to the rescue. Docking is used either to stick a control to a neighboring control's edge or the form's edge, or to force a control to fill all the available space not taken by other controls.

As with the Anchor property, the property browser provides a graphical tool to set a control's Dock property (shown in Figure 15.10).

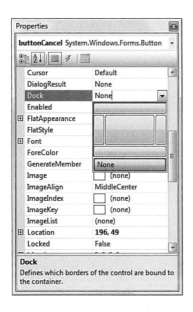

FIGURE 15.10    Setting the **Dock** property.

## Control Auto Scaling

The Windows Forms engine supports the capability to dynamically adjust a control's dimensions to preserve its original design proportions. This capability is useful if the form or control is displayed at runtime on a system with different display characteristics (resolution, DPI, and so on) than the system the form or control was designed on.

A simple example of this occurs when an application that uses a reasonable 9pt. font during design becomes almost unusable when displayed on a system whose default font size is larger. Because many UI elements auto-adjust based on the font of their displayed text (such as window title bars and menus), this can impact nearly every visual aspect of a form application.

Container controls (for example, those deriving from the ContainerControl class including the Form class and UserControl among others) starting with .NET 2.0 support two properties that enable them to counter these issues automatically without a lot of developer intervention: AutoScaleMode and AutoScaleDimensions. AutoScaleMode specifies an enumeration value indicating what the scaling process should use as its base reference (DPI or resolution). Table 15.2 shows the possible AutoScaleMode values.

TABLE 15.2    **AutoScaleMode** Enumeration Values

| Value | Description |
| --- | --- |
| Dpi | Scale relative to the resolution (96 DPI, 120 DPI, etc.) |
| Font | Scale relative to the dimensions of the font being used |
| Inherit | Scale according to the base class AutoScaleMode value |
| None | No automatic scaling is performed |

AutoScaleDimensions sets the dimensions (via a SizeF structure) that the control was originally designed to. This could refer to a font size or the DPI.

## Using Containers

Containers are .NET controls designed to hold other controls. You can use containers in conjunction with the Anchor and Dock control properties to create intricate design scenarios. Although there are various container controls, the ones most applicable to control layout are the FlowLayoutPanel, TableLayoutPanel, and SplitContainer classes.

Both the TableLayoutPanel and the FlowLayoutPanel classes derive from the more generic Panel class. The Panel class provides very high-level capabilities for grouping controls. This is beneficial from a placement perspective because you can aggregate a bunch of controls into one group by positioning them within a panel. This way, you can act on them as a group; for instance, disabling a panel control will disable all of its child controls. The TableLayoutPanel and FlowLayoutPanel build on that functionality by also providing the capability to dynamically affect the positioning of their child controls.

### The TableLayoutPanel

Consider a series of labels and text boxes for entering address information. They are typically arrayed in a column-and-row fashion. The TableLayoutPanel is ideal for implementing this behavior because it automatically forces the column and row assignment that you make for each of the controls. Figure 15.11 shows a series of label and text box controls embedded within a TableLayoutPanel. Notice that resizing the form (and thus the panel, which is docked to fill the form interior) causes the panel's controls to auto-adjust their alignment.

If an item within one of the cells extends beyond the cell's boundaries, it will automatically overflow within the cell. This provides you with the same layout capabilities that HTML provides for web browser–based interfaces.

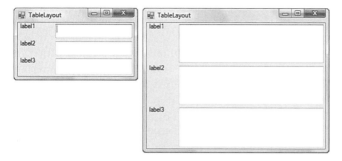

FIGURE 15.11   The **TableLayoutPanel**.

---

**NOTE**

When a control is added to a TableLayoutPanel, it is decorated with five additional properties: Cell, Column, Row, ColumnSpan, and RowSpan. These properties can be used to change the control's row/column position within the layout panel at runtime. The ColumnSpan and RowSpan properties are used the same way as their namesakes in the HTML world. In .NET, controls that imbue other controls with additional properties are called *extender providers*.

---

### The FlowLayoutPanel

The FlowLayoutPanel has a simpler layout algorithm: Items are ordered either vertically or horizontally by wrapping control sets across rows or columns as needed. The two screens shown in Figure 15.12 illustrate the effect of resizing a flow layout panel containing a series of radio buttons.

FIGURE 15.12   The **FlowLayoutPanel**.

### The SplitContainer

The SplitContainer control is a much enhanced alternative to the original Splitter control that was first included with .NET 1.0/1.1/Visual Studio 2003. This control represents the marriage of two panels and a splitter; the splitter separates the two panels either horizontally or vertically and allows a user to manually adjust the space (in the horizontal or vertical) that each panel consumes within the overall container.

Figure 15.13 shows the versatility of this control; two split containers, one embedded within a panel hosted by the other, are used to provide both vertical and horizontal resizing capabilities for the panels on a form (panel 2 isn't visible because it is the panel functioning as the container for the split container with panels 3 and 4). By dragging the split line to the right of panel 1, you can increase or decrease the horizontal real estate it occupies on the form. The same is true for the split line between panel 3 and panel 4: Dragging this will adjust the ratio of space that both panels vertically occupy in relation to one another.

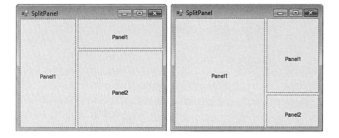

FIGURE 15.13   Resizing with the **SplitContainer**: a horizontal **SplitContainer** embedded in a vertical **SplitContainer**.

### The ToolStripContainer

Many applications support the capability to drag and dock a toolbar, menu, and the like to any side of a form: top, bottom, left, or right. Visual Studio itself is an example of just such an application. By grabbing and dragging a Visual Studio toolbar, you can reposition it, for example, to the left side of the form. The ToolStripContainer control enables this functionality in your applications as well; it is a combination of four panels, each positioned on the four different edges of the containing form. These panels are used to host ToolStrip controls (more on these in a bit) and—at runtime—allow users to move tool strips within and between the four panels.

> **NOTE**
>
> Although the ToolStripContainer provides a convenient vehicle for snapping tool strips to the sides of a form, there is unfortunately no built-in support for "floating" tool strips.

The design experience is simple: You can shuffle controls around to the four different panels depending on where you want them positioned within the parent form. Figure 15.14 shows a ToolStripContainer in design mode. The smart tag offers up control over the visibility of the top, left, right, and bottom panels. Each panel is hidden by default. You can click on any of the arrows on the sides of the container to expand the corresponding panel and give you room to place tool strips within the panel.

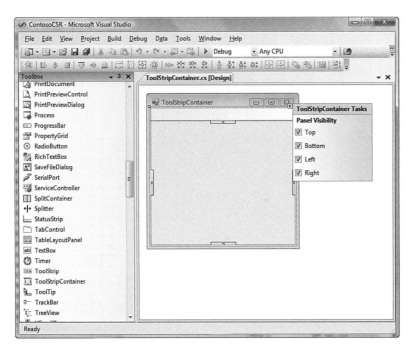

FIGURE 15.14  **ToolStripContainer** in design mode.

Although it is convenient to be able to place items in a ToolStripContainer within the designer, the real benefit that you get from the control is the automatic support for dragging and dropping between panels at runtime. This means that, without writing a single line of layout or positioning code, you have enabled functionality that allows users to place their menus or toolbars wherever they want within the form. Figure 15.15 shows a toolbar, hosted in a ToolStripContainer, that has been redocked from the top panel to the left panel at runtime.

FIGURE 15.15   A toolbar repositioned within a **ToolStripContainer**.

Multiple ToolStrip controls can also be stacked within any of the given panels in the ToolStripContainer. Figure 15.16 shows multiple command bars stacked within the rightmost panel. As noted later in the chapter, a control's z-order dictates its place within the stack.

FIGURE 15.16   Multiple toolbars stacked within the same panel.

---

**NOTE**

The sharing of space—vertically or horizontally—within a tool strip container is sometimes referred to as *rafting*: The tool strip controls are free to float anywhere within the panel.

---

There are a few other intricacies involved with form/control layout and positioning, but we have now covered the basics. With these concepts in hand and a general design for your form, you can start using the Windows Forms Designer.

## Control Appearance and Behavior

A control's appearance is set via the same set of basic properties used to control form appearance: items such as ForeColor, BackColor, and Font all make an appearance on most controls.

### Visual Styles

One item of interest, however, is the capability for a control to automatically alter its appearance to conform to the currently selected "Desktop Theme" if running on Windows XP or Windows Vista. This capability is enabled by a call to the Application.Enable VisualStyles method. This line of code is automatically included for you by default as the first line in the Main method. This location is ideal because it must be called before the controls in the application are actually created. If you remove the call, you can easily compare the appearance with and without the effects enabled. Figure 15.17 shows a form without visual styles enabled (left) alongside one with visual styles enabled (right).

FIGURE 15.17    The effects of **Application.EnableVisualStyles**.

### Tab Order

By default, the order in which the controls on a form receive focus (tab order) is the same as the order in which they were placed on the form. To explicitly set the tab order for all the controls on a form, the IDE has a tab order selection mode.

To enter tab order selection mode, select View, Tab Order from the menu. The Windows Forms Designer will annotate every control on the form with a number. This number represents that control's position within the overall tab order for the form. To set the tab order that you want, just click sequentially on the controls; their tab order number will automatically change as you click.

### ToolTips

ToolTips are small "balloons" that display text as a user moves his or her cursor over a control. Typically, they are used to provide helpful hints or descriptions of a control's purpose, action, and so on. ToolTips are implemented with the ToolTip class and can be assigned to controls at design time.

The ToolTip class is an example of an *extender provider* (see the previous note on extender providers in our discussion on the TableLayoutPanel control). When you add a ToolTip component to a form, every control on the form will now implement a ToolTip property that is used to assign a ToolTip to that specific control.

For illustration, if you wanted to add a ToolTip to a ToolStrip button, you would first drag the ToolTip component over to the form from the Toolbox. You would then select the ToolStrip button that you want to add the ToolTip to, and you would set its ToolTip property to reference the ToolTip instance on your form.

## Working with `ToolStrip` Controls

Many of the standard, core visual elements of a form will be realized with `ToolStrip` controls. A `ToolStrip` control functions as a container for other controls that derive from `ToolStripItem`; it can host various types of controls: buttons, combo boxes, labels, separators, text boxes, and even progress bars. The `ToolStrip` class itself is used to directly implement toolbars on a form and also functions as a base class for the `StatusStrip` control and the `MenuStrip` control.

`ToolStrip` controls come with an impressive list of built-in capabilities. They intrinsically support, for example, dragging an item from one tool strip to another, dynamically reordering and truncating items in the tool strip as users resize the strip or its parent form, and fully supporting different OS themes and rendering schemes.

All the different flavors of the `ToolStrip` control have some common traits:

▶ A design-time smart tag provides quick and easy access to common commands.

▶ In-place editing of child controls is supported (for example, a point-and-click interface is offered for adding, removing, and altering items within the `ToolStrip`, `StatusStrip`, or `MenuStrip`).

▶ An Items Collection Editor dialog box allows you to gain finer control over child control properties and also allows for add/reorder/remove actions against the child controls.

▶ Tool strips support a pluggable rendering model; you can change the visual renderer of a tool strip to a canned rendering object or to a custom object to obtain absolute control over the appearance of the tool strip.

From the initial form design, you know that you will need menus, toolbars, and status bars, so the `ToolStrip` control and its descendants will play a crucial role.

### Creating a Menu

`MenuStrip` controls enable you to visually construct a form's main menu system. Dragging and dropping this control from the Toolbox onto the blank form will automatically dock the menu strip to the top of the form (see Figure 15.18).

After you place this control on the form, selecting the `MenuStrip` control will activate the smart tag glyph (smart tags are covered in Chapter 8, "Working with Visual Studio's Productivity Aids"). Clicking on the smart tag allows you to quickly do three things:

▶ Automatically insert standard items onto the menu

▶ Change the menu's `RenderMode`, `Dock`, and `GripStyle` properties

▶ Edit the menu items

Leveraging the capability to automatically equip a menu strip with a standard set of menus shaves a few minutes of design time off the manual approach. Figure 15.19 shows the result.

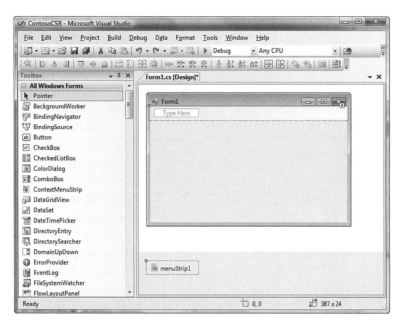

FIGURE 15.18    A menu positioned on the form.

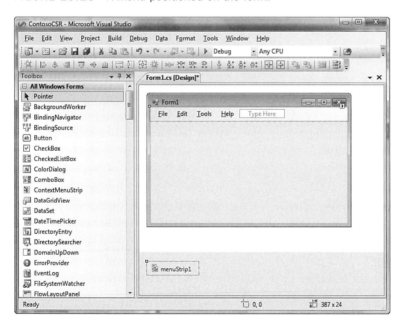

FIGURE 15.19    Menu with standard items.

Not only has the designer inserted the standard File, Edit, Tools, and Help top-level menu items, but it also has inserted subitems below each menu. Table 15.3 indicates the exact menu structure that results from using the menu's Insert Standard Items feature.

TABLE 15.3    Standard Menu Items

| Main Menu | Menu Items |
| --- | --- |
| File | New |
| | Open |
| | Save |
| | Save As |
| | Print |
| | Print Preview |
| | Exit |
| Edit | Undo |
| | Redo |
| | Cut |
| | Copy |
| | Paste |
| | Select All |
| Tools | Customize |
| | Options |
| Help | Contents |
| | Index |
| | Search |
| | About |

If you want to manually add menu items into the menu strip, you can use the placeholder block within the menu strip labeled with the text "Type Here." Every time you type in the placeholder block, additional placeholders become visible, and a menu item is added to the menu strip (see Figure 15.20).

**Creating a Toolbar**

The next item up for inclusion on the form is a toolbar. Toolbars in .NET 2.0 and later are implemented directly with ToolStrip controls. As mentioned before, `ToolStrip` controls can host various child controls; each inherits from the `ToolStripItem` base class. Figure 15.21 shows the controls that can be implemented inside a tool strip.

In fact, the interactive layout features of the tool strip work the same way as the menu strip: Dragging the control onto the form will result in a blank `ToolStrip` control docked to the top of the form just under the existing menu control, and you can quickly add a roster of standard items to the tool strip by using its smart tag and selecting Insert Standard Items.

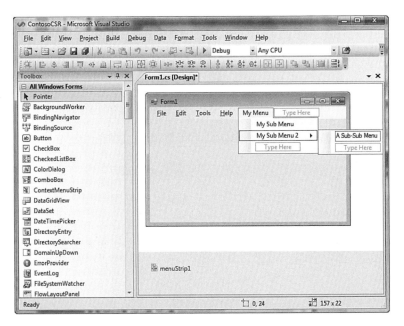

FIGURE 15.20 Manually adding menu items.

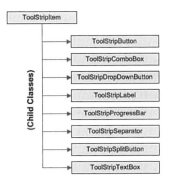

FIGURE 15.21 Classes inheriting from **ToolStripItem**.

---

**NOTE**

Controls use the concept of *z-order* to determine their "depth" on the form. If two controls occupy the same space on a form, the control's individual z-order determines which of the two controls is on top and which is on the bottom. You control this layering in the IDE by right-clicking a control and using the Send to Back and Bring to Front menu commands.

Z-order plays an important role in the placement of docked controls. Docked controls are arrayed in increasing order of their z index on the form. For instance, if you select the ToolStrip and issue the Send to Back command, the order of the MenuStrip and ToolStrip containers will be altered to place the ToolStrip first (at the top of the form) and the MenuStrip second (just below the ToolStrip instance).

Figure 15.22 shows the in-progress form with the added ToolStrip control.

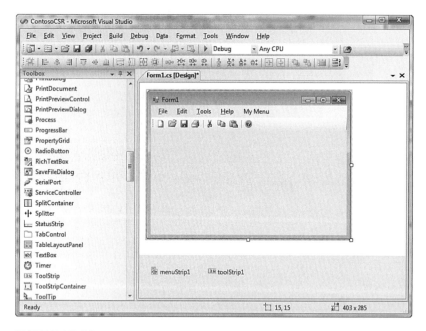

FIGURE 15.22    The main form with a complete menu and toolbar.

If you wanted to enable users to drag and drop the toolbar or menu onto one of the form's four sides, you would use the ToolStripContainer. In fact, there is a shortcut option here: You can take any of the ToolStrip controls currently on the form and add them to a ToolStripContainer with just a couple of clicks of the mouse. One of the items available via a tool strip's smart tag is the command Embed in a ToolStripContainer. If you issue this command against the toolbar that you just added to the sample form, Visual Studio will do two things for you: It will add a ToolStripContainer to the form, and it will place the selected ToolStrip into the container, specifically, in the top panel of the ToolStripContainer.

**Creating a Status Bar**

Status bars provide the user feedback on an application's current status, progress within an action, details in context with an object selected on a form, and so on. The StatusStrip control provides this functionality in starting with .NET 2.0/Visual Studio 2005, and it supplants the StatusBar control found in previous versions.

As with the other `ToolStrip` descendants, the `StatusStrip` control functions as a container; its capability to host labels in addition to progress bars, drop-downs, and split buttons makes it a much more powerful control than the `StatusBar`.

Figure 15.23 shows the fictional Contoso CSR form with a `StatusStrip` docked at the bottom of the form. In design mode, you see a drop-down button that holds a selection for each of the four supported child controls. For the purposes of this demonstration prototype, add a label control to report general application status and an additional label and progress bar to be used if you run into any long-running retrieval or edit operations.

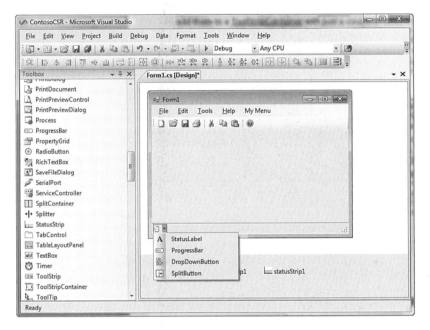

FIGURE 15.23    **StatusStrip** in design mode.

By default, child controls will be added in a left-to-right flow layout pattern within the `StatusStrip` pattern. With just six clicks (two per item), you can add these controls to the strip. The in-place editing capabilities are great for quickly building out the look and feel of the strip; for greater control of the strip's child controls, you can use the Items Collection Editor dialog box.

---

**TIP**

By right-clicking on any of the `StatusStrip` child controls and selecting Convert To, you can quickly change the type of the control. For instance, if you have a label control currently on the strip but you really want a drop-down button, you right-click the label and select Convert To, DropDownButton. This saves you the hassle of deleting the control and adding a new one.

---

**Editing the StatusStrip Items**  You use the StatusStrip's smart tag and select Edit Items to launch the Items Collection Editor dialog box. The editor provides direct access to all the hosted control's properties and also allows you to edit, delete, and reorder items within the status strip (see Figure 15.24).

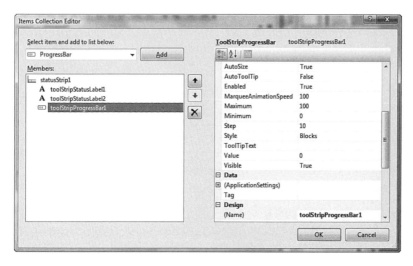

FIGURE 15.24   The Items Collection Editor.

By tweaking some properties here, you can improve the layout and appearance of your items. Figure 15.25 shows the default layout of the controls you added; ideally, you want the progress bar and its label control to sit at the far right of the status strip and the status label to sit at the far left to consume any remaining space.

FIGURE 15.25   Default **StatusStrip** items.

To make this happen, you need to set the Spring property to True for the leftmost label. This will cause the label to expand and contract to fill the available space on the status strip. Next, set its TextAlignment property to situate the text to the left of the label region and change the Text property to something more appropriate.

Figure 15.26 shows the fruits of our labor.

FIGURE 15.26   The final **StatusStrip** look and feel.

## Displaying Data

So far, we have only touched on form elements that provide the basic framework user navigation, status, commands, and so on. However, the capability to access, display, and edit data from an underlying data store (relational or otherwise) is the real value of an application like the fictional Contoso CSR application. We'll touch on the details of working with databases in the next chapter; here, we will describe some of the basic controls used to display data in a form.

### Hierarchical Data

The TreeView control is ideal for presenting data with hierarchical relationships and is thus a good candidate for housing the list of order records (which can be grouped by different criteria). First, add a SplitContainer control. This will partition the leftover interior space in the form into two discrete panels. Yet another panel will house the search function for orders; this will be docked to the top of the left split panel. A TreeView will dock-fill the remainder of this leftmost panel, and the right panel will house the data fields (text boxes, labels, radio buttons, and so on) for an individual CSR record.

TreeView controls present data as a list of nodes; each node can serve as a parent for additional nodes. Typically, with applications that front a database, you would build the contents of the TreeView by binding to a resultset from the database, or by programmatically looping through the resultset and adding to the TreeView's node list through its API. But you also have control over the TreeView content in the designer by launching the TreeNode Editor.

**The TreeNode Editor**   The TreeNode Editor (see Figure 15.27) is a dialog box that acts much the same as the Items Collection Editor examined previously. It enables you to add, edit, and remove items from the TreeView control. You launch the editor dialog box by selecting Edit Nodes from the TreeView's smart tag.

FIGURE 15.27   Using the designer to edit notes in the tree view.

Using the Add Root and Add Child buttons, you can insert new nodes into the tree's data structure at any given nesting level. Figure 15.27 shows manually inserted nodes with test data so that you can get an idea of what the order list would look like using the company as a parent node and order instances as child nodes under the corresponding company. Each item, or node, in the `TreeView` consists of two parts: an image and text. The image is optional; if you want to attach an icon to a node, you start by first assigning an `ImageList` control to the `TreeView` control.

**Using an ImageList**    `ImageList` controls function as an image provider for other controls. They maintain a collection of `Image` objects that are referenced by their ordinal position or key within the collection. Any control that provides an `ImageList` property can reference an `ImageList` component and use its images. `ListView`, `ToolStrip`, and `TreeView` are some examples of controls that can leverage the `ImageList` component.

> **NOTE**
>
> Visual Studio 2008 ships with a large library of images that you can use with the `TreeView` or any other control that requires these types of standard graphics such as toolbars and menus. By default, the image files are placed in `C:\Program Files\Microsoft Visual Studio 9.0\Common7\VS2008ImageLibrary`.

An `ImageList` doesn't have a visual presence on a form; in other words, you can't see the `ImageList` itself. Its sole use is as a behind-the-scenes component that feeds images to other controls. Dropping an `ImageList` onto the designer will put an instance of the component in the component tray (see Figure 15.28). You can then use the Images Collection Editor dialog box to add, edit, and remove the images hosted by the component. Changing the images associated with the image list will automatically change the images used by any controls referencing the `ImageList`.

Figure 15.29 shows a few images added for use in the `TreeView` control. To enable the `TreeView` to use these images, you have to do two things:

1. Assign the `TreeView.ImageList` property to point to the instance of the `ImageList` component (in this case, imageList1).

2. Set the image associated with a node either programmatically or via the TreeNode Editor dialog box.

With the `ImageList` component in place and the `TreeView` dropped in the `SplitContainer`'s left panel, the form is almost there from a design perspective. The remaining piece is the series of fields that will display the data for a record selected in the `TreeView` control.

You could add this piece by just dragging a bunch of text boxes and labels over into a `TableLayoutPanel` and then docking the whole mess in the open `SplitContainer` panel. But because you really want to treat this as one cohesive unit to simplify positioning, eventual data binding, and so on, you will instead create a user control for displaying a CSR record.

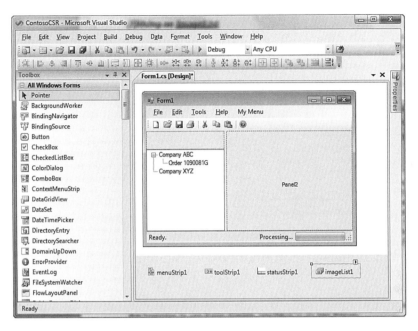

FIGURE 15.28   An **ImageList** added to the Forms Designer.

FIGURE 15.29   The Images Collection Editor.

### Tabular Data

The DataGridView control is the premium Visual Studio control for displaying data in a
tabular format. It provides a row/column format for displaying data from a wide variety of
data sources. Figure 15.30 shows a DataGridView with its smart tag menu opened; the
smart tag menu provides fast access to the column properties of the grid control and also
allows you to directly bind the DataGridView to a data source.

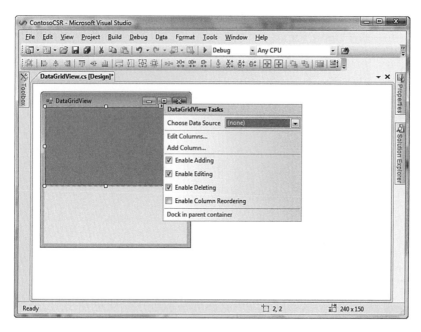

FIGURE 15.30    The **DataGridView** control.

**Data Sources**    The DataGridView control supports various possible data sources. For instance, scenarios like displaying name/value pairs from a collection are supported, in addition to mainstream support for datasets returned from a relational data store. If you select a data source for the grid, a column will be added to the grid for every column that appears in the data source, and the row data will automatically be provided inside the DataGridView control.

Data can be displayed in the grid control in an "unbound" mode as well; using the grid's row/column API, you can programmatically define the structure of the grid and add data to it at runtime.

**Cell Types**    Each individual cell in a DataGridView functions as if it is an embedded control. Each cell can express the underlying data that it contains in various ways; check boxes, drop-downs, links, buttons, and text boxes are all supported cell types. In addition to the data visualization possibilities, each cell also has its own set of events that can be hooked within your code. For example, you can hook the mouse enter and leave events for a specific cell.

We cover this control in depth in Chapter 18, "Working with Databases."

# Creating Your Own Controls

If none of the stock .NET controls will meet your specific needs, you can create your own controls for use on a Windows Form in three ways:

▶ You can subclass an existing control and modify or extend its behavior and appearance.

▶ You can create a user control by compositing together two or more existing controls.

▶ You can create a custom control from scratch, implementing your own visuals and behavior.

## Subclassing an Existing Control

Subclassing an existing control is the best approach if your needs are only slightly different from one of the standard .NET Framework controls. By inheriting from an existing control class, you are riding on top of its behavior and appearance; it's up to you to then add the specialized code to your new control class.

For example, suppose that you wanted a text box that would turn red anytime a numeric (that is, nonalphabetic) character was entered. This is easy to do with just a few lines of code sitting in the TextBox control's TextChanged event, but consolidating this behavior into its own class will provide a reuse factor.

You start by adding a new user control to the project. User controls actually inherit from the UserControl class; because you want to inherit from the TextBox class, you will need to change the class definition by using the code editor. After you do that, you can place the new component on a form and use its functionality.

### Working with an Inherited Control

Because TextBox already has a UI, you don't need to do anything with regard to the appearance of the control. In fact, it will work just like any other text box control within the Windows Forms Designer (see Figure 15.31).

The Properties window for the control behaves as expected, and double-clicking on the control will immediately take you to an open code editor window. In short, the design-time experience remains fully functional and requires no effort on the part of the developer.

## Designing a User Control

A user control is technically the same as any other class that you would author as a developer; because a user control has a visual aspect to it, Visual Studio provides a designer, just as with Windows Forms, to help in the drag-and-drop creation of the control.

User controls are composite controls; that is, they are constructed from one or more existing .NET controls. As with a derived control, their user interfaces inherit from the native controls they are composed of, making them simple to build and use in the designer.

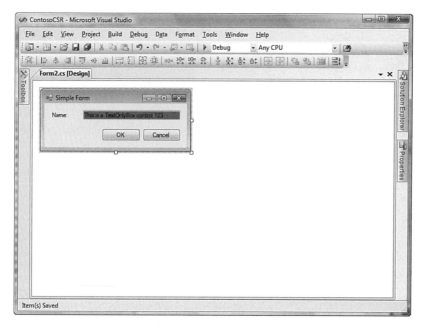

FIGURE 15.31    A derived control on a form.

There are two approaches to the user control creation process: You can create a separate Windows Control Library project, or you could simply add a user control class to an existing Windows Forms project.

Creating a separate project would allow the user control to live in its own assembly. If it is a separate assembly, you can treat the user control as the quintessential black box, giving you greater flexibility from a source control perspective and allowing you to share the control among multiple projects. For production scenarios, this is clearly the best route. However, for simple prototyping work, as you are doing here with the CSR form application, the ease and simplicity of just adding a new class to the existing project make this approach preferable to using the separate project approach. The class would live inside the same namespace as the form class.

If you were ever in a position to transition from prototyping to actual production development, nothing would preclude you from refactoring the control by simply copying the user control class file and embedding it in a separate control library project.

As soon as you add the user control class to the project, you are presented with the User Control Designer (see Figure 15.32). The designer works in exactly the same way as the Windows Forms Designer; to build the user control, you drag components or controls from the Toolbox onto its surface.

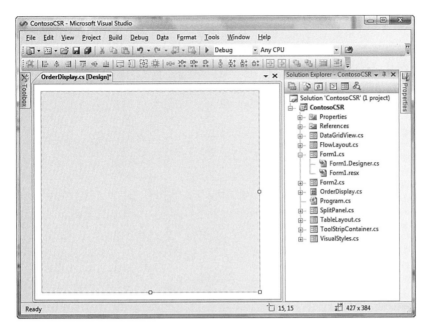

FIGURE 15.32   The User Control Designer.

### Adding Controls

Obviously, the controls that you use to build your composite control will entirely depend on its envisioned functionality. As an example, to create an order display control, you need to think about the underlying data structure of an order. An order record might contain the following:

▶ An order number

▶ A series of dates that capture the date the order was placed, date the order was shipped, and so on

▶ A list of items included on the order

▶ Billing information and shipping address

▶ Miscellaneous comments

Because this is a lot of information to try to cram onto one screen, you can turn to the TabControl. A tab control is another general-purpose container control that allows you to organize content across several pages that are accessed via tabs. Within each tab, you can leverage the TableLayoutPanel and implement most of the order fields with simple label and text box pairs.

The whole process of getting these controls into the user control works identically to the Windows Forms Designer: You drag and drop the controls from the Toolbox onto the user control design surface. Figure 15.33 shows the OrderDisplay user control with its user interface completed.

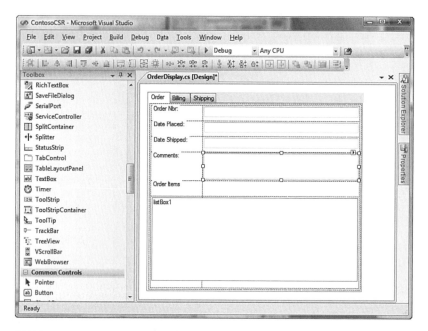

FIGURE 15.33   Designing a user control.

### Embedding the User Control

Now that you have a completed design for your user control, the only remaining step is to embed the control into your primary form. If you compile the project, Visual Studio will automatically recognize the user control class and include an entry for the control in the Toolbox. From there, you are just a drag and drop away from implementing the OrderDisplay control.

In Figure 15.34, you can see the OrderDisplay item in the Toolbox and the results of dragging it onto the form surface.

## Creating a Custom Control

Custom controls represent the ultimate in extensibility because they are built from scratch. As a result, they are relatively hard to develop because they require you to worry not only about functionality but also about every single aspect of the control's visual appearance. Because the physical user interface of the custom control needs to be drawn 100% by custom code, a steep learning curve is associated with authoring a custom control.

Because much of the work that goes into creating a custom control is at the code level, we won't try to tackle this subject with any useful degree of detail in this book. You should note, however, that the process starts the same way as with other control options: Visual Studio has a custom control project item template; adding this to your project will give you a baseline of code to start with. From there, it's up to you.

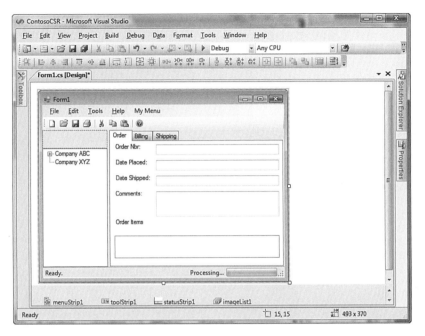

FIGURE 15.34   The user control in the Toolbox and on the form.

---
**NOTE**

The OnPaint event is where you place the code to draw your control's user interface. Although so-called "owner draw" controls can involve complex drawing code, the good news is that the Windows Forms Designer will leverage whatever code you place in the OnPaint event in order to render the control at design time. This means that you can still rely on the Windows Forms Designer to provide you with a WYSIWYG experience even with custom controls.

---

# Summary

In this chapter, we described the various design-time capabilities of the Windows Forms Designer tool. Windows Forms are a powerful presentation layer technology, and Visual Studio 2008 provides an array of tools for quickly building impressive, rich user interfaces based on this technology.

The role of the Windows Forms Designer, the Toolbox, and the Properties window were introduced in the context of delivering a modern, well-thought-out, standards-based user interface for a .NET Windows application. Using the tools documented here, you can wring the most out of your forms development experience.

# CHAPTER 16

# Creating Richer, Smarter User Interfaces

With .NET 3.0, Microsoft delivered a brand-new set of technologies for powering the presentation layer in your applications: the Windows Presentation Foundation (WPF). WPF was designed from the ground up to leverage the strengths of both the Windows Forms development world and the Web Forms development world. At the same time, WPF attempts to overcome many of the obstacles that developers face when trying to build rich, compelling user interfaces that involve media and highly customized user interfaces, and that exploit all the horsepower available in modern CPUs and graphics processors.

WPF is intended to be a unifying platform with built-in, first-class support for data binding, audio, video, and both 2D and 3D graphics. Because WPF likely represents a significant learning curve for both new and experienced developers, we will spend some time up front in this chapter discussing the basics before diving into the real target: how to use the Visual Studio WPF Designer tool (previously known by its code name "Cider") to build high-octane user interfaces for your Windows applications.

## The Windows Presentation Foundation Platform

As a brand-new presentation layer framework, WPF brings a lot of new concepts and new coding territory with it—and can represent a fairly significant learning curve for developers. But let's take a brief look at the overall architecture of the WPF platform, and then dissect the programming model.

Physically, WPF is implemented with a series of three .DLLs:

- ▶ WindowsBase.dll

- ▶ PresentationFramework.dll

- ▶ PresentationCore.dll

Every presentation layer framework has to eventually paint pixels onto a screen, and WPF is no different. Implemented within its binaries is a composition and rendering engine, which talks to your hardware through DirectX. In addition to the rendering layers, there is also obviously a rich programming model that is implemented with deep support for things such as layout, containership (the capability for one element to contain another), and events/message dispatches. In short, it does all the heavy lifting to ensure that some very complicated user interface scenarios can be rendered on the screen with enough performance to appeal to a wide range of solution scenarios.

Figure 16.1 shows the logical architecture of the various WPF components. The actual rendering "engine" is contained within the Media Integration Layer component; PresentationCore handles interop with the Media Integration Layer, and PresentationFramework contains all the other magic necessary to make WPF successful as an end-to-end platform such as layout, data binding, and event notifications.

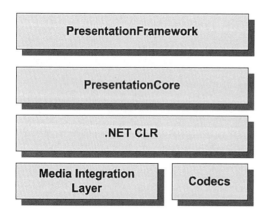

FIGURE 16.1    The components of a generic presentation layer framework.

**NOTE**

Most of WPF itself is implemented in managed .NET code. The exception is the Media Integration Layer. When it comes to rendering the UI to the screen, WPF needs to optimize for performance over nearly all other concerns, and thus the Media Integration Layer is implemented as native code.

All of these WPF components work in concert to deliver an impressive laundry list of improvements to the state of the art with regard to presentation layer design, construction, and runtime support with .NET. Here is a small sample:

▶ **Media**—WPF supports 2D and 3D graphics, as well as WMV, MPEG, and AVI video.

▶ **Data binding**—WPF was built from the start to fully support the entire spectrum of data binding scenarios, up to and including LINQ.

▶ **Windows Forms Interoperability**—WPF applications can host WinForms components and vice versa. This is comforting because it means developers won't need to abandon the hard-won knowledge that comes with WinForms programming for many years.

▶ **Document Support**—WPF has several native constructs for building document-centric applications. For instance, there is a `DocumentReader` class for displaying fixed-format documents, and a `FlowDocumentReader` class for displaying documents with a dynamic layout. Think of a newspaper article, for instance, that will automatically repaginate while remaining true to the column structure.

▶ **Animation**—Developers can create storyboard-based animations, and specify animation triggers and timers.

▶ **Control "look and feel"**—Controls in WPF have their appearance controlled by a template, which developers can replace or change to fully customize nearly every aspect of a control's "chrome."

▶ **Text**—There is rich typography support in WPF. Developers can manipulate a slew of font attributes (kerning; effects such as glow, drop-shadows, and motion blur; auto line spacing; etc.), and WPF renders its text using ClearType technology.

During the initial beta cycles, Microsoft produced a series of prototype applications to showcase the new technologies in .NET 3.0, including WPF. Figure 16.2 shows a screenshot from the healthcare prototype. Although a static shot in black and white doesn't do the application much justice, you can get a good sense for the possibilities: The user interface for this application would have been extremely difficult to implement using Windows Forms technology.

For the most part, developers are free to not worry so much about the low-level architectural details of WPF; the programming model—and the tools which help us leverage that model—is where most developers will focus their energies.

## Programming Model

The WPF class library consists of approximately 1,600 public types and more than 3,500 classes. As such, it has a considerably larger API surface than either ASP.NET or Windows Forms. As you would expect from a .NET class library, all of these classes can trace their ancestry back to `System.Object`. In addition, most WPF classes are based on so-called base elements: the `UIElement`, `FrameworkElement`, `ContentElement`, and `FrameworkContentElement` classes. These classes are responsible for basic item presentation and layout capabilities and are contained within the `System.Windows` namespace.

FIGURE 16.2 A WPF-based healthcare prototype application.

In addition to these four base element classes, there are a few other important base classes that drive a lot of the functionality found in WPF:

- **Visual**—This class is the core rendering unit within WPF; UIElement inherits from Visual as do the higher level classes such as Button.

- **DispatcherObject**—This class implements the WPF threading model.

- **Control**—This is the base class for controls in WPF.

- **Application**—The Application class encapsulates all WPF applications; it provides application lifetime services, including the basic concepts of Run (to start an application) and Exit (to quit an application).

As you would expect, the WPF class library also provides all the major controls that you would typically find in a Windows application such as buttons, labels, list boxes, and text boxes.

The following snippet shows a WPF button control being instantiated, and the text "Push Me" is assigned to the button. Note that the control constructs are all familiar but that the actual object model is slightly different; the Button object in WPF does not have a .Text property as we would expect from an ASP.NET or WinForms button. Instead, it exposes a .Content property.

```
System.Windows.Controls.Button btn = new Button();
btn.Content = "Push Me";
```

Besides procedural code like that shown here, WPF also allows us to create and manipulate objects in a declarative fashion using markup—specifically, by using XAML.

### Extensible Application Markup Language (XAML)

Extensible Application Markup Language, or XAML, is an XML dialect that can be used to describe the structure of a WPF application's presentation layer (for example, control instantiation, appearance, and layout).

XAML is a new "language," and is the principal way in which the various WPF tools create objects and set properties in a declarative fashion. As such, it is tempting to compare XAML to HTML: it certainly fills a similar role in that XAML and HTML are both declarative ways to describe objects. But XAML is actually tightly coupled to the .NET Framework. In fact, XAML is really a generic way to create and manipulate .NET objects. WPF tools, such as the WPF designer in Visual Studio, happen to leverage XAML, but strictly speaking, XAML is not a part of WPF. You can write an entire XAML application, for instance, using only the managed code language of your choice. But because XAML, as a programming model, brings several important advancements to the scene, it is heavily leveraged by all the Microsoft and non-Microsoft tools in the WPF world, and beyond. For instance, it is also used by Windows Workflow Foundation to describe workflows.

Just as we did previously, let's create a `Button` object and assign some text to the button—but this time, let's do all the work with XAML:

```
<Button Content="Push Me"></Button>
```

Alternatively, we could write this code like this:

```
<Button>Push Me</Button>
```

**NOTE**

XAML functionality is a subset of what is possible in .NET code. Or, to put this another way, anything you can do in XAML you can do in code, but not everything done in code can be done in XAML.

In a typical WPF application, XAML will coexist with managed code through the same partial class paradigm introduced with ASP.NET. In other words, we may have a `MainForm.xaml` file with the look and feel of a window, and a `MainForm.xaml.vb` file which contains code that reacts to a user's input on that form. We'll see more of this in action a little later in this chapter when we take a close look at the WPF designer.

If XAML isn't necessary to create a WPF application, why is it desired? Given the fact that you can accomplish the necessary tasks to create UI objects in XAML *or* in managed code, why is XAML even in the picture? There are a few areas where the declarative syntax becomes tremendously important.

**Syntax Simplicity**    As is true with all XML-based languages, XAML is relatively easy for applications to parse and understand—at least when compared to managed code. In fact, WPF has been a released technology for quite a while now, and Visual Studio is just now receiving the necessary tools to be able to do WYSIWYG design with XAML. This hasn't stopped WPF development in its tracks because developers have either handcrafted their XAML in a text editor (to be sure, not the most efficient approach, but it is possible) or turned to other lightweight tools that sprung up in the absence of full-fledged Visual Studio support, such as XAMLPad. This has allowed tool vendors, including Microsoft, to rapidly release products into the market that understand XAML. Adobe Illustrator, for example, has an XAML plug-in that allows you to emit XAML, and of course Microsoft has not one but two design tools that read and write XAML: Expression Design and Expression Blend.

The boundary between XAML and code also turns out to be a nice dividing line between appearance and behavior. In this scenario, XAML is used to create the UI objects and the general look and feel of the application, while procedural code is used to implement the business logic, and to react to a user's input. This leads us directly to the other important advantage of XAML: collaboration.

**Collaboration**    If we separate appearance and behavior, we can also reap the benefits of improved collaboration among project team members—specifically, collaboration between designers and developers. Before WPF, designers would rely on "flat" bitmaps created with drawing programs, or would even rely on applications such as PowerPoint to mock up the user experience for an application. When that design is eventually handed off to the developer for implementation, there is an inherent disconnect: Programming tools don't understand 2D bitmaps or PowerPoint storyboards. They understand code and objects. And in the reverse direction, we have the same problem: Tools made for designers don't understand managed code. A developer can't implement a form in Visual Basic, for instance, and hand it back to a designer for review and tweaking.

And so developers are forced to re-create, as best they can, the vision delivered from the design team. This is a decidedly second-rate way to design and build applications. But with XAML, this situation changes dramatically. Because designers can now use tools that express their design in XAML (such as Microsoft Expression Blend), the developer can simply open that XAML file and provide the coding "goop" necessary to flesh out the desired features. In the process, we have 100% preserved the fidelity of the designers' original vision because the developer's tools are talking the same languae. We also have full collaboration in the other direction: Changes that a developer makes to the designer's XAML can be instantly reviewed and tweaked within the designer's tools. This simple concept—the sharing of a codebase and language between design and development roles and tools—proves to be a powerful argument for leveraging XAML in your applications.

Having said that, it is important to realize that WPF is a version 1.0 technology, and can't compete, on various levels, with the functionality offered by the extensive controls community and built-in controls offered by the Windows Forms technology. But WPF does shine in those applications for which a premium is placed on the user experience. For this reason, we say that WPF is intended for "Experience First" applications—applications that can benefit from the unprecedented ease with which designers and developers can work together to build stunning, highly visual applications.

Now that we have covered the basics of WPF, let's see how we can start writing WPF applications using Visual Studio 2008.

# Introducing the WPF Designer

We first introduced the WPF designer back in Chapter 6, "Introducing the Editors and Designers." Let's recap the basics, and then move on to a more involved discussion of the WPF designer.

The WPF designer is the tool in Visual Studio that provides the WYSIWYG design surface for building WPF windows. In many ways, it behaves just like the designers we use for web forms and Windows forms. But it is in fact a brand-new tool, with some subtle differences over its IDE brethren. To see the designer in action, let's create a new project in Visual Studio. The project template we want to select is WPF Application, and it is located in the Windows category on the New Project dialog (see Figure 16.3).

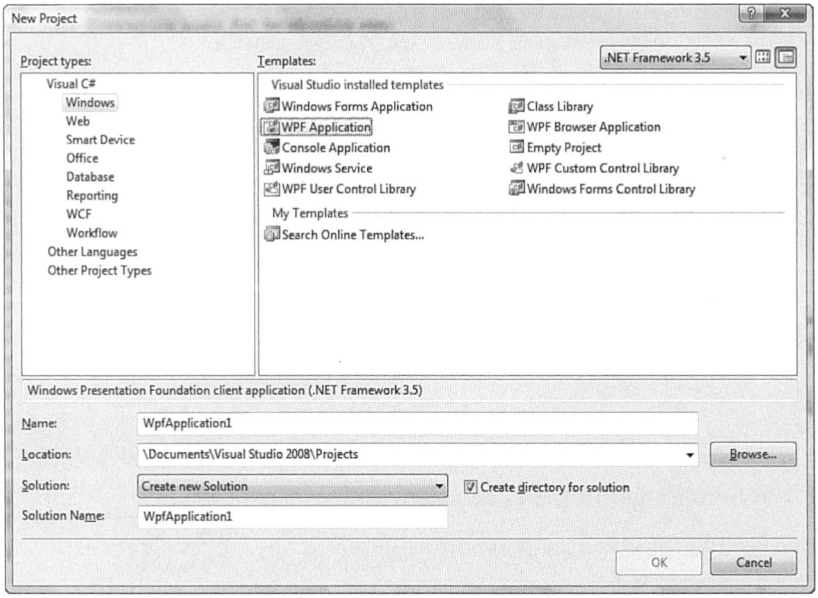

FIGURE 16.3    The WPF Application template.

This template will take care of adding the necessary WPF namespaces for us; the project will also include a file that implements the default window for the application:

Window1.xaml. Double-clicking on the Window1.xaml file will launch the designer, which is shown in Figure 16.4.

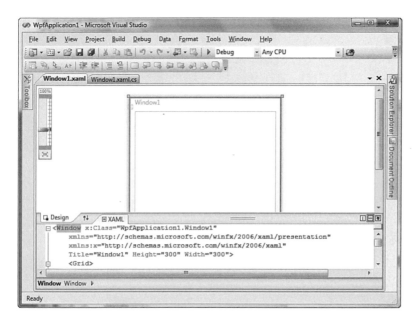

FIGURE 16.4    The WPF designer.

## XAML and Design Panes

The WPF designer offers two different views: the visual representation of the window, and the XAML that implements the window. You can make changes to the window and its controls by either editing the XAML or changing elements on the design surface. Either way, the designer keeps both panes in sync.

You can configure the position and layout of the XAML and design panes in the following ways:

- ▶ The Swap button swaps the positions of the XAML and design panes with one another.
- ▶ The Vertical Split button tiles the panes vertically.
- ▶ The Horizontal Split button tiles the panes horizontally.
- ▶ The Collapse/Expand Pane button minimizes or restores the bottom or leftmost pane (depending on the view mode you are in).

Figure 16.5 shows the location of these pane management buttons on the designer.

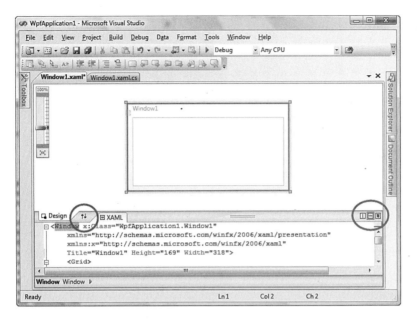

FIGURE 16.5    Configuring the WPF designer panes.

**TIP**

If you are lucky enough to have a multi-monitor setup, the vertical split view is particularly helpful because you can display your XAML code on one screen and your visual design surface on another.

We interact with the designer in the same way we interact with other design surfaces or code editors: Controls can be placed on the design pane from the toolbox and then manipulated, and we can use the XAML pane to handcraft or alter XAML (with complete IntelliSense and formatting).

For the most part, control placement and positioning works the same as it does in the Windows Forms designer. There are a few minor exceptions: The WPF designer has some unique visualizations for displaying snap lines and control sizing (see Figure 16.6).

### The Property Window

As expected, when you have a control selected in the designer, you can manipulate its attributes using the Properties window. The WPF Properties window has some surprises. For starters, it has only one display mode. Unlike in the WinForms or web property window, you can't sort the properties alphabetically—this window supports only the categorized view of properties. Additionally, the WPF Properties window has a header area that is used to name controls, or that you can use to search for properties of the control by typing in a search box. As you type, the window will automatically filter the property list to just those that match your search criteria. Figure 16.7 shows an image of the Properties window.

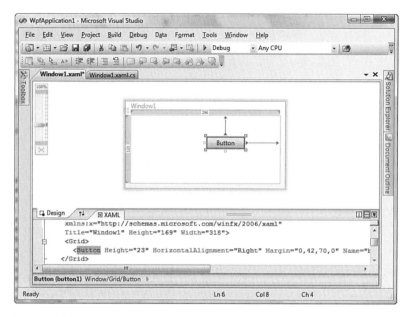

FIGURE 16.6    Sizing and positioning indicators.

FIGURE 16.7    The WPF designer Properties window.

**The Zoom Control**

One additional item is present with the WPF designer: a zoom slider control. Perched in the upper left of the design pane, this control can be used to zoom in or out on the current window from 10% to 2000% of the window's actual size. The shaded mark on the zoom control shows the 100% mark, and you can quickly toggle between 100% and 130% by clicking on the square button/region located at the bottom of the slider. Figure 16.8 shows the slider control, and Figure 16.9 shows our "Push Me" button at 3x magnification.

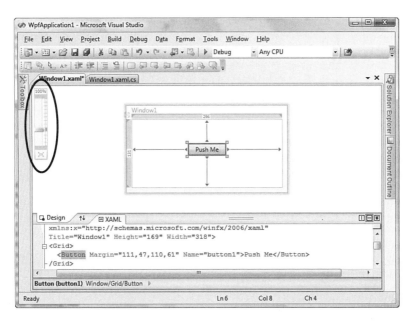

FIGURE 16.8   The zoom slider.

---

**TIP**

The zoom control is particularly useful when you have a complex form layout with a lot of snap lines and nested/layered controls amassed in a certain area. By zooming in on the area, you can get a crisp view of where things are positioned, and it becomes much easier to select or position the control you want instead of one of its neighbors. By zooming out, you can get a thumbnail look at your window to see how your overall look and feel is shaping up.

---

# Programming with WPF

With the basics out of the way, it's time for a more in-depth discussion of the various controls and technologies that you will typically encounter when creating a WPF-powered application. After firmly grounding ourselves in these topics, we will then move on to build a simple application, end to end, using the WPF designer.

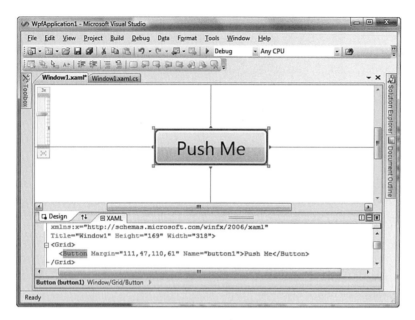

FIGURE 16.9    A button at 300% magnification.

## Layout

Because software needs to present controls and data on a screen for visual consumption by users, the layout—or how things are arranged onscreen—becomes an important design feature. Good layout systems not only have to enable developers to structure controls in a coherent fashion, but also need to be robust in terms of how they handle things such as window resizing and flow.

In WPF, layout is exercised through a set of container controls called panels. Each panel is uniquely suited for a specific layout scenario, and the capability to combine them with one another means that the layout system in WPF can handle a large number of different control organization scenarios. The key point to understand with panels is that, as containers, they are responsible for the positioning (and in some cases, the sizing) of all the controls placed within. This means that the individual child controls themselves don't need to be aware of the specific layout system they are participating in—which greatly simplifies the code and architecture.

Table 16.1 lists the available layout panel controls.

Let's examine these controls, and their subtypes, one by one.

### The Canvas Control

The Canvas control is unique among all the layout controls because it is the only one that actually performs no layout at all. It is functionally similar to the GroupBox control that you may have used with a Windows Forms project: Child objects that are placed within a Canvas control are placed using coordinates relative to the canvas itself. There is no automatic resizing, flow layout, or positioning done on behalf of the child controls by the canvas. If any such logic is needed, you will need to implement it yourself. This highlights the purpose of the Canvas control: providing the developer with the absolute control to position things as you want them positioned.

TABLE 16.1    The WPF Layout Panels

| Class | Description |
| --- | --- |
| Canvas | A container control with no built-in layout logic |
| DockPanel | Panel that enables docking of its child elements |
| Grid | A container control that allows child objects to be positioned within columns and rows |
| StackPanel | A container control that implements horizontal and vertical stacking behavior for its child controls |

In Figure 16.10, we have a Canvas control with four buttons in a unique arrangement. They are all positioned relative to the sides of the Canvas container in a diamond pattern.

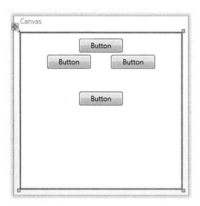

FIGURE 16.10    Elements docked using the DockPanel.

Here is the XAML:

```
<Window x:Class="ContosoAvalon.Canvas"
    xmlns="http://schemas.microsoft.com/winfx/2006/xaml/presentation"
    xmlns:x="http://schemas.microsoft.com/winfx/2006/xaml"
    Title="Canvas" Height="300" Width="300">
    <Canvas>
        <Button Canvas.Left="102" Canvas.Top="11" Height="23" Name="button1"
         Width="75">Button</Button>
        <Button Canvas.Left="47" Canvas.Top="38" Height="23" Name="button2"
         Width="75">Button</Button>
```

```
        <Button Canvas.Right="46" Canvas.Top="38" Height="23" Name="button3"
          Width="75">Button</Button>
        <Button Canvas.Left="102" Canvas.Top="99" Height="23" Name="button4"
          Width="75">Button</Button>
      </Canvas>
</Window>
```

Note that we have provided coordinates that are relative to a specified side of the canvas. If we resize the window, the buttons will move accordingly. Unless you absolutely need to manually specify control positions (as may be the case, for instance, if you are arranging controls in a nonstandard way or using controls to "draw" something in a window), it is recommended that you use one of the other panels that will automatically perform the layout you need.

### The DockPanel Control

Modern lines of business applications typically use some kind of docking arrangement for their controls: Toolbars may be docked at the top or sides of the window, a status bar may be docked at the bottom, and so forth. The DockPanel in WPF provides the capability to dock controls to one of the four sides of a window.

If we needed to create a window with a toolbar docked to the top and the left side of the window, with the remainder of the screen occupied by a canvas, we would do the following:

```
<Window x:Class="ContosoAvalon.DockPanel"
    xmlns="http://schemas.microsoft.com/winfx/2006/xaml/presentation"
    xmlns:x="http://schemas.microsoft.com/winfx/2006/xaml"
    Title="DockPanel" Height="300" Width="300">
    <DockPanel Name="dockPanel1">
        <ToolBar DockPanel.Dock="Top">
            <Button BorderBrush="Black">Button1</Button>
        </ToolBar>
        <ToolBar DockPanel.Dock="Left" MaxWidth="75">
            <Button BorderBrush="Black">Button2</Button>
        </ToolBar>
        <Canvas>
            <TextBlock>Canvas</TextBlock>
        </Canvas>
    </DockPanel>
</Window>
```

With the DockPanel, you can place more than one element in a certain dock position. Figure 16.11 shows six regions docked in a window: three of them are docked to the left, and three of them are docked to the top.

And here is the matching XAML:

```
<Window x:Class="ContosoAvalon.DockPanel"
    xmlns="http://schemas.microsoft.com/winfx/2006/xaml/presentation"
```

```
    xmlns:x="http://schemas.microsoft.com/winfx/2006/xaml"
    Title="DockPanel" Height="300" Width="300">
    <DockPanel Name="dockPanel1">
        <Button DockPanel.Dock="Left">Left #1</Button>
        <Button DockPanel.Dock="Left">Left #2</Button>
        <Button DockPanel.Dock="Left">Left #3</Button>
        <Button DockPanel.Dock="Top">Top #1</Button>
        <Button DockPanel.Dock="Top">Top #2</Button>
        <Button DockPanel.Dock="Top">Top #3</Button>
    </DockPanel>
</Window>
```

FIGURE 16.11    Multiple elements docked to the same side.

All the elements within a DockPanel are resized such that they stay docked in their designated position, and they entirely "fill" the window edge that they are docked to.

### The Grid Control

The Grid panel is used for row and column arrangements, similar to an HTML table or to the TableLayoutPanel control in WinForms.

One common use for the Grid control is with dialogs or data entry forms where labels and values exist side by side and row by row; we can use the columns in the grid to align items horizontally, and the rows to align items vertically.

Columns are created in a grid through the use of the Grid.ColumnDefinitions element. For example, this XAML snippet would create a grid with three columns:

```
<Grid>
    <Grid.ColumnDefinitions>
        <ColumnDefinition></ColumnDefinition>
        <ColumnDefinition></ColumnDefinition>
        <ColumnDefinition></ColumnDefinition>
    </Grid.ColumnDefinitions>
</Grid>
```

16

In a similar fashion, the `Grid.RowDefinitions` element defines the rows within a grid:

```
<Grid>
   <Grid.RowDefinitions>
      <RowDefinition></RowDefinition>
      <RowDefinition></RowDefinition>
      <RowDefinition></RowDefinition>
   </Grid.RowDefinitions>
</Grid>
```

The WPF designer also has interactive features that allow for row and column addition, deletion, and sizing. Figure 16.12 shows a two-column, six-row grid placed in a window. Note that the designer shows the grid lines demarcating the rows and columns, and that there is a shaded border area to the top and to the left of the `Grid` control. Not only does this border area show us the current size (width or height) of a column or row, but we also can use this border area to create new rows or columns by just clicking where we want to place the new element. We can also drag the row or column lines to increase or decrease the size of the row or column.

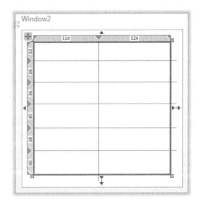

FIGURE 16.12   Working with a grid in the designer.

The dialog shown in Figure 16.13 is easily achieved using a `Grid` panel (the XAML is shown in Listing 16.1). Arguably, the `Grid` control is the most flexible and relevant of the panel controls for almost all layout scenarios. For this reason, when you add a new window project item to a WPF project, the window will by default already contain a `Grid` control.

FIGURE 16.13   Implementing a dialog with the Grid control.

LISTING 16.1   Implementing a Dialog with a **Grid** Panel

```
<Window x:Class="ContosoAvalon.Grid"
    xmlns="http://schemas.microsoft.com/winfx/2006/xaml/presentation"
    xmlns:x="http://schemas.microsoft.com/winfx/2006/xaml"
    Title="Grid" Height="300" Width="300">
  <Grid>
    <Grid.ColumnDefinitions>
      <ColumnDefinition Width="80*"></ColumnDefinition>
      <ColumnDefinition Width="*"></ColumnDefinition>
      <ColumnDefinition Width="*"></ColumnDefinition>
    </Grid.ColumnDefinitions>
    <Grid.RowDefinitions>
      <RowDefinition></RowDefinition>
      <RowDefinition></RowDefinition>
      <RowDefinition></RowDefinition>
      <RowDefinition></RowDefinition>
      <RowDefinition></RowDefinition>
      <RowDefinition></RowDefinition>
      <RowDefinition></RowDefinition>
      <RowDefinition></RowDefinition>
    </Grid.RowDefinitions>

    <Label Grid.Column="0" Grid.Row="0">Name:</Label>
    <Label Grid.Column="0" Grid.Row="1">Street:</Label>
    <Label Grid.Column="0" Grid.Row="2">City:</Label>
    <Label Grid.Column="0" Grid.Row="3">State:</Label>
    <Label Grid.Column="0" Grid.Row="4">Postal code:</Label>
    <Label Grid.Column="0" Grid.Row="5">Date Hired:</Label>

    <TextBox Margin="5,5" BorderBrush="Gray" Grid.Column="1" Grid.Row="0"
    Grid.ColumnSpan="2"></TextBox>
```

16

LISTING 16.1 Continued

```
      <TextBox Margin="5,5" BorderBrush="Gray" Grid.Column="1" Grid.Row="1"
      Grid.ColumnSpan="2"></TextBox>
      <TextBox Margin="5,5" BorderBrush="Gray" Grid.Column="1" Grid.Row="2"
      Grid.ColumnSpan="2"></TextBox>
      <ComboBox Margin="5,5" Grid.Column="1" Grid.Row="3"></ComboBox>
      <TextBox Margin="5,5" BorderBrush="Gray" Grid.Column="1" Grid.Row="4">
      </TextBox>
      <Label Grid.Column="1" Grid.Row="5">{Date}</Label>

      <Button Margin="5,5" Grid.Column="1" Grid.Row="6">OK</Button>
      <Button Margin="5,5" Grid.Column="2" Grid.Row="6">Cancel</Button>
   </Grid>
</Window>
```

There are three things to note in this XAML:

- We have used the concept of column spanning to get our controls to line up the way we want.

- We are using the Margin property on the child elements to give each label, text box, and so on, some room. Without a Margin specified, each control would automatically fill the bounds of the cell it resides in, meaning that we would have absolutely no border or gap between the controls (either horizontally or vertically).

- In the Grid's column definitions, we use an asterisk to denote a proportional size. In other words, the second and third columns equally share whatever space is left over after the first column has been rendered. We can adjust the proportion "ratio" by including a number as well (for example, ColumnDefinition.Width="2*").

### The StackPanel Control

StackPanel controls implement a vertical or horizontal stack layout for their child elements. Compared with the Grid control, this is a simple panel that supports very little tweaking: you can select to stack children horizontally or vertically using the Orientation property, and after that the panel takes care of everything else. Each element within the StackPanel will be resized/scaled to fit within the height (if stacked vertically) or width (if stacked horizontally) of the panel. Owing to the control's simplicity, the XAML is straightforward as well. Here, we are vertically stacking several check boxes, labels, a button, and a text box (see Figure 16.14 for the final product):

```
<StackPanel>
   <Label>Format Options:</Label>
   <CheckBox Margin="4" Height="16" Name="checkBox1">Perform Fast Format</CheckBox>
   <CheckBox Margin="4" Height="16" Name="checkBox2">Verify After Format</CheckBox>
   <CheckBox Margin="4" Height="16" Name="checkBox3">Enable Large Partition
    Support</CheckBox>
```

```
    <Label>Drive Label:</Label>
    <TextBox Margin="10,0" BorderBrush="Gray" Height="23" Name="comboBox2" />
    <Button Margin="80,20" Height="23" Name="button1" >Format</Button>
</StackPanel>
```

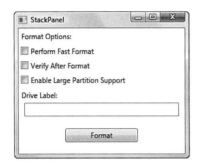

FIGURE 16.14   The StackPanel in action.

Another similar panel is the WrapPanel: this is essentially a StackPanel with additional behavior to wrap its children into additional rows or columns if there isn't enough room to display them within the bounds of the panel. See Figure 16.15 to see how the WrapPanel has auto-adjusted a series of buttons when its Window is sized smaller.

FIGURE 16.15   The WrapPanel.

## Styles and Templates

The capability to customize the look of a control in WPF, without losing any of its built-in functionality, is one of the huge advantages that WPF brings to the development scene. Consider the two slider controls in Figure 16.16: The top is the default style, and the bottom represents a restyled slider. Functionality is identical. We have simply changed the appearance of the control.

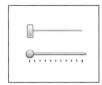

FIGURE 16.16   A restyled slider.

Style is an actual class (in the System.Windows namespace) that is used in association with a control; it groups property values together to allow you, as a developer, to set them once and have them applied to controls en masse instead of having to set them individually on each control instance. Suppose, for instance, that your application uses a nice grayscale gradient for its button backgrounds. In addition, each button has a white border, and renders its text with the Segoe UI font. We can manipulate each of these aspects using Button properties; but it would quickly become laborious to do this on every single button. A Style allows us to set all of these properties once, and then refer each button control to these properties by assigning the style to the button.

Here is the Style defined in XAML:

```
<Style x:Key="GradientButton" TargetType="Button">
    <Setter Property="Margin" Value="2"/>
    <Setter Property="BorderBrush" Value="White" />
    <Setter Property="FontFamily" Value="Segoe UI"/>
    <Setter Property="FontSize" Value="12px"/>
    <Setter Property="FontWeight" Value="Bold"/>
    <Setter Property="Foreground" Value="White" />
    <Setter Property="Background" >
        <Setter.Value>
            <LinearGradientBrush StartPoint="0,0" EndPoint="0,1" >
                <GradientStop Color="Gray" Offset="0.2"/>
                <GradientStop Color="DarkGray" Offset="0.85"/>
                <GradientStop Color="Gray" Offset="1"/>
            </LinearGradientBrush>
        </Setter.Value>
    </Setter>
</Style>
```

To assign this style to a button, it is as simple as this:

```
<Button Style="{StaticResource GradientButton}" Height="38" Name="button1"
Width="100">OK</Button>
```

This works very well for simplifying property sets. But what happens when we want to customize an attribute that isn't surfaced as a property? To continue with our button control, what if we wanted an oval shape instead of the standard rectangle? Because the Button class doesn't expose a property that we can use to change the background shape, we appear to be out of luck.

Enter the concept of templates. Templates allow you to completely replace the *visual tree* of any control giving you full control over every aspect of the control's user interface. A *visual tree* in WPF is the hierarchy of controls inheriting from the Visual class that provide a control's final rendered appearance. A good overview of WPF visual trees and logical trees can be found on http://www.msdn.microsoft.com: search for "Trees in WPF."

Earlier we mentioned that controls in WPF were "lookless"; templates are evidence of that fact. The functionality of a control exists separately from its visual tree. The default look for all the controls is provided through a series of templates, one per each Windows theme. This means that WPF controls can automatically participate in whatever OS theme you are running.

Templates are created via the `ControlTemplate` class. Within this class (or element, if we are implementing the template in XAML), we need to draw the visuals that will represent the button. The `Rectangle` class in WPF can be used to draw our basic background shape. By tweaking the `RadiusX` and `RadiusY` properties, we can soften the normal 90-degree corners into the desired elliptical shape:

```
<Rectangle RadiusX="25" RadiusY="25" Width="100" Height="50"
Stroke="Black" StrokeThickness="1">
```

We can also add some more compelling visual aspects such as a gradient fill to the button:

```
<Rectangle.Fill>
   <LinearGradientBrush>
     <LinearGradientBrush.GradientStops>
        <GradientStop Offset="0" Color="Gray" />
        <GradientStop Offset="1" Color="LightGray" />
     </LinearGradientBrush.GradientStops>
   </LinearGradientBrush>
</Rectangle.Fill>
```

To test the look and feel so far, type your "shape" XAML into the XAML editor, and tweak it as desired. After you are satisfied, you can copy and paste the XAML into the template. A better tool for designing user interfaces is Microsoft Expression Blend, but for simple design scenarios handcrafting the XAML or relying on Visual Studio's designer should be sufficient.

The text within the button is easily rendered using a `TextBlock` object:

```
<TextBlock Canvas.Top="5" Height="40" Width="100" FontSize="20"
TextAlignment="Center">OK</TextBlock>
```

16

After we are happy with the look and feel, we can "template-ize" this appearance by nesting everything within a `ControlTemplate` element. Because we will need to refer to this template later, we will provide a key/name:

```
<ControlTemplate x:Key="OvalButtonTemplate">
```

And finally, we embed the whole thing as a resource. A resource is simply a .NET object (written in XAML or code) that is meant to be shared across other objects. In this specific case, we want to be able to use this template with any button we want. Resources can be declared at any level within a WPF project: We can declare resources that belong to the overall window, or to any element within the window (such as a `Grid` panel), or we can store all of our resources in something known as a ResourceDictionary and allow them to be referenced from any class in our project. For this example, we'll stick to a simple resource defined in our parent window (for reference, this is the `Window.Resources` element that you see in the following code).

Listing 16.2 pulls this all together, and Figure 16.17 shows the resulting button.

FIGURE 16.17    A custom button template.

LISTING 16.2    Replacing a Button's Template

```
<Window x:Class="ContosoAvalon.CustomLook"
    xmlns="http://schemas.microsoft.com/winfx/2006/xaml/presentation"
    xmlns:x="http://schemas.microsoft.com/winfx/2006/xaml"
    Title="CustomLook" Height="300" Width="300"
    Background="#F8F8F8">
  <Window.Resources>
    <ControlTemplate x:Key="OvalButtonTemplate">
      <Canvas Width="100" Height="25" Margin="2">
        <Rectangle x:Name="BaseRectangle" Canvas.Top="0" RadiusX="25"
         RadiusY="25" Width="100" Height="40" Stroke="DarkGray"
         StrokeThickness="1">
          <Rectangle.Fill>
            <LinearGradientBrush>
              <LinearGradientBrush.GradientStops>
                <GradientStop Offset="0" Color="Gray" />
                <GradientStop Offset="1" Color="LightGray" />
              </LinearGradientBrush.GradientStops>
            </LinearGradientBrush>
          </Rectangle.Fill>
        </Rectangle>
```

```
        <TextBlock Canvas.Top="5" Height="40" Width="100" FontSize="20"
          TextAlignment="Center">OK</TextBlock>
      </Canvas>
    </ControlTemplate>
  </Window.Resources>
  <Canvas>
    <Button Canvas.Left="49" Canvas.Top="44" Height="38" Name="button1"
     Width="93" Template="{StaticResource OvalButtonTemplate}" />
  </Canvas>
</Window>
```

## Data Binding

Data binding, in its purest sense, is the capability of a control to be wired to a data source such that the control (a) displays certain items from that data source, and (b) is kept in synch with the data source. After the connection is made, the runtime handles all the work necessary to make this happen. It doesn't really matter where or how the data is stored: It could be a file system, a custom collection of objects, a database object, and so on.

So let's look briefly at how we can establish a data binding connection using WPF. The key class here is the System.Windows.Data.Binding class. This is the mediator in charge of linking a control with a data source. To successfully declare a binding, we need to know three things:

▶ What UI control property do we want to bind?

▶ What data source do we want to bind to?

▶ And, within the data source, what specific element or property or such holds the data we are interested in?

We can bind to either single objects (such as binding a string property on an object to a text box), or to collections of objects (such as binding a List<> collection to a list box). Either way, the mechanics remain the same:

```
Binding binding = new Binding();
binding.Source = _stringList;
listBox1.SetBinding(ListBox.ItemsSourceProperty, binding);
```

The preceding code snippet creates a Binding object, sets the source of the Binding object to our List<string> collection, and then calls SetBinding on our control (a ListBox), passing in the exact property on the control we want to bind to our data source, and the Binding object instance.

We can also assign data sources into a special object called the data context. Every FrameworkElement object, and those that derive from that class, implement their own DataContext instance. You can think of this as a global area where controls can go to get their data when participating in a data binding arrangement.

16

This ends up simplifying our data binding code quite a bit. We can set the context in our Window constructor like this:

```
this.DataContext = _stringList;
```

Now, we just point our ListBox to this data context using a tag within the ListBox's XAML element:

```
<ListBox Name="listBox1" ItemsSource="{Binding}" />
```

The binding object in this case will automatically hunt for objects stashed within a data context somewhere within the object tree. When it finds one, it will automatically bind the objects.

This works great for our simple List<string> example, but what if we are trying to bind a collection of custom objects to the list box? If we have a simple Employee class with a Name property and a PhoneNbr property, how could we bind to a collection of those objects and show the employee name? Our process would actually remain the same. If we create an Employee class, and then create a List<Employee> collection, all of this code still works. But there is a problem: Figure 16.18 highlights an issue we will have to solve.

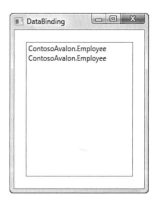

FIGURE 16.18    Binding to custom objects.

We haven't yet told the binding engine how exactly we want our data to be represented within the list box. By default, the binding process will simply call ToString on every object.

One quick remedy would be to simply override the ToString method:

```
public override string ToString()
{
    return _name;
}
```

This will correct the problem in this instance. But a more robust approach would involve the use of a DataTemplate. We'll cover that approach a little later, in the section "Building a Simple Image Viewer Application."

# Routed Events

The standard way that .NET classes and controls raise and handle events is essentially the way that you will perform these tasks in WPF. But the WPF libraries bring an important improvement to standard events: We call these *routed events*.

Consider a simple scenario: You have a Button control that consists of a background image and some text (see Figure 16.19). If you recall from our discussion of a controls template and visual tree, this means we actually have a few discrete elements that make up the button: a TextBlock, an Image, and the basic frame and background of the button.

FIGURE 16.19     A button with multiple elements.

These are separate objects/elements unto themselves. So the event situation becomes a little complex. It isn't enough to react to a click on the button background; we also have to react to a click on the button's text or the button's image. This is where routed events come into play. Routed events are capable of calling event handlers up or down the entire visual tree. This means we are free to implement an event handler at the Button level, and be confident that a click on the button's image or text will bubble up until it finds our event handler.

Routed events in WPF are broken down into three categories: bubbling events, tunneling events, and direct events:

▶ **Bubbling events**—These events travel up the visual tree starting at the initial receiving element.

▶ **Tunneling events**—These events start at the top of the control's visual tree and move down until they reach the receiving element.

▶ **Direct event**—These are the equivalent of "standard" .NET events: Only the event handler for the receiving element is called.

Events themselves, like nearly everything else in WPF, can be declared in XAML or in code. Here we have a button control with a MouseEnter event defined:

```
<Button MouseEnter="button1_MouseEnter" Height="23" Name="button1"
Width="75">OK</Button>
```

The event handler itself, in C#, looks like any other .NET event handler:

```
private void button1_MouseEnter(object sender, MouseEventArgs e)
{
    MessageBox.Show("MouseEnter on button1");
}
```

We have only scratched the surface on many of the basic programming concepts within WPF. But you should now be armed with enough knowledge to be productive writing a simple WPF application. Let's do just that, using the tools available to us in Visual Studio 2008.

# Building a Simple Image Viewer Application

To illustrate the role that Visual Studio plays in WPF application development, let's build a sample application from scratch. In the tradition of "experience first," for this example let's select something that can benefit from WPF's strong suits, namely visualizations and robust control layouts and templating.

Consider an image viewer application. We can use this application to view a list of image thumbnails and, after selecting a thumbnail, can view the image itself and even make changes to the image.

We'll target the rough design shown in Figure 16.20.

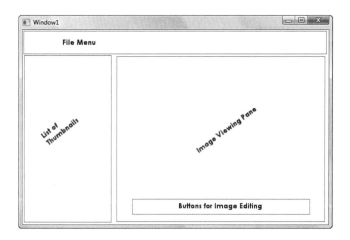

FIGURE 16.20    A sketch of an image viewer UI.

Here are our base requirements:

▶ When the application loads, it will parse the images contained in the specified folder.

▶ Every image will be listed in a list box; the list box will show image thumbnails and no text.

▶ When the user clicks on one of the items in the list box, the image viewing area will be populated with the selected image.

▶ The user can then choose to manipulate the image: a black and white effect can be applied, the image can be rotated clockwise or counterclockwise, the image can be flipped, and it can be mirrored.

▶ In general, we will try to use WPF's capabilities when possible to make the application more visually compelling; a standard battleship gray application is not what we are looking for here.

## Starting the Layout

After creating a new WPF project, we'll double-click the Window1.xaml file and start designing our user interface. To start, a Grid panel and some nested StackPanel or WrapPanel containers will provide the initial layout. We can use the Grid control that has been automatically placed on our window during project creation. Select the grid within the designer; you can do this by either clicking within the designer, or clicking within the <Grid> element in the XAML pane. With the Grid control selected, click in the header border once to create a column border. Place the border about halfway through the Grid's width so that it splits the grid about equally between two columns.

Now, click in the left border area of the Grid twice. This will create two rows. Drag the row splitters until our first row has a height of about 30, and our bottom row has a height of about 40. Your design surface should look something like that shown in Figure 16.21.

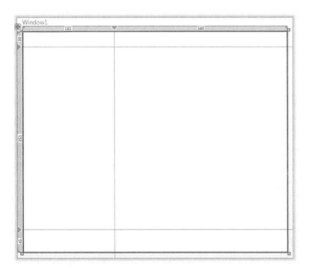

FIGURE 16.21   A window in progress.

Drag a ListBox into the middle row, left-hand column, and drag a menu control into the top row, left-hand column. Because we want our menu to span the entire width of the Grid, we will need to manually tweak the XAML at this point: Specify Grid.ColumnSpan= "2" within the Menu element. If there are any Margin settings in either the Menu or ListBox element, remove them. This will let the Menu control expand and contract as needed within the Grid, and will let the Menu fill the entire space allocated for the first row in the Grid. We know we need to provide folder selection capabilities, so we can title a main menu item as Folder, and include a sub-item under that titled Open:

```
<Menu Grid.Row="0" Grid.ColumnSpan="2" Height="22" Name="menu1"
VerticalAlignment="Top">
   <MenuItem Header="_Folder">
      <MenuItem Header="_Open..." Click="FolderOpenMenuItem_Click" />
   </MenuItem>
</Menu>
```

For the image view box, we will use an Image control. Drag one into the second row, right-most column—and, as before, remove any Margin settings.

And finally, drag a StackPanel into the third row, right-most column, remove any Margin settings, and set its Orientation property to Horizontal and the HorizontalAlignment property to Center. This panel is where we will place our image manipulation buttons, which you can add now as well. Drag four buttons into the StackPanel, and adjust their margins and height/width until you get the workable look and feel you are after.

---

**NOTE**

Most of these examples recommend using the XAML pane to tweak properties here and there, but remember that you can also use the Properties window to do this just as with any other project type. After you get used to XAML, however, you might find it faster to just add or change the elements you need right in the XAML pane. The IntelliSense makes this a very fast approach to UI design.

---

Your window should now look something like the one shown in Figure 16.22; here's a look at our XAML so far:

```
<Window x:Class="ImageViewer.Window1"
    xmlns="http://schemas.microsoft.com/winfx/2006/xaml/presentation"
    xmlns:x="http://schemas.microsoft.com/winfx/2006/xaml"
    Title="Window1" Height="464" Width="545">
   <Grid>
      <Grid.ColumnDefinitions>
         <ColumnDefinition Width="262*" />
         <ColumnDefinition Width="261*" />
      </Grid.ColumnDefinitions>
      <Grid.RowDefinitions>
         <RowDefinition Height="30" />
         <RowDefinition Height="352*" />
         <RowDefinition Height="45" />
      </Grid.RowDefinitions>
      <Menu Grid.Row="0" Grid.ColumnSpan="2" Height="22" Name="menu1"
       VerticalAlignment="Top">
         <MenuItem Header="_Folder" />
      </Menu>
      <ListBox Grid.Row="1" Name="listBox1" />
```

```
        <Image Grid.Column="1" Grid.Row="1" Name="image1" Stretch="Fill" />
        <StackPanel HorizontalAlignment="Center" Orientation="Horizontal"
         Grid.Column="1" Grid.Row="2" Name="stackPanel1">
            <Button Width="50" Margin="10,0">Button</Button>
            <Button Width="50" Margin="10,0">Button</Button>
            <Button Width="50" Margin="10,0">Button</Button>
            <Button Width="50" Margin="10,0">Button</Button>
    </Grid>
</Window>
```

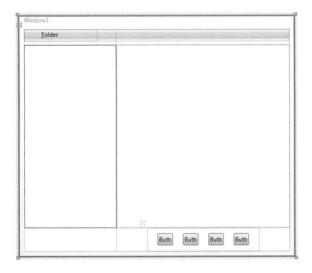

FIGURE 16.22    A draft layout.

## Storing the Images

With the UI elements in place, we can move on to the data binding issues (we'll come back later and give the UI more polish). The first task is to store the files in a collection of some sort. It turns out that there is a System.Windows.Media class that is suitable for our needs: BitmapSource. For a collection, a List<BitmapSource> object should work for the moment, but we will need some way to populate the list. So let's create a wrapper class that both loads the list and exposes it as a property. Add a new class to the project with the following code:

```
public class DirectoryImageList
{
    private string _path;
    private List<BitmapSource> _images = new List<BitmapSource>();

    public DirectoryImageList(string path)
    {
```

```
      _path = path;
      LoadImages();

  }

  public List<BitmapSource> Images
  {
     get { return _images; }
     set { _images = value; }
  }

  public string Path
  {
     get { return _path; }
     set
     {
        _path = value;
        LoadImages();
     }
  }

  private void LoadImages()
  {
     _images.Clear();
     BitmapImage img;

     foreach (string file in Directory.GetFiles(_path))
     {
        try
        {
           img = new BitmapImage(new Uri(file));

           _images.Add(img);
        }
        catch
        {
           // empty catch; ignore any files that won't load as
           // an image...
        }
     }
  }
}
```

The LoadImages method in the preceding code is where most of the important logic is found; it enumerates the files within a given directory and attempts to load them into a BitmapImage object. If it succeeds, we know that this is an image file. If it doesn't, we just ignore the resulting exception and keep on going.

Back in our Window1 class, we need to create some private fields to hold an instance of this new class, and to hold the currently selected path. This is something we will let the user change through a common dialog launched from the Folder, Open menu item.

Here are the fields:

```
private DirectoryImageList _imgList;
private string _path =
  Environment.GetFolderPath
          (Environment.SpecialFolder.MyPictures);
```

Note that we have defaulted our path to the Pictures folder. To load up the list object, we will write a ResetList method in our Window1 class (_imgList is declared in the code-behind file as our local DirectoryImageList instance):

```
private void ResetList()
{
   imgList = new DirectoryImageList(_path);
}
```

Referring to our earlier discussion on data binding, we will round things off by adding a few lines of code to the Window1 constructor: an initial call to ResetList, and a call to assign the data context to the Images property from the DirectoryImageList instance.

```
public Window1()
{
   InitializeComponent();
   ResetList();
   this.DataContext = _imgList.Images;
}
```

If we run the application now, we see a familiar site (as in Figure 16.23): The data binding is working, but isn't quite the presentation format we want.

## Binding to the Images

Because our earlier trick of overriding ToString won't give us the right data presentation (an image, after all, is not a string), we need to turn to data templates. The DataTemplate class is used to tell a control specifically how you want its data to be displayed. By using a data template within the visual tree of the control, you have complete freedom to present the bound data in any fashion you want.

16

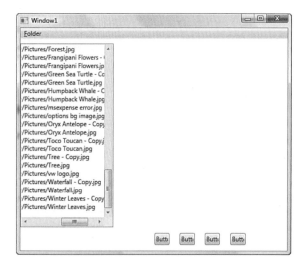

FIGURE 16.23   Initial binding.

For this application, we are looking for images in the ListBox. This turns out to be quite easy. Create a Window1.Resources element in XAML, and create a DataTemplate that sets up the exact visualization we need:

```
<Window.Resources>
    <DataTemplate x:Key="ImageDataTemplate">
        <Image Source="{Binding UriSource.LocalPath}" Width="125"
         Height="125" />
    </DataTemplate>
</Window.Resources>
```

Then assign the DataTemplate to the ListBox:

```
<ListBox Grid.Row="1" Name="listBox1" ItemsSource="{Binding}"
 ItemTemplate="{StaticResource ImageDataTemplate}"/>
```

In our data template, the Image element is expecting a source URI for each image. So we use the UriSource.LocalPath that is provided on the BitmapSource object.

Clicking on a thumbnail in the list box should cause the central Image control to display the indicated picture. By creating a SelectionChanged event handler and wiring it to the ListBox, we can update our Image.Source property accordingly.

The event is declared as expected in the ListBox element:

```
<ListBox SelectionChanged="listBox1_SelectionChanged" Grid.Row="1"
 Name="listBox1" ItemsSource="{Binding}"
 ItemTemplate="{StaticResource ImageDataTemplate}"/>
```

And for the event handler, we will cast the SelectedItem from the ListBox to its native BitmapSource representation, and assign it to our image control:

```
private void listBox1_SelectionChanged(object sender,
   SelectionChangedEventArgs e)
{
   image1.Source = (BitmapSource)((sender as ListBox).SelectedItem);
}
```

## Button Event Handlers and Image Effects

With the images successfully loaded into the list box, and displayed in the central Image control, we can turn our attention to our four image editing/effects features:

▶ Black and white filter

▶ Image blur

▶ Rotate

▶ Flip

Because these four functions are controlled by the four buttons, we will need to add some appropriate button images and events; we won't cover the button stylings here because they involve external graphics resources, but you can see how they turn out in the final screenshot (at the end of this chapter), or by downloading the source from this book's website.

The code for the events, however, is fair game. First, the XAML event declarations on each button:

```
<Button Click="buttonBandW_Click" Margin="20,0,0,0" Height="23"
 Name="buttonBandW" Width="30">Button</Button>

<Button Click="buttonBlur_Click" Margin="20,0,0,0" Height="23"
 Name="buttonBlur" Width="30">Button</Button>

<Button Click="buttonRotate_Click"  Margin="20,0,0,0" Height="23"
 Name="buttonRotate" Width="30">Button</Button>

<Button Click="buttonFlip_Click" Margin="20,0,20,0" Height="23"
Name="buttonFlip" Width="30">Button</Button>
```

Notice as you type these click events into the XAML pane that the XAML editor intervenes with IntelliSense pop-ups that not only complete our Click declaration, but also create the corresponding event handler in our code-behind class (see Figure 16.24)!

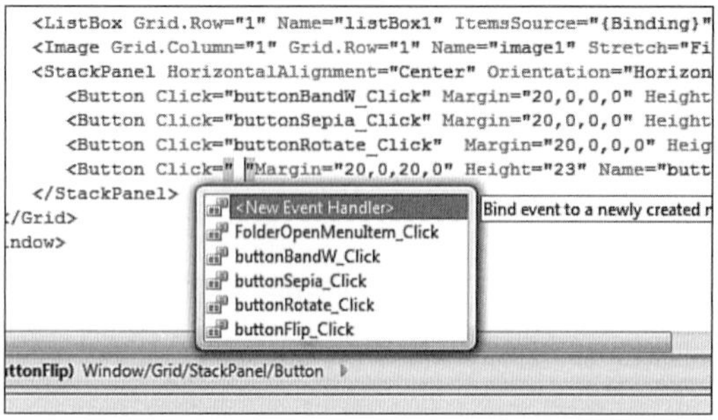

```
<ListBox Grid.Row="1" Name="listBox1" ItemsSource="{Binding}"
  <Image Grid.Column="1" Grid.Row="1" Name="image1" Stretch="Fi
<StackPanel HorizontalAlignment="Center" Orientation="Horizon
    <Button Click="buttonBandW_Click" Margin="20,0,0,0" Height
    <Button Click="buttonSepia_Click" Margin="20,0,0,0" Height
    <Button Click="buttonRotate_Click"  Margin="20,0,0,0" Heig
    <Button Click="  Margin="20,0,20,0" Height="23" Name="butt
  </StackPanel>
/Grid>                    <New Event Handler>      Bind event to a newly created r
.ndow>                    FolderOpenMenuItem_Click
                          buttonBandW_Click
                          buttonSepia_Click
                          buttonRotate_Click
                          buttonFlip_Click

ttonFlip) Window/Grid/StackPanel/Button ▶
```

FIGURE 16.24   The XAML editor IntelliSense in action.

To perform the image manipulations, we employ something known as a *transform*: the manipulation of a 2D surface to rotate, skew, or otherwise change the current appearance of the surface. We can handle our rotation feature directly with RotateTransform like this:

```
private void buttonRotate_Click(object sender, RoutedEventArgs e)
{
    CachedBitmap cache = new CachedBitmap((BitmapSource)image1.Source,
        BitmapCreateOptions.None, BitmapCacheOption.OnLoad);
    image1.Source = new TransformedBitmap(cache, new RotateTransform(90));
}
```

Our flip action ends up being just as easy, but uses a ScaleTransform instead:

```
private void buttonFlip_Click(object sender, RoutedEventArgs e)
{
    CachedBitmap cache = new CachedBitmap((BitmapSource)image1.Source,
        BitmapCreateOptions.None, BitmapCacheOption.OnLoad);
    ScaleTransform scale = new ScaleTransform(-1, -1, image1.Source.Width / 2,
        image1.Source.Height / 2);
    image1.Source = new TransformedBitmap(cache, scale);
}
```

The image blurring action is provided through a different mechanism known as a bitmap effect. By creating a new BlurBitmapEffect instance and assigning that to our image control, WPF will apply the appropriate algorithm to the bitmap to blur the picture:

```
image1.BitmapEffect = new BlurBitmapEffect();
```

## Path Selection with a Common Dialog

The last item on our to-do list is allowing the user to change the path of the picture files. WPF itself doesn't have any built-in dialog classes to manage this, but the System.Windows.Forms namespace has just what we need: the FolderBrowserDialog class. This is launched from within the event handler for our FolderOpenMenuItem click event:

```csharp
private void FolderOpenMenuItem_Click(object sender, RoutedEventArgs e)
{
    SetPath();
}

private void SetPath()
{
    FolderBrowserDialog dlg = new FolderBrowserDialog();
    dlg.ShowDialog();
    path = dlg.SelectedPath;
    ResetList();
}
```

See Figure 16.25 for a look at the dialog in action.

FIGURE 16.25   The Browse for Folders dialog.

When a user selects a folder, we update our internal field appropriately, reload the `DirectoryImageList` class with the new path, and then reset our window's `DataContext` property to reflect the change. This is a perfect example of how seamless it is to use other .NET technologies and class libraries from within WPF. By adding the appropriate namespace and reference to our project, we just instantiate this class like any other class in our solution.

**TIP**

Because there are a fair number of controls that share the same name between WPF and WinForms (the `ListBox` control is one example), if you find yourself using classes from the `System.Windows.Controls` and the `System.Windows.Forms` libraries, you will inevitably need to fully qualify some of your object names to avoid operating against the wrong class.

And with that, the application is functionally complete. For reference, we have provided the current state of the XAML and the code-behind listings in Listing 16.3 and Listing 16.4, respectively. If you really want to dissect this application, however, you should download the source code from this book's website. This will allow you to see the improvements made with graphics resources and general look and feel, producing the final polished version shown in Figure 16.26.

FIGURE 16.26    After the finishing touches.

LISTING 16.3    The Image Viewer XAML Code

```
<Window x:Class="ImageViewer.Window1"
    xmlns="http://schemas.microsoft.com/winfx/2006/xaml/presentation"
    xmlns:x="http://schemas.microsoft.com/winfx/2006/xaml"
    Title="Window1" Height="464" Width="545">
    <Window.Resources>
        <DataTemplate x:Key="ImageDataTemplate">
            <Image Source="{Binding UriSource.LocalPath}" Width="125" Height="125" />
        </DataTemplate>
    </Window.Resources>
    <Grid>
        <Grid.ColumnDefinitions>
            <ColumnDefinition Width="150" />
            <ColumnDefinition Width="378*" />
        </Grid.ColumnDefinitions>
        <Grid.RowDefinitions>
            <RowDefinition Height="30" />
            <RowDefinition Height="352*" />
            <RowDefinition Height="45" />
        </Grid.RowDefinitions>
```

```xml
<Menu Grid.Row="0" Grid.ColumnSpan="2" Height="22" Name="menu1"
VerticalAlignment="Top">
    <MenuItem Header="_Folder">
    <MenuItem Header="_Open..." Click="FolderOpenMenuItem_Click" />
    </MenuItem>
</Menu>

<ListBox SelectionChanged="listBox1_SelectionChanged" Grid.Row="1"
Name="listBox1" ItemsSource="{Binding}"
ItemTemplate="{StaticResource ImageDataTemplate}"/>
<Image Grid.Column="1" Grid.Row="1" Name="image1" Stretch="Fill" />
<StackPanel HorizontalAlignment="Center" Orientation="Horizontal"
Grid.Column="1" Grid.Row="2" Name="stackPanel1">
    <Button BorderThickness="0" Click="buttonBandW_Click"
    Margin="20,0,0,0" Height="23" Name="buttonBandW" Width="30">
      Button
    </Button>
    <Button Click="buttonBlur_Click" Margin="20,0,0,0" Height="23"
    Name="buttonBlur" Width="30">Button</Button>
    <Button Click="buttonRotate_Click"  Margin="20,0,0,0" Height="23"
    Name="buttonRotate" Width="30">Button</Button>
    <Button Click="buttonFlip_Click" Margin="20,0,20,0" Height="23"
    Name="buttonFlip" Width="30">Button</Button>
</StackPanel>
  </Grid>
</Window>
```

LISTING 16.4   The Image Viewer Code Behind C#

```csharp
<using System;
using System.Collections.Generic;
using System.Linq;
using System.Text;
using System.Windows;
using System.Windows.Controls;
using System.Windows.Data;
using System.Windows.Documents;
using System.Windows.Forms;
using System.Windows.Input;
using System.Windows.Media;
using System.Windows.Media.Effects;
using System.Windows.Media.Imaging;
using System.Windows.Navigation;
using System.Windows.Shapes;
```

16

LISTING 16.4    Continued

```csharp
namespace ImageViewer
{
    /// <summary>
    /// Interaction logic for Window1.xaml
    /// </summary>
    public partial class Window1 : Window
    {
        private DirectoryImageList _imgList;
        private string _path =
            Environment.GetFolderPath(Environment.SpecialFolder.MyPictures);

        public Window1()
        {
            InitializeComponent();
            ResetList();
            this.DataContext = _imgList.Images;
        }

        private void FolderOpenMenuItem_Click(object sender, RoutedEventArgs e)
        {
            SetPath();
        }

        private void SetPath()
        {
            FolderBrowserDialog dlg = new FolderBrowserDialog();
            dlg.ShowDialog();
            path = dlg.SelectedPath;
            ResetList();
        }

        private void ResetList()
        {
            if (IsValidPath(_path))
            {
                imgList = new DirectoryImageList(_path);
            }

            this.DataContext = _imgList.Images;

        }

        private bool IsValidPath(string path)
        {
            try
```

```
      {
         string folder = System.IO.Path.GetFullPath(path);
         return true;
      }
      catch
      {
         return false;
      }
}

private void buttonBandW_Click(object sender, RoutedEventArgs e)
{
   BitmapSource img = (BitmapSource)image1.Source;
   image1.Source =
      new FormatConvertedBitmap(img, PixelFormats.Gray16,
      BitmapPalettes.Gray256, 1.0);
}

private void buttonBlur_Click(object sender, RoutedEventArgs e)
{
   if (image1.BitmapEffect != null)
   {
      // if blur is current effect, remove
      image1.BitmapEffect = null;
   }
   else
   {
      // otherwise, add the blur effect to the image
      image1.BitmapEffect = new BlurBitmapEffect();
   }
}


private void buttonRotate_Click(object sender, RoutedEventArgs e)
{
   CachedBitmap cache =
      new CachedBitmap((BitmapSource)image1.Source,
      BitmapCreateOptions.None,
      BitmapCacheOption.OnLoad);

   image1.Source =
      new TransformedBitmap(cache, new RotateTransform(90));
}
private void buttonFlip_Click(object sender, RoutedEventArgs e)
{
```

LISTING 16.4    Continued

```
        CachedBitmap cache =
            new CachedBitmap((BitmapSource)image1.Source,
            BitmapCreateOptions.None,
            BitmapCacheOption.OnLoad);

        ScaleTransform scale =
            new ScaleTransform(-1, -1, image1.Source.Width / 2,
            image1.Source.Height / 2);

        image1.Source = new TransformedBitmap(cache, scale);

    }

    private void listBox1_SelectionChanged(object sender,
        SelectionChangedEventArgs e)
    {
        image1.Source =
            (BitmapSource)
            ((sender as System.Windows.Controls.ListBox).SelectedItem);
    }

    }
}
```

## Summary

In this chapter, you had a brief introduction to Microsoft's new presentation layer framework, the Windows Presentation Foundation. We investigated the overall framework architecture and its programming model, including the new concept of using declarative
markup to design and lay out a WPF client application's user interface. And we saw how
the Visual Studio WPF Designer can be used to quickly craft compelling user interfaces
using the same development processes we use when building Windows Forms or even
ASP.NET applications.

We spent some time discussing the basics of control layout—a central theme in WPF—and
covering the first-class data binding support that WPF enjoys.

As mentioned, developers trying to learn WPF will find that it is both a broad and deep
subject. It is highly recommended that you spend some time with MSDN resources (such
as the WPF developer center at http://www.msdn.microsoft.com/wpf) and then revisit this
chapter to get a full sense of the skills and knowledge required to come up to speed on
WPF development. Spending time with the design tools—free trials are available—is also
highly recommended. See http://www.microsoft.com/expression for more information.

# CHAPTER 17

# Creating Rich Browser Applications

Visual Studio 2008 is responding to the new push for what has been labeled Web 2.0. Web 2.0 brings together designers and developers. In this new web, you should expect to give users a rich degree of interaction with your site. Sites with just text, images, and hyperlinks that refresh every time the user clicks the mouse are being reworked to provide more user interaction similar to working in Windows. New sites are blurring the lines between web and Windows with these new technologies and using them to set themselves apart.

In this chapter, we will cover three browser-based technologies you can leverage in Visual Studio 2008 to create the next web. These include ASP.NET AJAX, WPF XAML browser application (XBAP), and Microsoft Silverlight. With AJAX, you can create a rich experience that targets standard browsers on all platforms. WPF browser applications allow you to leverage nearly the full power of Windows Presentation Foundation within the browser. Of course, this means having Windows on the client. Finally, Silverlight applications can run inside a browser plug-in and provide a rich experience similar to that with WPF. In addition, browser plug-ins are available for most browsers on most platforms.

## Building Active Client Applications in Standard Browsers

With Visual Studio 2008, you can now easily provide a high degree of user interaction within your ASP.NET applications. The tools include a set of controls, a code library, and access to a toolkit; all of these are available to help you embed client-side JavaScript in your user interface. This JavaScript can enable a richer user experience that includes modal dialogs, progress notification, partial-page updates, and much more. Collectively, this technology is known as Asynchronous JavaScript and XML (AJAX).

AJAX tries to break down the barrier between a thin, very dumb client and the server. In this way, it enables more real-time user interaction and at the same time offloads some of the server processing. Many activities can be done on the client without putting load on the server. In addition, in partial-page update scenarios, only the portion of the page being updated is sent to and from the server. This can increase the efficiency of the request and response.

The AJAX technology also allows you to continue to leverage the investments you've made in ASP.NET development. AJAX applications are built on the same ASP.NET control set you are used to. AJAX is simply an addition to these controls. In addition, because JavaScript is a standard (ECMAScript), it is part of all modern browsers (IE, Firefox, Safari) running on all platforms (Windows, Mac, and so on). Therefore, the web applications you build with it will work cross-platform, cross-browser.

> **NOTE**
>
> Many ASP.NET controls have been using JavaScript on the client to provide better user interaction for a long time now. These include the validation controls for doing client-side validation, the web part controls for doing drag and drop of web parts across zones, the menu control, the TreeView control to open and view nodes, the calendar control, and more. The AJAX controls and AJAX Toolkit are simply a formalization of a direction web development had been heading toward for years.

## The ASP.NET AJAX Controls

The ASP.NET AJAX controls are a set of four basic controls that serve one primary purpose: partial-page updates. Partial-page updates allow for a better user experience by not submitting and refreshing an entire page on every user request. Instead, these controls work together to allow portions of a page to submit and update independently. The ASP.NET controls manage this partial update process.

You use the ASP.NET AJAX controls when building a web page in the web form designer. You can drag them from the Toolbox onto your form and work with them as you would with other controls. Figure 17.1 shows you the list of AJAX controls available inside the Visual Studio Toolbox.

Table 17.1 provides a list of the AJAX controls and a description of each. This is simply a quick reference for you to understand how each control is differentiated. We will cover these in more depth in the coming sections.

FIGURE 17.1   The AJAX controls inside the Visual Studio Toolbox.

TABLE 17.1   ASP.NET AJAX Controls

| Control | Description |
| --- | --- |
| ScriptManager | All AJAX pages you write using the standard AJAX controls listed here require a single ScriptManager control on the page. It is used by ASP.NET to manage the other AJAX controls on the page, and handle partial-page rendering, globalization, localization, and more. |
| ScriptManagerProxy | A page may only contain a single ScriptManager control. Therefore, if you have a page whose master page may already define a ScriptManager, then you can use the ScriptManagerProxy control on the child page if you need to add script from the child page. The ScriptManagerProxy may also be used on user controls. |
| UpdatePanel | Use an UpdatePanel when you want to group items for partial-page update. Items inside an UpdatePanel that execute a post-back to the server do so only for the panel (and not the rest of the page). In this way, you get an easy model for updating only portions of your page from the server without executing a full page refresh in the browser. |

17

TABLE 17.1    Continued

| Control | Description |
| --- | --- |
| UpdateProgress | The UpdateProgress control allows you to provide the user with status information as a partial-page update is processing on the server. The UpdateProgress is used in conjunction with the UpdatePanel control. When a partial-page postback is started, progress indication is made to the user. When the postback is complete, the user is again notified. |
| Timer | The Timer control provides a client-side timer that lets you post-back the contents of an UpdatePanel at set intervals. |

## Creating an AJAX Page

You will find that the process of creating AJAX pages is very similar to creating standard pages. There are just a few things you need to worry about. In this section, you will walk through an example of creating a partial-page update. You will then build on this example to provide notification of server progress to the user's browser. Let's get started.

### Partial-Page Update

A partial-page update allows you to post only a portion of a page to the server, process it, and update only that portion in the user's browser. This cuts down on overhead and server processing, and users also end up with a better experience. Only the section of the page with which they are working gets updates. This seems natural and faster.

In this walk-through example, you will create a web page that allows users to search for customer orders. We will use the Northwind database as the source database. We will then build the page such that when results are displayed, a user can page through them. When they do, the data pages will be implemented as partial-page updates. This ensures that users do not feel as though they are performing a new search every time they select a new page of data.

To get started, create a simple ASP.NET website. By default, ASP.NET sites already support AJAX. Therefore, you do not need to do anything special beyond creating a basic ASP.NET site (see Chapter 14, "Creating ASP.NET Applications," for more info on creating websites). The following steps outline setting up the Default.aspx page on the site for the example:

1.  Add a ScriptManager to the page. Think of the ScriptManager as the common logic required by the UpdatePanel to process its partial-page update.

2.  Add an UpdatePanel to the page. The UpdatePanel will contain the portion of the page you want to partially update. The items placed inside the UpdatePanel will be posted back to the server independently of the rest of the page and thus updated independently. The user will not see a full page refresh.

3.  The next step is to lay out the portion of the page that sits outside the UpdatePanel. This will include a page title, some instructions, a text box for users to enter a portion of a customer's name, and a find button.

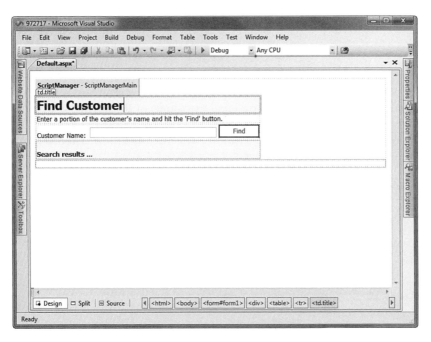

FIGURE 17.2   The beginnings of the partial-page update page.

Your page should now look something like the one shown in Figure 17.2. Notice the ScriptManager at the top of the page. The UpdatePanel control is below the text "Search results...." This text and everything above it will perform a full page post. Anything that happens inside the UpdatePanel will perform the partial-page post.

4. The next step is to configure a GridView control to access some data. To do so, drag a GridView control from the Data controls on the Toolbox onto the design surface and inside the UpdatePanel. You can use split view to verify that the control made it inside the UpdatePanel.

5. Use the quick tasks arrow on the upper right of the GridView control to set a data source. Use the Choose Data Source option and select a new data source. Follow along with the wizard: Select the database options for the data source and create a connection to the Northwind database.

When you get to the Configure the Select Statement option, select the radio button labeled Specify a Custom SQL Statement or Stored Procedure, and click the Next button. You can use the Query Builder tool to build a SQL statement that joins the Customers and Orders tables. The following code provides an example. Notice that the WHERE clause uses the parameter @cust along with the LIKE keyword to define a user-specified value for the search.

```
SELECT Customers.ContactName, Customers.CompanyName, Customers.Phone,
       Orders.OrderDate, Orders.RequiredDate, Orders.ShippedDate,
       Orders.ShipAddress, Orders.ShipCity, Orders.ShipVia,
       Orders.Freight, Orders.OrderID
```

17

```
FROM Orders INNER JOIN Customers ON Orders.CustomerID =
                        Customers.CustomerID
WHERE (Customers.ContactName LIKE @cust + '%')

ORDER BY Customers.ContactName, Orders.OrderDate
```

After defining the query, click the Next button on the wizard. You should now be on the Define Parameters page. Here you can define the source of the parameter you created in the prior SQL statement. For this example, indicate that the source is Form and the FormField is your text box used for data entry (TextBoxCustomer). Figure 17.3 shows an example of this setup.

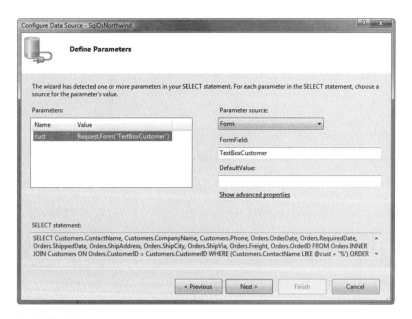

FIGURE 17.3    Defining the data-source parameter.

6. The next step is to configure paging for the GridView control. You can do so from the quick actions smart tag; select the check box EnablePaging.

7. As an optional step, you can make the GridView display a bit better. From the quick actions smart tag, choose AutoFormat to apply a format to the grid. You can also use the Edit Columns link to bring up the column editor. Here you can change the column header text for each column, change the column order, and set formatting options for date values and currency.

That's it. You now have a customer search page that displays customer and order results to a user based on their entry. When the user clicks one of the paging buttons, the page partially updates. Run the application and enter a couple of letters in the TextBoxCustomer field and click the Find button. In Figure 17.4, we've done just that. When a page link at the bottom of the page is selected, the grid is updated.

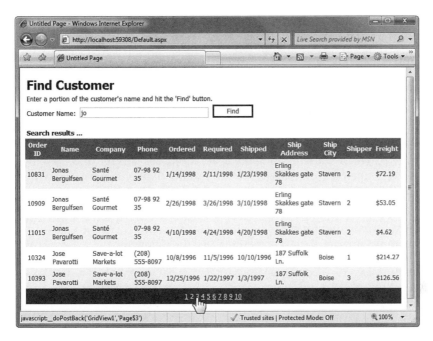

FIGURE 17.4 A partial-page update in action.

### Show Server Progress to the User

Users feel more comfortable when they get immediate feedback after clicking somewhere on a web page and initiating an action. Of course, many server operations can time many seconds and longer. A better experience is to let the user know you are working on their request when either retrieving pages that have long operations (above a second or so) or working across an occasionally slow network.

The ASP.NET Update progress control allows you to do just that. When a user clicks to execute a partial-page update, you can put up a wait notification or an animated .gif. Then, when the page has finished, the wait notification disappears and the partial page updates. Let's look at building this into our sample page.

In the preceding example, you implemented a partial-page update for paging a GridView. In this example, you will provide users with a progress indicator during paging. To get started, you will use the page created in the earlier walk-through. The following outlines the steps that should be applied to this page to implement progress notification.

1. The first step is to drag an UpdateProgress control to the page. Place the control under the GridView control but outside the UpdatePanel control. In this example, we will show the progress indicator below the data pager. In this way, the user will see a progress indicator in the same area where their attention is focused.

   You can place an UpdateProgress control anywhere on the page but not inside the UpdatePanel itself. When the partial-page postback triggers, the client will immediately kick off the progress notification.

**2.** Next, you need to set a few properties on the `UpdateProgress` control for the page. You need to set the `AssociatedUpdatePanelID` property to associate the `UpdateProgress` control to an `UpdatePanel` control. In this way, the two are linked. Because a given page may have multiple update controls, setting this property is required.

You can also set the `DisplayAfter` property to the number of milliseconds the client should wait before display notification. In this example, set the value low (`250` is a quarter of a second).

**3.** The last step is to define the message that is displayed to the user while they wait. You can put any HTML or markup inside the `UpdateProgress` control. You do so by dragging items onto the control in design view. In source view, you must create a `ProgressTemplate` node to house your markup.

In the example, you can put the text "Please wait...." Also, if you have an animated `.gif` file that cycles back and forth or in a circle, you can add it here. The `UpdateProgress` markup should look something like the following:

```
<asp:UpdateProgress ID="UpdateProgressResults" runat="server"
  AssociatedUpdatePanelID="UpdatePanelData" DisplayAfter="200"
  DynamicLayout="true">
  <ProgressTemplate>
    <div class="title" style="text-align: center; font-size: 10pt;" >
      <img src="images/rotation.gif" alt="waiting" />
      Please wait ...
    </div>
  </ProgressTemplate>
</asp:UpdateProgress>
```

**4.** Optional: If you are running this example locally, you might not see much in the way of wait times. Therefore, you might introduce a wait time just to see it work. Of course, you would never do such a thing in a real application. To do so, add code in the `PageIndexChanged` event of the `GridView` control to put the executing thread to sleep. The following code introduces a four-second delay:

```
protected void GridView1_PageIndexChanged(object sender, EventArgs e) {
  System.Threading.Thread.Sleep(4000);

}
```

You should now be able to run the application. When you click on a page in the data pager, you should see the "please wait" notification. Figure 17.5 shows this in action.

## The ASP.NET AJAX Control Toolkit Open-Source Library

Microsoft worked with the development community to introduce an early version of AJAX inside of Visual Studio back in the 2003/2005 versions. This support was referred to as ATLAS. From these early beginnings grew the AJAX Control Toolkit. Arguably, this toolkit represents one of the most successful open-source projects worked on jointly by a big company and the development community.

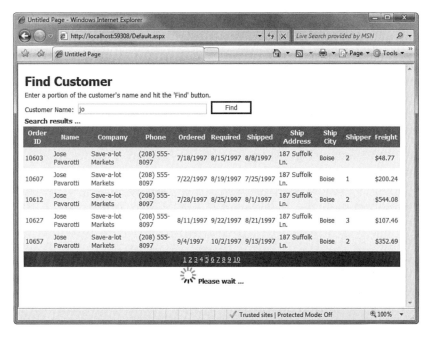

FIGURE 17.5   The AJAX progress notification running in a browser.

Inside the toolkit is a set of AJAX-based custom controls that provide many dynamic user activities inside the browser. There are controls for all sorts of features, including auto-complete as a user types, masked edit text boxes, password strength verification, modal pop-up dialogs, and many more. You can download the collection of controls either as full source or as a binary version. You can then leverage these controls inside your application.

**17**

> **NOTE**
>
> We discuss the ASP.NET Control Toolkit here because it has become a part of the Visual Studio developer's world. You can find tutorials and discussions on Microsoft's http://www.asp.net. You can get the source code at the http://www.codeplex.com site. In addition, the MSDN documentation discusses the controls and outlines how to work with the toolkit.

### Getting Started

The AJAX Control Toolkit source code and binary downloads are maintained on http://www.codeplex.com. There are versions that align with different versions of the .NET Framework. The latest of these aligns with .NET 3.5. You can download the source code or choose a no-source release version. Let's assume the latter because we are not covering the source code here.

After you have downloaded the zip and extracted it, you are left with a couple of things. The first is the actual toolkit. You can find it inside the `SampleWebSite\Bin` directory. This is a single `.dll` file that contains the controls. The sample web site itself shows a working example and documentation of each control in the toolkit. Finally, there is also a `.vsi` file for installing additional Visual Studio templates for creating new controls based on the toolkit's extender framework. We will skip these templates for now. Instead, let's look at how you can use the controls inside of Visual Studio. The following steps show you how to get started:

1. Create a new ASP.NET website with which to work. Alternatively, if you've created one for the previous walk-through, you can use it.

2. You want to add the controls to the Toolbox so that you can use them in your web site. First, however, right-click the Toolbox and choose Add Tab. This will give you a new area on the Toolbox in which to house the AJAX Control Toolkit controls. Name this tab AJAX Toolkit or something similar.

3. Next, right-click in the area inside the new tab and select Choose Items. This will allow you to select controls to add to this tab. Inside the Choose Toolbox Items, click the Browse button. Using the Open dialog, browse to the location where you unzipped the toolkit. Navigate to the `Bin` directory inside the `SampleWebSite` folder. Here you should see the `AjaxControlToolkit.dll` file. Select it and click the Open button and then the OK button. This will import the controls into the Toolbox.

The controls in the toolkit should now be ready for your use. Figure 17.6 shows the controls inside the Toolbox. Note that there are many controls listed here. Most of them provide a specific enough feature that you can understand them by name. Studying the sample website will also help you understand their capabilities.

### The Controls in the AJAX Control Toolkit

As you've seen, the controls inside the AJAX Control Toolkit have full design-time support. They can be worked with from the Toolbox and dragged onto your forms for use. Of course, it's important to know how you can leverage each control for your specific purpose.

Table 17.2 provides a high-level overview of some of the many controls in the Toolkit. Remember, these controls execute the vast majority of their functionality on the client. This gives the user a more interactive experience. Use the list in Table 17.2 as a reference and starting point when building these features into your applications.

### Using the Toolkit Controls on a Page

Refer to Table 17.2, immediately preceding. Notice that most of the controls in this table include the suffix `Extender`. This indicates that the control extends an existing ASP.NET control. Or, put a better way, the control works with another control to provide its functionality. For example, a `CalendarExtender` works with a `TextBox` control. Those controls in the library without this modifier exist as standalone controls.

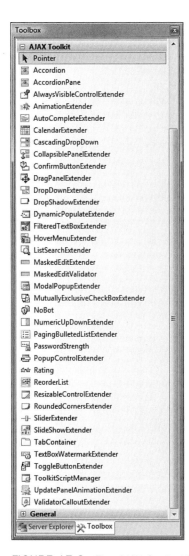

FIGURE 17.6    The AJAX Control Toolkit inside the Toolbox.

TABLE 17.2    ASP.NET AJAX Control Toolkit Controls

| Control | Description |
| --- | --- |
| Accordian | Use the `Accordian` control to display several sections of information (or panes) that have a title and content. However, only one of the `Accordian` sections is open at a given time. As one opens, the currently open one closes, giving an accordion-like effect for a user. |
| CollapsiblePanelExtender | The `CollapsiblePanelExtender` allows you to easily define a panel on your form that can be opened and closed by a user. The panel has a title bar that includes the expand and collapse button. |

17

TABLE 17.2    Continued

| Control | Description |
|---|---|
| AutoCompleteExtender | The AutoCompleteExtender control can respond to users' typing and provide them with options that they might be trying to type. It does so by attaching to a TextBox control and providing a pop-up panel with a list box. You populate the list box based on the user's typing as processed on the server. You might, for example, look up customer names as a user is entering an order. |
| CalendarExtender | Use the CalendarExtender control to attach a calendar picker to any ASP.NET text box. The control allows a user to browse a calendar and select a date for populating a text box. The calendar control shows up when the user sets focus to the text box or clicks a button. When the user has selected the date, the calendar disappears. |
| FilteredTextBoxExtender | The FilteredTextBoxExtender control allows you to indicate the type of data a user can enter into a given text box. You might, for example, restrict entry to only numeric characters, only letters, only lowercase letters, and so on. |
| HoverMenuExtender | The HoverMenuExtender control provides users with a small menu of actions based on where they hover their mouse on the page. You might, for instance, provide a menu for edit, delete, and modify when a user selects a given item in a list. You attach a HoverMenuExtender to a given control on the page. In this way, you can get the context of where the user was when he or she selected an action. |
| ListSearchExtender | The ListSearchExtender allows a user to type a letter in a ListBox or DropDownList and immediately select the first item in that list which starts with that letter. |
| MaskedEditExtender | The MaskedEditExtender control attaches to an ASP.NET text box and is used to both provide users with assistance when entering data and restrict the type of data they enter. For example, a user may need to enter a phone number in a certain format, such as *(area code)-exchange-number*. The MaskedEditExtender can enforce this format. |
| ModalPopupExtender | The ModalPopupExtender control allows you to create a window that pops up based on user action. This window will be modal on your page. That is, the page will be disabled and the user will have to respond to the dialog to continue. This control is great for confirming a user's request and allowing for complex data-entry scenarios where another form is required. |

| Control | Description |
|---------|-------------|
| ConfirmButtonExtender | The ConfirmButtonExtender control is another pop-up type control. Use it when you want to define a button whose action requires a confirmation by the user (see an example later in this chapter). |
| PasswordStrength | The PasswordStrength control attaches to a text box control and indicates visually to the user the strength of the password as the user enters it. You can use the control to set minimum password lengths, require not alphanumeric characters, and more. |
| ReorderList | The ReorderList control creates a data-bound list of items that a user can reorder inside the browser. Users select an item and move it above and below other items (without accessing the server, of course). New items can also be added to the list by users. |
| SliderExtender | The SliderExtender control works with an ASP.NET text box to capture user input. A user slides a graphical element up and down or left and right across a range. The text box is updated as the user moves the slider. |
| TabContainer | The TabContainer control allows you to group areas of functionality for a page into logical tabs. A user can then click on each tab and see the given functionality without refreshing from the server. Each TabContainer contains a TabPanel control. You place your ASP.NET controls onto the TabPanel control. |

17

The AJAX Toolkit makes it very easy to work with the controls—and even easier to work with the extender controls. To add an extender control to an ASP.NET control, you can use a smart tag action on the given control. The following directions outline adding a basic confirmation pop-up window to a button control:

1. Create a new page. Next, make sure your page has a ScriptManager control at the top of the page. Like the other AJAX controls, the Toolkit requires a ScriptManager.

2. Next, add a button to the page. You can double-click the button to add an event handler. In the event handler, you might set the Text property of the button to something different just to confirm that user cancellation is working. The following is an example:

```
protected void ButtonSave_Click(object sender, EventArgs e) {
    ButtonSave.Text = "Saved";
}
```

3. In design view, select the button and its smart tag. You will notice that there is an option for Add Extender. This option is added to Visual Studio by the AJAX Control Toolkit. Figure 17.7 shows an example. Select the option.

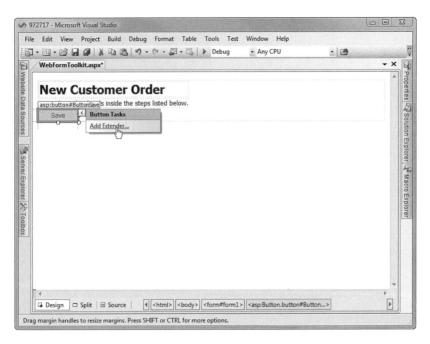

FIGURE 17.7    The Add Extender smart tag.

4. You should not be presented with the Choose an Extender dialog (see Figure 17.8). Here you will see all the extender controls listed. Select ConfirmButtonExtender. Notice that the ID is automatically set for the control based on the control you are extending. Click the OK button to continue.

5. The control has no visual representation because it simply extends the button control. Therefore, you need to either find it in the properties window or switch to split view. From either place, set the ConfirmText property to a message that confirms the user's operation. Notice too that the extender control's TargetControlID was automatically set to the ID of the control being extended (in this case, ButtonSave).

Now run the application. You should see your form display as you would expect. Click the Save button and you will be presented with a confirmation dialog, as shown in Figure 17.9. Clicking cancel will cancel the postback. Clicking OK will complete the postback on the server.

We've covered the AJAX basics that are built into Visual Studio 2008 and those that are available in the ASP.NET AJAX Toolkit. Our primary focus is on helping you use the AJAX controls to build better user experiences. Of course, there is more out there for those of you looking to build your own AJAX controls.

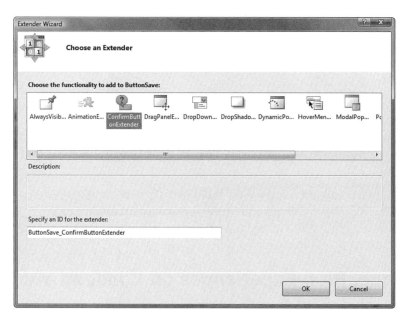

FIGURE 17.8    Selecting an extender control.

FIGURE 17.9    The **ConfirmButtonExtender** control in action.

As with ASP.NET server controls, Microsoft has provided a similar means for creating ASP.NET AJAX server controls. In fact, there is an ASP.NET AJAX Server Control template in Visual Studio to get you started. You can use it to build server controls that work with the `ScriptManager` and emit their own JavaScript out to the client. This process is a code-intensive one.

In addition, Visual Studio ships with the Microsoft AJAX library. This library wraps JavaScript into an easier-to-use, object-oriented structure for those looking to build more JavaScript into their controls and pages. The library ships with both a debug and a release version. In fact, the former is important in that Visual Studio 2008 has great support for debugging client-script.

There is also great community support out there for those looking to build ASP.NET AJAX controls. Check out both http://www.asp.net and http://www.codeplex.com for more information.

# Creating Unique, Rich Experiences on Windows via the Browser

In Chapter 16, "Creating Richer, Smarter User Interfaces," we walked through the process of creating Windows Presentation Foundation (WPF) applications using Visual Studio 2008. As you recall, these applications are based on XAML that is interpreted by the WPF portion of the .NET Framework and then rendered to screen. The WPF allows you to create user interfaces that leverage such things as vector-based graphics, scaling, and 3D effects in order to create unique user experiences for Windows. The applications we discussed in Chapter 16 are meant to be installed as standalone applications that run on the Windows operating system. However, similar WPF applications can be deployed to run in a user's web browser.

WPF applications built to target a web browser are also called XBAP (for XAML browser application). An XBAP can be deployed through a simple, ClickOnce URL and run as hosted inside the user's browser (the application does not leave the browser). Because of this, XBAP applications run inside a partial trust, security sandbox. For example, they do not have access to such things as the user's file system.

> **NOTE**
>
> WPF-based XBAP can run inside of both Internet Explorer and Firefox. This ensures a larger reach for your application because the vast majority of users are standardized on one or the other. An XBAP does, however, require Windows on the client along with the .NET Framework. If you need a fully cross-platform solution, you will have to build on ASP.NET or Silverlight.

## Choosing Between WPF Standalone and WPF XBAP

There are specific scenarios in which an XBAP application has an advantage over ASP.NET, WinForms, or a standard WPF application. For one, you can use XBAP to easily create a user experience that typically does not exist inside a browser application. This includes Windows-like menus, context menus (right-click), interactive drill-down data, real-time spell-checking, masked edit controls, data list scrolling, hotkeys and shortcuts, managing the user's cursor, and many more features. This type of rich user experience is typically limited to a standalone Windows client. However, with XBAP, you can run a client with these features hosted directly inside the browser. In this way, you get the added benefits of easy deployment (and update), the use of the browser's security sandbox, and communication with your server (and web services) via HTTP. And, if you need it, your XBAP application can access isolated storage to save and recall data securely on a user's machine.

An XBAP application is a type of WPF application. The two are based on the same .NET Framework code. However, they have their similarities and their differences. You want to understand these when you make a choice for building your next user interface. Table 17.3 should help illuminate the options you have when comparing one to the other.

TABLE 17.3   ASP.NET AJAX Controls

| Feature | WPF | XBAP |
|---------|-----|------|
| Installation | Typically installed on a user's machine using a `.msi` package or through ClickOnce.<br><br>Can be uninstalled through Add/Remove Programs. | Installed inside the browser's cache (not a direct install on the machine).<br><br>Installed via a ClickOnce URL. |
| User Access | A user can access via the Start menu, desktop shortcut, and so on.<br><br>An `.exe` file is installed in the `Program Files` folder. | Accessed via the browser shortcuts (favorites) over HTTP.<br><br>The `.exe` file is hosted in the browser. |
| Host/Process | Runs hosted in its own Windows process. | Hosted in the web browser's process. |
| Security | Typically runs with full trust on the user's machine. This means access to the registry, file system, and devices like printers. | Runs in a partial trust sandbox. By default, no access to remoting, reflection, the file system, printers, WCF services, the registry, and more. |
| WCF Support | Can fully communicate with WCF services. | Cannot call WCF services from a browser application. |
| New Windows | Creates new, child windows similar to any Windows application. | New windows are "navigated" to in the browser and not popped open like a Windows application. |

**17**

TABLE 17.3    Continued

| Feature | WPF | XBAP |
|---|---|---|
| Updating | Requires some update strategy to get updates to the client or for the client to request updates. | Easily updated as the user hits the server to access. New versions can be deployed once to the server and all clients will be updated. |
| Offline | A user typically has access to run the application when not connected to a server (offline). | Online only. Requires a connection to the server. |

## Creating a WPF Browser Application

Creating a WPF browser application is nearly the same as creating a standalone WPF application. Of course, there are a few things you need to consider to make sure your application is properly set up and configured to be deployed and run in a web browser. In this section, you will walk through the basic steps of creating, configuring, and debugging an XBAP. From there, we will discuss both security and deployment considerations.

To get started, you will create a basic WPF browser application. We will not discuss the basics of UI design, layout, and coding because they were discussed previously, in Chapter 16. The first step is to create a WPF project. There is a special template in Visual Studio 2008 for XBAP applications. This template is called WPF Browser Application. Using this template gives you a head start on getting your application configured to work in a browser. Figure 17.10 shows the New Project dialog with this template highlighted.

When you create a WPF browser application, you get a project built on a similar template to a standard WPF application. This includes a default WPF form file and an app.xaml for configuration. In a WPF application your new files are typically named WindowX.xaml by Visual Studio (where X represents a number). In a XBAP, Visual Studio calls your WPF forms pages (PageX.xaml).

Each of these files is built on a different base class. A window file, for example, derives from System.Windows.Window, whereas a page file is built on the class System.Windows.Controls.Page. The app.xaml configuration file is a good place to set the page that should be viewed when the user first hits the application. Here there is an attribute of the Application node called StartupUri. You set this value to the name of your startup form in your application, as the following markup from an App.xaml file shows:

```
<Application x:Class="WpfBrowserWorkQueue.App"
  xmlns="http://schemas.microsoft.com/winfx/2006/xaml/presentation"
  xmlns:x="http://schemas.microsoft.com/winfx/2006/xaml"
  StartupUri="Main.xaml">

</Application>
```

Your next step is to build your WPF application as you would any other. You want to pay close attention, however, to the security restrictions of the sandbox in which your application will be hosted (see below). Other than that, you can use the many WPF controls to lay out your user interface. This includes menus, context menus, shortcut keys, and more.

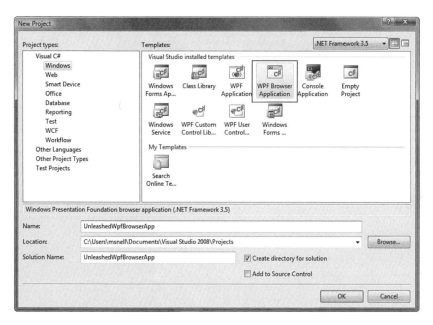

FIGURE 17.10   Creating a WPF browser application.

You can run and debug your XBAP application like any other .NET application. Simply set any breakpoints you want and click the Start Debugging (or Run) button. This will launch your application inside a browser. Figure 17.11 shows the beginnings of a help-desk work tracking system running as a WPF browser application. Notice that the application is hosted in IE. Also notice the use of a menu bar, a status bar, a toolbar, context menus, and related features of Windows.

After you have your XBAP built to your satisfaction, you will want to deploy it to a web server for user access. We will look at this process in a moment. First, however, you need to be aware of the security surrounding any XBAP application you build.

## Security Considerations

A WPF browser application gets installed from a web server. By default, applications that originate from web servers are not (and should not be) trusted. Trust, in this case, refers to an agreement between an application and a user with respect to the user's machine and devices. You do not want applications that originate from the Internet, for example, to simply have access to your file system. Therefore, WBF browser applications run in what's called a sandbox.

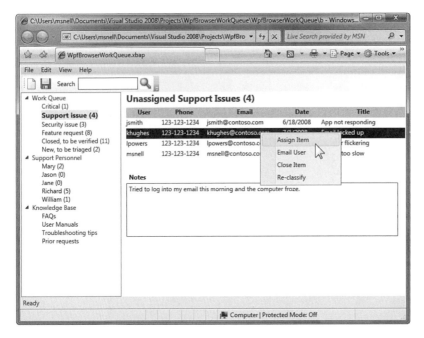

FIGURE 17.11    A WPF XBAP application running in the browser.

This sandbox is controlled by your browser's security. By default, an XBAP application runs in what's called the Internet zone. This zone is low-trust, high-security. Figure 17.12 shows the Internet zone from the perspective of Internet Explorer. In this way, an XBAP has similar rights as would any application originating from the Internet (and therefore should be as secure).

Clicking the Custom Level button shown in Figure 17.12 brings up the Security Settings dialog for the given zone. XBAP applications have their own basic settings. These are highlighted in Figure 17.13. You can disable XBAP applications or ask the user before running them. Be default, they are enabled in the Internet zone in IE.

When you run (or debug) your XBAP and it tries to go beyond the bounds of the sandbox, a security exception will be thrown. The user will see a message similar to that shown in Figure 17.14. Again, what your XBAP can do is controlled by the zone in which it resides. For the secure Internet zone, this means you need to avoid all the following when building your application:

▶ Remoting

▶ Private reflection

▶ Device driver access (like printers)

▶ Registry access

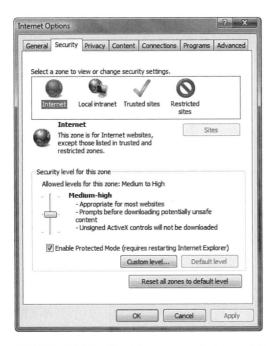

FIGURE 17.12    The Internet zone in Internet Explorer.

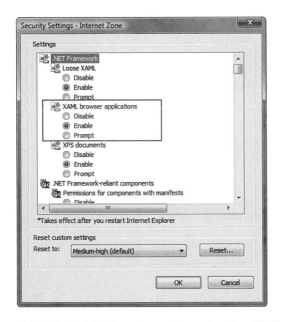

FIGURE 17.13    Security settings related to XBAP applications.

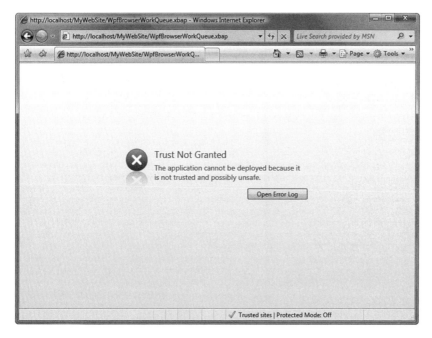

FIGURE 17.14   A Trust Not Granted user message.

▶ Interop with other code (not .NET)

▶ WCF service calls (HTTP and web service calls are allowed)

▶ File system access (you can write a secure upload similar to a web page upload; in addition, isolated storage on the client is available)

If you need access to any of these items, it is best to consider a different deployment strategy. For example, you might switch to a WPF application that is deployed through a browser (and ClickOnce) but installed on a user's machine rather than simply hosted in the browser. In this way, the .exe will be copied to the user's machine and installed as trusted (with access to the items previously listed).

It should be noted, however, that it is possible to run your XBAP application in a browser with full trust. This means giving your application rights inside the Local Intranet zone. A user will get a warning, but after the user confirms, the application will have full access to the user's machine from the browser. This should generally be avoided as a security best practice. If, however, it is used, it should be restricted to intranet applications at most.

You can use the Properties window for your WPF application to manage security. To do so, you right-click the project and choose properties. This will show you the property editor inside of Visual Studio 2008. Figure 17.15 shows the Security tab of this window. Notice that you can toggle between full trust (WPF standalone) and partial trust (XBAP). You can also set the zone in which the application will by default run.

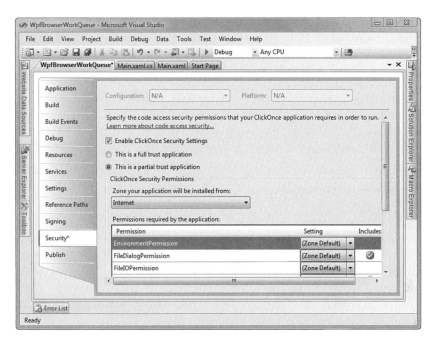

FIGURE 17.15   The Security tab for a WPF browser application.

### Security and Site Navigation

You should be aware of how navigation works between content in your application and between any websites and your application. Each scenario comes with its own security restrictions.

First, *application navigation security* refers to the security applied when your application navigates between one page (.xaml file) and another. This type of navigation is allowed without concern for additional security. For example, you can create a new .xaml page and navigate to it in code as shown here:

```
Page2 p = new Page2();
this.NavigationService.Navigate(p);
```

You might write this type of code in response to a user action such as a menu item select or button click. Alternatively, you can use the Hyperlink element to give users a weblike behavior when navigating between pages in your site. The following markup is an example:

```
<Hyperlink NavigateUri="Main.xaml">
  Back to Main
</Hyperlink>
```

The other type of navigation security is called *browser navigation security*. This refers to navigation that happens between a website and your application. This type of navigation is allowed provided that the user initiated the navigation from a hyperlink control in either the website or your WPF application. In this scenario, the content being linked to should also be in the same zone.

## Deploying a WPF Browser Application

Users access WPF browser applications from their web browser. Therefore, you must deploy them out to an IIS web server. You can then link to the XBAP from a standard HTML or ASP.NET page via a hyperlink. The application will then be installed in the browser via ClickOnce. The following list steps you through the deployment process:

1. When you are ready to deploy, the first step is to build your application. You typically set your build state to Release to ensure that you are not unnecessarily shipping debug code.

2. After you've built your application, you should see a number of files in the bin\release directory for your application. These files represent those you need to deploy. However, you can't simply copy these files out to your web server. You need a deployment file. To get this file, you need to run the Visual Studio Publish Wizard, which you can access via the Build menu (Build, Publish).

   The first step in this wizard is to set a directory to where you intend to publish the application. For now, leave this as publish\. This will create a directory in your application and put all the necessary files there. You can then copy them up to your web server. The next step in this wizard is to indicate how users will install the application. Here it is important that you indicate From a Web Site. Figure 17.16 shows an example. The next steps do not matter for XBAP applications; simply click Next and then Finish.

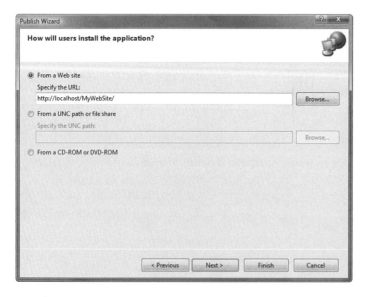

FIGURE 17.16    The Visual Studio Publish Wizard.

3. Next, navigate to the folder created in the prior step (...\publish\) to observe its contents. In this folder, you will see a couple of files and a folder containing other files. These items can be described this way:

Publish.htm: This is an HTML file that contains a hyperlink to install your application. You can use this file to test the publication of your application. However, you typically do not deploy this file. An example of the file is shown in Figure 17.17.

FIGURE 17.17   The HTML launch page for your XBAP.

ApplicationName.xbap: This file is called an XBAP manifest file where *ApplicationName* is the name of your Visual Studio project. The file is used to deploy your XBAP application. You create a web page (similar to publish.htm) to link to this file. IIS then passes this to ClickOnce to get the application installed.

Application Files\ApplicationName_version\ApplicationName.deploy: This is the ClickOnce deployment file. This file contains your .exe.

Application Files\ApplicationName_version\ApplicationName.manifest: This is a manifest file for your application and contains your application's metadata.

4. Your next step is to create an ASP.NET or HTML page for the user to initiate the installation. The important thing is that the page contains a hyperlink to the .xbap file. The following is an example:

```
<a href="WpfBrowserWorkQueue.xbap">Launch the Work Tracking System</a>
```

5. The next step is to make sure that IIS is configured correctly. If you are already running IIS 7, there is no need to do anything. If, however, you are running an older version of IIS, you need to register the MIME types in IIS as listed in Table 17.4. Figure 17.18 shows an example of adding MIME types to IIS.

TABLE 17.4    XBAP Required MIME Types

| Filename Extension | MIME Type |
| --- | --- |
| .application | application/x-ms-application |
| .deploy | application/octet-stream |
| .manifest | application/manifest |
| .xaml | application/xaml+xml |
| .xbap | application/x-ms-xbap |
| .xps | application/vnd.ms-xpsdocument |

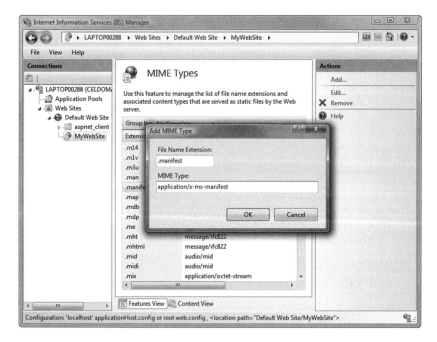

FIGURE 17.18    Adding MIME types to IIS.

6. Your next task is to make sure that you create a website for your application. This can be done by creating a virtual directory in IIS.

7. The virtual directory you created in the preceding step is, of course, mapped to a physical folder (typically C:\inetpub\wwwroot\SiteName\). You need to navigate back to the publish directory, copy the files from there, and paste them into the

physical folder of your website's virtual directory. You also need to paste your HTML file (`default.htm`) in the same folder.

All that is left is to run your application from a browser. When you do so, you should be presented with the default file for the site (typically `default.htm` for `default.aspx`). Figure 17.19 shows a launch page running at http://localhost/MyWebSite/.

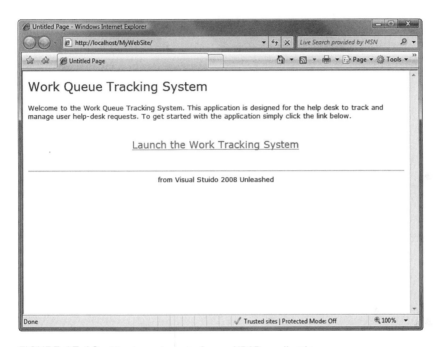

FIGURE 17.19  The launch page for an XBAP application.

Clicking the hyperlink in the center of the page will install the WPF application in the user's browser (with a progress bar provided by ClickOnce). Figure 17.20 shows the application deployed and running from this URL.

## Delivering Interactive Experiences Across Platforms

Microsoft is working to help developers and designers deliver a much richer (similar to WPF) user experience within a web browser over traditional ASP.NET, HTML sites, and even JavaScript. This new technology is called Silverlight. With it you can create media-rich sites that include brochure-ware, interactive games, new shopping and buying experiences, interactive training, and sites that deliver video and audio. It was built to allow you to create truly rich, truly unique user experiences over the web.

Because Microsoft Silverlight targets the web, it was built to work cross-platform and cross-browser. This means it works on Mac OS and Windows XP/Vista (there is even a Linux project underway by the community). In addition, it works on all modern browsers including IE 6 and 7, Firefox 2, and Safari. In all cases, it is a plug-in in the browser.

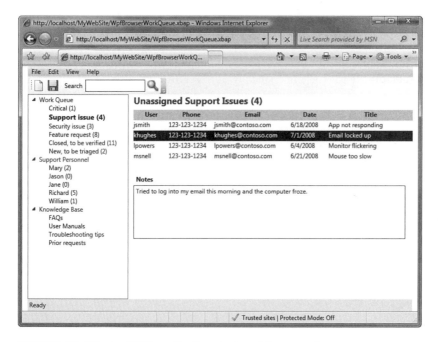

FIGURE 17.20    An XBAP application deployed from a web server.

The Silverlight plug-in runs a mini version of the .NET Framework. In this way, your development experience is similar to that of .NET. It does not, however, require the .NET Framework on the machine. Instead, everything that is required is in the plug-in.

You can write Silverlight applications similar to how you write WPF applications. The UI is marked up in XAML and the code-behind is C# or VB. You can also use AJAX, Python, or Ruby (and others) to work with Silverlight controls inside a website. In this section we will walk through writing a simple Silverlight application. We will then embed that application as part of a website. Let's get started.

## Getting Started with Silverlight

The first version of the Silverlight runtime is a released product; however, the tools are still catching up. This means there is no Silverlight in-the-box support in Visual Studio 2008. As of this writing (early 2008), there are alphas and betas of both a new runtime and a set of Silverlight tools. Here we discuss what is available. These items also serve as the basis for the content in this section. You will want to check whether new versions exist when you are ready to get started.

Your first step in building Silverlight applications is to set up your development environment. The best place to check for the latest design and development tools is http://www.silverlight.net. This site will give you links to download the latest runtime, design tools, and development templates and SDKs. In our examples for this book, this means the following set of tools:

- ▶ **Microsoft Silverlight 1.1 Alpha September Refresh**—Represents an Alpha release of the new (1.1) Silverlight runtime. This runtime is required to use the Alpha tools for Visual Studio 2008.

- ▶ **Microsoft Silverlight 1.1 Tools Alpha for Visual Studio 2008**—An Alpha release of the Silverlight tools for Visual Studio. This gives you project templates and the appropriate debugging support.

- ▶ **Microsoft ASP.NET Futures (July 2007)**—Provides a set of Silverlight-based ASP.NET controls that you can embed in your website.

- ▶ **Microsoft Silverlight 1.1 Software Development Kit Alpha September Refresh**—Provides the SDK for building Silverlight applications.

- ▶ **Expression Blend 2.0**—This tool provides designer support for building Silverlight (and WPF) applications. It is meant for designers. There is also a 1.0 version of the product. However, you really need the 2.0 version to build Silverlight applications.

> **NOTE**
>
> Not all of these tools are released products. They may be by the time you are reading this, in which case you can skip this note. However, at the time of writing, these products are early versions that contain quirks and bugs. They are not the type of polished, final tools that you might be used to. Therefore, they require patience when you are trying to get them to work.

**17**

To work alongside the pages that follow, you will need to download and install all the items in the previous list. This is a straightforward process and should not give you much trouble.

## Creating a Silverlight Application

It's important to note that there are multiple ways you can leverage Silverlight. You can create full-blown Silverlight applications. In this case, the application is launched inside a web browser and runs self-contained. Alternatively, you can create a web page that embeds Silverlight as part of the page. This might be for video or to use a Silverlight control. We will cover both. In this section, we will focus on building a Silverlight application.

### Defining a New Silverlight Project

Your first step to building a Silverlight application is to create a Silverlight project. In previous chapters, we discussed the developer-designer workflow that is now possible with Visual Studio and the Expression products. Silverlight is part of this workflow. Therefore, you can originate your Silverlight project in the tool that makes sense for your situation: Visual Studio 2008 or Expression Blend 2.

In Visual Studio 2008, you simply follow the standard File, New Project menu path. Provided that you installed everything from the previous section, you should see a Silverlight node in the New Project dialog (for both VB and C#). Figure 17.21 shows an example. Here you can select Silverlight Project to create an application or Silverlight Class Library to create a control or another library for use in a Silverlight application.

FIGURE 17.21    Creating a Silverlight project.

Expression Blend also has a Silverlight project template that works with either VB or C#. You can create a new project here or you can use Expression Blend to open your Visual Studio created project (or XAML files). To create a new project in Expression Blend, you again use the File, New Project menu items. This brings up the New Project dialog as shown in Figure 17.22. Notice that you can use this version of the tool to create both Silverlight 1.0 applications and Visual Studio 2008 (Orcas) applications targeted at a newer version of Silverlight (1.1 in the graphic, but 2.0 should be released by the time you read this). Notice too that you have your choice of C# or VB.

The project template created by both tools is pretty similar. They both create a solutions file and a project file. They both reference the same set of Silverlight libraries. In addition, they both embed the `Silverlight.js` file that includes JavaScript for working with your Silverlight application. And they both have a `Page.xaml` file as a starting point along with an HTML file for launching the `Page.xaml` file. Figure 17.23 shows the two project templates side by side.

FIGURE 17.22    Creating a new Silverlight project in Expression Blend 2.

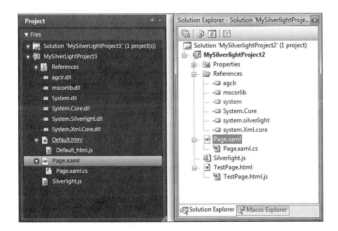

FIGURE 17.23    The Visual Studio 2008 and Expression Blend 2 Silverlight project templates.

### Building an Application

To build your application, you use the `.xaml` markup file to write your user interface and put any code you have in its code-behind. This should be a very familiar process. In the current release of the tools, however, Visual Studio does not have a visual designer for Silverlight XAML. This means no controls on the Toolbox and no WYSIWYG editor.

Instead, you have IntelliSense inside the editor. The good news is that Expression Blend does have a designer.

We, of course, will start in Visual Studio. In this example, you will create a simple slide-show application. It will allow a user to page forward and back through a set of images using Silverlight. As the user does so, the images will simply render (without page refresh). Follow these steps to create this application:

1. First, create a new project as described in the previous section.

2. Inside the `Page.xaml` file, add three `TextBlock` elements and an `Image` element. The three `TextBlock` elements will represent a title and a next and previous link. The `Image` element should represent the slide-show images. Listing 17.1 shows a sample of what your XAML should look like.

LISTING 17.1    The **`Page.xaml`** UI Markup

```
<Canvas x:Name="parentCanvas"
        xmlns="http://schemas.microsoft.com/client/2007"
        xmlns:x="http://schemas.microsoft.com/winfx/2006/xaml"
        Loaded="Page_Loaded"
        x:Class="MySilverlightProject2.Page;assembly=ClientBin/
➥MySilverlightProject2.dll"
        Width="400"
        Height="400"
        Background="White">

  <TextBlock x:Name="Title" Text="Image Slide Show" FontSize="18"
    Canvas.Left="10" Canvas.Top="10"></TextBlock>

  <Image x:Name="SlideImage" Source="" Canvas.Left="10" Canvas.Top="45"
        Height="250"></Image>

  <TextBlock x:Name="Previous" Text="\\ Previous" FontSize="12"
    Canvas.Left="10" Canvas.Top="300"></TextBlock>

  <TextBlock x:Name="Next" Text="Next //" FontSize="12"
    Canvas.Left="250" Canvas.Top="300"></TextBlock>

</Canvas>
```

3. For this example, we will use the sample images that ship with Windows. In Vista these can be found in the `Sample Pictures` folder. Create an images directory in your solution and copy these sample pictures into this directory.

4. Next you will add event handlers that respond to the user clicking the Next and Previous `TextBlock` elements. From within the XAML, add the appropriate attribute to each `TextBlock` element respectively:

```
<TextBlock x:Name="Previous"
   MouseLeftButtonDown="Previous_MouseLeftButtonDown" ...
<TextBlock x:Name="Next"

   MouseLeftButtonDown="Next_MouseLeftButtonDown" ...
```

5. We will now add some code in the code-behind to respond to these events. At the class level, we will keep track of the images in a string array as well as the selected image index. We will initialize the first image when the page loads, and in each TextBlock event we will change images. Listing 17.2 shows the code you might write to do so.

LISTING 17.2　The **Page.xaml** Code-Behind

```
using System;
using System.Windows;
using System.Windows.Controls;
using System.Windows.Documents;
using System.Windows.Ink;
using System.Windows.Input;
using System.Windows.Media;
using System.Windows.Media.Animation;
using System.Windows.Shapes;

namespace MySilverlightProject2 {

  public partial class Page : Canvas {

    //list of images
    string[] _images = new string[] {"Autumn Leaves.jpg", "Creek.jpg",
      "Desert Landscape.jpg", "Dock.jpg", "Forest Flowers.jpg",
      "Forest.jpg" };

    //used to track currently selected image
    int _selectedIndex = 0;

    public void Page_Loaded(object o, EventArgs e) {

      // Required to initialize variables
      InitializeComponent();

      //set start image
      SetUri();
```

17

LISTING 17.2   Continued

```
     }

   void Previous_MouseLeftButtonDown(object sender, MouseEventArgs e) {

     //check previous value
     if (_selectedIndex -1 >= 0) {
       _selectedIndex = _selectedIndex - 1;
     }
     //move to the previous image in the list
     SetUri();

   }

   void Next_MouseLeftButtonDown(object sender, MouseEventArgs e) {

     //check next value
     if (_selectedIndex + 1 < _images.GetLength(0)) {
       _selectedIndex = _selectedIndex + 1;
     }
     //move to the next image in the list
     SetUri();

   }

   private void SetUri() {
     Uri u = new Uri("images/" + _images[_selectedIndex],
       UriKind.Relative);
     SlideImage.Source = u;
   }

 }
}
```

6. Run the application to see it working in your browser. Notice that you can set break-points in the code-behind file and debug as you would any other application. Figure 17.24 shows an example of the application running in IE.

7. When you designed the Page.xaml file previously, you were limited by the Visual Studio designer. Recall that the designer-developer workflow means designers do the design and developers do the development. You can pass the .xaml file to a designer at this point to spruce things up.

   In this step, you will play the role of designer. You can right-click the .xaml file in Visual Studio to open it in Expression Blend 2. Figure 17.25 shows an example of this process.

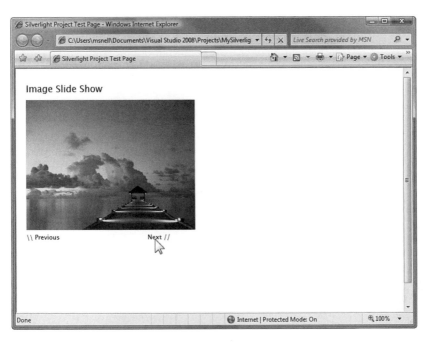

FIGURE 17.24   The initial Silverlight example running in a browser.

FIGURE 17.25   Launching the **.xaml** file in Expression Blend from Visual Studio.

Figure 17.26 shows the `Page.xaml` file open in Expression Blend. Notice that the entire project is open. This allows a designer to run the application to see the results of the changes. Notice too the split view of markup and designer.

FIGURE 17.26    The Silverlight markup inside Expression Blend.

8. You can now use the designer tools to change the XAML markup. Select an item in the designer and click the Properties pane (upper right). Here you can manipulate color, font, rendering, and so on. You can also position items relative to borders and each other using the designer.

Figure 17.27 shows an example. Here we've changed the title `TextBlock` to render on an angle, to be gradient filled, and to overlap the images. Notice too the next and previous `TextBlocks`. They also overlap the images. We also set their cursor to the hand cursor when a user hovers over them. All of this was set through the Properties pane.

Save the file and close Expression Blend. Return to Visual Studio and it should refresh your markup accordingly. The new markup might look as shown in Listing 17.3.

FIGURE 17.27    The revised Silverlight markup inside Expression Blend.

LISTING 17.3    The Revised **Page.XAML** from Expression Blend

```
<Canvas x:Name="parentCanvas"
  xmlns="http://schemas.microsoft.com/client/2007"
  xmlns:x="http://schemas.microsoft.com/winfx/2006/xaml"
  Loaded="Page_Loaded"
       x:Class="MySilverlightProject2.Page;assembly=ClientBin/
➡MySilverlightProject2.dll"
  Width="357"
  Height="354"
  Background="White">

  <Image x:Name="SlideImage" Source="images/Autumn Leaves.jpg"
    Width="337" Height="337" Canvas.Left="10" Canvas.Top="24"/>

  <TextBlock x:Name="Previous" Text="&lt;&lt; Previous" FontSize="14"
    Canvas.Left="10" Canvas.Top="300"
    MouseLeftButtonDown="Previous_MouseLeftButtonDown"
    Foreground="#FFFFFFFF" FontWeight="Bold" Cursor="Hand"></TextBlock>
```

17

LISTING 17.3   Continued

```
  <TextBlock x:Name="Next" Text="Next &gt;&gt;" FontSize="14"
    Canvas.Left="286.663" Canvas.Top="300"
    MouseLeftButtonDown="Next_MouseLeftButtonDown"
    Foreground="#FFFFFFFF" FontWeight="Bold" Cursor="Hand"></TextBlock>

  <TextBlock x:Name="Title" Text="Image Slide Show" FontSize="36"
    Canvas.Left="10.385"
    Canvas.Top="17.542" RenderTransformOrigin="0.5,0.5" Width="351.884"
    FontStretch="Expanded" FontStyle="Normal" FontWeight="Bold">
    <TextBlock.Foreground>
      <LinearGradientBrush EndPoint="0.5,1" StartPoint="0.5,0">
        <GradientStop Color="#FF0E2DF8" Offset="0"/>
        <GradientStop Color="#FFFFFFFF" Offset="1"/>
      </LinearGradientBrush>
    </TextBlock.Foreground>
    <TextBlock.RenderTransform>
      <TransformGroup>
        <ScaleTransform ScaleX="1" ScaleY="1"/>
        <SkewTransform AngleX="0" AngleY="0"/>
        <RotateTransform Angle="-7.595"/>
        <TranslateTransform X="0" Y="0"/>
      </TransformGroup>
    </TextBlock.RenderTransform>
</TextBlock>

</Canvas>
```

Finally, run the application in a web browser. You should get the new look and new behavior you've defined using Expression Blend. Figure 17.28 shows an example of the application running in IE.

## Using Silverlight on a Web Page

In the previous example, you built a standalone .xaml page that can be run in a browser using the Silverlight plug-in. This same XAML can be used inside an HTML or .aspx page. This section walks you through the process of embedding our prior example into a page on an ASP.NET website. The following steps walk through the highlights of this process:

1.  Create a Website application (File, New Project). You can do so in the same solution as your Silverlight application. In this way, you can link the two as they are related.

2.  Next you want to establish a link (similar to a reference) to your Silverlight application. Right-click your new website and choose Add Silverlight Link to do so. This will launch the Add Silverlight Link dialog, shown in Figure 17.29.

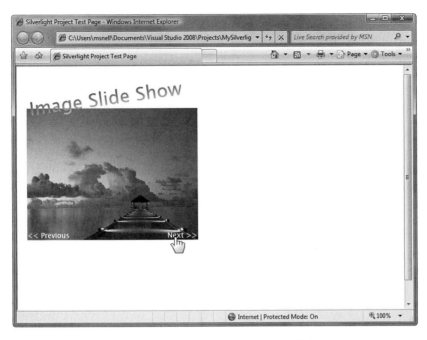

FIGURE 17.28   The revised Silverlight running in a web browser.

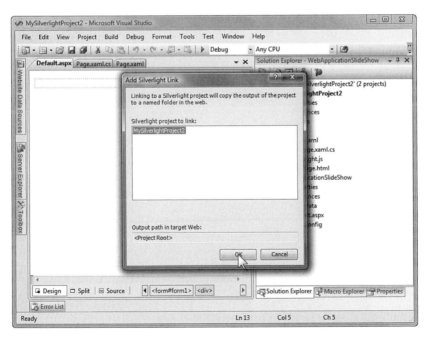

FIGURE 17.29   Adding a link from a website to a Silverlight project.

Linking the two projects will tell the compiler to push changes from the Silverlight project to the website project. The website project requires an actual copy of your Silverlight application. If you are not linking the two, you can just copy the files over to the website.

3. Launching the Silverlight application in your web page requires a little client-side JavaScript. Fortunately, the Silverlight application has all the code you need.

Look back at the Silverlight solution. Notice the Silverlight.js file. This should be copied into your website (the link should have taken care of that). Next, look at the page TestPage.html. It contains a code-behind file called TestPage.html.js. Inside here is auto-generated JavaScript that will load your Page.xaml file using the contents of Silverlight.js. Listing 17.4 shows this code.

Copy this code. Create a new file in your website called Default.aspx.js and paste this code into the file.

LISTING 17.4  The **createSilverlight** JavaScript Function

```
function createSilverlight()
{
  Silverlight.createObjectEx({
    source: "Page.xaml",
    parentElement: document.getElementById("SilverlightControlHost"),
    id: "SilverlightControl",
    properties: {
      width: "100%",
      height: "100%",
      version: "1.1",
      enableHtmlAccess: "true"
    },
    events: {}
  });

  // Give the keyboard focus to the Silverlight control by default
  document.body.onload = function() {
  var silverlightControl =
    document.getElementById('SilverlightControl');
  if (silverlightControl)
    silverlightControl.focus();
  }
}
```

4. You now need to link up this JavaScript into your web page (Default.aspx). In addition, you need to define a Silverlight host for the Silverlight XAML. To accomplish all of this, add the following script tags and style tag to the <head> section of your markup:

```
    <script type="text/javascript" src="Silverlight.js"></script>
    <script type="text/javascript" src="Default.aspx.js"></script>
    <style type="text/css">
       .silverlightHost { width: 357px; height: 354px; }
    </style>
```

5. Last, you need to lay out the rest of your ASP.NET page. This might mean a title, other controls, and so on. Somewhere on the page, however, you will write a call to the method inside the `Default.aspx.js` file `createSilverlight`. This will indicate where you want the `Page.xaml` embedded. Listing 17.5 shows some simple markup where the Silverlight control is embedded inside a table.

LISTING 17.5   The **Default.aspx** Markup

```
<%@ Page Language="C#" AutoEventWireup="true"
  CodeBehind="Default.aspx.cs"
  Inherits="WebApplicationSlideShow._Default" %>

<!DOCTYPE html PUBLIC "-//W3C//DTD XHTML 1.0 Transitional//EN"
  "http://www.w3.org/TR/xhtml1/DTD/xhtml1-transitional.dtd">

<html xmlns="http://www.w3.org/1999/xhtml" >
<head id="Head1" runat="server">
  <title>My Silverlight Page</title>
  <script type="text/javascript" src="Silverlight.js"></script>
  <script type="text/javascript" src="Default.aspx.js"></script>
  <style type="text/css">
    .silverlightHost { width: 357px; height: 354px; }
  </style>
</head>

<body style="font-family: Verdana; font-size: 12pt">
  <form id="form1" runat="server">
  <table>
      <tr>
          <td colspan="2">
              <div style="font-size: 18pt; color: Blue">
                  The Slide Show Viewer
              </div>
          </td>
      </tr>
      <tr><td colspan="2"><hr /></td></tr>
      <tr>
          <td valign="middle">
              <p>This Silverlight application allows you to traverse
              a set of images forward and backward.</p>
```

17

LISTING 17.5   Continued

```
            <p>Use the buttons at the bottom of the image to move
            Next and Previous through the images.</p>

        </td>
        <td>
            <div id="SilverlightControlHost" class="silverlightHost" >
                <script type="text/javascript">
                    createSilverlight();
                </script>
            </div>
        </td>
    </tr>
    <tr><td colspan="2"><hr /></td></tr>
    <tr>
        <td colspan="2">
            <div style="font-size: 9pt; text-align: right">
                from Visual Studio 2008 Unleashed
            </div>
        </td>
    </tr>
  </table>

  </form>
</body>
</html>
```

That's it. You should now be able to run the website and see the Silverlight embedded in the page. Figure 17.30 shows this running.

# Summary

In this chapter, we covered many new options for enabling rich client interaction inside a web browser. These included creating standard web pages that leverage AJAX, building rich Windows-like UIs with WPF inside a web browser running on a Windows Client, and building cross-platform, media-rich solutions based on the Silverlight browser plug-in. Which you use in your next application is really dependent on your content and your audience. The broadest possible user reach in order of most to fewest is ASP.NET and AJAX, then Silverlight, and finally WPF. However, the highest degree of user interaction is the opposite order: WPF, Silverlight, and then AJAX. You will want to consider carefully when starting your next browser-based UI project. The good news is that with these technologies, you can provide new and exciting experiences for your users.

FIGURE 17.30   The Silverlight application running embedded inside an ASP.NET web page.

# CHAPTER 18

# Working with Databases

This chapter is all about how you can manage databases and build data-aware applications using Visual Studio 2008 and SQL Server.

Five different Visual Studio tools allow you to interact with a database and assist with building applications that leverage data from a database:

▶ Solution Explorer

▶ Server Explorer

▶ Database Diagram Designer

▶ Table Designer

▶ Query and View Designer

Collectively, they are referred to as the *Visual Database tools*. We introduced a few of these tools earlier, in Chapter 5, "Browsers and Explorers." Now we have the opportunity to explore how developers can use these tools together to create database solutions.

We'll start by examining how to build databases and database objects with the Visual Database tools. From there, we can cover the specifics of creating data-aware applications with data-bound controls.

## Creating Tables and Relationships

The primary entities in any database are its tables. Tables are composed of a structure and data. Server Explorer is the Visual Studio instrument used to define or edit the structure or data of any table within a connected database. In fact, using Server Explorer, it is possible to create a new SQL Server database instance from scratch.

> **NOTE**
>
> As we noted in Chapter 5, the Express and Standard editions of Visual Studio refer to the Server Explorer as the Database Explorer. For simplicity, we will always refer to this window as the *Server Explorer* in this chapter.

## Creating a New SQL Server Database

Data connections are physical connections to a database. In Server Explorer, the Data Connections node has a list of every established database connection. To start the database creation process, right-click on the Data Connections node and select the Create New SQL Server Database option. In the resulting dialog box (see Figure 18.1), you will need to provide a server name, login credentials, and a name for the new database.

FIGURE 18.1    Creating a new SQL Server database.

This will immediately create the indicated database and add a connection to the new database under the Data Connections node. Figure 18.2 shows the newly created Contoso database added to the list of connections.

### Adding an Existing Database

Of course, you can also establish a connection to an existing database. Again, you right-click the Data Connections node; this time, though, you select the Add Connection option. The Add Connection dialog box (see Figure 18.3) is similar to the new database dialog box: You specify a data source, server name, login credentials, and database name/database filename to connect to the database.

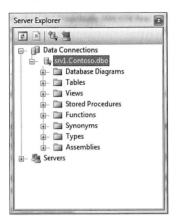

FIGURE 18.2    The new database added to the data connections.

FIGURE 18.3    Connecting to an existing database.

Under each connection are folders for the following classes of database objects:

▶ Database diagrams

▶ Tables

▶ Views

- ▶ Stored procedures

- ▶ Functions

- ▶ Synonyms

- ▶ Types

- ▶ Assemblies

These folders are the launching point for creating corresponding objects within the database.

## Defining Tables

The Table Designer is the Visual Studio tool you use to define or edit the definition for a table. Using the Server Explorer window, right-click the Tables folder under an existing connection and select Add New Table. The Table Designer will open in the main document pane of the IDE.

The designer is implemented in a tabular format; you add a row in the designer for every column you want to define in the table. For each table column, you specify a name, data type, and nullability. In addition to the tabular designer interface, a Properties window is present that provides complete access to all the different properties for any given column in a table (see Figure 18.4).

In addition to the basics, the Table Designer allows you to define a column, or group of columns, as part of the primary key for the table, or as part of an index.

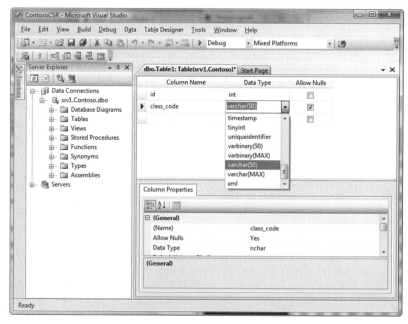

FIGURE 18.4   Defining a table's columns.

### Setting a Primary Key

With the Table Designer active in the IDE, a new Table Designer top-level menu item is available. You can use this menu, or the shortcut menu displayed whenever you right-click within the Table Designer, to access a list of useful actions. For instance, to create a primary key for the table, you would select the column or columns that constitute the key and then select Set Primary Key from the designer's menu. A key icon will indicate any primary keys defined in the table.

### Creating Indexes, Foreign Keys, and Check Constraints

Indexes, foreign keys, and check constraints are all created using the same interface and process: Select the appropriate action from the Table Designer menu; use the settings dialog box to first add the index, key, or constraint; and then set its properties in the property grid. As an example, to create an index across one or more columns in the table, select the Indexes/Keys item from the Table Designer menu. In the Indexes/Keys dialog box (see Figure 18.5), you can add a new index and then set its properties in the property grid.

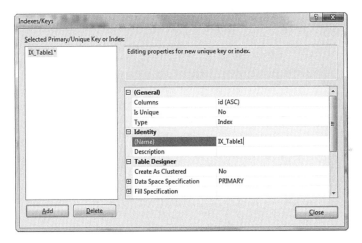

FIGURE 18.5   Creating an index.

Column population for the index is controlled with the index's `Columns` property; a separate Index Columns dialog box (see Figure 18.6) enables you to change the column membership and specify the sort order for each column.

## Using the Database Diagram Designer

The aforementioned Table Designer and dialog boxes allow you to define tables and table-related constructs on a table-by-table basis. The Database Diagram Designer provides the same functionality in a more visual format. It allows you to build a diagram of the whole database showing tables, table columns, keys, and table relationships, and also allows you to create each of these items from within the Diagram Designer tool.

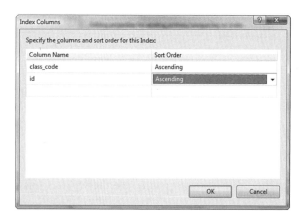

FIGURE 18.6    Column membership in an index.

Like the Table Designer, the Database Diagram Designer is implemented within the IDE's document pane. It has its own menu and toolbar associated with it; you can access many of the commands on the menu/toolbar through the designer's shortcut menu by right-clicking anywhere within the designer.

**TIP**

Within a diagram, you can change the view style on a per-table basis. Right-click the table and select one of the available Table views: Standard (shows column name, data type, and allow nulls), Column Names, Keys, Name Only, and Custom (you select the data you want to display). The Name Only view is particularly useful if you want to see an entire database diagram to get a sense of the relationships without necessarily caring about the table details themselves.

**Creating a Database Diagram**

To create a database diagram, right-click on the Database Diagrams node in the Server Explorer window and select Add New Diagram. A blank diagram will open, and the designer will immediately display a dialog box for adding tables to the diagram (see Figure 18.7).

After you've added a few tables, the diagram shows a graphical representation of the tables' columns and any relationships that the tables participate in. The diagram is fully interactive; you can directly edit column definitions, keys, relationships, and so on.

**TIP**

Here is a quick shortcut for adding groups of related tables: Add a table to the diagram, select it, and click on the Add Related Tables button in the designer's toolbar. This will automatically add to the diagram any table in the database that has a current relationship with the selected table.

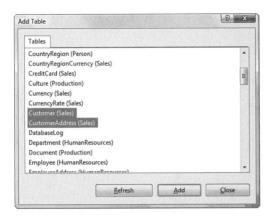

FIGURE 18.7  Adding tables to a diagram.

### Modifying Table Definitions

Tables can be edited "in-line" within the diagram. To change column details, you click within the table and then enter column name information or change the data type and nullability rules. To add a column, just fill out a new row within the table representation in the diagram.

### Building Table Relationships

Table relationships are easy to define within a diagram: Just drag and drop the primary key column from one table to the foreign key column on another table. This will automatically kick off two dialog boxes: Foreign Key Relationships and Tables and Columns (these are the same dialog boxes used to create foreign keys in the Table Designer). Figure 18.8 captures the foreign key and primary key assignments for the creation of a common one-to-many relationship between a category table and an order table. The order table has a category ID column (category_id) that will be foreign-keyed to the primary key on the category table (id).

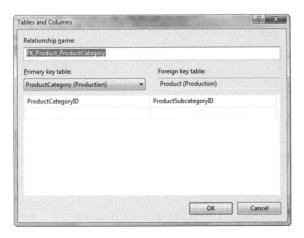

FIGURE 18.8  Creating a foreign key.

After committing the column assignments, you complete the relationship by changing any properties (if needed) on the relationship itself in the Foreign Key Relationships dialog box (see Figure 18.9).

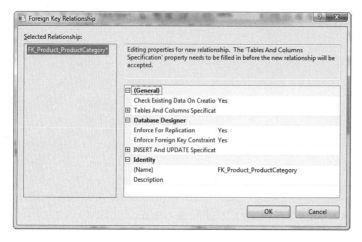

FIGURE 18.9    Creating a foreign key.

Relationships are depicted within the diagram as a line between the two tables. The line indicates the direction of the relationship by showing a key on the primary key side and an infinity symbol on the foreign key side (or the "many" side) of the relationship. Figure 18.10 illustrates the order category table to order table association as it would appear within the Database Diagram Designer.

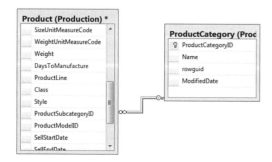

FIGURE 18.10    Two tables related in the Database Diagram Designer.

> **NOTE**
>
> By default, relationships will enforce referential integrity. That is, they will prevent any action (insert, update, delete) that would result in a mismatch of keys between the two related tables. This would include inserting a foreign key (FK) value when it doesn't exist as a primary key (PK) in the related table, changing a PK value that is referenced as a FK value, and so on.

You can control whether a relationship enforces referential integrity through the Enforce Foreign Key Constraint setting in the Foreign Key Relationship dialog box. Relationships that do not enforce referential integrity are depicted as banded lines instead of solid lines within the Diagram Designer. You should also note that the Diagram Designer will show only relationships that have been explicitly defined through the process covered in the preceding paragraphs. Just having similarly named foreign keys and primary keys will not automatically create a relationship for you.

In addition to one-to-many relationships, you can model one-to-one, many-to-many, and reflexive relationships using the Database Diagram Designer.

**One-to-One Relationships**    You build a one-to-one relationship in the same way you create a one-to-many relationship. The difference is this: One-to-one relationships are between two primary keys instead of a primary and a foreign key. If you drag a primary key column from one table to a primary key column on another table, this will automatically create a one-to-one association. These relationships are depicted with a key icon on both ends of the relationship line.

**Many-to-Many Relationships**    You create a many-to-many relationship with the help of a junction table. If you had to model a many-to-many association between an order table and an item table (an order can have many items, and an item can belong to many orders), you would first add a third table to the database to hold the foreign keys of this relationship.

After adding the junction table, you would then establish a one-to-many relationship between the order and orderitem table, and between the item and orderitem table. The last step is to define the multicolumn primary key on the junction table. Figure 18.11 shows the results in the diagram.

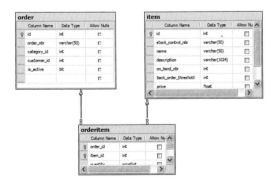

FIGURE 18.11    A many-to-many relationship.

18

**Reflexive Relationships**    A reflexive relationship is a relationship between a table and itself. A typical example used to illustrate reflexive relationship is that of a *part* table that relates back to itself to represent the fact that a part could be made up of other parts. In this case, the part table might carry a parent_part_id field that is meant to be a foreign key related to the employee table's primary key.

To create a reflexive relationship, select the primary key column and drag it back onto the same table. The configuration of the key associations and the relationship values is the same as with any other relationship. Figure 18.12 shows a diagram of a reflexive relationship.

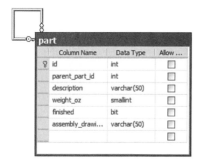

FIGURE 18.12    A reflexive relationship.

# Working with SQL Statements

There is full support within the Visual Database Tools set for crafting and executing SQL statements against a connected database. This includes support for compiling SQL statements as stored procedures, creating views and triggers, and writing user-defined functions.

## Writing a Query

The primary tool that facilitates the development of SQL statements is the Query/View Designer, which is a graphical tool that allows you to build queries with a point-and-click interface. After a query is constructed, this tool also allows you to view and interact with any results returned as a result of executing the query.

Now you're ready to put this tool through its paces.

Creating a new select query against a table is as simple as selecting the database in Server Explorer and then, under the Data menu, selecting New Query. An initial prompt gathers a list of the tables, views, functions, and/or synonyms to use as the target of the query (see Figure 18.13).

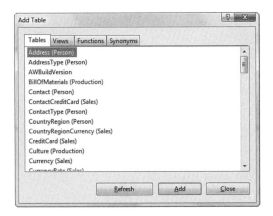

FIGURE 18.13   Adding tables to the query.

After you have selected the objects you want the query to target, the Query Designer will open. As Figure 18.14 illustrates, there are four separate panes to the designer:

▶ **Criteria pane**—This pane allows you to select, via a point-and-click diagram, the data columns to include in the select statement, sorting, and alias names.

▶ **Diagram pane**—This pane is similar to the diagram in the Database Diagram Designer; it graphically depicts the database object relationships. This makes creating joins a simple action of using existing relationships or creating new ones right within this tool.

▶ **Results pane**—After the query is executed, this pane holds any data returned as a result. Note that this pane is equipped with navigation controls to allow you to page through large resultsets.

▶ **SQL pane**—The SQL pane holds the actual SQL syntax used to implement the query. You can alter the statement manually by typing directly into this pane, or you can leverage the designer and let it write the SQL for you based on what you have entered in the diagram and criteria panes.

Each of these panes can be shown or hidden at will. Right-click anywhere in the designer and select the Pane fly-out menu to select or deselect the visible panes.

### Fine-Tuning the SQL Statement

To flesh out the select statement, you can indicate which columns from which tables you want returned by placing a check next to the column in the diagram pane. You use the criteria pane to specify a sort order, provide alias names for the return columns, and establish a filter for the resultset. As you select these different options, the designer turns them into SQL, visible in the SQL pane.

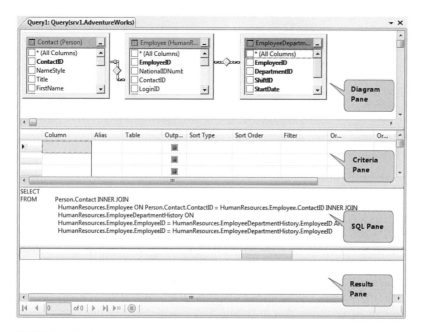

FIGURE 18.14   The Query/View Designer.

---

**NOTE**

We are using the AdventureWorks sample database in a SQL Server 2005 instance for most of this chapter. If you want to follow along, you can download a copy of this database and others by visiting http://www.codeplex.com/MSFTDBProdSamples. Many of the sample databases have been updated for SQL Server 2008 as well; you can access the different database samples by their corresponding SQL Server version by clicking on the All Releases link on the right of the CodePlex screen. AdventureWorks is also the sample database used by the SQL Server 2005 Books Online help collection.

---

Figure 18.15 shows the completed "Employee" query, with results visible in the bottom pane.

### Specifying Joins and Join Types

When you add multiple, related tables to the Query Designer, the designer uses their key relationships to automatically build a JOIN clause for the query. You also have the option to create joins on table columns that don't have an existing relationship. You do this the same way that you specify relationships in the Database Diagram Designer: You select and drag the column from one table to another within the diagram pane. The columns to be joined must be of compatible data types; you can't join, for instance, a varchar column with an integer column.

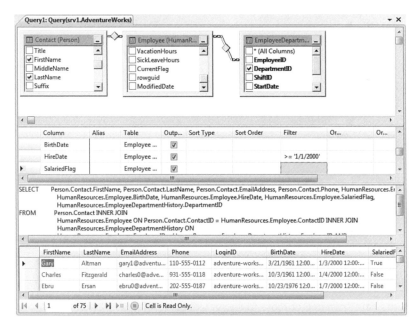

FIGURE 18.15    Querying for order information in the AdventureWorks database.

Joins are created using a comparison operator. By default, this is the equals operator; in other words, return rows where the column values are equal across the join. But you have control over the actual comparison operation used in the join. As an example, perhaps you want the resultset to include rows based on a join where the values in Table A are greater than the values in Table B on the joined columns. You can right-click the join relationship line in the diagram pane and select Properties to see the properties for the join; clicking the ellipsis button in the Join Condition and Type property will reveal the Join dialog box, shown in Figure 18.16.

### Other Query Types

By default, creating queries from the Server Explorer will result in a *select* query. But the Query Designer is equally adept at building other query types. If you want, for instance, an insert query, you can change the type of the query loaded in the designer by selecting Query Design, Change Type.

Table 18.1 shows the different query types supported by the designer.

---

**TIP**

If you just want to quickly see the data contents of any given table, you can right-click the table within the Server Explorer and then select Show Table Data. This will initiate a new Query/View Designer with a SELECT * statement for the given table. By default, only the results pane is visible. This functionality is ideal for testing scenarios in which you need to quickly edit data in the database or observe the effects of SQL statements on a table.

---

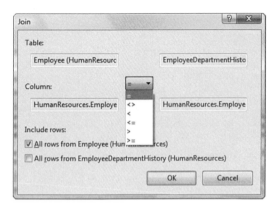

FIGURE 18.16    Setting join type and operator.

TABLE 18.1    Supported Query Types

| Query Type | Comments |
| --- | --- |
| Select | Returns data from one or more tables or views; a SQL SELECT statement |
| Insert Results | Inserts new rows into a table by copying them from another table; a SQL INSERT INTO ... SELECT statement |
| Insert Values | Inserts a new row into a table using the values and column targets specified; a SQL INSERT INTO ... VALUES statement |
| Update | Updates the value of existing rows or columns in a table; a SQL UPDATE ... SET statement |
| Delete | Deletes one or more rows from a table; a SQL DELETE statement |
| Make Table | Creates a new table and inserts rows into the new table by using the results of a select query; a SQL SELECT ... INTO statement |

## Creating Views

Views are virtual tables. They look and act just like tables in the database but are, in reality, select statements that are stored in the database. When you look at the content of a view, you are actually looking at the resultset for a select statement.

Because views are implemented as select statements, you create them using the Query/View Designer tool. In Server Explorer, right-click the Views folder under the database where you want to create the view. From there, you build the select statement just as you would for any other SQL statement.

Saving the view will refresh the database's copy of the view's select statement.

## Developing Stored Procedures

A stored procedure is a SQL statement (or series of statements) stored in a database and compiled. With SQL Server, stored procedures consist of Transact-SQL (T-SQL) code and have the capability to involve many coding constructs not typically found in ad hoc queries. For instance, you can implement error-handling routines within a stored procedure and even call into operating-system functions with so-called extended stored procedures.

For a given database, right-click the stored procedures folder in Server Explorer and select Add New Stored Procedure. A template for a stored procedure will open in the SQL Editor. The SQL Editor is a close sibling to Visual Studio's Code Editor; although it doesn't have IntelliSense, it does support syntax coloring, breakpoints, and the more general text-editing features (cut-copy-paste, word wrapping, and so on).

Figure 18.17 shows the beginnings of a stored procedure in the SQL Editor window.

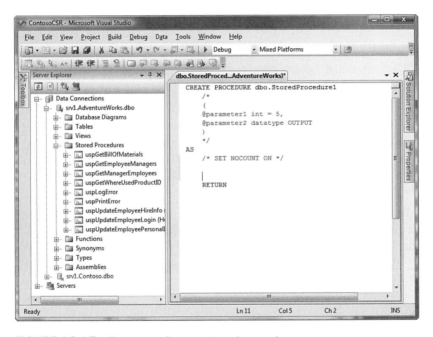

FIGURE 18.17   The start of a new stored procedure.

With the template loaded into the SQL Editor, writing a stored procedure involves typing in the lines of code and SQL that will perform the required actions. But stored procedure developers haven't been left out in the cold with regard to productivity in Visual Studio. You can leverage the power of the Query/View Designer to write portions of your stored procedure for you.

### Using the SQL Editor with the Query/View Designer

As you build the body of the procedure, the editor window will highlight and box in certain parts of the procedure. These boxed-in areas represent SQL statements that can be edited using the Query Designer. Consider the stored procedure featured in Figure 18.18.

18

FIGURE 18.18    SQL statements in a stored procedure.

This procedure, from the AdventureWorks database, essentially consists of two update queries. Both of them are contained within a blue-bordered box in the SQL Editor window. This is the editor's way of indicating that it has recognized a SQL statement within the procedure that can be designed using the Query/View Designer. If you right-click within the boxed-in area, the shortcut menu will include an option titled Design SQL Block. If you select this option, the Query/View Designer will open in a separate dialog box.

Figure 18.19 shows the first of the two update statements as they appear in the Query/View Designer. Using the same process outlined before for writing queries, you can construct the SQL within the relative luxury of the Query Designer's drag-and-drop interface. Clicking OK on the designer dialog box will save the query back into the stored procedure, updating the code in the editor window.

Notice that the Query Designer fully supports the use of parameters. When you fill in the parameter names in the New Value column (see the criteria pane in Figure 18.19), the designer is able to construct the appropriate SQL.

> **NOTE**
>
> The capability to create and edit stored procedures is supported only in Microsoft SQL Server. You cannot use the Visual Studio tools to create a procedure in, say, an Oracle database.

The Query Designer can also be pressed into play for inserting new blocks of SQL into a stored procedure (as opposed to editing existing SQL statements). First, in the SQL Editor window, right-click on the line within the procedure where you want to place the new query. From the pop-up menu, select Insert SQL. The Query/View Designer can now be used to craft the appropriate SQL. After you close out the dialog box by clicking OK, the new SQL will be inserted into the procedure and can be saved into the database.

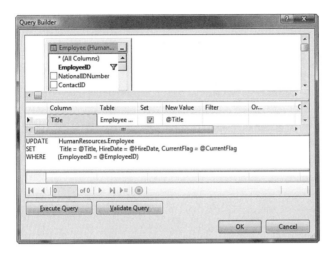

FIGURE 18.19    Designing a query for a stored procedure.

### Debugging Stored Procedures

In addition to coding stored procedures, you can leverage the Server Explorer tool to help you debug them. With the stored procedure open in the SQL Editor window, set a breakpoint in the procedure by clicking in the Indicator Margin (for more details on the Indicator Margin and general editor properties, see Chapter 6, "Introducing the Editors and Designers"). With a breakpoint in place, right-click on the stored procedure's name in the Server Explorer tree and select Step into Stored Procedure (see Figure 18.20).

The SQL Debugger is also parameter-friendly. If the stored procedure uses any parameters, the debugger will show a dialog box to capture values for the parameters (see Figure 18.21).

You can quickly cycle through the list of parameters, supplying appropriate values. After you click OK, the stored procedure will be executed. If you have set a breakpoint, execution will pause on the breakpoint (a yellow arrow is used to indicate the current line of execution within the editor, just the same as with the code editor window). With execution stopped, you can use the Locals and Watch windows to debug the procedure's code. See Chapter 10, "Debugging Code," for a more thorough treatment of the Locals and watch windows as debugging tools in Visual Studio.

The Debug menu is used to control execution and flow. If you select Continue, the procedure will continue running up to the next breakpoint (if present).

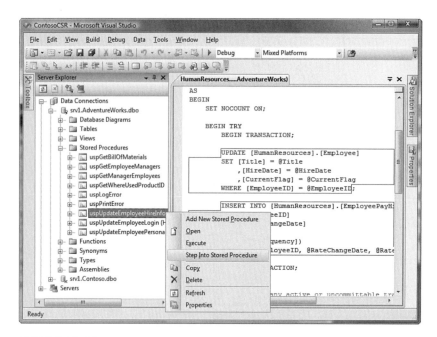

FIGURE 18.20     Debugging a stored procedure.

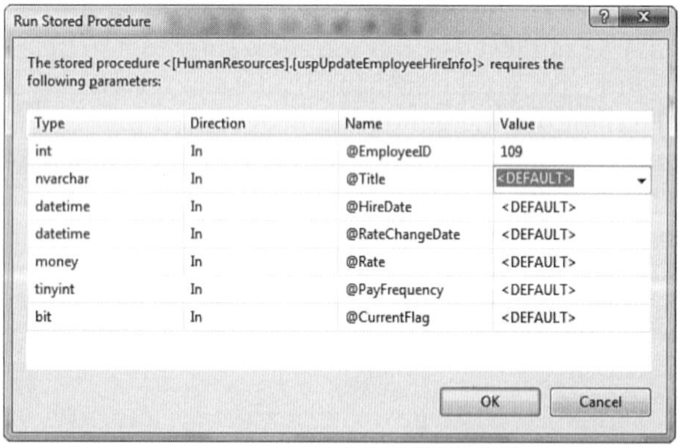

FIGURE 18.21     Entering parameter values in the SQL Debugger.

## Creating Triggers

Triggers are a type of stored procedure designed to run when the data in a table or view is modified. Triggers are attached to an individual table; when a query—an update, insert, or delete query—affects data in the table, the trigger will execute.

Because a trigger is really a stored procedure with a controlled execution time (hence the name *trigger*), it can have quite complex SQL statements and flow execution logic.

To create a trigger, use Server Explorer and locate the table to which the trigger is to be attached. Right-click the table name, select Add New Trigger, and then use the SQL Editor to write the SQL for the trigger. When the trigger is saved to the database, it will show up under its related table in Server Explorer (alongside the columns in the table). Figure 18.22 shows a simple trigger designed to raise an error if an update statement changes the Availability column in the Location table.

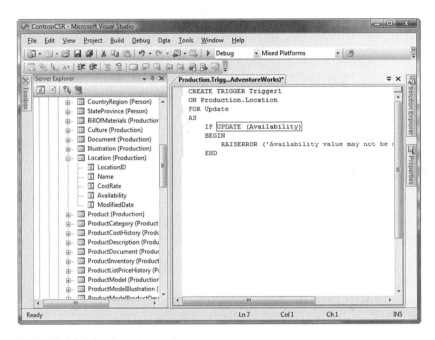

FIGURE 18.22   Creating a trigger.

## Creating User-Defined Functions

User-defined functions are bodies of code/SQL designed to be reusable across a variety of possible consumers: stored procedures, applications, or even other functions. In that respect, they are no different from functions written in C# or Visual Basic. They are routines that can accept parameters and return a value. User-defined functions return scalar values (for example, a single value) or a resultset containing rows and columns of data.

One example of a user-defined function might be one that accepts a date and then determines whether the day is a weekday or weekend. Stored procedures or other functions in the database can then use the function as part of their processing.

Because user-defined functions are T-SQL statements with a format similar to stored procedures, the SQL Editor again is the primary tool for writing them. For each data connection visible in Server Explorer, a Functions folder will contain any existing functions. To create a new function, you can right-click on this folder, select Add New, and then select the type of function to create. There are three options:

- ▶ **Inline Function**—Returns values as a resultset; the resultset is built from the results of a SELECT query.

- ▶ **Table-valued Function**—Returns values as a resultset; the resultset is built by programmatically creating a table within the function and then populating the table using INSERT INTO queries.

- ▶ **Scalar-valued Function**—Returns a single value.

After selecting the appropriate function type, template code for the function will be delivered inside a new SQL Editor window. Feel free to use the Query/View Designer to construct any required lines of SQL within the function.

For the specifics on how to write a function and put it to best use within the database, consult your database's documentation.

# Using Database Projects

Up to this point, we have discussed the use of the Visual Database Tools outside the context of a Visual Studio solution/project. Now let's investigate the role of the Database project type. Database projects hold a database connection (referred to as a *database reference*) and SQL scripts or queries that relate to that database. One benefit of housing scripts in a project like this is that they are available for storage in a source control system.

> **NOTE**
>
> Scripts are nothing more than SQL statements stored in a file. They are useful because they can be executed in batch to do such things as create tables in a brand-new database or add a canned set of stored procedures to a database. Because they are merely files, they can be transferred from computer to computer, enabling you to duplicate database structures across machines with ease.

The SQL scripts in the database project can create many of the database objects that we have already discussed: tables, views, triggers, stored procedures, and so on. Queries developed using the Query/View Designer can also be directly saved into a database project. In short, you use the Visual Database Tools in conjunction with a database project to create and save SQL scripts and queries.

## Creating a Database Project

To generate a database project, pick New Project from the File menu and then look under the Other Project Types category in the New Project dialog box (see Figure 18.23).

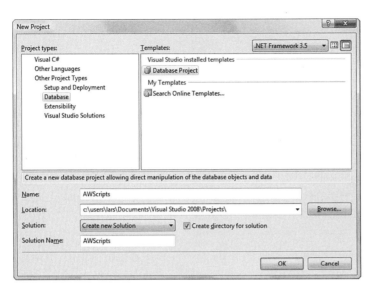

FIGURE 18.23    The database project type.

The project wizard will first prompt you for a database reference to add to the project; you do this by using the same set of dialog boxes used to add data connections in the Server Explorer (refer to Figure 18.3).

When created, the default project will have the structure shown in Figure 18.24.

As you can tell from this project structure, it has predefined folders for holding scripts, queries, and database references.

Scripts are added to the project in two ways. You can use the traditional "add new item" process just as you would with any other project. Select the item type (see Figure 18.25), and a script (or query) will be added to the project with the standard template skeleton

FIGURE 18.24    Database project structure.

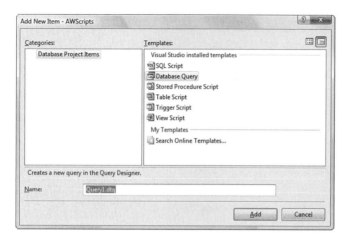

FIGURE 18.25    Database project items.

code added to the file for you. An easier way to create scripts, however, is to let the database tools do the work for you.

## Auto-Generating Scripts

There are two major types of auto-generated scripts: create scripts and change scripts. As their names imply, create scripts are used to create a new database object of some sort: a table, a stored procedure, and the like. Change scripts are used to update an existing database object.

### Create Scripts

Using Server Explorer, you can generate a create script for any object in the database. For example, to capture the create script for the BillOfMaterials table in the AdventureWorks database, you would right-click the table and select Generate Create Script to Project. All the SQL necessary to create the table (and its associated objects such as keys, indexes, and the like) will be written to a file under the Create Scripts folder in the current database project.

You even can script an entire database with one click: Instead of selecting an individual table, select the database node in Server Explorer and then select the Generate Create Script to Project command.

When the script is created, double-clicking on its file in the project will launch the SQL Editor with the script's content.

> **NOTE**
>
> As an indication of the manual work that script generation saves, consider this: The create script for the BillOfMaterials table weighs in at more than 120 lines of SQL.

### Change Scripts

The concept with change scripts is the same with two differences: Change scripts can be automatically generated only for tables, and the script will capture only changes made to the table instead of the creation of the table. The Table Designer provides easy access to change script generation. After making a change to the table within the designer, select Table Designer, Generate Change Script. The script will be constructed and placed within the Change Scripts folder in the current project.

> **NOTE**
>
> Because Visual Studio generates the change script by looking at your current edits and comparing them to the table structure as it exists in the database, you can generate a change script only before you have saved your changes down to the database.

## Executing a Script

After a script is created, you have the option to run the script against a database. You kick off script execution in the Solution Explorer by right-clicking on the script file. There are two options in the pop-up menu for running the script: a Run command and a Run On command. The Run command will run the script against the database specified in the default database reference. The Run On command allows you to manually specify which database, from the list of database references, should be the target of the script.

### Database References

If you recall from the Database Project Wizard, you are prompted for a database reference to include in the project. But database projects support the capability to have more than one reference. If you have more than one reference, you can specify which of the available references is the default reference by right-clicking on it in Solution Explorer and selecting Set As Project Default.

## Creating Database Objects in Managed Code

Database objects are commonly implemented using some dialect of the SQL language. This is true with SQL Server as well. SQL Server 2005, however, introduced the capability of authoring SQL objects in managed code. So, instead of using Transact SQL, you can actually write your stored procedures, queries, views, and so on using your favorite .NET language.

The key enabler in Visual Studio that makes this happen is the SQL Server Project. Not to be confused with the formerly discussed Database Project, the SQL Server Project is a language-specific project type that provides class templates for implementing managed code versions of database routines.

## Starting a SQL Server Project

In the Add New Project dialog box, SQL Server projects are located under the Database category within each language. Creating a new SQL Server project kicks off the same Add Database Reference dialog box that you have already seen with the Server Explorer and with the Database Project; the new project structure laid down by the project wizard is shown in Figure 18.26.

FIGURE 18.26    A SQL Server project.

The SQL Server project directly supports the creation of the following database objects:

▶ Stored procedures

▶ Triggers

▶ Aggregates

▶ User-defined functions

▶ User-defined types

The following sections look at how to go about creating a straightforward stored procedure.

## Creating a Stored Procedure in C#

First, you add a stored procedure item to your project by using the Project menu and selecting Add Stored Procedure. A new class will be added to the project. Listing 18.1 shows the base code that shows up within the new class file. You can add your custom code to the static void routine `UpdateEmployeeLogin`.

LISTING 18.1   The Start of a Managed Code Stored Procedure

```
using System;
using System.Data;
using System.Data.SqlClient;
using System.Data.SqlTypes;
using Microsoft.SqlServer.Server;


public partial class StoredProcedures
{
    [Microsoft.SqlServer.Server.SqlProcedure]
    public static void UpdateEmployeeLogin()
    {
        // Put your code here
    }
};
```

Managed code objects in SQL Server all leverage the .NET Framework data classes (that is, ADO.NET) to do their work. This means that stored procedures you write will end up instantiating and using classes such as SqlConnection and SqlCommand. The code you write is identical to data access code that you would write from within any other .NET project type: class libraries, web projects, and Windows forms projects. Because the common denominator is the use of ADO.NET classes, developers don't need to learn another language (like T-SQL) to perform work in the database.

> **NOTE**
>
> It's outside the scope of this chapter to cover the relative merits or disadvantages of writing your database objects in managed code as opposed to T-SQL. Check out the whitepaper available on MSDN titled "Using CLR Integration in SQL Server 2005," by Microsoft. Although fairly old (it was written in November 2004), it is a great treatment of this subject and is highly recommended reading.

Listing 18.2 shows a fleshed-out C# routine that will update the AdventureWorks Employee table with login information. None of this code is complicated and it can be easily understood (and written) by anyone with C# data access experience.

LISTING 18.2   Managed Code for Updating Employee Login Values

```
using System;
using System.Data;
using System.Data.SqlClient;
using System.Data.SqlTypes;
```

LISTING 18.2    Continued

```
using Microsoft.SqlServer.Server;


public partial class StoredProcedures
{
    [Microsoft.SqlServer.Server.SqlProcedure]
    public static void UpdateEmployeeLogin(SqlInt32 employeeId,
    SqlInt32 managerId, SqlString loginId, SqlString title,
    SqlDateTime hireDate, SqlBoolean currentFlag)
    {
        using (SqlConnection conn =
               new SqlConnection("context connection=true"))
        {
            SqlCommand UpdateEmployeeLoginCommand =
              new SqlCommand();

            UpdateEmployeeLoginCommand.CommandText =
                "update HumanResources.Employee SET ManagerId = " +
              managerId.ToString() +
                ", LoginId = '" + loginId.ToString() + "'" +
                ", Title = '" + title.ToString() + "'" +
                ", HireDate = '" + hireDate.ToString() + "'" +
                ", CurrentFlag = " + currentFlag.ToString() +
                " WHERE EmployeeId = " + employeeId.ToString();

            UpdateEmployeeLoginCommand.Connection = conn;

            conn.Open();
            UpdateEmployeeLoginCommand.ExecuteNonQuery();
            conn.Close();

        }
    }
};
```

One line of code, however, deserves a more detailed explanation. The SqlConnection object is created like this:

```
SqlConnection conn = new SqlConnection("context connection=true")
```

The connection string "context connection=true" tells the data provider engine that the connection should be created in the same context as the calling application. Because this routine will be running inside a database, that means you will be connecting to the host database and will run using the context (transactional and otherwise) of the calling application. Because you are piggybacking on the context of the database that the routine is running in, you don't need to hard-code a full SQL connection string here.

For comparison purposes, Listing 18.3 shows the same update query implemented in T-SQL.

LISTING 18.3    T-SQL for Updating Employee Login Values

```
ALTER PROCEDURE [HumanResources].[uspUpdateEmployeeLogin]
    @EmployeeID [int],
    @ManagerID [int],
    @LoginID [nvarchar](256),
    @Title [nvarchar](50),
    @HireDate [datetime],
    @CurrentFlag [dbo].[Flag]
WITH EXECUTE AS CALLER
AS
BEGIN
    SET NOCOUNT ON;

    BEGIN TRY
        UPDATE [HumanResources].[Employee]
        SET [ManagerID] = @ManagerID
            ,[LoginID] = @LoginID
            ,[Title] = @Title
            ,[HireDate] = @HireDate
            ,[CurrentFlag] = @CurrentFlag
        WHERE [EmployeeID] = @EmployeeID;
    END TRY
    BEGIN CATCH
        EXECUTE [dbo].[uspLogError];
    END CATCH;
END;
```

**18**

### Building and Deploying the Stored Procedure
When you build your SQL Server project, the typical compilation process takes place. Assuming that your code will build, you can now deploy the resulting assembly to the database. Use the Build menu to access the Deploy command.

After the assembly has been deployed, you can test it by calling it from an application or from a query window. For detailed information on how to call managed assemblies and write them, consult the SQL Server Books Online.

# Binding Controls to Data

You have now seen all the various ways you can use Visual Studio to create and manage databases. The following sections look at the tools available for consuming data within Windows forms or web applications.

## An Introduction to Data Binding

There is a common problem and solution pattern at hand with applications that front databases. Typically, data has to be fetched from the database into the application, and the application's user interface has to be updated to display the data in an appropriate manner. For large datasets, the concept of paging comes into play. Because it is inefficient to load in, say, a 100MB dataset, a paging mechanism needs to be pressed into action to allow the user to move forward and back through the data "stream." After the data has safely made it into the application's UI, the application-to-database flow needs to be handled. For any pieces of data that have been changed, those changes have to be reconciled and committed back into the database.

*Data binding* is the term given to the implementation of a design pattern that handles all facets of this round trip of data from a data structure, into an application's controls, and back again (see Figure 18.27). Although the data structure will most commonly be a database, it could be any sort of container object that holds data, such as an array or a collection. .NET further stratifies the concepts of data binding into *simple data binding* and *complex data binding*. Both of these terms refer to a control's intrinsic capabilities in the larger context of the data-binding process.

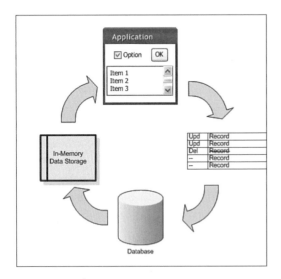

FIGURE 18.27   The data-binding process.

### Simple Data Binding

Simple data binding is the capability for a control to bind to and display a single data element within a larger dataset. A `TextBox` control is a great example of a control commonly used in simple data-binding scenarios. You might use a `TextBox`, for example, to display the last name of an employee as it is stored within the employee table of a database.

Support for simple data binding is widespread throughout both the Windows and web forms controls. When you use the built-in capabilities of the Windows and Web Forms Designer, it is trivial to add a group of controls to a form and simple-bind them to a dataset (more on this in a bit).

### Complex Data Binding

The term *complex data binding* refers to the capability of a control to display multiple data elements at one time. You can think of this as a "multirow" capability: If a control can be leveraged to view multiple rows of data at one time, it supports complex data binding.

The `DataGridView` control (for Windows forms) and `DataGrid` control (for web forms) are premier examples of controls that were purpose-built to handle tabular (multirow and multicolumn) data.

Although the internals necessary to implement data binding are messy, complex, and hard to understand, for the most part the Visual Studio tools have abstracted the cost of implementing data binding out to a nice, easy, drag-and-drop model. Now let's look at how to rapidly build out support for round-trip data binding.

## Auto-Generating Bound Windows Forms Controls

Although there are various ways to approach and implement data-bound controls with Visual Studio, they all involve the same basic two steps:

1. Establish a data source.
2. Map the data-source members to controls or control properties.

From there, the Visual Studio Form Designers are capable of generating the correct controls and placing them on the form. All the data-binding code is handled for you; all you need to worry about is the layout, positioning, and UI aspects of the controls.

As you might imagine, your form might have controls that use simple data binding or complex data binding or a mix of both. Now you're ready to look at the steps involved with creating a series of controls that will leverage both simple and complex data binding to display information from the AdventureWorks Employee table. In this scenario, you will work with the Windows Forms Designer. The ASP.NET Web Forms Designer works in a similar fashion, and you'll have a chance to investigate drag-and-drop approaches for data binding in the web environment in just a bit. As we have already established, the first step is selecting a data source.

### Selecting a Data Source

In Visual Studio, make sure you are working inside a Windows Application project and use the Data Sources window to select a data source. If this window isn't already visible, select Show Data Sources from the Data menu in the IDE. If your current project doesn't have any defined data sources, you will need to create one. Click the Add New Data Source button in the toolbar of the window to start the Data Source Configuration Wizard. On the first page of this wizard (see Figure 18.28), you select the type of the data source. There are three options here:

- ▶ **Database**—The data source resides as a table within a relational database.

- ▶ **Web Service**—The data source is a web service that will return the data to be bound to the form controls.

- ▶ **Object**—The data source is an object that will provide the data (this is useful in scenarios in which a business object from another layer of the application will be responsible for delivering the data to the form).

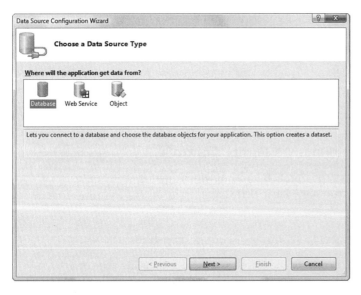

FIGURE 18.28    Choosing the data-source type.

Because the concepts of data binding are most easily understood within the context of a database, we will use the database data-source type as the underpinning for our walk-throughs in this chapter.

If you have selected the database data-source type, the second page of the wizard focuses on selecting a connection for the database. Any connections previously established for other data sources or for use in the Server Explorer will show up here by default in the drop-down (see Figure 18.29). You also have the option of specifying a new connection.

If the connection string to the database has private information such as a user password, you have the option at this point to exclude that information from the string.

The next step in the wizard allows you to save the connection string information to your application's local configuration file. Saving the information is usually a good idea because it allows you to tweak the string when needed (such as when changing database environments), but caution should be used if you have elected to store sensitive information in the string (refer to the previous wizard page).

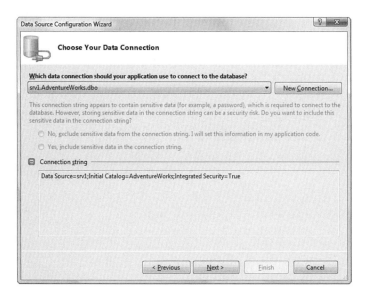

FIGURE 18.29    Selecting the connection.

On the final page of the wizard, shown in Figure 18.30, you indicate which of the objects in the database should be used for the source data. You can select from any of the data elements present in any of the various tables, views, stored procedures, or user-defined functions in the database. For the purposes of this example, select a few employee table data columns that are of interest: Employee ID, Title, BirthDate, Gender, HireDate, and ModifiedDate.

At the conclusion of the wizard, your selected data source will be visible in the Data Sources window (see Figure 18.31).

18

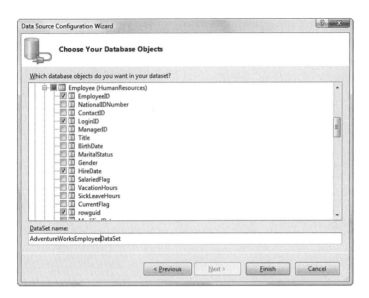

FIGURE 18.30    Selecting the data-source objects.

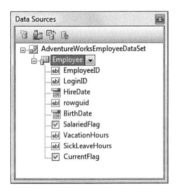

FIGURE 18.31    The Data Sources window.

With the data source in place, you're ready to move on to the next step: mapping the data-source elements to controls on your form.

### Mapping Data Sources to Controls

The really quick and easy way to create your data-bound controls is to let Visual Studio do it for you. From the Data Sources window, click on the drop-down button on the data-source name to reveal a menu (see Figure 18.32).

This menu enables you to set the control generation parameters and really answers the question of which controls you want generated based on the table in the data source. By setting this to DataGridView, you can generate a DataGridView control for viewing and editing your data source. The Details setting allows you to generate a series of simple data-bound controls for viewing or editing data in the data source. For this example, select

Details and then drag and drop the data source itself from the Data Sources window and onto a blank form.

FIGURE 18.32    Changing the data table mapping.

Figure 18.33 shows the results. In just two short steps, Visual Studio has done all the following for you:

- ▶ Auto-generated a set of Label, TextBox, and DateTimePicker controls
- ▶ Auto-generated a tool strip with controls for navigating among records in the data source, saving changes made to a record, deleting a record, and inserting a new record
- ▶ Created all the necessary code behind the scenes to establish a connection to the data source, read from the data source, and commit changes to the data source

You have essentially created an entire data-enabled application from scratch with absolutely no coding on your part.

The approach of using simple data binding may not fit into the user interface design, so you always have the option of working in the complex data-binding world and using the DataGridView as an alternative. Figure 18.34 shows the results of auto-generating a DataGridView instance using this same process.

**Customizing Data-Source Mappings**    Refer again to Figure 18.31 and look at the individual data elements that show up under the Employee data source. Each of these is displayed with a name and an icon. The name is, of course, the name of the data element as defined in the database. The icon represents the default mapping of that data type to a .NET control. For example, the Title field maps to a TextBox control, and the BirthDate field maps to a DateTimePicker control. Visual Studio actually attempts to provide the best control for any given data type. But feel free to manually indicate the specific control you want used. If you wanted to display the value of the Employee ID column in a label instead of a text box (in recognition of the fact that you cannot edit this value), it would be easy enough to change this before generating the controls by selecting the EmployeeID column in the Data Sources window and then clicking on the drop-down arrow to select Label instead of TextBox.

18

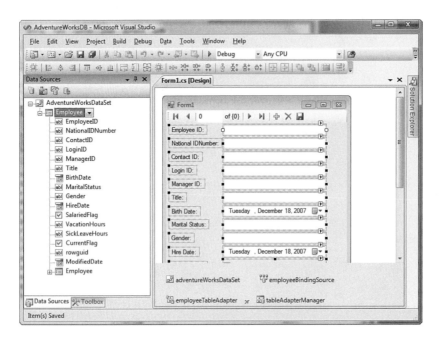

FIGURE 18.33    Auto-generated controls: viewing employee data.

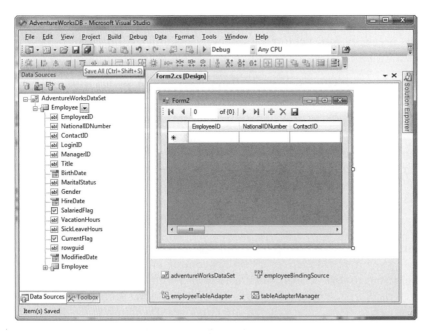

FIGURE 18.34    An auto-generated **DataGridView**.

In addition to changing the control to data type mapping on an individual level, you can affect the general default mappings that are in place by selecting the Customize option from that same drop-down menu. This will pop up the Visual Studio Options dialog box with the Windows Forms Designer page selected. Using the settings there (see Figure 18.35), you can specify the default control type that you want applied for each recognized data type.

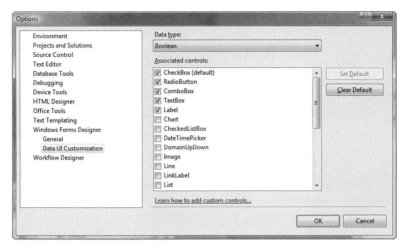

FIGURE 18.35    Customizing the data to control type mappings.

## Editing Typed DataSets

There is a designer provided solely for editing (and creating) typed datasets within Visual Studio: the DataSet Designer. This designer launches automatically when you open a DataSet project item such as the AdventureWorksEmployeeDataSet.xsd file that we just created when investigating data binding.

> **NOTE**
>
> Typed DataSet objects can be huge productivity enhancers over a normal dataset: Instead of using indexes into collections, you can reference tables and columns by their actual name. In addition, IntelliSense will work with typed DataSet members, making coding against large data hierarchies much easier.

The DataSet Designer can be used to easily tweak datasets by changing any of the various constituent parts including the queries used to populate the dataset. Figure 18.36 shows the previously created AdventureWorksEmployeeDataSet open in the DataSet Designer.

Note that each piece of the dataset is visually represented here, and we can interact with those pieces to effect changes. For instance, if we wanted to alter the query we originally constructed using the Data Set Configuration Wizard, we would simply right-click on the Employee table on the design surface and select Configure to relaunch the query editor.

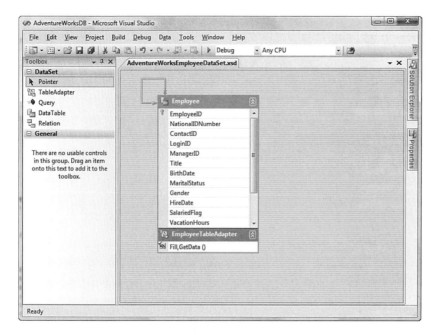

FIGURE 18.36   The Visual Studio DataSet Designer.

In the scenario we have been discussing, we are wiring the dataset directly to the results from a SQL query—but we can also use the DataSet Designer to create "unbound," new datasets. Adding a DataSet project item to our project will enable us to start with a blank slate, adding tables, queries, and so on to the dataset to satisfy any storage requirements (or data retrieval requirements) that our application may have. This is especially useful for applications that read and write data but don't necessarily interact with a database. These dataset files can be used as simple file storage that can easily be bound later to a relational database.

## Manually Binding Windows Forms Controls

In many situations, you don't want Visual Studio to create your data-bound controls for you, or you may need to bind existing controls to a data source. Data binding in these cases is just as simple and starts with the same step: creating or selecting a data source. Some controls, such as the DataGridView, have smart tag options for selecting a data source. Others don't have intrinsic data dialog boxes associated with them but can be bound to data just as easily by working, again, with the Data Sources window.

### Binding the DataGridView

Grab a DataGridView from the Toolbox and drag it onto the form's surface. After you've created the control, select its smart tag glyph and use the drop-down at the top of the task list to select the data source to bind to (see Figure 18.37).

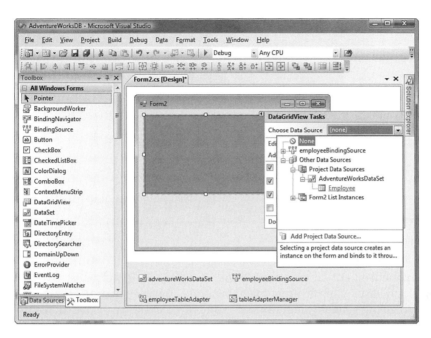

FIGURE 18.37   Selecting the **DataGridView**'s data source.

With a data source selected, you have again managed to develop a fully functional application with two-way database access. All the code to handle the population of the grid and to handle committing changes back to the database has been written for you.

**Customizing Cell Edits**   The power of the DataGridView lies in its capability to both quickly bind to and display data in a tabular format and also to provide a highly customized editing experience. As one small example of what is possible in terms of cell editing, follow through with the Employee table example. When you auto-generated form controls to handle Employee table edits, you ended up with DateTimePicker controls to accommodate the date- and time-based data in the table. With the DataGridView, the cell editing experience is a simple text box experience: Each cell contains text, and you can edit the text and save it to the database. But you can provide a more tailored editing experience. You can use various stock controls (such as the DataGridViewButtonColumn, DataGridViewComboBoxColumn, and others that inherit from DataGridViewColumn; see Chapter 15, "Building Windows Forms Applications") to display data within the columns of the grid.

For instance, you can use the DataGridViewComboBoxColumn class to provide a drop-down edit for the Gender column in the grid. To do this, you first need to change the default column type. Select the grid control, open the smart tag glyph, and select the Edit Columns action. In the Edit Columns dialog box, find the column for the employee gender data and change its column type to DataGridViewComboBoxColumn (see Figure 18.38).

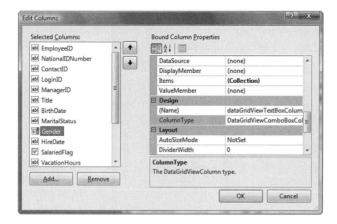

FIGURE 18.38    Changing the column type.

With the column type changed, you now need to specify how the grid should retrieve the list of possible values to display in the drop-down; the grid is smart enough to already know to use the underlying gender values from the table to select the one value to display in the grid. To handle the list of possible values, you could hard-code them in the column (see the Items property in Figure 18.38), or you could wire up a separate query—something along the lines of SELECT DISTINCT(Gender) FROM Employees—and have that query provide the list of possible values. Because constructing another query or data source is easy and doesn't lead to a brittle hard-coded solution, that's the approach we'll investigate here. To create a query to feed the combo-box column, you can visit the Data Sources window, select the Add New Data Source action, and follow the same steps you followed before to add the original Employee data source. This time, though, select only the Gender column.

After the data source is created, right-click on the data source and select Edit DataSet with Designer. We'll use the DataSet Designer to modify our query appropriately. In the designer (see Figure 18.39), you can see the Fill query and TableAdapter used to populate the dataset. If you click on the query (that is, click on the last row in the table graphic in the designer window), you can use the Properties window to directly edit the SQL for the query. By modifying this to reflect SELECT DISTINCT syntax, you can return the valid gender values for inclusion in the grid.

Figure 18.40 shows the results of these efforts. If you need to implement a cell edit control that doesn't currently exist, you need to create your own by inheriting from the DataGridViewColumn base control. This employee grid could benefit from a DateTimePicker control for the date- and time-based data such as birth date and hire date.

> **NOTE**
>
> If you look in the MSDN documentation, there is a specific example of creating a DataGridViewDateTimePickerColumn control and then wiring it up within the grid. Search for the phrase "How to: Host Controls in Windows Forms DataGridView Cells."

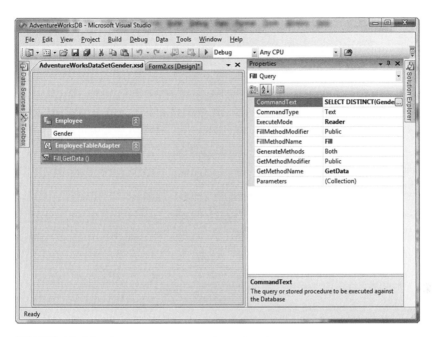

FIGURE 18.39   Changing the query for a data source.

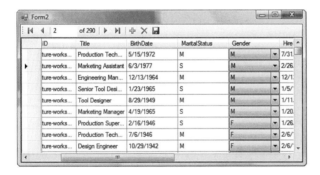

FIGURE 18.40   A drop-down within a **DataGridView**.

### Binding Other Controls

For other controls that don't have convenient access to binding via their smart tag, you can leverage the Data Sources window. Drag a data source from the Data Sources window and drop it onto an existing control. The designer will create a new binding source, set it appropriately, and then make an entry in the control's DataBinding collection. If you try to drag a data element onto a control that doesn't match up (for instance, dragging a character field onto a check box), the drop operation won't be allowed.

## Data Binding with Web Controls

Although the general concepts remain the same, data-binding web-based controls is a slightly different game than in the Windows forms world. The first obvious difference is that data sources for web forms are implemented by data-source controls in the System.Web.UI.WebControls namespace; there is no concept of the Data Sources window with web applications. Because of this, instead of starting with a data source, you instead need to start with a data control and then work to attach that control to a data source.

### Selecting a Data Control

There are five primary controls you will work with in a web application to deliver data-bound functionality:

▶ **GridView** Control—Provides a tabular presentation similar to the DataGridView control.

▶ **DetailsView** Control—Displays a single record from a data source; with a DetailsView control, every column in the data source will show up as a row in the control.

▶ **FormView** Control—Functions in the same way as the DetailsView control with the following exception: It doesn't have a built-in "default" for the way that the data is displayed. Instead, you need to provide a template to tell the control exactly how you want the data rendered onto the web page.

▶ **Repeater** Control—Simply renders a list of individual items fetched from the attached data source. The specifics of how this rendering looks are all controlled via templates.

▶ **DataList** Control—Displays rows of information from a data source. The display aspects are fully customizable and include header and footer elements.

For demonstration purposes, continue working with the AdventureWorks employee table and see how you can implement a data-bound web page for viewing employee records.

**Using the GridView**    First, with a web project open, drag a GridView control from the Toolbox onto an empty web page. The first thing you will notice is that the GridView's smart tag menu is just as efficient as the DataGridView's menu. You are directly prompted to select (or create and then select) a data source as soon as you drop the control onto the web page surface (see Figure 18.41).

Selecting the <New Data Source...> option will use a similar data-source wizard (refer to Figure 18.28) to collect information about your data source and add it to the project.

Once again, because of the data-binding support in the designer, you now have a fully functional application without writing a line of code. Figure 18.42 shows this admittedly ugly web page with live employee data.

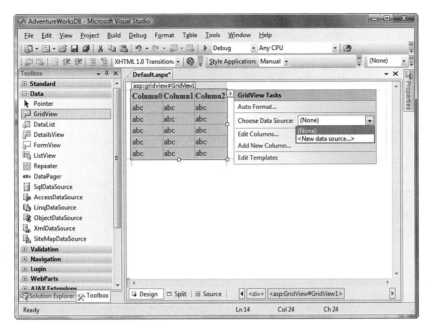

FIGURE 18.41 Selecting the **GridView**'s data source.

| EmployeeID | Title | BirthDate | Gender | HireDate | SalariedFlag | VacationHours | SickLeaveHours |
|---|---|---|---|---|---|---|---|
| 1 | Production Technician - WC60 | 5/15/1972 12:00:00 AM | M | 7/31/1996 12:00:00 AM | ☐ | 21 | 30 |
| 2 | Marketing Assistant | 6/3/1977 12:00:00 AM | M | 2/26/1997 12:00:00 AM | ☐ | 42 | 41 |
| 3 | Engineering Manager | 12/13/1964 12:00:00 AM | M | 12/12/1997 12:00:00 AM | ☑ | 2 | 21 |
| 4 | Senior Tool Designer | 1/23/1965 12:00:00 AM | M | 1/5/1998 12:00:00 AM | ☐ | 48 | 80 |
| 5 | Tool Designer | 8/29/1949 12:00:00 AM | M | 1/11/1998 12:00:00 AM | ☐ | 9 | 24 |
| 6 | Marketing Manager | 4/19/1965 12:00:00 AM | M | 1/20/1998 12:00:00 AM | ☑ | 40 | 40 |
| | Production | 2/16/1946 | | 1/26/1998 | | | |

FIGURE 18.42 Employee records in the **GridView**.

Thankfully, you can just as easily put some window dressing on the table and make it look nice. By using the GridView's smart tag menu again, you can select the Auto Format option to apply several flavors of window dressing to the table (see Figure 18.43). And, of course, by applying a style sheet, you can really impact the look and feel of the page.

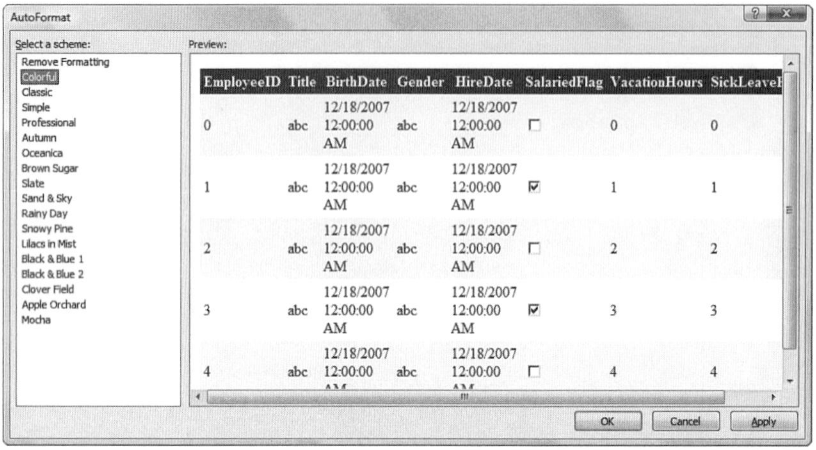

FIGURE 18.43    Autoformatting options for the **GridView** control.

**Updating Data with the GridView**    Creating the web grid was easy, and no data access coding was required on your part. However, there is one thing missing here: How can you update data back to the database? The GridView you currently have is great for static reporting, but what if you want to edit data within the grid just as you did earlier in the Windows forms application? The key here is a set of properties on the GridView: AutoGenerateEditButton and AutoGenerateDeleteButton. When you set these properties to True, the GridView will automatically include an Edit link and a Delete link. The Edit link comes fully baked with rendering code so that when it is clicked, that particular row in the grid will become editable. In Figure 18.44, notice that by setting the AutoGenerateEditButton to True and then clicking on one of the edit links, you now have a fully interactive set of columns that you can use to modify the record's data.

After changing the data in one or more of the columns, you can click on the Update link to send the data back to the database. For the update to work, however, you need to explicitly tell the data-source control (in this case, a SqlDataSource control) which query to use for processing updates. This is done with the SqlDataSource.UpdateQuery property. By specifying a parameterized UPDATE query in this property, you have fully informed the data source on how to deal with updates. You can take advantage once more of the Query Builder window to write this query for you: Select the data-source control on the web form, and in the Properties window select the UpdateQuery property. This will launch the Query Builder window and allow you to construct the parameterized update command (see Figure 18.45).

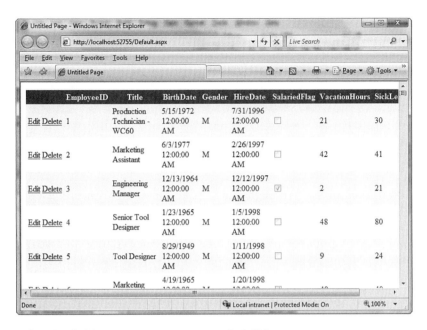

FIGURE 18.44    Editing a record in the **GridView**.

FIGURE 18.45    Specifying an **UpdateCommand** query.

With that last piece of the puzzle in place, you now have a fully implemented and bound grid control that pages data in from the database and commits changes back to the database.

---

**NOTE**

To implement delete capabilities for a record, you perform the same steps using the `DeleteQuery` property and setting the `AutoGenerateDeleteButton` to True.

---

**Data-Source Controls**

As mentioned, data sources are surfaced through one or more data-source controls placed onto the web form. In the `GridView` example, the designer actually adds a `SqlDataSource` control to the form for you (based on your creation of a new DB-based data source). But there is nothing preventing you from adding one or more data-source controls to a web page directly. Just drag the control from the Toolbox onto the form surface. Table 18.2 itemizes the available data-source controls.

After configuring the data source, you can then visit any data-aware control and bind it to the source.

TABLE 18.2    Data-Source Controls

| Control | Description |
| --- | --- |
| ObjectDataSource | Exposes other classes as data sources. |
| SqlDataSource | Exposes a relational database as a data source. Microsoft SQL Server and Oracle databases can be accessed natively; ODBC and OLE DB access is also supported. |
| AccessDataSource | Exposes a Microsoft Access database as a data source. |
| XmlDataSource | Exposes an XML file as a data source. |
| SiteMapDataSource | A special-case data source that exposes an ASP.NET site map as a data source. |

# Object Relational Mapping

We have spent most of this chapter covering the "standard" process for creating .NET applications that read and write data that resides in a database. Although Visual Studio and the ADO.NET libraries themselves do a lot to abstract away the difficult pieces of that process, problems still remain. In fact, there is one common problem that developers writing database-driven applications face: the mismatch between an application's normal object-oriented programming model, implemented in C# or Visual Basic, and the relational programming model surfaced in databases or datasets, implemented primarily with SQL.

In the object-oriented world, we manipulate objects via methods and properties, and each object itself can be (and often is) a parent or container for other objects. The relational database world is much more straightforward: Entities are implemented as row/column-based tables, and each "cell" in a table holds simple scalar values. The core issue is that you must change programming models when dealing with an application's internal framework or the relational database used as its data store—and translating from one to the other isn't a straightforward task.

As a simple example, rows from an invoice table are easily fetched into a dataset object using the various data-binding tools and classes discussed previously. But deriving a "native" `Invoice` object from the dataset involves two-way, manual translation and manipulation to get the core values to translate across this object/relational barrier. This highlights several issues: Do you abandon the dataset approach and read directly from the database into your applications' objects? Do you eschew the object approach and try to use the `DataSet` component throughout all layers of your application? Or is a hybrid approach best, maintaining strongly typed object collections in addition to the datasets?

Ideally, application developers would be free to work with and manipulate objects within the program's object model and have those objects and changes automatically stored in the database with little or no intervention. Not only does this keep the focus on core, well-understood object design patterns, but it also lets the individual developer work with his core language strength without having to learn or become expert in SQL. Pursuit of this goal would obviously require some sort of standard approach, and tooling support, for mapping objects to and from their equivalents within the relational database. And this is exactly what object/relational mapping tools do.

The term object/relational mapping (or O/R mapping) is used to refer to this general process of translating objects to and from databases. O/R mapping tools have been on the market for years now, and thankfully Microsoft has finally delivered O/R mapping support directly in the .NET Framework and in Visual Studio. This technology is called LINQ to SQL. Let's briefly discuss the LINQ to SQL concept, and then look at the Visual Studio tool—the O/R Designer—that aids in this overall task.

## An Overview of LINQ

As discussed in Chapter 3, ".NET Framework and Language Enhancements in 2008," LINQ is an acronym for "Language Integrated Query." It is a component of the .NET Framework 3.5 that adds SQL-like querying capabilities to .NET objects. Specifically, it extends the core .NET languages—Visual Basic and C#—and the runtime to try to erase the object-to-database-entity barrier. Visual Basic and C# both support new query operators that operate over objects similar to the way SQL operates over tables in a database.

For example, you could query for all approved invoice objects like this:

```
var approved =
    from invoice in invoices
    where (invoice.Approved) == true
```

```
   select invoice;

foreach (Invoice invoice in approved)
{
    // do some work here
}
```

And runtime support is introduced for physically translating objects and methods to and from their database equivalents (primarily through the use of code attributes, as you will see in a moment). This is a simple example of a class method mapped to a SQL Server stored procedure:

```
[Function(Name="HR.uspDeleteEmployee")]
public int uspDeleteEmployee([Parameter(Name="EmployeeID", DbType="Int")]
                            System.Nullable<int> employeeID)
{
   IExecuteResult result = this.ExecuteMethodCall(this,
           ((MethodInfo)(MethodInfo.GetCurrentMethod())), employeeID);
   return ((int)(result.ReturnValue));
}
```

LINQ comes in several different flavors, each targeted at a specific mapping problem:

▶ **LINQ to SQL**—This enables you to map objects to database entities.

▶ **LINQ to XML**—This enables you to query XML documents and map objects to XML document elements.

▶ **LINQ to Objects**—This specifically refers to the inclusion of .NET language syntax that allows queries to be written over collections of objects (as in our previous example with the approved invoices).

LINQ is a fairly broad and deep set of technology pieces, and covering even one in depth is outside of the scope of this book. We will, however, dig into the primary Visual Studio tool used when writing LINQ to SQL applications: the O/R Designer.

## Mapping Using the O/R Designer

The first step in creating a LINQ to SQL application is typically the construction of an object model that is based on a given database definition. This is the exact function of the O/R Designer: It allows you to select a database and generate an object model that maps to the database's structure. Table 18.3 shows how the database components are mapped to object components.

### Adding Database Entities

The O/R Designer is the design surface for project items known as LINQ to SQL Classes, and so the first step in using the designer is to add a new LINQ to SQL Class project item to a project. Figure 18.46 shows where this project item lives in the Add New Item dialog.

TABLE 18.3   Default Database to Object Mappings

| Database | Application Object |
|---|---|
| Table | Class |
| Table Column | Class Property |
| Foreign Key Relationship | Association |
| Stored Procedure/Function | Class Method |

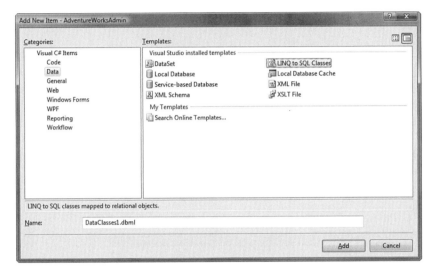

FIGURE 18.46   Adding a LINQ to SQL Classes item.

After you've selected the LINQ to SQL Classes item and added it to the project, the O/R Designer immediately launches (see Figure 18.47).

There isn't much to see yet because we haven't selected which database entities we want to represent within our object model. This involves the use of the second primary tool for performing the O/R mapping: Server Explorer.

By selecting a valid data source in Server Explorer, we can simply drag and drop a table over onto the left-hand side (the "data class" side) of the O/R Designer (see Figure 18.48).

Although nothing obvious happens after the table is dragged onto the data class pane (beyond having its visual representation in the designer), in reality potentially thousands of lines of code have been automatically generated to implement a class structure that mimics the table structure. In addition, all the attribute-based wiring has been implemented so that the LINQ engine can understand and process updates between the class object and the table's rows and columns.

18

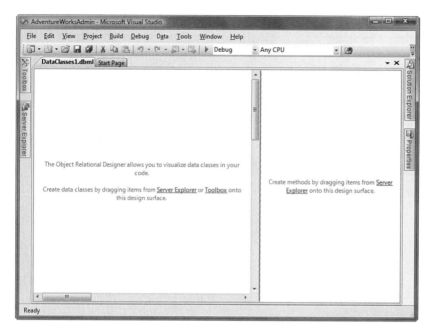

FIGURE 18.47    The O/R Designer surface.

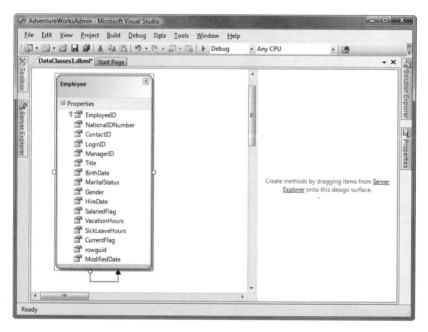

FIGURE 18.48    An entity added to the O/R Designer.

This exact process is also used to create methods within our object model. We can, for instance, drag a stored procedure over onto the right-hand pane of the designer (the "methods" pane) to map a method within our object model to the stored procedure (see Figure 18.49).

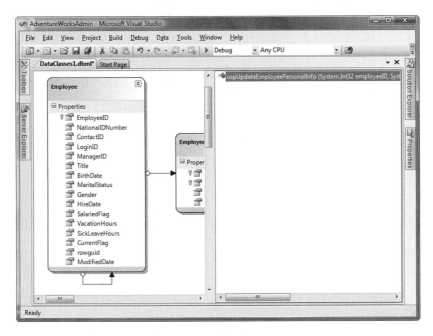

FIGURE 18.49    A method in the O/R Designer.

## LINQ Code

Let's examine exactly what has taken place behind the scenes as a result of the drag-and-drop operation between Server Explorer and the O/R Designer.

For one, the connection string necessary to open a connection to the selected database is automatically stored in the app.config (or web.config) file for you. This is then leveraged by LINQ to make calls into the database when needed. In addition, a new class has been defined. Here is a snippet from the Employee class showing its constructor:

```
public Employee()
{
   this._Employees = new EntitySet<Employee>
                    (new Action<Employee>(this.attach_Employees),
                     new Action<Employee>(this.detach_Employees));
 this._Employee1 = default(EntityRef<Employee>);
 OnCreated();
}
```

18

**NOTE**

The O/R Designer actually "de-pluralizes" entity names for you automatically. Many HR databases, for instance, may choose to implement an employee table and call it "employees" because it stores the data records for more than one worker. In an attempt to further push through the object model to data model impedance mismatch, the O/R Designer will actually create a class called "Employee" and *not* "Employees"; this correlates much better with the true intent of the class (which is to contain a single row/instance from the table and not the entire table).

You can see that LINQ marks up the object model with attributes to perform the magic linking between the objects and the database: Via the `Table` attribute, this class has been identified as a direct map to the HumanResources.Employee table.

Each column in the Employee table has also been implemented as a property on the `Employee` class. This snippet shows the `EmployeeID` property:

```
[Column(Storage="_EmployeeID", AutoSync=AutoSync.OnInsert,
DbType="Int NOT NULL IDENTITY", IsPrimaryKey=true, IsDbGenerated=true)]
public int EmployeeID
   {
     get
     {
       return this._EmployeeID;
     }
     set
     {
       if ((this._EmployeeID != value))
       {
          this.OnEmployeeIDChanging(value);
          this.SendPropertyChanging();
          this._EmployeeID = value;
          this.SendPropertyChanged("EmployeeID");
          this.OnEmployeeIDChanged();
       }
     }
   }
```

Beyond the `Employee` object, there has also been code generated for the data context. Here is a snippet of the class definition created automatically for us:

```
[System.Data.Linq.Mapping.DatabaseAttribute(Name="AdventureWorks")]
public partial class DataClasses1DataContext : System.Data.Linq.DataContext
   {
```

```
private static System.Data.Linq.Mapping.MappingSource mappingSource =
      new AttributeMappingSource();

   #region Extensibility Method Definitions
   partial void OnCreated();
   partial void InsertEmployee(Employee instance);
   partial void UpdateEmployee(Employee instance);
   partial void DeleteEmployee(Employee instance);
   #endregion

 public DataClasses1DataContext(string connection) :
   base(connection, mappingSource)
 {
  OnCreated();
 }
 public System.Data.Linq.Table<Employee> Employees
 {
  get
  {
   return this.GetTable<Employee>();
  }
 }
}
```

You can think of DataContext as the LINQ manager: It handles the connection back to the database, manages the in-memory entities, and marshals the calls necessary for data updates and any issues that might arise from concurrency and locking conflicts. In total, more than 500 lines of functioning code were emitted to make this all work. So, how do you actually use a LINQ object within your application? Read on.

**Working with LINQ Objects**
The goal with LINQ, again, is simplicity: LINQ classes look and behave just like any other class in our object model. We can create a new employee object, and set its properties like this:

```
Employee emp = new Employee();


emp.BirthDate = new DateTime(1965, 4, 4);
emp.Gender = 'F';
emp.LoginID = "templogin";
emp.MaritalStatus = 'M';
emp.Title = "Project Resource Manager";
...
```

To commit this new Employee object to the Employee table, we need to add the object to the Employees collection held by our data context, and then call the SubmitChanges method. Remember that the type is simply the default name given by the O/R Designer to our data context class; we can change this to anything we want.

```
DataClasses1DataContext db = new DataClasses1DataContext();
db.Employees.InsertOnSubmit(emp);
db.SubmitChanges();
```

In a similar fashion, employees can be removed from the collection (and then from the database):

```
db.Employees.DeleteOnSubmit(emp);
db.SubmitChanges();
```

We have really just scratched the surface here with regard to the intricacies and complexities of O/R application development using LINQ; but hopefully this overview of the O/R Designer can be used as a starting point for your O/R explorations in Visual Studio.

# Summary

In this chapter, you read about the broad and deep support that Visual Studio 2008 has for building and managing databases. We discussed the suite of Visual Database tools, available right within the IDE, that function in synergy with one another and with the various Visual Studio designers to provide a seamless experience for writing queries, creating table structures, and crafting stored procedures. We also investigated the newfound support for writing SQL Server database procedures and functions using entirely managed code.

We spent some time discussing the basics of data binding—how it is a core problem space with many application development efforts and how the Visual Studio Web and Windows Form Designers and controls provide first-class support for simple to complex data-binding scenarios. In particular, we examined the role that the designers play in the data-binding world by enabling developers to rapidly build forms-based applications with sophisticated data needs without writing a single line of code.

And finally, we examined the built-in support that Visual Studio provides for mapping entire object models to a database using the O/R Designer and the technology known as LINQ.

Hopefully, by exposing you to all of these great built-in tools, we have started you on the road to becoming even more efficient in leveraging Visual Studio across a range of database interactions.

# CHAPTER 19

# Service-Oriented Applications

$S$ervices have transformed the way we think of the Web and how we leverage it to build software. Prior to services, the Web was mostly a means to deliver cross-platform user interfaces with low deployment costs. Of course, that was a huge deal (and remains so) for both Internet and intranet applications. Services have shown a similar potential to change the way we build our applications both for the Web and across networks.

At their core, services represent an interface (or set of methods) that provide black-box-like access to shared functionality using common formats and protocols. By this definition, a service should be loosely coupled with its clients and work across boundaries. These boundaries have, for a long time, prevented the true promise of reusable application components like services. By working across boundaries such as process, machine, language, and operating system, services can truly be leveraged by the many potential clients that an organization may have today and tomorrow. Visual Studio 2008 and the .NET Framework 3.5 enable developers to create service-oriented applications without having to dig into the inner workings of such things as SOAP, HTTP, Remoting, and WSDL. Instead, you can focus on creating services that solve your specific business problems. You can then let the framework worry about your needs with respect to formats and protocols.

In this chapter, we first cover the fundamental concepts behind service-based applications. We will then cover the two primary service technologies built into Visual Studio: ASP.NET web services and Windows Communication Foundation (WCF). The former allows you to build standard web services hosted by ASP.NET. The latter is Microsoft's new service infrastructure that allows you to configure how your services are hosted and accessed. For each section we will discuss both creating services and writing clients to consume them.

## Service Fundamentals

A service defines a contract between a calling client and the service itself. In English, this contract states something like this: "If you send me data in this format, I will process it and return you the results in this other format." The format of this data and the communication parameters of these calls are all based on open standards such as XML and SOAP. Similar standards allow a client to often "discover" a web service and its contract and then work with it. These service standards apply across technology boundaries and therefore make services very attractive for exchanging data between heterogeneous environments.

To help frame the benefits of services, it can be helpful to think of them within the context of the problems they were designed to solve. For example, many large companies have multiple applications that need to access and update similar information. They might, for instance, rely on customer data records inside a customer relationship management (CRM) system, an order-processing application, a shipping tool, a financial system, and a reporting package. In this case, the customer record is duplicated per system. This means the data may be contradictory (or out-of-date) in any one system. Companies might have band-aids in place such as batch processing that tries to keep the data in synch on a daily basis. Figure 19.1 illustrates this problem example.

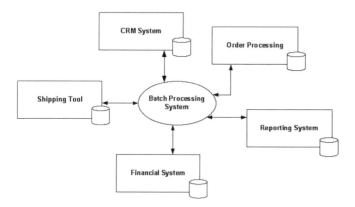

FIGURE 19.1   Common needs, heterogeneous applications.

What's worse, a company might have multiple systems that offer the same functionality (like two CRM systems). This can happen if the company has grown through acquisition and merger activities, or if each department has chosen its own technology. In fact, even if a company wrote all of these applications from scratch, you often see duplicate (or very similar) code in each application for doing the same thing. This code, of course, has to be maintained and changes to it can often have unintended consequences on the other systems.

These problems are what service-oriented solutions are intended to solve. Consider that each of the applications in the prior example may work on different servers running different code on different operating systems. They often even have different database technologies. Therefore, a reusable component that could be plugged into each application could not be easily created. Even if it did, the need to centralize this information into a common view would still exist. For example, an update to a customer record in one system needs to somehow be recorded in the other systems.

What is required to solve this type of problem is a common, shared interface into a centralized view of a customer. This interface should be able to work across application boundaries such as protocols, data types, and processes. Architects recognized this problem but did not see a viable solution until the advent of the Web. With web technologies, the HTTP protocol was ubiquitous. Servers could now talk to each other. Then along came the XML standard for describing messages. With these two technologies (HTTP and XML), applications running on different platforms now had a way to communicate. They could now send and receive structured messages over a common protocol, and thus web services were born.

## Why ASP.NET Web Services and WCF

Web services still maintain a dominant role in building service applications. They are great for communicating across the Internet. However, they are not always the most efficient means of communication. For example, if both the client and the service exist on the same technology (or even the same machine), they can often negotiate a more efficient means to communicate (such as Remoting). Service developers found themselves making the same choices they were trying to avoid. They now would have to choose between creating efficient, internal services and being able to have the broad access found over the Internet. And, if they had to support both, they might have to create multiple versions (or at least proxies) to their service. This is the problem Microsoft has solved with Windows Communication Foundation (WCF).

With WCF, you can create your service without concern for boundaries. You can then let WCF worry about running your service in the most efficient way, depending on the calling client. To manage this task, WCF introduces the concept of endpoints. Your service may have multiple endpoints (configured at design time or after deployment). Each endpoint indicates how the service might support a calling client over the web, via Remoting, through MSMQ, and more. WCF allows you to focus on creating your service functionality. It worries about how to most efficiently speak with calling clients. In this way, a single WCF service can efficiently support many different client types.

Consider our example from before. The customer data is shared among the applications. Each application might be written on a different platform, and it might also exist in a different location. You can extract the customer interface into a WCF service that provides common access to shared customer data. This centralizes the data. In addition, by using WCF, you can configure the service endpoints to work in the way that makes sense to the calling client. Figure 19.2 shows our example with centralized access of customer data in a WCF service.

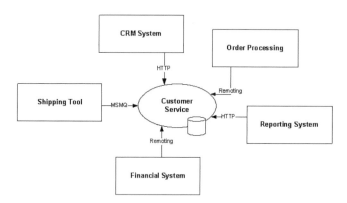

FIGURE 19.2    A service-oriented view of customer data.

In the coming sections we will cover creating both web services and those built on WCF. Visual Studio 2008 and the .NET Framework do a lot to abstract the intricacies or "plumbing" of building services away from everyday programming tasks. The result is a more productive development experience. You spend less time worrying about how to create a proper SOAP message or building communications channels and more time developing real business value.

# ASP.NET Web Service Applications

Before getting started, it is important that developers understand the key concepts and standard terms around web services. This knowledge ensures that you know what is happening in your application. It also helps when you are reading the .NET documentation and articles related to building web service applications. Therefore, we have put together the following glossary of key terms related to web services:

▶ **Web Service**—A web service represents a cohesive set of application logic that performs actions and provides data. A web service groups this logic as methods that can be called over HTTP. Not all services are web services; only those that work over the Internet are considered web services.

▶ **Web Service Method (or Web Method)**—A web service method represents a method exposed by a web service. A web method can take parameters and return a response.

▶ **XML (Extensible Markup Language)**—XML is used to both represent and describe data in a platform-neutral manner. XML can be used to represent both simple and complex data elements and relationships. It is the XML standard that makes web services possible.

▶ **WSDL (Web Service Description Language)**—WSDL is used to describe the contents of a web service and its web methods. The WSDL provides the message data contracts that allow clients to work with a given service.

▶ **XSD (XML Schema Document)**—XSD contains a set of predefined types (string, decimal, and so on) and a standard language for describing your own complex types. An XML Schema Document (also referred to as an XSD) uses these types to describe (and restrict) the contents of an XML message.

▶ **SOAP (Simple Object Access Protocol)**—SOAP is an XML-based protocol for communicating between client and web service. It is helpful to think of SOAP as representing the format of the messages as they pass over the wire. SOAP wraps XML messages (in envelopes) for communication across the Web. Most SOAP messages are sent over HTTP. However, they can also be sent with transport protocols such as SMTP and FTP.

▶ **HTTP (Hypertext Transfer Protocol)**—HTTP represents the communication protocol used by web services to transfer SOAP-formatted (or encoded) messages. HTTP is also the way standard web page requests (GET and POST) communicate.

▶ **UDDI (Universal Description, Discovery, and Integration)**—UDDI is used to define a registry of web services. This capability is useful for the publication of services for developers to find and consume.

▶ **URI (Uniform Resource Identifier)**—URIs provide a means for locating items on the web. In most cases, URIs are URLs (uniform resource locators) that point to a given service.

▶ **DISCO (Discovery Document)**—A DISCO file provides information that links to other key elements of a web service. This includes links to XSDs, SOAP bindings, and namespaces. A program can use a DISCO file to determine how to work with a given web service.

▶ **WS-\***—This term represents the overall standards for web services.

▶ **WSE (Web Service Enhancements)**—This is Microsoft's implementation of WS-\* standards. WSE 3.0 is the latest version. It enables web service transactions and enhanced security. WSE can be downloaded and acts as an add-in to Visual Studio.

Visual Studio makes building web services a similar experience as you would get when developing other classes and components. In this way, the complexities of SOAP, WSDL, XSD, and the like are abstracted (and auto-generated by the tool). You still have access and control over these low-level items if you need them. However, for the most part, you define a web service the same way you create a class. You then define web methods similar to the way you would define methods on a class. Visual Studio takes on the job of creating the appropriate schema contract for your method signatures and describing your web services in terms of WSDL. The .NET Framework then worries about properly packaging your data into a SOAP message and transmitting it across HTTP.

Web services in .NET are built and delivered on the same framework that delivers ASP.NET websites. This means that web services share the same server technology (Internet Information Services, or IIS) as well as the same objects, such as Application, Session, and Context. In this way, developers who are familiar with delivering ASP.NET applications can leverage this experience for web services. You can take advantage of the built-in state management, authentication services, and performance of ASP.NET, for instance.

A web service in .NET is simply a web address to a web service file that contains the extension .asmx. The service has a standard http://... address. This file is used as the URI for the web service (similar to a web page). You write your code "behind" this file, and Visual Studio and .NET do the rest by attaching the appropriate WSDL and enabling the SOAP calls over HTTP. Let's take a closer look at how to leverage Visual Studio and ASP.NET to deliver web services.

## The ASP.NET Web Service Project Template

A web service can be added to any ASP.NET web project. Visual Studio also provides a web service–specific project template. This template is useful if you intend to create an entire service layer or want to separate your services from any user interface elements. You create a project from this template the same way you define other web projects: Selecting File, New, Website will launch the Add New Project dialog box, as shown in Figure 19.3. Here, you can select the template ASP.NET Web Service Application to define a web service–specific project.

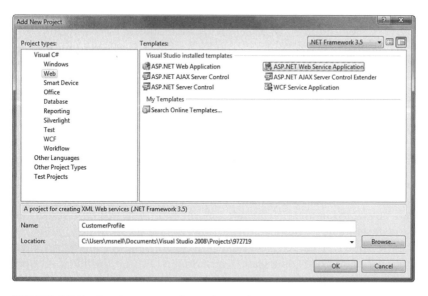

FIGURE 19.3   Create a new web service project.

As with defining a new website, you can indicate the location of the web service. You can choose a location by using the file system or by browsing to a web server using HTTP, or by leveraging FTP to indicate where to store the web service. In addition, you can define the default language in which the web service should be programmed.

### Web Service Files

The actual web service project that is created through the web service template contains exactly one service, a config file, and a set of standard references. The service is referenced by an .asmx file. Again, this file is used as the URI (and URL) for the web service. The actual contents of this file are shown in Figure 19.4.

The .asmx file in the figure has a design view for adding components, a markup view (shown) for seeing the ASP.NET service definition, and the code-behind (or code) view. You can switch views by right-clicking the .asmx file. The markup view shows a single directive WebService. This directive indicates that the web service file is a pointer to the code for the service. The CodeBehind attribute indicates this information. Here, it points to the code file called Service1.asmx.cs; this is the code-behind file shown under the Service1.asmx file in the Solution Explorer. This is where the application logic for the service resides. Finally, this directive uses the Class attribute to indicate a class contained inside Service1.asmx.cs; this class is the web service. The methods in this class are the web methods.

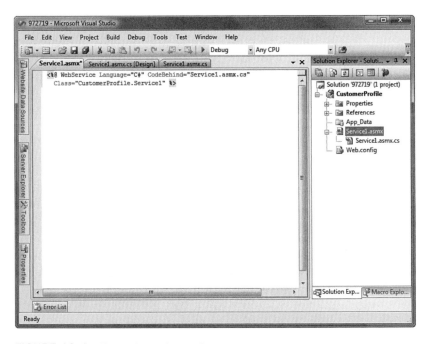

FIGURE 19.4  The web service project.

**NOTE**

You can actually choose to define a web service as a single file. In this case, both the directive and the code are stored together (instead of the code-behind model).

Figure 19.5 shows the contents of `Service1.asmx.cs`. First, note that this class is just a standard C# class (it could also be VB). It has `using` statements, the class definition, a method, and some attributes. The web service programming model should be very familiar to .NET developers.

Of course, you still have to let .NET know that this code is a web service. There are two ways the code does this. First, it uses attributes. The `Service1` class in Figure 19.5 is decorated with the `WebService` attribute. This defines the class as a web service. Notice also that the `HelloWorld` method has the `WebMethod` attribute applied. This attribute indicates that this method is a web method that can be called for the web service.

Another way this class indicates itself as a web service is through inheritance. The class inherits `System.Web.Services.WebService`. This is actually optional. You could define a class as a web service without inheriting from `WebService`. However, through this inheritance, the class will actually have full access to the ASP.NET features such as `Session` and `Context` objects. Having access to these objects provides many of the familiar ASP.NET features to web service developers.

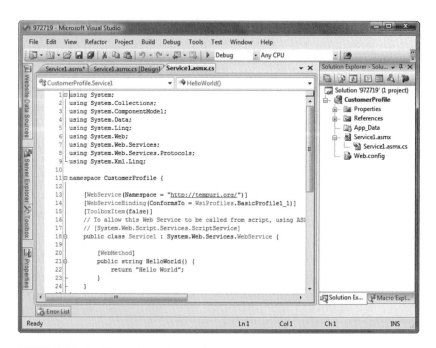

FIGURE 19.5    The web service code.

## Creating an ASP.NET Web Service

Thus far, you've looked at the standard web service files created by the Visual Studio web service template. Now you're ready to explore developing an actual web service with Visual Studio 2008. For this example, you will develop a CustomerProfile web service. This web service will provide methods for retrieving customer information from a data store and saving changes to that information. Along the way, you will look at the finer points of developing a .NET web service. The following steps outline this process:

1. To create the web service, add a new web service to an ASP.NET Web Service Application template. Call this service CustomerProfile.asmx.

2. Next, remove the HelloWorld sample method and in its place create methods called GetCustomerProfile, SaveCustomer, and DeleteCustomer. Each method should be marked with the [WebMethod] attribute.

3. Add a new class library project to your solution. Call this project BusinessEntities. This project will contain the actual definition for a simple Customer class with a set of properties. Listing 19.1 shows an example of this code.

LISTING 19.1   The **BusinessEntities.Customer** Class

```
using System;

namespace BusinessEntities {

  public class Customer {

    public string Id { get; set; }
    public string Name { get; set; }
    public string Email { get; set; }
    public string AddressLine1 { get; set; }
    public string AddressLine2 { get; set; }
    public string City { get; set; }
    public string State { get; set; }
    public string PostalCode { get; set; }
    public string Phone { get; set; }
    public bool ContactEmail { get; set; }
    public bool ContactPhone { get; set; }

  }
}
```

4. Next, create a second class library project called EntityServices and add a class called CustomerProfile to this library. The EntityServices namespace will provide the actual implementation of the code that executes on behalf of the service's SaveCustomer web method. The service is actually a proxy for the

`EntityServices.CustomerProfile.SaveCustomer` method. This latter method does the work to actually save the customer.

This proxy implementation pattern is optional. You could define all your execution logic right inside the web service. However, we are showing this example for two reasons. The first is that most applications leverage some existing code. It can be useful to build a proxy to expose this existing code through web services. The second point is that this is just good design. Having the implementation code inside a separate object can lead to reuse, enable easier unit testing, and enable client scenarios that are more traditional (and do not rely on web services).

5. Create a database to which the customer profile information will be retrieved and saved. This has little to do with the web service but helps round out the example. A customer table is all that is required. Figure 19.6 shows an example of a customer table added to a `Customer.mdf` database file in the `EntityServices` project.

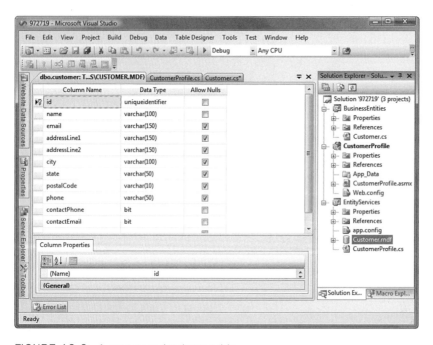

FIGURE 19.6   A customer database table.

6. You can now write the methods for retrieving, saving, and deleting a customer. First, add a reference from the `EntityServices` project to the `BusinessEntities` project. Next, add a `SaveCustomer`, `GetCustomer`, and `DeleteCustomer` method to the `CustomerProfile` class in the `EntityServices` class library project you created. Listing 19.2 shows some basic sample code that works with the database table you created previously.

LISTING 19.2   The **EntityServices.CustomerProfile** Class

```
using System;
using System.Collections.Generic;
using System.Data.SqlClient;
using System.Data;
using System.Text;
using BusinessEntities;

namespace EntityServices {
  public class CustomerProfile {

    string _dbConnect = @"Data Source=.\SQLEXPRESS;AttachDbFilename=C:\...\
➥Customer.mdf;Integrated Security=True;User Instance=True";

    public Customer GetCustomer(string customerId) {

      StringBuilder sql = new StringBuilder("SELECT id, name, email, ");
      sql.Append("addressLine1, addressLine2, city, state, postalCode, ");
      sql.Append("phone, contactPhone, contactEmail ");
      sql.Append("FROM customer WHERE id = @id");

      using (SqlConnection cnn = new SqlConnection(_dbConnect)) {

        SqlCommand cmd = new SqlCommand(sql.ToString(), cnn);
        cmd.CommandType = CommandType.Text;
        cmd.Parameters.Add(new SqlParameter("id", customerId));

        cnn.Open();
        SqlDataReader dr = cmd.ExecuteReader();
        dr.Read();
        Customer c = new Customer();
        c.AddressLine1 = dr["addressLine1"].ToString();
        c.AddressLine2 = dr["addressLine2"].ToString();
        c.City = dr["city"].ToString();
        c.ContactEmail = (bool)dr["contactPhone"];
        c.ContactPhone = (bool)dr["contactEmail"];
        c.Email = dr["email"].ToString();
        c.Id = dr["id"].ToString();
        c.Name = dr["name"].ToString();
        c.Phone = dr["phone"].ToString();
        c.PostalCode = dr["postalCode"].ToString();
        c.State = dr["state"].ToString();

        return c;
```

LISTING 19.2    Continued

```
    }
  }

  public void SaveCustomer(Customer customer) {

    StringBuilder sql = new StringBuilder();
    SqlCommand cmd = new SqlCommand();

    //determine if update or save
    if (customer.Id == null) {
      //assume insert
      sql.Append("INSERT INTO customer (id, name, email, addressLine1, ");
      sql.Append("addressLine2, city, state, postalCode, phone, ");
      sql.Append("contactPhone, contactEmail) ");
      sql.Append("VALUES(@id, @name, @email, @addressLine1, ");
      sql.Append("@addressLine2, @city, @state, @postalCode, @phone, ");
      sql.Append("@contactPhone, @contactEmail)");
      cmd.Parameters.Add(new SqlParameter("@id",
        Guid.NewGuid().ToString()));

    } else {
      //assume update
      sql.Append("UPDATE customer set name=@name, email=@email, ");
      sql.Append("addressLine1=@addressLine1, ");
      sql.Append("addressLine2=@addressLine2, city=@city, ");
      sql.Append("state=@state, postalCode=@postalCode, ");
      sql.Append("phone=@phone, contactPhone=@contactPhone, ");
      sql.Append("contactEmail=@contactEmail ");
      sql.Append("WHERE id=@id ");
      cmd.Parameters.Add(new SqlParameter("@id", customer.Id));
    }

    //add additional parameters
    cmd.Parameters.Add(new SqlParameter("@name", customer.Name));
    cmd.Parameters.Add(new SqlParameter("@email", customer.Email));
    cmd.Parameters.Add(new SqlParameter("@addressLine1",
      customer.AddressLine1));
    cmd.Parameters.Add(new SqlParameter("@addressLine2",
      customer.AddressLine2));
    cmd.Parameters.Add(new SqlParameter("@city", customer.City));
    cmd.Parameters.Add(new SqlParameter("@state", customer.State));
    cmd.Parameters.Add(new SqlParameter("@postalCode",
      customer.PostalCode));
    cmd.Parameters.Add(new SqlParameter("@phone", customer.Phone));
```

```
      cmd.Parameters.Add(new SqlParameter("@contactPhone",
        customer.ContactPhone));
      cmd.Parameters.Add(new SqlParameter("@contactEmail",
        customer.ContactEmail));

      using (SqlConnection cnn = new SqlConnection(_dbConnect)) {
        cmd.CommandType = CommandType.Text;
        cmd.CommandText = sql.ToString();
        cmd.Connection=cnn;
        cnn.Open();
        cmd.ExecuteNonQuery();
      }
    }

    public void DeleteCustomer(string customerId) {

      string sql = "delete from customer where id = @id";

      using (SqlConnection cnn = new SqlConnection(_dbConnect)) {
        SqlCommand cmd = new SqlCommand(sql, cnn);
        cmd.CommandType = CommandType.Text;
        cmd.Parameters.Add(new SqlParameter("@id", customerId));
        cnn.Open();
        cmd.ExecuteNonQuery();
      }

    }
  }
}
```

7. Again, the EntityServices class serves as a proxy for the web service. You can now add a reference from the web service project to both the BusinessEntities and EntityServices projects.

8. The last step is to write the code for the web service itself. This includes a method for GetCustomerProfile that takes the parameter customerId and returns a Customer instance. Also, create a SaveCustomer method that takes an instance of the Customer class but does not return a value. Finally, create a DeleteCustomer method that takes a customerId. Listing 19.3 shows the sample code for the service.

LISTING 19.3  Customer Profile Web Service

```
using System;
using System.Collections;
using System.ComponentModel;
using System.Data;
```

LISTING 19.3    Continued

```csharp
using System.Linq;
using System.Web;
using System.Web.Services;
using System.Web.Services.Protocols;
using System.Xml.Linq;
using BusinessEntities;

namespace CustomerProfile {

  [WebService(Namespace = "http://tempuri.org/")]
  [WebServiceBinding(ConformsTo = WsiProfiles.BasicProfile1_1)]
  [ToolboxItem(false)]
  public class CustomerProfile : System.Web.Services.WebService {

    [WebMethod(Description = "Used to return a customer's profile.")]
    public Customer GetCustomerProfile(string customerId) {

      EntityServices.CustomerProfile custProfile =
        new EntityServices.CustomerProfile();

      return custProfile.GetCustomer(customerId);
    }

    [WebMethod(Description = "Saves a customer")]
    public void SaveCustomer(BusinessEntities.Customer customer) {

      EntityServices.CustomerProfile custProfile =
        new EntityServices.CustomerProfile();

      custProfile.SaveCustomer(customer);
    }

    [WebMethod(Description = "Deletes a customer")]
    public void DeleteCustomer(string customerId) {

      EntityServices.CustomerProfile custProfile = new
        EntityServices.CustomerProfile();

      custProfile.DeleteCustomer(customerId);
    }

  }
}
```

---

**TIP**

When you're building a web service, it is best to group functionality into coarse-grained interfaces. You don't want web methods that do a number of fine-grained operations such as setting properties before calling a method. This chatty nature can be expensive when communicating across the Internet.

Of course, this approach is also contrary to most object-oriented application designs. Therefore, the use of a proxy object to bundle operations around a business object is ideal. The business object can be serialized and passed across the wire. On the other side, it can be deserialized and then worked with in an in-process manner (in which chatty calls are not expensive).

---

Now that you have built a simple web service, let's take a look at what defines this class as a web service. We will return to this service example in a moment.

### The WebService Attribute Class

The WebService attribute class (also called WebServiceAttribute) can be used to provide additional details about a given web service. You may apply this attribute when declaring a class as a web service. However, the attribute is not required. It merely gives context about a web service. For example, we used the WebService attribute on the CustomerProfile class declaration to provide details about the web service's namespace.

The following are the descriptive elements you can define with the WebService attribute class:

- ▶ **Description**—Used to define a description of the web service. This description will be provided to consumers of your web service and in related documentation. You should always supply this web service description.

- ▶ **Namespace**—Used to declare the namespace for your web service (tempuri.org by default). This is similar to namespaces as you know them inside .NET. However, these namespaces are meant to be unique across the web on which they operate. Therefore, you should always define a namespace using a URL that you own and control. This can be a company Internet address, for example.

- ▶ **Name**—Used to define a different name for your web service. The name of your web service need not be restricted to the naming confines of .NET. Therefore, you can use this parameter to create a new name for your web service.

### The WebService Class

The WebService class represents the base class for .NET web services. This is not to be confused with the WebService attribute class (see the preceding section). You derive from this class in order to use the common ASP.NET objects (Session, Application, Context, and so on). However, it is not mandatory that you do so. Visual Studio enforces this inheritance when you define a new web service, but you can remove this code if you have no intention of leveraging the ASP.NET objects within your web service. If you choose to derive from `WebService`, you access these ASP.NET objects the same way you would inside any web application.

### The WebMethod Attribute Class

The `WebMethod` attribute class is used to indicate that a method in your service should be exposed via the web service. This declaration is mandatory for all methods that you intend to make available through the web service.

There are various parameters you can set when defining a web method. These parameters control how the web method operates. For the example, you will simply set the `Description` parameter to document a description of the method. However, the following list provides a more comprehensive list of parameters on the `WebMethod` attribute:

- ▶ **Description**—Used to provide a description of the web method. This description will appear to calling clients and on help documentation related to the web method.

- ▶ **EnableSession**—Used to indicate whether session states should be enabled for the given web method. Setting this value to `True` allows you to store and retrieve items in the session. If you set this parameter to `True` and inherit from `WebService`, you access the session from the `Session` object (`WebService.Session`). If you are not inheriting from `WebService`, you can still set this parameter to `True`. However, to get to the session object, you will have to traverse the `HttpContext.Current.Session` path.

- ▶ **CacheDuration**—Used to indicate that the results of the web service should be cached for a specific duration. You set the duration (in seconds) for this parameter. Enabling this cache will result in the caching of the response for every unique set of parameters passed to the web service (similar to ASP.NET output caching).

- ▶ **MessageName**—Used to define an alias or separate name for a given web method. This capability is useful if you intend to have overloaded methods that .NET supports but web services do not. In this way, you can keep your overloaded methods and then apply a unique name to each one using this parameter.

- ▶ **BufferResponse**—Used to indicate whether the entire response should be buffered in the server's memory before passing it back across the wire to the calling client. The default setting for this parameter is `True`. If you set it to `False`, the response will be buffered in chunks of 16KB, with each chunk being sent to the client one at a time.

- ▶ **TransactionOption**—Used to indicate whether the web service should be the root of a transaction. By default, web services cannot be enlisted in other transactions. They can, however, invoke objects that participate in a transaction along with the single web service.

### Viewing the Formal Web Service Description

Visual Studio and the .NET Framework enable you to view a given web service inside the web browser. This capability can be useful for both testing a web service and discovering how one works (the messages they require and return). To access a web service, you first build (compile) it in Visual Studio and then access the `.asmx` file in a browser.

Figure 19.7 shows the `CustomerProfile` web service example in a browser window. Notice that all methods of the service are listed. Each method's description is also provided. This is the same description entered in the web method definition (`WebMethodAttribute`).

To see the actual formal description of the web service as it is defined in WSDL, you can select the link Service Description from the top of the page shown in Figure 19.7. When you click this link, the `WSDL` parameter is passed to the `.asmx` file on the `QueryString`. This tells ASP.NET to return the WSDL of the service.

This WSDL is generated for you. It conforms to the WSDL standards and can therefore be used by clients that want to access your service. These clients use this WSDL to understand how your web service operates.

---

**NOTE**

.NET ships with a tool named `Disco.exe`. Visual Studio uses this tool to generate files related to the understanding and discovery of web services. You too can leverage this tool from the command line to generate these documents and store them for examination and use.

The documents created by `Disco.exe` serve as the input for client applications that consume the web service. These client applications are created using a related tool called `WSDL.exe`.

---

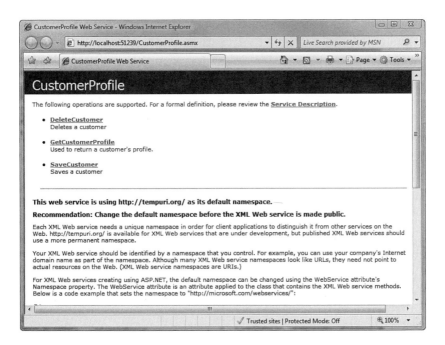

FIGURE 19.7    Navigating to the web service through a browser.

You can find the complete listing of the WSDL for the `CustomerProfile` service in Listing 19.4. This listing is easier to view in a browser (where you get color-coding and a treelike structure to navigate the XML). However, the listing is provided here for your reference. As you scan it, notice how each service is defined. Also notice how the `Customer` complex type is embedded inside the WSDL. This complex type was generated based on the sample `Customer` object (`BusinessEntities.Customer`). Recall that this type is a return value to one method and a parameter to another. You can see that .NET is converting this to an XML type for use by web services.

LISTING 19.4   The Web Service WSDL

```
<wsdl:definitions xmlns:soap="http://schemas.xmlsoap.org/wsdl/soap/"
xmlns:tm="http://microsoft.com/wsdl/mime/textMatching/"
xmlns:soapenc="http://schemas.xmlsoap.org/soap/encoding/"
xmlns:mime="http://schemas.xmlsoap.org/wsdl/mime/"
xmlns:tns="http://tempuri.org/" xmlns:s="http://www.w3.org/2001/XMLSchema"
xmlns:soap12="http://schemas.xmlsoap.org/wsdl/soap12/"
xmlns:http="http://schemas.xmlsoap.org/wsdl/http/"
targetNamespace="http://tempuri.org/"
xmlns:wsdl="http://schemas.xmlsoap.org/wsdl/">
  <wsdl:types>
    <s:schema elementFormDefault="qualified" targetNamespace="http://tempuri.org/">
      <s:element name="GetCustomerProfile">
        <s:complexType>
          <s:sequence>
            <s:element minOccurs="0" maxOccurs="1" name="customerId"
            type="s:string" />
          </s:sequence>
        </s:complexType>
      </s:element>
      <s:element name="GetCustomerProfileResponse">
        <s:complexType>
          <s:sequence>
            <s:element minOccurs="0" maxOccurs="1" name="GetCustomerProfileResult"
            type="tns:Customer" />
          </s:sequence>
        </s:complexType>
      </s:element>
      <s:complexType name="Customer">
        <s:sequence>
          <s:element minOccurs="0" maxOccurs="1" name="Id" type="s:string" />
          <s:element minOccurs="0" maxOccurs="1" name="Name"
            type="s:string" />
          <s:element minOccurs="0" maxOccurs="1" name="Email"
            type="s:string" />
          <s:element minOccurs="0" maxOccurs="1" name="AddressLine1"
```

```
              type="s:string" />
          <s:element minOccurs="0" maxOccurs="1" name="AddressLine2"
            type="s:string" />
          <s:element minOccurs="0" maxOccurs="1" name="City"
            type="s:string" />
          <s:element minOccurs="0" maxOccurs="1" name="State"
            type="s:string" />
          <s:element minOccurs="0" maxOccurs="1" name="PostalCode"
            type="s:string" />
          <s:element minOccurs="0" maxOccurs="1" name="Phone"
            type="s:string" />
          <s:element minOccurs="1" maxOccurs="1" name="ContactEmail"
            type="s:boolean" />
          <s:element minOccurs="1" maxOccurs="1" name="ContactPhone"
            type="s:boolean" />
        </s:sequence>
      </s:complexType>
      <s:element name="SaveCustomer">
        <s:complexType>
          <s:sequence>
            <s:element minOccurs="0" maxOccurs="1" name="customer"
              type="tns:Customer" />
          </s:sequence>
        </s:complexType>
      </s:element>
      <s:element name="SaveCustomerResponse">
        <s:complexType />
      </s:element>
      <s:element name="DeleteCustomer">
        <s:complexType>
          <s:sequence>
            <s:element minOccurs="0" maxOccurs="1" name="customerId"
              type="s:string" />
          </s:sequence>
        </s:complexType>
      </s:element>
      <s:element name="DeleteCustomerResponse">
        <s:complexType />
      </s:element>
    </s:schema>
  </wsdl:types>
  <wsdl:message name="GetCustomerProfileSoapIn">
    <wsdl:part name="parameters" element="tns:GetCustomerProfile" />
  </wsdl:message>
  <wsdl:message name="GetCustomerProfileSoapOut">
    <wsdl:part name="parameters" element="tns:GetCustomerProfileResponse" />
```

LISTING 19.4    Continued

```xml
    </wsdl:message>
    <wsdl:message name="SaveCustomerSoapIn">
      <wsdl:part name="parameters" element="tns:SaveCustomer" />
    </wsdl:message>
    <wsdl:message name="SaveCustomerSoapOut">
      <wsdl:part name="parameters" element="tns:SaveCustomerResponse" />
    </wsdl:message>
    <wsdl:message name="DeleteCustomerSoapIn">
      <wsdl:part name="parameters" element="tns:DeleteCustomer" />
    </wsdl:message>
    <wsdl:message name="DeleteCustomerSoapOut">
      <wsdl:part name="parameters" element="tns:DeleteCustomerResponse" />
    </wsdl:message>
    <wsdl:portType name="CustomerProfileSoap">
      <wsdl:operation name="GetCustomerProfile">
        <wsdl:documentation xmlns:wsdl="http://schemas.xmlsoap.org/wsdl/">Used to
return a customer's profile.</wsdl:documentation>
        <wsdl:input message="tns:GetCustomerProfileSoapIn" />
        <wsdl:output message="tns:GetCustomerProfileSoapOut" />
      </wsdl:operation>
      <wsdl:operation name="SaveCustomer">
        <wsdl:documentation xmlns:wsdl="http://schemas.xmlsoap.org/wsdl/">Saves a
customer</wsdl:documentation>
        <wsdl:input message="tns:SaveCustomerSoapIn" />
        <wsdl:output message="tns:SaveCustomerSoapOut" />
      </wsdl:operation>
      <wsdl:operation name="DeleteCustomer">
        <wsdl:documentation xmlns:wsdl="http://schemas.xmlsoap.org/wsdl/">Deletes a
customer</wsdl:documentation>
        <wsdl:input message="tns:DeleteCustomerSoapIn" />
        <wsdl:output message="tns:DeleteCustomerSoapOut" />
      </wsdl:operation>
    </wsdl:portType>
    <wsdl:binding name="CustomerProfileSoap" type="tns:CustomerProfileSoap">
      <soap:binding transport="http://schemas.xmlsoap.org/soap/http" />
      <wsdl:operation name="GetCustomerProfile">
        <soap:operation soapAction="http://tempuri.org/GetCustomerProfile"
          style="document" />
        <wsdl:input>
          <soap:body use="literal" />
        </wsdl:input>
        <wsdl:output>
          <soap:body use="literal" />
        </wsdl:output>
      </wsdl:operation>
```

```
  <wsdl:operation name="SaveCustomer">
    <soap:operation soapAction="http://tempuri.org/SaveCustomer"
      style="document" />
    <wsdl:input>
      <soap:body use="literal" />
    </wsdl:input>
    <wsdl:output>
      <soap:body use="literal" />
    </wsdl:output>
  </wsdl:operation>
  <wsdl:operation name="DeleteCustomer">
    <soap:operation soapAction="http://tempuri.org/DeleteCustomer"
      style="document" />
    <wsdl:input>
      <soap:body use="literal" />
    </wsdl:input>
    <wsdl:output>
      <soap:body use="literal" />
    </wsdl:output>
  </wsdl:operation>
</wsdl:binding>
<wsdl:binding name="CustomerProfileSoap12" type="tns:CustomerProfileSoap">
  <soap12:binding transport="http://schemas.xmlsoap.org/soap/http" />
  <wsdl:operation name="GetCustomerProfile">
    <soap12:operation soapAction="http://tempuri.org/GetCustomerProfile"
      style="document" />
    <wsdl:input>
      <soap12:body use="literal" />
    </wsdl:input>
    <wsdl:output>
      <soap12:body use="literal" />
    </wsdl:output>
  </wsdl:operation>
  <wsdl:operation name="SaveCustomer">
    <soap12:operation soapAction="http://tempuri.org/SaveCustomer"
      style="document" />
    <wsdl:input>
      <soap12:body use="literal" />
    </wsdl:input>
    <wsdl:output>
      <soap12:body use="literal" />
    </wsdl:output>
  </wsdl:operation>
  <wsdl:operation name="DeleteCustomer">
    <soap12:operation soapAction="http://tempuri.org/DeleteCustomer"
      style="document" />
```

LISTING 19.4    Continued

```
      <wsdl:input>
        <soap12:body use="literal" />
      </wsdl:input>
      <wsdl:output>
        <soap12:body use="literal" />
      </wsdl:output>
    </wsdl:operation>
  </wsdl:binding>
  <wsdl:service name="CustomerProfile">
    <wsdl:port name="CustomerProfileSoap" binding="tns:CustomerProfileSoap">
      <soap:address location="http://localhost:51239/CustomerProfile.asmx" />
    </wsdl:port>
    <wsdl:port name="CustomerProfileSoap12"
      binding="tns:CustomerProfileSoap12">
      <soap12:address
        location="http://localhost:51239/CustomerProfile.asmx" />
    </wsdl:port>
  </wsdl:service>
</wsdl:definitions>
```

**Viewing the Web Method**

When you click on the web method name in the page as shown in Figure 19.7, ASP.NET generates a web form for you to use to test the given web service method. This form is accessed from the .asmx file (URI) with the QueryString parameter op (operation). You pass the name of the web method to this parameter. For the example, look at the web method named GetCustomerProfile. Figure 19.8 shows this web form.

The top part of the form allows you to enter parameters for the web method and then invoke the actual web method using the HTTP POST protocol. This protocol is just one way to invoke the web method. Recall that you also use SOAP. This page shows actual examples of a SOAP request and response as well as the HTTP samples. These examples can be useful if you want to see how messages should be constructed for these protocols.

As an example, Listing 19.5 shows a SOAP 1.2 message request for this web method. Notice that it indicates that the <customerId> element must be passed to the method. This is of the primitive type int.

LISTING 19.5    SOAP 1.2 Request

```
POST /CustomerProfile.asmx HTTP/1.1
Host: localhost
Content-Type: application/soap+xml; charset=utf-8
Content-Length: length
```

```
<soap12:Envelope xmlns:xsi="http://www.w3.org/2001/XMLSchema-instance"
xmlns:xsd="http://www.w3.org/2001/XMLSchema"
xmlns:soap12="http://www.w3.org/2003/05/soap-envelope">
  <soap12:Body>
    <GetCustomerProfile xmlns="http://tempuri.org/">
      <customerId>string</customerId>
    </GetCustomerProfile>
  </soap12:Body>
</soap12:Envelope>
```

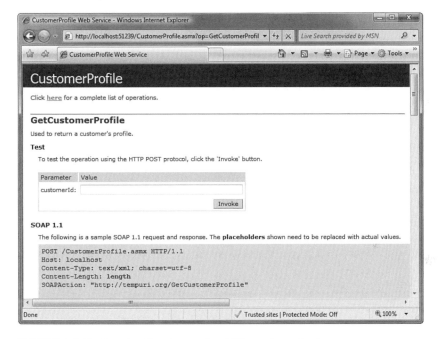

FIGURE 19.8    The **GetCustomerProfile** web method.

Listing 19.6 shows the correlated SOAP response from the call. Notice here that the SOAP
result is contained in the element <GetCustomerProfileResult>.

LISTING 19.6    SOAP 1.2 Response

```
HTTP/1.1 200 OK
Content-Type: application/soap+xml; charset=utf-8
Content-Length: length

<soap12:Envelope xmlns:xsi="http://www.w3.org/2001/XMLSchema-instance"
xmlns:xsd="http://www.w3.org/2001/XMLSchema"
xmlns:soap12="http://www.w3.org/2003/05/soap-envelope">
```

LISTING 19.6    Continued

```
  <soap12:Body>
    <GetCustomerProfileResponse xmlns="http://tempuri.org/">
      <GetCustomerProfileResult>
        <Id>string</Id>
        <Name>string</Name>
        <Email>string</Email>
        <AddressLine1>string</AddressLine1>
        <AddressLine2>string</AddressLine2>
        <City>string</City>
        <State>string</State>
        <PostalCode>string</PostalCode>
        <Phone>string</Phone>
        <ContactEmail>boolean</ContactEmail>
        <ContactPhone>boolean</ContactPhone>
      </GetCustomerProfileResult>
    </GetCustomerProfileResponse>
  </soap12:Body>
</soap12:Envelope>
```

#### Invoking the Web Method

To invoke the web method, you enter a value for the parameters and click the Invoke button (as shown in Figure 19.8). Doing so executes the web service and returns the results. The results are sent back as XML (as defined by the message). Remember, this invocation is HTTP POST. Figure 19.9 shows the results from the example.

> **NOTE**
>
> You can use this method only to invoke web methods that take simple (primitive) data types as parameters. If your web method takes a complex type (SaveCustomer, for example), then you can still see the request/response examples but cannot invoke the web method in this manner.

## Consuming an ASP.NET Web Service

A web service can be consumed by any client capable of calling the service and managing its results. Visual Studio makes this task easy. It allows you to set a *service reference* to any service. This process is similar to setting a reference to another .NET library or COM component. After you define this service reference, Visual Studio generates a local proxy class for consuming the service. This allows you to program against the proxy class and not worry about writing service-specific code. Service references can be set inside most any .NET application, including Windows forms, WPF, console applications, and more. Let's take a look at this process.

FIGURE 19.9  **GetCustomerProfile** results.

### Defining a Service Reference

You define a service reference for your project by selecting the Add Service Reference option from the context menu for a given project. This will launch the Add Service Reference dialog box. You use this dialog box to browse to a service and add that service as a reference.

This dialog has been revamped from prior versions of Visual Studio. It represents a unification of all service references including ASP.NET web services and those built on WCF. Figure 19.10 shows the initial screen of the Add Service Reference dialog. From here you can type in the URI address of your service or click the Discover button to find services that already exist in your solution. After you've located services, you can see them on the list on the left. You can select the service interface and see its operations on the right. At the bottom of the form, you can set the namespace for your service reference. This defines the namespace that Visual Studio will use when generating service proxy code for you.

Clicking the Advanced button at the bottom of the Add Service Reference dialog brings up the Service Reference Settings dialog, shown in Figure 19.11. From here you can control how Visual Studio will generate your proxy code. This includes the collections you want to map to and the scope of your proxy methods (public or private).

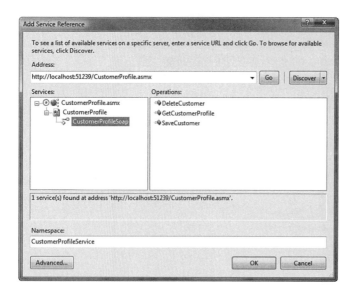

FIGURE 19.10   The Add Service Reference dialog box.

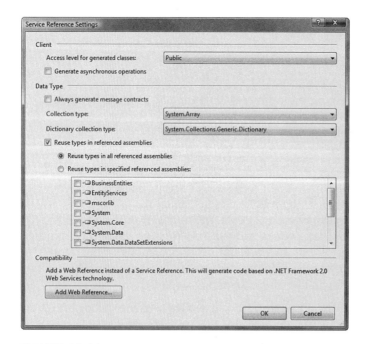

FIGURE 19.11   The Service Reference Settings dialog box.

Notice the Add Web Reference button at the bottom of the Service Reference Settings form. This allows you to create a web reference in the prior (.NET 2.0) style. Figure 19.12 shows an example. Prior to WCF, this was the principal means of setting a service reference as there were only web services. This too generates a proxy class for you, the namespace of which is defined by the content of the Web Reference Name text box.

Thinking back to the example, you will bind a Windows form application called CustomerManager to the CustomerProfile ASP.NET web service defined previously. For this example, assume that the Windows form application will exist independently of the service (in a separate process) and that the web service will be used by multiple, disparate clients.

---

**NOTE**

Note that if the client had direct access to the EntityService library, you would be better off bypassing the web service and setting a direct reference to EntityServices (and thus skip the overhead of the web service). For now, however, assume that they are separate processes and create a reference to the web service. When we discuss WCF, we will look at creating a single service to efficiently handle both local clients and those that call out of process.

---

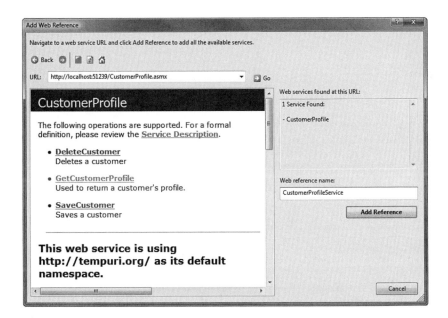

FIGURE 19.12   The Add Web Reference dialog box.

In our example, both the Windows form application and the service are in the same solution. Therefore, you can use the Add Service Reference dialog and click the Discover button to find the service. This is shown back in Figure 19.10. Set the service namespace to CustomerProfileService and click the OK button to close the dialog and generate the code used for the reference.

**Viewing the Web Reference**

You can now program against the service proxy that was generated for you. You can also see the generated code. From the Solution Explorer, select the option to Show All Files. Then, navigate to the Service References folder. Here you can see the CustomerProfileService reference. Figure 19.13 shows this along with the proxy service class open in the editor. This proxy class is a C# class that represents the service. The intent of the class is to encapsulate and abstract the intricacies of calling this service. This allows developers to work with the service the same way they might work with any other .NET component or class. The contents of the proxy class include methods that mimic the web methods and objects that are used for the parameters (such as the Customer object in the example).

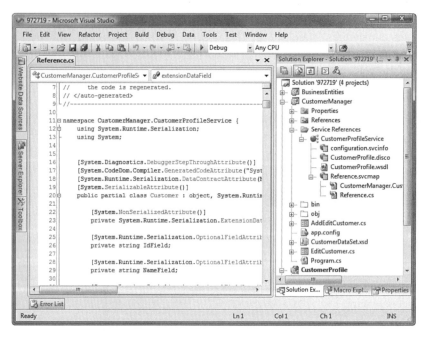

FIGURE 19.13    The web reference.

---

**TIP**

If you update or modify your web service, you will need to update the service reference. To do so, you right-click the service reference and choose Update Service Reference. This will instruct Visual Studio to refresh the reference and regenerate files as necessary.

### Calling the Web Service

You can call the web service the same way you would call any other .NET class. This capability is courtesy of the proxy class that was generated for you. However, it does require that you understand a little bit about WCF as the proxy generated is based on this technology.

We will cover WCF in the coming section. However, for now, we will focus on creating a SOAP client version of the `CustomerProfileService`. To do so, you reference the `CustomerProfileService` namespace and then create a new instance of the `CustomerProfileSoapClient` class. This is demonstrated here:

```
CustomerProfileService.CustomerProfileSoapClient cp =
  new CustomerProfileService.CustomerProfileSoapClient();
```

This class will give you access to the `GetCustomerProfile`, `DeleteCustomer`, and `SaveCustomer` web methods (via the proxy). To wire up these methods to the CustomerManager application, we will create a form that shows all customers in a list and provides buttons for Edit, New, and Delete. This is shown in Figure 19.14.

Let's look at what happens when a user clicks the Edit button. This will launch the `AddEditCustomer.cs` Windows form and pass it the user-selected `customerId` on the constructor. This method creates an instance of the proxy class `CustomerProfileSoapClient` and then calls `GetCustomerProfile`. Listing 19.7 shows this constructor of this form for your review.

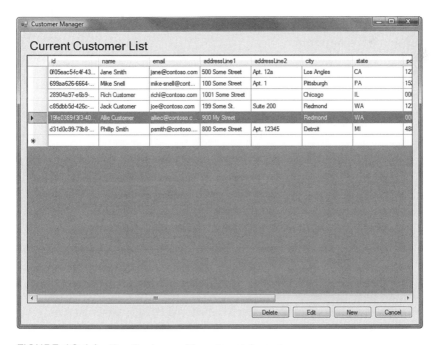

FIGURE 19.14   The Customer Manager main page.

LISTING 19.7    Calling the **GetCustomerProfile** Web Method

```
public AddEditCustomer(string customerId) {

  InitializeComponent();

  _editMode = EditMode.Update;
  labelTitle.Text = "Edit Existing Customer";

  _customerId = customerId;

  //get the customer record
  CustomerProfileService.CustomerProfileSoapClient cp =
  new CustomerProfileService.CustomerProfileSoapClient();

  CustomerProfileService.Customer c =
    cp.GetCustomerProfile(_customerId);

  //set text box labels
  textBoxName.Text = c.Name;
  textBoxEmail.Text = c.Email;
  textBoxPhone.Text = c.Phone;
  textBoxPostalCode.Text = c.PostalCode;
  textBoxState.Text = c.State;
  textBoxCity.Text = c.City;
  textBoxAddress1.Text = c.AddressLine1;
  textBoxAddress2.Text = c.AddressLine2;
  checkBoxContactEmail.Checked = c.ContactEmail;
  checkBoxContactPhone.Checked = c.ContactPhone;

}
```

The calls to DeleteCustomer and SaveCustomer are very similar (you can examine them by downloading the code for this book). A call is made to the CustomerProfileSoapClient proxy and you then work with the proxy to call the appropriate web method. Figure 19.15 shows the final results. Here the Customer dialog is shown in response to the user clicking the Edit button. If the user clicks the Save button here, the SaveCustomer web method will be called and the customer list refreshed.

---

**NOTE**

To debug your ASP.NET web service from a client application, you need to either be running the service in the same solution or attach to the ASP.NET worker process responsible for hosting the service. Refer to Chapter 10, "Debugging Code," for details on doing just that.

---

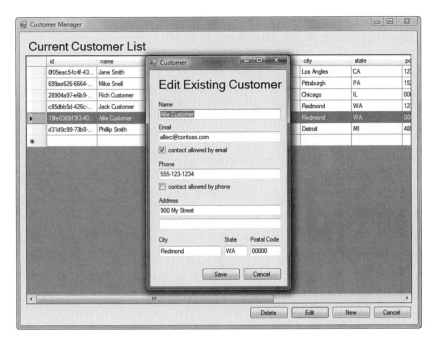

FIGURE 19.15   The customer profile service in action.

## Managing ASP.NET Web Service Exceptions

.NET can make it easy to forget that you are calling a web service. When you deal with proxy classes, you often get used to working with a web service as if it were no different from any other method. However, this can be dangerous. Web methods are different. One big difference is the way in which you throw exceptions from a web service. The following sections explore how to throw exceptions.

### Creating a Web Service Exception

Fortunately, the SOAP specification describes how an exception is thrown over the Web through this protocol. These exceptions can be business logic exceptions or those generated by .NET when processing a call. The important point is that if you wrap these exceptions appropriately, the client should be able to understand how to manage them.

.NET provides the SoapException object for wrapping an exception for SOAP transmission. This class has a number of parameters that you may not be used to working with when throwing exceptions. The parameters and properties include the following:

▶ **Message**—Used to define a descriptive message of the exception. If you are passing a standard .NET exception through SOAP, you can set the Message property to the Message property of the standard exception.

▶ **Code**—Used to indicate whether the error was server or client related. You set the property to ServerFaultCode if the client passed the message correctly but the server failed to process the request (was down or broken). You set this value to `ClientFaultCode` if the client passed a bad message or bad parameter values.

▶ **Actor**—Used to set the value to the URI of the web service. The actor is the code that caused the exception.

▶ **Detail** (Optional)—Used to pass more information about a given error. The `Detail` property can include nothing or as much detail as you want to include about the exception.

Listing 19.8 shows a new version of the `GetCustomerProfile` web method. This version checks to see whether the customer exists. If not, it throws a `SoapException` with the `Code` property set to `ClientFaultCode`.

LISTING 19.8    Creating a SOAP Exception

```
[WebMethod(Description = "Used to return a customer's profile.")]
public Customer GetCustomerProfile(string customerId) {

  EntityServices.CustomerProfile custProfile =
    new EntityServices.CustomerProfile();

  Customer customer = custProfile.GetCustomer(customerId);
  if (customer == null) {
    SoapException soapEx = new SoapException("Could not find Customer",
      SoapException.ClientFaultCode, Context.Request.Url.AbsoluteUri.ToString());
    throw soapEx;
  }

  return customer;
}
```

# WCF Service Applications

Like web services, Windows Communication Foundation (WCF) services have their own set of terms. It is important that you have a baseline understanding of these before discussing the key concepts around WCF service applications. The following list details these key terms related to WCF services.

> **NOTE**
>
> It is not imperative that you understand all of these terms to work with WCF. However, it can be helpful to have a cursory understanding when you are creating and configuring these services.

▶ **WCF Service**—A WCF service is a set of logic that you expose to multiple clients as a service. A service may have one or more service operations (think *methods*). A WCF service is exposed to clients through one or more endpoints that you define. Each endpoint has a binding and behaviors (see the "Endpoint" entry in this list). In this way, you can create a single service and configure it to work efficiently with multiple clients (such as HTTP, TCP, and Named Pipes).

▶ **WCF Client**—A WCF client is an application generated by Visual Studio to call a WCF service. You can create a WCF client by adding a service reference to a client application. The client application is the actual application that will consume the results of the WCF service. Think of the WCF client as the go-between or proxy that helps connect your client code to the WCF service.

▶ **Host**—A host is a process that runs (or hosts) the WCF service. This process controls the lifetime of the service. This is similar to how ASP.NET provides a host for web services. You can write your own service host or allow a service to be self-hosted.

▶ **Contract**—Contracts define your WCF services. This is essentially the public contract you guarantee between your service and any clients. There is a service contract that defines the content of the service (such as its operations). There is also an operation contract for each service operation. This contract indicates the parameters and return type of the service operation. There are also message, data, and fault contracts.

▶ **Endpoint**—Endpoints are configured for each service operation. An endpoint is where messages for your service are sent and received. Each endpoint defines both an address and binding for communicating with a service. For example, you might have one endpoint that works with SOAP over HTTP. You might have another endpoint for the same service that allows the service to work with MSMQ. In this way, you can add and configure endpoints to your service independently of actually coding the service. This ensures that your service can be configured to work efficiently with both existing and new clients.

▶ **Address**—An address is a unique URI for a given service. The address is used by calling clients to locate the service. The URI also defines the protocol that is required to reach the address such as HTTP or TCP. Each endpoint you define for your service can have its own address.

▶ **Behaviors**—A behavior defines how an entire service, a specific endpoint, or a specific service operation behaves. You can define behaviors for such things as security credentials and service throttling.

▶ **Binding, Binding Element, and Channel**—Endpoints have bindings that define how the endpoint communicates. A binding includes information about transport, encoding, and security. For example, you can configure an endpoint's binding to work with the HTTP transport encoded as text.

A binding is made up of binding elements. Each element represents a single portion of the binding. You might, for example, have a binding element for the encoding and another for the transport. Binding elements and their configuration are implemented as channels. The binding elements are stacked together to create this channel. In this way, the channel represents the actual implementation of the binding.

Visual Studio provides various tools that make building WCF services easier. The basic steps are to define a WCF project, create a service contract (as an interface), implement the service contract, and then configure communication endpoints for the service. You then write a client to consume the service (via its endpoints). Finally, you pick a hosting model for your service and deploy it accordingly. Let's take a look at each of these steps.

## The WCF Project Template

You can use Visual Studio to create a WCF service project in much the same way as you define other projects. Selecting File, New, Project will launch the Add New Project dialog. From here you can select the WCF node under either C# or Visual Basic. This will allow you to choose a WCF service project template. Figure 19.16 shows this dialog. From this dialog you can define the service name and the location of the code.

Notice that there are a few WCF service templates. These templates allow you to create WCF services based on your specific needs. There are two templates for working with Windows workflow: Sequential Workflow Service Library and State Machine Workflow Service Library. The Syndication Service Library allows you to create a syndication service like an RSS feed. The standard template, WCF Service Library, is where we will focus our attention here.

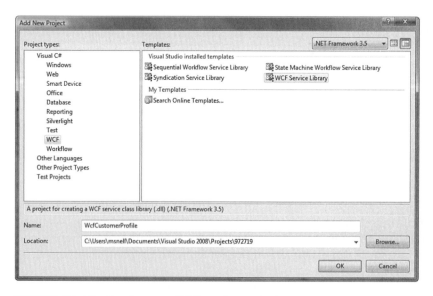

FIGURE 19.16    Create a new WCF service project.

There is another WCF service project template. It can be found under the Web node in the Add New Project dialog. This template creates a WCF service hosted by ASP.NET and IIS (similar to a standard web service).

### WCF Service Library Files

The actual WCF Service Library project that is created through the Visual Studio template contains an interface for defining your service contract, a service class for implementing the interface, an App.config file for configuring the service, and references to other .NET libraries. Figure 19.17 shows a new project based on the template. Here the start of the CustomerProfileService interface is depicted in the code window.

The service interface class (shown as ICustomerProfileService.cs in the figure) is an interface you use to define your service contract. A contract includes the service operations and the data contract. Having the interface split into a separate file helps abstract all the WCF attributes and contract items away from your actual service logic.

The class is defined as a WCF service through the use of the ServiceContract attribute at the top of the class. In addition, the service operations (or service methods) are indicated as such through the OperationContract attribute applied to the method (GetCustomerProfile).

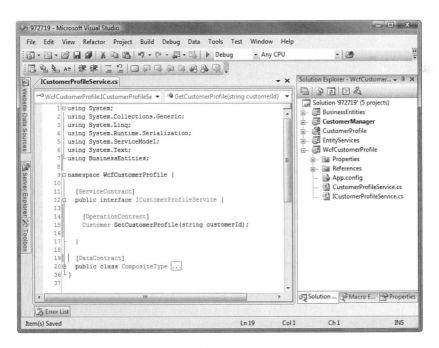

FIGURE 19.17   The WCF Service Library project.

The actual service class (listed in the Solution Explorer as `CustomerProfileService.cs`) implements the service interface. This is where you place your service logic, whether that logic contains real business functionality or calls out to another library that contains the actual implementation code. Figure 19.18 shows a representation of a service class. Note that this class is just a standard C# class (it could also be VB) that implements the service interface. This programming model should be very familiar.

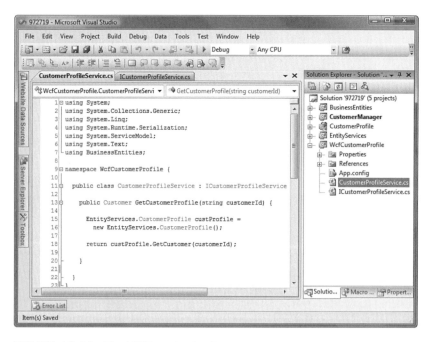

FIGURE 19.18    The WCF service implementation code.

## Creating a WCF Service

Now that you've seen the standard WCF service project template, it's time to walk through creating an actual WCF service with Visual Studio 2008. For this example, we will develop a WCF version of the `CustomerProfile` service we created earlier in the web service section. Like that service, this service will access the `Customer` object defined in a `BusinessEntities` library (Listing 19.1) and the `EntityServices` implementation code (Listing 19.2). The latter provides methods to retrieve customer information from a data store and save changes to that information. The following steps outline the process of exposing this functionality as a WCF service:

1. Start by creating a new WCF Service Library project. Call the service in this library `CustomerProfileService` (and its interface `ICustomerProfileService`).

2. Add references to both `EntityServices` and the `BusinessEntities` class libraries from the prior, web service walk-through.

**3.** Open the `ICustomerProfileService` file. Remove the sample code in the file and in its place add method definitions for `GetCustomerProfile`, `SaveCustomer`, and `DeleteCustomer`. Each method definition should be marked with the `[OperationContract]` attribute. Your code should look similar to that in Listing 19.9.

LISTING 19.9   The **ICustomerProfileService** Interface Definition

```
using System;
using System.Collections.Generic;
using System.Linq;
using System.Runtime.Serialization;
using System.ServiceModel;
using System.Text;
using BusinessEntities;

namespace WcfCustomerProfile {

  [ServiceContract]
  public interface ICustomerProfileService {

    [OperationContract]
    Customer GetCustomerProfile(string customerId);

    [OperationContract]
    void DeleteCustomer(string customerId);

    [OperationContract]
    void SaveCustomer(Customer customer);

  }
}
```

**4.** Next, open the `CustomerProfileService.cs` class file. Here you will implement the code for the interface defined in the preceding step. To start, highlight the `ICustomerProfileService` interface implementation at the class level. You should see a small smart tag. Click it and choose Implement Interface 'ICustomerProfileService'. This will stub out your service methods. You will then add code similar to that in Listing 19.10.

LISTING 19.10   The **CustomerProfileService** Implementation Code

```
using System;
using System.Collections.Generic;
using System.Linq;
using System.Runtime.Serialization;
using System.ServiceModel;
```

LISTING 19.10  Continued

```
using System.Text;
using BusinessEntities;

namespace WcfCustomerProfile {

  public class CustomerProfileService : ICustomerProfileService {

    public Customer GetCustomerProfile(string customerId) {

      EntityServices.CustomerProfile custProfile =
        new EntityServices.CustomerProfile();

      return custProfile.GetCustomer(customerId);

    }

    public void DeleteCustomer(string customerId) {

      EntityServices.CustomerProfile custProfile = new
        EntityServices.CustomerProfile();

      custProfile.DeleteCustomer(customerId);

    }

    public void SaveCustomer(Customer customer) {

      EntityServices.CustomerProfile custProfile =
        new EntityServices.CustomerProfile();

      custProfile.SaveCustomer(customer);

    }

  }
}
```

5.  The last step is to mark the Customer object you created in the first example as seri-
    alizable. This class was inside the BusinessEntities library. Doing so tells WCF it
    can serialize the data inside the class for passing between client and service. To do
    so, you use the DataContract attributes of the System.Runtime.Serialization
    namespace (you may need to add a reference to this namespace). You mark the class
    as a DataContract and each property as a DataMember. Listing 19.11 shows this code.

LISTING 19.11   Marking the Customer Class as a **DataContract**

```
using System;
using System.Runtime.Serialization;

namespace BusinessEntities {

[DataContract]
  public class Customer {

    [DataMember]
    public string Id { get; set; }

    [DataMember]
    public string Name { get; set; }

    [DataMember]
    public string Email { get; set; }

    [DataMember]
    public string AddressLine1 { get; set; }

    [DataMember]
    public string AddressLine2 { get; set; }

    [DataMember]
    public string City { get; set; }

    [DataMember]
    public string State { get; set; }

    [DataMember]
    public string PostalCode { get; set; }

    [DataMember]
    public string Phone { get; set; }

    [DataMember]
    public bool ContactEmail { get; set; }

    [DataMember]
    public bool ContactPhone { get; set; }

  }
}
```

That's it. You now have a simple WCF service you can configure with specific endpoints for various calling clients. We will now take a look at using Visual Studio to test the WCF service.

### Running and Testing Your WCF Service

Visual Studio 2008 ships with a host application that you can use to host, run, and test your services. You set your service application as the startup project in Visual Studio (right-click, Set as Startup Project). You can then run the application in debug mode. This will launch the host application as well as create a client for testing your service. Figure 19.19 shows the host service. It is accessible from the system tray.

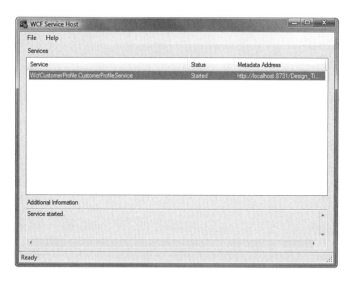

FIGURE 19.19   The WCF host service.

The WCF test client presents your service and its operations. Figure 19.20 shows the service written in the example running inside this test client. Notice the ICustomerProfileService interface. You can expand this to see your service operations. If you double-click a given service, you get the test client on the right. Here we have selected the service operation GetCustomerProfile.

To invoke the service, you enter its parameters in the Request section and click the Invoke button. In our example, this means entering a customerId value and returning a Customer object. Figure 19.21 shows the results of our test.

You can also toggle your results between the Formatted view (shown in Figure 19.21) and an XML view. The XML view can be useful when debugging. Clicking the XML tab at the bottom of the WCF test client toggles the two views. Figure 19.22 shows the same results in XML.

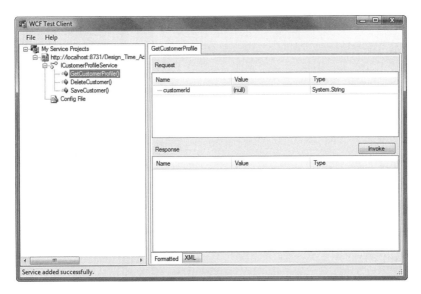

FIGURE 19.20   The WCF test client.

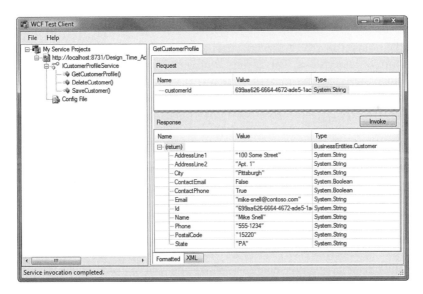

FIGURE 19.21   The service invoked with the WCF test client.

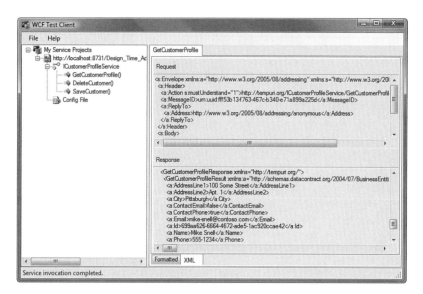

FIGURE 19.22 The WCF test client results in XML.

## Configuring a WCF Service

You've seen the basics for creating a WCF service. After your service exists, you can edit its configuration to support various clients. This means adding endpoints and related configuration information. Remember, the promise of WCF is that you can create a single service and then optimize it to work with multiple clients. One client might access via HTTP, another through TCP, and yet another with Named Pipes. You can support all of these clients (and more) through configuration.

Recall that the WCF Service Library template contained an App.config file. This file is where you define your service configuration. Fortunately, Microsoft created the Service Configuration Editor tool to help you. To access this tool, right-click the App.config file and choose Edit WCF Configuration. This will launch the tool as shown in Figure 19.23.

---

**TIP**

This same editor can be used to edit WCF configuration files outside of Visual Studio. This can be helpful if your edits are post-development. Simply run the tool SvcConfigEditor.exe to launch the same dialog.

---

You can use the tool to set individual settings on specific elements of your configuration. However, the tool is best used through its wizards. In fact, there is a wizard for defining a new endpoint. The following steps guide you through creating a new TCP endpoint for the CustomerProfileService. We will use this endpoint when we create a client to call the service.

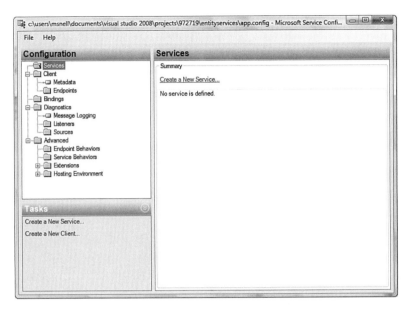

FIGURE 19.23   The WCF Configuration Editor.

**1.** To get started, select the Endpoints folder. From the Tasks pane, select Create a New Service Endpoint. Figure 19.24 shows this action. This will launch the new endpoint dialog.

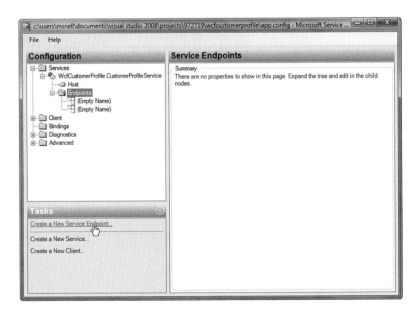

FIGURE 19.24   Launch the New Service Endpoint Element Wizard.

2. The first step in the wizard is to select the service for which you are defining the new endpoint. Figure 19.25 shows this step. You will select our service from the example, `ICustomerProfileService`.

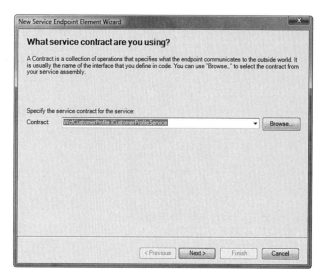

FIGURE 19.25    Define the service contract for the endpoint.

3. The next step is to select the communication mode of the service. You can choose from TCP, HTTP, Named Pipes, MSMQ, and Peer to Peer. For the purposes of the example, you will choose TCP. Figure 19.26 illustrates this step.

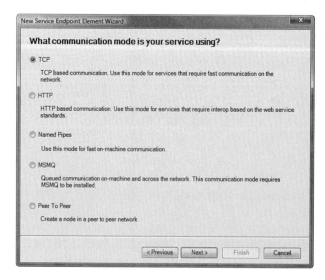

FIGURE 19.26    Set the endpoint's communication.

4. Next, you need to specify an address (or URI) for locating the service. In the example, set this to `net.tcp://localhost/CutomerProfileService`. We will host the service at this address. Calling clients will then be able to reach the service from here. Figure 19.27 shows entering this value.

5. This should complete the New Service Endpoint Element Wizard. You should see a summary of the endpoint (as shown in Figure 19.28). Click the Finish button to complete the operation.

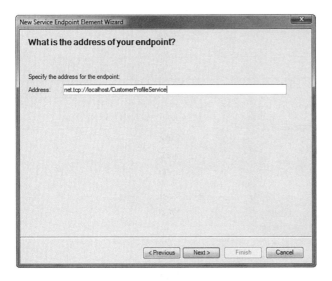

FIGURE 19.27   Set the address of the endpoint.

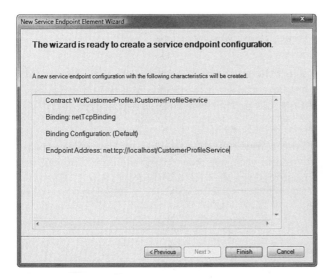

FIGURE 19.28   The New Service Endpoint Element Wizard summary.

6. Next, we need to make sure that port sharing is enabled for the service. This allows multiple clients to access the same TCP port on the machine. To do so, select the Bindings folder from the configuration tree. In the Tasks pane select New Binding Configuration. This will launch a dialog that asks you to select a binding type (see Figure 19.29). Select netTcpBinding and click OK.

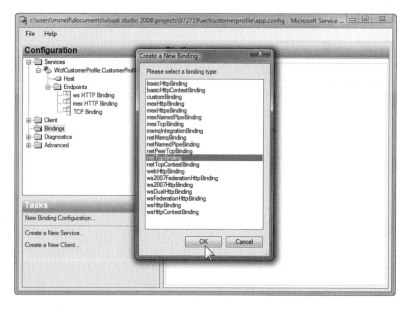

FIGURE 19.29    Creating a new binding configuration.

7. In the Binding properties window find the property PortSharingEnabled and set its value to True. This is shown in Figure 19.30. Also, set the binding's name to Port Sharing Binding.

8. Next, in the configuration tree, select the endpoint you created through the wizard. Find its BindingConfiguration property and set it to the name of the binding configuration you previously created (should be PortSharingBinding). Figure 19.31 shows an example.

You can now close the Configuration Editor. You should be able to open the App.config file and see the <netTcpBinding> element and your new <endpoint> element. You can run the service as before. This time, you should see the host for both the HTTP and TCP endpoints as shown in Figure 19.32.

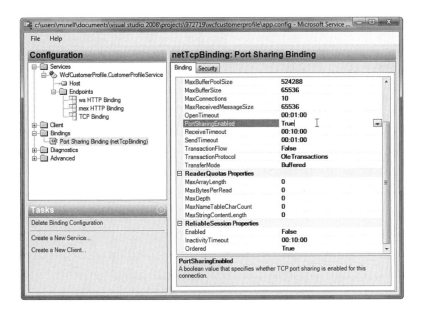

FIGURE 19.30  Set **PortSharingEnabled** to True.

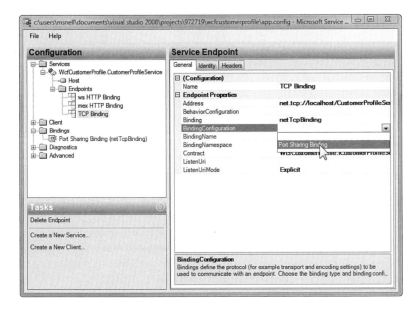

FIGURE 19.31  Selecting the **BindingConfiguration** for the endpoint.

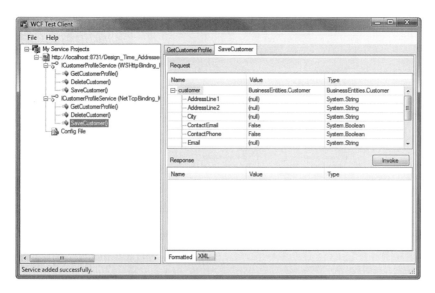

FIGURE 19.32    The new endpoint inside the WCF test client.

**TIP**

To get this to work properly on Windows Vista, you may have to enable TCP port sharing on the machine. You can do so using the command line (as administrator) sc.exe config NetTcpPortSharing start= demand.

We will now look at creating a client to call this service through this new endpoint.

## Consuming a WCF Service

You consume a WCF service in a similar manner as described previously when consuming a web service. You start by adding a service reference to your project. The following list walks you through this process:

1. Make sure that the CustomerManager application in your solution contains no service references. If it does still contain the reference you created in the previous section on ASP.NET web services, remove it. Also, be sure to remove the App.config file because it may contain service configurations. It will be re-created.

2. Right-click the project and choose Add Service Reference. This will launch the Add Service Reference dialog, shown in Figure 19.33. You can use the Discover button to find the WCF service in the solution. Set the namespace for the reference to CustomerServiceProfile and click the OK button.

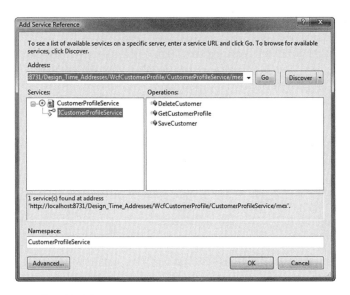

FIGURE 19.33    The Add Service Reference dialog.

3. You should now have a new service reference and a new App.config file. You can use the WCF Configuration Editor for client configuration files as well. Right-click the App.config file in the CustomerManager application and choose Edit WCF Configuration to open the configuration (as shown in Figure 19.34). Select the Client folder. Note that there are two client endpoints: one for HTTP and one for TCP. Note their names (you'll need them shortly) and close the editor.

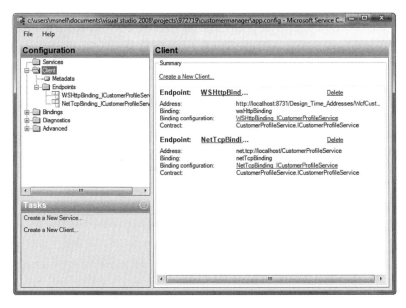

FIGURE 19.34    The WCF client configuration file open in the editor.

4. The final step is to change the way you create an instance of the service. Look back at the code in Listing 19.7. Here you created an instance of `CustomerProfileSoapClient`. You need to change this code to create an instance of `CustomerProfileServiceClient`. This is an instance of the WCF client generated by the service reference. Recall that there are two endpoints for this service. You pass the endpoint you want to use into the constructor of the service. This is done by the name of the endpoint, as shown here:

```
CustomerProfileService.CustomerProfileServiceClient cp =
    New CustomerProfileService.CustomerProfileServiceClient(
    "WSHttpBinding_ICustomerProfileService");
```

That should be it. In this code, you indicate that you want to work with the HTTP endpoint. The host Visual Studio generates will work easily with HTTP endpoints. You can now run the CustomerManager application and connect directly to your WCF service.

Of course, this still leaves a step undone. Just as Visual Studio can't host your websites, it is also not a long-term host for your services. You need to pick a host, deploy the service to that host, and then change the way the client accesses the service. Let's look at the options for doing so.

## Hosting and Deploying a WCF Service

For your services to accept requests, they have to be active and running. This means they need to be hosted in some runtime environment. Recall that when we covered web services, they were hosted for us by IIS. You can host your WCF services there too. However, there are additional options available to you.

You want to pick your host based on your needs. For example, if you have a peer-to-peer application, you may already know that each peer can host its own services. You also need to consider issues such as deployment, flexibility, monitoring, process lifetime management, security, and more. The following provides a brief overview of the WCF host options available to you:

▶ **Self-Hosted**—A self-hosted service contains the service within a running executable. The executable is managed code you write. You simply also embed one or more services within the executable. In this way the service is self-hosted. It does not require an additional process to execute. Instead, its lifetime is managed by the lifetime of the executable. When the executable is running, the service is listening for requests and responding accordingly. If not, the service is out of commission.

Self-hosted services are great when your clients need to communicate with one another. This is the case with peer-to-peer applications like Microsoft's Groove. Each client has services that can speak with the other clients.

To create a self-hosted service, you create an instance of the `ServiceHost` class inside your application. This class is passed an instance of your service. You then call the `Open` method of `ServiceHost` to begin hosting the service. When finished, you call the `Close` method.

▶ **Windows Service**—You can host your WCF service inside a Windows service application. A Windows service application is one that is installed as a service on a given machine. A Windows service can be configured to start, stop, and start up again on system reboot. In this way, they are very reliable and robust when you need services to simply stay up and running. They are also supported on all versions of Windows and Windows server.

To create a Windows service to host your WCF service, you create a class derived from `ServiceBase`. You then override the `OnStart` and `OnStop` methods in order to set up your service host. In the `OnStart` method you create a global `ServiceHost` instance and then call the `Open` method to begin listening for requests. You then simply call the `Close` method in the `OnStop` method.

Finally, you create an installer class for your service to install it in a machine's service directory. This class derives from the `Installer` class. You then compile the code and run `installutil` to get the service installed on a machine.

▶ **IIS**—IIS can host your WCF services. In this way you can take advantage of the many features built into this platform, including monitoring, high availability, high scalability, and more. However, only the HTTP transport is available when your service is hosted in IIS. This can be a limiting factor for many.

To host your WCF service in IIS, you first create a new IIS folder and configure it as an application. You then create a `.svc` file to represent your service. If you use the WCF template found under the web projects, you have this by default. This file needs to contain a directive for ASP.NET to see your service. The following is an example:

```
<%@ServiceHost language=c# Debug="true"
    Service="WcfCustomerProfile.CustomerProfileService"%>
```

You can then deploy your service to an `App_Code` subdirectory within the IIS application's folder. This includes the service implementation class, its interface, and the configuration file.

▶ **WAS (Windows Process Activation Service)**—WAS is new to Windows Server 2008 (and available on Windows Vista). WAS gives you the benefits of IIS (health monitoring, process recycling, message-based activation, and so on) without the limitations of HTTP only. WAS works with HTTP, TCP, Named Pipes, and MSMQ. In addition, WAS does not require that you write hosting code (like the self-hosted and Windows Service options). Instead, you simply configure WAS to be a good host of your service.

As you can see, there are many options for hosting your service. Each has its own plusses and minuses with respect to setup, coding, configuration, and deployment. Depending on your needs, you will want to spend some time learning more about your host options. You can find a how-to on each option inside MSDN. Simply search for "WCF Hosting Options" and you should find how-to's on each host just discussed.

# Summary

This chapter presented both ASP.NET web services and those built on WCF. You saw how .NET abstracts the programming of services and provides tools to make your life easier. In this way, you can concentrate on building business functionality (and not writing plumbing code). Some key points in this chapter include the following:

▶ Web services are based on open standards. .NET adheres to these standards to ensure that heterogeneous applications can all work together with web services.

▶ An ASP.NET web service consists of an .asmx file that points to the code behind the service. A web service works only across HTTP. This .asmx file represents the URI to the service.

▶ A WCF service can be created with multiple endpoints to efficiently support multiple clients across different communication protocols. WCF services work across HTTP, TCP, Named Pipes, and more.

▶ You consume a service by adding a service reference. This generates a local proxy client for your code to call.

# CHAPTER 20

# Embedding Workflow in Your Applications

There are many types of applications you might encounter as a developer. You might build user interface controls, websites, rich clients, frameworks, services, data-driven reports, and more. There is a specific class of applications, however, that are created to manage a business process. A business process might involve many other applications, systems, and people. You may have even written an application like this. For example, you might have a library for processing an order. There may be a method on this library that knows how to identify the order, read some state out of the database, and respond accordingly to the current request. It is likely that this code works with other code libraries, services, and systems. This type of code can be referred to as a workflow application.

A workflow is simply a set of steps that must be logically processed in order to realize a specific business goal or task. There are workflows everywhere. For example, processing documents such as expense reports, timesheets, purchase orders, invoices, and appropriations requests all represent possible workflows. In addition, tasks such as renting a movie, processing a loan, and reserving a hotel room are also workflows. You may have already written code like these examples (whether or not you called it a workflow).

This chapter covers the fundamental concepts of building workflows using Visual Studio and Windows Workflow Foundation (WF). Here we will cover building both sequential and state-driven workflows. We will also look at your options for hosting workflows and calling them from a client application.

> **NOTE**
>
> You can build Windows Workflow applications using both Visual Studio 2005 and 2008. The tools ship "in the box" in 2008. For 2005, you need to download the Windows Workflow Extensions. The Windows Workflow class libraries ship inside both .NET 3.0 and 3.5. The latter provides a few enhancements with respect to workflows and WCF. For the most part, however, you can build the same workflows using 3.0.

# Windows Workflow Fundamentals

You should think of a workflow as a series of steps that are interrelated to solve a specific business problem. These steps might call external code or services to accomplish their tasks. They typically also involve human intervention such as approval or some related form of processing. When a task is complete, the next task in the workflow gets executed until the specific instance has completed. The workflow may have to pause during execution while waiting for a message or a user response. The workflow may be short-lived or long-running, spanning days or even months. In this way, a workflow mimics the needs of the actual business process.

Microsoft Windows Workflow Foundation (WF) provides a set of tools for expressing workflows graphically and a runtime to formalize the process of executing workflow code. You use these tools to map the steps of a business process to connected activities that get executed by the workflow runtime. Let's take a look at how this works.

## The Components of a Workflow

Before you begin developing workflows, it's important that you understand the components that work together to help you build and run them. The first is a designer that allows you to visually build code to represent your workflow. Using the designer is a similar experience to building a Windows or ASP.NET form. You could do any of them with only code but the tools make it much easier.

When complete, your workflow is compiled into an assembly. This assembly is used by a host application to a create specific instance of your workflow based on a client request. Figure 20.1 shows a visual representation of this process.

Notice that the figure on the left represents a workflow. This is compiled into an assembly. The assembly is then referenced by a host application that you create. This host application can be an ASP.NET site, a web service, a Windows Service, or any other .NET process. The host is responsible for managing client requests with respect to the workflow.

The host manages requests by creating an instance of the WorkflowRuntime object. It is this object that creates instances of your workflow. It uses the workflow scheduler to run the workflow on a specific thread and return you a pointer (GUID) to the workflow. You can then use this GUID to retrieve the running instance of the workflow from the runtime. The runtime either calls the scheduler service (not shown) for in-memory workflows or uses the persistence service to reactivate a saved workflow.

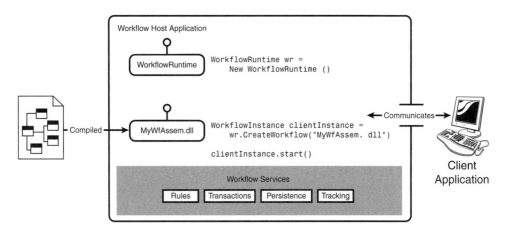

FIGURE 20.1    The components of a Windows Workflow.

Clients communicate with a host through whatever mechanism you choose. In fact, you can combine the client and host as a single application. This can be useful for testing purposes and in applications in which workflows are relevant only when the client is running (and thus do not support multiple workflows). More common scenarios for communicating with clients is to create a Windows Service host application that works with Remoting or WCF as the communication channel. You can also communicate with workflows in a website process or expose them through a web service over HTTP.

Now that you have a good foundation, let's look at the tools Visual Studio exposes for building workflows. We will return to each of these concepts in the coming sections and demonstrate how they operate.

## Workflow Project Templates

Recall that there are two primary workflow types: those driven by sequence alone and those that work in response to the state changes on a central document or data record. These types are understood by the workflow runtime. In fact, a workflow created as a state machine derives from the class StateMachineWorkflowActivity, whereas a sequential workflow implements the SequentialWorkflowActivity class.

These workflow types are also reflected in the tools. When you create a new workflow project, for instance, you are asked to select a project type based on these types. Figure 20.2 shows the Add New Project dialog with the Workflow node selected. You can, of course, create workflow projects in either Visual Basic or C#.

Many of the project templates in the figure show two related templates: one for state machine and one for sequential. Choosing your type simply creates a project that includes a file that implements the appropriate class. You can add any type of workflow to any workflow project. You can also start with an empty workflow project to which you simply add workflow items.

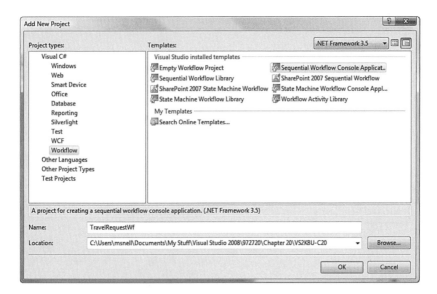

FIGURE 20.2    Adding a new workflow.

There are workflow project templates that also include a host application. These are identified as the Console application workflows for both sequential and state machine. A project of this type will include a simple host application that creates an instance of your workflow. You can use this project type during design to run and test your workflow as you build it. When you are ready to release, however, you will typically remove the Console application and switch this to a library (.dll) project.

A new workflow project also sets up the appropriate workflow references in the .NET Framework. The key namespaces that encapsulate workflow classes include System.Workflow.Activities for housing the various workflow activities, System.Workflow.Runtime for containing the runtime classes associated with a workflow, and System.Workflow.ComponentModel, which includes the base classes used to construct workflow activities.

## The Workflow Designer

When you create a new workflow project, it is, by default, opened in the Workflow designer. This tool allows you to graphically express your workflow in terms of activities, states, and connections. You also use the tool to work with each activity to configure its properties and set up code relationships. Figure 20.3 shows an example of the Windows Workflow designer inside of Visual Studio 2008.

Notice first the center of the screen. This is the design surface for a workflow. This is a sequential workflow in the process of being created. There is a start arrow at the top of this workflow, as well as an end icon at the bottom to indicate when the workflow is completed. In the lower right of this designer are three tools: Print Preview, Zoom, and Pan. Workflows are visual representations of how your code maps to a business process and therefore are often printed for review and sharing. The zoom and pan features are useful because a workflow can become quite large and therefore you need to be able to find and focus in on different areas.

You drag activities to the design surface from the Workflow Toolbox shown on the left of the screen. Notice the many activities that can be used to express a workflow. We cover these in a moment.

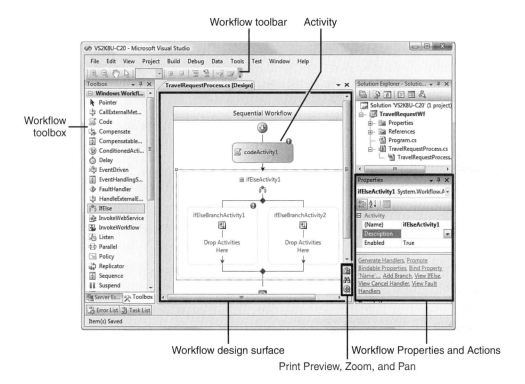

FIGURE 20.3    The Workflow tools.

### The Workflow Properties Window

The bottom right of Figure 20.3 shows the Properties window for the selected workflow activity. In this case, a CodeActivity is selected. The Properties window is the primary means of naming activities, accessing their configuration, and connecting them to code. The bottom of the Properties window contains a set of actions that are relevant to the selected activity. Here you can generate event handlers, view additional properties, manage conditional branches (if applicable), and more. If you forget how to do something, chances are you can find a link to the action in this window.

### The Workflow Toolbar

The Workflow toolbar (shown at the top of Figure 20.3) enables you to zoom in and out and pan across workflows. You can also use the plus and minus icons to expand and collapse nested activities such as the IfElse activity shown in the previous figure. The

20

icons that look like Visual Studio's comment/uncomment icons are for disabling and enabling activities. You simply select an activity and click the Disable button to comment it out.

You can also use the two buttons on the right end of the toolbar to work with custom workflow themes. A workflow theme allows you to change the appearance of the workflow in the designer. You can change colors, fonts, line weights, and much more. The second button from the far right on the toolbar launches the Theme Configuration tool, shown in Figure 20.4. Notice here that the Code Activity is being changed to have a white background and a dotted outline. Your theme will be stored in a .wtm (workflow theme) file. The last button on the toolbar launches the Options dialog and selects the Workflow Designer, Themes options. Here you can select a specific theme file for your workflow.

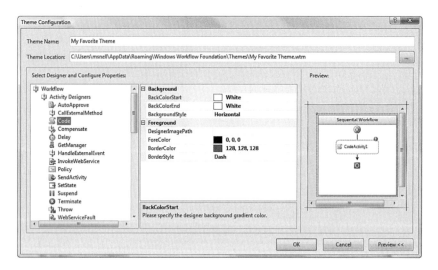

FIGURE 20.4    Configuring a custom theme for your workflow.

## The Workflow Item Templates

You add items to a workflow as you would any other project (right-click the project file, choose Add, and select New Item). This will launch the Add New Item dialog with the Workflow node selected, as shown in Figure 20.5.

From this dialog, you can add a new activity, sequential workflow, and state machine workflow. The workflows are just an additional workflow in the project like the ones we've been discussing. An activity item allows you to create a custom activity for use in your workflow. There is also a project library for creating shared activities (this is similar to a user or custom control).

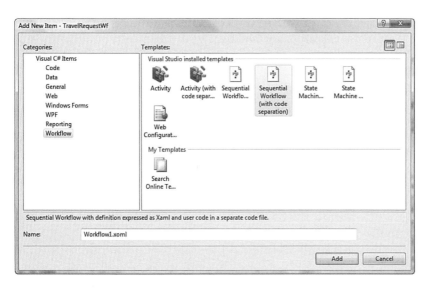

FIGURE 20.5   The workflow item templates.

There are two versions of each item type. One version of each item template is marked
with the text "(with code separation)." You can see this in the selected item in the figure.
These item templates allow you to express a workflow using XAML markup code instead
of designer-generated C# or VB. A workflow expressed as XAML has the .xoml extension
so as not to confuse it with .xaml files in WPF. You still use the designer to create an
XAML-based workflow. However, some developers might find it easier to work with
markup if they need to edit the workflow inside the code. In the end, all workflows get
compiled into an assembly. The following shows the designer-generated markup for a
simple sequential workflow expressed as XAML:

```
<SequentialWorkflowActivity x:Class="TravelRequestWf.Workflow1"
  x:Name="Workflow1"
  xmlns:x="http://schemas.microsoft.com/winfx/2006/xaml"
  xmlns="http://schemas.microsoft.com/winfx/2006/xaml/workflow">
  <CodeActivity x:Name="codeActivity1" />
  <IfElseActivity x:Name="ifElseActivity1">
    <IfElseBranchActivity x:Name="ifElseBranchActivity1">
      <CallExternalMethodActivity x:Name="callExternalMethodActivity1" />
    </IfElseBranchActivity>
    <IfElseBranchActivity x:Name="ifElseBranchActivity2">
      <CodeActivity x:Name="codeActivity2" />
    </IfElseBranchActivity>
  </IfElseActivity>
</SequentialWorkflowActivity>
```

20

When expressed as a partial class, the designer generates the same workflow as follows (inside the <workflowName>.Designer.cs (or .vb) file):

```
namespace TravelRequestWf {
  partial class TravelRequestProcess {

    private IfElseBranchActivity ifElseBranchActivity2;
    private IfElseBranchActivity ifElseBranchActivity1;
    private IfElseActivity ifElseActivity1;
    private CodeActivity codeActivity2;
    private CallExternalMethodActivity callExternalMethodActivity1;
    private CodeActivity codeActivity1;

    [System.Diagnostics.DebuggerNonUserCode]
    private void InitializeComponent() {
      this.CanModifyActivities = true;
      this.codeActivity2 = new
        System.Workflow.Activities.CodeActivity();
      this.callExternalMethodActivity1 =
        new System.Workflow.Activities.CallExternalMethodActivity();
      this.ifElseBranchActivity2 =
        new System.Workflow.Activities.IfElseBranchActivity();
      this.ifElseBranchActivity1 =
        new System.Workflow.Activities.IfElseBranchActivity();
      this.ifElseActivity1 =
        new System.Workflow.Activities.IfElseActivity();
      this.codeActivity1 =
        new System.Workflow.Activities.CodeActivity();
      //
      // codeActivity2
      //
      this.codeActivity2.Name = "codeActivity2";
      //
      // callExternalMethodActivity1
      //
      this.callExternalMethodActivity1.Name = "callExternalMethodActivity1";
      //
      // ifElseBranchActivity2
      //
      this.ifElseBranchActivity2.Activities.Add(this.codeActivity2);
      this.ifElseBranchActivity2.Name = "ifElseBranchActivity2";
      //
      // ifElseBranchActivity1
      //
```

```
        this.ifElseBranchActivity1.Activities.Add(this.callExternalMethodActivity1);
        this.ifElseBranchActivity1.Name = "ifElseBranchActivity1";
        //
        // ifElseActivity1
        //
        this.ifElseActivity1.Activities.Add(this.ifElseBranchActivity1);
        this.ifElseActivity1.Activities.Add(this.ifElseBranchActivity2);
        this.ifElseActivity1.Name = "ifElseActivity1";
        //
        // codeActivity1
        //
        this.codeActivity1.Name = "codeActivity1";
        //
        // TravelRequestProcess
        //
        this.Activities.Add(this.codeActivity1);
        this.Activities.Add(this.ifElseActivity1);
        this.Name = "TravelRequestProcess";
        this.CanModifyActivities = false;
    }
  }
}
```

**TIP**

For those who want to develop in code and not use visual tools, you can see that this is possible. In fact, you can combine the `InitializeComponents` method and activity declarations as shown previously with your workflow class in a single file (as the compiler does when compiling the two partial classes).

## The Workflow Activities

You map the steps of your business process to a set of activities that define your workflow. You might have activities that call internal code, reach out to web services, or call a member of a referenced assembly. Your activities might branch based on data passed to the workflow. You might use the activities to execute tasks in parallel. The activities in Windows Workflow provide a rich set of tools creating a business process in code.

The set of activities for sequential and state machine workflows are nearly all the same. This stands to reason because a state machine workflow is simply another way to look at the sequences of a business process. Each state contains sequences instead of there being a single, long sequence. There are a few additional activities for working with setting states and kicking off activities.

**20**

Table 20.1 lists the most common activities you will use to create your workflows. Each activity is listed with its icon from the toolbar. In addition, a brief description of each is provided.

TABLE 20.1    Key Workflow Activities on the Toolbox

| Activity | Description |
| --- | --- |
| CallExternalMethod | The CallExternalMethod activity is used to call a method on a referenced .NET assembly. The method is external to the workflow. |
| Code | The CodeActivity is used to call code contained within your workflow. You connect this activity to a method in the code associated with your workflow. |
| Delay | The Delay activity is used to induce a pause in your workflow. |
| EventDriven | The EventDriven activity is used to connect events that implement the IEventActivity interface. The EventDriven activity can nest other activities that need to run as part of the event. |
| HandleExternalEvent | The HandleExternalEvent activity is used to allow an external application to call into your activity (like waiting for an approval). Your workflow is paused on this activity until the event is raised. |
| IfElse | The IfElse activity is used to provide conditional branching. The conditions may be based on expressions or a rule set that can be managed outside of the workflow itself. |
| InvokeWebService | The InvokeWebService activity is used to call out to a web service from your workflow. |
| InvokeWorkflow | The InvokeWorkflow activity can be used to asynchronously invoke another workflow from within a workflow. |
| Parallel | The Parallel activity is used to group two or more sequences of activities that can execute in parallel.<br><br>Note that workflows are single-threaded in nature. Therefore, parallel activities are executed in more of a round-robin approach than true multithreading. |
| SetState | The SetState activity is used inside state machine workflows only. It allows you to transition from one state in a workflow to another. |
| StateInitialization | The StateInitialization activity can be used to provide a sequence of activities that execute when a specific state is first entered in a state machine workflow. |
| StateFinalization | The StateFinalization activity is used to execute a set of activities just before a state transitions from one state to another. |
| While | The While activity can be used to execute a loop over another activity until a specific condition is met. A While activity can contain only a single activity. If you need to loop over multiple activities, make this single activity a SequenceActivity (which itself can contain multiple child activities). |

| Activity | Description |
|---|---|
| ReceiveActivity | The `ReceiveActivity` is used to receive data using WCF. |
| SendActivity | The `SendActivity` is used to send data using WCF. |

You now have the fundamentals of Windows Workflow down. It's time to put this knowledge to use by creating first a sequential workflow and then one driven by state.

# Creating a Sequential Workflow

A sequential workflow is a lot like a flowchart. Processing starts at the top and works its way down. Along the way, different decisions are made and the workflow branches accordingly. The workflow may loop back on itself, but it will eventually end. Sequential workflows are much like what you would draw on a whiteboard when describing your business process (a lot of boxes and arrows).

The best way to understand how a Windows Workflow is built is to create one surrounding a real business process. In the following sections, you will walk through the core steps required to create any Sequential Workflow.

## Designing the Workflow

Workflows start with a concept in a diagram, on paper, or on a whiteboard. You then use the design tools to map this concept to workflow activities. For this example, consider that you are working for a large company that needs to automate and track the process of handling business travel requests.

A user initiates a travel request by filling out a form (the form could be on a website, created from an InfoPath form, inside a rich client application, and so on). The form is connected to travel vendors and internal logic that calculates the total cost of the travel: airfare, rental car, per diem, parking, and mileage. Users are also asked to write a travel justification.

If the request is under $1,500 and the requestor is a manager or above, the request is automatically approved. If, however, the request is over $1,500 or the requestor is not a manager, it requires an approval from a higher-level manager. In this case, the user's direct manager is notified of the request. The manager can log in to a system where he or she can review the request and approve or reject it. After it's approved, the travel reservations are made through the appropriate vendors and the requestor is notified with the appropriate travel details. There is a web service application for handling vendor reservations.

The actual application to log the request and do the approval is external to the actual workflow, as is the host. We will look at creating both client and host in a later section. For now, you will simulate the client inside a Console application setup to host the workflow. The following steps walk through using Visual Studio 2008 to build a workflow for this process:

1. Create a new Sequential Workflow Console application project called
   `TravelRequestWf` in either Visual Basic or C#. This example will use C# but the same
   concepts and visual design applies. We will use the Console application version to
   test and run the workflow without having to create a separate host and client.

2. Rename the default workflow in the project template (`Workflow1`) to
   `TravelRequestProcess`. By default, Visual Studio will create a code-based workflow.
   However, this example works with either code-based or XAML-based workflows.

3. When the travel request workflow is first created, it requires some information
   about the request: user requesting travel and total travel cost. In addition, a travel
   request id should be passed to the workflow to link out to details of the request in
   the database, should this be necessary.

   All of this data will be passed as parameters to the workflow from the host application.
   The `WorkflowRuntime` maps these parameters to properties on your workflow. You can
   then use these properties within the workflow (as both input and output parameters).

   To add the properties, right-click your workflow and choose View Code. You can
   then add the properties to your `TravelRequestProcess` class. Your properties should
   look similar to the following:

   ```
   namespace TravelRequestWf {
     public sealed partial class TravelRequestProcess :
       SequentialWorkflowActivity {

       public TravelRequestProcess() {
         InitializeComponent();
       }

       public string TravelRequestor { get; set; }
       public double TravelCost { get; set; }
       public int TravelRequestId { get; set; }


     }
   }
   ```

4. You can now start designing the workflow. Double-click the workflow file to open it
   in the designer. The first activity you need to add is one to notify the manager of the
   approval. Assume that this code exists in an external assembly (as it is reused across
   multiple applications). Therefore, drag a `CallExternalMethod` activity to the design
   surface and connect it to the workflow line that connects the start and end icons.

   Use the Properties pane (right-click the shape and select Properties) to set the name
   of this activity to `GetUserProfile`. No need to configure this activity now; you will
   configure all activities as a separate step.

5. For the next step in the workflow, you need to determine whether the user making
   the request is a manager. To do so, add an `IfElse` activity to the design surface
   under the `CallExternalMethod` activity. Use the Properties pane to set the `Name` of
   this activity to `ifUserManager`.

You will use the left side of the IfElse activity branch for the condition when the user is a manger. Select this branch and name it ifManager. Select the right-side branch and name it elseNotManager.

Your design surface should look similar to what's shown in Figure 20.6.

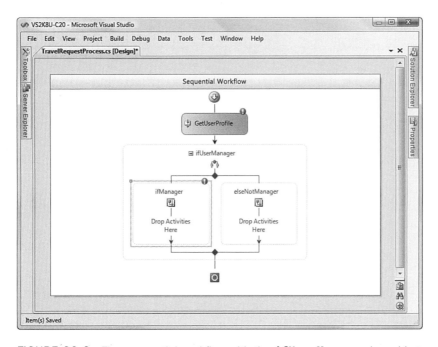

FIGURE 20.6    The sequential workflow with the **ifUserManager** branching.

6. On the branch that executes when a user is a manager, there is another condition to check. Here you need to add another IfElse activity to determine whether the request is over $1,500. Name this activity ifOverThreshold. Use the left side of the branch to represent true and the right side to represent false. Name the branches ifOver and elseAutoApprove, respectively.

In the branch that represents the approval required for a manager, add a CallExternalMethod activity and name it NotifyManager. This will use a shared library to notify a manager that an approval is required. Under this, you need to add an activity to process the approval. For this, you will drag a HandleExternalEvent activity to the design surface. This will pause the workflow and await an event from an outside application that will contain the approval details. Name this activity awaitApprovalForManager.

On the auto approve branch, you need to tell the workflow that the request has been approved. To do so, add a Code activity. This will be used to call an internal method to the workflow and set the approval status accordingly. Name this activity setAutoApprove.

Your workflow should now look similar to that shown in Figure 20.7.

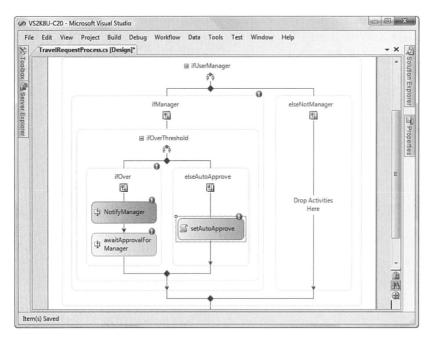

FIGURE 20.7    The manager approval conditions.

7. You now need to configure the branch that executes if the user making the request
   is not a manager. You first need to add a CallExternalMethod activity called
   NotifyManager2. Next add a HandleExternalEvent activity under this and call it
   awaitManagerApproval.

   Your workflow should now look similar to what's shown in Figure 20.8.

8. For the last step in the design, you need to add an activity to determine the outcome
   of the approval. For this, add another IfElse activity under the previous activity and
   just before the workflow endpoint. Name this activity checkApproval. Name the left-
   side branch ifApproved and the right-side branch ifRejected.

   Inside the approved branch add an InvokeWebService activity to call the service that
   works with the vendor sites to set the travel accommodations (dismiss the web reference dialog for now). Name this invokeTravelReservations. Under that, add a
   CallExternalMethod that will notify the user of the travel confirmation number. Call
   this SendConfirmationNotice.

   Inside the rejected branch, add a CallExternalMethod that will notify the user that
   the travel has been rejected. Call this SendRejectionNotice.

   This section of your workflow should look as shown in Figure 20.9.

Your workflow is now designed. The next step is to configure the activities you just placed
on the workflow in terms of the code they call, the events they handle, and the rules they
process. We will walk through each activity type and discuss how it is configured.

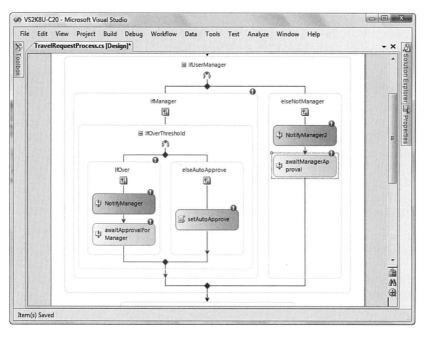

FIGURE 20.8    Adding the manager approval for requests from nonmanagers.

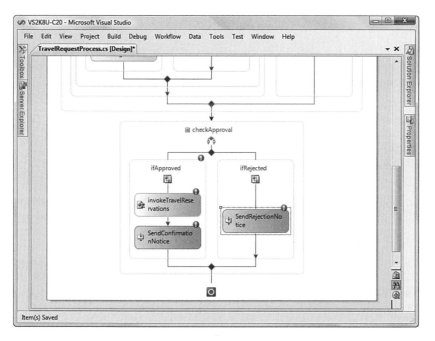

FIGURE 20.9    The approval-processing section of the workflow.

20

**Configure the `CallExternalMethod` Activities**

To start, you will configure all the `CallExternalMethod` activities. These all follow a similar pattern. After you've done one, you can do them all.

To set up a workflow to call out to external code, you must first define an interface tagged with the `ExternalDataExchangeAttribute` attribute. The workflow will be configured to call this interface. The host application will then implement that same interface as a class and then register an instance of the implementation with the runtime. The runtime will then call the instance accordingly. We will look at the host and client in a moment. For now, let's define the interfaces and configure the activities:

1. Add an interface to the workflow project (using the Add Item Dialog) and call it `IUserProfile`. This will define the signature of the method, `IsUserManager`, which takes a `userId` as a string. Your code should look as follows:

```
using System;
using System.Collections.Generic;
using System.Linq;
using System.Text;
using System.Workflow.Activities;

namespace TravelRequestWf {
  [ExternalDataExchange]
  public interface IUserProfile {
    bool IsUserManager(string userId);
  }

}
```

2. Add another interface to the workflow project and call it `INotification`. This will define the signature for the various notification methods. This code should look as follows:

```
using System;
using System.Collections.Generic;
using System.Linq;
using System.Text;
using System.Workflow.Activities;

namespace TravelRequestWf {

  [ExternalDataExchange]
  public interface INotification {

    void NotifyPendingApproval(string userId);
    void RejectTravel(string userId, int travelId);
    void NotifyUser(string userId, string message);
    void SendConfirmation(string userId, string confirmationNumber);

  }

}
```

3. Open the workflow in the designer. Select the `GetUserProfile` activity and view its properties. Click the ellipsis button on the `InterfaceType` property. This will launch the Browse and Select a .NET type dialog, which allows you to select an interface that this method will call. Figure 20.10 shows an example. Select the `IUserProfile` interface you just created.

4. Next, select the `MethodName` from the drop-down list. Select `IsUserManager`.

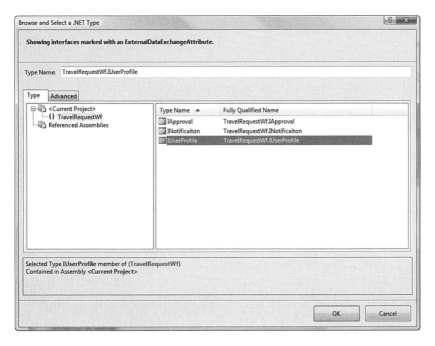

FIGURE 20.10    Setting the **InterfaceType** property of the **CallExternalMethod** activity.

5. You should now see two additional properties in the Properties pane: `userId` and `ReturnValue`. The `userId` is the parameter of the `IsUserManager` method. Click the ellipsis button next to the parameter to bring up the dialog shown in Figure 20.11. From here you can select the properties you defined earlier on your object. Select `TravelRequestor`. Recall that this property will be set when the workflow is first started.

6. Next, you need to do the same thing to map the `ReturnValue` of the `IsUserManager` method call to a local property. First add a new property to the workflow (using the code-behind file) of type Boolean. Call it `IsUserManager`. Select the `ReturnValue` property from the Properties pane and select the bind property action from the bottom of the pane. This will bring up the property binding dialog as before. Select the `IsUserManager` property.

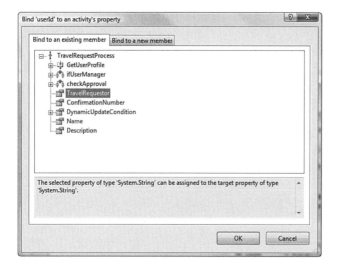

FIGURE 20.11    Mapping the parameter of the method call to a property of the workflow.

Notice that the red exclamation point icon is now gone from the activity. This indicates that the activity was configured without error. You will want to repeat these steps for the other `HandleExternalMethod` activities: `NotifyManager`, `NotifyManager2`, `SendConfimation`, and `SendRejectionNotice`. The following are tips for doing so:

▶ Assume that the `NotifyPendingApproval` method takes the requestor's id and looks up the manager.

▶ When using the `NotifyUser` method, simply type a string literal for the message property.

▶ Create a new property in your workflow for housing the confirmation number returned by the travel web service. This can be bound to the `confirmationNumber` parameter of the `SendConfirmation` method.

## Configure a `CodeActivity`

You can configure a code activity simply by double-clicking it to generate and connect to a method on your workflow. Alternatively, you can use the property window to set the `ExecuteCode` property.

Select the `CodeActivity`, `setAutoApprove` and double-click it. Inside the code editor, add a local field to track the approval status of the workflow. Next, set this field to `true` inside the `setAutoApprove` activity. Your code should look as follows:

```
private bool _isApproved = false;
private void setAutoApprove_ExecuteCode(object sender, EventArgs e) {
  _isApproved = true;
}
```

## Configure the `IfElse` Activities and Use the `RuleConditionEditor`

Your next task is to configure the `IfElse` conditions. You can create two types of conditions: code conditions and declarative rule conditions. The former allows you to write code in your workflow that sets the condition. The latter uses the rules engine to manage the conditions. For this example, you will configure declarative rule conditions:

1. Open the workflow in the designer. First, you will configure the `ifUserManager` branches. Select the `ifManager` branch and view its properties. Select the `Condition` property. Set it to declarative rule condition. This will give you two additional properties under the `Condition` property: `ConditionName` and `Expression`.

2. Click the ellipsis button in `ConditionName` to launch the Select Condition dialog. Here, click the New button in the toolbar to create a new condition. This brings up the Rule Condition Editor dialog, shown in Figure 20.12.

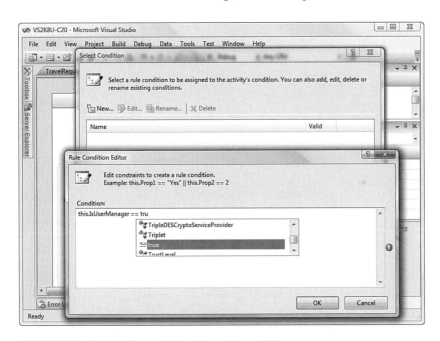

FIGURE 20.12   Adding a declarative rule condition.

3. Set the condition to a Boolean expression that evaluates the content of the local property, `IsUserManager`, to see whether it's true. Notice that you get IntelliSense in this window. Click OK and choose Rename to name the condition `IsManager`. Click OK again to close the Select Condition dialog. You've now configured the `ifManager` branch of the `ifUserManager IfElse` activity.

4. Repeat this process for the `elseNotManager` branch. Evaluate the `IsUserManager` property to see whether it's false. Name this rule `NotManager`. This step is optional

20

because the `else` condition would execute automatically if the other condition proves false.

5. Repeat this process for the `ifOverThreshold`, `ifOver` branch. Set the condition for this branch to evaluate as `this.TravelCost >= 1500` and name it `OverThreshold`. There is no need to explicitly configure the `else` branch because this will be executed if the condition in the other branch is false.

6. Repeat the procedure for the `checkApproval`, `ifApproved` branch. Set the condition for this branch to evaluate as `this._isApproved = true` and name it `IsApproved`. Again, there is no need to explicitly configure the `else` branch.

All `IfElse` activities should now be configured. No error icons should exist on these activities or their branches.

## Configure an `InvokeWebService` Activity

You now need to add a web service to simulate making the reservations. For this, add an ASP.NET Web Service project to your solution. Create a single method (ReserveTravel) to take the id of the travel request record and return a confirmation number. Your code should look as follows:

```
namespace TravelReservationService {


  [WebService(Namespace = "http://tempuri.org/")]
  [WebServiceBinding(ConformsTo = WsiProfiles.BasicProfile1_1)]
  [ToolboxItem(false)]
  public class Reservation : System.Web.Services.WebService {


    [WebMethod]
    public string ReserveTravel(int travelId) {

      //test code to return travel confirmation
      return "7XCV89432";
    }
  }
}
```

Return to your workflow and add a reference to this web service. Use the Advanced button on the Add Service Reference dialog to add a standard web service reference (instead of a WCF client reference). This will keep things simple for this example. You can name this reference, `TravelReservationService`. You are now ready to configure this `InvokeWebService` activity.

You configure the `InvokeWebService` activity to call the proxy class that was generated when you set the web reference. To do so, follow these steps:

1. First, select the `invokeTravelReservations` activity and view its properties.

2. Select the `ProxyClass` property and set it to `TravelRequestWf.`
   `TravelReservationService.Reservation` (it should appear in the drop-down).

3. Set the method name to `ReserveTravel`.

4. Use the properties pane to bind the `travelId` parameter to the `TravelRequestId`
   property of the workflow. Follow the same process for the return value of the
   method. Bind it to the `ConfirmationNumber` property.

Your configuration should look like that shown in Figure 20.13.

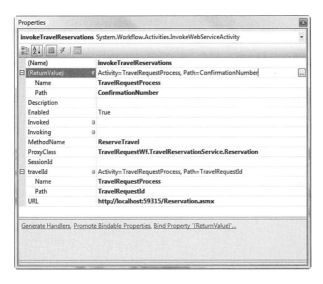

FIGURE 20.13   The **invokeTravelReservations** web service configuration.

## Configure the `HandleExternalEvent` Activities

The last activities you need to configure are the two `HandleExternalEvent` activities. Recall
that these activities are to wait for an external communication indicating that an approval
was sent. This is similar to an external application calling a method on your workflow.
However, due to the nature of the workflow (database persistence, long-running, runtime
driven, and so on), you cannot simply call a method as you would to another class.
Instead, you use the `HandleExternalEvent` activities. To get these configured, you will have
to write some code. This is, however, a common pattern for communicating into workflows and you will find yourself repeating it often.

The following steps walk you through configuring the `HandleExternalEvent` activities:

1. Create an interface that defines the event that external callers will use. Add an interface to your workflow project and name it `IApproval`.

2. Add a using statement, `System.Workflow.Activities`, to the top of the file.

3. Create an event in the interface called that uses the delegate `EventHandler<T>` and name it `Approval`, as shown here:

   ```
   event EventHandler< ExternalDataEventArgs > Approval;
   ```

   As you can see, typically this delegate takes `ExternalDataEventArgs` as a parameter. If you simply need to know that the event was raised, you could use this argument. However, because here we need to know whether the user actually approved or rejected the travel request, we need to pass data into the event.

4. Inside the same file, create a new class derived from `ExternalDataEventArgs`. Call this class `ApprovalEventArgs`. This class should expose a property for passing the approval. You should also create a constructor that takes an `instanceId` and passes it to the base class. Finally, mark this class as `[Serializable]` to allow the workflow runtime to serialize it as necessary.

5. Change the argument of the interface event's delegate to use this `ApprovalEventArgs`.

6. Mark the interface with the `[ExternalDataExchange]` attribute in order for the workflow to recognize it. Your file should now look as follows:

   ```
   using System;
   using System.Collections.Generic;
   using System.Linq;
   using System.Text;
   using System.Workflow.Activities;

   namespace TravelRequestWf {

     [Serializable]
     public class ApprovalEventArgs : ExternalDataEventArgs {

       public bool IsApproved { get; set; }

       public ApprovalEventArgs(Guid instanceId)
         : base(instanceId) {
       }

     }

     [ExternalDataExchange]
     interface IApproval {
       event EventHandler<ApprovalEventArgs> Approval;
     }
   }
   ```

7. Return to the workflow designer. Select the `awaitApprovalForManager` activity and view its properties. First, set the `InterfaceType` property to the one just defined. Figure 20.14 shows the dialog to do so.

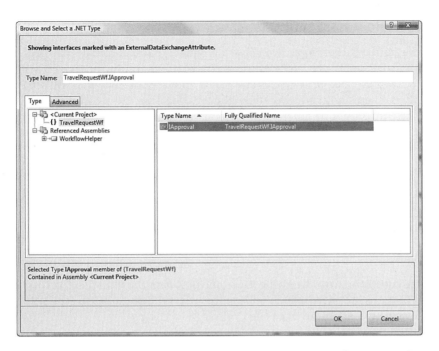

FIGURE 20.14    Selecting the **InterfaceType** for the **HandleExternalEvent** activity.

8. Next, set the EventName property to the Approval event. This should add the parameters e and sender to the Properties pane. These are the parameters that will be sent by the event. You could create a property here to bind to the e value and then use it in the conditions. However, we will simply write this code when the event is fired.

   Select the Invoked handler in the Properties window and choose the Generate Handlers action from the bottom of the pane (or double-click the actual activity in the designer). Here you need to write code to cast the event args and set the approval condition field. Your code should look as follows:

```
private void awaitApprovalForManager_Invoked(
  object sender, ExternalDataEventArgs e) {

  ApprovalEventArgs approvalArgs = (ApprovalEventArgs)e;
  this._isApproved = approvalArgs.IsApproved;


}
```

9. Repeat this process for the awaitManagerApproval activity. We can use the same event interface because only one will be waiting at any given time.

Your workflow should now be fully configured and usable. You now need to set up the client to call into the workflow and raise the appropriate events.

20

## Defining the Workflow Host and Client

Recall that when we started this example, we chose a template that included a Console application. This Console application includes the client (as itself) and the host code, and embeds a workflow in its process. Of course, many of the applications you write will separate these three things (client, host, and workflow library). However, the actual code to write the host and client will not be different from what you'll see in this example except for setting up communication channels (which has little to do with workflows). Therefore, this single Console application provides a good overview of how both host and client work.

### The Client

The client application in our example is very simple. Data is input into the console and responses are written back to the console. You could easily replace the console with a Windows UI to get the input and display to a user. Of course, doing so teaches nothing additional about workflow.

The console-specific code is mixed with host code. Some of it is in the Main method (of Program.cs); other portions are encapsulated outside the method. For clarity, the following shows how we will get the user's input from the Console:

```
private static string _userName;
private static double _travleCost;
private static int _requestId;

private static void EnterTravelRequest() {

  //define the workflow parameters
  Console.Write("Enter a user name (>6 = manager): ");
  _userName = Console.ReadLine();

  Console.Write("Enter travel cost (double): ");
  string cost = Console.ReadLine();
  _travleCost = double.Parse(cost);

  Console.Write("Enter travel id (int): ");
  string id = Console.ReadLine();
  _requestId = int.Parse(id);
}
```

> **NOTE**
>
> In this example, host and client (and workflow) are embedded. By host and client, therefore, we mean the host-related code and client-related code.

**The Host**

The host portion of the workflow is where we want to focus our attention. The host, of course, needs to reference the Windows Workflow namespaces and the actual workflow library itself. In our example, the combined template takes care of both of these requirements.

When the application starts, the host needs to create an instance of the `WorkflowRuntime` class in order to create workflows and manage them. You typically do so with a `using` statement as shown here:

```
using (WorkflowRuntime workflowRuntime = new WorkflowRuntime()) {
}
```

The runtime is then available during the lifetime of the application. The next step is to start the runtime. You can either explicitly call the `StartRuntime` method to do so, or wait until the first workflow is created and started. This will start the workflow runtime automatically. For our example, we will choose the latter method.

You can create an instance of a workflow by calling the `CreateWorkflow` method off the runtime object. This will return you a type of `WorkflowInstance` with which you can work. Into this method, you pass the type of workflow you want to create. The following is an example:

```
WorkflowInstance instance = workflowRuntime.CreateWorkflow(
  typeof(TravelRequestWf.TravelRequestProcess));
```

You use the `InstanceId` property of the `WorkflowInstance` object to identify the workflow to the runtime. The runtime can host multiple instances. Therefore, this id is important in identifying a running workflow that a client is working with or requesting. A running workflow is one that is in progress. It may be in memory or persisted to the database. This property is of type `Guid` and can be retrieved like this:

```
Guid wfId = instance.InstanceId;
```

**Passing Parameters to the Workflow**

The host is also responsible for passing parameters into a workflow when it is first created. A client may typically send these parameters into the host, but it is the host that sends them into the workflow. To do so, you must first set up public properties of the workflow. Any parameter passed to the workflow with the same name as one of those public properties will be automatically bound to that property. Recall that we did this previously.

Parameters are passed in to a workflow as a key-value Dictionary collection that contains an item for each property you want to set. The key values will be of type `string` and will hold the property names. The values will be of type `object` because a parameter can be of any type. You create the Dictionary collection as shown here:

```
Dictionary<string, object> myDictionary = new Dictionary<string, object>();
```

In our example, we have three properties set up for which we need initial values: TravelRequestor, TravelCost, and TravelRequestId. You saw previously how the client Console application got this information from the user. We need to map these inputs to items in the dictionary collection in this way:

```
Dictionary<string, object> wfParams = new Dictionary<string, object>();
wfParams.Add("TravelRequestor", _userName);
wfParams.Add("TravelCost", _travleCost);
wfParams.Add("TravelRequestId", _requestId);
```

Finally, you use an overload of the CreateWorkflow method in the host to pass the parameters at the same time the runtime is creating an instance of the workflow. The following shows an example:

```
//create an instance of the workflow
WorkflowInstance instance = workflowRuntime.CreateWorkflow(
  typeof(TravelRequestWf.TravelRequestProcess), wfParams);
```

These parameters will now have their value set when the workflow runs.

### Setting Up Code for the Workflow to Call

You now need to define some code to get called for the CallExternalMethod activities. Remember that you added interfaces to the workflow when configuring these items. Here you will implement these interfaces and then add an instance of your new class to the workflow runtime:

1. Create a new class file and call it UserProfile.

2. Inside the class, implement the IUserProfile interface.

3. Add a simple means to determine whether the user is a manager (remember, this is test code). Here is an example:

```
using System;
using System.Collections.Generic;
using System.Linq;
using System.Text;
using System.Workflow.Activities;

namespace TravelRequestWf {

  //host implementation of workflow interface
  public class UserProfile : IUserProfile {

    public bool IsUserManager(string userId) {
      //test code to return true based on size of user id
      return (userId.Length > 6);
    }
  }
}
```

4. Add another class to the library and call it Notification.

5. Implement the INotification interface within this new class.

6. For testing purposes the methods you create will simply write to the Console so you can verify that they are being called. These methods should look like this:

```
using System;
using System.Collections.Generic;
using System.Linq;
using System.Text;
using System.Workflow.Activities;

namespace TravelRequestWf {

  //host implementation of workflow interface
  class Notification : INotification {

    //note: test code only

    public void NotifyPendingApproval(string userId) {
      Console.WriteLine("Approval pending. UserId: " + userId);
    }

    public void RejectTravel(string userId, int travelId) {
      Console.WriteLine("User travel rejected. UserId: " + userId
        + " TravelId: " + travelId.ToString());
    }

    public void NotifyUser(
      string userId, string message) {
      Console.WriteLine("User travel approved. UserId: " + userId
        + " TravelId: " + message);
    }

    public void SendConfirmation(string userId,
      string confirmationNumber) {
      Console.WriteLine("Travel confirmed. UserId: " + userId +
        " Confirmation number: " + confirmationNumber);
    }

  }
}
```

7. You now need to connect these classes to the workflow. Recall that the workflow is simply configured to work with the interface. It will actually check the runtime for an instance of a class that implements this interface. Open the host (Program.cs) to set up this communication.

Following the creation of the `WorkflowRuntime`, create an instance of the `ExternalDataExchangeService`. You will then add this service to the runtime and then add your class to this service. The following shows the code:

```
//create a data exchange object
ExternalDataExchangeService exchangeServ = new
➥ExternalDataExchangeService();
workflowRuntime.AddService(exchangeServ);

//set up CallExternalMethod communication
exchangeServ.AddService(new UserProfile());

exchangeServ.AddService(new Notification());
```

The host is now configured to allow the workflow to call out to it. You now need to make sure that the host can call events on the workflow.

**Raising Events from the Client to the Workflow**
The last step before running the workflow is to create the communication from the host to the running workflow through the event model. Recall that we already defined an interface that set up the call contract from host to workflow. We did so when we configured the `HandleExternalEvent` activities. This interface contract was called `IApproval`.

Follow these steps to implement this communication contract in the host application:

1. Create a new class in the application and call it `ManageApproval`.

2. Implement the `IApproval` interface created previously. This means you have to define a handler for the `Approve` event. In addition, the class needs to be marked `Serializable`. The following shows an example:

```
[Serializable]
class ManageApproval : IApproval {
  public event EventHandler<ApprovalEventArgs> Approval;

}
```

3. Next, create a method in the class that will trigger the event. This method should be called from the client to approve the travel (or reject it). It should set the results into the `ApprovalEventArgs` that the `Approval` event takes and then raise the event passing itself as the sender. Here is an example:

```
public void ApproveTravel(int travelId,
  bool isApproved, Guid wfInstanceId) {

  //verify there is a subscriber to the event
  if (Approval != null) {

  //create new event args and set approval
  ApprovalEventArgs approvalArgs = new ApprovalEventArgs(wfInstanceId);
  approvalArgs.IsApproved = isApproved;
```

```
            //invoke the event passing self
            Approval(this, approvalArgs);


        }
    }
```

4. You need to register an instance of this new class with the data exchange service on the workflow. This will allow events to be connected between host and workflow. Add the following code to the Main method (after the calls you made previously to AddService):

```
//set up HandleExternalEvent communication
ManageApproval approvalMgr = new ManageApproval();

exchangeServ.AddService(approvalMgr);
```

5. You now need to add some client code (also to the Main method of Program.cs). This will allow you to enter an approval condition.

   Recall that the workflow is to notify the appropriate approver. This approver would then come into a client application. This application would verify the approver as the right approver and then allow the approver to approve. However, our simple Console application needs to simulate this with some test code. It has to simulate the Boolean logic in the workflow that predicts approval. In a robust solution, the client application would know this based on some information set (maybe in the database) by the workflow.

   Based on this information, you can ask the user to enter an approval into the console and then call the ApproveTravel method of the ManageApproval class. This will then be raised to the waiting workflow. To this method, you must pass the simulated travel request id, the approval status (true or false), and the instance id of the workflow in question. The following code demonstrates this:

```
approvalMgr.ApproveTravel(_requestId, true, instance.InstanceId);
```

The complete listing for the host and client code is shown in Listing 20.1.

LISTING 20.1    The Full Host/Client Application Code

```
using System;
using System.Collections.Generic;
using System.Linq;
using System.Text;
using System.Threading;
using System.Workflow.Runtime;
using System.Workflow.Runtime.Hosting;
using System.Workflow.Activities;

namespace TravelRequestWf {
  class Program {
```

LISTING 20.1   Continued

```
private static AutoResetEvent _waitHandle = new AutoResetEvent(false);
private static string _userName;
private static double _travleCost;
private static int _requestId;

private static void EnterTravelRequest() {

  //define the workflow parameters
  Console.Write("Enter a user name (>6 = manager): ");
  _userName = Console.ReadLine();

  Console.Write("Enter travel cost (double): ");
  string cost = Console.ReadLine();
  _travleCost = double.Parse(cost);

  Console.Write("Enter travel id (int): ");
  string id = Console.ReadLine();
  _requestId = int.Parse(id);

}

static void Main(string[] args) {

  using (WorkflowRuntime workflowRuntime = new WorkflowRuntime()) {

    //create a data exchange object
    ExternalDataExchangeService exchangeServ =
      new ExternalDataExchangeService();
    workflowRuntime.AddService(exchangeServ);

    //set up CallExternalMethod communication
    exchangeServ.AddService(new UserProfile());
    exchangeServ.AddService(new Notification());

    //set up HandleExternalEvent communication
    ManageApproval approvalMgr = new ManageApproval();
    exchangeServ.AddService(approvalMgr);

    //wire-up workflow events
    workflowRuntime.WorkflowCompleted += OnWorkflowComplete;
    workflowRuntime.WorkflowTerminated += OnWorkflowTerminated;

    //get user input
    EnterTravelRequest();
```

```csharp
      //set up parameters
      Dictionary<string, object> wfParams = new Dictionary<string, object>();
      wfParams.Add("TravelRequestor", _userName);
      wfParams.Add("TravelCost", _travleCost);
      wfParams.Add("TravelRequestId", _requestId);

      //await user's orders
      Console.WriteLine("Hit enter to start the workflow.");
      Console.ReadLine();

      //create an instance of the workflow
      WorkflowInstance instance = workflowRuntime.CreateWorkflow(
        typeof(TravelRequestWf.TravelRequestProcess), wfParams);

      //start the workflow
      instance.Start();
      Console.WriteLine("Workflow Started: " + instance.InstanceId.ToString());

      //pause to let the workflow catch up
      Thread.Sleep(300);

      //guess if the workflow is waiting on approval (test code)
      if(IsWaitingOnApproval()) {
        Console.Write(
          "Enter 'approve' to approve travel, or anything else to reject: ");
        string approval = Console.ReadLine();

        if(approval == "approve") {
          approvalMgr.ApproveTravel(_requestId, true, instance.InstanceId);
        } else {
          approvalMgr.ApproveTravel(_requestId, false, instance.InstanceId);
        }
      }

    _waitHandle.WaitOne();
    Console.WriteLine("");
    Console.WriteLine("Hit enter to exit.");
    Console.ReadLine();

  }
}

private static bool IsWaitingOnApproval() {

  //this is simulation/test code and not a real client
```

20

LISTING 20.1   Continued

```
    //determine if the workflow is waiting for an approval
    UserProfile userProfile = new UserProfile();

    //if the user is not a manager then approval req.
    if (!userProfile.IsUserManager(_userName)) {
      return true;
    } else if (_travleCost > 1500) {
        return true;
      } else {
        return false;
      }
  }

  private static void OnWorkflowComplete(object sender,
    WorkflowCompletedEventArgs e) {
    Console.WriteLine("Workflow Completed: " +
      e.WorkflowInstance.InstanceId.ToString());
    _waitHandle.Set();
  }

  private static void OnWorkflowTerminated(object sender,
    WorkflowTerminatedEventArgs e) {
    Console.WriteLine("Workflow Completed: " +
      e.WorkflowInstance.InstanceId + ". Message: " +e.Exception.Message);
    _waitHandle.Set();
  }

  }
}
```

## Running Your Workflow

You should now have created a working, sequential workflow that includes all three parts of a workflow application: workflow, host, and client. These parts are conceptual in our single application. However, you could split them out into their own pieces depending on your needs. For clarity, the following list names the conceptual parts (by file) as broken down across workflow, host, and client:

▶ **Workflow**—TravelRequestProcess, IApproval, INotification, IUserProfile.

▶ **Host**—Partially embedded in Program.cs, ManageApproval, Notification.

▶ **Client**—Program.cs (contains user input but also contains host code).

You can now run the workflow and test it out. It should compile and then present you with a Console application for entering travel request information. You can enter the information and start the workflow. The logic will execute accordingly, and if an approval is required, you will be prompted to enter one. Figure 20.15 shows a pass through the workflow.

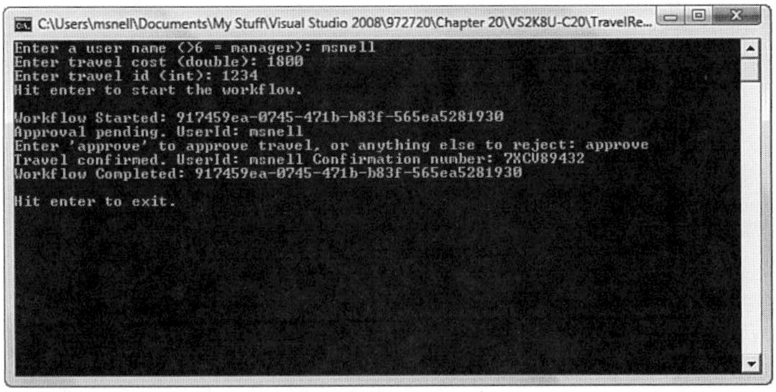

FIGURE 20.15    The running workflow.

### Debug a Workflow

You can set breakpoints in your code in any project in your solution, and you can step through code as you would any other application. In addition, you can visually step through the executing workflow.

To set a breakpoint on your workflow, first select the activity on which you want to break. Right-click this activity and choose Breakpoint, Insert Breakpoint. This will put a red breakpoint icon on the activity. Now, when you run the workflow, it will stop on this activity. You can then use the immediate window and the step commands as you would with code.

Figure 20.16 shows an example of the travel request workflow open in the debugger. You can see that the Locals window shows the parameters mapped to the workflow.

---

**TIP**

Windows Workflow provides activities for handling errors. There is a FaultHandler activity that works much like a Try...Catch block in your code.

---

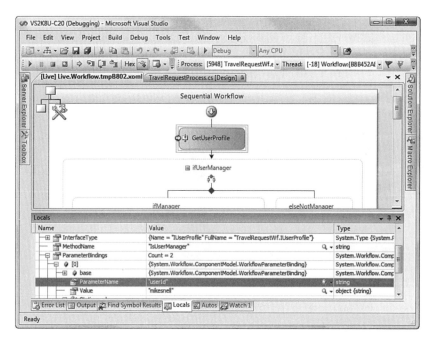

FIGURE 20.16   The travel request workflow running in the debugger.

# Creating a State Machine Workflow

The good news is that state machine workflows work much like their sequential counter-parts. Therefore, what you've learned previously applies to these types of workflows as well, and thus we won't repeat it. Instead, we will focus on the differences between the two workflow types.

The principal difference between a sequential workflow and a state machine is conceptual. Both have a start and a finish; both execute steps in sequence. However, a state machine workflow is focused on a single element as it moves through states. This might be a document or a database record. Sequences are executed when the state changes (leaving an existing state or entering a new one). Inside the state, you can do everything a sequential workflow does: branching, waiting for events, calling external methods, and so forth.

Let's take a look at creating a simple state machine workflow.

## Designing a State Machine Workflow

For this example, assume that you now have to process user expense reports from the travel the user requested in the prior example. Here, a user will create an expense report and be able to save somewhere as a draft. When the expense report is ready, the user will submit it to a manager for approval (through a client application). It will then enter the workflow in a submitted state. A manager will then approve or reject the report. If approved, it will go to the approved state. If rejected, the workflow will notify the user and it will complete the instance of the workflow. The user may resubmit later if required. After the report has been approved, a notice will be sent to the finance department indicating that payment is required. After payment is processed, the user will be notified of the check number of the payment and the report will move into its final state, completed.

> **NOTE**
>
> We are intentionally focusing on the state machine–specific items in this section. If you find yourself not following a concept, return to the sequential example and reread that section for additional detail.

The following steps walk through using Visual Studio 2008 to design this state machine workflow for this process:

1. Create a new state machine workflow Console application project called `ExpenseReportWf` in either Visual Basic or C#. This example uses VB (as the other used C#). However, the same concepts and visual design apply. We will use the Console application version to test and run the workflow without having to create a separate host and client.

2. Rename the default workflow in the project template (`Workflow1`) to `ExpenseReport`. By default, Visual Studio will create a code-based workflow. However, this example works with either code-based or XAML-based workflows.

3. When the `ExpenseReport` workflow is first created, it requires some information about the expense report: the user submitting and an identifier to link back to the actual expense report (through a client application). This information will be passed as parameters to the workflow from the host application.

   Add properties to the workflow for these parameters (`UserId` as `String` and `ExpenseReportId` as `Guid`). Your code should look as follows:

   ```vb
   Private _userId As String
   Public Property UserId() As String
     Get
       Return _userId
     End Get
     Set(ByVal value As String)
       _userId = value
     End Set
   End Property

   Private _expenseReportId As Guid
   Public Property ExpenseReportId() As Guid
   ```

**20**

```
Get
    Return _expenseReportId
End Get
Set(ByVal value As Guid)
    _expenseReportId = value
End Set

End Property
```

4. Open the state machine workflow in the designer. Select the state on the designer and view its properties. Set the name property of this state to Submitted.

This state will represent the actions that take place when the workflow starts. Therefore, right-click this state and choose Set as Initial State to indicate that this is the state of the workflow when it starts. You should see a green arrow to the left of the state.

5. Now add a State activity from the Toolbox for the remaining states: Approved, Rejected, Paid, and Completed. Set their name properties appropriately. Right-click the Completed state and choose Set as Completed State. This indicates that this state represents that the workflow has completed. Figure 20.17 shows an example of what your workflow should look like.

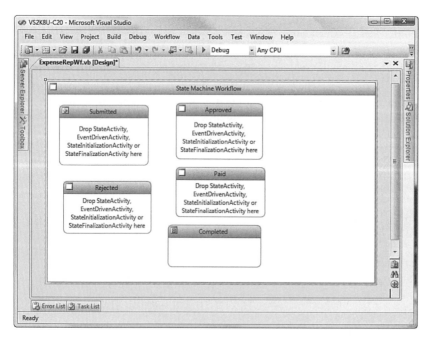

FIGURE 20.17   The states on the state machine workflow designer.

# Initializing and Transitioning States

Recall that each state executes a series of activities that typically transition to other states. For this to work, you add either a StateInitialization or StateFinalization activity to the state. The former is used to process activities when the state is entered. The latter is optionally used to process transitions for when the state exits (and before the next state starts).

### Design the Submitted State

Follow these steps to configure the Submitted state's initialization and transition:

1. Configure the Submitted state. Add a StateInitialization activity to it and set its name to submittedInit.

2. Double-click this StateInitialization activity to open up the Submitted state's designer. There is a bread-crumb control in the upper left to get you back to the ExpenseReport designer. This also works well when you have substates inside of states.

3. Add a CodeActivity to the submittedInit activity and name it NotifyManager. Here, we will skip the CallExternalMethod activities because they were presented in the sequential example. Instead, you will write code that will simulate sending a notice to the manager that an approval is pending.

4. Add a handler to this activity using the property window and set its code to write the notice to the console. Note that you would not do this in a real workflow. This code simply simulates a real notice. The following is an example of the code:

   ```
   Private Sub NotifyManager_ExecuteCode(ByVal sender As System.Object, _
     ByVal e As System.EventArgs)
       Console.WriteLine("Expense report approval required: " & UserId)

   End Sub
   ```

5. Return to the designer. The Submitted state's StateInitialization design should look like that found in Figure 20.18. Click the ExpenseReport link in the upper left to return to the main state machine design.

6. You now need to add an EventDriven activity under the Submitted state's StateInitialization activity. Name it eventDrivenApproval. A StateInitialization activity cannot handle external events so this activity is required for managing the event that will be fired by the host for a manager's approval.

7. Double-click this event to open it in the designer.

8. At the top of the event, add a HandleExternalEvent activity that will wait for a manager's approval. Name this activity waitMgrApproval. We will return to configure this activity in a moment.

9. Add an IfElse activity under the HandleExternalEvent activity. Name it ifApproved. Name the left branch isApproved. Name the right branch notApproved. You will configure these in a moment.

10. Add a SetState activity to each branch in the IfElse activity. SetState is used to transition to the next state.

20

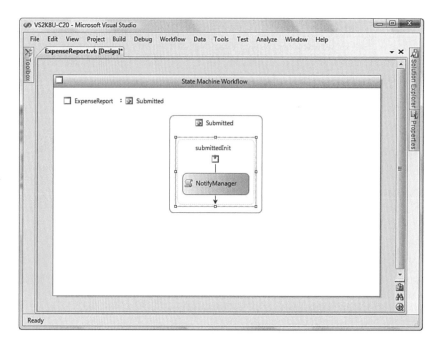

FIGURE 20.18    The **Submitted** state's **StateInitialization** design.

**11.** Select the left branch's `SetState` activity and open its properties. Name it `setApproved` and set its `TargetStateName` property to `Approved` via the drop-down.

**12.** Name the `SetState` activity in the right branch `setRejected` and set its `TargetStateName` to `Rejected`.

The workflow for the `EventDriven` activity is now designed. Your workflow should look similar to that found in Figure 20.19. You now need to configure the `HandleExternalEvent` and `IfElse` activities.

### Configure the Submitted State

The `eventDrivenApproval` design still has some unfinished business. First, we need to set up the communication pattern for sending messages into a workflow via an event. This will allow you to complete the configuration of the `waitMgrApproval` `HandleExternalEvent` activity.

Recall from the sequential workflow that the first step in this process is to set up an interface declared in the workflow. The host application will create an implementation class using this interface and then pass an instance of it into the workflow runtime.

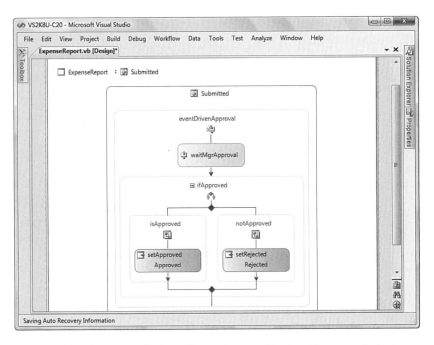

FIGURE 20.19   The **Submitted** state's **eventDrivenApproval** design.


Follow these steps to configure the workflow for communication into this event:

1. Create a new Visual Basic code file and call it `IApproval.vb`.

2. In the new file, create a new class that inherits from `ExternalDataEventArgs`. Name this class `ApprovalEventArgs`. Add a property called `IsApproved` (of type Boolean) to this class. This property will hold the approval.

3. Add an interface for the event that will be raised to the workflow. Name this interface `IApproval`. The event should be of type `EventHandler<T>`. You should type it as the new event args class.

   Your code should look as follows:

```
Imports System.Workflow.Activities


<ExternalDataExchange()> _
Public Interface IApproval
    Event Approval As EventHandler(Of ApprovalEventArgs)
End Interface


<Serializable()> _
Public Class ApprovalEventArgs
  Inherits ExternalDataEventArgs
```

**20**

```
Public Sub New(ByVal instanceId As Guid)
  MyBase.New(instanceId)
End Sub

Private _isApproved As Boolean
Public Property IsApproved() As Boolean
  Get
    Return _isApproved
  End Get
  Set(ByVal value As Boolean)
    _isApproved = value
  End Set
End Property


End Class
```

4. Return to the workflow and open its code-behind. Add a property that will be bound to the event args sent in to the HandleExternalEvent activity. Name this property ApprovalEventArg. Your property should look as follows:

```
Private _approvalEventArgs As ApprovalEventArgs
Public Property ApprovalEventArg() As ApprovalEventArgs
  Get
    Return _approvalEventArgs
  End Get
  Set(ByVal value As ApprovalEventArgs)
    _approvalEventArgs = value
  End Set

End Property
```

5. Return to the workflow designer for the Submitted state's eventDrivenApproval activity. Use the property window to configure the HandleExternalEvent activity waitMgrApproval to use this new interface. Set the InterfaceType property, the EventName, and map the event arg e to the new property you just created. Your configuration should look like the one in Figure 20.20.

6. The last step to configure the Submitted state activity is to set the IfElse condition branches. Select the left branch (isApproved). From the property window, indicate that the Condition is a Declarative Rule Condition. In the ConditionName property, open the condition rule manager. Set the Rule Condition to evaluate the contents of the ApprovalEventArg property you just bound to. This condition should read as follows:

```
this._approvalEventArgs.IsApproved
```

7. Name the condition ApprovedCondition. This completes the Submitted state. Return to the main screen of the state machine workflow.

You should now see the lines going from Submitted to Approved and Rejected. These represent the transitions (as shown in Figure 20.21). You now need to configure the other states.

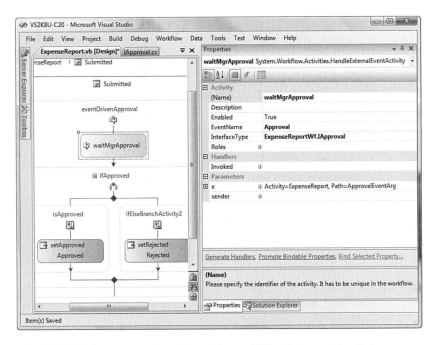

FIGURE 20.20    The configuration of the **waitMgrApproval** activity.

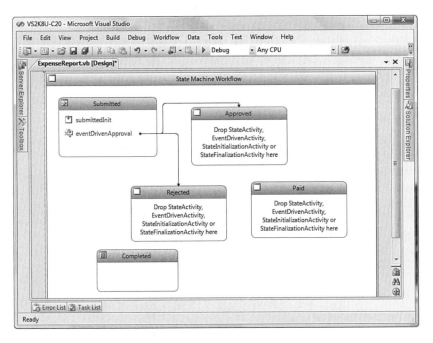

FIGURE 20.21    The state machine workflow with the **Submitted** state transitions.

**Design and Configure the Approved State**

The Approved state follows a similar pattern to the Submitted state. You need to add both a StateInitialization and an EventDriven activity to the state. The following steps you through:

1. Add a StateInitialization activity and call it approvedInit. Double-click it to open its design.

2. Add a CodeActivity named NotifyFinance and again write out to the console a simulated notification to the finance department that an expense report is ready to be paid. In reality, this might be data sent into a financial system. Your code should look as follows:

```
Private Sub NotifyFinance_ExecuteCode( _
  ByVal sender As System.Object, ByVal e As System.EventArgs)
    Console.WriteLine("Finance notice. ExpenseId: " _
                    & _expenseReportId.ToString())

End Sub
```

3. Return to the state diagram. Add an EventDriven activity called eventDrivenPayment. Double-click it to open its design.

4. Add a HandleExternalEvent activity for waiting for the payment notification from the finance system. Name this activity waitForPaymentNotice.

5. Under that, add a SetState activity called setPaid. Use the property window to set the state of the workflow to Paid after payment has been received.

6. To configure the HandleExternalEvent activity, create a new code file similar to the IApproval.vb file created earlier. Call this file IPaymentNotice. This file will contain an interface with an event to be fired by the finance system. When it's fired, the check number assigned to the expense report payment will be sent. This code should look as follows:

```
Imports System.Workflow.Activities


<ExternalDataExchange()> _
Public Interface IPaymentNotice
  Event Approval As EventHandler(Of PaymentNoticeEventArgs)
End Interface

<Serializable()> _
Public Class PaymentNoticeEventArgs
  Inherits ExternalDataEventArgs

  Public Sub New(ByVal instanceId As Guid)
    MyBase.New(instanceId)
  End Sub


  Private _checkNumber As Integer
```

```vb
Public Property CheckNumber() As Integer
  Get
    Return _checkNumber
  End Get
  Set(ByVal value As Integer)
    _checkNumber = value
  End Set
End Property


End Class
```

7. Use this code to configure the HandleExternalEvent activity for the Approved state's EventDriven activity. Map the event args from the event e to a new property on the workflow of type PaymentNoticeEventArgs (you can call this property, paymentNoticeArgs). The state's activity should look like that shown in Figure 20.22.

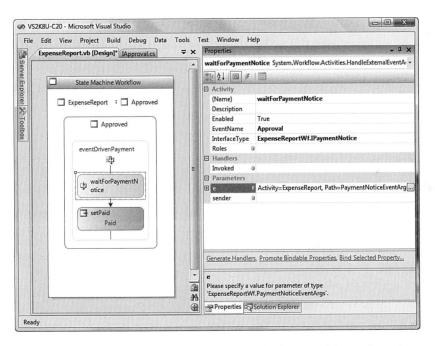

FIGURE 20.22   The **Approved** state's **EventDriven** activity configuration.

### Design and Configure the Rejected State

Inside the Rejected state, you will simply notify the user of the rejection and mark the workflow complete. The following steps you through setting the Rejected state's workflow:

1. Start by adding a StateInitialization activity to the Rejected event. Name it rejectInit. Double-click it to open it in the designer.

2. Add a `CodeActivity` to the `Rejected` state's `StateInitialization` and name it `NotifyRejection`. Add a handler for this code activity and write a rejected notification out to the Console as shown here:

```
Private Sub NotifyRejection_ExecuteCode( _
  ByVal sender As System.Object, ByVal e As System.EventArgs)
    Console.WriteLine("Expense report rejected. ExpenseId: " _
                    & _expenseReportId.ToString())

  End Sub
```

3. Add a `SetState` activity called `SetComplete` and set the `TargetStateName` to the `Completed` state. This tells the runtime that the workflow has completed successfully.

### Design and Configure the Paid State

You can repeat the preceding steps for the `Paid` state. The following outlines them:

1. Add a `StateInitialization` activity called `paidInit`. Double-click it to open it in the designer.

2. Add a `CodeActivity` to the `Paid` state's `StateInitialization` and name it `NotifyUser`. Add a handler for this code activity and write the notification out to the Console. Include the check number in the message as shown here:

```
Private Sub NotifyUser_ExecuteCode(ByVal sender As System.Object, _
                                  ByVal e As System.EventArgs)
    Console.WriteLine("Expense report paid. CheckNumber: " _
                    & _paymentNoticeArgs.CheckNumber.ToString())

  End Sub
```

3. Add a `SetState` activity called `setComplete2` and set the `TargetStateName` to the `Completed` state.

The workflow is now designed and configured. The final design view with all transitions is shown in Figure 20.23.

## Defining the Client and Host

In this section, we will set up the client and host for the state machine workflow. Remember, these two items are conceptually different and can be physically separated. We are simply combining them to test the workflow and focus on its concepts (and not those of a client application or Windows service, for example).

The following steps you through coding the client/host application:

1. Open the `Module1.vb` file that contains the Console application.

2. You need to define parameters that will be passed into the workflow. First, add two local fields at the class level for holding these values as shown here:

```
Shared _userId As String
Shared _expenseReportId As Guid
```

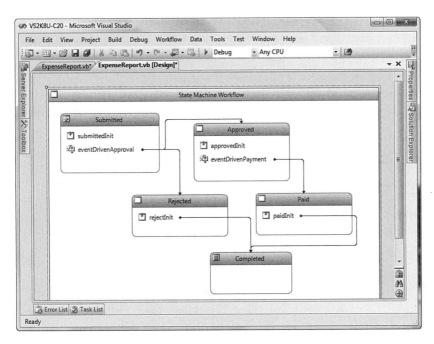

FIGURE 20.23  The **ExpenseReport** workflow transitions.

Near the top of Sub Main, add a user prompt to input the simulated user id. Your code should read as follows:

```
Console.Write("Enter user name: ")

_userId = Console.ReadLine()
```

Next, add a Dictionary collection object definition to house the parameters that will be passed to the workflow. Add this definition before the workflow instance is created. The code should read as follows:

```
Dim wfParams As New Dictionary(Of String, Object)
wfParams.Add("UserId", _userId)
Dim expenseId As Guid = Guid.NewGuid()

wfParams.Add("ExpenseReportId", expenseId)
```

Finally, change the CreateWorkflow method call to take these parameters. The code is as follows:

```
workflowInstance = _

    workflowRuntime.CreateWorkflow(GetType(ExpenseReport), wfParams)
```

3. Add a console message inside the OnWorkflowCompleted event handler as shown here:

```
Shared Sub OnWorkflowCompleted(ByVal sender As Object, _
                          ByVal e As WorkflowCompletedEventArgs)
```

**20**

```
    WaitHandle.Set()
    Console.WriteLine("Workflow Completed")

End Sub
```

4. You now need to set up the call for the approval required of the submit state. Start by adding a new class called ManageApproval.vb. Here you will implement the approval event from the IApproval interface created earlier. You also need a method to allow the approval to happen. This code should read as follows:

```
<Serializable()> _
Public Class ManageApproval
    Implements IApproval

    Public Event Approval(ByVal sender As Object, _
        ByVal e As ApprovalEventArgs) Implements IApproval.Approval

    Public Sub ApproveExpenseReport(ByVal expenseReportId As Guid, _
        ByVal isApproved As Boolean, ByVal wfInstanceId As Guid)

        Dim appArgs As New ApprovalEventArgs(wfInstanceId)
        appArgs.IsApproved = isApproved
        RaiseEvent Approval(Me, appArgs)

    End Sub

End Class
```

5. Open Module1.vb, and right under the creation of the WorkflowRuntime, create a new instance of the ManageApproval class and register it with the workflow runtime like this:

```
'create a data exchange object
Dim exchangeServ As New ExternalDataExchangeService()
workflowRuntime.AddService(exchangeServ)

'set up HandleExternalEvent communication
Dim approvalMgr As New ManageApproval()

exchangeServ.AddService(approvalMgr)
```

6. You now need to process the approval based on the user's input. Add the following code to Module1.vb to do so (under the call to workflowInstance.Start):

```
'wait for workflow to throw notice event
Thread.Sleep(300)

'get approval
Console.Write( _
    "Enter 'approve' to approve, or anything else to reject: ")
```

```
    Dim approval As String = Console.ReadLine()
    If approval = "approve" Then
      approvalMgr.ApproveExpenseReport(expenseId, True, _
                                     workflowInstance.InstanceId)
    Else
      approvalMgr.ApproveExpenseReport(expenseId, False, _
                                     workflowInstance.InstanceId)

    End If
```

7. We now need to follow a similar set of steps to register the finance department's payment notice. Start by creating a new file called `ManagePayment.vb`. In this class, implement the `IPaymentNotice` interface as shown here:

```
<Serializable()> _
Public Class ManagePayment
  Implements IPaymentNotice

  Public Event Approval(ByVal sender As Object, _
    ByVal e As PaymentNoticeEventArgs) _
    Implements IPaymentNotice.Approval

  Public Sub ProcessPayment(ByVal expenseReportId As Guid, _
    ByVal checkNumber As Integer, ByVal wfInstanceId As Guid)

    Dim payArgs As New PaymentNoticeEventArgs(wfInstanceId)
    payArgs.CheckNumber = checkNumber
    RaiseEvent Approval(Me, payArgs)

  End Sub

End Class
```

8. Return to `Module1.vb` and register an instance of this new class with the runtime like this:

```
Dim paymentMgr As New ManagePayment()

exchangeServ.AddService(paymentMgr)
```

9. Inside the approved section of the `If...Else` block in the Console application, add a prompt to simulate the finance department entering the check number (see Listing 20.2).

The complete listing for the host and client code is shown in Listing 20.2.

LISTING 20.2   The Full Host/Client Application Code

```
Module Module1
  Class Program
```

LISTING 20.2   Continued

```
Shared WaitHandle As New AutoResetEvent(False)
Shared _userId As String
Shared _expenseReportId As Guid

Shared Sub Main()

   Using workflowRuntime As New WorkflowRuntime()
      AddHandler workflowRuntime.WorkflowCompleted, _
        AddressOf OnWorkflowCompleted
      AddHandler workflowRuntime.WorkflowTerminated, _
        AddressOf OnWorkflowTerminated

      'create a data exchange object
      Dim exchangeServ As New ExternalDataExchangeService()
      workflowRuntime.AddService(exchangeServ)

      'set up HandleExternalEvent communication
      Dim approvalMgr As New ManageApproval()
      exchangeServ.AddService(approvalMgr)
      Dim paymentMgr As New ManagePayment()
      exchangeServ.AddService(paymentMgr)

      Console.Write("Enter user name: ")
      _userId = Console.ReadLine()

      Dim wfParams As New Dictionary(Of String, Object)
      wfParams.Add("UserId", _userId)
      Dim expenseId As Guid = Guid.NewGuid()
      wfParams.Add("ExpenseReportId", expenseId)

      Dim workflowInstance As WorkflowInstance
      workflowInstance = workflowRuntime.CreateWorkflow( _
      GetType(ExpenseReport), wfParams)

      workflowInstance.Start()
      Console.WriteLine("Workflow Started: " + _
                       workflowInstance.InstanceId.ToString())

      'wait for workflow to throw notice event
      Thread.Sleep(300)

      'get approval
      Console.Write( _
```

```vbnet
                "Enter 'approve' to approve, or anything else to reject: ")
        Dim approval As String = Console.ReadLine()
        If approval = "approve" Then
          approvalMgr.ApproveExpenseReport(expenseId, True, _
                                    workflowInstance.InstanceId)

          'wait for finance department notice
          Thread.Sleep(300)

          Console.Write("Enter check number (int): ")
          Dim checkNbr As String = Console.ReadLine()
          paymentMgr.ProcessPayment(expenseId, Integer.Parse(checkNbr), _
                            workflowInstance.InstanceId)

        Else
          approvalMgr.ApproveExpenseReport(expenseId, False, _
                                    workflowInstance.InstanceId)
        End If

        WaitHandle.WaitOne()
        Console.WriteLine("")
        Console.WriteLine("Hit enter to exit.")
        Console.ReadLine()

      End Using

    End Sub

    Shared Sub OnWorkflowCompleted(ByVal sender As Object, _
                                   ByVal e As WorkflowCompletedEventArgs)
      WaitHandle.Set()
      Console.WriteLine("Workflow Completed")
    End Sub

    Shared Sub OnWorkflowTerminated(ByVal sender As Object, _
      ByVal e As WorkflowTerminatedEventArgs)
      Console.WriteLine(e.Exception.Message)
      WaitHandle.Set()
    End Sub

  End Class

End Module
```

20

## Running the State Machine Workflow

You can now run the workflow application. It starts by prompting for a user name from the user. After this is entered, the expense report is considered submitted. A notice is sent indicating that the workflow has started. An approval is then indicated as required and a prompt given to the user to enter the approval. If it's rejected, the workflow completes as planned.

If the expense report is approved, a notice is sent to the finance manager and the user is asked to enter a check number. The workflow is then marked paid and a user is notified of the check number. The workflow then completes. Figure 20.24 shows an example of the Console application running through these steps in the debugger.

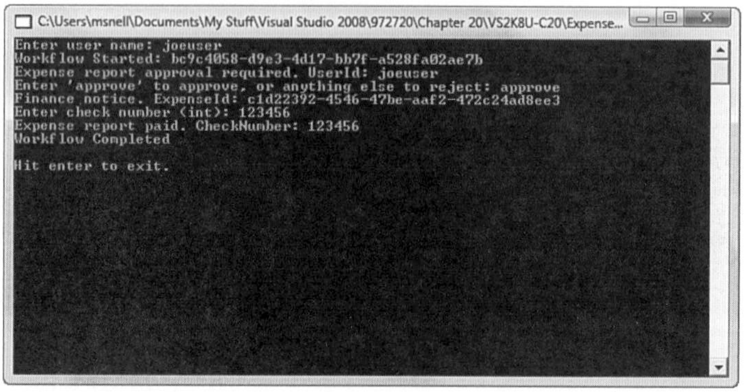

FIGURE 20.24    The application results in a Console window.

You can add breakpoints and step through state machine workflows just as you did with the sequential workflows. Your breakpoint may be on a state activity or any activity within the state.

# Summary

This chapter presented the core fundamental concepts for building applications that work with Windows Workflow Foundation. These included the components of all workflow applications: client, host, and workflow. A client is any application that calls into a host to work with a workflow instance. A workflow is a set of steps that solve a business problem. Your workflow is compiled and hosted inside a host application. The host application manages calls between the client and the workflow runtime.

We also covered the Visual Studio design tools. This included the core shapes for creating workflows such as CodeActivity, HandleExternalEvent, SetState, and IfElse. We also discussed how to create your own theme for the look and feel of a workflow.

In the later sections of the chapter, we covered a detailed walk-through of both a sequential and a state machine workflow. The former is a set of activities linked together with a beginning and an end. The latter is a workflow based on a single element's states (`Submitted`, `Approved`, `Rejected`, `Archived`, and so on). The code for these walk-throughs can be found on the website for this book.

It's important to note that this chapter is only the core of Windows Workflow. We hope it lays a foundation for you to explore additional concepts and services provided by the foundation, including persisting a workflow to a SQL Server database, adding the tracking service to monitor the activities of an executing workflow, creating compensating transactions for rolling back long-running workflows, and developing your own custom activities that can be reused across workflows.

CHAPTER 21

# Developing Office Business Applications

Microsoft Office is the well-known, best-selling suite of information worker productivity applications. We are all familiar with the word processing, spreadsheet, email, and form features provided by Microsoft Word, Microsoft Excel, Microsoft Outlook, and Microsoft InfoPath. But these applications are capable of more than just their stock features: They are a development platform unto themselves, a platform that can be extended and customized to build out line-of-business applications that leverage and build on the best-of-breed features offered by each application.

For instance, a purchase-order application could leverage the end user's familiarity with Microsoft Word to allow for data entry using a Word form, and reports and charts can be generated against purchase-order history using Excel.

In the past, the primary tool for extending Microsoft Office applications has been Visual Basic for Applications (VBA). With VBA, developers and even end users could create a broad range of solutions from simple macros to more complicated features that implement business logic and access data stored in a database. VBA offers a simple "on ramp" for accessing the object models exposed by every application in the extended suite of Microsoft Office: Project, Word, Outlook, InfoPath, PowerPoint, Publisher, and so on.

But starting with the first release of the Visual Studio Tools for Office (VSTO), developers now have a robust way to create Office solutions in managed code—Visual Basic and Visual C#—from directly within Visual Studio.

Visual Studio 2008 was released with the third generation of VSTO, which allows you to target the latest release of

Office, Microsoft Office 2007. The topic of using VSTO for Office development is a large topic that has entire books devoted to it; in this chapter we hope to simply introduce the concepts involved with VSTO and show how the Visual Studio Office project types can be used to quickly create powerful applications that leverage the existing power of Word, Excel, and Outlook. Some subjects we will cover include these:

▶ Creating custom action panes

▶ Creating custom task panes

▶ Customizing the Office Ribbon

We specifically do not attempt to cover the object automation models for any of the Office applications, beyond the minimum necessary to understand the preceding concepts. For a more complete treatment of Office as a development platform, we recommend the VSTO team blog at http://blogs.msdn.com/vsto/, the book *VSTO for Mere Mortals™: A VBA Developer's Guide to Microsoft Office Development Using Visual Studio 2005 Tools for Office,* by Kathleen McGrath and Paul Stubbs (Addison-Wesley Professional, 2007), and of course the various MSDN sections that cover VSTO (see the Visual Studio Tools for Office topic).

Let's kick things off with a quick run-through of the various Office features that are available for customization.

**NOTE**

Although you can use Visual Studio 2008 to target both Office 2003 and Office 2007, we discuss only Office 2007 projects in this chapter.

# An Overview of Office Extension Features

Because each Office application has a unique and very specialized function, it should come as no surprise that the ways in which you can customize an Office application will depend on which Office application we are specifically talking about. Although they all share a common, general layout for their user interface, there are intricacies involved with each of them that dictate different capabilities from within VSTO.

For instance, both Excel and Word deal with files as their central work piece, whereas Outlook deals with emails (which may be stored locally or on a server or both). So we can apply document-level extensions to Excel and Word, but this is not possible in Outlook. Conversely, the Outlook object model supports the concept of form regions, a concept absent in Excel and Word.

## Office Features

Table 21.1 provides a matrix of the various features available for customization/extension within each Office application. We'll discuss each of these in the next section.

TABLE 21.1   Microsoft Office Extension Points

| Application | Feature |
|---|---|
| Microsoft Excel 2007 | Actions pane |
| | Task pane |
| | Data cache |
| | Ribbon |
| | Smart tags |
| Microsoft InfoPath 2007 | Task pane |
| Microsoft Outlook 2007 | Task pane |
| | Outlook form regions |
| Microsoft PowerPoint 2007 | Task pane |
| Microsoft Word 2007 | Actions pane |
| | Task pane |
| | Data cache |
| | Ribbon |
| | Smart tags |

Some of these features are document-level features, and others are application-level features. The difference between the two is largely one of scope. Document-level customizations are attached to, and live with, a specific document, whether a Word .doc/.docx file or an Excel spreadsheet file. In contrast, application-level features are more global in reach and are implemented as add-ins to a specific Office application, in exactly the same way that add-ins are created and implemented for Visual Studio itself (see Chapter 13, "Writing Add-ins and Wizards").

We will look at the mechanics of how solutions are document-level or application-level differentiated in just a bit when we overview the VSTO project types. First, let's examine the features mentioned in Table 21.1. Understanding these features is key to determining how you might leverage Office using VSTO in your solutions.

### Task Panes and Actions Panes

*Task panes* in Office are used to expose commands and features that are central to the task at hand without disrupting the user from focusing on the currently loaded document. See Figure 21.1 for a screenshot of a Microsoft Word 2007 task pane for merging form letters. This task pane is able to guide the user through a series of steps while still allowing the loaded letter document to be visible. Task panes exist at the application level. *Actions panes*, on the other hand, are a type of task pane implemented at the document level.

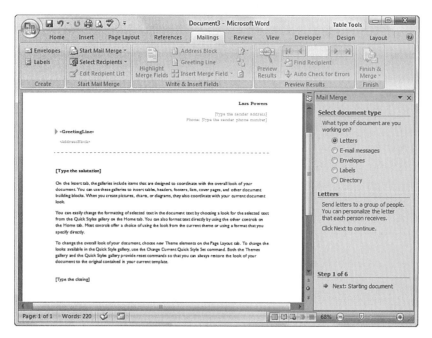

FIGURE 21.1    A Microsoft Word 2007 task pane.


**Data Cache**

A *data cache* refers to the capability of VSTO to store data locally within a document. This cache is also sometimes referred to as a data island. Because VSTO can read and write to the data cache, it is a useful tool for storing information needed by your Office add-in, or for shadowing data that resides in a database but is needed in certain disconnected scenarios.


**Ribbon**

The Ribbon is a new user interface element that premiered with Microsoft Office 2007. It represents a new way to present features to users without using the traditional toolbars and menus. Commands in the Ribbon are grouped by task category, and within each task category commands are visually grouped with other similar commands. So with Word, for instance, we have a Review tab that consolidates all the commands related to document review. Because the Ribbon makes the most used commands immediately visible and available, the Ribbon attempts to avoid the problems caused by the menu bar paradigm in which items could be grouped and nested several layers deep within the menu system.

The tabs of the Ribbon and the command groupings within a tab are free to change from application to application depending on the context. Figure 21.2 compares the Ribbon home tab for Word and PowerPoint.

Microsoft Word 2007

Microsoft PowerPoint 2007

FIGURE 21.2   The Microsoft Word 2007 and PowerPoint 2007 Ribbons.

### Smart Tags

*Smart tags* in Office function in a similar way to the smart tags present in the Visual Studio IDE (see Chapter 8, "Working with Visual Studio's Productivity Aids," to refresh your memory). Word is capable of recognizing various pieces of content as it is typed into a document, such as names, dates, financial symbols, and telephone numbers. When one of these items is recognized, it is flagged with a dotted purple underline. Hovering over that underline will display the smart tag icon, which can then be used to access a cascading menu with various options on ways to interact with that data. For instance, you may want to add someone's telephone number to your contact list. This action is easily executed from the smart tag menu for a telephone number (see Figure 21.3).

With VSTO, you can create your own smart tag recognizers and commands associated with them.

FIGURE 21.3   A smart tag menu in Microsoft Word 2007.

## Visual Studio Office Project Types

In general, there is a project type or family of project types available per Office application. In Figure 21.4, we see the various project types available by expanding first your
chosen language node and then the Office node within the New Project dialog.

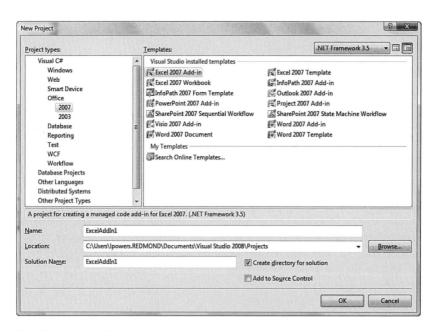

FIGURE 21.4    Office project types in Visual Studio.

Note that we have the option of targeting either Microsoft Office 2003 or Microsoft Office
2007 applications. For the most part, the approach and capabilities will remain the same
between the two, excepting of course the new features available in Office 2007 (not the
least of which is the new Ribbon user interface).

For Word and Excel, you will see two project types each: an add-in template and a document-level template (for Word, this is referred to as the Word 2007 Document project
template, and for Excel, this is referred to as the Excel 2007 Workbook project template).
As previously discussed, the difference between an application-level add-in and a document extension is one of scope: When you compile a VSTO project, just as with every
other project type in Visual Studio, a managed code assembly is generated. That assembly
can be attached or linked to an Office application (for example, Word or Excel), or to an
Office document (for example, a .doc/.docx file or a .xls/.xlsx file). Document-level
assemblies are loaded only when the document is loaded and are limited in scope to the
document. Application-level add-ins are loaded during application startup (although this
can be controlled by the user) and are more global in their reach.

**NOTE**

Although Visual Studio 2008 fully supports Microsoft Office projects right out of the box (at least with the Visual Studio Professional version), you will also obviously need to have a copy of Microsoft Office installed on your computer and potentially various other components. See the MSDN article "How to: Install Visual Studio Tools for Office" for an in-depth look at VSTO requirements.

# Creating an Office Add-in

To start creating your own Office add-in, create a new project in Visual Studio by selecting any of the Office add-in project types. Figure 21.5 shows the basic project structure created with a Word add-in project. We have a single code-file that establishes the startup entry point for the add-in, and provides us with the namespaces we need in order to access the Word automation object model.

There isn't anything terribly compelling about the developer experience so far. But VSTO provides a powerful set of visual designers you can use to craft your Office solution just as you would any other project in Visual Studio. To access these, we will need to add a project item that has an associated designer. To start, let's see how to create a customized ribbon.

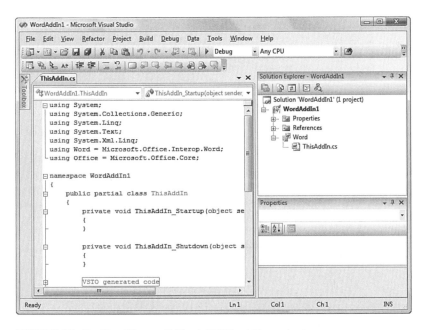

FIGURE 21.5   The Microsoft Word 2007 add-in project.

## Customizing the Ribbon

Ribbon support within a VSTO project is enabled by adding a Ribbon project item to the project. Right-click on the project within Solution Explorer, and select Add New Item. In the Add New Item dialog (see Figure 21.6), you will see two different Ribbon templates available for selection: Ribbon (Visual Designer) and Ribbon (XML). As their names suggest, the Visual Designer template will provide you with a WYSIWYG design surface for creating your ribbon customizations. Because this design surface can't be used to build certain types of more advanced ribbon features, the Ribbon (XML) item template is provided to allow you to handcraft ribbon features in XML. You will need to use the Ribbon (XML) item if you want to do any of the following:

▶ Add a built-in (as opposed to custom) group to a custom tab

▶ Add a built-in control to a custom group

▶ Customize the event handlers for any of the built-in controls

▶ Add or remove items from the Quick Access Toolbar

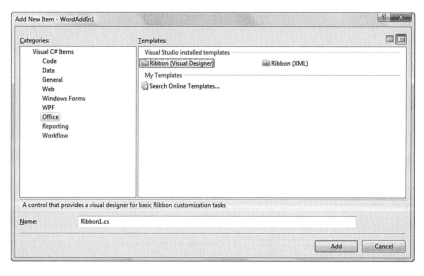

FIGURE 21.6   Office project item templates.

For our purposes, let's select the Ribbon (Visual Designer) item and add it to our project. This will add the Ribbon1.cs file to our project. In a fashion similar to Windows Forms, this file has a designer and a code-behind file attached to it.

The design surface we are presented with is an exact replica of an empty ribbon (see Figure 21.7).

Ribbons are composed of several elements: Tabs are used to provide the high-level task grouping of features, groups are used within each tab to provide more granular sectioning of the features, and controls reside within the groups to build out the custom user interface for the add-in.

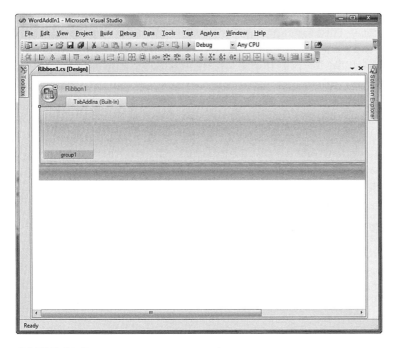

FIGURE 21.7   The Ribbon design surface.

With the Ribbon designer loaded, we now have access to ribbon-specific controls over in the toolbox (see Figure 21.8). Adding controls to the ribbon or adding new groups is as simple as dragging the desired control over to the ribbon or group tab.

FIGURE 21.8   Office Ribbon controls in the IDE toolbox.

## Adding Items to the Ribbon

To demonstrate, we will create our own custom group within the Add-Ins tab. Because we are presented with one group already by default, we can rename it to something more appropriate for our add-in. All the items in the ribbon are modified via the properties window just as with all other Visual Studio project types. We simply click on the group, and then set its label property.

Groups act as containers on the design surface, allowing us to now drag and drop a button into the group. Figure 21.9 shows the beginnings of a custom ribbon for a purchasing system integration add-in. We have added two buttons, changed their `ControlSize` property to `RibbonControlSizeLarge`, set their label property to the text we want displayed in the button, and added some images to the buttons as well.

---

### TIP

The images used in this example were taken from the Visual Studio 2008 Image Library, but there is actually a cool way to reuse any of the icons that you see within Office. First, download the Icons Gallery Add-In from the Microsoft Download Center (search for "2007 Office System Add-In: Icons Gallery"). This download will place an Excel file on your drive that, when opened, will display a gallery of the Office icons (see the Developers tab in the Excel Ribbon).

By hovering over an image of interest, you will see its *imageMso value.* This is a string that can be plugged directly into a Ribbon button's *OfficeImageId* property. As long as an image isn't already set for the button, this will cause the identified Office icon to be used. This is a real boon for UI design given the hundreds and hundreds of high-quality icons already available within Office. The image won't show in design-time, but will display correctly at runtime.

---

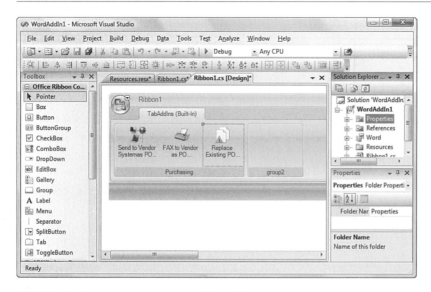

FIGURE 21.9   Creating a custom Office Ribbon.

If you wanted to add more groups to our Ribbon, this involves more of the same drag-and-drop action from the toolbox. You can change the order of the groups in the Ribbon by selecting and then dragging a group to the left or right of any other existing groups.

> **NOTE**
>
> You will notice that there is already a default tab implemented on the ribbon called TabAddIns (Built-In). When you're creating a ribbon for your add-in, its groups will automatically be displayed under the Add-Ins tab within the target Office application. If you wanted to add items to a built-in tab, or create your own tab that doesn't map to the built-in Add-Ins tab, you would have to use the Ribbon (XML) item to achieve that level of customization.

### Handling Ribbon Control Events

Handling the events for our buttons is easy: again, the idea behind VSTO is to provide Office customization capabilities using the same development paradigms already present in Visual Studio. This means we can simply double-click on a button to have the IDE automatically create and wire up an event-handler routine, ready to accept whatever code we need to write to implement the button's behavior.

To test this out, let's add the following to the Replace PO button:

```
private void buttonReplacePO_Click(object sender,
    RibbonControlEventArgs e)
{
    MessageBox.Show("buttonReplacePO_Click fired!");
}
```

If we run the project now by pressing F5, Word will automatically launch; we can see our ribbon customizations by clicking on the Add-Ins tab. Clicking on the Replace PO button yields the results shown in Figure 21.10.

## Customizing the Task Pane

Task panes don't have a dedicated visual designer because they are implemented through the creation of a user control, which already has a design surface. To add a custom task pane to our Word add-in, right-click the project, select Add New Item, and then select the User Control item.

> **NOTE**
>
> Because action panes are document-level concepts, we will discuss those separately in the section "Creating an Office Document Extension" later in this chapter. The same general development process will be followed.

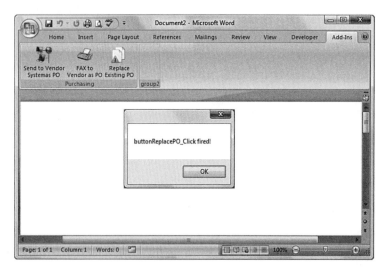

FIGURE 21.10   Testing a Ribbon button.

After the user control is added and the designer is loaded, we can set about creating the UI and code-behind for the task pane. The only VSTO-specific action item here is wiring the task pane user control into Word's object model. All of that work is accomplished in code within the add-in class. First, to make our life a bit easier, we will add a using statement to our add-in class:

```
using Microsoft.Office.Tools;
```

Then, we declare two local objects, one for the task pane and one for the user control:

```
private PurchaseOrderTaskControl poUserControl;
private CustomTaskPane poTaskPane;
```

And finally, we need the code to add the custom task pane to the application instance. We'll put this in the Startup event (for this example, ThisAddIn_Startup) so that the task pane is immediately available and visible when you run the add-in:

```
poUserControl = new PurchaseOrderTaskControl();
poTaskPane = this.CustomTaskPanes.Add(poUserControl, "Purchase Orders");
poTaskPane.Visible = true;
```

If you build and run the project now, you should see your task pane within the Word environment (see Figure 21.11).

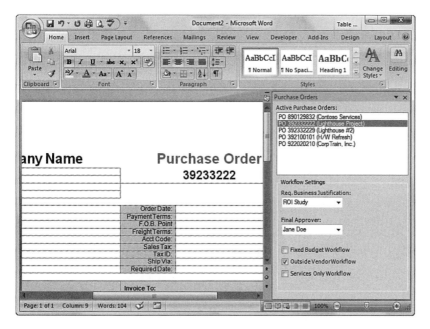

FIGURE 21.11   A custom task pane in Microsoft Word 2007.

## Creating Outlook Form Regions

Outlook add-ins are capable of adding form regions to any *message class* within Outlook. A message class is best thought of as the various entities that Outlook defines; these include notes, tasks, email, and so on.

Form regions are implemented by first creating an Outlook add-in project, and then adding an Outlook Form Region item. This will trigger the form region wizard, which captures the information necessary to auto-generate a region class file. The first screen in the wizard is used to indicate whether you want to create a brand-new form region or use an existing one that was designed in Outlook itself. The second page in the wizard, shown in Figure 21.12, specifies where the region presents itself. There are four options here, with a graphic that illustrates the positioning behavior of the region.

The third page of the wizard (see Figure 21.13) queries for the name of the region, and which *inspector* display modes the region should support. *Inspector* is the Outlook term for the window used to view and edit a specific message class. For instance, when you compose a new email message in Outlook, you are actually seeing the email inspector in action.

The fourth and final page of the wizard (see Figure 21.14) associates the form region with any of the built-in Outlook message classes, or a custom message class implemented by a third party.

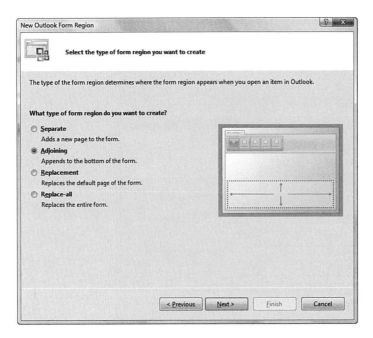

FIGURE 21.12    Possible Outlook form region types.

FIGURE 21.13    Inspector display mode support.

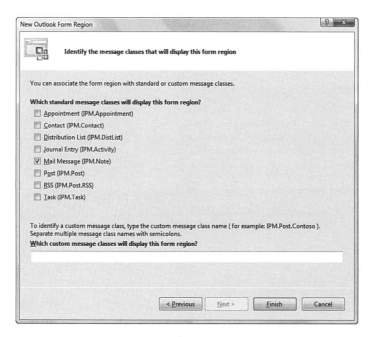

FIGURE 21.14   Associating the region with a message class.

When finished, Visual Studio will generate the code to match the form region properties provided in the wizard. You are now ready to construct the user interface for your region.

The visual designer for an Outlook Form Region looks identical to the UserControl designer: It is essentially a blank canvas that you drag controls onto. As with the other add-in types, your add-in class is where you will link the user interface of your form region to Outlook's object model to perform the actual work of the add-in.

Figure 21.15 shows a completed Outlook form region attached to the mail message class (IPM.Notes).

# Creating an Office Document Extension

There are various ways to customize Office documents themselves. You can host controls in a document, create action panes specific to a document, implement your own smart tags, and store data within a document.

A document-level project is created using the same process we used for add-ins. This time, however, you will select an Excel 2007 Workbook or Word 2007 Document project type. These project types use designers that represent the look and feel of an Excel workbook or a Word document.

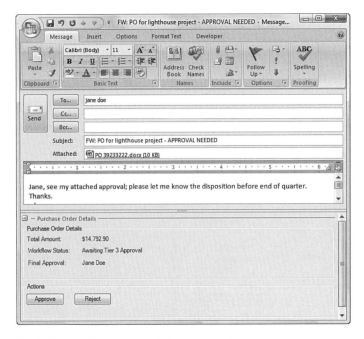

FIGURE 21.15   An Outlook form region in action.

## Hosting Controls

Both Word and Excel have host items that function as containers for control and code. A host item is essentially a proxy object that represents a physical document within either application. These are key to document-level customizations. For Word, we have the `Microsoft.Office.Tools.Word.Document` object, and for Excel, we have the `Microsoft.Office.Tools.Excel.Worksheet` object. Within Visual Studio, we build functionality using these host items through the use of designers. Each host item can host both Windows Forms controls and native Office controls.

> **NOTE**
>
> There is actually a third host item that represents an Excel workbook: `Microsoft.Office.Tools.Excel.Workbook` is a host item for enabling workbook-level customization, but is not an actual controls container. Instead, Workbook functions as a component tray and can accept components such as a DataSet.

### Windows Forms Controls

Windows Forms controls can be added onto the document design surface just as if you were designing a Windows Forms application. In this example, we will use an Excel workbook. The Excel 2007 Workbook project template automatically adds an `.xslx` file to our project, which will include three worksheets, each represented by its own class (these are the host items we discussed previously). These sheets have defined events for startup and shutdown, enabling us to perform work as the worksheet is first opened or closed.

The design surface for the worksheet looks identical to how the worksheet looks in Excel. From here, we can add Windows Forms controls to the worksheet by using the Visual Studio toolbox, and implement code in the code-behind file to customize the action of those controls. Figure 21.16 shows a workbook designer in the IDE with a few controls added.

---

**NOTE**

Creating an Office document project requires that your system allow access to the Microsoft Office Visual Basic for Applications project system. Normally, this type of access is disabled for security reasons. If access is disabled, Visual Studio will prompt you to enable it before creating your Office project.

---

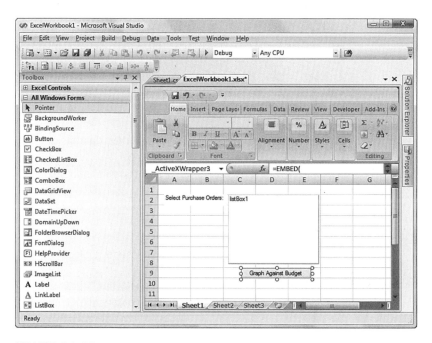

FIGURE 21.16    Customizing an Excel worksheet.

### Host Controls

*Host controls* is the term applied to native Office controls. These controls actually extend objects found in the Word or Excel object models to provide additional capabilities such as event handling and data binding. Building out a document using host controls follows the same process as with Windows Forms controls. With a document-level project loaded, you will see a tab in the Visual Studio toolbox that stores the host controls for the specific application that is targeted. For Excel, there will be an Excel Controls tab, and for Word a Word Controls tab.

Table 21.2 itemizes the available host controls for both Excel and Word.

TABLE 21.2    Microsoft Office Extension Points

| Project Type | Host Control | Function |
| --- | --- | --- |
| Excel 2007 Workbook | ListObject | Displays data in rows and columns |
| Excel 2007 Workbook | NamedRange | Represents an Excel range; can be bound to data and expose events |
| Word 2007 Document | Bookmark | Represents a Word book-mark |
| Word 2007 Document | BuildingBlockGalleryContentControl | Document building blocks are pieces of a document meant to be reused (a cover page, header, and so on)—this control displays a list of building blocks that users can insert into a document |
| Word 2007 Document | ComboBoxContentControl | A standard combo box |
| Word 2007 Document | DatePickerContentControl | A standard date picker control |
| Word 2007 Document | DropDownListContentControl | A drop-down list of items |
| Word 2007 Document | PictureContentControl | Represents a document region that displays an image |
| Word 2007 Document | PlainTextContentControl | Represents a block of text |
| Word 2007 Document | RichTextContentControl | Represents a block of text; can contain rich content |

## Creating an Actions Pane

In addition to customizing the interaction with users within a document, Windows Forms controls are used to craft custom actions panes. Actions panes should be used to provide contextual data and command options to users as they are editing/viewing a document (either a Word document or an Excel workbook file).

There are several reasons why you would elect to implement your document interface using an action pane. One reason is that the actions pane is "linked" to the document but is not an actual part of the document—the contents of the actions pane won't be printed when the document is printed. Another reason to implement an actions pane is to preserve the application's document-centric focus: You can read and page through an entire document while keeping the information and commands in the action pane in full view at all times.

Physically, actions panes are created with user controls and are represented by an Actions Pane Control item. Adding this item to your document project will create a user control class; you simply build out the user interface of the control as normal. In general, though, you will likely want to dynamically add or remove controls from the actions pane depending on what the user is doing within the document that is open in Word or Excel. Providing this level of contextual relevance is the strong point and target of the actions pane in the first place.

> **TIP**
>
> By leveraging Windows Forms to Windows Presentation Foundation interop, it is also possible to include WPF controls within an action pane. For more information on hosting WPF controls within a user control, see the MSDN documentation for the Windows Forms ElementHost class.

### Controlling Stacking Behavior

Because the actions pane functions as a toolbar container that can be docked and moved around by the user, there is a complete control layout engine for dictating how the controls within the actions pane should be displayed. The ActionsPane.StackOrder property works with a StackStyle enum to control layout behavior. The various StackStyle values are documented for you in Table 21.3.

As we did with the custom task pane, after you have assembled a user control that you want to surface within the actions pane, you need to create a field variable to hold an instance of the control, and then add the control to the action pane.

TABLE 21.3  **StackStyle** Values

| Value | Description |
| --- | --- |
| FromBottom | Controls are stacked starting from the bottom of the actions pane |
| FromLeft | Controls are stacked starting from the left of the actions pane |
| FromRight | Controls are stacked starting from the right of the actions pane |
| FromTop | Controls are stacked starting from the top of the actions pane |
| None | No stacking is performed (order and layout are manually controlled) |

So in the ThisWorkbook class, we would add the following declaration:

```
private ActionsPaneControl1 approvalPane = new ActionsPaneControl1();
```

And the following line of code will add our user control to the workbook's action pane:

```
this.ActionsPane.Controls.Add(approvalPane);
```

Figure 21.17 shows a custom actions pane alongside its worksheet.

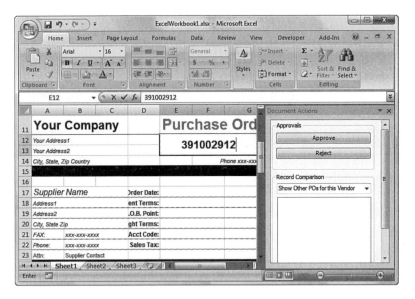

FIGURE 21.17   A custom actions pane in Excel.

## Storing Data in the Data Cache

The data cache is a read/write location within an Office Word document or Excel workbook that can be leveraged by your Office application to store needed data. One common scenario is to bind host controls or Windows Forms controls in an actions pane or on a document surface to a data set stored in the document's data island.

Physically, this data island is implemented as an XML document that is embedded within the Office document. This XML container can host any data type that meets the following two requirements:

▶ It has to be implemented as a read/write public field on the host item (for example, the Word ThisDocument or Excel ThisWorkbook class).

▶ It must be serializable (the runtime uses the XmlSerializer to verbalize the object within the data island).

Most of the built-in .NET types meet these requirements. If you have written a custom type that also adheres to these requirements, it too can be stored within the data island.

Adding data to the data cache is easy. You mark the data type you want to store with the CachedAttribute attribute; assuming that the type meets the data cache requirements, and that you have created an instance of the type within your document-level VSTO project, it will automatically be added to the data island.

DataSet objects turn out to be useful for conveyance within a data island. To declare a DataSet as cached, we would write the following:

```
[Microsoft.VisualStudio.Tools.Applications.Runtime.Cached()]
public DataSet poDataSet;
```

This declaratively instructs the VSTO runtime to serialize the object and add it to the current document's data cache. The DataSet itself can be populated however you see fit.

There is also a way to imperatively cache an object in a document. Each host item exposes an IsCached method and a StartCaching method. By combining the two, you can check to see whether an object is already in the cache, and, if it isn't, add it to the cache. Using these two methods, we might end up with the following code to store our poDataSet object in a document:

```
if (!this.IsCached("poDataSet"))
{
    this.StartCaching("poDataSet ");
}
```

If you use the StartCaching() method, there is no need for the class to be decorated with the Cached attribute, but the object does still need to adhere to the other requirements for Office data island serialization. You can also use the StopCaching method on the host item to tell the VSTO runtime to remove the object from the document's data cache.

---

**TIP**

There is yet a third way to place an object into the data cache: the properties window. If you use the Data Sources window to add a data set to your project, you can then create an instance of the data set, and then select it in the designer. In the properties window for the data set instance, set the Cache in Document property to True. You will also need to change the access type of the data set instance to Public.

---

### Accessing the Data Cache

Many times, an Office business application will rely on a server to function as a central repository for documents. This introduces a dilemma: the Office applications such as Word and Excel are not designed to be run in a server environment where many instances may need to be spooled up to serve multiple requests for document-level extensions. So far, we have been using objects within the Office object model to extend Office. And this implies that Office is installed on the machine running your assembly—something that is certainly not the case for typical server installations. Thankfully, one of the primary goals for document-level Office architecture is to enable the clean separation of data from the view of the data. Or, put another way, the VSTO architecture defines a way to access a document without actually using the Office client application. Instead, the VSTO runtime itself is used.

The key to accessing a document server side is the `ServerDocument` class. This class, which is part of the VSTO runtime and lives in the `Microsoft.VisualStudio.Tools.Applications` namespace, allows programmatic access to a document's data cache on machines that do not have Office installed. The process running on the server passes the path for the needed document into the `ServerDocument`'s constructor, and then uses the `CachedDataHostItem` class and the `CachedDataItem` class to obtain either the schema or the XML or both from the document's data island.

As long as the target computer has the VSTO runtime installed, the following code could be used to access the purchase order data from a server-side purchase order spreadsheet:

```
string poFile = @"C:\ServerData\po39233202.xls";
ServerDocument poDoc = null;

poDoc = new ServerDocument(poFile);

CachedDataHostItem dataHostItem =
    sd1.CachedData.HostItems["ExcelWorkbook1.DataSheet1"];

CachedDataItem dataCache = dataHostItem.CachedData["CachedPO"];

//The dataCache.Xml property will contain the XML
//from the specified data island
```

Using the `dataCache.Xml` property, you can now deserialize back into the source data type, view the data, and so on.

## Implementing Your Own Smart Tags

Office smart tags procedurally work like this: As a user types in an open document, the text is "tokenized" and then compared to all the terms/expressions that any of the smart tags in Office recognize. If the text is recognized by a smart tag, a list of actions is provided to the user (and displayed using the UI described previously when we first introduced the smart tag concept). So we have two parts to the process: recognition and action.

Using VSTO, you can create your own smart tags that define which text they will recognize, and define the list of possible action items that will be presented on recognition to the user.

Both Word and Excel implement classes that derive from the `Microsoft.Office.Tools.SmartTagBase` base class. For Word, this is the `Microsoft.Office.Tools.Word.SmartTag` class, and for Excel, this is the `Microsoft.Office.Tools.Excel.SmartTag` class. Both of these classes implement two important properties defined on the `SmartTagBase` class: `Terms` and `Expressions`. If your smart tag needs to match on simple text tokens, you can add them to the `Terms` collection. If more complicated matching is required, the `Expressions` property will accept a regular expression to perform its matching.

To determine how to configure your smart tag object, a little knowledge is needed concerning how Office applications tokenize text. For instance, if a user types `PO29302` into Word, the parser will automatically create two tokens out of that text: token 1 will be `PO` and token 2 will be `29302`. Adding the string `PO` to the `Terms` collection would cause this text to be recognized by our smart tag because one of the tokens matches our term. We could also write a more complicated and robust regular expression that matches on "the letters PO preceded by one or more spaces, followed by any number of numerical digits, and then followed by one or more spaces" by using this: `\sPO[0-9]*\s`.

After you have determined what you want to match text-wise with your smart tag, you need to determine the list of actions available to users who click on the smart tag. If we wanted to match on a purchase order number using the regex just shown, and then offer a user the ability to see the purchase orders details (perhaps within an actions pane or with an Outlook forms region), we would define that action using the `Action` class (again, available in both Word and Excel). The `Action` class provides an event that we can hook to perform the custom work of performing the indicated action:

```
// Create the action object
DisplayPO = new Action("Display PO details");

// Add the action to the smart tag
POSmartTag.Actions = new Action[] { DisplayPO };
```

Listing 21.1 puts all of this together in a region that can be copied and pasted into a Word document class (for example, `ThisDocument`) to create a custom smart tag, and Figure 21.18 shows the smart tag in action.

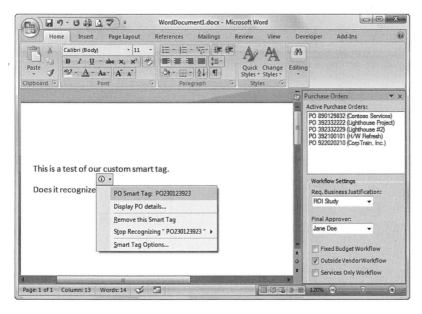

FIGURE 21.18   A custom smart tag in action.

LISTING 21.1    A Word Document Project with Custom Smart Tag

```csharp
using System;
using System.Collections.Generic;
using System.Data;
using System.Linq;
using System.Text;
using System.Text.RegularExpressions;
using System.Windows.Forms;
using System.Xml.Linq;
using Microsoft.VisualStudio.Tools.Applications.Runtime;
using Tools = Microsoft.Office.Tools.Word;
using Office = Microsoft.Office.Core;
using Word = Microsoft.Office.Interop.Word;

namespace WordDocument1
{
    public partial class ThisDocument
    {

        private void AddPOSmartTag()
        {
            // Create the smart tag object
            Tools.SmartTag poSmartTag =
                new Tools.SmartTag(
                    "www.contoso.com#POSmartTag",
                    "PO Smart Tag");

            // We want to match on a regex:
            poSmartTag.Expressions.Add(new Regex(@"\sPO[0-9]*\s"));

            // Define an action for the smart tag
            Tools.Action displayDetails =
                new Tools.Action("Display PO details...");

            // Add the action to the smart tag
            poSmartTag.Actions =
                new Tools.Action[] { displayDetails };

            // Add the smart tag to the document
            this.VstoSmartTags.Add(poSmartTag);

            // Wire up event handlers for the smart tag action
            displayDetails.Click += new
                Tools.ActionClickEventHandler(
```

```csharp
            displayDetails_Click);
    }


    void displayDetails_Click(object sender,
        Tools.ActionEventArgs e)
    {
        // code would go here to reach out to the purchasing
        // system and surface the information in the current
        // document
    }



    private void ThisDocument_Startup(object sender,
        System.EventArgs e)
    {
        AddPOSmartTag();
    }



    private void ThisDocument_Shutdown(object sender,
        System.EventArgs e)
    {

    }

    #region VSTO Designer generated code

    /// <summary>
    /// Required method for Designer support - do not modify
    /// the contents of this method with the code editor.
    /// </summary>
    private void InternalStartup()
    {
        this.Startup +=
            new System.EventHandler(ThisDocument_Startup);
        this.Shutdown +=
            new System.EventHandler(ThisDocument_Shutdown);
    }

    #endregion
}
}
```

# Summary

In this chapter, we covered the capabilities present in Visual Studio 2008 for building on top of Microsoft Office applications and customizing their behavior at both the application level and the document level. In our discussion of Office add-ins, we covered the capability to add your own items, tabs, and groupings to the Ribbon, the construction of Outlook forms regions, and the development of custom task panes. In our discussion of Office document-level extensions, we illustrated the concepts behind hosting Windows Forms controls and native Office controls on a document's surface, building custom actions panes to provide context-aware actions and information to users, and using the data cache architecture to both read and write data to Office documents on the client and server side.

Last, we presented how to craft your own smart tags.

Although we focused on only a few of the Office applications that can be customized using VSTO, we hope we have provided enough information around VSTO's projects and designers to get you started on your own investigation into Visual Studio and Office as a development platform.

# PART VI

# Visual Studio Team System

## IN THIS PART

# CHAPTER 22

# Team Collaboration and Visual Studio Team System

We have spent most of this book specifically describing how to best press Visual Studio into action for writing a variety of application types: Windows forms applications, web applications, database-connected applications, class libraries, and so on. And in our discussion of the various Visual Studio tools that enable those development scenarios, we have focused squarely on the role of the developer in writing quality code quickly using the Visual Studio IDE. But to talk solely about coding is to miss the larger picture. Software development projects involve other equally important roles and skill sets. Software projects are also a whole lot more complicated than simply producing code; they have a life all their own that involves variables across various work activities.

Visual Studio Team System is the graduation of Visual Studio from a developer-focused integrated development environment to a collaborative suite of tools that targets all the different roles involved on a software project, and enables productive work across all phases of the Software Development Life Cycle (SDLC). In this chapter, we will look at this suite of collaborative tools collectively referred to as *Visual Studio Team System (VSTS)*. We will first establish some baseline knowledge of SDLCs to provide context for the problems faced by development teams. Then we will discuss exactly what we mean when we refer to the Visual Studio Team System and take a brief tour through the Team System toolset. The balance of the chapters in this book will look in detail at the various scenarios enabled through VSTS.

> **NOTE**
>
> Be watchful: VSTS can be used to refer to two similar but different concepts. Here, we use it to describe all the client and server software that the Visual Studio Team System comprises. VSTS, however, is also commonly used to refer to Visual Studio Team Suite. This is a SKU of Visual Studio that includes the capabilities of all the various Visual Studio editions (Development Edition, Database Edition, Architecture Edition, and so on).

# A View of Software Development Projects

Software development projects are complex projects that involve various moving parts: Yes, developers are an important component of the software development machinery, but they are far from the only component. With any sufficiently sized project, architects are also involved. They act as the keepers of the technical blueprint for a solution and work closely with developers to ensure that the blueprint is achievable in code and that it matches the requirements and expectations of the project. Testers are also involved. They test the validity of the code produced by the developers against a gamut of quality benchmarks. And finally, one or more individuals are usually needed to manage the logistics of the project: who is working on what, schedule achievement, and general process management.

In addition to the different roles and skill sets involved, any given project progresses through a series of phases from inception to completion. Over time, the software industry has evolved various models that are useful in describing the software development life cycle and the interactions between the various roles and parties.

Microsoft has developed its own series of models and guidance around the SDLC and the involved roles called the *Microsoft Solutions Framework*. The Microsoft Solutions Framework, or MSF, is in its fourth major incarnation. It documents a process model for describing the phases and activities within the SDLC and a team model for describing the roles that participate on the software development project team. It is also a collection of best practices, project-specific guidance, and templates.

The MSF is available in two flavors: MSF for Agile Software Development (MSF Agile) and MSF for Capability Maturity Model Integration Process Improvement (MSFCMMI). A basic understanding of MSF is important to this discussion of Visual Studio Team System for two reasons:

▶ To understand the value of VSTS, you first have to understand the problem space presented with software development projects; by using a common set of terms and semantics to describe this problem space, you'll have a much easier time understanding the benefits that the Visual Studio Team System brings to the table.

▶ In addition, VSTS is capable of using template models that actually impact tool behavior within Visual Studio. MSF Agile and MSF for CMMI are two templates delivered by Microsoft for direct use with Visual Studio Team System.

## MSF Agile

MSF Agile maps the concepts of a solutions framework into the values favored by an agile development methodology. Although it is hard to come up with a universal definition of what makes a development process agile, in general these methodologies can be said to adhere to and prize the following characteristics:

- Individuals and interactions trump processes and tools.

- Valid, quality software is valued over comprehensive documentation.

- Collaboration with the customer and between team members is advocated over contract negotiation.

- The project team is empowered to react to change as opposed to following a pre-scriptive project plan.

### The MSF Agile Process Model

The MSF v4 Agile process model deals with the development process in terms of tracks, checkpoints, and work products. *Tracks* are a set of activities (some sequential, known as *workstreams*; others not). *Checkpoints* are consensus points where the team collaboratively examines progress and determines whether to continue on the current path, change paths, or stop altogether. *Work products* is the term given to the tangible outputs from one or more activities; these are the source code, documents, spreadsheets, and so on that are generated throughout the course of a project.

The MSF Agile model also incorporates the concept of cycles. *Cycles* represent the frequency with which activities are performed. For instance, a daily build is an example of a cycle that involves a discrete set of activities that, in turn, result in a discrete set of work products.

### The MSF Agile Team Model

Beyond the activities you expect to see within an SDLC, it is also useful to understand the interaction between the various roles you encounter on a software project. The MSF Agile team model represents the project team as a set of different constituencies. The needs of each constituency are represented by its team members, and all members are considered to be peers on the project team. No one role is more important than another. Figure 22.1 documents the Agile team model.

## MSF for CMMI

The Software Engineering Institute's Capability Maturity Model (CMM) is "a reference model of mature practices in a specified discipline, used to improve and appraise a group's capability to perform that discipline" (see http://www.sei.cmu.edu). The Capability Maturity Model for Integration (CMMI) is a collection of four CMMs focused on the disciplines of software engineering, systems engineering, integrated product and process development, and supplier sourcing. MSF v4 for CMMI (MSFCMMI) is a framework tied directly to this four-discipline CMMI.

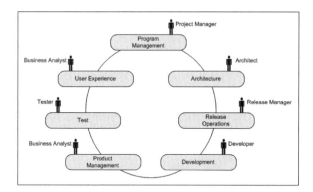

FIGURE 22.1    Constituencies and roles in the MSF Agile team model.

### The MSF for CMMI Process Model

Just like MSF Agile, the MSF for CMMI process is described in terms of tracks and checkpoints. The tracks within MSFCMMI are more formally defined, and the checkpoints are also all well-defined with expected deliverables.

Figure 22.2 shows the tracks and checkpoints espoused by the MSF for CMMI process model.

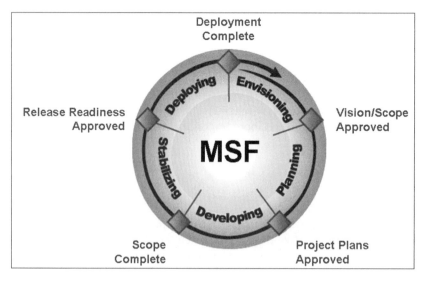

FIGURE 22.2    Tracks and checkpoints in MSF for CMMI.

These tracks are a recognition of the fact that although there are many competing models for the SDLC, they really all distill down to project activities spread across the natural rhythm of the project process:

1. First, all the parties involved need to agree on the vision for the project. What are they setting out to achieve? How will they know whether they are successful?

2. After a common vision has been agreed on, boundaries have been set, and goals have been documented, the project team needs to agree on both what they are going to build and how they are going to build it.

3. Then the plans are put into action, and the software application is actually architected, designed, and written.

4. As various components of the system are written, they need to be tested to ensure that they are actually realizing the requirements of the project and that they meet the project team's commitments with respect to quality.

5. And finally, after all the parts have been written, tested, and approved, the software application has to actually be deployed so that it can be used.

These phases are termed, respectively, *Envisioning, Planning, Developing, Stabilizing*, and *Deploying*. Each of these phases has a different set of anticipated work activities, work outputs, and culminating checkpoints.

### The MSF for CMMI Team Model

The MSFCMMI team model is identical in principle and structure to the MSF Agile team model, but it defines and maps many more roles. Compare Figure 22.1 with Figure 22.3.

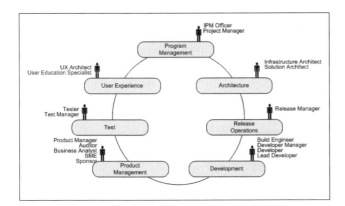

FIGURE 22.3    Constituencies and roles in the MSF for CMMI team model.

# Introducing the Visual Studio Team System

Only three variables in play at any given time affect the impact and success of a software project: speed, quality, and money. Put another way, you can "improve" the success of any given application by delivering the application faster, by delivering a better application, or by spending less money to develop the application. If you truly want to optimize against this "faster, better, cheaper" troika, you need to look beyond the role of the developer and the singular process of writing code and start to contemplate how you can enable the other roles and skill sets that are prevalent in the software development life cycle. You also have to pay attention to more than just the development phase of any project. You need to pay attention to project planning, initial architecture analysis, test suites, and work item management.

Visual Studio Team System recognizes this basic premise and elevates the role of Visual Studio in the software development process by providing a suite of interconnected tools that focus on all roles and all phases of the SDLC.

Visual Studio Team System is the name applied to a set of Visual Studio versions, each of which targets a different role in the software development process. From a product capabilities perspective, you can think of Visual Studio Team System as a team-focused superset of the other available Visual Studio versions such as Visual Studio Professional or Visual Studio Standard (see Figure 22.4).

Earlier, we discussed the MSF team models: Visual Studio Team System provides tools useful for the architect, developer, tester, and project manager roles. This means that separate products are tailored to the architect, developer, and tester work sets: Visual Studio Team Architect, Visual Studio Team Developer, and Visual Studio Team Test. Project managers are enabled via a set of add-ins, utilities, and reporting functions delivered with the Visual Studio Team Foundation Server. Team Foundation Server also functions as the keystone collaboration and storage component within the team system. Each of these different products surfaces role- and track/activity-specific tools within the familiar IDE.

> **NOTE**
>
> Keep in mind the superset relationship between the Visual Studio Team System products (such as Architecture Edition) and the other Visual Studio versions: The VSTS versions add capabilities (specific to a role) over and above the features and functions found in Visual Studio Professional. Another way to think about it is like this: Anything you can do in Visual Studio Professional, you can also do in Visual Studio Team System Architecture Edition (or Development Edition, or Test Edition, and so on).

Let's look at the different VSTS products and how they map into the software development process/team model space.

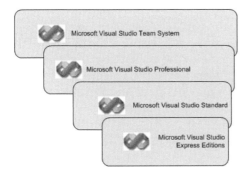

FIGURE 22.4   The Visual Studio versions.

## Visual Studio Team System Architecture Edition

Visual Studio Team System Architecture Edition is, obviously, focused on the architect role. Part of an architect's job is to help the development team and the project management team crisply communicate the design of a system. The design and architecture of a system are typically visualized through the use of models; models are a superb way to construct and think about all the different aspects and variables involved in a large system and from that perspective are great documentation vehicles. Their historical problem is that they are difficult to translate into code and must then be updated to match the code any time the code base changes.

Visual Studio Architecture Edition provides the architect with tools that overcome those problems. Specifically, four designers—the Distributed Application Designer, Logical Infrastructure Designer, Deployment Designer, and Class Designer—work together to deliver dynamic models of a software system. Besides working together in an integrated fashion, these designers are also capable of synchronizing with the system's code.

This is the key benefit realized within Visual Studio Team Architect:

- ▶ You can visually author code using the Class Designer.

- ▶ You can describe the network infrastructure using the Logical Infrastructure Designer.

- ▶ The Distributed Application Designer enables you to construct services-based architectures around the code described in the Class Designer.

- ▶ The Deployment Designer enables you to deploy a specific system or subsystem into the specified environment that was described using the Logical Infrastructure Designer.

- ▶ Changes made to any of the models in these designers are immediately recognized and synchronized with the code base.

We cover these four designers in depth in Chapter 27, "Architecture Edition."

## Visual Studio Team System Development Edition

Visual Studio Professional already does a terrific job as an integrated development environment; its code-authoring editors and designers are both powerful and easy to use. The Visual Studio Team System Development Edition extends the embrace of the developer role by delivering tools to validate code. Using VS Team Developer, you can verify the performance and quality of your code. This edition provides static and dynamic code analysis tools, code profiling, code coverage, and unit-testing facilities.

### Static Code Analysis

Static code analysis is a design-time check of source code that goes beyond the syntax-checking capabilities of the compiler. In fact, if we extend that analogy, if compiler checks are analogous to spelling checks in a word processor, then static code analysis is similar in concept to grammar checking in a word processor: It attempts to determine the meaning of your code and then highlight areas of concern.

Code analysis happens at build/compile time; the various analysis checks are controlled on the Code Analysis tab on the project properties dialog box (as shown in Figure 22.5).

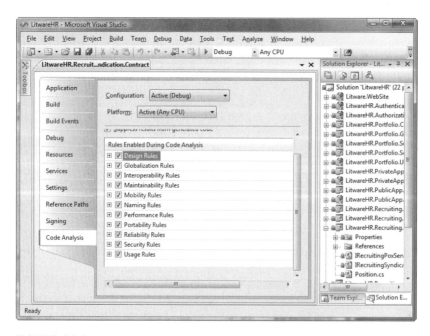

FIGURE 22.5    Controlling code analysis options.

### Dynamic Code Analysis and Code Profiling

Just as static code analysis works against your code at design time, dynamic code analysis works against your code at runtime. Code profiling analyzes your code to give you information on how your application is running. There are two code profilers. A sampling profiler polls your application and retrieves information about it. An instrumented profiler injects probes into your code at compile time; these probes emit data, which is collected by the profiler.

### Code Metrics

Code Metrics are a way of objectively generating statistics about your code. In VSTS Development Edition, the Code Metrics tool is used to generate a picture of how complex and maintainable the code base is. Among the measurements available in the Code Metrics tool are these:

- **Maintainability Index**—A value (from 0 to 100) that represents how easy it is to maintain your code; the higher the number, the more maintainable your code is.

- **Cyclomatic Complexity**—A value indicating the structural complexity of your code. It is derived by examining the count of different code paths possible within the flow of the program.

- **Depth of Inheritance**—A value generated by counting, for each class, its relative depth from the root of your class hierarchy.

- **Class Coupling**—A value used to determine the relative coupling that exists in the application (as a rule, low coupling is the goal).

- **Lines of Code**—A value that indicates the traditional count of lines of executing code within the application.

### Code Coverage and Unit Testing

Code coverage and unit testing work together. Unit testing is accomplished via an attribute-based framework (similar to that employed by JUnit and NUnit, if you are familiar with those tools).

After creating a test, you can use the test facilities to determine which lines of code were actually covered by the test. This is done interactively in the code editor window (tested lines of code are shaded green, missed lines of code shaded red) and via a Code Coverage Results window. Creating unit tests and test projects is actually supported from within Visual Studio 2008 Professional, but VSTS Test Edition provides the following capabilities over and above those found in VS Pro:

- The capability to create web, database, manual, and load unit tests

- The capability to run tests remotely

- The capability to manage work items related to a test

In addition, code coverage features are available only in VSTS.

## Visual Studio Team System Test Edition

Visual Studio Team System Test Edition picks up the testing activities where the Development Edition leaves off. In addition to the same profiling, unit testing, and code coverage tools, this edition has tools for load-testing web applications, running and analyzing unit tests, and managing test cases.

### Creating Tests

You can create tests of the following types within VSTS Test Edition:

- **Unit Tests**—These are the same unit tests supported by VSTS Development Edition.

- **Web Tests**—These are a series of HTTP requests designed to web application functionality; they could be used in performance or stress-testing cycles.

- **Load Tests**—Load tests are used to simulate traffic against a website (see the following section).

- **Manual Tests**—Certain tests may be impossible to automate or script (such as user interaction with the applications UI). In these cases, a manual test can be generated. Manual tests in VSTS are nothing more than Word documents that outline the discrete tasks that constitute a test. Even though the tests are manual, by capturing the task sequence and results in a document, you can manage and view the test along with the other tests in the system.

- **Generic Tests**—Generic tests are simply wrappers around any other tests that return a pass or fail result. This type of test is useful as an extensibility mechanism because it allows you to wrap tests that aren't covered by the native test types in VSTS.

- **Ordered Tests**—Ordered tests are similar to generic tests. They are wrappers around a series of other tests that must run in sequence.

**Load Tests**    Load tests are somewhat unique: VSTS can create a logical testing unit called a *rig*. Rigs are client computers (known as *agents*) and a controller used to generated load demand against a system. There are full management capabilities in Visual Studio Team Test to create agents, assign them to a controller, encapsulate a group of agents and a controller as a rig, and run and monitor tests from the rig.

Tests are globally managed and controlled using the Test List Editor (see Figure 22.6).

We cover load tests in Chapter 28, "Test Edition."

## Visual Studio Team System Database Edition

Visual Studio Team System Database Edition attempts to fold data developers and database administrators into the overall SDLC by providing tools that treat database objects the same way that other project artifacts are treated. For instance, using the VSTS Database Edition, you can place database objects under source code control and test stored procedures. The following subsections cover the major toolsets delivered with VSTS Database Edition.

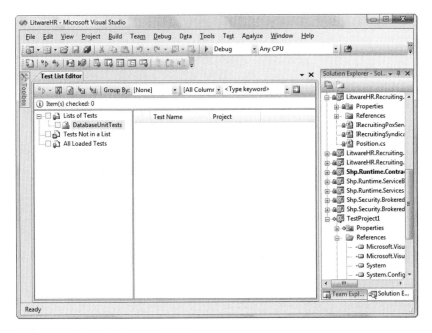

FIGURE 22.6    The Test List Editor.

### Unit Test

Unit testing is just as important with databases as it is with applications. You will want to verify that your database API (consisting of stored procedures, triggers, and functions), data structures (tables and views), and even table-level or user-level security can pass functional testing with unit tests. Unit tests defined against database objects are treated the same as all other unit tests within Visual Studio Team System, which in turn means that they can be included within any defined test suites.

### T-SQL Editor

The T-SQL Editor brings additional capabilities to Visual Studio's current SQL designer, including support for multithreaded stored procedure execution, better handling and display of multiple result sets, and an improved developer experience with syntax highlighting, script language selection, and query statistics.

### Database Projects

Data developers can script database schema and metadata into the new database project, and place those objects in version control. This allows team members to work against database definitions in an offline mode (for example, without a direct connection to the product or test SQL Server)—a huge benefit that allows teams to develop and test schema changes before committing them to the server.

### Schema and Data Changes

VSTS Database Edition has both a schema comparison and a data comparison tool. These allow you to see at a glance the specific differences between any two different versions of a database schema or dataset.

We discuss the Database Edition in Chapter 29, "Database Edition."

## Team Foundation Server

The individual team products can all function individually, but adding Team Foundation Server (TFS) allows the entire team to collaborate seamlessly across work activities and tracks. It even has its own set of enabling technologies. Although TFS serves all the individual roles and constituencies, the project manager role in particular is shored up by the tools provided with Team Foundation Server.

> **NOTE**
>
> Team Foundation Server requires Microsoft SQL Server 2005.

### Source Control

Team Foundation Server includes a brand-new source control engine that far exceeds Visual Source Safe's capabilities when used with large development teams. The TFS source control engine uses SQL Server 2005 as its backing store instead of the file system and is very scalable up to the largest development teams. In addition to native support for access over HTTP/HTTPS, the TFS source control system also supports check-in policies and *shelving*:

▶ Check-in policies allow you to add rules that are run on check-in to ensure that procedures and best practices are enforced. A common example of this is a check-in policy that requires a clean bill of health from the static code analyzer before the check-in is allowed.

▶ Shelving is a technique whereby you can check in a file to a "shelveset" instead of checking in to the live source code tree. This allows you to check in a work in progress without overwriting the work in progress that is maintained on the main source code branch for your project.

> **NOTE**
>
> Although most users will leverage the TFS source system within Visual Studio, it also ships with a standalone user interface that can provide administrator- and contributor-level functionality to individuals who don't own Visual Studio Team System.

Source control is covered in Chapter 24, "Source Control."

### Work Item Tracking

A work item is the atomic unit within VSTS for tracking and managing activities and work products within the context of a project. Work items can be assigned to any role within the project team and can be assigned to a specific workflow. Work items are powerful in that they can be related to a multitude of items to create a web of connected work products. For example, you may create a work item for a bug report and then link that bug report to a checked-in source code file, a developer, a tester, and the test case that revealed the bug.

A set of Microsoft Office add-ins ships with Team Foundation Server to allow project managers to tie into work items from within Office. For instance, a project manager can use the Microsoft Word add-in to generate a status report directly linked to work items in the TFS database. Or the project manager can use the Microsoft Project add-in to automatically generate and sync work items with the action items in the Microsoft Project plan file.

Although simple in concept, work items are the single most important collaboration element in VSTS. Consider an end-to-end scenario: You are assigned a work item to fix a bug in your code. You would first review the work item, check out the section of offending code, make the fix, and then use the VSTS development/test tools to automatically run the tests that cover that code section. From there, you would check the changed code back into the source repository. The test team would then pick up the ball. When the fix makes it into a build, that build is also linked to the work item. All the while, notifications are sent to interested parties so that others can track the progress of the work item through its workflow.

We cover work items in depth in Chapter 25, "Work Item Tracking."

### Build Automation

Team Foundation Build is a part of the Team Foundation Server. It enables release management roles to run tests against a code base, build the code base, release the code base to a file server, and generate reports about the build and distribute them to the team.

Team Foundation Build is a tool and graphical user interface that sits over the top of the MSBuild tool. Chapter 30, "Team Foundation Build," has all the details on using the TFS build automation features.

### Reports

Because all the work items and other work products in VSTS are stored in a SQL Server 2005 database, TFS is able to leverage the SQL Server 2005 Reporting Services and the SQL Server 2005 Analysis Services to deliver reports about build quality, work item progress, test results, build results, and so on.

### The Project Portal

Team Foundation Server uses the project template to generate a Windows SharePoint site containing the correct document libraries and document templates that map to the chosen project type. For instance, creating a project based on the MSF Agile template will produce a SharePoint site with artifact document templates specifically generated for the agile process.

By using the SharePoint site as a universal portal, even non–Visual Studio project stakeholders can interact with the VSTS work items and participate in project collaboration.

# Summary

Visual Studio Team System focuses on enabling all tracks of the SDLC, not just the development track. A holistic approach toward managing progress through the SDLC is key. VSTS extends the reach of Visual Studio from the developer to include other pivotal roles in the SDLC such as architects, business analysts, QA, and project management, and by doing so aims to do the following:

- ▶ Avoid unplanned scope increases
- ▶ Improve communication
- ▶ Minimize duplication of effort
- ▶ Optimize resources
- ▶ Streamline the development process
- ▶ Manage and mitigate risks
- ▶ Facilitate postmortem analysis and capture of best practices

In this chapter, you learned that VSTS is a set of different Visual Studio versions, each targeted at a different role within the SDL landscape. These VS versions are available separately or in a package known as the Visual Studio Team Suite. There is also a server-side component known as the Team Foundation Server that sits in the middle of a VSTS deployment. Because these tools all work together in an integrated fashion, Visual Studio Team System enables consistent support of work activities ranging from architecture to development to test, and management of the work items associated with each.

In the following chapters, we will look at the individual tools associated with Visual Studio Team System and see how they can be utilized within the fabric of a development team.

# CHAPTER 23

# Managing and Working with Team Projects

The preceding chapter described the cohesive tools ecosystem delivered with Visual Studio Team System. Now, it's time to look at the specifics involved with the Team Foundation Server.

You can think of Team Foundation Server as the central collaborative hub in a Visual Studio Team System environment: Visual Studio provides role-specific tools for architects, developers, testers, and managers, whereas Team Foundation Server provides the central repository and information-sharing services necessary to bind a project team together into one cohesive unit. In this chapter, we will focus on implementing a Team Foundation Server setup and leveraging its team-enabling capabilities.

## Anatomy of Team Foundation Server

As discussed in Chapter 22, "Team Collaboration and Visual Studio Team System," Team Foundation Server (TFS) serves as the core collaboration hub for the Visual Studio Team System. It is TFS that enables source control, work item tracking, project alerts, reporting, and a host of other collaboration features.

You can best think of TFS as a suite of web services running over the top of a data store. Physically, this means that TFS functionality is surfaced through Windows IIS web services, with data storage, warehousing, analysis, and reporting services provided by SQL Server 2005. These two parts of TFS are referred to as the *application tier* and the *data tier*. These tiers are logical and physically can map onto one or more servers. Some organizations deploy both of these tiers onto a single server, whereas others deploy the application tier into a web farm and the data tier onto several SQL Server installations.

## The Application Tier

The application tier is composed of a set of web services (running under ASP.NET/ Microsoft Internet Information Services) that provide source code control, work item tracking, reporting, and core TFS functionality. Figure 23.1 shows the general structure of a TFS application server.

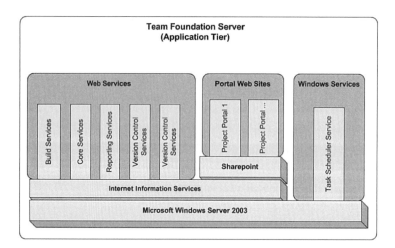

FIGURE 23.1   Team Foundation Server: application.

The tier web services on the application tier act as wrappers over the top of the TFS API, which provides the actual functionality delivered by TFS. These services are hosted in virtual directories under the root Team Foundation Server website. Figure 23.2 shows these web service directories within IIS Manager.

Within each service directory, there are one or more web service endpoints. The list is provided in Table 23.1.

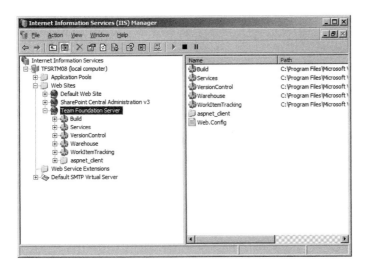

FIGURE 23.2   Team Foundation Server web services.

TABLE 23.1   Application Tier Web Services

| Service Directory | Web Service(s) |
| --- | --- |
| Build Services | BuildController |
| | BuildStore |
| | Integration |
| | PublishTestResultsBuildService |
| Core Services | EventService |
| | AuthorizationService |
| | CommonStructureService |
| | GroupSecurityService |
| | ProcessTemplate |
| | ProjectMaintenance |
| | Registration |
| | ServerStatus |
| Warehouse | WarehouseController |
| Version Control | Administration |
| | Integration |
| | ProxyStatistics |
| | Repository |
| Work Item Tracking | ClientService |
| | ConfigurationSettingsService |
| | ExternalServices |
| | Integration |
| | SyncEventsListener |

> **TIP**
>
> In general, you don't need to worry about the TFS web services. They function as the server's API, which is used by various TFS tools such as the Team Explorer. However, if you want to extend TFS functionality, the web services are a great place to start. Documentation on the TFS web services is spotty, but you can find some information on extending and integrating with TFS in the Visual Studio 2008 SDK (see http://msdn.microsoft.com/vstudio/extend/default.aspx). You can also get a small glimpse of web service functionality by simply calling the web service from your browser. This will give you a brief description of the service and a list of its supported methods.

In addition to these web services, a Windows service is also deployed and run on TFS application tier servers: the task scheduler service. The task scheduler service—which runs under the name `TfsServerScheduler`—is a generic service for scheduling various TFS tasks. For example, the VSTS build system leverages this service to schedule builds.

> **NOTE**
>
> Team Foundation Build is the server application designed to run and manage automated software builds. It relies on its own service, the Team Build Service, which runs independently from the task scheduler. The Team Build Service can be deployed onto the application tier server but doesn't have to be. It also can be deployed on a client or on a standalone server.

## The Data Tier

The data tier is essentially a SQL Server 2005 machine. It acts as the data repository for TFS and provides analysis and reporting services that are directly leveraged by Team Foundation Server (see Figure 23.3).

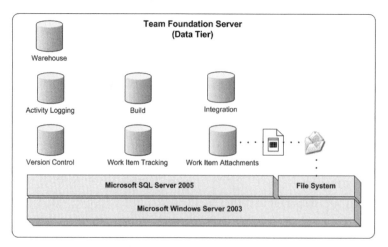

FIGURE 23.3    Team Foundation Server: data tier.

Physically, TFS stores its data across seven different databases:

- An activity log database (`TfsActivityLogging`)

- A build database (`TfsBuild`) that holds data related to system builds such as build steps and build quality indicators

- An "integration" database (`TfsIntegration`) that stores core team project information, security settings, and event registrations

- A version control database (`TfsVersionControl`)

- A data warehouse database (`TfsWarehouse`) that serves as the analysis and reporting store

- A work item database (`TfsWorkItemTracking`) that stores work items

- A work item attachment database (`TfsWorkItemTrackingAttachments`) that has a single table, `Attachments`, that serves as a collection of pointers to the work item attachment files

Work item attachments are actually stored in the file system.

It is important to note that the relationship between TFS and SQL Server is a close one: TFS relies on and requires SQL Server Analysis Services and SQL Server Reporting Services to complete its various reporting requirements.

## Security

Team Foundation Server uses the traditional and well-understood model of users and groups to implement security. Two broad categories of users need to be accommodated: server administrators and project members. Server administrators are responsible for the administration of all the TFS components from the web service configurations within IIS to the database setup under SQL Server. Project members are those users who compose a project team. Although these broad categories may overlap, and certainly there is nothing preventing someone from sharing server administration responsibilities with project management responsibilities, they are served by different groups within a default Team Foundation Server install.

### Global Security Groups

Global security groups are the high-level, universal groups that broadly organize users into administrator- or user-level permission sets: The Team Foundation Administrators group has full rights to all pieces of the TFS deployment, and the Team Foundation Valid Users group contains the user population that is allowed to access the resources of a Team Foundation Server.

Team Foundation Valid Users are further broken down at the project level by the project security groups.

**Project Security Groups**

For each individual project, TFS defines permissions and access levels by classifying users into three groups: project administrators, contributors, and readers. Each of these groups has a decreasing level of privileges with respect to one another (see Figure 23.4).

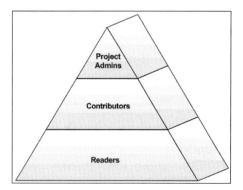

FIGURE 23.4    Team Foundation Server security roles.

**Project Administrators**    Project administrators have permission to manage individual projects en masse. They control content in the project portal sites, determine team membership, set security parameters, and have full control over a project's work items.

**Contributors**    Contributors represent the bulk of the team members; they are the individuals responsible for executing the project and therefore are imbued with permissions to add, edit, and delete work items in a given project, and can view information published on the project portal site.

**Readers**    Readers are individuals who have a vested interest in looking at project artifacts but don't contribute principally to the project. As the group name implies, they have only view permissions and will primarily interact with project data through the project portal site.

**Mapping Roles to Groups**

In Chapter 22, we covered two of the project process models that are supported. TFS uses *process templates* to describe how to physically implement a particular process using the components of TFS and Visual Studio Team System. We cover process templates in more depth in the following section; they are important to mention here because security is one area covered by a process template. It effectively takes the roles defined by the process and maps them into the security groups that TFS cares about. Table 23.2 shows how the MSF Agile and MSF CMMI roles map into the three project-level groups used by the Foundation Server security subsystem.

TABLE 23.2    MSF Roles and TFS Security Groups

**MSF Agile Roles**

| Role | Group |
| --- | --- |
| Architect | Contributor |
| Business Analyst | Contributor |
| Developer | Contributor |
| Project Manager | Project Administrator |
| Release Manager | Project Administrator |
| Tester | Contributor |

**MSF for CMMI Roles**

| Role | Group |
| --- | --- |
| Auditor | Contributor |
| Build Engineer | Project Administrator |
| Business Analyst | Contributor |
| Developer | Contributor |
| Development Manager | Project Administrator |
| Infrastructure Architect | Contributor |
| IPM Officer | Contributor |
| Lead Developer | Project Administrator |
| Product Manager | Contributor |
| Project Manager | Project Administrator |
| Release Manager | Project Administrator |
| Solution Architect | Contributor |
| Sponsor | Reader |
| Subject Matter Expert | Reader |
| Test Manager | Project Administrator |
| Tester | Contributor |
| User Education Architect | Contributor |
| User Experience Specialist | Contributor |

# Managing a Team Project

Now that you have a decent understanding of what Team Foundation Server looks like from an architectural perspective, you're ready to see how you can create and host a *team project* within TFS. The term *team project* is used to distinguish a TFS-based collaboration project from a Visual Studio project.

The first step is installing the Team Foundation Server client software; this is available on the Team Foundation Server install media. After this software has been installed on your machine, several additions are made to Visual Studio to allow it to interact with a Team Foundation Server: A new option under the Tools menu will allow you to connect to a

Team Foundation Server, a new Team menu is added to the Visual Studio menu bar, and new options are available under the File menu. We'll get to the Team menu in just a bit. In addition to these Visual Studio enhancements, various Microsoft Office add-ins are installed; they allow you to surface certain TFS capabilities, such as work item tracking, within applications like Microsoft Word, Microsoft Excel, or even Microsoft Project.

## Creating a New Team Project

Creating a new team project works much the same as creating a new Visual Studio project: From the File menu, choose New, Team Project. The New Team Project Wizard will start.

> **NOTE**
>
> If you don't see the Team Project option available under the Visual Studio File menu, you may not have the Team Foundation Server client software installed. Another possibility is your choice of VS environment settings. Your Visual Studio environment settings will alter the way your File menu is structured. For instance, if you have the Visual Basic Development settings profile loaded, you will see the New Team Project option located directly under the File menu instead of under the New submenu. You can change environment settings by using the Import and Export Settings Wizard (which you access by choosing Tools, Import and Export Settings).

The wizard will collect all the information needed to create the various TFS structures used by a team project, including the databases and websites.

### Selecting a Team Project Name

On the first page of the wizard (see Figure 23.5), you are prompted to select a name for the team project. Keep in mind that the name you choose here will, in one form or another, be embedded in many of the TFS structures from database names to SharePoint websites. Therefore, you need to select a name that doesn't conflict with any of the current projects hosted in the target TFS server.

### Selecting a Process Template

The second page of the wizard (see Figure 23.6) asks you to identify a process template. As we have mentioned, the default selections here are the MSF Agile template and the MSF for CMMI template.

Your template selection will drive many of the behaviors in the Team System environment. For instance, the default work items, documents, and team roles that are populated when you start a new team project are all based on the information contained within the process template.

### Naming the Project Portal

The next page is used to name the project portal website (see Figure 23.7). The project portal is a Windows SharePoint Services website designed to be the one-stop shop for all of a team project's collateral from the standard work items and documents to team announcements, links, and process guidance information.

FIGURE 23.5    Selecting a project name.

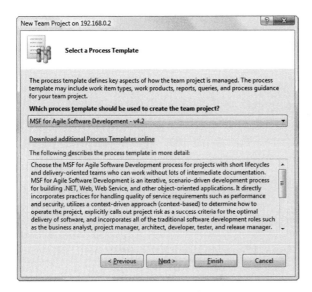

FIGURE 23.6    Choosing a process template.

FIGURE 23.7    Naming the project portal.

The portal name will default to the team project name that you specified on the initial wizard page; you can change it to something else, keeping in mind that the project portal has a potentially larger and more diverse audience than the other team project entry points.

### Specifying Source Control Settings
The source control settings page (see Figure 23.8) enables you to control how this new project should be configured with regard to its source control repository. You have the option to create a new folder under the root source control tree, create a new branch under an existing source control folder, or leave the source control creation for a later date.

### Confirming Your Settings
At this point, the wizard will display a confirmation page of the settings you have chosen. Clicking Finish will start the project generate process on the server. A progress page will show you which process is currently running. After everything has been created, a final notice page (see Figure 23.9) will confirm that the team project has been created and offer you the option of viewing the project process guidance (more on the guidance page later in this chapter).

You have now successfully created a new team project within TFS. The next step is to add team members to the project.

FIGURE 23.8    Source control settings.

FIGURE 23.9    Final confirmation.

## Adding Users to a Project Team

As a project administrator, you have access to the security groups that control access to your projects. In Visual Studio, you can access the group membership settings through the Team Explorer tool or through the Team menu. Take a moment to briefly examine the

Team Explorer window. As a project administrator or contributor, you will want to thoroughly understand the various Team Explorer features. And indeed, in later sections of this chapter and later chapters in this book, we will provide even more focus on this tool and its use scenarios. For now, though, a high-level acquaintance is sufficient.

### Working with the Team Explorer Window

When you are connected, display the Team Explorer window by selecting View, Team Explorer within Visual Studio. The Team Explorer window is a full-fledged tool window that operates just like other tool windows such as the Solution Explorer.

With a connection established to a running TFS application tier server, you will see various nodes within the Team Explorer window (see Figure 23.10). The top-level node represents the Team Foundation Server itself. Below this node are the various projects available on that server. And within each project are folders for Work Items, Documents, Reports, Team Builds, and Source Control. Also, below the server node is a Favorites folder.

FIGURE 23.10    The Team Explorer window.

**Team Project Folders**    Just as with the Solution Explorer, the folders within team project nodes serve to organize the artifacts generated within the team project. Each of the folders provides a context menu: Just right-click on the folder to access the valid actions for that particular node. Figure 23.11 shows the context menu for the Work Items node.

Double-clicking on any of the items within the project will load that item into its appropriate window within Visual Studio. We'll cover how to view and create items within a project in the section "Contributing to a Project Team," later in this chapter.

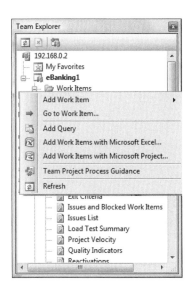

FIGURE 23.11    The Team Explorer context menu for the Work Items node.

**Team Explorer Favorites**    The Favorites folder holds shortcuts to other nodes within the Team Explorer window. Typically, you would place links to frequently used project nodes here because they may be buried within the tree structure or at the end of a long list of explorer items.

The quickest way to add a shortcut is simply to drag the target node into the Favorites folder.

### Controlling Project Groups
As we explained earlier in the discussion on the TFS security model, access to TFS functionality is controlled by privilege levels and permissions that are doled out based on group membership. Put another way, what you can do and see within a team project is based on what group your user ID belongs to. The Project Group Membership dialog box can be accessed by project administrators and is used to control group membership.

There are two ways to access this dialog box: through the Team menu or through the Team Explorer window. On the Team menu (shown in Figure 23.12), select Team Project Settings, Group Membership. Using Team Explorer, you perform the identical action by right-clicking on the project node to access the Team Project Settings menu items.

**Adding Users to a Group**    The Project Group Membership dialog box is the principal mechanism for adding or removing users from a project group (see Figure 23.13).

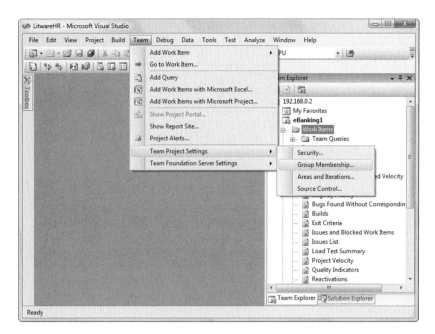

FIGURE 23.12    The Visual Studio Team menu.

FIGURE 23.13    The Project Group Membership dialog box.

To add a new user to an existing group, select the group and then click on the Properties button. This will launch a properties window for that group (see Figure 23.14).

From the properties window, make sure you have the Members tab selected, select the Windows User or Group radio button, and then click the Add button. This will yield the standard Windows user selection dialog box (see Figure 23.15). Selecting a user here and clicking OK will add that user to the group.

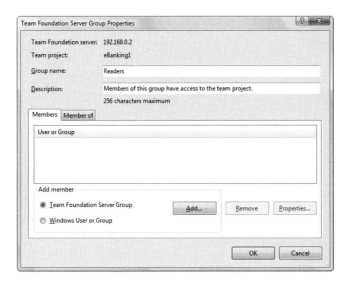

FIGURE 23.14    Project group properties.

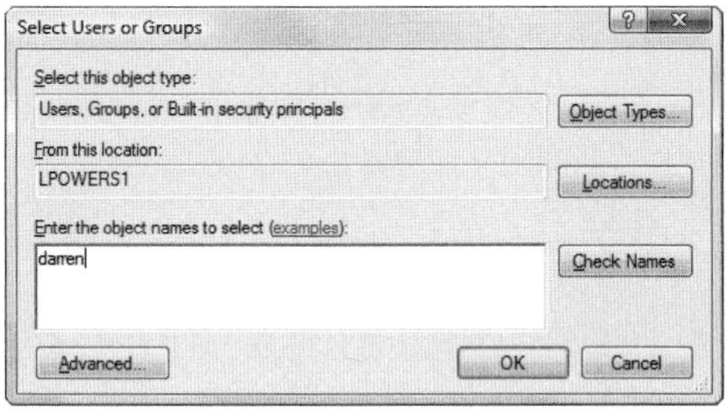

FIGURE 23.15    Selecting users and groups.

**Adding Custom Groups**    Some organizations may want to implement their own group scheme within TFS. There is nothing that prevents you from adding your own groups or, in fact, deleting the default groups that are part of the TFS setup.

To add a new group, you start at the same Project Group Membership dialog box shown in Figure 23.13. Instead of clicking on the Properties button, however, click the New button. In the resulting window (see Figure 23.16), you can enter a name for the new group and a description.

**Fine-tuning Permissions**    Each group has a default set of permissions applied to it. As a project administrator or TFS administrator, you can change the permissions associated with each group. From the Team menu, select Team Project Settings, Security. The security dialog box (see Figure 23.17) will enable you to fine-tune the exact permissions associated with any of the project-level or global security groups on the Team Foundation Server machine.

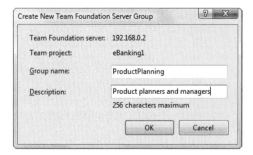

FIGURE 23.16    Creating a new project group.

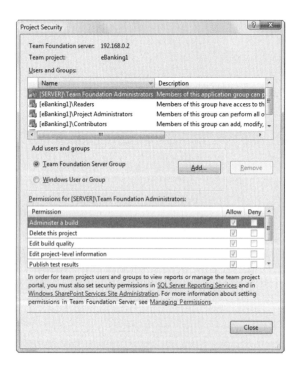

FIGURE 23.17    Setting group permissions.

## Controlling Project Structure and Iterations

Besides controlling access to a project, another responsibility of the project administrator is to define the structural aspects of a project and also control the number of *iterations* planned for a project.

From the previous discussions on the Software Development Life Cycle (SDLC) process in Chapter 22, you know that different methodologies have different approaches to the development process. But in general, an iteration is a complete work cycle that results in a working release of the software. Subsequent iterations build on the previously generated artifacts and lessons learned until, finally, enough iterations have been processed to achieve a releasable product. Using the team settings in Visual Studio, project administrators can control how many iterations any given project will progress through.

In addition to iterations, TFS supports the concept of *areas*. Areas are simply logical ways to group work efforts within the project. For software development projects, an area may define the boundary of a functional group or feature set.

Both areas and iterations are controlled using the same Areas and Iterations dialog box (reached through Team Project Settings, Areas and Iterations).

## 23

### Adding or Changing Project Areas

Figure 23.18 shows the Areas and Iterations dialog box, with the Area tab active. This is the work surface used for creating and structuring areas within a project. For instance, you may want to flesh out some project structure by creating Web UI, Web Services, and Database areas. You could then further subdivide these functional areas into specific breakouts for each major component.

Areas are depicted within a tree control in the dialog box. To add a new area, first select the parent area and then click on the Add New Node button (on the toolbar within the Area tab). You can then edit the area's name inline within the tree. Removing a node is as simple as selecting it and then clicking on the Delete Node button in the toolbar. Nodes can also be moved within the tree hierarchy. First, select the node you want to move and then use the four buttons on the right of the dialog box's toolbar to move them up within their siblings list or move the node up or down within the parent-child relationship.

FIGURE 23.18   Adding areas to a project.

Any areas created are then used to help structure the work items for the project. In that way, they can function as a mechanism for organizing work against these functional area breakouts.

> **NOTE**
>
> Because areas will likely be very specific to a given project, no areas are created by default when you instantiate a new team project.

### Adding or Changing Iterations

Iterations are handled in exactly the same fashion as areas. First click on the Iteration tab and then add or move nodes as necessary. Unlike with areas, the process template that you have selected for the current project will initially default to a number of iterations. As an example, the MSF Agile project already has three iterations defined (see Figure 23.19).

**FIGURE 23.19**   Managing project iterations.

# Contributing to a Project Team

Team members interact with a team project in various ways that will differ depending on the unique role of that user. The following sections cover how team contributors can use the Visual Studio Team Explorer to interface with a Team Foundation Server.

## Connecting to a Team Foundation Server

Before using the Team Explorer tool, you will first need to connect to a Team Foundation Server—specifically, an application tier server.

From the Tools menu in Visual Studio, select Connect to Team Foundation Server. This will launch a dialog box that shows any "known" TFS instances (see Figure 23.20). You can either select from this list or, if your intended server isn't shown, you can add it to the list by clicking on the Servers button.

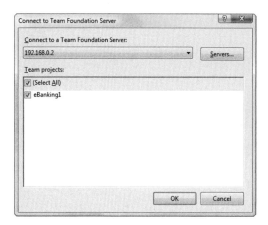

**FIGURE 23.20**   Connecting to a Team Foundation Server.

To add a new TFS server to the dialog box, click on the Add button and fill out the HTTP connection properties: server name, port, and protocol.

Select one of the listed servers, select one or more of the projects hosted on that server, and then click OK.

Assuming that the project administrator has added your credentials to that project's groups, you are now wired into the selected TFS team projects and can use Team Explorer to access the items within those projects.

## Using Team Explorer

You have already had a decent look at the Team Explorer tool; it provides an interactive, organized view of items within a particular project. As a project contributor, you can edit or view those items or create new items within the various categories (for example, work items, reports, and documents).

Using Team Explorer isn't complicated: By right-clicking on a node, you get a context-sensitive menu with the various actions that correspond to the folder's content. For instance, you can upload a document in this fashion by right-clicking on one of the document folders. Or you can create a new work item.

Dedicated chapters following this one discuss work item, build, and source control management.

## Using the Project Portal

As we stated previously, the project portal is the nexus of all the various components of a project. Because it is a SharePoint Services–based site, it follows the standard composition theme for a SharePoint site: It is composed of a mix of standard web parts—links, announcements, and so on—and TFS-specific web parts to provide users a holistic view of the current state of the project (see Figure 23.21).

FIGURE 23.21  Connecting to projects on a Team Foundation Server.

You can visit the project portal from a web browser by manually navigating to the site; by default, it is located at http://<tfs app server>/sites/<project name>/default.aspx. You can automatically navigate there by right-clicking on a project in Team Explorer or selecting the Team menu. Both have a Show Project Portal option, which will launch a new browser window pointed at the portal site.

Contributors will typically use the portal site to gain access to team project documents from outside Visual Studio and check on announcements, general progress reports, and the like. The portal site will also be heavily used by users in the "reader" role because it represents the only way to access team project information without using Team Explorer.

Default web parts are available for viewing build information, checking on remaining work, seeing bug rates, and looking at the open issues list. You can also gain access to the entire roster of reports (served up from SQL Server Reporting Services) or look at process guidance.

### Process Guidance

*Process guidance* refers to a collection of HTML-based material that describes and documents the SDLC process. For each team project, guidance specific to the process used by that project is made available within the project portal site: Just click on the Process Guidance link in the left navigation bar.

Figure 23.22 shows the process guidance material for an MSF CMMI-based project.

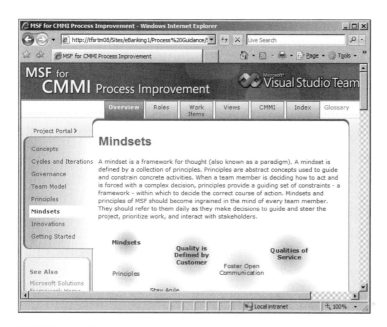

FIGURE 23.22   Project process guidance.

## Using Microsoft Office

Microsoft Office is the third tool you can use to work with items stored in a Team Foundation Server. Through various add-ins and templates, you can use Office applications such as Word, Excel, and Project to talk directly to a TFS server and update items stored there.

The use of Microsoft Word is limited to working with the various document templates (`.dot` files) that are included with the MSF Agile and MSF for CMMI process templates. Microsoft Project and Microsoft Excel offer actual integration with TFS and allow you to manage work items directly from these Office applications.

### Managing Work Items with Project and Excel

After the Team Foundation Server client software is installed, a new toolbar and Team menu will appear in the Office application. Figure 23.23 shows Microsoft Project with the TFS add-in installed. Using the toolbar or the Team menu, you can connect to a Team

Foundation Server (using the same process you saw in Figure 23.19) and then import work items from TFS into the project. After editing the project plan in Microsoft Project, you can then push those work item changes back into TFS by using the Publish button.

You also can access several custom project views via the MS Project View menu.

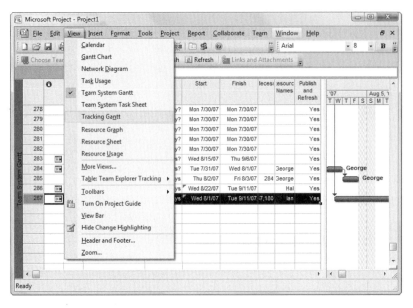

FIGURE 23.23    Microsoft Project working with TFS.

Similar capabilities are present with Microsoft Excel. You can use the Team menu to retrieve a list of work items, import them into Excel, and even make round-trip changes back to the TFS database (see Figure 23.24). We will cover both Excel and Project integration in more depth in Chapter 25, "Work Item Tracking."

---

**NOTE**

Microsoft also provides a centralized project collaboration server called Microsoft Office Project Server. Team Foundation Server can integrate with Microsoft Office Project Server 2007 through a separate connector that is available at http://www.codeplex.com/pstfsconnector. Release 1 is designed to work with Team Foundation Server 2005, and Release 2 is designed to work with Team Foundation Server 2008.

---

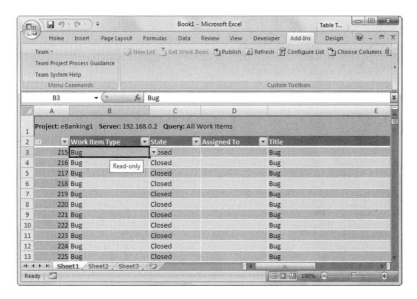

FIGURE 23.24    Using Microsoft Excel to manage work items.

## Using Project Alerts

Alerts are email notifications that are sent from the TFS server whenever a specific event occurs. Project team members can subscribe to the alerts that they need to react to by using the Project Alerts dialog box. From the Team menu in Visual Studio, select Project Alerts. The dialog box that is displayed shows all the possible alert categories; from there, you can type in your email address (or someone else's) to receive a notification when that event transpires (see Figure 23.25).

You can elect to receive alerts in HTML or plain-text format. When an alert arrives in your Inbox, you can view the basics of the alert and then follow the embedded links to get more detail. As an example, if you receive an alert because someone has changed one of your work items, you can actually retrieve information about exactly who changed the work item and which items were changed.

## Working with Project Reports

For the most part, you handle project reports in the same way as any of the other project artifacts such as documents or work items: You can double-click on a report within Team Explorer (or select a report from the project portal) to view its content. Figure 23.26 shows a report on requirements opened within Visual Studio.

Remember that the reporting feature of TFS relies on SQL Server Reporting Services. We cover some of the basics in the following sections.

FIGURE 23.25    Managing project alerts.

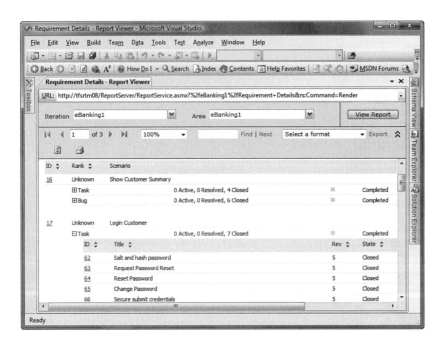

FIGURE 23.26    Viewing a TFS report in Visual Studio.

### Using the Data Warehouse
Reports are generated directly from an OLAP cube derived from the TfsWarehouse relational database (see Figure 23.27). This allows reports to deliver information across several different sources and aggregate information on builds, tests (including test cases, code coverage, and load testing), source control, and work items.

### Designing Reports
Team members can take an existing canned report and alter it to suit their needs. You can also build custom reports from scratch. Again, owing to the SQL Server Reporting Services dependency, the best way to do this is to actually use the Report Designer inside Visual

Studio. Create a new Report Server project (under the Reporting category) in Visual Studio (see Figure 23.28). If the Business Intelligence Reports category isn't visible to you, you will need to install the SQL Server Business Intelligence Server Studio from the SQL Server install media.

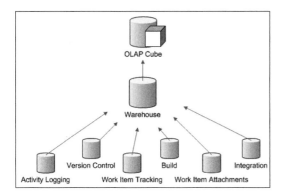

FIGURE 23.27   The reporting database relationship.

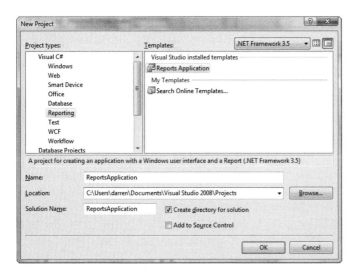

FIGURE 23.28   Creating a new report project.

After creating the project, you can add a new Report project item and use the Report Wizard to graphically build your report. Figure 23.29 shows a report being built to disseminate build information for the project.

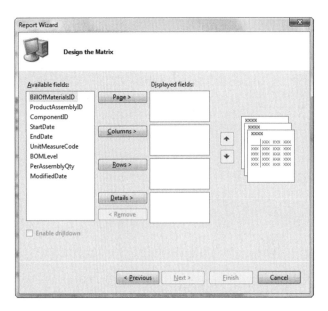

FIGURE 23.29    Building a custom report.

# Summary

Team Foundation Server is the core set of application and data tier components that enable collaboration within team projects. In this chapter, we reviewed the system architecture of the data tier and application tier of the Team Foundation Server. We also discussed how security is handled within a TFS deployment.

We covered how project managers interact with a Team Foundation Server and tools such as Team Explorer to create new team projects, manage process templates, assign team members to a project, and maintain the project portal site. For project contributors, you learned how to effectively work as part of a team and use the various TFS features to participate within the overall project process by using the Team Explorer, the project portal, and even Microsoft Office.

In the following chapters, you will build on this knowledge by digging deeper into the process for managing work items, working with the TFS source control system, and managing builds. You will also examine how architects and developers can use the VSTS modeling features, how testers can use Visual Studio Test Edition to conduct unit and load testing and manage test cases, and how data developers and DBAs can leverage the database-focused tools found in VSTS Database Edition.

CHAPTER 24

# Source Control

This chapter covers source control with Visual Studio
Team System: specifically, the source control system and
repository provided by Team Foundation Server and its integration with Visual Studio.

The premise of source control is relatively simple: On a software project, there is a need to centrally store and control
access to the files that constitute the core artifacts. In other
words, a source control system centrally manages access not
just to source code files, but also to any other file-based artifact produced during the execution of the project. These
artifacts could include items such as requirements documents, network diagrams, and test plans.

---

**NOTE**

The terms *source control* and *version control* are synonymous, at least as far as this book is concerned.
Although the term *version control* is in some ways
preferable because it alludes to the fact that there is
more than just source code being controlled, we use
the term *source control* in this chapter so that we conform to the majority of the MSDN documentation on
team systems—even though the source control database in the Team Foundation Server data tier is, ironi-
cally, named TfsVersionControl.

---

The job of a source control system can be broken down into
the following responsibilities:

▶ It centrally stores files in a secure and reliable fashion.

- ▶ It provides a way to bundle sets of file versions together to constitute a "release."

- ▶ It allows multiple users to interact with the same file at the same time through the concepts of check-in, checkout, and merging.

- ▶ It keeps track of which changes were made to a file, who made them, when they were made, and why.

The source control system that ships as part of Team Foundation Server and Visual Studio handles all those requirements and more. It is a robust client/server-based solution specifically targeted at the source control needs of large enterprise-level development teams.

# The Basics of Team Foundation Source Control

The source control system that ships as a part of VSTS and Team Foundation Server is a brand-new system from Microsoft; it is not an enhanced version of Microsoft's previous source control system, Visual Source Safe. Team Foundation Source Control (TFSC) was built from the ground up to be an enterprise-class system capable of handling hundreds or even thousands of concurrent users.

> **NOTE**
>
> Visual Source Safe (VSS) has not, in fact, gone away. A new version, VSS 2005, was produced in conjunction with Visual Studio 2005, and it remains the preferred source control mechanism for individual developers or small teams (those with five or fewer members).

TFSC was built around some fundamental design goals:

- ▶ To provide a scalable solution for enterprise-class development teams

- ▶ To provide a reliable solution

- ▶ To allow the system to be accessed remotely using the HTTP/HTTPS web protocols

- ▶ To allow more than one developer at a time to work on a source file

- ▶ To provide a completely integrated user experience from within Visual Studio

From a high level, the following sections cover the basics of the Team Foundation source control system before moving on to more in-depth topics relating to actually interacting with the system.

## Basic Architecture

Because the Team Foundation source control system is merely another service provided by TFS, it rides on top of the same three-tier architecture. It relies on SQL Server as the database to house the source control repository, exposes access to the repository through a set of services hosted on a TFS application tier server, and leverages Visual Studio as the client. Figure 24.1 shows a diagram depicting this system architecture.

FIGURE 24.1    The Team Foundation Source Control System.

In support of its design goals, this architecture allows the TFS source control system to scale up by adding additional servers on the application tier. In addition, storage space can be increased by adding additional storage devices to the database server or adding additional database servers.

> **TIP**
>
> For geographically dispersed teams, Team Foundation supports the capability to use proxy servers to cache source control data on servers that are local to a particular team segment. Proxy server settings are controlled via the Team Foundation Settings dialog box and are handled by the Team Foundation administrators. For more details on how to configure proxy servers to increase performance, see the MSDN documentation and search for the phrase "How to: Configure Team Foundation Source Control to Use Proxy Server."

## Security Rights and Permissions

TFSC uses the same Windows integrated security system as the application tier Team Foundation Server that it is hosted on. This means that the same user/group model is used to determine permission levels specific to source control operations and that the same process for adding and removing users is used. In other words, TFSC does not maintain its own specific user base or security system; it participates in the larger Team Foundation Server infrastructure. In general, a user will play either a *contributor* or an *administrator* role in the source control system.

The contributor group is usually filled by team members in the developer, tester, sponsor, or other role. These individuals will interact with the source control system to perform a basic set of common tasks: checking out files for modification, checking in changes made to a file, viewing a file in the repository, and adding or deleting files to the repository.

Administrators, as the name implies, are more focused on maintaining the source control server as a whole. Administrators manage access to the source repository and are tasked with maintaining the integrity and security of any items in the repository. Administrators may also have project-specific tasks such as determining when a new branch should be created in the project tree and handling merges between branches. Membership in this group is typically limited to the global TFS administrators and team roles such as project manager or project lead.

At the permission level, TFSC supports various granular rights that can be assigned or denied to an individual user or a group of users. The specific permissions/rights supported by TFSC are documented in Table 24.1.

TABLE 24.1    Team Foundation Source Control Permissions

| Permission | Description |
| --- | --- |
| *File/Folder Permissions* | |
| AdminProjectRights | User can set permission levels for users/groups. |
| Checkin | User can check in a file to the source control repository. |
| CheckinOther | User can check in another user's file to the source control repository. |
| Label | User can label an item. |
| LabelOther | User can label another user's item. |
| Lock | User can lock an item. |
| PendChange | User is able to check out, add, delete, branch, merge, or undelete. |
| Read | User can read the contents of a file or folder. |
| ReviseOther | User can change another user's changeset comments or check-in notes. |
| UndoOther | User can undo another user's pending changes. |
| UnlockOther | User can remove a lock that another user has placed on an item. |
| *Global Permissions* | |
| AdminConfiguration | User can function as an administrator and change the basic source control settings. |
| AdminConnections | User can stop any in-progress source control action. |
| AdminShelvesets | User can delete another user's shelveset. |
| AdminWorkspaces | User can edit another user's workspace. |
| CreateWorkspace | User can create a workspace. |
| UseSystem | User can access the source control system (this is the base-level permission required to use any portion of the TFSC system). |

Armed with this basic understanding of the Team Foundation source control system, you're ready to look at the tooling integrated into Visual Studio that allows VS users to perform basic and advanced source control tasks.

## Getting Started with Team Foundation Source Control

You will use two primary tools within Visual Studio to perform both basic and advanced source control tasks: Solution Explorer (a tool we discuss in many chapters in this book) and the Source Control Explorer tool. Solution Explorer can be used to directly manage solution and project items under source control. Source Control Explorer provides many of the same functions and also allows you to browse the Team Foundation Source Control items stored in the TFS data tier.

Before you can use either of these tools, however, or use any of the Visual Studio source control–specific features, you have to ensure that Visual Studio is configured for use with Team Foundation Server.

## Configuring Visual Studio

Visual Studio source control settings are configured from the Options dialog box. Select Tools, then Options, and then navigate to the Source Control page. From there, you use the drop-down to select the source control system that you want to use; Visual Studio Team Foundation Server is one option in this list (see Figure 24.2) and, in this case, is the option to select.

With TFS selected as the source control provider, you automatically can use VS as a source control client whenever you connect to a Team Foundation Server. From within Visual Studio, you can do the following:

- ▶ Browse Team Projects and workspaces

- ▶ Examine the individual files within the source repository

- ▶ Retrieve and check out files from the source repository

- ▶ Check in changes made to a file or reverse changes made to a file

- ▶ View the change history associated with a file

We'll cover all these actions and more a bit later in this chapter. For now, it's time to get comfortable with the Source Control Explorer user interface.

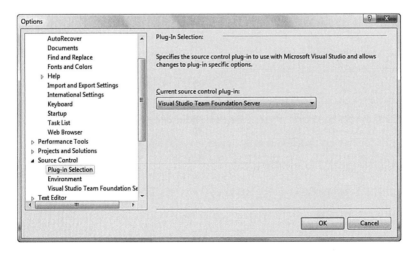

FIGURE 24.2   Selecting the source control system in Visual Studio.

## Using the Source Control Explorer Window

Figure 24.3 shows the Source Control Explorer (SCE) window open in Visual Studio. You can see that the SCE is hosted as a document window (as opposed to a tool window), that it has several different panes in which source control information is visible, and that these panes are arranged so that the window looks similar to the Windows File Explorer window.

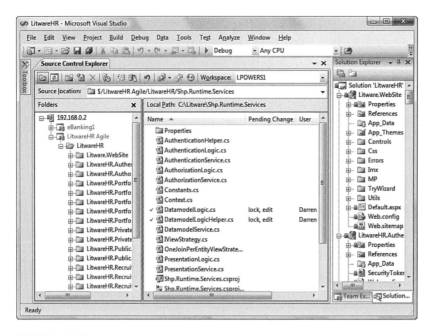

FIGURE 24.3    The Source Control Explorer window.

### The Toolbar

The toolbar on the SCE window provides easy access to common activities. Moving left to right, these buttons allow you to do the following:

▶ Hide or show the folders pane

▶ Refresh the contents of all the panes (for example, requery the server)

▶ Create a new folder within the source control tree structure

▶ Add files to the source control repository

▶ Remove files from the source control repository

▶ Retrieve the latest version of the file from the server (this command functions recursively; by selecting the root of the source control tree, you can retrieve the latest version of *all* the files)

▶ Check out a file for editing

▶ Check in changes made to a file

▶ Undo changes made to a file

▶ Compare the server copy of a file with the local copy

The toolbar also has two drop-downs you can use to change the workspace you are working in (more on workspaces in a bit) or change your location within the source control tree.

### The Folders Pane

The folders pane contains a hierarchical view of the server source control "folders" in the selected *workspace*. If you are familiar with Visual Source Safe terminology, you'll understand that a workspace is analogous to a working folder; it is a local working area on your hard drive that is mapped to a specific source control project on the server. When you retrieve files from the server, they are placed in the local folder that you have associated with the workspace. Because workspaces map onto your local file system, and because projects are naturally organized in a hierarchical fashion in terms of the artifacts they generate, it is natural that the view you use to look into a workspace is a folder/file view *even though the files are actually stored in a set of tables in a SQL Server database*.

### The Files Pane

Each time you select a folder in the folders pane, the files pane will refresh to show you any files (or subfolders) that exist in that workspace/folder. Notice that the files pane uses specific icon overlays to indicate the status of a particular file. For instance, a red check mark is used to indicate a file that you have already checked out, whereas a yellow plus sign indicates a file or folder that is waiting to be added to the source repository on the server. These same icons are used by the Solution Explorer window.

## Managing Workspaces

As we have mentioned, workspaces are areas in your local file system. Any local copies of files under source control are stored in a workspace. Local copies of files are created the first time you connect to a source repository. From then on, your local files become your working set; whenever you modify one of the local files, the changes you have made are marked as pending within the workspace, and not committed to the TFSC server until you explicitly elect to do so during a check-in. Put another way, a workspace is like a sandbox. You can do anything you want to the files in your workspace without worrying about affecting other team members or damaging the viability of the project.

> **NOTE**
>
> Workspaces can be owned by only one user on the local machine. This means that if there are multiple user accounts on one machine, and each of those accounts participates in a TFS Team Project, each would have its own workspaces.

### Creating a Workspace

Besides having Visual Studio configured for source control, the other requisite step for interacting with the source control server is to create a workspace on your computer. Without one, you won't be able to retrieve any files from the source repository, and therefore you won't be able to view those files or make changes to them—which is the whole point of being a team member in the first place.

To create a new workspace, select File, Source Control, Workspaces. This will start the Manage Workspaces dialog box (see Figure 24.4).

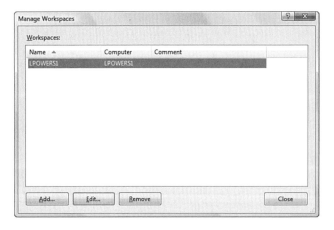

FIGURE 24.4    Managing workspaces.

From here, click on the Add button to open the Add Workspace dialog box (see Figure 24.5). In this dialog box, you provide the required information about the workspace and map the server-side source to a client-side folder.

After giving the workspace a name and indicating the owner and local machine name for it, you need to map a local folder to the source tree on the server. In the Working Folders table at the bottom of the dialog box, click in the Source Control Folder column on the line "Click here to enter a new working folder." This will create a new line in the table; you will now need to click on the ellipses button in the Source Control Folder column and select the source control project folder from the server that you want to mirror within your workspace (see Figure 24.6).

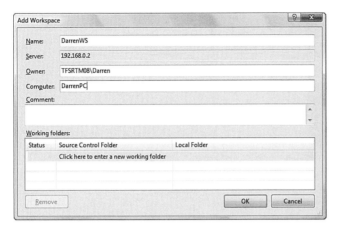

FIGURE 24.5    Creating a workspace.

Browse for Folder

Team Foundation Server:

192.168.0.2

Folders:

LitwareHR
  Litware.WebSite
  LitwareHR.Authentication.SvcHost
  LitwareHR.Authorization.SvcHost
  LitwareHR.Portfolio.Contract
  LitwareHR.Portfolio.Gateways
  LitwareHR.Portfolio.SecureHost
  LitwareHR.Portfolio.Services
  LitwareHR.Portfolio.UnSecureHost

Folder path:

$/LitwareHR Agile/LitwareHR/LitwareHR.Portfolio.Contract

FIGURE 24.6    Selecting the server source project.

**NOTE**

Don't get confused about the concept of project folders on the source control server. Although source control is implemented with a relational database, and not the file system, you still interact with the TFSC's repository as if it were a hierarchical folder-like store of the various projects and items stored in the source control system.

The last step is to select a folder from your file system that will function as the root level for your new workspace. Click in the Local Folder column, click on the ellipses button, and then select the local folder to link to the server source repository (see Figure 24.7). Clicking OK will bring you back to the Add Workspace dialog box.

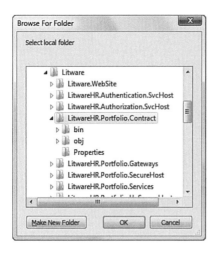

FIGURE 24.7     Selecting the local folder.

Click OK on the Add Workspace dialog box to actually create the workspace.

With the workspace established, you can now view the workspace using the Source Control Explorer. To open it, on the View menu, select Other Windows and then select Source Control Explorer.

Every workspace will initially be empty. If a file exists on the server but not locally, its filename will be grayed out. Figure 24.8 shows the workspace immediately after creation; all the files are grayed out, indicating that these are server-only copies at this point.

To actually populate the local workspace with the files from the Team Foundation source repository, you need to execute a Get Latest command. To do this, make sure you have the right workspace selected in the SCE's Workspace drop-down (refer to Figure 24.3), select the server project folder in the folders pane, and then click on the Get Latest (Recursive) button in the SCE's toolbar (again, see Figure 24.3).

## Adding Files to Source Control

Of course, you might be the one tasked with initially placing the source code files under source control. Suppose, for instance, that you have an existing Visual Studio solution that you need to place under source control. The same steps apply in terms of creating a workspace, but there won't be any files on the server yet—they will all be local. The source control system won't know anything about them, even though you may have mapped your local workspace folder onto the folder containing your solution files. In this case, you need to take the local files and add them to the server.

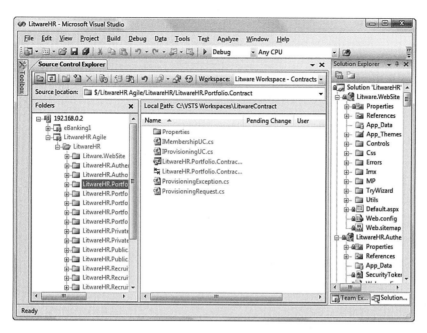

FIGURE 24.8    Server-side files in the Source Control Explorer.

The Solution Explorer is the tool used to do this: Right-click on the solution node in the Solution Explorer window and select Add Solution to Source Control.

At this point, the files will be placed into the pending changes list as *adds*. This means that the next time you perform a check-in, you will have the option of completing the operation and physically adding the files to the server. After the adds have been committed, the files will be available for checkout.

Using the Solution Explorer is the easiest way to add solutions and projects en masse to the source control system, but you can also use the Source Control Explorer to place files under source control. This is the preferred way to handle nonproject-related items. To add a file with the Source Control Explorer, follow these steps:

1.  Open the Source Control Explorer window.
2.  Using the folders pane, browse to the Team Project source folder where you want to place the file.
3.  Select the file, choose Source Control, and then Add to Source Control.
4.  In the dialog box, click OK. Figure 24.9 shows the Add to Source Control dialog box.

Again, as with the Solution Explorer, this procedure really only flags the file or files as pending adds. You must complete the operation by checking in the files. In the next section, we'll examine the check-in process and tool support from beginning to end.

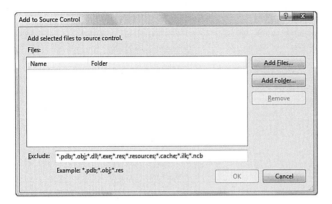

FIGURE 24.9    Adding files using the Source Control Explorer.

# Editing Files Under Source Control

So far, we have examined the fundamentals of getting the client workspace set up and using both the Solution Explorer and the Source Control Explorer to retrieve files from the Team Foundation source server or add files to the server. Now let's get to the heart of the source control mechanism: change management.

## Retrieving a File from the Source Repository

There are two ways to pull a file from the server source repository and place it into the local workspace: by using a Get Latest command or by using the Check Out command. Get Latest, as you saw in the previous examples relating to workspace management, simply retrieves the current version of the file as it exists on the server and copies it down into your workspace. You use the Check Out command to tell the system that you not only want the latest version of the file, but also intend to make changes to the file. This can mean one of two things depending on whether the TFSC system has been configured for exclusive or shared access: If it's exclusive, a lock will be placed on the file and no one else will be able to make changes as long as it is checked out by you. If it's shared, others are permitted to make changes to the file; these changes will later be merged with any changes you make to generate a new version that will ultimately be the one stored in the source repository.

> **NOTE**
>
> The exclusive versus shared access setting is actually dictated by the process template being used within your Team Project. For more information on process templates, consult Chapter 23, "Managing and Working with Team Projects," or the MSDN documentation for Team Foundation Server.

## Checking in Your Changes

When you are done with your changes, it is time to check those changes back into the source server. There are three ways to do this: You can right-click on the file in the Solution Explorer, you can right-click on the file in the Source Control Explorer, or you can use the Pending Changes window.

Using the Solution Explorer window, you right-click on the file you want to check in and select the Check In command from the context menu. The Check In dialog box, shown in Figure 24.10, is where the action happens. This dialog box contains a list of all the files currently available for check-in. Each file can be selected or deselected using a check box (the file you previously selected will already have its selection check box checked for you). You simply select any of the files you want included in the check-in process and then click on the Check In button. Notice that you can provide a comment as well (which is always a best practice to provide the check-in with some historical context on the reason for the change/check-in).

Buttons in the top toolbar allow you to control how the files are viewed, hide or show the comment area, or even filter the list of files based on the solution.

You can access this same window from the Source Control Explorer window: Select your file or files, right-click, and select the Check In command to view the Check In dialog box.

On the left side of the Check In dialog box are buttons—referred to as *channels*—used to place the dialog box into different modes. Besides the Source Files channel (which is shown in Figure 24.10), you can select channels for working with Work Items, Check-In Notes, and Policy Warnings. Before we get into these topics, let's examine the third way to check changes back into the source repository: through the Pending Changes window.

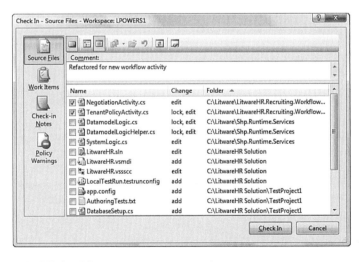

FIGURE 24.10   The Check In dialog box.

### Checking Changes with the Pending Changes Window

The Pending Changes window is implemented as a tool window in Visual Studio. You open it by selecting View, Other Windows, Pending Changes. You can also launch the window by right-clicking on any item within the Solution Explorer and selecting View Pending Changes.

As its name implies, this window, shown in Figure 24.11, contains a list of all pending changes within your current workspace. Every file you have checked out is visible in the window.

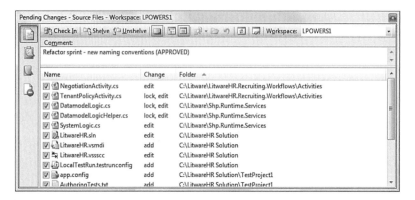

FIGURE 24.11    Viewing Pending Changes.

The Pending Changes window is structured identically to the Check In window and supports the same channels. There are just a few minor differences with the toolbar, which supports two new buttons: Shelve and Unshelve. We cover shelving later in this chapter.

### Understanding Check-In Policies

Project teams have different rules that users need to follow in determining whether a check-in is appropriate. For instance, checking in a class file that doesn't compile probably isn't a good idea. Anyone else performing a Get Latest operation or Check Out on the file would have his or her project "broken" because of your changes. Team Foundation Source Control recognizes the importance of vetting check-ins and provides a way to enforce certain rules on check-in through the use of check-in policies.

Three check-in policies are available out of the box with TFS:

- ▶ **Code Analysis Policy**—Ensures that certain code analysis tests have been run against the code before a check-in is allowed.

▶ **Testing Policy**—Ensures that certain tests (selected from a list of all known tests) have been run against the code before check-in.

▶ **Work Items Policy**—Requires that one or more work items be associated with a check-in.

Check-in policies are typically set up and configured on a per-project basis by project administrators; a default set of selected policies is usually turned on by the TFS process template currently in use. To configure which policies are in effect for your current project, you would access the Team Foundation Server source control settings available by selecting Team, Team Project Settings, Source Control Settings. The Source Control Settings window (see Figure 24.12) has a Check-in Policy tab, which allows you to select the specific policies to be enforced for the current project.

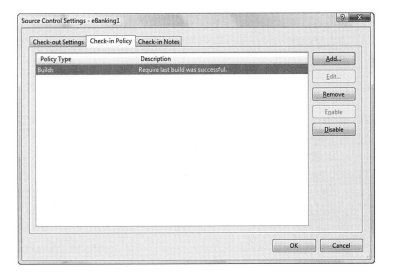

FIGURE 24.12    Adding a Check-in Policy to the current project.

Each policy may require additional settings. For instance, adding the Code Analysis policy will spawn yet another dialog box used to specify the exact code analysis tests that should be required (see Figure 24.13).

If check-in policies are in effect, select the Policy Warnings channel (in either the Check-In or the Pending Changes window), and you will see any policy violations. As an example, Figure 24.14 shows the policy warnings that result from enabling the Code Analysis policy and then attempting to check in a VB class file without running the Code Analyzer.

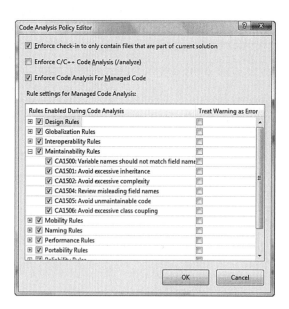

FIGURE 24.13    Configuring the Code Analysis Check-in Policy.

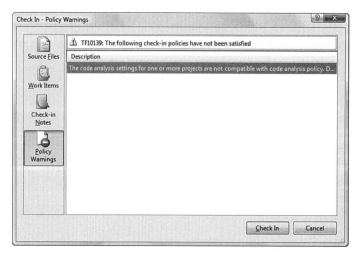

FIGURE 24.14    Policy warnings.

If you were to try to check in these files, a Policy Failure dialog box would launch (see Figure 24.15). You can choose to either abort the check-in and satisfy the policy, or override and provide a comment that explains your decision to circumvent the policy.

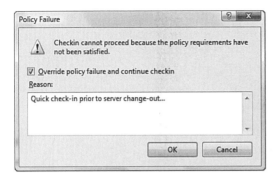

FIGURE 24.15   Overriding a policy failure.

**Adding a Check-in Note**

*Check-in notes* are short pieces of text you can attach to the check-in items during the check-in process. Check-in notes become a part of the file's historical metadata, are stored in the source repository, and can be viewed later so that you can get a sense for an item's change history.

A check-in note consists of a category name or prompt and the actual note text. By default, there are three note categories: security reviewer, code reviewer, and performance reviewer. When performing a check-in, you can click on the Check-in Notes channel button to enter notes. Each note prompt/category will appear with a corresponding text box that holds the text of the note (see Figure 24.16).

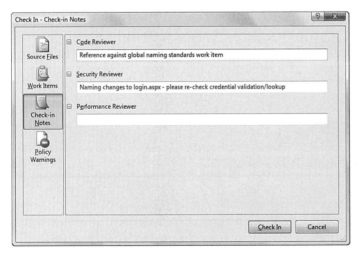

FIGURE 24.16   Adding notes to a check-in.

Check-in notes can be required for a project, and you can also add your own check-in note categories. These settings are managed from the Source Control Settings dialog box, which we covered during our discussion of check-in policy management. The Check-in Notes tab (see Figure 24.17) allows you to add or remove note categories.

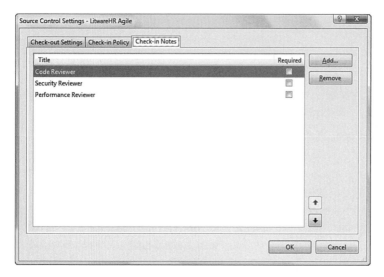

FIGURE 24.17    Managing Check-in Notes for a project.

For example, you could add a new note prompt for a knowledge base article number. Just click on the Add button, fill in the category/prompt text, and then select whether the note should be required (see Figure 24.18).

FIGURE 24.18    Adding a new Check-in Note category.

### Using Work Items

The last check-in feature we'll cover is the concept of relating check-ins to work items. *Work items*, which we cover in depth in the next chapter, are used to represent tasks within the project, from bug reports to traditional "to do" items. Work items can be linked to various artifacts within the Team Foundation system; check-ins are merely one of those items.

To associate a check-in with a work item, select the Work Items channel and then select from the list of available work items. By associating work items with a check-in, you help to integrate the various work sets from across the project into one cohesive representation of the project's progress. Consider, for example, a developer who has created a class library as part of her project tasks. After testing, she determines that one of her classes isn't responding as expected to one of the test cases. Instead of reporting an exception, the class is swallowing the exception. A bug is filed in the team system as a work item. To fix this problem, the developer checks out the class file, fixes the bug, and then checks the file back in. In the check-in dialog, she has the option of simply associating the work item to the check-in, or going one step further and indicating that this check-in actually resolves the bug documented in the work item (see Figure 24.19).

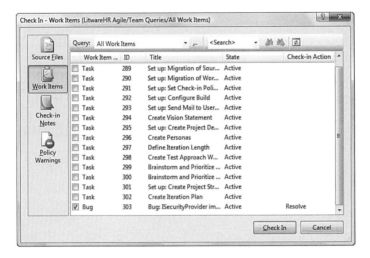

FIGURE 24.19   Associating a work item.

The work items that appear in the list are actually returned from a query that is run against the work item database. You can change the query by using the drop-down at the top of the Work Items channel window, or you can even perform a search across all work items. As mentioned, work items, queries, and many more work item topics are covered in Chapter 25, "Work Item Tracking."

## Understanding the Concept of Changesets

Until now, our discussion of the checkout/check-in process has been fairly simplistic, focusing on checking out a file, making changes, and then checking that file back in. In reality, what we have been talking about is the concept of *changesets*. A changeset is a compilation of *all* the information associated with a check-in operation.

To extend the prior bug-fix example, you may check out three different files to fix a bug. When you perform a check-in, you will check in all three of these files at the same time and associate their check-in with the bug work item. This is where the changeset concept comes into play: The changeset bundles these three files into a single entity. In other words, the bug is, rightly, associated with the three files as a whole. It is associated with the changeset. Any related work items, notes, and metadata about the code change (date, time, user) are all associated with the changeset as a whole, and not to the individual files.

---

**NOTE**

It is worth noting that check-ins and, by extension, changesets are atomic in nature. That is, Team Foundation Server guarantees that the entire changeset was committed in its entirety; you would never, for instance, attempt a check-in of three files and have only two of those files succeed in the transaction. All three of them go, or (in the case of an error) none of them goes.

---

The diagram in Figure 24.20 shows how changesets figure into the overall source control process.

Each changeset is assigned an incremental, numeric ID.

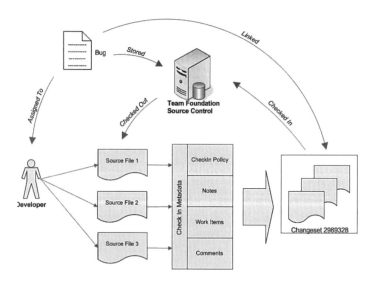

FIGURE 24.20    Changesets.

## Shelving Your Code

Sometimes, developers may need to set aside their current work or move on to other tasks before the files are ready for check-in. For instance, you may be in the middle of working on some code files when an urgent bug is logged that requires your attention. Or perhaps you haven't quite completed a required code change before leaving on vacation. In these scenarios, you don't want to check in your work because it is incomplete. You also don't want to leave the work checked out locally onto your box for what may be a lengthy period. Shelving allows you to take some or all of your pending changes and store them back into the TFS source repository database without checking them in.

Shelving works in a similar way to the check-in process, and is handled by the Shelve window. To open the Shelve window, you can click on the Shelve button in the Pending Changes window, or you can click on the Shelve Pending Changes button in the Source Control Explorer. Alternatively, you can use the Solution Explorer: Right-click on a file and select Shelve Pending Changes.

When you shelve your code, you are creating a *shelveset*, which is identical to a changeset but applies to shelved code only. You will be prompted to name your shelveset so that it can be retrieved later. Figure 24.21 shows code files being shelved from the Shelve window.

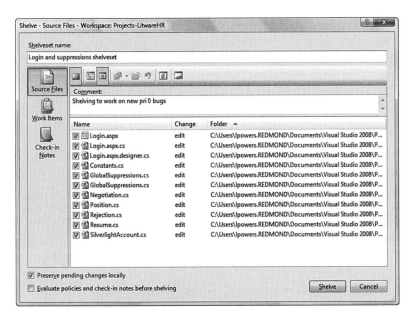

FIGURE 24.21    Shelving code changes.

### Unshelving Files

After a shelveset has been created, you have the option to unshelve that shelveset at any point in time. This will return all the shelved files into your workspace. Click on the Unshelve button in the Pending Changes window to launch the Unshelve window.

All your previously created shelvesets will be visible; you simply select the one you want and click the Unshelve button (see Figure 24.22). Note that you can change the owner name field and initiate a new search for any shelvesets that belong to that user.

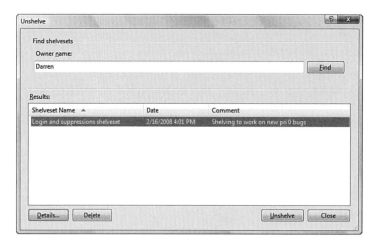

FIGURE 24.22    Unshelving code changes.

## Merging Changes

When we introduced the checkout process, we mentioned that checkouts can be exclusive or shared. In the case of shared checkouts, in which more than one person is actively changing the same file, Team Foundation provides a way to merge those changes into a new changeset that will replace the current file version on the server.

Let's examine a common scenario: Developer A checks out a class file and works on a method within the class. While the file is checked out, Developer B is assigned a bug and has to work on a different method contained in the same code file. Developer B then checks out the file and works on his method. Developer A checks in her changes, and then a day later Developer B checks in his changes. At this point, a conflict exists: Because Developer B never had a copy of the source file in his workspace with Developer A's changes, something needs to be done to merge the two files. This situation is handled with the merge tool.

When Developer B starts to check in his file, Team Foundation source control will automatically detect a conflict. This will result in the Resolve Conflicts window being displayed (see Figure 24.23).

To resolve the conflicts in the identified file, you click on the Resolve button, which launches yet another screen—the Resolve Version Conflict window, shown in Figure 24.24—that provides some more details on the file conflict and offers some options for rectifying the conflict.

There are four options available for proceeding:

▶ Allow Visual Studio to automatically merge the changes.

▶ Merge the changes in the two files using the merge tool.

▶ Undo the changes that were made to the local copy of the file.

▶ Undo the changes that were made to the server copy of the file.

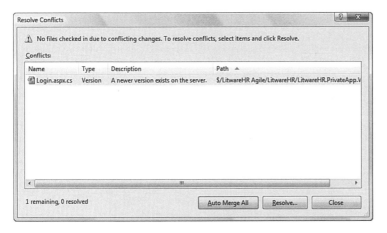

FIGURE 24.23   The Resolve Conflicts window.

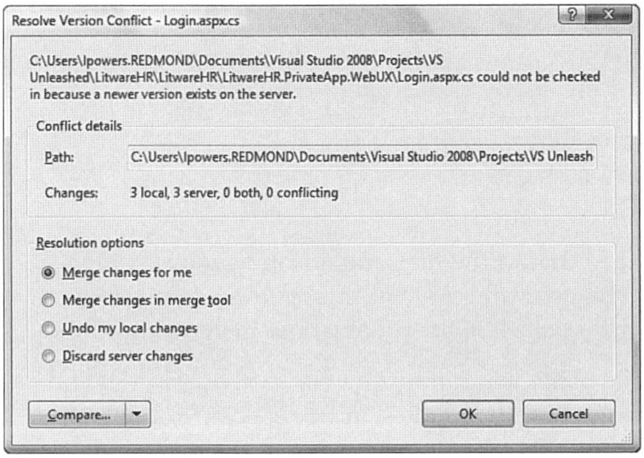

**24**

FIGURE 24.24   The Resolve Version Conflict window.

In all but the simplest cases, you will need to use the merge tool to explicitly tell Visual Studio how to handle the conflict. To assist with understanding the nature of the conflict, you can also launch the File Comparison tool from this window.

### Comparing File Differences

The File Comparison tool, shown in Figure 24.25, provides a simple side-by-side view of the two files, the server file and the local file, and visually highlights the textual differences between the two through a highlighting scheme. Blue represents changed text, green represents inserted text, and red represents deleted text.

You can't actually edit the files using this tool; that needs to take place with the merge tool.

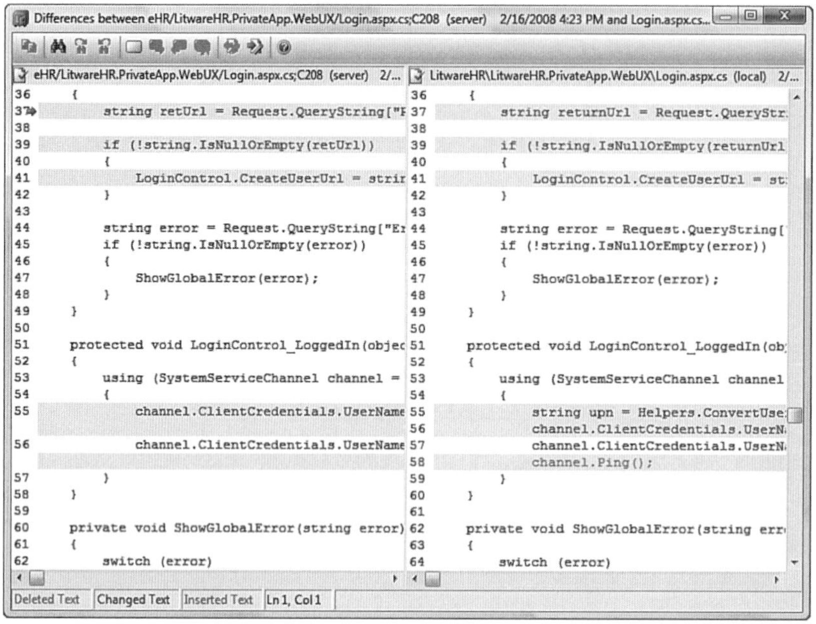

FIGURE 24.25    Using the File Comparison tool.

### Using the Merge Tool

The merge tool provides a view similar to that in the file comparison window: It highlights the textual differences between the two windows. But this tool shows a third view as well: the results of a merged file. See Figure 24.26 for a look at the merge tool window.

By moving the cursor in the merged file pane, you can move your current position and then insert changes from either of the two conflicting files. In this specific example, we wanted to add two methods to the merged file. One method exists in the server copy, and the other method exists in the local copy. To create the merged file, you would first select the change highlighted in the server copy (upper-left pane). This will insert that block of changed text into the blank merged copy (bottom pane). You can then reposition the cursor location to some point after the newly added method text and then click on the highlighted, changed text in the local copy (upper-right pane). The merge tool will add this text into the merged file as well, resulting in the desired outcome: a new version of the source file that combines the content of the server copy and the local copy.

# Branching and Merging

*Branching* and *merging* refer to two different but related processes for managing the source code tree within the Team Foundation Server repository. These operations are often performed by development teams that need to execute on different versions of the code in parallel and then, at some point, bring those changes back together for a release path through the source tree.

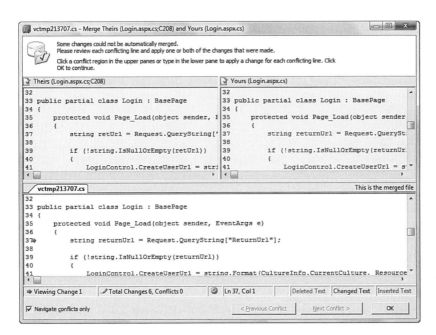

FIGURE 24.26   Merging changes.

Owing to both the nature of iterative development and the circumstances of the modern software market, development teams often have complex needs in terms of maintaining their source code tree. The source code tree is essentially a hierarchical look at the various code files that constitute a solution by version. To solidify the idea behind branching, let's discuss the problem space in the context of a work scenario.

Assume that a development team is hard at work on a market-revolutionizing piece of software. Part of the team's product plan involves a rapid version 1.0 release to really nail the fundamentals, with a very quick follow-up that contemplates some of the more diffi-cult design problems. The product management team decides to tackle this effort with two different development teams. One will start the initial architecture and development work for version 1.0. When enough architecture, design, and code base exists, the second team will start working on version 2.0. Because their development phases overlap, in a sense, their source code will as well.

Consider the diagram in Figure 24.27; it depicts a versioned view of the source tree and highlights the need for the version 2.0 efforts to work from, or branch from, the initial 1.0 efforts. Then, at some point, the fully complete 1.0 bits will be merged into the 2.0 tree. Notice as well that the product team anticipates a patch release to address the inevitable issues in the 2.0 code base. These changes will also need to branch and merge in the source tree.

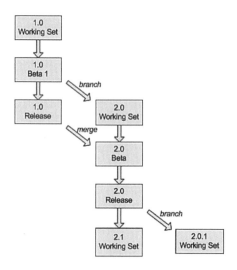

FIGURE 24.27    Branching and merging a source tree.

## Branching

Branching, just as it sounds, is the act of copying code from the current source tree and putting that code into a new branch of the tree. An easy way to understand this concept is to think of this space in terms of folders: To branch is to take a current folder of code (called the source) and create a new folder with a copy of the source's code (called the target). In other words, you can think of branching as a file system copy operation: You take the files in one location and make a copy of them in another location. Development is then free to continue within both folders in a parallel fashion.

Branching in Team Foundation is performed using the Source Control Explorer. You first need to navigate to the source folder on the server; then you right-click on the folder and select Branch. In the Branch dialog box (see Figure 24.28), you provide a name for the new branch (or target folder) and select a version of code from the source folder. Click OK to create the branch; it will be immediately visible in the Source Control Explorer.

FIGURE 24.28    Branching source using the Source Control Explorer.

## Merging

Merging is the opposite of branching: Instead of forking one element of the source tree, it combines two elements of the source tree into one.

As with branching, you kick off the process from the Source Control Explorer. Right-click one of the source folders that will participate in the merge and then select Merge.

The Source Control Merge Wizard (see Figure 24.29) will collect all the needed information about the merge operation. Specifically, you will be asked to provide

- ► The source branch

- ► The target branch

- ► The changes you want to merge (all within the source branch or only specific changesets)

- ► The source versions you want to merge

Clicking Finish at the end of the wizard will complete the merge.

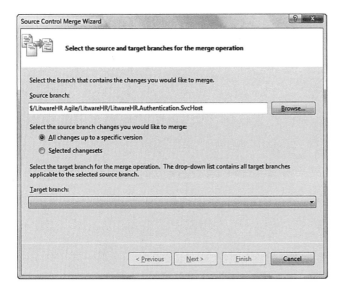

FIGURE 24.29    Using the Source Control Merge Wizard.

# Summary

In this chapter, we took an end-to-end look at the tools and capabilities of the Team Foundation source control system. We presented the architecture of the server-side aspects and discussed how Team Foundation leverages Windows and SQL Server to provide an eminently reliable and scalable infrastructure for source control services.

We described the basic concepts behind source control and investigated how Team Foundation delivers on those essentials.

In addition, we painted a picture of the powerful suite of tools that Visual Studio Team System users have at their disposal for handling policy compliance, branching and merging, and source management. We also examined how to use the source control tools for various tasks:

▶ Setting up new workspaces

▶ Checking out files from the source repository

▶ Checking in changesets

▶ Shelving file changes

▶ Resolving check-in conflicts

▶ Branching and merging the source tree

Because all these tools are integrated into the Visual Studio IDE, and because the source control system itself is integrated into the larger concepts of process management, Team Foundation source control truly provides a seamless experience with the rest of the project development tasks and activities.

# CHAPTER 25

# Work Item Tracking

The process of developing software on a team can be as difficult as writing the actual code. Developers want to be free to focus on writing great code. However, clients, project sponsors, project managers, testers, and others are just as interested in tracking the progress of that code and determining the overall state of the project. Keeping everyone in the loop requires time-consuming meetings. These meetings generate reports that are often out of synch with what is really happening before the target audience has a chance to review them.

A similar challenge is getting actual, meaningful metrics. This can be problematic at best. Project managers are often left to interpret the ramblings of team members as they take turns reporting their progress in weekly meetings. This data, by its very nature, represents only a small view of reality on the project. Therefore, in the absence of real statistical measures, a divide begins to open between what is happening on a project and what is being reported.

Many software development shops have become good at managing this divide. They become better and better at estimating, reporting, and tracking progress. To do so, they have implemented methodologies such as Agile, SCRUM, RUP, MSF, CMMI, and Extreme Programming. These methodologies have been an important part of helping the software development process to mature. However, the tools to support these methodologies within a development platform are just now taking hold.

With Team Foundation Server and work item tracking, you can get back to writing great code while still providing the information on the state and progress of that code. Just as importantly, other team members can provide you with key information within the IDE. This includes test results, requirements management, scenarios, and more.

This chapter focuses squarely on work items as they are the bit of information that gets tracked in the software process and provide the much-needed metrics on that process. We will look at work items from the perspective of various team members in the Software Development Life Cycle (SDLC). We will then explore the tools built into Visual Studio 2008 for working with and customizing work items.

---

**NOTE**

Review Chapter 22, "Team Collaboration and Visual Studio Team System," for a better understanding of the methodologies that ship with TFS. This chapter focuses specifically on work items and how they relate to the development process and Visual Studio 2008. Where appropriate, we discuss work items in context with MSF Agile and CMMI. However, work items are only part of the overall methodology picture.

When you define a project website, Team System creates pages that define process guidance around the selected methodology. These pages are required reading and can provide a quick reference if you ever lose your context within the methodology.

---

# Understanding Work Items

A *work item* in Visual Studio Team System is just what it sounds like: a definition of work for a development project. A work item is responsible for recording that work, allowing the work to be assigned, tracked, related to other work, and reported on. Like a project task, a work item has a title and description of the work to be done. It has a current owner, a history, related information, an associated life cycle (or workflow), and a current state. The difference, however, is that unlike with a simple project task, all the work item information is maintained in a central server and is at once accessible to all team members as work happens. It is for this reason that work items are the fundamental driver behind the power of communication and collaboration in Team System.

## Understanding the Role of Work Items and the SDLC

The actual work items themselves can be defined to represent the wide variety of work executed on any given project. Work items can be created for project requirements, tasks, change requests, code reviews, bugs, and so on. Work items provide enough customization to cover the entire SDLC and its associated roles. They can be created by, assigned to, and worked on by developers, architects, business analysts, testers, and project managers. For these reasons, work items are the core nugget for driving a software project forward. All work can be done through, and tracked by, a work item.

To get the most out of Team Foundation Server and its reports, you need to track all work done on a project through a work item. Before starting work, all team members should ask themselves, "What work item am I using to track this work?" This, coincidentally, is also good project management. Project managers can only predict work they can see and track.

## Picking the Work Item Set for Your Project

Most projects that leverage Team Systems will use a set of predefined work items. Each work item set covers the SDLC for a given development methodology. You can create custom work items and even custom methodologies for Team Systems (more on these later). However, the most common scenario is to define a project based on one of the methodologies that ship with Team Systems: MSF for Agile Software Development and MSF for CMMI Process Improvement (both discussed in Chapter 22).

Team Systems generate a set of work item definitions for your project when you choose the methodology you want to employ on your new project. The actual work items associated with a methodology are based on the driving principles behind the given methodology. These work items define the fields, states, and transitions of the work that will be done on the project. In addition, they generate the metrics for reports that let team members know the state of the project at any given time. Let's explore these core work items across both methodologies that ship with TFS.

Due to the success of Visual Studio Team System, additional third-party add-ons have been developed. These include additional project methodologies that include associated work items and reports. We suggest you start by understanding those that ship with Team Systems. You can then look to see whether another methodology suites your team better.

### MSF for Agile Work Items

The MSF Agile methodology is driven by scenarios. Scenarios describe what the application must do from a user's perspective. They also define various service-level requirements for performance and security. They are meant to get the team working together with customers on a common vision while staying flexible with respect to change. Ultimately, the scenarios drive the tasks that will be executed by the team to realize the customer's vision.

This is the full set of work items for the MSF Agile methodology:

▶ Scenario

▶ Quality of Service Requirement

▶ Task

- Bug

- Risk

Let's look at each of these work items in more depth.

**Scenario Work Item**    A scenario defines a user's interaction with the system to complete a specific goal or task. If you have ever created or worked with use cases, scenarios will seem very familiar. Typically, a scenario will define a common, successful path to achieve a user's goal. In addition, it may relate to alternative scenarios that define alternative (sometimes unsuccessful) paths through the system.

MSF process guidance suggests that the team initially brainstorm the list of possible scenarios for the system. Of course, these scenarios should relate to the overall vision of the project. Each scenario is then assigned to a business analyst (or customer/subject-matter expert) to define and describe. Ultimately, the scenarios will be broken down into tasks that the team members can complete to realize the given scenario (and thus the project's vision).

The key fields defined for a scenario include the following:

- **Description**—This field provides a high-level overview of the given scenario. MSF Agile recommends that the actual scenario be created as a Word document (a template is provided for this inside the project portal).

- **History**—This field tracks the scenario as changes are made.

- **Rank**—This field is used by the team to indicate the priority relative to other scenarios in the system.

- **Integration build**—This field is used to indicate the actual build where the scenario is implemented. This is important information for the test team.

- **Rough order of magnitude**—This field is used to indicate the relative complexity of the scenario. It may seem early to start estimating. However, this important information can be used to determine whether a scenario should move forward (before additional time and money are spent).

**Quality of Service (QoS) Requirement Work Item**    A QoS requirement defines how a given system should operate after it is complete. These work items come in the form of load, performance, platform, stress, security requirements, and the ubiquitous "other" category. Their purpose is to get the team on the same page with respect to what is expected overall for the system. For instance, a QoS requirement might define that all user interaction in the user interface can be performed in less than a second. This requirement might dictate that the team creates a rich client application rather than a browser-based client.

The fields used to define a QoS requirement are nearly identical to those of a scenario. The MSF Agile process guidance suggests that the QoS requirement is fully defined inside the fields of the work item. You can attach additional documents to your QoS requirements, but there should not be a specific need to do so (as is the case with a scenario).

**Task Work Item**   A task work item is just what it sounds like: a project task that signals a team member to execute some work on the project. Like other work items, tasks are assigned to team members. However, task items are typically the work items that make the project schedule. For example, there may be a task to create a new scenario. This task might be assigned to a business analyst on the team.

When you define a task, you select the discipline to which the task belongs. Disciplines are similar to the roles on the project; they include architecture, development, project management, release management, requirements, and testing. These disciplines help to imply meaning behind the state, which describes the current progress of a task (more on this in a moment).

**Bug Work Item**   A bug work item is used to report a problem with the system. Typically, testers and users report issues. These are recorded and then assigned for fixing. The bug work item allows for defect management and tracking in Team Systems.

The following are a few key fields related to a bug work item:

▶ **Priority**—The priority field indicates whether the bug is a showstopper or something minor.

▶ **Found in build/resolved in build**—The build fields allow you to indicate which version of the code the bug was originally found in and where it was fixed. This ensures that the developers and testers stay on the same page.

▶ **Test name/test path**—The test fields allow you to indicate which actual tests were used to produce the bug. This information can help a developer reproduce the bug.

▶ **Triage**—The triage field is used to indicate whether the bug has been approved to work on or requires further investigation. Bugs are typically triaged by a project manager. They may be sent for additional investigation and estimation before being assigned to get fixed.

**Risk Work Item**   A risk work item allows the team to proactively track and manage project risk. Risks to a project represent anything that might have a negative impact on the project in terms of quality, cost, schedule, and so on.

You define a risk by indicating its description (and related fields). Some additional key fields include severity and rank. Severity indicates the likelihood of the risk to occur along with the impact of that risk. Severity is defined as critical, high, medium, or low.

### MSF for CMMI Work Items

The MSF for CMMI methodology is not unlike that of MSF Agile. In fact, they share some of the same core principles and ideas regarding quality, customers, and adaptation to change. The CMMI methodology, however, helps development teams to be assessed by a third party in terms of their commitment to process and continuous improvement. It is not meant to be a larger or more complex process. It, too, should be lightweight and sized to fit the project.

## 25

The work items that drive MSF for CMMI are also similar to those found in the MSF for Agile method. For example, MSF for CMMI also drives a project through requirements and tasks.

The full set of work items for MSF for CMMI includes the following:

▶ Requirement

▶ Task

▶ Change request

▶ Risk

▶ Review

▶ Bug

▶ Issue

Let's examine each of these items in turn.

**Requirement Work Item**    We've discussed how MSF for Agile defines two work items for defining requirements (scenario and QoS). MSF for CMMI, on the other hand, defines a single requirement work item. When you create a new requirement work item under MSF for CMMI, you define the requirement's type. You can then delineate between a scenario and a QoS requirement. In fact, the requirement work item for CMMI has seven types by default: functional, interface, operational, quality of service, safety, scenario, and security.

Some additional fields of note for the requirement work item include the following:

▶ **Subject matter experts**—This section allows you to choose up to three people who can provide additional expert-level information with respect to the given requirement.

▶ **Impact assessment**—This field allows you to indicate the overall impact of the given requirement if it is not realized or implemented.

▶ **User acceptance test (UAT)**—This field allows you to track whether the requirement is ready for UAT or has passed/failed UAT.

**Task Work Item**    The task work item is meant to trigger a team member to execute work and to track that work. For example, an architect may break down a scenario requirement into a number of developer implementation tasks. These tasks are assigned and tracked by the project manager. Tasks can be assigned to all roles on the project.

**Change Request Work Item**    The change request work item allows you to track and manage the inevitable on all software projects: change. Some projects might simply roll with the changes. Other, more formal projects will require documentation of the change and an assessment of its impact. This change will then be presented to a change control board for a decision. When the decision is made to accept the change, a new set of task work items will result, altering the baseline schedule and costs.

Typically, a business analyst (or similar) creates the change request work items and obtains impact and analysis relative to the request. This information is stored in a few key areas on the work item:

- ▶ **Description**—This field is used to describe the request.

- ▶ **Justification**—This field tells readers why the request is being logged and the value it brings to the overall project.

- ▶ **Analysis**—This section of the work item lets you address the impact of the request across five key project elements: architecture, user experience, test, development, and technical documentation.

**Risk Work Item**    The risk work item allows team members to log items that have a potential to impact the project in a negative way. The MSF for CMMI risk work item allows users to enter a mitigation plan along with events that might trigger that plan. In addition, users document a contingency plan that describes what to do in the event that the risk actually presents itself on the project.

**Review Work Item**    The review work item allows you to document the outcome of a given code or document review. A best practice on most development projects is to do a review of scenarios, requirements, design, and code. These reviews may be offline or done as a meeting. In addition, these reviews may be iterative in that they continue to occur until the item passes the review. All of this can be tracked by the review work item.

The review work item has a type field to indicate whether the review was a meeting or done offline. In addition, there are fields to indicate who did the review (or attended the meeting). These fields allow for up to eight iterations through a given review. The results of the review are tracked via the minutes field. This is where a reviewer might document requested action items relative to the review.

**Bug Work Item**    A bug work item allows team members to indicate perceived problems with the system. These bugs are documented, triaged, prioritized, and categorized by severity.

**Issue Work Item**    The issue work item allows team members to log issues that are blocking progress on the project. These are not risks. Rather, issues are real things that require actions (not potential risks). After an issue is identified, a set of tasks should be created to resolve the issue.

The issue work item allows for the definition of priority, impact to project, escalation, and corrective action. Priority indicates the order in which issues should be dealt with. The impact of the issue is defined in terms of critical, medium, high, or low. The escalate field indicates whether the issue should be escalated because it is blocking the project in some manner. Finally, corrective action allows you to define the agreed-to plan for solving the issue.

## Identifying Work Item Commonalities

You should now have a basic understanding of the many work items defined by both MSF methodologies. Again, you choose a single methodology for your project and inherit the work item set associated with your choice. By examining all work items across both methodologies, you've seen that there are many similarities between the two. In fact, work items in general have a lot in common with one another.

Work item commonalities are not an accident. The term *work item* itself is a generic abstraction, the concrete implementation of which are the various work items we've been discussing (bug, task, risk, and so on). Work items are created and managed by a work item framework. Therefore, when you understand how a work item works in that framework, you will essentially understand how they all work. The following sections define and discuss those commonalities.

> **NOTE**
>
> For the remainder of this chapter, we will discuss and present sample work items from the MSF for CMMI methodology. Everything we discuss is still applicable to MSF for Agile. However, focusing on a single methodology will simplify discussion. In addition, you should find it easy to move from the MSF for CMMI methodology concepts to MSF for Agile (if required).

### Work Item Areas and Iterations

Work item areas and iterations allow you to categorize and group work and define when that work will be executed. This information is defined for your entire project (typically by the project manager). Areas and iterations are typically project-specific and are therefore not predefined by the methodology. Each work item is then classified in terms of its area and iteration.

Although we covered the basics of areas and iterations in Chapter 23, "Managing and Working with Team Projects," let's dig deeper and see how they directly relate to work items and project management.

You define areas and iterations through the Areas and Iterations dialog box, which you can access from Visual Studio's Team Explorer. To open it, you right-click the team project you want to define and then choose Team Project Settings, Areas and Iterations. Figure 25.1 provides an example of accessing this dialog box.

**Areas**    An area represents a category used to group work. Many times this is referred to as a module or feature set. For example, a project may break down work by defining a user account profile module, an order entry module, an order history module, or an inventory module. These modules or areas are used to group tasks and other work items in the system. This capability is useful for reporting and tracking. Areas can also be defined in a hierarchical structure. This allows for the definition of subareas and the like.

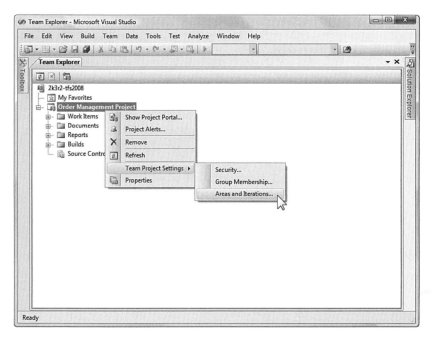

FIGURE 25.1    Accessing the Areas and Iterations dialog box.

You create areas using Visual Studio Team Explorer and the Areas and Iterations dialog box. You've already seen how to access this dialog box. Figure 25.2 shows the dialog box along with a definition of a few areas (modules) for a sample project.

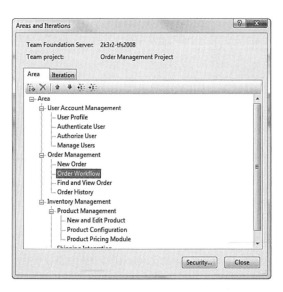

FIGURE 25.2    Defining the areas for a project.

Notice that you can define areas in a hierarchy. This allows for the creation of areas and subareas (modules and submodules). The toolbar in this dialog box allows you to position each item in the correct order and hierarchy.

Notice the Security button at the bottom of the dialog box. It allows you to configure the security associated with this area. For example, you can indicate who on the team is allowed to create, edit, and view work items associated with a given area.

Clicking the Security button brings up the Project Security dialog box. It is important to note that this dialog box is specific to the actual node (area) you have selected. For example, if you select the User Profile node and click this button, you will be defining security for the area User Profile. Figure 25.3 shows this dialog box and the permissions that can be set.

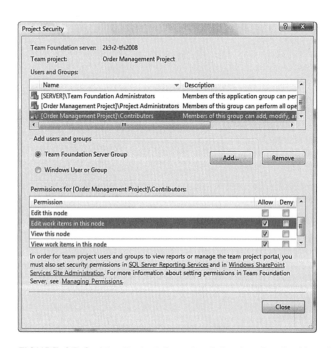

FIGURE 25.3   The Project Security dialog box for the User Profile area.

**Iterations**   An iteration represents a time period on the project in which you will execute some portion of the work. The intent of an iteration is to time-box some set of work items that will be delivered in a specific window of time. You may define 30-day sprints, for example. In addition, iterations may overlap one another for various reasons. Typically, this is the result of a handoff between team members or groups on the project.

For example, suppose you define four iterations for your project. Each iteration may be defined as a 30-day time-box. You would go through the full life cycle of development for a subset of functionality during each of these iterations. You might define two to four areas or modules to be developed during each iteration.

Suppose you start the first iteration by doing architecture and design for the first two modules. After those modules are designed, the iteration might continue with the designers passing the specification off to the development team. The designers might then begin working on the next iteration. When the first iteration is developed and unit-tested, it might be passed to a quality assurance team. At this time, the developers might begin working on coding the design for the second iteration. This process would continue through the iterations. Notice how each iteration overlaps the others.

Clearly, this process requires a mature team and toolset to work smoothly. In addition, there can be many variations on these cycles. Team Systems allows you to define the iterations for your project and then classify work items in terms of their iteration. Figure 25.4 shows the Iteration tab on the Areas and Iterations dialog box.

Notice that you can define sub-iterations under a given iteration. This capability can be helpful for certain reporting purposes. However, we've discovered that most teams find it sufficient to have four to six top-level iterations for the project. Each might be time-boxed into eight-week increments: two weeks for design, four weeks for development, and two more weeks for integration and user acceptance testing.

---

**TIP**

If you modify areas or iterations, you will have to execute a refresh in Team Explorer before these changes are reflected in the work item definitions.

---

FIGURE 25.4    Defining the iterations for a project.

### Work Item States and Transitions

Work items are tracked through the State and Reason fields. Together, these fields define the state in which a work item exists at any given time, the state to which it can transition (move), and the reason the work item might move from one state to another. This seemingly simple process is used to track all work items in Team Systems. Let's look at an example of how this works.

For this example, we will look at the states of a bug work item. Figure 25.5 shows the state diagram for a bug (from the process guidance).

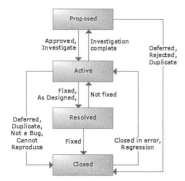

FIGURE 25.5    The Bug States and Transitions diagram from the MSF for CMMI process guidance.

The boxes on the state diagram indicate the states in which a bug can exist. The arrows represent the transitions between the states. An arrow from one state to another indicates a possible transition. The verbiage associated with the transition represents the reason behind the transition.

As an example, suppose you have a bug in the Active state. This bug could be transitioned back to the Proposed state or on to Resolved or Closed. Moving the bug back to Proposed would be valid only when the bug was moved to Active for the purpose of doing more investigation. When that investigation is complete, it would move back to Proposed so that it could be triaged. If the bug is moved to Resolved, it was either fixed or determined not to be a bug (as designed). If the bug is moved to Closed from Active, the possible reasons include that it was deferred, was a duplicate item, was not really a bug, or cannot be reproduced.

All work items in Team Systems work in this manner. Again, the work item State and Reason fields make this workflow easy to manage. In fact, the work item editor inside Team Explorer enforces these transitions and reasons. It will allow a work item to move only to a valid state, and the transition reasons are also enforced. Figure 25.6 demonstrates this through a bug work item moving from the Active state to Closed. When doing so, you must select a reason (as shown).

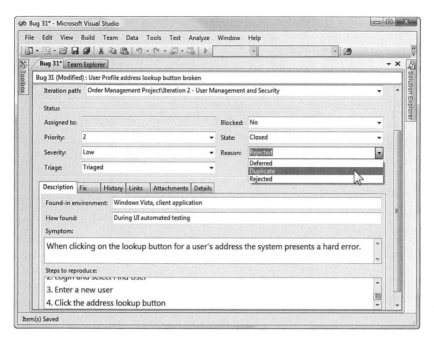

FIGURE 25.6    Moving a bug from Active to Closed.

### Tracking Work Item History

As a work item is changed, Team System automatically logs the history of that change. You can review an item's history through the History tab on the given work item. Each change is stored in an entry. The entries are categorized by date and time of change, along with the name of the person who executed the change. Figure 25.7 shows a bug work item's history.

Notice that in Figure 25.7, you can determine which fields changed between work item history records. In addition, users can enter their comments in this tab (Type your comment here). These comments are embedded in the work item history. This allows for a recorded discussion relative to the given work item.

Figure 25.8 shows another history record for the same item. This record was the result of moving the bug from Closed back to Active. Note the comment in the history record. Also notice that only the fields that are changed are tracked in the history.

### Linking Work Items

Often you will need to link work items together. Linking these items helps provide a better understanding of the system and the work that is being created. It keeps people on the same page and facilitates better reporting. As an example, suppose you write a user scenario. It would be good to know which requirements were created as a result of the scenario. You might also like to know which tasks were generated from each requirement.

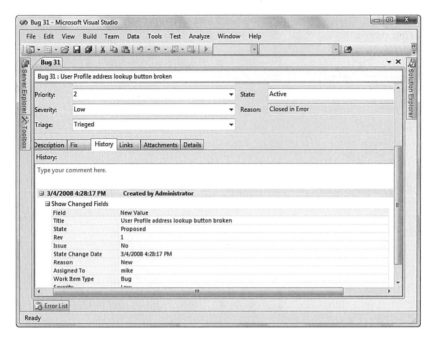

FIGURE 25.7    Tracking history for a work item.

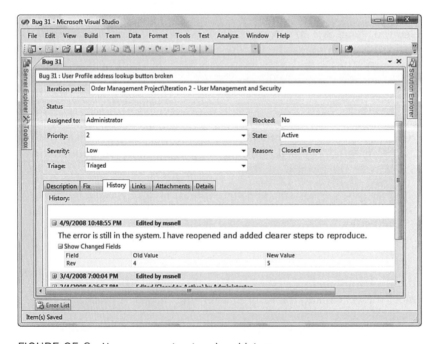

FIGURE 25.8    User comments stored as history.

If you take this example even further, you might want to link issues and change requests to tasks and/or requirements.

Ultimately, you can then use metrics to determine the success of a given requirement or scenario. A scenario that resulted in no change requests and fewer issues means that the scenario was well written, understood, and agreed to by the team, whereas a scenario that ended up spawning many issues and change requests could mean that the scenario was not understood, not agreed to, or poorly written.

As another example, if you have a task that is blocked because of an issue or risk, you might want to link that task to the work items that were created to unblock the task.

You define a work item link using the Links tab for the given work item. This tab presents the various links already established for the work item. You can view, edit, and delete an existing link. You can also establish a new link from here. Figure 25.9 shows the Add Link dialog box.

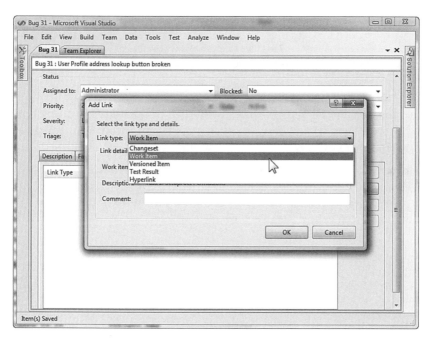

FIGURE 25.9    Adding a link to a work item.

Notice that when adding a link to a work item, you are asked to browse to that work item. Clicking the Browse button will bring up the Choose Related Work Item dialog box, shown in Figure 25.10. From here, you can search the work item database and find those items you want to link. In the example used for these dialog boxes, a bug is being linked to a related development task.

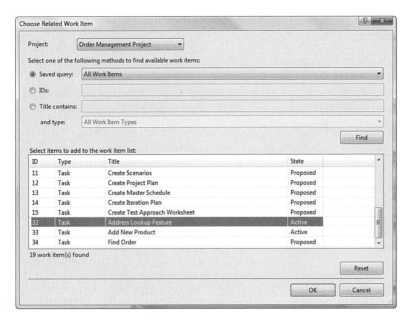

FIGURE 25.10    Finding the work item to link.

After you've selected the link and clicked OK, you are returned to the Add Link dialog box (see Figure 25.11). The work item ID and description are populated for you. You can add a comment to the link and then click OK to establish your link.

Not all links are between two work items. You can establish a link from a work item to other things, too. This includes linking a work item to a web page (hyperlink), a source control changeset, a versioned item, or a test result. You use a similar set of dialog boxes for each of these additional items.

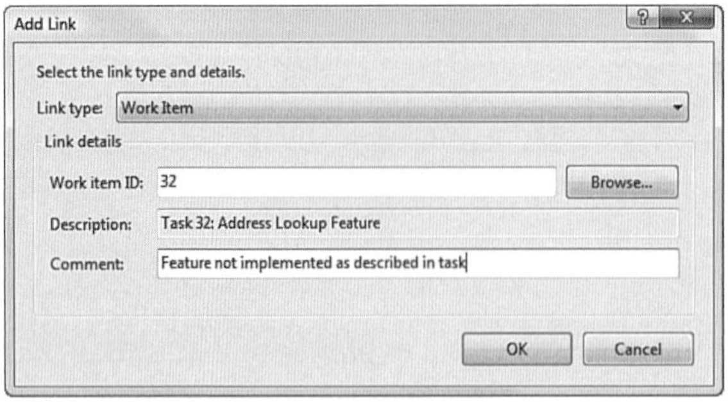

FIGURE 25.11    Adding a work item link.

**Attaching Files**

You can also attach files directly to work items. This capability is useful if, for example, you want to attach a screenshot to a bug or perhaps the Word document associated to a scenario.

The interface for attaching files is similar to that of establishing links. An Attachments tab lists all attachments. From here, you can add, delete, view, and update file attachments to work items.

# Using Team Explorer to Manage Work Items

If you install one of the Team editions of Visual Studio, you have the right license to connect to Team Foundation Server. However, you may not have the tools. You need to install the Team Explorer client tools. You can find this install on the Team Foundation Server media. These tools are the principal means for interacting with work items using Visual Studio. The following sections cover the basic functionality of these tools. Following this discussion, we will illustrate how various project roles work using these same tools.

## Creating a New Work Item

You can create a new work item through Team Explorer or the Team menu. When you do so, you must choose the work item type. Again, the types available for your project are dependent on methodology and customizations that might have been made. Figure 25.12 shows how to create a new task work item using the Team menu.

When you select the work item type, you are presented with a screen to define the work item. From here, you can define the work item's title, assign the work item, enter a description, add attachments, and so on. Figure 25.13 shows the definition of a new task work item. Notice the task work item's Discipline field. Here, you can indicate whether this is a development task, business analysis, test, and so on.

Figure 25.14 shows the Details tab on the work item. It contains some key functionality that we have not yet discussed. Most of these features apply to all work items. Features include scheduling the task, identifying its related build, indicating that it requires review, and associating it to a test (not shown).

A work item task is scheduled through estimation. The person assigned the work item should indicate the number of hours estimated and the number of hours completed; then the number of hours remaining is estimated as Estimate to Complete. This information is used by Project and other applications to show scheduling. From this data, you can calculate how you are tracking against your estimate, how much of the time has elapsed, and what remains. The start and finish dates are entered as tasks are started and finished.

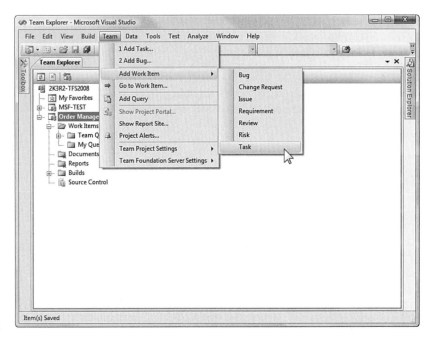

FIGURE 25.12    Creating a new work item.

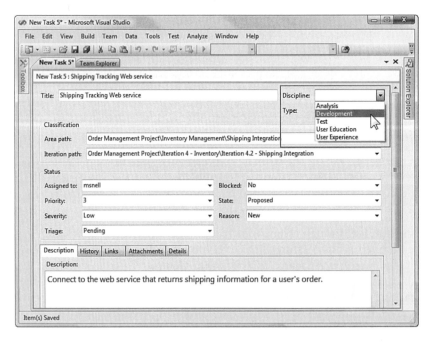

FIGURE 25.13    A new work item's dialog box.

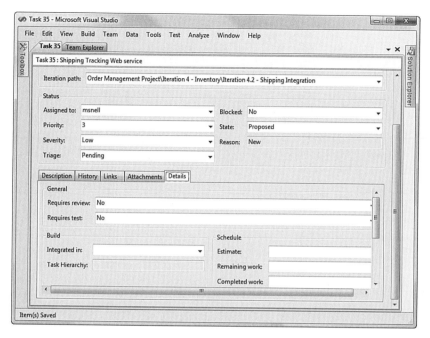

FIGURE 25.14    Work item details.

## Finding and Filtering Work Items

You often need to find the work item or work item set with which you want to work. For doing so, Team Explorer provides a query engine. Each query is run against the work item database and returns a subset of information. In this way, you can quickly zero in on your next task.

A number of default queries ship out of the box (dependent on chosen methodology). You can find them under the folder heading Team Queries. Figure 25.15 illustrates a set of queries for an MSF for CMMI project.

Team queries are shared across project team members. That is, each team member sees the list of team queries. If you have proper credentials, you can define a new team query. In this way, you can write queries of which everyone can take advantage.

You also have a folder to store your personal set of queries. This folder is aptly named My Queries. It is useful for storing queries that are pertinent to you. For instance, you might create queries associated with your user ID, or you might simply write a few queries specific to your job function.

### Running a Query and Viewing Results

To run a query, you select it in the Team Explorer tree and choose Run Query from the Team menu (or press F5). You can also right-click the query and choose View Results or Open. There is also a toolbar for work item queries. You can run a query from here by clicking the Run Query button.

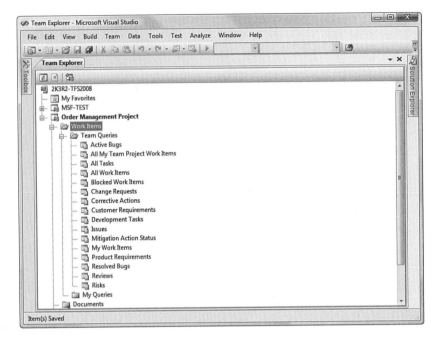

FIGURE 25.15   Work item team queries.

The results of your query are displayed in a list that includes the work item's ID, its type, state, and title. As you scroll through items in this list, the selected work item's details are displayed at the bottom of the screen. You have full interaction with a work item from this screen. Figure 25.16 shows a sample result set.

You can customize the list that is returned as a result of the query. To do so, you click the Column Options toolbar item (far right) or select this option from the context menu to bring up the Column Options dialog box. With it, you can determine which fields you want in the list and each field's width using the Fields tab. You can even define a multi-column sort from here by using the Sorting tab. Figure 25.17 shows this dialog box.

---

**TIP**

The changes you make in the Column Options dialog box can be saved back to the query definition.

---

### Creating a Custom Query

You can create custom queries for Team Explorer. These queries can be created for the entire team (Team Queries) or just yourself (My Queries). To create a custom query, you select the Add Query menu option from either the Team menu or the context menu for the given folder under which you want to store the new query.

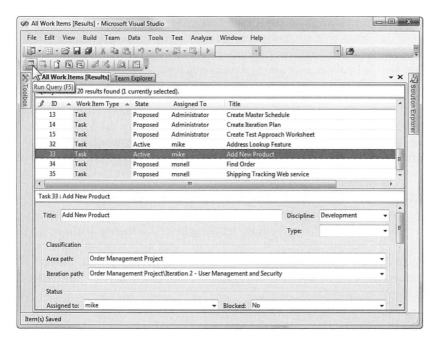

FIGURE 25.16    View query results.

FIGURE 25.17    Customizing query results.

Selecting this option brings up the query view. From here, you define filter clauses that allow you to narrow your query to just those items for which you are searching. Each clause in your query defines a field, an operator, and a value (think WHERE clause in SQL). In addition, you can relate clauses to one another using AND and OR conditions. Let's look at an example.

Suppose that you have been identified to triage all bugs that are proposed. This makes you the central person for determining who should work on a bug, whether the bug requires more research, whether the bug is actually a bug, and so on. To do this work, you might want to define a query in your My Queries that allows you to view all proposed bugs for a specific area in the system.

When setting the filter for this query, you define three clauses. The first is for the Work Item Type field. You are interested only in bugs, so you set the operator to = and the Value field to Bug. This will return all work items whose type is a bug. You then add another clause to your filter for the state of the bug. You need to see only bugs that are in the state of Proposed. This clause is inclusive, so you set the And/Or field to And. Lastly, you add another And option and choose the Area Path field and set it appropriately. Figure 25.18 shows this filter example using the tool.

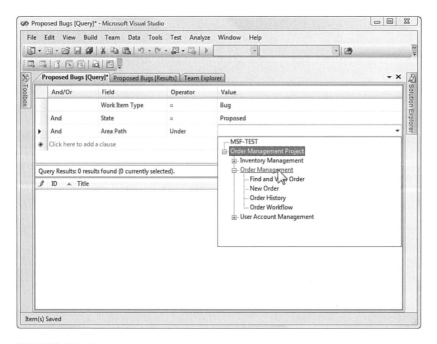

FIGURE 25.18    Defining a new query.

Next, to select the fields that are shown as a result of your query, you use the Column Options dialog box, which also allows you to indicate a sort order. This is the same dialog box we discussed previously (refer to Figure 25.17). You can then run your query and test the results. When you're happy, you can name it and save it for future use.

**NOTE**

You edit queries using the same interface. To open a query for edit, select the View Query option from the context menu for the given query.

# Understanding Team Role Perspectives

As we've discussed, work items are the key collaborative element that connects all team members on the project. They are used to communicate tasks, status, issues, risks, and so on. They also emit status information and define metrics for reporting. Work items touch the entire team. Therefore, in the following sections, we will cover how some of the key roles across the SDLC interact with work items. We will present a few common activities per role and then demonstrate how those activities are realized through work items.

The roles we will discuss include project manager, business analyst, developer, and tester. There are many more roles defined for most processes (including MSF). However, in general, these roles tend to interact the most with work items on any given software project.

**25**

**NOTE**

Only the roles of architect, developer, database developer, and tester are assumed to have an installed version of a Visual Studio team client. Other team members (such as business analysts, project managers, and customers) will connect to the project using tools such as Excel and Project. They can also view reports and information via the project team site (portal). Of course, each of these team members should have a client access license (CAL) for Team Foundation Server.

There is also a web-based client that allows access to Work Items. It is available as a separate download. Simply search Microsoft.com for the product "Visual Studio Team System Web Access 2008 Power Tool."

## Project Vision

It is helpful to discuss each role's interaction with work items in the context of an actual project. So for this section, we will assume the following as the parameters and vision that define the sample project:

▶ There is an existing e-commerce application.

▶ A project has been envisioned to develop an application that allows both sales and customer service representatives (CSRs) to proactively manage the user accounts in this e-commerce system.

▶ Sales will interact with customer accounts to offer special direct marketing. They would also like to do data mining to prioritize top accounts.

▶ CSRs will manage user accounts and handle customer requests. They need to be able to look up information, change orders, determine tracking information, and so on.

We will use this as the basis for describing how various roles work on this project through work items. Let's first look at the project manager's role.

> **NOTE**
>
> MSF defines actual workstreams to group activities by role. It is recommended that you become familiar with these workstreams, their activities, and their associated roles. In addition, MSF illustrates how a work item is used inside each workstream. Our approach is simpler: We want to show common activities by role and illustrate how work items come into play and how those work items are reflected in Visual Studio and Team Explorer.

## Project Manager

For this example, assume that you are the project manager (PM) who is in charge of the project. It is therefore your responsibility to set up the project in Team Systems, select a methodology, control security, and so on. Given that many PMs have little experience with Visual Studio, you may want to assign a technical lead to aid with these tasks.

We will not cover these project setup tasks here. Instead, assume that a project has been defined with the MSF for CMMI methodology, security is in place for each role, and the iterations and areas have been defined similar to those found in Figures 25.2 and 25.4. We will now focus on a few common tasks the PM will execute involving work items.

### Identifying the PM's Work Items

In general, project managers focus on tasks, risks, and issues on a day-to-day basis. Many are also occasionally concerned with requirements, reviews, and bugs. For this example, we will discuss the former set and cover the latter with other, more pertinent roles.

### Using Excel

As the PM, you may have a copy of Team Explorer (this is recommended). From here, you can query and update work items as we have discussed. Many project managers, however, also like to work with lists of information in both Excel and Project. Team Explorer has support for two-way integration with these products, as we introduced in Chapter 23. You therefore can view, create, and update work items using these common Office tools. Of course, this feature is not limited to project managers; we simply will walk through a few scenarios pertinent to their role.

**Viewing Open Issues**    For this example, assume that you, as the project manager, want to view the list of active issues on the project, update them, and then publish this list back to server.

To start, you launch Excel. Provided that you have installed the Team Explorer tools, you will have a Team toolbar inside Excel. This toolbar provides interaction with a team server.

From this toolbar, you click New List to launch the Connect to Team Foundation Server dialog box. This allows you to select a TFS server and a project on that server.

Next, you are presented with the New List dialog box. From here, you can indicate whether you want to query for work items or create an input list. Query allows you to get back a list, work with the list items, and then update the server. We will look at the Input list in a moment. Recall that you want to work with the current issues on this project. For this reason, you will select Query List and choose the Issues List from the Query drop-down (which includes the list of both team and private queries). Figure 25.19 shows this interaction.

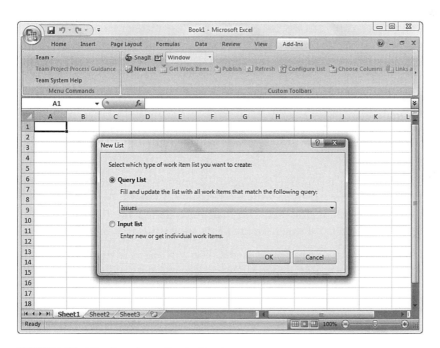

FIGURE 25.19   Opening a list in Excel.

When the query runs, you are then presented with all open issues on the project. Using the features of Excel, you can filter and sort this list. Figure 25.20 shows the results of the query.

25

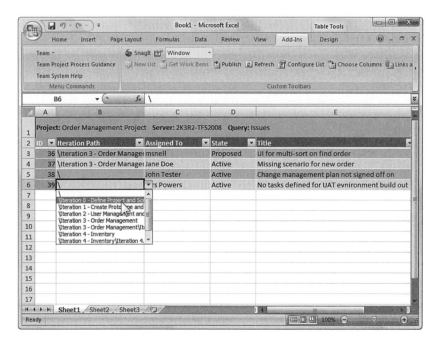

FIGURE 25.20    The list of issue work items in Excel.

Notice that the Team Add-in toolbar now has many more active buttons. From here, you can publish changes you make to the list, refresh the list from the server, configure the list, determine which columns you want to view, and manage links and attachments to the various work items in the list.

Let's suppose that you, as the project manager, need to update the Escalation field and the Target resolution date for these items. To do so, you click the Choose Columns item on the toolbar to bring up the related dialog box. This dialog box allows you to determine which fields are displayed in the Excel sheet. Figure 25.21 shows this task in action.

The next step is to update the data for the work items. The good news is that Excel provides drop-downs for data entry that match the work item drop-downs in Team Explorer. This ensures that the data conforms to the right business rules and eases the data entry.

For changes, assume that you updated the escalation fields and target resolution dates and changed the status of the Proposed work item to Active (and assigned it). You also have to enter a new issue. You can do so at the bottom of the list.

When adding a new issue to the list, you will go to the Choose Columns dialog box, select the work item type (Issue in this case), and then click the Add Required button. This will push all the required fields to the form.

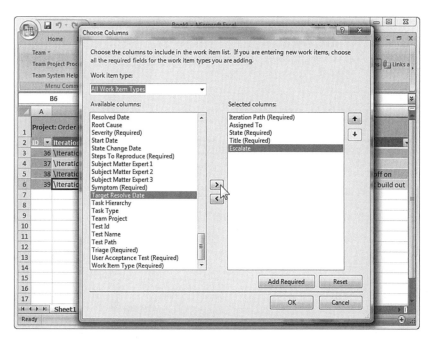

FIGURE 25.21    Selecting work item fields to display in Excel.

**TIP**

Because you work with multiple types of work items in Excel, one of the required fields is Work Item Type. It is important to *set this field first* when entering a new work item. This way, all other fields in the row will be updated as to allowed values. You will then get the correct data entry experience.

Now that you are finished doing updates and have even added a new issue to the list, the next step is to publish these items to the server. To do so, you click the Publish button on the toolbar. This will start the synchronization process.

Note that you may run into errors when publishing. If problems are detected, you will be presented with the Work Item Publishing Errors dialog box. This dialog box lists the results of the operation and shows the work items that have errors. Figure 25.22 shows the work items that did not successfully publish.

You can click the Edit Work Item button to resolve the errors for each item. Clicking this button brings up the work item in the standard view (not Excel). The errors are listed at the top of the form, and the fields in error are also highlighted. From here, you can make your fixes and then click the Close button. Figure 25.23 shows an error with the State field being fixed. A new work item must start in the state Proposed, and not Active. You will click the Publish button on the Work Item Publishing Errors dialog box after each error is fixed.

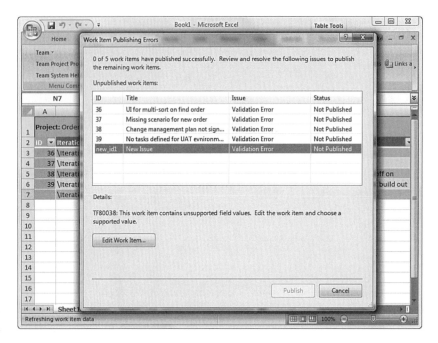

FIGURE 25.22    Publishing errors.

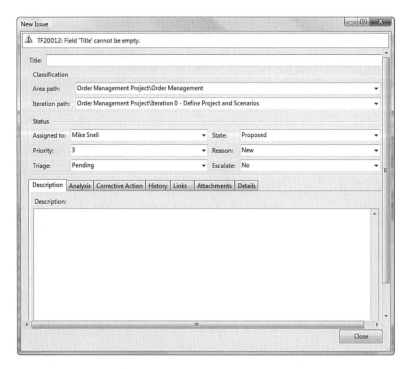

FIGURE 25.23    Resolving a publishing error.

**NOTE**

You can add links and attachments to work items from Excel. The interface is similar to that of Team Explorer's. However, you can only do so after a work item is published. Therefore, if you create a new work item in Excel, you will need to publish before adding attachments and links. After the item is published, you can make your additions. You will then have to republish to post those additions.

**Creating a Risk List**    For the next example, suppose that you, as the PM, want to create a project risk list in Excel. Each risk will be entered in a blank worksheet and then published to the Team Foundation Server. The steps involved in this task are not unlike what we discussed previously. To create a risk list in Excel, follow these steps:

1. Open Excel and select the New List menu option from the Team drop-down on the Add-In toolbar.

2. Connect to the TFS server and a valid project.

3. On the New List dialog box (see Figure 25.19), select Input List to indicate that you do not want to start with a query or set of work items. Rather, you simply want to have the correct schema for entering items.

4. You will be presented with an Excel sheet that allows you to enter work items. One of the fields is Work Item Type. Selecting this field will define the data entry for the remaining fields on the sheet.

5. In the example, you want to enter Risk work items. Therefore, you need to click the Choose Columns button from the toolbar. This will invoke the Choose Columns dialog box (see Figure 25.21). From here, remove all existing columns. Then, choose the Risk work item type and click the Add Required button (you can then order the columns as you like). Then click OK to be taken back to the Excel sheet.

6. Enter the risks associated with the project.

7. When the risk list is complete, click the Publish button to update the server.

These steps allow any team member to create work items in Excel and then publish them to the server.

**TIP**

You may want to save your Excel workbooks after they're created. Doing this can be a great way to get team members to use work items in Excel. You define a workbook for risks, for instance, and then publish that workbook to the project portal. Team members can now simply open the workbook, add or edit the given item, and then publish to the server. The MSF for Agile project portal has a couple of examples of this.

**Using Project**

Work items can also be viewed, edited, created, and scheduled using Microsoft Project. The integration of work items and Project is nearly identical to that of Excel. As an example, suppose that you, as the PM, need to schedule the tasks on the project.

First, you may run a query inside Team Explorer. Next, you select the Open Selection in Project item from the toolbar. Selecting this item will open a new project file and feed it the selected tasks from the query. Within Project, you are free to do project-related tasks. This includes rolling up tasks under a group name, defining the hours for a task and its predecessors, and so on. Figure 25.24 shows an example of the sample project's task work items being scheduled in Project.

You then click the Publish button after scheduling is complete. This will update the team server. The synchronization will update all rows marked as Publish and Refresh (see Figure 25.24). Therefore, for rows that do not map to work items, simply mark these accordingly.

The schedule information for each task is now available inside each work item. For example, if developers open a development task work item, they can click on the Details tab to see the remaining work and scheduled start and end dates. Figure 25.25 shows an example.

Project managers can save their schedules and use them as a basis to receive updates to tasks from the developers. This way, they can handle work items with the tool they're most comfortable using.

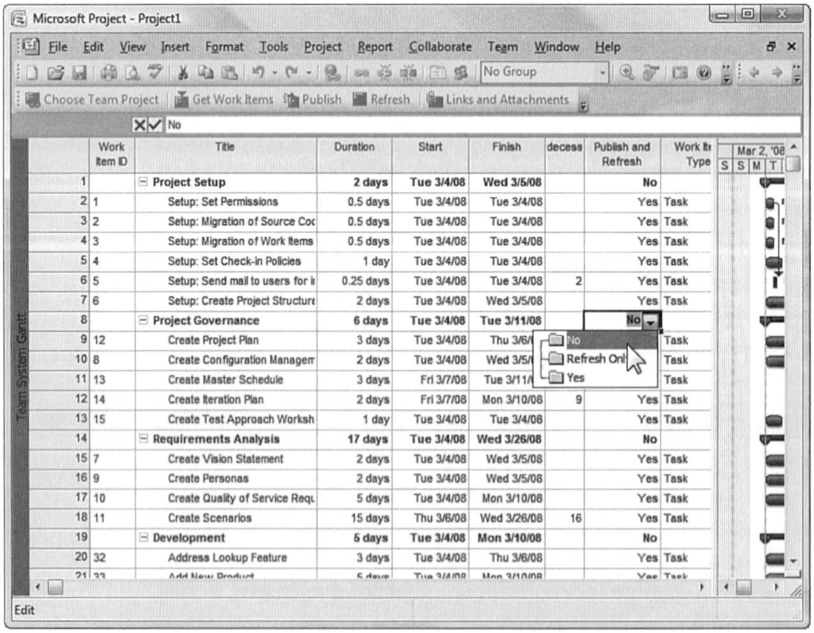

FIGURE 25.24    Working with task work items in Project.

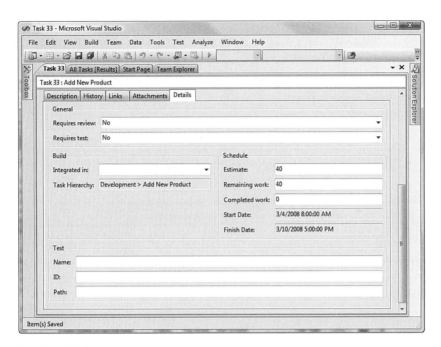

FIGURE 25.25    A scheduled work item.

## Business Analyst

A business analyst's (BA's) primary interaction with work items will be to define require-ments and user scenarios. These items will represent the interaction with the system that a user must have to consider the project a success. Therefore, these scenarios are typically defined at the beginning of an iteration. The scenarios drive other work items such as development tasks. Let's look at a standard method that a BA might follow with respect to work items and a project.

For this example, imagine that you are now the business analyst. Your first step is to meet with stakeholders and brainstorm possible user scenarios. Suppose that this meeting defined 25 possible scenarios. The first step would be to create Requirement work items of type Scenario for each of these 25 possible scenarios. This will allow for the work items to be named, assigned, and tracked. In addition, the PM can now track these work items on the schedule as you estimate the time required to complete each scenario.

Next, you begin to write the various scenarios. You can query the set of scenarios to deter-mine which are of the highest priority and do those first. When writing a simple scenario, you can use the Description tab on the work item. You can write longer, more complex scenarios using a Word document. Let's look at an example of doing so.

Suppose that you have a work item for the scenario titled Login Scenario. When you write this scenario, you use a scenario Word template for the project. You then upload this scenario to the project. You can do so using the project portal or through Team Explorer.

Suppose that you used Team Explorer. From here, you expand the Documents folder and then right-click the Requirements folder. You then choose Upload Document to navigate to the document and upload it to the server.

This document is uploaded to the same library used by the project portal. There are simply two views: one from Team Explorer and one from the portal. Figure 25.26 shows the scenario document in both views.

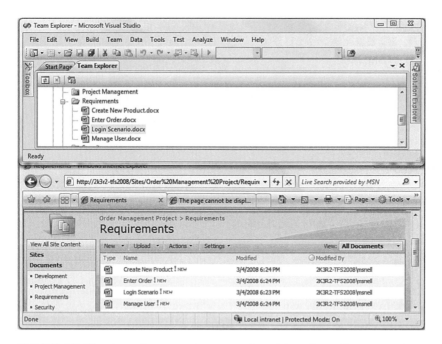

FIGURE 25.26    A requirements document viewed from Team Explorer and the portal.

Finally, you will want to link the scenario document to the work item. It may seem intuitive for you, as the BA, to use the Link tab for this work. However, this is not the case. Instead, this link is made through the Attachment tab. You add an attachment and navigate to the document stored on the portal (see Figure 25.27). Adding this attachment actually defines a link between the work item and the file. This way, if the file is updated from the portal, the updates are reflected when the file is opened from the work item.

## Developer

Developers get their task lists from the work items database. In addition, they use work items to get clarification on requirements, user scenarios, bugs, and so on. Developers are probably the prime consumers of work items in Team Systems. We have already discussed the majority of these scenarios. Therefore, we will focus on one primary activity of the developer: associating code to work items.

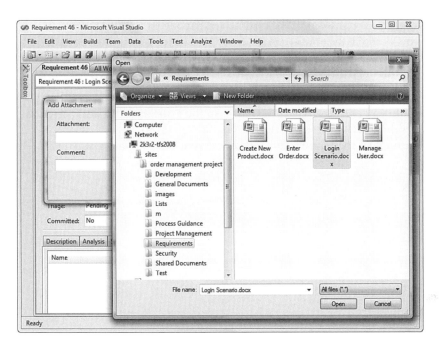

FIGURE 25.27    Linking to a scenario document on the project portal.

Associating work items and code provides vital statistics to Team Foundation Server. It allows for reporting on code churn, task progress, and bug status. In addition, it provides a vital link when going back over code and doing maintenance. The capability to look at a piece of code and then read the associated requirements, tasks, and scenarios is extremely helpful.

> **TIP**
>
> It is a best practice to create a check-in policy that forces developers to associate all check-ins with one or more work items. This ensures that development work is properly tracked (and therefore can be reported on).

### Associating Code and Work Items Through Check-In

The principal means for a developer to associate code with a work item is to do so during the source control check-in procedure. We cover source control in Chapter 24, "Source Control." However, it is important to illustrate this process here from the perspective of work items.

As an example, suppose that you are the project's technical lead and have been assigned the task for generating the skeletal structure of the application. Of course, this task would be a work item. Your activity as the tech lead might include creating the solution and the projects and scripting out code stubs for many of the items in the project.

When the code is complete, you would check in the entire code structure. During the check-in process, you would associate the check-in to the task for generating the code structure. You would do so by clicking the Work Items icon on the Check In dialog box. Selecting this option will open a window that allows you to query and search for work items to associate to code. Figure 25.28 shows this example in progress.

After you find the task, you click the check box to make the association. In addition, you can indicate whether the check-in resolves the given task. You do this by setting the Check-In Action (far right in the figure). This indication automatically marks the task's status as Resolved.

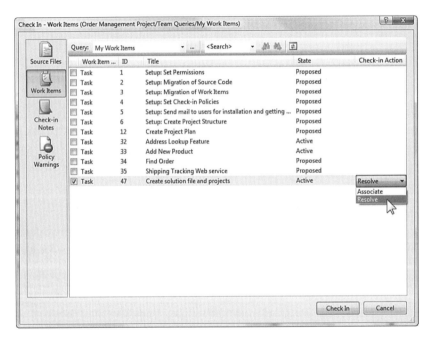

FIGURE 25.28    Linking a changeset to a work item.

Finally, this process also creates a link back to the work item. When you open the work item and click the Links tab, you will see the changeset that was checked in as part of the previous process. This linked changeset represents the history of what code was resolved or checked in relative to this work item. Figure 25.29 shows this link and the open changeset.

**TIP**

You will most often link check-ins to multiple work items. This capability is fully supported and a best practice. For instance, if your check-in resolves a bug, is related to a requirement, and resolves a task that was created to fix the bug, you will want to relate to all three work items.

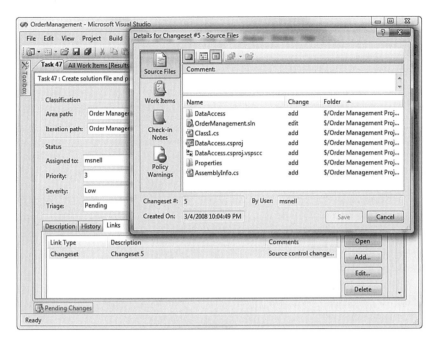

FIGURE 25.29   The changeset link on the work item.

### Linking Code to Work Items

You can also associate code to a work item through the Link tab on the work item. This capability can be useful if you want to make the association outside a check-in (or you forget).

To link the code this way, navigate to the work item and select the Links tab. Click the Add button to bring up the Add Link dialog box. In this dialog box, select Versioned Item from the Link Type field. Then, next to the Item field, click the Browse button. Figure 25.30 shows an example.

For this example, your task is to create a `Customer` class. The class is created and checked in. It now needs to be manually associated with the work item. After clicking the Browse button, you can navigate the source tree to find the correct code files with which to associate the item. Figure 25.31 shows this process in action. After making a selection, you can then indicate whether the link should always point to the latest version or a changeset.

## Tester

A tester interacts with work items by writing and tracking bugs and issues for the project. You have seen examples of these tasks. What we want to discuss here is how a tester might associate a test to work items.

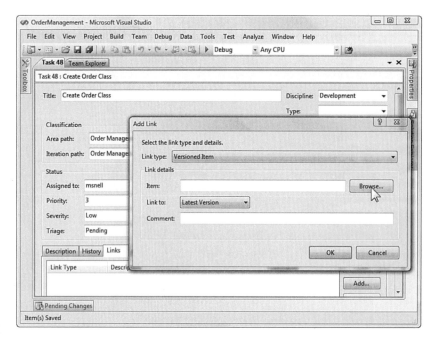

FIGURE 25.30    Adding a versioned item link to a work item.

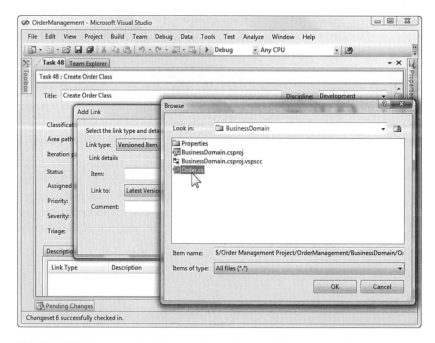

FIGURE 25.31    Selecting the versioned item to link to a work item.

As a simple example, let's look at the Requirement work item. Each requirement in the system should be verified by someone representing the user. This is referred to as a user acceptance test (UAT). The Details tab of the Requirement work item has a space to track the UAT status. Figure 25.32 shows an example. In this way, the team knows which requirements have made it all the way through UAT (and are thus ready to ship).

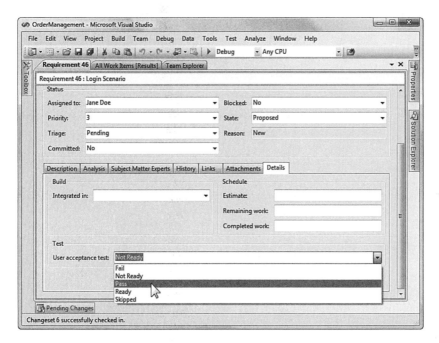

FIGURE 25.32   Setting the UAT results for a requirement.

Testers may also be asked to indicate which test satisfies a given requirement or task. For example, suppose that you, as the tester, have a development task to create the Customer class. This work item might indicate on the Details tab that a test is required before the item can be resolved. In this case, the item's test details must be filled out.

You add test details to a task work item in the Test group on the Details tab. Unfortunately, there is no way to associate tests and work items from within the IDE. Instead, this is currently a manual process. The test information you need to enter includes the name of the test, its ID, and a path to the test. This information is available from the Test Manager screen. Figure 25.33 shows a horizontal split between the Test Manager and the details of a given work item.

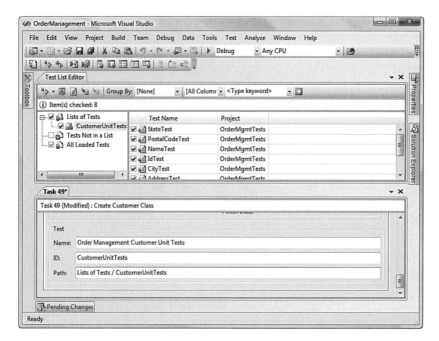

**FIGURE 25.33** Filling in the test details for a task.

# Customizing Work Items

You can customize and extend the features of Team Systems in several places. Customizing is the process of taking the existing functionality and tweaking it to fit your needs. This is the typical scenario for most development shops. Extending involves using the Team System API and report engine to write new functionality into Team Systems. The following are all possible customization and extension points:

- ▶ **Process Methodology**—You can customize the existing methodologies or write your own. This includes changing the workflows of work items.

- ▶ **Work Items**—You can edit the existing work items (add new fields and data) or create your own new work items.

- ▶ **Reporting**—You can create new reports and customize existing ones.

- ▶ **Project Portal**—You can modify the project portal to contain your own templates and default project documents.

We cannot cover all these extension points here. Instead, we will look at two common scenarios related to work items: seeding your process with standard work items for a project and customizing an existing work item.

## Seeding the Process with Work Items

When you create a new project based on one of the MSF methodologies, the team server is seeded with an initial set of work items. These items represent common tasks required for the execution of the project. Some of these tasks involve starting the project moving (such as creating a project plan and master schedule).

This initial set of work items is part of the overall methodology. A common request is to seed your own tasks (work items) into an existing methodology. Let's look at how this is done.

> **NOTE**
>
> You can apply this process of adding work items to a methodology to extend the methodology in other directions as well. You can even use it as a basis for writing your own methodology.

### Downloading (Exporting) a Methodology

Methodologies in Team Systems are defined as process templates. A process template is a set of files that Team Systems can use to define a given process or methodology. As we have discussed, Team Systems ships with two process templates: MSF for Agile and MSF for CMMI. As you tweak your process, you will want to tweak these templates to stay in tune.

You use the Process Template Manager to modify a process template. This tool lets you export a process, tweak it, and then reimport it. You can access this tool from Team Explorer. Figure 25.34 shows the menu structure for accessing the tool.

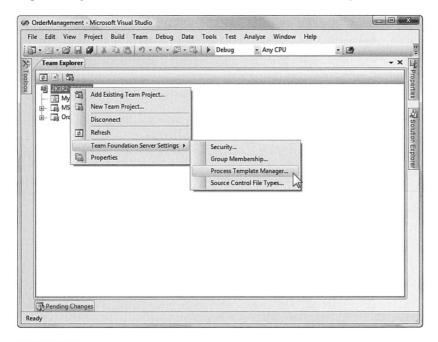

FIGURE 25.34   Accessing the Process Template Manager.

The Process Template Manager presents the process templates installed on your TFS. From here, you can export (download), import (upload), set one process as the default, and even delete a process if needed. Figure 25.35 shows this dialog box.

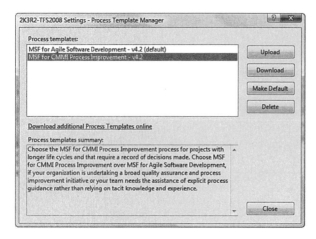

FIGURE 25.35    The Process Template Manager.

For this example, you will export the MSF for CMMI process template. You will then add a few custom work items to this template and reimport.

The Process Template Manager saves all the files that define the process to a folder upon download. This folder contains XML files that define a lot of the process. It also contains the default documents, queries, and process guidance associated with the methodology. Figure 25.36 shows the folder structure that defines the CMMI process.

Notice that the file you will be working with in this example, WorkItems.xml, has been highlighted. You will edit this file in Visual Studio. Figure 25.37 shows the file open in the IDE.

There are three sections to this file: work item type definitions, work items, and queries. The type definitions section indicates the location of the XML files used to describe each work item. The work items section identifies the set of seed work items to be loaded at project creation (this is the focus). The query section lists the location of each query file to be loaded as part of the methodology.

### Adding Work Items to the Methodology

Again, the focus in this example is the set of work items to be seeded for the project. If you look at an existing work item, you can understand its structure. This will help you create a few new tasks and tweak existing ones. The following represents the task titled "Setup: Set Permissions" (we've truncated the description):

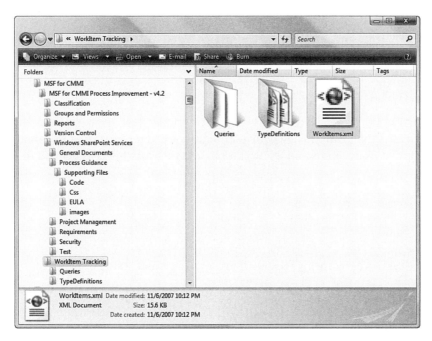

FIGURE 25.36    The exported process template.

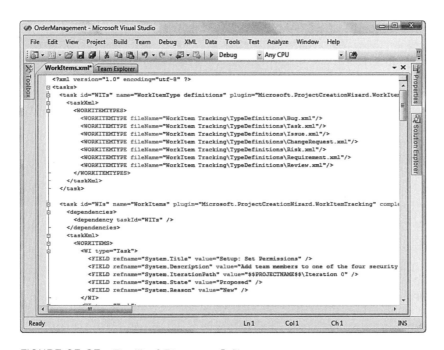

FIGURE 25.37    The **WorkItems.xml** file.

```
<WI type="Task">
  <FIELD refname="System.Title" value="Setup: Set Permissions" />
  <FIELD refname="System.Description" value="Add team members to ... " />
  <FIELD refname="System.IterationPath" value="$$PROJECTNAME$$\Iteration 0" />
  <FIELD refname="System.State" value="Proposed" />
  <FIELD refname="System.Reason" value="New" />
</WI>
```

You can see that to seed the methodology with additional work items, you need to define a type, title, description, state, and so on. Now you can add the work items as defined in Listing 25.1.

LISTING 25.1   New Tasks to Be Seeded

```
<WI type="Task">
  <FIELD refname="System.Title" value="Setup: Execute setup checklist" />
  <FIELD refname="System.Description" value="Fill out the Excel file,
➥'ProjectStartupChecklist.xls' from the portal." />
  <FIELD refname="System.IterationPath" value="$$PROJECTNAME$$\Iteration 0" />
  <FIELD refname="System.State" value="Proposed" />
  <FIELD refname="System.Reason" value="New" />
</WI>
<WI type="Task">
  <FIELD refname="System.Title" value="Create billing report" />
  <FIELD refname="System.Description" value="Fill out the Excel file,
➥'ProjectBillingReport.xls' from the portal." />
  <FIELD refname="System.IterationPath" value="$$PROJECTNAME$$\Iteration 0" />
  <FIELD refname="System.State" value="Proposed" />
  <FIELD refname="System.Reason" value="New" />
</WI>
<WI type="Task">
  <FIELD refname="System.Title" value="Enter project in Time Tracking Sys" />
  <FIELD refname="System.Description" value="Go to TimeTrack2008 and enter new
➥project information." />
  <FIELD refname="System.IterationPath" value="$$PROJECTNAME$$\Iteration 0" />
  <FIELD refname="System.State" value="Proposed" />
  <FIELD refname="System.Reason" value="New" />
</WI>
```

**Uploading (Importing) the Methodology**

The next step is to import the refined methodology. To do so, you return to the Process Template Manager and choose Upload. You are then presented with a folder selection screen. You use this screen to navigate to the folder that contains the updated methodology.

The process template name is very important. If the name matches the name of an existing process template, the Template Manager will ask to overwrite the existing template. This is great if it is your intention. However, if you want to keep the Visual Studio core templates, you should rename your process template before uploading.

You rename the process template at the top of the `ProcessTemplate.xml` file found in the root folder for the template. You can also use this file to change the process template description that shows up in the Template Manager. Figure 25.38 shows the uploaded process template.

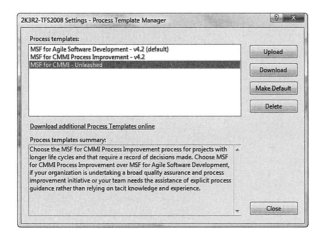

FIGURE 25.38    The newly uploaded process template.

**NOTE**

If you choose to overwrite an existing process, this will not affect projects that are already defined by this process. Instead, these projects use a copy of this core methodology. What you will overwrite is the core that drives new projects.

You can now use your newly customized process to create new projects. You can use this same process of export, tweak, and import to make all kinds of modifications to team systems. You can also use the import to load third-party processes. Figure 25.39 shows the results of this work: a new project with a new set of seed work items.

## Customizing an Existing Work Item

You can customize the definition for an existing work item by using the same steps outlined in the preceding section: export, tweak, and import. Customizing existing work items is probably the most common Team System customization. Let's look at an example.

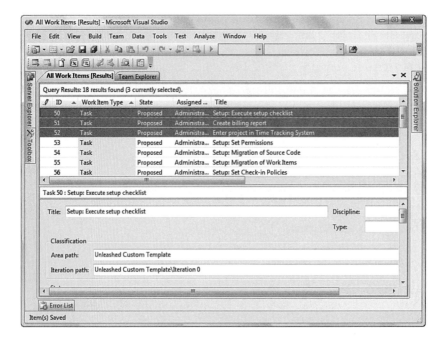

FIGURE 25.39    The new tasks in a new project.

Suppose that you want to customize the Bug work item. You want to add a field to indicate bug type. This will allow the person triaging bugs to categorize them. You can then
report and prioritize bugs that are of type error versus cosmetic and the like.

To make your edits, you again would export a methodology. For this example, use the one
you exported previously (CMMI). You then navigate to the work item type definitions
(\WorkItem Tracking\TypeDefinitions). This folder contains definitions for each work
item defined by the process. Of course, you are interested in the Bug.xml file.

This definition file contains the core fields defined for bugs as well as common fields that
apply to most work items. The definition is long and does not bear repeating here. You
will add your new field to the core fields area in this XML. Listing 25.2 represents the
new field.

LISTING 25.2    A New Field Inside **Bug.xml**

```
<FIELD name="Bug Type" refname="Unleashed.BugType" type="String"
  reportable="dimension">
  <HELPTEXT>Represents the type of bug</HELPTEXT>
  <REQUIRED/>
  <ALLOWEDVALUES>
```

```
    <LISTITEM value="Error"/>
    <LISTITEM value="Requirement"/>
    <LISTITEM value="Change"/>
    <LISTITEM value="Navigation"/>
    <LISTITEM value="Text"/>
    <LISTITEM value="Cosmetic"/>
  </ALLOWEDVALUES>
  <DEFAULT from="value" value="Error"/>
</FIELD>
```

This field is added to the Fields section of the XML. Notice that you restrict the values
that can be entered in this field by using the AllowedValues node. This will tell Team
Systems to display this field as a drop-down list for users. This field is also marked as
required (<REQUIRED/>) and has a default value set using the Default element. Finally, the
field definition indicates that the field is reportable. This tells Team System to include this
field when doing analysis for reports.

You must also define how the field should appear on the form. You do this inside the
Form section of the XML. You want the field to appear at the top of the form to the right
of the Title field. To accomplish this, you add a column to the Group element that
contains the Title field. Listing 25.3 illustrates adding the Bug Type field to this group.

LISTING 25.3    Adding the Field to the Form

```
<Group>
  <Column PercentWidth="70">
    <Control Type="FieldControl" FieldName="System.Title" Label="&Title:"
      LabelPosition="Left"/>
  </Column>
  <Column PercentWidth="30">
    <Control Type="FieldControl" FieldName="Unleashed.BugType" Label="&Bug Type:"
      LabelPosition="Left"/>
  </Column>
</Group>
```

Finally, you upload the new process template. Figure 25.40 shows the results of this
work.

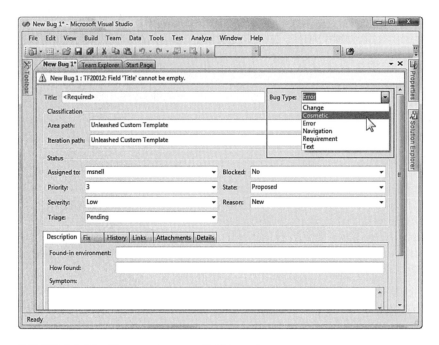

FIGURE 25.40    The new bug type field in action.

# Summary

Work items are the driving force behind team collaboration using Team Systems. If used correctly, they can define all work and then track the progress and related metrics associated to that work. In this chapter, we discussed the many work items defined by both MSF for Agile and MSF for CMMI. We covered the basics behind these items, including workflow, work item history, linking, file attachments, and more.

Work items are also integrated into the IDE. You can query them and work on them directly inside Visual Studio. This capability provides a great experience for developers and testers. For example, you saw how developers can associate work items to their code during the check-in process.

Team Systems provides integration with Excel and Microsoft Project for nondevelopers (such as project managers). Work items can be pulled into these tools, updated (even new ones can be added), and then published back to the server. This chapter presented both these scenarios.

Finally, in this chapter, we showed a few of the ways you might customize work items and Team Systems to meet the needs of your team. We demonstrated the process of downloading, tweaking the XML, and then uploading the results as a new process inside TFS.

# Development Edition

$V$isual Studio Team Systems Development Edition provides a set of team-oriented tools that work on top of the Professional Edition product. As discussed in other chapters, developers working with team systems will be able to use the TFS source control features and work with Team Explorer to track their work.

In addition to these features, Development Edition provides various key tools for the team developer. These include performance profiling that allows you to create a performance report against running code. This report can be used to pinpoint performance issues. There is also the static code analyzer, which allows you to execute automated code reviews against common best practices for .NET. Development Edition also now includes a code measurement tool for finding those areas of your code that need additional scrutiny.

In this chapter, we will cover all of these items. In addition, we will discuss using the class designer to visually develop your code. This can both increase productivity and help you understand existing code. We will also cover creating developer unit tests and verifying their effectiveness.

> **NOTE**
>
> We cover both the Class Designer and Unit Testing in this chapter. However, these features are not specific to Visual Studio Team Systems 2008 Development Edition. Microsoft has made both of these available to all developers using Visual Studio Professional or a Team Edition.

# Visually Developing Code

Many developers are used to seeing things as diagrams. It is useful to think of your application as classes with specific semantics and relationships with one another. Many developers have been creating these types of diagrams for some time using the Unified Modeling Language (UML) or something similar. These tools and modeling languages offer a great, abstract view of systems. However, they are difficult to keep in synch as your objects change. They also do not offer much assistance in terms of productivity or refactoring.

The Visual Studio 2008 Class Designer provides a graphical means for writing and modifying the classes that make up your business domain. You can use it to define classes and their relationships, add properties and methods to those classes, and modify elements within a property or method; it even allows for the refactoring of code. An added benefit of the designer is that it enables the rapid discovery of code. With the Class Designer, you can drop a few key classes on a model, let the tool determine the relationships that exist in the code, and quickly discover (with visual reference) how an application works.

The Class Designer's greatest strength lies in what it can do over and above representing your objects visually. It provides a real-time view of your code, along with the capability to edit this view. With the Class Designer, you can both model your application and visually develop code at the same time.

> **TIP**
>
> The Class Designer is a great way to come up to speed on existing code. With it, you can open an existing set of objects and quickly find out how they work with one another.

## The Class Designer

The class diagram allows you to get a view of your code as it exists statically (or at rest). You also get real-time synchronization between the model and the actual code. You should think of the class designer more as a visual code editor and less like a diagram. If you make a change to code, that change is reflected in the diagram. When you change the diagram, your code changes too.

### Creating a Class Diagram

There are a couple of ways to create a class diagram. The first is to add a class diagram to your project from the Add New Item dialog box. Here, you select a class diagram template (.cd) and add it to the project. You can then add items to this diagram from the Toolbox or from existing classes in the Solution Explorer.

The second way to add a class diagram to a project is to choose View Class Diagram from the context menu for a given project. In this way, Visual Studio will generate a class diagram from an existing project. This option is shown in Figure 26.1.

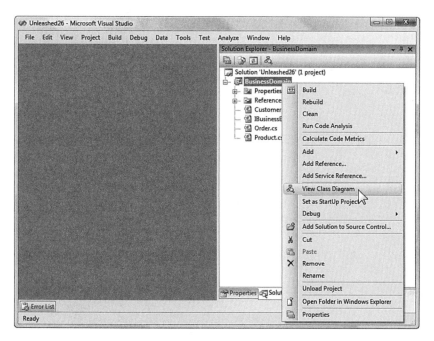

FIGURE 26.1    The Class Designer.

In either case, you end up with a .cd file in your project that represents the visual model of your classes. Clearly the View Class Diagram option saves you the time of dragging everything onto the diagram. Figure 26.2 shows an example of the Class Designer file. We will cover each window shown in this designer.

### Displaying Members

You use the arrow icon (points up or down) in the upper-right corner of each object in the designer to toggle whether to show or hide its members. This capability is helpful if you need to fit a lot of classes on a screen or if you are interested only in members of a particular class.

You can also use the Class Designer toolbar to indicate how members are grouped for display and what additional information is shown. For example, you can sort members alphabetically, group them by their kind (property, method, and so on), or group by access (public, private, and so on). You can then indicate whether you want to display just member names, their name and type, or the full signature.

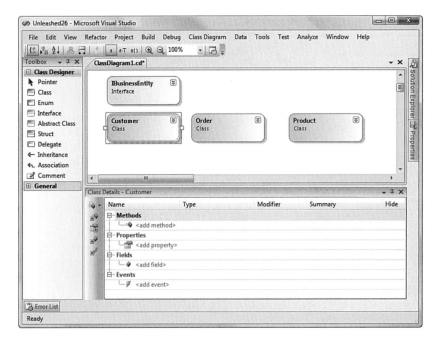

FIGURE 26.2    The Class Designer.

## Adding Items to the Diagram

You add items to the Class Designer by using either the Toolbox or the Solution Explorer. The Toolbox is for adding new items. You use the Solution Explorer to add existing classes to the diagram. In both scenarios, you simply drag and drop the item onto the Class Designer window. If the item already exists, Visual Studio will build out the class details for you. In fact, if the class file contains more than one class, each class will be placed as an object on the diagram.

Figure 26.3 shows an example of the Class Designer Toolbox tools. Notice that you can define all object-oriented concepts here, including classes, interfaces, inheritance, and so on.

When you add a new item such as a class or struct to the designer, it will prompt you for its name and location. You can choose to generate a new file to house the item or place it in an existing file. Figure 26.4 shows the New Class dialog box. Here, you can give the class a name, set its access modifier, and indicate a filename.

---

### TIP

The Class Designer can automatically add related classes to the diagram. For example, suppose you add a class from the Solution Explorer. If you want to show classes that inherit from this class, you can right-click the class and choose Show Derived Classes. This will add to the model all classes that derive from the selected class.

---

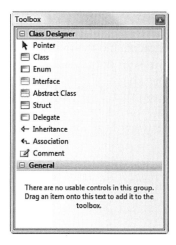

FIGURE 26.3   The Class Designer Toolbox.

FIGURE 26.4   Adding a new class to the designer.

## Defining Relationships Between Classes

One of the biggest benefits of the class diagram is that it visually represents the relationships between classes. These relationships are much easier to see in a diagram than through code. The following relationships can be represented:

- ▶ **Inheritance**—Indicates if a class inherits from another class.

- ▶ **Interface**—Indicates if a class implements one or more interfaces.

- ▶ **Association**—Indicates an association between classes.

Let's look at implementing each of these relationships through an example.

## Inheritance

First, let's look at inheritance with the class designer. Suppose that you have a base class called Product. This class represents a generic product in your system. You then want to create a concrete Book class that inherits from Product. To do this with the Class Designer, you make sure that both classes are on the screen. You then select the Inheritance tool from the Class Designer Toolbox. This tool has its own special icon that shows an arrow pointing upward. This visual cue indicates that you want to draw the inheritance from the implementation class to the base class. Figure 26.5 shows this drawing in action.

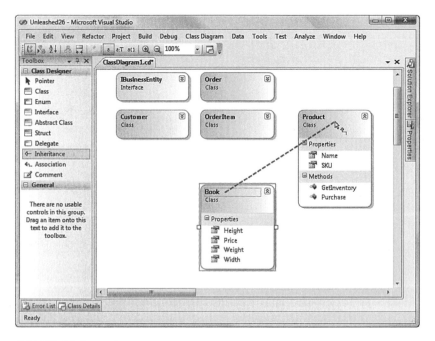

FIGURE 26.5    Defining inheritance.

When the drawing is complete, the inheritance arrow should point toward the base class. Figure 26.6 shows an example. Also, notice that the Book class now contains an icon indicating that it inherits Product.

## Interface

The next visual relationship we'll look at is an interface. For this example, suppose that all the business entities in your system implement a similar contract. This contract may define properties for ID and name. It may also define methods such as Get, Delete, and Save.

To implement this interface, you again use the Inheritance tool from the Class Designer Toolbox. You drag it from the class doing the implementation toward the interface. Figure 26.7 shows the result of an implemented interface. Notice the lollipop icon above the Customer class; it denotes the interface implementation.

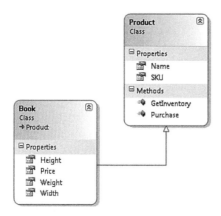

FIGURE 26.6    Inheritance defined.

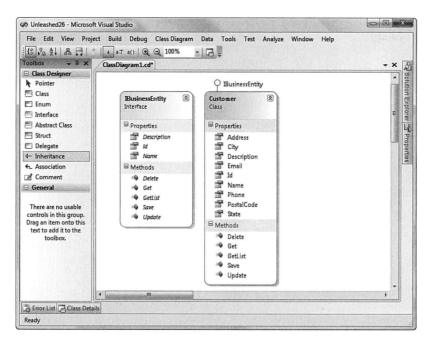

FIGURE 26.7    Implementing an interface.

### Association

The final relationship to look at is association. This relationship is typically a very loose one in the UML world. However, in the Class Designer, an association is very real. Typically, this means that two classes have an association through the use of one of the classes. This relationship is also optional in terms of viewing. It can exist, but you do not have to show it in the diagram.

For example, suppose that you have an Order object. This object might expose an OrderStatus property. Suppose that it also has a property for accessing the Customer record associated with the order. These two properties are associations. You can leave them as properties, or you can choose to show them as associations.

You can also draw these property associations on the diagram. To do so, you select the Association tool from the Toolbox. This tool has the same icon as Inheritance. You then draw the association from the class that contains the association to the class that is the object of the association. You can also right-click the actual property that represents the association and choose Show as Association from the context menu (or Show as Collection Association for associations that are part of a collection). Figure 26.8 shows an example.

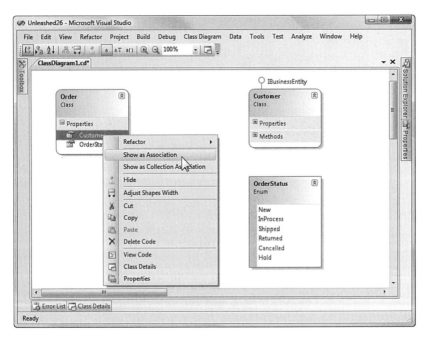

FIGURE 26.8    Showing as an association.

The result is that the association property is displayed on the association arrow. This indicates that the class from where the association originates contains this property (it is shown only on this line, however). Figure 26.9 illustrates this.

## Defining Methods, Properties, Fields, and Events

The most exciting part of the Class Designer is that it allows you to do more than define classes and relationships. You can actually stub out code and do refactoring (see Chapter 9, "Refactoring Code," for details).

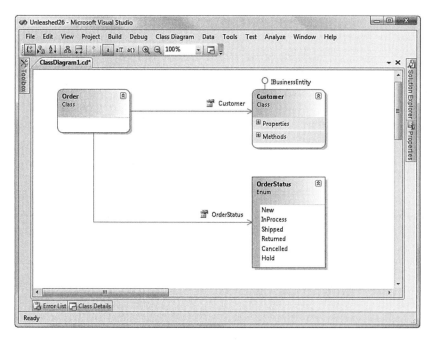

FIGURE 26.9    Creating an association.

**26**

There are two ways to add code to your classes, structs, interfaces, and the like. The first is to type directly into the designer. For example, if you are in the Properties section of a class, you can right-click and choose to add a new property. This will place the property in your class and allow you to edit it in the diagram. This method works for other class members as well. It does have a couple of drawbacks, however. You can't, for instance, define a full method signature or indicate access levels. For that, you need the Class Details window.

The Class Details window allows you to fully define methods, fields, properties, and events for a class. It also works with other constructs such as interfaces, delegates, and enums. To use this window, you right-click a class and choose Class Details from the context menu. Selecting this menu item brings up the Class Details editor for the selected class. Figure 26.10 shows the Class Details editor in action.

Notice that when working in the Class Details window, you still get IntelliSense. In this example, the Cancel method is being added to the Order class. You can indicate a return type for the method with the Type column. You can define the access modifier with the Modifier column. You can also set the parameters of the method. In this case, the method takes the parameter reasonCode.

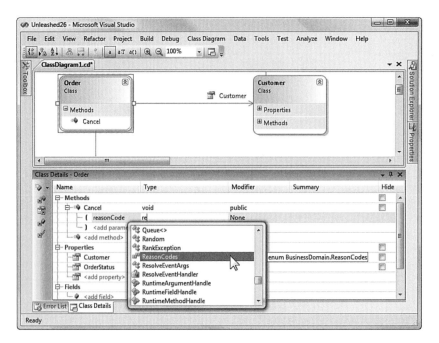

FIGURE 26.10    The Class Details window.

Finally, there are the Summary and Hide columns. The Hide column indicates whether you want to show an item on the diagram. This capability allows you to hide various members when printing or exporting as an image. The Summary column allows you to add your XML documentation to the class. Clicking the ellipsis button (not shown) in this field brings up the Description dialog box. Here, you can enter your XML summary information for the given member. Figure 26.11 shows an example for the Cancel method.

# Developer Unit Testing

Developers have always been responsible for testing their code before its release to the testers. In the past, this meant walking through every line of code in the debugger (including all conditions and errors). Going through all the code made for a fine goal but was not always realized (and very difficult to verify). In fact, the entire exercise was often skipped during code changes and updates. The result was lower-quality builds sent to the testers.

Clearly, this system highlights a need to automate unit testing. As a result, unit test frameworks were developed. The first such framework for .NET was NUnit, which is an open-source project that allows you to write code that tests other code. A similar framework was built into Visual Studio 2005 and is also now in 2008. With it, developers can write unit tests that call their code and test possible conditions and outcomes.

FIGURE 26.11    The Description dialog box for a method.

**NOTE**

Unit testing with Visual Studio 2008 is not specific to the Development Edition of the product. It is available in Professional and above.

The unit test framework in Visual Studio allows you to build tests as you build your application. Alternatively, if you subscribe to test-driven development, you can write your tests before you write your code. In either case, a disciplined approach to unit testing can lead toward building a full set of tests in unison with your application.

This full set of tests can often represent a regression test for most components or even the entire system. The result is increased confidence in activities that were previously very high-risk, such as last-minute fixes, refactoring, and late additions. When these activities occur, you can leverage your full set of unit tests to find out what, if anything, was broken as a result of the change.

**NOTE**

Database unit testing is specific to the Database Edition and is therefore covered in Chapter 29, "Database Edition." Automated testing that is typically performed by testers with Team System Test Edition is covered in Chapter 28, "Test Edition."

## A Sample Unit Test

Before we go too much further, it makes sense to look at unit tests to better understand them. Remember, a unit test is simply test code you write to call your application code. This test code asserts that various conditions are either true or false as a result of the call to your application code. The test either passes or fails based on the results of these assertions. If, for example, you expect an outcome to be true and it turns out false, then a test fails. Let's look more closely at a real example.

Suppose that you have a web service that returns a customer's profile from the database. This web service takes the customer's ID as a parameter. You might write a simple test to call this web service and pass a known ID from the database. This test might then confirm that what is returned not only works but also is correct. Listing 26.1 shows an example of such a test.

LISTING 26.1    A Sample Unit Test

```
[TestMethod()]
public void GetCustomerProfileTest() {
  CustomerProfile custProfileService = new CustomerProfile();
  int customerId = 1234;
  Customer customer = custProfileService.GetCustomerProfile(customerId);
  Assert.AreEqual(customer.Id, 1234);
}
```

Notice that this code is similar to other C# code. You mark the method as a test by adding the TestMethod attribute. Inside the code, you create the object and make the method call. If this call fails (or any exception is thrown), the test fails. You then do an assertion in the test to make sure that the object returned matches the expected results. If this assertion is false (the values are not equal), the test fails. If it is true, the test succeeds. You might add a few more assertions to round out this test. In addition, you might create some additional tests for this method. However, you should now have an understanding of the basics of a unit test. We will dig a little deeper in a moment.

## Writing Effective Unit Tests

The more unit tests you write, the better you get at writing them. There are a few tenants (or best practices) to keep in mind in order to write effective unit tests. They include the following:

▶ Each unit should be tested independently. If your method has multiple possible, expected outcomes, you need a unit test for each.

▶ Unit tests should exist independently from other tests. A unit test should not require other tests (or a sequence of tests) to be run prior to its executing.

▶ Unit tests should cover all cases. An effective set of unit tests covers every possible condition for a given method, including bounds checks, null values, exceptions, conditional logic, and so on.

▶ Unit tests should run (and rerun) without additional configuration. You should be able to run your unit tests easily. If you create an environment that requires configuration every time you run unit tests, you decrease the likelihood they will be run (or written) by the team.

▶ Test a standard application state. If your unit tests work with application data, for example, you should reset this data to common state prior to each unit test's executing. This way, you ensure that tests are not causing errors in other tests. You also give developers a common platform on which to test.

These best practices represent a few guidelines for writing effective tests. As you write more and more tests, you may come up with your own effective unit test tenets.

## Using Unit Test Classes and Methods

Visual Studio 2008 provides the `Microsoft.VisualStudio.TestTools.UnitTesting` namespace, which contains the attribute classes used to define tests. Attributes are used to decorate classes and methods for execution by the unit test framework. Table 26.1 presents a list of common attribute classes used for unit testing.

The `UnitTesting` namespace also includes the `Assert` static type. This object contains methods for evaluating whether the results of a test were as expected. Table 26.2 lists some key assertion methods.

**26**

TABLE 26.1    Visual Studio Test Attribute Classes

| Test | Description |
| --- | --- |
| TestClass | Used to indicate that a class is a test class containing unit tests. |
| TestMethod | Used to decorate a method as a unit test. Test methods must have no return value (void) and cannot expect parameters (because there is nothing to pass parameters to the method). |
| TestInitialize | Used to indicate that a given method should be run before each test. This capability is useful if you need to reset the system state before each test. |
| TestCleanup | Used to indicate that the method should be run after each test. You can use this method to do any cleanup after each test. |
| ClassInitialize | Used to indicate that the method should be run once before any tests in the class are run. |
| ClassCleanup | Used to indicate that the method should run once after all tests in the class are executed. |
| ExpectedException | Used to indicate that a given test is expected to throw a certain exception. This capability is useful for testing expected error conditions. |

TABLE 26.2  Test Assertions

| Test | Description |
| --- | --- |
| AreSame/AreNotSame | Used to test whether two objects are the same object (or not) |
| AreEqual/AreNotEqual | Used to test whether two values are equal to one another (or not) |
| IsNull/IsNotNull | Used to test whether an object contains a null reference (or not) |
| IsInstanceOfType/IsNotInstanceOfType | Used to determine whether an object is of a specified type (or not) |
| IsTrue/IsFalse | Used to test whether a condition is true (or false) |

Many of the methods listed in Table 26.2 contain multiple overloads. These overloads allow you to compare various data types to one another, generic collections, and more. In addition, there are overloads that allow you to simply do the assert and those that both do the assert and allow you to enter a message that is displayed when the assertion fails.

The UnitTesting namespace also contains additional assertion classes. The CollectionAssert class is used to verify the contents of collections. As an example, you can call the Contains method to assert whether a given collection contains a specific element. The StringAssert class contains methods for matching strings and portions of strings. You can use the StartsWith method, for example, to assert whether a string begins with a certain set of characters.

## Creating Unit Tests

There are a few ways you can initiate the creation of unit tests. You can do so manually by creating a class file and adding the appropriate references, attributes, and the like. You can also add a unit test item to a test project via the Test menu or the context menu associated with a test project. These methods create blank unit tests to which you can add your code.

Visual Studio also provides a means of automating the creation of unit tests. You can right-click an existing class and choose Create Unit Tests from the context menu. In this case, Visual Studio will actually generate a set of unit tests based on the code in your class. You can also right-click a test project and choose Add, Unit Test. This will allow you to select classes in the solution for which you want to generate unit tests.

What gets generated is more than just stub code. Visual Studio actually examines the methods and properties in your class and writes out real, possible tests. Of course, you have to finish adding the appropriate values and assertions, but what is generated is a nice start.

Let's look at an example. Suppose that you have a Customer object that contains standard properties such as Name, Address, Phone, and Email. It also can contain methods such as

Save, Update, and Delete. Also, suppose that you choose to add a new unit test to your test project. Visual Studio will present the Create Unit Tests dialog box. Figure 26.12 shows an example.

FIGURE 26.12   Unit Test Creation dialog box.

In this dialog box, you can select the members that need to have tests generated. For this example, the members of the Customer object have been selected. The Settings button opens a dialog box that allows you to indicate various settings for generating your unit tests. Figure 26.13 shows an example of this dialog box. Notice you can use the macro text [File], [Class], and [Method] to indicate that Visual Studio should use key portions of the class to name portions of the test.

Visual Studio generates a test for every method and every property in the object. As an example, consider the Name property. Listing 26.2 shows what Visual Studio generated as a unit test for this property. Notice that this test creates a new instance of the Customer object. It then attempts to set the value of the Name property. Finally, it confirms that this property set was successful via the assertion. This is a valid property test. All that is left for a developer is to put a valid value into the variable expected (note the TODO) and remove the Assert.Inconclusive call.

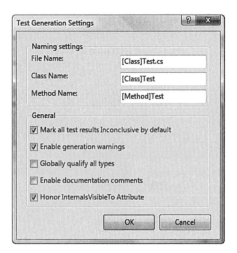

FIGURE 26.13    The Test Generation Settings dialog box.

LISTING 26.2    A Sample of an Auto-Generated Unit Test

```
[TestMethod()]
public void NameTest() {
  Customer target = new Customer(); // TODO: Initialize to an appropriate value
    string expected = string.Empty; // TODO: Initialize to an appropriate value
    string actual;
    target.Name = expected;
    actual = target.Name;
    Assert.AreEqual(expected, actual);
    Assert.Inconclusive("Verify the correctness of this test method.");
}
```

## Running Unit Tests

You can run your tests from the Test Tools toolbar or the Test menu. You have a couple of options: Run with the debugger or run without it. The former allows you to break into the debugger if a test fails. This capability can be useful if you are troubleshooting code through tests. The latter is a more likely scenario. You simply want to run your set of unit tests and determine their results.

The Test Tools toolbar runs all tests in a given project. You will want to use the Test List Editor to run a group, list, or subset of tests. For example, if you simply want to run the Customer unit tests, you can open the Test List Editor from the Test menu.

From the Test List Editor window, choose Class Name from the Group By list. This will allow you to zero in on just the CustomerTest tests. You can highlight all of these tests and check their box for execution, as shown in Figure 26.14.

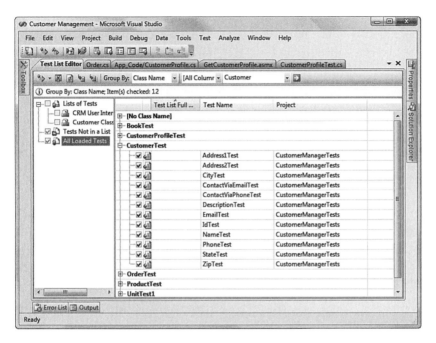

FIGURE 26.14    Selecting tests in the Test List Editor, All Loaded Tests pane.

You could also enter a filter to find tests you want to run. To do so, you enter your search criteria in the rightmost text box of the Test List Editor toolbar. You then click the green arrow to apply the filter. If your test list will be run often, you can create an actual new list to store the list of tests you want to run as a group. You can do so by right-clicking Lists of Tests in the Test List Editor explorer and then selecting New Test List. Here you can add new tests to a list and save the list for future reference.

When you have the list of tests you want to run, you can do so from the toolbar on the Test List Editor. You choose the Run Checked Tests option to do so.

> **NOTE**
>
> When you run a test project, only the test project is recompiled. If you make changes to a project you are testing, you must recompile that project. This approach is different from "running" applications with the debugger and can therefore take some time to get used to.

**Viewing Test Results**

The Test Results window provides an overview of which tests passed and which failed. Figure 26.15 shows this window in action. Notice that the given test run is considered failed if one or more tests fail. In this case, 11 of 12 tests passed. However, the overall test failed due to the one test failure.

You can navigate through the results in the Test Results window. If you double-click a test, you are presented with statistics relative to the test. The top of Figure 26.15 shows the failure information for the CityTest; this includes the error message and stack trace.

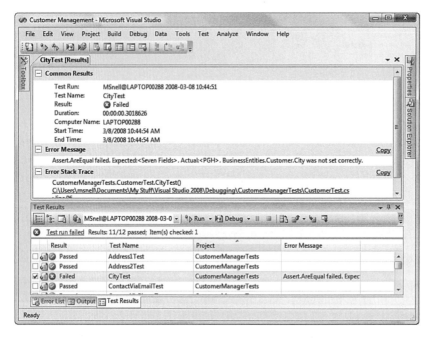

FIGURE 26.15    Test results.

You can also publish the results of your testing to Team Foundation Server. Doing so provides vital statistics on the quality of a given build, including which tests were run and what the results were. In addition, you can right-click a test and generate a Team Systems work item. This capability is useful if you have a failure. You can right-click it and log it as a bug or task for someone to fix. Figure 26.16 shows an example of logging a bug against the test results.

When you add a Bug work item based on a test, part of the work item is filled in for you by Visual Studio. This includes the Test information. Figure 26.17 shows the result of adding the CityTest as a Bug work item. Note that the path to the test, its name, and its ID are auto-filled by the tool.

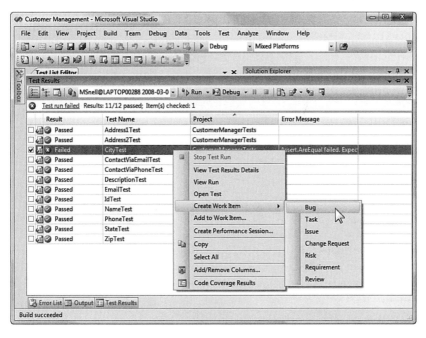

FIGURE 26.16   Logging a work item against a unit test result.

**26**

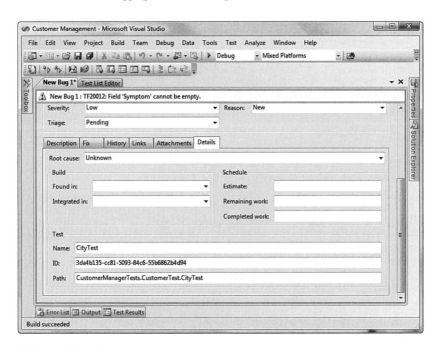

FIGURE 26.17   The Test information inside the Bug work item.

## Code Coverage Analysis

Automated unit tests are wonderful. However, you also need some assurance that the unit tests cover all the code in the system. This is true especially for project managers and other stakeholders. They need a measure of how much code is being tested. They cannot simply rely on the word of the developers (who are often also unsure).

Visual Studio provides code coverage analysis to help solve this issue. This analysis matches unit tests to code and indicates what code is being covered and what code is not. The result is a shared view into the state of testing. For example, all your tests may pass; however, it makes for a different interpretation of the report if only 30% of your code is being called by those tests.

### Configuring Code Coverage

Looking at code coverage can help developers write effective unit tests. It can also help to measure those tests. You configure (or turn on) code coverage for a given assembly from the .testrunconfig file (found in the Solution Items folder). Figure 26.18 shows this file. In this example, code coverage is turned on for the BusinessEntities.dll project.

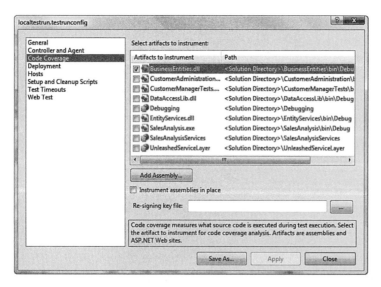

FIGURE 26.18    Configuring code coverage.

### Evaluating Code Coverage

The next step is to rerun your tests. Visual Studio then captures the coverage data. This data is then presented to you in the Code Coverage Results window. You can access this window from the toolbar on the Test Results window. Figure 26.19 shows an example of these test results.

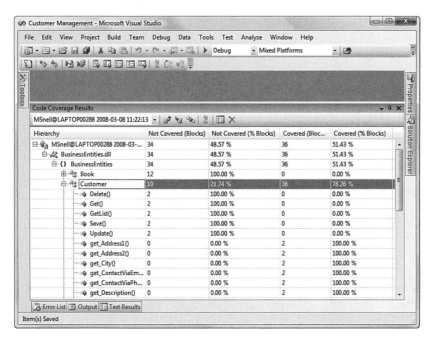

FIGURE 26.19   Code coverage results.

Notice that only approximately 78% of the code is covered inside the Customer class. You can navigate through this list to find gaps. Plus, you can quickly see that several methods do not have unit tests (0% coverage).

You can navigate to this code directly from the coverage window. In fact, you can turn on code-coloring from the Coverage toolbar. Code-coloring highlights in blue the code that is being called by the test. It turns red the code that is not called. These colors give you an easy way to find dead spots in your testing. Figure 26.20 shows an example of this coloring (although the distinction is difficult to see in this black-and-white book). The Id property is covered by the executing tests, but the method below it is not.

# Performance Profiling

Visual Studio provides a tool for profiling your application for performance. With it, you can analyze your application for performance issues and take action to remediate any issues found. Performance profiling and reporting is done within the IDE.

The primary vehicle within Visual Studio for evaluating and analyzing performance issues in code is a performance session. You create a performance session to profile your application. The process of *profiling* involves the following actions:

1. Configuring an application for performance analysis.
2. Collecting the performance data.
3. Viewing/analyzing the collected data.

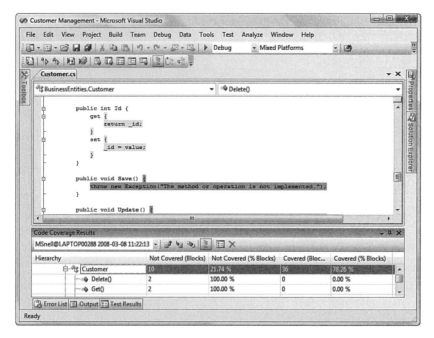

FIGURE 26.20    Code coverage coloring.

The Performance Explorer in Visual Studio provides a point-and-click interface for establishing performance sessions and analyzing the resulting datasets. It has a simple interface with a toolbar and a client area where data is displayed. The Performance Explorer is capable of displaying and managing multiple performance sessions at a time.

> **NOTE**
>
> Performance profiling is now supported for 64-bit as well as 32-bit machines.

## Creating a Performance Session

You access the Performance Explorer from the View menu (View, Other Windows, Performance Explorer). This opens an explorer window similar to the Solution Explorer or Server Explorer. You can also get to the Performance Explorer action items from the Analyze menu. This lets you launch the performance analyzer, look at code metrics (more on this later), and compare reports.

The Performance Explorer window has a toolbar at the top that contains various useful items. Figure 26.21 shows an overview of this toolbar.

The toolbar enables you to create a new performance session via either the Performance Wizard or the New Performance Session button. Table 26.3 describes these buttons and the others found in Figure 26.21.

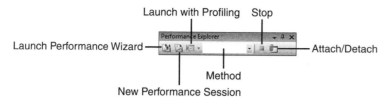

FIGURE 26.21   The Performance Explorer toolbar.

TABLE 26.3   Performance Explorer Toolbar Buttons

| Button | Action |
| --- | --- |
| Launch Performance Wizard | Launches the Performance Wizard to create a new performance session. |
| New Performance Session | Creates a new, empty performance session. |
| Launch with Profiling | Runs a performance session against the specific target. |
| Stop | Stops a currently running performance session. |
| Attach/Detach | Attaches or detaches a profiler to/from a currently running process. This action is valid and will appear only when the Sampling method is selected in the Method drop-down. |
| Method | Allows you to specify the profiling method (either Sampling or Instrumentation) for a performance session. |

The Performance Wizard will collect information concerning all the following:

▶ The type of the assembly you are gathering data about

▶ The location of the assembly

▶ The method of performance profiling to implement

**TIP**

If a solution is currently loaded into Visual Studio, you can select one of its projects as the target of the performance session instead of browsing to an assembly on disk.

Performance profiling is conducted using either sampling or instrumentation. Sampling is used to profile an entire application; instrumentation is used to specifically target an individual module within an application.

After the basic session information has been collected, the wizard will close and the Performance Explorer will show a tree view of the session data. This tree view is organized into two major parent nodes: Targets (the assemblies or modules you identified in the wizard) and Reports (the actual performance data collected against the targets). Figure 26.22 shows a performance session as viewed within the Performance Explorer.

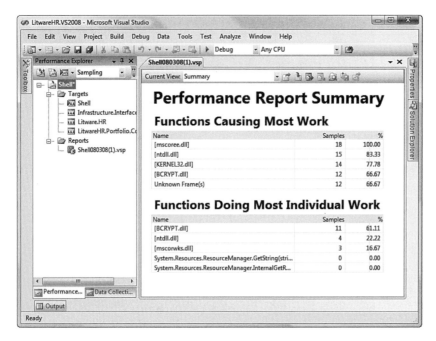

FIGURE 26.22   A performance session in the Performance Explorer.

The Performance Explorer can display multiple sessions at one time. The shortcut menu for a session exposes several useful commands, including those to launch the session, set the session as the current session, and edit the properties for the session.

## Configuring a Session

To edit the individual properties of any given session, right-click on the session node (in the example shown in Figure 26.22, this is the node titled Shell), and select the Properties command. The Properties dialog box exposes various basic and advanced properties for the selected session.

### General Properties

The General Properties property page enables you to set general instrumentation properties. You can select the profiling method (sampling or instrumentation) and also enable/disable memory profiling during the session.

Two check boxes control the collection of object allocation and lifetime statistics. If the Collect .NET Object Allocation Information box is not checked, the Allocation subreport will not be available for analysis. If the Also Collect .NET Object Lifetime Information box is not checked, the Objects Lifetime subreport will not be available.

You can also control how reports are named and stored:

▶ **Report Location**—The physical folder used to save the performance report.

▶ **Report Name**—The name of the report.

▶ **Automatically Add New Reports**—If checked, will cause new reports to automatically appear under the Reports node within the Performance Explorer.

▶ **Append Incrementing Number**—If checked, will cause an incrementing number to be appended to the report name and filename to prevent name collisions.

▶ **Use a Timestamp**—If checked, will use a timestamp basis for the report number.

### Launch Properties

The Launch Properties page controls the binaries launched and their order. The available binaries appear in a list. Check those to launch in the performance session and use the up and down arrows to change the launch order.

### Sampling Properties

Sampling events are the mechanism by which performance sessions collect data at specified intervals during a target run. Use the Sampling Properties page to change the sampling event used by the profiler. You can also change the sampling interval (the time distance between sampling events). For example, you could decide to do a performance sample after every five page faults. You would configure this by selecting Page Fault as the sample event and changing the sampling interval to 5.

If you select the Performance Counter sample event, you can then select from a list of all the available performance counters. Figure 26.23 shows an example of sampling based on hardware interrupts. Note that the Summary section (toward the bottom of the dialog box) provides a plain-text description of the selected sampling event and interval.

### Binary Properties

As part of the instrumentation process, probes are automatically inserted into the session targets and assemblies. The Binary Properties property page will override this behavior and force the profiler to first make a copy of the binaries and place them in a specified directory before changing them. The following are the binary property options:

▶ **Relocate Instrumented Binaries**—If checked, will cause the target binaries to be copied to a directory before instrumentation. The original binaries will not be touched.

▶ **Location to Place the Instrumented Binaries**—Specifies a physical location for the instrumented binaries.

### Instrumentation Properties

You use the Instrumentation Properties property page to indicate executables or batch files that you want to run before or after a session's instrumentation. You could use this, for example, to make certain environment changes to a machine prior to profiling and then to return the machine to its prior state after profiling has completed. The following are the instrumentation options:

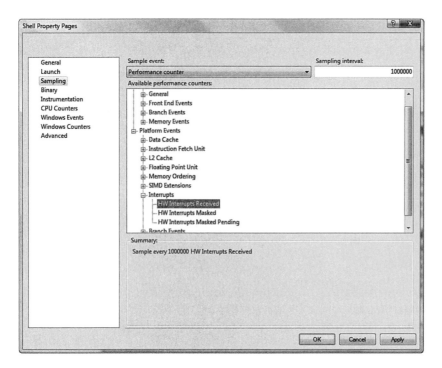

FIGURE 26.23   Configuring sample events for a performance session.

▶ **Pre-Instrument Command Line**—Command to issue before instrumentation; this is typically used to specify a .cmd/.bat or executable to run prior to the session instrumentation.

▶ **Pre-Instrument Description**—A free-form description of the pre-instrument command.

▶ **Pre-Instrument Exclude**—Checking this box will cause the session to skip the pre-instrument command that you have specified (but will not remove it from the text box).

▶ **Post-Instrument Command Line**—Command to issue before instrumentation; this is typically used to specify a .cmd/.bat or executable to run prior to the session instrumentation.

▶ **Post-Instrument Description**—A description of the post-instrument command.

▶ **Post-Instrument Exclude**—Checking this box will cause the session to skip the post-instrument command that you have specified (but will not remove it from the text box).

### CPU Counters Properties

CPUs generally implement their own performance counters. By checking the box on the CPU Counters property page, you are asking the profiler to collect data directly from one or more of these counters. To select a counter, expand the available counters tree until the counter of interest is shown, highlight the counter, and then click on the arrow button to transfer it to the list of selected counters. Figure 26.24 shows how to select CPU performance counters.

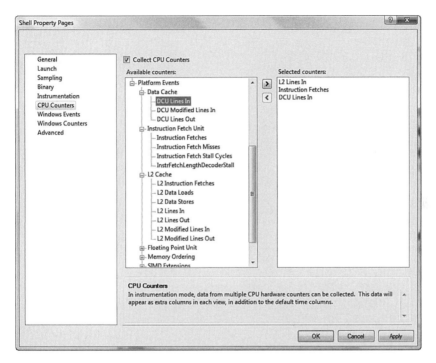

FIGURE 26.24    Selecting CPU performance counters.

**NOTE**

The counters available are hardware dependent and will vary by chip type and manufacturer.

### Windows Events Properties

.NET applications, and the runtime itself, are capable of registering and exposing various event trace providers. The Performance Explorer can collect data from these providers during a performance session (see Figure 26.25).

### Windows Counters Properties

You can collect Windows performance counter data as part of the application profiling. This includes counters for ASP.NET, the .NET CLR, the database, and many more. Figure 26.26 shows the configuration of these counters.

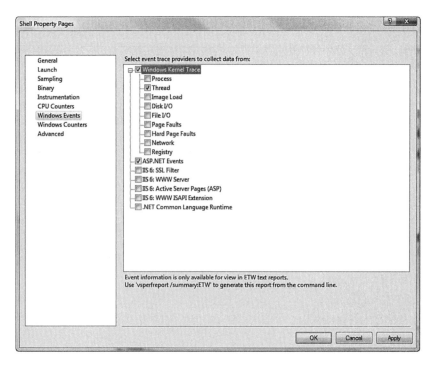

**FIGURE 26.25**    Collecting data from event trace providers.

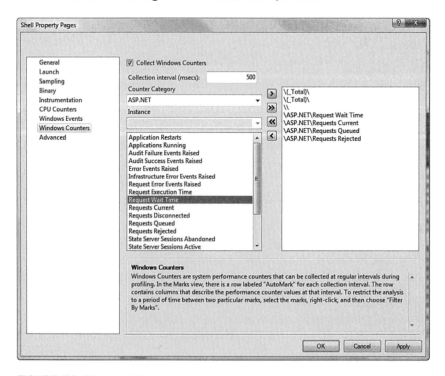

**FIGURE 26.26**    The Windows Counters properties.

### Advanced Properties

The VSInstr command-line tool is used to instrument and run profiling sessions within the IDE. This takes place behind the scenes when you use the Performance Explorer to create and run those sessions. Sometimes, though, you might need to pass command-line options to the VSInstr tool. The Advanced Properties page is used to do just that.

## Session Targets

Each session can have multiple targets; only one target, however, will be profiled when the session is run. The "launch" target is denoted with a green "run" triangle. Right-clicking on a target brings up the shortcut menu for targets. From this menu, you can remove the target from the list, set the target as the launch target, or edit the properties of the target. The properties selection will launch an Object Property dialog box in which you can specify more advanced information that is not collected by the Performance Wizard.

### Launch Properties

Use the Launch property page to indicate executables or batch files that you want to run before or after a session's instrumentations. The following are the launch properties:

- ▶ **Override Project Settings**—Checking this box enables you to manually specify the target executable and arguments.

- ▶ **Executable to Launch**—The executable assembly to launch as the target of the session.

- ▶ **Arguments**—Arguments to be passed to the target executable.

- ▶ **Working Directory**—The working directory for the target executable.

### Instrumentation Properties

The Instrumentation Properties page is identical in form and function to the Instrumentation Properties page in the Session Properties dialog box (discussed previously).

### Advanced Properties

This page is identical in form and function to the Advanced Properties page in the Session Properties dialog box (discussed previously).

## Reports

The Reports node of the Performance Explorer tree (refer back to Figure 26.22) contains the analysis reports generated as the result of running a profile against a target. Clicking on a report will display its contents in a multitabbed window, similar to a Visual Studio editor window.

Report data can be exported into more consumable formats: Right-click on a report node and select Export Report from the shortcut menu. The Export Report dialog box, shown in Figure 26.27, launches. When exporting a report, you can you select the desired subreports and the export format (CSV or XML).

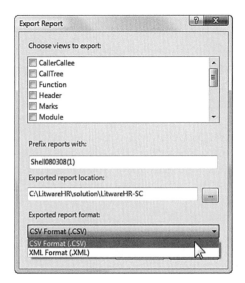

FIGURE 26.27    Exporting a report.

## Understanding Performance Reports

The reports generated from a performance session will vary in their form and content depending on whether the session was an instrumentation or sample session. The profile data is organized across several subreports. With the exception of the Summary, each subreport is displayed in a tabular format with columns and rows; the columns represent the various data collection points (such as Number of Calls or Application Exclusive Time). The rows represent the entities specific to the subreport. For the Functions subreport, for example, these will be functions.

---

**TIP**

You can sort a specific subreport by clicking on a column heading. This will toggle between an ascending and descending sort on that column's data. This capability is obviously very useful on reports such as the Functions report: You can sort descending by the Number of Calls column to get a great sense of which routings are being used the most within a given application or module.

---

Table 26.4 provides an exhaustive list of all the possible data points within each performance report.

There are a total of six subreports (also referred to as *views*) within a performance report. Each subreport has a small set of data points displayed by default. You can add or remove data points (effectively adding or removing columns in the subreport) by right-clicking in the report (or on any of the column headers) and selecting Add/Remove Columns. A list of all valid data points for the current subreport will display, enabling you to simply check the ones you want to view. Refer to Table 26.4.

TABLE 26.4    Performance Report Columns

| Column | Subreport | Description |
|---|---|---|
| Application Exclusive Time | Functions, Caller/Callee | Execution time for a function that does not include the time for instrumentation, callees from the function, or transition events. |
| Application Inclusive Time | Functions, Caller/Callee | Same as the Application Exclusive Time sample, except callee times are included. |
| AVG Application Exclusive Time | Functions, Caller/Callee, Call Tree | The average Application Exclusive Time for all instances of a function within a given time range. |
| AVG Application Inclusive Time | Functions, Caller/Callee, Call Tree | The average Application Inclusive Time for all instances of a function within a given time range. |
| AVG Elapsed Exclusive Time | Functions, Caller/Callee, Call Tree | The average Elapsed Exclusive Time for all instances of a function within a given time range. |
| AVG Elapsed Inclusive Time | Functions, Caller/Callee, Call Tree | The average Elapsed Inclusive Time for all instances of a function within a given time range. |
| Class Name | Allocation | The name of the class. |
| Class Token | Allocation, Objects Lifetime | A metadata identifier for a class. |
| Elapsed Exclusive Time | Functions, Caller/Callee | Time for execution of a function; includes transition events but does not include time for any called functions. |
| Elapsed Inclusive Time | Functions, Caller/Callee | Time for execution of a function including transition events and execution time for all called functions. |
| Exclusive Allocations | Functions, Caller/Callee, Call Tree | Object allocations made in a function; excludes all called functions. |

26

TABLE 26.4    Continued

| Column | Subreport | Description |
|---|---|---|
| Exclusive Allocations % | Functions | Exclusive Allocations expressed as a percentage of all total allocations. |
| Exclusive Bytes Allocated | Functions, Caller/Callee, Call Tree | Bytes allocated in a function; excludes bytes allocated in any called function. |
| Exclusive Bytes % | Functions, Caller/Callee, Call Tree | Exclusive Bytes expressed as a percentage of all total bytes allocated. |
| Exclusive Samples | Functions, Caller/Callee | All samples made in a function; excludes samples in any called function. |
| Exclusive Transitions | Caller/Callee, Call Tree | Total number of transition events that occurred in a function, excluding any called functions. |
| Exclusive Transitions % | Functions, Caller/Callee, Call Tree | Inclusive Transitions expressed as a percentage of all total transition events. |
| Function Address | Functions, Caller/Callee, Call Tree, Allocation | The memory address of a function in hex. |
| Function Name | Functions, Caller/Callee, Call Tree, Allocation | The name of the function. |
| Gen 0 Bytes Collected | Objects Lifetime | Total number of bytes collected by the .NET Garbage Collector for a specific generation. |
| Gen 1 Bytes Collected | Objects Lifetime | Total number of bytes collected by the .NET Garbage Collector for a specific generation. |
| Gen 2 Bytes Collected | Objects Lifetime | Total number of bytes collected by the .NET Garbage Collector for a specific generation. |
| Gen 0 Instances Collected | Objects Lifetime | Total number of object instances collected by the .NET Garbage Collector for a specific generation. |

| Column | Subreport | Description |
|---|---|---|
| Gen 1 Instances Collected | Objects Lifetime | Total number of object instances collected by the .NET Garbage Collector for a specific generation. |
| Gen 2 Instances Collected | Objects Lifetime | Total number of object instances collected by the .NET Garbage Collector for a specific generation. |
| Inclusive Allocations | Functions, Caller/Callee, Call Tree | Object allocations made in a function, including all called functions. |
| Inclusive Allocations % | Functions | Inclusive Allocations expressed as a percentage of all total allocations. |
| Inclusive Bytes Allocated | Functions, Caller/Callee, Call Tree | Bytes allocated in a function, including all bytes allocated in all called functions. |
| Inclusive Bytes % | Functions, Caller/Callee, Call Tree | Inclusive Bytes expressed as a percentage of all total bytes allocated. |
| Inclusive Samples | Functions, Caller/Callee | All samples made in a function, including all samples made in all called functions. |
| Inclusive Transitions | Caller/Callee, Call Tree | Count of transition events occurring in a function, including all transition events occurring in all called functions. |
| Inclusive Transitions % | Functions, Caller/Callee, Call Tree | Inclusive Transitions expressed as a percentage of all total transition events. |
| Instances | Allocation, Objects Lifetime | Total number of instances for a given object. |
| Instances Alive at End | Objects Lifetime | Total number of instances of a given object still alive (loaded in memory) at the time when the performance session ended. |

26

TABLE 26.4 Continued

| Column | Subreport | Description |
|---|---|---|
| Large Object Heap Bytes Collected | Objects Lifetime | Total number of large object instance bytes, placed on the heap, that were collected by the .NET Garbage Collector. |
| Large Object Heap Instances Collected | Objects Lifetime | Total number of large object instances, placed on the heap, that were collected by the .NET Garbage Collector. |
| Line Number | Functions, Caller/Callee, Call Tree, Allocation | The starting line number of a function (within the context of a source file). |
| MAX Application Exclusive Time | Functions, Caller/Callee, Call Tree | The largest Application Exclusive Time recorded during the performance session for all instances of a function. |
| MAX Application Inclusive Time | Functions, Caller/Callee, Call Tree | The largest Application Inclusive Time recorded during the performance session for all instances of a function. |
| MAX Elapsed Inclusive Time | Functions, Caller/Callee, Call Tree | The largest Elapsed Inclusive Time recorded during the performance session for all instances of a function. |
| MAX Elapsed Exclusive Time | Functions, Caller/Callee, Call Tree | The largest Elapsed Exclusive Time recorded during the performance session for all instances of a function. |
| MIN Application Exclusive Time | Functions, Caller/Callee, Call Tree | The smallest Application Exclusive Time recorded during the performance session for all instances of a function. |
| MIN Application Inclusive Time | Functions, Caller/Callee, Call Tree | The smallest Application Inclusive Time recorded during the performance session for all instances of a function. |

| Column | Subreport | Description |
|---|---|---|
| MIN Elapsed Inclusive Time | Functions, Caller/Callee, Call Tree | The smallest Application Inclusive Time recorded during the performance session for all instances of a function. |
| MIN Elapsed Exclusive Time | Functions, Caller/Callee, Call Tree | The smallest Application Exclusive Time recorded during the performance session for all instances of a function. |
| Module Identifier | Functions, Caller/Callee, Call Tree | Within a process, a sequential number assigned to modules as they are loaded. |
| Module Name | Functions, Caller/Callee, Call Tree, Allocation | The name of the module. |
| Module Path | Functions, Caller/Callee, Call Tree, Allocation | Physical path to the module. |
| Number of Calls | Functions, Caller/Callee, Call Tree | Number of calls made to a function. |
| Parent Function Address | Call Tree | Address in memory of the caller function (in hex). |
| Percentage of Calls | Functions, Caller/Callee, Call Tree | Number of calls made to a function as a percentage of all calls made to all functions. |
| Process ID | Functions, Caller/Callee, Call Tree, Allocation, Objects Lifetime | Numeric ID for a given process. |
| Process Name | Functions, Caller/Callee, Call Tree, Allocation, Objects Lifetime | The name of the process. |
| Root Application Exclusive Time | Caller/Callee | The Application Exclusive Time for the root function of the selected function. |
| Root Application Inclusive Time | Caller/Callee | The Application Inclusive Time for the root function of the selected function. |
| Root Elapsed Exclusive Time | Caller/Callee | The Elapsed Exclusive Time for the root function of the selected function. |

26

TABLE 26.4    Continued

| Column | Subreport | Description |
|---|---|---|
| Root Elapsed Inclusive Time | Caller/Callee | The Elapsed Inclusive Time for the root function of the selected function. |
| Root Node Recursive | Functions, Caller/Callee, Call Tree | For a given function, indicates whether it was called directly or indirectly in the recursive chain. |
| Source File Name | Functions, Caller/Callee, Call Tree, Allocation | Source file that contains the given function. |
| Time Exclusive CAP Overhead | Functions, Caller/Callee, Call Tree | The total time for all probes within the exclusive time of the function that were called by the parent function. |
| Time Inclusive CAP Overhead | Functions, Caller/Callee, Call Tree | The total time for all probes within the inclusive time of the function that were called by the parent function. |
| Total Bytes Allocated | Allocation, Objects Lifetime | For a given data type or class instance, total number of bytes allocated. |
| Type | Caller/Callee, Allocation | A number indicating caller/callee relationship: 0—Root function 1—Calling function 2—Called function |
| Unique ID | Functions, Caller/Callee, Call Tree | A number, in hex, used to identify a function. |
| Unique Process ID | Functions, Caller/Callee, Call Tree, Allocation, Objects Lifetime | A sequential number (unsigned integer) assigned to a process in order of its activation. |
| % Application Exclusive Time | Functions, Caller/Callee, Call Tree | Application Exclusive Time for a given function expressed as a percentage of the sum of all function application exclusive times. |

| Column | Subreport | Description |
|---|---|---|
| % Application Inclusive Time | Functions, Caller/Callee, Call Tree | Application Inclusive Time for a given function expressed as a percentage of the sum of all function application inclusive times. |
| % Elapsed Exclusive Time | Functions, Caller/Callee, Call Tree | Elapsed Exclusive Time for a given function expressed as a percentage of the sum of all function elapsed exclusive times. |
| % Elapsed Inclusive Time | Functions, Caller/Callee, Call Tree | Elapsed Inclusive Time for a given function expressed as a percentage of the sum of all function elapsed inclusive times. |
| % of Total Bytes | Allocation, Objects Lifetime | A measure of the Total Bytes Allocated divided by the total bytes allocated for all data types or class instances during the performance session. |
| % Time Exclusive CAP Overhead | Functions, Caller/Callee, Call Tree | The Time Exclusive CAP Overhead expressed as a percentage of the sum of all exclusive CAP overhead timings. |
| % Time Inclusive CAP Overhead | Functions, Caller/Callee, Call Tree | The Time Inclusive CAP Overhead expressed as a percentage of the sum of all inclusive CAP overhead timings. |

**26**

### Summary Subreport

The Summary subreport provides a summary of function statistics such as most-called functions and longest-running functions. Double-clicking on one of the listed functions will jump immediately to the function data in the Functions subreport (see the following section).

This tab is most useful in gaining an at-a-glance feel for performance hot spots within the profiled application or module.

## Functions Subreport

The Functions subreport provides an exhaustive list of all functions that were called during the profile session. Each function is presented with timing data and, in the case of an instrumentation session, the number of calls made into that function.

## Caller/Callee Subreport

The Caller/Callee tab presents caller/callee information in three separate panes. The middle pane contains a selected, called function. Functions that appear in the top pane are functions that called the selected function (the caller function), and functions that appear in the bottom pane are functions that were called by the target function (the callee function).

This view is fully dynamic: Clicking on any of the functions that appear in any of the three panes will cause that function to be selected and thus placed in the middle pane, with the caller and callee panes changing to reflect the new selected function.

## Hotpathing with the Call Tree Subreport

The Call Tree view shows you a trace of the call tree generated during the performance session. Each function call is represented within the call tree, and you can expand or collapse lists of called functions within a given root function.

You can reposition any calling function into the root node by using the right-click shortcut menu and selecting Set Root. You can redisplay the true root node by selecting Reset Root from the shortcut menu.

This view is particularly useful to gain insight into inclusive/exclusive function timings. These timings help you understand where your application is spending the most time. In fact, there is now a Hotpathing option to help you pinpoint this information. Figure 26.28 shows the Call Tree view of the performance profile report. Here you can see the flame icon on the toolbar. When you click this option, the report will be filtered to show areas in your application that are taking the most time executing. These areas will also be highlighted by a flame icon as shown.

## Allocation Subreport

The Allocation subreport is a list of the types/objects allocated during the performance session. Each type is displayed along with the function or functions responsible for its allocation.

The default columns within this view can be used to identify any types or function areas that are memory intensive.

## Objects Lifetime Subreport

The Objects Lifetime view is similar to the Allocation view but instead focuses on the timed lifetime of all types/objects allocated during the session. Each class is represented as a row in the subreport.

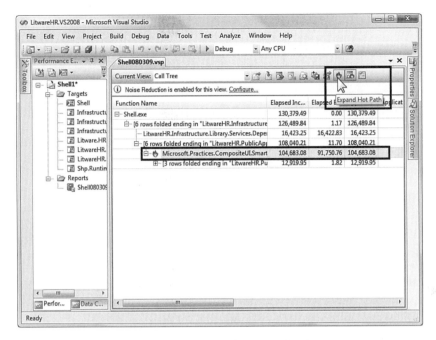

FIGURE 26.28   Hotpathing to an area of your application.

**NOTE**

Although having a large number of data points is useful when performance is being analyzed, two data points stand out as great tripwires for finding code that isn't behaving as expected: Number of Calls and Elapsed Exclusive Time. If a function is looping more than expected or is taking longer to execute than expected, these two data points (both present by default on the Functions view) should immediately help you to identify those routines.

### Report Comparison

You can also use Visual Studio to compare one report against another. You do so from the Analyze menu, Compare Performance Reports option. This brings up the dialog shown in Figure 26.29. Here you set a baseline report and a report to which you want to compare.

The results of a simple comparison are shown in Figure 26.30. Here you can see the change between the very first execution of a simple .NET application and its second run. The data that gets compared, of course, is dependent on the data you have configured the profiler to collect.

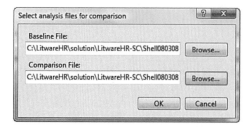

FIGURE 26.29    Select performance reports to compare.

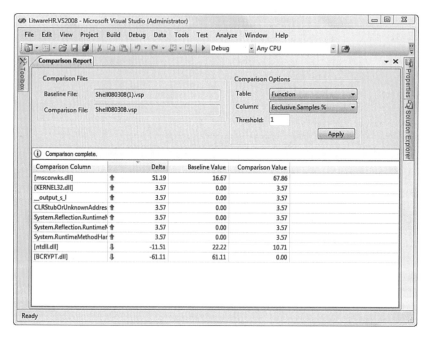

FIGURE 26.30    Viewing report comparisons.

# Code Analysis

As discussed in Chapter 24, "Source Control," you can define specific policies that affect what code developers are allowed to check in to the solution. These check-in policies allow you to define the best practices to which you plan to adhere and then ensure that these policies are being enforced. One important check-in policy in this regard is the code analysis policy. The code analyzer is able to examine your code against a set of predetermined, specific best practices in order to prevent issues before they happen. This tool can be used with source control check-in policies or on its own.

## Configuring Rules to Enforce

You configure the set of rules you intend to enforce on a per-project basis. This allows you to control which rules will be applied for a specific project type in your solution. For example, you might have one set of rules for your user interface and a slightly different configuration for your middle-tier code. The good news is that your settings persist. In addition, they get checked in to the solution and then propagated to other developers. In this way, you can define a common set of rules to be checked for each team member's code and make sure that they get enforced.

Rules are configured through the Project Properties dialog (right-click the project file and select Properties). In this window, you select the Code Analysis tab on the left side to see your options. Figure 26.31 shows an example of this.

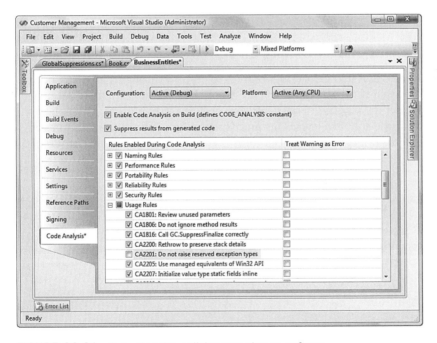

FIGURE 26.31    Selecting the policies you plan to enforce.

At the top of the Code Analysis configuration window, you can indicate the type of build to which your configuration applies. This way you can have one configuration during debugging and another during release. In fact, you might want to turn code analysis off during debugging. The check box Enable Code Analysis on Build allows you to do just that. With this option checked, Code Analysis runs every time you build your solution. Otherwise, it runs only when you tell it to.

There is a list of rules that the static code analyzer uses when reviewing your code. This list is categorized by such items as design, globalization, interoperability, maintainability, mobility, naming, and security. Each category contains rules that apply to that category. You can review this list and select only the ones you want to enforce.

Each rule is identified by a unique id. This id is linked to additional details about the rule, its enforcement, and suggestions on how you might write your code to comply with the rule. Notice in Figure 26.31 that CA2201 is being turned off from Code Analysis. This rule is a Usage rule that says .NET reserved exceptions should not be in your code. In this case, violations of this rule will be ignored.

> **NOTE**
>
> The Code Analyzer now includes rules that can spell-check your code. For example, rule CA1703 checks resource strings for proper spelling. Rule 1704 makes sure that your identifiers like class names are spelled correctly.

## Treating Rule Violations as Coding Errors

Recall from Chapter 24 that you can configure rules to enforce through a check-in policy. These policies are created through Team Explorer (right-click the project, choose Source Control Settings, select the Check-in Policy tab, and click the Add button). The policies defined here apply at the solution level. This means that all projects in the solution get the same Code Analysis policy. The policy editor is the same as discussed previously; in this case, it simply applies across all projects in the solution.

You might then have both a global setting that defines a group of analysis rules and a project-specific group. The project-specific group will apply during development. However, the solution policy will be enforced at the time of check-in. You can replace your project-specific policy settings with those of the check-in policy through the Analyze menu. Figure 26.32 shows your options. You can replace your settings or merge the two rule sets.

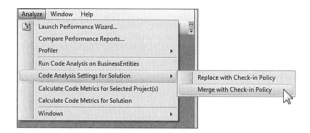

FIGURE 26.32    Replacing or merging code analysis rule sets.

## Treating Rule Violations as Coding Errors

By default, violations to the code analysis rules are treated as warnings by the IDE. That means your code will still compile and run without exception, but you will get a list of warning messages.

You can select the Treat Warning as Error option next to a given rule to change this behavior. This setting tells the compiler to treat the given rule as an error and not just a simple warning.

Figure 26.33 shows an example of setting this value for the performance rule CA1822. This rule states that class members that do not require an object should be marked as static (to improve performance). Issues of this type will now be marked as errors (and not just warnings) by the code analyzer. We will look at this in a moment.

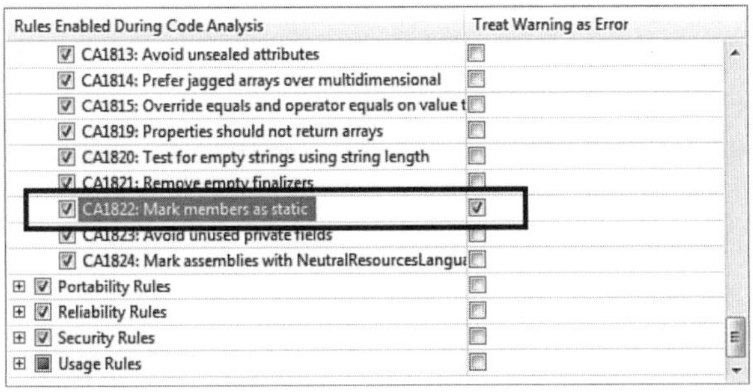

| Rules Enabled During Code Analysis | Treat Warning as Error |
|---|---|
| ☑ CA1813: Avoid unsealed attributes | ☐ |
| ☑ CA1814: Prefer jagged arrays over multidimensional | ☐ |
| ☑ CA1815: Override equals and operator equals on value t☐ | |
| ☑ CA1819: Properties should not return arrays | ☐ |
| ☑ CA1820: Test for empty strings using string length | ☐ |
| ☑ CA1821: Remove empty finalizers | ☐ |
| ☑ CA1822: Mark members as static | ☑ |
| ☑ CA1823: Avoid unused private fields | ☐ |
| ☑ CA1824: Mark assemblies with NeutralResourcesLangua☐ | |
| ⊞ ☑ Portability Rules | ☐ |
| ⊞ ☑ Reliability Rules | ☐ |
| ⊞ ☑ Security Rules | ☐ |
| ⊞ ☑ Usage Rules | ☐ |

FIGURE 26.33    Marking a rule to be treated as an exception.

## Suppressing Rules

There are several ways in which you can suppress rules. One is by simply turning them off for the given project through the properties window (as we've seen). Another is to apply the SuppressMessage attribute to your code.

The SuppressMessage attribute allows you to indicate a specific rule to be suppressed (via category and id), a reason for suppressing the rule, and the scope of the suppression (entire assembly, namespace, module, member, type, resource, or parameter). If you leave the scope out, the scope will be applied at the level of the attribute. If, for example, you apply the attribute to a method, it will apply only to that method.

You must indicate at minimum both the rule category and its id. For example, to suppress the rule that states you should avoid out parameters (ByRef in VB), you would apply the following attribute at the offending method:

```
[SuppressMessage("Microsoft.Design", CA1021)]
```

You could add a justification message to this suppression to give a reason for the suppression.

---

**NOTE**

You want to suppress rules sparingly. The intent of Code Analysis is to find issues with the code. If you suppress the messages it raises, you can defeat its purpose and weakens its ability to help you write better code.

---

You can also mark items as suppressed right from the code analysis results window. Here you can select an item and choose the Suppress Message(s) option, as shown in Figure 26.34. Some items can be suppressed in source code and others must be global. In this instance the suppression would be at the assembly level.

When you suppress messages at the assembly level, Visual Studio adds a global suppression file to your project. This file contains calls to the SuppressMessage attribute that apply for the entire assembly. Figure 26.35 shows this in action. Note that Visual Studio also applies a strikethrough to the actual rule being suppressed.

---

**TIP**

You can also choose to suppress results from generated code. Refer to Figure 26.31, shown earlier. Notice the check box that allows you to turn off code analysis for the code generated by Visual Studio. This is off by default.

---

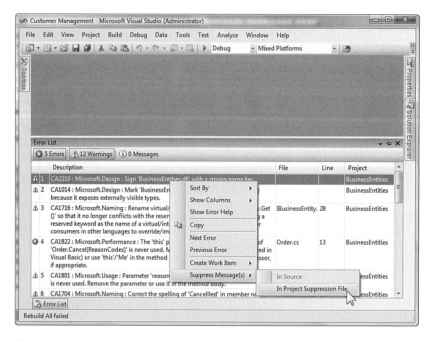

FIGURE 26.34    Suppressing a rule from within the code analysis results.

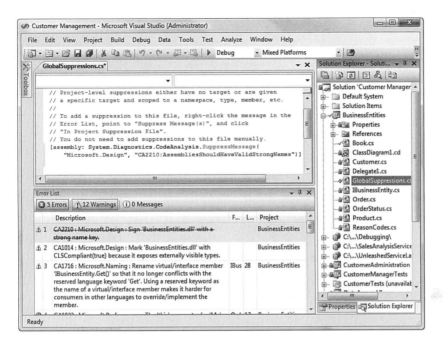

FIGURE 26.35    A **GlobalSupression.cs** file.

## Doing the Analysis

You can manually run code analysis by right-clicking a project and choosing Run Code Analysis. You can also access this option from the Analyze menu, as shown in Figure 26.36. In addition, if you configure code analysis to run on each build, executing a build or running the application will also execute the analysis.

## Viewing the Results

You view the results of code analysis in the Error List window. This window shows you errors, warnings, and messages generated by the compiler and static code analyzer. The dialog should be familiar to all .NET developers. Figure 26.37 shows an example of the static code analysis results.

Recall that back in Figure 26.33, we marked CA1822 to be treated as an error. You can see here that there are five occurrences of this issue, all treated as errors. The rest of the issues (minus those we suppressed) are shown as warnings.

From this window, you can review the issue, get help on how you might fix it, create an associated work item (bug), or suppress the item. You can also link directly to the source code in question by double-clicking it.

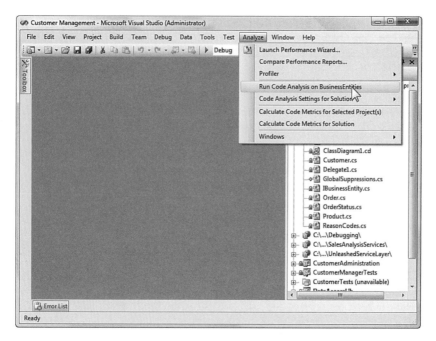

FIGURE 26.36    Running code analysis.

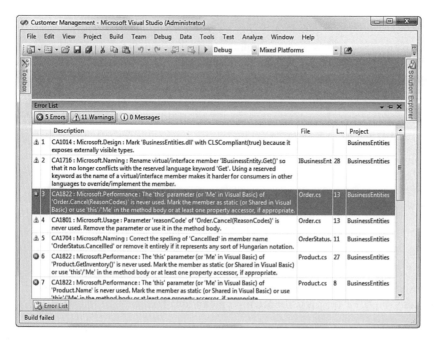

FIGURE 26.37    The code analysis results.

## Prescriptive Guidance for Remediation

You right-click an item in the error list and choose Show Error Help to find out more details on how you might fix the issue. Each static code analysis item has an associated entry in the MSDN Library. You can look up these entries by number from the Index. Figure 26.38 shows the help for the rule CA1822. You'll notice a cause, a description, and guidance on how to fix the violation. There is also information on when you might suppress the given issue.

In this example, we can simply mark the given code as a static method and the rule will be satisfied.

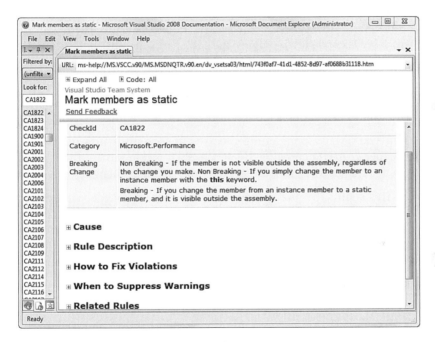

FIGURE 26.38    The code analysis rule help.

# Code Metrics

Code metrics is a new tool built into Visual Studio Team System 2008 Development Edition. It is designed to measure your code across a set of categories. These measurements rate your code for such things as maintainability and complexity. The intent is to provide insight into those areas of your code that pose a potential risk to the project. You can then zero in on these areas and apply additional development and testing to increase your score and lower your risk.

## The Measurements

There are five key areas of your code that get measured. Each is meant to provide you with a specific rating to help you understand how your code stacks up. The following lists these key areas and gives a brief description of each:

- ▶ **Maintainability**—This calculation evaluates your code and rates it for maintainability. For example, if you have a lot of indirection and layers in your code, it might be difficult to understand and to test and thus you will have a lower score. A high score represents a high degree of maintainability (and thus a lower degree of complexity). The scale for maintainability is 0 to 100 (where 100 is a perfect score).

- ▶ **Cyclomatic Complexity**—This calculation rates your code for overall complexity. Your code is evaluated for flow between objects. The more code paths, the higher the complexity. This score is constrained only by the code paths in your application.

- ▶ **Depth of Inheritance**—This rating checks your code for the number of classes required to reach the root of the hierarchy. If you have many objects that inherit from one another, you will have a higher depth of inheritance rating. This typically means your code will be more difficult to understand and maintain.

- ▶ **Class Coupling**—The class coupling rating checks your code to see how interdependent it is. This higher degree of coupling, the less likely it is that pieces of the code will be able to be reused and the more brittle the code will be to changes.

- ▶ **Lines of Code**—This counts the number of IL (intermediate language) code lines. Look for classes and methods with a high number. You might target these to break them up in order to increase possible reuse, reduce duplicate code, and increase maintainability.

## Running Code Metrics

You can choose to calculate code metrics either for just the selected projects in the Solution Explorer or for the entire solution. You do so from the Analyze menu. Figure 26.39 shows an example. Clicking either of these options starts the analysis and brings up the code metrics results window.

Code metrics can take some time to execute. You might simply choose to run them for one project at a time (and not the entire solution).

## Working with the Results

The code metric results are shown in a hierarchical view. The hierarchy moves from project to namespace to class to member. The code metrics results are aggregated at each level. This allows you to scan the list looking for issues and then drill down into a given area to find the root cause of the issue.

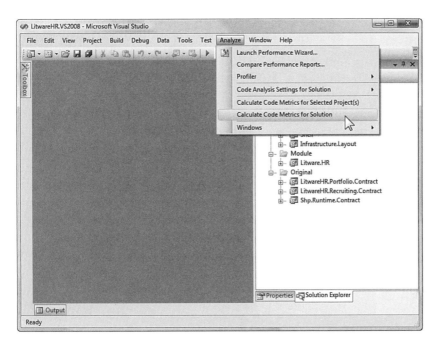

FIGURE 26.39     Starting the code metrics running from the Analyze menu.

26

You should keep in mind that all scores should be compared only to scores at the given level. For example, a complexity score of 10 might be considered high for a single method. However, when aggregated across a namespace, a score five times this might be normal.

Figure 26.40 shows an example of the Code Metrics Results window. Here you can see that the source code is being rated against each of the measurements listed previously. In this case, we are drilling down on an issue where maintainability is low, complexity is a bit high for a single method, the lines of code are relatively high compared to other methods, and the class coupling is very high. This method might be a good candidate for focused refactoring and additional testing. Of course, you can go to it by double-clicking the item in the Code Metrics Results window.

You can use the toolbar in the Code Metrics Results window to filter your results to find specific areas of your code that need attention. To set a filter, you choose a measurement from the Filter list. You then set Min and Max values for the filter. For example, Figure 26.41 shows a filter for areas of the code where the Maintainability Index is lower than 50.

You can also use the toolbar to export the results to Microsoft Excel or to create a work item to address an issue.

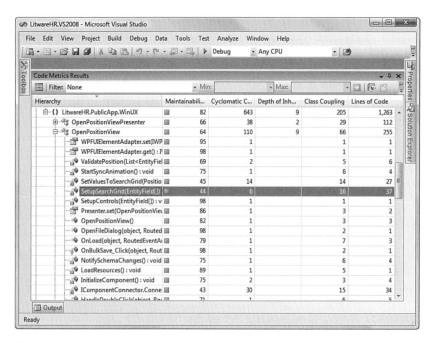

FIGURE 26.40    The Code Metrics Results window.

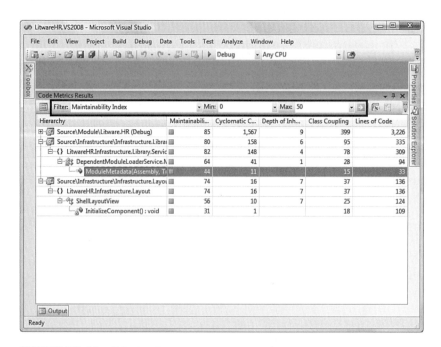

FIGURE 26.41    Filtering the measurement results.

# Summary

In this chapter, you saw many of the features of Visual Studio Team Systems Development Edition that enhance the professional development experience. This tool builds on the other features discussed in prior sections of the book, including source control and policy enforcement. Specifically, this chapter looked at how the Development Edition can be used to do the following:

▶ Create visual models of your classes that stay in synch with your code.

▶ Develop tests that verify the execution of the code you write. This includes checking those tests for the percent of code that is covered (and not covered).

▶ Profile your code for performance bottlenecks.

▶ Analyze your code against a set of rules for such things as globalization, security, design, and performance.

▶ Measure your code against complexity, maintainability, lines of code, and more.

# Architecture Edition

Most developers will agree that having a solid architecture and visualization of your code will lead to a better overall product and development experience. More often than not, however, architecture documents are created at the beginning of the project (if at all) in a tool like Visio only to become quickly outdated during the build phase. It seems there is never time enough to go back and update the diagrams. You are left to watch them rapidly deteriorate into "original design" or "system vision" documents—new labels put on what once represented the actual, physical structure of the application. Round-trip synchronization between the modeling tool and the development project was supposed to solve this problem. However, this solution was laden with its own issues—the principal among them is that developers want to see their code in their code window or IDE, not in yet another tool.

Visual Studio 2008 is Microsoft's first step toward moving software modeling out of this documentation mode and into the IDE. Having the models in the IDE means they are closer to the code and systems you write. This helps ensure that these models are useful to the development process and the team. It also provides a better chance that they stay in synch with the project.

In this chapter, we focus on the models and related tools used to develop software with Visual Studio 2008. These models include the following diagrams:

▶ **Application**—The application diagram is used to define the components that make up your application.

▶ **System**—The system diagram is used to group applications into systems for deployment purposes.

▶ **Class**—The class diagram is used to visualize code and make changes to its structure (see Chapter 26, "Development Edition," for more details).

▶ **Logical Datacenter**—The logical datacenter diagram is used to define the infrastructure that will house your application.

▶ **Deployment**—The deployment diagram represents the logical deployment of your systems into the datacenter.

Each of these diagrams has an associated set of tools or a designer that can be used to create and edit the diagrams. We cover each of the architecture diagrams and their related tools through the rest of this chapter.

> **NOTE**
>
> Everything we discuss in this chapter is related to the Visual Studio Team System 2008 Architecture Edition product (or Team Suite).

# Team Architect Artifacts

Visual Studio Team Architect installs a couple of additional project templates and a few new item templates. These templates are focused on a single role called *architect*. However, in most organizations there is a split between infrastructure and application architects. These are typically two distinct roles played by people with different skill sets. For example, the infrastructure architect is often concerned with server software, networks, firewalls, and VPNs. The application architect, on the other hand, is more involved in determining whether an application's interface will be web or Windows, whether it will leverage web services, what external interfaces it will connect to, and so on. Visual Studio Team Architect tries to unite these roles and increase the communication between them.

## Project Templates

Team Architect defines project templates for both the application and infrastructure architects. These templates can be found in the New Project dialog box under the Distributed Systems project types. Figure 27.1 shows an example of this dialog box.

Both the Application Design template and the System Design template are meant for the application architect. The former allows you to model an application, whereas the latter allows you to group portions of an application model into interconnected systems. You can start with one of these project types. However, you cannot add this project type to existing solutions. Instead, for existing solutions, you can only add the diagram files to the solution itself (as it is already established).

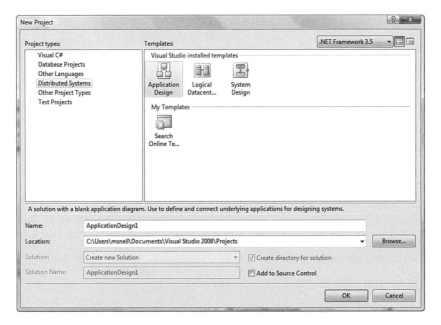

FIGURE 27.1    The Distributed Systems templates.

---

**NOTE**

You can have only one application diagram per solution. The reason is that the contents of this file should represent the entirety of your solution.

---

The Logical Datacenter template is for the infrastructure architect. Visual Studio creates a new solution with a blank Logical Datacenter Diagram file when this project type is selected. It, too, cannot be added to existing solutions. Instead, you can add the diagram itself to the solution (and not the project).

## Item Templates

Visual Studio Team Architect provides three items templates: Application Diagram (.ad), Logical Datacenter Diagram (.ldd), and System Diagram (.sd). These templates can be added to existing solutions from the Add New Item dialog box. Figure 27.2 shows an example of this dialog box in action.

All distributed system diagrams are added to the Solution Items folder in the Solution Explorer. The reason is that they refer to the entire solution and are not project specific.

A couple of diagrams that may seem to be missing from the item templates list are the class diagram (.cd) and the deployment diagram (.dd). The class diagram, as we have stated, is not solely tied to Team Architect. It can be added to a project from the New Item Template dialog box. We cover this topic in Chapter 26.

27

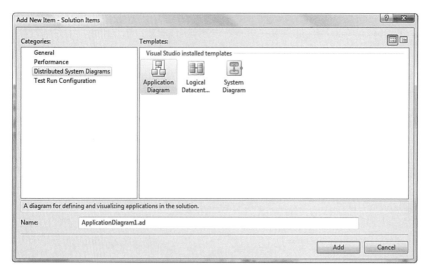

FIGURE 27.2    The team architect diagrams.

The deployment diagram does not have an item template. It can be created only through the logical datacenter diagram (see "Deploying Your Application" later in this chapter).

# Designing Your Application

The Application Designer allows architects to create a system definition model (SDM) that defines how different "applications" are combined for a given solution. An application in this sense refers to a website, web service, database, and so on. For example, a single solution might include a website that talks to multiple web services. These web services in turn might be communicating with a database or message queue. The Application Designer allows for this type of modeling. An architect can indicate which applications communicate with one another and can define the constraints between these relationships.

Typically, the first step in designing an application is for the application architect to define the components that make up the application, the communication between those components, and their settings and constraints. The application diagram directly supports this activity. Doing this step first in the process allows the application architect to lay out the components of the system and have those elements verified for deployment by a logical datacenter diagram. When verified, these components can then generate stub projects and code for the solution. This will give the development team a head start.

The following lists the logical order of using the diagrams in Visual Studio 2008 to build a new application:

1. Create an application diagram to define the clients, services, components, and communication paths of the application.
2. Group applications together to form systems with the System Designer.
3. Create a logical datacenter diagram that represents the infrastructure in which the application will be deployed.
4. Use the Deployment Designer to verify that your application definition (diagram) will deploy in the logical infrastructure.
5. Use your application diagram to generate the project stubs for your solution.

We will walk through each of these steps throughout the rest of this chapter. Our examples will follow the design of an application that represents a customer management system for an existing e-commerce application.

---

**TIP**

Visual Studio will generate the model of your application if you add an application diagram to the existing application. This can be a great way to understand the relationship between components of an application. It is also a great place to start when you're working with an existing application to extend its functionality.

In fact, all application models are synchronized with the solution that contains them. This ensures that the models stay in step with the code base.

---

**27**

## Working with the Application Diagram

You've seen how to add an application diagram to a solution. Now you're ready to look at the application diagram in greater detail. Figure 27.3 shows an open application diagram in the IDE using the Application Designer toolset.

The four main parts of the Application Designer are the diagram itself, the Toolbox items, the Settings and Constraints window, and the Diagram menu. These four items allow you to design the details of your application. Now let's look at each of these in more detail.

### The Diagram Menu

The Diagram menu is active only when you have an architectural diagram loaded in the active window. The contents of the menu change depending on what type of diagram you have loaded. In fact, even the application Diagram menu changes depending on what is selected in the actual diagram. Figure 27.4 shows an example of this menu for an application diagram with a web service application selected.

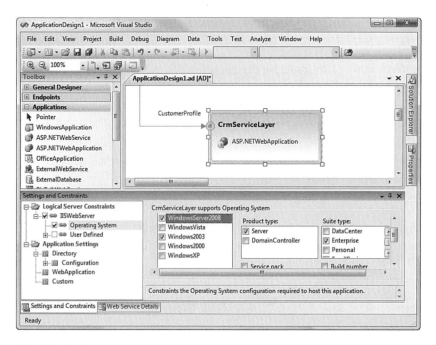

FIGURE 27.3 The Application Designer.

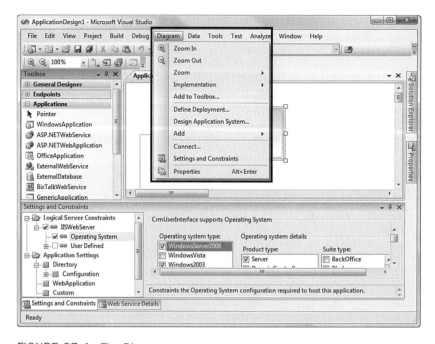

FIGURE 27.4 The Diagram menu.

Some key features of this menu worth discussing are Define Deployment, Design Application System, and Add to Toolbox. The Define Deployment menu item enables you to select the deployment details of the application. We will cover this item later when we discuss the deployment diagram. The Design Application System menu item allows you to create a system from components of your application. We'll cover this item in the next section. Finally, the Add to Toolbox menu item allows you to take an existing application, endpoint, or group of applications and create a reusable Toolbox item from it. This capability can be useful if you are consistently reusing an element across diagrams.

### Application Designer Toolbox

The Application Designer Toolbox provides access to the items that can be added to the application diagram. These items are grouped into three sections: General Designer, Endpoints, and Applications. The General Designer section contains elements that are common to many of the architect designers. The Endpoints section groups the endpoint connections that define the communication between applications. Finally, the Applications section groups the various applications that can be defined on the diagram. Figure 27.5 shows this Toolbox.

FIGURE 27.5   The Application Designer Toolbox.

For the most part, these Toolbox items are aptly named, and you should have no problem using them. We will cover adding applications and using the endpoints in the coming section.

> **NOTE**
>
> The applications in the Toolbox are clients, web services, or databases. There is no support for adding frameworks or class libraries to the Application Designer. These items are not part of the Application Designer by design.

### The Application Diagram

The application diagram represents the canvas for the application architect. It is here that you drag applications from the Toolbox and connect them together to form a solution. Figure 27.6 shows an application diagram in progress.

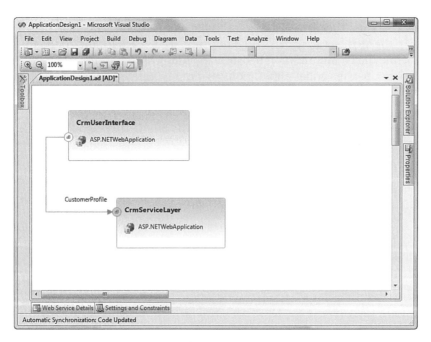

FIGURE 27.6    The application diagram.

There are two ASP.NET web application items on the diagram. The top one, CrmUserInterface, represents the web-based user interface screens for the customer management sample application. The one below that, CrmServiceLayer, is a web service for the CustomerProfile service. Notice that after they are placed on the diagram, it is difficult to distinguish between a web application and web service; this is by design because either application could contain both .aspx and .asmx files.

There is also an arrow that connects the two applications. This arrow is a Connection item; it is used to connect endpoints of an application. Notice that each application has an associated endpoint. Each endpoint is a web service endpoint. The CrmUserInterface endpoint has a hollow or white background, indicating that it is the client endpoint. The

CrmServiceLayer endpoint is solid to indicate that it represents the server. The arrow also indicates the direction of caller (client) to server. Finally, the arrow contains a decorator or label. This label indicates the web service that connects the two applications (CustomerProfile). This relationship will become a web reference upon implementation.

Now let's look at adding a couple of new applications to the diagram and connecting them.

**Adding Applications**    You add applications to the diagram through drag and drop. For the example, you will add an external database to which the service layer can connect. This external database belongs to the existing e-commerce application that the CRM application extends. You will also add a Windows user interface to allow the sales and marketing team to do their data analysis work. Figure 27.7 shows the results of this work.

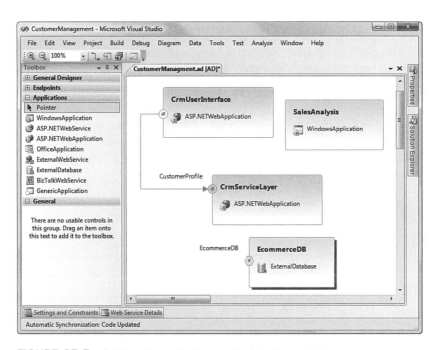

FIGURE 27.7    Additional applications added to the model.

**Connecting Applications**    Now you're ready to add endpoints to the applications and connect them. The Toolbox shows three endpoints, but there is actually a fourth one: DatabaseServerEndpoint. This endpoint exists on database applications by default. It can also be dragged to connecting applications. The following list describes the possible endpoints for connecting applications in the diagram:

▶ .NETWebServiceEndpoint—Used to connect to SOAP-based web services. Each web service endpoint represents an actual web service. You can create a one-to-one relationship between web service application and web service endpoint. Or you can create as many endpoints as you need for your web service application.

▶ WebContentEndpoint—Used to connect to web-based content through HTTP (such as files).

▶ GenericEndpoint—Used to set an endpoint without specifying an exact communication protocol. It defines a connection but not the mechanics of the connection.

▶ DatabaseServerEndpoint—Used to connect to a database server.

You will use these endpoints to connect applications. First, the SalesAnalysis Windows client application will need to connect to the CrmServiceLayer through a web service endpoint. Next, the CrmServiceLayer will require a connection to the EcommerceDB database.

First, you add all the endpoints to the various applications. Next, to connect the endpoints, you can use the Connection item from the Toolbox. Alternatively, you can hold down the Alt key and select and drag the endpoint from one application to another.

When you connect an application to a database application, Visual Studio presents you with the Connection Properties dialog box for establishing a connection to an actual database. You can cancel this step or define the actual connection details if they are set up.

Figure 27.8 shows the applications connected. Notice the addition of a new web service layer: SalesAnalysisServices. The SalesAnalysis client application will connect to both the CRM layer and this newly defined layer. Also, notice the endpoint names. You can turn these labels off for each endpoint, show for each, or show for only one endpoint. The labels connecting to a web service represent the actual web service's name that is defined by the endpoint.

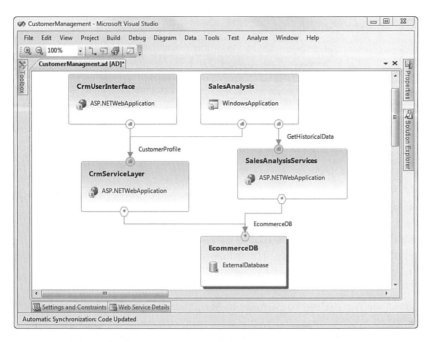

FIGURE 27.8  The connected applications.

### Application Settings and Constraints

Each application on the diagram has a set of properties, settings, and constraints. This metadata helps further define how this application will be built and deployed. For example, suppose that the web user interface must be deployed on a Windows 2008 Enterprise server that is running the .NET Framework version 3.5.

To indicate this setting, you would select the `CrmUserInterface` application from the diagram, right-click, and choose Settings and Constraints. Visual Studio will present the related window in the IDE. Figure 27.9 shows this window and the related setting.

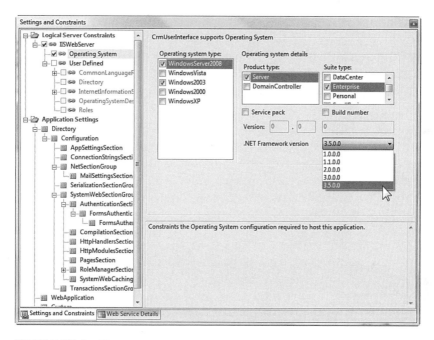

FIGURE 27.9    The Settings and Constraints window.

Notice that the Settings and Constraints window is split between Logical Server Constraints and Application Settings. The former represents the server on which the application will be deployed. Constraints entered here will be enforced when you try to deploy against a logical datacenter diagram. The Application Settings section is essentially the configuration file for the application. You can set all related settings here. These settings will be emitted when you implement the application diagram.

On the right side of the screen, you modify the settings. Notice in the example that the operating system, server type, suite type, and .NET Framework version have been selected.

**Application Properties**    You can define additional implementation details about the application using the Properties window. Again, select an application from the diagram, right-click, and choose Properties. This will open the Properties window for the given application. Of course, the settings in this window are dependent on the type of application selected.

As an example, assume that the development team for the SalesAnalysis Windows client application intends to work in Visual Basic. You can add this implementation detail in the Properties window. This setting will affect how Visual Studio creates the project when implementing the diagram. Figure 27.10 shows this process in action.

FIGURE 27.10   The application Properties window.

**Web Service Settings**   Recall that each endpoint on a web service application represents an actual web service that will be implemented. The Application Designer allows you to indicate the implementation details of each of these web services. You will later generate, or stub out, all of this code.

To add these details, you select a web service endpoint, right-click, and choose Define Operations from the context menu. Selecting this menu item will open the Web Service Details window. Figure 27.11 shows an example of this window along with the web service's Properties window.

When defining web service details, you can add operations, set their return types, and indicate parameters. You can also define summary information that will be used for the XML documentation of the web service.

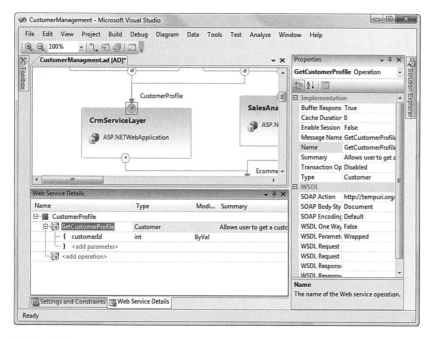

FIGURE 27.11    The Web Service Details window.

# Defining a System

We have now described the basic application architecture. The next step is to compose actual systems using the System Designer. The concept and use of system diagrams can be difficult to grasp. They are also somewhat optional, which adds to their being obtuse. Simply put, a system is an actual configuration of one or more applications you intend to deploy.

This definition may already seem confusing given that an application diagram already represents the configuration (settings and constraints) of the applications you intend to deploy. This is what makes system diagrams optional. You can simply use the application diagram and move it into your infrastructure. However, there is a real use for system diagrams.

System diagrams can group applications into a system. The only reason to do so is for actual deployment. Also, a system is based on the original application architecture. However, the system diagram can be reconfigured for the actual deployment.

It helps to think of an example. Suppose you intend to deploy your service layer twice: once in your intranet zone and again in your Internet zone. The base application architecture does not change. What changes are the settings for a specific deployment. Therefore, you can create two systems, one for each deployment. Each system draws on the base application architecture. In addition to allowing configuration overrides, the system diagram enables you to control which portions of the application actually are deployed in any system.

## System Diagram

There are a couple of ways to add a system diagram to your solution. You can use the item template, as described earlier; or you can select one or more applications, right-click, and choose Design Application System. In either case, you will be working with the applications defined in your application diagram. Recall that a given solution may contain only one application diagram. All system diagrams will use the applications defined in this diagram. Figure 27.12 shows an example of selecting three applications and starting creating a system design based on this selection.

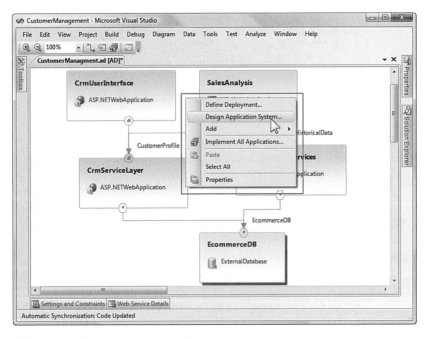

FIGURE 27.12    Defining an application system.

The System Designer contains a System View window and the System Designer (SD) window. The System View is like a Toolbox of items that can be added to the SD window. Its contents are directly linked to your application architecture diagram. Each application you defined there is available to be added to the system from the System View window. Figure 27.13 shows an example of a system in the designer.

Notice that this system view is not unlike the view you had on the application diagram. The difference here is that this view is constrained to this single system. You also have access to the Settings and Constraints window from this designer. This will allow you to do the setting overrides for the system, as discussed.

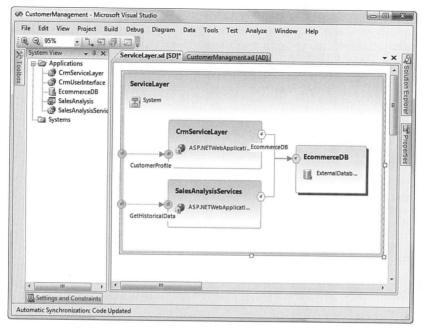

FIGURE 27.13   The System Designer.

### Creating Proxy Endpoints

The outer box of the System Designer represents the way in which you intend to expose the system for communication from other applications and systems. Notice that in Figure 27.13, there are two endpoints on this outer box: One points to the CrmServiceLayer and one points to the SalesAnalysisServices application. These endpoints are called *proxy endpoints*; they allow you to define the communication that is allowed to the system.

The proxy endpoints are not on the outer system box by default. You must explicitly select and drag the application endpoints to the other box to create these proxy endpoints.

### Connecting Applications to Systems

You can use the System Designer to connect an application inside a system to another, previously defined system. This way, you can reuse the configuration of the system for defining new systems.

As an example, suppose you want to define a system for the sales client application. Recall that this is a Windows-based client that connects to the service layer. It would be useful to create one or more systems for the actual deployment of this client. However, each system will talk to a deployed version of the service layer system.

Therefore, you add a new system diagram to the solution. On this diagram, you will drag the SalesAnalysis application. The System View tool window also gives you access to the other systems you have created. Under the Systems folder, you will see the ServiceLayer system created in the prior example. You will drag this onto the designer as well.

27

The ServiceLayer shape is represented as a system (and not an application). You have access only to the proxy endpoints exposed by the system. You will use the SalesAnalysis endpoints to connect to the two proxy endpoints of the ServiceLayer system. The diagram will enforce that you connect the proper endpoints (based on the Web Service Description Language, or WSDL).

Figure 27.14 shows the completed system diagram. We will come back to these diagrams when we deploy the application into the logical datacenter.

---

**TIP**

It is helpful to remember that the systems defined here do not physically exist. Rather, they define application configurations at the time of deployment.

---

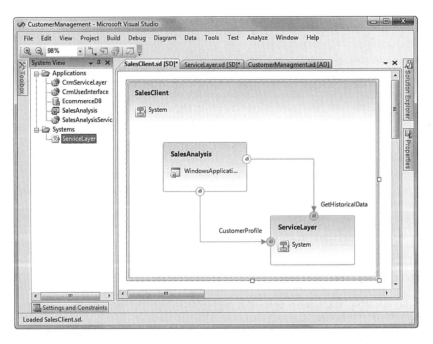

FIGURE 27.14    Creating a system that uses another system.

# Defining Your Infrastructure

An important, and often overlooked, step in any software project is ensuring that what the development team plans to build will deploy in the production infrastructure. This includes hardware, software versions, configuration of that software, and communication between the various servers involved. The sooner you can get a comfort level (or identify the risks), the more likely it is that your project will succeed.

It is the job of the application architect and the infrastructure architect to make sure that they get on the same page, while the design is simply that, a page. When that design moves from paper to code, the wrong infrastructure assumptions can cause costly delays (or worse) in deployment.

Modeling your datacenter can streamline communications between the infrastructure and development teams. Visual Studio 2008 allows you to define the boundaries within your datacenter (zones), the traffic allowed between these boundaries, and the servers contained within each boundary. In addition, constraints can be applied to items within this logical model, including versions of software on machines, types of traffic allowed on the machine, application pools, global assembly cache information, session state management, and the like. Finally, these models can be signed and versioned (as they seldom change), and the application design can be vetted against this logical model.

## Logical Datacenter Diagram

The logical datacenter diagram (.1dd) allows you to represent an infrastructure environment in a model. In fact, for most projects, you may want to represent more than one infrastructure model. Perhaps a development, staging, and production infrastructure will exist. Knowing the anomalies between these infrastructures can be very helpful. Having this logical representation allows you to test whether your application, as modeled, will deploy.

The current version of the Logical Datacenter Designer is not a networking diagram or even a similar tool. Those tools are still important for the infrastructure team. This diagram is less for the infrastructure team and more for the application architect's benefit. The infrastructure team may be concerned about switches, routers, firewalls, trusts, virus protection, VLANs, and so on (as well they should be). The logical datacenter diagram does not represent this information. It is meant solely to logically represent servers and their related software configuration and their allowed connection points. This gives the application architect and the infrastructure team confidence that a new application project will be deployable in the environment.

The logical nature of this designer is evident from the first use. For example, a logical server in the datacenter diagram would be an IIS web server, a database server, a generic server, and so on. These logical servers do not have physical mappings. Instead, one IIS server might represent an entire farm of web servers, or a database and web server may be deployed on the same box. This information is important to the infrastructure team but is not as relevant to the application architect's need to ensure that the new project will deploy correctly.

Instead, the focus is on software, configuration of that software, and communication channels between servers. For example, as an application architect, you may need to ensure that your production environment supports the 2.0 version of the .NET Framework, or that the IIS server that hosts your web services is capable of communicating with your database. These are the types of details that can be embedded in a logical datacenter diagram.

**27**

### Logical Datacenter Diagram Toolbox

The Logical Datacenter Designer Toolbox provides the access to the items that can be added to the logical datacenter diagram. These items are grouped into three sections: General Designer, Endpoints, and Logical Servers. The General Designer section contains elements common to many of the architect designers. The Endpoints section groups the endpoint connections that define the communication between servers in the datacenter. Finally, the Logical Servers section groups the various logical servers and zones that can be defined on the diagram. Figure 27.15 shows a visual representation of this Toolbox.

FIGURE 27.15   The Logical Datacenter Designer Toolbox.

### Defining Zones

A zone in a logical datacenter is used to group servers and provide an abstraction of the same. Zones do not, by default, represent any one thing or group of things. You are free to define zones to group servers as you see fit. You can even nest zones within other zones to represent complex relationships.

The principal benefit of using a zone is to indicate what type of communication (traffic) is allowed in and out of the zone. The servers within the zone may talk to one another, but connecting to the zone can be a different story. As an example, a zone can be used to represent any number of things, including an intranet, an extranet, the Internet, a firewall, or a VPN.

As an example, say you want to define zones that will host servers to support the application and systems you have defined previously. You will want a client zone to represent the Windows client application for the sales analysis tool. You will also create an Internet or public access zone for the CRM user interface, as well as to expose a set of proxies for the service layer. Next, you will define a zone for the intranet; you will call this zone ServiceLayer. Finally, you will create a zone for the database. Figure 27.16 shows an example of these zones.

The next step is to add servers to these zones. After you do this, you'll define the connections between the zones and servers within the zones. You will then work to set the constraints on both servers and zones.

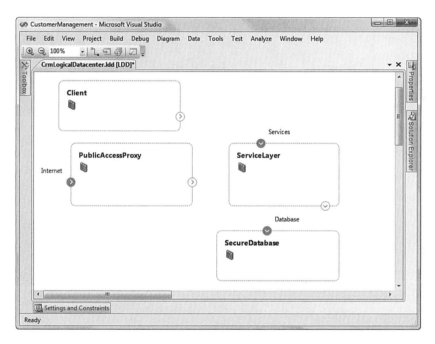

FIGURE 27.16    Logical datacenter zones.

### Adding Servers

Servers do not have to be added to a zone. They can be added directly to the diagram. However, it helps to think of servers inside communication zones or boundaries. Therefore, the example will use the zones you defined earlier when adding servers.

The Logical Datacenter Designer allows you to use a few different server types on your diagram. These server types and their descriptions are listed here:

▶ WindowsClient—Represents a user's machine or desktop running Windows.

▶ IISWebServer—Represents a Windows web server running IIS.

▶ DatabaseServer—Represents a server in the datacenter that is running a relational database.

▶ GenericServer—Represents custom or other types of servers in the datacenter.

For the example, you will end up with one logical server per zone. Many times you will have more than one server in a zone. For example, if you have both an application server and a front-end web server in your intranet, you might define them in the same zone. The servers would talk to one another, but the zone boundary would dictate the incoming and outgoing traffic. Figure 27.17 focuses back on the example.

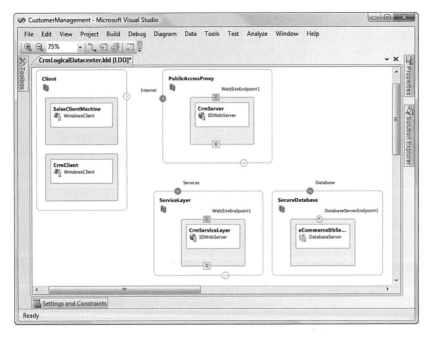

FIGURE 27.17    Logical datacenter zones and servers.

This diagram shows the five added servers. The Client zone contains two servers—one to represent each type of client that will connect to the solution. These are not really servers. Rather, they represent an application host that also has configuration implications. Next, the logical database server was added to the SecureDatabase zone. Then two web servers were added. The web server in the PublicAccessProxy zone is meant to host the CrmUserInterface application. In addition, this server has proxy web services that call into the server in the ServiceLayer zone. These are used for the SalesClient application. The next step is to connect the communication channels between these servers and zones.

## Connecting Servers and Zones

Servers and zones are connected via endpoints. Endpoints define the type of traffic (and related constraints) that is allowed for a zone or server. If a zone endpoint, for instance, allows only inbound web traffic, no other open communication method is allowed into that zone. The servers in the zone may have their own endpoints and communicate with one another using different traffic patterns.

The Logical Datacenter Designer allows you to define a few different endpoints. These are the endpoints and their descriptions:

- ▶ ZoneEndPoint—Represents the traffic flow into and out of zones. These endpoints also indicate the direction of that traffic using arrows. An arrow pointing into a zone or server represents inbound traffic, whereas an arrow pointing out of a zone or server represents outbound traffic. An arrow pointing in both directions represents bidirectional traffic. ZoneEndPoints can also be constrained to indicate what type of traffic is allowed.

- ▶ HTTPClientEndpoint—Used to constrain communication to a web server from a client.

- ▶ WebSiteEndpoint—Used to manage server traffic for a web server.

- ▶ DatabaseClientEndpoint—Used to manage communication to a database server from a client.

- ▶ GenericClientEndpoint—Used to manage client communication to a generic server.

- ▶ GenericServerEndpoint—Used to manage traffic allowed on a generic server.

For the example, your goal is to wire up the zones and servers within the zones. When there is traffic coming into a zone, typically that traffic is destined for a server (and not simply routed through the zone). The same is true on the outbound side. The outbound traffic from a zone typically originates from a server.

Figure 27.18 shows the endpoints added to the diagram and connected accordingly.

The following provides a step-by-step walk-through illustrating how to connect the items in the diagram:

1. In each of the client servers (or hosts), add an HTTPClientEndpoint. This allows these machines to talk using the HTTP protocol. You then connect these endpoints to the outbound traffic for the Client zone.

2. Connect the inbound traffic endpoint for the PublicAccessProxy zone to a WebSiteEndpoint on the logical web server (CrmServer). This allows you to then connect the outbound traffic from the Client zone to the Internet endpoint of the PublicAccessProxy zone. The HTTP client traffic is now routed to a web server.

3. Follow a similar pattern for the server in the ServiceLayer zone. You connect the inbound zone endpoint to the WebSiteEndpoint of the CrmServiceLayer server. You then connect the HTTPClientEndpoint on the CrmServer to the outbound endpoint for the PublicAccessProxy zone. You could then connect the two zones (outbound PublicAccessProxy to inbound ServiceLayer).

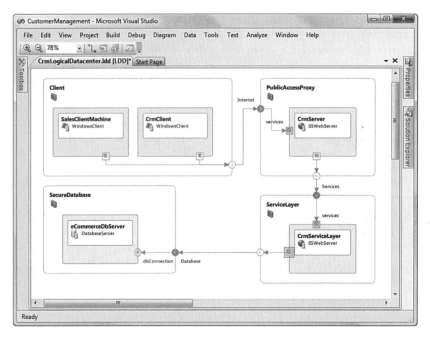

FIGURE 27.18    Logical datacenter connected zones and servers.

4. Remove the HTTPClientEndpoint from the CrmServiceLayer server. You replace it with a DatabaseClientEndpoint. You then connect the inbound zone endpoint for the SecureDatabase zone to the database server. The last step is to connect the ServiceLayer zone outbound endpoint to the inbound endpoint of the SecureDatabase zone.

### Defining Settings and Constraints

Configuring the zones and the servers is the final step. The logical datacenter diagram will then represent your infrastructure—at least for the purpose of the application architect. This architect can then use this zone to determine whether the proposed architecture will fit with the real infrastructure environment. Of course, the logical datacenter diagram works only if it truly matches your physical system configurations.

**Configuring a Zone**    There are several settings you can control with respects to zones. These settings include the capability to constrain the types of logical servers that can be added to the zone, the communication allowed in and out of the zone, whether zones can be nested within the zone, and the capability to define custom settings. The Datacenter Designer respects these constraints. It will not allow you, for instance, to add a web server to a zone that is configured for database servers only.

As an example, each zone defined previously should be constrained as to what servers are allowed in the zone. The client zone should allow only clients, the two zones that partici-pate in web traffic should allow only web servers, and the database zone should be constrained to database servers. You set these types of constraints in the Settings and Constraints window (just as in the application diagram). Figure 27.19 shows an example.

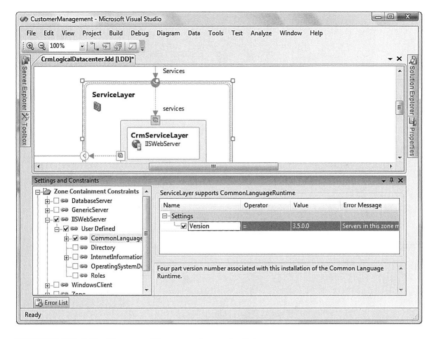

FIGURE 27.19   Zone settings and constraints.

In the example, the ServiceLayer zone has been selected. Notice on the left side of the Settings and Constraints window that servers other than an IISWebServer have been disabled (and thus disallowed) to be in this zone. Next, for this type of server, another constraint has been added: Web servers in this zone must be running version 3.5 of the .NET Framework.

For each constraint you set, you can craft a custom error message that is displayed when this constraint is broken. To do so, you click the ellipsis button in the Error Message field for the constraint. This brings up the dialog box shown in Figure 27.20. Here, you can set the error message. Notice that you can use the macro text to show special fields for the given message.

**Configuring a Server**   You configure servers in the same manner. You select each and then control their settings through the Settings and Constraints window. From here, you can indicate the types of applications that are allowed to run on the server, the constraints for each, and the various server settings.

Figure 27.21 shows an example. The CrmServiceLayer server has been selected. To restrict this server to running ASP.NET and web service applications, you can use the check boxes on the left side of the window.

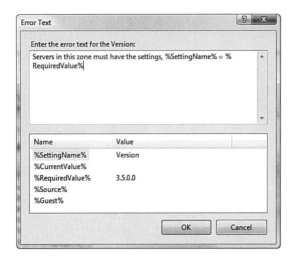

FIGURE 27.20    A custom constraint error message.

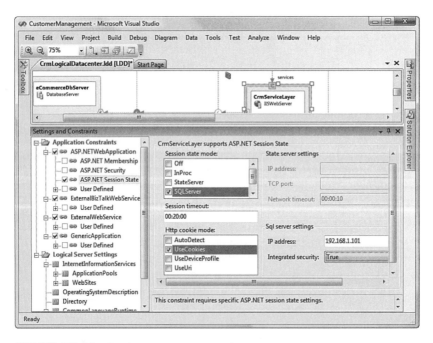

FIGURE 27.21    Setting a server constraint.

Next, you can define various settings for the server. Notice that the ASP.NET Session State parameter has been selected (left side, settings tree). You can now use the configuration area on the right side of the dialog box to control these constraints. Figure 27.21 indicates that session state is managed via SQL Server.

Again, your settings should closely match the servers in your environment. These settings will be used to restrict what the application architect can deploy.

**Importing Server Settings**   The datacenter diagram is a logical representation of your servers. However, you can use an import feature to point a server at a real, physical machine and import its settings. This capability can be helpful if you have access to servers that already represent the correct environment.

You access this feature from the Diagram menu with the Import Settings item. Selecting this menu item launches the Import IIS Settings Wizard. The imported settings apply to the server you have selected in the diagram. The wizard will walk you through the import.

Figure 27.22 shows the key step in the wizard. Here, you provide login credentials to the server. You also indicate which settings you want to import. If you import website settings, the diagram tool can add a new endpoint for each website on your server. You can also pick and choose which sites to import on another screen in the wizard.

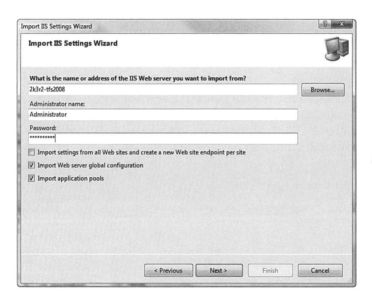

FIGURE 27.22   The Import IIS Settings Wizard.

# Deploying Your Application

The application and Logical Datacenter Designers would be little more than pretty pictures if it were not for the Deployment Designer. This tool allows you to test your application's deployment against your logical datacenter. The intent of modeling the logical infrastructure is to avoid problems that might arise during deployment of an application. It can be extremely frustrating to get your application built and tested in one environment only to see it fail to deploy in the production environment. Often these issues are not found until late in the project and end up causing great delays and other headaches.

If you've been doing development for a while, you've undoubtedly come across the statement "Deploy early, deploy often." This adage is in direct response to those who have experienced these headaches. You can be thankful that the Deployment Designer was built to try to avoid these types of issues. It allows you to deploy as often as you like.

The tool verifies that you are allowed to make a deployment, allows you to drag and drop an application to a valid server, and verifies the deployment via a deployment compiler. For example, the tool does not allow you to place a web application on a database server that does not allow web traffic. In addition, during compilation, the deployment tool can determine whether the target server has the required software to run your application. Errors are output into a task list similar to coding errors. The intended effect is that deployment errors are found before code is moved onto production servers, where errors can get very costly.

## Deployment Diagram

The Deployment Designer tool ties together the application and the logical datacenter diagrams. With it, you can use an application diagram to do a test deployment against your logical infrastructure. This test deployment will show where the application should run smoothly when you deploy it and where errors exist.

To start, you need to create a deployment diagram (.dd). You can do so from an existing application diagram. With it open, you can use the Diagram menu or the context menu and choose the Define Deployment option. Selecting this menu item brings up the Define Deployment dialog box (see Figure 27.23). From here, you select a logical datacenter diagram that represents the environment to which you want to test deploy.

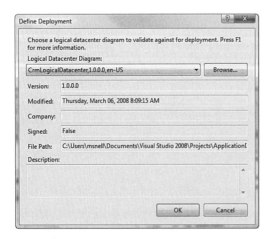

FIGURE 27.23   The Define Deployment dialog box.

Visual Studio then brings up the deployment diagram. Remember, it is meant to be a marriage between your logical datacenter and application diagrams. Figure 27.24 shows an example. Notice that the diagram itself looks mostly like your infrastructure. The reason is that you are deploying your application into this diagram. Each server in the infrastructure has a box below it to which you can add an application. The applications from the application diagram are listed in the tree (System View) on the left side of the figure. Finally, notice that each application is added to its respective server.

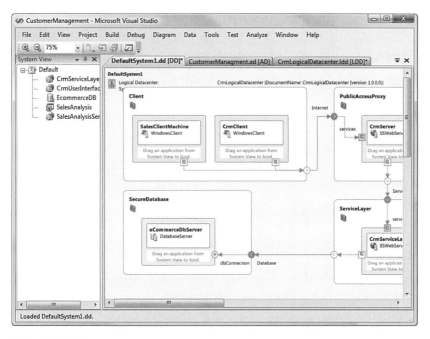

FIGURE 27.24   The deployment diagram.

## Validating Deployment

The next step is to test the deployment. Some testing occurs when applications are added to the servers. The Deployment Designer will not allow you to add applications if you are breaking a hard rule in the deployment. For example, you cannot add a web application to the database server.

To validate the deployment, you choose the Validate Diagram option from the Diagram or context menu. This checks the configuration of your applications against all the pieces of the infrastructure diagram. It then generates a set of warnings and errors for you to review. Figure 27.25 shows the results of the example. You can see that there were no errors but plenty of warnings to work on.

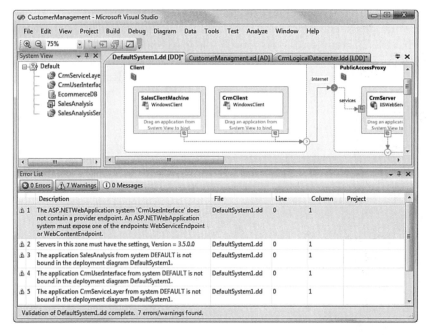

FIGURE 27.25    Warnings generated from the validate diagram.

## Deployment Report

You can also generate a report that details your deployment. This lengthy document indicates every aspect of the application, datacenter, and deployment.

You can set a few options for generating the report. For example, you can indicate whether you want to see copies of the diagrams in the report. You set these options from the Properties window of the deployment diagram itself.

To access the report generation tool, you use the Diagram or context menu and choose the Generate Deployment Report option. Selecting this menu item creates the detailed report. Figure 27.26 shows a sample portion of the report. The contents of this report are all-inclusive. You may prefer to pull a few sections out and paste them into a smaller report for archiving.

# Implementing Your Application

After you have the application designed and tested through deployment, the next step is to set up the actual project for the development team. The application architect performs this task. The Application Designer allows the architect to implement the applications defined in the diagram. This implementation is used to generate projects with the appropriate settings, references, and template files.

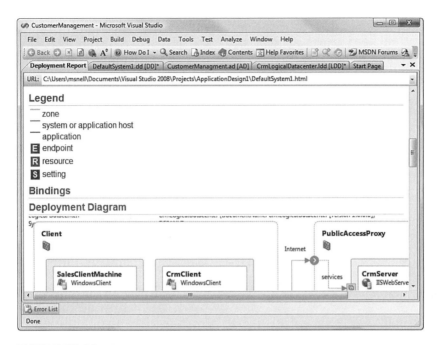

FIGURE 27.26    The deployment report.

## Setting Implementation Properties

Before generating the actual projects, you will want to define the implementation details of each application on the diagram. You can do this through the Properties window. When you're viewing properties for a given application, the Properties window will present an Implementation subsection. The properties in this section are based on the type of application you are configuring. Figure 27.27 shows the implementation properties for a web application.

Notice that you can set the language with which the application will be built. You can also define the project template, the default namespace, and so on.

You select each application and set its implementation properties in turn. When you're happy with these implementation details, it's time to generate the actual implemented templates.

## Generating Projects

You do the actual implementation through the Implementation menu option on the Diagram menu. With it, you can choose to implement all applications on the diagram or only a single application.

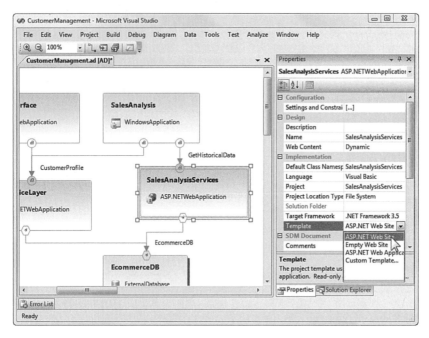

FIGURE 27.27    Setting implementation details.

Note that if you're working in a solution that already contains some of the applications used for the application diagram, those applications will not be available for implementation (because they are already implemented). This happens to be the case with the example here. If you choose Implement All Applications, a confirmation dialog box is presented. Figure 27.28 shows the example. Notice that only two additional applications will be added to the existing solution.

FIGURE 27.28    The Confirm Application Implementation dialog box.

When complete, the new projects are generated with their properties and references set. You can now begin coding against your application architecture. Figure 27.29 shows the results of the implementation in the Solution Explorer.

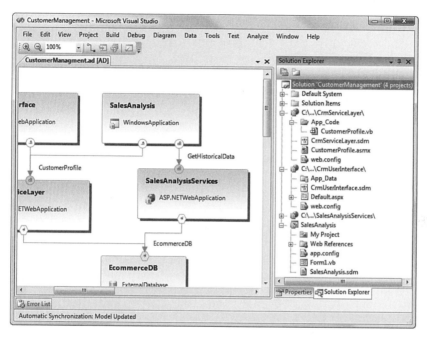

FIGURE 27.29   The implemented applications.

# Summary

You have seen how Visual Studio Team Architect can be used to move software modeling beyond just raw documentation. The models you create with it are much more: They are real tools that help increase productivity and reduce errors.

In this chapter, you looked at the standard approach for modeling applications. You first created an application diagram to represent the interfaces, services, and database that existed in the example. You then created a system diagram to group key application elements. Next, you learned how the logical datacenter diagram can be used to represent a physical infrastructure environment. This diagram became the basis of a test deployment for the application. Finally, you saw how the Class Designer can be leveraged to build diagrams and code at the same time.

These tools form the basis for modeling with Visual Studio 2008. They also represent a milestone step in what is sure to be a great future for visually modeling applications and code.

# CHAPTER 28

# Test Edition

Testing is one of the most important parts of the Software Development Life Cycle (SDLC). All too often, however, testing is pushed to the back of the project as a last-minute exercise. Or, just as bad, developers are put in charge of testing their own code. In either case, you can expect poor results. If you have ever released software like this, you know that the release is just a point in time on a calendar. When users get hold of the application, the real testing begins. In fact, this is where we get alpha and beta releases. Developers and testers do not have the tools to be confident in a release of software. Therefore, they throw it over the wall with a name like *alpha release* to get a read on everything that is actually wrong with the code. The tags *alpha* and *beta* mean that the users can't get too mad when things break. This typical cycle is changing, however.

Visual Studio Team System 2008 Test Edition provides developers and testers with tools that allow for repeatable, automated tests. These tools bring testing into all phases of the SDLC (including development). The tools allow you to test early and test often. The result is an increased confidence in the software. This confidence can turn the tables on the alpha and beta releases. Instead of users fettering out the errors, they can focus on usability and requirements mapping. The result is an application delivered with predictability and fewer bugs.

In this chapter, we focus on the testing tools built into Visual Studio 2008 Team System Test Edition. They include test case management, web testing, load testing, and others. This chapter will get you well on your way to creating software of a higher quality.

> **NOTE**
>
> Developer unit testing is covered in Chapter 26, "Development Edition." Database unit testing is covered in Chapter 29, "Database Edition."

# Creating, Configuring, and Managing Tests

Testing is no longer a manual process tracked inside an Excel spreadsheet. Instead, testing is now built into the Visual Studio IDE. Here, you can create test projects and tests. You can control, configure, and manage these in a central area. You can also execute tests and publish the results to Team Foundation Server (TFS). In the following sections, we'll look at the basics of test projects, test management, and testing configuration.

## Test Projects

You define tests inside test projects. This is a familiar paradigm for all Visual Studio users: Create a project, add items to that project. In this way, you can group test items under one or more projects. You can also check that project (and associated items) into source control as you would any other project.

In most cases, you create a single test project for an application. That is, if your application is contained within a single solution, you would add a test project to that solution. Of course, there are exceptions. For larger projects, you may want to break out the test project by component, module, or even iteration.

### Creating a Test Project

You create a test project like any other. You can choose New Project from the File menu, or you can right-click a solution and indicate the same. In either case, you are presented with the New Project dialog box. Figure 28.1 shows an example.

From the New Project dialog box, you navigate to the Test node. This will allow you to use the Test Project template. Notice that when adding a new test project, you can indicate whether Visual Studio should create a new solution or add your new project to the existing solution.

### Configuring the Creation of Test Projects

By default, when you create a new test project, a new manual test and unit test are added to the project. Your project template also gets an automatic reference to the UnitTestFramework namespace. Figure 28.2 shows the Solution Explorer with a new test project, along with all its related files.

The Test Project template is actually configurable. To configure it, you can bring up the Options dialog box (by selecting Tools, Options) and select the Test Project node under Test Tools. Figure 28.3 shows an example.

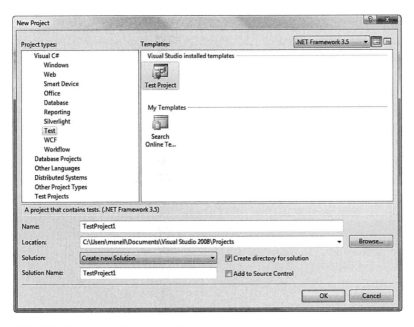

FIGURE 28.1    Creating a new test project.

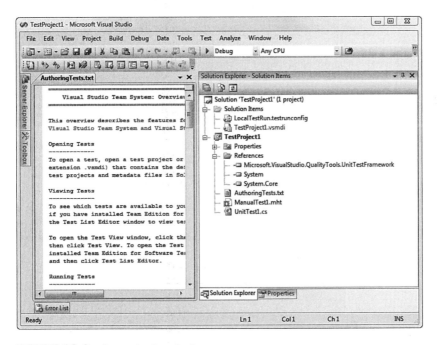

FIGURE 28.2    A new test project.

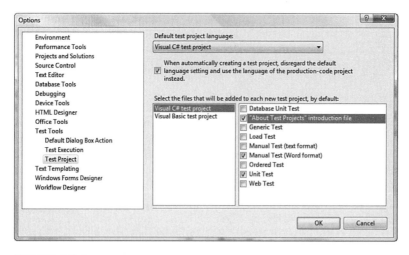

FIGURE 28.3   New test project options.

From this Options dialog box, you can indicate the default test project type (C#, VB, and so on). You can also indicate the default items that are added to the test project upon creation. Notice that the default settings include a unit test, a manual test, and an introductory file. You can override these settings by toggling the check boxes.

## Test Items

Various test item templates are defined for Visual Studio. Each represents a different test or a version of a test. These items are added to a test project. Each is a file that can be versioned inside source control. Figure 28.4 shows the Add New Test dialog box.

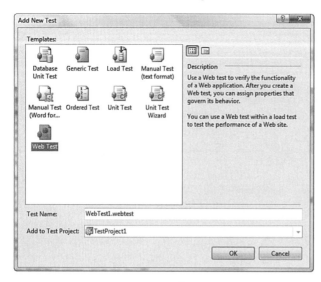

FIGURE 28.4   The Add New Test dialog box.

The figure shows the full list of the test items available. We will cover each one throughout this chapter. However, Table 28.1 provides a brief overview of each test item.

TABLE 28.1   Visual Studio Test Items

| Test | Description |
|------|-------------|
| Database Unit Test | A database unit test is one that can be run against your SQL code and stored procedures. See Chapter 29 for more information. |
| Generic Test | A generic test is an application or third-party tool that should be treated like a test. The generic test wraps this application. |
| Load Test | A load test is used to test your application's behavior when many concurrent users are accessing it. |
| Manual Test (text format) | A manual test is a set of steps that must be performed by a tester. This test is described as text. When the test is run, a tester has to indicate the results of the manual test. |
| Manual Test (Word format) | A manual test (see above) is written using Microsoft Word. |
| Ordered Test | An ordered test allows you to execute existing tests in a set order. |
| Unit Test | A unit test is a bit of code that executes a portion of your application and asserts the results. See Chapter 26 for more information. |
| Unit Test Wizard | The Unit Test Wizard allows you to automatically generate unit tests for existing code. |
| Web Test | A web test is used to test your web application. These tests can be recorded and then seeded with data to exercise an entire web user interface. |

## Managing Tests

The larger the project, the more tests you will have. It is not uncommon for a project to have hundreds of tests. Each unit test, web test, load test, or manual test needs to be managed. Thankfully, Visual Studio provides the Test List Editor tool to solve this issue. With it, you can organize tests into lists, group tests together, filter which test details you want to view, search for tests, run a group of tests, and more. It is the principal tool for the tester to bring order to his or her work. You access this tool from the Test menu (by selecting Test, Windows, Test List Editor) or from the Test Tools toolbar. Figure 28.5 shows the Test List Editor window in the IDE.

Notice the selection tree to the left. This allows you to view lists of tests, create new lists, and select the tests to run as a group. The tests themselves are shown in the list to the right.

You can group the test list by namespace, project, host type, class name, and so on using the Group By option on the Test List Editor toolbar. This toolbar also allows you to filter the list by a column value. Of course, you can also run the selected tests from this toolbar (the icon on the far left).

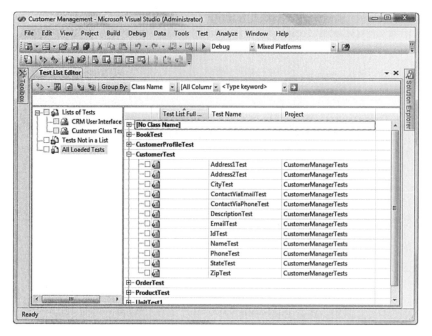

FIGURE 28.5    The Test List Editor.

## Lists of Tests

The Lists of Tests node in the test list tree view allows you to choose groups of tests to run and create new lists of tests. These lists are persisted for reuse across test sessions. You can define your own custom lists and then add tests to those lists. Perhaps the biggest benefit to test lists is that you can run a list as a single unit. This gives you control over which tests to group together to form, for instance, a module test.

To define a test list, you can right-click the Lists of Tests node on the Test List Editor navigation tree view. You can also select Create New Test List from the Test menu. Selecting this menu option brings up the Create New Test List dialog box. Figure 28.6 shows this dialog box in action.

In the Create New Test List dialog box, you define the list name, provide a description, and indicate where the list should exist in the test list hierarchy. Finally, you add tests to the list through drag and drop in the IDE.

You can define the tests to add to the test list by defining a filter. For example, suppose that you want to add all unit tests to the newly created list. You can use the Test List Editor toolbar to set the filter column to Test Type and then enter the keyword Unit Test. You then click the green arrow to filter the list. You will now have only Unit Tests in your selection. You can select all these items and drag them to the new list of tests. Figure 28.7 illustrates this example. Alternatively, you can select the items in a filtered list and right-click to define a new list from the selected items.

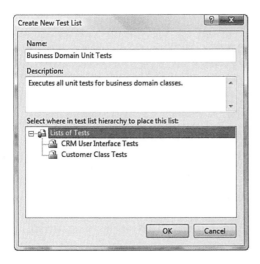

FIGURE 28.6    The Create New Test List dialog box.

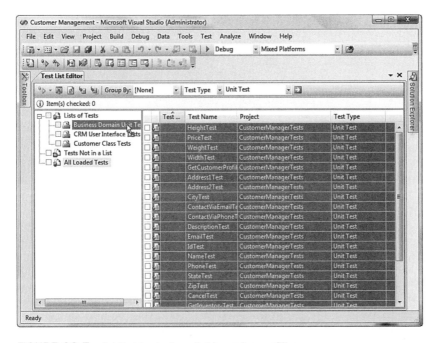

FIGURE 28.7    Adding tests to a list based on a filter.

**TIP**

A test may exist in one or more lists. This capability can be very helpful. You can reuse tests across lists and then execute that list as a group. For example, you may put a specific unit test in a regression test list you create and then reuse it again in a specific module test.

## Testing Configuration

When you create a test project, Visual Studio adds a test configuration file to the solution. This file, with the extension .testrunconfig, can be found under the Solution Items folder. You use this configuration file to set various settings related to code coverage, web tests, test setup and cleanup, and so on. An example of the dialog box is shown in Figure 28.8. We will refer to this configuration as we move through the chapter.

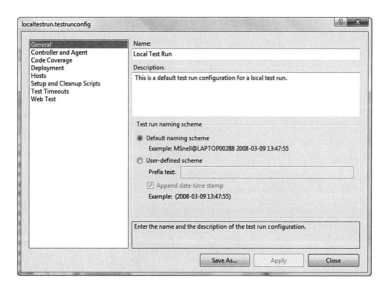

FIGURE 28.8    The .testrunconfig editor.

# Web Testing

Testing a web user interface does not have to be a manual process. In fact, if it is, testers cannot be expected to test every permutation of a data-driven user interface. Instead, they often test a common path through the system and rely on and hope that the other combinations produce similar results.

Visual Studio 2008 provides the web test tools for automating web testing. These tools enable you to record navigation paths through your site, manage these requests, bind requests to data in a database, and then run the tests over again. You can also review and save the test results to TFS in order to report on the quality of a given build.

### Recording a Web Test

You create a new web test by adding a web test item template to a test project. When you do this, Visual Studio automatically launches the web test recording tool in the browser. The intent of this tool is to allow a tester to record a set of web requests in the system. This recording will serve as the basis for defining the web test.

As an example, suppose that you want to define a web test for a Customer Manager application. Assume that the current release being tested contains web forms that allow a user to find customers and edit their profiles. The tester would then navigate to each of these features in turn using the recorder. Figure 28.9 shows an example.

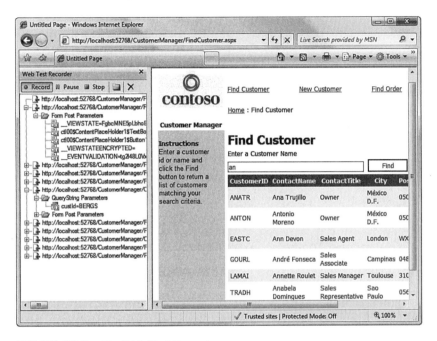

FIGURE 28.9    The Web Test Recorder.

Notice the recording being captured on the left. The Web Test Recorder provides a toolbar for pausing your recording, stopping it, deleting a request from the list, and adding comments (or notes) in between requests. Finally, notice that the details of requests containing QueryStrings and form posts are captured. We will cover more on this in a moment.

Visual Studio writes the requests to the web test upon stopping the recording. The complete set of requests is captured and contained within the test. Figure 28.10 shows the details of the sample web test inside the web test viewer.

Notice the web test toolbar above the web test list. The buttons on this toolbar allow you to (from left to right) rerun the test, bind the test to a data source, set user credentials for test execution, do more recording, set a web test plug-in, set a request plug-in, generate code from the web test, parameterize web servers, promote dynamic parameters to web test parameters, and create a performance profiling session from the web test. We will cover most of these items in the following sections.

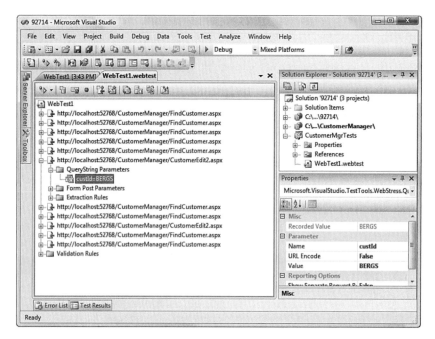

FIGURE 28.10    The recorded web test.

## Managing Web Test Requests

The requests in the web test can be manipulated. You can move them up and down in the list (they are run in order), delete them, and add new requests between them. When you define an effective web test, you should be sure to cover all requests and possible request conditions. However, you often end up with a lot of redundancy in your recorded requests. Therefore, it makes sense to go through each request and pare down your test to the essentials.

In the example, you want the following list of requests:

- ▶ The initial request of `FindCustomer.aspx`.

- ▶ A form post on `FindCustomer.aspx` that searches for customers by clicking the Find button.

- ▶ Another form post for `FindCustomer.aspx` that happens when the user clicks the edit button on a customer in the GridView. This post redirects to `CustomerEdit2.aspx` and passes the customer ID on the `QueryString`.

- ▶ A single request and post for `CustomerEdit2.aspx` that shows the customer to the users and saves the details of the customer when the user clicks the Save button.

You can see that this list covers all the bases for the pages we are testing. Figure 28.11 shows the list cleaned up inside the IDE.

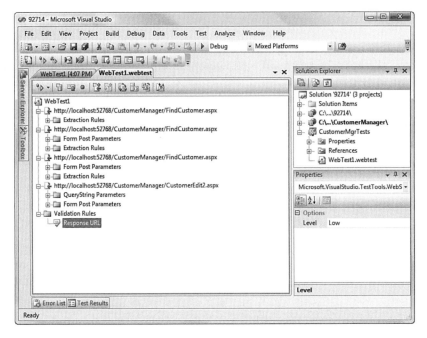

FIGURE 28.11   Cleaned-up web tests.

## Running the Web Test and Viewing Results

You can run your web test from the web test toolbar. When you do so, Visual Studio executes each request and captures all statistics relative to the same. This includes the outcome of the request, its size, the response time, and the actual details of what happened. Figure 28.12 shows the results of the web test created earlier.

Notice that you can navigate each request and view its details. These details can be stored for later review. This provides proof of what exactly happened when the test ran. You have access to the actual HTML that was returned, the request details, the response details, the context of the request, and other details such as exceptions and extraction rules (we will look at these rules in a moment).

## Seeding a Web Test with Data

The real power of the automated web test is the capability to seed it with data from a database. In this way, you can test many more possible permutations of your web application. This is simply not practical when you're doing manual testing.

Using the example, you have a few options for database seeding. First, say you want to be able to call the edit profile screen for each user in the database. You then might also want to save those profiles back to the database. As another option, you might also seed the find pages with data elements and filter the lists accordingly. Running this small number of tests with a lot of data rows should give the web interface a good workout.

28

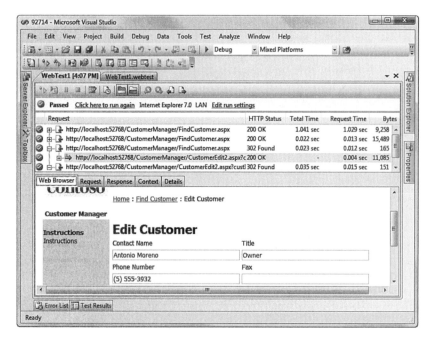

FIGURE 28.12    Web test results.

### Defining the Web Test Data Source

The first step is to define a source for the data that will seed your web test. You can do this from the web test toolbar (database icon). Clicking this toolbar button brings up the New Test Data Source Wizard. The first step in this wizard allows you to choose from a database source, a CSV file, or an XML file. Figure 28.13 shows an example.

In this example, we will create two data sources. First, we will create a CSV file to contain search strings for testing the find customer feature. The second step is to select a CSV file. For our example, assume that we have a simple CSV file that contains an entry for every letter of the alphabet. Figure 28.14 shows this file in the data source wizard.

We also will add a Database data source using the same wizard. This data source will connect to the Customers table. We will use this information to pass each customer in the database to the edit customer page in the site. When complete, the data sources are listed inside the actual web test. Figure 28.15 shows this.

These data sources are specific to each test. That is, they do not have an effect on any other portion of your code. Also, notice that in the Figure 28.15 the Customers table is selected and its properties are shown. Here, you can set how data is accessed or loaded for each web test. You can have that data pulled in one of the following ways:

▶ **Random**—Access rows in the table randomly.

▶ **Sequential**—Access each row in the table in order. After the entire table has been executed, the process will start over (loop) for the duration of a load test.

▶ **Unique**—The same as sequential without the looping.

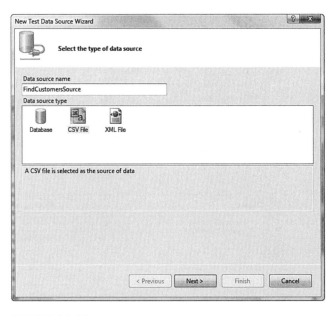

FIGURE 28.13    The New Test Data Source Wizard.

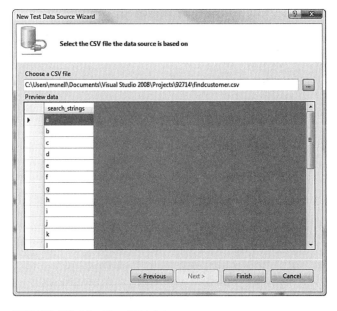

FIGURE 28.14    The CSV data source.

28

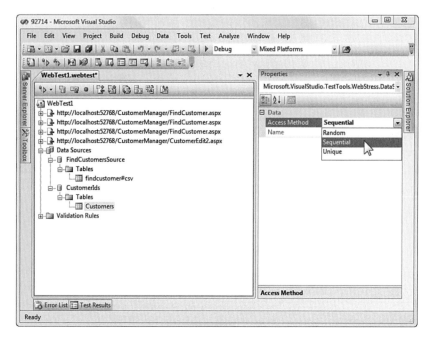

FIGURE 28.15 Web test data sources.

This access method setting is more important in a load test in which the test is executed over a duration of time. In a web test, you will indicate how many (or all) rows you want to execute as part of the test.

### Binding Form Posts to Data

The next step is to bind the tests to the data. Typically, binding is done to the query string parameters and the form post values. Let's first look at binding to form post parameters. First, suppose that you want to execute a search for each item in the CSV file. You can do so by binding the find customer page's search text box to the column of data in the CSV file. Figure 28.16 shows an example.

In this configuration, the form will post the value of the CSV file as if a user entered it in the text box. For this test, we also want to simulate a user selecting the first item returned in the grid view. This can be done by navigating the form post parameters of the FindCustomer.aspx page. Refer to Figure 28.17 for an example. Here you can see that __EVENTARGUMENT=EditItem$0 is set. The text, EditItem, is actually the command text set for the grid view's button. The number indicates the item selected by the user. We set this to zero to choose the first item. If no items are returned, the test will result in an error.

We also set the custId binding of the query string to empty for the CustomerEdit2.aspx page. This allows the selection to post and pass through to the page. You can see this also in Figure 28.17.

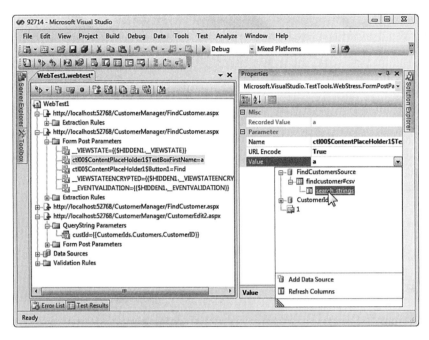

FIGURE 28.16     Binding to form post parameters.

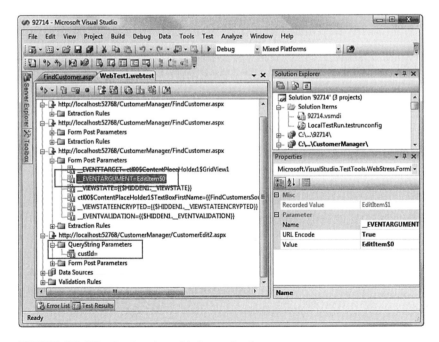

FIGURE 28.17     Setting the grid view selection.

Before you run the test, you must tell the tool to run your web test once per row in the database. You can also determine a fixed count for your web test. You modify this setting through the .testrunconfig file. Figure 28.18 shows an example. Here, you select the option button One Run Per Data Source Row.

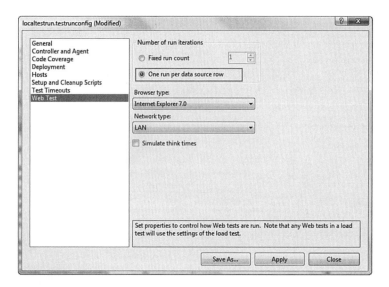

FIGURE 28.18    Configuring the web test to run once per data row.

When you run the test, you will get a run for each letter in the alphabet (26) as stored in the CSV file. You can see this from Figure 28.19. Notice that the results are for run 26 (and the letter z). Notice also the failure messages. You can use the Next and Previous Error search buttons (red circle with white "x") in the toolbar to quickly navigate any errors. In our case, errors were generated when we told the test to select the first item in the grid view and no rows were returned by the search.

### Binding Query Strings to Data

To bind to a query string parameter, you select the parameter from beneath the given request in the web test. You then view the properties of the parameter. Here, you can set the value property to a field in the database. Figure 28.20 shows an example of binding the custId query string parameter of the customer edit page to the database table Customers.CustomerID field.

In this example, imagine that you want to hit the customer edit page for every item in the database. You want to verify that the item opens and displays correctly. You also want to execute a save for each of these items. In our case, we will do so with a single Customers table. However, you could have one table that was for read data and another that you bound to for the changes.

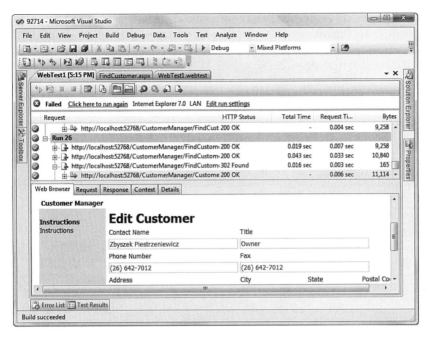

FIGURE 28.19   Viewing the results.

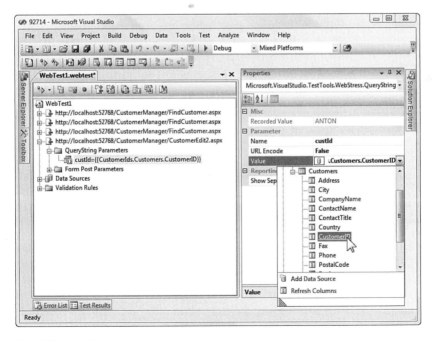

FIGURE 28.20   Binding the test to database data.

You already saw the first step in Figure 28.20. Here we bound the database record for each customer to the query string parameter. This will allow the form to load appropriately. However, we need data inside our form post. Therefore, we will bind the same database items to the post of the customer edit page. Figure 28.21 shows each of these items bound accordingly.

When you run this new test, you will get an execution for each customer record in the database (in this example, this means 91 records). Of course, you can use any test result to generate the appropriate work item to get any problem fixed.

---

**TIP**

Visual Studio provides complete control over the web tests for those testers who can write code. On the web test toolbar, there is an option to generate code. Selecting this option will create a class file that represents the web test. The web test uses the `Microsoft.VisualStudio.TestTools.WebTesting` namespace and can be coded manually or edited from this generated code.

---

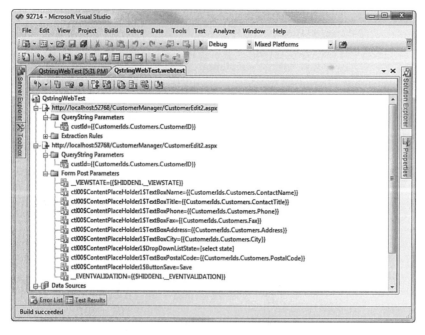

FIGURE 28.21    Binding the test to database data.

## Extracting Values from Web Tests

You can further refine your web tests by creating your own extraction rules. These rules allow you to extract key information from the request and save it as part of the test results. As an example, you might want to extract the values inside an HTML attribute such as an anchor tag's URL or a button's name. Other examples might include extracting text from the page, form field values, values of hidden fields, and so on. Figure 28.22 shows an example of the extract rule dialog.

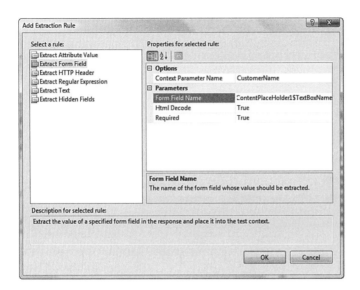

FIGURE 28.22    Defining the extraction rule.

You access this dialog box by right-clicking a web test request and choosing Add Extraction Rule. From here, you can define various rule types. For this example, say you are creating a rule to extract the value from a form field, TextBoxName. Notice that we have set this rule's Context Parameter Name to CustomerName. This name will allow us to identify the parameter in the test results.

Figure 28.23 shows these results. On the Context tab, you can find the extracted values. Also, on the Details tab (not shown), you can review the results of your extraction tests. If an extraction fails, for instance, then an error is raised on the Details tab.

**Linking Pages with Extracted Values**
In addition to viewing these extracted values, you can use this information to link requests together. You can pull a value from one page and then pass it to another. For example, when defining the extraction rule, you gave the parameter the name CustomerName. This name becomes a variable name that you can use inside the Properties window when binding test items to values.

## Requesting Validation Rules

You can also add validation rules to each of the requests in your web test. Validation rules allow you to check a page (or request) for certain expected values. These additional tests are run against the request. Validation rules include the capability to check for expected form field values, verify HTML tags, check expected request times, and more.

28

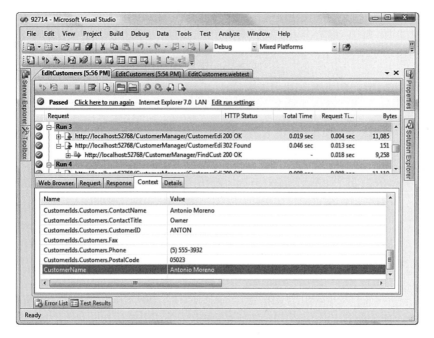

FIGURE 28.23    Viewing the extracted value.

You add a validation rule by right-clicking a web test request and choosing Add Validation Rule. Selecting this option brings up the Add Validation Rule dialog box. Here, you can define the rule type and its parameters. As an example, following the search invocation by the user on the FindCustomer.aspx page, if data is present, an edit hyperlink will appear. We can then add a Find Text validation rule to determine whether rows were returned from the search. To do so, you create a FindText validation rule and enter the appropriate parameters. Figure 28.24 shows an example.

> **NOTE**
>
> Validation rules can sometimes have an effect on performance. Therefore, you can use the Level property to indicate when a given validation rule should run. Typically, you set your validation rules to High, and then on a load test, you indicate that you want to run tests on a Low level to get a more accurate view of performance.

The results of the validation rule are shown on the Details tab for the request. Figure 28.25 shows the results of the sample validation rule.

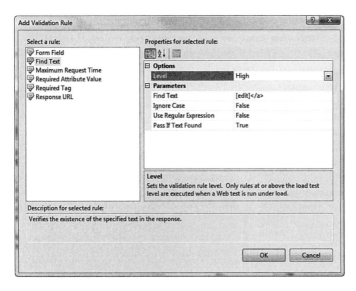

FIGURE 28.24    Defining a validation rule.

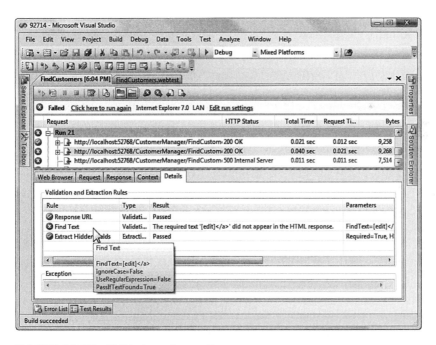

FIGURE 28.25    Validation rule results.

# Load Testing

It is important to know how your application handles user load. Typically, you will define a performance benchmark for the application. This benchmark is best represented in terms of the number of users that an application can support at a given time (concurrent users). Without load testing, it is very difficult to know whether you have reached your goal. Clearly, you do not want to wait until after deployment to find out whether you've fallen short of your benchmark.

Visual Studio Team Test provides a load testing tool to do just that. With it, you can create a load test. The load test can be configured to simulate multiple users accessing a site concurrently. While the load test runs, you capture instrumentation output from the environment. This data lets you know how the environment and your application held up under stress.

## Creating a Load Test

Visual Studio provides a load test wizard to walk you through the process of creating a load test. The good news is that load tests leverage the web and unit tests you've already defined for the initial stages of application testing. By walking through the wizard steps, you can select the existing tests you will use to simulate load and then configure the actual load. The load test is then added to a testing project where it, too, can be saved, edited, versioned, and run over and over again.

Let's walk through an example with the New Load Test Wizard. You will simulate load on the customer management application and will leverage the web tests created previously. Recall that these tests simulated searching for customers and editing those customers. Each test was also fed from the database.

### Starting the New Load Test Wizard

You launch the New Load Test Wizard by simply adding a load test to a test project. The first screen of the wizard is introductory in nature. Figure 28.26 shows an example.

### Defining Your Load Scenario

You define a name for your scenario on the second screen of the New Load Test Wizard. This name is simply a label for the test to help others understand exactly what you want to test. For this example, we will load test the `FindCustomer.aspx` and `EditCustomer2.aspx` pages. Therefore, we will call this scenario Find and Edit Customers.

The second screen also allows you to define a *think time* profile. Think times represent the time a user might spend thinking between requests. This time is used to read the page, fill it out, and so on. Think times are important in that you want to simulate actual users with your load test. You have a few options here.

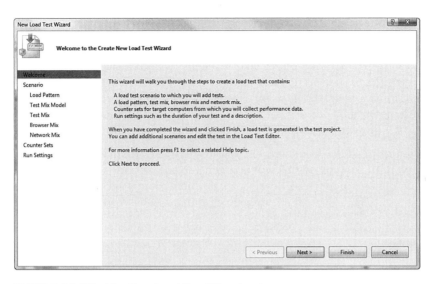

FIGURE 28.26    The New Load Test Wizard welcome screen.

You can use recorded think times. These times were recorded when you created the web test. Therefore, this is a great option. You can smooth out these recorded think times by indicating a standard distribution based on the recorded think times. Last, you can turn off think times altogether. This setting is useful only if you are trying to spike load on the server (and not simulate users).

Finally, the second screen allows you to indicate the time between test iterations. This value is in seconds. It is useful if you know something about your users. For example, if you know that approximately every five seconds, a user initiates a find-and-edit customer process, you could indicate that number here. Figure 28.27 shows the sample setup for the scenario.

### Defining a Load Pattern for Your Test

The next wizard screen is used to indicate a pattern for the load test. You have a couple of options here: constant load and stepped load. The first allows you to execute the test with a steady, constant load of users. For standard load testing scenarios, this is sufficient. You already have think times for the users. If you want to test how the system performs with a constant target load, you would use this setting.

Stepping the load represents using a load test to stress-test your application. For example, you might be trying to determine how the system behaves as more and more users are added to the load. This capability is great if you are trying to stress your application to find its breaking point or bottleneck relative to server and application stress. To define your stepped load, you indicate a starting number of users and a maximum number of users to be stepped up to. You then indicate the time period (duration) between each jump (or step) and the size of each step. Figure 28.28 shows an example of a stepped load.

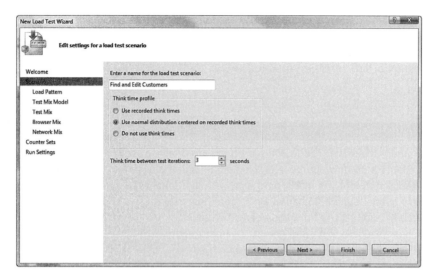

FIGURE 28.27    Defining the scenario using the New Load Test Wizard.

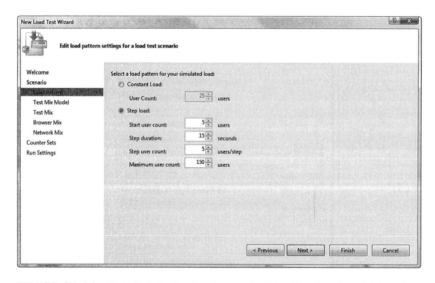

FIGURE 28.28    Defining the load pattern using the New Load Test Wizard.

### Choosing the Test Mix to Simulate Load

The next wizard screen allows you to determine how you intend to mix your load tests. You have three options: by total number of tests, by number of users, and by user pace. Here's the breakdown:

▶ **Total number of tests**—This allows you to set a percentage for each test in your application. If you have three tests, for instance, you could set one to be run 25%

of the time, another to run 40% of the total tests, and the last to run the remainder (or 35%).

▶ **Number of users**—This allows you to indicate that your test should be run by user distribution (and not test distribution). For example, using this model you might indicate that 7 out of 10 users should be searching while the other 3 are buying. If you have a test that represents each, you would set 70% of the users to always run the search test and 30% of the users to run the buy test.

▶ **User pace**—This setting allows you to indicate that each test should be run a specified number of times over the course of an hour. Test are run by all users in this time period. If you know, for example, that every hour 100 users search your application and 10 users buy, you could set up a test for each condition and set the pace accordingly.

Figure 28.29 shows an example of this dialog. In our example, we have selected the Based on the Number of Virtual Users option. Whatever you select here drives the configuration of the next screen.

In the next screen, you choose the tests to run to simulate the user load based on the user mix you selected previously. You can add multiple web tests and unit tests based on your scenario. You can then choose the percentage distribution based on your mix model.

In our example, we have a web test to simulate editing customers and another for searching for them. We will assume that we know that for every five lookups, we get one edit. In this case, we will distribute these two tests across our load test. The find customer web test would represent 80% of the load, and the edit customer test would be the other 20%. Figure 28.30 shows an example of this distribution.

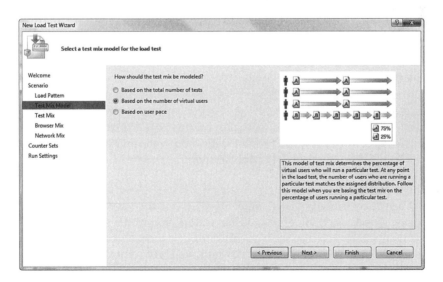

FIGURE 28.29   Defining the load test mix model.

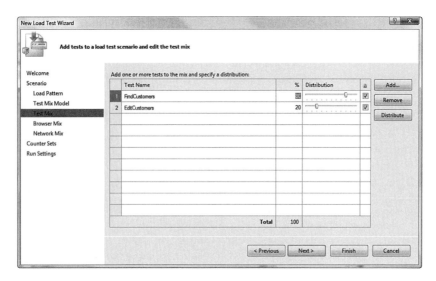

FIGURE 28.30    Defining the test mix distribution.

> **NOTE**
>
> Remember to set your web test data source to pull data randomly or sequentially from the database. If you use the Unique setting, each row will be pulled from the database once and the load test will report an error, indicating that there was insufficient data to finish the test.

### Indicating a Browser Mix

The next screen of the load test allows you to simulate the browsers that users might use to visit your application. Again, you can distribute these browsers across a percentage. Figure 28.31 shows an example.

### Indicating a Network Mix

Next, you indicate the user's network mix. If you know that 100% of the users are on the LAN, you can indicate that information here. If, however, a portion of the user base comes from outside the LAN, you can set up that distribution on this page. Of course, setting up the distribution this way requires you to have some data about your user base (or do projections). Figure 28.32 shows an example of this screen.

### Choosing Computers to Monitor

The next screen in the wizard is used to determine which servers the load test should monitor. If your application is distributed on multiple servers, you would indicate the details of these computers here. You also want to indicate the controller computer. This is the computer running the tests. Of course, for best results, you will want the controller computer and the server computers to be physically different machines.

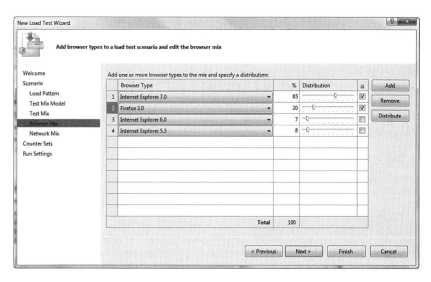

FIGURE 28.31 Defining the browser mix.

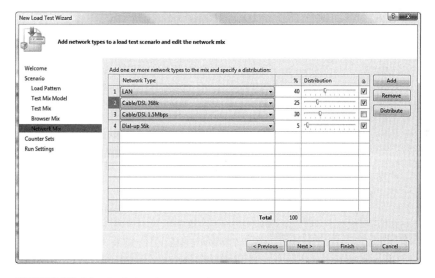

FIGURE 28.32 Defining the network mix using the New Load Test Wizard.

In addition, for each computer you intend to monitor, you can define a counter set. A counter set represents a standard set of performance indicators you want to monitor. There are counter sets for IIS, SQL, and so on. Figure 28.33 shows an example of the Counter Sets screen.

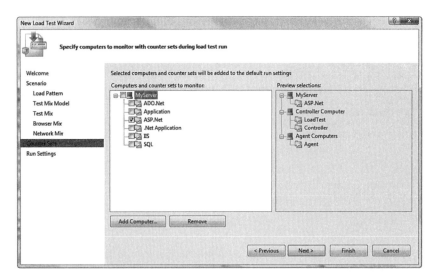

FIGURE 28.33   Defining counters using the New Load Test Wizard.

### Indicating Execution Timings and Run Settings

The final screen of the wizard is used to define configuration settings for the load test. These settings include the timings, the number of errors to trap, and the validation level. Recall the validation level from the web tests; this is the level of validations to run to simulate load. If, for example, you define a number of validations for your web test, these validations take away from performance and have nothing to do with simulating actual users. Therefore, you can indicate a level here that excludes these validations.

In addition, you can use this screen to set a warm-up duration for your tests during which your tests will run but data will not be collected. You can also set the total test duration or the number of iterations that should execute. Finally, you can set the sampling rate, which indicates how often data is captured. Figure 28.34 shows an example of this final screen in the wizard.

## Reviewing and Editing a Load Test

When the wizard finishes, it creates a .loadtest file. This file can be opened and edited within the IDE. Figure 28.35 shows an example of the file open in the IDE. Notice that each section defined in the wizard is represented here.

If you need to edit an item, you can select it and modify its settings through the Properties window. You can also right-click a section and bring up an editor. For example, if you want to change the Network mix, you can right-click this section and choose Edit Network Mix to bring up a dialog box that looks just like the wizard page for this setting.

Also, notice the rightmost icon in the load test editor's toolbar. This allows you to use the load test to start a performance profiling session (as discussed in Chapter 26).

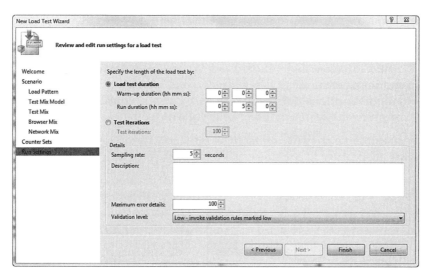

FIGURE 28.34    Configuring run settings using the New Load Test Wizard.

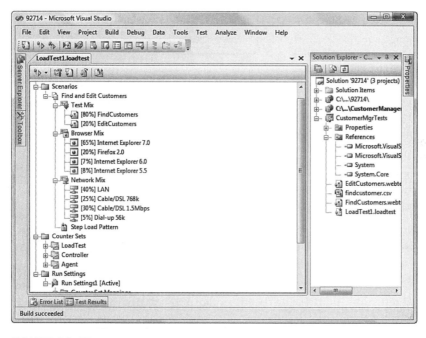

FIGURE 28.35    The load test viewer.

## Running Load Tests and Reviewing Results

You are finally ready to run the load test. When you click the Run button on the load test page, Visual Studio opens the load test monitor window. This window is shown in Figure 28.36. Here the system is still running the set of tests.

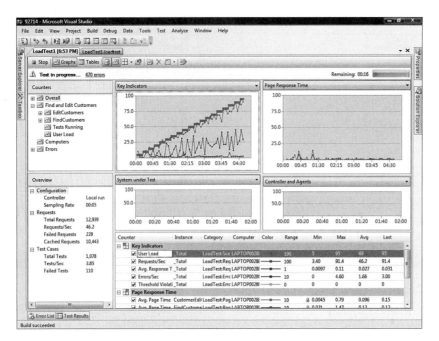

FIGURE 28.36    Monitoring a load test.

If you have used the Performance Monitor in Windows, you will find similarities with this screen. At the center of the monitor is a set of graphs that track important counters (you can change the layout of the grid and number of graphs to show). By default, there is a graph for Key Indicators, Page Response Time, System Under Test, and Controller and Agents.

The counters being tracked by each graph are listed at the bottom of the screen, along with their general statistics. It is helpful to select one of these counters to see the line of the graph highlighted. For example, in the image the User Load indicator is selected. You can see that this load is being stepped up over time.

There are a couple of other windows here. The Counters window to the left allows you to navigate counters and add them to the monitor. The Overview window shows a summary view of the tests. You can locate some key statistics in this window, such as the total requests, requests per second, and use of the cache.

Last, when the load test stops running, the data is stored. You can work with this data and review it in detail. In addition, you can look for trends and breaking points. You can also review errors that occurred during execution. Figure 28.37 shows an example of the report. You can also view this data as graphs and tables using the toolbar at the top. And, of course, you can export the data as required.

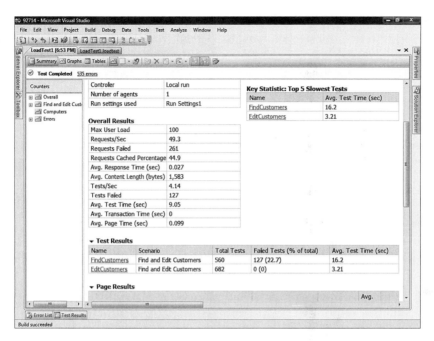

FIGURE 28.37   The test report.

# Manual Tests

Even with all the automated testing inside Team Test, a user will still need to perform some tests manually. The good news is that these tests can be defined for the project and tracked just like other tests.

## Creating a Manual Test

You create a manual test by adding the manual test item to a test project. A manual test can be defined as a text file or a Word document. Manual tests have the extension .mht and are stored inside the test project.

As an example, suppose that you want a tester to view a page in your application to confirm its layout across browsers. You can define a manual test to do just that. Figure 28.38 shows an example. You give the test a title and indicate the steps to execute the test.

## Executing a Manual Test

You run a manual test the same way you run all other tests. In fact, if you execute a manual test as part of a group (using the Test List Editor), that manual test will be presented to the tester for completion. In addition, the details of the manual test's execution will be saved as part of the test results. This ensures that all test results make it back to the team.

28

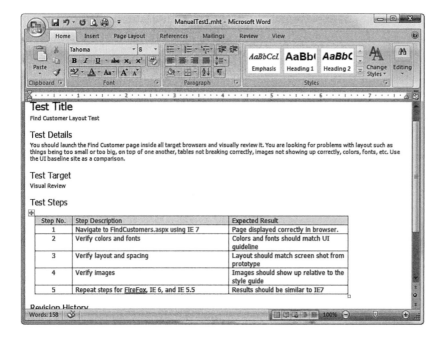

FIGURE 28.38    A manual test in Word.

Figure 28.39 shows the sample manual test inside the IDE. Notice that the tester must indicate the test results (pass/fail). The tester can also add comments here. In addition, the actual test that the tester must perform is shown in the space at the bottom of the window.

# Generic Tests

A generic test is used to wrap existing test code and have that code executed as part of the testing system. Performing a generic test ensures that the result of these test scripts will be published along with the other application test results.

You create a generic test by adding it to a test project. Figure 28.40 shows some of the fields used to define generic tests.

Generic tests are outside the bounds of a typical testing scenario for most applications. It is good to know, however, that they exist in case you ever need them. For more information, including a detailed walk-through of generic tests, you can search the MSDN documentation for "Generic Tests."

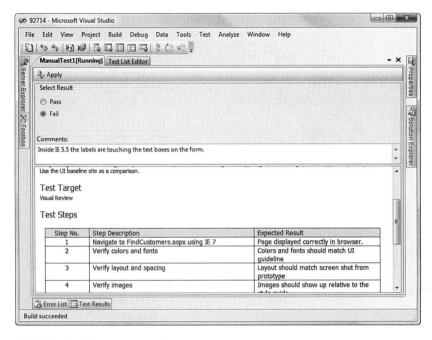

FIGURE 28.39    Executing the manual test.

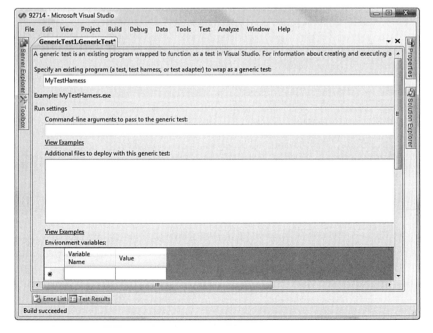

FIGURE 28.40    A generic test.

# Ordered Tests

The last test we need to look at is the ordered test. An ordered test is simply a test you create that groups and orders other tests. This type of test can be useful if you want to define an overall module test, for instance. The ordered test is treated as a single test even though it groups many tests. This is also true for the results of an ordered test. The ordered test either fails or succeeds.

## Creating an Ordered Test

You add an ordered test to a test project just like any other test. You can then use the ordered test definition window to add any type of test to the ordered test, with the exception of a load test. Load tests are outside the bounds of an ordered test.

Figure 28.41 shows an example of an ordered test. You can select tests from the left and add them to the ordered test on the right. You can then choose the order in which these items get executed. Finally, you can indicate whether the ordered test should continue upon the first failure.

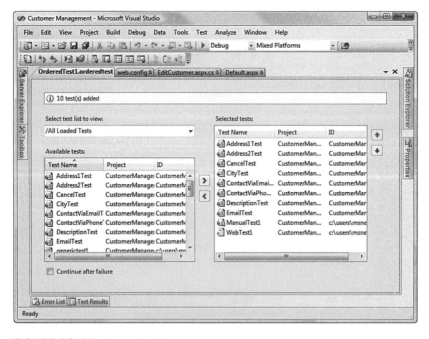

FIGURE 28.41   An ordered test.

# Summary

You have seen how developers can build unit tests to increase the quality of their code and the code they deliver to production. You have also seen the power of Visual Studio Team Test to create web tests, load tests, manual tests, generic tests, and ordered tests. Some key points in this chapter include the following:

- ▶ You can define a test project to group test items.
- ▶ The Test List Editor enables you to review and group tests inside the IDE.
- ▶ You configure test settings through the `.testrunconfig` file.
- ▶ You can record a navigation path through a web application and save these requests as a web test.
- ▶ The parameters of a web test can be seeded from a data source.
- ▶ You can leverage your web and unit tests to define load tests.
- ▶ Load tests can be configured to simulate actual users visiting your site.
- ▶ You can define a manual test for execution by a tester. The results of this test can be maintained along with those of the other tests.
- ▶ You can create an ordered test to treat a group of tests as a single, atomic test.

> **NOTE**
>
> One item that is beyond the scope of this book is the new Visual Studio 2008 Test Load Agent product. This product is not included in Team Suite. You can use it to simulate user loads in your test environment that will match the anticipated loads in the production environment. Test Load Agent is capable of using multiple client computers to execute tests; these clients then report data back to a central controller. For more information, see http://msdn2.microsoft.com/en-us/vsts2008/products.

28

# Database Edition

Visual Studio Team System Database Edition is the newest edition of the VSTS development environments. It was originally released after the first set of Visual Studio 2005 Team System versions to accommodate a very specific need in the development environment that was underserved by current toolsets: that of the database administrator (DBA) and database developer.

In general, VSTS has moved the focus away from individual developer productivity and has broadened the scope to try to optimize for team productivity. This is an important distinction. And as we look at development teams, the role of the "database professional" was left out of the Visual Studio Team System vision. VSTS Database Edition corrects that flaw.

There are a few core issues in the database development world that VSTS Database Edition hopes to tackle:

▶ **Database schema changes**—Schema changes to a database can be problematic; typically, schema changes are implemented by DBA against live production databases or through scripts that are then run against the live production database. The potential for error, and the corresponding implications to the system, are high.

▶ **Test and development reproduction**—Testers and developers need to work against copies of the production database—but understanding the differences between different versions of the same database is difficult, and the process has not historically been served by tools hosted right within the IDE.

▶ **Testing against database changes**—Just as with bugs in the application layer of a system, it is true that finding and fixing bugs late in the project life cycle is exponentially more costly than finding them early in the project life cycle.

This chapter introduces the tools delivered with Visual Studio Team System Database Edition. These tools aim to fold the DBA and database developer into the same software development life-cycle process that application developers, testers, and architects participate in, and surrounds those database professionals with tools specific to the problems in this space. And VSTS Database Edition does all of this while recognizing the needs and workflows that are specific and native to the database world.

Because this tool, and thus this chapter, caters to the database developer role, we will assume a base level of understanding around core database concepts such as tables, views, stored procedures, triggers, and constraints, and the issues surrounding the maintenance of those items.

# The Database Project System

The center of gravity for VSTS Database Edition is the database project. A database project is essentially an offline version of a database. It mirrors a database through a set of .SQL files that contain the schema and object definitions for things such as tables, indexes, and stored procedures. The database project acts as the nucleus for the database development life cycle, or DDLC (depicted in Figure 29.1). A typical workflow enabled with VSTS Database Edition might go something like this:

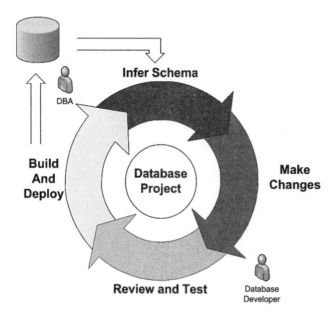

FIGURE 29.1    The database development life cycle.

▶ The DBA, who is typically the only person on a project team with access to the production database, uses VSTS Database Edition to create an initial database project and reverse engineer a production database into that project.

▶ The DBA is also typically responsible for generating test data sets for use in non–production databases.

▶ From there, the database developer gets involved. The database developer works within the confines of the database project to write the database code, changes schema items as needed to implement the required functionality, and writes unit tests that validate those changes.

▶ When done with a set of changes, the database developer checks the schema changes into the Team Foundation Server source control system.

▶ The DBA is then reinjected into the process. The DBA reviews the changes, compares the changes to the schema and data already in production, builds a deployment package containing those changes, and then oversees the deployment of those changes in a moderated way into production.

With VSTS Database Edition, this entire workflow is enabled from right within the Visual Studio IDE.

Because a database project is only a representation of a real database, changes can be made to the project without impacting the physical database. And because these changes are made to discrete sets of files—files that can participate in the same source/version control system as all other files in VSTS—the database developer can participate in the same work item tracking process as other members of the project team.

Because an understanding of the database project is crucial to executing tasks in VSTS Database Edition, we'll start our exploration with the process for creating a database project.

## Creating a Database Project

Database projects use the same project template system and "new project" process as all other Visual Studio project types. This means that we launch the creation process by selecting File, New, and then selecting one of the templates located in the Data Projects category on the New Project dialog. VSTS 2008 ships with support for SQL Server 2000 and SQL Server 2005, and because these require different parsing and tooling support, they are both represented by different templates. In fact, we have two templates to pick from for both SQL Server 2000 and SQL Server 2005: One template will use a wizard to guide us through creating the project, and the other will create an empty or blank project that will then require some manual configuration (see Figure 29.2).

Let's select the SQL Server 2005 Wizard template, and walk through the wizard screens one by one.

29

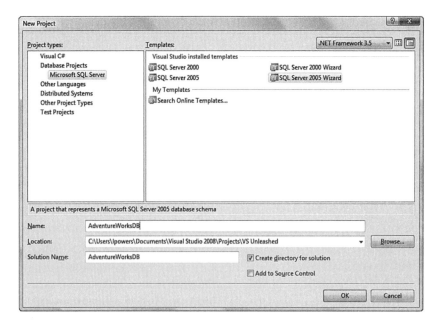

FIGURE 29.2    The database project templates.

To be able to parse and validate the objects within a database project, Visual Studio needs to communicate with a local instance of SQL Server: This can be SQL Server 2005 Express Edition, SQL Server 2005 Developer Edition, or SQL Server 2005 Enterprise Edition. If you do not have a local instance of SQL Server running, you will see a dialog at the start of the new project process prompting you to supply the path to a valid SQL Server local instance. Note that all the VSTS products ship with SQL Server Express Edition.

### Project Properties

After we're past the initial welcome screen, we are prompted to specify how we want the project to be organized and which schema to use (see Figure 29.3). There are two options for organizing the project: by object type and by schema. With the Organize My Project by Object Type option selected, Visual Studio will create a schema objects folder with subfolders for your database objects such as tables and stored procedures. The Organize My Project by Schema option will group your project objects by the schema type that they belong to. For most database implementations, the default By Object Type setting is the most useful.

This page of the wizard is also used to collect data on whether we want to enable full text search or enable SQL CLR support (which essentially allows the use of CLR types and functions within the database), and whether the files generated by Visual Studio will include the database schema name as a prefix in the filename. Note that support for full text search is not a viable option if you are using SQL Server Express.

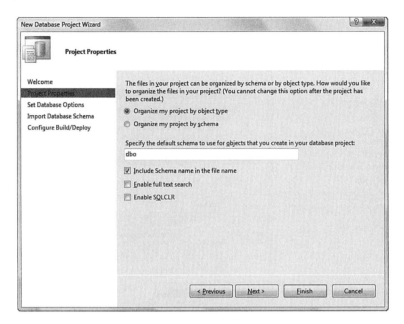

FIGURE 29.3   Project organization options.

### Database Options

The next page of the wizard specifies the collation type to use, and various collation and storage settings (see Figure 29.4). Again, leaving these at their default is normal. In fact, in the next page of the wizard, you will have the option to import these settings from the live database (in addition to its schema).

### Import Database Schema

This page is where VSTS Database Edition really starts to enable the DDLC: Although we can create an "empty" database project, most database developers will want to build their initial project from an existing database. This preserves the concept of a production database being the "one version of the truth." This is a recognition of the fact that we really want our test and development database environments to mirror the production environment in terms of structure. By reverse engineering a database into its component objects, Visual Studio allows us to create copies of a database, and that, in turn, allows developers to work in their own private sandbox without worrying about impacting the product data store. Figure 29.5 shows the import schema page.

> **NOTE**
>
> Checking the box Override Database Configuration with Imported Schema Settings will cause Visual Studio to ignore the database options specified in the preceding screen, and instead infer the settings from the database that you are about to import.

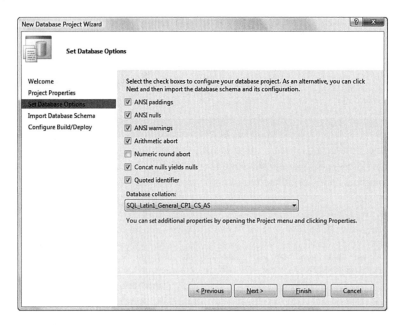

FIGURE 29.4    Database settings.

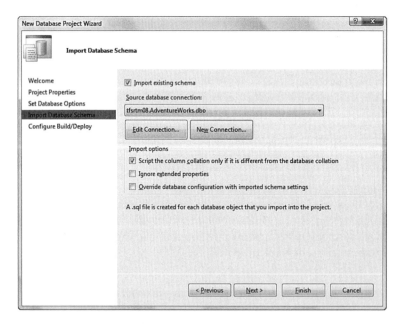

FIGURE 29.5    Importing a database schema.

Specify a connection to the database you want to reverse engineer, and then continue on to the next, and final, page of the wizard.

### Configure Build and Deploy

The last page of the project wizard (see Figure 29.6) determines how Visual Studio will build and deploy the database project. Of particular interest here are the target database settings. There are two basic deployment scenarios: You can specify a new database, or you can specify an existing database as the target. This allows database developers to either create a brand-new database instance based on the schema defined in the project, or update an existing database to use the schema defined in the project.

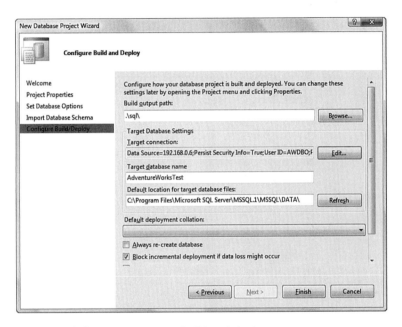

FIGURE 29.6    Configuring the build and deploy process.

We specify the target database by providing a connection, a database name, and a location for the database files on the server. This last piece of information is defaulted to the location specified by the source database (which Visual Studio queried based on the information provided on the prior screen).

Table 29.1 describes the options on the Configure Build and Deploy screen.

TABLE 29.1    Build and Deploy Options

| Setting | Description |
| --- | --- |
| Build Output Path | The path where Visual Studio will place the actual build script; you can specify a relative path here, which will be relative to the database project's path. |

TABLE 29.1    Continued

| Setting | Description |
| --- | --- |
| Target Connection | The connection information for the database you want to deploy to. If you leave this blank, Visual Studio will use the local instance of SQL Server that is being used for design validation (see the earlier note on the requirement for a local instance of SQL Server). |
| Target Database Name | The name of the database to deploy to; if the database doesn't exist, it will be created. |
| Default Location for Target Database Files | The path on the SQL Server where the local database files are kept. |
| Default Deployment Collation | The collation to use during the deployment. You can elect to not script any collation, to use the collation defined on the project, or to use the collation defined on the target database. |
| Always Re-create Database | If this box is checked, the database will be dropped and then re-created during the deployment process. Clearing the check box tells the deployment process to update the existing database. |
| Block Incremental Deployment If Data Loss Might Occur | If this box is checked and you are deploying to an existing database, schema changes that could result in data loss (such as narrowing the width of a numeric field) will cause the deployment to stop with an error message. |
| Back Up Database Before Deployment | Indicates whether the deployment script should back up the target database before updating its schema. |

This is the last page of the wizard; at this stage, Visual Studio has all the information needed to create the initial project. Clicking on the Finish button will kick off the project generation within Visual Studio. Figure 29.7 is a screenshot of the schema import in progress, and Figure 29.8 shows the end result: a fully populated database project within Visual Studio.

Note that the database schema objects reside under a root Schema Objects folder, and within that folder they are organized in a more granular manner by their type. Each object in the database—be it a table, a stored procedure, an index, a key, or a constraint—is represented by a single .sql file. In addition to the schema files, we also have folders for holding data generation plans (more on these later in this chapter), and pre- and post-deployment scripts. Scripts placed into the pre- and post- folders will be executed just before, or immediately after, deployment.

**TIP**

Pre- and post-deployment scripts are useful when you're deploying into a test environment. You can use predeployment scripts to initialize the environment, and post-deployment scripts to clean up after the deployment has finished.

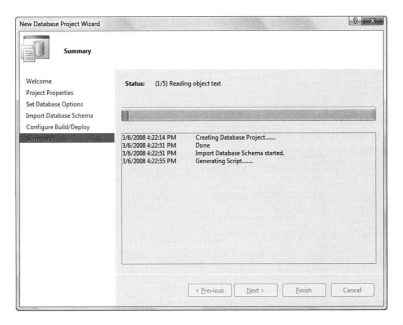

FIGURE 29.7    Importing the AdventureWorks schema.

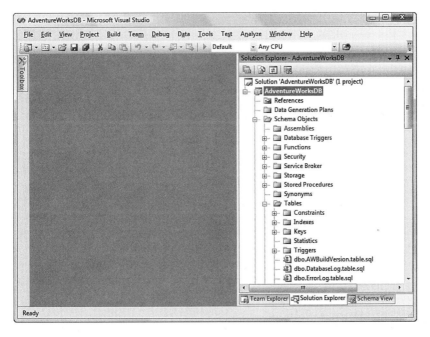

FIGURE 29.8    A complete database project.

## The Schema View

In addition to the familiar Solution Explorer view, database projects also have a Schema View window (shown in Figure 29.9).

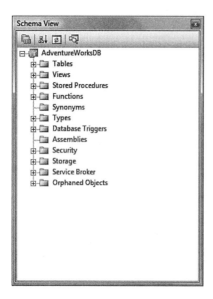

FIGURE 29.9    The database project Schema View.

This explorer window looks similar to the Solution Explorer layout (especially if you have opted to organize your database project by object type and not schema), but it goes a step further to make SQL Server developers feel right at home in the IDE: It was designed to closely mimic the look and feel of the SQL Management Studio tool, right down to the icons used for the individual project items. In Figure 29.10, we compare the view from SQL Management Studio's Object Explorer with the Visual Studio Schema Explorer.

Because the Schema View window focuses exclusively on database objects, you won't find things like data generation plans here, or pre- and post-deployment scripts. The Schema View window also has a cool feature that visually indicates whether a syntax error exists in any of the database objects. For instance, if we were to double-click on the dbo.uspGetBillOfMaterials object and then change its SQL to something invalid, we would get a visible notification of the problem right within Schema View (see Figure 29.11).

Now that we know our way around the database project system, we can explore the database-specific tools in VSTS Database Edition.

Schema View

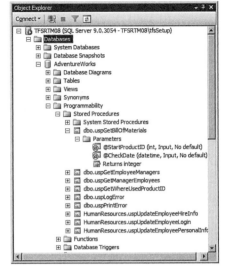

SQL Management Studio

FIGURE 29.10   The Schema View compared to the view from SQL Server Management Studio.

FIGURE 29.11   An error indicator in the Schema View window.

29

> **NOTE**
>
> Although the Schema View window is a powerful tool to use when managing database objects, it also has one annoying issue: It does not have a horizontal scrollbar like the Solution Explorer does. This means that if you have long object names, you will actually need to widen the window in order to see the full name. Hopefully this is something that will be fixed in a future service pack.

# Comparing Schemas

The Schema Comparison tool is used to compare the structure of two databases. It is also capable of comparing the schema represented in a database project and a live database. This is a crucial feature for enabling the DDLC: Database developers (and DBAs) need to understand the differences between schema sets in order to understand the changes that need to be propagated from development to test, or from test to production.

> **NOTE**
>
> The Schema Comparison tool is used behind the scenes during the schema import process. For a new database project, this means comparing the schema of the project (which is blank—no objects exist) to a database and generating a script to account for the differences. The end result, of course, is the wholesale copy of a database's schema into a database project.

Besides simply comparing two different schemas to see where they are different, you can also directly synch one schema to another using this tool.

The Schema Comparison tool is launched from the Data menu: Select Schema Compare and then New Schema Comparison. The New Schema Comparison dialog (see Figure 29.12) is used to specify the two entities to compare. We have the option of selecting a database project or database as the source, and a project or database as the target (note that you can't compare two projects: Database to database, project to database, or database to project are the valid scenarios that the tool can handle).

In this example, we are comparing the schema for the AdventureWorks OLTP database with the AdventureWorks data warehouse database. After selecting our target and source, we launch the comparison activity by clicking OK. The arrow button in the middle of the dialog is used to swap the target and source information.

> **TIP**
>
> The Schema Comparison tool can even be used to compare SQL Server databases of different versions. This is a huge benefit for development organizations that are developing on SQL Server 2005 but running SQL Server 2000 in production—or for groups that want to move databases from SQL Server 2000 to SQL Server 2005 while making enhancements to the schema along the way.

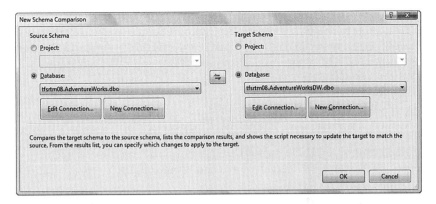

FIGURE 29.12    Configuring a data comparison.

After the comparison is done running, we can see the results in the IDE (see Figure 29.13). The top pane of the comparison window shows a hierarchical view of all the database objects in both databases. Each object is shown under its owning database and an update action is also displayed. The update action is the required action to make the target database look like the source database schema-wise.

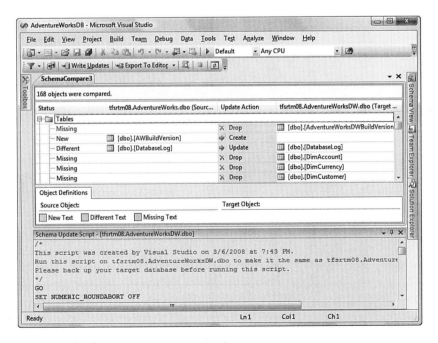

FIGURE 29.13    Data comparison results.

So in the sample comparison shown in Figure 29.13, we have a dbo.DatabaseLog table that exists in both databases, and therefore its update action is set to Update. In the case of dbo.AWBuildVersion, which exists in the source but not in the target, the update action is set to Create: We need to take the source schema for this table and use it to create a new, identical table in the target database.

## Viewing Object Definitions

If we click on a row in the comparison table, we will see side-by-side comparisons of the selected object's schema in the Object Definitions pane. This pane isn't fully visible in Figure 29.13; in Figure 29.14, we have opened up the pane a bit more to show the information displayed there.

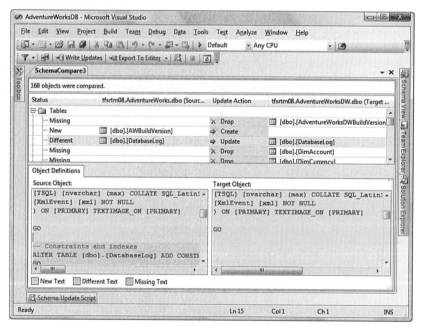

FIGURE 29.14    Comparing object definitions.

For the source and target database, each object's schema, in SQL, will appear. The SQL text will be shaded according to the legend provided in the IDE: New Text is text that exists in the source but not in the target, Different Text is text that exists in both the target and the source but is different between the two, and Missing Text is text that is in the target but not in the source. Viewing individual object definitions is a great way to get detail on the exact SQL-level differences between two objects. In the example shown in Figure 29.14, we see a block of text that is flagged as New Text.

## The Schema Update Script

The bottom pane of the Schema Comparison window shows us the script that was generated based on the comparison process. This script, which is not editable on this screen, contains the actual SQL commands we would need to run in order to make the target database identical from a schema perspective to the source database. We can edit this script on a per-object basis by clicking on Update Action in the comparison results table. This will reveal a drop-down that allows us to select the default action (based on the comparison), or to set the action to Skip. By skipping an object, we remove any script from the update script affecting that object (whether it is in the source or target).

Figure 29.15 shows the update script generated from our database-to-database comparison.

---

**TIP**

You may want to use the Skip action for things such as users, logins, and filegroups. These are typically things that shouldn't be mirrored, especially if you are running a data comparison with the intent of pushing changes from a test database to a production database.

---

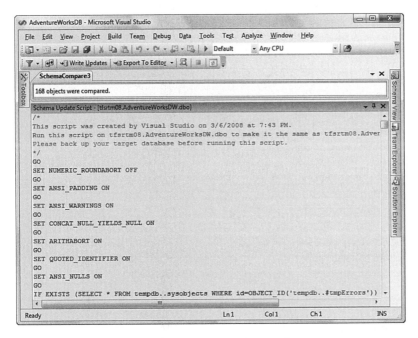

FIGURE 29.15    Previewing the schema update script.

29

### Executing the Update Script

With the update script prepared, you now have the option to actually execute the script against the target database. Again, this has the end goal of conforming the target database schema to that of the source database. You can run the script directly from within the Schema Comparison tool, export the script to a file (which can then be run from various tools that understand T-SQL), or open the script in the T-SQL editor and run it from there.

All of these options are easily executed using the Schema Comparison windows' toolbar, or by using the Data, Schema Compare menu. The Write Updates action runs the update script immediately against the target database; the Export to Editor and Export to File actions handle the task of opening the script in an editor or writing it out to a file.

## Comparison Options

You can control how the Schema Comparison tool conducts its comparison by using the Options dialog. Select Tools, Options, and then navigate to the Schema Compare page under the Database Tools section. This screen, shown in Figure 29.16, allows you to tweak how the comparison works, and which objects are used in the comparison. For instance, you can check the box labeled Ignore Filegroups to tell the comparison tool that you want to exclude SQL Server filegroups from the comparison. Most of the options here are self-explanatory, but the VSTS help topic "Options (Database Tools/Schema Compare)" has detailed explanations for all the settings.

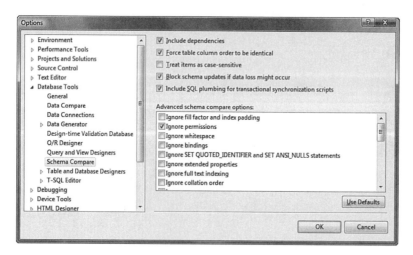

FIGURE 29.16    Setting comparison options.

# Comparing Data

Besides being able to compare schemas across databases and database projects, VSTS Database Edition also ships with a data comparison tool. The process here is nearly identical to the schema comparison process. First, we launch the comparison through the Visual Studio Data menu by selecting Data Compare and then New Data Comparison. A simple two-page wizard/dialog will collect the needed information. First, just as with the schema comparison operation, we need to indicate the source and target database. Note that we don't have the option of comparing database projects because they don't contain any data—they contain only schema. Figure 29.17 shows the target and source database configurations page.

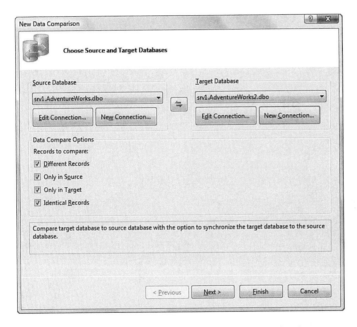

FIGURE 29.17    Selecting the target and source databases.

We also have the option at this stage of selecting exactly which records we want to compare across the two databases:

▶ All records that are different

▶ Records that exist only in the source database

▶ Records that exist only in the target database

▶ All records that are identical

By selecting all of these options, we are indicating that we want to compare every single record in the two databases.

Next, we need to indicate which tables and views we want to include in the comparison. simply place a check next to every object that should be part of the compare (see Figure 29.18).

FIGURE 29.18    Selecting the tables and views to compare.

With that, the Data Comparison tool has all the information it needs to start. After the comparison is complete, the Data Comparison window will be displayed. This has a very similar layout to the Schema Comparison window just discussed. The top pane shows a per-table or view tally of the number of records that are the same, are different, exist only in the source, or exist only in the target. A section of the window shows the details of the data differences, and at the bottom there is again a pane to use for previewing the data update script (see Figure 29.19).

## Viewing Record-Level Details

Clicking on one of the rows will show the physical rows that are physically different for the selected entity. They will appear under one of tab headings that organize them by the type of difference. In Figure 29.20, we can see that the HumanResources.Employee table has 13 rows in the source database that don't exist in the target database. Clicking on this table entry will show the exact records that are different under the Only In Source tab.

The record details table also allows us to manually deselect any rows we don't want to update. By removing the check from the Update column, we can indicate those rows that we don't want updated or inserted into the target database.

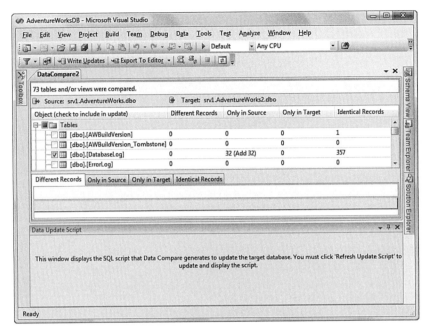

FIGURE 29.19    Data comparison results.

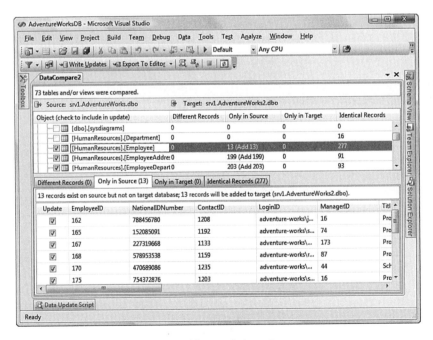

FIGURE 29.20    Selecting the tables and views to compare.

## Previewing and Executing the Update Script

The Data Update Script is the logical equivalent in the Data Comparison window to the Schema Update Script present in the Schema Comparison window: It shows the SQL statements necessary to update the target database so that it mirrors the source database in terms of data.

Initially, this window will be blank. You must force the script to be generated by selecting the Data menu and then selecting Data Compare, Refresh Update Script. Figure 29.21 shows the update script for our AdventureWorks comparison. The comments at the top of the script are interesting because they reveal the true robust nature of the script: It is intelligent enough to drop table foreign key constraints before performing the required data inserts or updates. They are then re-created after the data has been pushed into the selected tables or views.

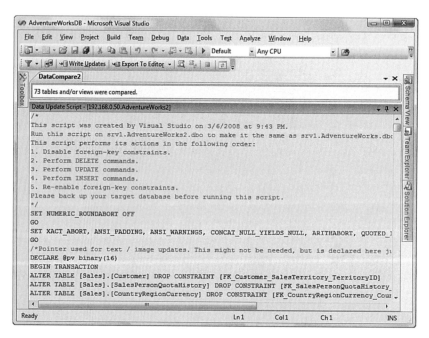

FIGURE 29.21    Selecting the tables and views to compare.

Our options for running the update script remain the same: We can execute the script directly or export it to a file or to the T-SQL editor for action.

# Rename Refactoring

VSTS Database Edition has taken the first small step toward introducing refactoring concepts to the database development community. We spend a whole chapter in this book (Chapter 9, "Refactoring Code") talking about all the great built-in refactoring support that Visual Studio Professional has for Visual C# and Visual Basic code. In VSTS Database Edition, support has been introduced for "Rename" refactoring of database objects.

When you make a change to an object's name, just as with rename refactoring in VB or C#, a preview is given of all the discrete items in the database schema that will need to be changed to accommodate the name change. To do this, the rename refactoring engine runs along the entire dependency change for any given object to ensure that all references to the object will also be updated.

Let's assume, for instance, that we want to change the name of the HumanResources. Employee table in the AdventureWorks database. In the Schema View window, right-click on the table and then select Refactor, and then Rename. This displays the Rename dialog (see Figure 29.22).

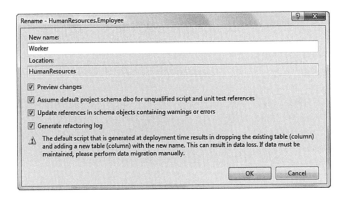

FIGURE 29.22   The Rename dialog.

## Rename Options

In the Rename dialog, we select the new name of the object, and also specify a few options for how the refactor should work:

▶ We can preview the required changes to the schema files.

▶ For any database objects that aren't already prefixed with a schema name, we can prepend the "dbo" schema name by default.

▶ If we have any schema files that are currently in an invalid state (for instance, a table definition schema that is in progress and doesn't currently have valid syntax), we can elect to still run the rename process within those files.

▶ We can generate a log of the changes made.

Clicking OK will display a window allowing us to preview all the changes that are necessary to execute the rename command.

## Previewing the Schema Changes

The Preview Changes window (see Figure 29.23) consists of two areas: The top list shows all the objects affected by the rename command, and the bottom area highlights the actual SQL changes that will be made. By clicking on an object in the top list, we can see the exact updates that the refactoring engine will be applying to that object's schema SQL. It is important to remember that we are changing only the schema files in our database project, not the schema of a live database. Again, this is the power of the database project: We are able to make changes in a safe environment before testing them, checking them in, and then moving those changes to a physical database.

> **NOTE**
>
> The great thing about rename refactoring is that it is capable of looking at not only schema object dependencies, but also any other dependent object stored in the project, such as a data generation plan or unit tests (more on these features next).

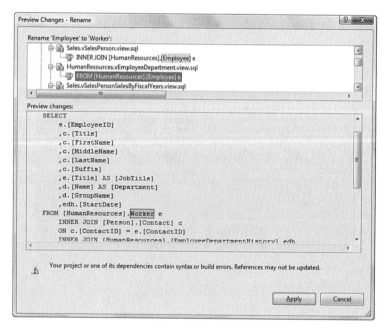

FIGURE 29.23    The Rename-Preview Changes dialog.

# Unit Tests

We cover the unit testing framework in Visual Studio (and VSTS) in depth in Chapter 26, "Development Edition," and in Chapter 28, "Test Edition." VSTS Database Edition builds on top of the existing unit test framework in Visual Studio to deliver unit testing capabilities specific to databases. Unit tests in a database project are focused on validating the correctness of the schema. That is, they are meant to ensure that changes made to the database don't break existing code or don't break the implicit "contract" between the application tier and the database tier. As such, they are not at all different with regard to expected results from the unit tests written for the application tier in VB or C#. The difference that is key for database developers is that the test designer in VSTS Database Edition is SQL focused. Unit tests can be constructed in T-SQL, as well as in VB or C#.

## Creating Unit Tests

There are two ways for you to create unit tests for a database. We can use the standard Test menu, and select New Test to launch the Add New Test dialog. The Database Unit Test template is the one we want for creating our data-focused unit tests (see Figure 29.24).

After we click OK on the Add New Test dialog, a new test project will be created and added to the current solution. The test designer will already be open and ready for action. But VSTS Database Edition provides an easier way to create unit tests from within the Schema View window. Right-click on the object you want to test, and then select Create Unit Tests.

The resulting dialog, shown in Figure 29.25, allows us to select any of the schema items in our database project and insert a new unit test class for that item. We can either add the unit test class to an existing test project in the current solution, or create a new VB- or C#-based test project in the current solution.

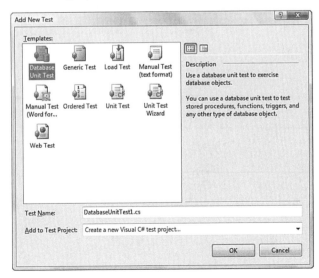

FIGURE 29.24   Creating a database unit test.

FIGURE 29.25    Selecting objects to test.

We had mentioned earlier that unit tests in VSTS Database Edition can be written in T-SQL as well as VB or C#. So, why then do we have options only for C# and Visual Basic in the Add New Test dialog? The reason is this: Although we can write unit tests in T-SQL, these are actually translated into VB or C# managed code tests. For the DBA or database developer, you don't need to worry about the VB or C# code that is generated—unless you want to!

The advantage to creating unit tests via the Schema View window as opposed to the Test menu is that VSTS Database Edition will automatically create a T-SQL stub to use as a starting point for the test. They aren't particularly complete, but they do improve productivity by at least relieving you of some of the typing necessary to write a test. Stubs can be created for the following items:

▶ Stored procedures

▶ Functions

▶ Triggers

▶ Arbitrary SQL (that is, any "compilable" chunk of SQL)

### Creating a Test Project

If there are no current test projects within the current solution, Visual Studio will create one for you based on your selection in the output drop-down (refer to Figure 29.25). When the project is created, you will be prompted for a database connection to use for the test project. Figure 29.26 shows a window where you will enter this information. This window also shows another important feature of the database unit test feature: You can specify a second data connection to use for *validation* of test results. This allows you to specify a typical user-privileged connection for running the tests (this is the primary connection), and a higher-level database owner or admin privileged connection to validate the tests (this is the secondary connection).

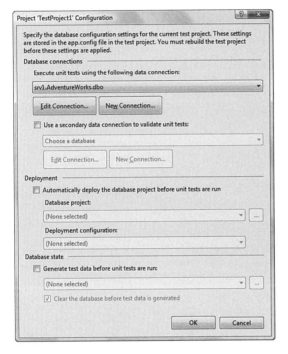

FIGURE 29.26    Selecting the primary and secondary database connections.

## The Database Unit Test Designer

The unit test designer depicted in Figure 29.27 shows a unit test stub for the dbo.uspGetManagerEmployees stored procedure.

In this case, let's assume that we want to test the validity of the selected stored procedure. Because we know that the test data loaded into the database, we also know that we should expect exactly 20 rows to be returned if we pass in a manager ID of 16 to this stored procedure. To craft a unit test around this assumption, we first need to set the input parameter to the desired value of 16. This is easily done by editing the T-SQL of the unit test, and setting @ManagerId to the value like this:

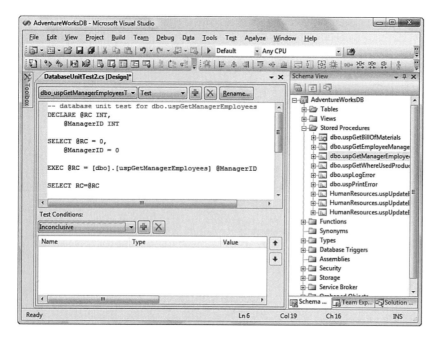

**FIGURE 29.27**    The unit test designer.

```
SELECT @RC = 0, @ManagerID = 16
```

We now need a test condition that will look for the expected row count. In the bottom pane of the designer, select the Row Count value in the Test Conditions drop-down, and click on the plus sign. This will add the condition to the conditions list. With the condition added, we now need to set the actual condition value. Double-click on the condition row to show the condition properties window. In this window, we can set the value of the Row Count property to 20. Figure 29.28 shows the condition added and configured for our test.

### Running the Database Unit Test

We are now ready to run the test and see the results. Open the Test View window by selecting the Test menu, then Windows, then Test View. Select the test we just created in the test list, and then click on the Run Selection button at the top of the Test View window. Visual Studio will immediately run the test script against the database, and will show the results in the Test Results window. In Figure 29.29, we can see that the test has run successfully, but that our stored procedure did not pass the test.

To get further details about the test failure, double-click on the result line in the Test Results window. We can clearly see that the stored procedure returned only 12 rows from the target table, instead of the expected 20 (see Figure 29.30).

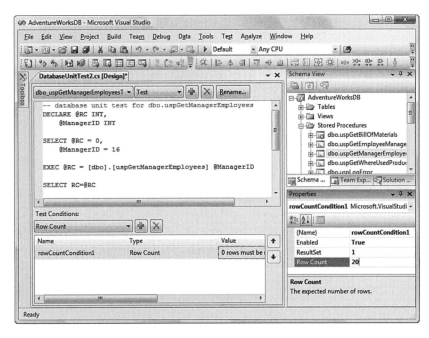

FIGURE 29.28    Adding a condition to the test.

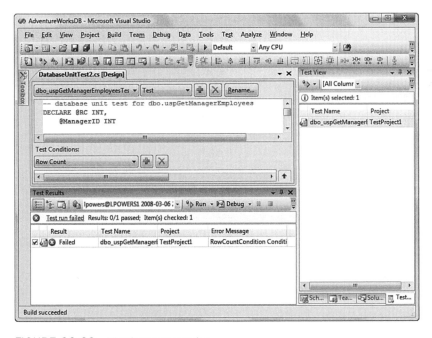

FIGURE 29.29    Viewing test results.

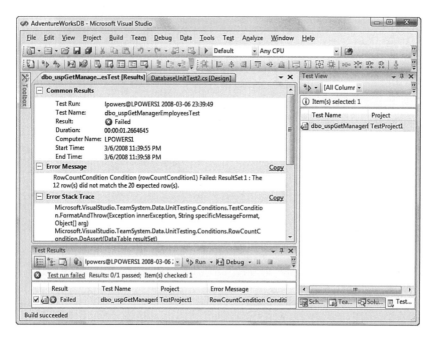

FIGURE 29.30    Viewing test results.

# Generating Data

Yet another key activity within the DDLC is the creation of test data. It goes without saying that you can't really test either the application tier or the database tier of a database application without having data in the database. This is a common problem area with database projects. Ideally, you'd like to test with the production data, but there are all sorts of concerns that crop up around using these data sets. Production data often contains confidential information or personally identifiable information that is simply not legally available. The work required to produce a "sanitized" version of data from a production database is often staggering, and fraught with the potential to stray from the volume and unique data relationships present in the production database.

This is where the VSTS Database Edition data generator comes into play. It acts as a companion to the schema import tool: If we inspect a production database and reverse engineer its schema, we will want to do the same with the data. The data generator leverages the data profile found on a production database to create its own algorithm for generating random, but relevant, data in a target database.

## Creating a Data Generation Plan

A data generation plan is an object we can add to our database projects to generate test data sets. These plans will show up in the Solution Explorer window under the Data Generation Plans folder. To add a plan to your project, right-click on the project name, select Add New Item, and then select the Data Generation Plan template under the Data Generation Plans category (see Figure 29.31).

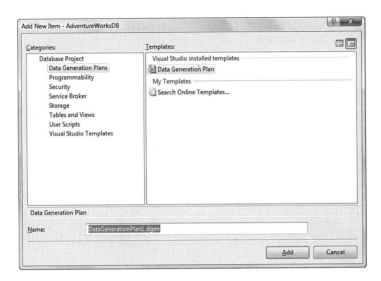

FIGURE 29.31   Adding a data generation plan.

After the plan object has been added to the project, it will inspect the project's schema objects, and then load them into the Data Generation Plan Designer window (see Figure 29.32). The designer window is where we control all the aspects of the data generation plan. The top pane of the designer shows us all the table objects in our project. We can elect to include or not include any given object in the data generation plan by the check box next to each object's name.

In addition to displaying the table name, we also see a number representing the number of rows to be inserted into the table. By default, the plan will insert 50 rows into every table. We can change this number to any value we like by typing in a different value in the table cell. There is also a Related Table column, and a Ratio to Related Table column. These are important settings to understand, so let's discuss the concept of ratios in some detail.

### Table Ratios

In a database that has a one-to-many table relationship, there will typically be a somewhat standard ratio of rows from the one side of the relationship to the many side of the relationship. One concrete example is that of an order table that has a one-to-many relationship with an order line item table. If orders placed with the company have an average of three items, we would say that the average ratio is 1:3 of order rows to order line item rows. The data generator is capable of taking these types of relationships into account.

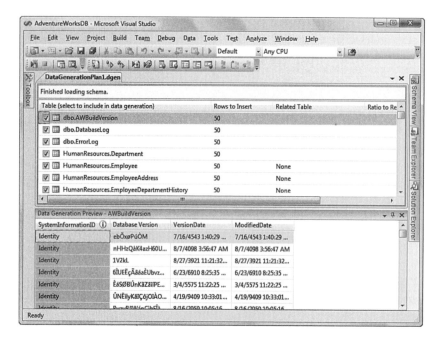

FIGURE 29.32    The Data Generation Plan Designer.

In the table list, we can specify a related table by clicking in the Related Table column. The list of available tables will be populated based on the foreign keys and relationships defined in the database's schema. After a related table has been selected, we have the option of then specifying a ratio—this number will automatically adjust the number of rows to insert into the "many" table based on the provided ratio.

For example, in the AdventureWorks database, we have a Purchasing.PurchaseOrderHeader table and a Purchasing.PurchaseOrderDetail table. These two tables are related (every header has one or more details), and they are related at a rough average of 2:1. That is, for every one header row, there are approximately two detail rows. Figure 29.33 shows this ratio accounted for within the designer. Note that it has automatically calculated 100 rows for us by applying that ratio to the default of 50 rows.

## Previewing the Generated Data

The bottom pane of the data generation designer shows us a preview of the data for any table we select in the top pane. For instance, by selecting the Person.Contact table, we are able to see the rows for insert that were automatically generated by the data generator (see Figure 29.34).

To understand how these values were produced, and how you can tweak that process, we need to introduce the concept of *data generators*.

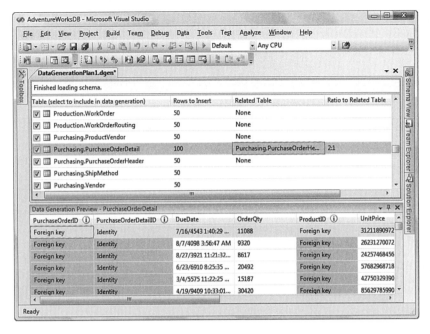

FIGURE 29.33     Adding a data generation plan.

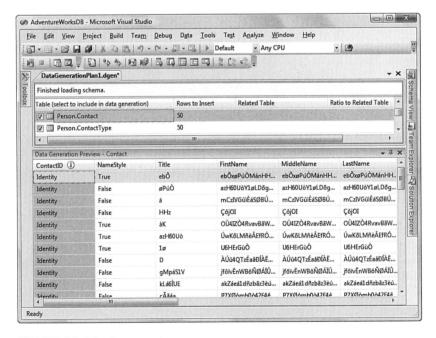

FIGURE 29.34     Data preview.

**Configuring the Data Generators**

Data generators are components that create data aligned to a specific type; VSTS Database Edition has generators for all the basic data types:

▶ Strings (ASCII and Unicode)

▶ Numbers (tinyint, smallint, int, bigint, real, float, decimal, numeric, money)

▶ Binary (varbinary, image)

▶ Date and time

▶ Uniqueidentifier (GUID)

▶ Bit

In addition, there are also generators for more complex types, such as these:

▶ Foreign keys

▶ Regular expressions

▶ Query-based data (these are known as "data bound" generators)

Each generator bases its output on random seed values and is matched to the target schema. So, for our Contact table example, we see that no values were generated for the ContactID column because the database schema has defined that as an identity column; the database itself will provide the values for the column. And in general, as you look through the sample data, you will see numbers where you expect numbers, strings where you expect strings, and date/time stamps where you expect date/time data. But the data isn't perfect. For instance, we can see that the name columns contain data that is string-oriented but far from an actual name. And the ModifiedDate column has some fairly strange dates in there like "8/1/6169 5:13:59 PM." So while the defaults have gotten us close, we aren't all the way there yet. To change the data to a more realistic model, we need to set some properties on the individual generators.

**Changing Generator Properties**    To change a generator, we first need to open the Column Details window within the Data Generation Plan Designer. You can either right-click within the data preview window and select Column Details, or click the Column Details button in the designer's toolbar.

The Column Details window enumerates all the columns in the table. When we click on a column, we get a property window with various settings for the generator attached to that column. As an example, if we want to change the dates generated for the ModifiedDate column, we can click on that column in the column list and then set the Max and Min values for the date/time generation to more realistic values (see Figure 29.35).

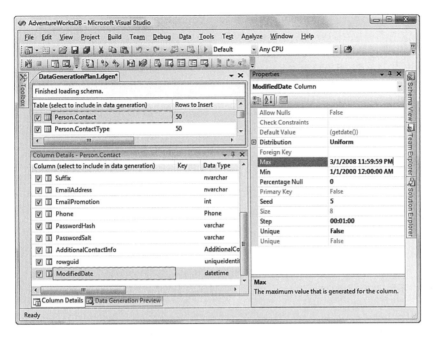

FIGURE 29.35    Changing the date/time generator settings.

> **TIP**
>
> Each generator type will have its own unique properties that can be configured. So for numeric generators, we can set a min and max value. Besides controlling things like min and max values or the seed value, we can also specify a distribution for string generators by setting a min and max length for the generated strings.
>
> One particularly useful property for numeric and date/time generators is the Distribution property. This is used to set the statistical distribution curve for the generated data. For instance, if we wanted to generate data for an age column in a person table, we might want those values to be distributed along a bell-like curve. By setting the Distribution to Normal instead of Uniform, we can approximate this type of statistic.

### Using a Complex Generator

As mentioned, we also have the ability to implement more complicated generators. Let's take the Title column in our Contact table as an example. Ideally, we would like the generator attached to that column to generate Mr, Mrs, Ms, or Dr. Because the basic string generator doesn't know how to do this, we can instead use a regular expression generator.

To change the generator assigned to a column, scroll over to the Generator column in the Column Details window. Clicking in the column will reveal a drop-down with all the supported generator types. In this case, we will select Regular Expression. With the generator now changed over, we can use the property window to enter our expression syntax to generate believable titles (see Figure 29.36).

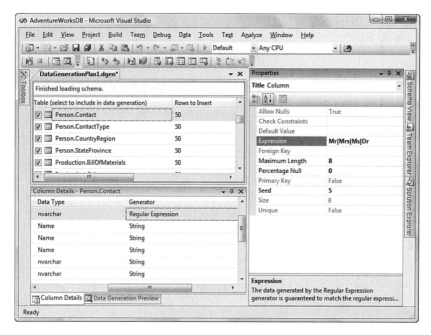

FIGURE 29.36    Changing the generator assignment.

If we now switch back to the Data Generation Preview tab, we can see that the sample data has already been updated based on the generator settings (see Figure 29.37).

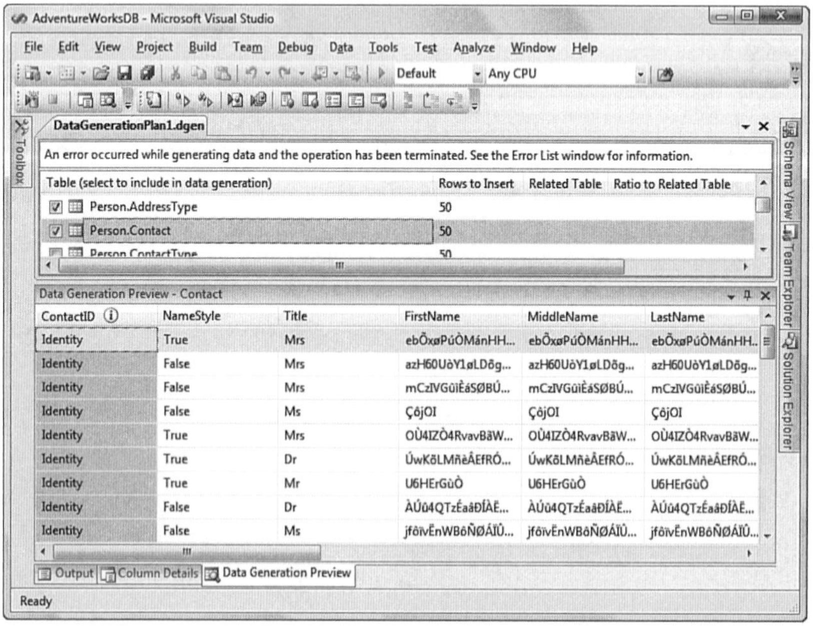

FIGURE 29.37    The regular expression generator in action.

## Generating the Data

After we have our data generation plan configured the way we want, the last step is to actually run the plan against a database. The easiest path here is to click on the Generate Data button on the Data Generator toolbar. You will need to first specify the database connection to use (which in turn identifies the target database). From there, you will be asked whether you want to clear any existing rows in the table before generating the new data. With those two dialogs answered, the generation process will start.

This operation is multithreaded; typically, several tables will be updating at the same time. During the entire process, the designer window will be updated to show you the progress of each table: A check mark indicates a successful generation, and a triangle indicates an in-progress or scheduled generation (see Figure 29.38).

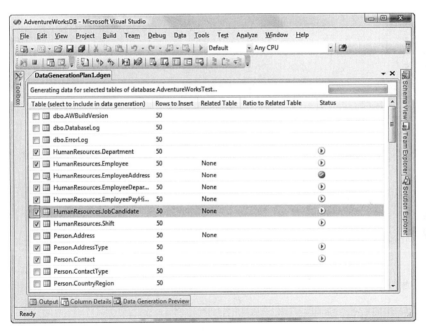

FIGURE 29.38   The regular expression generator in action.

29

# Building and Deploying

The final item we haven't covered is the actual act of updating a schema in a database with the schema in a database project. This uses the familiar build-and-deploy paradigm leveraged by other Visual Studio project types. In the context of a database project, the build process will parse all the SQL files and identify any files that have SQL syntax errors. If the build is clean, the deployment will actually update the target database with the schema (or create a new database if the target database doesn't exist).

We specified the default target database when we ran through the initial project creation wizard. You can also change this information at any time by right-clicking on the project in the Solution Explorer window and selecting Properties to open the properties window. The Build tab (see Figure 29.39) holds the settings that dictate how we build and which database we deploy to.

> **NOTE**
>
> You don't have to use Visual Studio to do the actual schema deployment. By building the database project, you are generating a SQL script file with all the necessary SQL commands. You can execute that script file from within any tool that understands T-SQL (including SQL Enterprise Manager itself). This is useful in situations in which the actual schema change will be implemented by someone in the DBA role, who may or may not have VSTS Database Edition installed, or who may have a specific tool that he or she is required to use for schema propagation.

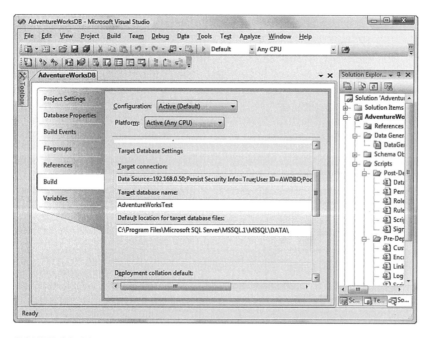

FIGURE 29.39    The Build tab.

# Summary

In this chapter, you have seen how database developers and database administrators can use the VSTS Database Edition tools to conquer many of the common problems faced by these roles within the context of an end-to-end database development life cycle. Specifically, we looked at how the Database Edition IDE can be used to do the following:

- Reverse engineer a database into a database project

- Make changes to the schema files in a database project, and even store those files within source control

- Compare both the schema and data of two databases or, for schemas, a database project and a database

- Create unit tests and validate those tests against the objects in a database project

- Generate sophisticated data generation plans

- Build and deploy a database project schema to a live database

CHAPTER 30

# Team Foundation Build

The last Visual Studio Team System tool we will cover in this book is Team Foundation Build (TFB). It is distributed as part of Team Foundation Server and, like the other tools we have discussed, is an integrated part of the overall project experience offered by VSTS.

As projects march through their life cycle, you reach a point at which it is time to pull together all the various components, compile them, distribute them, and test them. This overall process is known as a *build*. And as you will see, building software is much more than simply compiling source code into executable binaries. In fact, builds can be amazingly complex and can involve a huge amount of manual work by various members of the project team. This process presents some unique issues:

▶ The lack of a comprehensive, universal set of build tools that integrate with the project environment leads to unpredictable and unrepeatable ad hoc build processes.

▶ Monitoring the build process and gaining an understanding of the health of any given build can be difficult.

▶ Typically, no mechanisms are available to troubleshoot problems when they occur within a build.

Team Foundation Build is intended to automate many aspects of the build process and address the problems listed here by providing the entire project team with a holistic set of tools for creating and analyzing builds.

This chapter covers the capabilities of the Team Foundation Build tool. It overviews the basics of build systems, discusses how a typical build process is accommodated within Visual Studio Team System, and details the ways you can interact with the build tools from within Visual Studio.

# An Overview of Team Foundation Build

Many development organizations leverage a build lab to create both public and private builds of their software releases. Distilled to its basics, a build lab is a set of hardware and software resources that take all the source code files from the team project, centralize them on a build server, and then compile the system with all the latest changes. Ideally, this build is then packed up and copied over to a central, accessible location that everyone on the team can access. Quality Assurance (QA) resources are then free to run their test suites against the software and determine what sorts of changes need to be fed back to the development team.

Team Foundation Build's stated goal is to provide a build lab in a box. In essence, it strives to eliminate much of the manual work from the build process while at the same time enabling team members to gain information about the health of a particular build. The Team Foundation Build platform provides various benefits to the project team:

▶ It enables a build process to be constructed and initiated quickly and easily from within Visual Studio.

▶ It provides a repeatable, continuous process for building the software upon certain activities such as check-ins or timed intervals.

▶ It provides the project team with the tools necessary to determine the overall health of the build.

▶ It allows for build-to-build comparison for a historical look at overall project progress as each build is created and tested.

## Team Foundation Build Architecture

Team Foundation Build services are provided by four subsystems within the Visual Studio Team System ecosystem: client tools, build services, build web services, and build repository. Each plays a specific role in the high-level build process. Figure 30.1 identifies how these components work with one another.

Each of these four components plays a key role in ensuring that your builds happen on a reliable basis. The following list describes the components from Figure 30.1:

▶ **Build Client Tools (Visual Studio)**—This will define a build (which can be versioned and stored in the Team Foundation Source Control system) and then initiate the build.

▶ **Build Web Services**—This component exists on the Team Foundation Server application tier. Its job is to listen for any build requests that come through from the Team Build client tools; it then passes off the build request to the Build Services (build server).

▶ **Build Agents**—This represents the actual build servers in your application. These agents have the build services running on them. They are the workhorses that execute the actual builds. They do so by first examining the specific build definition. They then grab the necessary files from the source control system, compile the source files, runs tests, and publish results to the build repository. Notifications of the build completion can then be sent to the team. In addition, the build agents will publish the build out to a specified location.

▶ **Build Repository**—The Team Foundation Server data tier fills its typical role as data repository. The build details and log events are all stored here. This allows the build client to view and analyze a given build.

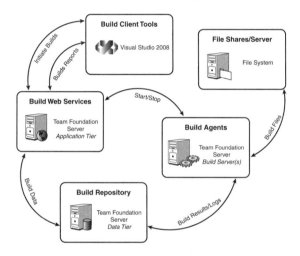

FIGURE 30.1    The Team Foundation Build system.

---

**NOTE**

The diagram presented in Figure 30.1 is a logical architecture. The Team Foundation system can be physically structured in various ways. For example, although it makes sense to have a dedicated build server for larger projects, you could host the build server on the same machine that is hosting the Team Foundation Server application tier or, for that matter, the data tier. For very large projects, on the other hand, it may make sense to have an entire farm of Build machines running the build server components.

---

**The Team Build Client**

Team Explorer, hosted inside Visual Studio, functions as the primary client for the Team Foundation Build system. Within Team Explorer, builds are managed and configured through the Builds node. Under the Builds node, every defined build within the scope of the current team project is visible. Each of these entities represents various settings, including which files should be incorporated in the build, what tests should be run as part of the build, where the build should be published, and so on. Figure 30.2 shows a list of build definitions within the Team Explorer window.

FIGURE 30.2 Builds within the Team Explorer window.

> **NOTE**
>
> You must be a member of the Build Services group inside of TFS for the specific project whose builds you want to manage.

### The Application Tier

The Team Foundation Server application tier exposes Team Foundation Build as a set of four web services (see Chapter 23, "Managing and Working with Team Projects," for a look at all the web services implemented by the TFS application tier machine):

- The Build Controller web service exposes the API for managing and controlling builds. It is capable, for instance, of issuing start and stop commands to build agents.

- The Build Store web service provides methods for saving and retrieving build information to the TFS data tier.

- The Build Integration web service allows the build server and other clients to interface with other team project entities.

- The Publish Test Results web service is the API used to distribute test results run against the build to the project team as a whole.

The application tier also contains the source code control access and other key project definitions like code analysis and test information. These are all, of course, vital to the build process.

### The Build Agents

Build agents represent a server (or servers) capable of executing a build and dropping the results into a shared directory. The build agent (also called build server) is the core engine that really implements the build process.

The build process starts from a call from the team build client (or through a scheduled process) to the application tier. Inside the application tier, there is a running service called the Team Build Service. Its job is to issue commands out to a build agent to actually execute the build. Of course, these commands are based on information retrieved from the build database.

The build agent then executes the build scripts and drops the build on the appropriate share. It logs its progress back to the application tier and notifies it when the build is complete. It also works with the application tier to write the build results out to the TFS data store for tracking purposes.

> **NOTE**
>
> We are discussing each of these items as separate components. However, it is important to remember that each could exist on the same machine.

**The Build Repository**

The build repository is implemented by the Team Foundation Server data tier within its own SQL Server database called TfsBuild. This database contains tables that store information related to build definitions, test results, and related work items.

As an example of the information stored here, Figure 30.3 shows the data model for a few of the core tables used to define a build. This includes the build definition table that stores your build definitions, the build agent table that stores information about a build computer, and the build table for storing actual instances of a given build.

Now that you have the fundamentals in hand, it's time to see how to manage the build process within the Visual Studio Team System.

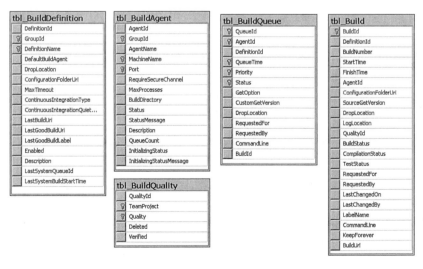

FIGURE 30.3    Partial data model for the Build database.

30

# Creating a New Build

Team Foundation Build uses the concept of build definitions. A build definition is simply the container for all the configuration information related to a build. In essence, it defines all the different parts of a particular build.

You create a new build definition by using the Team Explorer window. Right-click the Builds node and then select New Build Definition. This will launch the build definition wizard, which will guide you through the process of defining a workspace, selecting a file to be built, configuring test and analysis, defining the build agent, and scheduling the build. After you've completed the wizard, it will write the build configuration into a specific file format used by the build engine. The following sections step you through the build definition wizard.

## Naming the Build

The first step is to provide a name for the build. This is the same name that is reflected within the Team Explorer Builds node and in the build reports. Figure 30.4 shows the first page in the build definition wizard.

Note that we will progress through this screen using the links on the left side (general, workspace, and so on). This UI is not a true wizard.

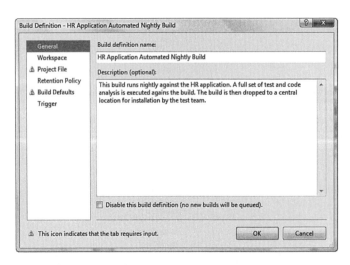

FIGURE 30.4   Specifying the build definition name.

## Selecting Project Files to Build

The second screen in the Build Definition window is the Workspace screen. Here you can configure the build to be based on one or more source control folders. You might have multiple instances (branches) of the same code in different folders. Or you might need to get source code from multiple projects within the source control system to complete your build.

Each source control folder can be mapped to a folder on the build computer (called local folder). Figure 30.5 shows an example of setting the build working folders. Here there is a single source control folder mapped to a single local folder on the build server.

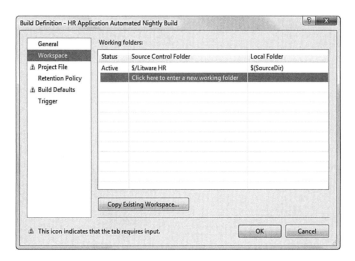

FIGURE 30.5    Specifying a source control workspace for the build server.

## Defining the Build Project File

You now need to select a place to store the actual build project. Remember, this build project will be versioned. Therefore, you need to select a folder in the version control system where you want to store the project. You do so via the Browse button next to the Version Control Folder option, as shown in Figure 30.6.

After you select a location, you need to click the Create button on the same screen to generate a TFSBuild.proj file. Clicking this button will launch the MSBuild Project File Creation Wizard.

### Setting Build Order
The MSBuild Project File Creation Wizard allows you to set the order of the items you intend to build, their configuration, and other options. The first screen allows you to set an order of the solutions you are building (as selected in the workspace). Figure 30.7 shows this screen. Notice the arrows on the right. This allows you to move items up and down the list if there are dependencies between them and build order is important.

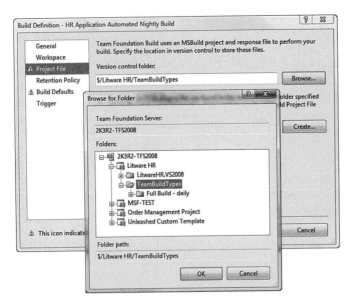

FIGURE 30.6    Selecting a source control location for the build project.

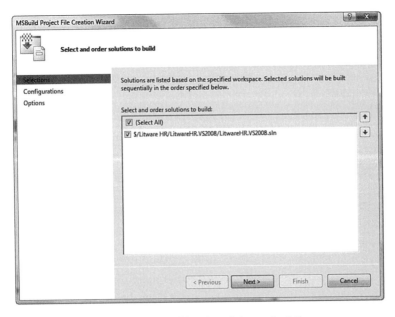

FIGURE 30.7    Defining the build order of dependent items.

### Defining Build Configurations

You next need to set the build configuration. It dictates parameters for the build, such as whether this is a release or debug build, and what the target CPU platform is. You can specify multiple configurations on this screen. Figure 30.8 shows an example.

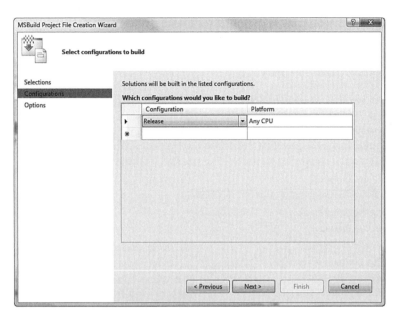

FIGURE 30.8   Defining the build configuration.

### Selecting Build Analysis and Tests

Tests can be run as part of the build process. This next page of the wizard (see Figure 30.9) gathers information on which tests should be run as part of the build process. You can select a test metadata file from within the Team Project. Alternatively, you can have the build system detect test assemblies and execute them accordingly.

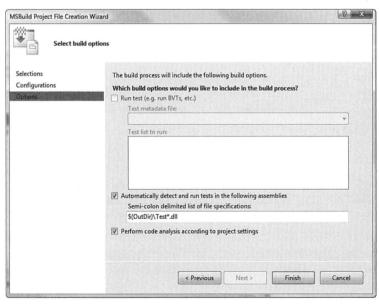

FIGURE 30.9   Options for testing the build.

By using the bottom check box, you can elect to run static code analysis against the source files included in the build.

## Defining the Build Retention Policy

The build retention policy allows you to indicate how many builds should be held on the server at any given time. This policy allows the build system to clean up old builds and thus recover space on your build server. The retention policy can be set based on the outcome of the build: failed, stopped, partially succeeded, or succeeded. For each, you can indicate how many builds you want to keep around. Figure 30.10 shows an example.

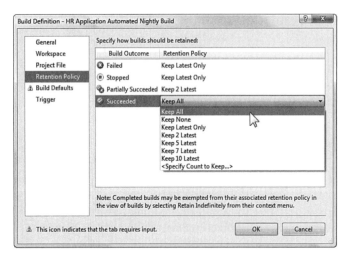

FIGURE 30.10    Setting the build retention policy.

## Defining the Build Agent Configuration

The next step is to tell Team Foundation Build which server to use as the Build Agent (see Figure 30.11). Remember, you must prepare this server as a build server by running the appropriate setup files from the Team Foundation Server install media; this will deploy the build service onto the server (which must, of course, be running before you can start a build).

Build agents are added to TFS and can be reused across builds. You can also use the New button on the screen in Figure 30.11 to define a new build agent. This launches the Build Agent Properties dialog, shown in Figure 30.12. Here you can set the name of the build agent computer, the port on which to communicate, the working directory, and more. Notice also that you can now initiate builds across a secure channel.

The build engine now needs to know where to place the build files locally on the build server and where the build output should be published so that the team can access it. This parameter is set back on the Build Defaults page as shown in Figure 30.11. Note that you can define a file share here as the place to write the build so that others can access it.

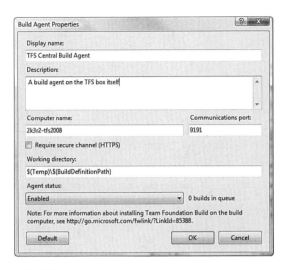

FIGURE 30.11    Setting the build defaults.

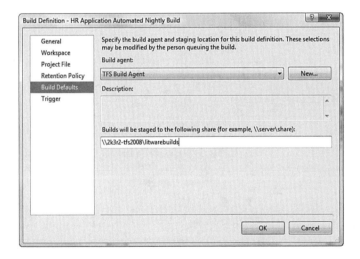

FIGURE 30.12    Defining a new build agent.

## Scheduling the Build or Setting Build Triggers

The final screen in the Build Definition window is the Trigger screen. Here you can indicate when you would like to automatically trigger a build. You can set a build to run every time a source is checked into the server (also called continuous integration). You can also indicate that builds should happen, one after another, based on check-ins relative to executing builds. In this case, if a build is already running and one or more check-ins happen, a new build is not started until the old build completes.

You can also schedule a build to run from this interface. Here you can set the days of the week and a time to run a build. Figure 30.13 shows this as an example.

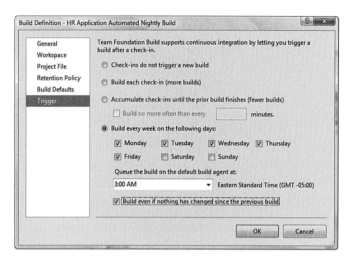

FIGURE 30.13    Triggering a build to run nightly.

Finishing the build definition will do two things: It will write the various build settings into an XML file called TFSBuild.proj, and it will add that XML file to the source control system at the location specified during the build definition.

For instance, Figure 30.14 shows a build project (TFSBuild.proj) at the root of the folder labeled TeamBuildTypes. There is another build project inside the folder, Full Build - daily.

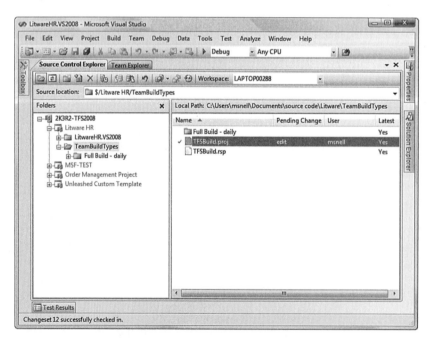

FIGURE 30.14    Build definition files in the Source Control Explorer.

# Editing a Build Definition

You can edit a build definition file from within Team Explorer. Simply right-click the build name and choose Edit Build Definition. An example is shown in Figure 30.15. This will bring up the same screens used to create the build.

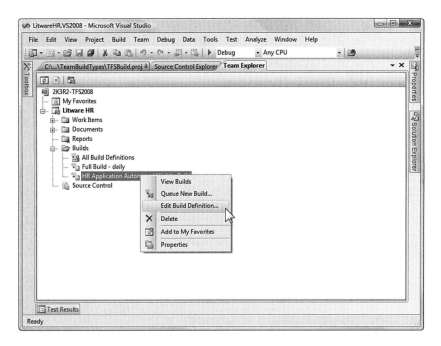

FIGURE 30.15    Launching the build editor.

## The TFSBuild.proj Project File

The good news is that you can edit all common elements of a build using the build definition editor. However, you can often do more to customize your build process by editing the build project's XML directly. The XML in the build project files is extremely well commented, and the files are fairly short.

To open the build project file in Visual Studio, you navigate to the specific TFSBuild.proj file in Source Control Explorer and double-click on the filename. Reading through this XML file, you will notice that it has captured all the major build type information categories within its individual nodes: There are nodes for storing general build, solution, configuration, location, and test option information.

---

**TIP**

It is fairly straightforward to extend any given build type with custom tasks that will run during the build process. Because a task is really just a body of code that is executed during the build, creating a new task involves writing code to implement your custom action. For information on how to extend a build using custom tasks, see the MSDN topic "Walkthrough: Customizing Team Foundation Build."

---

## The Role of MSBuild

As mentioned earlier, the core of the TFS build server is a technology called MSBuild. This build engine is implemented in a single executable, `msbuild.exe`. Although MSBuild ships with Visual Studio, it does not have any dependencies on the IDE, which means you can run the file on machines that don't have the development environment installed.

MSBuild works by taking in an XML file that describes the sequence of events for the build. It then processes those events in the order specified. MSBuild is a robust engine in that it can handle conditional builds, incremental builds, and dependencies between targets and builds. Because the `TFSBuild.proj` file conforms to the MSBuild specifications for its input file, Team Foundation Build is able to simply pass this file over for execution when the build is kicked off. In summary, Team Foundation Build overlays the MSBuild engine with a user interface and a series of functions to integrate the build into the overall fabric of the project team (thus allowing for notifications, changeset selections, and so on).

# Starting a Build

With one or more builds defined, team members can initiate any of them at any time by manually invoking them from the Team Explorer. Of course, they can also simply wait for them to run based on their present trigger as discussed previously.

To invoke a build from Visual Studio Team Explorer, right-click on the build definition and select Queue New Build. This will send a message to the build queue on the application tier indicating that the build should be run on the given build agent.

As you can see from Figure 30.16, the Queue Build dialog box will provide the opportunity to select a build definition and change some of the settings contained within that build definition. This includes the machine to use to conduct the build, the drop folder on that machine, and the priority of the build relative to other builds in the queue.

After a build has been started, it will proceed through its steps until failure or success. Figure 30.17 shows the general process that each build will follow.

As the build progresses through its various steps, the build engine constantly writes and logs information about its progress back to the build repository, enabling interested team members to monitor its progress at runtime from within Visual Studio.

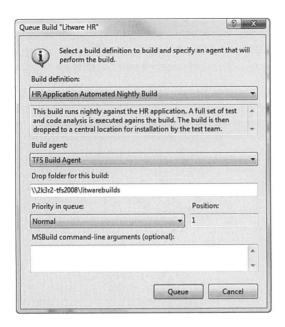

FIGURE 30.16    Queuing a build to run.

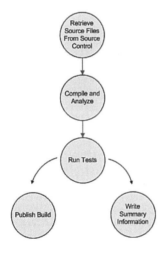

FIGURE 30.17    The general build process.

# Monitoring and Analyzing Builds

Build information is provided in Visual Studio through the Team Build Explorer. This browser window provides a list of completed or in-flight builds, and it functions as the principal mechanism for viewing build progress or completed summary reports.

## Introducing the Team Build Explorer

The Team Build Explorer, shown in Figure 30.18, provides a snapshot of any build by indicating whether it succeeded, failed, or is in progress; the name of the build; the quality of the build; and the date it was completed.

---

**TIP**

If you or other members of the project team want to be notified when a build has been completed, you can use the Team Foundation Server project alerts feature. TFS defines two build-related events you can subscribe to: Build Completed and Build Quality Changed.

---

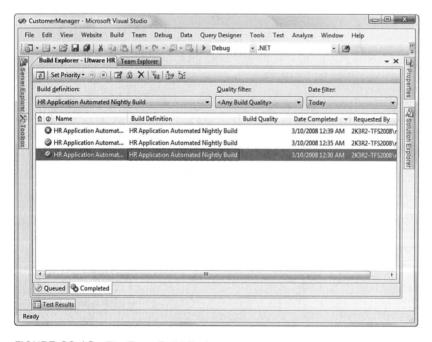

FIGURE 30.18    The Team Build Explorer.

The browser enables you to access the report for a specific build and set the build's quality state.

### Setting a Build's Quality State

Team Foundation Build comes with a stock set of quality states that the QA group can select from when indicating the quality of a given build:

▶ Initial Test Passed

▶ Lab Test Passed

▸ Ready for Deployment

▸ Ready for Initial Test

▸ Rejected

▸ Released

▸ UAT Passed

▸ Under Investigation

As part of the build process, the QA group would visit the Team Build Browser and change a build's quality state to indicate to the rest of the team what their tests have found. You can do this quite easily by clicking in the column and selecting one of the states, as shown in Figure 30.19.

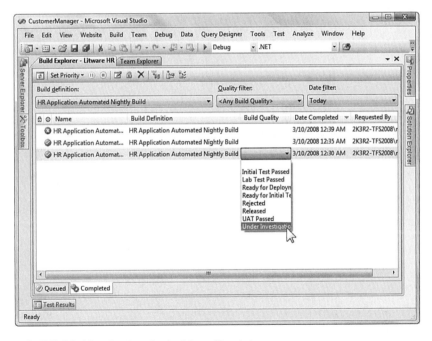

FIGURE 30.19   Setting the build quality state.

In addition to the stock quality states, you can also add your own. Just select the Manage Build Qualities button on the Build Explorer toolbar. Using the Edit Build Qualities dialog box (see Figure 30.20), you can add new states or remove one of the existing ones.

30

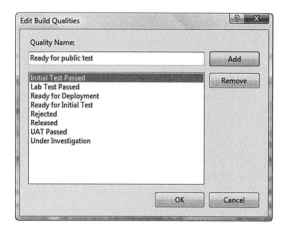

FIGURE 30.20   Adding a new build quality state.

## The Build Report

To view reports for both in-progress and completed builds, you double-click the build within the Team Build Browser.

Each report is hosted within a document window opened in Visual Studio and has the following sections:

▶ **Summary**—Summarizes the details of the build and includes data points such as the build name, the person who requested the build, the machine that executed the build, the current quality state of the build, and a link to the build log.

▶ **Build Steps**—Contains a list (which is dynamic if the build is in progress) that provides date and timestamp information for each stage of the build.

▶ **Result Details**—Contains errors and warnings generated by the build, the results of any tests run with the build, and the code coverage results.

▶ **Associated Changesets**—Contains a hyperlinked list of any changesets that were a part of the build.

▶ **Associated Work Items**—Provides a hyperlinked list of any work items that were associated with the build.

Figure 30.21 shows a build report open in Visual Studio.

Work items once again provide a correlation mechanism for associating builds and other team project artifacts. For example, consider the following chain of information:

1. A developer fixes a bug and checks in its changes to the source control system.

2. The bug work item with the changeset is created from the check-in.

3. Because the changeset is associated with the work item, and builds work against changesets within the source repository, you can now easily tell which bugs have been fixed in what build.

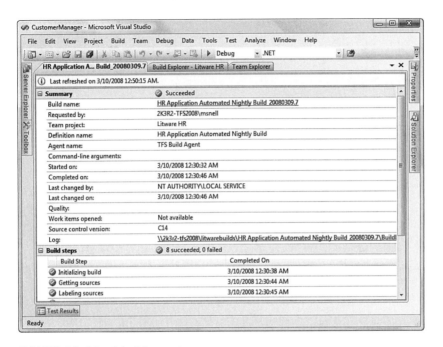

FIGURE 30.21    A build report.

# Summary

In this chapter, we covered the use of Team Foundation Build to automate and manage simple to complex build processes within a team project. Team Foundation Build allows you to treat builds as an integral piece to the team project.

On the server, Team Foundation Build provides a database, build engine, and common web services interface for defining, executing, and analyzing software builds. This chapter presented the logical and physical architecture of the Team Foundation Build components and showed how they coexist within the larger Visual Studio Team System technical framework. By using loosely coupled tiers, Team Foundation Build enables you to scale out build environments by assigning build server functionality to a shared server, a dedicated server, or even multiple servers in a farm configuration.

On the client, a series of windows integrated into Visual Studio allows team members in all roles to easily participate in the build process. In this chapter, we described how the Team Explorer is used to define new build types and run those builds from within the IDE. And finally, this chapter toured the capabilities of the Team Build Browser to monitor and analyze the results of builds.

30

# Index

AutoScaleDimensions property (form controls), 590
AutoScaleMode property (form controls), 590
AutoSize property (form design), 579

# B

BackColor property (forms), 583
behaviors, 781
best practices, 1006-1007
beta releases, 1079
Bin folder (website projects), 510
Binary Properties property page, 1019
binding. *See also* data binding
    defined, 782
    extracted values to web test requests, 1097
    query strings to data, 1094-1096
    tests to data, 1092-1094
bindings. *See* key bindings
bookmarks, 166-170
Bookmarks window, 169-170
brace matching (productivity tool), 277-279
Branch dialog box, 946
branching source code tree, 944-946
Break All command, 337
breaking execution for exceptions, 320-321
Breakpoint Condition dialog box, 344-345
Breakpoint Filter dialog box, 346
Breakpoint Hit Count dialog box, 347
breakpoints, 340. *See also* Run To Cursor command; tracepoints
    Breakpoints window, 341
    clearing, 327
    conditions, 343-345
    configuring, 180, 325
    controlling flow of code, 180-181
    defined, 178
    on file locations, 346
    filters, 346
    hit count, 347
    icons for, 341

indicator margin, 166
    setting, 179-180, 324, 340
Breakpoints window, 341
browsers
    defined, 135
    Object Browser. *See* Object Browser
    output for web form applications, 204-205
    selecting for load tests, 1104
    targeting, 204
bubbling events (WPF), 637
bug reports, sending via Help menu, 223-224
bug work items
    MSF for Agile, 953
    MSF for CMMI, 955
build agents, 1155-1156, 1162
build and deploy options (database projects), 1121-1122
Build Configuration property page, 116
Build Events property page, 130
Build menu, 62
Build property page, 130
build servers, 1155-1156
Build Solution Action section (build options for website projects), 515
build triggers, 1163-1164
building database projects, 1149-1150
builds, 1153. *See also* Team Foundation Build
    build reports, 1170-1171
    build repository, 1155-1157
    automation, 893
    configuration, 116, 513-515, 1160
    creating
        configuring build agents, 1162
        defining build project file, 1159, 1162
        defining build retention policy, 1162
        naming builds, 1158
        scheduling the build, 1163-1164
        selecting project files, 1158
    definitions, 1158
    editing
        build project file, 1165
        MSBuild, role of, 1166
    events, 130
    extending with custom tasks, 1166

# D

# E

**Edit and Continue feature (debugger), 355-356**

**Edit menu, 60, 257-259**

editing

  builds

    build project file, 1165

    MSBuild, role of, 1166

  custom component set (Object Browser), 153

  in Document Outline, 157

  files in source control. *See source control, files*

  load tests, 1106

  markup, 202

  recorded macros, 427-430

  styles, 539-541

  text documents, 402-403, 406-408

  typed DataSets, 731-732

  variables in Locals or Autos windows, 350

  .vstemplate XML file, 236-237

  XML documents, 184

  XSLT styles sheets, 185-186

**editors.** *See names of specific editors*

**EditorZone control, 553**

**EditPoint object**

  adding text, 405

  editing text, 406

  properties/methods, 403

  repositioning, 407

**element styles.** *See style rules*

**embedded XML, 96-97**

**embedding**

  resources (WPF), 634

  user controls, 610

**Empty Web Site template, 501**

**enabling**

  TCP port sharing, 796

  website debugging, 318-319

**Encapsulate Field refactoring tool, 312-314**

**Encapsulte Field dialog box, 313-314**

**ending debug sessions, 339**

**endpoints**

  connecting applications in application diagram, 1055-1056

  connecting servers to zones, 1067-1068

  defined, 781

  defining, 790-796

  proxy endpoints, 1061

**enhancements.** *See new features of Visual Studio 2008*

**EnvDTE/EnvDTE80 assemblies, 366**

**environment settings**

  changing, 902

  configuring IDE, 54-56

**EnvironmentEvents module, 431**

**errors.** *See also exceptions*

  productivity tools. *See productivity tools*

  publishing errors (work items), 975

**evaluating code coverage analysis, 1014-1015**

**event handlers, 416.** *See also events*

  color palette example (add-ins), 462-463, 466-469

  creating, 584

  for image viewer application example (WPF), 645

  in macros

    adding event declarations, 434

    event definitions, 431

    initializing event object, 435-436

    writing event handler, 433-434

  removing arguments from, 97

**Event Logs node (Server Explorer), 149**

**event model**

  ASP.NET, 518, 523-526, 562

  workflows, 828-829

**EventDriven activity, 810**

**events.** *See also event handlers*

  defining in Class Designer, 1002-1004

  event declarations, adding to macros, 431, 434

  event model

    ASP.NET, 518, 523-526, 562

    workflows, 828-829

  event objects, initializing, 435-436

# G

# H

# I

## J–K

## L

# M

# T

# V

# UNLEASHED

Unleashed takes you beyond the basics, providing an exhaustive, technically sophisticated reference for professionals who need to exploit a technology to its fullest potential. It's the best resource for practical advice from the experts, and the most in-depth coverage of the latest technologies.

**ASP.NET 3.5 Unleashed**
ISBN: 0672330113

## OTHER UNLEASHED TITLES

**ASP.NET 3.5 AJAX Unleashed**
ISBN: 0672329735

**C# 3.0 Unleashed**
ISBN: 0672329816

**LINQ Unleashed**
ISBN: 0672329832

**Microsoft Dynamics AW 5.0 Programming Unleashed**
ISBN: 0672330105

**Microsoft Dynamics CRM 4.0 Unleashed**
ISBN: 0672329700

**Microsoft Exchange Server 2007 Unleashed**
ISBN: 0672329204

**Microsoft Expression Blend Unleashed**
ISBN: 067232931X

**Microsoft ISA Server 2006 Unleashed**
ISBN: 0672329190

**Microsoft Office Project Server 2007 Unleashed**
ISBN: 0672329212

**Microsoft SharePoint 2007 Development Unleashed**
ISBN: 0672329034

**Microsoft Small Business Server 2003 Unleashed**
ISBN: 0672328054

**Microsoft SQL Server 2005 Unleashed**
ISBN: 0672328240

**Microsoft XNA Unleashed**
ISBN: 0672329646

**System Center Operations Manager 2007 Unleashed**
ISBN: 0672329557

**VBScript, WMI and ADSI Unleashed**
ISBN: 0321501713

**Windows Communication Foundation Unleashed**
ISBN: 0672329484

**Windows PowerShell Unleashed**
ISBN: 0672329530

**Windows Server 2008 Unleashed**
ISBN: 0672329301

**Silverlight 1.0 Unleashed**
ISBN: 0672330075

**Windows Presentation Foundation Unleashed**
ISBN: 0672328917

## SAMS

informit.com/sams

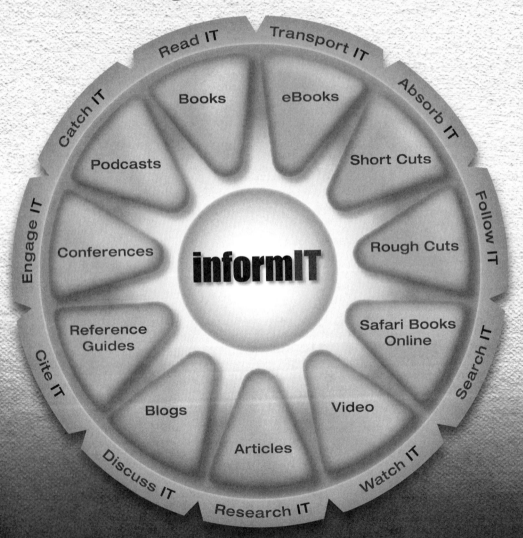

# Learn IT at InformIT

## Go Beyond the Book

Read IT · Transport IT · Absorb IT · Follow IT · Search IT · Watch IT · Research IT · Discuss IT · Cite IT · Engage IT · Catch IT

- Books
- eBooks
- Short Cuts
- Rough Cuts
- Safari Books Online
- Video
- Articles
- Blogs
- Reference Guides
- Conferences
- Podcasts

**informIT**

**11 WAYS TO LEARN IT** at **www.informIT.com/learn**

The online portal of the information technology
publishing imprints of Pearson Education

 Addison · Cisco Press · EXAM/CRAM · IBM · QUE ·  SAM

**BOOKS ONLINE**

ENABLED

# THIS BOOK IS SAFARI ENABLED

## INCLUDES FREE 45-DAY ACCESS TO THE ONLINE EDITION

The Safari® Enabled icon on the cover of your favorite technology book means the book is available through Safari Bookshelf. When you buy this book, you get free access to the online edition for 45 days.

Safari Bookshelf is an electronic reference library that lets you easily search thousands of technical books, find code samples, download chapters, and access technical information whenever and wherever you need it.

**TO GAIN 45-DAY SAFARI ENABLED ACCESS TO THIS BOOK:**

- Go to **informit.com/safarienabled**

- Complete the brief registration form

- Enter the coupon code found in the front of this book on the "Copyright" page

If you have difficulty registering on Safari Bookshelf or accessing the online edition, please e-mail customer-service@safaribooksonline.com.

# Safari Library
## Subscribe Now!
### http://safari.informit.com/library

**Safari's entire technology collection is now available with no restrictions. Imagine the value of being able to search and access thousands of books, videos, and articles from leading technology authors whenever you wish.**

## EXPLORE TOPICS MORE FULLY

Gain a more robust understanding of related issues by using Safari as your research tool. With Safari Library you can leverage the knowledge of the world's technology gurus. For one flat, monthly fee, you'll have unrestricted access to a reference collection offered nowhere else in the world—all at your fingertips.

With a Safari Library subscription, you'll get the following premium services:

- Immediate access to the newest, cutting-edge books—Approximately eighty new titles are added per month in conjunction with, or in advance of, their print publication.

- Chapter downloads—Download five chapters per month so you can work offline when you need to.

- Rough Cuts—A service that provides online access to prepublication information on advanced technologies. Content is updated as the author writes the book. You can also download Rough Cuts for offline reference

- Videos—Premier design and development videos from training and e-learning expert lynda.com and other publishers you trust.

- Cut and paste code—Cut and paste code directly from Safari. Save time. Eliminate errors.

- Save up to 35% on print books—Safari Subscribers receive a discount of up to 35% on publishers' print books.